Vietnam, Cambodia, Laos & Northern Thailand

Vietnam
p46

Laos
p272

Northern
Thailand
p359

Cambodia
p170

THIS EDITION WRITTEN AND RESEARCHED BY

Greg Bloom,
Austin Bush, Iain Stewart, Richard Waters

Contents

LUANG PRABANG,
LAOS P295

HANOI, VIETNAM P50

FOTOTRAV / GETTY IMAGES ©

YELLOW DOG / GETTY IMAGES ©

Contents

UNDERSTAND

SURVIVAL
GUIDE

SPECIAL FEATURES

**Hue's Imperial Enclosure
3D Illustration** 90

**Temples of Angkor
3D Illustration** 210

**Wat Phra Kaew & Grand
Palace 3D Illustration** . . 364

**Wat Pho
3D Illustration** 366

Welcome to the Mekong Region

The Mekong. It's an exotic name guaranteed to fire up the imagination. Riding high on the global hot list, it is home to such iconic sights as Angkor Wat, Halong Bay and Luang Prabang.

A River Runs Through It

One of the world's great rivers, the Mekong winds its way down from the foothills of Tibet to the South China Sea, encompassing some of the most diverse backdrops in Asia. Its dramatic journey southward takes in remote national parks and immense waterfalls in Laos, traditional towns and 21st-century cities in Thailand, freshwater dolphins and forgotten temples in Cambodia and a patchwork of emerald greens in Vietnam's Mekong Delta.

Old Asia, New Asia

Experience old Asia and new Asia jostling for space. One minute it's Bangkok, riding the Skytrain to a state-of-the-art shopping mall, the next it's an elephant careering through the jungle in Cambodia. In the cities, the pace of life runs at a dizzying speed, matched only by the endless rush of motorbikes and call of commerce. In the countryside, life seems timeless, the rural rhythms the same as they have been for centuries, with pyjama-clad peasants tending the fields and monks wandering the streets in search of alms.

Memorable Journeys

Travelling in the Mekong region is as much about the journey as the destination, although it is not always as smooth as the brochures would have you believe. Float down the river by slow boat from Huay Xai to Luang Prabang, passing by distant minority villages in a land that time forgot. Ride a bicycle around the ancient temples of Angkor. Or explore the bustling backstreets of old Asia from the comfort of a *cyclo* (bicycle rickshaw). Experience some rough with the smooth for the real flavour of the Mekong region.

The Spirit of the Mekong

Quench your thirst for adventure with some adrenalin-fuelled activities in the jungle before relaxing on a beautiful beach overlooking the South China Sea. Delve deeper to discern the mosaic of ethnicities and learn about their cultures and lifestyles. The people are irrepressible, the experiences unforgettable and the stories impossible to re-create, but sometime during your journey, the Mekong and its people will enter your soul. Go with the flow and let the Mekong's spirit course through your veins.

Why I Love Vietnam, Cambodia, Laos & Northern Thailand

By Greg Bloom, Author

My love affair with the Mekong region began in July 1997. An overnight bus from Bangkok and the next morning I'm in Vientiane. It's traffic- and tourist-free – the opposite of Bangkok. And it's surely the most relaxed place on earth. The next month is a somnolent, seemingly interminable journey north to Muang Sing, along misty mountain roads and swollen rivers coloured caramel by the monsoon. Inevitably, I would return to the region. I now live in Cambodia, where the icons of Mekong life – exuberant temples, radiant green rice fields, glistening water buffalo, sugar palms and mangosteens – are on full display. I returned to Laos for the first time in 16 years to research this book. It's still the most relaxed place on earth.

For more about our authors, see page 528

Above: Halong Bay (p68), Vietnam

Vietnam, Cambodia, Laos & Northern Thailand

ELEVATION

	3300m
	2700m
	2100m
	1500m
	900m
	600m
	300m
	0

Hanoi (Vietnam)
The historic heartbeat of Vietnam (p50)

Halong Bay (Vietnam)
See nature at its outrageous best (p68)

Hainan Island (China)

Phong Nha-Ke Bang National Park (Vietnam)
Stunning cave systems (p83)

Vieng Xai Caves (Laos)
If these cave walls could talk (p314)

Vang Vieng (Laos)
Outdoorsy pursuits have pushed the party aside (p289)

Sukhothai (Thailand)
Cycle through Thailand's golden age (p434)

CHINA

MYANMAR (BURMA)

LAOS

VIENTIANE

HANOI

Gulf of Tonkin

Halong Bay

Mekong

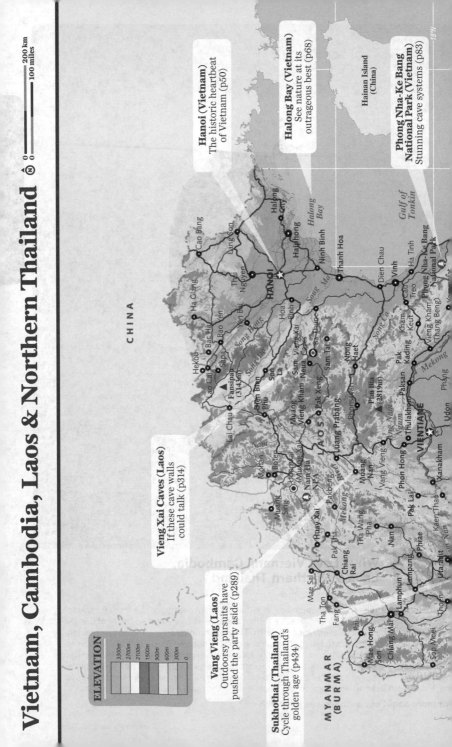

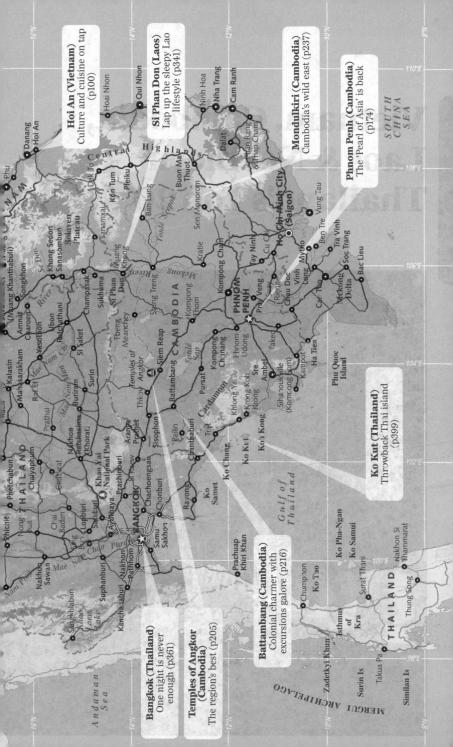

Hoi An (Vietnam)
Culture and cuisine on tap (p100)

Si Phan Don (Laos)
Lap up the sleepy Lao lifestyle (p341)

Mondulkiri (Cambodia)
Cambodia's wild east (p237)

Phnom Penh (Cambodia)
The 'Pearl of Asia' is back (p174)

Ko Kut (Thailand)
Throwback Thai island (p399)

Bangkok (Thailand)
One night is never enough (p361)

Temples of Angkor (Cambodia)
The region's best (p205)

Battambang (Cambodia)
Colonial charmer with excursions galore (p216)

Vietnam, Cambodia, Laos & Northern Thailand's Top 20

Temples of Angkor (Cambodia)

1 One of the world's most magnificent sights, the temples of Angkor (p205) are even better than the superlatives. Choose from Angkor Wat (below), the world's largest religious building; Bayon, one of the world's weirdest; or Ta Prohm, where nature runs amok. Siem Reap is the base from which to explore the world's grandest collection of temples and is a buzzing destination with a superb selection of restaurants and bars. Beyond the temples you'll find floating villages on Tonlé Sap lake, adrenalin activities such as quad biking and microlighting, and cultured pursuits such as cooking classes and birdwatching.

Luang Prabang (Laos)

2 Hemmed in by the Mekong River and Nam Khan (Khan River), this timeless city (p295) of temples is a travel editor's dream; rich in royal history, saffron-clad monks, stunning river views, world-class French cuisine and the best boutique accommodation in Southeast Asia. Hire a bike and explore the tropical peninsula's backstreets; take a cooking class or an elephant trek; or just ease back with a restful massage at one of the many affordable spas. Prepare to adjust your timetable and stay a little longer than planned.

Halong Bay (Vietnam)

3 The stunning combination of karst limestone peaks and sheltered, shimmering seas makes Halong Bay (p68) one of Vietnam's top tourist draws, but with more than 2000 islands there's plenty of superb scenery to go around. Definitely book an overnight cruise and make time for your own special moments on this World Heritage wonder – rising early for an ethereal misty dawn, or piloting a kayak into grottoes and lagoons. If you're hankering for more karst action, move on to the less touristy but equally spectacular Lan Ha Bay.

Bangkok (Thailand)

4 The original City of Angels lives up to its hype as one of Southeast Asia's most buzzing cities. Excuses to delay your trip upcountry include the city's excellent-value accommodation, cheap and spicy eats, unparalleled shopping and a rowdy but fun nightlife scene. Bangkok (p361) also functions as the unofficial gateway to the rest of the region, with cheap flights, cosy train rides, modern buses and a variety of other convenient and comfortable transport options to your next destination - when you finally decide to leave, that is.

Si Phan Don (Laos)

5 Legends don't happen by accident. Laos' hammock-flopping mecca as been catering to weary travellers for ears. While these tropical islands (p341) unded by the waters of the Mekong e best known as a happy haven for tatonic sun-worshippers, more active uls are spoiled for choice. Between bing and cycling through paddy fields, ab a kayak or fish with the locals, round-g off your day with a sunset boat trip to e the rare Irrawaddy dolphin.

Hoi An (Vietnam)

6 Vietnam's most cosmopolitan town (p100), this beautiful, ancient port is replete with gourmet Vietnamese restaurants, hip bars and cafes, quirky boutiques and expert tailors. Immerse yourself in history in the warrenlike lanes of the Old Town, shop till you drop, tour the temples and pagodas, dine like an emperor on a peasant's budget (and learn how to cook like the locals). Then hit glorious An Bang beach, wander along the riverside and bike the back roads. Yes, Hoi An has it all.

Sukhothai (Thailand)

7 Northern Thailand isn't just about hill tribes and trekking. A visit to the awesome ruins of Thailand's 'golden age' at Sukhothai (p434) and Si Satchanalai-Chaliang Historical Parks (p437) also throws a bit of history into the mix. The ruins range from towering Buddha statues to ancient kilns, many of which are amazingly well preserved. Best seen by bicycle, these two parks offer self-guided exploration at its best, and are good outdoor alternatives for those less inclined to the north's more adrenalin-based options.

Phong Nha-Ke Bang National Park (Vietnam)

8 Picture jungle-crowned limestone hi rainforest, turquoise streams and tr ditional villages. Then throw in the globe's most impressive cave systems – Phong N Cave, the ethereal beauty of Paradise Cav and the cathedral-like chambers of Son Doong (below), the world largest cave, an you can see why Phong Nha-Ke Bang (p8 is Vietnam's most rewarding national par to explore. Accommodation options are fast improving, and as it's a little way off th main tourist trail it's a great place to expe ence rural Vietnam at its most majestic.

SHUTTERWORX / GETTY IMAGES ©

Top: Elephant, Mondulkiri

Mondulkiri & Ratanakiri (Cambodia)

9 Eventually the endless rice fields and sugar palms of the Cambodian lowlands give way to the rolling hills of the wild northeast. Spend days trekking amid threatened forests and ethnic minority villages where animism and ancestor worship are still practised. Elephant treks are possible, or visit them in their natural element at the Elephant Valley Project (p237). Add freshwater dolphins and a collection of thunderous waterfalls to the mix and you have the right recipe for adventure.

Phnom Penh (Cambodia)

10 The Cambodian capital (p174) is a chaotic yet charming city that has thrown off the shadows of the past to embrace a brighter future. Boasting one of the most beautiful riverfronts in the region, Phnom Penh is in the midst of a boom, with designer restaurants, funky bars and hip hotels ready to welcome the adventurous. Experience emotional extremes at the inspiring National Museum and the depressing Tuol Sleng Museum. Once the 'Pearl of Asia', Phnom Penh is regaining its shine.

Above: Royal Palace, Phnom Penh

WWW.JETHUYNH.COM / GETTY IMAGES ©

Ho Chi Minh City (Vietnam)

11 Increasingly international, but still unmistakably Vietnamese, the former Saigon's visceral energy will delight big-city devotees. HCMC (p129) doesn't inspire neutrality; either you'll be drawn into its thrilling vortex and hypnotised by the perpetual whir of its orbiting motorbikes, or you'll find the whole experience just too overwhelming. Dive in to be rewarded with a wealth of history, delicious food and a vibrant nightlife that sets the standard for Vietnam. The heat is always on in Saigon; loosen your collar and enjoy.

Sihanoukville (Cambodia)

12 Its reputation for backpacker hedonism notwithstanding, the real appeal of Sihanoukville (p243) is its beaches. Many are on nearby islands such as Koh Rong and Koh Rong Samloem, where resorts are creating a buzz for their laid-back bungalow vibe. On the Cambodian mainland, it's only 5km from Sihanoukville's grittier central beach, Occheuteal, to Otres Beach, still mellow and sublime. More central Victory Beach, Independence Beach, Sokha Beach and even Occheuteal also have their charms – and their own personalities.

Khmer Temple Trail (Thailand)

13 If you want to see Angkor Wat, but don't want the crowds, consider following northeastern Thailand's informal Angkor temple trail from Phimai (p401) to Phanom Rung (p404). The area's Khmer-era ruins cover the spectrum from immaculate to rubble, and visiting them is a good excuse to explore Thailand on rented wheels. In addition to taking in some pretty impressive history, a visit offers a unique chance to experience the laid-back rural lifestyle and unique culture of this little-visited region.
Above right: Phanom Rung Historical Park

attambang (Cambodia)

14 This is the real Cambodia, far from the jet-set destinations of Phnom nh and Siem Reap. Unfurling along the nks of the Sangker River, Battambang 216) is one of the best-preserved colonial-a towns in the country. Streets of charm-g French shophouses host fair-trade cafes here you can arrange bike excursions. eyond Battambang lies the Cambodian untryside and a cluster of ancient temples at mercifully lack the crowds of Angkor at. Further afield lies the world-class Prek al Bird Sanctuary on Tonlé Sap lake.

Vang Vieng (Laos)

15 The riverine jewel in Laos' karst country, Vang Vieng (p289) sits under soaring cliffs beside the Nam Song (Song River) and has an easy, outdoorsy vibe. Since the party crowd was moved on in 2012, tranquillity reigns, with more family-oriented visitors dropping in to soak up well-organised activities such as trekking, hot-air ballooning, caving and climbing, not forgetting the main draw: tubing. Smart boutique hotels and quality restaurants are blossoming too. There's never been a better time to visit.

Ko Chang & Ko Kut (Thailand)

16 These islands are a world apart from the mayhem of Thailand's more popular western gulf islands. Mountainous and mellow, they are closer to the up-and-coming Cambodian islands to the south. Ko Chang's beaches (p395) have developed, but the interior remains vast and wild. Take a jungle trek (and cooling waterfall swim) or ride an elephant through pristine rainforest. Sleepy Ko Kut (p399) has some of the most heavenly stretches of sand in Thailand, fine snorkelling and a jungle-clad interior.

Below: Ban Bang Bao, Ko Chang

Hanoi Old Quarter (Vietnam)

17 Don't worry, it happens to everyone when they first get to Hanoi (p50): getting agreeably lost in the city's ancient Old Quarter, a frantic commercial labyrinth where echoes of the past are filtered and framed by a 21st-century energy. Discover Vietnam's culinary flavours and aromas at street level, perched on a tiny chair eating iconic Hanoi dishes like *pho bo, bun cha* and *banh cuon*. Later at night, join the socialising throngs enjoying refreshingly crisp *bia hoi* (local beer) at makeshift street-corner bars

 EKKACHAI PHOLROJPANYA / GETTY IMAGES ©

TIM BARKER / GETTY IMAGES ©

ieng Xai aves (Laos)

18 This is history writ large in stone. 1 area of outstanding tural beauty, Vieng Xai 314) was home to the thet Lao communist adership during the US mbing campaign of 64–73. Laos became e most heavily bombed untry in the world at this ne and the leadership rrowed into these natu- l caves for protection. A perb audio tour brings e experience alive. hen the bombers buzz erhead to a soundtrack Jimi Hendrix you'll be cking for cover in the d Prince's lush garden.

Chiang Rai Province (Thailand)

19 The days of the Golden Triangle opium trade are over, but intrigue still lingers at Chiang Rai (p437) in the form of fresh-air fun such as trekking and self-guided exploration. It's also a great destination for cultural experiences ranging from a visit to an Akha village to a stay at the Yunnanese-Chinese hamlet of Mae Salong. From the Mekong River to the mountains, Chiang Rai is arguably Thailand's most beautiful province, and if you've set your sights further, it's also a convenient gateway to Laos and China.

Top right: Doi Pha Tang, Chiang Rai province

Gibbon Experience (Laos)

20 Here's your chance to become the Silver Surfer as you whiz high above the forest floor attached to a zipline. These brilliantly engineered cables – some more than 500m long – span forest valleys in the lush Bokeo Nature Reserve (habitat of the black-crested gibbon and Asiatic tiger). Your money goes towards protecting the eponymous endangered primate and your guides are former poachers turned rangers. Zip into and bed down in vertiginously high tree-houses by night, listening to the call of the wild. This is Laos' premier wildlife and adrenalin high (p323).

Need to Know

For more information, see Survival Guide (p483)

Currency
Cambodia: riel (r)
Laos: kip (K)
Thailand: baht (B)
Vietnam: dong (d)

Language
Cambodia: Khmer
Laos: Laotian
Thailand: Thai
Vietnam: Vietnamese

Visas
Cambodia: US$20
on arrival
Laos: US$30–42
on arrival
Thailand: 15-day visa
waivers on arrival
Vietnam: US$45–95
in advance

Money
ATMs widely available in
Thailand and Vietnam,
and in most Cambodian
and Laotian provincial
capitals. Credit cards accepted at most midrange
and top-end hotels.

Mobile Phones
Roaming possible, but
expensive. Local SIM
cards and unlocked
mobile phones available.

Time
Indochina Time (GMT/
UTC plus seven hours).

When to Go

Hanoi
• GO Mar–May

Luang Prabang
GO Oct–Feb

Bangkok
GO Nov–Mar

Siem Reap
• GO Nov–Mar

Ho Chi Minh City
GO Nov–Mar
•

■ Tropical climate, wet & dry seasons
■ Warm to hot summers, mild winters

High Season (Dec–Mar)

➡ Cool and dry in the southern Mekong region.

➡ Cold in Hanoi and the mountains of Laos and Vietnam.

➡ Watch out for Chinese New Year in January/February, when everyone is on the move.

Shoulder (Apr–May & Oct–Nov)

➡ April to May is sweltering hot in the south.

➡ October and November offer good trekking, lush landscapes and a pleasant climate.

➡ Songkram (April) is a blast, but Cambodia, Laos and Thailand begin to slow down.

Low Season (Jun–Sep)

➡ Wet season means emerald green landscapes, and respite from the searing sun.

➡ Big hotel discounts in touristy spots like Angkor Wat.

➡ Thailand remains busy as Western visitors flock for summer holidays.

Useful Websites

Lonely Planet (www.lonelyplanet.com) The online authority in the Mekong region.

Travelfish (www.travelfish.org) Opinionated articles and reviews about the region.

Mekong Tourism (http://mekongtourism.org) Updated links to latest regional travel news and trends.

Golden Triangle Rider (www.GT-rider.com) The motorbiking website for the Mekong region.

Important Numbers

Always remember to drop the initial 0 from the mobile prefix or regional (city) code when dialling into Cambodia, Laos, Thailand or Vietnam from another country.

Cambodia code	⤴855
Laos code	⤴856
Thailand code	⤴66
Vietnam code	⤴84

Exchange Rates

Cambodia	US$1	4000r
Laos	US$1	7800K
Thailand	US$1	30B
Vietnam	US$1	21,000d

For current exchange rates see www.xe.com.

Daily Costs

Budget: Less than US$50

➡ Dorm bed: US$2–3

➡ Cheap guesthouse room: US$5–10

➡ Local meals and street eats: US$1–2

➡ Local buses and trains: US$2–3 per 100km

Midrange: US$50–150

➡ Air-con hotel room: US$15–50

➡ Decent local restaurant meal: US$5–10

➡ Short cab ride: US$2.50–5

➡ Local tour guide per day: US$20

Top End: More than US$150

➡ Boutique hotel or resort: US$50–500

➡ Gastronomic meal with drinks: US$25–75

➡ 4WD rental per day: US$60–120

Getting Around

Trains, planes, automobiles and boats are all viable options.

Air Budget flights plentiful in Thailand; elsewhere air travel overpriced, routes limited.

Boat Losing popularity as roads improve, but still popular on a few routes.

Bus The reliable war horse of the region, will likely be your main form of transport.

Motorbike Great for localised travel; rentals cheap and widely available.

Train Alternative to buses in Thailand and Vietnam; nonexistent in Laos and Cambodia.

Travelling Responsibly

Much of the Mekong region is extremely poor, so consider how you might put a little back into the countries you visit. Staying longer, travelling further and avoiding package tours all help. On shorter stays, consider spending money in local markets and in restaurants and shops that assist disadvantaged locals.

For tips on travelling responsibly while still having the trip of a lifetime, try the following websites:

Friends International (www.friends-international.org) Supports marginalised children and their families across Southeast Asia and runs the global **ChildSafe Network** (www.thinkchildsafe.org) to encourage travellers to behave responsibly with children.

Mekong Responsible Tourism (www.mekongresponsibletourism.org) Runs a list of responsible tour operators and tours in the Mekong region, plus tips on travelling in ways that are culturally sensitive and benefit local communities and the environment.

Ecotourism Laos (www.ecotourismlaos.com) Has comprehensive information on Laos' protected areas, indigenous groups and endangered species, plus a useful 'Do's and Don'ts' section for travelling in the Mekong region.

For much more on **getting around**, see p498

If You Like...

Temples & Tombs

Cambodia is the temple heavyweight but Laos and Thailand are dotted with elegant wats and ancient stupas, while Vietnam has emperors' tombs and pagodas that are a world apart from their Mekong neighbours.

Angkor, Cambodia The one and only, the temples that put all others in the shade. (p205)

Wat Xieng Thong, Laos The jewel in the crown of Luang Prabang's temples, with its roofs sweeping majestically low to the ground. (p297)

Hue, Vietnam Vietnamese emperors constructed dazzling monuments around Hue. Don't miss Tu Duc and Minh Mang. (p85)

Sukhothai, Thailand The ancient capital of one of Thailand's first home-grown kingdoms. (p434)

Prasat Preah Vihear, Cambodia The most mountainous of all Khmer temples, perched imperiously on the cliff-face of the Dangkrek Mountains. (p224)

Wat Phu Champasak, Laos The ancient Khmers once held sway over much of the Mekong region, with hilltop Wat Phu one of their bastions. (p340)

Beautiful Beaches

Vietnam, Cambodia and Thailand all boast lengthy and beautiful coastlines with hidden lagoons, coves, tropical islands and infinite stretches of sand.

Ko Kut, Thailand A paradise island where the crowds are thin, the water aquamarine and clear, the beaches wide and long. (p399)

Phu Quoc, Vietnam Stretching for many kilometres, Long Beach offers white sand in profusion, while Sao Beach is a quieter stretch of sand. (p151)

Otres Beach, Cambodia Tranquillity and 5km of white sand, just 15 minutes from the backpacker party town of Sihanoukville. (p244)

Mui Ne, Vietnam Squeaky sands along the shore, towering sand dunes nearby and expanses of empty beaches up the coast. (p117)

Koh Rong, Cambodia Largely undeveloped island off Sihanoukville has myriad empty beaches and a happy backpacker vibe. (p251)

Ko Samet, Thailand Bangkok expats and locals in the know flock here for good reason: 14 gorgeous white-sand beaches just a half-day from the Thai capital. (p391)

Fabulous Food

There's no surer way to spice up your life than with a culinary odyssey through the Mekong region. Learn the tricks of the trade with a cooking class.

Bangkok, Thailand Food capital of the Mekong region; take a hands-on cooking class at Helping Hands. (p372)

Phnom Penh, Cambodia Dine to make a difference at one of Phnom Penh's many training restaurants to help the disadvantaged. (p174)

Hanoi, Vietnam Dive into Hanoi's famous street-food scene at stalls specialising in *bun cha* (barbecued pork), sticky rice creations, fried eels or crab noodle soup. (p50)

Vientiane, Laos Not just Laos' capital, but its culinary capital – think Laotian home cooking with a Gallic flare. (p273)

IF YOU LIKE... SURREAL SCULPTURE

Buddha Park near the Lao capital Vientiane is one of the more trippy sights in the region. (p277)

Siem Reap, Cambodia Browse the lively restaurants of the Old Market area and choose from exotic barbecues, mod Khmer cuisine or stop-and-dip food stalls. (p194)

Ho Chi Minh City, Vietnam Foodie paradise: roadside stalls, swish gourmet restaurants, to-die-for Vietnamese eateries and international cuisine. (p129)

Luang Prabang, Laos Discover the art of making *mok pa* (steamed fish in banana leaves) at Tamarind, home to traditional Lao cuisine. (p300)

Markets

From ethnic-minority meets in the highlands to floating wholesalers on the river, the Mekong region does markets like nowhere else.

Bac Ha, Vietnam See the unique costume of the Flower Hmong at one of the most colourful markets in Southeast Asia. (p76)

Luang Prabang, Laos The candlelit Handicraft Night Market is an endless ribbon of colourful textiles, paper lanterns and ethnic motifs. (p303)

Chiang Mai, Thailand The weekend 'Walking Streets' offer the chance to shop till you drop, with a bit of culture thrown in for good measure. (p418)

Mekong Delta's floating markets, Vietnam Get up early and experience the Delta's famous floating markets. (p147)

Russian Market, Cambodia Phnom Penh's premier shopping destination; if it's available in Cambodia, it's somewhere here. (p188)

Muang Sing, Laos The new market is a blaze of colour and activity in the early morning as ethnic minorities hit the town to trade. (p321)

Top) Bac Ha (p76), Vietnam
Bottom) Wat Chang Lom, Sukhothai (p434), Thailand

Spectacular Treks

Thailand is the original trekking hot spot but these days all countries of the Mekong offer great hiking featuring mountains, minority cultures and – if you're lucky – rare wildlife.

Sapa, Vietnam Join chatty Hmong guides to explore the ethnic minority villages, framed by cascades of verdant rice terraces, around Sapa. (p77)

Khao Yai National Park, Thailand Spot elephants, monkeys, snakes and creepy-crawlies on treks in Thailand's oldest national park. (p402)

Nam Ha National Protected Area (NPA), Laos This national park offers responsibly coordinated trekking and is one of the best places to see towering original-growth forest. (p317)

Chiang Rai, Thailand Home to a diversity of ethnic groups, the hills around Chiang Rai are one of Thailand's best areas for trekking. (p437)

Mondulkiri, Cambodia Try a trek with a difference or 'walking with the herd' at the Elephant Valley Project. (p237)

Cuc Phuong, Vietnam Hike through wildlife-rich forests and up to tribal villages in Cuc Phuong National Park. (p67)

Cycling & Motorbiking

Adventure motorbiking is huge, including along the legendary Ho Chi Minh Trail in Vietnam and Laos. Cyclists can experience highs in the region's many mountain ranges, or lows along the pancake-flat trails of the Mekong River.

Northwest Loop, Vietnam The spectacular road between Dien Bien Phu and Sapa offers glorious mountain scenery, river valleys and tribal villages. (p77)

Nong Khiaw, Laos Base for adventure cycling trips through beautiful scenery, with responsible local operators. (p305)

Sukhothai, Thailand Explore the first Thai capital, with its 200 temples and stupas, on two wheels. (p435)

Preah Vihear Province, Cambodia Ride Route 66 from Beng Mealea to the lost jungle temple of Preah Khan in northern Cambodia – not for novices.

Tha Khaek, Laos A great place to hire dependable dirt bikes to take you round The Loop and to Tham Kong Lo. (p327)

Kayaking

Kayaks are a perfect (carbon-free) way to explore the region's diverse water systems – from karst-studded Halong Bay and the meandering Mekong River to the islands off southern Cambodia and Thailand's eastern seaboard.

Don Det, Laos Tours out of Don Det in Si Phan Don (4000 Islands) take in fishing villages, million-dollar sunsets, rare Irrawaddy dolphins and thunderous rapids. (p343)

> ### IF YOU LIKE... WHITE-WATER RAFTING
> Thailand's whitest waters are found at the end of the rainy season on the Mae Nam Wa in remote Nan Province. (p445)

Cat Ba, Vietnam Halong Bay's largest and most developed island is the perfect base for paddling excursions in the bay. (p69)

Stung Treng, Cambodia From the dolphin pools on the Lao border, paddle downstream through bird-infested flooded forests, where the Mekong is at its most brilliant. (p231)

Ko Chang, Thailand Propel yourself and a closed-top sea kayak along the clear waters that surround Ko Chang. (p395)

Diving & Snorkelling

Thailand is the dive capital for those exploring the south, but Vietnam also offers a number of decent underwater destinations.

Con Dao Islands, Vietnam Unquestionably the best diving and snorkelling in Vietnam, with bountiful marine life, fine reefs and even a wreck dive. (p120)

Nha Trang, Vietnam The country's most popular diving and snorkelling centre, with several reputable dive operators and fun boat trips for the non-diving fraternity. (p110)

Sihanoukville, Cambodia At Cambodia's most established dive centre, the best action takes place around the more isolated islands far from the coast. (p243)

Phu Quoc, Vietnam Visibility can be a challenge, but there are nice coral gardens and impressive marine life at some sights. (p151)

Ko Rang Protected Marine Park, Thailand The best diving in the eastern Gulf of Thailand is around the uninhabited island of Ko Rang, near Ko Chang. (p396)

Month by Month

Tet/Chinese New Year January/February

Khmer/Lao/Thai New Year April

Rocket Festival May

Pchum Ben September/October

Loi Krathong November

January

This is peak tourist season with the region just about as busy as it gets as Europeans and North Americans escape the cold winter. For serious revellers, January also sees the rare occurrence of two new-year celebrations in a month.

✡ Tet

The Big One! Vietnamese Lunar New Year is Christmas, New Year and birthdays all rolled into one. Travel is difficult at this time, as transport is booked up and many businesses close. Falls in late January or early February.

✡ Chinese New Year

Always occurring at the same time as Vietnamese New Year, these festivities are headline news in major cities in the region such as Phnom Penh and Bangkok. Expect businesses to close for a few days and dragon dances to kick off all over town.

February

Still peak season for the region, and the coastline is busy with sun-seekers. Inland the first round of rice harvesting is over, but in parts of Vietnam and Thailand they are already onto round two.

✡ Bun Wat Phu Champasak

The three-day Wat Phu Champasak Festival has an atmosphere somewhere between a kids' carnival and music festival. The central ceremonies performed are Buddhist, culminating with a dawn parade of monks receiving alms, followed that evening by a candlelit *wien thien* (circumambulation) of the lower shrines.

✡ Makha Bucha

One of three holy days marking important moments of Buddha's life, Makha Bucha falls on the full moon of the third lunar month and commemorates Buddha preaching to 1250 enlightened monks who came to hear him 'without prior summons'. It's mainly a day for temple visits.

✡ Flower Festival

Chiang Mai displays its floral beauty during this three-day event. Flower-bedecked floats parade through town.

April

The hottest time of year, so book an air-con room. New year is ushered in all over the region, including Cambodia, Laos and Thailand. The accompanying water fights are a guaranteed way to keep cool.

✡ Songkran

Songkran, the Thai New Year, is a no-holds-barred countrywide water fight that has to be seen to be believed. Bangkok and Chiang Mai are some of the most raucous battlegrounds. Like Lao and Khmer new year, it always falls in mid-April.

✡ Pi Mai Lao

Lao New Year is one of the most effusive, fun-splashed events in the Lao calendar as houses and Buddha statuary are cleaned, and the country engages in a week-long national water fight with water pistols and buckets of H_2O tossed with great mirth at passers-by. Protect your camera and join in the fun.

✿✿ Chaul Chnam

Khmer New Year is a more subdued event than in neighbouring Laos and Thailand, but water fights still kick off in much of the countryside. It is mainly a family time when city dwellers return to the place of their ancestry to meet distant relatives.

✿✿ Liberation Day

April 30 marks the date in 1975 when Saigon fell to the north and was renamed Ho Chi Minh City. It's celebrated by the Communist Party; expect the reaction to be more subdued in the south.

May

The hottest time of year in many parts of the region; escape to northern Vietnam for springlike weather. This is low season, when visitor numbers drop and prices follow.

✿✿ Chat Preah Nengkal

The Royal Ploughing Ceremony in Cambodia determines the forthcoming harvest for the year. If the royal oxen eat, the harvest will be bountiful; should they refuse, it may spell drought. Also celebrated at the Royal Palace in Bangkok.

✿✿ Rocket Festival

Villagers craft bamboo rockets *(bang fai)* and fire them into the sky to provoke rainfall in the hope that it will bring a bountiful rice harvest. Mainly celebrated in northeastern Thailand and Laos; things can get pretty wild with music, dance and folk theatre. Dates vary from village to village.

✿✿ Visaka Bucha

The holy day of Visaka Bucha falls on the 15th day of the waxing moon in the sixth lunar month and commemorates Buddha's birth, enlightenment and *parinibbana* (passing away). Activities centre around the temple.

June

The wet season begins in much of the Mekong region. Expect brief daily downpours, but much of the time it should be dry. River levels begin to rise again.

✿✿ Hue Festival (Biennial)

Vietnam's biggest cultural event (www.huefestival. com) is held every two years (next is 2016 and 2018). Most of the art, theatre, music, circus and dance performances, including many international acts, are held inside Hue's Citadel.

✿✿ Phi Ta Khon

The Buddhist holy day of Bun Phra Wet is given a Carnival makeover in Dan Sai village in northeastern Thailand. Revellers disguise themselves in garish 'spirit' costumes and

parade through the village streets wielding wooden phalluses and downing rice whisky. Dates vary. (p419)

July

A mini-high in the midst of the low season, the summer months see Europeans head to the region to coincide with long summer holidays back home. The rain keeps falling.

✿✿ Khao Phansaa

Early in the monsoonal rains, Buddhist monks retreat into monasteries in Cambodia, Laos and Thailand. This is the traditional time for young men to enter the monkhood or when monks begin a retreat for study and meditation. Worshippers offer candles and donations to the temples and attend ordinations.

September

The height of the wet season: if places like Bangkok or Phnom Penh are going to flood this is when it usually happens. Occasional typhoons sweep in across Vietnam, wreaking havoc.

✿✿ Pchum Ben

A sort of Cambodian All Souls' Day – respects are paid to the dead through offerings made at wats to resident monks. Often falls in October. Trung Nguyen is a similar festival celebrated in Vietnam, usually in the preceding month.

October

The rains are easing off and farmers prepare for the harvest season. A series of festivals fall around this time and the temples are packed as monks emerge from their retreat.

✵ Bon Om Tuk

Cambodia's Water Festival, held mainly in Phnom Penh, celebrates Jayavarman VII's victory over the Chams in 1177 and the reversal of the Tonlé Sap river. After a stampede killed 347 people in 2010, it was cancelled from 2011 to 2013, but hopes are that it will resume.

✵ Ork Phansaa

The end of the Buddhist Lent (three lunar months after Khao Phansaa) is marked by the *gà·tĭn* ceremony, in which new robes are given to monks by merit-makers. The peculiar natural phenomenon known as the '*naga* fireballs' (p416) coincides with Ork Phansaa.

November

The cool, dry season begins and is an ideal time for lush landscapes. In the far north of the region, temperatures begin to drop.

✵ Loi Krathong

Join Thais in launching floating candles during the festival of Loi Krathong, usually held in early November. In Chiang Mai, the banana-leaf boats are replaced by *yêe peng* (floating paper lanterns).

✵ Bun Pha That Luang

That Luang Festival is tied to the November full moon. Based in Vientiane and lasting a week, this celebration involves music, a lot of drinking, processions to That Luang, fireworks and a cast of many thousands who flock to the capital.

✵ Surin Elephant Roundup

Held on the third weekend of November, Thailand's biggest elephant show celebrates this northeastern province's most famous residents. The event in Surin begins with a colourful elephant parade culminating in a fruit buffet for the pachyderms. (p405)

December

Peak tourism season is back and the weather is fine, so the chances of a white Christmas are very slim unless you happen to be climbing Vietnam's highest peak, Fansipan.

✵ Christmas

We wish you a merry Christmas. Most of the region has adopted Christmas in some shape or form, but for the sizeable Catholic population of Vietnam it is serious business, with important services in churches and cathedrals across the country.

✵ Ramadan

Observed in the Cham areas of Cambodia and Vietnam during October, November or December, the Muslim fasting month requires that Muslims abstain from food, drink, cigarettes and sex between sunrise and sunset.

✵ Lao National Day

This 2 December holiday celebrates the 1975 victory over the monarchy with parades and speeches. Lao national and communist flags are flown around the country. Celebration is mandatory.

Plan Your Trip
Itineraries

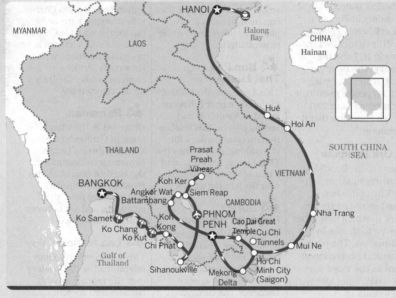

5 WEEKS **The Classic**

Cut a swathe through the fertile belly of the region, taking in iconic temples, verdant landscapes, lush forests and heavenly beaches along with the Mekong's three main metropolises: Bangkok, Phnom Penh and Ho Chi Minh City (Saigon).

Like so many Southeast Asian journeys, yours begins in **Bangkok**. Acclimatise with the sights, sounds, smells and divine culinary flavours of the City of Angels before heading south for some beach time on **Ko Samet**, **Ko Chang** and/or **Ko Kut**.

From here it's an easy hop into Cambodia. You'll land in **Koh Kong**, gateway to the lush Cardamom Mountains. Explore them from idyllic rainforest lodges or the fabulous community-based ecotourism project in **Chi Phat**.

Now make the easy trip to party-happy **Sihanoukville**. Beach bums should budget a few days on offshore islands such as Koh Rong or Koh Rong Samloem before hopping on a plane for the short flight to **Siem Reap**, gateway to the incredible temples of Angkor. See the mother of all temples, **Angkor Wat**, the world's largest religious building; the Bayon with its

Halong Bay (p68), Vietnam

enigmatic faces; and jungle-clad Ta Prohm. Venture further to encounter the usurper capital of **Koh Ker** or the spectacular mountaintop temple of **Prasat Preah Vihear**.

In the wet season, the boat trip from Siem Reap to colonial-flavoured **Battambang** is not to be missed. From Battambang continue south by bus to experience the contrasts of **Phnom Penh**, then make your way to **Ho Chi Minh City** by direct bus or by boat via Chau Doc and the **Mekong Delta**. From HCMC, go underground at the **Cu Chi Tunnels**, then join the faith-

ful at the **Cao Dai Great Temple** before setting your sights on the South China Sea. **Mui Ne** is the logical first stop, especially for kitesurfers. From here, take as long as you want to drift north to Hanoi. Required stops include **Nha Trang**, Vietnam's biggest party beach as well its dive capital; the graceful old port of **Hoi An**, which is loaded with cultural and historic interest and boasts an amazing dining scene; and **Hue**, the old imperial capital and cultural hub of central Vietnam. Wind up with some sea kayaking or a junk cruise among the karsts in **Halong Bay**.

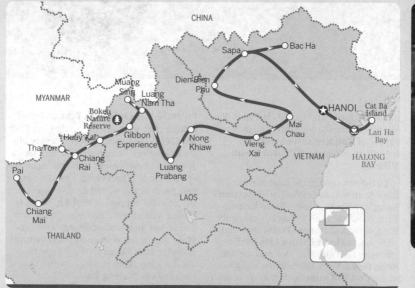

Highland Adventure

4 WEEKS

This itinerary takes you from northern Thailand to Halong Bay, Vietnam, via the rugged and thrilling northern route. Traversing the Mekong's highest mountains, you'll get up close and personal with colourful hill tribes and have a range of outdoor adventures at your disposal.

Start in **Chiang Mai**, where every activity known to athletes – mountain biking, kayaking, abseiling, trekking, ziplining – has a following. Take the winding road to **Pai**, a mountain retreat that proves the hippy trail is alive and well. Then head on to **Tha Ton**, the entry point for rafting trips down to **Chiang Rai**, itself a good base for responsible trekking. Cross into Laos and check out the **Gibbon Experience** at Bokeo Nature Reserve before heading for **Luang Nam Tha**. Spend a day or two trekking with the award-winning Nam Ha Ecoguide Service, before continuing to **Muang Sing**, surrounded by diverse minority villages.

Head south to beautiful **Luang Prabang** on the banks of the Mekong to soak up the culture, before boomeranging north once more to **Nong Khiaw**. From here an adventurous overland trail runs east to Vietnam via **Vieng Xai** and the Pathet Lao Caves, a sort of Cu Chi Tunnels cast in stone. Once over the border in **Mai Chau**, try the northwest loop through **Dien Bien Phu** to experience incredible scenery and dramatic mountain passes.

Sapa, an old French hill station, is the gateway to the minority communities of this region. Consider a side trip to **Bac Ha**, home to the colourful Flower Hmong folk and great walking country. Head south to **Hanoi**, where you'll appreciate that you bought ethnic souvenirs from the minority people and not in the designer boutiques of the Old Quarter.

Still haven't had your fill of adventure? Set off for **Halong Bay**. Take to the waters of **Lan Ha Bay** by local boat to see the 'new' Halong Bay without the tourists. Boating, kayaking and camping are possible, and there are some beautiful hidden coves. Then leave the water behind and head to the spectacular limestone outcrops of **Cat Ba Island**. Experienced craggers will find challenging routes here, and there's instruction available for novice climbers as well.

Top: Rice terraces near Sapa (p77), Vietnam
Bottom: Lanterns, Hanoi (p50), Vietnam

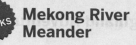

6 WEEKS
Mekong River Meander

This trip follows the famous river downstream from northern Laos all the way to its terminus in Vietnam's Mekong Delta. En route you'll encounter a wide range of landscapes, cultures and adventures as you slice through all four countries of the Mekong region.

Leave behind the bustle of **Bangkok** and make a beeline for **Chiang Rai** near the Golden Triangle, where the borders of Laos, Myanmar (Burma) and Thailand converge. Crossing the Mekong into Laos at **Huay Xai** is like stepping back in time. Take a slow boat down the Mekong to **Luang Prabang**, stopping overnight in **Pak Beng**. Soak up the magic before leaving the river for some relaxation in **Vang Vieng**.

Continue to **Vientiane** and reunite with the mighty waterway. The Lao capital is a sleepy place with some great cafes, restaurants and bars, which you won't be encountering for a while after here. Board a bus and follow the river southeast, stopping off in **Tha Khaek** and **Savannakhet** before arriving in **Pakse**. Visit the imposing Khmer sanctuary of **Wat Phu Champasak**, in the shadow of Lingaparvata Mountain; explore the villages of the **Bolaven Plateau**; or enjoy the islands of **Si Phan Don**.

Cross into Cambodia. If you missed the Irrawaddy dolphins near Don Khon in Si Phan Don, you can see them near the border at **Preah Rumkel**, or a few hours further south in the laid-back Mekong riverside town of **Kratie**. From Kratie, consider peeling off to visit the mountains of **Mondulkiri Province**, home to elephants, hill tribes and pristine nature.

Weeks in rural provinces will have you happy to see **Phnom Penh**, where the Mekong merges with another vital regional waterway, the Tonlé Sap. Take a sunset boat cruise or participate in an aerobics session on the riverfront promenade. When you're recharged, board a fast boat downstream to **Chau Doc**, Vietnam, gateway to the Mekong Delta. Check out **Can Tho**, the Delta's commercial heart. Hotfoot it to **Ho Chi Minh City** for some fun; delve deeper into the delta with a homestay around **Vinh Long**, or make for the tropical retreat of **Phu Quoc Island**, a well-earned reward for following the mother river.

Top: Mekong River, Laos
Bottom: Katu village girl, Bolaven Plateau (p346), Laos

Off the Beaten Track: Vietnam, Cambodia, Laos & Northern Thailand

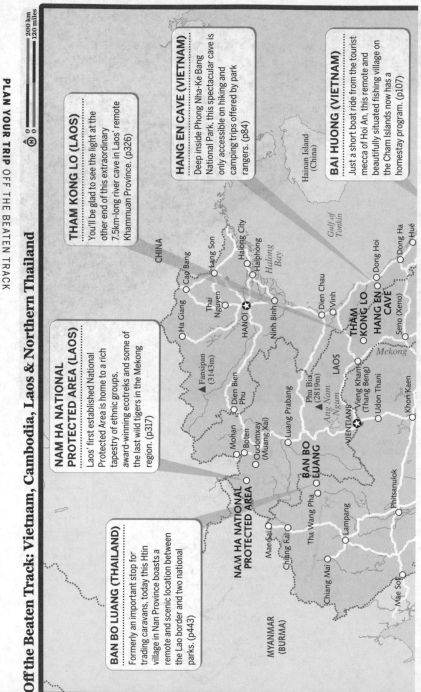

THAM KONG LO (LAOS)

You'll be glad to see the light at the other end of this extraordinary 7.5km-long river cave in Laos' remote Khammuan Province. (p326)

HANG EN CAVE (VIETNAM)

Deep inside Phong Nha-Ke Bang National Park, this spectacular cave is only accessible on hiking and camping trips offered by park rangers. (p84)

BAI HUONG (VIETNAM)

Just a short boat ride from the tourist mecca of Hoi An, this remote and beautifully situated fishing village on the Cham Islands now has a homestay program. (p107)

NAM HA NATIONAL PROTECTED AREA (LAOS)

Laos' first established National Protected Area is home to a rich tapestry of ethnic groups, award-winning ecotreks and some of the last wild tigers in the Mekong region. (p317)

BAN BO LUANG (THAILAND)

Formerly an important stop for trading caravans, today this Htin village in Nan Province boasts a remote and scenic location between the Lao border and two national parks. (p443)

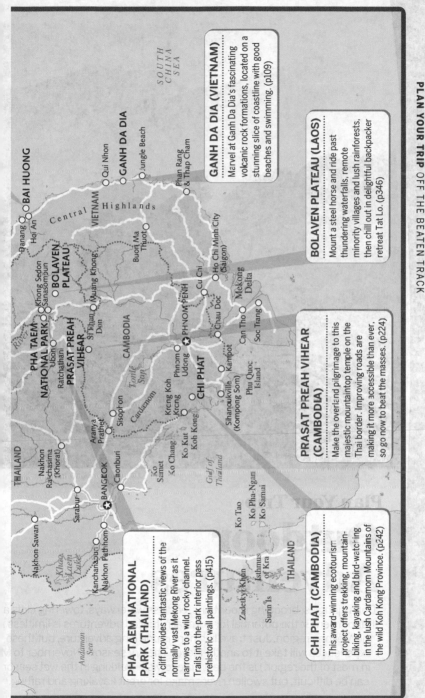

GANH DA DIA (VIETNAM)

Marvel at Ganh Da Dia's fascinating volcanic rock formations, located on a stunning slice of coastline with good beaches and swimming. (p109)

BOLAVEN PLATEAU (LAOS)

Mount a steel horse and ride past thundering waterfalls, remote minority villages and lush rainforests, then chill out in delightful backpacker retreat Tat Lo. (p346)

PRASAT PREAH VIHEAR (CAMBODIA)

Make the overland pilgrimage to this majestic mountaintop temple on the Thai border. Improving roads are making it more accessible than ever, so go now to beat the masses. (p224)

CHI PHAT (CAMBODIA)

This award-winning ecotourism project offers trekking, mountain-biking, kayaking and bird-watching in the lush Cardamom Mountains of the wild Koh Kong Province. (p242)

PHA TAEM NATIONAL PARK (THAILAND)

A cliff provides fantastic views of the normally vast Mekong River as it narrows to a wild, rocky channel. Trails into the park interior pass prehistoric wall paintings. (p415)

Hills around Chiang Mai (p418), Northern Thai

Plan Your Trip

Outdoor Adventures

Dense jungles, brooding mountains, endless waterways, towering cliffs a
hairpin bends: the potential for adrenalin-fuelled adventures is limitless i
the Mekong region. Just travelling here is one long adventure, but these
experiences will take it to another level. The dry season (November to M
in most of the region) is the best time to visit. Trekking in the wet seasor
can be difficult, but swollen rivers make for great kayaking and rafting.

Best Outdoors

Best Trekking

Sapa Superlative views but very popular.

Nam Ha National Protected Area (NPA) Responsible treks in old-growth forest.

Chiang Rai Fascinating hill-tribe terrain.

Ratanakiri Disappear for days in Virachey National Park.

Best Cycling

Mekong Delta Backroads through Vietnam's rice bowl.

Sukhothai Pedal into Thai history.

Muang Sing Cycle by ethnic minority villages.

Angkor Free wheel past ancient wonders.

Best Motorbiking

Mondulkiri Mountains, jungle and a variety of rides.

Luang Namtha Dramatic scenery, fecund forests and minority villages.

Nan Plenty of jungles and parks to explore.

Dien Bien Phu Accessed by precarious mountain roads with glorious views

Best Diving & Snorkelling

Con Dao Remote underwater adventures.

Nha Trang Vietnam's most popular diving.

Koh Rong Head well offshore to dive Cambodia.

Trekking

Trekking is a huge draw in all four countries. Hike one to several days to minority hill-tribe villages, walk a half-day through the jungle to pristine waterfalls, or launch an assault on Fansipan (3143m), the region's highest mountain. The scenery – think plunging highland valleys, tiers of rice paddies and soaring limestone mountains in much of Laos, Thailand and Vietnam – is often remarkable.

Trekking companies are recommended in the relevant sections. You may need special permits, especially if you plan to spend the night in remote mountain villages in parts of Laos and Vietnam.

Prices, including all food, guides, transportation, accommodation and park fees, start at around US$25 per day for larger groups. For more specialised long treks into remote areas, prices can run into several hundred US dollars.

Cambodia

Trekking in northeast Cambodia is beginning to take off in the provinces of **Mondulkiri** (p237) and **Ratanakiri** (p232) thanks to their wild natural scenery, abundant waterfalls and ethnic minority populations. Remote **Virachey National Park** (p236) in Ratanakiri offers the possibility of multiday trips. Some of the most accessible trekking is in the **Cardamom Mountains** (p242) near Koh Kong.

Laos

Trekking through the mountains and forests of Laos is almost a mandatory part of any visit to the country. And thanks to projects aimed at getting money into poor communities, there are now a dozen or more areas you can choose from. **Luang Namtha** (p317) has developed an award-winning ecotourism project for visits to local ethnic minority villages in Nam Ha NPA. In southern Laos, **Xe Pian NPA**, close to Pakse, is great for elephant treks and general hikes. **Dong Natad NPA** has treks through beautiful landscapes, organised by Savannakhet's Eco Guide Unit (p334).

Thailand

The northern Thai cities of **Chiang Mai** (p418) and **Chiang Rai** (p437) are very popular for treks, often in combination with white-water rafting and elephant rides. **Pai** (p432) has also emerged as an alternative place to trek. Many of these treks are run by ethical operators with sustainable trips to help disadvantaged minority peoples, but there are a lot of cowboys out there. At up-and-coming **Pha Taem National Park** (p415), the centrepiece is a long cliff with views over to Laos and a collection of prehistoric rock paintings that are at least 3000 years old.

Vietnam

Vietnam's trekking mecca is **Sapa** (p77). The scenery is remarkable, with majestic mountains, impossibly green rice paddies and some fascinating tribal villages. But the main trails are incredibly popular and some villagers see hiking groups on an hourly basis. **Bac Ha** (p76) is at a lower elevation, less rainy and the trails here are not as heavily tramped. **Phong Nha-Ke Bang National Park** (p83) is just opening up to tourism. Adventure tour operators in **Hoi An** (p100) also offer some intriguing treks in the tribal areas west of town.

Cycling

For hard-core cyclists, the mountains of northern Vietnam and northern Laos are the ultimate destination. For those who like a more gentle workout, meandering along Mekong villages is memorable, particularly in the Mekong Delta in Vietnam. Biking around Angkor is a great way to get around, and Thailand's northeast can be

Cai Be floating market (p147), Mekong Delta, Vietr

rewarding thanks to good roads and light traffic.

Throughout the region, basic bicycles can be rented for US$1 to US$3 per day and good-quality mountain bikes cost US$10 to US$15. When it comes to cycling tours, Bangkok-based **Spice Roads** (www.spiceroads.com) is the acknowledged expert for the Mekong region and Asia beyond, but there are good local operators in each country.

For some laughs, as well as the lowdown on cycling in the Mekong region, visit the website www.mrpumpy.net. Visit the FAQ sections for to-the-point information on what to take and packing your bike on an aeroplane.

SAFETY GUIDELINES FOR HIKERS

➡ Don't stray from established paths, as there are landmines and unexploded ordnance (UXO) in parts of Cambodia, Laos and Vietnam.

➡ Guides are worth hiring; they're inexpensive, speak the language and understand indigenous culture.

➡ Dogs can be aggressive; a stout stick may come in handy.

➡ Boots with ankle support are a great investment.

➡ Carry a mosquito net if trekking in malarial zones of the region.

➡ Consider quality socks and repellent to reduce the likelihood of leeches.

➡ Carry water purification tablets if you have a weak constitution.

➡ Invest in some snack bars or energy snacks to avoid getting 'riced out' on longer treks.

Motorbiking

For those with a thirst for adventure, motorbike trips into remote areas of the region are unforgettable. The mobility of two wheels is unrivalled. Motorbikes can traverse trails that even the hardiest 4WD cannot follow, and put you closer to the countryside – its smells, people and

Cycling in Laos

scenery – compared with getting around by car or bus. Just remember to watch the road, even when the passing scenery is sublime. Motorbiking is still *the* mode of transport for many Mekong residents, so you'll find repair shops everywhere.

Motorbikes are widely available for rent throughout the region. Daily charges start at US$4 to US$10 for 100cc bikes and rise to US$15 to US$50 for 250cc dirt bikes or road bikes. One-way bike rentals are often available in Laos and Cambodia (for an extra fee of course!).

Specialist motorcycle touring companies can organise multiday trips into remote areas using the roads less travelled. Costs for these trips range from US$50 up to US$150 a day or more for the premium tours, depending on accommodation.

Based in Vientiane, the **Midnight Mapper** (p292) is a new GPS service that hires out satellite navigation machines with your route especially programmed in.

Hiring bikes in Thailand usually requires a licence. You rarely need to show a licence to rent a bike in Laos, Cambodia or Vietnam (although actually driving a bike technically requires one). However, in all four countries you almost always need to leave a passport to hire a bike. This can cause problems if you get into an accident in remote Laos or Cambodia and need to be evacuated out of the country (usually to Thailand or Vietnam) to receive adequate medical care. An alternative is to leave a several-hundred dollar deposit to cover the value of the bike.

Boat Trips

With the Mekong cutting a swathe through the heart of the region, it's hardly surprising to find that boat trips are a major drawcard here. There are opportunities to explore small jungled tributaries leading to remote minority villages in Cambodia and Laos. It is possible to explore cave systems by boat in Vietnam, as well as experience the bustle of a floating market in the Mekong Delta. Whole villages float on the waters of Tonlé Sap lake in Cambodia. Cruising the waters of Vietnam's Halong Bay on a junk is one of the most iconic boat trips in the region.

PHOTO TAKEN BY ALAN / ALAN / GETTY IMAGES ©

Boats on the Mekong River

Kayaking & Rafting

There has been an explosion in popularity in kayaking in the past few years. In Vietnam, many standard **Halong Bay** tours now include kayaking through the karsts, or you can choose a kayaking specialist and paddle around majestic limestone pinnacles, before overnighting at a remote bay. Other kayaking destinations in Vietnam include **Cat Ba** (p69), **Phong Nha** (p83), **Dalat** (p122) and rivers of the **Hoi An** (p100) region. In Laos you'll find easy to adrenalin-level kayaking trips offered in **Luang Prabang** (p295), **Nong Khiaw** (p305), **Vang Vieng** (p289) and on **Don Det** (p343) in Si Phan Don (4000 Islands). In Cambodia, you'll find mellow river paddling trips offered in **Stung Treng** (p231), **Kratie** (p228), **Battambang** (p216) and **Kampot** (p252). Sea kayaking opportunities abound on Cambodia's **Otres Beach** (p244), **Koh Rong** and **Koh Rong Samloem** (p251), and over the border on **Ko Chang** (p395), Thailand. Kayaking starts from US$5/20 per hour/day.

Though white-water rafting is in its infancy in the Mekong region and the rivers are fairly tame most of the year, things can get a little more vigorous in the wet season. Rafting in Vietnam is available out of **Dalat** (p122) and **Nha Trang** (p110). In Thailand, it is possible to include rafting on treks out of **Chiang Mai** (p418) or **Chiang Rai** (p437) or, for something more specialised, try a two- to three-day rafting trip out of **Nan** (p445) or **Pai** (p432).

It is also possible to make some functional boat trips that offer beautiful scenery. The two-day boat trip from Huay Xai and the Golden Triangle down to Luang Prabang includes a stunning stretch of the Mekong. Travelling by boat from Chau Doc in the Mekong Delta to Phnom Penh offers a tantalising glimpse of rural life, or go one better with a boat cruise from Ho Chi Minh City to Siem Reap.

ZIPLINING IN LAOS

Ziplining has, well, quite literally taken off in Laos. The **Gibbon Experience** (p323) in Bokeo Nature Reserve pioneered the use of ziplines to explore the jungle canopy. Visitors hang from a zipline and glide through the forest where the gibbons roam. Overnight in treehouses and test-drive the new Gibbon Spa for a massage in the most memorable of locations.

Ecotourism pioneer **Green Discovery** offers an alternative zipline experience for thrill-seekers in southern Laos. **Tree Top Explorer** (p337) is an exciting network of vertiginous ziplines passing over the semi-evergreen canopy of the south's Don Hua Sao NPA. You can ride so close to a giant waterfall you will taste the spray on your lips. Feel the wind on your face on its longest 450m ride, then flop into bed in your comfortable 20m-high treehouse.

Above: Kayaker, Halong Bay (p68), Vietnam

Right: White-water rafting, Pai River (p432), Thailand

JOHN BORTHWICK / GETTY IMAGES ©

Diving & Snorkelling

Compared with destinations like Indonesia and the Philippines, diving and snorkelling opportunities in the Mekong region are limited. Southern Thailand (not covered in this book) has great diving for those heading south from Bangkok. Vietnam, and to a lesser extent Cambodia, have growing dive industries.

The **Con Dao Islands** (p120) offer unquestionably the best diving and snorkelling in Vietnam, with bountiful marine life, fine reefs and even a wreck dive. Two professional dive schools are based here, though it's much more costly than the rest of Vietnam. The most popular place to dive in Vietnam is **Nha Trang** (p110), with plenty of reputable dive operators, whose equipment and training is up to international standards. **Phu Quoc Island** (p151) has some beautiful coral gardens full of marine life, although visibility can be a challenge. Hoi An's two dive schools head to the lovely **Cham Islands** (p107), where the focus is on macro life.

In Cambodia, the best diving is on the islands off the south coast. **Sihanoukville** (p243) has several dive operators, but you're better off basing yourself on **Koh Rong** or **Koh Rong Samloem** (p251) to be closer to the action. Overnights on a boat are possible further offshore near **Koh Tang** or **Koh Prins** (p244).

Responsible Diving

Please consider the following tips when diving and help preserve the ecology and beauty of reefs:

➡ Avoid touching or standing on living marine organisms or dragging equipment across a reef. Polyps can be damaged by even the gentlest contact. If you must hold on to a reef, only touch exposed rock or dead coral.

➡ Be conscious of your fins. Even without contact, the surge from fin strokes near a reef can damage delicate organisms. Take care not to kick up clouds of sand, which can smother organisms.

➡ Practise and maintain proper buoyancy control. Major damage can be done by divers descending too fast and colliding with the reef.

➡ Resist the temptation to collect or buy coral or shells or to take souvenirs from marine archaeological sites (mainly shipwrecks).

➡ Ensure that you take home all your rubbish, and any litter you may find as well. Plastics in particular are a serious threat to marine life.

➡ Do not feed fish.

➡ Minimise your disturbance of marine animals. *Never* ride on the backs of turtles.

Kitesurfing & Windsurfing

In Vietnam, **Mui Ne Beach** (p117) is the undisputed top spot for Asian wind chasers. You can kitesurf in Mui Ne year-round (rare for Southeast Asia), although it is best in the dry season (November to April). **Nha Trang** (p110) and **Vung Tau** are other possibilities. In Cambodia, **Otres Beach** (p244) and **Kampot** (p252) have nascent kitesurfing scenes.

If you've never kitesurfed before, go for a taster lesson (US$80 to US$100) before you enrol in a lengthy course – a three-day course costs around US$275 to US$385.

Surfing

Unfortunately, *that* wave scene in *Apocalypse Now* was shot in the Philippines. The Mekong region is hardly known for surfing, but if you need your fix you can find swell at certain times of the year. Finding a board can be decidedly more problematic, however.

With a 3000km coastline, Vietnam is the obvious top candidate. Your best bet is **Danang** (p97), where there's a small scene and some surf shops with boards for hire. Board hire costs US$5 to US$20 per day, while a two-hour surfing lesson will set you back about US$25. The peak season is December to March, when the waves

---

DIVING & SNORKELLING COSTS

Discover Scuba US$60–80

Two fun dives US$70–80 (US$160 in Con Dao)

PADI Open Water US$350–500

Snorkelling day trip US$20–40

Windsurfers, Mui Ne (p117), Vietnam

arc small but steady. July to November is fickle, but occasional typhoons passing offshore can produce clean peaks over 2m; watch for pollution after heavy rains.

In Cambodia, we have heard of waves happening on Sihanoukville's Otres Beach during the June-to-October wet season, when the southwest monsoon winds are raging, but it's a choppy onshore break. There are a few surfboards and stand-up paddle boards available for rent.

Rock Climbing

When it comes to organised rock climbing, Thailand has the most on offer, but the region is liberally peppered with karsts and climbing in Laos and Vietnam has really taken off. In Vietnam, the pioneers and acknowledged specialists are Asia Outdoors (p70), a highly professional outfit based on Cat Ba that offers instruction for beginners and dedicated trips for rock hounds. In **Dalat** (p122) there are a couple of good adventure tour operators offering climbing and canyoning too.

In Laos, **Vang Vieng** (p289) has some of the best climbing in Southeast Asia with 200 routes – many of them bolted – up the limestone cliffs, along with excellent instructors and safe equipment. Most routes are rated between 4a and 8b. Adam's Rock Climbing School (p291) is the only dedicated climbing outfit in town, with experienced guides and sturdy kit. **Nong Khiaw** has attracted the adventure specialist Green Discovery (p306), with climbs up the limestone karsts under close and experienced instruction.

Climbing costs in the region start from about US$25 to US$30 and rise for more specialised climbs in the Halong Bay area or for instruction.

Wildlife-Watching

While wildlife-spotting may not be quite as straightforward as in the Serengeti, it is still possible to have some world-class encounters in the Mekong region.

You can lean more about gibbon behaviour with a dawn trek to a habituated family in **Cat Tien National Park** (p128),

Vietnam. Listen to the forest slowly come alive with their calls before watching the family go about their everyday lives.

And the **Veun Sai-Siem Pang Conservation Area** (p236) in Cambodia's Ratanakiri Province is home to several hundred northern buff-cheeked gibbons, a species that was only discovered in 2010. Sleep in the jungle and awake before dawn to see and hear semi-habituated families.

At Thailand's remote **Khao Yai National Park** (p402), the massive jungle is home to one of the world's largest monsoon forests. Here you can track shy wildlife, including more than 200 elephants, or hike to hidden waterfalls.

You can learn about the life of the Laotian elephant at the superb **Elephant Conservation Center** (ECC; ☎020-2302 5210; www.elephantconservationcenter.com; 1-day visit US$60, 3-day experience US$175, 6-day ecoexperience US$399), near **Sainyabuli**. Walk with the elephants, learn the art of the mahout and see young jumbos in the nursery. At the Elephant Valley Project (p237) in Cambodia's **Mondulkiri**, you can see these majestic animals in their natural environment by 'walking with the herd' in lush jungles.

Off land, the freshwater Irrawaddy dolphin is one of the rarest mammals on earth, with fewer than 100 inhabiting

Khao Yai National Park (p402), Thail

stretches of the Mekong. Kayak with a small pod on the Lao–Cambodia border, or further south near **Kratie** (p228), northeast Cambodia.

Countries at a Glance

Many a Mekong adventure begins or ends in Bangkok. It works as a convenient launch pad into hilly northern Thailand, the beaches of the eastern Gulf, or Laos and Cambodia to the east.

Laos is the remote backwater of Indochina. Diverse minorities and national parks ensure it is the ecotourism darling of the region. Cambodia is best known for the Angkorian temples around Siem Reap, but also features outstanding beaches on the south coast, fine food in Phnom Penh and wildlife-watching opportunities in the mountainous east. A range of excellent community-based ecotourism initiatives bring much-needed income to more remote areas.

Vietnam is catching up with Thailand fast. Spiralling cities, designer dining and ultra luxury beach resorts point to the future. War relics and traditional minority lifestyles are reminders of the past.

Vietnam

Beaches
Food
History

Blissful Beaches

Vietnam has a voluptuous coastline. Hoi An, Mui Ne and Nha Trang are the big hitters, but there are hundreds of kilometres of empty beaches to discover, including islands such as Phu Quoc and Con Dao.

Delectable Dining

You don't have to be a gastronome to experience the culinary delights of Vietnam. Surf the streets for sumptuous local snacks, discover the bounty of the sea along the lengthy coastline or learn the secrets of the kitchen with a cooking class.

Historic Cities

Explore the bustling Old Quarter of 1000-year-old Hanoi, discover the tombs and royal relics of imperial Hue, and browse the backstreet galleries, cafes and bars of delightful Hoi An – in Vietnam you are literally spoilt for choice when it comes to cities with a story to tell.

p46

Cambodia

Architecture
Good-Cause Tourism
Nature

Ancient Temples

Heard enough about Angkor Wat? Well, don't forget the pre-Angkorian capital of Sambor Prei Kuk, the region's first temple city, or the jungle temples of Preah Vihear Province.

Return the Hospitality

There are many ways to give something back to the communities you visit in Cambodia. Dine at sumptuous training restaurants lending a helping hand to ex-street kids, buy designer dresses stitched by disabled seamstresses or try a community homestay deep in the countryside.

Jungle Adventures

While it's being cut down at an alarming rate, jungle pursuits remain a huge part of travel in remote Cambodia. Bike into the Cardamom Mountains from a base in Chi Phat or trek through the remote and unexplored Virachey National Park in Ratanakiri.

p170

Laos

Forests
Minority Cultures
Jungle Adventures

Wild Ecotrekking

With around 20 National Protected Areas, Laos has more dense forest per square kilometre than anywhere else in Southeast Asia and is begging to be explored. Award-winning ecotreks take you deep into the jungle realm of the clouded leopard, wild elephant and Asiatic tiger.

Meet the Locals

More than 65 tribes compose Laos' colourful ethnic quilt. In the rugged north, rural homestay programs allow you to encounter animism and observe cultures which have changed little in the last century.

Have a Swinging Time

Glide like gibbons on one of a number of tree-canopy ziplines, that take you up close to nature and jaw-dropping jungle views. By night sleep in a tree house and listen for the pre-dawn call of gibbons.

p272

Northern Thailand

Food
Shopping
Communities

Fire up the Taste Buds

Start getting your taste buds in shape, as everything you've heard about Thai food is true. From spicy stir-fries to sadistic salads, chillies form their own food group for Thais.

Markets to Megamalls

Believe us, you've never encountered commerce the way they do it in Thailand. From the megamalls of Bangkok to Chiang Mai's more sedate Saturday and Sunday Walking Streets, you'll inevitably leave Thailand with a souvenir or five.

A Visit Upcountry

Provincial Thailand invites you to see the countryside from the saddle of a motorcycle, live in a homestay in rice-growing country or trek to a remote hill-tribe village. Prerequisites include a Thai phrasebook and a willingness to live like a local; the memories come effortlessly.

p359

On the Road

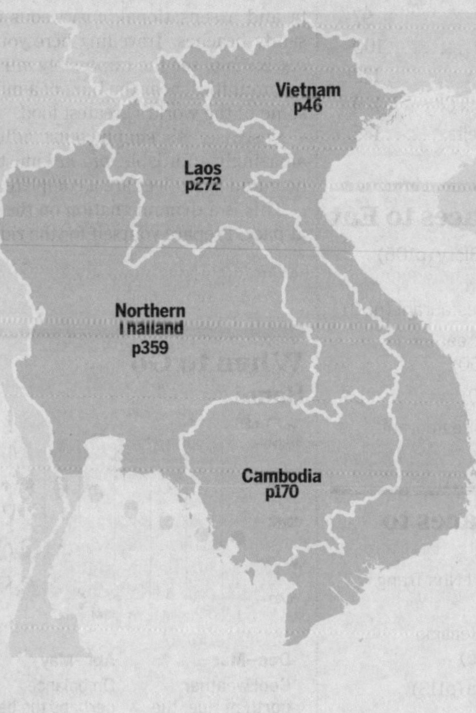

Vietnam
p46

Laos
p272

Northern
Thailand
p359

Cambodia
p170

Vietnam

🔊 84 / POP 92.5 MILLION

Includes ➡

Best Places to Eat

➡ Morning Glory (p106)

➡ Hill Station
Signature Restaurant (p80)

➡ Hanoi's street-food
kitchens (p60)

➡ May (p140)

➡ Lac Canh Restaurant
(p115)

Best Places to Stay

➡ Mia Resort Nha Trang
(p114)

➡ An Bang Seaside
Village (p105)

➡ Sunny Sea (p113)

➡ Sofitel Metropole
Hotel (p58)

➡ Madame Cuc 127 (p137)

Why Go?

Astonishingly exotic and utterly compelling, Vietnam is a kaleidoscope of vivid colours and subtle shades, grand architecture and deeply moving war sites.

Nature has blessed Vietnam with soaring mountains in the north, emerald-green rice paddies in the Mekong Delta and a sensational, curvaceous coastline with ravishing sandy beaches. Travelling here you'll witness children riding buffalo, see the impossibly intricate textiles of hill-tribe communities, hear the buzz of a million motorbikes and eat some of the world's greatest food.

Costwise, it's simply outstanding value: dining out is amazingly affordable, *bia hoi* must be the world's cheapest beer and spa prices are a complete bargain.

This is a dynamic nation on the move, where life is lived at pace. Prepare yourself for the ride of your life.

When to Go
Hanoi

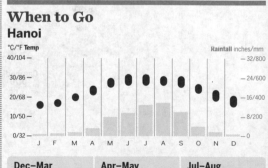

Dec–Mar	Apr–May	Jul–Aug
Cool weather north of Hue; the winter monsoon brings cloud and drizzle.	On balance perhaps the best time to tour the whole nation.	High season on the central coast, with balmy temperatures.

VIETNAM

Connections

Vietnam shares a long border with Laos, with seven possible crossings. Visas for Laos are available at all border posts for most nationalities for between US$30 and US$40, payable in US dollars (other currencies may be accepted too). A passport photo is also required. Crossing from Laos to Vietnam, you must have a visa organised in advance; visas are not available at the border.

There are five main border crossings between Vietnam and Cambodia and many other minor ones. Cambodian visas are available on arrival (US$20) for most nationalities (photo required). Vietnamese visas must be arranged in advance.

ITINERARIES

One Week

Begin in **Hanoi**, immersing yourself in Old Quarter life and touring the capital's sights and famous museums for a couple of days. Then make a day-trip to **Halong Bay** to lap up the surreal karst scenery from the deck of a boat, ideally with a cold beer in hand. Move down to **Hue** to explore the imperial citadel and any number of wonderful pagodas on the banks of the Perfume River. Then shift to **Hoi An** for two days of foodie treats, old-world ambience and beach time. Finish off with a night in **Ho Chi Minh City (HCMC)**.

Two Weeks

Acclimatise in the capital, **Hanoi**. See the sights, then wine and dine. Tour incomparable **Halong Bay** by boat, then take in the extraordinary caves and karsts of **Phong Nha**. **Hue**, city of pagodas and tombs, beckons next before pushing on to charming **Hoi An**. Rest up here, and hit lovely An Bang beach nearby if the climate is benign. Party in **Nha Trang**, Vietnam's beach king, then continue south to idyllic **Mui Ne Beach**. Round things off Saigon-style in Vietnam's liveliest metropolis, **HCMC**.

Internet Resources

→ **Vietnam Coracle** (vietnamcoracle.com) Excellent independent travel advice.

→ **The Word** (www.wordhcmc.com) Based in HCMC, this superb magazine has comprehensive coverage and features.

→ **Thanh Nien News** (www.thanhniennews.com) Government-approved news, but includes diverse and interesting content.

→ **Lonely Planet** (www.lonelyplanet.com/vietnam) Destination information, hotel bookings, traveller forum and more.

NEED TO KNOW

→ **Currency** Dong (d)

→ **Language** Vietnamese

→ **Money** ATMs are widespread

→ **Visas** Required in advance for most nationalities

→ **Mobile phones** Prepay SIM cards for a few dollars

Fast Facts

→ **Area** 329,566 sq km

→ **Capital** Hanoi

→ **Emergency** Police ☏113

Exchange Rates

Australia	A$1	19,045d
Cambodia	10,000r	53,250d
Euro Zone	€1	28,960d
Laos	10,000K	26,330d
Thailand	100B	65,105d
UK	£1	35,110d
USA	US$1	21,085d

Set Your Budget

→ **Budget hotel room** US$8–18

→ **Memorable restaurant meal** US$8–20

→ **Beer in bar** from US$1

→ **Short taxi ride** US$2

Vietnam Highlights

1 Take a trip back in time in **Hoi An's** (p100) maze of cobbled lanes

2 Get seduced by **Hanoi's** (p50) blend of Parisian-style grace and Asian pace

3 Be spellbound by the natural wonder of **Halong Bay** (p68)

4 Discover limestone highlands riddled with extraordinary cave systems in **Phong Nha-Ke Bang National Park** (p83)

5 Be delighted by **Ho Chi Minh City's** (p129) visceral energy and vibrant nightlife

6 Explore the dramatic **Northwest Highlands** (p75), which is dotted with tribal villages

7 Climb and sail those karst peaks on **Cat Ba Island** (p69)

8 Lie back on the pristine beach or kitesurf sick waves in **Mui Ne** (p117)

9 Visit idyllic, remote beaches and dive sites in the **Con Dao Islands** (p120)

10 Follow in the footsteps of emperors in majestic **Hue** (p85)

Hanoi

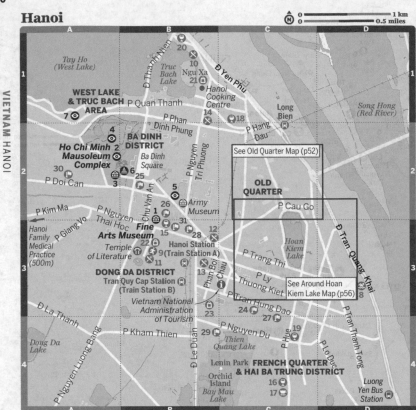

HANOI

📵 04 / POP 6.7 MILLION

The grand old dame of the Orient, Hanoi is the most graceful, atmospheric and captivating capital city in the region. Here, exotic old Asia blends seamlessly with the dynamic face of the continent, an architectural museum piece evolving in harmony with its history, rather than bulldozing through it.

A mass of motorbikes swarms the tangled web of streets of the Old Quarter, a cauldron of commerce for almost 1000 years and still the best place to check the pulse of this resurgent city. Hanoi has it all: ancient history, a colonial legacy and a modern outlook. There's no better place to untangle the paradox that is contemporary Vietnam.

Known by many names down the centuries, Thang Long (City of the Soaring Dragon) is the most evocative, and let there be no doubt that this dragon is on the up.

👁 Sights

Hanoi's sights are scattered throughout the city, but the logical place to start exploring is the Old Quarter.

👁 Old Quarter

This is the Asia we dreamed of from afar. Steeped in history, pulsating with life, bubbling with commerce, buzzing with motorbikes and rich in exotic scents, the Old Quarter is Hanoi's historic heart. Hawkers pound the streets bearing sizzling, smoking baskets that hide a cheap meal. *Pho* (noodle soup) stalls and *bia hoi* (draught beer) dens hug every corner, resonant with the sound of gossip and laughter. It's modern yet medieval, and there's no better way to spend some time in Hanoi than walking these streets, simply soaking up the sights, sounds and smells.

Hanoi

★**Bach Ma Temple** BUDDHIST TEMPLE
(Map p52; cnr P Hang Buom & P Hang Giay; ⊙8-11am & 2-5pm Tue-Sun) FREE In the heart of the Old Quarter, the small Bach Ma Temple is said to be the oldest temple in the city, though much of the current structure dates from the 18th century and a shrine to Confucius was added in 1839. It was originally built by Emperor Ly Thai To in the 11th century to honour a white horse that guided him to this site, where he chose to construct his city walls.

Memorial House HISTORIC BUILDING
(Map p52; 87 P Ma May; admission 5000d; ⊙8.30am-5pm) One of the Old Quarter's best-restored properties, this traditional merchants' house is sparsely but beautifully decorated, with rooms set around two courtyards and filled with fine furniture. Note the high steps between rooms, a traditional design incorporated to stop the flow of bad energy around the property.

There are crafts and trinkets for sale here, including silver jewellery, basketwork and Vietnamese tea sets, and there's usually a calligrapher or other craftsperson at work too.

◎ Around Hoam Kiem Lake

★**National Museum of Vietnamese History** MUSEUM
(Map p56; www.nmvnh.org.vn; 1 P Trang Tien; adult/student 20,000/10,000d; ⊙8am-noon & 1.30-5pm, closed first Mon of the month) The wonderful architecture of the history museum was formerly home to the École Française d'Extrême-Orient in Vietnam. It is an elegant, ochre-coloured structure built between 1925 and 1932. French architect Ernest Hébrard was among the first in Vietnam to incorporate a blend of Chinese and French design elements. Highlights include bronzes from the Dong Son culture (3rd century BC to 3rd century AD), Hindu statuary from the Khmer and Champa kingdoms, and beautiful jewellery from imperial Vietnam.

More recent history includes the struggle against the French and the story of the Communist Party. The breezy garden cafe is a lovely spot for a drink.

★**Hoa Lo Prison Museum** HISTORIC BUILDING
(Map p56; ☎04-3824 6358; cnr P Hoa Lo & P Hai Ba Trung; admission 15,000d; ⊙8am-5pm) This thought-provoking site is all that remains of the former Hoa Lo Prison, ironically nicknamed the 'Hanoi Hilton' by US prisoners of war (POWs) during the American War. Most exhibits relate to the prison's use up to the mid-1950s, focusing on the Vietnamese struggle for independence from France. A gruesome relic is the ominous French guillotine, used to behead Vietnamese revolutionaries. There are also displays focusing on the American pilots who were incarcerated at Hoa Lo during the American War.

These include Pete Peterson (the first US ambassador to a unified Vietnam in 1995)

Old Quarter

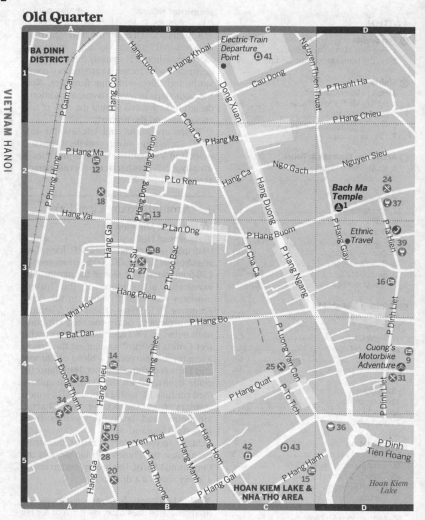

and Senator John McCain (the Republican nominee for the US presidency in 2008). McCain's flight suit is displayed, along with a photograph of Hanoi locals rescuing him from Truc Bach Lake after being shot down in 1967.

★ **Hoan Kiem Lake**   LAKE
(Map p56) Legend claims in the mid-15th century Heaven sent Emperor Le Thai To (Le Loi) a magical sword, which he used to drive the Chinese from Vietnam. After the war a giant golden turtle grabbed the sword and disappeared into the depths to restore the

weapon to its divine owners, inspiring the name Ho Hoan Kiem (Lake of the Restored Sword). Every morning at around 6am local residents practise traditional t'ai chi on the shore.

Ngoc Son Temple   BUDDHIST TEMPLE
(Jade Mountain Temple; Map p56; Hoan Kiem Lake; adult/student 20,000/10,000d; ⊗7.30am-5.30pm) Hanoi's most visited temple sits pretty on a delightful little island in the northern part of Hoan Kiem Lake. An elegant scarlet bridge, Huc (Rising Sun) Bridge, constructed in classical Vietnamese

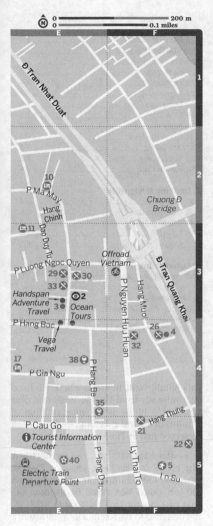

role in Vietnamese society and culture. Labelled in English and French, it's the memories of the wartime contribution by individual heroic women that are most poignant. There is a stunning collection of propaganda posters, as well as costumes, tribal basketware and fabric motifs from Vietnam's ethnic minority groups.

St Joseph Cathedral CHURCH
(Map p56; P Nha Tho; ⊙main gate 5am-noon & 2-7.30pm) FREE The striking neo-Gothic St Joseph Cathedral was inaugurated in 1886, and boasts a soaring facade that faces a little plaza. Its most noteworthy features are its twin bell towers, elaborate altar and fine stained-glass windows. Mass times are listed on a sign on the gates to the left of the cathedral. The main gate is only open when Mass is held.

Guests are welcome at other times of the day, but must enter via the compound of the Diocese of Hanoi, the entrance to which is a block away at 40 P Nha Chung.

⊙ Other Areas

★**Temple of Literature** CONFUCIAN TEMPLE
(Map p50; ☎04-3845 2917; P Quoc Tu Giam; adult/student 20,000/10,000d; ⊙8am-5pm) About 2km west of Hoan Kiem Lake, the Temple of Literature is a rare example of well-preserved traditional Vietnamese architecture. This highly impressive temple was dedicated to Confucius in 1070 by Emperor Ly Thanh Tong and later established as a university for the education of mandarins. Its roofed gateways, low-eaved buildings and five courtyards are typical of 11th-century courtly architecture.

In 1484, Emperor Le Thang Tong ordered the establishment of stelae honouring the men who had received doctorates in triennial examinations dating back to 1442. Each of the 82 stelae that stands here is set on a stone tortoise.

★**Ho Chi Minh Mausoleum Complex** HISTORICAL SITE
(Map p50; entrance cnr P Ngoc Ha & P Doi Can) To the west of the Old Quarter, Ho Chi Minh's mausoleum is an important place of pilgrimage for many Vietnamese.

In the tradition of Lenin, Stalin and Mao, Ho's mausoleum is a monumental marble edifice. Contrary to his desire for a simple cremation, the structure was constructed from materials gathered from all over

style and lined with flags, connects the island to the lake shore.

Inside you'll find some fine ceramics, a gong or two, some ancient bells and a glass case containing a stuffed lake turtle, which is said to have weighed a hefty 250kg.

The nearby **Martyrs' Monument** was erected as a memorial to those who died fighting for Vietnam's independence.

Vietnamese Women's Museum MUSEUM
(Map p56; www.baotangphunu.org.vn; 36 P Ly Thuong Kiet; admission 30,000d; ⊙8am-5pm) This excellent museum showcases women's

Old Quarter

Vietnam between 1973 and 1975. Set deep in the bowels of the building in a glass sarcophagus is the frail, pale body of Ho Chi Minh. The mausoleum is closed for about two months each year while his embalmed body goes to Russia for maintenance.

Within the complex are Ho Chi Minh's mausoleum, stilt house and the Presidential Palace and Ho Chi Minh Museum.

Ho Chi Minh Museum   MUSEUM
(Map p50; ☑04-3846 3757; www.baotanghochi minh.vn; admission 25,000d; ⊙8-11.30am daily & 2-4.30pm Tue-Thu, Sat & Sun) The huge concrete Soviet-style Ho Chi Minh Museum is a triumphalist monument dedicated to the life of the founder of modern Vietnam and to the onward march of revolutionary socialism. Mementos of Ho's life are showcased and there are some fascinating photos and official documents relating to the overthrow of the French and the rise of communism.

Ho Chi Minh's Stilt House   HISTORIC SITE
(Nha San Bac Ho; Map p50; admission 25,000d; ⊙summer 7.30-11am & 2-4pm, winter 8-11am & 1.30-4pm, closed Mon, closed Fri afternoon)

This humble stilt house is where Ho lived intermittently from 1958 to 1969. In a neat garden, the house is an interpretation of a traditional rural dwelling, and has been preserved just as Ho left it.

One Pillar Pagoda   BUDDHIST TEMPLE
(Map p50; P Ong Ich Kiem; admission 25,000d; ⊙summer 7.30-11am & 2-4pm, winter 8-11am & 1.30-4pm, closed Mon, closed Fri afternoon; ⏹) Built by Emperor Ly Thai Tong (r 1028–54) and designed to represent a lotus blossom, a symbol of purity, rising from a sea of sorrow.

★**Vietnam Museum of Ethnology** MUSEUM
(☑04-3756 2193; www.vme.org.vn; Đ Nguyen Van Huyen; admission 40,000d, guide 100,000d, camera fee 50,000d; ⊙8.30am-5.30pm Tue-Sun) Occupying a modern structure, the terrific collection here features well-presented tribal art, artefacts and everyday objects gathered from across the nation. Displays are well labelled in Vietnamese, French and English. For anyone with an interest in Vietnam's minorities, it's an essential visit. It's in the Cau Giay district, 7km from the city centre and around 200,000d each way in a taxi.

★ **Fine Arts Museum** MUSEUM
(Map p50; www.vnfam.vn; 66 P Nguyen Thai Hoc; adult/concession 20,000/7,000d; ⊗8.30am-5pm) Hanoi's excellent Fine Arts Museum is housed in two buildings that were once the French Ministry of Information. Artistic treasures from Vietnam abound, including ancient Champa stone carvings and some astonishing effigies of Quan Am, the thousand-eyed, thousand-armed Goddess of Compassion. Look out for the remarkable lacquered-wood statues of robed Buddhist monks from the Tay Son dynasty as well.

Imperial Citadel HISTORIC SITE
(Map p50; www.hoangthanhthanglong.vn; main entrance 19C P Hoang Dieu; ⊗8.30-11.30am & 2-5pm, closed Mon & Fri) FREE Added to Unesco's World Heritage List in 2010 and reopened in 2012, Hanoi's Imperial Citadel was the hub of Vietnamese military power for over 1000 years. Ongoing archaeological digs of ancient palaces, grandiose pavilions and imperial gates are complemented by fascinating military command bunkers from the American War – complete with maps and 1960s communications equipment – used by the legendary Vietnamese General Vo Nguyen Giap. The leafy grounds are also an easy-going antidote to Hanoi's bustle.

Tay Ho LAKE
(West Lake; Map p50) The city's largest lake, Tay Ho is 15km in circumference and ringed by upmarket suburbs. On the south side, along Đ Thuy Khue, are seafood restaurants, and to the east, the Xuan Dieu strip is lined with restaurants, cafes, boutiques and luxury hotels. You'll also find two temples on its shores, the Tay Ho and Tran Quoc pagodas. A pathway circles the lake, making for a great bicycle ride. To rent a bike contact the **Hanoi Bicycle Collective** (www.thbc.vn; 44 Ngo 31, Xuan Dieu, Tay Ho; bike rental per day from 100,000d; ⊗8am-8pm Tue-Sun).

☆ **Activities**

La Siesta Spa SPA
(Map p52; ☑04-3935 1632; www.zenspa.vn/lasiesta; 32 P Lo Su) Spa, massage and beauty treatments across two floors of the Hanoi Elegance Diamond Hotel.

MOD Palace Hotel SWIMMING
(Map p50; ☑04-3825 2896; 33C P Pham Ngu Lao; admission 65,000d; ⊗6am-8pm) In central Hanoi, the MOD Palace offers day use of its pool, which is big enough for laps.

Zenith Yoga YOGA
(Map p52; ☑0904 356 561; www.zenithyoga vietnam.com; 16 P Duong Thanh; one-off class 250,000d) Yoga, Pilates and meditation classes are all available at this centrally located studio. Downstairs is the Zenith Cafe (p58) with lots of soothing teas and healthy vegetarian food. There's another Zenith Yoga **branch** (Map p50; 111 P Xuan Dieu) near Tay Ho.

🍴 **Courses**

Hanoi Cooking Centre COOKING
(Map p50; ☑04-3715 0088; www.hanoicooking centre.com; 44 P Chau Long; per class US$55) Excellent interactive classes including market visits and a special kids' club. Also runs a highly recommended walking tour exploring Hanoi's street-food scene.

Hidden Hanoi COOKING, LANGUAGE
(☑0912 254 045; www.hiddenhanoi.com.vn; 147 P Nghi Tam, Tay Ho; per class with/without market tour US$55/45) Offers cooking classes from its kitchen near the eastern side of Tay Ho. Options include seafood and village food menus.

Highway 4 COOKING
(Map p52; ☑04-3715 0577; www.highway4.com; 3 Hang Tre; per class US$50) Classes incorporate a *cyclo* (bicycle rickshaw) ride and market tour.

🛏 **Sleeping**

Most budget and midrange visitors make for the Old Quarter or the neighbouring Hoan Kiem Lake area for accommodation. Luxury places tend to be further afield.

🛏 **Old Quarter**

May De Ville Backpackers HOSTEL $
(Map p52; ☑04-3935 2468; www.maydevilleback packershostel.com; 1 Hai Tuong, P Ta Hien; dm US$6, d US$30-35; ✳@ ⚡) A short walk from Ta Hien's bars, May De Ville is one of Hanoi's best hostels. Dorms are spotless and there's also a movie room. Doubles are good value.

Hanoi Backpackers 2 HOSTEL $
(Map p52; ☑04-3935 1890; www.hanoibackpackers hostel.com; 9 Ma May; dm US$7.50, tw & d US$25; ✳@ ⚡) Options range from spotless dorms to designer doubles, and there's a restaurant and bar downstairs. The relaxed team at reception arranges well-run tours including excursions to Halong Bay and Sapa.

Around Hoan Kiem Lake

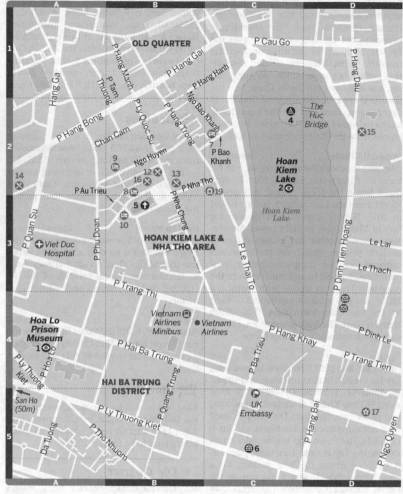

Hanoi Hostel 1 HOSTEL **$**
(Map p52; ☏0972 844 804; www.vietnam-hostel.
com; 91C P Hang Ma; dm/d/tr US$6/16/21; 🛜)
Well run and clean with lots of tours on tap
and plenty of information about onward
travel to China and Laos. Look forward
to a more local location outside of Hanoi's
backpacker scrum.

Hanoi Hostel 2 HOSTEL **$**
(Map p52; ☏0972 844 804; www.vietnam-hostel.
com; 32 P Hang Vai; dm/d/tr US$6/18/21; 🛜)
More tours, traveller information and clean
rooms at the Hanoi Hostel's second Old

Quarter location. A private family room for
four people (US$25) is also available.

Hanoi Rendezvous Hotel HOTEL **$**
(Map p52; ☏04-3828 5777; www.hanoirendezvous
hotel.com; 31 Hang Dieu; dm/s/d/tr US$7.50/
25/30/35; 🕸@🛜) Deliciously close to several brilliant street-food places, Hanoi Rendezvous features spacious rooms, friendly
staff and well-run tours to Halong Bay, Cat
Ba Island and Sapa.

⭐**Hanoi Elite** BOUTIQUE HOTEL **$$**
(Map p52; ☏04-3828 1711; www.hanoielitehotel.
com; 10/5032 Dao Duy Tu; r US$50-55; 🕸@🛜)

VIETNAM HANOI

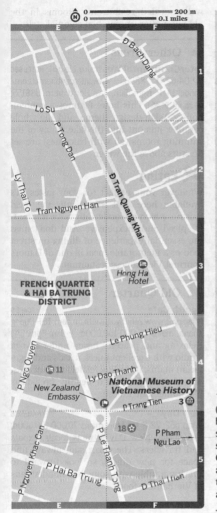

0 — 200 m
0 — 0.1 miles

Ð Bach Dang

Lo Su

P Tong Dan

Ly Thai To

Tran Nguyen Han

Ð Tran Quang Khai

Hong Ha Hotel

FRENCH QUARTER & HAI BA TRUNG DISTRICT

Le Phung Hieu

P Ngo Quyen

11

New Zealand Embassy

Ly Dao Thanh

National Museum of Vietnamese History 3

P Trang Tien

18

P Pham Ngu Lao

P Nguyen Khac Can

P Hai Ba Trung

P Le Thanh Tong

D Thai Tran

Around Hoan Kiem Lake

Top Sights
1	Hoa Lo Prison Museum	A4
2	Hoan Kiem Lake	C2
3	National Museum of Vietnamese History	F4

Sights
4	Ngoc Son Temple	C2
5	St Joseph Cathedral	B3
6	Vietnamese Women's Museum	C5

Sleeping
7	6 on Sixteen	C2
8	Cinnamon Hotel	B2
9	Hanoi Backpackers Hostel	B2
10	Joseph's Hotel	B3
11	Sofitel Metropole Hotel	E4

Eating
12	Banh Ghoi	B2
13	Hanoi House	B2
14	Hanoi Social Club	A2
15	Pho Thin	D2
16	The Cart	B2

Entertainment
17	Cinematheque	D5
18	Hanoi Opera House	F5

Shopping
19	Things of Substance	C2

★ **Calypso Legend Hotel** BOUTIQUE HOTEL $$
(Map p52; 04-3935 2751; www.calypsolegend hotel.com; 11A Trung Yen, P Dinh Liet; r US$50-58, ste US$80-85; ❄❋@☎) Tucked away in a small lane, it's a bit of a mission to find the Calypso Legend, but definitely worth it. Red and white combines for romantic decor, and the reception team is unfailingly friendly and helpful.

Tirant Hotel HOTEL $$
(Map p52; 04-6269 8899; www.tiranthotel. com; 38 Gia Ngu; s/d from US$55/65; ❋@☎) Trendy decor, switched-on staff who speak excellent English and spacious bedrooms all conspire to make this one of central Hanoi's best hotels. The buffet breakfast is definitely worth lingering for.

Art Hotel HOTEL $$
(Map p52; 04-3923 3868; www.hanoiarthotel. com; 65 P Hang Dieu; s/d from US$30/45; ❋@☎) The young, friendly and welcoming crew at the Art Hotel make this well-located spot really stand out. Rooms are spacious with spotless bathrooms and wooden floors,

Features cool and classy decor, top-notch staff and the kind of touches – rainforest shower heads, breakfasts cooked to order and in-room computers – you'd expect from more expensive accommodation.

★ **Art Trendy Hotel** HOTEL $$
(Map p52; 04-3923 4294; www.arttrendyhotel. com; 6 Hang But; r US$45-70; ❄❋@☎) Rooms are stylish and relatively spacious, and there's a real can-do attitude and friendly style from all the exceptional staff here. Each room has a laptop, and breakfast includes warm baguettes, omelettes and fresh fruit.

and within a 30m radius you'll find some of Hanoi's best opportunities for partaking in the city's great street food.

Around Hoan Kiem Lake

Madame Moon Guesthouse   GUESTHOUSE $
(Map p52; 04-3938 1255; www.madammoonguesthouse.com; 17 Hang Hanh; r US$23-27; ✲@🕸) Keeping it simple just one block from Hoan Kiem Lake, Madame Moon has surprisingly chic rooms and a (relatively) traffic-free location in a street filled with local cafes and bars.

Hanoi Backpackers Hostel   HOSTEL $
(Map p56; 04-3828 5372; www.hanoibackpackershostel.com; 48 P Ngo Huyen; dm/r US$7.50/25; ✲@🕸) An efficient, perennially popular hostel now occupying two buildings on a quiet lane. It's impressively organised, with custom-built bunk beds and lockers, and the dorms all have en-suite bathrooms.

★6 on Sixteen   BOUTIQUE HOTEL $$
(Map p56; 04-6673 6729; www.sixonsixteen.com; 16 P Bao Khanh; r US$72; ✲@🕸) Adorned with designer textiles, ethnic art and interesting locally made furniture, 6 on Sixteen has a welcoming ambience. There are just six concisely decorated rooms, but lots of shared areas. Book a balcony room as rooms at the back have tiny windows.

Cinnamon Hotel   BOUTIQUE HOTEL $$
(Map p56; 04-3938 0430; www.cinnamonhotel.net; 26 P Au Trieu; r US$58-65; ⊖✲@🕸) A hip hotel overlooking St Joseph Cathedral. The design is outstanding, combining the historic features of the building – wrought iron and window shutters – with Japanese-influenced interiors and modern gadgetry. There's also a small bar-restaurant.

Joseph's Hotel   HOTEL $$
(Map p56; 04-3939 1048; www.josephshotel.com; 5 P Au Trieu; r from US$40; ✲@🕸) Tucked away in a quiet lane behind St Joseph Cathedral, this compact 10-room hotel features pastel tones, mod-Asian decor and breakfasts cooked to order. Try to secure a room with views of the church's nearby towers.

★Sofitel Metropole Hotel   HOTEL $$$
(Map p56; 04-3826 6919; www.sofitel.com; 15 P Ngo Quyen; r from US$220; ✲@🕸) A refined place to stay, the Metropole boasts an immaculately restored colonial facade, mahogany-panelled reception rooms and well-regarded restaurants. Rooms in the old wing offer unmatched colonial style.

Other Areas

InterContinental Westlake Hanoi   HOTEL $$$
(04-6270 8888; www.intercontinental.com/hanoi; 1A P Nghi Tam, Tay Ho; d from US$155; ⊖✲@🕸) This hotel features a contemporary Asian-design theme, and the whole complex juts out into the lake. Many of the stunning rooms (all with balconies) are set on stilts above the water.

Eating

Whatever your budget (or your tastes) it's available here. Get stuck into the local cuisine, which is wonderfully tasty, fragrantly spiced and inexpensive. And don't miss the essential experience of dining on street food or a memorable meal in one of Hanoi's gourmet Vietnamese restaurants.

Old Quarter

Zenith Cafe   CAFE $
(Map p52; www.zenithyogavietnam.com; 16 P Duong Thanh; mains 45,000-100,000d; ⊙9am-6pm; 🍴) Relaxing and peaceful haven under a yoga studio with excellent juices, salads and vegetarian mains, including felafel and hummus, goat-cheese pizzas and healthy breakfasts like homemade muesli.

New Day   VIETNAMESE $
(Map p52; 72 P Ma May; mains 70,000-100,000d; ⊙8am-late) New Day attracts locals, expats and travellers. The eager staff always find space for new diners, so look forward to sharing a table with some like-minded fans of Vietnamese food.

Nola   CAFE $
(Map p52; 89 P Ma May; snacks 30,000-60,000d; ⊙9am-midnight) Retro furniture is mixed and matched in this bohemian labyrinth tucked away from Ma May's tourist bustle. Pop in for a coffee and banana bread, or return after dark for one of Hanoi's best little bars.

Highway 4   VIETNAMESE $$
(Map p52; 04-3926 0639; www.highway4.com; 3 P Hang Tre; mains 125,000-275,000d; ⊙noon-late) This is the original location of a family of restaurants pioneering the development of Vietnamese cuisine. Try bite-sized snacks like *nem ca xa lo* (catfish spring rolls). There's another **branch** (Map p52; 25 P Bat Su) in the Old Quarter.

Yin & Yang VIETNAMESE $$
(Map p52; 78 P Ma May; mains 100,000-130,000đ; ☺8am-late; 🖥) This atmospheric spot along touristy Ma May stands out with well-priced versions of Vietnamese classics like *bun cha* (barbecued pork) and banana flower salad. Don't leave town without having a Yin & Yang mojito.

Cha Ca Thang Long VIETNAMESE $$
(Map p52; 📞04-3824 5115; 21 P Duong Thanh; cha ca fish 180,000đ; ☺10am-3pm & 5-10pm) *Cha ca* is an iconic Hanoi dish: bring along your DIY cooking skills here and grill your own succulent fish with a little shrimp paste and plenty of herbs.

Foodshop 45 INDIAN $$
(Map p52; www.foodshop45.com; 32 P Hang Buom; meals 100,000-150,000đ; ☺10am-10.30pm) A new Old Quarter branch now showcases Hanoi's best Indian food. This spot is definitely convenient, but the lakeside location of the original **Foodshop 45** (Map p50; 📞04-3716 2959; www.foodshop45.com; 59 P Truc Bach; meals 100,000-150,000đ; ☺10am-10.30pm) is more atmospheric. Either way, the curries are great, and the beers are exceedingly well chilled.

Quan Bia Minh VIETNAMESE $$
(Map p52; 7A P Dinh Liet; mains 90,000-130,000đ; ☺8am-late) This *bia hoi* joint has evolved into an Old Quarter favourite with well-priced Vietnamese food and excellent service led by the eponymous Mrs Minh.

Green Mango MEDITERRANEAN $$
(Map p52; 📞04-3928 9917; www.greenmango. vn; 18 P Hang Quat; meals 200,000-250,000đ; ☺noon-late) A hip restaurant-cum-lounge has a real vibe as well as great cooking. The stunning dining rooms, complete with rich silk drapes, evoke the feel of an opium den, while the huge rear courtyard comes into its own on summer nights. Menu-wise there's everything from pizza and pasta to mod-Asian fusion creations.

✕ Around Hoan Kiem Lake

Hanoi House CAFE $
(Map p56; www.thehanoihouse.com; 48A P Ly Quoc Su; snacks 40,000-60,000đ; ☺8.30am-11pm; 🖥) A chic and bohemian cafe with superb upstairs views of St Joseph Cathedral. Chill out on the impossibly slim balcony with excellent juices and Hanoi's best ginger tea.

The Cart CAFE $
(Map p56; www.thecartfood.com; 10 Tho Xuong; snacks & juices 40,000đ-80,000đ; ☺7.30am-5pm; 🖥🖊) Superlative pies, excellent juices and smoothies, and interesting baguette sandwiches feature at this little haven of Western comfort food tucked away near St Joseph Cathedral.

Hanoi Social Club CAFE $$
(Map p56; www.facebook.com/TheHanoiSocial-Club; 6 Hoi Vu; mains 95,000-160,000đ; ☺8am-11pm) On three funky levels with retro furniture, this is the city's most cosmopolitan cafe. Also works as a good spot for a beer or wine and hosts regular gigs and events (check its Facebook page).

✕ Greater Hanoi

Net Hue VIETNAMESE $
(Map p50; cnr P Hang Bong & P Cam Chi; snacks & mains from 35,000đ; ☺11am-9pm) Net Hue is well priced for such comfortable surroundings. Head to the top floor for the nicest ambience and enjoy Hue-style dishes like *banh nam* (steamed rice pancake with minced shrimp).

Quan An Ngon VIETNAMESE $
(Map p50; www.ngonhanoi.com.vn; 15 Phan Boi Chau; dishes 60,000-120,000đ; ☺11am-11pm) A number of small kitchens turn out street-food specialities from across Vietnam. To avoid the rush, try to visit just outside the busy lunch and dinner periods, or consider Quan An Ngon's newest **branch** (Map p50; www.ngonhanoi.com.vn; 34 P Phan Đinh Phung; dishes 60,000-120,000đ; ☺11am-11pm) in a lovely French villa just north of the Old Quarter.

★ KOTO CAFE $$
(Map p50; 📞04-3747 0338; www.koto.com.au; 59 P Van Mieu; meals 120,000-160,000đ; ☺7.30am-10pm, closed dinner Mon; 😊) This is a stunning four-storey modernist cafe-bar-restaurant overlooking the Temple of Literature, where the short menu has everything from excellent Vietnamese food to beer-battered fish and chips. KOTO is a not-for-profit project providing career training and guidance to disadvantaged children and teens.

★ Quan Kien VIETNAMESE $$
(📞0983 430 136; www.quankien.com; 143 P Nghi Tam; mains 80,000-130,000đ; ☺11am-11pm) An interesting spot for cuisine from the Hmong, Muong and Tai ethnic minorities.

DON'T MISS

THE OLD QUARTER'S TOP STREET FOOD

Instead of just walking on by (and wondering what might have been), squat down on one of those teeny-tiny plastic stools next to a smoking charcoal burner and chow down with the masses. Many stalls have been operating for decades, and most specialise in just one dish. Note that opening hours can be somewhat flexible. Around 40,000d to 60,000d should be sufficient per person.

Bun Cha Nem Cua Be Dac Kim (Map p52; 67 P Duong Thanh; ⊙11am-7pm) Visiting Hanoi and not eating *bun cha* (barbecued pork) should be classed as a capital offence.

Banh Cuon (Map p52; 14 P Hang Ga; ⊙8am-3pm) Gossamer-light *banh cuon* – steamed rice crêpes filled with minced pork, mushrooms and ground shrimp.

Pho Thin (Map p56; 61 Dinh Tien Hoang; ⊙6am-3pm) Excellent *pho bo* (beef noodle soup).

Banh Ghoi (Map p56; 52 P Ly Quoc Su; ⊙10am-7pm) Deep-fried pastries crammed with pork, vermicelli and mushrooms.

Bun Oc Saigon (Map p52; cnr P Nguyen Huu Huan & Hang Thung; ⊙11am-11pm) Shellfish specials here include *bun oc* (snail noodle soup) with a hearty dash of tart tamarind.

Bun Bo Nam Bo (Map p52; 67 P Hang Dieu; ⊙11am-10pm) *Bun bo nam bo* (dry noodles with beef) is a zingy southern Vietnamese dish mixed with bean sprouts, garlic, lemongrass and green mango.

Xoi Yen (Map p52; cnr P Nguyen Huu Huan & P Hang Mam; ⊙7am-11pm) Sticky rice topped with goodies including sweet Asian sausage, gooey fried egg and slow-cooked pork.

Mien Xao Luon (Map p52; 87 P Hang Dieu; ⊙7am-2pm) Crunchy fried eels prepared three different ways.

Bun Rieu Cua (Map p52; 40 P Hang Tre; ⊙7-9am) Crab noodle soup laced with fried shallots and garlic, and topped with shrimp paste and chilli.

Try the grilled chicken with wild pepper, traditional Vietnamese *ruou* (Vietnameseswine) made from apricots or apples, and more challenging snacks like grilled ants' eggs and crickets.

Southgate FUSION $$
(Map p50; ☎04-3938 1979; www.southgatehanoi.com; 28 Tong Duy Tan; tapas 90,000-120,000d, mains 150,000-275,000d; ⊙11.30am-midnight Sun-Wed, to 2am Thu-Sat) Tempting fusion tapas and superb desserts – including thyme, honey and yoghurt panna cotta – feature at this stylish restaurant and bar in a wonderfully restored colonial villa.

The Matchbox EUROPEAN, VIETNAMESE $$
(Map p50; ☎04-3734 3098; www.thematchbox.vn; 40 Cao Ba Quat; mains 100,000-290,000d; ⊙8am-10.30pm) Well-priced food with a Mediterranean spin. Pop in for a plate of pasta and a glass of wine, or linger longer over excellent steaks and Australian red wine.

Puku CAFE $$
(Map p50; 18 Tong Duy Tan; mains 70,000-125,000d; ⊙24hr; ☻☎) Kiwi cafe culture with great burgers, Mexican wraps and all-day eggy breakfasts. The coffee is terrific; upstairs shows big-screen live sports.

🍷 Drinking & Nightlife

Hanoi has sophisticated bars, congenial pubs, grungy clubs and *bia hoi* joints by the barrel-load. Cafes come in every persuasion too, from old-school to hip young thing.

Ha Tien in the Old Quarter has a choice of bars and is a good starting or finishing point for a crawl.

Bars

Bar Betta BAR, CAFE
(Map p50; www.facebook.com/barbetta34; 34 Cao Ba Quat; ⊙9am-midnight) Retro decor and a Jazz Age vibe combine with good cocktails, coffee and cool music in this breezy French colonial villa. Two-for-one beers are available from 3pm to 7pm, and the rooftop terrace is essential on a sultry Hanoi night.

Manzi Art Space BAR, CAFE
(Map p50; www.facebook.com/manzihanoi; 14 Phan Huy Ich, Ba Dinh; ⊙cafe 9am-midnight,

shop 10am-6pm) Part cool art gallery and part chic cafe and bar in a restored French villa. Hosts diverse exhibitions of painting, sculpture and photography, and the compact courtyard garden is perfect for a coffee or glass of wine.

Summit Lounge BAR
(Map p50; 20th fl, Sofitel Plaza, 1 Đ Thanh Nien; ⊙4.30pm-late) It's official. The best views in town are from this 20th-floor lounge bar. Order a (pricey) cocktail or beer, grab a spot on the outside deck and take in Truc Bach Lake and great vistas of the city.

Cama ATK BAR
(Map p50; www.cama-atk.com; 73 P Mai Hac De; ⊙6pm-midnight Wed-Sat) Bohemian bar run by CAMA (Hanoi's Club for Art and Music Appreciation). Check the website for what's on, which includes everything from Japanese funk and dancehall DJs through to experimental short films.

Quan Ly BAR
(Map p50; 82 P Le Van Hu; ⊙10am-9pm) One of Hanoi's most traditional *ruou* bars. Kick off with the ginseng one and work your way up to the gecko variation. There's also cheap beer and good Vietnamese food on offer.

Blah Blah BAR
(Map p52; 59B P Hang Be; ⊙7am-late) Hanoi's cosiest bar, so you'll definitely have to chat to other fellow travellers. The music's decent and we're big fans of the Friday night pub quiz at 8pm.

Cheeky Quarter BAR
(Map p52; ☑0936 143 3999; 1 P Ta Hien; ⊙noon-4am) Sociable bar where table footy (foosball) is taken very seriously, and the tunes are contemporary: drum 'n' bass or house music.

Le Pub PUB
(Map p52; ☑04-3926 2104; 25 P Hang Be; ⊙7am-late) A great place to hook up with others. There's a cosy, tavern-like interior (with big screens for sports fans), a street-facing terrace and a rear courtyard.

Mao's Red Lounge BAR
(Map p52; 5 P Ta Hien; ⊙noon-late) Classic dive bar with dim lighting and air thick with tobacco smoke. Drinks are well priced and the music's usually good.

Cafes

Café Duy Tri CAFE
(43A P Yen Phu) In the same location since 1936, this caffeine-infused labyrinth is a Hanoi classic. Try the delicious *ca phe sua chua* (iced coffee with yoghurt).

Cafe Pho Co CAFE
(Map p52; 11 P Hang Gai) This place has plum views over Hoan Kiem Lake. Enter through the silk shop and then via a courtyard. For something deliciously different, try the *ca phe trung da* (coffee topped with a silky-smooth beaten egg white).

Cong Caphe CAFE
(Map p50; 152 P Trieu Viet Vuong) Settle in to the eclectic beats and kitsch communist memorabilia at Cong Caphe.

☆ Entertainment

Cinematheque CINEMA
(Map p56; ☑04-3936 2648; 22A P Hai Ba Trung) This Hanoi institution is a hub for art-house film lovers, and there's a great little cafe-bar here too. It's nominally 'members only', but a 50,000d one-off membership usually secures visitors an always-interesting themed double bill.

Hanoi Rock City LIVE MUSIC
(www.hanoirockcity.com; 27/52 To Ngoc Van, Tay Ho) Hanoi Rock City is tucked away down a residential lane about 7km north of the city near Tay Ho, but it's a journey well worth taking for an eclectic mix including reggae, Hanoi punk and regular electronica nights. A few international acts swing by; check the website or www.newhanoian.xemzi.com.

Hanoi Opera House OPERA
(Map p56; ☑04-3993 0113; 1 P Trang Tien) This French-colonial 900-seat venue was built in 1911. Performances of classical music and opera are periodically held here in the evenings. Check the website www.ticketvn.com for upcoming events.

Municipal Water Puppet Theatre THEATRE
(Map p52; ☑04-3824 9494; www.thanglongwaterpuppet.org; 57B P Dinh Tien Hoang; admission 60,000-100,000d, camera/video 20,000/60,000d; ⊙performances 3.30pm, 5pm, 6.30pm, 8pm & 9.15pm daily, & 10.30am Sat, 9.30am Sun) These shows are a real treat for children. Multilingual programs allow the audience to read up on each vignette as it's performed. Book well ahead, especially during high season.

🛍 Shopping

The Old Quarter is brimming with temptations; price labels signal set prices. As you wander around you'll find cosmetics, fake sunglasses, luxury food, T-shirts, musical instruments, herbal medicines, jewellery, spices, propaganda art, fake English Premier League football kits and much, much more.

Art & Handicrafts

For ethnic minority garb and handicrafts P Hang Bac and P To Tich are good hunting grounds.

North and northwest of Hoan Kiem Lake around P Hang Gai, P To Tich, P Hang Khai and P Cau Go are dozens of shops offering handicrafts (lacquerware, mother-of-pearl,inlay and ceramics) as well as artwork and antiques.

Private art galleries are concentrated on P Trang Tien, between Hoan Kiem Lake and the Opera House.

Viet Art Centre   ART
(Map p50; 📞04-3942 9085; www.vietartcentre.vn; 42 P Yet Kieu; ☉9am-5pm) Contemporary Vietnamese art, including paintings, photography and sculpture.

Craft Link   HANDICRAFTS
(Map p50; 📞04-3843 7710; www.craftlink.com.vn; 43 P Van Mieu; ☉9am-6pm) A not-for-profit organisation near the Temple of Literature that sells quality tribal handicrafts and weavings at fair-trade prices.

Books

Bookworm   BOOKS
(Map p50; www.bookwormhanoi.com; 44 Chau Long; ☉9am-7pm) Stocks over 10,000 new and used English-language books. There's plenty of fiction and it's good on South Asian history and politics.

Markets

Dong Xuan Market   MARKET
(Map p52; ☉6am-7pm) There are hundreds of stalls here and it's a fascinating place to

---

THE 36 STREETS

In the 13th century, Hanoi's 36 guilds established themselves in the city, each taking a different road – hence the original name '36 Streets'. *Hang* means 'merchandise' and is usually followed by the name of the product that was traditionally sold in that street. Thus, P Hang Gai translates as 'Silk Street'.

---

explore if you want to catch a flavour of Hanoian street life. It's 900m north of Hoan Kiem Lake.

Silk Products & Clothing

P Hang Gai, about 100m northwest of Hoan Kiem Lake, and its continuation, P Hang Bong, are good places to look for embroidery and silk (including tailored clothes). Also check out the chic boutiques in the streets around St Joseph Cathedral.

Tan My Design   CLOTHING
(Map p52; www.tanmydesign.com; 61 P Hang Gai; ☉8am-8pm) Stylish clothing, jewellery and accessories, homewares and bed linen.

Things of Substance   CLOTHING
(Map p56; 📞04-3828 6965; 5 P Nha Tho; ☉9am-6pm) Tailored fashions and some off-the-rack items at moderate prices. The staff are professional and speak decent English.

ℹ Information

EMERGENCY
Ambulance (📞115)
Fire (📞114)
Police (📞113)

INTERNET ACCESS
Virtually all budget and midrange hotels offer free internet, with computers in the lobby and wi-fi. You'll find several cybercafes on P Hang Bac in the Old Quarter; rates start at 5000d per hour.

INTERNET RESOURCES
To get the most out of Hanoi, try the following websites:

Hanoi Grapevine (www.hanoigrapevine.com) Information about concerts, art exhibitions and cinema.

TNH Vietnam (www.tnhvietnam.xemzi.com) The premier online resource for visitors and expats; good for up-to-date restaurant and bar reviews.

The Word (www.wordhanoi.com) Online version of the excellent, free monthly magazine *The Word*.

MEDICAL SERVICES
Hanoi Family Medical Practice (📞04-3843 0748; www.vietnammedicalpractice.com; Van Phuc Diplomatic Compound, 298 P Kim Ma; ☉24hr) This practice includes a team of well-respected international physicians and dentists and has 24-hour emergency cover. Prices are high, so check that your medical travel insurance is in order.

SOS International Clinic (📞04-3826 4545; www.internationalsos.com; 51 Xuan Dieu;

SCAM ALERT!

Hanoi is a very safe city on the whole and crimes against tourists are extremely rare. That said, the city certainly has its share of scams. Make sure you report scams to the **Vietnam National Administration of Tourism** (Map p50; ☎04-3942 3760; www. vietnamtourism.gov.vn; 80 Quan Su), which might well pressure the cowboys into cleaning up their act.

➡ **Fake Hotels** Beware of taxis and minibuses at the airport that take unwitting tourists to the wrong hotel. Invariably, the hotel has appropriated the name of another popular property and will then attempt to swindle as much of your money as possible. Check out a room before you check in, and walk on if you have any suspicions.

➡ **Hotel Tours** Some budget-hotel staff have been verbally aggressive and threatened physical violence towards guests who've declined to book tours through their in-house tour agency. Don't feel pressured, and if it persists find another place to stay.

➡ **Women** Walking alone at night is generally safe in the Old Quarter, but you should always be aware of your surroundings. Hailing a taxi is a good idea if it's late and you have a long walk home.

➡ **The Kindness of Strangers** There's a scam going on around Hoan Kiem Lake in which a friendly local approaches you, offering to take you out. You end up at a karaoke bar or a restaurant, where the bill is upwards of US$100. Gay men have been targeted in this way. Exercise caution and follow your instincts.

⊙24hr) English, French, German and Japanese are spoken and there is a dental clinic. It's 5km north of central Hanoi near Tay Ho West Lake.

MONEY
Hanoi has many ATMs. On the main roads around Hoan Kiem Lake are international banks where you can change money and get cash advances on credit cards.

POST
Domestic Post Office (Buu Dien Trung Vong; Map p56; ☎04-3825 7036; 75 P Dinh Tien Hoang; ⊙7am-9pm)

International Postal Office (Map p56; ☎04-3825 2030; cnr P Dinh Tien Hoang & P Dinh Le; ⊙7am-8pm) The entrance is to the right of the domestic office.

TELEPHONE
Guesthouses and internet cafes are convenient for local calls. For international services, internet cafes using Skype offer the cheapest rates.

TOURIST INFORMATION
Tourist Information Center (Map p52; ☎04-3926 3366; P Dinh Tien Hoang; ⊙9am-7pm) City maps and brochures, but privately run with an emphasis on selling tours. In the cafes and bars of the Old Quarter, look for the excellent local magazine *The Word*.

TRAVEL AGENCIES
Hanoi has hundreds of budget travel agencies. It's not advisable to book trips or tickets through guesthouses and hotels. Dealing

directly with tour operators will give you a much better idea of what you'll get for your money, and how many other people you'll be travelling with. Try to seek out tour operators that stick to small groups.

Successful tour operators often have their names cloned by others looking to trade on their reputation, so check addresses and websites carefully.

Ethnic Travel (Map p52; ☎04-3926 1951; www.ethnictravel.com.vn; 35 P Hang Giay; ⊙9am-6pm Mon-Sat, 10am-5pm Sun) Off-the-beaten-track trips across the north in small groups including activity-based trips (hiking, cycling and cooking). Offers Bai Tu Long Bay tours.

Handspan Adventure Travel (Map p52; ☎04-3926 2828; www.handspan.com; 78 P Ma May; ⊙9am-8pm) Sea-kayaking trips in Halong Bay and around Cat Ba Island, jeep tours, mountain biking, trekking. Includes remote areas like Moc Chau, and the *Treasure Junk* for cruising Halong Bay. Also has offices in Sapa and HCMC.

Ocean Tours (Map p52; ☎04-3926 0463; www.oceantours.com.vn; 22 P Hang Bac; ⊙8am-8pm) Well-organised tour operator with Halong Bay and Ba Be National Park options, and 4WD road trips around the northeast.

Vega Travel (Map p52; ☎04-3926 2092; www. vegatravel.vn; cnr P Ma May & 24A P Hang Bac; ⊙8am-8pm) Well-run tours around the north and throughout Vietnam with excellent guides and drivers.

ℹ Getting There & Away

AIR

Hanoi has fewer international flights than Ho Chi Minh City (HCMC), but with a change of aircraft in Hong Kong or Bangkok you can get almost anywhere.

Vietnam Airlines (Map p56; ☎1900 545 486; www.vietnamair.com.vn; 25 P Trang Thi; ⊙8am-5pm Mon-Fri) Links Hanoi to destinations throughout Vietnam including Dalat, Danang, Dien Bien Phu, HCMC, Hue and Nha Trang, all served daily.

Jetstar Airways (☎1900 1550; www.jetstar.com) Operates low-cost flights to Danang, HCMC and Nha Trang.

VietJet Air (☎1900 1886; www.vietjetair.com) This low-cost airline has flights to Hanoi, Nha Trang, Danang, Dalat and Bangkok.

BUS

Hanoi has four main long-distance bus stations, each serving a particular area. It's a good idea to arrange your travel the day before you want to leave. The stations are pretty well organised with ticket offices, displayed schedules and fixed prices.

Gia Lam Bus Station (☎04-3827 1569; Đ Ngoc Lam) 3km northeast of the centre on the far bank of the Song Hong (Red River). Serves points east and northeast of Hanoi.

BUSES FROM HANOI

Gia Lam Bus Station

DESTINATION	COST (D)	DURATION (HR)	FREQUENCY
(Bai Chay) Halong City	120,000	3½	every 30min
Haiphong	70,000	2	frequent
Lang Son	100,000	4	every 45min
Mong Cai	260,000	8	hourly (approx)
Lao Cai	250,000	9	6.30pm, 7pm (sleeper)
Sapa	300,000	10	6.30pm, 7pm (sleeper)
Ba Be	180,000	6	noon

Luong Yen Bus Station

DESTINATION	COST (D)	DURATION (HR)	FREQUENCY
HCMC	920,000	40	7am, 10am, 2pm, 6pm
Haiphong	100,000	3	frequent
Lang Son	100,000	3½	frequent
Cat Ba Island	240,000	5	5.20am, 7.20am, 11.20am, 1.20pm

My Dinh Bus Station

DESTINATION	COST (D)	DURATION (HR)	FREQUENCY
Dien Bien Phu	375,000	11	11am, 6pm
Hoa Binh	55,000	3	frequent
Son La	170,000	7	frequent to 1pm

Giap Bat Bus Station

DESTINATION	COST (D)	DURATION (HR)	FREQUENCY
Ninh Binh	70,000	2	frequent 7am-6pm
Dong Hoi	380,000	8	sleepers noon-6.30pm
Dong Ha	380,000	9	sleepers noon-6.30pm
Hue	380,000	10	sleepers noon-6.30pm
Danang	380,000	12	sleepers noon-6.30pm

TRAINS FROM HANOI

DESTINATION	STATION	COST SOFT SEAT/SOFT BERTH (D)	DURATION (HR)
Danang	Hanoi	615,000/942,000	15½-21
Haiphong	Long Bien & Gia Lam	55,000/65,000	2½-3
HCMC	Hanoi	1,175,000/1,690,000	30-41
Hue	Hanoi	535,000/844,000	12-16
Lao Cai	Tran Quy Cap	232,000/478,000	8½-9½
Nha Trang	Hanoi	996,000/1,607,000	19-28

Luong Yen Bus Station (Map p50; ☑04-3942 0477; cnr Tran Quang Khai & Nguyen Khoai) 3km southeast of the Old Quarter and serves destinations to the south and the east, including sleeper buses to Hue and transport to Cat Ba Island.

Note that taxis at Luong Yen are notorious for their dodgy meters. Walk a couple of blocks and hail one off the street.

My Dinh Bus Station (☑04-3768 5549; Đ Pham Hung) 7km west of the city and provides services to the west and the north, including sleeper buses to Dien Bien Phu.

Giap Bat Bus Station (☑04-3864 1467; Đ Giai Phong) 7km south of the train station and used by some buses from Ninh Binh and the south.

Tourist-style minibuses can be booked through most hotels and cafes. Popular destinations include Halong Bay and Sapa. Prices are usually about 30% to 40% higher than the regular public bus, but include a hotel pick-up.

Open-tour bus tickets are available in Hanoi for destinations including Ninh Binh and Hue.

Buses also connect Hanoi with China. Two daily services (at 7.30am and 7.30pm) to Nanning (450,000d, eight hours) leave from the private terminal of **Hong Ha** (Map p56; ☑04-3824 7339; 204 Đ Tran Quang Khai). Tickets should be purchased in advance and you may be asked to show your Chinese visa.

CAR & MOTORCYCLE

Car hire is best arranged via a travel agency or tour operator. The roads in the north are in pretty good shape but expect an average speed of 35km to 40km per hour. You'll definitely need 4WD. Daily rates start at about US$110 a day (including driver and petrol).

Try Hanoi motorbike tour operators for reliable machines.

TRAIN

The main **Hanoi train station** (Ga Hang Co; Train Station A; ☑04-3825 3949; 120 Đ Le Duan; ☺ticket office 7.30am-12.30pm & 1.30-7.30pm) is at the western end of P Tran Hung Dao. Trains from here go to destinations south.

To the right of the main entrance of the train station is a separate ticket office for northbound trains to Lao Cai (for Sapa) and China. Note that all northbound trains leave from a separate station (just behind the main station) called **Tran Quy Cap station** (Train Station B; ☑04-3825 2628; P Tran Quy Cap; ☺ticket office 4am-6am & 4pm-10pm).

To make things even more complicated, some northbound (Lao Cai and Lang Son included) and eastbound (Haiphong) trains depart from **Gia Lam** (Đ Ngoc Lam) on the eastern side of the Song Hong (Red River), and **Long Bien** on the western (city) side of the river. Be sure to ask where you need to go to catch your train.

Schedules, fares, information and advance bookings are available at Vietnam Railways (p169) and Vietnam Impressive (p169), two dependable private booking agents.

It's best to buy tickets at least one day before departure to ensure a seat or sleeper. Travel agents will book train tickets for a commission.

❶ Getting Around

BICYCLE

Many Old Quarter guesthouses and cafes rent bikes for about US$2 per day. Good luck with that traffic.

BUS

Plenty of local buses (fares from 3000d) serve routes around Hanoi but very few tourists bother with them.

CYCLO

A few *cyclo* drivers still frequent the Old Quarter. Settle on a price first and watch for overcharging.

Aim to pay 30,000 to 50,000d for a short journey; night rides cost more.

ELECTRIC TRAIN

Hanoi's ecofriendly **electric train** (per car six passengers) 250,000d; ☺8.30am-10.30pm) is actually a pretty good way to get your bearings. It traverses a network of 14 stops in the Old Quarter and around Hoan Kiem Lake. Catch one at the northern end of the lake; a circuit takes around 40 minutes.

MOTORCYCLE

Offers for *xe om* (motorbike taxi) rides are ubiquitous. A short ride should be about 20,000d, about 5km around 70,000d.

Forget getting around Hanoi by motorbike unless you're very familiar with the city – traffic is relentless, road signs are missing, road manners are non-existent and it's dangerous.

TAXI

Taxis are everywhere. Flag fall is around 20,000d, which takes you 1km or 2km; every kilometre thereafter costs around 15,000d. Some dodgy operators have high-speed meters, so use the following reliable companies:

Mai Linh Taxi (📞04-3822 2666)
Thanh Nga Taxi (📞04-3821 5215)

AROUND HANOI

Ninh Binh

📞 030 / POP 134,000

Ninh Binh, 93km south of Hanoi, isn't a destination in itself, but it's a good base for exploring some quintessentially Vietnamese karst scenery and bucolic countryside (including Tam Coc and Cuc Phuong National Park). However, Ninh Binh has become a big destination for domestic tourists and many of its attractions are heavily commercialised.

🛏 Sleeping & Eating

Accommodation is excellent value here. Most places can arrange tours, and hire out motorbikes and bicycles.

Restaurant choices are very limited, but try the local speciality, *de* (goat meat), usually served with fresh herbs and rice paper. There are also lots of restaurants serving delicious *oc luoc xa* (snails cooked with lemongrass and chilli) in the lanes north of Đ Luong Van Tuy.

Thanh Thuy's Guest House & New Hotel   GUESTHOUSE $
(📞030-387 1811; www.hotelthanhthuy.com; 53 Đ Le Hong Phong; r with fan/air-con from 150,000/250,000d; ❋@🛜) Set well back from the road, this guesthouse's courtyard and restaurant are a great place to meet other travellers. Offers good-value, clean rooms, some with balcony. They also run tours.

Kinh Do Hotel   HOTEL $
(📞030-389 9152; http://kinhdohotel.vn; 18 Đ Phanh Dinh Phung; s/d 140,000/250,000d; ❋@🛜) The service here is excellent – management goes the extra mile, even offering free pick-ups from the bus/train station – and the spacious, clean rooms with high ceilings represent fine value.

★**Thuy Anh Hotel**   HOTEL $$
(📞030-387 1602; www.thuyanhhotel.com; 55A Đ Truong Han Sieu; r old wing US$15-25, r new wing US$25-35; ❀❋@🛜) A well-run place with good-value rooms in the old wing and spotless, tastefully furnished and comfortable rooms in the new wing. The restaurant serves good Vietnamese and Western-style food (including complimentary breakfasts).

ℹ Information

You'll find a cluster of internet cafes on Đ Luong Van Tuy and several ATMs on Đ Tran Hung Dao.

ℹ Getting There & Away

Public buses leave regularly from Giap Bat and Loung Yen bus terminals in Hanoi (70,000d, 2½ hours). The bus station is on the east side of the Van River. Ninh Binh is also a hub on the open-tour bus route.

Ninh Binh is a scheduled stop for some trains travelling between Hanoi and HCMC, but travelling by road is faster.

Around Ninh Binh

Tam Coc

Known as 'Halong Bay on the Rice Paddies' for its huge rock formations jutting out of paddies, Tam Coc has breathtaking scenery.

The only way to see Tam Coc is by **rowboat** (per boat 1/2 people 110,000/140,000d) on the Ngo Dong River. The boats take you through karst caves on this beautiful two-hour trip. Boats seat two passengers (and have no shade); arrive before 9am to beat the crowds, as it can be a bit of a circus thanks to the pushy vendors.

Tam Coc is 9km southwest of Ninh Binh. By car or motorbike, follow Hwy 1 south and turn west at the turn-off.

Chua Bai Dinh

A vast (modern) Buddhist temple complex, **Chua Bai Dinh** (🕑7am-5.45pm) FREE attracts thousands of Vietnamese visitors. Cloister-like walkways pass 500 stone *arhats* (statues of enlightened Buddhists). They line the route up to the triple-roofed Phap Chu pagoda, which contains a 10m-high 100-tonne bronze Buddha. Chua Bai Dinh is 11km northwest of Ninh Binh.

Hoa Lu

Hoa Lu was the capital of Vietnam under the Dinh (968–80) and Le dynasties (980–1009). The **ancient citadel** (admission 10,000d), most of which, sadly, has been destroyed, once covered an area of about 3 sq km.

There is no public transport to Hoa Lu, which is 12km north of Ninh Binh.

Cuc Phuong National Park

♩030 / ELEV 150-648M

One of Vietnam's most important reserves is this **national park** (☑030-384 8006; www. cucphuongtourism.com; adult/child 40,000/ 20,000d). Ho Chi Minh personally took time off from the war in 1963 to dedicate the area as a national park, Vietnam's first. The hills are laced with many grottoes, and the climate is subtropical at the park's lower elevations.

There are excellent trekking opportunities in the park, including a hike (8km return) to an enormous 1000-year-old tree (*Tetrameles nudiflora,* for botany geeks), and to a Muong village where you can also go rafting. A guide is mandatory for longer treks.

◉ Sights

Endangered Primate Rescue Center   CONSERVATION CENTRE

(☑030-384 8002; www.primatecenter.org; ☺9.30-11.30am & 1.30-4.30pm) The Endangered Primate Rescue Center is home to over 140 creatures from 15 species of gibbon, langur and loris. The gibbon is a long-armed, fruit-eating ape; the langur is a long-tailed, tree-dwelling monkey; and the loris is a smaller nocturnal primate with large eyes.

Turtle Conservation Center   CONSERVATION CENTRE

(☑030-384 8090; www.asianturtlenetwork.org; ☺9-11am & 2-4.45pm) The Turtle Conservation Center houses over 1000 turtles from 20 of Vietnam's 25 native species. This includes animals that were confiscated from smugglers. China generates the demand, for culinary and medicinal value.

🛏 Sleeping & Eating

There are three accommodation areas in the park.

At the visitor centre are dark, basic rooms (US$8 per person) and decent en-suite guesthouse rooms (US$25 to US$30); 2km away you'll find attractive bungalows (US$35) overlooking Mac Lake.

The main park centre, 18km from the gate, has simple rooms (US$8 per person), large four-bed rooms (US$25) and a few bungalows (r US$32).

You'll find restaurants (meals 25,000-50,000d) in all three locations. It's important to call ahead and place your order for each meal (except breakfast).

Cuc Phuong can get very busy at weekends and holiday time, when you should make a reservation.

❶ Getting There & Away

Cuc Phuong National Park is 45km west of Ninh Binh; there are irregular bus connections (28,000d, 1½ hours).

NORTHERN VIETNAM

Welcome to the roof of Vietnam, where the mountains of the Tonkinese Alps soar skyward, delivering some of the most spectacular scenery in the country. The attractive old French hill station of Sapa remains the main base in the far north, but nearby Bac Ha is a less-visited alternative for trekking and exploring hill-tribe villages. South of here, the sublime scenery and idyllic lakes of Ba Be National Park are well worth a diversion.

Bizarre but beautiful, Halong Bay is geology gone wild, with hundreds of limestone pinnacles emerging from the waters. North of Halong Bay is the less-visited Bai Tu Long

---

BAI TU LONG BAY

The area immediately northeast of Halong Bay is part of **Bai Tu Long National Park** (☑033-379 3365), which is blessed with spectacular limestone islands every bit as beautiful as its more famous neighbour Halong.

Hanoi travel agencies including Ethnic Travel (p63) run trips into the Bai Tu Long area. Or for more flexibility head overland to Cai Rong and visit the outlying islands by boat from there.

Bay, where nature's spectacular show continues all the way to the Chinese border. Or head to rugged Cat Ba, a verdant island renowned for its hiking, biking, sailing, and world-class rock climbing.

Halong Bay

Majestic and mysterious, inspiring and imperious, Halong Bay's 3000 or more incredible islands rise from the emerald waters of the Gulf of Tonkin. A Unesco World Heritage Site, this mystical seascape of limestone islets is a vision of breathtaking beauty. The islands are dotted with wind-and-wave-eroded grottoes, many now illuminated with technicolor lighting effects. Sadly, litter and trinket-touting vendors are now also part of the experience.

From February through until April, the weather is often cold and drizzly, and the ensuing fog can cause low visibility, although the temperature rarely falls below 10°C. Tropical storms are frequent during the summer months (July to September).

Most visitors sensibly opt for tours that include sleeping on a boat in the bay. Some dodge the humdrum gateway Halong City completely and head for Cat Ba Town, from where trips to less-visited, equally alluring Lan Ha Bay are easily set up.

Halong Bay Management Department (📞033-384 6592; www.halong.org.vn; 166 Đ Le Thanh Tong), 2km west of Halong City, regulates independent cruises on the bay. It's easy to hook up with other people to share a boat with here; rates start at around 50,000d per hour.

Halong City

📞 033 / POP 198,000

Halong City is the main gateway to Halong Bay. Overdeveloped but underloved, the seafront is blighted by high-rise hotels. That said, it has good-value accommodation and

its waterside setting is breathtaking on a fine day.

An elegant suspension bridge connects the western, touristy side of town (known as Bai Chay) with the much more Vietnamese entity (Hon Gai) to the east.

🛏 Sleeping & Eating

The 'hotel alley' of Đ Vuon Dao has more than 50 minihotels, most of them almost identical with comfortable doubles for around US$15. Midrange and top-end hotels are scattered along Đ Halong.

For cheap, filling food there are modest places at the bottom of Đ Vuon Dao with English menus. Seafood lovers should gravitate to the harbourfront Đ Halong, where there's a cluster of good places.

Thanh Hue Hotel   HOTEL $
(📞033-384 7612; Đ Vuon Dao; r US$12-18; ❋ @ 🛜) Look for the powder-blue paint job on this good-value hotel. Most rooms have cracking views of the bay from their balconies.

Novotel   HOTEL $$$
(📞033-384 8108; www.novotelhalongbay.com; Đ Halong; r from US$110; ❂ ❋ @ 🛜 ☲) This hip hotel fuses Asian and Japanese influences with contemporary details. The rooms are simply stunning, with teak floors, marble bathrooms and sliding screens to divide living areas. Facilities include an oval infinity pool, an espresso bar and a great restaurant.

Asia Restaurant   VIETNAMESE $
(📞033-384 6927; 24 Đ Vuon Dao; mains 60,000-100,000d; ⊙10am-10pm) A clean, attractive place that's geared to travellers' tastes, with good Vietnamese food and a smattering of Western favourites.

❶ Getting There & Away

The bus station is 6km south of central Bai Chay, just off Hwy 18. Getting to Cat Ba Island from Halong City can be a pain.

BUSES FROM HALONG CITY

DESTINATION	COST (D)	DURATION (HR)	FREQUENCY
Hanoi	120,000	3½	frequent
Haiphong	70,000	1½	frequent to 3pm
Mong Cai	90,000	4	every 40min to 3pm
Van Don	60,000	1½	approx hourly
Lang Son	110,000	5½	11.45am, 12.45pm
Ninh Binh	94,000	3	every 1½ hours

DON'T MISS

CRUISING THE KARSTS: TOURS TO HALONG BAY

Halong Bay tours sold out of Hanoi start from US$50 per person for a dodgy day trip, rising to around US$200 for two nights on the bay with kayaking. For around US$90 to US$110, you should get a worthwhile overnight cruise.

We get many complaints about poor service, bad food and rats running around boats, but these tend to be on the ultra-budget tours. Spend a little more and enjoy the experience a whole lot more. Most tours include transport, meals and, sometimes, island hikes or kayaking.

Boat tours are sometimes cancelled in bad weather – ascertain in advance what a refund will be. You should also take real care with your valuables if on a day trip (most overnight cruises have lockable cabins).

If you've got more time and want to experience Halong Bay without the crowds, consider heading to Cat Ba Island. From there, tour operators concentrate on Lan Ha Bay, which is relatively untouched and has sublime sandy beaches.

Cat Ba Island

☑ 031 / POP 14,500

Rugged, craggy and jungle-clad Cat Ba, the largest island around Halong Bay, is emerging as northern Vietnam's adventure-sport and ecotourism mecca. There's a terrific roll-call of activities here – sailing trips, birdwatching, biking, hiking and rock climbing – and some fine tour operators organising them.

Lan Ha Bay, off the eastern side of the island, is especially scenic and offers numerous beaches to explore. You could spend a year here discovering a different islet every day, while swimming and snorkelling the bay's turquoise waters. While the vast majority of Halong Bay's islands are uninhabited vertical rocks, Cat Ba has a few fishing villages, as well as a fast-growing town.

Much of Cat Ba Island was declared a national park in 1986 in order to protect the island's diverse ecosystems and wildlife, including the endangered golden-headed langur, the world's rarest primate. There are beautiful beaches, numerous lakes, waterfalls and grottoes in the spectacular limestone hills.

In recent years Cat Ba Town has experienced a hotel boom, and a chain of ugly concrete hotels now frames a once-lovely bay. But its ugliness is skin deep, as the rest of the island and Lan Ha Bay are so alluring.

◉ Sights

Lan Ha Bay   BAY

(admission 30,000d) The 300 or so karst islands of Lan Ha Bay are south and east of Cat Ba Town. Geologically they are an extension of Halong Bay, but these islands lie in a different province of Vietnam. The limestone pinnacles and scenery are just as beautiful as Halong Bay, but these islands have the additional attraction of numerous white-sand beaches.

Lan Ha Bay is a fair way from Halong City, so not as many tourist boats venture to this side of the bay. In short, Lan Ha Bay has a more isolated, off-the-beaten-track appeal.

Sailing, kayaking and rock-climbing trips here are best organised in Cat Ba Town. With hundreds of beaches to choose from, it's easy to find your own private patch of sand for the day. Camping is permitted on gorgeous Hai Pai Beach (also known as Tiger Beach).

Cat Ba National Park   NATIONAL PARK

(☑031-216 350; admission 30,000d; ☺sunrise-sunset) This accessible national park is home to 32 types of mammal and 70 bird species. Mammals in the park include langurs and macaques, wild boar, deer, civets and several species of squirrel, including the giant black squirrel. The golden-headed langur is officially the world's most endangered primate with around 65 remaining, most in this park. Birds include hawks, hornbills and cuckoos.

There's good trekking including a challenging 18km hike through the park up to one of the mountain summits. This is not an easy walk, and is much harder and more slippery after rain. Shorter hiking trails are less hardcore.

To reach the park headquarters at Trung Trang, take a green QH public bus from the docks at Cat Ba Town (20,000d,

20 minutes); buses leave at 8am and 11am. Or *xe om* charge 80,000d one-way.

Hospital Cave
HISTORIC SITE

(☎ 031-368 8215; admission 15,000d; ⊙ 7am-4.30pm) Hospital Cave served both as a secret, bomb-proof hospital during the American War and as a safe house for VC leaders. Built between 1963 and 1965 (with assistance from China), this incredibly well-constructed three-storey feat of engineering was in constant use until 1975.

A guide (most know a few words of English) will show you around the 17 rooms, point out the old operating theatre and take you to the huge natural cavern that was used as a cinema (and even had its own small swimming pool).

The cave is about 10km north of Cat Ba Town.

Cat Co Cove
BEACH

A 15-minute walk southeast from Cat Ba Town, the three Cat Co Cove beaches boast white sand and good swimming, although debris and rubbish in the water can be a problem on some days. The prettiest is Cat Co 2, backed by limestone cliffs, and the site of Cat Ba Beach Resort. Cat Co 1 and 3 also have resorts.

🏃 Activities

Cat Ba is a superb base for adventure sports.

Mountain Biking

Hotels can arrange Chinese mountain bikes (around US$4 per day); Blue Swimmer rents Trek bikes for US$12 per day.

One possible route traverses the heart of the island, past Hospital Cave down to the west coast's mangroves and crab farms, and then loops back to Cat Ba Town past tidal mudflats and deserted beaches.

Rock Climbing

Cat Ba Island and Lan Ha Bay's spectacular limestone cliffs make for world-class rock climbing amid stunning scenery. Asia Outdoors uses licensed and certified instructors and remains the absolute authorities.

Full-day climbing trips including instruction, transport, lunch and gear start at US$60 per person. Climbing and boat trips incorporate kayaking, beach stops and exploring the amazing karst landscape.

Sailing & Kayaking

Blue Swimmer offers sailing excursions to myriad islands around Cat Ba, often including kayaking and sleeping on a private beach.

Plenty of hotels in Cat Ba Town rent kayaks (half-day around US$8). Blue Swimmer's cost a little more, but are ideal for exploring the Cat Ba coast independently.

Sailing excursions on gorgeous Lan Ha Bay and full-day trips on a Chinese junk to Long Chau lighthouse, built by the French in the 1920s, are also possible.

Trekking

Most of Cat Ba Island consists of protected tropical forest. Asia Outdoors and Blue Swimmer both offer a great hike around Cat Ba Island, including taking in Butterfly Valley.

👉 Tours

Tours of the island and boat trips around Halong Bay are offered by nearly every hotel in Cat Ba. Typical prices are around US$20 for day trips including kayaking and US$80 for two-day, one-night tours.

We receive unfavourable feedback – cramped conditions and dodgy food – about some of these trips. Good adventure tour operators understand travellers' needs and will steer you away from the tourist trail to really special areas of Cat Ba, Lan Ha Bay and beyond.

★ Asia Outdoors
ROCK CLIMBING

(☎ 031-368 8450; www.asiaoutdoors.com.vn; Ð 1-4, Cat Ba Town) Climbing instruction is Asia Outdoors' real expertise, but it also offers excellent, well-structured boating, kayaking, biking and hiking trips. Rock up to its office in Noble House (at 6pm every night) to see what's planned.

★ Blue Swimmer
SAILING, KAYAKING

(☎ 0915 063 737, 031-368 8237; www.blueswimmersailing.com; Ben Beo Harbour) A very well-organised, environmentally conscious outfit with superb sailing and kayaking trips, trekking and mountain-biking excursions.

Cat Ba Ventures
BOAT TOUR, KAYAKING

(☎ 0912 467 016, 031-388 8755; www.catbaventures.com; 223 Ð 1-4, Cat Ba Town) This locally owned and operated company offers boat trips out to Halong Bay, kayaking and hiking. Excellent service from Mr Tung is reinforced by numerous reader recommendations.

🛏 Sleeping

Most of the island's hotels are concentrated along the bayfront in Cat Ba Town. Room rates fluctuate greatly between high-season summertime and the slower winter months.

🛏 Cat Ba Town

Thu Ha HOTEL $
(☑ 031-388 8343; Đ 1-4, Cat Ba Town; r US$12-20; ❄☎) With air-con, wi-fi and a seafront location, the Thu Ha offers great value. Negotiate hard for a front room and wake up to sea views.

Le Pont HOSTEL $
(☑ 0165 662 0436; jim.lepontcatba@gmail.com; 62-64 Đ Nui Ngoc; dm US$5, d & tw US$15-20; @☎) The best spot in town for budget-wise backpackers with cheap dorms and OK double and twin rooms. The rooftop bar and terrace is a handy place to meet fellow travellers.

Duc Tuan Hotel HOTEL $
(☑ 031-388 8783; www.catbatravelservice.com; 210 Đ 1-4, Cat Ba Town; r US$12-20; ❄☎) Simple but colourfully furnished rooms feature at this family-owned spot on the main drag. The rooms at the back are quieter, but lack windows.

Cat Ba Dream HOTEL $
(☑ 031-388 8274; www.catbadream.com.vn; 226 Đ 1-4, Cat Ba Town; r US$15-25; ❄@☎) Slightly more expensive than Cat Ba's ultra cheapies, Cat Ba Dream is a good addition to the town's seafront cavalcade of accommodation. Angle for a front room with sea views.

Cat Ba Beach Resort RESORT $$
(☑ 031-388 8686; www.catbabeachresort.com; Cat Co 2 Beach; bungalows from around US$80; ❄☎) Recently opened on Cat Co 2 beach, Cat Ba Beach Resort has manicured tropical grounds and accommodation ranging from seafront bungalows to shared houses sleeping up to eight. Kayaking, windsurfing and a sauna are all on tap, and there's a breezy open-sided bar-restaurant with water views. Check online for good discounts.

Hung Long HOTEL $$$
(☑ 031-626 9269; 268 Đ 1-4; d US$80; ❄☎) At the quieter southeastern end of Cat Ba Town, Hung Long has very spacious rooms, many with excellent views.

🛏 Around Cat Ba Island

Ancient House Homestay HOMESTAY $
(☑ 0916 645 858, 0915 063 737; www.catba-homestay.com; Ang Soi village; shared house s/d US$17/25, private house d US$50; ☎) Around 3km from Cat Ba Town, this beautiful wooden heritage home has a high-ceilinged interior. A second adjacent house is available for more private use. Cookery classes, biking, sailing and kayaking can all be arranged.

Whisper of Nature GUESTHOUSE $
(☑ 031-265 7678; www.vietbungalow.com; Viet Hai Village; dm/d US$12/28) Offers concrete-and-thatch bungalows grouped around a stream on the edge of the forest. Getting there is an adventure in itself, with the final stage a bike ride through lush scenery. Ask about transport when you book.

Cat Ba Eco Lodge GUESTHOUSE $$
(☑ 031-368 8966; www.suoigoicatbaresort.vn; Xuan Dam village; s/d from US$35/45; ❄☎) This eco-resort celebrates a wonderfully quiet village location 12km from Cat Ba Town. Spacious wooden stilt houses sit around a breezy bar and restaurant. Pick-ups can be arranged from the ferry or Cat Ba Town.

🛏 Nearby Islands

Cat Ba Sandy Beach Resort RESORT $$
(☑ 0989 555 773; www.catbasandybeachresort.com; Nam Cat Island; d from US$45; ❄) This island's prescription for relaxation includes simple bungalows plus posher villas with private facilities – all located under looming, indigo limestone cliffs. Spend your days swimming and kayaking, and kick back with seafood barbecues and beach bonfires after dark. It's included on itineraries arranged by Cat Ba Ventures and Hanoi's Vega Travel (p63).

Monkey Island Resort RESORT $$
(☑ 04-3926 0572; www.monkeyislandresort.com; d US$60-100; ❄) There's a nicely social vibe going down at Monkey Island with a nightly seafood buffet, cool R&B beats, and a bar with a pool table. Accommodation is in comfortable private bungalows, and beach barbecues, kayaks and volleyball keep the holiday spirit alive. Free transfers from Cat Ba Town.

Cat Ong Beach Cottages BUNGALOWS $$$
(📱 0983 234 628; www.catongisland.com; Cat Ong Island; r US$75-150; 📶) Located on a private island a short ride from Cat Ba Town, these beautiful, traditionally-built cottages enjoy a wonderful beachfront location. A seafood barbecue is served on the sand every night and boat transfers are included.

🍴 Eating & Drinking

There are a few good places dotted along Cat Ba Town's seafront strip, and the floating restaurants offshore are also worth a visit.

On the seafront, two good places for a drink are **Good Bar** (Đ 1-4; ◷noon-late), which is a social HQ for travellers with pool tables and a lively vibe, and the tiny, Kiwi-owned **Flightless Bird** (📱031-388 8517; Đ 1-4,; ◷noon-11pm; 📶). Just inland, **Rose Bar** (15 Đ Nui Ngoc; ◷noon-3am; 📶) has lots of happy-hour specials and *shisha* (water pipe) action.

Green Bamboo Forest VIETNAMESE $
(Đ 1-4; meals 80,000-120,000d; ◷7am-11pm) This is a friendly and well-run waterfront eatery that also acts as a booking office for Blue Swimmer. Our pick of the restaurants along the seafront, and the quieter location is also a bonus.

Family Bakery BAKERY $
(196 Đ 1-4, Cat Ba Town; dishes 80,000-120,000d; ◷7am-4pm) Friendly spot that opens early for goodies like Turkish bread and almond pastries. Pop in for a coffee, crème caramel or a croissant before the bus-ferry-bus combo back to Hanoi.

Vien Duong VIETNAMESE $$
(12 Đ Nui Ngoc, Cat Ba Town; meals from 120,000d; ◷11am-11pm) One of the most popular of the seafood spots lining Đ Nui Ngoc, and often heaving with Vietnamese tourists diving into local crab, squid and steaming seafood hotpots. Definitely not the place to come if you're looking for a quiet night.

ℹ Information

The best impartial tourist advice is at Asia Outdoors; Cat Ba Ventures is also very helpful.

Agribank has a branch 1km north of town and an ATM on the harbourfront.

Most accommodation, seafront cafes and restaurants offer wi-fi access.

ℹ Getting There & Away

Cat Ba Island is 45km east of Haiphong and 30km south of Halong City. Various boat and bus combinations make the journey, starting in either Hanoi or Haiphong. It's possible to travel by boat from Halong City to Cat Ba Island, but it's a journey often blighted by scams.

TO/FROM HANOI

The easiest way to/from Hanoi is via the city's Luong Yen bus station. From here, **Hoang Long** (📱031-268 8008) offers a combined bus-boat-bus ticket (240,000d, five hours) straight through to Cat Ba Town. Buses depart Hanoi at 5.20am, 7.20am, 11.20am and 1.20pm, and return from Cat Ba Town at 7.15am, 9.15am, 1.15pm and 3.15pm.

TO/FROM HAIPHONG

A fast hydrofoil departs Haiphong's Ben Binh harbour and goes straight to Cat Ba Town. This takes around 50 minutes (200,000d). Cat Ba–

HALONG BAY TO CAT BA ISLAND (WITHOUT THE HASSLE)

Warning! Travelling from Halong City to Cat Ba Island can be fraught with hassles.

Tourist boats (US$10, four hours) depart from Halong Bay around 1pm for Cat Ba Island. The trouble is they dock at Gia Luan, which is 40km from Cat Ba Town – and local taxi and *xe om* mafia frequently demand up to US$50 for the ride. There *is* actually a local bus (20,000d) at 5pm – the QH Green Bus – but this usually departs just before the boats arrive. Funny that…

Many boat owners in Halong Bay are part of the scam, so check if onward transport to Cat Ba Town is included. Some operators, including Cat Ba Ventures (p70), do include it.

An alternative route is taking the **passenger and vehicle ferry** (per person 40,000d; one hour; ◷on the hour 5am-5pm May-Sep & 8am, 11.10am & 3pm Oct-Apr) that travels from the resort island of Tuan Chau to Gia Luan. (A taxi from Halong City to Tuan Chau is around 150,000d, *xe om* 50,000d.) You can then catch a QH Green bus (departures at 6am, 9.30am, 1.10pm, 4pm and 5pm for 20,000d) to Cat Ba Town.

To travel in the other direction contact Cat Ba Ventures in Cat Ba Town for the latest information.

bound hydrofoils depart from Haiphong at 7am, 9am, 1pm and 3pm, and return from Cat Ba Town at 8am, 10am, 2pm and 4pm.

⊙ Getting Around

Rented bicycles are a good way to explore.

Motorbike rentals (with or without driver) are available from most of the hotels from US$5 per day.

Haiphong

🕿 031 / POP 1.69 MILLION

Vietnam's third-largest city, Haiphong has a graceful air and its verdant tree-lined boulevards conceal some classic colonial-era structures. It's an important seaport, industrial centre and transport hub, but few visitors linger long.

⊙ Sights

Though there isn't a whole lot to see in Haiphong, its slow-paced appeal is enhanced by the French colonial architecture lining the streets.

★ Haiphong Museum   MUSEUM
(66 P Dien Bien Phu; admission 5000d; ⊙8am-12.30pm & 2-4pm Mon-Fri, 7.30-9.30pm Wed & Sun) In a splendid colonial building, the Haiphong Museum concentrates on the city's history. Some displays have English translations and the museum's garden harbours a diverse collection of war detritus.

★ Opera House   HISTORIC BUILDING
(P Quang Trung) With a facade embellished with white columns, Haiphong's neoclassical Opera House dates from 1904. Unfortunately, it is not usually possible to view the interior.

🛏 Sleeping & Eating

For more stylish cafes and restaurants, take a wander along P Minh Khai.

Duyen Hai Hotel   HOTEL $
(🕿 031-384 2134; 6 Đ Nguyen Tri Phuong; r 250,000-400,000d; ❄🛜) With a recently renovated reception area and decent rooms, Duyen Hai offers fair value and is handily near Lac Long bus station and Ben Binh harbour.

Bao Anh Hotel   HOTEL $$
(🕿 031 382 3406; www.hotelbaoanh.com; 20 P Minh Khai; r 400,000-700,000d; ❄@🛜) Refurbished in minimalist style, the Bao Anh features a great location in a leafy street framed

by plane trees and buzzy cafes. It's a short walk to good beer places if you're after something stronger. Reception is definitely open to negotiation.

★ Big Man Restaurant   RESTAURANT $$
(🕿 031-384 2383; 7 P Tran Hung Dao; mains from 100,000d; ⊙11am-11pm) This sprawling restaurant has an outdoor terrace and an extensive menu with good seafood and excellent Vietnamese salads. It also doubles as a microbrewery, with light and dark lager.

⊙ Information

There are internet cafes on P Dien Bien Phu; many cafes have free wi-fi. ATMs dot the city centre.

⊙ Getting There & Away

Vietnam Airlines (🕿 031-3810 890; www.viet-namair.com.vn; 30 P Hoang Van Thu), **Jetstar Pacific** (🕿 1900 1550; www.jetstar.com) and **Vietjet Air** (🕿 1900 1886; www.vietjetair.com) have flights across the nation.

There are also boat connections to Cat Ba.

Buses for Hanoi (100,000d, two hours) leave from the **Tam Bac bus station** (P Tam Bac), 4km from the waterfront. Buses heading to points south including Ninh Binh (110,000d, 3½ hours, every 30 minutes) leave from **Niem Nghia bus station** (Đ Tran Nguyen Han). **Lac Long bus station** (P Cu Chinh Lan) has buses to Halong City (70,000d, 1½ hours).

There are four trains a day to Hanoi (55,000d to 65,000d, 2-3 hours) from **Haiphong train station** (Đ Pham Ngu Lao).

Ba Be National Park

🕿 0281 / ELEV 145M

Boasting mountains high, rivers deep, and waterfalls, lakes and caves, **Ba Be National Park** (🕿 0281-389 4014; admission 20,000d per person) is an incredibly scenic spot. The region is surrounded by steep peaks (up to 1554m), while the park contains tropical rainforest with more than 400 plant species. Wildlife in the forest includes bears, monkeys, bats and lots of butterflies. Surrounding the park are Tay minority villages, whose people live in stilt homes.

Ba Be (Three Bays) is actually three linked lakes, with a total length of 8km and a width of about 400m. The Nang River is navigable for 23km between a point 4km above Cho Ra and the **Dau Dang Waterfall** (Thac Dau Dang), which is a series of spectacular cascades between sheer walls of rock. **Puong**

Cave (Hang Puong) is about 30m high and 300m long, and passes completely through a mountain. A navigable river flows through the cave.

Park staff can organise tours, starting at about US$35 per day for solo travellers, less for a group. Boat trips (hire around 650,000d) take around seven hours to take in most sights; canoeing, cycling, boating and walking excursions are also possible. Tay-owned Ba Be Center Tourism (☑ 0281-389 4721; www.babecentertourism.com; Bolu village) arranges homestays, boat trips and trekking and kayaking.

🛏 Sleeping & Eating

There are two accommodation options not far from the park headquarters.

Park Guesthouse (☑ 0281-389 4026) has semi-detached bungalows (350,000d) and rooms (220,000d) that are fairly basic. Meals (from 50,000d) are available here – place your order a few hours ahead.

Homestays in stilt houses (per person 70,000d) at Pac Ngoi village on the lakeshore are very popular. The park office can help organise this. Meals (40,000d to 60,000d), which can include fish from the lake, are available.

GETTING TO CHINA: NORTHEAST BORDERS

Lang Son to Pingxiang

Getting to the border The Friendship Pass at the Dong Dang/Pingxiang border crossing is the most popular crossing in the far north. The border post itself is at Huu Nghi Quan (Friendship Pass), 3km north of Dong Dang town. Frequent minibuses travel between Lang Son and Dong Dang. From Dong Dang a *xe om* to Huu Nghi Quan is around 30,000d and a taxi around 60,000d. From Lang Son count on about 140,000d for a taxi or 70,000d for a *xe om*.

At the border The border is open 24 hours. To cross the 500m to the Chinese side, you'll need to catch one of the electric cars (10,000d). You'll also need a pre-arranged visa for China.

Moving on On the Chinese side, it's a 20-minute drive to Pingxiang by bus or shared taxi. Pingxiang is connected by train and bus to Nanning (three hours).

Mong Cai to Dongxing

Getting to the border The Mong Cai/Dongxing border crossing is in the extreme northeastern corner of Vietnam. The crossing is around 3km from the Mong Cai bus station; around 20,000d on a *xe om* or 40,000d in a taxi.

At the border The border is open daily between 7am and 10pm Vietnam time. Note that China is one hour ahead of Vietnam. You'll need to have a pre-arranged visa for China.

Moving on Across the border in Dongxing, frequent buses run to Nanning in China's Guangxi province.

Lao Cai to Kunming

Getting to the border The Chinese border at the Lao Cai/Hekou border crossing is about 3km from Lao Cai train station, a journey done by *xe om* (around 25,000d) or taxi (around 50,000d).

At the border The border is open daily between 7am and 10pm Vietnam time. Note that China is one hour ahead of Vietnam. You'll need to have a pre-arranged visa for China, and border-crossing formalities usually take around one hour. Note that travellers have reported Chinese officials confiscating Lonely Planet *China* guides at this border, so you may want to try masking the cover.

Moving on The new Hekou bus station is around 6km from the border post. There are regular departures to Kunming, including sleeper buses that leave at 7.20pm and 7.30pm, getting into Kunming at around 7am. There are also earlier departures.

Only cash is accepted; the nearest ATM and internet access are in Cho Ra.

ⓘ Getting There & Around

Ba Be National Park is 240km from Hanoi and 18km from Cho Ra.

Most visitors get here by chartered vehicle from Hanoi (six hours) or on a tour.

A noon bus (180,000d, six hours) leaves Hanoi's Gia Lam bus station for Cho Ra, where you'll have to overnight before continuing to Ba Be by *xe om* (100,000d).

Mai Chau

📞 0218 / POP 47,500

In an idyllic valley, Mai Chau is surrounded by lush paddy fields and the rural soundtrack is defined by gurgling irrigation streams and birdsong. Dozens of local families have signed up for a highly successful homestay initiative, and for visitors the chance to sleep in a traditional stilt house is a real appeal – though note that the villages are on the tour-group agenda. If you're looking for hardcore exploration, this is not the place, but for biking, hiking and relaxation, Mai Chau fits the bill nicely.

⊙ Sights & Activities

There's fine walking past rice fields and trekking to minority villages. A typical trek further afield covers 7km to 8km; a local guide costs about US$10. Most homestays also rent bikes to explore the village at your own pace.

A popular 18km trek is from Lac village (Ban Lac) in Mai Chau to Hmong Xa Linh village, near a mountain pass (elevation 1000m) on Hwy 6. This trek takes in a 600m climb in altitude and usually involves an overnight stay.

Many travel agencies in Hanoi run inexpensive trips to Mai Chau.

🛏 Sleeping & Eating

Most visitors stay in Thai stilt houses (per person incl breakfast around 200,000d) in the villages of Lac or Pom Coong, just a five-minute stroll apart. All the stilt-house homestays have electricity, running water, hot showers, mosquito nets and roll-up mattresses.

Most people eat where they stay. Establish the price of meals first as some places charge up to 150,000d for dinner. Warning:

cheesy song-and-dance routines follow dinner at some places.

★ **Mai Chau Nature Lodge** BUNGALOWS $$
(📞0946 888 804; www.maichaunatureplace.com; Lac Village; dm/d US$5/40) Private bungalows with bamboo furniture and local textiles. Dorms are also available, and there are free bikes to explore the surrounding countryside.

Mai Chau Lodge HOTEL $$$
(📞0218-386 8959; www.maichaulodge.com; Mai Chau; r US$150; 🌀@🛜🏊) Contemporary accommodation with wooden floors and designer lighting, all trimmed with local textiles; most rooms have balconies with rice-paddy views.

ⓘ Getting There & Around

Direct buses to Mai Chau leave Hanoi's My Dinh bus station at 6am, 8.30am and 11am (100,000d, 3¾ hours). Alternatively, catch a regular Son La or Dien Bien Phu bus to Tong Dau junction (100,000d, 3½ hours). From the junction *xe om* charge 25,000d.

Lao Cai

📞 020 / POP 46,700

One of the gateways to the north, Lao Cai lies at the end of the train line, 3km from the Chinese border. The town has no sights but is a major hub for travellers journeying between Hanoi, Sapa and the Chinese city of Kunming.

There are ATMs next to the train station, plus internet cafes close by. You'll find inexpensive hotels around the station including Nga Nghi Tho Huong (📞020-383 5111; 342A P Nguyen Hue; r 180,000-300,000d; 🌀🛜).

ⓘ Getting There & Around

Nine daily buses (250,000d, nine hours) ply the Hanoi–Lao Cai route, but virtually everyone prefers the train.

Minibuses for Sapa (50,000d, one hour) wait by the train station while services to Bac Ha (60,000d, 2½ hours) leave at 6.30am, 8.15am, 9am, 11.30am, noon, 2pm and 3pm from a terminal next to the Red River bridge.

Rail tickets to Hanoi (8½ to 10 hours) start at 135,000d for a hard seat (bad choice) and run to 515,000d for an air-con soft sleeper, rising by about 15% at weekends. Several companies operate special private carriages with comfortable sleepers, including the affordable **ET Pumpkin** (www.et-pumpkin.com) and the more expensive **Victoria Express** (www.victoriahotels-asia.com).

Bac Ha

☑ 020 / POP 7400

An unhurried and friendly town, Bac Ha makes a relaxed base for exploring the northern highlands and hill-tribe villages. The atmosphere is very different from Sapa, and you can walk the streets freely without being accosted by hawkers. The climate here is also noticeably warmer than in Sapa.

Bac Ha has a certain charm, though its stock of traditional old adobe houses is dwindling and being replaced by concrete structures. Wood-smoke fills the morning air and chickens and pigs poke around the back lanes. For six days a week Bac Ha slumbers, but its lanes fill up to choking point each Sunday when tourists and Flower Hmong flood in for the weekly market.

◉ Sights

While you're here, check out the outlandish **Vua Meo** ('Cat King' House; ⊘7.30-11.30am & 1.30-5pm) **FREE**, a palace constructed in a bizarre 'oriental baroque' architectural style.

Bac Ha's **Sunday market** is a riot of colour and commerce, and while the influx of day-trippers from Sapa is changing things, it's still a worthwhile and relatively accessible place to visit. The *ruou* corn hooch produced by the Flower Hmong is so potent it can ignite; there's an entire area devoted to it at the Sunday market.

Beyond town lie several interesting markets. Tour operators in Bac Ha can arrange day trips to those listed here.

Can Cau Market   MARKET

(⊘6am-1pm Sat) A Saturday morning market 20km north of Bac Ha that spills down a hillside with food stalls on one level and livestock at the bottom of the valley, including plenty of dogs. Locals will implore you to drink the local *ruou* with them and you can't fail to be impressed with the costumes of the Flower Hmong and Blue Hmong (look out for the striking zigzag costume of the latter).

Some trips from Bac Ha include the option of an afternoon trek (for those still standing after *ruou* shots) to the nearby village of Fu La.

Coc Ly Market   MARKET

(⊘6am-1pm Tue) The impressive Coc Ly market attracts Dzao, Flower H'mong, Tay and Nung people from the surrounding hills. It's about 35km southwest of Bac Ha along reasonably good roads.

Lung Phin Market   MARKET

(⊘6am-1pm Sun) Lung Phin market is between Can Cau market and Bac Ha, about 12km from town. It's less busy than other markets, with a really local feel, and is a good place to move on to once the tour buses arrive in Bac Ha from Sapa.

⚡ Activities

There's great hiking to hill-tribe villages around Bac Ha. The Flower Hmong village of **Ban Pho** is one of the nearest to town, from where you can walk to the Nung settlement of **Na Kheo** then head back to Bac Ha. Other nearby villages include **Trieu Cai**, an 8km return walk, and **Na Ang**, a 6km return walk; it's best to set up a trip with a local guide.

Tour guides in Bac Ha can arrange visits to rural schools as part of a motorbike or trekking day trip. There's also a **waterfall** near Thai Giang Pho village, about 12km east of Bac Ha, which has a pool big enough for swimming.

Take a peek at the website www.bachatourist.com for more inspiration. It's operated by English-speaking **Mr Nghe** (☑0912 005 952; www.bachatourist.com; Green Sapa Tour, Đ Tran Bac), Bac Ha's one-man tourism dynamo. Many hotels also offer excursions.

🛏 Sleeping & Eating

Room rates tend to increase on weekends, when tourists arrive for the Sunday market. Weekday rates are quoted here.

Hoang Vu Hotel   GUESTHOUSE $

(☑020-388 0264; www.bachatourist.com; 5 Đ Tran Bac; r from US$8) It's nothing fancy, but the spacious rooms offer good value (all have TV and fan). The best spot in town for budget travellers.

Sunday Hotel   HOTEL $

(☑020-384 1747; 1 Đ Vu Cong Mat; r 200,000-350,000d; ❄🛜) Bac Ha's newest opening, on the edge of the market and main square, is colourful and bright. Look forward to good value and clean rooms.

EXPLORING THE FAR NORTH BY MOTORBIKE

With spectacular scenery and relatively minimal traffic, the northwest loop from Hanoi up to Lao Cai, over to Dien Bien Phu and back to the capital is a truly memorable motorbike ride.

Hanoi is the place to start making arrangements. Consider joining a tour or hiring a guide, who will know the roads and can help with mechanical and linguistic difficulties.

Get acquainted with your bike first and check current road conditions and routes. Most motorbikes in Vietnam are under 250cc. Japanese road and trail bikes (US$20 to US$30 per day) are good choices as they tend to be reliable and have decent shock absorbers and seat cushioning. You'll suffer on a moped given the rough roads.

Essentials include a good helmet, a local mobile phone for emergencies, rain gear, a spare parts and repair kit (including spark plugs, spanners, inner tube and tyre levers), an air pump and decent maps. Knee and elbow pads and gloves are also a good idea.

Highways can be hell in Vietnam, so let the train take the strain on the long route north to Lao Cai. Load your bike into a goods carriage while you sleep in a berth. You'll have to (almost) drain it of petrol.

If you're planning on riding from Dien Bien Phu via Muong Lay and Lai Chau on Hwy 12 to Sapa, check road conditions first. At the time of writing, the 40km after Muong Lay to Lai Chau was very rough with many roadworks. Highway 12 was scheduled to be completed by August 2014, so it should be OK once this edition is published.

Take it slowly, particularly in the rain. Do not ride during or immediately after heavy rainstorms as this is when landslides might occur; many mountain roads are quite new and the cliff embankments can be unstable. Expect to average about 35km per hour. Only use safe hotel parking. Fill up from petrol stations where the petrol is less likely to have been watered down.

If running short on time or energy, remember that many bus companies will let you put your bike on the roof of a bus, but get permission first from your bike rental company.

Recommended specialists in Hanoi include **Cuong's Motorbike Adventure** (Map p52; ☑ 0913 518 772; www.cuongs-motorbike-adventure.com; 46 P Gia Ngu; ◷8am-6pm) and **Offroad Vietnam** (Map p52; ☑ 0913 047 509; www.offroadvietnam.com; 36 P Nguyen Huu Huan; ◷8am-6pm Mon-Sat).

Ngan Nga Bac Ha
HOTEL $

(☑ 020-380 0286; www.nganngabachahotel.com; 117 Ngoc Uyen; r US$18-20; ☎) This friendly place is above a popular restaurant that does a roaring trade in tasty hotpots for travellers and the occasional tour group.

Congfu Hotel
HOTEL $$

(☑ 020-388 0254; www.congfuhotel.com; 152 Ngoc Uyen; r US$30; ✴@☎) This place has 21 attractive rooms and its restaurant (meals from 60,000d) is one of the best in town. Book rooms 205, 208, 305 or 308 for windows overlooking Bac Ha Market.

Hoang Yen Restaurant
VIETNAMESE $

(Đ Tran Bac; mains 60,000-100,000d; ◷7am-10pm; ☎) Hoang Yen's menu includes tasty breakfast options and a good-value set menu for 140,000d. Cheap beer and wi-fi access are both available. It's on Bac Ha's main square.

ℹ Information

There's an ATM at the Agribank and wi-fi access at Hoang Yen Restaurant.

ℹ Getting There & Away

Buses run to Hanoi (400,000d, 11 hours, 8pm) and Lao Cai (60,000d, 2½ hours, 6am, 8am, noon, 1pm & 2pm). Tours to Bac Ha from Sapa cost from US$20 per person; on the way back you can bail out in Lao Cai and catch the train back to Hanoi. A motorbike/taxi to Lao Cai costs US$25/70, or to Sapa US$30/80.

Sapa

☑ 020 / POP 38,000 / ELEV 1650M

Perched on a steep slope, Sapa overlooks a plunging valley of cascading rice terraces, with mountains towering above the town on all sides. Founded as a French hill station in 1922, Sapa is the premier tourist

Sapa

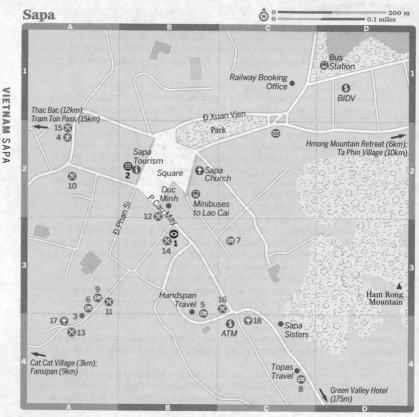

Map labels:
- Bus Station
- Railway Booking Office
- BIDV
- Đ Xuan Vien
- Park
- Thac Bac (12km); Tram Ton Pass (15km)
- 15
- 4
- Sapa Tourism
- 2
- Square
- Sapa Church
- 10
- Duc Minh
- P Cau May
- Đ Phan Si
- 12
- Minibuses to Lao Cai
- Hmong Mountain Retreat (6km); Ta Phin Village (10km)
- 14
- 1
- 7
- Ham Rong Mountain
- 9
- 6
- 11
- Handspan Travel
- 5
- 16
- 17
- 3
- 13
- ATM
- 18
- Sapa Sisters
- Cat Cat Village (3km); Fansipan (9km)
- Topas Travel
- 8
- Green Valley Hotel (175m)

destination in northern Vietnam. Views of this epic scenery are often subdued in thick mist rolling across the peaks, but even if it's cloudy Sapa is a fascinating destination, especially when local hill-tribe people fill the town with colour.

The town's colonial villas fell into disrepair during successive wars with the French, Americans and Chinese, but following the advent of tourism, Sapa has experienced a renaissance. The downside is a hotel building boom, including numerous soaring concrete constructions.

Inherent in this prosperity is cultural change for the hill-tribe people. The Hmong are canny (though very persistent) traders and will urge you to buy handicrafts and trinkets. Many have had little formal education, yet all the youngsters have a good command of English, French and a handful of other languages.

Sapa is known for its cold, foggy winters (down to 0°C). The dry season for Sapa is approximately January to the end of June.

◉ Sights

Surrounding Sapa are the Hoang Lien Mountains, including **Fansipan**, which at 3143m is Vietnam's highest peak. The trek from Sapa to the summit and back can take several days. Some of the better-known sights around Sapa include the epic **Tram Ton Pass**, the pretty **Thac Bac** (Silver Falls), and **Cau May** (Cloud Bridge), which spans the Muong Hoa River.

★ Sapa Market   MARKET
(⊙6am-2pm) Hill-tribe people from surrounding villages go to the Sapa market most days to sell handicrafts and ethnic-style clothing. Saturday is the busiest day, and every day the market's food stalls are popular for breakfast and lunch. The loca-

tion of the town's market may change in the next few years.

Sapa Museum MUSEUM
(103 Đ Xuan Vien; ⊙7.30-11.30am & 1.30-5pm) FREE Excellent showcase of the history and ethnology of the Sapa area including colonial times. Exhibitions demonstrate the differences between the various ethnic minority people of the area.

🏃 Activities

★ **Sapa O'Chau** HIKING
(☑020-377 1166; www.sapaochau.com; 8 Đ Thac Bac; ⊙6.30am-6.30pm) Excellent day walks, longer homestay treks and Fansipan hikes are offered. Profits from this tour agency provide training to Hmong children in a learning centre. Volunteers are welcome.

Indigo Cat CRAFT
(http://indigocat.dznly.com; 46 Đ Phan Si; per person per project 100,000d; ⊙9am-7pm) Learn traditional Hmong weaving at this craft shop co-owned by a Hmong-Swiss couple. Bags and iPad covers are popular.

Hill Station Signature Restaurant COOKING
(☑020-388 7112; www.thehillstation.com; 37 Đ Phan Si; per person US$29; ⊙from 9am) Cooking classes feature five local dishes, and are conducted by an English-speaking Hmong chef. Includes local rice wine and dishes like smoked buffalo and homemade tofu.

🛏 Sleeping

Green Valley Hotel HOSTEL $
(☑0979 110 800; sapagreenvalleyhotel@gmail.com; 45 Đ Muong Hoa; dm US$4, s US$7-10, d & tw US$10-15; @🛜) Sapa's only true backpacker hostel is this welcoming spot with great views. Motorcycles can be rented for US$5 per day, and there's a cosy on-site bar with pool table.

Casablanca Sapa Hotel BOUTIQUE HOTEL $
(☑0974 418 111; www.sapacasablanca.com; Đ Dong Loi; r US$22-30; @🛜) One of Sapa's first boutique hotels has a new lease on life thanks to the friendly family owners. Look forward to colourful decor and good hospitality from Mr Tom.

Luong Thuy Family Guesthouse GUESTHOUSE $
(☑020-387 2310; www.familysapa.com; 28 Đ Muong Hoa; s/d from US$15/18, @🛜) This friendly guesthouse is slightly away from the hubbub of downtown Sapa. There are valley views from front balconies.

Cat Cat View Hotel HOTEL $$
(☑020-387 1946; www.catcathotel.com; 46 Đ Phan Si; budget r US$10, s/d from US$30/35; @🛜) This excellent spot has 40 rooms over nine floors, many with great views. There's something for every budget, with homely, comfortable pine-trimmed accommodation; the cheaper rooms are the best value.

Sapa Luxury Hotel HOTEL $$
(☑020-387 2771; www.sapaluxuryhotel.com; 36 Đ Phan Si; s/d/tr from US$28/28/35; @🛜) One of the newer hotels has spacious rooms with wooden floors and trendy Asian decor.

★ **Hmong Mountain Retreat** ECOLODGE $$
(☑020-650 5228; www.hmongmountainretreat.com; 6 Ban Ho Rd, Lao Chai; d/f incl breakfast US$59/120) 🌿 Accommodation in bungalows or a restored Hmong house is simple, but the real attraction is sleeping above a cascade of rice paddies several kilometres out of Sapa. The retreat's restaurant (crafted from an 80-year old tribal house) features locally sourced ingredients.

Cha Pa Garden
BOUTIQUE HOTEL $$

(☏020-387 2907; www.chapagarden.com; 23B P Cau May; r US$65-82; ❄@☎) Cha Pa occupies a sensitively restored colonial villa amid lush and private gardens in the heart of Sapa. There are just four rooms, all presented in contemporary style, with wooden floors, uncluttered lines and hip bathrooms.

★ Topas Eco Lodge
ECOLODGE $$$

(☏020-387 2404; www.topasecolodge.com; bungalows US$115-140; @☎) ✐ Overlooking a plunging valley, this ecolodge has 25 lovely stone-and-thatch bungalows, each with front balconies to make the most of the magnificent views. The whole project is sustainable and environmentally friendly, with solar energy providing the power. Hiking, biking and market tours are all available.

✗ Eating

For eating options on a tight budget, cheap Vietnamese restaurants are huddled below the market, and night market stalls south of the church serve *bun cha* (barbecued pork).

Vietnamese-style hotpot is a very popular local dish; try the area just south of the bus station.

Little Sapa
VIETNAMESE $

(18 P Cau May; mains 50,000-80,000d; ⏰8am-10pm) One of the better-value eateries along touristy P Cau May, Little Sapa also lures in locals. Steer clear of the largely mediocre European dishes and concentrate instead on the Vietnamese menu.

Sapa O'Chau
CAFE $

(www.sapaochau.org; 8 Đ Thac Bac; snacks from 20,000d; ⏰6.30am-6.30pm) Cosy cafe that's also the best place to ask about trekking, homestays and volunteering opportunities with Sapa O'Chau. Don't miss warming up with a cup of ginger tea sweetened with Sapa mountain honey.

Sapa Market
VIETNAMESE $

(P Cau May; dishes around 30,000d; ⏰6am-1pm; ✐) Lots of local food stalls and a good alternative to another hotel breakfast or for a cheap and authentic lunch.

Baguette & Chocolat
CAFE $$

(☏020-387 1766; Đ Thac Bac; cakes from 30,000d; snacks & meals 70,000-160,000d; ⏰7am-10pm) Head to this elegant converted villa for a fine breakfast, open sandwich, baguette or tasty slab of gateau.

★ Hill Station Signature Restaurant
HMONG $$

(www.thehillstation.com; 37 Đ Phan Si; meals 90,000-180,000d; ⏰7am-10.30pm) Cool Zen decor and superb views showcase Hmong ethnic minority cuisine. Dishes include chicken with wild ginger, ash-baked trout in banana leaves, and traditional Hmong-style black pudding. Tasting sets of local rice and corn wine are also of interest to curious travelling foodies.

Village Noshery
CAFE $$

(www.saparooms.com/village_noshery; 42 P Cau May; tapas 60,000-80,000d; mains 70,000-110,000d; ⏰6.30am-11pm) Stylish cafe with decent Vietnamese food, including tapas-sized plates of interesting snacks like barbecued beef in betel leaves. Noodle dishes, soups and spring rolls are also available, and it's a top place for an end-of-day beer or cocktail. Coffee and cake is another post-trekking option. Upstairs are double rooms (US$30 including breakfast).

Nature View
VIETNAMESE $$

(51 Đ Phan Si; mains 90,000-150,000d; ⏰8am-10pm; ✐) You've got to love the photos of the owner's kids on the walls at this friendly spot with great valley views. Look forward to decent Vietnamese and European food and just maybe Sapa's best fruit smoothies. Those who aren't fans of tofu should try the sizzling tofu with lemongrass and be converted. Don't worry – it's not all vegetarian food.

☙ Drinking & Nightlife

Mountain Bar & Pub
BAR

(2 Đ Muong Hoa; ⏰noon-11pm) Dangerously strong cocktails, cold beer and ultra-competitive games of table football conspire to make this Sapa's go-to place for a great night out. Try the warm apple wine for some highland bliss.

Color Bar
BAR

(www.facebook.com/colorbar; 56 Đ Phan Si; ⏰noon-11pm) Owned by a Hanoi artist, this rustic and atmospheric spot ticks all the boxes with reggae, table football, *shisha* and ice-cold Bia Lao Cai.

❶ Information

Internet access, including complimentary wi-fi, is available at hotels, restaurants and cafes around town.

BIDV (✆020-387 2569; Đ Ngu Chi Son) Has an ATM and will exchange cash.

Duc Minh (✆020-387 1881; www.ducminh travel.com; 10 P Cau May) Friendly English-speaking operator organising transport, treks to hill-tribe villages and assaults of Fansipan.

Handspan Travel (✆020-387 2110; www. handspan.com; Chau Long Hotel, 24 Dong Loi) Offers trekking and mountain-biking tours to villages and markets.

Main Post Office (Đ Ham Rong)

Sapa Sisters (www.sapasisters.webs.com; Luong Thuy Family Guesthouse, 28 Đ Muong Hoa) Trekking and homestays with a group of savvy and knowledgeable Hmong girls.

Sapa Tourism (✆020-387 3239; www.sapa-tourism.com; 103 Đ Xuan Vien; ⊙7.30-11.30am & 1.30-5pm) Helpful English-speaking staff offering details about transport, trekking and weather. Internet access is free for 15 minutes, and the organisation's website is also a mine of useful information.

ℹ Getting There & Away

The gateway to Sapa is Lao Cai, 38km to the west. Minibuses (50,000d, 1½ hours) make the trip regularly until mid-afternoon.

A (return) minibus to Bac Ha for the Sunday market is around US$30 per person; departure from Sapa is at 6am and from Bac Ha at 1pm. It's cheaper to go by public minibus, changing in Lao Cai.

Direct sleeper buses for Hanoi (300,000d, 10 hours) depart from Sapa's main square, and there's a 5pm sleeper bus to Halong City (500,000d, 13 hours). Services to Dien Bien Phu will resume when highway improvements are finished (scheduled for late 2014).

Most hotels and travel agencies can book train tickets from Lao Cai to Hanoi.

ℹ Getting Around

Downtown Sapa can be walked in 20 minutes. For excursions further out, you can hire a motorbike from US$5 per day, or take one with a driver from US$15.

Dien Bien Phu

✆0230 / POP 72,700

On 7 May 1954, French colonial forces were defeated by the Viet Minh in a decisive battle at Dien Bien Phu (DBP), signalling an end to the days of their Indochine empire.

Previously just a minor settlement, DBP only became a provincial capital in 2004. Boulevards and civic buildings have been constructed and the airport now has daily flights from Hanoi. With the nearby border with Laos now open to foreigners, many travellers are passing through the city.

⊙ Sights

★**Dien Bien Phu Museum**   MUSEUM
(✆0230-382 4971; Đ 7-5; admission 5000d; ⊙7-11am & 1.30-5pm) Commemorating the 1954 battle, this well-laid-out museum features an eclectic collection. Alongside weaponry and guns, there's a bicycle capable of carrying 330kg of ordnance, and photographs and documents, some with English translations. At the time of writing, a new modern structure to house the collection was under construction.

★**Bunker of Colonel de Castries**   WAR MEMORIAL
(admission 5000d; ⊙7-11am & 1.30-5pm) Across the river, the command bunker of Colonel Christian de Castries has been recreated. A few discarded tanks linger nearby, and you'll probably see Vietnamese tourists mounting the bunker and waving the Vietnamese flag, re-enacting an iconic photograph taken at the battle's conclusion.

★**A1 Hill**   WAR MEMORIAL
(admission 3000d; ⊙7-11am & 1.30-5pm) More tanks and a monument to Viet Minh casualties on this former French position, known to the French as Eliane and to the Vietnamese as A1 Hill. The elaborate trenches at the heart of the French defences have also been recreated.

🛏 Sleeping

Viet Hoang 2   GUESTHOUSE $
(✆0989 797 988; 69 Đ Phuong Thanh Binh; r 250,000-350,000d; ❄@🖂) Tucked away opposite the bus station, this guesthouse is the newer and much cleaner offshoot of the older, nearby Viet Hoang 1 (rooms 150,000d to 200,000d). The extra dong are definitely worth it.

Binh Long Hotel   GUESTHOUSE $
(✆0230-382 4345; 429 Đ Muong Thanh; d & tw US$10; ❄🖂) On a busy junction in the thick of things. The twin rooms aren't exactly huge, but the owners know about onward transport to Sapa and Laos.

Muong Thanh Hotel   HOTEL $$
(✆0230-381 0043; www.muongthanhthanhnien. com; Đ Muong Thanh; r US$50-80; ❄🖂🏊) The

modern rooms here include satellite TV, elegant furniture and marble bathrooms. Added attractions include a swimming pool watched over by a not-so-scary concrete dragon.

🍴 Eating & Drinking

Dining options are limited. Muong Thanh Hotel has a good restaurant. For a cheap bite, check out the pho stalls and simple restaurants opposite the bus station. *Bia hoi* gardens on Đ Hoang Van are ideal for a local brew or two.

ⓘ Information

Internet cafes are on Đ Hoang Van Thai.

Agribank (☑ 0230-382 5786; Đ 7-5) Has an ATM and changes US dollars.

ⓘ Getting There & Away

AIR

Vietnam Airlines (☑ 0230-382 4948; www. vietnamairlines.com; Nguyen Huu Tho; ⊘7.30-11.30am & 1.30-4.30pm) operates one flight daily between DBP and Hanoi. The office is near the airport, about 1.5km from the town centre, along the road to Muong Lay.

BUS

DBP's bus station is on Hwy 12.

CAR & MOTORBIKE

The 480km drive from Hanoi to DBP on Hwys 6 and 279 takes around 11 hours.

Note that north of DBP, the road between Muong Lay and Lai Chau was subject to many roadworks at the time of research.

GETTING TO LAOS: NORTHERN BORDERS

Dien Bien Phu to Muang Khua

Getting to the border Buses from Dien Bien Phu to Muang Khua (110,000d) leave daily at 5.30am. It's advisable to book your ticket the day prior to travelling. This bus takes you through the Tay Trang/Sop Hun border crossing and drops you off in Muang Khua in Laos. The journey typically takes between seven and eight hours, but can be longer depending on the roads and border formalities. Other destinations in Laos from DBP include Luang Prabang (495,000d, 6am), Nam Tha (350,000d, 6.30am) and Udomxai (230,000d, 7.30am).

At the border The Lao border at Tay Trang, 35km from Dien Bien Phu, is open daily between 7am and 7pm. Crossing into Laos most travellers can get a 30-day visa on arrival (US$30 to US$42, depending on your nationality). Have photo ID and additional cash (around US$5) on hand for occasional local administrative fees.

Moving on From Muang Khua there are buses to Udomxai.

For more information about crossing this border in the other direction, see p309.

Thanh Hoa to Sam Neua

Getting to the border Those seeking a backwoods adventure can try the Na Meo/Nam Xoi border crossing. If at all possible take a direct bus and avoid getting onward transport on the Vietnamese side of the border where foreigners are seriously ripped off. There's a daily 8am bus from Thanh Hoa's western bus station (Ben Xe Mien Tay) to Sam Neua (310,000d), but expect overcharging.

At the border The border is open from 7am to 5pm. Lao visas are available here. Readers have reported no hassle from border officials, but they may try to offer you bad rates for all currencies – you'll get a better deal in Na Meo hotels. It's best not to get stuck on the Laos side of the border as transport is extremely irregular and there's no accommodation. Na Meo has several basic, serviceable guesthouses.

Moving on There's unbelievable overcharging on this route (unless you're on a direct bus). Vietnamese bus drivers demand up to US$50 for the trip to Thanh Hoa (it should cost about US$8).

For more information about crossing this border in the other direction, see p314.

BUSES FROM DIEN BIEN PHU

DESTINATION	COST (D)	DURATION (HR)	FREQUENCY
Hanoi	375,000	11½	frequent 4.30am-9pm
Lai Chau	130,000	6-7	frequent 5am-1.15pm
Muong Lay	57,000	3-4	6.30am, 2.30pm, 4pm
Son La	97,000	4	4.30am, 8am, noon, 2pm

CENTRAL VIETNAM

With ancient history, compelling culture, incredible food and terrific beaches, central Vietnam is one of the must-see regions of the country. This is a region that packs in Hue (the country's former imperial capital), the DMZ battle sites, and Hoi An, an exquisite architectural gem that time forgot. Throw in the ancient religious capital of My Son, the extraordinary cave systems of Phong Nha and nature reserves so dense that scientists discover new creatures in them every few years, and the region's appeal is overwhelming.

Danang and Hue airports are the perfect gateways for visitors who want to avoid long overland journeys.

Phong Nha–Ke Bang National Park

A Unesco World Heritage Site, the remarkable Phong Nha-Ke Bang National Park FREE contains the oldest karst mountains in Asia and is riddled with hundreds of cave systems.

Its collection of stunning dry caves, terraced caves, towering stalagmites and glistening crystal-edged stalactites represents nature on a very grand scale indeed.

Serious exploration only began in the 1990s, led by the British Cave Research Association and Hanoi University. Cavers first penetrated deep into Phong Nha Cave, one of the world's longest systems. In 2005 Paradise Cave was discovered, and in 2009 a team found the world's largest cave – Son Doong.

Huge caverns and unknown cave networks are being discovered each year. Above ground, most of this mountainous 885 sq km national park is near-pristine tropical evergreen jungle, over 90% of which is primary forest. More than 100 types of mammal (including 10 species of primate, tigers, elephants and the saola, a rare Asian antelope), 81 types of reptile

and amphibian, and 300 varieties of bird have been logged in Phong Nha.

Until recently, access was strictly controlled by the Vietnamese military. Things are relaxing, but officially you are not allowed to hike here without a licensed tour operator.

The Phong Nha region is changing fast, with more and more accommodation options opening. Son Trach village (population 3000) is the main centre, but it's a tiny place – there's only one ATM and transport connections are poor.

◉ Sights & Activities

Paradise Cave　　　　　　　　　　CAVE
(Thien Dong; adult/child under 1.3m 120,000/ 60,000d; ⊘7.30am-4.30pm) Deep in the national park, surrounded by forest and karst peaks, this remarkable cave system extends for 31km, though most people only visit the first kilometre or so.

Once you're inside, the sheer scale of Paradise Cave is truly breathtaking, as wooden staircases descend into a cathedral-like space replete with colossal stalagmites and glimmering stalactites of white crystal that resemble glass pillars.

Commendably, development has been sensitive. But in the last few years, visitor numbers have soared – spoiling the whole experience. Try to get here as early as you can to beat the crowds.

To really explore Paradise Cave, consider booking Phong Nha Farmstay's 7km trek (2,650,000d, minimum two people), which penetrates deep into the cave and includes a swim through an underground river and lunch under a light shaft.

Paradise Cave is about 14km southwest of Son Trach.

Tu Lan Caves　　　　　　　　　　CAVE
A spectacular excursion, the Tu Lan cave trip begins with a countryside hike then a swim (with headlamps and life jackets) through two spectacular river caves before emerging in an idyllic river valley. Then there's more hiking through dense forest to

a 'beach' where rivers merge that's an ideal campsite. There's wonderful swimming here in vast caverns.

Moderate fitness levels are necessary. Tu Lan is 65km north of Son Trach and can only be visited on a guided tour.

Phong Nha Caves & Boat Trip CAVE
(adult/child 50,000/25,000d; boat 300,000d; ⊙7am-4pm) The spectacular boat trip through Phong Nha Cave is a highly enjoyable experience, though quite touristy, beginning in Son Trach village. You cruise along the Son River past bathing buffalo, jagged limestone peaks and church steeples to the cave's gaping mouth – Phong Nha means 'Cave of Teeth', but the 'teeth' (stalagmites) by the entrance are long gone. Then the engine is cut and you're transported to another world as you're paddled through cavern after garishly illuminated cavern.

Hang En CAVE
This gigantic cave is very close to Hang Son Doong. Getting here involves a trek through dense jungle, valleys and the Ban Doong minority village. You stay overnight in the cave or minority village.

Tours (4,600,000d per person, minimum two people) here are run by Phong Nha-Ke Bang National Park rangers.

🛏 Sleeping & Eating

There are a dozen or so guesthouses (all 200,000d) and cheap eateries in Son Trach village.

Easy Tiger HOSTEL $
(☑052-367 7844; www.easytigerphongnha.com; Son Trach; dm 160,000d; ❄@🛜) Owned by the Farmstay crew, this great new hostel has comfortable dorms, a great bar-restaurant area, a pool table and excellent travel info. A swimming pool is planned.

Thanh Dat GUESTHOUSE $
(☑052-367 7069; Son Trach; r 250,000d; ❄🛜) On the main drag in Son Trach, this is the most welcoming locally owned place. Rooms are clean and it's owned by a family who speak some English.

HANG SON DOONG: WORLD-CLASS CAVE

Ho Khanh, a hunter from a jungle settlement close to the Vietnam–Laos border, would often take shelter in the caves that honeycomb his mountain homeland. He stumbled across gargantuan **Hang Son Doong** (Mountain River Cave) in the early 1990s, but the sheer scale and majesty of the principal cavern (more than 5km long, 200m high and, in some places, 150m wide) was only confirmed as the world's biggest cave when British explorers returned with him in 2009.

The expedition team's biggest obstacle was to find a way over a vast overhanging barrier of muddy calcite they dubbed the 'Great Wall of Vietnam' that divided the cave. Once they did, its true scale was revealed – a cave big enough to accommodate a battleship. Sections of it are pierced by skylights that reveal formations of ethereal stalagmites that cavers have called the Cactus Garden. Some stalagmites are up to 80m high. Colossal cave pearls have been discovered, measuring 10cm in diameter, formed by millennia of drips, as calcite crystals fused with grains of sand. Magnificent rimstone pools are present throughout the cave.

Hang Son Doong is one of the most spectacular sights in Southeast Asia, and the government only approved very restricted access to the cave system in June 2013. The only specialist operator permitted (by the Vietnamese president no less) to lead tours here is Son Trach–based Oxalis (p85). Son Doong is no day-trip destination, it's in an extremely remote area and the only way to visit is by booking a seven-day expedition with around 16 porters. It costs US$3000 per person, with a maximum of eight trekkers on each trip.

Is it worth it? Well, *National Geographic* photographer Carsten Peter, whose photographs first unveiled the majesty of the cave to the world (and who has climbed Everest and K2), described it as the most impressive natural sight in the world.

Note that you may come across tour agencies professing to sell tours of Hang Son Doong on the internet. The only licensed operator with access is Oxalis. Other agencies promise to take you to Hang Son Doong but actually set up a trip to Hang En instead (which is mighty impressive, but not Son Doong).

★ **Phong Nha Farmstay**   GUESTHOUSE **$$**
(☑ 052-367 5135; www.phong-nha-cave.com; Cu Nam village; r 500,000-900,000d; f 1,500,000d; ⊖✳@🛜🏊) The Farmstay has views overlooking an ocean of rice paddies and smallish but neat rooms, with high ceilings and shared balconies. The bar-restaurant with pool table has tasty Asian and Western grub (meals 40,000d to 120,000d) and a gregarious vibe. Tours are outstanding. It's in Cu Nam village, 9km east of Son Trach.

Phong Nha Lake House Resort   HOTEL **$$**
(☑ 052-367 5999; www.phongnhalakehouse.com; Khuong Ha; dm/d/villas US$10/35/50; ✳🛜) Impressive new lakeside resort owned by an Australian-Vietnamese couple with an excellent dorm, spacious and stylish rooms and lovely villas. A pool, jacuzzi and spa are planned. The huge wooden restaurant is a traditional structure from rural Vietnam. It's 7km east of Son Trach.

★ **Jungle Bar**   CAFE, BAR **$**
(Son Trach; meals 25,000-50,000d; ⊙7am-midnight; 🛜) Run by Hai, a switched-on, English-speaking local, this cool cafe-bar offers cheap grub (including breakfasts and vegetarian choices), fresh juices, travel info, bike rental and a welcoming atmosphere. In the evening it's more of a bar, with lounge music, cocktails and an open mike some nights.

ℹ Information

In Son Trach, head to the Jungle Bar where owner Hai (an ecologist) is a superb source of independent travel information. He can book train and bus tickets, organise tours and rent bikes and motorbikes. Staff at Phong Nha Farmstay and Easy Tiger hostel are also extremely well informed and can assist with information and transport.

There's an ATM in Son Trach and some places have wi-fi.

ℹ Getting There & Around

The coastal city of Dong Hoi, 166km north of Hue on Hwy 1 and on the north–south train line, is the main gateway to Phong Nha. The park abuts Son Trach village, 50km northwest of Dong Hoi.

Local buses (45,000d, two hours) offer irregular connections between Dong Hoi and Son Trach. There's also a bus link (120,000d, 1¼hr) between Dong Hoi train station, the Farmstay and Son Trach. It leaves Dong Hoi daily at 6.30am and 8.00am and returns from Son Trach (via Farmstay) at 6pm and 8pm. A tour bus (500,000d, five hours) also links Son Trach, the Farmstay and Hue, stopping at the Ben Hai River Museum and

---

WORTH A TRIP

NUOC MOOC ECO-TRAIL

A beautiful riverside retreat inside the Phong Nha–Ke Bang National Park, the wooden walkways and paths of the **Nuoc Mooc Ecotrail** (adult/child 6-16yr 30,000/50,000d; ⊙7am-5pm) extend over a kilometre through woods to the confluence of two rivers. It's a gorgeous place for a swim, where you can wallow hippo-style in turquoise waters with a limestone-mountain backdrop. Bring a picnic. Nuoc Mooc is 12km southwest of Son Trach.

Vinh Moc Tunnels. It leaves Son Trach at 6.30am daily and returns from Hue at 1pm. Tickets on these buses to/from Hue and Dong Hoi can be booked via the Farmstay, Easy Tiger or Hue Backpackers.

Hotels can organise lifts in private cars from Dong Hoi (400,000d to 500,000d); they work together so rides can be shared between travellers.

Organised tours are an excellent way to explore the park – those run by Phong Nha Farmstay are recommended (1,000,000d by minibus). **Oxalis** (☑ 052-367 7678; www.oxalis.co.vn; Son Trach) is a highly professional adventure tour operator specialising in caving and trekking expeditions; it is the only outfit licensed to conduct tours to Hang Son Doong.

It's possible to rent a bike and explore the region yourself, though road signs are lacking. But with a sense of adventure, some wheels and a map (ask at Jungle Bar) it's perfectly doable.

Hue

☑ 054 / POP 388,000

Hue is the intellectual, cultural and spiritual heart of Vietnam. Palaces and pagodas, tombs and temples, culture and cuisine, history and heartbreak – there's no shortage of poetic pairings to describe Hue.

A World Heritage Site, the capital of the Nguyen emperors is where tourists come to see the decaying, opulent royal tombs and the grand, crumbling Citadel. Most of these architectural attractions lie along the northern side of the Song Huong (Perfume River). For rest and recreation, plus a little refreshment, the south bank is where it's at.

The city hosts a biennial arts festival, the **Festival of Hue** (www.huefestival.com), on even-numbered years, featuring local and international artists and performers.

Hue

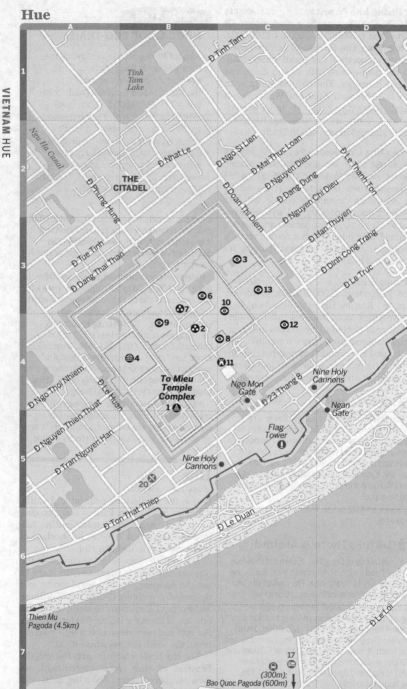

Tinh
Tam
Lake

Ngu Ha Canal

Đ Tinh Tam

Đ Nhat Le

Đ Ngo Si Lien

Đ Mai Thuc Loan

Đ Nguyen Dieu

Đ Dang Dung

Đ Le Thanh Ton

THE
CITADEL

Đ Phung Hung

Đ Doan Thi Diem

Đ Nguyen Chi Dieu

Đ Tue Tinh

Đ Dang Thai Than

Đ Han Thuyen

Đ Dinh Cong Trang

Đ Le Truc

3

13

6
10
7
9
2
8
12

4

To Mieu
Temple
Complex

11

Ngo Mon
Gate

Nine Holy
Cannons

1

Đ 23 Thang 8

Ngan
Gate

Flag
Tower

Đ Ngo Thoi Nhiem

Đ Le Huan

Đ Nguyen Thien Thuat

Nine Holy
Cannons

Đ Tran Nguyen Han

2

Đ Ton That Thiep

Đ Le Duan

Đ Le Loi

Thien Mu
Pagoda (4.5km)

17
(300m);
Bao Quoc Pagoda (600m)

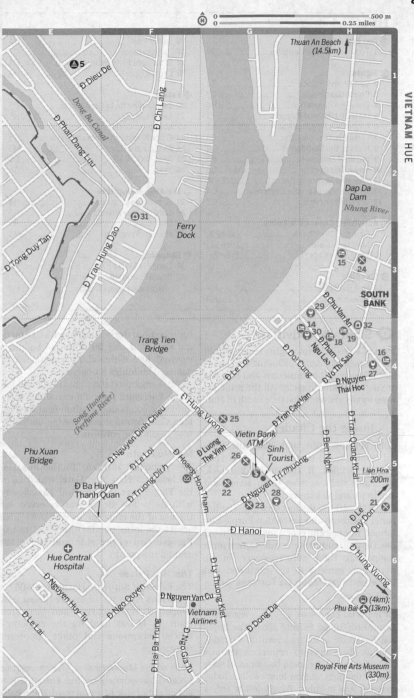

Hue

◉ Sights & Activities

Most of Hue's principal sights reside within the moats of its Citadel, including the Imperial Enclosure. Other museums and pagodas are dotted around the city. All the principal royal tombs are some distance south of Hue.

◎ Inside the Citadel

Built between 1804 and 1833, the Citadel (Kinh Thanh) is still the heart of Hue. Heavily fortified, it consists of 2m-thick, 10km-long walls, a moat (30m across and 4m deep), and 10 gateways.

The Citadel has distinct sections. The Imperial Enclosure and Forbidden Purple City formed the epicentre of Vietnamese royal life. On the southwestern side were temple compounds. There were residences in the northwest, gardens in the northeast and in the north the **Mang Ca Fortress** (still a military base).

★**Imperial Enclosure**   HISTORIC SITE
(admission 105,000d; ⊙ 7am-5.30pm) The Imperial Enclosure is a citadel-within-a-citadel, housing the emperor's residence, temples and palaces and the main buildings of state within 6m-high, 2.5km-long walls. Today much of it is in ruins. What's left is only a fraction of the original – the enclosure was

badly bombed during the French and American wars, and only 20 of its 148 buildings survived. Restoration and reconstruction of damaged buildings is ongoing.

We've organised the sights inside the Imperial Enclosure as you'll encounter them inside the compound, beginning at the Ngo Mon Gate entrance and moving anticlockwise around the enclosure.

Ngo Mon Gate   GATE
The principal entrance to the Imperial Enclosure is Ngo Mon Gate, which faces the Flag Tower. The central passageway with its yellow doors was reserved for the use of the emperor, as was the bridge across the lotus pond. Others had to use the gates to either side and the paths around the pond.

Thai Hoa Palace   PALACE
The Palace of Supreme Harmony (1803) is a spacious hall with an ornate timber roof supported by 80 carved and lacquered columns. It was used for the emperor's official receptions and other important ceremonies.

Halls of the Mandarins   HISTORIC BUILDING
Located immediately behind Thai Hoa Palace on either side of a courtyard, these halls

were used by mandarins as offices and to prepare for court ceremonies.

Behind the courtyard are the ruins of **Can Chanh Palace**, where two wonderful long galleries, painted in gleaming scarlet lacquer, have been reconstructed.

Emperor's Reading Room HISTORIC BUILDING
(Thai Binh Lau) The exquisite (though crumbling) little two-storey Emperor's Reading Room was the only part of the Forbidden Purple City to escape damage during the French reoccupation of Hue in 1947. It's currently being renovated and not open to visitors, but it's worth checking out the Gaudiesque roof mosaics.

Royal Theatre HISTORIC BUILDING
(Duyen Thi Duong; ☑ 054-351 4989; www.nhanhac. com.vn; tickets 70,000d; ⊙ performances 9am, 10am, 2.30pm & 3.30pm) The Royal Theatre, begun in 1826 and later home to the National Conservatory of Music, has been rebuilt on its former foundations. Cultural performances here last 30 minutes.

Almost nothing remains of the **Thai To Mieu temple complex**, now a plant nursery, and the former **University of Arts**.

Co Ha Gardens GARDEN
Occupying the northeast corner of the Imperial Enclosure, these delightful gardens were developed by the first four emperors of the Nguyen dynasty, but fell into disrepair. They've been beautifully recreated in the last few years, and are dotted with little gazebo-style pavilions (one a cafe) and ponds.

Forbidden Purple City RUIN
(Tu Cam Thanh) There's almost nothing left of the once-magnificent Forbidden Purple City, once reserved solely for the personal use of the emperor.

Dien Tho Residence HISTORIC BUILDING
The stunning, partially ruined Dien Tho Residence (1804) once comprised the apartments and audience hall of the Queen Mothers of the Nguyen dynasty.

Just outside is an enchanting **pleasure pavilion**, a carved wooden building set above a lily pond. This has now been transformed into a delightful little cafe.

★**To Mieu Temple Complex** BUDDHIST TEMPLE
Taking up the southwest corner of the Imperial Enclosure, this highly impressive walled complex has been beautifully restored.

The imposing three-tiered **Hien Lam Pavilion** , dating from 1824, sits on the south side of the complex. On the other side of a courtyard is the solemn **To Mieu Temple**, housing shrines to each of the emperors, topped by their photos.

Between these two temples are **Nine Dynastic Urns** (*dinh*), cast between 1835 and 1836, each dedicated to one Nguyen sovereign.

Nine Holy Cannons CANNON
Located just inside the Citadel ramparts are the Nine Holy Cannons (1804), symbolic protectors of the palace and kingdom. Each brass cannon is 5m long and weighs about 10 tonnes.

◉ Outside the Citadel

★**Royal Tombs** HISTORIC BUILDINGS
(⊙6.30am-5.30pm summer, 7am-5pm winter) The tombs of the rulers of the Nguyen dynasty (1802–1945) are extravagant mausoleums, spread out along the banks of the Perfume River 2km to 16km south of Hue. The three listed here are particularly impressive, but there are many more.

The **Tomb of Tu Duc** (admission 80,000d), built between 1864 and 1867, is one of the most impressive. Emperor Tu Duc designed it himself, but the enormous expense and the forced labour used in its construction spawned a coup plot that was discovered and suppressed. Tu Duc lived a life of imperial luxury and carnal excess (he had 104 wives and countless concubines), though no offspring.

Renowned for its architecture and sublime natural setting, the **Tomb of Minh Mang** (admission 80,000d) was planned during his reign (1820–40) but built by his successor, Thieu Tri. It's on the west bank of the Perfume River, about 12km from Hue and surrounded by a forest.

The hillside **Tomb of Khai Dinh** (admission 80,000d), 10km south of Hue, is a synthesis of Vietnamese and European elements. Most of the tomb's grandiose exterior is covered in blackened concrete, creating an unexpectedly Gothic air, while the interiors resemble an explosion of colourful mosaic.

While many of the tombs can be reached by boat, you'll have more time to enjoy them by renting your own bicycle or motorbike. Alternatively, hire a *xe om* or car and driver for the day.

Hue's Imperial Enclosure

EXPLORING THE SITE

An incongruous combination of meticulously restored palaces and pagodas, ruins and rubble, the Imperial Enclosure is approached from the south through the outer walls of the Citadel. It's best to tackle the site as a walking tour, winding your way around the structures in an anticlockwise direction.

You'll pass directly through the monumental **Ngo Mon Gateway ❶** where the ticket office is located. This dramatic approach quickens the pulse and adds to the sense of occasion as you enter this citadel-within-a-citadel. Directly ahead is the **Thai Hoa Palace ❷** where the emperor would greet offical visitors from his elevated throne. Continuing north you'll step across a small courtyard to the twin **Halls of the Mandarins ❸**, where mandarins once had their offices and prepared for ceremonial occasions.

To the northeast is the Royal Theatre, where traditional dance performances are held several times daily. Next you'll be able to get a glimpse of the Emperor's Reading Room built by Thieu Tri and used as a place of retreat. Just east of here are the lovely Co Ha Gardens. Wander their pathways, dotted with hundreds of bonsai trees and potted plants, which have been recently restored.

Guarding the far north of the complex is the Tu Vo Phuong Pavilion, from where you can follow a moat to the Truong San residence and then loop back south via the **Dien Tho Residence ❹** and finally view the beautifully restored temple compound of To Mieu, perhaps the most rewarding part of the entire enclosure to visit, including its fabulous **Nine Dynastic Urns ❺**.

TOP TIPS

Allow half a day to explore the Citadel. Drink vendors are dotted around the site, but the best places to take a break are the delightful Co Ha Gardens, the Tu Vo Phuong Pavilion and the Dien Tho Residence (the latter two also serve food).

Dien Tho Residence
This pretty corner of the complex, with its low structures and pond, was the residence of many Queen Mothers. The earliest structures here date from 1804.

Tu Vo Phuong Pavilion

Truong San Residence

❹

To Mieu Temple Complex

Nine Dynastic Urns
These colossal bronze urns were commissioned by Emperor Minh Mang and cast between 1835 and 1836. They're embellished with decorative elements including landscapes, rivers, flowers and animals.

Tu Vo Phuong Pavilion

The two-storey Tu Vo Phuong Pavilion, elevated above a moat, was once a defense bastion for the northern part of the Imperial Enclosure. It combines both European and Vietnamese architectural styles (note the elaborate roof dragons).

Halls of the Mandarins

Unesco-sponsored conservation work is ongoing in the eastern hall here to preserve the elaborate ceiling and wall murals.

**Emperor's
Reading Room**

**Co Ha
Gardens**

**Royal
Theatre**

③

②

①

Ngo Mon Gateway

A huge, grandiose structure that guards the main approach to the Imperial Enclosure, this gateway has a fortified lower level and a more architecturally elaborate upper part. It dates from 1833.

Thai Hoa Palace

Be sure to check out this palace's incredible ironwood columns, painted in 12 coats of brilliant scarlet and gold lacquer. The structure was saved from collapse by restoration work in the 1990s.

★ Thien Mu Pagoda
BUDDHIST TEMPLE

FREE Built on a hill overlooking the Perfume River, 4km southwest of the Citadel, this pagoda is an icon of Vietnam and as potent a symbol of Hue as the Citadel. The 21m-high octagonal tower, **Thap Phuoc Duyen**, was constructed under the reign of Emperor Thieu Tri in 1844. Each of its seven storeys is dedicated to a *manushi-buddha* (a Buddha that appeared in human form).

Since the 1960s it has been a flashpoint for political demonstrations.

Royal Fine Arts Museum
MUSEUM

(150 Đ Nguyen Hue; ⊘ 6.30am-5.30pm summer, 7am-5pm winter) **FREE** This recently renovated museum is located in the baroque-influenced An Dinh Palace, commissioned by Emperor Khai Dinh in 1918 and full of elaborate murals, floral motifs and *trompe l'œil* details. Emperor Bao Dai lived here with his family after abdicating in 1945. Inside you'll find some outstanding ceramics, paintings, furniture, silverware, porcelain and royal clothing, though information is a little lacking.

Dieu De National Pagoda
BUDDHIST TEMPLE

(Quoc Tu Dieu De; 102 Đ Bach Dang) **FREE** Overlooking Dong Ba Canal, this pagoda was built under Emperor Thieu Tri's rule (1841–47) and is famous for its four low towers, one to either side of the gate and two flanking the sanctuary.

Dieu De was a stronghold of Buddhist and student opposition to the South Vietnamese government and the American War, and many arrests were made here when police stormed the building in 1966.

Bao Quoc Pagoda
BUDDHIST TEMPLE

(Ham Long Hill) **FREE** Founded in 1670, this hilltop pagoda is on the southern bank of the Perfume River and has a striking triple-gated entrance reached via a wide staircase. On the right is a centre for training monks, which has been functioning since 1940.

To get here, head south from Đ Le Loi on Đ Dien Bien Phu and take the first right after crossing the railway tracks.

☞ Tours

Most hotels and travellers' cafes offer shared tours hitting the main sights (from as little as US$4 to around US$18 per person). These tours usually run from 8am to 4pm. There are many different itineraries; some of the better ones start with a morning river cruise, stopping at pagodas and temples, then after lunch you transfer to a minibus to hit the main tombs and then return to Hue by road.

OFF THE BEATEN TRACK

TOMBS & DUNES

From the centre of Hue it's only 15km north to the sands of **Thuan An Beach** where there's a large resort hotel. If you continue southeast from here there's a beautiful, quiet coastal road to follow with very light traffic (so it's ideal for bikers). The route actually traverses a narrow coastal island, with views of the Tam Giang–Cau Hai lagoon on the inland side and simply stunning sandy beaches and dunes on the other. This wonderful coastal strip is virtually undeveloped, but between September and March the water's often too rough for swimming.

From Thuan An the road winds past villages alternating with shrimp lagoons and vegetable gardens. Thousands and thousands of garishly colourful and opulent graves and family temples line the beach, most the final resting places of Viet Kieu (overseas Vietnamese). Little tracks cut through the tombs and sand dunes to the ocean. Just pick a spot and the chances are you'll have a beach to yourself.

At glorious **Phu Thuan** beach (about 7km southeast of Thuan An) you pass the lovely Beach Bar Hue (p93). Around 8km further south there are the remains of Phu Dien, a small Cham temple half-buried in a sand dune.

Continuing southeast a narrow but paved road weaves past fishing villages, shrimp farms, more giant sand dunes and the settlement of **Vinh Hung** until you reach the mouth of another river estuary at **Thuon Phu An**, where there's a row of seafood restaurants. This spot is 40km from Thuan An. Cross the Tu Hien bridge here and you can continue around the eastern lip of the huge Cau Hai lagoon and link up with Hwy 1.

On the cheaper options you'll often have to hire a motorbike to get from the moorings to the tombs, or walk (in the heat of the day).

It's perfectly possible to rent a *xe om* or your own bike and do a DIY tour.

Cafe on Thu Wheels TOUR
(☑054-383 2241; minhthuhue@yahoo.com; 10/2 Đ Nguyen Tri Phuong) Inexpensive cycle, motorcycle (from US$10 per person) and car tours (DMZ from US$40 per person) around Hue and beyond, run by Minh, who is a great character.

Stop & Go Café TOUR
(☑054-382 7051; www.stopandgo-hue.com; 3 Đ Hung Vuong) Personalised motorbike and car tours around Hue. Guided trips to Hoi An stopping at beaches are also recommended.

Mandarin Café TOUR
(☑054-382 1281; www.mrcumandarin.com; 24 Đ Tran Cao Van) Boss Mr Cu organises transport and tours.

🛏 Sleeping

All the following places are in the city, except Beach Bar Hue.

⭐**Huenino** GUESTHOUSE $
(☑054 625 2171; www.hueninohotel.com; 14 Đ Nguyen Cong Tru; r US$14-24; ❄✳@🛜) Family-owned, this warm, welcoming guesthouse has an artistic flavour with stylish furniture, artwork and smallish rooms with minibar, cable TV and good-quality beds. A generous breakfast is included.

⭐**Jade Hotel** GUESTHOUSE $
(☑054-393 8849; www.jadehotelhue.com; 17 Đ Nguyen Thai Hoc; r US$15-25; ❄✳@🛜) You'll find simply excellent service standards at this fine place; staff are very sweet and welcoming. Rooms enjoy soft comfy mattresses and there's a nice lobby-lounge for hanging out.

⭐**Beach Bar Hue** HOTEL $
(☑0908 993 584; www.beachbarhue.com; Phu Thuan beach; dm/bungalow 250,000/600,000d, meals 100,000d; ❄🛜) With excellent dorms and bungalows geared to backpackers, this place sits pretty on a sublime stretch of sand (with no hawkers...for now).

Hue Backpackers HOSTEL $
(☑054-382 6567; www.vietnambackpackerhostels. com; 10 Đ Pham Ngu Lao; dm US$8-12, r US$18; ✳@🛜) Backpacker mecca thanks to its cen-

tral location, eager-to-please staff, good info and sociable bar-restaurant. Dorms (some with queen-sized beds) are well designed and have air-con and lockers.

Moonlight Hotel Hue HOTEL $$
(☑054-397 9797; www.moonlighthue.com; 20 Pham Ngu Lao; r US$44-65, ste US$70-140; ❄✳@🛜🛁) A 'new generation' Hue hotel where the rooms boast a very high spec for the modest bucks charged. All come with polished wooden floors, marble-clad bathrooms (with tubs) and lavish furnishings. Pay a bit more for a balcony with a Perfume River view. Breakfast is great but the pool area is small and covered.

Orchid Hotel HOTEL $$
(☑054-383 1177; www.orchidhotel.com.vn; 30A Đ Chu Van An; r US$30-75; ❄✳@🛜🛁) This is a very well-run modern hotel rightly renowned for its warm service; staff really make an effort here. The accommodation is excellent: all options have laminate flooring, bright scatter cushions and a DVD player, while some pricier rooms even have a jacuzzi with city views.

Gold Hotel HOTEL $$
(☑054-381 4815; www.goldhotelhue.com; 28 Đ Ba Trieu; r US$35-42, ste US$60-80; ✳@🛜🛁) Impressive new hotel a short walk or *cyclo* (pedicab) ride from the river. It has a main restaurant area and immaculately presented modern rooms with superb bathrooms (all have tubs).

⭐**Pilgrimage Village** RESORT HOTEL $$$
(☑054-388 5461; www.pilgrimagevillage.com; 130 Đ Minh Mang; r/bungalows from US$110/153; ❄✳@🛜🛁) Designed around a verdant valley that includes a 40m pool, lotus ponds and a state-of-the-art spa and yoga space, this feels more like a Zen eco-retreat than a hotel. There's a fine restaurant, lovely breakfast room and bar. Located about 3km from the centre of Hue.

La Residence HOTEL $$$
(☑054-383 7475; www.la-residence-hue.com; 5 Đ Le Loi; r from US$155; ❄✳@🛜🛁) Once the French governor's residence, this wonderful hotel resonates with art-deco class, with its original features and period detailing. Rooms are sumptuously appointed, the restaurants are excellent and service is polished and professional.

✖ Eating

We have famed fussy-eater Emperor Tu Duc to thank for the culinary variety of Hue, and an imperial cuisine banquet is usually a memorable experience.

Royal rice cakes, the most common of which is *banh khoai,* are well worth seeking out here.

Lien Hoa VEGETARIAN $

(3 Đ Le Quy Don; meals 30,000-55,000d; ⊙11am-9.30pm; 🖉) Nononsense, very local Vietnamese vegie restaurant renowned for providing filling food at rock-bottom rates. Fresh *banh beo* (steamed rice pancakes), noodle dishes, crispy fried jackfruit and eggplant with ginger all deliver. The menu has very rough English translations.

GETTING TO LAOS: CENTRAL BORDERS

Dong Ha to Savannakhet

Getting to the border The Lao Bao/Dansavanh border crossing, on the Sepon River (Song Xe Pon), is one of the most popular and least problematic border crossings between Vietnam and Laos. Buses to Savannakhet in Laos run from Hue via Dong Ha and Lao Bao. From Hue, there's a 7am air-con bus (340,000d, 9½ hours), on odd days only, that stops in Dong Ha at the Sepon Travel office around 8.30am to pick up more passengers. It's also easy to cross the border on your own; Dong Ha is the gateway. Buses leave the town to Lao Bao (55,000d, two hours) roughly every 15 minutes. From here *xe om* charge 12,000d to the border. You can check schedules and book tickets at Tam's Cafe.

At the border The border posts (open 7am to 6pm) are a few hundred metres apart. Lao visas are available for most nationalities for between US$30 and US$40.

Moving on *Sŏrngtǎaou* head regularly to Sepon, from where you can get a bus or another *sŏrngtǎaou* to Savannakhet.

For more information about crossing this border in the other direction, see p333.

Vinh to Vieng Khan & Tay Son

Getting to the border The Cau Treo/Nam Phao border crossing has a dodgy reputation with travellers on local non-direct buses, who report chronic overcharging and hassle (such as bus drivers ejecting foreigners in the middle of nowhere unless they cough up extra bucks). Stick to direct services. Most transport to Phonsavan in Laos uses the Nong Haet/Nam Can border further north. Buses leave Vinh at 6am (on Monday, Wednesday, Friday and Saturday) for Vieng Khan in Laos (280,000d). There are also regular local buses from Vinh to Tay Son (70,000d, two hours) and then irregular services from Tay Son on to the border at Cau Treo. Otherwise *xe om* ask for around 170,000d for the ride.

At the border The border is open from 7am to 6pm. Lao visas are available for most nationalities for between US$30 and US$40.

Moving on A jumbo or *sŏrngtǎaou* between the border and Lak Sao runs to about 50,000 kip (bargain hard).

For more information about crossing this border in the other direction, see p329.

Vinh to Phonsavan

Getting to the border The often mist-shrouded Nam Can/Nong Haet border crossing is 250km northwest of Vinh. Direct buses from Vinh's marketplace leave daily for Phonsavan in Laos (320,000d, 12 hours). It's possible to travel independently from Vinh to Muong Xen by bus and then take a motorbike (around 170,000d) uphill to the border, but we strongly recommend you take the direct option due to overcharging and hassle.

At the border The border post is open from 7am to 5pm. Lao visas are available for most nationalities for between US$30 and US$40.

Moving on Transport on the Laos side to Nong Haet is erratic, but once you get there you can pick up a bus to Phonsavan.

For more information about crossing this border in the other direction, see p313.

Take
JAPANESE $

(34 Đ Tran Cao Van; meals 60,000-140,000d; ⊙11.30am-9.30pm) An authentic Japanese restaurant with tasteful furnishings (lanterns, calligraphy wall hangings and even fake cherry blossom) and a winsome menu of sushi, tempura and yakitori dishes.

Restaurant Bloom
CAFE $

(14 Đ Nguyen Cong Tru; meals from 35,000-80,000d; ⊙7am-9.30pm; 🖥) Ideal for pasta, a sandwich, baguette or homemade cake (baked on the premises), this likeable little cafe employs disadvantaged youths and graduates of the ACWP (Aid to Children Without Parents) training program. Food is MSG-free.

Mandarin Café
VIETNAMESE $

(☑054-382 1281; 24 Đ Tran Cao Van; mains from 26,000d; 🖥☑) Owner-photographer Mr Cu, whose inspirational pictures adorn the walls, has been hosting backpackers here for years, and his relaxed restaurant has lots of vegetarian and breakfast choices. Also operates as a tour agency.

Stop & Go Café
INTERNATIONAL $

(3 Đ Hung Vuong; meals 20,000-60,000d; ⊙7am-10pm; 🖥) Atmospheric little place with decent Vietnamese and backpacker fare: *banh beo*, beef noodle soup, tacos, pizza and pasta, and filling Western breakfasts. It's worth dropping by for the excellent travel information.

Omar Khayyam's Indian Restaurant
INDIAN $$

(☑054-382 1616; www.omarkhayyamhue.com; 34 Đ Nguyen Tri Phuong; mains 48,000-170,000d; ⊙noon 10pm, 🖥) If you're after a spice fix, this Indian has curries, samosas and vegie dishes. Imported Australian lamb is used for the full-flavour rogan josh, or order a thali (set meal from 145,000d) for a real treat.

★ Les Jardins de la Carambole
FRENCH, VIETNAMESE $$$

(☑054-354 8815; www.lesjardinsdelacarambole. com; 32 Dang Tran Con; meals US$12-30; ⊙7am-11pm; 🖥) A memorable dining experience, this incredibly classy and refined French restaurant occupies a gorgeous colonial-style building in the Citadel quarter. The menu majors in Gallic classics, and there's a lengthy wine list and informed service. It's just the place for a romantic meal – arrive

BACH MA NATIONAL PARK

A French-era hill station known for its cool weather, **Bach Ma National Park** (Vuon Quoc Gia Bach Ma; ☑054-387 1330; adult/child/under 6yr 40,000/20,000d/free) is 45km southeast of Hue. The road to the summit has recently been upgraded.

There's some decent trekking in the lower levels through subtropical forest to villages on the fringes of the park. You can book village and birdwatching **tours** and English- or French-speaking guides (250,000d per day) at the visitor centre. Unexploded ordnance is still in the area, so stick to the trails. There's a **guesthouse** at the park entrance.

by *cyclo* and it's easy to roll back the years to Indochine times.

🍷 Drinking & Nightlife

★ Brown Eyes
BAR

(Đ Chu Van An; ⊙5pm-late; 🖥) The most popular late-night bar in town, with a good blend of locals and traveller-revellers and a party vibe. DJs drive the dance floor with R&B, hip hop and house music anthems. It's open 'till the last one passes out'.

DMZ Bar
BAR

(www.dmz.com.vn; 60 Đ Le Loi; ⊙7am-1am; 🖥) Ever-popular riverside bar with a free pool table, cold Huda beer, cocktails (try a watermelon mojito) and a good craic most nights. Happy hour is 3pm till 8pm.

Hue Backpackers
BAR

(10 Đ Pham Ngu Lao; ⊙6am-11pm; 🖥) There's always a buzz about this backpackers' drinking den, which packs 'em in with its infused vodkas and happy hour (8pm to 9pm).

Café on Thu Wheels
BAR

(10/2 Đ Nguyen Tri Phuong; ⊙6.30am-11pm; 🖥) Hole-in-the-wall bar par excellence. Graffiti-splattered walls, a sociable vibe and good info from the feisty owner, Thu, and her family. They also offer good tours.

🛍 Shopping

Spiral Foundation Healing the Wounded Heart Center
HANDICRAFTS

(☑054-383 3694; www.hwhshop.com; 23 Đ Vo Thi Sau; ⊙8am-6pm) Gorgeous eco-friendly

TRANSPORT FROM HUE

DESTINATION	AIR	BUS	CAR & MOTORBIKE	TRAIN
Danang	N/A	US$3.50, 3hr, frequent	2½-4hr	US$3.50-6, 2½-4hr, 7 daily
Dong Hoi	N/A	US$4-7, 4hr, 12 daily	3½hr	US$5-11, 3-5½hr, 7 daily
Hanoi	from US$30, 1hr, 3 daily	US$20-32, 13-16hr, 9 daily	16hr	US$24-42, 12-15½hr, 6 daily
HCMC	from US$34, 1¼hr, 4 daily	US$26-42, 19-24hr, 9 daily	22hr	US$32-55, 19½-23hr, 5 daily
Ninh Binh	N/A	US$14-22, 10½-12hr, 8 daily	11hr	US$19-35, 10-13hr, 5 daily
Vinh	N/A	US$9-17, 7½-9hr, 7 daily	7hr	US$23-38, 6½-10hr, 5 daily

handicrafts (including picture frames from recycled beer cans) made by disabled artisans. Profits aid heart surgery for children.

Dong Ba Market   MARKET
(Đ Tran Hung Dao; ⊙ 6.30am-8pm) Just north of Trang Tien Bridge, this is Hue's largest market, selling anything and everything.

ⓘ Information

There are lots of internet cafes on the tourist strips of Đ Hung Vuong and Đ Le Loi.
Hue Central Hospital (Benh Vien Trung Uong Hue; ☑ 054-382 2325; 16 Đ Le Loi; ⊙ 6am-10pm)
Post Office (8 Đ Hoang Hoa Tham; ⊙ 7am-5.30pm Mon-Sat)
Sinh Tourist (☑ 054-382 3309; www.thesinhtourist.vn; 7 Đ Nguyen Tri Phuong) Books open-tour buses and buses to Laos.
Vietin Bank ATM (12 Đ Hung Vuong)

ⓘ Getting There & Away

AIR

Vietnam Airlines (☑ 054-382 4709; 23 Đ Nguyen Van Cu; ⊙ closed Sun) has two daily flights to both Hanoi and HCMC. **VietJet Air** (☑ 1900 1886; www.vietjetair.com) also connects Hue with HCMC and the capital.

Phu Bai airport is 14km south of town. Metered taxis meet all flights and cost about 190,000d to the centre, or use the minibus service for 50,000d. Vietnam Airlines also runs an airport shuttle, which can collect you from your hotel (tickets 60,000d).

BUS

The main bus station is 4km southeast of the centre on the continuation of Đ Hung Vuong.

An Hoa bus station (Hwy 1), northwest of the Citadel, serves northern destinations, including Dong Ha.

From here, one daily bus at 11.15am (look for 'Phuc Vu' in the windscreen) heads for Phong Nha Farmstay and Son Trach (150,000d, four hours). There's also a useful minibus connection (500,000d, five hours) between Hue Backpackers and Phong Nha Farmstay/Son Trach village, leaving the hostel in Hue at 1pm and stopping at the Vinh Moc Tunnels and the Ben Hai River Museum. Entrance tickets and a guide at the tunnels are included.

Hue is a regular stop on open-tour bus routes. Most drop off and pick up passengers at central hotels.

The Mandarin and Stop & Go cafes can arrange bookings for the bus to Savannakhet, Laos.

TRAIN

Hue train station (☑ 054-382 2175; 2 Đ Phan Chu Trinh) is at the southwestern end of Đ Le Loi.

ⓘ Getting Around

Bicycles (US$1 to US$2), motorbikes (from US$5) and cars (from US$40 per day) can be hired through hotels and tour operators. **Mai Linh** (☑ 054-389 8989) has air-con taxis with meters. *Cyclos* and *xe om* will find you when you need them – and when you don't.

Around Hue

Demilitarised Zone (DMZ)

From 1954 until 1975, the Ben Hai River served as the dividing line between South Vietnam and North Vietnam. The DMZ, 90km north of Hue, consisted of the area 5km on either side of the line.

Many of the 'sights' around the DMZ are places where historical events happened, and may not be worthwhile unless you're into war history. To make sense of it all, and to avoid areas where there's still unexploded ordnance (UXO), take a guide. Group day tours from Hue cost from US$15 for a budget bus trip to up to US$120 for a specialised car tour with a Viet vet.

◉ Sights

Vinh Moc Tunnels
HISTORICAL SITE

(admission 20,000d; ⊙7am-4.30pm) A highly impressive complex of tunnels 110km northwest of Hue, Vinh Moc is the remains of a coastal North Vietnamese village that literally went underground in response to unremitting American bombing. More than 90 families disappeared into three levels of tunnels running almost 2km in all, and continued to live and work while bombs rained down around them.

Most of the tunnels are open to visitors, and are kept in their original form (except for electric lights, a luxury the villagers certainly didn't have).

Khe Sanh Combat Base
HISTORIC SITE

(museum 20,000d; ⊙museum 7am-5pm) The site of the most famous siege of the American War: about 500 Americans, 10,000 North Vietnamese troops and uncounted civilian bystanders died around this remote highland base. Today the site is occupied by a small **museum**. Khe Sanh is 3km north of the small town of Huong Hoa.

Truong Son National Cemetery
CEMETERY

An evocative memorial to the legions of North Vietnamese soldiers who died along the Ho Chi Minh Trail, this cemetery is a sobering sight. More than 10,000 graves dot these hillsides, each marked by a simple white tombstone headed by the inscription *liet si* (martyr).

Danang

☑0511 / POP 992,000

Nowhere in Vietnam is changing as fast as Danang. For decades it had a reputation as a slightly mundane provincial backwater, but big changes are ongoing. The Han riverfront is resplendent with gleaming new modernist hotels and restaurants. Beachside, five-star hotel developments are emerging on the My Khe strip, andnd a revamped international airport opened in 2012.

Danang still has few conventional sights, except for an outstanding museum. For most travellers, a day or two is enough.

🛏 Sleeping

An excellent selection of new minihotels has opened along the riverside in central Danang, though good budget hotels aren't as easy to find.

🛏 City Centre

Zion Hotel
HOTEL $

(☑0511-382 8333; www.sion.com.vn; 121/7 Hoang Van Thu; s US$15, d US$20-25; ❖@🛜) There's a scarlet theme running through this new excellent-value hotel from the lobby to the inviting, modern rooms. Boasts a convenient location and staff are eager to please.

Bao Ngoc Hotel
HOTEL $

(☑0511-381 7711; baongochotel@dng.vnn.vn; 48 Đ Phan Chu Trinh; r US$18-22; ❖@🛜) Spacious, carpeted and comfortable rooms full of solid, dark-wood furniture; some have sofas. The ageing five-storey building also retains a glint of colonial character, with its chocolate-brown French-style shutters.

New Moon Hotel
HOTEL $$

(☑0511-382 8488; www.newmoonhotel.vn; 126 Đ Bach Dang; r 440,000-1,100,000d; ❖@🛜) Modern minihotel with a selection of inviting rooms in different price categories, all with flat-screen TV, minibar, wi-fi and en-suite marble bathrooms. The river-view options enjoy incredible vistas.

DON'T MISS

MUSEUM OF CHAM SCULPTURE

Danang's jewel is its famed **Museum of Cham Sculpture** (Bao Tang; 1 Đ Trung Nu Vuong; admission 30,000d; ⊙7am-5pm). This classic, colonial-era building houses the finest collection of Cham sculpture to be found anywhere on earth. More than 300 pieces on display include altars, lingas, garudas, apsaras, Ganeshas and images of Shiva, Brahma and Vishnu – all dating from the 5th to 15th centuries. These intricately carved sandstone pieces come from Cham sites all over Vietnam.

Guides hang out at the museum's entrance.

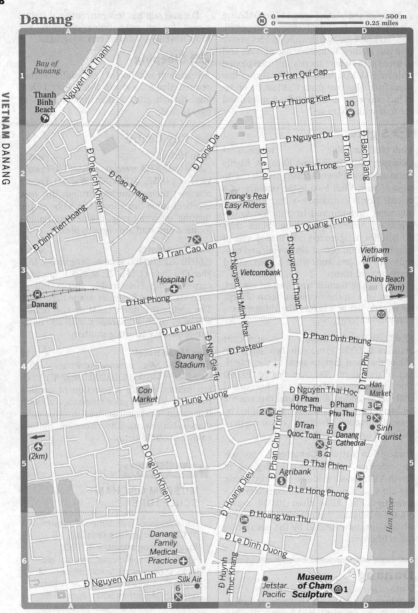

Danang

VIETNAM DANANG

Rainbow Hotel HOTEL $$

(📞0511-382 2216; www.rainbowhotel.com.vn; 220 Đ Bach Dang; r 630,000-1,100,000d; ❄@🛜) Enjoy a prime riverfront location at modest rates. Contemporary decor and flooring, artwork, modern furniture and all mod cons.

China Beach

Eena Hotel HOTEL $

(📞0511-222 5123; www.geocities.jp/eenahotel; Khu An Cu 3, My Khe; s 150,000-400,000d; d & tw 350,000-800,000d; ❄@🛜) This Japanese-

Danang

owned minihotel is a great base with its immaculately clean and spacious white rooms. There's a lift, fast wi-fi, friendly English-speaking staff and a good free breakfast.

🍴 Eating & Drinking

Quan Com Hue Ngon   VIETNAMESE, BARBECUE $
(65 Tran Quoc Toan; meals 50,000-80,000d; ⊙ 3-9pm) Fab new barbecue place, all charcoal smoke and sizzling meats, where you grill your own. There's a street terrace, and the welcoming English-speaking owner will help with the menu.

Com Tay Cam Cung Dinh   VIETNAMESE $
(K254/2 Đ Hoang Dieu; dishes 15,000-40,000d; ⊙ 11am-8pm) This simple place is good for local dishes including *hoanh thanh* – a wonton-like combination of minced pork and shrimp. It's down a little alley.

★ Waterfront   INTERNATIONAL, BAR $$
(☎ 0511-384 3373; www.waterfrontdanang.com; 150-152 Đ Bach Dang; meals 95,000-360,000d; ⊙ 10am-11pm; 🛜) Riverfront lounge/restaurant that gets everything right on every level. It works as a stylish bar for a chilled glass of NZ sauvignon blanc and also as a destination restaurant for a memorable meal (book the terrace deck for a stunning river vista). The menu features imported meats, Asian seafood and terrific 'gourmet' sandwiches.

Le Bambino   FRENCH, INTERNATIONAL $$
(☎ 0511-389 6386; www.lebambino.com; 122/11 Đ Quang Trung; meals 120,000-300,000d; ⊙ 11.30am-1.30pm & 4.30-10pm Mon-Sat, 4.30-10pm Sun; 🛜) Atmospheric place run by a French-Vietnamese couple who have crafted a great menu that takes in French classics, pub food, barbecued meat (try the ribs) and a few Vietnamese favourites. Eat inside or around the pool, and don't neglect the wine list or the cheese selections, both superb.

★ Luna Pub   BAR
(www.lunadautunno.vn; 9A Tran Phu; ⊙ 11.30am-late; 🛜) Half-bar, half-Italian restaurant, this hot new hang-out is a cool warehouse-sized space with an open frontage, a DJ booth in the cabin of a truck, cool music, an amazing drinks selection and some *shisha* smoking action. Also popular with the expat crowd for its authentic Italian food (pizza, pasta, salads and more).

ℹ Information

Cafes and hotels have wi-fi; there are internet cafes scattered all over Danang. Consult the website www.indanang.com for reviews and information.

Agribank (202 Đ Nguyen Chi Thanh; ⊙ 7.30am-3.30pm Mon-Sat) ATM and exchange service.

Danang Family Medical Practice (☎ 0511-358 2700; www.vietnammedicalpractice.com; 50-52 Đ Nguyen Van Linh; ⊙ 7am-6pm) Set up like a mini-hospital with inpatient facilities, this is an excellent practice run by an Australian doctor.

Hospital C (Benh Vien C; ☎ 0511-382 1483; 122 Đ Hai Phong; ⊙ 24hr) The most advanced hospital in Danang.

Main Post Office (64 Đ Bach Dang; ⊙ 7am-5.30pm) Near the Song Han Bridge.

Sinh Tourist (☎ 0511-384 3258; www.thesinhtourist.vn; 154 Đ Bach Dang) Books open-tour buses and tours, and offers currency exchange.

Trong's Real Easy Riders (☎ 0903 597 971; www.easyridervn.com; 12/20 Nguyen Thi Minh Khai) A motorbike collective that operates out of Danang. A four-day trip to the central highlands costs US$280; day trips are also possible.

ℹ Getting There & Away

AIR

Danang's international airport has **Silk Air** (☎ 0511-356 2708; www.silkair.com; HAGL Plaza Hotel, 1 Đ Nguyen Van Linh) flights to Singapore and Siem Riep, Lao Airlines flights to Pakse, Savannakhet and Vientiane, and there are a few connections to China including a Dragon Air flight to Hong Kong. For domestic destinations, **Jetstar Pacific** (☎ 0511-358 3538; www.jetstar.com; 307 Đ Phan Chu Trinh) and **VietJet Air** (☎ 1900 1886; www.vietjetair.com) have daily flights from Danang to HCMC and Hanoi, while **Vietnam Airlines** (☎ 0511-382 1130; www.vietnamairlines.com; 35 Đ Tran Phu) flies to lots of cities nationwide.

BUS

The **bus station** (📞 0511-382 1265; Đ Dien Bien Phu) is 3km west of the city centre and has services to all major towns.

For Laos, there are three weekly services to Savannakhet at 8pm (340,000d, 14 hours) and a daily service to Pakse at 6.30am (330,000d, 13 hours). Buses to the Lao Bao border crossing alone are 128,000d (six hours); you may have to change buses at Dong Ha.

Yellow public buses to Hoi An (18,000d, one hour, hourly) travel along Đ Bach Dang in the heart of town.

Sinh Tourist open-tour buses operate twice daily to both Hue (80,000d to 89,000d, 2½ hours) and Hoi An (70,000d, one hour).

TAXI & MOTORBIKE

A taxi to Hoi An officially costs around 400,000d but most will drop to 330,000d, while *xe om* charge around 120,000d. A ride to the airport is around 55,000d. Call **Mai Linh** (📞 0511-356 5656) for a cab.

TRAIN

Danang train station is 1.5km from the city centre on Đ Hai Phong. The train ride to Hue is one of the best in the country – it's worth taking as an excursion in itself.

AROUND DANANG

About 10km south of Danang are the striking **Marble Mountains** (admission 15,000d; ⏰ 7am-5pm), which consist of five craggy marble outcrops topped with jungle and pagodas. With natural caves sheltering small Hindu and Buddhist sanctuaries and stunning views of the ocean and countryside, they're worth taking the time to explore.

China Beach (Bai Non Nuoc), once an R&R hang-out for US soldiers during the war, is actually a series of beaches stretching 30km between Hoi An and Danang. For surfers, China Beach's break gets a decent swell from mid-September to December. There's a mean undertow, so take care.

Buses and minibuses between Danang and Hoi An can drop you at the entrance to the Marble Mountains and China Beach, and it's easy to find onward transport.

Hoi An

📞 0510 / POP 122,000

Graceful, historic Hoi An is Vietnam's most atmospheric and delightful town. Once a major port, it boasts the grand architecture and beguiling riverside setting that befits its heritage, but 21st-century curses of traffic and pollution are almost entirely absent.

In the Old Town, an incredible legacy of tottering Japanese merchant houses, Chinese temples and ancient tea warehouses has been preserved and converted into stylish restaurants, wine bars and a glut of tailor shops. And yet, down by the market and over in neighbouring An Hoi Peninsula, you'll find life has changed little.

Travel a few kilometres further – you'll find some superb bicycle, motorbike and boat trips – and some of central Vietnam's most enticing bucolic scenery and beaches are within easy reach.

Hoi An's riverside location makes it particularly vulnerable to flooding during the wet season (October and November). It's common for the waterfront to be hit by sporadic floods of about 1m and a typhoon can bring levels of 2m or more.

◎ Sights

◎ Hoi An Old Town

A Unesco World Heritage Site, Hoi An Old Town levies an admission fee to most of its

TRANSPORT FROM DANANG

DESTINATION	AIR	BUS	CAR & MOTORBIKE	TRAIN
Dong Hoi	N/A	US$8-13, 6½hr, 7 daily	6-7hr	US$10-17, 5½-8½hr, 6 daily
Hanoi	from US$36, 70min, 9 daily	US$24-34, 16-19hr, 7 daily	19hr	US$28-45, 14½-18hr, 6 daily
HCMC	from US$33, 75min, 18 daily	US$24-39, 19-25hr, 9 daily	18hr	US$31-50, 17-22hr, 5 daily
Hue	N/A	US$3-4, 3hr, every 20min	2½-4hr	US$3.50-6, 2½-4hr, 6 daily
Nha Trang	from US$38, 30min, 2 daily	US$15-22, 10-13hr, 8 daily	13hr	US$18-29, 9-12hr, 5 daily

historic buildings, which goes towards funding the preservation of the town's architecture. Buying the ticket (www.hoianworldheritage.org.vn; tickets 120,000d) gives you a choice of five heritage sites to visit, including a traditional musical concert or stage play. Booths dotted around the Old Town sell tickets.

★ Japanese Covered Bridge BRIDGE

(Cau Nhat Ban) FREE This beautiful little bridge is emblematic of Hoi An. A bridge was first constructed here in the 1590s by the Japanese community in order to link them with the Chinese quarters across the stream.

The structure is very solidly constructed because of the threat of earthquakes. Over the centuries the ornamentation has remained relatively faithful to the original understated Japanese design. The French flattened out the roadway for their motor vehicles, but the original arched shape was restored in 1986.

★ Assembly Hall of the Fujian Chinese Congregation TEMPLE

(Phuc Kien Hoi Quan; opposite 35 Ð Tran Phu; admission by Old Town ticket; ⊙ 7am-5.30pm) Originally a traditional assembly hall, this structure was later transformed into a temple for the worship of Thien Hau (Tianhou), a deity from Fujian province. The gaudy, green-tiled triple gateway dates from 1975.

The mural on the right-hand wall depicts Thien Hau, her way lit by lantern light as she crosses a stormy sea to rescue a foundering ship. Opposite is a mural of the heads of the six Fujian families who fled from China to Hoi An in the 17th century.

★ Tan Ky House HISTORIC BUILDING

(101 Ð Nguyen Thai Hoc; admission by Old Town ticket; ⊙ 8am-noon & 2-4.30pm) Built two centuries ago by an ethnically Vietnamese family, this gem of a house has been lovingly preserved through seven generations.

Look out for signs of Japanese and Chinese influences on the architecture. Japanese elements include the ceiling (in the sitting area), which is supported by three progressively shorter beams, one on top of the other. Under the crab-shell ceiling are carvings of crossed sabres wrapped in silk ribbon. The sabres symbolise force, the silk represents flexibility.

Tran Family Chapel HISTORIC BUILDING

(21 Ð Le Loi; admission by Old Town ticket; ⊙ 7.30am-noon & 2-5.30pm) Built for worshipping family ancestors, this chapel dates back to 1802. It was commissioned by Tran Tu, one of the clan who ascended to the rank of mandarin and served as an ambassador to China. His picture is to the right of the chapel.

The architecture of the building reflects the influence of Chinese (the 'turtle' style roof), Japanese (triple beam) and vernacular (look out for the bow-and-arrow detailing) styles.

Quan Cong Temple CONFUCIAN TEMPLE

(Chua Ong; 24 Ð Tran Phu; admission by Old Town ticket) This small temple dates from 1653 and is dedicated to Quan Cong, an esteemed Chinese general who is worshipped as a symbol of loyalty, sincerity, integrity and justice. His partially gilded statue, made of papiermâché on a wooden frame, is on the central altar at the back of the sanctuary.

Chinese All-Community Assembly Hall HISTORIC BUILDING

(Chua Ba; ☑ 0510-861 935; 64 Ð Tran Phu; ⊙ 8am-5pm) FREE Founded in 1773, the beautifully restored main temple here is a total assault on the senses with great smoking incense spirals, demonic-looking deities, dragons and lashings of red lacquer – it's dedicated to Thien Hau.

Museum of Trading Ceramics MUSEUM

(80 Ð Tran Phu; admission by Old Town ticket; ⊙ 7am-5.30pm) Occupies a simply restored wooden house and contains artefacts from all over Asia, with oddities from as far afield as Egypt. The small exhibition on the restoration of Hoi An's old houses provides a useful crash course in Old Town architecture.

🏃 Activities

Diving & Snorkelling

Two reputable dive schools offer trips to the Cham Islands (p107). Both charge very similar rates: two fun dives are US$75 to US$80. The diving is not world-class, but can be intriguing, with good macro life – and the day trip to the Cham Islands is superb. Snorkellers pay US$30 to US$40. Trips only leave between February and September; conditions are best in June, July and August.

Blue Coral Diving DIVING

(☑ 0510-627 9297; www.divehoian.com; 77 Ð Nguyen Thai Hoc) A friendly, professional outfit with an 18m dive boat and additional

Hoi An

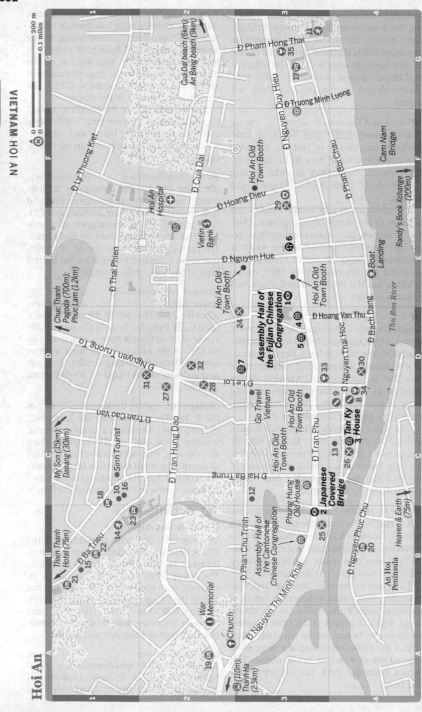

200 m
0.1 miles

Đ Pham Hong Thai

Cua Dai beach (6km);
An Bang beach (9km)

Đ Nguyen Duy Hieu

Đ Truong Minh Luong

Đ Ly Thuong Kiet

Đ Cua Dai

Đ Hoang Dieu

Hoi An Old
Town Booth

Đ Phan Boi Chau

Cam Nam
Bridge

Hoi An
Hospital

Vietin
Bank

Đ Nguyen Hue

Hoi An Old
Town Booth

Thu Bon River

Randy's Book Xchange
(200m)

Đ Thai Phien

Chuc Thanh
Pagoda (700m);
Phuc Lam (1.2km)

**Assembly Hall of
the Fujian Chinese
Congregation**

Hoi An Old
Town Booth

Boat
Landing

Đ Hoang Van Thu

Đ Nguyen Truong To

Đ Bach Dang

Đ Le Loi

Đ Nguyen Thai Hoc

**Tan Ky
House**

Go Travel
Vietnam

Hoi An Old
Town Booth

Đ Tran Hung Dao

Đ Tran Phu

Sinh Tourist

Đ Hai Ba Trung

Đ Tran Cao Van

My Son (35km);
Danang (30km)

**Japanese
Covered
Bridge**

Phung Hung
Old House

Đ Phan Chu Trinh

Assembly Hall of
the Cantonese
Chinese Congregation

Đ Ba Trieu

Thien Thanh
Hotel (75m)

Đ Nguyen Phuc Chu

Heaven & Earth
(75m)

An Hoi
Peninsula

War
Memorial

Church

Đ Nguyen Thi Minh Khai

(110m);
Thanh Ha
(2.5km)

Hoi An

⊙ Top Sights
1	Assembly Hall of the Fujian Chinese Congregation..........E3
2	Japanese Covered Bridge B3
3	Tan Ky House C4

◎ Sights
4	Chinese All-Community Assembly Hall..........D3
5	Museum of Trading Ceramics..........D3
6	Quan Cong Temple..........E3
7	Tran Family Chapel..........D3

✪ Activities, Courses & Tours
8	Blue Coral Diving..........D4
9	Cham Island Diving Center..........D4
10	Hoi An Motorbike Adventures..........C1
11	Life Spa..........G3
12	Love of Life..........C3
13	Morning Glory Cooking School..........C4
14	Palmarosa..........B1
15	Phat Tire Ventures..........B1
16	Vietnam Jeeps..........C1

⬒ Sleeping
17	Ha An Hotel..........G3
18	Hoa Binh Hotel..........C1
19	Hoang Trinh Hotel..........A2
20	Long Life Riverside..........B4
21	Phuong Dong Hotel..........B1
22	Thien Nga Hotel..........B1
23	Vinh Hung 3 Hotel..........B1

⊗ Eating
24	Bale Well..........D3
25	Ca Mai..........B3
26	Cargo Club..........C4
27	Ganesh Indian Restaurant..........D2
28	Little Menu..........D2
29	Mermaid Restaurant..........F3
	Morning Glory Street Food Restaurant..........(see 13)
30	Phone Café..........D4
31	White Sail Cafe..........D2
32	White Sail Seafood..........D2

⊙ Drinking & Nightlife
33	Before & Now..........D3
	Dive Bar..........(see 9)
	Q Bar..........(see 9)
34	White Marble..........D4
35	Why Not?..........G3

⊙ Shopping
	Reaching Out..........(see 26)

speedboat. Chief instructor is Steve Reid from the UK.

Cham Island Diving Center   DIVING
(☑0510-391 0782; www.chamislanddiving.com; 88 Đ Nguyen Thai Hoc) Run by a friendly, experienced team, this dive shop's mantra is 'no troubles, make bubbles'. They've a large boat and also a speedboat for zippy transfers.

Massage & Spa

★ **Palmarosa**   SPA
(☑0510-393 3999; www.palmarosaspa.vn; 90 Đ Ba Trieu; 1hr massage from US$21; ⊙10am-9pm) A cut above the competition, this highly professional spa offers a full range of massages (including Thai and Swedish), scrubs and facials, as well as hand and foot care.

Countryside Charm   SPA
(Duyen Que; ☑0510-350 1584; www.spahoian.vn; 512 Đ Cua Dai; 1hr massage from US$16; ⊙8am-11pm) On the beach road, this treatment centre has fairly functional premises, but you'll find staff are well trained and know their stuff. A 70-minute hot-stone massage is US$22.

Life Spa   SPA
(☑0510-391 4555, ext 525; www.life-resorts.com; Life Heritage Resort, 1 Đ Pham Hong Thai; 1hr massage from US$58) This luxury hotel's spa is a lovely place to unwind, and has the full gamut of treatments and massages, including anti-oxidant facials (US$52), sea-salt scrubs (US$26) and hot-stone therapies (US$57).

☞ Courses

Green Bamboo Cooking School   COOKING
(☑0905 815 600; www.greenbamboo-hoian.com; 21 Đ Truong Minh Hung, Cam An; per person US$35) Directed by Van, a charming local lady, these courses are more personalised than most. Groups are limited to a maximum of 10, and take place in Van's spacious home (5km east of the centre).

Morning Glory Cooking School   COOKING
(☑0510-224 1555; www.restaurant-hoian.com; 106 Đ Nguyen Thai Hoc; half-day course US$27) Coordinated by the acclaimed Trinh Diem Vy, owner of several restaurants in town, or one of her protégés, these classes concentrate on local recipes including *cao lau* and 'white rose'. Note that classes can have up to 30 people.

Red Bridge Cooking School COOKING

(☑ 0510-393 3222; www.visithoian.com/redbridge; Thon 4, Cam Thanh) At this school, going to class involves a relaxing 4km cruise down the river. There are half-day (US$29) and full-day (US$47) courses, both of which include market visits. As an added sweetener, there's a 20m swimming pool at the school! It's 4km east of the centre.

✲✲ Festivals & Events

Full Moon Festival CULTURAL

(☻5-11pm) Takes place on the 14th day of every lunar month. These festive evenings feature traditional food, song and dance, and games along the lantern-lit streets in the town centre.

🛏 Sleeping

Hoi An is awash with excellent accommodation options.

Nhi Trung Hotel HOTEL $

(☑ 0510-386 3436; 700 Đ Hai Ba Trung; r US$17-27; ❄@🛜) Around 1.5km north of the Old Town, this well-run hotel has spacious, light rooms, some with balconies, that represent excellent value. The free breakfast (pancakes, omelettes, fruit) is superb.

Sunflower Hotel HOTEL $

(☑0510-393 9838; www.sunflowerhotelhoian. com; 397 Cua Dai; dm US$7, r US$20-22; ❄@🛜🏊) This popular place is 2km east of the centre with a hostel vibe that draws lots of young backpackers. Dorms are decent and the buffet breakfast will set you up for the day.

Phuong Dong Hotel HOTEL $

(☑0510-391 6477; www.hoianphuongdonghotel. com; 42 Đ Ba Trieu; s/d/tr US$13/16/20; ❄@🛜) It's nothing fancy, but a safe budget bet: plain, good-value rooms with comfortable mattresses, reading lights, fridge and aircon. The owners rent motorbikes at fair rates, too.

Hoang Trinh Hotel HOTEL $

(☑0510-391 6579; www.hoianhoangtrinhhotel. com; 45 Đ Le Quy Don; s/d/tr US$20/25/30; ❄@🛜) Well-run hotel with helpful, friendly staff where travellers are made to feel welcome. Rooms are quite 'old school' Vietnamese but spacious and clean. A generous breakfast and pick-up are included.

Hoa Binh Hotel HOTEL $

(☑0510-391 6838; www.hoianbinhhotel.com; 696 Đ Hai Ba Trung; dm US$9, r US$15-25; ❄@🛜🏊) A good selection of modern rooms, all with minibar, cable TV and air-con, and a reasonable dorm. The inclusive breakfast is good, but the pool is covered by a roof.

★ Vinh Hung Emerald Resort HOTEL $$

(☑0510-393 4999; www.vinhhungemeraldresort. com; Minh An, An Hoi; r US$48-65, ste US$80; ❂❄🛜🏊) Beautifully designed new hotel with a riverside location in An Hoi, and modernist rooms that represent exceptional value for money. All rooms face the lovely central pool or have a terrace facing the river. There's a fitness centre and small spa.

★ Ha An Hotel HISTORIC HOTEL $$

(☑0510-386 3126; www.haanhotel.com; 6-8 Đ Phan Boi Chau; r US$60-120; ❄@🛜) Elegant and refined, the Ha An feels more like a colonial mansion than a hotel. All rooms have nice individual touches – a textile wall hanging or painting – and views over a gorgeous central garden. The helpful, well-trained staff make staying here a very special experience.

Thien Nga Hotel HOTEL $$

(☑0510-391 6330; thienngahotel@gmail.com; 52 Đ Ba Trieu; r US$35; ❄@🛜🏊) This place has a fine selection of rooms: most are spacious, light and airy and have a balcony and a minimalist feel (though the bathrooms are more prosaic). Book one at the rear if you can for garden views. The pool is covered by a roof, though.

Vinh Hung 3 Hotel HOTEL $$

(☑0510-391 6277; www.hoianvinhhung3hotel.com; 96 Đ Ba Trieu; r US$37-43; ❄@🛜🏊) This fine minihotel has modish rooms that have huge beds, dark-wood furniture, writing desks and satellite TV. All bathrooms are sleek and inviting, and breakfast is included.

Thien Thanh Hotel HOTEL $$

(Blue Sky Hotel; ☑0510-391 6545; www.hoian-thienthanhhotel.com; 16 Đ Ba Trieu; r US$40-60, ste US$68; ❄@🛜🏊) Staff are dressed in traditional *ao dai* at this atmospheric hotel and maintain good service standards. The spacious, inviting and well-equipped rooms enjoy a few Vietnamese decorative flourishes, DVD players and bathtubs.

Long Life Riverside HOTEL **$$**
(☎0510-391 1696; www.longlifehotels.com; 61
Đ Nguyen Phuc Chu; r US$42-75 ste US$90;
❄@🛜🛗) Impressive hotel with a peaceful
riverside setting in An Hoi Peninsula. Rooms
are spacious, with modern furnishings, a
computer and state-of-the-art bathrooms
complete with jazzy jacuzzi-style bathtubs.

★**An Bang
Seaside Village** BUNGALOW, VILLA **$$$**
(☎0126 944 4567; www.anbangseasidevillage.
com; An Bang Beach; villas US$53-138; ❄🛜) One
of *the* best beachside locations in Vietnam,
these wonderful cottages and villas are superbly situated between the coastal trees
on glorious An Bang beach, close to restaurants. Each of the six units combines modern (polished concrete) and natural materials beautifully, and boasts stylish furnishings and lots of space. They're serviced daily
and breakfast is included.

★**Hoi An Chic Hotel** HOTEL **$$$**
(☎0510-392 6799; www.hoianchic.com; Đ Nguyen
Trai; r US$96; ❄❄@🛜🛗) Surrounded by rice
fields, halfway between the town and the
beach, Hoi An Chic enjoys a tranquil, near-
rural location. A lot of thought has gone into
the design, with hip, colourful furnishings,
outdoor bathrooms and an elevated pool.
There's a free shuttle (in an original US
jeep!) to town. It's 3km east of the centre.

🍴 Eating

Hoi An offers a culinary tour de force, in-
cluding several amazing local specialities.
Be sure to try *banh bao* ('white rose'), an
incredibly delicate dish of steamed dump-
ling stuffed with minced shrimp. *Cao lau,*
doughy flat noodles mixed with croutons,
bean sprouts and greens, topped with pork
slices and served in a savoury broth, is also
delicious. The other two culinary treats are
fried *hoanh thanh* (wonton) and *banh xeo*

TOURS AROUND HOI AN

The evergreen, quintessentially Vietnamese countryside and rural lanes around Hoi
An beg to be explored, and you'll find several excellent tour operators offering trips in
the region.

Motorbike and bicycle trips are wildly popular and there's no better way to appreciate
the countryside than on two wheels. Jeep tours are another option.

The idyllic Cham Islands (p107) make another perfect day trip destination during the
March to September season. Both Hoi An dive schools run tours.

Hoi An Motorbike Adventures (☎0510-391 1930; www.motorbiketours-hoian.com;
111 Ba Trieu) Specialises in tours on cult Minsk motorbikes. The guides really know the
terrain and the trips make use of beautiful back roads and riverside tracks.

Phat Tire Ventures (☎0510-653 9839; www.ptv-vietnam.com; 62 Ba Trieu) Offers a terrif-
ic mountain-bike trip to the My Son ruins that takes in country lanes and temple visits.

Hoi An Free Tour (☎0979 587 744; www.hoianfreetour.com) Ride on a bike around the
fringes of Hoi An with students. You get to meet the locals and see village life; they get to
practise their English.

Taste of Hoi An (☎0905 382 783; www.tasteofhoian.com) Walk the streets to meet the
vendors, then munch your lunch in an ancient (air-conditioned!) Hoi An townhouse.

Heaven & Earth (☎0510-386 4362; www.vietnam-bicycle.com; 57 Đ Ngo Quyen, An Hoi;
tours US$15-19) Cycling tours are well thought out and not too strenuous; they explore
the Song Thu River delta area.

Love of Life (☎0510-393 9399; www.hoian-bicycle.com; 95B Đ Phan Chu Trinh; tours US$19)
Has good bicycle tours along quiet country lanes past vegetable gardens and fishing
villages, and walking tours of Hoi An.

Vietnam Jeeps (☎0510-391 1930; www.vietnamjeeps.com; 111 Ba Trieu) Heading up into
the hills behind Hoi An, this group offers tours in original US jeeps to a Co Tu tribal vil-
lage. There are hot springs and great hikes in the region.

Hoi An Eco Tour (☎0510-392 8900; www.hoianecotour.com.vn; Phuoc Hai village; tours
US$38-72) Offers cultural activities along the river: you can fish, paddle a basket boat,
ride a buffalo or learn about wet rice planting.

(crispy savoury pancakes rolled with herbs in fresh rice paper).

★ Mermaid Restaurant
VIETNAMESE $

(☎ 0510-386 1527; www.restaurant-hoian.com; 2 Đ Tran Phu; most dishes 38,000-95,000d; ⊙ 10.30am-10pm) For local specialities, you can't beat this modest little restaurant, owned by local legend Vy. Hoi An's holy culinary trinity (*cao lau*, white rose and *banh xeo*) are all superb, as are the special fried wontons.

Bale Well
VIETNAMESE $

(45-51 Đ Tran Cao Van; meals 45,000-85,000d; ⊙ 11.30am-10pm) Down a little alley near the famous well, this local place is renowned for one dish: barbecued pork, served up satay-style, which you then combine with fresh greens and herbs to create your own fresh spring roll.

Little Menu
VIETNAMESE $

(www.thelittlemenu.com; 12 Đ Le Loi; dishes 50,000-135,000d; ⊙ 7am-9.30pm; 🐾) English-speaking owner Son is a fantastic host at this great little restaurant with an open kitchen and short menu – try the fish in banana leaf or duck spring rolls.

Phone Café
VIETNAMESE $

(80b Đ Bach Dang; dishes 22,000-62,000d; ⊙ 7am-9pm) This humble-looking place serves up the usual faves, plus some good clay-pot specialities.

★ Morning Glory Street Food Restaurant
VIETNAMESE $$

(☎ 0510-224 1555; www.restaurant-hoian.com; 106 Đ Nguyen Thai Hoc; dishes 45,000-130,000d; ⊙ 8am-11pm; 🐾🌿) An outstanding restaurant in historic premises that concentrates on street food and traditionally prepared dishes (primarily from central Vietnam). Highlights include the pork-stuffed squid, and shrimp mousse on sugar-cane skewers. There's an excellent vegetarian selection (try the smoked eggplant), including many wonderful salads.

★ Cargo Club
INTERNATIONAL, VIETNAMESE $$

(☎ 0510-391 0489; www.restaurant-hoian.com; 107 Đ Nguyen Thai Hoc; dishes 35,000-105,000d; ⊙ 8am-11pm; 🐾) Remarkable cafe-restaurant, serving mainly Western food, with a terrific riverside location – the upper terrace has stunning views. The breakfasts are legendary (try the eggs Benedict), the patisserie and cakes are to die for, and fine dining dishes seriously deliver, too.

Ganesh Indian Restaurant
INDIAN $$

(☎ 0510-386 4538; www.ganeshindianrestaurant. com; 24 Đ Tran Hung Dao; meals 65,000-135,000d; ⊙ noon-10.30pm; 🐾🌿) A highly authentic, fine-value North Indian restaurant where the tandoor oven pumps out perfect naan bread and the chefs' fiery curries don't pull any punches. Plenty of vegetarian choices, and great lassis.

White Sail Cafe
VIETNAMESE, SEAFOOD $$

(Canh Buom Trang; 134 Đ Tran Cao Van; meals 50,000-155,000d; ⊙ 7am-10pm; 🐾) Enjoyable little restaurant serving authentic Vietnamese food including great squid (stuffed or salt 'n' pepper), smoked eggplant with tamarind and caramelised prawns. Prices are moderate, though the kitchen can struggle a bit at busy times.

White Sail Seafood
SEAFOOD $$

(47/6 Trang Hung Dao; dishes 45,000-140,000d; ⊙ 11.30am-10pm) Very local, no-frills place in someone's scruffy backyard, where it's all about the freshness of the seafood. Little English is spoken, but the cooking is first-rate. Not to be confused with the tourist-geared White Sail Cafe.

Ca Mai
VIETNAMESE $$

(45 Đ Nguyen Thi; meals 90,000-170,000d; ⊙ 7am-10pm; 🐾) Casual new cafe which has something for everyone with Hoi An specialities and pan-Asian dishes including great tempura and Peking duck. The cocktails here are amazing (happy hour is 5 pm to 7pm).

🍷 Drinking & Nightlife

★ Dive Bar
BAR

(88 Đ Nguyen Thai Hoc; ⊙ 8am-midnight; 🐾) The best bar in town, with a great vibe thanks to the welcoming service, contemporary electronic tunes and sofas for lounging. There's also a cocktail garden and bar at the rear, a pool table and pub grub.

Why Not?
BAR

(10B Đ Pham Hong Thai; ⊙ 5pm-late; 🐾) Great late-night bar 1km east of the centre, run by a friendly local character. There's a popular pool table and usually a party vibe in the air. Yes, things can get very messy.

White Marble
BAR

(www.visithoian.com; 99 Đ Le Loi; ⊙ 11am-11pm; 🐾) Wine-bar-cum-restaurant in historic premises with an unmatched selection of wines (many are available by the glass, from US$4) and refined ambience.

Q Bar
LOUNGE, BAR

(94 Đ Nguyen Thai Hoc; ☺noon-midnight; ☏) Q Bar offers stunning lighting, lounge music and electronica, and the best (if pricey at around 100,000d) cocktails and mocktails in town. Draws a cool crowd and it's gay-friendly.

Before & Now
BAR

(www.beforennow.com; 51 Đ Le Loi; ☺7am-midnight; ☏) Popular but slightly bland travellers' bar, complete with pool table. Happy hour is from 6pm to 9pm.

🔒 Shopping

Tailor-made clothing is one of Hoi An's best trades, and there are more than 200 tailor shops in town that can whip up suits, shirts and much more.

Hoi An also boasts some interesting art galleries, especially on the west side of the Japanese Covered Bridge.

Metiseko
CLOTHING, ACCESSORIES

(Map p52; www.metiseko.com; 03 Chau Thuong Van; ☺9am-9.30pm) Lots of stylish, organic and eco-friendly spins on clothing, homewares and accessories. Both cotton and silk are harnessed for Metiseko's chic collections.

⭐ Reaching Out
SOUVENIRS, CLOTHING

(www.reachingoutvietnam.com; 103 Đ Nguyen Thai Hoc; ☺8am-8pm) Excellent fair-trade gift shop that stocks good-quality silk scarfs, clothes, jewellery, hand-painted Vietnamese hats, handmade toys and teddy bears. The shop employs and supports artisans with disabilities.

Randy's Book Xchange
BOOKS

(www.randysbookxchange.com; To 5 Khoi Xuyen Trung; ☺9.30am-6pm Mon-Sat) More than 5000 used books for sale or exchange; also offers digital downloads.

ℹ Information

For the most part, Hoi An is very safe at any hour. However, late-night bag snatchings in the unlit market have been known and women should avoid walking home alone late at night.

Virtually all hotels have lobby computers and free wi-fi. The website www.livehoianmagazine.com is excellent for cultural content, features and reviews.

WORTH A TRIP

CHAM ISLANDS

A breathtaking cluster of granite islands offshore from Hoi An, the beautiful **Cham islands** make a wonderful excursion. In the last year or two the serenity of the islands has been compromised (on weekends and Vietnamese holidays) by boatloads of day tripping tourists from the mainland, so try to plan your visit accordingly. It will have to be between February to September, as the ocean is usually too rough at other times.

The best trips include some diving or snorkelling the Cham's (modest) coral reefs and a visit to the main island of **Hon Lao**. The islands are protected as a marine park and the underwater environment includes 135 species of soft and hard coral and varied macro life.

Bai Lang, Hon Lao's pretty little port, is the only real settlement. Drop by the curious temple **Ong Ngu**, which is dedicated to whales (locals worshipped them as oceanic deities). There are two good, simple guesthouses in town: **Luu Ly** (☏0510-393 0240; r with shared bathroom 220,000d) and **Thu Trang** (☏0510-393 0007; r with shared bathroom 220,000d) both serve meals. A dirt track heads southwest from Hon Lao for 2km past coves to a fine, sheltered beach, home to **Cham Restaurant** (☏0510-224 1108; meals 50,000-120,000d; ☺10am-5pm).

Tiny **Bai Huong**, a fishing village 5km southeast of Bai Lang, is an idyllic but isolated spot where an excellent new **homestay** (☏0120 237 8530; www.homestaybaihuong.com; per person 100,000d, meals 30,000-70,000d) initiative has been set up. Facilities are basic, and little or no English is spoken by locals, but it's certainly the perfect place to get away from it all.

Most visitors arrive on **tours** (US$30 to US$80) organised by dive schools in Hoi An. There's also a scheduled daily boat connection from Đ Bach Dang in Hoi An (20,000d, two hours, 7.30am). Note foreigners are routinely overcharged. Boats do not sail during heavy seas. Bring a copy of your passport and visa.

Hoi An Hospital (☎0510-386 1364; 4 Đ Tran Hung Dao; ⊙6am-10pm) If it's anything serious, head for Danang.

Hoi An Police Station (☎0510-386 1204; 84 Đ Hoang Dieu)

Main Post Office (6 Đ Tran Hung Dao; ⊙7am-5pm)

Min's Computer (2 Truong Minh Luong; per hr 5000d; ⊙7.30am-9pm) Lots of terminals; you can also print, scan, burn and Skype here.

Sinh Tourist (☎0510-386 3948; www.thesinh-tourist.vn; 587 Đ Hai Ba Trung; ⊙7.30am-6pm) Books reputable open-tour buses.

Vietin Bank (☎0510-386 1340; 4 Đ Hoang Dieu; ⊙8am-5pm Mon-Fri, 8.30am-1.30pm Sat) With ATM.

❶ Getting There & Away

Most north–south bus services do not stop at Hoi An, but you can head for the town of Vinh Dien (10km to the west) and catch one there. If you're heading for Hue or Nha Trang, open-tour buses are easier.

Hoi An bus station (96 Đ Hung Vuong), 1km west of the centre, mainly serves local destinations including Danang (18,000d, one hour).

The nearest airport and train station are both in Danang. **Go Travel Vietnam** (☎0510-392 9115; info@go-travel-vietnam.com; 61A Phan Chau Trinh; ⊙9am-9pm) offers shuttle bus transfers between Hoi An and Danang airport and train station five times per day (80,000d, one hour).

❶ Getting Around

Metered taxis and motorbike drivers wait for business over the bridge in An Hoi. Call **Hoi An Taxi** (☎0510-391 9919) or **Mai Linh** (☎0510-392 5925) for a pick-up.

Many hotels offer bicycles/motorbikes for rent from 20,000/100,000d per day.

Around Hoi An

Beaches

The nearest beach to Hoi An, **Cua Dai** is subject to intense development and the domain of hard-selling beach vendors. There are seafood restaurants here.

Just 3km north of Cua Dai, **An Bang** is fast emerging as one of Vietnam's most happening and enjoyable beaches. It's easy to see what all the fuss is about – you're greeted with a wonderful stretch of fine sand, a huge empty ocean and an enormous horizon, with only the distant Cham Islands in-terrupting the seaside symmetry. You'll find lots of cool little beachfront bar-restaurants serving European cuisine. **Le Banyan Bar** (meals 130,000-240,000d; ⊙10am-10pm; ☎). **Soul Kitchen** (☎0906 440 320; www.soulkitch-en.sitew.com; meals 80,000-180,000d; ⊙10am-10pm Tue-Sun, 10am-6pm Mon; ☎) and **La Plage** (☎0510-392 8244; www.laplagehoian.com; snacks/meals 70,000/130,000d; ⊙8am-10pm; ☎) offer terrific European food.

The coastline immediately to the north of An Bang remains pristine, a glorious broad beach lined with casuarina and pandan trees and dotted with the curious coracles of local fishermen.

My Son

The ancient Cham city of **My Son** (admission 100,000d; ⊙6.30am-4pm) is one of the most stunning sights in the area, and another Unesco World Heritage Site. The ruins are nestled in a lush valley surrounded by hills and the massive Hon Quap (Cat's Tooth Mountain). My Son became a religious centre under King Bhadravarman in the late 4th century and was occupied until the 13th century – the longest period of development of any city in the Mekong region.

My Son's temples are in poor shape today after American bombing devastated the temples – only about 20 structures survive where at least 68 once stood. Note that only a handful of the monuments are properly labelled and there are virtually no information panels on site.

Look out for temples **C1**, an 8th-century structure used to worship Shiva; **B1**, dedicated to Bhadresvara; **B5**, built in the 10th century, which has some original Cham masonry; and **B3**, which has an Indian-influenced pyramidal roof typical of Cham towers.

Buildings **D1** and **D2** were once meditation halls and now house small displays of Cham sculpture.

Group A was almost completely destroyed by US bombs. **A1** was previously My Son's largest temple, reaching 24m, but only its foundations remain.

The ruins are 55km southwest of Hoi An. Day tours to My Son can be arranged in Hoi An for US$4 to US$8, not including admission, and some trips return to Hoi An by boat. Independent travellers can hire a motorbike, *xe om* or car. Get here early (preferably pre-dawn) or late in the afternoon to beat the tour groups.

SOUTHEAST COAST

Vietnam has an incredibly curvaceous coastline and it's in the southeast region that it is at its most alluring, with sweeping sands, towering cliffs and concealed bays. Many of the voluptuous beaches along this stretch are yet to be developed. Not for long.

Nha Trang, Mui Ne and Con Dao are the key destinations, but the beach breaks come thick and fast in this part of the country. If your idea of paradise is reclining in front of turquoise waters and weighing up the merits of a massage or a mojito, then you have come to the right place.

On hand to complement the sedentary delights are activities to set the pulse racing, including scuba diving, snorkelling, surfing, windsurfing and kitesurfing. Action or inaction, this region bubbles with opportunities.

Quy Nhon

🖉 056 / POP 292,000

This sprawling city is not a destination in itself, but it's still worth a stop. Close by are some blissful beaches, the countryside is dotted with ancient Cham temples and you'll find some excellent seafood.

◎ Sights & Activities

The long sweep of Quy Nhon's **beachfront** extends from the port in the northeast to the hills in the south: a beautiful stretch of sand. **Queen's Beach** is popular with locals and has great views back over Quy Nhon. It's just over the hill to the south of town. **Quy Hoa Beach** is a popular weekend hang-out for the city's small expat community.

The partially ruined **Thap Doi Cham Towers** (admission 10,000d; ◷ 8-11am & 1-6pm) sit in a pretty little park. They're about 1.5km south of Quy Nhon, beyond Queen's Beach.

⏢ Sleeping & Eating

Anh Vy Hotel　　　　　　　　HOTEL $
(🖉 056-384 7763; 8 Đ An Duong Vuong; r 160,000-250,000d; 🕸◎🛜) Owned by a very friendly lady, and offering excellent travel information and bikes for hire. Boasts clean rooms with satellite TV; those with sea views cost a little more.

Hotel Au Co – Ben Bo Bien　　　HOTEL $
(🖉 056-374 7699; hotel_auco@yahoo.com; 8 & 24 Đ An Duong Vuong; r 160,000-300,000d; 🕸◎🛜)

VIETNAM QUY NHON

GANH DA DIA

A smaller version of Ireland's Giant's Causeway, Ganh Da Dia is a spectacular outcrop of volcanic rock that juts into the ocean south of Quy Nhon. Half the fun is simply getting there, as the scenery in this coastal region is superb.

Ganh Da Dia is signposted from the small town of Chi Thanh, 68km south of Quy Nhon. Heading down Hwy 1, take the turn just past the river bridge on the northern side of town. The route to the coast meanders for 13km through a delightful pastoral landscape of rice paddies and farming villages.

Consisting of hundreds of interlocked columns of volcanic rock, Ganh Da Dia was created millions of years ago as fluid molten basalt cooled. Some of the best sections are formed of incredibly regular pentagonal- and hexagonal-sided horizontal rocks. The Vietnamese call this place 'the cliff of stone plates,' and it's regularly used by Buddhist monks for ceremonies.

You can bathe in the tiny rocky cove next to Ganh Da Dia, but the drop-dead gorgeous sandy beach on the south side of the bay, a five-minute walk away, is even more inviting. Fresh coconuts and snacks are sold by local villagers at the car park.

Continuing south (and avoiding Hwy 1) you can take a lovely coastal road to Tuy Hoa. Head inland (west) from Ganh Da Dia for 3.5km and then a side (paved) road heads south through sand dunes, past cacti and agave to the fishing village of **An Hai**, where a row of seafood restaurants face the O Loan estuary and make an ideal pit stop.

From An Hai, it's 27km south to Tuy Hoa. The route has a few twists and turns, but the kilometre waymarks, which indicate the distance to Tuy Hoa, help guide you the right way.

Tuy Hoa is on Hwy 1, for all points north and south.

Under the same ownership, these two hotels confusingly share the same name. That one of number 8 is slightly more atmospheric, with clean rooms (some with sea views and balconies). No. 24 is even more kitsch (some rooms even have fake plastic trees!). Bicycles (35,000d per day) and motorbikes (150,000d) are available for rent. Mr Thoai, the friendly owner, speaks good English.

Hoang Yen Hotel   HOTEL $$
(☑ 056-374 6900; www.hoangyenhotel.com.vn; 5 Đ An Duong Vuong; r 500,000-710,000d; ✢ @ 🛜 ✈) A 10-storey concrete hotel overlooking the beach with good-value rates given the rooms' specs and space. Secure a sea view, as the rates aren't much higher and include breakfast.

Barbara's: The Kiwi Connection   CAFE $
(12 Đ An Duong Vuong; mains 35,000-80,000d; ⊘ 7am-10pm; 🛜) Barbara has moved on and the cafe has a new location, but this place remains a popular meeting point thanks to the reliable travel information and Western grub. Rooms are also available.

★ C.ine   SEAFOOD $$
(☑ 056-651 2675; 94 Xuan Dieu; dishes 50,000-150,000d; ⊘ 11am-10pm) This likeable and very popular seafood restaurant has gingham tablecloths and views over the bay. Feast on delectable dishes including sweet soft-shell crab and green-mango prawn salad.

❶ Information

Barbara's: The Kiwi Connection (☑ 056-389 2921; www.barbaraquynhon.weebly.com; 12 Đ An Duong Vuong ; 🛜) Free tourist information including bus and train timetables and tickets, city and countryside tours, bike and motorbike hire, local maps and internet access.

Main Post Office (197 Đ Phan Boi Chau; ⊘ 6.30am-10pm)

Vietcombank (148 Đ Le Loi; ⊘ 7.30am-3pm Mon-Sat) With ATM.

❶ Getting There & Away

AIR

Vietnam Airlines (☑ 056-382 5313; www.vietnamairlines.com; 1 Đ Nguyen Tat Thanh) has flights to HCMC and Hanoi from Phu Cat airport, 32km north of the city. There are minibus transfers (40,000d) for passengers between Vietnam Airlines' office and the airport.

BUS

Quy Nhon bus station (☑ 056-384 6246; Đ Tay Son) is on the south side of town. Buses run very regularly towards Danang and Nha Trang and irregularly to towns to the west including Buon Ma Thuot and Pleiku.

There's also a connection to Pakse in Laos (from 388,000d, 20 hours, four per week).

TRAIN

The nearest main-line station is Dieu Tri, 10km west of the city.

Nha Trang
☑ 058 / POP 375,000

Welcome to the beach capital of Vietnam. Loud and proud (say it!), the high-rise, high-energy resort of Nha Trang enjoys a stunning setting: ringed by a necklace of hills, with a sweeping crescent beach, the city's turquoise bay is dotted with tropical islands.

Nha Trang is a party town at heart, like any self-respecting resort should be. Forget the curfews of the capital; people play late here. Or if cocktail buckets and shooters aren't your flavour, try the natural mud baths or visit the imposing Cham towers.

This part of the country has its very own microclimate and the rains tend to come from October until December.

❂ Sights

★ Nha Trang Beach   BEACH
Forming a magnificent sweeping arc, Nha Trang's 6km-long golden sand beach is the city's trump card. Various sections are des-

TRANSPORT FROM QUY NHON

DESTINATION	AIR	BUS	CAR & MOTORBIKE	TRAIN (SOFT SEAT)
Danang	115,000d, 6hr, 14-17 daily	7hr	5½hr, from 198,000d, 3 daily	N/A
HCMC	from 730,000d, 1hr, 1 daily	330,000d, 16hr, 10 daily	18hr	from 340,000d, 10hr, 3 daily
Hanoi	from 1,300,000d, 1½hr, 6 weekly	from 520,000d, 23hr, 7 daily	around 26hr	from 750,000d, 17hr, 3 daily

ignated for swimmers, where you won't be bothered by jetskis or boats. The turquoise water is fabulously inviting, and the promenade a delight to stroll.

Two popular lounging spots are the Sailing Club and Louisiane Brewhouse. If you head south of here, the beach gets quieter and it's possible to find a stretch of sand to yourself.

★ **Po Nagar Cham Towers**   BUDDHIST TEMPLE

(Thap Ba, Lady of the City; admission 21,000d; ⊙6am-6pm) Built between the 7th and 12th centuries, these four Cham Towers are still actively used for worship by Cham, ethnic Chinese and Vietnamese Buddhists. Originally the complex had seven or eight towers, but only four towers remain, of which the 28m-high North Tower (Thap Chinh; AD 817) – with its terraced pyramidal roof, vaulted interior masonry and vestibule – is the most magnificent.

The towers stand on a granite knoll 2km north of central Nha Trang on the banks of the Cai River.

Long Son Pagoda   BUDDHIST TEMPLE

(⊙7.30-11.30am & 1.30-5.30pm) FREE This striking pagoda was founded in the late 19th century. The entrance and roofs are decorated with mosaic dragons constructed of glass and ceramic tile while the main sanctuary is a hall adorned with modern interpretations of traditional motifs.

Behind the pagoda is a huge white **Buddha** (Kim Than Phat To) seated on a lotus blossom. Around the statue's base are firering relief busts of Thich Quang Duc and six other Buddhist monks who died in self-immolations in 1963.

The pagoda is about 400m west of the train station, just off Ð 23 Thang 10.

Alexandre Yersin Museum   MUSEUM

(☎058-382 2355; 10 Ð Tran Phu; admission 28,000d; ⊙7.30-11am & 2-4.30pm Mon-Fri, 8-11am Sat) Highly popular in Vietnam, Dr Alexandre Yersin (1863–1943) founded Nha Trang's Pasteur Institute in 1895. He learned to speak Vietnamese fluently, introduced rubber and quinine-producing trees to Vietnam, and discovered the rat-borne microbe that causes bubonic plague. You can see Yersin's library and office at this small, interesting museum; displays include laboratory equipment (such as astronomical instruments) and a fascinating 3D photo viewer.

Tours are conducted in French, English and Vietnamese, and a short film on Yersin's life is shown.

Long Thanh Gallery   ART GALLERY

(☎058-382 4875; www.longthanhart.com; 126 Ð Hoang Van Thu; ⊙8am-5.30pm Mon-Sat) FREE This gallery showcases the work of Vietnam's most prominent photographer. Long Thanh developed his first photo in 1964 and continues to shoot extraordinary black-and-white images of everyday Vietnamese moments and compelling portraits. The powerful images capture the heart and soul of Vietnam.

Do Dien Khanh Gallery   ART GALLERY

(☎058-351 2202; www.ddk-gallery.com; 126B Ð Hong Bat; ⊙8am-6pm Mon-Fri) FREE Do Dien Khanh is a talented photographer whose portraits of surrounding Cham communities are hauntingly beautiful.

🏃 Activities

Diving

Nha Trang is Vietnam's most popular scuba diving centre. February to September is considered the best time to dive, while October to December is the worst. There are around 25 dive sites in the area. Some have good drop-offs and there are underwater caves to explore. Frankly, it's not world-class diving, but the waters support a reasonable number of small reef fish.

A two-dive boat trip costs between US$60 and US$85; snorkellers typically pay US$15 to US$20. Most dive operators also offer a range of dive courses too.

Be aware that there are some dodgy dive shops not following responsible diving practices and even using fake PADI/SSI accreditation – stick to reputable operators.

Mark Scott Dive Center   DIVING

(☎0122 903 7795; www.divingvietnam.com; 24/4 Ð Hung Vuong) Owned by a larger-than-life Texan, an instructor since 1991, this new school has quickly established an excellent reputation. SSI courses are offered.

Angel Dive   DIVING

(☎058-352 2461; www.angeldivevietnam.info; 1/33 Ð Tran Quang Khai) Reliable operator with English, French and German instruction, plus the choice of PADI or SSI certification.

Rainbow Divers   DIVING

(☎058-352 4351; www.divevietnam.com; 90A Ð Hung Vuong) This large, well-established PADI dive school is part of a nationwide chain. There is also a popular restaurant and bar.

Nha Trang

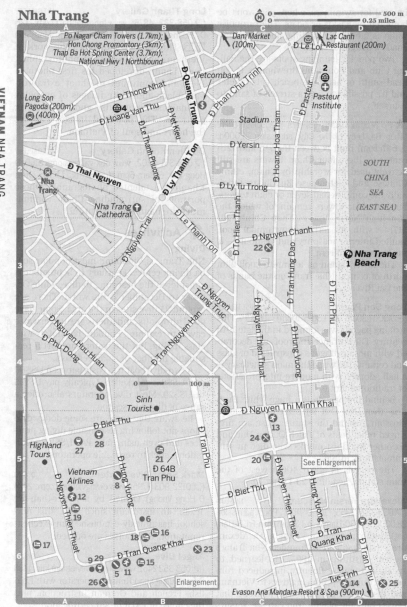

Other Activities

Vietnam Active ADVENTURE SPORTS
(☎058-351 5821; www.vietnamactive.com; 47 B1 Nguyen Thien Thuat) Offers a diverse range of excellent activities, including mountain-biking trips (from US$45 for four people).

Stretch those aching limbs afterwards at one of its Hatha or Ashtanga yoga classes.

Shamrock Adventures RAFTING, KAYAK
(☎058-352 7548; www.shamrockadventures.vn; Đ Tran Quang Khai; trips per person incl lunch from

Nha Trang

US$40) Offers white-water rafting (though it's not that dramatic by international standards), which can be combined with some mountain-biking, kayaking and fishing trips.

Thap Ba Hot Spring Center THERMAL BATHS
(☎058-383 4939; www.thapbahotspring.com.vn; 25 Ngoc Son; ☺7am-7.30pm) The original hot thermal mud centre. For 250,000/500,000d you get a single/double wooden bathtub full of gooey mud, or it's 120,000d per person for a communal slop-up. Located 7km northwest of Nha Trang (130,000d in a taxi).

Su Spa SPA
(☎058-352 3242; www.suspa.vn; 93 Đ Nguyen Thien Thuat; ☺8am-9.30pm) One of the most

expensive spas in town, but it's stylishly designed and offers good scrubs, rubs, tubs and body massages (from US$24).

Vy Spa SPA
(☎0128 275 8662; 78B Đ Tue Tinh; ☺8am-9pm) This is a simple, fine-value place that's not really a 'spa' (more a converted store), but the massages and treatments are superb value and professional. Choose from Vietnamese, Thai or Swedish massages (all around 200,000d per hour) or try a facial (150,000d) or scrub.

🛏 Sleeping

★ **Sunny Sea** HOTEL $
(☎058-352 5244; www.sunnyhotel.com.vn; 64B/9 Đ Tran Phu; r US$10-15; ❄@🛜) An exceptional place owned by a welcoming local couple (a doctor and nurse) and Kim, the ever-helpful receptionist. Recently renovated, the rooms boast new mattresses, minibar, modern bathrooms and some have a balcony. The location is great, on a quiet lane just off the beach, and there's a lift.

Sao Mai Hotel HOTEL $
(☎058-352 6412; www.saomainhatranghotel.com; 99 Đ Nguyen Thien Thuat; dm US$6, r US$12-25; ❄@🛜) Long-standing budget favourite that's moved a little upmarket but remains superb value, with friendly management and 32 immaculately clean, spacious rooms. The five-bed dorm has air-con, en-suite bathroom and lockers.

Mojzo Inn HOSTEL $
(☎0988 879 069; 120/36 Đ Nguyen Thien Thuat; dm US$7, r US$16-19; ❄@🛜) The name is more cocktail list than hotel bed, but this funky new hostel gets most things right, with well-designed dorms and a lovely cushion-scattered lounge area.

Ngoc Thach HOTEL $
(☎058-352 5988; ngocthachhotel@gmail.com; 6I Quan Tran, Đ Hung Vuong; r US$15-18; ❄🛜) A great deal, the spacious, modern rooms (some with balcony) here are in excellent shape and have a real sparkle considering the modest tariffs. There's a lift.

Le Duong HOTEL $$
(5 & 6 Quan Tran, Đ Hung Vuong; r 450,000-700,000d; ❄🛜) This inviting new modern hotel has 50 beautifully presented, spacious rooms with pale furniture and white linen that represent excellent value. Prices are flexible to a degree, depending on demand.

BEAUTIFUL BEACHES

There are many pristine stretches of sand along the southeast coast, some of which see very few tourists. Here's our top five from north to south:

My Khe Located near the site of the infamous My Lai Massacre, My Khe (not to be confused with the other My Khe Beach near Danang) is a great beach, with fine white sand and clear water.

Vung Ro Bay The most easterly point on the mainland and famed for its beautiful and isolated bays, which hide some unspoilt beaches.

Whale Island Off the coast to the north of Nha Trang, Whale Island is a tiny speck on the map, home to the lovely and secluded **Whale Island Resort** (☑058-384 0501; www.whaleislandresort.com; s/d from US$33/45; 🐎) and a great spot for diving.

Doc Let Within commuting distance of busy Nha Trang, the beachfront is long and wide, with chalk-white sand and shallow water, and there are several blissful resorts.

Ninh Van Bay This place doesn't really exist – except in an alternate reality populated by European royalty, film stars and the otherwise rich and secretive. It's home to the **Six Senses Ninh Van Bay** (☑058-3524 268; www.sixsenses.com; villas US$690-1240; ⊜❋@🐎❄).

Golden Summer Hotel   HOTEL $$
(☑058-352 6662; www.goldensummerhotel.com.vn; 22-23 Tran Quang Khai; r US$25-50; ❋🐎) Modish new hotel, with a super-stylish lobby and inviting, modern rooms all with nice artistic touches such as statement photography on the walls. The location is excellent with myriad restaurants and the beach a short stroll away.

Summer Hotel   HOTEL $$
(☑058-352 2186; www.thesummerhotel.com.vn; 34C Ð Nguyen Thien Thuat; r US$32-106; ❋@🐎❄) Smart three-star hotel with affordable prices and very comfortable rooms. The pool is on the rooftop.

★ Mia Resort Nha Trang   HOTEL $$$
(☑058-398 9666; www.mianhatrang.com; Bai Dong, Cam Hai Dong; r/villa US$210/270; ⊜❋@🐎❄) Prepare yourself: the sense of occasion as you check in at Mia's alfresco reception is quite something, high above a horizon-filling expanse of ocean. The sky-high standards continue effortlessly through the resort, with superb accommodation units (each with sea view and outdoor bathrooms). There's a 40m pool and a stunning waveside restaurant. Oh, and the setting – nestled in a private cove beach – is breathtaking.

Evason Ana Mandara Resort & Spa   RESORT HOTEL $$$
(☑058-352 2522; www.evasonresorts.com; Ð Tran Phu; villa US$279-537; ❋@🐎❄) Exuding taste, this fine hotel consists of a charming cluster of spacious oceanside villas that have a colonial feel thanks to the classic furnishings and four-poster beds.

✗ Eating

Nha Trang is a diner's delight, with a diverse mix of international flavours.

For authentic Vietnamese food, try **Dam Market** (Ð Trang Nu Vuong; ⊙6am-4pm), which has a colourful collection of stalls, including *com chay* (vegetarian) options.

Nha Hang Yen's   VIETNAMESE $
(3/2A Tran Quang Khai; dishes 55,000-120,000d; ⊙7am-9.30pm; 🐎) Stylish restaurant with a hospitable atmosphere and a winning line-up of delectable clay-pot, noodle and rice dishes. Lilting traditional music and waitresses in *ao dai* add to the vibe.

Hy Lap   GREEK $
(1 Ð Tran Quang Khai; meals 30,000-75,000d; ⊙noon-10pm) Casual, inexpensive hole-in-the-wall run by an extremely welcoming Cretan couple. Only six tables (all outside), but good for moussaka, souvlaki or a salad.

Au Lac   VEGETARIAN $
(28C Ð Hoang Hoa Tham; meals 15,000-30,000d; ⊙11am-7pm; ✗) Long-running vegan and vegetarian near the corner of Ð Nguyen Chanh. A mixed plate is just about the best-value meal you can find in Nha Trang.

★**Lac Canh Restaurant** VIETNAMESE **$$**
(44 Ð Nguyen Binh Khiem; dishes 30,000-150,000d; ⊙11am-8.45pm) A totally local experience, this bustling, smoky, scruffy and highly enjoyable place is crammed most nights with groups firing up the table-top barbecues (beef is the speciality, but there are other meats and seafood). Closes quite early.

★**Nha Trang Xua** VIETNAMESE **$$**
(Thai Thong, Vinh Thai; dishes 52,000-210,000d; ⊙8am-9.30pm; 🛜) A classic Vietnamese restaurant set in a beautiful old house in the countryside surrounded by rice paddies around 7km west of town (100,000d in a taxi). Think refined menu, beautiful presentation and atmospheric surrounds. Highlights include the Vietnamese salads, five-spice beef and seafood.

Lanterns VIETNAMESE **$$**
(www.lanternsvietnam.com; 34/6 Ð Nguyen Thien Thuat; dishes 48,000-158,000d; ⊙7.30am-9.30pm; 🚭🛜🎜) This restaurant supports local orphanages and provides scholarship programs. Flavours are predominantly Vietnamese, such as lemon and chilli pork and tofu curry. Cooking classes and tours are also offered.

Louisiane Brewhouse INTERNATIONAL **$$**
(www.louisianebrewhouse.com.vn; 29 Ð Tran Phu; mains 62,000-360,000d; ⊙7am-1am; 🛜) It's not only the beer that draws a crowd here, as there is an eclectic menu with breakfast classics, superb salads, fish and seafood (red snapper is 140,000d), and Vietnamese, Japanese and Italian dishes. The beachside setting is superb, with tables grouped around a pool and giant copper beer vats.

🍷 **Drinking & Nightlife**

There have been a number of reports of dodgy cocktail buckets (laced with moonshine or drugs) doing the rounds in bars and clubs. Keep an eye on what goes into the bucket or avoid them completely – you don't want your night to end in paranoia, illness or robbery.

★**Guava** LOUNGE BAR
(www.guava.vn; 17 Ð Biet Thu; ⊙7am-1am; 🛜) Groovy Guava is the only game in town for quality electronic music – DJs spin house and lounge here on weekends. There's always a friendly vibe, good service and a busy pool table. Choose from sunken sofas inside or a leafy garden patio at the rear.

TRIPPING THE BAY BY BOAT

The 71 offshore islands around Nha Trang are renowned for their remarkably clear water. Boat trips to these islands – booze cruises and snorkelling excursions, from just 150,000d – are wildly popular with young backpackers.

Most of these trips are extremely touristy, involving whistle-stop visits to the Tri Nguyen **Aquarium** (Ho Ca Tri Nguyen; admission 50,000d), some snorkelling on a degraded reef, and a bit of beach time (beach admissions 30,000d). The booze cruises feature (very) organised entertainment with a DJ on the deck (or a cheesy boy band) and lots of drinking games.

Keep the following tips in mind:

➡ Choose the right tour. Some are geared towards Asian families, others are booze cruises.

➡ Remember sunscreen and drink plenty of water.

➡ Entrance charges are not usually included.

➡ If you're more interested in snorkelling than drinking, the dive schools' trips will be more appropriate.

Some decent boat-trip operators include the following:

Funky Monkey (📞058-352 2426; www.funkymonkeytour.com.vn; 75A Ð Hung Vuong; cruise incl pick-up 100,000d) Backpacker fun-geared trip including live entertainment.

Nha Trang Tours (📞058-352 4471; www.nhatrangtour.com.vn; 1/24 Ð Tran Quang Khai) Budget party-themed booze cruises for US$8 or snorkelling trips for around US$15.

Khanh Hoa Tourist Information (📞058-352 8000; khtourism@dng.vnn.vn; Ð Tran Phu; cruise incl lunch 349,000d) Boat trips to beautiful Van Phong Bay.

GETTING TO CAMBODIA & LAOS

Pleiku to Ban Lung (Cambodia)

Getting to the border Remote and rarely used by foreigners, the Le Thanh/O Yadaw border crossing lies 90km from Pleiku and 64km from Ban Lung, Cambodia. From Pleiku there's a daily Noi Thinh bus at 7.30am (60,000d, two hours) from the main marketplace on Đ Tran Phu direct to the Cambodian border at Le Thanh. You can also get to Le Thanh by buses from the main bus terminal, travelling via Moc Den (40,000d, two hours, four daily), from where local buses (20,000d, 15km) head to the border. Get as early a start as you can.

At the border Cambodian visas (US$20) are issued at the border (you'll need a passport-sized photo).

Moving on From O Yadaw, on the Cambodian side of the border, local buses (US$8) or motorbikes (around US$25) head to Ban Lung. There are far fewer transport options in the afternoon.

For more information about crossing this border in the other direction, see p235.

Kon Tum to Attapeu (Laos)

Getting to the border The Bo Y/Phou Keua border crossing is 86km northwest of Kon Tum and about 119km southeast of Attapeu (Laos). From Pleiku bus station, Mai Linh buses leave daily at 6.30am for Attapeu (250,000d, seven hours), continuing to Pakse (420,000d, 11½ hours). Kon Tum Tourist can arrange for you to join the bus when it passes through Kon Tum at around 8.15am.

Crossing the border independently can be a challenge. On the Vietnamese side, the nearest major town is Ngoc Hoi, which can be reached by bus from Kon Tum (34,000d, 1½ hours). You'll have to catch a minibus from Ngoc Hoi to the border (12,000d, 30 minutes). On the Lao side, things are even quieter and you'll be at the mercy of passing traffic to hitch a ride onwards.

At the border Vietnamese visas aren't available at this border, but Lao visas are available for most nationalities (between US$30 and US$42).

Moving on Buses from Pleiku arrive in Attapeu around 1.30pm, where a free lunch is included as part of your fare if you're travelling with Mai Linh. You'll arrive in Pakse around 6pm.

For more information about crossing this border in the other direction, see p347.

Sailing Club   BAR, CLUB
(www.sailingclubnhatrang.com; 72-74 Đ Tran Phu; ☺7am-2am) The Sailing Club is the definitive Nha Trang nightspot with a good mix of locals and foreigners. It's an upmarket venue, with expensive drinks, DJs and bands, and draws the city's beautiful crowd.

Oasis   BAR
(3 Đ Tran Quang Khai; ☺7am-2am; ☎) Buzzing bar on a corner plot with large garden terrace that's popular for bucket-downing and *shisha*-puffing. Happy hour runs right through from 4pm to midnight. It's a good choice for big sporting events.

Crazy Kim Bar   BAR
(http://crazykimvietnam.wordpress.com; 19 Đ Biet Thu; ☺8am-midnight; ☎) Regular themed party nights, devilish cocktail buckets,
shooters, cheap beer (from 25,000d), good tunes and tasty grub. Home to the commendable 'Hands off the Kids!' campaign, working to prevent paedophilia.

ℹ Information

Nha Trang has dozens of internet cafes and most hotels and bars have free wi-fi. ATMs are widespread too.

Highland Tours (☎058-352 4477; www.highlandtourstravel.com; 54G Đ Nguyen Thien Thuat) Affordable tours in the Central Highlands.

Main Post Office (4 Đ Le Loi; ☺6.30am-8pm)

Pasteur Institute (☎058-382 2355; 10 Đ Tran Phu; ☺7-11am & 1-4.30pm) Offers medical consultations and vaccinations. Located inside the Alexandre Yersin Museum.

Sinh Tourist (☑ 058-352 2982; www.thesinh tourist.vn; 2A Đ Biet Thu) Inexpensive local tours as well as open-tour buses.

Vietcombank (17 Đ Quang Trung; ⊘ 7.30am-4pm Mon-Fri) Has an ATM.

DANGERS & ANNOYANCES

Though Nha Trang is generally a safe place, be very careful on the beach during the day (theft) and at night (robbery). Pickpocketing is a perennial problem. Bags with valuables left behind in bars for 'safekeeping' are regularly relieved of cash and phones. Drive-by bag snatching is on the rise – take great care on the back of *xe om*. And note the warning about cocktail buckets.

① Getting There & Away

AIR

Vietnam Airlines (☑ 058-352 6768; www. vietnamairlines.com; 91 Đ Nguyen Thien Thuat) connects Nha Trang with Hanoi (three daily flights) and HCMC and Danang daily. **Jetstar Pacific** (www.jetstar.com) offers cheap flights to Hanoi.

BUS

Phia Nam Nha Trang bus station (Đ 23 Thang 10) has regular buses to Danang. Heading south, there are sleeper buses to HCMC from 7pm.

Open-bus tours are the best option for Mui Ne (four to five hours). Open buses also head to Dalat (five hours) and Hoi An (11 hours).

TRAIN

Nha Trang train station (☑ 058-382 2113; Đ Thai Nguyen; ⊘ ticket office 7-11.30am, 1.30-6pm & 7-9pm) is in the middle of town.

① Getting Around

Cam Ranh international airport is 30km south of the city via a beautiful coastal road. A shuttle bus runs the route (60,000d), leaving from the site of the old airport (near 86 Đ Tran

Phu) two hours before scheduled departure times, taking about 40 minutes. Taxis cost 380,000/300,000d to/from the airport.

Cyclos and *xe om* cost 20,000d for a short-ish ride. Hotels and cafes rent bicycles from 30,000d per day. **Mai Linh** (☑ 058-382 2266) taxis are safe and reliable.

Mui Ne

☑ 062 / POP 16,000

Once upon a time, Mui Ne was an isolated stretch of sand, but it was too beautiful to be ignored – it's now a string of resorts. Mercifully, most of these are low-rise and set amid pretty gardens by the sea. The original fishing village is still here, but tourists outnumber locals these days. Mui Ne is definitely moving upmarket, as more exclusive resorts open their doors, but there is still a (kite) surfer vibe to the town.

Mui Ne is the adrenalin capital of southern Vietnam – windsurfing and kitesurfing are huge here. Surf's up from August to December. It's also the 'Sahara' of Vietnam, with the most dramatic sand dunes in the region looming large.

◉ Sights

Sand Dunes   BEACH

Mui Ne is famous for its enormous red and white sand dunes. The white dunes are the more impressive, the near-constant oceanic winds sculpting the sands into wonderful Saharaesque formations. But as this is Vietnam (not deepest Mali), there's little chance of experiencing the silence of the desert.

Prepare yourself for the hard-sell as children press you to hire a plastic sledge to ride the dunes. Litter can be a problem too.

TRANSPORT FROM NHA TRANG

DESTINATION	AIR	BUS	CAR & MOTORBIKE	TRAIN
HCMC	from US$28, 1hr, 6 daily	US$10-14, 11hr, 13 daily	10hr	US$11-17, 7-9hr, 6 daily
Mui Ne	N/A	US$8, 6hr, open buses only	5hr	N/A
Dalat	N/A	US$7, 5hr, 17 daily	4hr	N/A
Quy Nhon	N/A	US$6.50, 5hr, hourly	4hr	US$5.50-8, 4hr, 5 daily
Danang	from US$55, 1hr, 1 daily	US$11-14, 12hr, 13-16 daily	11hr	US$16-26, 9-11hr, 5 daily

VIETNAM MUI NE

Mui Ne Beach

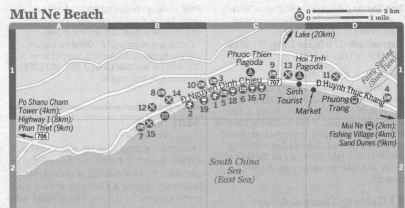

Po Shanu Cham Towers   HINDU TEMPLE
(Km 5; admission 5000d; ⏰ 7.30-11.30am & 1.30-4.30pm) West of Mui Ne, the ruins of the three Po Shanu Cham towers occupy a hill near Phan Thiet, with sweeping views of the town and a cemetery filled with candylike tombstones.

Activities

Surfpoint Kiteboarding
School   KITESURFING, SURFING
(☎ 0167 342 2136; www.surfpoint-vietnam.com; 52A Đ Nguyen Dinh Chieu; 5hr course incl all gear US$250; ⏰ 7am-6pm) With well-trained instructors and a friendly vibe, it's no surprise Surfpoint is one of the best-regarded kite schools in town. A three-hour taster costs US$145. Surfing lessons on softboards are offered (from US$50) when waves permit.

Jibes   KITESURFING
(☎ 062-384 7405; www.windsurf-vietnam.com; 84-90 Đ Nguyen Dinh Chieu; ⏰ 7.30am-6pm) Set up in 2000, this is the original kitesurfing school, offering lessons and renting state-of-the-art gear, including windsurfs, surfboards, kitesurfs and kayaks.

Sankara Kitesurfing Academy   KITESURFING
(☎ 0914 910 607; www.muinekiteschool.com; 78 Đ Nguyen Dinh Chieu) This school is run by experienced kitesurfers and offers kitesurfing lessons and equipment rentals. Lessons start at US$99 for two hours, or US$270 for five hours.

Courses

Taste of Vietnam   COOKING
(☎ 0916 655 241; www.c2skykitecenter.com/cooking-school; Sunshine Beach Resort, 82 Đ Nguyen Dinh Chieu; ⏰ 9am-12.30pm) Well-regarded Vietnamese cooking classes by the beach. Pay US$30 and a market visit is included. Make sure you have a light breakfast first as there are lots of delicacies to try!

🛌 Sleeping

Coco Sand Hotel
GUESTHOUSE $
(☎ 0127 364 3446; cocosandcatdua@yahoo.com.vn; 119 Đ Nguyen Dinh Chieu; r US$12-15; ❄ 🤖) Down a lane on the inland side of the main drag, these simple, clean rooms are quite spacious and excellent value. The owners are all smiles and there's a little garden with hammocks.

Mui Ne Backpackers
GUESTHOUSE $
(☎ 062-384 7047; www.muinebackpackers.com; 88 Đ Nguyen Dinh Chieu; dm US$6-10; r US$20-60; ❄ @ 🤖 ≋) Popular with young travellers for its sociable vibe and shoreside location;the dorms (with en-suite bathrooms and good mattresses) are a good bet, though the rooms are little pricey and quite plain. Lots of tours; transport tickets can be arranged.

Song Huong Hotel
HOTEL $
(☎ 062-384 7450; www.songhuonghotel.com; 241 Đ Nguyen Dinh Chieu; r inc breakfast US$12-20; ❄ 🤖) Run by welcoming family owners, this hotel is set well back from the road and boasts spacious, airy rooms in a modern house.

Lu Hoang Guesthouse
HOTEL $
(☎ 062-350 0060; 106 Đ Nguyen Dinh Chieu; r US$16-22; ❄ @ 🤖) This guesthouse has been lovingly decorated and several rooms include a sea view and breezy balconies, plus all have spotless bathrooms. The charming owners really make an effort here.

Duy An Guesthouse
GUESTHOUSE $
(☎ 062-384 7799; 87A Đ Huynh Thuc Khang; s/d US$12/15; ❄ @ 🤖) Close to the western end of the strip, the Duy An has friendly owners who speak good English. Room options include quads and there are bikes for hire.

Mui Ne Hills 1
BOUTIQUE HOTEL $$
(☎ 0908 052 350; www.muinehills.com; 69 Đ Nguyen Dinh Chieu; r US$40-55; ❄ @ 🤖 ≋) High above the coast, this fine villa-style hotel has wonderful vistas from its pool. Rooms are superb value, all with contemporary design touches and full facilities, but it's the personal touch from staff and owners that guests rightly rave about. Note that it's located up a dusty, very steep lane.

Xin Chao
BOUTIQUE HOTEL $$
(☎ 062-374 3086; www.xinchaohotel.com; 129 Đ Nguyen Dinh Chieu; r US$20-50; ❄ @ 🤖 ≋) Impressive new hotel (owned by kitesurfers) set well back from the busy coastal road. A lot of thought has gone into the design, with rooms grouped around a pool at the rear, and a small lounge area (with pool table) and roadside bar-restaurant that add to the appeal.

Full Moon Beach Hotel
HOTEL $$
(☎ 062-384 7008; www.fullmoonbeach.com.vn; 84 Đ Nguyen Dinh Chieu; r from US$56; ❄ @ 🤖 ≋) An artistically designed place where the committed owners have consistently upgraded the facilities to keep up with the competition. Features a bamboo-shaded pool, rooms with four-poster beds and terracotta tiling, and an oceanfront bar. However, it's a little overpriced; try to negotiate a discount.

★ Mia Resort
BOUTIQUE HOTEL $$$
(☎ 062-384 7440; www.miamuine.com; 24 Đ Nguyen Dinh Chieu; r US$90, bungalows US$130-190; ❄ @ 🤖 ≋) Everything is right at this stylish beachfront hotel. The gorgeous accommodation features designer furnishings dotted around a beautiful tropical garden. The pool area is particularly attractive, facing the ocean and bordered by the excellent Sandals restaurant, and the friendly, efficient staff really give the hotel that little extra polish that is lacking elsewhere.

🍴 Eating

As Mui Ne is an upmarket resort rather than a backpacker stronghold, it's one of the most expensive places to dine out in Vietnam.

★ Com Chay Phuoc
VEGETARIAN $
(15B Đ Huynh Thuc Khang; meals 20,000d; ⊙ 7am-9pm; 🖋) An exceptional little vegetarian place owned by Di, the ever-helpful English-speaking owner. There's no menu, but always four or five freshly cooked Vietnamese dishes. You eat on bamboo tables in very clean surrounds. It's right opposite the Eiffel Tower of the Little Paris resort, on the far east of the strip.

Phat Hamburgers
INTERNATIONAL $
(253 Đ Nguyen Dinh Chieu; burgers 55,000-95,000d; ⊙ 11am-9.30pm; 🤖) Roadside burger joint with variety of options, from gourmet to classic, served with great fries. Sip on a shake (try the chocolate and mint) for the full experience.

Lam Tong
VIETNAMESE, SEAFOOD $
(92 Đ Nguyen Dinh Chieu; dishes 28,000-115,000d; ⊙ 11.30am-9.30pm) You're eating under a corrugated roof, and staff can be brusque

verging on rude, but this beachfront restaurant serves good seafood, Vietnamese classics, and some vegetarian dishes.

Peaceful Family Restaurant VIETNAMESE $
(Yen Gia Quan; 53 Đ Nguyen Dinh Chieu; dishes 30,000-70,000d; ⊙7am-9.30pm) The family as this long-running local restaurant serve up traditional Vietnamese cuisine under a breezy thatched roof. Prices are pretty reasonable and the service is always efficient and friendly.

★ **Sandals** INTERNATIONAL $$
(24 Đ Nguyen Dinh Chieu, Mia Resort; meals 90,000-350,000d; ⊙7am-10pm; 🖭) This outstanding hotel restaurant is the most atmospheric place in town. It's particularly romantic at night, with tables set around the shoreside pool or in the elegant dining rooms. Waiting staff are knowledgeable, attentive and welcoming. The menu is superb with everything from pasta dishes to Malay-style *laksa* executed and presented beautifully. Peruse the extensive wine list or enjoy a fresh juice.

Rung Forest VIETNAMESE $$
(65A Đ Nguyen Dinh Chieu; dishes 70,000-200,000d; ⊙5-10pm) An incredible building, with trees screening tables from the road and lots of tribal art, masks and statues. The menu includes good claypots and hotpots, seafood and some Western options.

🍷 Drinking & Nightlife

Joe's Café BAR
(www.joescafegardenresort.com; 86 Đ Nguyen Dinh Chieu; ⊙7am-1am; 🖭) Mui Ne's premier live music (every night at 7.30pm) hang out with a sociable bar area, tables under trees, lots of drink specials, an extensive food menu and a pool table. Draws a slightly older crowd.

Fun Key BAR
(124 Đ Nguyen Dinh Chieu; ⊙10am-1am; 🖭) With a faintly boho ambience, this bar is popular with the backpacker crowd. Overlooks the ocean and has drink promotions to rev things up.

Dragon Beach BAR, NIGHTCLUB
(120-121 Đ Nguyen Dinh Chieu; ⊙8am-2am) With a great shoreside location that catches the sea breeze, this place has the most happening dance floor in town. Western and local DJs play deep house, techno and drum 'n' bass. There's a chill-out deck with cushions to one side. Happy hour is 8pm to 10pm.

Wax BAR
(68 Đ Nguyen Dinh Chieu; ⊙noon-late; 🖭) A well-established beach bar, Wax has happy hour until midnight when they light up the beach bonfire. Drunken bopping and beachside flopping draw the crowds.

ℹ Information

A great resource for information on Mui Ne is www.muinebeach.net.

Internet and wi-fi are widely available and there are several ATMs.

Main Post Office (348 Đ Huynh Thuc Khang; ⊙7am-5pm) In Mui Ne village.

Sinh Tourist (www.thesinhtourist.vn; 144 Đ Nguyen Dinh Chieu) Operates out of Mui Ne Resort, booking open-tour buses and trips around Mui Ne and offering credit-card cash advances.

ℹ Getting There & Around

Mui Ne is connected to Hwy 1 via branch roads to the north and south, but few regular buses serve the town.

Open-tour buses are the best option for Mui Ne. Several companies have daily services to/from HCMC (120,000d to 149,000d, six hours), Nha Trang (120,000d, five hours) and Dalat (110,000d, four hours). Sleeper buses usually cost more: Sinh Tourist's prices are HCMC (209,000d), Nha Trang (209,000d), Hoi An (378,000d) and Hue (477,000d).

Phuong Trang (www.futabuslines.com.vn; 97 Đ Nguyen Dinh Chieu) has four to five comfortable buses a day running between Mui Ne and HCMC (135,000d).

Local buses run from nearby Phan Thiet to Mui Ne. **Mai Linh** (☐062-389 8989) operates metered taxis. *Xe om* charge 20,000d to 40,000d for rides up and down the coast.

Con Dao Islands

🖉 064 / POP 5500

Isolated from the mainland, the Con Dao Islands are one of the star attractions in Vietnam. Once the Devil's Island of Indochina – the preserve of political prisoners and undesirables – this place is now turning heads thanks to its striking natural beauty. Con Son, the largest of this chain of 15 islands and islets, is ringed with lovely beaches, coral reefs and scenic bays, and remains partially covered in thick forests. Hiking, diving and deserted beaches are all a big draw.

More than three-quarters of the land area in the island chain is part of Con Dao National Park, which protects Vietnam's most important **sea turtle nesting grounds**.

⊙ Sights

All the following sights are in Con Son Town, share the same opening hours and are covered by a single ticket costing 20,000d, which you can purchase at Phu Hai. There are 11 former prisons on Con Son.

Phu Hai Prison   HISTORIC SITE
(⊙7-11.30am & 1-5pm) The largest of the 11 jails on the island, this prison dates from 1862. Thousands of prisoners were held here, with up to 200 prisoners crammed into each detention building. During the French era all prisoners were kept naked, chained together in rows, with one small box serving as a toilet for hundreds. One can only imagine the squalor and stench. Today, emaciated mannequins that are all too lifelike recreate the era.

Tiger Cages   HISTORIC SITE
The notorious cells dubbed 'tiger cages' were built in 1940 by the French to incarcerate nearly 2000 political prisoners. There are 120 chambers with ceiling bars, where guards could poke at prisoners like tigers in a Victorian zoo. Prisoners were beaten with sticks from above, and sprinkled with quick lime and water (which burnt their skin and caused blindness).

Hang Duong Cemetery   CEMETERY
Some 20,000 Vietnamese prisoners died on Con Son, and 1994 of their graves can be seen at the peaceful Hang Duong cemetery, located at the eastern edge of town. Sadly, only 700 of these graves bear the name of the victim.

Vietnam's most famous heroine, Vo Thi Sau (1933–52), was buried here, the first woman executed by a firing squad on Con Son, on 23 January 1952.

Revolutionary Museum   MUSEUM
(⊙7-11am & 1.30-5pm) Located in the former French commandant's residence, this museum has exhibits on Vietnamese resistance against the French, communist opposition to the Republic of Vietnam, and the treatment of political prisoners. You'll also find a painting of Vo Thi Sau (facing death with her head held high), a diorama of the Con Daos, and some stuffed wildlife, including boa constrictors, lizards and monkeys.

Beaches   BEACH
Arguably the best all-round beach, **Bai Dam Trau** is a secluded cove at the southern end of the island. Other options include tiny **Bai Nhat**, though it's exposed only during low tide. **Bai Loi Voi** is another possibility.

🏊 Activities

Con Dao offers the most pristine marine environment in the country. Diving is possible year-round, but for ideal conditions and good visibility, January to June is considered the best time.

There are lots of treks around Con Son Island, as much of the interior remains heavily forested. It's necessary to take a national park guide (180,000d to 300,000d) when venturing into the forest. Trekking destinations include **Bamboo Lagoon** (Dam Tre), **Ong Dung Bay** and **So Ray**.

★ Dive! Dive! Dive!   DIVING
(☎064-383 0701; www.dive-condao.com; Đ Nguyen Hue; ⊙8am-9pm) An experienced, conservation-minded American-run operation, offering both PADI and SSI courses. Two dives are US$160 and snorkelling tours cost US$40 (including equipment).

A TEENAGE ICON

If breeze is blowing from the north, you can probably smell the incense from a specific grave in Con Son's cemetery: the tomb of **Vo Thi Sau**, a national icon.

A teenage resistance fighter executed in Con Dao during the French occupation, Vo Thi Sau was politically active from a very early age. She killed a French captain in a grenade attack at the age of 14, and was only captured years later following a second assassination attempt, after which she was taken to Con Dao and executed at the age of 19.

Visit Con Son Town's Hanh Duong cemetery at midnight and you'll find crowds of people packed around her grave, saying prayers and making offerings. The Vietnamese believe that this is the most auspicious time to pay respects and venerate the spirit of this national heroine, who was killed in the early hours of 23 January 1952.

🛏 Sleeping & Eating

Nha Nghi Thanh Xuan GUESTHOUSE $

(☑ 064-383 0261; 44 Đ Ton Duc Thang; r 350,000-450,000d; 🖥) Painted in marine blue, this guesthouse has rooms with good mattresses and duvets; the upstairs rooms are light and airy. The owners speak little or no English.

Hai Nga Mini Hotel HOTEL $

(☑ 064-363 0308; 7 Đ Tran Phu; r 400,000-600,000d; 🌸@🖥) A good option for sharers, some rooms here sleep up to five people, and all have air-con. Run by a friendly family who can speak some English and German.

Con Dao Sea Cabanas HOTEL $$

(☑064-383 1555; www.condaoseacabanas.com/en; Đ Nguyen Duc Thuan; r 650,000-750,000d; 🌸@🖥) Well worth considering, these two rows of cute A-frame bungalows enjoy a nice position right by a stretch of beach. Frills (if not thrills) include satellite TV, two beds, a porch, a minibar and showers with a view of the night sky.

★ Six Senses Con Dao BOUTIQUE HOTEL $$$

(☑ 064-383 1222; www.sixsenses.com; Dat Doc Beach; villas from US$685; 🌸@🖥🌊) Bagging an unmatched position on the island's best beach, this ultra-luxe hotel is in a class (and location) of its own. There are 50 or so ocean-facing timber-clad beach units fusing contemporary style with rustic chic, each with its own pool, giant bathtub and Bose stereo.

Quan Thanh Huyen VIETNAMESE $$

(Khu 3, Hoang Phi Yen; meals 70,000-160,000d; ☺noon-9pm) South of town by a water-lily-filled lake, this lovely little restaurant enjoys a great setting, with gazebos next to the water and an orchestra of croaking frogs. Offers authentic Vietnamese cuisine including hotpots and snakehead fish straight from the lake.

Thu Tam VIETNAMESE $$

(Đ Nguyen Hue; mains 25,000-170,000d; ☺11.30am-9pm) On the Con Son strip, offering fresh seafood from bubbling tanks. Shellfish comes in many shapes and sizes, or go for a huge fish to feed a family.

ℹ Information

Larry of Dive! Dive! Dive! is a great contact, and very knowledgeable about the islands; he'll give you a map and chat for free and can organise motorbikes for hire.

There are three ATMs in Con Dao. Internet access and wi-fi are available at hotels.

The **National Park HQ** (☑ 064-383 0669; www.condaopark.com.vn; 29 Đ Vo Thi Sau; ☺7-11.30am & 1.30-5pm daily) is a good place to get information about excursions and hikes.

ℹ Getting There & Around

Vasco (☑ 064-383 1831; www.vasco.com.vn; 44 Đ Nguyen Hue) offers three flights daily from HCMC. The tiny airport is 15km from Con Son Town centre. Big hotels provide free airport transfers; you can hitch a ride on one of these for about 50,000d.

Ferries connect Con Son island with Vung Tau, with sailings three to four times a week. Facilities are basic and the crossing can be very rough leading to frequent cancellations. The ferries (at 5pm, seat/berth 145,000/275,000d, 12 hours) depart from Ben Dam port, 12km south of Con Son Town.

Boat trips (2,000,000d to 5,000,000d per day) can be arranged through the national park office or Dive! Dive! Dive!

Bicycles (US$2) and motorbikes (from US$7) are available for rent from hotels.

SOUTHWEST HIGHLANDS

There's a rugged charm to this distinctly rural region, with pine-studded hilltops soaring over intensively farmed fields and remote, bumpy roads meandering through coffee plantations.

Looking for big nature? Check out Cat Tien National Park, where there are gibbons, crocodiles and elusive tigers.

Dalat, a former French hill station that still boasts plenty of colonial charm, makes a great base. An adventure-sports mecca, it offers myriad biking and hiking trips for daytime thrills and atmospheric restaurants and bars for after-dark chills.

Dalat

☑ 063 / POP 215,000 / ELEV 1475M

Dalat is the alter-ego of lowland Vietnam. The weather is spring-like cool instead of tropical hot. Days are fine, but nights can be chilly. The town is dotted with elegant French colonial villas instead of squat socialist architecture, and farms are thick with strawberries and flowers, not rice.

Dalat is small enough to remain charming, and the surrounding countryside is blessed with lakes, waterfalls, evergreen forests and gardens. The town is a big draw for domestic tourists for whom it's a honeymoon capital. For travellers the moderate climate is ideal for adrenalin-fuelled activities – mountain biking, hiking, canyoning and climbing.

⊙ Sights

Perhaps there's something in the cool mountain air that fosters the distinctly artistic vibe that veers towards cute kitsch in Dalat.

Hang Nga Crazy House NOTABLE BUILDING
(☑ 063-382 2070; 3 Đ Huynh Thuc Khang; admission 40,000d; ⊙ 7am-7pm) A free-wheeling architectural exploration of surrealism, Hang Nga Crazy House defies definition. Joyously designed, outrageously artistic, this private home is a monument to the creative potential of concrete, with sculptured rooms connected by super-slim bridges and an excess of cascading lava-flow-like shapes. Think Gaudí on acid.

Wander around as you please; getting lost is definitely part of the experience.

A note of caution for those with young kids: the Crazy House's maze of precarious tunnels, walkways and ladders are certainly not child safe. Be extra vigilant.

Bao Dai's Summer Palace HISTORIC BUILDING
(off Đ Trieu Viet Vuong; admission 15,000d; ⊙ 7am-5pm) A faded art-deco-influenced villa, this was one of three palaces Bao Dai (the last emperor of the Nguyen dynasty) kept in Dalat. The building's design is striking, though it's in serious need of restoration and the once-modern interior is distinctly scruffy, with tatty net curtains and chipped furniture. Bao Dai's imposing office, with its royal and military seals and flags, is still impressive.

Truc Lam Pagoda & Cable Car BUDDHIST TEMPLE
(Ho Tuyen Lam; cable car (one-way/return adult 50,000/70,000d, child 30,000/40,000d; ⊙ cable car 7.30-11.30am & 1.30-5pm) For a spiritual recharge, visit Truc Lam Pagoda, which enjoys a hilltop setting and has splendid gardens. It's an active monastery (ask about meditation sessions) and the grounds are expansive enough to escape the odd tour group. Be sure to arrive by cable car (the terminus is 3km south of the centre), which soars over majestic pine forests.

From the monastery it's a 15-minute walk down to the shore of **Tuyen Lam Lake** (actually a reservoir), where there are cafes and boats for hire. Both the pagoda and lake can also be reached by road via turn-offs from Hwy 20.

Lam Dong Museum MUSEUM
(☑ 063-382 0387; 4 Đ Hung Vuong; admission 10,000d; ⊙ 7.30-11.30am & 1.30-4.30pm Mon-Sat) Housed in a modern pink building, this hillside museum displays ancient artefacts and pottery, costumes and musical instruments of local ethnic minorities, and propaganda about the government support for their mountain neighbours. There are informative exhibits about Alexandre Yersin and the history of Dalat on the upper level.

Xuan Huong Lake LAKE
Created by a dam in 1919, this banana-shaped lake was named after an anti-authoritarian 17th-century Vietnamese poet. The lake can be circumnavigated along a scenic 7km sealed path that passes the flower gardens, golf club and Dalat Palace hotel.

🏃 Activities

Crémaillère TRAIN TRIP
(Ga Da Lat; 1 Đ Quang Trung; ⊙ 6.30am-5pm) The Crémaillère is a cog railway that linked Dalat and Thap Cham–Phan Rang from 1928 to 1964. It's about 500m east of Xuan Huong Lake. The line has now been partially repaired and is a tourist attraction. You can ride 8km down the tracks to Trai Mat village, where you can visit the ornate Linh Phuoc Pagoda.

There are five scheduled trains to Trai Mat (return ticket 124,000d, 30 minutes, 8km) every day between 7.45am and 4.05pm.

★ Phat Tire Ventures ADVENTURE TOUR
(☑ 063-382 9422; www.ptv-vietnam.com; 109 Đ Nguyen Van Troi) A highly professional and experienced operator with mountain-biking trips from US$49, trekking from US$31, kayaking from US$39, canyoning from US$45 and white-water rafting (US$72) in the wet season. Combined bike-riding/rafting trips to Mui Ne (US$115) are definitely the best way to hit the coast.

Groovy Gecko Adventure Tours ADVENTURE TOUR
(☑ 063-383 6521; www.groovygeckotours.net; 65 Đ Truong Cong Dinh) Experienced agency operated by a lively young team with prices

starting at US$35 for rock climbing, canyoning or mountain biking, and two-day treks from US$59.

Pine Track Adventures ADVENTURE TOUR
(☑ 063-383 1916; www.pinetrackadventures.com; 72B Đ Truong Cong Dinh) Run by an enthusiastic local team, this operator offers canyoning, trekking, biking and some excellent multi-sport packages. A six-day trip taking in Dalat and the ride down to Mui Ne is US$510.

🛏 Sleeping

⭐ Dreams Hotel GUESTHOUSE $
(☑ 063-383 3748; dreams@hcm.vnn.vn; 138-140 Đ Phan Dinh Phung; r US$20-25; ⊜@🖭) An incredibly hospitable guesthouse owned by a family that looks after its guests with affection and care. Boasts spotless rooms, a legendary breakfast spread, and hot tub and sauna.

Thien An Hotel HOTEL $
(☑ 063-352 0607; thienanhotel@vnn.vn; 272A Đ Phan Dinh Phung; s US$18, d US$22-25; @🖭) Superb, welcoming family hotel providing spacious and well-equipped rooms, glorious breakfasts (including Vegemite and Marmite), a cosy atmosphere and high levels of cleanliness. Free bicycles provided.

Le Phuong Hotel HOTEL $
(☑ 063-382 3743; www.lephuonghotel.com; 80 Đ Nguyen Chi Thanh; s 300,000d, d 350,000-500,000d; ❋@🖭) From the gleaming lobby to the stylish, spacious minimalist rooms, this family-run hotel is a great deal. Cleanliness standards are high and it's conveniently located.

Green City HOTEL $
(☑ 063-382 7999; www.dalatgreencityhotel.com; 172 Đ Phan Dinh Phung; s/d/tw US$17/19/21; ❋@🖭) New place switched on to travellers' needs with attractive, well-presented rooms, all with fine wooden beds, fresh linen, TV and minibar. Loafers will love the sofa-strewn lobby.

⭐ Dreams 3 HOTEL $$
(☑ 063-383 3748, 063-382 5877; dreams@hcm. vnn.vn; 138-140 Đ Phan Dinh Phung; r US$30-35; ⊜❋@🖭) This commodious new venture owned by the amazing 'Dreams Team' offers incredibly tasteful accommodation. All rooms have high-quality mattresses and modish bathrooms, and some have a balcony. On the top floor there's a jacuzzi, steam room and sauna; a restaurant is planned.

The only downer is the location on a traffic-heavy street.

Dalat Train Villa APARTMENTS $$
(☑ 063-381 6365; www.dalattrainvilla.com; 1 Đ Quang Trung; apt US$70; ⊜🖭) A stunning French-era villa that's been sensitively converted into four apartments, perfect for families or groups. Each unit has a lounge, small kitchen and large-screen TV. There's a converted train-carriage cafe on your doorstep for meals. About 2km east of the centre.

Dalat Hotel du Parc HOTEL $$
(☑ 063-382 5777; www.hotelduparc.vn; 7 Đ Tran Phu; s & d US$50-70, ste US$110; ❋@🖭) A respectfully refurbished 1932 building that offers colonial-era style at enticing prices. The old lobby lift sets the tone and the spacious rooms include classy furnishings and polished wooden floors. However, it's slightly lacking in facilities.

⭐ Ana Mandara Villas Dalat BOUTIQUE HOTEL $$$
(☑ 063-355 5888; www.anamandara-resort.com; Đ Le Lai; r US$82-102, ste from US$138; ⊜❋@🖭) Elegant property spread across 17 lovingly restored French colonial villas. Rooms are finished in period furnishings and each villa has a lounge with fireplace and the option of private dining. The spa is glorious. It's quite a hike from the centre.

Dalat Palace COLONIAL HOTEL $$$
(☑ 063-382 5444; www.dalatpalace.vn; 12 Đ Tran Phu; s US$246-306, d US$260-320, ste US$446-510; ⊜❋@🖭) With unimpeded views of Xuan Huong Lake, this *grande dame* of hotels has lashings of wood panelling and period class. The opulence of French-colonial life has been splendidly preserved: claw-foot tubs, fireplaces, chandeliers and paintings. However it can be achingly empty at times, and consequently can lack ambience. Online deals can reduce rates to around US$130.

🍴 Eating

There are vegetarian food stalls and cheap eats in the market area.

⭐ Trong Dong VIETNAMESE $
(☑ 063-382 1889; 220 Đ Phan Dinh Phung; mains 40,000-80,000d; ⊙11.30am-9.30pm) Intimate restaurant run by a very hospitable team where the menu has been creatively

Dalat

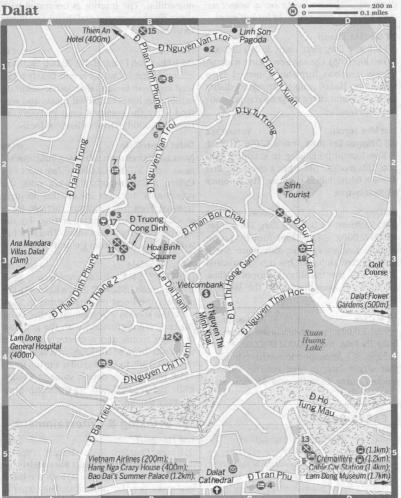

Dalat

Activities, Courses & Tours
1	Groovy Gecko Adventure Tours	B3
2	Phat Tire Ventures	C1
3	Pine Track Adventures	B3

Sleeping
4	Dalat Hotel du Parc	C5
5	Dalat Palace	D5
6	Dreams 3	B2
7	Dreams Hotel	B2
8	Green City	B1
9	Le Phuong Hotel	B4

Eating
10	Da Quy	B3
11	Goc Ha Thanh	B3
12	Lan Mot Nguoi	B4
13	Le Rabelais	D5
14	Nhat Ly	B2
15	Trong Dong	B1
16	V Cafe	C3

Drinking & Nightlife
17	The Hangout	B3

Entertainment
18	Escape Bar	D3

designed – shrimp paste on a sugarcane stick and beef wrapped in *la lut* leaf excel.

★ Goc Ha Thanh   VIETNAMESE $

(53 Đ Truong Cong Dinh; mains 35,000-119,000d; ⊙7am-10pm; 🖥) Casual new place with attractive bamboo furnishings owned by a welcoming Hanoi couple. Strong on dishes such as coconut curry, hotpots, clay pots, stir fries and noodles.

Lan Mot Nguoi   VIETNAMESE $

(58 Đ Nguyen Chi Thanh; meals 32,000-68,000d; ⊙10am-10pm) Specialising in steaming hotpots, this modern place has a casual air and draws a faithful local clientele. Try the spicy seafood hotpot.

Da Quy   VIETNAMESE, WESTERN $

(Wild Sunflower; 49 Đ Truong Cong Dinh; dishes 30,000-72,000d; ⊙8am-10pm) Run by Loc, a friendly English speaker, this place has a sophisticated ambience but unsophisticated prices. Try the traditional claypot dishes, a hotpot or something from the Western menu.

★ V Cafe   INTERNATIONAL $$

(☑063-352 0215; www.vcafedalatvietnam.com; 1/1 Đ Bui Thi Xuan; meals 80,000-170,000d; ⊙7am-10.30pm; 🖥) Atmospheric bistro-style place that serves international cuisine, such as chicken curry Calcutta and Mexican-style quesadillas. The interior is decorated with stunning photography and there's live music most nights.

Nhat Ly   VIETNAMESE $$

(88 Đ Phan Dinh Phung; dishes 35,000-130,000d; ⊙11am-9.30pm) Nhat Ly serves hearty highland meals on tartan tablecloths, including sumptuous hotpots, grilled meats and seafood – try the steamed crab in beer (1kg costs 280,000d). Draws plenty of locals.

Dalat Train Cafe   CAFE $$

(www.dalattrainvilla.com; 1 Đ Quang Trung; snacks/meals from 50,000/90,000d; ⊙7am-10pm; 🖥) Calling all trainspotters! Don't miss the opportunity to step inside this lovingly restored French-era railway carriage for a snack or meal in a unique setting. Try the blue-cheese burger or a salad. There's a full wine list. It's 100m from the train station.

★ Le Rabelais   FRENCH $$$

(☑063-382 5444; www.dalatresorts.com; 12 Đ Tran Phu; meals US$29-85; ⊙7am-10pm; 🖥) For arguably the finest colonial setting in Vietnam, the signature restaurant at the Dalat Palace is *the* destination with the grandest of dining rooms and a spectacular terrace that looks down to the lakeshore. Set dinner menus (US$65 to US$85) offer the full treatment, but lunch is decent value at US$29, while high tea is US$16. It's frequently pretty empty though.

🍷 Drinking & Entertainment

The Hangout   BAR

(71 Đ Truong Cong Dinh; ⊙11am-11pm; 🖥) Popular hangout for some of Dalat's Easy Riders, as well as visiting backpackers, with a relaxed vibe and a popular pool table. The owner is an excellent source of local information.

★ Escape Bar   LIVE MUSIC

(Basement, Blue Moon Hotel, 4 Đ Phan Boi Chau; ⊙4pm-midnight; 🖥) Outstanding live-music bar, owned by blues guitarist Curtis King, who performs here most nights with a rotating band (from 9pm). Sunday is a jam session. The bar's decor, all 1970s chic and 'groovy baby' furnishings, suits the sonics perfectly.

🔒 Shopping

Hoa Binh Square and the **market** building adjacent to it are the places to purchase ethnic handicrafts, including Lat rush baskets

---

EASY DOES IT

For many travellers, the highlight of their trip to the central highlands is an off-the-beaten-track motorcycle tour with an **Easy Rider** (guide-rider). The flip side to the popularity of the Easy Riders is that now everyone claims to be one. In central Dalat, you can't walk down the street without being invited (sometimes harassed) for a tour.

Rider-guides can be found in hotels and cafes in Dalat. Read testimonials from past clients. Check the bike over. Test-drive a rider first before committing to a longer trip. Then discuss the route in detail – for scenery the new coastal highways that link Dalat to Mui Ne and Nha Trang, plus the old road to the coast via Phan Rang, are wonderful.

Rates start at US$25 for a day tour, or US$50 to US$70 per day for longer journeys.

AROUND DALAT

Curtis King is a Dalat-based musician and restaurant/hotel owner who's been visiting the city since 2001. He filled us in on his favourite experiences in and around Dalat.

Best Road Trips There are basically six different routes leading out of Dalat, all spectacular in their own way, in particular the roads heading to the coast – the road to Nha Trang is truly stunning.

Best Waterfalls Dalat and the surrounding areas are home to some of the country's most beautiful waterfalls. Slightly off the beaten path, Elephant Falls and Tiger Den Falls are highly impressive, or head to those along Hwy 20.

Best Train Experiences Being a big railway fan, it was the Dalat train station and the local tourist train that really got my attention when I first came here in 2001. The train ride to Trai Mat, although it only takes about 30 minutes, is so evocative of colonial times. Then stop by the Dalat Train Cafe for a drink in a classic railway carriage.

that roll up when empty. Coffee is another smart purchase.

ℹ️ Information

Dalat has numerous ATMs and internet cafes. Wi-fi is available in most hotels and cafes.

Lam Dong General Hospital (☎063-382 1369; 4 Đ Pham Ngoc Thach; ⊕24hr)

Main Post Office (14 Đ Tran Phu; ⊕7am-6pm)

Sinh Tourist (☎063-382 2663; www.thesinhtourist.vn; 22 Đ Bui Thi Xuan) Tours, including city sightseeing trips, and open-tour bus bookings.

Vietcombank (6 Đ Nguyen Thi Minh Khai; ⊕7.30am-3pm Mon-Fri, to 1pm Sat) With ATM.

ℹ️ Getting There & Around

Vietnam Airlines (☎063-383 3499; www.vietnamairlines.com; 2 Đ Ho Tung Mau) has daily services to HCMC, Danang, and Hanoi. **Vietjet Air** (☎1900 1886; www.vietjetair.com) also flies daily to Hanoi.

Lien Khuong Airport is 30km south of the city. Vietnam Airlines operates a shuttle bus (40,000d, 30 minutes) timed around flights. Taxis cost about 250,000d.

Dalat's modern **long-distance bus station** (Đ 3 Thang 4) has timetables and booking offices; it's about 1.5km south of Xuan Huong Lake by road. From here there are express buses to HCMC, other cities in the highlands, Danang and Nha Trang. **Phuong Trang** (☎063-358 5858) operates smart double-decker buses, including several sleeper services, to HCMC (US$11, seven to eight hours, roughly hourly).

Dalat is a major stop for open-tour buses. The Sinh Tourist has daily buses to Mui Ne (129,000d, four hours), Nha Trang (129,000d, five hours) and HCMC (179,000d, eight hours).

Car rental with a driver starts from about US$40 a day. Full-day tours with local motorbike guides (from US$25) are a great way to see the area, as many of the sights lie outside Dalat's centre. Many hotels offer bicycle and motorbike hire. For a taxi call **Mai Linh** (☎063-352 1111).

Around Dalat

Waterfalls

Dalat's waterfalls are obviously at their gushing best in the wet season but still flow when it's dry. Most tend to focus on commerce rather than nature – Prenn and Cam Ly Falls are two to avoid.

An uneven and sometimes hazardous path heads down to **Elephant Falls** FREE, which are best seen from below. The falls are near Nam Ban village, 30km west of Dalat.

Datanla Falls (admission 10,000d; bobsled ride adult one-way/return 30,000/40,000d) are 7km southeast of Dalat off Hwy 20. It's a nice walk through the rainforest and a steep hike downhill to the falls. You can also take a bobsled ride down a winding elevated track. On weekends expect crowds and loud music.

The largest waterfall in the Dalat area, **Pongour Falls** (admission 10,000d; ⊕7am-4pm) are about 55km in the direction of HCMC. The stepped falls are beautiful at any time, but most spectacular during the wet season when they form a full semicircle.

Dambri Falls (admission 10,000d), 75km from Dalat, are the tallest falls (90m) in the area – walking down to feel the spray from the bottom is divine. You can trek your way down and take the cable car back up.

You'll need your own wheels to access these waterfalls.

CENTRAL HIGHLANDS

It's easy to get off the beaten track in this scenic part of the country. Only Dalat makes it onto most tourists' radars, meaning that the rest of the region still offers adventure in abundance. This is a great part of the country to see from the back of a motorbike.

The upgrading of the historic **Ho Chi Minh Trail** has made it easier than ever to visit out-of-the-way places such as **Kon Tum**, one of the friendliest cities in Vietnam, with several fascinating churches in town and hill-tribe villages close by.

Buon Ma Thuot is the major city in the region, but the biggest buzz you'll get is from the coffee beans. Nearby **Yok Don National Park** (☑ 0500-378 3049; www.yokdon-nationalpark.vn; admission free as part of package) is home to 38 endangered mammal species, including plenty of elephants and a handful of tigers. Impressive waterfalls in this area include **Gia Long** and **Dray Nur Falls** along the Krong Ana River.

Bidoup Nui Ba National Park

Occupying a densely forested highland plateau, this **national park** (☑ 063-374 7449; www.bidoupnuiba.gov.vn) encompasses evergreen and coniferous woodlands, bamboo groves and grasslands at altitudes between 650m and 2288m.

Bidoup Nui Ba has 96 endemic plants, including the Dalat pine, and nearly 300 species of orchids. Yellow-cheeked gibbons can be heard in the early morning if you're fortunate, while the national park is also home to black bears and the vampire flying frog (which was only discovered in 2010).

Hill-tribe guides are available for hiking and there's an impressive visitor centre, 32km north of Dalat, with interactive displays about the flora and fauna and K'Ho hill-tribe crafts and culture.

The pleasant 3.5km trail from the visitor centre to a waterfall only fringes the national park; to penetrate deep inside Bidoup Nui Ba consider one of three other options, which include ascents of Lang Biang and Bidoup mountains. The longer trails do not start from the visitor centre itself, but staff there can organise guides and logistics.

There are five comfortable **bungalows** (300,000d), each with three en-suite rooms at the visitor centre, as well as a **canteen** (meals 30,000d to 70,000d).

Cat Tien National Park

One of the outstanding natural spaces in Vietnam, Unesco-listed **Cat Tien National Park** (☑ 061-366 9228; www.cattiennationalpark.vn; adult/child 50,000/20,000d; ☉ 7am-10pm) 🐾 comprises an amazingly biodiverse area of lowland tropical rainforest. The hiking, mountain biking and birdwatching are outstanding.

Fauna in the park includes 326 bird species, 100 mammals (including elephants), 79 reptiles plus an incredible array of insects, including 400 or so species of butterfly. Leopards are also believed to be present, though the last rhino was killed by poachers in 2010. Call ahead for reservations, as the park can accommodate only a limited number of visitors.

◉ Sights & Activities

Cat Tien National Park can be explored on foot, by mountain bike, by 4WD and also by boat along the Dong Nai River. There are many well-established hiking trails in the park, though you will need a **guide** (from 250,000d).

Trips to the **Crocodile Swamp** (Bau Sau; admission 140,000d, guide fee 300,000d, boat trip 350,000d), taking in a three-hour jungle trek, are popular. **Night safaris** (from 300,000d) are another option, although deer are the only animals usually seen. There's also a small bear sanctuary for animals rescued from the bile trade. Wherever you decide to go, be sure to book a guide in advance and take plenty of insect repellent.

Dao Tien Endangered Primate Species Centre (www.go-east.org; adult/child incl boat ride 150,000/50,000d; ☉ 8am & 2pm) is located on an island in the Dong Nai River. It's a rehabilitation centre hosting gibbons, langurs and loris that have been confiscated as pets or from traffickers.

A **Wild Gibbon Trek** (ecotourism@cattiennationalpark.vn; per person US$60, maximum 4 people) runs daily and involves a 4am start to get out to the gibbons in time for their dawn chorus. Relax in a hammock as the forest slowly comes alive with their calls before watching the family go about their everyday lives. The trip finishes with a guided tour of the primate species centre. Book ahead.

🛏 Sleeping & Eating

In Jun village by the park entrance, **Sinthai Ho Lak** (📞 0905 424 239; per person US$5) offers comfortable communal longhouse accommodation and meals.

⭐**Forest Floor Lodge** (📞 061-366 9890; www.vietnamforesthotel.com; luxury tents from US$136, houses/studios from US$136/152; ❄ @ 🛜) is a fine privately run ecolodge that has lovely safari tents overlooking the Dong Nai River and a range of rooms set in reclaimed traditional wooden houses. There's a great **restaurant** (meals from 75,000d).

Cat Tien National Park (📞 061-366 9228; namcattien@yahoo.com.vn; small/big tents 220,000/350,000d; bungalows from 580,000d; ❄) offers basic bungalow rooms and tented accommodation close to the park headquarters. There are two small **restaurants** (meals 35,000-200,000d) here. Avoid weekends and holidays if possible.

❶ Getting There & Around

Cat Tien is 125km north of HCMC and 175km south of Dalat. Turn off Hwy 20 at Tan Phu and it's another 25km up a paved access road to the entrance. Buses between Dalat and HCMC pass the access road. Waiting motorbikes (around 170,000d) will then take you to the park entrance.

Bicycles are available for hire in the park, from 20,000d per day.

HO CHI MINH CITY (SAIGON)

📞 08 / POP 7.4 MILLION

Ho Chi Minh City (HCMC) is a metropolis on the move and we're not just talking about the city's motorbikes. Yes, Saigon is Vietnam at its most dizzying, a high-octane city of commerce and culture that has driven the whole country forward with its limitless energy and booming economy.

Wander through alleys to ancient pagodas or teeming markets, past ramshackle wooden shops selling silk and spices, before fast-forwarding into the future beneath skyscrapers and mammoth malls.

Whether you want to relive the colonial experience in sumptuous French-era hotels or crash in the cheapest guesthouse, seek out the classiest restaurants or indulge in street food, shop designer boutiques or join the scrum of the markets, Saigon has it all. Put simply, there's nowhere else quite like it.

◉ Sights

◉ Reunification Palace & Around

⭐**War Remnants Museum** MUSEUM
(Bao Tang Chung Tich Chien Tranh; Map p130; 📞 08-3930 5587; 28 Đ Vo Van Tan, cnr Đ Le Quy Don; admission 15,000d; ❧ 7.30am-noon & 1.30-5pm) Once known as the Museum of Chinese and American War Crimes, the War Remnants Museum is consistently popular with Western tourists. Few museums anywhere drive home so effectively the brutality of war and its many civilian victims. Many of the atrocities documented here were well publicised, but rarely do Westerners get to hear the victims of US military action tell their own stories.

While the displays are one-sided, many of the most disturbing photographs illustrating American atrocities are from US sources, including those of the infamous My Lai Massacre.

Upstairs, look out for the **Requiem Exhibition** compiled by legendary war photographer Tim Page.

⭐**Reunification Palace** HISTORIC BUILDING
(Dinh Thong Nhat; Map p130; 📞 08-3829 4117; Đ Nam Ky Khoi Nghia; adult/child 30,000/3000d; ❧ 7.30-11am & 1-4pm) Built in 1966 to serve as South Vietnam's Presidential Palace, today this landmark is known as the Reunification Palace. It's an outstanding example of 1960s architecture, with an airy and open design. The first communist tanks in Saigon crashed through the gates of this building on the morning of 30 April 1975, when Saigon surrendered to the North. The building is a time warp, having been left just as it looked on that momentous day. English- and French-speaking guides are available.

Ho Chi Minh City

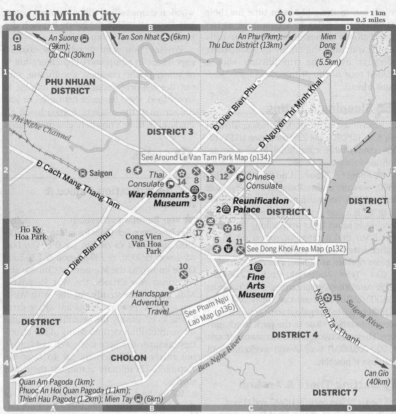

★**Fine Arts Museum** ART GALLERY
(Bao Tang My Thuat; Map p130; 97A Đ Pho Duc Chinh; admission 10,000d; ⊙9am-5pm Tue-Sun) With its airy corridors and breezy verandas, this elegant 1929 colonial-era yellow-and-white building is stuffed with period details; it's exuberantly tiled throughout and home to some fine (albeit deteriorated) stained glass, as well as one of Saigon's oldest lifts. Hung from the walls is an impressive selection of art, including thoughtful pieces from the modern period.

Mariamman Hindu Temple HINDU TEMPLE
(Chua Ba Mariamman; Map p130; 45 Đ Truong Dinh; ⊙7.30am-7.30pm) There may only be a small number of Hindus in HCMC, but this colourful slice of southern India is also considered sacred by many ethnic Vietnamese and Chinese. The temple was built at the end of the 19th century and dedicated to the Hindu goddess Mariamman.

◉ Dong Khoi Area

HCMC Museum MUSEUM
(Bao Tang Thanh Pho Ho Chi Minh; Map p132; www.hcmc-museum.edu.vn; 65 Đ Ly Tu Trong; admission 15,000d; ⊙8am-5pm) A grand, neoclassical structure built in 1885 and once known as Gia Long Palace (and later the Revolutionary Museum), HCMC's city museum is a singularly beautiful and impressive building, telling the story of the city through archaeological artefacts, ceramics, old city maps and displays on the marriage traditions of its various ethnicities.

★**Notre Dame Cathedral** CATHEDRAL
(Map p132; Đ Han Thuyen; ⊙mass 9.30am Sun) Built between 1877 and 1883, Notre Dame Cathedral rises up romantically from the heart of HCMC's government quarter. A brick neo-Romanesque church with two 40m-high square towers, it looks like it's been beamed in from Normandy.

Ho Chi Minh City

The walls of the interior are inlaid with devotional tablets and some stained glass survives.

★ Central Post Office   HISTORIC BUILDING
(Map p132; 2 Cong Xa Paris) HCMC's striking French post office was designed by Gustave Eiffel and built between 1886 and 1891. Painted on the walls of its grand concourse are fascinating historic maps of South Vietnam and Saigon.

Around Le Van Tam Park

★ Jade Emperor Pagoda   TAOIST TEMPLE
(Phuoc Hai Tu, Chua Ngoc Hoang; Map p134; 73 Đ Mai Thi Luu; ⊙7am-6pm, on 1st & 15th of lunar month 5am-7pm) FREE Built in 1909 in honour of the supreme Taoist god (the Jade Emperor or King of Heaven, Ngoc Hoang), this is one of the most spectacularly atmospheric temples in HCMC, stuffed with statues of phantasmal divinities and grotesque heroes. The pungent smoke of incense *(huong)* fills the air, obscuring the exquisite woodcarvings.

★ History Museum   MUSEUM
(Bao Tang Lich Su; Map p134; Đ Nguyen Binh Khiem; admission 15,000d; ⊙8-11.30am & 1.30-5pm Tue-Sun) Built in 1929 by the Société des Études Indochinoises, this notable Sino-French museum houses a rewarding collection of artefacts illustrating the evolution of the cultures of Vietnam, from the Bronze Age Dong Son civilisation (which emerged in 2000 BC) and the Funan civilisation (1st to 6th centuries AD), to the Cham, Khmer and Vietnamese.

Highlights include valuable relics taken from Cambodia's Angkor Wat, a fine collection of Buddha statues, the perfectly preserved mummy of a local woman who died in 1869, excavated from Xom Cai in District 5, and some exquisite stylised mother of pearl Chinese characters inlaid into panels. Also housing a branch of the shop Nguyen Freres (p142), the museum is just inside the main gate to the city's botanic gardens and zoo.

Botanic Gardens   GARDENS
(Thao Cam Vien; Map p134; 2 Đ Nguyen Binh Khiem; admission 8000d; ⊙7am-7pm) These fantastic, lush gardens are very agreeable for strolling beneath giant tropical trees. Avoid the miserable zoo.

Cholon

The Cholon district is about a kilometre southwest of the Pham Ngu Lao area.

Thien Hau Pagoda   TAOIST TEMPLE
(Ba Mieu, Pho Mieu, Chua Ba Thien Hau; 710 Đ Nguyen Trai) FREE This gorgeous 19th-century temple is dedicated to the goddess Thien Hau (Tianhou) and attracts a mix of worshippers and visitors, who mingle beneath the large coils of incense suspended overhead. It is believed that Thien Hau can travel over the oceans on a mat and ride clouds to save people in trouble on the high seas.

★ Phuoc An Hoi
Quan Pagoda   TAOIST TEMPLE
(184 Đ Hong Bang) FREE Stands as one of the most beautifully ornamented constructions in the city. Of special interest are the many small porcelain figures, the elaborate brass ritual objects and the fine woodcarvings on the altars, walls and hanging lanterns. This pagoda was built in 1902 by the Fujian Chinese congregation.

Quan Am Pagoda   BUDDHIST TEMPLE
(Chua Quan Am; 12 Đ Lao Tu) FREE One of Cholon's most active and colourful temples,

VIETNAM HO CHI MINH CITY (SAIGON)

Dong Khoi Area

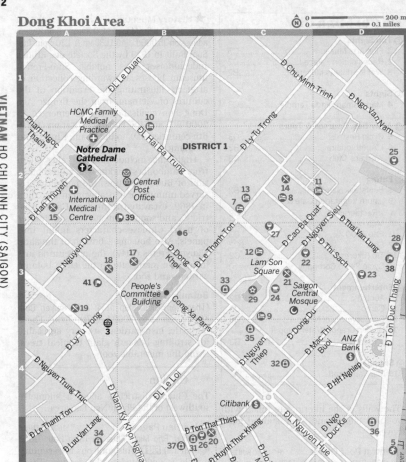

this shrine was founded in the early 19th century. It's named after the Goddess of Compassion, whose full name is Quan The Am Bo Tat, literally 'the Bodhisattva who listens to the cries of the world' (觀世音菩薩 in Chinese characters).

◎ Greater Ho Chi Minh City

Giac Lam Pagoda   BUDDHIST TEMPLE
(Chua Giac Lam; 118 Đ Lac Long Quan, Tan Binh District; ⊘6am-noon & 2-8.30pm) Believed to be the oldest temple in HCMC, Giac Lam

(1744) is a fantastically atmospheric place set in peaceful, garden-like grounds. The Chinese characters that constitute the temple's name (覚林寺) mean 'Feel the Woods Temple' and the looming Bodhi tree (a native fig tree, sacred to Buddhists) in the front garden was the gift of a Sri Lankan monk in 1953.

Prayers are held daily from 4am to 5am, 11am to noon, 4pm to 5pm and 7pm to 9pm.

About 3km from Cholon, Giac Lam Pagoda is best reached by taxi or *xe om*.

Dong Khoi Area

🏃 Activities

Massage

HCMC offers some truly fantastic settings for pampering – the perfect antidote to a frenetic day dodging motorbikes. While many midrange and upmarket hotels offer massage service, some are more legitimate than others.

L'Apothiquaire   SPA
(La Maison de L'Apothiquaire; Map p130; ☏ 08-3932 5181; www.lapothiquaire.com; 64A Đ Truong Dinh, District 3; ⊙ 8.30am-9pm) Long considered the city's most elegant spa, L'Apothiquaire is housed in a pretty white mansion and offers body wraps, massages, facials, foot treatments and herbal baths.

**Vietnamese Traditional
Massage Institute**   MASSAGE
(Map p136; ☏ 08-3839 6697; 185 Đ Cong Quynh, District 1; per hr in fan/air-con room 50,000/60,000d, per hr sauna 40,000d; ⊙ 8.30am-8pm) Not the classiest act in town, but it offers inexpensive, no-nonsense massages performed by

well-trained blind masseurs from the HCMC Association for the Blind.

River Cruises

Les Rives   DINNER CRUISE
(Map p132; ☏ 0128 592 0018; www.lesrivesexperience.com; Bach Dang Pier; sunset cruise 7,380,000d, Mekong Delta adult/child 2,263,000/1,697,000d) Sunset boat tour (minimum two people) at 4pm along canals beyond the city edges, including light dinner and guide.

Bonsai River Cruise   DINNER CRUISE
(Map p132; ☏ 08-3910 5095; www.bonsaicruise. com.vn; tickets US$36) Set on-board a striking wooden boat painted like a dragon, the Bonsai's dinner cruises feature live music. The price includes a welcome drink, canapés, buffet dinner, soft drink and, incongruously, a head and shoulder massage.

Tau Sai Gon   DINNER CRUISE
(☏ 08-3823 0393; www.tausaigon.com) Saigon Tourist's large floating restaurant takes to the waters every evening, offering both an Asian and European menu. There's a

Around Le Van Tam Park

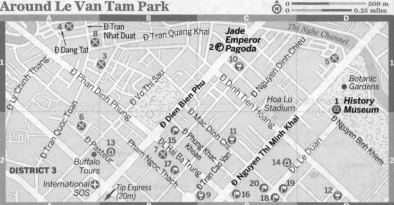

Around Le Van Tam Park

fixed charge for the Sunday buffet lunch (150,000/100,000d per adult/child; departing 11.30am, returning 1.30pm).

Swimming Pools & Water Parks

Workers' Club   SWIMMING
(Map p130; 55B Đ Nguyen Thi Minh Khai, District 3; admission 18,000d; ⊙6am-7pm) The swimming pool of the old Cercle Sportif still has its colonnades and some art-deco charm.

🍴 Courses

Saigon Cooking Class   COOKING
(Map p132; ☑08-3825 8485; www.saigoncooking class.com; 74/7 ĐL Hai Ba Trung, District 1; per adult/child under 12 US$39/25; ⊙10am & 2pm Tue-Sun) Watch and learn from the chefs at Hoa Tuc as they prepare three mains (including *pho bo* – beef noodle soup – and some of their signature dishes) and one dessert. A market visit is optional

(US$45/28 per adult/child under 12, including a three-hour class).

Vietnam Cookery Centre   COOKING
(Map p132; ☑08-3512 7246; www.vietnamcookery. com; 362/8 Đ Ung Van Khiem, Binh Thanh District) Offers introductory classes, market visits and VIP premium classes.

Cyclo Resto   COOKING
(Map p130; ☑08-6680 4235; www.cycloresto. com; 3-3A Đ Dang Tran Con; classes US$23) Fun and informative three-hour cooking class including a trip to **Thai Binh Market** (Map p136) by *cyclo*.

🧭 Tours

XO Tours   TOURS
(☑0933 083 727; www.xotours.vn; from US$38) Wearing *ao dai* (traditional dress), these girls run scooter/motorbike foodie, sights

and Saigon-by-night tours: super hospitable and fantastic fun.

Saigon Street Eats
TOURS

(☎0908 449 408; www.saigonstreeteats.com; from US$50) Highly entertaining three- to four-hour scooter foodie tours around the streets and backstreets of town. Select your tour according to taste: morning *pho* tours, lunchtime vegie, or evening seafood tours and prepare for some fun surprises.

Back of the Bike Tours
TOURS

(☎0935 046 910; www.backofthebiketours.com) Hop on the back of a motorbike and dine like a local on the wildly popular four-hour Street Food tours, or lasso in the sights of Saigon. Excellent guides.

Vietnam Vespa Adventure
TOURS

(Map p136; ☎0122 299 3585; www.vietnam-vespaadventure.com; 169A Đ De Tham) Zooming out of Cafe Zoom (Map p136; 169A Đ De Tham; mains 30,000-70,000d; ☺breakfast, lunch & dinner), Vietnam Vespa Adventure offers entertaining, guided city tours on vintage scooters. Embracing food, drink and music, the Saigon after Dark tour is excellent.

🎊 Festivals & Events

Saigon Cyclo Challenge
CHARITY RACE

(☺mid-Mar) Professional and amateur *cyclo* drivers find out who's fastest; money raised is donated to local charities.

🛌 Sleeping

Budget travellers often head straight to the Pham Ngu Lao area. Those seeking upscale digs go to Dong Khoi, home to the city's best hotels, restaurants and bars.

🛌 Dong Khoi Area

The Dong Khoi area is home to most of HCMC's top-notch hotels but also some excellent midrange options.

Spring Hotel
HOTEL $$

(Map p132; ☎08-3829 7362; www.springhotel vietnam.com; 44-46 Đ Le Thanh Ton; s US$35-45, d US$40 50, ste US$75-100; ❄@☎) An old favourite, this welcoming hotel is handy for dozens of restaurants and bars on the popular Le Thanh Ton and Hai Ba Trung strips. Rooms are a little dated, but bas-reliefs and moulded cornices add a touch of class.

Asian Ruby
HOTEL $$

(Map p132; ☎08-3827 2837; www.asianruby hotel.com; 26 Đ Thi Sach; d US$70-90; ❄☎) This comfortable, spick-and-span midrange hotel is a gem, with a top location and polite staff, although for space it's worth outlaying an extra US$20 to upgrade to a deluxe room.

King Star Hotel
HOTEL $$

(Map p132; ☎08-3822 6424; www.kingstarhotel. com; 8A ĐL Thai Van Lung; r US$50-90; ❄@☎) Completely refurbished, this spruce hotel verges on the boutique-business look. The decoration is contemporary and all rooms have flat-screen TVs and snazzy showers, but the cheapest have no window.

A & Em Hotel
HOTEL $$

(Map p132; ☎08-3825 8529; www.a-emhotels. com; 60 Đ Le Thanh Ton; r US$40-85) For a taste of overblown style, Asian bling and pseudo-luxury – putti-adorned phones, baroque-style furniture, ostentatious cornicework – the tall and slender A & Em has smallish but clean rooms. Cheaper rooms come without window or wardrobe. Many branches around town.

★ Park Hyatt Saigon
HOTEL $$$

(Map p132; ☎08-3824 1234; www.saigon.park. hyatt.com; 2 Lam Son Sq; r from US$300; ❄@☎☲) Sumptuously decorated with traditional Vietnamese-style furniture and objets d'art, this is the jewel in Saigon's hotel crown, matching a prime location opposite the Opera House with exemplary service, fastidiously attired staff, lavishly appointed rooms, an inviting pool, the ac-

---

DON'T MISS

SKY-HIGH SAIGON

Opened in late 2010, the magnificent Carlos Zapata–designed Bitexco Financial Tower (Map p132; www.saigonskydeck.com; 2 Đ Hai Trieu; adult/child 200,000/130,000d; ☺9.30am-9.30pm) peaks at 262m and dwarfs all around it. It's meant to be shaped like a lotus bulb, but we can't help thinking it looks a little like a CD rack with a tambourine shoved into it. That tambourine is actually the Saigon Skydeck, on the 48th floor. The views are, of course, extraordinary (on a clear day).

Pham Ngu Lao

Pham Ngu Lao

🟢 Activities, Courses & Tours
1 Vietnam Vespa Adventure	B2
2 Vietnamese Traditional Massage Institute	A6

🛏 Sleeping
3 Bich Duyen Hotel	A4
4 Blue River Hotel	A4
5 Cat Huy Hotel	A5
6 Diep Anh	A3
7 Giang Son	A4
8 Giang Son 2	A4
9 Hong Han Hotel	B5
10 Madame Cuc 127	B6
11 Ngoc Minh Hotel	A4
12 PP Backpackers	A4

🍽 Eating
13 Baba's Kitchen	B3
14 Café Zoom	B2
15 Coriander	B5
16 Dinh Y	A6
17 Five Oysters	B5
18 Margherita & An Lac Chay	A1
19 Sozo	B3

🍸 Drinking & Nightlife
20 Go2	B2
21 God Mother Bar	B6
22 Le Pub	A2
23 Spotted Cow	B3

🛍 Shopping
24 Blue Dragon	B2
25 Hanoi Gallery	B3
26 SahaBook	A2

claimed Xuan Spa and highly regarded (yet affordable) restaurants.

Intercontinental Asiana Saigon   HOTEL **$$$**
(Map p132; ☑08-3520 9999; www.intercontinental.com; cnr ĐL Hai Ba Trung & ĐL Le Duan; r from US$189; ❄@🛜🏊) Modern and tasteful without falling into generic blandness, rooms here have separate shower cubicles and free-standing baths, and many enjoy supreme views. A neighbouring tower of apartment-style residences caters to longer stayers.

Caravelle Hotel   HOTEL **$$$**
(Map p132; ☑08-3823 4999; www.caravellehotel.com; 19 Lam Son Sq; r from US$310; ❄@🛜🏊) 🌿 One of the first luxury hotels to reopen its doors in postwar Saigon, the five-star Caravelle is a classic operation. Rooms in the modern 24-floor block are quietly ele-gant, with two rooms bigger than the

others on each floor (ask); the priciest rooms and suites are in the historic 'signature' wing.

Pham Ngu Lao

Saigon's backpacker ghetto has more than 100 places to stay, most between US$10 and US$35. There are also some excellent midrange deals here, with most minihotels priced at US$25 to US$55.

★ Madame Cuc 127   GUESTHOUSE $
(Map p136; ☑08-3836 8761; www.madamcuc hotels.com; 127 Đ Cong Quynh; s US$20, d US$25-30; ❈@☎) The original and by far the best of the three hotels run by the welcoming Madame Cuc and her friendly and fantastic staff. Rooms are clean and spacious.

Giang Son   GUESTHOUSE $
(Map p136; ☑08-3837 7547; www.guesthouse. com.vn; 283/14 Đ Pham Ngu Lao; r US$16-28; ❈@☎) Tall and thin, with three rooms on each floor, a roof terrace and charming service, Giang Son's sole downer is that there's no lift. Consider upgrading to a room with window.

Hong Han Hotel   GUESTHOUSE $
(Map p136; ☑08-3836 1927; www.honghan.net-firms.com; 238 Đ Bui Vien; r US$20-25; ❈@☎) Another corker guesthouse (seven floors, no lift), Hong Han has front rooms with ace views and smaller, quieter and cheaper rear rooms plus free breakfast served on the 1st-floor terrace.

Bich Duyen Hotel   GUESTHOUSE $
(Map p136; ☑08-3837 4588; bichduyenhotel@ yahoo.com; 283/4 Đ Pham Ngu Lao; r US$17-30; ❈@☎▥) On the same slender lane as Giang Son, this spruce 15-room place follows a similar template. The US$25 rooms are worth the extra money for a window. There's no lift.

Giang Son 2   GUESTHOUSE $
(Map p136; ☑08-3920 9838; www.guesthouse. com.vn; 283/24 Pham Ngu Lao; r US$18-25) Son of Giang Son some may say, with a more contemporary finish. Two double rooms come with balcony and staff are excellent. No lift.

PP Backpackers   HOSTEL $
(Map p136; ☑1262 501 823; Đ 283/41 Pham Ngu Lao; dm US$6, d US$16-18; ❈@☎) Very helpful, friendly and efficient staff at this cheap and welcoming hostel where you can nab a dorm bed for US$6 or fork out a bit more for an affordable double room.

Diep Anh   GUESTHOUSE $
(Map p136; ☑08-3836 7920; dieptheanh@hcm. vnn.vn; 241/31 Đ Pham Ngu Lao; r US$20; ❈@☎) A step above most Pham Ngu Lao guesthouses, figuratively and literally (think one thousand-yard stairs), Diep Anh's tall and narrow shape makes for light and airy upper rooms. The gracious staff ensure they are well kept.

Blue River Hotel   HOTEL $$
(Map p136; ☑08-3837 6483; www.blueriver hotel.com; 283/2C Đ Pham Ngu Lao; r US$25-40; ❈@☎) This welcoming and well-run 10-room place offers clean, spacious rooms, each with neat furnishings and a safe. A kitchen for guests' use is available, as is a piano (and more brand-new rooms across the way).

Cat Huy Hotel   HOTEL $$
(Map p136; ☑08-3920 8716; www.cathuyhotel. com; 353/28 Pham Ngu Lao; r US$28-34; ❈☎) Stuffed away down an alley, this lovely 10-room hotel has modern, swish and chic accommodation. The cheapest rooms are windowless, others have balconies. Airport pick-up is US$15. No lift.

Ngoc Minh Hotel   HOSTEL $$
(Map p136; ☑08-3837 6407; www.ngocminhhotel. net; 283/11 Đ Pham Ngu Lao; r US$20-35; ❈@☎) This bright and friendly guesthouse has 19 clean and well-presented rooms with all mod-cons, a rooftop terrace decorated with blooming orchids and a lift. It's just east and across the road from the Blue River Hotel.

Other Neighbourhoods

★ Ma Maison Boutique Hotel   HOTEL $$$
(☑08-3846 0263; www.mamaison.vn; 656/52 Cach Mang Thang Tam, District 3; s US$50-75, d US$75-120; ❈☎) Down a peaceful lane off a busy arterial route, friendly Ma Maison is halfway between the airport and the city centre, and partly in the French countryside, decor-wise. Wooden shutters soften the exterior of the modern, medium-rise block, while in the rooms, painted French provincial–style furniture and first-rate bathrooms add a touch of panache.

✗ Eating

Hanoi may consider itself more cultured, but HCMC is Vietnam's culinary capital. Delicious regional fare is complemented by a well-developed choice of international restaurants, with Indian, Japanese, Thai, Italian and East-West fusions well represented. Unsurprisingly, given its heritage, HCMC has a fine selection of French restaurants, from the casual bistro to haute cuisine.

Good foodie neighbourhoods include the Dong Khoi area, which has a high concentration of top-quality restaurants, as well as the bordering sections of District 3. Pham Ngu Lao's eateries are generally less impressive. There are also a few escapes further afield for those who are willing to explore.

Markets have a good selection of stalls whipping up tasty treats. Ben Thanh's night market is particularly good.

The largest concentration of vegetarian restaurants is around the Pham Ngu Lao area.

✗ Reunification Palace & Around

Quan An Ngon VIETNAMESE $
(Map p132; 138 Đ Nam Ky Khoi Nghia; mains from 35,000d; ☺6.30am-11pm) Always heaving with locals and foreigners alike, this is a popular place for the taste of street food in stylish surroundings, set in a leafy garden ringed by food stalls and hung with lanterns. Each cook serves up a specialised traditional dish.

Cyclo Resto Company VIETNAMESE $
(Map p130; www.cycloresto.com.vn; 3-3A Đ Dang Tran Con; five courses US$6; ☺9am-9pm) The makeshift feel at this super-duper upstairs place detracts nothing from some of the best-value food in town, cooked to absolute perfection. For US$6 you get five fabulous Vietnamese dishes; the popular cooking course is US$23.

Beefsteak Nam Son VIETNAMESE $
(Map p130; 157 Đ Nam Ky Khoi Nghia; mains from 50,000d; ☺6am-10pm; ☎) For first-rate, affordable steak in a simple setting, this is a superb choice. Local steak, other beef dishes (such as the spicy beef soup *bun bo Hue*), imported Canadian fillets and even

cholesterol-friendly ostrich are on the well-priced menu.

Pho 2000 VIETNAMESE $
(Map p130; ☑08-3822 2788; 1-3 Đ Phan Chu Trinh; mains 42,000-58,000d; ☺6am-2am) Near Ben Thanh Market, Pho 2000 is where former US president Bill Clinton stopped by for a bowl.

★ **...hum Vegetarian Cafe & Restaurant** VEGETARIAN $$
(Map p130; ☑08-3930 3819; www.hum-vegetarian.vn; 32 Đ Vo Van Tan; mains 65,000-150,000d; ☺7am-10pm) Even if you're not a vegetarian, this serene and elegant restaurant requires your attention. Everything – from the charming service to the delightful Vietnamese dishes and peaceful outside tables – makes dining here an occasion to savour.

Shri JAPANESE FUSION $$
(Map p130; ☑08-3827 9631; 23rd fl, Centec Tower, 72-74 Đ Nguyen Thi Minh Khai; mains 200,000-400,000d; ☺11am-midnight; ☎☎) Perched up a tower block, romantic Shri looks out onto some of the choicest views in town. Book ahead for a terrace table or settle for the dark, industrial-chic dining room. Two menus run side by side: Japanese-influenced Western mains and a traditional (and considerably cheaper) Japanese section.

✗ Dong Khoi Area

★ **Nha Hang Ngon** VIETNAMESE $
(Map p132; ☑08-3827 7131; 160 Đ Pasteur; mains 35,000-205,000d; ☺7am-10pm; ☎☎) Thronging with locals and foreigners, this is one of HCMC's most popular spots, with a large range of the very best street food in stylish surroundings. It's set in a leafy garden ringed by food stalls, with each cook serving up a specialised traditional dish, ensuring an authentic taste.

★ **Temple Club** VIETNAMESE $
(Map p132; ☑08-3829 9244; 29 Đ Ton That Thiep; mains 59,000-98,000d; ☺11.30am-10.30pm; ☎☎☑) This classy establishment, housed on the 2nd floor of a beautiful colonial-era villa decorated with spiritual motifs and elegant Chinese characters, offers a huge selection of delectable Vietnamese dishes, including vegetarian specialities, alongside a spectrum of spirited cocktails.

Huong Lai   VIETNAMESE $
(Map p132; 38 Đ Ly Tu Trong; mains 49,000-150,000d) A must for finely presented, traditional Vietnamese food, the airy and high-ceilinged loft of an old French-era shophouse is the setting for dining with a difference. Staff are from disadvantaged families or are former street children and receive on-the-job training, education and a place to stay.

3T Quan Nuong   VIETNAMESE $
(Map p132; ☑ 08-3821 1631; 29 Đ Ton That Thiep; mains 85,000-280,000d; ⊘ 4 11pm) This breezy alfresco Vietnamese barbecue restaurant on Temple Club rooftop is in many a Saigon diners' diary: choose your meat, fish, seafood and vegies and flame them up right there on the table.

Hoa Tuc   VIETNAMESE $
(Map p132; ☑ 08-3825 1676; 74/7 DL Hai Ba Trung; mains 50,000-190,000d; ⊘ 10.30am-10.30pm; ☻☎) In the trendy courtyard of the former opium refinery, Hoa Tuc offers atmosphere and style to match the excellence of its food. Signature dishes include spicy beef salad with kumquat, baby white eggplant and lemongrass. Home chefs can pick up tricks at an in-house cooking class.

Au Parc   CAFE $
(Map p132; www.auparcsaigon.com; 23 Đ Han Thuyen; mains 160,000-260,000d; ⊘ 7am-11pm; ☻☎) The laptop and tablet crowd flocks to this slender two-floor cafe for its Mediterranean and Middle Eastern salads, quiches, baguettes, focaccias, pasta, mezze and light grills, from breakfast and brunch to dinner. There's a lounge upstairs.

5Ku Station   BARBECUE $
(Map p132; 29 Đ Thai Van Lung; meals from around 50,000d; ⊘ 5pm-late) Hopping with evening diners, this chain of makeshift-looking alfresco barbecue restaurants is fun, boisterous, outgoing and tasty. Grab yourself a wooden box seat and a cold beer and chow down on barbecue and hotpot alongside a mix of locals, travellers and expats. Branches move about so check on the latest address.

Xu   VIETNAMESE $$
(Map p132; ☑ 08-3824 8468; www.xusaigon.com; 1st fl, 75 DL Hai Ba Trung; 3-course set lunch Mon-Fri 290,000d, mains from 100,000d; ⊘ 11am-2.30pm & 6-11pm; ☎) This super-stylish restaurant-lounge serves up a menu of Vietnamese-inspired fusion dishes. It's pricey, but well worth the flutter for top service, a classy wine list and a happening lounge-bar. For a gastronomic adventure, embark on the tasting menu (850,000d).

★**Cirrus**   INTERNATIONAL $$$
(Map p132; www.cirrussaigon.com; 51st fl, Bitexco Financial Tower, 2 Đ Hai Trieu; 3-course dinner 980,000d; ☻☎) Elevate yourself out of the hectic whirl at street level to the 51st floor of HCMC's tallest tower for a sure-fire combination of supreme food, tantalising views, impeccable service and stylish ambience.

✗ Around Le Van Tam Park

★**Cuc Gach Quan**   VIETNAMESE $
(Map p134; ☑ 08-3848 0144; en.cucgachquan.com; 10 Đ Dang Tat; mains 50,000-200,000d; ⊘ 9am-midnight) It comes as little surprise that the owner is an architect when you step into this cleverly renovated old villa. The decor is rustic *and* elegant, which is also true of the food, which excels. This is no secret hideaway: book ahead.

Pho Hoa   VIETNAMESE $
(Map p134; 260C Đ Pasteur; mains 45,000-50,000d; ⊘ 6am-midnight) This long-running establishment is more upmarket than most but is definitely the real deal – as evidenced by its popularity with regular local patrons.

Banh Xeo 46A   VIETNAMESE $
(Map p134; ☑ 08-3824 1110; 46A Đ Dinh Cong Trang; mains 25,000-50,000d; ⊘ 10am-9pm; ☑) Locals will always hit the restaurants that specialise in a single dish and this renowned spot serves some of the best *banh xeo* (rice-flour pancakes with bean sprouts, prawns and pork). Vegetarian versions available.

Tib   VIETNAMESE $
(Map p134; ☑ 08-3829 7242; www.tibrestaurant.com.vn; 187 Đ Hai Ba Trung; mains 70,000-285,000d; ☎) Visiting presidents and prime ministers have slunk down this lantern- and fairy-light-festooned alley and into this atmospheric old house to sample Tib's imperial Hue cuisine. Although you could probably find similar food for less money elsewhere, the setting is wonderful. **Tib Express** (Map p130; 162 Đ Nguyen Dinh Chieu; mains 28,000-50,000; ☑) and **Tib Vegetarian** (Map p134; 11 Đ Tran Nhat Duat; mains 30,000-40,000; ☑) offer a cheaper, more relaxed take on the same.

★ **May** VIETNAMESE **$$**
(Map p134; www.may-cloud.com; 3/5 Hoang Sa; mains 55,000-220,000d; ⏰10.30am-11.30pm) Tucked away down a small alley in an old French villa and overseen by endlessly obliging staff, sublime May is a sensory and culinary sensation, with diners testifying to some of the best Vietnamese food in town, if not the entire country. MSG-free.

Pham Ngu Lao Area

★ **Baba's Kitchen** INDIAN **$**
(Map p136; ☑08-3838 6661; 164 Đ Bui Vien; mains 50,000-210,000d; ⏰11am-11pm; ▨) It's worth going out of your way to secure a table here. Two-storey Baba's has set Bui Vien alight with its fine flavours, aromas and spices of India. There's ample vegetarian choice.

Coriander THAI **$**
(Map p136; 16 Đ Bui Vien; mains 40,000-180,000d; ⏰11am-2pm & 5-11pm) The menu here is stuffed with authentic Siamese delights, including lovely fried *doufu* (tofu), zesty green curry and claypot seafood fried rice.

Five Oysters VIETNAMESE **$**
(Map p136; 234 Bui Vien; mains from 35,000d; ⏰9.30am-11pm) With a strong seafood slant and friendly service, light and bright Five Oysters is frequently packed. Feast on oysters (25,000d), grilled octopus, seafood soup, snail pie, *pho*, fried noodles, grilled mackerel with chilli oil and more.

Dinh Y VEGETARIAN **$**
(Map p136; 171B Đ Cong Quynh; mains from 25,000d; ⏰6am-9pm; ▨) Run by a friendly Cao Dai family, this humble eatery is in a very 'local' part of PNL near Thai Binh Market. The food is delicious and cheap and there's an English menu.

**Margherita &
An Lac Chay** INTERNATIONAL, VEGETARIAN **$**
(Map p136; 175/1 Đ Pham Ngu Lao; mains 25,000-77,000d; ⏰8am-10pm; ▨) Another golden oldie, Margherita cooks up Vietnamese, Italian and Mexican food at a steal. Head up the stairs at the rear of the dining room to An Lac Chay, a purely vegetarian restaurant – with an entirely separate kitchen.

Mon Hue VIETNAMESE **$**
(Map p130; ☑08-6240 5323; 98 Đ Nguyen Trai; mains 29,000-150,000d; ⏰6am-11pm) Hue's famous cuisine comes to HCMC's hungry hordes through this chain of eight restaurants. This handy branch offers a good introduction for travellers who don't make it to the old capital.

Sozo CAFE **$**
(Map p136; www.sozocentre.com; 176 Đ Bui Vien; cookies 25,000d; ⏰7am-10.30pm; 🐾) This charming cafe in the Pham Ngu Lao backpacker ghetto has excellent smoothies, doughy cinnamon rolls, homemade cookies, other sweet treats, bags of style, and trains and employs disadvantaged Vietnamese.

🍸 Drinking & Nightlife

Action is concentrated around the Dong Khoi area, with everything from dives to designer bars. However, places in this area generally close around 1am while Pham Ngu Lao rumbles on into the wee hours.

HCMC's hippest club nights include the semi-regular **Everyone's a DJ** (www.everyonesadjvietnam.wordpress.com) loft party, **dOse** and **The Beats Saigon** (www.the-beats-saigon.com).

🍷 Reunification Palace & Around

Cloud 9 BAR
(Map p134; 6th fl, 2 bis Cong Truong Quoc Te; ⏰5.30pm-midnight) Fashionable young things flock to the rooftop bar, while dance music pounds in the room below.

🍷 Dong Khoi Area

Many of Dong Khoi's coolest bars double as restaurants or hover at the top of hotels.

★ **2 Lam Son** COCKTAIL BAR
(Map p132; www.saigon.park.hyatt.com; 2 Lam Son Sq, enter ĐL Hai Ba Trung; ⏰5pm-late) A chic blend of wood, glass and steel, the Park Hyatt's ground floor cocktail bar is a super-stylish meeting ground for Saigon's makers and shakers, with an intimate lounge level slung out above.

★ **Vesper** BAR
(Map p132; Ground fl, Landmark Bldg, 5B Đ Ton Duc Thang; ⏰10am-late Mon-Sat) From the sinuous curve of the hardwood bar to the smoothly arranged bottles on the shelves, soft chill-out rhythms, funky caramel leather furniture and fine tapas menu, Vesper is a cool spot by the river. There's a roadside terrace, but traffic noise is epic.

Apocalypse Now NIGHTCLUB
(Map p132; ☑ 08-3824 1463; 2C Đ Thi Sach; ⊙ 7pm-2am) A sprawling place with a big dance floor and an outdoor courtyard, it's quite a circus, with a cast comprising travellers, expats, Vietnamese movers and shakers, plus the odd hooker (some odder than others). Others have come and gone, but 'Apo' has been around since the early days and remains one of the must-visit clubs.

Vasco's BAR, NIGHTCLUB
(Map p132; www.vascosgroup.com; 74/7D ĐL Hai Ba Trung; ⊙ 4pm-late; 🛜) One of the hippest hangouts in town: downstairs is a breezy spot for cocktails and pizza, while the upstairs nightclub-like space regularly hosts DJs and live bands.

Temple Club Bar & Lounge BAR
(Map p132; 29 Đ Ton That Thiep; ⊙ 11.30am-midnight) For the ultimate colonial chill-out, sip a G&T in this elegant shrine to Indochine. Frequently deserted, the lounge is one of the quietest, most tranquillising and civilised corners of HCMC.

Alibi COCKTAIL BAR
(Map p132; www.alibi.vn; 5A Đ Nguyen Sieu; ⊙ 10am-late; 🛜) A happening New York–style bar, with black-and-white photographs and a central table, Alibi turns out creative cocktails and, upstairs, excellent fusion food.

Lush BAR, NIGHTCLUB
(Map p134; www.lush.vn; 2 Đ Ly Tu Trong; ⊙ 7.30pm-late) This bar's decor is very manga, with cool graphics plastering the walls. DJs spin most nights, with Fridays devoted to hip hop.

Fuse NIGHTCLUB
(Map p132; 3A Đ Ton Duc Thang; ⊙ 7pm-late) Small club, loud techno.

🍸 Around Le Van Tam Park

★ Decibel BAR
(Map p134; 79/2/5 Đ Phan Kê Bính; ⊙ 7.30am-midnight Mon-Sat) This small, two-floor restaurant-cafe-bar is a super-relaxed choice for a coffee or cocktail, with a fine cultural vibe, film nights and art events.

Hoa Vien MICROBREWERY
(Map p134; www.hoavien.vn; 18 bis/28 Nguyen Thi Minh Khai; ⊙ 8am-midnight; 🛜) An unexpected find in the backstreets of HCMC, this Czech restaurant brews up fresh pilsner daily.

GAY & LESBIAN HCMC

There are few openly gay venues in town, but most of HCMC's popular bars and clubs are generally gay-friendly. Apocalypse Now sometimes attracts a small gay contingent among an otherwise straight crowd, as does Le Pub in Pham Ngu Lao. In the same area, the **God Mother Bar** (Map p136; www.godmothersaigon.com; 129 Đ Cong Quynh) is a gay-friendly venue. The most happening night out is the monthly **Bitch Party** (www.bitch partysaigon.com; admission incl 1st drink 100,000d), which moves around. **Centro Cafe** (Map p132; ☑ 08-3827 5946; 11-13 Lam Son Sq; 🛜) attracts a gay crowd on Saturday nights.

🍸 Pham Ngu Lao Area

Le Pub PUB
(Map p136; ☑ 08-3837 7679; www.lepub.org; 175/22 Đ Pham Ngu Lao; ⊙ 9am-2am; 🛜) The name says it all – British pub meets French cafe-bar – and the pomegranate-coloured result, ranging over three floors, is a hit. An extensive beer list, nightly promotions, cocktail jugs and pub grub draw in the crowds.

Go2 BAR
(Map p136; 187 Đ De Tham; ⊙ 24hr; 🛜) There's no better street theatre than watching the crazy Bui Vien goings-on from the outside seats of this all-night venue, which also has a trashy club upstairs.

Spotted Cow SPORTS BAR
(Map p136; 111 Đ Bui Vien; ⊙ 11am-midnight) Fun, Aussie-run, bovine-themed sports bar on Bui Vien with lots of drink specials.

☆ Entertainment

Pick up *The Word HCMC, Asialife HCMC* or *The Guide* to find out what's on during your stay in Saigon, or log onto www.anyarena.com or www.thewordhcmc.com.

Live Music

★ Acoustic LIVE MUSIC
(Map p130; ☑ 08-3930 2239; 6E1 Đ Ngo Thoi Nhiem; ⊙ 7pm-midnight; 🛜) Don't be misled by the name: most of the musicians are plugged in and dangerous when they take to the intimate stage here. And judging by the

numbers that pack the floor, the crowd just can't get enough. It's at the end of the alley, by the upended VW Beetle.

★**Cargo** LIVE MUSIC
(Map p130; Đ 7 Nguyen Tat Thanh; ⊙ 3pm-midnight Wed-Sun) Hugely popular spacious warehouse venue for up-and-coming local acts, regional bands and DJ events backed up by a great sound system; it's across the river in District 4.

Municipal Theatre CONCERT HALL
(Map p132; ☎08-3829 9976; Lam Son Sq) The French-era Opera House is home to the HCMC Ballet and **Ballet & Symphony Orchestra** (www.hbso.org.vn) and hosts performances by visiting artists.

Conservatory of Music CONCERT HALL
(Nhac Vien Thanh Pho Ho Chi Minh; Map p130; ☎08-3824 3774; 112 Đ Nguyen Du) Performances of both traditional Vietnamese and Western classical music are held here.

Water Puppetry

Golden Dragon Water Puppet Theatre WATER PUPPETS
(Map p130; ☎08-3930 2196; www.goldendragonwaterpuppet.com; 55B Đ Nguyen Thi Minh Khai; US$7.50) The main water-puppet venue, with shows starting at 5pm, 6.30pm and 7.45pm and lasting about 50 minutes.

🛍 Shopping

Among the tempting wares to be found in Saigon are embroidered silk shoes, miniature *cyclos*, fake Zippos engraved with GI philosophy and toy helicopters made from beer cans. Boutiques along Đ Le Thanh Ton and Đ Pasteur sell handmade ready-to-wear fashion. In Pham Ngu Lao, shops sell ethnic-minority fabrics, handicrafts, T-shirts and various appealing accessories.

Ben Thanh Market (Cho Ben Thanh; Map p132; Đ Le Loi, ĐL Ham Nghi, ĐL Tran Hung Dao & Đ Le Lai) is the best place to start. Part of the market is devoted to normal everyday items, but the lucrative tourist trade also has healthy representation.

🛍 Dong Khoi Area

Mekong Quilts HANDICRAFTS
(Map p132; ☎08-2210 3110; www.mekong-quilts.org; 1st fl, 68 Đ Le Loi, District 1; ⊙9am-7pm) 🍃 For beautiful handmade silk quilts, sewn by the rural poor in support of a sustainable income.

Dogma SOUVENIRS
(Map p132; www.dogmavietnam.com; 1st fl, 43 Đ Ton That Thiep; ⊙9am-10pm) Specialises in reproduction propaganda posters, emblazoning their revolutionary motifs on coffee mugs, coasters, jigsaws and T-shirts.

Mai Lam CLOTHING
(Map p132; www.mailam.com.vn; 132-134 Đ Dong Khoi; ⊙9am-9pm) Vibrant, colourful, creative and highly inspiring, Mai Lam carries beautiful (but pricey) hand-stitched men's and women's clothing and accessories.

Nguyen Freres ANTIQUES, HANDICRAFTS
(Map p132; ☎08-380 3070; 2 Đ Dong Khoi) A spellbinding selection of ceramics, chopsticks, Buddha heads, bags, scarves, textiles and more.

Mystere HANDICRAFTS
(Map p132; 141 Đ Dong Khoi; ⊙9am-10pm) Attractive lacquerware, fabrics and jewellery sourced from ethnic minority peoples and hill tribes.

Khai Silk CLOTHING
(Map p132; ☎08-3829 1146; www.khaisilkcorp.com; 107 Đ Dong Khoi; ⊙9.30am-8pm) This is one of several branches in HCMC of the nationwide silk empire. Expensive but high quality.

Song Handmade CLOTHING
(Map p132; www.maisonsong.com; 63 Đ Pasteur) Specialising in sophisticated linens and cottons for men and women.

🛍 Around Le Van Tam Park

Thu Quan Sinh Vien BOOKS
(Map p134; 2A ĐL Le Duan; ⊙8am-10pm; 🛜) This upmarket store stocks imported books and magazines in English, French and Chinese and has a cafe.

Orange CLOTHING, ACCESSORIES
(Map p134; 238B Đ Pasteur; ⊙9am-10pm) Funky T-shirts and bags.

🛍 Pham Ngu Lao Area

Hanoi Gallery PROPAGANDA POSTERS
(Map p136; 79 Đ Bui Vien; ⊙9am-10pm) Fans of socialist realism should visit this very cool little store selling both original (so we're told) propaganda posters (US$600) and A3 prints (US$8).

SahaBook BOOKS
(Map p136; www.sahabook.com; 175/24 Đ Pham
Ngu Lao; ⏱9am-5.30pm Mon-Fri) Authentic
Lonely Planet guidebooks with readable
maps.

Blue Dragon HANDICRAFTS
(Map p136; 1B Đ Bui Vien; ⏱8.30am-10.30pm)
Souvenirs including cinnamon-bark boxes,
ethnic bags, jewellery, horn bracelets and
clothing.

Other Neighbourhoods

Mai Handicrafts HANDICRAFTS
(Map p130; ☎08-3844 0988; www.maihandicrafts.
com; 298 Đ Nguyen Trong Tuyen, Tan Binh District;
⏱10am-7pm Mon-Sat) 🍃 A fair-trade shop
dealing in ceramics, ethnic fabrics and other
gift items that, in turn, support disadvantaged families and street children. To get
here, head northwest on ĐL Hai Ba Trung,
which becomes Đ Phan Dinh Phung and
turn left on Đ Nguyen Trong Tuyen.

ⓘ Information

For up-to-date information on what's going on in
town, check out **The Word HCMC** (www.word
hcmc.com) or **Asialife HCMC** (www.asialifeh-
cmc.com), both quality listings magazines.

DANGERS & ANNOYANCES

Be careful in the Dong Khoi area and along the
Saigon riverfront, where motorbike 'cowboys'
operate and specialise in bag and camera
snatching. Be aware of common taxi and *xe om*
scams.

EMERGENCY

Ambulance (☎115)
Police (☎113)

INTERNET ACCESS

Internet cafes are everywhere in HCMC. Many
hotels, cafes, restaurants and bars offer free
wi-fi.

MEDICAL SERVICES

HCMC Family Medical Practice (Map p132;
☎24hr emergency 08-3822 7848; www.
vietnammedicalpractice.com; rear, Diamond
Department Store, 34 ĐL Le Duan; ⏱24hr)
Well-run practice.

International Medical Centre (Map p132;
☎08-3827 2366, 24hr emergency 08-3865
4025; www.cmi-vietnam.com; 1 Đ Han Thuyen;
⏱24hr) A nonprofit organisation with English-
speaking French doctors.

International SOS (Map p134; ☎08-3829
8424; www.internationalsos.com; 167A Đ Nam

Ky Khoi Nghia; ⏱24hr) An international team
of doctors who speak English, French, Japanese
and Vietnamese.

MONEY

There are ATMs and exchange counters (most
offering decent rates) in the airport hallway of
arrivals, just after clearing customs.
ANZ Bank (Map p132; ☎08-3829 9319; 11 Me
Linh Sq) With ATM.
Citibank (Map p132; 115 Đ Nguyen Hue)
Sacombank (Map p136; ☎08-3836 4231;
www.sacombank.com; 211 Đ Nguyen Thai Hoc)
With ATM.

POST

Central Post Office (Map p132; 2 Cong Xa
Paris; ⏱7am-9.30pm)

TRAVEL AGENCIES

There are lots of travel agents offering tours
of the Mekong Delta and other jaunts beyond
HCMC. Some of the better ones include the
following:
Handspan Adventure Travel (Map p130;
☎08-3925 7605; www.handspan.com; 10th fl,
Central Park Bldg, 208 Nguyen Trai) Excellent,
high-quality tours.
Sinhbalo Adventures (Map p136; ☎08-3837
6766; www.sinhbalo.com; 283/20 Đ Pham
Ngu Lao) For customised tours, this is a great
choice. Also offers cycling and innovative
special-interest journeys to the Mekong Delta
and further afield.
Sinh Tourist (Map p136; ☎08-3838 9593;
www.thesinhtourist.vn; 246 Đ De Tham;
⏱6.30am-10.30pm) Well-organised budget
tour agency, runs its own open-tour buses.
Buffalo Tours (Map p134; ☎08-3827 9170;
www.buffalotours.com; 157 Đ Pasteur;
⏱8.30am-5pm Mon-Fri, to 2.30pm Sat) Top-
end tour agency.
Cafe Kim Tourist (Map p136; ☎08-3836
5489; www.thekimtourist.com; 270 Đ De Tham;
⏱7am-9pm)

ⓘ Getting There & Away

AIR

Vietnam Airlines (☎08-3832 0320;
www.vietnamairlines.com) Flies to/from Hanoi,
Haiphong, Vinh, Dong Hoi, Hue, Danang, Quy
Nhon, Nha Trang, Dalat and Phu Quoc Island.
VietJet Air (☎1900 1886; www.vietjetair.com)
An expanding number of internal flights, includ-
ing Danang and Hanoi.
Jetstar Pacific Airlines (☎1900 1550; www.
jetstar.com) Destinations including Hanoi,
Haiphong, Vinh, Hue and Danang.

Vietnam Air Service Company (VASCO; www.vasco.com.vn) Flies to/from Con Dao Islands and Ca Mau.

BOAT

Hydrofoils (adult/child 200,000/100,000d, 1¼ hours) depart for Vung Tau almost hourly from **Bach Dang jetty** (Map p132; Đ Ton Duc Thang). There are three main companies here:

Greenlines (☑08-3821 5609; www.greenlines.com.vn)

Petro Express (☑08-3821 0650)

Vina Express (☑08-3825 3333; www.vinaexpress.com.vn)

BUS

Intercity buses operate from three main bus stations around HCMC. Local buses (3000d) travelling to the intercity bus stations leave from the local bus station opposite Ben Thanh Market.

An Suong bus station Buses to Tay Ninh and points northeast of HCMC; located in District 12, west of the centre. Buses to/from Cu Chi leave from here, but tours are far more convenient.

Mien Dong bus station Buses heading north of HCMC; located about 5km from downtown on Hwy 13. Express buses depart from the east side of the station, and local buses connect with the west side of the complex.

Mien Tay bus station Serves all the main Mekong Delta towns; located about 10km southwest of Saigon in An Lac.

Open-tour buses depart and arrive in the Pham Ngu Lao area. Destinations include Mui Ne (US$5 to US$10), Nha Trang (US$7 to US$20), Dalat (US$8 to US$15), Hoi An (US$15 to US$37) and Hanoi (US$25 to US$49).

There are plenty of international bus services connecting HCMC and Cambodia, most with departures from the Pham Ngu Lao area. **Sapaco** (Map p136; ☑08-3920 3623; www.sapacotour-ist.vn; 309 Pham Ngu Lao) has nine direct daily services to Phnom Penh (230,000d, six hours, departing between 6am and 3pm), as well as one to Siem Reap (430,000d, 12 hours, 6am).

CAR & MOTORCYCLE

Hotels and travellers' cafes can arrange car rentals (from US$40 per day). Pham Ngu Lao is the neighbourhood to look for motorbike rentals (US$5 to US$10 per day).

TRAIN

In Pham Ngu Lao, purchase tickets from **Hoa Xa Agency** (Map p136; ☑08-3836 7640; 275C Đ Pham Ngu Lao; ◷7.30am-6pm) or from most travel agents for a small fee. Trains from **Saigon train station** (Ga Sai Gon; ☑08-3823 0105; 1 Đ Nguyen Thong , District 3; ◷ticket office 7.15-11am & 1-3pm) head north to various destinations.

❶ Getting Around

TO/FROM THE AIRPORT

Tan Son Nhat Airport is 7km northwest of central HCMC. Metered taxis are your best bet and cost around 180,000 to/from the centre. English-speaking controllers will shuffle you into a waiting cab and tell the driver your destination. The driver may try to claim your hotel of choice is closed, burned down, dirty and dangerous, or anything to steer you somewhere else for a commission. Stick to your guns.

Air-conditioned buses (route 152; 5000d, every 15 minutes, 6am to 6pm) also run to and from the airport. These make regular stops along Đ De Tham (Pham Ngu Lao area) and along Đ Dong Khoi.

BICYCLE

Bicycles are available for hire (US$2) from many budget hotels and cafes. Use parking lots to safeguard against theft.

CAR & MOTORCYCLE

HCMC is *not* the place to learn to ride a motorbike. They are nevertheless available for hire around Pham Ngu Lao for US$5 to US$10 per day.

CYCLO

Cyclos are an interesting way to get around town, but overcharging tourists is the norm. Short hops should be 20,000d to 25,000d.

TAXI

Metered taxis cruise the streets. Flagfall is around 15,000d for the first kilometre and most rides in the city centre cost just two or three bucks.

Mai Linh Taxi (☑08-3838 3838)

XE OM

Xe om drivers hang out on parked bikes touting for passengers. From 20,000d for short rides.

TRANSPORT FROM HO CHI MINH CITY

DESTINATION	AIR	BUS	TRAIN
Dalat	50min, from US$39	7hr, US$8-15	N/A
Nha Trang	55min, from US$44	12hr, US$10-20	6½hr, US$17-31
Hue	80min, from US$37	29hr,US $26-37	18hr,US$26-64
Hanoi	2hr, from US$70	41hr, US$35-49	30hr, US$49-93

GETTING TO CAMBODIA: HCMC TO PHNOM PENH

Getting to the border The busy Moc Bai/Bavet border crossing is the fastest land route between HCMC and Phnom Penh. Pham Ngu Lao traveller cafes sell through bus tickets (US$10 to US$15) to Phnom Penh; buses leave from Pham Ngu Lao between 6am and 3pm. Reliable bus companies include **Mekong Express** (www.catmekong express.com), **Sapaco** (www.sapacotourist.vn) and the cheaper **Kumho Samco** (www.kumhosamco.com.vn). Allow six hours for the entire trip.

At the border Cambodian visas (US$20) are issued at the border (you'll need a passport-sized photo).

Moving on Most travellers have a through bus ticket from HCMC to Phnom Penh, a further four-hour bus ride away.

For more information about crossing this border in the other direction, see p192.

AROUND HO CHI MINH CITY

Cu Chi

If the tenacious spirit of the Vietnamese could be symbolised by a single place, then Cu Chi would be it. Its fame is such that it's become a place of pilgrimage for many Vietnamese and a must-see for travellers.

⊙ Sights

Cu Chi Tunnels　　　　　　　　　HISTORIC SITE
(www.cuchitunnel.org.vn; adult/child 80,000/20,000d) These tunnels are the stuff of legend due to their role facilitating Viet Cong control of a large rural area only 30km from Saigon. At its height, the tunnel system stretched from Saigon to the Cambodian border.

Two sections of this remarkable tunnel network (which are enlarged and upgraded versions of the real thing) are open to the public. One is near the village of Ben Dinh and the other is 15km beyond at Ben Duoc.

Visits to both sites usually start with an extremely dated propaganda video before guides in army greens lead small groups through some short sections of tunnel. Both sites have gun ranges attached where you shell out a small fortune to shell up and fire genuine AK-47s and machine guns. You pay per bullet, so be warned.

Cu Chi Wildlife Rescue Station　　　　　　　WILDLIFE
(www.wildlifeatrisk.org; adult/child US$5/free; ⊙7.30-11.30am & 1-4.30pm) Just a few kilometres down the road from the tunnels of Ben Dinh, this small centre is dedicated to the protection of wildlife that has been confiscated from owners or illegal traders. Animals here include bears, otters and gibbons. There is an informative display on the rather depressing state of wildlife in Vietnam, including the 'room of death' featuring a host of traps and baits. It's tough to navigate these back roads solo, so talk to a travel agent about incorporating it into a Cu Chi Tunnels trip.

Tay Ninh

☑ 066 / POP 129,000

Tay Ninh town, capital of Tay Ninh Province, serves as the headquarters of Cao Dai, one of Vietnam's most interesting indigenous religions. The **Cao Dai Great Temple** was built between 1933 and 1955. Victor Hugo is among the Westerners especially revered by the Cao Dai; look for his likeness at the Great Temple.

Tay Ninh is 96km northwest of HCMC. The Cao Dai Holy See complex is 4km east of Tay Ninh. One-day tours from Saigon, including Tay Ninh and the Cu Chi Tunnels, cost from US$7.

Beaches

There are several beach resorts within striking distance of downtown Saigon, although most travellers make for Mui Ne. If time is short and you want a quick fix, consider Vung Tau, which you can reach by hydrofoil.

MEKONG DELTA

The 'rice bowl' of Vietnam, the Mekong Delta is a landscape carpeted in a dizzying variety of greens and slashed with mighty waterways. It's a water world where boats, houses, restaurants and even markets float upon the innumerable rivers, canals and streams that flow through the region like arteries. At times you can quite simply lose sight of land.

The area is both riparian and deeply rural, but it's also one of Vietnam's most densely populated regions, with nearly every hectare intensively farmed. Visitors can dwell on southern charm in little-visited riverside cities, sample fruits traded in the colourful floating markets, or feast on home-cooked delicacies before overnighting as a homestay guest. Mangrove forests, sacred Khmer pagodas and off-the-beaten-track attractions round out the picture.

Those seeking tropical hideaways can come ashore on Phu Quoc, a divine forested island fringed with white-sand beaches and crisscrossed with empty dirt roads that simply beg for DIY motorbike exploration.

My Tho

📞 074 / POP 172,000

Gateway to the Mekong Delta for day trippers to the region, the slow-paced capital of Tien Giang Province is an important market town, but to visit floating markets you'll need to continue on to Can Tho.

On the riverfront, the **My Tho Tourist Boat Station** (8 Đ 30 Thang 4) is home to several tour companies offering cruises to the neighbouring islands and through the maze of small canals. Destinations usually include a coconut-candy workshop, a honey farm (try the banana wine) and an orchid garden. A 2½-hour boat tour costs around 350,000d for one person or 450,000d for two. Prices drop if you can join a group.

🛏 Sleeping

Song Tien Annex HOTEL $
(📞073-387 7883; www.tiengiangtourist.com; 33 Đ Thien Ho Duong; r 450,000-500,000d; ✳🖤) Rooms at this becalming, clean and tidy hotel have hardwood floors, natty extras such as bathrobes and hair dryers, lovely bathrooms with freestanding claw-footed bathtubs, and modern furniture.

Song Tien HOTEL $$
(📞073-387 2009; www.tiengiangtourist.com; 101 Đ Trung Trac; r 450,000-850,000d; ✳🖤) This friendly, smart and well-looked-after hotel has decent-enough rooms with satellite TV and minibars. Check the rooms: cheaper ones are windowless with occasional traces of mould.

✗ Eating

My Tho is well known for a special vermicelli soup called *hu tieu My Tho,* which is richly garnished with fresh and dried seafood, pork, chicken, offal and fresh herbs. Carnivores will enjoy **Hu Tieu 44** (44 Đ Nam Ky Khoi Nghia; soups 20,000d), while vegetarians should try **Hu Tieu Chay 24** (24 Đ Nam Ky Khoi Nghia; mains 10,000-14,000d).

Ngoc Gia Trang VIETNAMESE $
(📞073-387 2742; 196 Đ Ap Bac; mains 45,000-150,000d; ⊘8am-9pm) This friendly spot is down a lane off the main road into My Tho from HCMC, with tables set alongside ponds amidst lots of greenery, and excellent, beautifully presented seafood.

ⓘ Getting There & Away

New bridges and roads have considerably shortened travel distances to My Tho. The **bus station** (Ben Xe Tien Giang; 42 Đ Ap Bac) is 3km west of the town centre on Đ Ap Bac, the main road to HCMC. Buses head to HCMC's Mien Tay bus station (35,000d, around 75 minutes), Can Tho (50,000d), Cao Lanh (32,000d), Chau Doc (51,000d) and Ca Mau (123,000d).

Ben Tre

📞 075 / POP 120,000

Famous for its *keo dua* (coconut candy), Ben Tre's sleepy waterfront is lined with ageing villas and is easy to explore on foot, as is the rustic settlement across the bridge to the south of the centre. Located off the main trail, it receives far fewer visitors than My Tho and makes a lovely stop on a Mekong tour.

Ben Tre Tourist (📞075-382 9618; www.ben-tretourist.vn; 65 Đ Dong Khoi; ⊘7-11am & 1-5pm) rents out bikes and motor boats (US$12 per hour) and arranges excursions, including a bike tour to coconut, guava and grapefruit groves.

Hung Vuong (📞075-382 2408; 166 Đ Hung Vuong; d/tw/ste 350,000/370,000/530,000d; ✳🖤) has an attractive riverfront plot plus

A NIGHT ON THE MEKONG

Spending the night on board a boat on the Mekong River is a good way to explore more of the waterways that make up this incredible region and helps bring you closer to life on the river. The more interesting options for overnighting on the Mekong include the following:

Bassac (☑ 0710-382 9540; www.transmekong.com; overnight US$232) Offers a range of beautiful wooden boats for small groups. The standard itinerary is an overnight between Cai Be and Can Tho, but custom routes are possible.

Exotissimo (☑ 08-3827 2911; www.exotissimo.com; overnight 4,123,000-12,659,000d) Up-market single- or multiday tours of the delta by boat.

Le Cochinchine (☑ 08-3993 4552; www.lecochinchine.com; price on application) Cruises on a luxurious converted rice barge and a traditional sampan that are akin to floating hotels.

Mekong Eyes (☑ 0710-246 0786; www.mekongeyes.com; price on application) A stunningly converted traditional rice barge that travels between Can Tho and Cai Be. It's also available for charter.

large clean rooms while **Nam Son** (☑ 075-382 2873; 40 Đ Phan Ngoc Tong; mains 20,000-60,000d) is famous for grilled chicken.

Buses leave regularly from the bus terminal 5km northeast of town for HCMC (67,000d, last bus between 4pm and 5pm), Can Tho (55,000d), Ca Mau (103,000d) and Ha Tien (134,000d). The last buses to HCMC depart between 4pm and 5pm.

Slow boats can be rented at the public pier near the market from 90,000d per hour.

Vinh Long

☑ 070 / POP 133,000

It may not be the largest town in the Mekong Delta, but as a major transit hub Vinh Long can be noisy and chaotic nonetheless. Escape to the riverfront, where there are plenty of cafes and restaurants. Vinh Long is the gateway to island life and some worthwhile sites, including the Cai Be floating market, abundant orchards and atmospheric homestays, which can be a highlight of a Mekong journey.

What makes a trip to Vinh Long worthwhile are the beautiful islands in the river. Charter a boat through **Cuu Long Tourist** (☑ 070-382 3616; www.cuulongtourist.com; 2 Đ Phan B Chau; ⊙ 7am-5pm) for around US$14 per person.

The bustling **Cai Be floating market** (⊙ 5am-5pm) is worth including on a boat tour from Vinh Long. It's best to arrive early in the morning. Wholesalers on big boats

moor here, each specialising in one or a few types of fruit or vegetable.

We suggest you don't stay in town; instead opt for a homestay. **Dong Khanh** (49 Đ 2 Thang 9; mains from 30,000d; ⊙ 6am-6pm) offers lots of hotpots and rice dishes.

Frequent buses go between Vinh Long and HCMC (90,000d, three hours), from the terminal in the middle of town. Buses to other locations, including Can Tho (40,000d), leave from a provincial bus station 3km south of town.

Can Tho

☑ 071 / POP 1.1 MILLION

The epicentre of the Mekong Delta, Can Tho feels like a veritable metropolis after exploring the backwaters. As the political, economic, cultural and transportation centre of the Mekong Delta, Can Tho hums with activity. It's a buzzing town with a waterfront lined with sculpted gardens and an appealing blend of narrow backstreets and wide boulevards that make for some rewarding exploration.

Can Tho also makes the perfect base for visiting nearby floating markets. **Cai Rang** is the biggest floating market in the Mekong Delta, 6km from Can Tho towards Soc Trang. Although the lively market goes on until around noon daily, show up before 9am for the best photo opportunities. You can hire boats (about 100,000d per hour) here. Cai Rang is one hour away by boat, or you can drive to Cau Dau Sau boat landing, where you can get a **rowing boat** (per hr around 90,000d) to the market, 10 minutes away.

Less crowded and less motorised is the **Phong Dien market**, with more stand-up rowboats. It's best between 6am and 8am. Twenty kilometres southwest of Can Tho, it's easy to reach by road and you can hire a boat on arrival.

🛏️ Sleeping

★ **Xoai Hotel** HOTEL $
(📞 0907 652 927; www.hotelxoai.com; 93 Đ Mau Than; s US$10, d US$14-26, tw US$19; ❀@🛜) Fantastic value at this friendly, efficient hotel with bright, mango-coloured (the hotel name means 'Mango Hotel'), airy rooms. Helpful staff speak excellent English and there's a roof terrace with hammocks.

★ **Kim Tho Hotel** HOTEL $$
(📞 071-381 7517; www.kimtho.com; 1A Đ Ngo Gia Tu; r 950,000-1,400,000d; ❀🛜) A smart boutique-style hotel, with stylish rooms throughout and designer bathrooms. Cheaper rooms are on lower floors, but superior rooms have hardwood flooring and the pricier river-view rooms are still a great deal. There's a rooftop coffee bar.

★ **Victoria Can Tho Resort** RESORT $$$
(📞 071-381 0111; www.victoriahotels.asia; Cai Khe Ward; r US$91-230, ste US$277-310; ❀@🛜🏊) With particularly gracious service, this hotel defines style and sophistication in the Mekong Delta. Designed with a French colonial look, the rooms – along stunning corridors – are set around an inviting pool that looks out over the river. Facilities include an excellent restaurant, an open-air bar and a spa.

🍴 Eating & Drinking

Sao Hom VIETNAMESE, INTERNATIONAL $
(50 Đ Hai Ba Trung; mains 45,000-160,000d; ⊙8am-11pm) Set in the former market and overseen by staff in *ao dai,* Sao Hom has an atmospheric, breezy riverside setting, and is a great spot for lunch or a morning coffee.

Mekong VIETNAMESE, INTERNATIONAL $
(38 Đ Hai Ba Trung; mains from 25,000d; ⊙7am-8pm; 🍴) Looking onto busy Hai Ba Trung, this travellers' favourite has a good blend of local and international food at reasonable prices. Try the lovely sour soup with fish (40,000d); good vegie selection.

ℹ️ Information

There are plenty of ATMs and internet cafes dotted around town.

Can Tho Tourist (📞071-382 1852; www.canthotourist.com.vn; 50 Đ Hai Ba Trung) Helpful staff speak both English and French here and decent city maps are available, as well as general information on attractions in the area. There is also a booking desk for Vietnam Airlines and Jetstar.

OFF THE BEATEN TRACK

MEKONG DELTA

It's not hard to get off the beaten track in the Mekong Delta, as most tourists are on hit-and-run day trips from HCMC or passing through on their way to or from Cambodia. Here are some lesser-known regional gems:

➡ Check out some Khmer culture in **Tra Vinh**, home to a significant population of Cambodians and their beautiful temples.

➡ The Khmer kingdom of Funan once held sway over much of the lower Mekong; its principal port was at **Oc-Eo**, located near Long Xuyen. Archaeologists have found ancient Persian and Roman artefacts here.

➡ Birding enthusiasts will want to make a diversion to **Tram Chin Reserve** near Cao Lang, a habitat for the rare eastern sarus crane. These huge birds are depicted on the bas-reliefs at Angkor and only found here and in northwest Cambodia.

➡ The small and secluded beach resort of **Hon Chong** has the most scenic stretch of coastline on the Mekong Delta mainland. The big attractions here are Chua Hang Grotto, Duong Beach and Nghe Island.

ℹ️ Getting There & Away

AIR

Can Tho's new airport 10km northwest of the centre has **Vietnam Airlines** (📞 071-384 4320; 64 Đ Nguyen An Ninh) flights to Phu Quoc (from 610,000d, daily), Con Dao (1,300,000d, four per week), HCMC, Danang and Hanoi.

BOAT

Boat services include hydrofoils to Ca Mau (150,000d, three to four hours), passing through Phung Hiep.

BUS

Can Tho has two bus stations. The **old bus station** (Ben Xe Khach Can Tho; cnr Đ Nguyen Trai & Đ Hung Vuong) is centrally located on the northern edge of the city centre, with regular buses to HCMC's Mien Tay bus station (100,000d to 110,000d), Cao Lanh (60,000d), Ben Tre (70,000d), My Tho (70,000d), Ca Mau (90,000d), Chau Doc (60,000d) and Long Xuyen (40,000d). The **new bus station** is in the southwest, with buses to HCMC (110,000d), Ca Mau (110,000d) and Dalat (320,000d).

Chau Doc

📞 076 / POP 112,000

Draped along the banks of the Hau Giang River (Bassac River), Chau Doc sees plenty of travellers washing through on the river route between Cambodia and Vietnam.

A likeable little town with significant Chinese, Cham and Khmer communities, Chau Doc's cultural diversity – apparent in the mosques, temples, churches and nearby pilgrimage sites – makes it fascinating to explore even if you're not bound for Cambodia. Taking a boat trip to the Cham communities across the river is another highlight, while the bustling market and intriguing waterfront provide fine backdrops to a few days of relaxation.

🛏️ Sleeping & Eating

Good local eateries in Chau Doc include **Bay Bong** (22 Đ Thuong Dang Le; mains 40,000-80,000d; ⏰9am-8pm), with excellent hotpots and soups, and **Thanh Tinh** (42 Đ Quang Trung; mains 30,000-80,000d; ⏰6am-7pm; 🌿) for vegetarian food.

★**Trung Nguyen Hotel**   HOTEL **$**
(📞076-386 6158; trunghotel@yahoo.com; 86 Đ Bach Dang; s/d/tw US$14/16/20; ❄️@🛜) One of the better budget places, with more mid-range trim. Rooms are more decorative than the competition, with balconies overlooking the market. It's a busy corner site, so pack earplugs.

Chau Pho   HOTEL **$$**
(📞076-356 4139; www.chauphohotel.com; Đ 88 Trung Nu Vuong; r US$32-50; ❄️🛜) This solid, friendly midrange hotel with tennis courts has 50 well-presented rooms over five floors, some with balcony. Deluxe rooms are far more pleasant than the cheaper options.

★**Victoria Chau Doc Hotel**   HOTEL **$$$**
(📞076-386 5010; www.victoriahotels.asia; 32 Đ Le Loi; r/ste from US$110/175; ❄️@🛜🏊) Victoria delivers classic colonial charm, overseen by *ao dai*–clad staff. With a striking location on the riverfront, the grand rooms here have dark-wood floors and furniture, and inviting bathtubs. The swimming pool overlooks the busy river action and there's a small spa upstairs.

ℹ️ Information

Mekong Tours (📞 076-356 2828; www.mekongvietnam.com; 14 Đ Nguyen Huu Canh; ⏰8am-8pm) is a reliable travel agent offering boat/bus transport to Phnom Penh, Mekong boat trips, and cars with drivers.

ℹ️ Getting There & Away

Buses to Chau Doc depart HCMC's Mien Tay station (130,000d, six hours).

Ha Tien

📞 077 / POP 95,000

Ha Tien may be part of the Mekong Delta, but lying on the Gulf of Thailand it feels a world away from the rice fields and rivers that typify the region. Dramatic limestone formations define the area, pepper-tree plantations dot the hillsides and the town itself has a sleepy tropical charm.

It's a transport hub for road links to the Cambodia border at Xa Xia–Prek Chak and boats to Phu Quoc.

🛏️ Sleeping & Eating

Be sure to try the local coconut; its flesh is mixed with ice and sugar and served in restaurants all over town.

Hai Phuong HOTEL **$**
(☎077-385 2240; So 52, Đ Dong Thuy Tram; r 200,000-700,000d; ❄️🛜) Friendly and family-run, this smart six-level hotel is in good nick and some rooms have excellent river views from their balconies.

Ha Tien Hotel HOTEL **$$**
(☎077-395 2093; 36 Đ Tran Hau; s 390,000-690,000d, d 440,000-790,000d, tr 590,000d; ❄️🛜) A rambling place exuding a faded sense of midrange grandeur, this clean and central hotel has polite staff and spacious rooms, some with terrace.

Xuan Thanh VIETNAMESE **$**
(20 Đ Tran Hau; mains 35,000-200,000d; ⏰6am-9pm) You know you've hit the coast when shrimp is the cheapest dish on the menu, which also runs to seafood and grills. Try the delicately flavoured steamed fish with ginger and onion.

GETTING TO CAMBODIA: SOUTHERN BORDERS

Chau Doc to Phnom Penh

Getting to the border One of the most enjoyable ways to enter Cambodia is via the Vinh Xuong/Kaam Samnor border crossing located just northwest of Chau Doc along the Mekong River. Several companies in Chau Doc sell boat journeys from Chau Doc to Phnom Penh via the Vinh Xuong border. **Hang Chau** (☎Chau Doc 076-356 2771, Phnom Penh 855-12-883 542; www.hangchautourist.com.vn; per person US$24) boats depart Chau Doc at 7.30am from a pier at 18 Đ Tran Hung Dao, arriving at 12.30pm. The more upmarket **Blue Cruiser** (☎HCMC 08-3926 0253, Phnom Penh 855-236-333 666; www.bluecruiser.com) leaves the Victoria Hotel pier at 7am, costing US$55. It takes about five hours, including the border check. Also departing from this pier at 7am are Victoria Speedboats (US$97, five hours), exclusive to Victoria Hotel guests.

At the border If leaving Vietnam, Cambodian visas are available at the crossing, but minor overcharging is common (plan on paying around US$24).

For more information about crossing this border in the other direction, see p192.

Chau Doc to Takeo

Getting to the border Eclipsed by the newer crossing of Xa Xia near Ha Tien, the Tinh Bien/Phnom Den border crossing is less convenient for Phnom Penh–bound travellers, but may be of interest for those who savour the challenge of obscure border crossings. Buses from Chau Doc to Phnom Penh (US$15 to US$21, five hours) depart at 7.30am and can be booked through Mekong Tours in Chau Doc. Roads to the border are terrible.

At the border Cambodian visas can be obtained here, although it's not uncommon to be charged US$25, several dollars more than the official rate.

Moving on Most travellers opt for a through bus ticket from Chau Doc.

For more information about crossing this border in the other direction, see p192.

Ha Tien to Kep

Getting to the border The Xa Xia/Prek Chak border crossing connects Ha Tien with Kep and Kampot on Cambodia's south coast, making a trip to Cambodia from Phu Quoc via Ha Tien, or vice versa, that much easier. Direct minibuses leave Ha Tien for Cambodia at around 1pm, heading to Kep (US$12, one hour, 47km), Kampot (US$15, 1½ hours, 75km), Sihanoukville (US$20, four hours, 150km) and Phnom Penh (US$18, four hours, 180km). Bookings can be made through Ha Tien Tourism (which also operates through the Oasis bar), which can arrange the Cambodian visa too. It's far better to change money in Ha Tien than at the border.

At the border Cambodian visas (US$20) are issued at the border (you'll need a passport-sized photo).

Moving on As it costs only slightly more than taking local transport and is far comfier, most travellers opt for a through minibus ticket.

For more information about crossing this border in the other direction, see p258.

★ Oasis
BAR

(☎077-370 1553; www.oasisbarhatien.com; 42 Đ Tuan Phu Dat; ☉9am-9pm; ☜) Run by Ha Tien's only resident Western expat and his Vietnamese wife, this friendly little bar is not just a great spot for a cold beer or coffee, it's also great for impartial travel information. The menu runs to all-day, real-deal, full-English breakfasts, caramelised onion soup, mango shakes and more.

ℹ Getting There & Away

Passenger ferries dock at the ferry terminal, opposite the Ha Tien Hotel. See Phu Quoc (p155) for ferry information.

Buses connect HCMC (from 140,000d, 10 hours) and Ha Tien, and also run to destinations including Chau Doc (70,000d), Rach Gia (50,000d) and Can Tho (110,000d). Ha Tien's bus station is on the road to Mui Nai Beach and the Cambodian border.

Rach Gia

☏ 077 / POP 206,000

Rach Gia is something of a boom town, flush with funds from its thriving port and an injection of Viet Kieu (overseas Vietnamese) money. The population here includes significant numbers of ethnic Chinese and ethnic Khmers. Most travellers give the busy centre short shrift, heading straight to Phu Quoc Island. Those who do linger can explore the lively waterfront and bustling backstreets, where there are some inexpensive seafood restaurants to be found.

🛏 Sleeping & Eating

Kim Co Hotel
HOTEL $

(☎077-387 9610; www.kimcohotel.com; 141 Đ Nguyen Hung Son; r 350,000-400,000d; ❄☜) Centrally located, trim and tidy Kim Co is a masterclass in pastel shade. Bright and cheerful rooms have clean bathrooms, but most face the corridor, so pull the shades for privacy.

Hong Yen
HOTEL $

(☎077-387 9095; 259 Đ Mac Cuu; r 150,000-250,000d; ❄@☜) Stretching over four pink floors, Hong Yen is a likeable minihotel with sizeable, clean rooms and friendly owners. There's a lift and some rooms have balconies.

Hai Au
VIETNAMESE, INTERNATIONAL $

(2 Đ Nguyen Trung Truc; mains 60,000-120,000d; ☉6am-10pm; ☜) A fancy restaurant by local standards, this cavernous eatery with chandeliers has a great location by the Cai Lon River. Seafood is popular, including crayfish and crab, and Western-style dishes also feature.

ℹ Information

Banks, ATMs and internet cafes are scattered around town.

Kien Giang Tourist (Du Lich Lu Hanh Kien Giang; ☎077-386 2081; ctycpdu lichkg@vnn.vn; 5 Đ Le Loi; ☉7am-5pm) is the provincial tourism authority.

ℹ Getting There & Around

Vietnam Airlines has daily flights to and from HCMC (from 1,100,000d) and Phu Quoc Island (from 800,000d). The airport is 10km southeast of the centre; a taxi into town will cost around 80,000d.

Boats to Phu Quoc Island leave from the centrally located ferry terminal at the western end of Đ Nguyen Cong Tru. three hydrofoils leave daily for Ca Mau (110,000d, three hours) from the **Rach Meo ferry terminal** (☎077-381 1306; Đ Ngo Quyen), about 2km south of town.

There are regular services to Ca Mau (50,000d, three hours), Ha Tien (38,000d, two hours) and other cities in the region from the **central bus station** (260A Đ Nguyen Binh Khiem) north of town. A taxi into town will cost around 20,000d.

Phu Quoc Island

☏ 077 / POP 89,000

Fringed with idyllic beaches and with large tracts still covered in dense, tropical jungle, Phu Quoc is morphing from a sleepy backwater into a favoured escape. Beyond the chain of resorts lining Long Beach, it's still largely undeveloped. Dive the reefs, kayak bays, explore back roads by motorbike – or live the life of a lotus eater by lounging on the beach, indulging in a massage and dining on fresh seafood.

Despite increasing development (including a new international airport), close to 70% of the island is protected as Phu Quoc National Park.

Phu Quoc's wet season is from July to November; the peak season for tourism is between December and March.

◉ Sights & Activities

Deserted white-sand beaches form a ring around Phu Quoc.

Duong Dong   TOWN

The island's main town and chief fishing port is not that exciting, though the filthy, bustling market is interesting. The old bridge in town is a great vantage point to photograph the island's fishing fleet crammed into the narrow channel. Take a peek at **Cau Castle** (Dinh Cau; Đ Bach Dang) `FREE`, actually more of a temple-cum-lighthouse, built in 1937 to honour Thien Hau (Tianhou), the Chinese goddess of the sea.

Phu Quoc is famous for the quality of its *nuoc mam* (fish sauce), and the factory **Nuoc Mam Hung Thanh** (⊘8-11am & 1-5pm) `FREE` exports all over the world.

Long Beach   BEACH

(Bai Truong) Long Beach is draped invitingly along the west coast from Duong Dong almost to An Thoi port. Development concentrates in the north near Duong Dong, where the recliners and rattan umbrellas of the various resorts rule; like all beaches in Vietnam, these are the only stretches that are kept clean. With its west-facing aspect, sunsets can be stupendous.

Sao, Khem & Vong Beaches   BEACH

With white sand like powdered ivory, the delightful curve of beautiful **Sao Beach** (Bai Sao) bends out alongside a sea of mineral-water clarity just a few kilometres from An Thoi, the main shipping port at the southern tip of the island. There are a couple of beachfront restaurants, where you can settle into a deck chair or partake in water sports.

To the south is undeveloped **Khem Beach** (Bai Dam), one of the most beautiful beaches on the island, but also one of the few remaining areas that's under military control. Consequently, it's generally closed to the public.

Around 10km north along the east coast is attractive **Vong Beach** (Bai Vong), where the fast boats from the mainland dock.

Phu Quoc National Park   NATIONAL PARK

About 90% of Phu Quoc is forested and the trees and adjoining marine environment enjoy official protection (in 2010 it was declared a Unesco Biosphere Reserve). There are a few primitive dirt roads, but no real hiking trails.

Vung Bau, Dai & Thom Beaches   BEACH

Still retaining their isolated, tropical charm, these northern beaches are rarely peopled, let alone crowded. A newer road follows the coast along **Vung Bau** (Bai Vung Bau) and **Dai** (Bai Dai) beaches, cutting down on motorbike time and red dust in your face. The road from Dai to **Thom** (Bai Thom) via Ganh Dau is very beautiful, passing through dense forest with tantalising glimpses of the coast below.

Cua Can & Ong Lan Beaches   BEACH

The most accessible of the northern beaches, **Cua Can** (Bai Cua Can) is about 11km from Duong Dong. It remains mercifully quiet during the week, but can get busy at weekends. Just south of here is **Ong Lan** (Bai Ong Lan), with a series of sandy bays sheltered by rocky headlands. Several midrange resorts in this area service those wanting to get away from it all.

🏃 Activities

Diving & Snorkelling

There's plenty of underwater action around Phu Quoc, but only during the dry months (from November to May). Two fun dives cost from US$40 to US$80; four-day PADI Open Water from US$320 to US$360; snorkelling trips from US$20 to US$30. The following schools are based in the Doung Dong area.

Rainbow Divers   DIVING, SNORKELLING

(☑ 0913 400 964; www.divevietnam.com; 11 Đ Tran Hung Dao; ⊘9am-6pm) A PADI outfit with a wide range of diving and snorkelling trips.

Flipper Diving Club   DIVING

(www.flipperdiving.com; 60 Đ Tran Hung Dao; ⊘9am-9pm) Multilingual PADI dive centre for everything from novice dive trips to full instructor courses.

Searama   DIVING, SNORKELLING

(☑ 0126 479 1922; www.searama.com; 98B Đ Tran Hung Dao) French- and English-speaking operators; tends to be a bit cheaper than the competition.

Fishing & Boat Trips

Jerry's Jungle & Beach Tours   BOAT TOUR, HIKING

(☑ 0938 226 021; jerrysjungletours@gmail.com; day trips from US$25) Archipelago explorations by boat, snorkelling, fishing, day and multi-day trips to islands, motorbike tours, bouldering, bird-watching, hiking and cultural tours around Phu Quoc.

Anh Tu's Tours BOAT TOUR
(☑ 077-399 6009; anhtupq@yahoo.com) Snorkelling, squid fishing, island tours, plus motorbike rental.

John's Tours BOAT TOUR
(☑ 0919 107 086; www.johnsislandtours.com; 4 Đ Tran Hung Dao) Cruises include snorkelling, island-hopping and squid-fishing trips.

🛏 Sleeping

Accommodation prices yo-yo depending on the season. Price fluctuations are more extreme than anywhere else in Vietnam, but tend to affect budget and midrange places more than the top-end resorts.

🛏 Duong Dong

Sea Breeze HOTEL $
(Gio Bien; ☑ 077-399 4920; www.seabreezephuquoc.com; 62A Đ Tran Hung Dao; r with fan from US$15, air-con US$25-40; ✳🤶) Clean, modern and attractive rooms; accommodation roadside is noisier at this curvaceous hotel.

Hiep Phong Hotel GUESTHOUSE $
(☑ 077-384 6057; nguyet_1305@yahoo.com; 17 Đ Nguyen Trai; r US$15-20; ✳@🤶) A very friendly, family-run minihotel in the middle of town. The rooms include satellite TV, fridge and hot water.

🛏 Long Beach

Mushrooms GUESTHOUSE $
(☑ 0126 471 4249; 170 Đ Tran Hung Dao; dm US$6, d US$10-15) This spruce, clean and colourful outfit on the far side of the road has epic-and-span four- and six-bed dorms and a couple of decent doubles, one sans shower.

Lien Hiep Thanh Hotel RESORT HOTEL $
(☑ 077-384 7583; lienhiepthanh2007@yahoo.com.vn; 118/12 Đ Tran Hung Dao; r with fan US$15-20, air-con US$30-60; ✳🤶) This friendly place has simple rooms and bungalows amid trees and a great strip of beach. Beachfront rooms include air-con and hot water, and there's a small restaurant.

Sea Star Resort RESORT HOTEL $$
(☑ 077-398 2161; www.seastarresort.com; r US$36-46, bungalows US$60-85; ✳@🤶) A fun and friendly place to stay, this extensive compound includes 37 rooms and bungalows, many fronting on to a manicured stretch of sand with sea-view balconies. Cheapest rooms are conjoined in a block

and prices drop by about 20% in the low season.

Beach Club RESORT HOTEL $$
(☑ 077-398 0998; www.beachclubvietnam.com; Ap Cua Lap, Xa Duong To; r US$30-40; 🤶) Run by an English-Vietnamese couple, this is a great escape from the main-drag bustle, with tightly grouped and well-kept rooms and bungalows on a small plot, plus a breezy beachside restaurant.

★ Mai House RESORT HOTEL $$$
(☑ 077-384 7003; maihouseresort@yahoo.com; 118 Đ Tran Hung Dao; r with fan US$75, air-con US$95-240; ✳@🤶) Dappled with palm shade, Mai House offers one of the most exquisite settings on Long Beach, nailing the whole tropical-paradise vibe with its well-tended gardens, open-sided restaurant and loungers shaded by rattan umbrellas. The food is excellent and the beach is gorgeous.

★ La Veranda RESORT HOTEL $$$
(☑ 077-398 2988; www.laverandaresort.com; 118/9 Đ Tran Hung Dao; r US$275-375; ✳@🤶) With grounds shaded by palms, this is the most elegant place to stay on the island, designed in colonial style and small enough to remain intimate, with just 44 rooms. The beach is adorable and for food you can choose between a cafe on the lawn and the **Pepper Tree Restaurant** (mains US$6-20; ⊘6.30am-11pm) upstairs.

🛏 Around the Island

★ Bamboo Cottages & Restaurant RESORT HOTEL $$
(☑ 077-281 0345; www.bamboophuquoc.com; r US$50-95; ✳@) Run by a friendly family, Bamboo Cottages has Vung Bau Beach largely to itself. The focal point is a big open-sided restaurant and bar, with the beach at its doorstep. Set around the lawns, the attractive, lemon-coloured villas have private, open-roofed bathrooms with solar-powered hot water. The family supports an education scholarship for local kids in need.

Freedomland HOMESTAY $$
(☑ 077-399 4891; www.freedomlandphuquoc.com; 2 Ap Ong Lang, Xa Cua Duong; bungalow US$30-60; ⊘Oct-Jun; @🤶) With an emphasis on socialising – including fun, communal dinners – Freedomland has 11 basic bungalows

(mosquito nets, fans, no hot water) scattered around a shady plot. It's a popular choice, particularly with solo budget travellers. Shut in the wet season.

Mango Garden   B&B **$$**
(⌘077-629 1339; mangogarden.inn@gmail.com; r US$35-50; ☺Oct-Mar; ✻❀☎) Best suited to those with their own (two) wheels, this isolated B&B is reached by a bumpy dirt road (turn left just before Sao Beach). Run by a Vietnamese-Canadian, it features gorgeous flower and mango gardens. There's motorbike rental, 24-hour solar-powered hot water, fishing and snorkelling trips. Book well ahead.

★**Chen Sea Resort & Spa**   RESORT HOTEL **$$$**
(⌘077-399 5895; www.centarahotelsresorts.com; bungalows US$234-473; ✻@☎✖) Tranquil 36-room Chen Sea has lovely villas with sunken baths and deep verandahs, designed to resemble ancient terracotta-roofed houses. An infinity pool faces the resort's beautiful sandy beach. Borrow a bike, kayak or catamaran – or settle into the spa or the open-sided restaurant.

✖ Eating

Most hotels have their own lively cafes or restaurants in-house.

Duong Dong's **night market** (Đ Vo Thi Sau; ☺5pm-midnight) is one of the most atmospheric (and affordable) places to dine, with a delicious range of Vietnamese seafood, grills and vegetarian options.

The seafood restaurants in the fishing village of Ham Ninh also offer an authentic local experience and taste; try **Kim Cuong I** (⌘077-384 9978; mains 30,000-300,000d).

✖ Duong Dong

★**Buddy Ice Cream**   ICE CREAM **$**
(www.visitphuquoc.info; 26 Đ Nguyen Trai; mains 25,000-130,000d; ☺8am-10pm; ☎) With the coolest music in town, this cafe is excellent for sides of free internet and tourist info. Fill up with New Zealand ice-cream combos, toasted sandwiches, fish and chips, thirst-busting fruit juices, shakes, smoothies, all-day breakfasts, comfy sofas and a book exchange.

✖ Long Beach

★**The Spice House at Cassia Cottage**   VIETNAMESE **$**
(www.cassiacottage.com; 100C Đ Tran Hung Dao; mains from 74,000d; ☺7-10am & 11am-10pm) Nab a beachside high-table, order a papaya salad, grilled garlic, a cinnamon-infused okra or a delectable fish curry and time dinner to catch the sunset at this excellent restaurant.

Alanis Deli   CAFE **$**
(98 Đ Tran Hung Dao; pancakes from 75,000d; ☺8am-10pm) Fab caramel pancakes and coffees plus ace breakfasts and friendly service.

Oasis   VIETNAMESE, WESTERN **$**
(118/5 Đ Tran Hung Dao; mains from 55,000d; ☺7am-10pm, bar till later; ☎) On the lane leading to La Veranda and Rory's Beach Bar, Oasis feeds ravenous travellers with a menu embracing shepherd's pie, shrimp spring rolls, apple pie and winning all-day breakfasts.

Mondo   TAPAS **$**
(82 Đ Tran Hung Dao; tapas 35,000-105,000d; ☺7am-10pm Tue-Sun) Serving traditional

---

DON'T MISS

AN THOI ISLANDS

Just off the southern tip of Phu Quoc Island, these 15 islands and islets can be visited by chartered boat. It's a fine area for sightseeing, fishing, swimming and snorkelling. Hon Thom (Pineapple Island) is about 3km in length and is the largest in the group. Other islands include Hon Dua (Coconut Island), Hon Roi (Lamp Island), Hon Vang (Echo Island), Hon May Rut (Cold Cloud Island), the Hon Dams (Shadow Islands), Chan Qui (Yellow Tortoise) and Hon Mong Tay (Short Gun Island). As yet, there is no real development on the islands, but expect some movement in the next few years.

Most boats depart from An Thoi on Phu Quoc, but you can make arrangements through hotels and resorts on Long Beach. You can also inquire at the dive operators, as they have boats heading down there regularly for diving. Boat trips are seasonal and generally do not run during the wet season.

Spanish tapas and other Western treats plus all-day breakfasts, Mondo is a dependable Long Beach slot, with imported beers (Chimay, Duvel).

Itaca Resto Lounge FUSION $$
(www.itacalounge.com; 125 Đ Tran Hung Dao; mains 200,000-300,000d; ⊘4pm-1am) This popular restaurant boasts a winning Mediterranean-Asian fusion menu (with tapas). The ambience is charming.

Around the Island

Sakura VIETNAMESE $
(mains from 45,000d; ⊘10am-10pm) This simple wood restaurant is run by the very fluent English-speaking Kiem. Food is scrumptious, but bring a fly swat and repellent.

Drinking & Nightlife

Both these place are on Long Beach.

★Le Bar BAR
(118/9 Đ Tran Hung Dao; ⊘6am-11pm; 🖭) With its gorgeous tiled floor, art-deco furniture and colonial charms, this highly elegant and well-poised upstairs lounge-bar at La Veranda is a superb spot for a terrace sundowner.

★Rory's Beach Bar BAR
(118/10 Đ Tran Hung Dao; ⊘9am-late) Phu Quoc's liveliest and most fun beach bar draws a steady torrent of travellers and island residents down the path to its seaside perch.

ℹ Information

There are ATMs in Duong Dong and in many resorts on Long Beach. Buddy Ice Cream offers free internet and wi-fi.

ℹ Getting There & Away

AIR

Demand can be high in peak season, so book ahead.

Vietnam Airlines (☑077-399 6677; www.vietnamairlines.com; 122 Đ Nguyen Trung Truc) Flies to/from Rach Gia, Can Tho, Hanoi and HCMC.

VietJet Air (☑1900 1886; www.vietjetair.com) Flies to/from HCMC.

BOAT

Fast boats connect Phu Quoc to both Ha Tien (1½ hours) and Rach Gia (2½ hours). Phu Quoc travel agents, such as **Green Cruise** (☑077-397 8111; www.greencruise.com.vn; 14 Đ Tran Hung

Dao, Duong Dong), have the most up-to-date schedules and can book tickets.

Also from Ha Tien, a massive 400-passenger car ferry (departing 8.20am from Ha Tien and 2pm from Phu Quoc; per passenger/motorbike/car 165,000d/100,000d/US$50) departs daily.

Rach Gia has two reputable operators servicing the route:

Savanna Express (☑077-369 2888; www.savannaexpress.com; adult/child 330,000/250,000d) Departs Rach Gia at 8.05am and Phu Quoc at 1.05pm; 2½ hours.

Superdong (☑Phu Quoc 077-398 0111, Rach Gia 077-387 7742; www.superdong.com.vn; to Rach Gia adult/child 320,000/250,000d, to Ha Tien adult/child 215,000-230,000/160,000d) Departs Rach Gia and Phu Quoc at 8am, 9am, 12.40pm and 1pm. Departs Ha Tien at 8am and 1pm and leaves Phu Quoc at 8.30am and 1.30pm.

ℹ Getting Around

The island's brand-new Phu Quoc International Airport is 10km out of town. A taxi will cost around US$8 to Long Beach.

If you can ride a bicycle in the tropical heat over these dusty, bumpy roads, more power to you. Bicycle rentals are available through most hotels from US$3 per day.

There is a skeletal bus service between An Thoi and Duong Dong. Buses run perhaps once every hour or two. A bus (20,000d) waits for the ferry at Bai Vong to take passengers to Duong Dong. Several hotels operate shuttles or will offer free transfers for guests.

You won't have to look for the motorbike taxis – they'll find you. For short runs, 20,000d should be sufficient. Otherwise, figure on around 50,000d for about 5km.

Motorbikes can be hired from most hotels and bungalows for around US$7 (semi-automatic) to US$10 (automatic) per day.

Mai Linh (☑077-397 9797) is a reliable taxi firm; their drivers always use the meter. It costs about 250,000d from Duong Dong to the dock at Vong Beach.

UNDERSTAND VIETNAM

Vietnam Today

Vietnam has had a good couple of decades; a period of rising, sustained growth has benefited most. The standard of living has risen markedly, as cities have been transformed, education and healthcare have improved and the tourism sector continues to thrive.

Yet a growing disconnection between a heavy-handed state and its people is evident, with widespread resentment regarding rampant corruption and evidence of growing, if limited, political dissent.

Politics & Economics

Vietnam's political system could not be simpler: the Communist Party is the sole source of power. Officially, according to the Vietnamese constitution, the National Assembly (or parliament) is the country's supreme authority, but in practice it's a tool of the Party and carefully controlled elections ensure 90% of delegates are Communist Party members.

The state still controls around two-fifths of the economy. More than 100 of the 200 biggest companies in Vietnam are state-owned and the key sectors of oil production, shipbuilding, cement, coal and rubber are government controlled. Many of these state-controlled businesses are in deep trouble and haemorrhaging money.

Corruption scandals are frequent.

North & South

The Vietnamese economy has been buoyant for 20 years, but some areas are more buoyant than others. In 2013, Ho Chi Minh City's economy was growing at almost double the national rate (8.1% compared to 4.3%). It's the south that's benefited most from inward investment as Viet Kieu (overseas Vietnamese, the vast majority of whom are southerners) have returned and invested in the region. The government is aware of these divisions and tries to balance the offices of state, so if the prime minister is from the south, the head of the Communist Party is from the north.

When it comes to the older generation, the south has never forgiven the north for bulldozing their war cemeteries, imposing communism and blackballing whole families. The north has never forgiven the south for siding with the Americans against their own people. Luckily for Vietnam, the new generation seems to have less interest in the country's harrowing history.

Vietnam's Place in the World

Today, relations with the USA are politically cordial and economically vibrant (bilateral trade was worth US$24.9 billion in 2012). The US and Vietnamese militaries hold annual Defense Policy Dialogue talks. Vietnam's suppression of political dissent and issues of freedom of speech and religion remain areas of contention though. For the Vietnamese, the legacy of Agent Orange and dioxin poisoning remains unresolved – the USA has never paid compensation to the up to four million victims of dioxin poisoning resulting from aerial bombing during the American War.

The situation with Vietnam's traditional historic enemy, China, is far more complicated, and occasionally fraught. On the plus side trade is booming (though more one-way than the Vietnamese would like) and borders are hyper busy. Chinese is the second-most popular foreign language studied in Vietnam. However, the Spratly Islands, rich in oil deposits, remain a potential flashpoint, with both nations – in addition to several others – claiming sovereignty. There have been regular protests in Hanoi against the Chinese occupation of the islands.

Vietnam enjoys good relations with most Southeast Asian countries, but there are ongoing tensions with Laos over the construction of dams on the Mekong River.

State of the Nation

Overall, most Vietnamese are pretty happy with their lot – for now. The last couple of decades have transformed the nation as blue-chip finance has flooded into a red-flag communist society and comrades have become entrepreneurs. The country is stable. However, this status quo is very much dependent on the economy and with declining rates of growth, the situation is less rosy than it was a few years ago.

History

Vietnam has a history as rich and evocative as anywhere on earth. Sure, the war with the USA captured the attention of the West, but centuries before that the Vietnamese were scrapping with the Chinese, the Khmers, the Chams and the Mongols. Vietnamese civilisation is as sophisticated as that of its mighty northern neighbour, China, from which it drew many of its influences under a 1000-year occupation. Later came the French and the humbling period of colonialism from which Vietnam was not to emerge until the second half of the 20th century. The Americans were simply the last in a long line of invaders who had come and gone throughout the centuries – no matter what was required or how long it took, they too were vanquished. If only the military planners in Washington had paid a little more attention to the history of this proud nation, the trauma and tragedy of a long war might have been avoided.

Early Vietnam

The sophisticated Indianised kingdom of Funan flourished from the 1st to 6th centuries AD in the Mekong Delta area. Archaeological evidence reveals that Funan's busy trading port of Oc-Eo had contact with China, India, Persia and even the Mediterranean. Between the mid-6th century and the 9th century, the Funan empire was absorbed by the pre-Angkorian kingdom of Chenla.

Meanwhile, around present-day Danang, the Hindu kingdom of Champa emerged in the late 2nd century AD. Like Funan, it adopted Sanskrit as a sacred language and borrowed heavily from Indian art and culture. By the 8th century Champa had expanded to include what is now Nha Trang and Phan Rang. The Cham warred constantly with the Vietnamese to the north and the Khmers to the south and ultimately found themselves squeezed between these two great powers.

Chinese Occupation

The Chinese conquered the Red River Delta in the 2nd century BC and over the following centuries attempted to impress a centralised state system on the Vietnamese. There were numerous small-scale rebellions against Chinese rule – which was characterised by tyranny, forced labour and insatiable demands for tribute – between the 3rd to 6th centuries, but all were defeated.

However, the early Viets learned much from the Chinese, including advanced irrigation for rice cultivation and medical knowledge, as well as Confucianism, Taoism and Mahayana Buddhism. Much of the 1000-year period of Chinese occupation was typified by Vietnamese resistance while at the same time adopting many Chinese cultural traits.

In AD 938, Ngo Quyen destroyed Chinese forces on the Bach Dang River, winning independence and signalling the start of a dynastic tradition. During subsequent centuries the Vietnamese successfully repulsed foreign invaders, including the Mongols, and absorbed the kingdom of Champa in 1471 as they expanded south.

Contact with the West

In 1858 a joint military force from France and the Spanish colony of the Philippines stormed Danang after several missionaries were killed. Early the next year, Saigon was seized. By 1883 the French had imposed a Treaty of Protectorate on Vietnam. French rule often proved cruel and arbitrary. Ultimately, the most successful resistance came from the communists, first organised by Ho Chi Minh in 1925.

During WWII, the only group that significantly resisted the Japanese occupation was the communist-dominated Viet Minh. When WWII ended, Ho Chi Minh – whose Viet Minh forces already controlled large parts of the country – declared Vietnam independent. French efforts to reassert control soon led to violent confrontations and full-scale war. In May 1954, Viet Minh forces overran the French garrison at Dien Bien Phu.

The Geneva Accords of mid-1954 provided for a temporary division of Vietnam

DISSENT & THE NET

Dubbed the 'bamboo firewall', the entire nation's internet operates behind a state-controlled security system that blocks anything – including Facebook – that might potentially lead to trouble. In September 2013 the Vietnamese government introduced new rules restricting all use of websites and online social media to the exchange of 'personal information' only.

Political dissent is a complete no-no and arrests and trials are common. Bloggers are particularly vulnerable, with 46 sentenced to prison for 'anti-state propaganda' in 2013, including Le Quoc Quan, a democracy activist and prominent Catholic.

All newspapers and television channels are state-run.

at the Ben Hai River. When Ngo Dinh Diem, the anti-communist Catholic leader of the southern zone, refused to hold the 1956 elections, the Ben Hai line became the border between North and South Vietnam.

The American War

Around 1960, the Hanoi government changed its policy of opposition to the Diem regime from one of 'political struggle' to one of 'armed struggle'. The National Liberation Front (NLF), a communist guerrilla group better known as the Viet Cong (VC), was founded to fight against Diem.

An unpopular ruler, Diem was assassinated in 1963 by his own troops. When the Hanoi government ordered North Vietnamese Army (NVA) units to infiltrate the South in 1964, the situation for the Saigon regime became desperate. In 1965 the USA committed its first combat troops, soon joined by soldiers from South Korea, Australia, Thailand and New Zealand in an effort to bring global legitimacy to the conflict.

As Vietnam celebrated the Lunar New Year in 1968, the VC launched a surprise attack, known as the Tet Offensive, marking a crucial turning point in the war. Many Americans, who had for years believed their government's insistence that the USA was winning, started demanding a negotiated end to the war. The Paris Agreements, signed in 1973, provided for a ceasefire, the total withdrawal of US combat forces and the release of American prisoners of war.

Reunification

Saigon surrendered to the NVA on 30 April 1975. Vietnam's reunification by the communists meant liberation from more than a century of colonial oppression, but it was soon followed by large-scale internal repression. Hundreds of thousands of southerners fled Vietnam, creating a flood of refugees for the next 15 years.

Vietnam's campaign of repression against the ethnic Chinese, plus its invasion of Cambodia at the end of 1978, prompted China to attack Vietnam in 1979. The war lasted only 17 days, but Chinese-Vietnamese mistrust lasted for well over a decade.

Post–Cold War

After the collapse of the Soviet Union in 1991, Vietnam and Western nations sought rapprochement. The 1990s brought foreign investment and Association of Southeast Asian Nations (Asean) membership. The US established diplomatic relations with Vietnam in 1995, and in 2000 Bill Clinton became the first US president to visit north Vietnam. George W Bush followed suit in 2006, as Vietnam was welcomed into the World Trade Organisation (WTO) in 2007.

Relations have also greatly improved with the historic enemy, China. China may still secretly think of Vietnam as 'the one that got away', but Vietnam's economic boom has caught Beijing's attention and trade and tourism are booming across mutual borders.

People & Culture

People

The Vietnamese are battle-hardened, proud and nationalist, as they have earned their stripes in successive skirmishes with the world's mightiest powers. But that's the older generation, which remembers every inch of the territory for which it fought. For the new generation, Vietnam is a place to succeed, a place to ignore the staid structures set in stone by the communists, and a place to go out and have some fun.

As in other parts of Asia, life revolves around the family; there are often several generations living under one roof. Poverty, and the transition from a largely agricultural society to that of a more industrialised nation, is changing the structure of the modern family unit as more people head to the bigger cities to seek their fortune. Women make up 52% of the nation's workforce but are not well represented in positions of power.

Vietnam's population is 84% ethnic Vietnamese (Kinh) and 2% ethnic Chinese; the rest is made up of Khmers, Chams and members of more than 50 minority peoples, who mainly live in highland areas.

Religion

Over the centuries, Confucianism, Taoism and Buddhism have fused with popular Chinese beliefs and ancient Vietnamese animism to form what's collectively known as the Triple Religion (Tam Giao). Most Vietnamese people identify with this belief system but, if asked, they'll usually say they're Buddhist. Vietnam also has a significant percentage of Catholics (8% to 10% of the total population).

The unique and colourful Vietnamese sect Cao Daism was founded in the 1920s. It combines secular and religious philosophies of the East and West, and is based on seance messages revealed to the group's founder, Ngo Minh Chieu.

There are also small numbers of Muslims (around 60,000) and Hindus (50,000).

Arts

CONTEMPORARY ART

It is possible to catch modern dance, classical ballet and stage plays in Hanoi and Ho Chi Minh City (HCMC).

The work of contemporary painters and photographers covers a wide swath of styles and gives a glimpse into the modern Vietnamese psyche.

Youth culture is most vibrant in HCMC where there is more freedom for musicians and artists. There are small hip-hop, rock, punk, reggae and DJ scenes. Hot bands include rock band Microwave, metal merchants Black Infinity, the punk band Giao Chi and alt-roots band 6789. Skank The Tank and Sub Elements are two leading reggae sound systems based in Hanoi.

ARCHITECTURE

The Vietnamese were not great builders like their neighbours the Khmer. Most early Vietnamese buildings were made of wood and other materials that proved highly vulnerable in the tropical climate. The grand exceptions are the stunning towers built by Vietnam's ancient Cham culture. These are most numerous in central Vietnam. The Cham ruins at My Son are a major draw.

SCULPTURE

Vietnamese sculpture has traditionally centred on religious themes and has functioned as an adjunct to architecture, especially that of pagodas, temples and tombs.

The Cham civilisation produced exquisite carved sandstone figures for its Hindu and Buddhist sanctuaries. The largest single collection of Cham sculpture is at the Museum of Cham Sculpture in Danang.

WATER PUPPETRY

Vietnam's ancient art of *roi nuoc* (water puppetry) originated in northern Vietnam at least a thousand years ago. Developed by rice farmers, the wooden puppets were

---

THERE'S SOMETHING FISHY AROUND HERE...

Nuoc mam (fish sauce) is the one ingredient that is quintessentially Vietnamese and it lends a distinctive character to Vietnamese cooking. The sauce is made by fermenting highly salted fish in large ceramic vats for four to 12 months. Connoisseurs insist high-grade sauce has a much milder aroma than the cheaper variety. Dissenters insist it is a chemical weapon. It's very often used as a dipping sauce, and takes the place of salt on a Western table.

---

manipulated by puppeteers using water-flooded rice paddies as their stage. Hanoi is the best place to see water-puppetry performances, which are accompanied by music played on traditional instruments.

Food & Drink

Vietnamese food is one of the world's greatest cuisines; there are said to be nearly 500 traditional dishes. It varies a lot between north, central and south. Soy sauce, Chinese influence and hearty soups like *pho* typify northern cuisine. Central Vietnamese food is known for its prodigious use of fresh herbs and intricate flavours; Hue imperial cuisine and Hoi An specialities are key to this area. Southern food is sweet, spicy and tropical; its curries will be familiar to lovers of Thai and Cambodian food. Everywhere you'll find Vietnamese meals are superbly prepared and excellent value.

Fruit

Aside from the usual delightful Southeast Asian fruits, Vietnam has its own unique *trai thang long* (green dragon fruit), a bright fuchsia-coloured fruit with green scales. Grown mainly along the coastal region near Nha Trang, it has white flesh flecked with edible black seeds, and tastes something like a mild kiwifruit.

Meals

Pho is the noodle soup that built a nation and is eaten at all hours of the day, but especially for breakfast. *Com* are rice dishes.

You'll see signs saying *pho* and *com* everywhere. Other noodle soups to try are *bun bo Hue* and *hu tieu*.

Spring rolls (*nem* in the north, *cha gio* in the south) are a speciality. These are normally dipped in *nuoc mam* (fish sauce), though many foreigners prefer soy sauce (*xi dau* in the north, *nuoc tuong* in the south).

Because Buddhist monks of the Mahayana tradition are strict vegetarians, *an chay* (vegetarian cooking) is an integral part of Vietnamese cuisine.

Snacks

Street stalls or roaming vendors are everywhere, selling steamed sweet potatoes, rice porridge and ice-cream bars even in the wee hours.

There are also many other Vietnamese nibbles to try:

Bap xao Made from fresh, stir-fried corn, chillies and tiny shrimp.

Bo bia Nearly microscopic shrimp, fresh lettuce and thin slices of Vietnamese sausage rolled up in rice paper and dipped in a spicy-sweet peanut sauce.

Sinh to Shakes made with milk and sugar or yoghurt, and fresh tropical fruit.

Sweets

Many sticky confections are made from sticky rice, like *banh it nhan dau,* made with sugar and bean paste and sold wrapped in banana leaf.

Most foreigners prefer *kem* (ice cream) or *yaourt* (yoghurt), which is generally of good quality.

Try *che,* a cold, refreshing sweet soup made with sweetened beans (black or green) or corn. It's served in a glass with ice and sweet coconut cream on top.

Drink

ALCOHOLIC DRINKS

Memorise the words *bia hoi,* which mean 'draught beer' – it's probably the cheapest beer in the world. Starting at around 5000d a glass, anyone can afford a round. Places that serve *bia hoi* usually also serve cheap food.

Several foreign labels brewed in Vietnam under licence include Tiger, Carlsberg and Heineken.

National and regional brands include Halida and Hanoi in the north, Huda and Larue in the centre, and BGI and 333 (*ba ba ba*) in the south of the country.

Wine and spirits are available but at higher prices. Local brews are cheaper but not always drinkable.

NONALCOHOLIC DRINKS

Whatever you drink, make sure that it's been boiled or bottled. Ice is generally safe on the tourist trail, but not guaranteed elsewhere.

Vietnamese *ca phe* (coffee) is fine stuff and there is no shortage of cafes in which to sample it.

Foreign soft drinks are widely available in Vietnam. An excellent local treat is *soda chanh* (carbonated mineral water with lemon and sugar) or *nuoc chanh nong* (hot, sweetened lemon juice).

Environment

Environmental consciousness is low in Vietnam. Rapid industrialisation, deforestation and pollution are major problems facing the country.

RHINO HORN & VIETNAM

International pressure is growing. In 2013 the WWF and Traffic (the wildlife trade monitoring network) launched a campaign in Vietnam to counter rhino horn sale and consumption, declaring that the country needed to 'clean up its act'. Some Vietnamese still believe rhino horn can do everything from increasing libido to cure cancer. Even the tragic news about the extinction of the rhino in Vietnam has failed to curb domestic demand.

Vietnamese gangs have stolen antique rhino horns from museum displays across Europe, and provoked a rhino poaching crisis in South Africa.

A media campaign was launched in 2013 to try to change mindsets and make the consumption of rhino horn unacceptable. **ENV** (Education for Nature-Vietnam; www.envietnam.org) is coordinating the efforts. For more information consult Save the Rhino (www. savetherhino.org) and the **Rhinose Foundation** (www.rhinoseday.com).

Unsustainable logging and farming practices, as well as the extensive spraying of defoliants by the US during the American War, have contributed to deforestation. This has resulted not only in significant loss of biological diversity, but also in a harder existence for many minority people.

The country's rapid economic and population growth over the last decade – demonstrated by the dramatic increase in industrial production, motorbike numbers and helter-skelter construction – has put additional pressure on the already-stressed environment.

The Land

Vietnam stretches more than 1600km along the east coast of the Indochinese peninsula. The country's land area is 329,566 sq km, making it slightly larger than Italy and a bit smaller than Japan.

As the Vietnamese are quick to point out, it resembles a *don ganh* – the ubiquitous bamboo pole with a basket of rice slung from each end. The baskets represent the main rice-growing regions of the Red River Delta in the north and the Mekong Delta in the south.

Of several interesting geological features found in Vietnam, the most striking are its spectacular karst formations (limestone peaks with caves and underground streams). The northern half of Vietnam has a spectacular array of karst areas, particularly around Halong Bay, Tam Coc and Phong Nha.

Wildlife

We'll start with the good news. Despite some disastrous bouts of deforestation, Vietnam's flora and fauna is still incredibly exotic and varied. The nation has an estimated 12,000 plant species, only 7000 of which have been identified, and more than 275 species of mammal, 800 species of bird, 180 species of reptile and 80 species of amphibian.

The other side of the story is that despite this outstanding diversity, the threat to Vietnam's remaining wildlife has never been greater due to poaching, hunting and habitat loss. Three of the nation's iconic animals – the elephant, saola and tiger – are on the brink. It's virtually certain that the last wild Vietnamese rhino was killed inside Cat Tien National Park in 2010. And for every trophy animal there are hundreds of other less 'headline' species that are being cleared from forests and reserves for the sake of profit (or hunger).

Many officials still turn a blind eye to the trade in wildlife for export and domestic consumption, though laws are in place to protect the animals. Poachers continue to profit from meeting the demand for exotic animals for pets and traditional medicines.

National Parks

There are 31 national parks, covering about 3% of Vietnam's total territory. In the north the most interesting and accessible include Cat Ba, Bai Tu Long, Ba Be and Cuc Phuong.

Heading south Phong Nha-Ke Bang, Bach Ma National Park, Yok Don National Park and Cat Tien National Park are well worth investigating.

SURVIVAL GUIDE

❶ Directory A–Z

ACCOMMODATION

In general, accommodation in Vietnam offers superb value for money and excellent facilities. In big cities and the main tourism centres you'll find everything from hostel dorm beds to uber-luxe hotels. Cleanliness standards are generally good and there are very few real dumps.

Most hotels in Vietnam quote prices in Vietnamese dong and/or US dollars. Prices are quoted in dong or dollars in reviews in this book based on the preferred currency of the particular property.

Hostel dorm beds (around US$4 to US$7) are usually the cheapest options, but these only exist in a few backpacker centres such as Nha Trang, Ho Chi Minh City (HCMC), Hue and Hanoi. Family-run guesthouses are great value; they often have private bathrooms and room rates range from US$8 to US$20. A step up from the guesthouses, minihotels typically come with more amenities, such as satellite TV.

When it comes to midrange places, flash a bit more cash and three-star touches are available, such as chic decor or access to a swimming pool.

At the top end you'll find everything from faceless but comfortable business hotels to colonial places resonating with history and lovely boutique hotels.

Be aware that some hotels apply a 10% sales tax. Check carefully before taking a room to avoid any unpleasant shocks on departure.

Accommodation is at a premium during Tet (Vietnamese New Year; late January or early

February), when the whole country is on the move and overseas Vietnamese flood back into the country. Prices can rise by 25% or more. Christmas and New Year represent another high season.

Homestays

Homestays are popular in parts of Vietnam. Often the accommodation is in a long-house or communal space with people sleeping on roll-up mattresses.

Areas that are well set up include the Mekong Delta, the White Thai villages of Mai Chau, Ba Be and the Cham Islands.

Price Ranges

The following price ranges refer to a double room with bathroom in high season. Dorm-bed prices are given individually.

$ less than 525,000d (US$25)

$$ 525,000d to 1,575,000d (US$24 to US$75d)

$$$ more than 1,575,000d (US$75)

ACTIVITIES

Vietnam's roads, rivers, sea and mountains have ample opportunity for active adventures.

Asia Outdoors (☎031-368 8450; www. asiaoutdoors.com.vn) Climbing instruction is Asia Outdoors' real expertise, but it also offers excellent, well-structured boating, kayaking, biking and hiking trips.

Handspan Adventure Travel (☎04-3926 2828; www.handspan.com) If you're really keen on kayaking in Halong Bay, contact specialist operator Handspan which runs professionally organised trips, has qualified guides and operates two beach camps.

Sinhbalo Adventures (www.sinhbalo.com) Specialises in cycling tours to the Mekong Delta and beyond, plus trips to the central and northern highlands.

BOOKS

➜ *The Quiet American* (Graham Greene; 1955) Classic account of Vietnam in the 1950s as the French empire is collapsing.

➜ *The Sorrow of War* (Bao Ninh; 1994) A deeply poignant tale told from the North Vietnamese perspective.

➜ *Shadows and Wind* (Robert Templer; 1999) Snappily-written exploration of Vietnam.

➜ *Catfish & Mandala* (Andrew X Pham; 1999) Biographical tale of a Vietnamese-American.

➜ *Vietnam: Rising Dragon* (Bill Hayton; 2010) Candid assessment of the nation today.

CHILDREN

Children get to have a good time in Vietnam. There are some great beaches, but pay close attention to any playtime in the sea, as there are some strong rip tides.

Kids generally enjoy local cuisine, which is rarely too spicy; the range of fruit is staggering. Western comfort food from home (pizzas, pasta, burgers and ice cream) is available in most places.

Baby supplies are available in the major cities. Cot beds are rare, and car safety seats virtually non-existent. Breastfeeding in public is fine.

The main worry throughout Vietnam is keeping an eye on what infants put in their mouths: remember dysentery, typhoid and hepatitis are common. Keep hydration levels up, and apply sunscreen regularly.

ELECTRICITY

220V, 50 cycles. Sockets are two pin, round head.

EMBASSIES & CONSULATES

Australian Embassy (☎04-3774 0100; www. vietnam.embassy.gov.au; 8 Đ Dao Tan, Ba Dinh District, Hanoi)

Australian Consulate (Map p132; ☎08-3521 8100; 5th fl, 5B Đ Ton Duc Thang, HCMC)

Cambodian Embassy (Map p50; camemb. vnm@mfa.gov.kh; 71A P Tran Hung Dao, Hanoi)

Cambodian Consulate (Map p134; ☎08-3829 2751; 41 Đ Phung Khac Khoan, HCMC)

Canadian Embassy (Map p50; www.canada international.gc.ca/vietnam; 31 Đ Hung Vuong, Hanoi)

Canadian Consulate (Map p132; ☎08-3827 9899; www.canadainternational.gc.ca/vietnam; 10th fl, 235 Đ Dong Khoi, HCMC)

Chinese Embassy (Map p50; ☎04-8845 3736; http://vn.china-embassy.org/chn; 46 P Hoang Dieu, Hanoi)

Chinese Consulate (Map p130; ☎08-3829 2457; 39 Đ Nguyen Thi Minh Khai, HCMC)

French Embassy (Map p50; ☎04-3944 5700; www.ambafrance-vn.org; P Tran Hung Dao, Hanoi)

French Consulate (Map p134; 27 Đ Nguyen Thi Minh Khai, HCMC)

German Embassy (Map p50; ☎04-3845 3836; www.hanoi.diplo.de; 29 Đ Tran Phu, Hanoi)

German Consulate (Map p134; ☎08-3829 1967; www.hanoi.diplo.de; 126 Đ Nguyen Dinh Chieu, HCMC)

Japanese Embassy (☎04-3846 3000; www. vn.emb-japan.go.jp; 27 P Lieu Giai, Ba Dinh District, Hanoi)

Japanese Consulate (Map p132; ☎08-3822 5341; 13-17 ĐL Nguyen Hue, HCMC)

Laotian Embassy (Map p50; ☎04-3942 4576; www.embalaohanoi.gov.la; 22 P Tran Binh Trong, Hanoi)

Laotian Consulate (Map p132; ☎08-3829 7667; 93 Đ Pasteur, HCMC)

Netherlands Embassy (Map p50; ☎04-3831 5650; www.netherlands-embassy.org; 6th fl, Daeha Office Tower, 360 Kim Ma St, Ba Dinh, Hanoi)

Netherlands Consulate (Map p134; ☎08-3823 5932; Saigon Tower, 29 ĐL Le Duan, HCMC)

New Zealand Embassy (Map p56; ☎04-3824 1481; www.nzembassy.com/viet-nam; Level 5, 63 P Ly Thai To, Hanoi)

New Zealand Consulate (Map p132; ☎08-3827 2745; 8th fl, The Metropolitan, 235 Đ Dong Khoi, HCMC)

Thai Embassy (Map p50; ☎04-3823 5092; www.thaiembassy.org; 3-65 P Hoang Dieu, Hanoi)

Thai Consulate (Map p130; ☎08-3932 7637; 77 Đ Tran Quoc Thao, HCMC)

UK Embassy (Map p56; ☎04-3936 0500; ukinvietnam.fco.gov.uk; Central Bldg, 31 P Hai Ba Trung, Hanoi)

UK Consulate (Map p134; ☎08-3829 8433; 25 ĐL Le Duan, HCMC)

US Embassy (☎04-3850 5000; vietnam. usembassy.gov; 7 P Lang Ha, Ba Dinh District, Hanoi)

US Consulate (Map p134; ☎08-3822 9433; hochiminh.usconsulate.gov; 4 ĐL Le Duan, HCMC)

FOOD & DRINK

The following price ranges refer to a typical meal (excluding drinks). Unless otherwise stated, taxes are included in the price.

$ less than 105,400d (US$5)

$$ 105,400d to 316,300d (US$5 to US$15)

$$$ more than 316,300d (US$15)

GAY & LESBIAN TRAVELLERS

Vietnam is pretty hassle-free for gay travellers. There's not much in the way of harassment, nor are there official laws on same-sex relationships.

Hanoi's first Gay Pride march was held in 2012. Indeed, in 2013 the government started a consultation process about legalising same-sex marriages.

Checking into hotels as a same-sex couple is perfectly OK. But be discreet – public displays of affection are not socially acceptable whatever your sexual orientation.

Check out **Utopia** (www.utopia-asia.com) to obtain contacts and some useful travel information.

INSURANCE

Insurance is a *must* for Vietnam, as the cost of major medical treatment is prohibitive. A travel insurance policy to cover theft, loss and medical problems is the best bet.

Some insurance policies specifically exclude such 'dangerous activities' as riding motorbikes, diving and even trekking. Check that the policy covers an emergency evacuation in the event of serious injury.

Worldwide travel insurance is available at www.lonelyplanet.com/travel-insurance. You can buy, extend and claim online anytime – even if you're already on the road.

LEGAL MATTERS

If you lose something really valuable such as your passport or visa, you'll need to contact the police. Few foreigners experience much hassle from police and demands for bribes are rare – it's a different story for the Vietnamese though...

The Vietnamese government is seriously cracking down on the burgeoning drug trade. You may face imprisonment and/or large fines for drug offences, and drug trafficking can be punishable by death.

MAPS

The road atlas *Tap Ban Do Giao Thong Duong Bo Viet Nam* is the best available, but the latest roads are not included. It's available in bookstores including Fahasa and costs 220,000d.

MONEY

Vietnam's official currency is the dong (d). For the last few years the dong has been fairly stable at around 21,000d to the dollar. US dollars are also widely used.

Tipping isn't expected, but it's appreciated.

ATMs

ATMs are widespread. They're present in virtually every town in the country and accept foreign cards. Watch out for stiff withdrawal fees (typically 20,000d to 30,000d) and low withdrawal limits – most are around 3,000,000d, but Agribank allows up to 6,000,000d.

Bargaining

For *xe om* and *cyclo* trips, as well as anywhere that prices aren't posted, bargaining is possible. In tourist hotspots, you may be quoted as much as five times the going price, but not everyone is trying to rip you off. In less-travelled areas, foreigners are often quoted the Vietnamese price, but you can still bargain a little bit.

Credit & Debit Cards

Visa and MasterCard are accepted in most top hotels, upmarket restaurants and shops but not in many budget places. Commission charges (around 3%) sometimes apply.

For cash advances, try branches of Vietcombank in cities or Sinh Tourist travel agencies. Expect at least a 3% commission for this service.

OPENING HOURS

Vietnamese people rise early and consider sleeping in to be a sure indication of illness.

Lunch is taken very seriously and many government offices close between 11.30am and 2pm.

Banks 8am to 3pm weekdays, to 11.30am Saturday

Offices and museums 7am or 8am to 5pm or 6pm; museums generally close on Monday

Restaurants 11.30am to 9pm

Shops 8am to 6pm

Temples and pagodas 5am to 9pm

PHOTOGRAPHY

Memory cards are pretty cheap in Vietnam. Most internet cafes can also burn photos onto a CD or DVD to free up storage space. Photo-processing shops and internet cafes in bigger cities can burn digital photos onto DVDs. Colour print film is widely available; slide film is available in HCMC and Hanoi.

Vietnam's gorgeous scenery and unique character makes for memorable photographs. Inspiration will surely strike when you see a row of colourfully dressed hill-tribe women walking to market, but remember to maintain an appropriate level of respect for the people and places you visit. Ask permission before snapping a photo of someone.

PUBLIC HOLIDAYS

Politics affects everything, including many public holidays, in Vietnam. If a Vietnamese public holiday falls on a weekend, it is observed on the following Monday.

New Year's Day (Tet Duong Lich) 1 January

Vietnamese New Year (Tet) A three-day national holiday; late January or February

Anniversary of the Founding of the Vietnamese Communist Party (Thanh Lap Dang CSVN) 3 February – the date the Party was founded in 1930

Hung Kings Commemorations (Hung Vuong) 10th day of the 3rd lunar month; late March or April

Liberation Day (Saigon Giai Phong) 30 April – the date on which Saigon's surrender is commemorated nationwide as Liberation Day

International Workers' Day (Quoc Te Lao Dong) 1 May

Ho Chi Minh's Birthday (Sinh Nhat Bac Ho) 19 May

Buddha's Birthday (Phat Dan) Eighth day of the fourth lunar month (usually June)

National Day (Quoc Khanh) 2 September – commemorates the Declaration of Independence by Ho Chi Minh in 1945

SAFE TRAVEL

All in all, Vietnam is an extremely safe country to travel in. Sure, there are scams and hassles in some cities, particularly in Hanoi and Nha Trang, but overall the police keep a pretty tight grip on social order and we very rarely receive reports about muggings, armed robberies and sexual assaults.

Watch out for petty theft. Drive-by bag snatchers on motorbikes are not uncommon, and thieves patrol buses, trains and boats. Don't be flash with cameras and jewellery.

Since 1975 many thousands of Vietnamese have been maimed or killed by rockets, artillery shells, mortars, mines and other ordnance left over from the war. Stick to defined paths and *never* touch any suspicious war relic you might come across.

TELEPHONE

A mobile (cell) phone with a local SIM card and a Skype account will allow you to keep in touch economically with anyone in the world.

International Calls

It's usually cheapest to use a mobile phone to make international phone calls – rates can be as little as US$0.10 a minute.

Many budget hotels also operate cheap webcall services, as do post offices.

Of course, using services such as Skype costs next to nothing, and many budget and midrange hotels now have Skype and webcams set up for their guests.

Directory assistance (☎116)

General information (☎1080)

International operator (☎110)

International prefix (☎00)

Time (☎117)

Local Calls

Phone numbers in Hanoi, HCMC and Haiphong have eight digits. Elsewhere around the country phone numbers have seven digits. Telephone area codes are assigned according to the province.

Local calls from hotels are often free – though confirm this first!

Mobile Phones

Vietnam has an excellent, comprehensive cellular network. The nation uses GSM 900/1800, which is compatible with most of Asia, Europe and Australia, but not with North America.

Viet Sim Cards

It's well worth getting a local SIM card if you're planning to spend any time in Vietnam: you'll be able to send texts (SMS) anywhere in the world for between 500d to 2500d per message. Local handsets are available for as little as US$30, often with US$15 of credit included.

There are three main mobile phone companies (Viettel, Vinaphone and Mobifone), all with offices nationwide.

Roaming

If your phone has roaming, it's easy enough (although it can be outrageously expensive) to use your handset in Vietnam – particularly if you use the internet.

TIME

Vietnam is seven hours ahead of Greenwich Mean Time/Universal Time Coordinated (GMT/UTC); there's no daylight-saving or summer time.

TOILETS

Western-style sit-down toilets are the norm but the odd squat bog still survives in some cheap hotels and bus stations. Hotels usually supply a roll of toilet paper, but it's wise to bring your own while on the road.

TOURIST INFORMATION

Tourist offices in Vietnam have a different philosophy from the majority of tourist offices worldwide. These government-owned enterprises are really travel agencies whose primary interests are booking tours and turning a profit.

Travellers' cafes, travel agencies and your fellow travellers are a much better source of information than most of the so-called tourist offices.

VISAS

Most nationalities need a visa (or approval letter) in order to enter Vietnam. Entry and exit points include Hanoi, HCMC and Danang airports, or any of the plentiful land borders shared with Cambodia, China and Laos.

Tourist visas are valid for a 30- or 90-day stay (and can be single or multiple entry). Online visa agents provide a more efficient, cheaper and quicker service than Vietnamese embassies for those flying into Vietnam.

If you plan to exit Vietnam and enter again from Cambodia or Laos, arrange a 90-day multiple-entry visa (around US$110).

In our experience, personal appearance influences the reception you'll receive from airport immigration – try your best to look 'respectable'.

Visa Extensions

If you've got the dollars, they've got the rubber stamp. Tourist-visa extensions officially cost as little as US$10, but it's advisable to pay more and go via a travel agency as the bureaucracy is deep. The process can take seven days, and extensions are 30 to 90 days.

Extensions are best organised in major cities such as HCMC, Hanoi, Danang and Hue.

Multiple-Entry Visas

It's possible to enter Cambodia or Laos from Vietnam and then re-enter without having to apply for another visa. However, you must apply for a multiple-entry visa *before* you leave Vietnam.

If you arrived in Vietnam on a single-entry visa, multiple-entry visas are easiest to arrange in Hanoi or HCMC, but you will have to ask a visa or travel agent to do the paperwork for you. Agents charge about US$45 for the service and visa fees are charged on top of this – the procedure takes up to seven days.

Multiple-entry visas are easiest to arrange in Hanoi or HCMC, but you will almost certainly have to ask a travel agent to do the paperwork for you. Travel agents charge about US$45, and the procedure takes up to seven days.

Visa on Arrival

Citizens of the following countries do not need to apply in advance for a Vietnamese visa if arriving by air. Always double-check visa requirements before you travel as policies change regularly.

COUNTRY	DAYS
Myanmar, Brunei	14
Thailand, Malaysia, Singapore, Indonesia, Laos, Cambodia	30
Philippines	21
Japan, South Korea, Russia, Norway, Denmark, Sweden, Finland	15

VOLUNTEERING

Opportunities for voluntary work are quite limited in Vietnam as there are so many professional development staff based here.

For information, chase up the full list of nongovernment organisations (NGOs) at the **NGO Resource Centre** (04-3832 8570; www.ngocentre.org.vn; Room 201, Bldg E3, 6 Dang Van Ngu, Trung Tu Diplomatic Compound, Dong Da, Hanoi), which keeps a database of all of the NGOs assisting Vietnam. **Service Civil International** (www.sciint.org) has links to options in Vietnam.

You can donate your skills, time or money to **KOTO** (www.koto.com.au), which helps give street children career opportunities in its restaurants in Hanoi or HCMC; a three-month minimum commitment is required.

Volunteers for Peace (www.vpv.vn) is always looking for volunteers to help in an orphanage on the outskirts of Hanoi.

WOMEN TRAVELLERS

While it always pays to be prudent (avoid dark lonely alleys at night), foreign women rarely report problems in Vietnam. That said, you may receive unwanted (although usually pretty harmless) advances if travelling alone. Be aware that exposing your upper arms (by wearing a vest top) will attract plenty of attention – local women rarely expose much flesh.

East Asian women travelling in Vietnam may want to dress quite conservatively. Very occasionally some ill-educated locals may think an Asian woman accompanying a Western male could be a Vietnamese prostitute.

Most Vietnamese women enjoy relatively free, fulfilled lives and a career. The sexes mix freely and society does not expect women to behave in a subordinate manner.

WORK

At least 90% of foreign travellers seeking work in Vietnam end up teaching English, though there is some demand for French teachers too. Pay can be as low as US$7 per hour at a university and up to US$20 per hour at a private academy.

It's best to arrange a business visa if you plan on job hunting.

❶ Getting There & Away

Most travellers enter Vietnam by plane or bus, but there are also train links from China and boat connections from Cambodia via the Mekong River.

Flights, car hire and tours can be booked online at www.lonelyplanet.com/bookings.

ENTERING VIETNAM

Formalities at Vietnam's international airports are generally smoother than at land borders. Crossing overland from Cambodia and China is now also relatively stress-free. Crossing the border between Vietnam and Laos can be slow.

AIR

Airports

There are three main international airports in Vietnam and a few others (Hue, Phu Quoc) which see the odd charter.

Tan Son Nhat Airport (☏ 08-3845 6654; www. tsnairport.com; Ho Chi Minh City) Vietnam's busiest international air hub.

Noi Bai Airport (☏ 04-3827 1513; Hanoi) Serves the capital.

Danang Airport (☏ 0511-383 0339) International flights to China, Laos and Cambodia.

Airlines

Vietnam Airlines (www.vietnamairlines.com. vn) is the state-owned flag carrier and has flights to many international destinations on modern airplanes.

LAND & RIVER

Vietnam shares land border crossings with Cambodia, China and Laos. Vietnam visas were not available at any land borders at the time of research.

Cambodia

Cambodia and Vietnam share a long frontier with seven (and counting) border crossings. One-month Cambodian visas are issued on arrival at all border crossings for US$20, but overcharging is common except at Bavet (the most popular crossing).

There's also a river border crossing between Cambodia and Vietnam at Kaam Samnor–Vinh Xuong on the banks of the Mekong. Regular fast boats ply the route between Phnom Penh in Cambodia and Chau Doc in Vietnam via this border.

Most Cambodian border crossings are generally open daily between 8am and 8pm.

China

There are three border checkpoints where foreigners are permitted to cross between Vietnam and China: Lao Cai, Huu Nghi Quan (the Friendship Pass) and Mong Cai.

International trains link China and Vietnam, connecting Hanoi with Nanning in Guangxi Province – and even on to Beijing!

VIETNAM VISA AGENTS

If you're flying into Vietnam it's usually easiest and cheapest to get your visa approved through an online visa-service company. This system does *not* operate at land border crossings.

They will need passport details, and will email you an approval document two to three days later (one day for rush service), which you need to print and bring with you to the airport. On arrival, present the approval document and passport picture, then pay a stamping fee (US$45 for single-entry, US$65 to US$95 for multiple-entry visas). Many travellers prefer this method since they don't have to deal with bureaucratic hassles or give up their passport, and it's usually cheaper than using a Vietnamese embassy based in the West.

Recommended companies include **Vietnam Visa Choice** (www.vietnamvisachoice. com) and **Vietnam Visa Center** (www.vietnamvisacenter.org).

It is necessary to arrange a Chinese visa in advance.

Laos

There are seven (and counting) overland crossings between Vietnam and Laos. Thirty-day Lao visas are now available at all borders. All of the border crossings between north and central Vietnam and Laos have a degree of difficulty. Lao Bao is the simplest route.

The golden rule is to try to use direct city-to-city bus connections between the countries, as potential hassle will be greatly reduced. If you travel step-by-step using local buses expect hassle and transport scams (eg serious overcharging) on the Vietnamese side. Devious drivers have even stopped in the middle of nowhere to renegotiate the price.

Transport links on both sides of the border can be very hit and miss, so don't use the more remote borders unless you have plenty of time to spare.

ⓘ Getting Around

AIR

Vietnam has good domestic flight connections, and very affordable prices (if you book early). Airlines accept bookings on international credit or debit cards. However, note that cancellations are not unknown.

Vietnam Airlines (www.vietnamairlines.com.vn) The leading local carrier with the most comprehensive network and best reliability.

Vietjet Air (⌁1900 1886; www.vietjetair.com) A new, privately owned airline with an expanding number of internal flights.

Jetstar Pacific (www.jetstar.com/vn/en/home) This budget airline has very affordable fares, though only serves the main cities.

Vasco (www.vasco.com.vn) Flies to the Con Dao Islands from HCMC.

BICYCLE

Bikes are a great way to get around Vietnam, particularly when you get off the main highways.

The main hazard is the traffic, and it's wise to avoid certain areas (notably Hwy 1). Some of the best cycling is along quiet coastal roads in central Vietnam, in the southwest highlands and up in the northern mountains (although you'll have to cope with some big hills).

Purchasing a good bicycle in Vietnam is hit and miss. It's recommended that you bring one from abroad, along with a good helmet and spare parts.

Bicycles can also be hired locally from guesthouses for about US$2 per day, while good-quality mountain bikes cost US$10 to US$12.

BOAT

The extensive network of canals in the Mekong Delta makes getting around by boat feasible in the far south. Travellers to Phu Quoc Island can catch ferries from Ha Tien or Rach Gia.

In the country's northeast, hydrofoils connect Haiphong with Cat Ba Island (near Halong Bay), and cruises on Halong Bay are extremely popular. Day trips to islands off the coast of Nha Trang, to the Chams off Hoi An, and in Lan Ha Bay are also good excursions.

BUS

Vietnam has an extensive network of buses that reach the far-flung corners of the country. Modern buses, operated by myriad companies, run on all the main highways.

Many travellers (perhaps the majority) never actually visit a Vietnamese bus station at all, preferring to stick to the convenient, tourist-friendly open-tour bus network.

Whichever class of bus you're on, bus travel in Vietnam is never speedy; reckon on just 50kmh on major routes including Hwy 1.

Bus Stations

Many cities have several bus stations, so make sure you get the right one! Bus stations all look chaotic but many now have ticket offices with official prices and departure times displayed.

Reservations & Costs

Always buy a ticket from the office, as bus drivers are notorious for overcharging. Reservations aren't usually required for most of the frequent, popular services between towns and cities.

On rural runs, foreigners are typically charged anywhere from twice to 10 times the going rate. As a benchmark, a typical 100km ride is between US$2 and US$3.

Deluxe Buses

On most popular routes, modern air-conditioned Korean and Chinese deluxe buses offer comfortable reclining seats or sleeper beds for really long trips. Deluxe buses are nonsmoking. On the flip side, most of them are equipped with blaring TVs and some with dreaded karaoke machines.

Open Tours

Connecting backpacker haunts across the nation, open tour buses are wildly popular in Vietnam. These air-con buses depart from convenient, centrally located departure points and allow you to hop-on, hop-off at any major city along the main north-to-south route.

Prices are reasonable. A through ticket from Ho Chi Minh City (Saigon) to Hanoi costs between US$25 and US$49, while Nha Trang to Hoi An is around US$12.

Travellers' cafes, tour agencies and budget hotels sell tickets. **Sinh Tourist** (☑ 08-3838 9597; www.thesinhtourist.com) started the concept and has a good reputation.

Local Buses

Local buses in the countryside are slow and stop frequently. Conductors tend to routinely overcharge foreigners on these services, so they're not popular with travellers.

CAR & MOTORCYCLE

Having your own wheels gives you maximum flexibility to visit remote regions and to stop when and where you please. Car hire always includes a driver. Motorbike hire is good value and this can be self-drive or with a driver.

Driving Licence

In order to drive a car in Vietnam, you need a Vietnamese licence and an International Driving Permit (IDP). However, all rental companies only rent out cars with drivers.

When it comes to renting motorbikes, the whole situation is a grey area. An IDP and a motorbike licence (which includes a test in the Vietnamese language) is officially required, but the reality on the ground is that foreigners are never asked for it by police, and no rental places ever ask to see one.

Fuel

Unleaded gasoline costs 25,000d per litre. Even isolated communities usually have someone selling petrol by the roadside.

Hire

The major considerations are safety, the mechanical condition of the vehicle, the reliability of the rental agency, and your budget.

Car & Minibus

Renting a vehicle with a driver and guide is a realistic option even for budget travellers, provided there are enough people to share the cost.

Costs per day:
Standard model US$50 to US$100
4WD/Minibus US$90 to US$130

Motorbike

Motorbikes can be rented from virtually anywhere, including cafes, hotels and travel agencies. Some places will ask to keep your passport as security. Ask for a signed agreement stating what you are renting, how much it costs, the extent of compensation and so on.

It is compulsory to wear a helmet when riding a motorbike in Vietnam, even when travelling as a passenger.

Costs per day:
Moped (semi-auto) US$4 to US$6
Moped (fully auto) US$6 to US$10
Trail and road bikes from US$15 to US$30

Plenty of local drivers will be willing to act as a chauffeur and guide for around US$10 to US$20 per day.

Insurance

If you are travelling in a tourist vehicle with a driver, then it is almost guaranteed to be insured. When it comes to motorbikes, many rental bikes are not insured and you will have to sign a contract agreeing to a valuation for the bike if it is stolen.

Road Conditions & Hazards

Road safety is definitely not one of Vietnam's strong points. Vehicles drive on the right-hand side (in theory). Size matters and small vehicles get out of the way of big vehicles. Even Hwy 1 is only a two-lane highway for most of its length and high-speed head-on collisions are all too common.

MOTORBIKE TOURS

Specialised motorbike tours offer an unrivalled way to explore Vietnam's scenic excesses on traffic-light back roads. A little experience helps, but many of the leading companies also offer tuition for first-timers.

Explore Indochina (☑ 09-1309 3159; www.exploreindochina.com) Expertly arranged trips on vintage Urals or modified Minsks. Jeep tours are also offered.

Free Wheelin' Tours (www.freewheelin-tours.com) Trips and custom-made tours utilising the company's own homestays.

Hoi An Motorbike Adventure (www.motorbiketours-hoian.com; tours US$40-1050) Specialises in short trips on well-maintained Minsk bikes.

Offroad Vietnam (☑ 04-3926 3433; www.offroadvietnam.com) Well-organised tours to remote areas of northern Vietnam. Also rents quality Honda road and trail bikes (from US$20 per day)

In general, the major highways are hard surfaced and reasonably well maintained, but seasonal flooding can be a problem. Non-paved roads are best tackled with a 4WD vehicle or motorbike. Mountain roads are particularly dangerous: landslides, falling rocks and runaway vehicles can add an unwelcome edge to your journey.

LOCAL TRANSPORT

➡ **Cyclos** are bicycle rickshaws. Drivers hang out in touristy areas and some speak broken English. Bargaining is imperative; settle on a fare before going anywhere. A short ride costs 10,000d to 30,000d in most towns.

➡ **Taxis** with meters are found in all cities and are very, very cheap by international standards and a safe way to travel around at night. Average tariffs are about 10,000d to 15,000d per kilometre. Only travel with reputable or recommended companies. **Mai Linh** (www.mailinh.vn) and **Vinasun** (www.vinasuntaxi.com) are excellent nationwide firms.

➡ **Xe om**, or motorbike taxis, are everywhere. Fares are comparable with those for a *cyclo*. Drivers hang out around street corners, markets, hotels and bus stations. They will find you before you find them...

TOURS

The following are Vietnam-based travel agencies that offer premium tours throughout Vietnam. Handspan Adventure Travel (p162) also runs innovative trips to seldom-visited regions.

Buffalo Tours (Map p52; www.buffalotours. com) Offers diverse and customised trips including a nine-day Gourmet Vietnam tour.

Ocean Tours (🕿04-3926 0463; www.ocean tours.com.vn) Well-organised tour operator with Halong Bay and Ba Be National Park options, and 4WD road trips around the northeast.

TRAIN

The Vietnamese railway system, operated by **Vietnam Railways** (Duong Sat Viet Nam; 🕿04-3747 0308; www.vr.com.vn), is an ageing, slow but fairly dependable service, and offers a relaxing way to get around the nation. Travelling in an air-con sleeping berth sure beats a hairy overnight bus journey along Hwy 1. And of course there's some spectacular scenery to lap up.

Routes

The main line connects HCMC with Hanoi. Three rail-spur lines link Hanoi with other parts of northern Vietnam: Haiphong, Lang Son, and Lao Cai.

The journey between Hanoi and HCMC takes from 30 to 41 hours, depending on the train.

Classes & Costs

Trains classified as SE are the smartest and fastest. There are four main ticket classes: hard seat, soft seat, hard sleeper and soft sleeper. These are also split into air-con and non air-con options. Presently, air-con is only available on the faster express trains. Hard-seat class is usually packed, and is tolerable for day travel, but expect plenty of cigarette smoke.

Ticket prices vary depending on the train; the fastest trains are the most expensive.

Reservations

Reservations should be made at least one day in advance, especially for sleeping berths. You'll need to bring your passport when buying train tickets.

Schedules, fares, information and advance bookings are available at **Vietnam Railway** (www.vietnam-railway.com) and **Vietnam Impressive** (www.vietnamimpressive.com), two dependable private booking agents. They'll deliver tickets to your hotel in Vietnam, free of charge (or can send them abroad using DHL for a fee).

Many travel agencies, hotels and cafes also sell train tickets for a small commission.

Cambodia

♪ 855 / POP 15.5 MILLION

Includes ➡

Best Places to Eat

Best Places to Stay

Why Go?

Ascend to the realm of the gods at Angkor Wat, a spectacular fusion of spirituality, symbolism and symmetry. Descend into the darkness of Tuol Sleng to witness the crimes of the Khmer Rouge. This is Cambodia, a country with a history both inspiring and depressing, a captivating destination that casts a spell on all those who visit.

Fringed by beautiful beaches and tropical islands, sustained by the mother waters of the Mekong River and cloaked in some of the region's few remaining emerald wildernesses, Cambodia is an adventure as much as a holiday. This is the warm heart of Southeast Asia, with everything the region has to offer packed into one bite-sized chunk.

Despite the headline attractions, Cambodia's greatest treasure is its people. The Khmers have been to hell and back, but thanks to an unbreakable spirit and infectious optimism, they have prevailed with their smiles and spirits largely intact.

When to Go

Phnom Penh

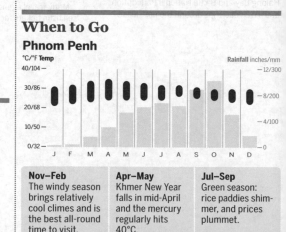

Nov–Feb	Apr–May	Jul–Sep
The windy season brings relatively cool climes and is the best all-round time to visit.	Khmer New Year falls in mid-April and the mercury regularly hits 40°C.	Green season: rice paddies shimmer, and prices plummet.

Connections

By air, Cambodia can be reached from most major Asian hubs, but there are no direct flights from North America or Europe. The country shares several border crossings with Vietnam and Thailand, both of which can be reached painlessly and cheaply by bus from various Cambodian cities. Buses to Thailand generally require a change at the border, while Vietnam-bound buses are usually through buses. The two most popular bus routes are Siem Reap to Bangkok and Phnom Penh to Ho Chi Minh City (Saigon). The latter can also be done by boat. To get to Laos overland, you must travel via the fairly remote Nong Nok Khiene/Trapeang Kriel crossing, which connects Stung Treng in northeast Cambodia with southern Laos.

ITINERARIES

One Week
Soak up the sights, sounds and smells of **Phnom Penh**, Cambodia's dynamic and fast-changing capital. Travel by road to **Siem Reap**, gateway to the majestic temples of **Angkor**, passing by the pre-Angkorian temples of Sambor Prei Kuk or taking a longer detour via the charming colonial-era city of **Battambang**. Explore Angkor in depth; no one does temples quite like Cambodia.

Two Weeks
After exploring Phnom Penh and Siem Reap for a week, hit the provinces. Those heading to Thailand should head south to Cambodia's up-and-coming coastline. Soak up the languid charms of **Kampot** and **Kep**, then head to **Sihanoukville**, where dreamy islands lurk offshore. Try some adrenalin adventures around **Koh Kong** before exiting the country. Laos- or Vietnam-bound travellers can easily spend a week in the wild east, trekking in **Ratanakiri** or **Mondulkiri** and tracking rare Irrawaddy dolphins on the Mekong River around **Kratie** or **Stung Treng**.

Internet Resources

➡ **Phnom Penh Post** (www.phnompenhpost.com) The online version of Cambodia's newspaper of record.

➡ **Cambodia Daily** (www.cambodiadaily.com) Hard-hitting journalism; most articles are truncated online, so buy the print version (1800r).

➡ **Khmer440** (www.khmer440.com) The expats' forum of choice, plus travel news and events listings.

➡ **Cambodia Tribunal Monitor** (www.cambodiatribunal.org) Detailed coverage of the Khmer Rouge trials.

➡ **Andy's Cambodia** (http://blog.andybrouwer.co.uk) Gateway to all things Cambodian; includes a popular blog.

NEED TO KNOW

➡ **Currency** Riel (r)

➡ **Language** Khmer

➡ **Money** ATMs common in major cities

➡ **Visas** Available on arrival for most nationalities

➡ **Mobile phones** Prepaid SIM cards are cheap, but you need a passport to register

CAMBODIA

Fast Facts

➡ **Area** 181,035 sq km

➡ **Capital** Phnom Penh

➡ **Country Code** ☏855

➡ **Emergency** Police ☏117

Exchange Rates

Australia	A$1	3580r
Euro Zone	C$1	5440r
Laos	10,000K	4970r
Thailand	10B	1220r
UK	£1	6595r
USA	US$1	3960r
Vietnam	10,000d	1880r

Set Your Budget

➡ **Budget hotel room** US$5–15

➡ **Decent restaurant meal** US$5–10

➡ **Beer in bar** US$1–2

➡ **Short moto ride** US$0.50

Cambodia Highlights

1 Discover the eighth wonder of the world, **Angkor** (p205)

2 Enjoy the 'Pearl of Asia', **Phnom Penh** (p174), with striking museums, a sublime riverside setting and happening nightlife

3 Island-hop around **Sihanoukville** (p243) and soak up the city's hedonistic vibe

4 Wander around the lush **Battambang** (p216) countryside, climbing hilltop temples and exploring caves

5 Explore wild **Mondulkiri** (p237), a land of rolling hills, thundering waterfalls and indigenous minorities

6 Slip into the soporific pace of riverside **Kampot** (p252)

7 Make the pilgrimage to the awe-inspiring hilltop temple of **Prasat Preah Vihear** (p224)

8 Explore the bucolic Mekong islands and dolphin pools around **Kratie** (p228) by bicycle and boat

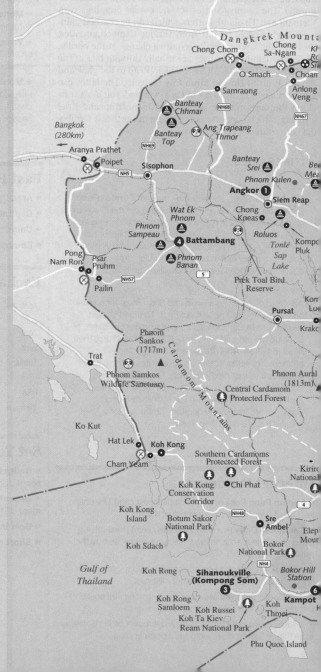

PHNOM PENH

♪ 023 / POP 1.5 MILLION

Phnom Penh (ភ្នំ ពេញ): the name can't help but conjure up an image of the exotic. The glimmering spires of the Royal Palace, the fluttering saffron of the monks' robes and the luscious location on the banks of the mighty Mekong – this is the Asia many dreamed of when first imagining their adventures overseas.

Once the 'Pearl of Asia', Phnom Penh's shine was tarnished by war and revolution. But that's history and the city has risen from the ashes to take its place among the 'in' capitals of Asia, with an alluring cafe culture, bustling bars and a world-class food scene. Whatever your flavour, no matter your taste, it's all here in Phnom Penh.

◉ Sights

★ **Royal Palace** PALACE
(ព្រះវិមានព្រះកែវមរកត; Map p176; Sothearos Blvd; admission incl camera/video 25,000r, guide per hr US$10; ☺ 8-11am & 2-5pm) With its classic Khmer roofs and ornate gilding, the Royal Palace dominates the diminutive skyline of Phnom Penh. It is a striking structure near the riverfront, bearing a remarkable likeness to its counterpart in Bangkok.

Being the official residence of King Sihamoni, parts of the massive palace compound are closed to the public. Visitors are only allowed to visit the throne hall and a clutch of buildings surrounding it. Adjacent to the palace, the **Silver Pagoda** (Map p180; Sothearos Blvd; included in admission to Royal Palace; ☺ 7:30am-11am & 2.30-5pm) complex is also open to the public.

Visitors need to wear shorts that reach to the knee, and T-shirts or blouses that reach to the elbow; otherwise they will have to rent an appropriate covering. The palace

ℹ STREET NUMBERS

Phnom Penh's sequentially numbered streets may be a paragon of logic, but when it comes to house numbering, utter chaos reigns. It's not uncommon to find a row of adjacent buildings numbered, say, 13A, 34, 7, 26. Worse, several buildings on the same street, blocks apart, may have adopted the same house number! When you're given an address, try to get a cross-street, such as 'on St 240 near St 51'.

gets very busy on Sundays when countryside Khmers come to pay their respects, but this can be a fun way to experience the place, thronging with locals.

★ **National Museum of Cambodia** MUSEUM
(សារមន្ទីរជាតិ; Map p176; www.cambodiamuseum.info; cnr St 13 & St 178; admission US$5; ☺ 8am-5pm) The National Museum of Cambodia is home to the world's finest collection of Khmer sculpture, a millennium's worth and more of masterful Khmer design. Housed in a graceful, traditionally designed terracotta structure (built 1917–20), it provides the perfect backdrop to an outstanding array of delicate objects.

The museum comprises four pavilions, facing the beautiful central courtyard. Start left and continue in a clockwise, chronological direction. Most interesting are the pre-Angkorian and Angkorian collections, which include an imposing eight-armed Vishnu statue from the 6th century found at Phnom Da; several striking statues of Shiva from the 9th, 10th and 11th centuries; a giant pair of wrestling monkeys (Ko Ker, 10th century); and the sublime, oft-copied statue of a seated Jayavarman VII (r 1181–1219) meditating.

No photography is allowed except in the central courtyard.

★ **Tuol Sleng Museum** MUSEUM
(សារមន្ទីរទួលស្លែង; Map p180; cnr St 113 & St 350; admission US$2, guide US$6; ☺ 7am-5.30pm) In 1975, Tuol Svay Prey High School was taken over by Pol Pot's security forces and turned into a prison known as Security Prison 21 (S-21). This soon became the largest centre of detention and torture in the country. At the height of its activity, some 100 victims were killed every day.

The prison has been turned into the Tuol Sleng Museum, which serves as a testament to the crimes of the Khmer Rouge. Like the Nazis, the Khmer Rouge leaders were meticulous in keeping records of their barbarism. Each prisoner who passed through S-21 was photographed, sometimes before and after torture. The long corridors are hallways of ghosts containing haunting photographs of the victims, their faces staring back eerily from the past. Tuol Sleng is not for the squeamish.

French-Cambodian director Rithy Panh's powerful 1996 film *Bophana*, which tells the true story of a beautiful young woman and a regional Khmer Rouge leader who fall in

Phnom Penh

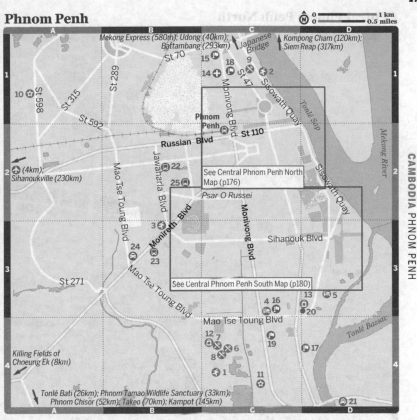

Phnom Penh

🎯 Activities, Courses & Tours
1 Cooperation Committee for Cambodia	C4
2 Cruising Boats	C1
3 Offroad Cambodia	B3

🛏 Sleeping
4 Rambutan	C3
5 Sofitel Phnom Penh Phokeethra	D3

🍽 Eating
6 Alma Cucina Mexicana	C4
7 Café Yejj	C4
8 Sesame Noodle Bar	C4
9 Tepui	C1

🎭 Entertainment
10 Apsara Arts Association	A1
11 Sovanna Phum Arts Association	C4

🛍 Shopping
Nyemo	(see 7)
Rajana	(see 7)
12 Russian Market	C4
13 Watthan Artisans	D3

ℹ Information
14 Calmette Hospital	C1
15 French Embassy	C1
16 Lao Embassy	C3
17 Thai Embassy	D4
18 UK Embassy	C1
19 Vietnamese Embassy	C4

ℹ Transport
20 Cambodia Angkor Air	D3
21 Chbah Ampeau Taxi Park	D4
Kampot Express	(see 3)
22 Kim Seng Express	B2
23 Olympic Express	B3
24 Psar Dang Kor Taxi Park	B3
25 Rith Mony	B2

Central Phnom Penh North

See Central Phnom Penh South Map (p180)

love and are consequently executed at S-21 prison, screens here at 10am and 3pm daily.

Killing Fields of Choeung Ek　MUSEUM
(វាលពិឃាតជើងឯក; admission incl audio tour US$5; ⊙ 7.30am-5.30pm) Most of the 17,000 detainees held at the S-21 prison were executed at Choeung Ek, 14km southwest of Phnom Penh. Prisoners were often bludgeoned to death to avoid wasting precious bullets.

It is hard to imagine the brutality that unfolded here when wandering through this peaceful, shady, former longan orchard, but the memorial stupa soon brings it home, displaying more than 8000 skulls of victims and their ragged clothes.

A trip out here will cost US$5 round trip on a *moto* (motorcycle taxi) or about US$10 by *remorque* (motorcycle-pulled trailer). Drivers start at US$15 to US$20.

Wat Phnom　BUDDHIST TEMPLE
(វត្តភ្នំ; Map p176; admission temple/museum US$1/2; ⊙ temple 7am-6.30pm, museum 7am-6pm) Wat Phnom, meaning Hill Temple, is appropriately set on the only hill (more like a mound at 27m) in Phnom Penh. The wat

main building is a stupa containing an eyebrow hair of Buddha with an inscription in Pali (an ancient Indian language) over the entrance.

Independence Monument MONUMENT

(វិមានឯករាជ្យ; Map p180; cnr Norodom & Sihanouk Blvds) Soaring over the city's largest roundabout is the grand Independence Monument, built in 1958 to commemorate Cambodia's 1953 independence from France and now also a memorial to Cambodia's war dead. Modelled on the central tower of Angkor Wat, it was designed by leading Khmer architect Vann Molyvann.

🏃 Activities

Don't miss the quirky and colourful **aerobics** sessions that take place in parks around the city at dawn and again at dusk. The riverfront opposite Blue Pumpkin and Olympic Stadium are two good places to jump in and join the fun.

Most pool-equipped boutique hotels will let you **swim** for about US$5 and/or a food purchase. The great pool at the **Himawari Hotel** (Map p180; ☎ 023-214555; 313 Sisowath Quay; admission weekday/weekend US$7/8) is another option.

Boat Cruises

Sunset boat trips on the Tonlé Sap and Mekong Rivers are highly recommended. A slew of **cruising boats** (Map p175) are available for hire on the riverfront about 500m north of the tourist boat dock. Just rock up and arrange one on the spot for US$15 to US$20 an hour, depending on negotiations and numbers. Bring your own drinks.

Public river cruises are another option. They leave every 30 minutes from 5pm to 7.30pm from the **tourist boat dock** (Map p176; 93 Sisowath Quay) and last about 45 minutes (US$5 per head).

Cooking Classes

Cambodia Cooking Class COOKING COURSE (Map p180; ☎ 012 524801; www.cambodia-cooking-class.com; booking office 67 St 240, classes near Russian embassy; half/full day US$15/23) Learn the art of Khmer cuisine through Frizz Restaurant. Reserve ahead.

Cycling

You can hire a bike and go it alone or opt for something more organised – Vicious Cycle and Offroad Cambodia both run daily group tours to Udong or Koh Dach, departing before 8am.

is revered by locals, who flock here to pray for good luck. Legend has it that in 1373 the first temple was built by a lady named Penh to house four Buddha statues that she found floating in the Mekong. A statue of a smiling and rather plump Lady Penh is in a pavilion behind the *vihara* (temple sanctuary).

Wat Ounalom BUDDHIST TEMPLE

(វត្តឧណ្ណាលោម; Map p176; Sothearos Blvd; ⊙6am-6pm) **FREE** This wat is the headquarters of Cambodian Buddhism. It received a battering during the Pol Pot era, but today the wat has come back to life. Behind the

Central Phnom Penh North

◎ **Top Sights**
1 National Museum of Cambodia E5
2 Royal Palace F5

◎ **Sights**
3 Wat Ounalom...F4
4 Wat Phnom...C2

◎ **Activities, Courses & Tours**
Bodia Spa.....................................(see 53)
5 Cyclo Centre C5
6 Daughters E5
7 Nail Bar..E4
8 Seeing Hands Massage.......................D2
9 Seeing Hands Massage.......................D2
10 Vicious Cycle E3

◎ **Sleeping**
11 11 Happy Backpacker.............................E3
12 Amanjaya Pancam Hotel F4
13 Blue Lime E5
14 Eighty8 Backpackers B1
15 Monsoon Hotel E3
16 Natural House Boutique Hotel.............E4
17 Natural Inn Backpacker Hostel...........E4
18 Osaka Ya E3
19 Raffles Hotel Le Royal B1
20 The Billabong...C5
21 The Quay..F4

◎ **Eating**
22 Armand's... D2
23 Beirut..E2
24 Blue Pumpkin F3
25 Bopha Phnom Penh Restaurant..........E2
Cantina...(see 27)
26 Friends...E5
27 Happy Herb Pizza....................................F4
28 Metro...F3
29 Pop Café F5
30 Psar Kandal..E4
31 Romdeng.. C5
32 Sam Doo Restaurant..............................B4
33 Sher-e-Punjab E3

Sugar 'n Spice Cafe........................ (see 6)
34 Thai Huot B3
35 Van's Restaurant.....................................D2
36 Warung Bali...F4

◎ **Drinking & Nightlife**
37 Dusk Till Dawn C5
Elephant Bar ....(see 19)
38 FCC..F4
39 Heart of Darkness D5
40 Howie Bar D5
41 Pontoon C5
42 Rainbow Bar...D4
43 Slur D5
44 Zeppelin Café D5

◎ **Entertainment**
45 Flicks 2 ....E3
46 Plae Pakaa E5

◎ **Shopping**
47 Ambre C5
Daughters .... (see 6)
48 D's Books.. F4
Friends n' Stuff ....(see 26)
49 KeoK'jay...E2
50 Night Market..E2
51 Psar Thmei..C4

◎ **Information**
52 ANZ Royal Bank......................................F3
53 U-Care Pharmacy....................................F4

◎ **Transport**
54 Angkor Motorcycles...............................D5
55 CTT Net...E3
56 Giant Ibis..E2
57 Mekong Express......................................E2
58 Neak Krorhorm..E2
59 Rith Mony..E2
60 Seila Angkor E4
61 Vannak Bikes Rental E3
62 Virak Buntham...E2

Offroad Cambodia   CYCLING
(Map p175; ☏088 855 5123; www.offroad-cambo
dia.com; 2 St 215) Rents quality Trek mountain
bikes for US$7 per day and runs a variety of
day and multiday tours.

Vicious Cycle   CYCLING
(Map p176; ☏012 430622; www.grasshopperad-
ventures.com; 23 St 144; road/mountain bike per
day US$4/8) Plenty of excellent mountain
and other bikes available here. Vicious represents well-respected Grasshopper Adventures (p198) in Phnom Penh.

Massage & Meditation

Free one-hour Vipassana meditation sessions take place in the central *vihara* of **Wat
Langka** (Map p180; cnr St 51 & Sihanouk Blvd) at
6pm on Monday, Thursday and Saturday,
and at 8am on Sunday.

Spa Bliss   SPA
(Map p180; ☏023-215754; www.blissspacambo
dia.com; 29 St 240; massages from US$22) One
of the most established spas in town, set in
a lovely old French house on the popular
St 240.

Bodia Spa
SPA

(Map p176; ☑023-226199; www.bodia-spa.com; cnr Sothearos Blvd & St 178; massages from US$26; ☺10am-11pm) About the best rub-downs in town, in a Zen-like setting (albeit with some street noise).

Seeing Hands Massage
MASSAGE

(Map p176; 12 St 13; ☺7.30am-10pm) Helps you ease those aches and pains; helps blind masseurs stay self-sufficient. Massages average US$7 per hour. There are several other cooperatives around town including **St 108** (Map p176; 34 St 108; ☺8am-9pm).

Nail Bar
MASSAGE

(Map p176; www.mithsamlanh.org; Friends n' Stuff store, 215 St 13; 30/60min massages US$4/7; ☺11am-9pm) Cheap manicures, pedicures, foot massages, hand massages and nail painting, all to help Mith Samlanh train street children in a new vocation.

Daughters
SPA

(Map p176; ☑077 657678; www.daughtersofcambodia.org; 65 St 178; 1hr foot spa US$10; ☺9am-5.30pm Mon-Sat) Hand and foot massages administered by participants in this NGO's vocational training program for at-risk women. Shorter (15- to 30-minute) treatments available.

☞ Tours

Cyclo Centre
TOURS

(Map p176; ☑097 700 9762; www.cyclo.org.kh; 95 St 158; per hour/day from US$3/12) Dedicated to supporting *cyclo* (pedicab) drivers in Phnom Penh, these tours are a great way to see the sights.

Kingdom Brewery
TOURS

(☑023-430180; 1748 NH5; tours US$6; ☺1-5pm Mon-Fri) Tours include two beers and you don't even have to book ahead – just show up. It's exactly 1km north of the Japanese Bridge on NH5.

🛏 Sleeping

Accommodation in Phnom Penh, as in the rest of the country, is terrific value no matter your budget and there are hundreds of guesthouses and hotels to choose from.

The traditional backpacker area around Boeng Kak ('The Lake') all but died when the lake was filled in with sand in 2011. Four miniature Khao San Rd backpacker colonies have emerged in its wake:

➡ St 172, between St 19 and St 13 (the most popular area);

➡ St 258 near the riverfront;

➡ The Psar O Russei area west of busy Monivong Blvd; and

➡ St 278 (aka 'Golden St') in the trendy Boeng Keng Kang (BKK) district south of Independence Monument.

🛏 Central Phnom Penh North

Many travellers target the riverfront, but hotels along the river can be noisy and/or windowless. A few superb options exist at the top end, but worthwhile pickings are much slimmer in the budget and midrange categories. You'll find much better value off the river. The blocks running west of the river from St 104 to about St 144 contain pockets of sleaze.

★ Eighty8 Backpackers
HOSTEL $

(Map p176; ☑023-500 2440; www.88backpackers.com; 98 St 88; dm US$5-7, d US$20-24; ❄@🔊🏊) The swimming pool and the premises – a magnificent, rambling villa – set this place apart from the rest of Phnom Penh's hostels. The courtyard is anchored by a big, sturdy bar, with billiards and plenty of places to lounge. Dorm rooms come in air-con and fan varieties, and there's a female dorm.

Osaka Ya
GUESTHOUSE $

(Map p176; ☑023-650 9423; www.osakayaguesthouse.com; 171 Sisowath Quay; r US$15-25; ❄🔊) This Japanese-run high-rise raises the bar for budget riverside lodging. Osaka Ya is allergic to the stank and mould that plague other hotels of this ilk. Here you swathe yourself in imported linens and watch crisp flat-screen TVs. Tasteful and spotless.

11 Happy Backpacker
HOSTEL $

(Map p176; ☑088 777 7421; happy11gt@hotmail.com; 87-89 St 136; dm US$5, r US$8-30; ❄@🔊) The sprawling rooftop bar/restaurant/chill-out area here has cosy chairs, a pool table and a flat-screen TV. Mellow by day, fun by night. The white-tiled rooms hardly compare but are clean and have no major problems.

★ Blue Lime
BOUTIQUE HOTEL $$

(Map p176; ☑023-222260; www.bluelime.asia; 42 St 19z; r incl breakfast US$45-80; ❄@🔊🏊) Blue Lime is a popular boutique hotel offering smart, minimalist rooms and a leafy pool area done just right. The pricier rooms are

Central Phnom Penh South

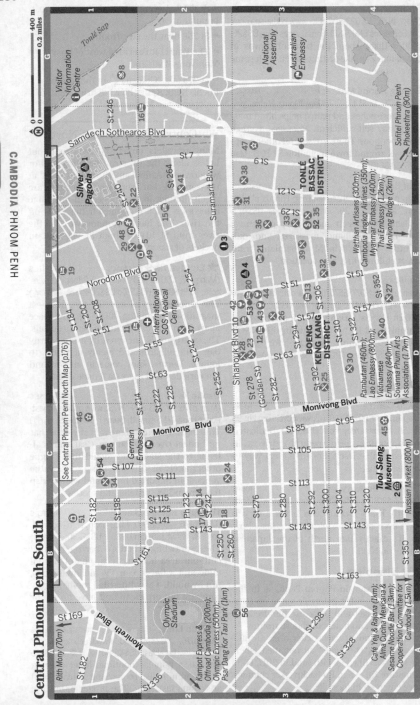

See Central Phnom Penh North Map (p176)

CAMBODIA PHNOM PENH

400 m
0.2 miles

Tonlé Sap

Visitor
Information
Centre

National
Assembly

Australian
Embassy

Silver
Pagoda

St 246

Samdech Sothearos Blvd

St 7

St 264

St 240

Suramarit Blvd

TONLÉ
BASSAC
DISTRICT

St 19

St 21

St 29

Norodom Blvd

St 254

St 51

St 306

St 352

St 51

BOENG
KENG KANG
DISTRICT

St 184
St 200
St 208
St 51

International
SOS Medical
Centre

St 55

St 242

St 252

Sihanouk Blvd

St 278
(Golden St)

St 282

St 57

St 294

St 57

St 322

St 310

Watthan Artisans (300m);
Cambodia Angkor Airlines (350m);
Myanmar Embassy (400m);
Thai Embassy (1.2km);
Monivong Bridge (2km)

Sofitel Phnom Penh
Phokeethra (90m)

Rambutan (460m);
Lao Embassy (800m);
Vietnamese
Embassy (840m);
Sovanna Phum Arts
Association (1.7km)

St 63

St 222
St 228

St 242

St 302

St 63

German
Embassy

Monivong Blvd

Monivong Blvd

St 85

St 95

St 214

St 46

St 107
St 54
St 34

St 111

St 24

St 105

St 113

Tuol Sleng
Museum

Russian Market (800m)

St 115
St 125
St 141

Ph 232
St 242

St 276

St 280

St 292
St 300
St 304
St 310
St 320

St 45

St 182
St 198
St 51

St 143
St 250
St 260

St 163

St 143

St 143

Café Yejj & Rajana (1km);
Alma Cucina Mexicana &
Sesame Noodle Bar (1.3km);
Cooperation Committee for
Cambodia (1.5km)

Russian Market (1.5km)

St 161

Olympic Stadium

Monireth Blvd

St 169

Rith Mony (70m);

St 182

Kampot Express & Offroad Cambodia (200m);
Olympic Express (500m);
Psar Dang Kor Taxi Park (1km)

St 336

St 298

St 328

St 350

St 56

Central Phnom Penh South

CAMBODIA PHNOM PENH

true gems, with private plunge pools, four-poster beds and contemporary concrete love seats. No kids allowed.

Natural House Boutique Hotel HOTEL $$
(Map p176; ☎097 263 4160; www.naturalhouse.asia; 52-54 St 172; r incl breakfast US$20-35; ❄️🛜) The best-looking US$20 rooms in the St 172 area are here. Plush bedding and kitchenettes in all rooms are the highlights. Across the road is Natural House's newly opened **Natural Inn Backpacker Hostel** (Map p176; ☎097 263 4160; www.naturalhouse.asia; off St 172; dm US$3-8; ❄️🛜).

Monsoon Hotel BOUTIQUE HOTEL $$
(Map p176; ☎023-989856; www.monsoonhotel.com; 53-55 St 130; r incl breakfast US$39-45; ❄️@🛜) Blink and you'll miss this little oasis on chaotic St 130. Hidden inside are

attractive rooms with pleasing murals and polished-concrete walls and floors. A super price considering the sophistication of the design and a location so close to the river.

The Billabong BOUTIQUE HOTEL $$
(Map p176; ☎023-223703; www.thebillabonghotel.com; 5 St 158; s/d/tr incl breakfast from US$34/55/80; ❄️@🛜🏊) Near Psar Thmei but an eddy of calm by comparison, Billabong has a big open courtyard and 41 stylish rooms set around a large swimming pool. Standard rooms are smallish.

★ **Raffles Hotel Le Royal** HOTEL $$$
(Map p176; ☎023-981888; www.raffles.com/phnompenh; cnr Monivong Blvd & St 92; r from US$299; ❄️@🛜🏊) A grandee from the golden age of travel, this is one of Asia's opulent addresses.

Indulgent diversions include two swimming pools, a gym, a spa, and bars and restaurants with lavish dining and drinking.

The Quay
BOUTIQUE HOTEL $$$

(Map p176; ☎023-224894; www.thequayhotel.com; 277 Sisowath Quay; r/ste incl breakfast from US$60/110; ❄@ 🛜) The Quay is a temple of contemporary style right on the riverfront. The long, narrow suites have fabulous desks if you want to work, and flat-screen TVs if you don't. Standard quarters are much smaller but equally slick. Ascend to the rooftop Chow bar to catch breezes off the Tonlé Sap.

Amanjaya Pancam Hotel
BOUTIQUE HOTEL $$$

(Map p176; ☎023-214747; www.amanjaya-pancam-hotel.com; 1 St 154; r incl breakfast US$135-185; ❄@ 🛜) One of Phnom Penh's original Asian Zen–style boutiques, Amanjaya boasts a superb riverfront location and spacious, stylish rooms with dark-wood floors, elegant Khmer drapes and tropical furnishings.

🛏 Central Phnom Penh South

Hotels in this zone are ideally positioned within a short *remorque* ride of the riverfront action and well south of the chaos and girlie bars of the north-central area. The BKK district south of Independence Monument is the flashpacker zone.

★Mad Monkey
HOSTEL $

(Map p180; ☎023-987091; www.phnompenh-hostels.com; 26 St 302; dm US$7, r with/without bathroom US$20/15; ❄@ 🛜) This colourful and arty hostel is justifiably popular. The spacious dorms have air-con and sleep six to 20; the smaller ones have double-wide bunk beds that can sleep two (US$9 per couple). Private rooms vary, so check out a few. The rooftop bar above quiet St 302 is a nice draw.

Top Banana Guesthouse
HOSTEL $

(Map p180; ☎012 885572; www.topbanana.biz; 9 St 278; dm US$6, r US$7-20; ❄@ 🛜) Great bar, so-so hostel has long been the mantra here. Now a facelift has seen the rooms improved. The brilliant location high above Golden St and comfy open-air chill-out area remain the top selling points, however. Book way ahead.

Same Same Backpackers
HOSTEL $

(Map p180; ☎077 717174; theatoch@yahoo.com; 5 St 258; dm US$4, d with fan/air-con from US$7/10; ❄@ 🛜) Nothing fancy, just simple rooms priced right on the well-located mini backpacker strip known as St 258.

★Pavilion
BOUTIQUE HOTEL $$

(Map p180; ☎023-222280; www.thepavilion.asia; 227 St 19; r incl breakfast US$50-100, apt US$110-120; ❄@ 🛜) Housed in an elegant French villa, this immensely popular and atmospheric place helped popularise the Phnom Penh poolside boutique hotel. Rooms have stunning furniture, personal computers and iPod docks. Recently expanded to 27 rooms; some of the newer rooms include a private plunge pool. No children allowed.

★Villa Langka
BOUTIQUE HOTEL $$

(Map p180; ☎023-726771; www.villalangka.com; 14 St 282; r incl breakfast US$48-120; ❄@ 🛜) One of the first players in the poolside-boutique game, it's now firmly cemented as a Phnom Penh favourite. Rooms ooze postmodern panache. The leafy pool area is perfect.

★Rambutan
BOUTIQUE HOTEL $$

(Map p175; ☎017 992240; www.rambutanresort.com; 29 St 71; r incl breakfast US$55-120; ❄🛜) Sixties-groovy, gay-friendly and extremely well run, this striking villa once belonged to the American Embassy. The soaring original structure and a newer wing shade a boot-shaped swimming pool. Concrete floors set an industrial tone in the 19 smart rooms.

Khmer Surin Boutique Guesthouse
BOUTIQUE HOTEL $$

(Map p180; ☎012 731909; www.khmersurin.com.kh; 11A St 57; r incl breakfast US$50-60; ❄🛜) The 19 rooms in this sumptuous villa come with flat-screen TVs, leafy and lavish balconies, and bathrooms that would put most four-star properties to shame. With all the museum-quality furniture lying around, rooms might seem busy to some.

Circa 51
BOUTIQUE HOTEL $$

(Map p180; ☎012 585714; www.circa51.com; 155 St 222; s/d incl breakfast from US$46/56; ❄🛜) In a classic '60s villa, Circa 51 has just 10 rooms and they are lovely, with ambient lighting, cool furniture, minimalist art, flat-screen TVs and silk robes. A banyan tree shades the luscious pool area within arm's length of the bar.

Anise
HOTEL $$

(Map p180; ☎023-222522; www.anisehotel.com.kh; 2C St 278; s incl breakfast US$42-72, d US$47-77; ❄@ 🛜) If the leafy-boutique-hotel-around-the-pool thing isn't for you, Anise is the best midrange high-rise in town. Indigenous textiles and handsome wood trim add character to rooms that already boast extras like DVD players. Pricier rooms are gargantuan. Free laundry.

The Plantation   BOUTIQUE HOTEL **$$$**
(Map p180; ☏ 023-215151; www.theplantation.asia; 28 St 184; r incl breakfast US$85-100; ❋ @ 🛜 ≋) This is the unmatched Pavilion group's largest and most ambitious property. It's more impersonal than its kin, but it still has the goods: high ceilings, top-grade furniture and fixtures, open-plan bathrooms and balconies (pay more to have one overlooking the glorious pool area).

Sofitel Phnom Penh Phokeethra   HOTEL **$$$**
(Map p175; ☏ 023-999200; www.sofitel.com; 26 Sothearos Blvd; r from US$210; ❋ @ 🛜 ≋) Phnom Penh's latest five-star property boasts spacious rooms and a gazillion facilities, including numerous tennis courts and several restaurants. Absolutely first-class, but it feels somewhat large and impersonal and the location isn't perfect.

Psar O Russei Area

The guesthouses in this budget-friendly zone are particularly appealing – you won't come close to finding better US$15 air-con rooms elsewhere in the centre.

★ Narin Guesthouse   GUESTHOUSE **$**
(Map p180; ☏ 099 881133; www.naringuesthouse.com; 50 St 125; r with fan/air-con US$12/17; ❋ @ 🛜) One of the stalwarts of the Phnom Penh guesthouse scene. Rooms are smart, bathrooms smarter still and there is a super relaxed open-air restaurant-terrace for taking some time out.

Smiley's Hotel   HOTEL **$**
(Map p180; ☏ 012 365959; smileyhotel.pp@gmail.com; 37 St 125; s with fan US$6, d US$15-20; ❋ @ 🛜) Smiley's is a huge seven-storey hotel with a choice of 40 spacious rooms that border on chic. The US$20 rooms have big flat-screen TVs. Includes a lift.

Star Wood Inn   HOTEL **$**
(Map p180; ☏ 023-223253; www.starwood-inn.com; 74 St 141; r with fan/air-con US$10/15; ❋ @ 🛜) More clean and sleek rooms for a ridiculously low price here. Rooms have either twin or king beds with attractive runners. Amenities vary from room to room: some have balconies, and air-con rooms include flat-screen TVs. No lift.

✖ Eating

For foodies, Phnom Penh is a real delight, boasting a superb selection of restaurants that showcase the best in Khmer cooking, as well as the greatest hits from the region and the world.

✖ Central Phnom Penh North

★ Sam Doo Restaurant   CHINESE **$**
(Map p176; 56-58 Kampuchea Krom Blvd; mains US$2.80-5; ⊙ 7am-2am) Many Chinese Khmers swear that this upstairs eatery near Central Market has the best food in town. The signature 'Sam Doo fried rice', hotpots and dim sum are recommended.

Beirut   MIDDLE EASTERN **$**
(Map p176; ☏ 023-720011; 117 Sisowath Quay; dishes US$3-7; ⊙ 11am-10.30pm; 🛜🍴) Lilliputian eatery with super deals on wraps, kebabs and saucy appetisers like hummus with pita bread, plus *shisha* (water pipes) for US$6 to US$8.

Cantina   MEXICAN **$**
(Map p176; 347 Sisowath Quay; mains US$4-6; ⊙ 2.30-11pm, closed Sat; 🛜) This is the spot for tostadas, fajitas and other Mexican favourites, all freshly prepared. It's also a journo hang-out and a lively bar with expertly made margaritas and tequilas.

Warung Bali   INDONESIAN **$**
(Map p176; 25 St 178; dishes US$1.50-3; ⊙ 8.30am-9pm) At Warung Bali you'll encounter spicy Indonesian favourites like fish in sweet soy-bean sauce and beef *rendang* (beef cooked in coconut milk and spices). It's busy and fragrant.

Thai Huot   SUPERMARKET **$**
(Map p176; 103 Monivong Blvd; ⊙ 7.30am-8.30pm) This is the place for French travellers who are missing home, as it stocks many French products, including Bonne Maman jam and Hénaff pâté. Additional location in **BKK** (Map p180; cnr St 63 & St 352; ⊙ 7.30am-8.30pm).

Sher-e-Punjab   INDIAN **$$**
(Map p176; ☏ 023-216360; 16 St 130; mains US$3-7; ⊙ 11am-11pm; 🍴) The top spot for a curry fix according to many members of Phnom Penh's Indian community; the tandoori dishes are particularly good. Even the prawn dishes cost under US$6.

Bopha Phnom Penh Restaurant
CAMBODIAN $$

(Map p176; Sisowath Quay; mains US$5-10; ⏰6am-11pm; 🛜) Also known as Titanic, this place is right on the river and designed to impress, with Angkorian-style carvings and elegant wicker furniture. The menu is thick with the exotic, especially water buffalo, plus Western food for the less adventurous.

Pop Café
ITALIAN $$

(Map p176; ✉012 562892; 371 Sisowath Quay; pasta dishes US$6-9; ⏰11am-2pm & 6-10pm) Owner Giorgio welcomes diners as if they are coming to his own home for dinner, making this a popular spot for authentic Italian cooking. Thin-crust pizzas, homemade pastas and tasty gnocchi – it could be Roma.

Blue Pumpkin
CAFE $$

(Map p176; 245 Sisowath Quay; mains US$3-7; ⏰6am-11pm; 🛜) The beloved Siem Reap import with the alluring white upholstery is wildly popular for its healthy breakfasts, pastas, sandwiches and the capital's best ice cream. Other branches can be found in BKK (Map p180; 12A St 57; ⏰6am-10pm; 🛜) and at Monument Books (p188).

Happy Herb Pizza
PIZZERIA $$

(Map p176; ✉012 921915; 345 Sisowath Quay; medium pizzas US$6-8.50; ⏰8am-11pm; 🛜) No, happy doesn't mean it comes with free toppings; it means pizza à la ganja. The non-marijuana pizzas are also pretty good, but don't involve the free trip. Delivery available.

★Tepui
LATIN AMERICAN $$$

(Map p175; ✉023-991514; 45 Sisowath Quay, cnr St 84; mains US$12-20; ⏰5-10.30pm Mon-Sat) Based in the Chinese House, one of the city's true colonial-era masterpieces, Tepui's highlights include red snapper ceviche, Brazilian beef tenderloin and calamari black-ink paella, plus creative specials and cocktails.

★Van's Restaurant
FRENCH $$$

(Map p176; ✉023-722067; 5 St 13; mains US$16-43; ⏰11.30am-2.30pm & 5-10.30pm) Located in one of the city's grandest buildings, the former Banque Indochine; you can still see the old vault doors en route to the refined dining room upstairs. Dishes are presented with decorative flourish and menu highlights include langoustine ravioli, tender veal and boneless quail.

Armand's
FRENCH $$$

(Map p176; ✉015 548966; 33 St 108; meals US$12-25; ⏰from 6pm, closed Mon) The best steaks in town are served flambé style by the eponymous owner of this French bistro. The steaks are nonpareil, and every item on the chalkboard menu shines. Space is tight so book ahead.

Metro
FUSION $$$

(Map p176; ✉023-222275; 271 Sisowath Quay; small plates US$4-8, large plates US$8-24; ⏰9.30am-1am; 🛜) The trendiest spot on the riverfront strip thanks to a striking design and an adventurous menu that includes beef with red ants and tequila black-pepper prawns. Also does a mean eggs Benedict for brunch.

✕ Central Phnom Penh South

★Asian Spice
ASIAN $

(Map p180; 79 St 111; mains US$2.30-2.80; ⏰6am-9pm; 🛜) The house speciality is the zesty Singapore *laksa* (yellow curry noodles), but you'll also find spicy Indonesian, Malaysian and Cambodian fare. One of Phnom Penh's best bargains.

The Vegetarian
CAMBODIAN $

(Map p180; 158 St 19; mains US$1.75-2.50; ⏰10.30am-8.30pm Mon-Sat; ✏) All dishes at the Vegetarian are US$2.50 or under and it doesn't skimp on portions either. Noodles and fried rice are the specialities.

Ayotaya
THAI $

(Map p180; 58 St 302; dishes US$3.50-4.50; ⏰10.30am-2pm & 5-9pm Mon-Sat) No punches are pulled for tourists here. Besides the trademark pad thai, you'll find delicious papaya salads, zippy red curry and scrumptious lime-steamed fish.

Mama Restaurant
CAMBODIAN $

(Map p180; 10C St 111; mains US$1.50-4; ⏰7.30am-8.30pm) This long-running backpacker cafe in the heart of the Psar O Russei area serves tasty French-influenced Khmer food, plus shepherd's pie. Try the beef stew.

★Malis
CAMBODIAN $$

(Map p180; 136 Norodom Blvd; mains US$6-12; 🛜) The leading Khmer restaurant in the Cambodian capital, Malis is a chic place to dine alfresco. The original menu includes beef bites in bamboo, goby with Kampot peppercorns, and traditional soups and salads.

Piccola Italia Da Luigi
PIZZERIA $$

(Map p180; ✉017 323273; 36 St 308; pizzas US$4.50-9; ⏰11am-2pm & 6-10pm) A bustling curbside eatery, just like in Italy, Luigi's makes some of the best pizza in Phnom Penh. Also has a small deli attached if you're in the mood for some zingy antipasti. Reservations are a good idea.

Java Café
CAFE $$

(Map p180; www.javaarts.org; 56 Sihanouk Blvd; mains US$4-8; ⏰7am-10pm; 🛜📶) Consistently popular thanks to a breezy balcony and a creative menu that includes crisp salads, delicious homemade sandwiches, burgers and coffee from several continents. The upstairs area doubles as an art gallery, downstairs as a bakery.

Flavours of India
INDIAN $$

(Map p180; 📱023-990455; 158 St 63; mains US$4-6; ⏰9.30am-10.30pm; 🛜) Popular with the South Asian community, this place specialises in North Indian and Nepalese cuisine. Ask the staff to spice it up or they will spice it down for tourists.

Freebird
AMERICAN $$

(Map p180; 69 St 240; mains US$5-15; ⏰7am-11pm; 🛜) An American-style bar-diner with a great selection of burgers, wraps, salads and Tex-Mex. The steak 'n' cheese sandwich and chilli con carne are the highlights.

Sushi Bar
JAPANESE $$

(Map p180; 2D St 302; sushi sets from US$6; ⏰11am-10pm; 🛜) Purists will scoff at the low sushi prices, but it's always packed for a reason. Definitely the best place in town for quick-and-easy raw fish.

ARTillery
CAFE $$

(Map p180; St 240½; mains US$4-6; ⏰7.30am-9pm Tue-Sun, to 5pm Mon; 🛜📶) Healthy salads, sandwiches, shakes and snacks like hummus and felafel are served in this creative space on an artsy alley off St 240. Also has a small raw-food menu. Another **branch** (Map p180; 13 St 278; ⏰7.30am-5pm) is on St 278.

⭐Deco
EUROPEAN $$$

(Map p180; 📱017 577327; cnr St 352 & St 57; mains US$9-13; ⏰noon-2pm & 5-10pm) With an enviable setting in an impeccably restored '60s modernist house, Deco is one of Phnom Penh's most sophisticated restaurants. The rotating menu might include duck breast or Kampot crab cakes at any given time, and the creative cocktails are legendary.

🍴 Russian Market Area

⭐Café Yejj
CAFE $

(Map p175; www.cafeyejj.com; 170 St 450; mains US$3.50-6; ⏰8am-9pm; 🛜📶) 🍃 An air-con escape upstairs from Russian Market, this cafe uses many organic ingredients to prepare pastas, salads, wraps and soups. Promotes fair trade and responsible employment.

Sesame Noodle Bar
NOODLES $

(Map p175; www.sesamenoodlebar.com; 9 St 460; mains US$3.75-4.50; ⏰11.30am-2.30pm & 5-9.30pm; 📶) A Japanese-American duo is

---

LOCAL FLAVOURS

Markets

Phnom Penh's many markets all have large central eating areas where stalls serve up local faves like noodle soup and fried noodles during daylight hours. Most dishes cost a reasonable 4000r to 6000r. The best market for eating is Russian Market (p188), with an interior food zone that's easy to find and a nice variety of Cambodian specialities. Psar Thmei (p188) and Psar O Russei (p189) are other great choices. **Psar Kandal** (Map p176; btwn St 144 & St 154) gets going a little later and is an early-evening option.

Khmer Barbecues

After dark, Khmer eateries scattered across town illuminate their Cambodia Beer signs, hailing locals in for grilled strips of meat or seafood and generous jugs of draught beer. Khmer barbecues are literally all over the place, so it won't be hard to find one. A few recommended local eateries:

Sovanna (Map p180; 2C St 21; mains US$2-3; ⏰6-11am & 3-11pm) Always jumping with locals and even a smattering of expats who have made this their barbecue of choice.

Red Cow (Map p180; 126 Norodom Blvd; mains US$2.50-7; ⏰4-11pm) Grills up everything imaginable — eel, eggplant, frog, pig intestine, quail — and also serves curries and other traditional Khmer dishes.

Sonivid (Map p180; 39 St 242; meals US$5-10; ⏰3pm-midnight) Steamed or fried crab, squid, fish and shellfish are the speciality at this wildly popular corner eatery.

TOP FIVE: GOOD-CAUSE DINING

These fantastic eateries act as training centres for young staff and help fund worthy causes in the capital.

Friends (Map p176; ✆ 012 802072; www.friends-international.org; 215 St 13; tapas US$4-7, mains from US$6; ⊗ 11am-9pm; ☎) One of Phnom Penh's best-loved restaurants, it offers former street children a headstart in the hospitality industry. Tasty tapas bites, heavenly smoothies and creative cocktails.

Sugar 'n Spice Cafe (Map p176; www.daughtersofcambodia.org; 65 St 178; sandwiches US$3.50-7; ⊗ 9am-6pm Mon-Sat; ☎) This fantastic cafe on the top floor of the Daughters visitor centre features soups, smoothies, coffee drinks and fusion-y mains served by former sex workers being trained by Daughters to reintegrate into society.

Romdeng (Map p176; ✆ 092 219565; 74 St 174; mains US$5-8; ⊗ 11am-9pm; ☎) Part of the Friends' extended family, this elegant restaurant specialises in Cambodian country fare, including a famous *amok* (fish baked with coconut and lemongrass in banana leaves). The place to sample deep-fried tarantulas or stir-fried tree ants with beef and holy basil.

Hagar (Map p180; 44 St 310; lunch/dinner buffet US$6.50/11; ⊗ 7am-2pm & 6-9pm Thu-Sat, 7am-2pm Sun-Wed) Proceeds from the all-you-can-eat buffets here go towards assisting destitute or abused women. The spread is usually Asian fusion or barbecue, except for Wednesday lunches and Thursday dinners, when Hagar lays out its legendary Italian buffet.

Le Lotus Blanc (Map p180; 152 St 51; mains US$4-8.50; ⊗ 7am-10pm Mon-Sat; ☎) This suburban restaurant acts as a training centre for youths who previously scoured the city dump. Run by French NGO Pour un Sourire d'Enfant (For the Smile of a Child), it serves classy Western and Khmer cuisine.

---

behind Russian Market's trendiest lunch spot. Cold noodle dishes arrive in vegetarian or egg varieties and come heaped with an egg and carmelised pork or grilled tofu. Simply delicious.

Alma Cucina Mexicana　MEXICAN $
(Map p175; 43A St 454; meals US$3-5; ⊗ 7am-2pm; ☎) The scrumptious rotating menu of home-cooked Mexican faves might include chorizo quesadillas one day, *bistec encebollado* (steak and onions) the next. The *huevos rancheros* breakfasts are legendary.

🍷 Drinking & Nightlife

Phnom Penh has some great bars and clubs and it's definitely worth planning at least one big night on the town.

Many venues are clustered around the intersection of St 51 and St 172, where seemingly everybody ends up late at night. Golden St (St 278) is popular, and the riverfront also has its share of bars. Two-for-one happy hours are a big thing in Phnom Penh so it pays to get started early.

For the lowdown on club nights, check out **Phnom Penh Underground** (www.phnom-penh-underground.com), a roving party

of sorts that promotes gigs for various electro troupes in Phnom Penh and beyond.

★FCC　BAR
(Foreign Correspondents' Club; Map p176; 363 Sisowath Quay; ⊗ 6am-midnight; ☎) A Phnom Penh institution, the 'F' is housed in a colonial gem with great views and cool breezes. One of those must-see places in Cambodia, almost everyone swings by for a drink – happy hours are 5pm to 7pm and 10pm to midnight. If the main bar is too crowded, head up to the rooftop, which often sees live music at weekends.

★Heart of Darkness　NIGHTCLUB
(Map p176; 26 St 51; ⊗ 8pm-late) Everybody should stop in at least once just to bask in the aura and history of the legendary 'Heart'. It has evolved into a nightclub more than a bar over the years, attracting all – and we mean *all* – sorts.

★Elephant Bar　BAR
(Map p176; St 92; ⊗ 2pm-midnight Mon-Fri, noon-midnight Sat & Sun) The Raffles' atmospheric bar has been drawing journos, politicos, and the rich and famous for more than 80 years. Singapore slings and all drinks are half-price during happy hour (4pm to 9pm).

Equinox   BAR
(Map p180; 3A St 278; ☺8am-late; 🐸) At the heart of the action on St 278, this is a popular place with a lively outdoor bar downstairs and bands upstairs from Thursday to Saturday.

Slur   BAR
(Map p176; 28 St 172; ☺11am-2am) Slur consistently draws some of Phnom Penh's best musical talent. Worth stopping by to see who's on stage and throw back a Jägerbomb.

Zeppelin Café   BAR
(Map p176; 109 St 51; ☺6.30pm-late) Who says vinyl is dead? It lives on here thanks to this old-school rock bar with a serious 60s and '70s music collection.

Howie Bar   BAR
(Map p176; 32 St 51; ☺7pm-6am) Friendly, fun and unpredictable, 'way-cool' Howie is the perfect spillover when the famous Heart of Darkness is packed.

Pontoon   NIGHTCLUB
(Map p176; www.pontoonclub.com; 80 St 172; admission weekends US$3-5, weekdays free; ☺9.30pm-late) The city's premier nightclub often sees big foreign acts on the decks. Thursday is gay-friendly night, with a 1am lady-boy show.

Top Banana   BAR
(Map p180; 9 St 278) There's no question where the top backpacker party spot in Phnom Penh is. The rooftop bar of this guesthouse goes off practically every night of the week.

Dusk Till Dawn   BAR
(Map p176; 46 St 172) Also known as Reggae Bar because of the clientele and the music, the rooftop party here often lasts well into the evening. Ride the lift to the top floor in the tall building opposite Pontoon.

Rainbow Bar   BAR
(Map p176; 134 St 136) Phnom Penh's friendliest, most laid-back gay bar, with a 10pm drag show every night.

Score   BAR
(Map p180; ☎023-221357; 5 St 282; ☺8am-late) With its ginormous screen, this spacious sports bar is the best place to watch the big game. Several pool tables tempt those who would rather play than watch.

☆ Entertainment

For the ins and outs of the entertainment scene, grab a copy of free listings newspaper the *Advisor* or check out '7 Days' in the Friday issue of the *Phnom Penh Post*. Online, try www.ladypenh.com, www.khmer440.com or www.lengpleng.com.

★Meta House   CINEMA
(Map p180; www.meta-house.com; 37 Sothearos Blvd; ☺4pm-midnight Tue-Sun; 🐸) This German-run open-air theatre screens art-house films, documentaries and shorts from Cambodia and around the world most evenings at 4pm (admission free) and 7pm (admission US$2). Films are sometimes followed by Q&As with those involved.

★Plae Pakaa   PERFORMING ARTS
(Fruitful; Map p176; ☎023-986032; National Museum, St 178; adult/child US$15/6; ☺7pm Mon-Sat Oct-Mar, Fri & Sat May-Sep, closed Apr) Plae Pakaa is a series of three rotating, hour-long performances put on by **Cambodian Living Arts** (CLA; Map p180; ☎017 998570; www.cambodianlivingarts.org; 128 Sothearos Blvd) that showcase various Khmer traditional arts and customs.

Flicks   CINEMA
(Map p180; www.theflicks-cambodia.com; 39B St 95; tickets US$3.50; 🐸) It shows at least two movies a day in an uber-comfortable air-conditioned screening room. You can watch both on one ticket. A second **Flicks** (Map p176; 90 St 136) is downstairs at 11 Happy Backpacker.

French Institute   CINEMA
(Institut Français; Map p180; ☎023-213124; www.institutfrancais-cambodge.com; 218 St 184) Has frequent movie screenings in French during the week, usually kicking off at 6.30pm, as well as a French library, bookstore and gallery space.

Apsara Arts Association   DANCE
(Map p175; ☎012 979335; www.apsara-art.org; 71 St 598; tickets US$6-7) 🎭 Alternate performances of classical dance and folk dance most Saturdays at 7pm (call to confirm). It's in Tuol Kork district, in the far north of the city.

Sovanna Phum Arts Association   PERFORMING ARTS
(Map p175; ☎023-987564; www.shadow-puppets.org; 166 St 99, btwn St 484 & St 498; adult/child US$5/3) 🎭 Traditional shadow-puppet, classical dance and drum shows are held here at 7.30pm every Friday and Saturday.

Shopping

An affirmation of identity, the *krama* (checked scarf) is worn around the neck, shoulders and waist of nearly every Khmer. The scarves make superb souvenirs or gifts, as do Cambodia's sculptures and handicrafts.

Bookshops

Monument Books BOOKSTORE
(Map p180; 111 Norodom Blvd; ⊙7am-8.30pm) This is the best-stocked bookshop in town, with almost every Cambodia-related book available, plus a superb maps and travel section, plus a wi-fi-enabled branch of Blue Pumpkin cafe.

D's Books BOOKSTORE
(Map p176; 7 St 178; ⊙9am-9pm) The largest chain of secondhand bookshops in the capital, with a good range of titles. There's a second **branch** (Map p180; 79 St 240; ⊙9am-9pm) on trendy St 240.

Clothing

Ambre CLOTHING
(Map p176; ☎023-217951; 37 St 178; ⊙10am-6pm) Leading Cambodian fashion designer Romy-da Keth has turned this striking French-era mansion into a showcase for her stunning silk collection.

Couleurs d'Asie ACCESSORIES
(Map p180; www.couleursdasie.net; 33 St 240; ⊙8am-7pm) Couleurs d'Asie is a great place for gift shopping, with lots of kids' clothes, silks, chunky jewellery, beautiful bags, knick-knacks and fragrant soaps, lotions, incense and oils.

KeoK'jay CLOTHING
(Map p176; www.keokjay.com; cnr St 110 & Sisowath Quay; ⊙11am-10pm) Original women's clothing and accessories stitched by HIV-positive women.

Markets

Bargains galore can be found at Phnom Penh's vibrant markets. Navigating the labyrinths of shoes, clothing, bric-a-brac and food is one of the most enjoyable ways to earn a foot massage.

Russian Market MARKET
(Psar Tuol Tom Pong; Map p175; ⊙6am-5pm) The Russians' retail outlet of choice back in the 1980s, this is the one market all visitors should explore during a trip to Phnom Penh. It includes designer clothing labels hot out of the factory, bootleg music and films, and carvings in wood, stone or bronze. Bargain hard, as hundreds of tourists pass through here every day. It is located in the far south of the city, about four blocks south of Mao Tse Toung Blvd.

Psar Thmei MARKET
(Central Market; Map p176; ⊙6.30am-5.30pm) Often referred to as Central Market, this art-deco landmark resembles a Babylonian ziggurat. It houses an array of stalls selling jewellery, clothing and curios. The food sec-

---

TOP FIVE: GOOD-CAUSE SHOPPING

The stores here sell high-quality silk items and handicrafts to provide the disabled and disenfranchised with valuable training for future employment, plus a regular flow of income to improve lives.

Daughters (Map p176; www.daughtersofcambodia.org; 65 St 178; ⊙9am-6pm Mon-Sat) Fashionable clothes, bags and accessories made with ecofriendly cotton and natural dyes by former prostitutes and victims of sex trafficking.

Friends n' Stuff (Map p176; 215 St 13; ⊙11am-9pm) The closest thing to a charity shop or thrift store in Phnom Penh, with a good range of new and secondhand products sold to generate money to help street children.

Nyemo (Map p175; 41 St 450; ⊙8am-5pm) Quality silk and soft toys for children. It helps disadvantaged women return to work.

Rajana (Map p175; www.rajanacrafts.org; 170 St 450; ⊙7am-6pm Mon-Sat, 10.30am-5pm Sun) Promoting fair wages and training, Rajana has fine jewellery, bamboo crafts, quality T-shirts, kids' clothing, good-looking skirts and dresses – you name it.

Watthan Artisans (Map p175; www.wac.khmerproducts.com; 180 Norodom Blvd; ⊙8am-6.30pm) Silk and other products, including wonderful contemporary handbags, made by landmine and polio victims.

tion is enormous, with produce spilling onto the streets.

Psar O Russei MARKET
(Map p180; ⊙6.30am-5.30pm) Housed in a sprawling mall-like space, this less-touristy market is the place to come if you want to lose the legion of attentive *remorque* drivers. It is a complete rabbit warren, selling everything you can think of and some things you can't.

Night Market MARKET
(Psar Reatrey; Map p176; cnr St 108 & Sisowath Quay; ⊙5-11pm Fri-Sun) A cooler alfresco version of Russian Market, the Night Market mainly sells souvenirs, silk and knick-knacks. Bargain vigorously, as prices can be on the high side.

ℹ Orientation

The riverfront Sisowath Quay, lined with myriad restaurants and a brand-new promenade, is where most visitors gravitate. The city sprawls west from there. The main thoroughfares, Sihanouk Blvd and Norodom Blvd, intersect a few blocks west of the river at lotus-flower-like Independence Monument, a useful landmark.

ℹ Information

DANGERS & ANNOYANCES
Phnom Penh is not as dangerous as people imagine, but it is important to take care. Armed robberies do sometimes occur, but statistically you would be very unlucky to be a victim. More common is bag snatching (see the boxed text).

The riverfront area of Phnom Penh, particularly places with outdoor seating, attracts many beggars, as do Psar Thmei and Russian Market. Generally, however, there is little in the way of push and shove.

EMERGENCY
Ambulance (⊡119, in English 023-724891)
Fire (⊡in Khmer 118)
Police (⊡117)

INTERNET ACCESS
Internet cafes are everywhere and usually charge US$0.50 to US$1 per hour. Pretty much all hotels and most cafes and restaurants offer wi-fi connections, usually free.

MEDICAL SERVICES
Calmette Hospital (Map p175; ⊡023-426948; 3 Monivong Blvd; ⊙24hr) The best of the local hospitals, with the most comprehensive services and an intensive-care unit.

> ### BAG SNATCHING
> Bag and phone snatching has become a real problem in Phnom Penh. Hot spots include the riverfront and busy areas around popular markets, but there is no real pattern and the speeding motorbike thieves, usually operating in pairs, can strike any place, any time. Countless expats and tourists have been injured falling off their bikes in the process of being robbed. Keep your valuables close or concealed and be prepared to let go rather than be dragged into the road. Keep shoulder bags in front of you when riding on *motos* (motorcycle taxis). These guys are real pros and only need one chance.

International SOS Medical Centre (Map p180; ⊡012 816911, 023-216911; www.international sos.com; 161 St 51; ⊙8am-5.30pm Mon-Fri, 8am-noon Sat, 24hr emergency) Top clinic with a host of Western doctors, and with prices to match.
Tropical & Travellers Medical Clinic (Map p176; ⊡023-306802; www.travellersmedical-clinic.com; 88 St 108; ⊙9.30-11.30am & 2.30-5pm Mon-Fri, 9.30-11.30am Sat) Well-regarded clinic run for more than a decade by a British general practitioner.
U-Care Pharmacy (Map p176; 26 Sothearos Blvd; ⊙8am-10pm) International-style pharmacy with a convenient location near the river.

MONEY
There are exchange services and banks with viable ATM machines all over Phnom Penh (including the airport).
ANZ Royal Bank (Map p176; 265 Sisowath Quay; ⊙8.30am-4pm Mon-Fri, 8.30am-noon Sat) With multiple locations, it offers cash advances and ATM withdrawals at US$4 per transaction.
Canadia Bank (Map p176; cnr St 110 & Monivong Blvd; ⊙8am-3.30pm Mon-Fri, 8-11.30am Sat) Canadia Bank ATMs around town incur no transaction charges. This flagship branch changes travellers cheques of several currencies for a 2% commission. Additional branches at Sorya Shopping Centre (Map p176; Sorya Shopping Centre, cnr St 63 & St 154) and on Norodom Blvd (Map p180; Norodom Blvd).

POST
Central Post Office (Map p176; St 13; ⊙8am-6pm) A landmark in a charming building just east of Wat Phnom.

TOURIST INFORMATION

There is not much in the way of official tourist information in the Cambodian capital, but private travel agencies are everywhere and are usually happy to dispense advice. The *Phnom Penh Visitors' Guide* (www.canbypublications. com) has good maps and is brimming with useful information on the capital.

Visitor Information Centre (Map p180; Sisowath Quay; ⊙8am-5pm Mon-Sat) Located on the riverfront near the Chatomuk Theatre. While it doesn't carry a whole lot of information, it does offer free internet access, free wi-fi, air-con and clean public toilets.

TRAVEL AGENCIES

Travel agencies abound on the riverfront. Most offer a city tour plus the standard day tours, and can sort you out with bus and boat tickets to just about anywhere.

Reliable operators:

Hanuman Travel (Map p180; ☑023-218396; www.hanumantravel.com; 12 St 310) Guides in several languages, tours and more, all over the country.

Palm Tours (Map p180; ☑023-726291; www. palmtours.biz; 1B St 278; ⊙8am-9pm) Efficient Volak and her team are a great option for bus tickets (no commission) and the like. In the heart of all the action on St 278.

ℹ Getting There & Away

AIR

Many international air services run to/from Phnom Penh. Domestically, **Cambodia Angkor Air** (Map p175; ☑023-666 6786; www.cambodia angkorair.com; 206A Norodom Blvd) flies four to six times daily to Siem Reap (about US$100, 30 minutes) and three times a week to Sihanoukville (about US$120, 30 minutes).

BOAT

Between August and March, speedboats depart daily to Siem Reap (US$35, five to six hours) at 7am from the tourist boat dock at the eastern end of St 104, but the tickets are overpriced compared with the bus.

Following the Mekong to Chau Doc in Vietnam is a gorgeous way to go.

BUS

All major towns in Cambodia, plus regional hubs Bangkok, Ho Chi Minh City (Saigon) and Pakse, are accessible by air-conditioned bus from Phnom Penh. Most buses leave from company offices, which are generally clustered around Psar Thmei or located near the corner of St 106 and Sisowath Quay.

Not all buses are created equal. Buses run by Capitol Tour and Phnom Penh Sorya are usually among the cheapest. Giant Ibis runs upscale 'VIP' buses with plenty of legroom and dysfunctional wi-fi, but they are about double the average price. Virak Buntham is the night bus specialist.

Most of the long-distance buses drop off and pick up in major towns along the way, such as Kompong Thom en route to Siem Reap, Pursat on the way to Battambang, or Kompong Cham en route to Kratie. However, the full fare is usually charged anyway. Another popular bus route is to Ho Chi Minh City.

Capitol Tour (Map p180; ☑023-724104; 14 St 182)

Giant Ibis (Map p176; ☑023-999333; www. giantibis.com; 3 St 106; ☎)

GST (US Liang Express Bus; Map p176; ☑023-218114; 13 St 142)

Mekong Express (☑023-427518; www. catmekongexpress.com; 2020 NH5) Also has a riverside booking office (Map p176; Sisowath Quay).

Olympic Express (Map p175; ☑092 868782; 70 Monireth Blvd)

Phnom Penh Sorya (Map p176; ☑023-210359; Psar Thmei area)

Rith Mony (Map p175; ☑097 888 9447; St 169) Also has a riverfront terminal (Map p176; ☑017 525388; 24 St 102).

Sapaco (Map p180; ☑023-210300; www. sapacotourist.com; Sihanouk Blvd)

Virak Buntham (Kampuchea Angkor Express; Map p176; ☑016 786270; St 106)

EXPRESS VAN

Express vans are an option to most cities. These shave hours off average trip times, but are cramped and often travel at ulcer-inducing speeds.

Several of the big bus companies also run vans, most famously Mekong Express. It's a good idea to book express vans in advance.

Companies:

CTT Net (Map p176; ☑023-217217; 223 Sisowath Quay)

Kampot Express (Map p175; ☑077 555123; kampotexpress@gmail.com; 2 St 215)

Kim Seng Express (Map p175; ☑012 786000; 506 Kampuchea Krom Blvd)

TRANSPORT FROM PHNOM PENH

Bus

DESTINATION	COST (US$)	DURATION (HR)	COMPANIES	FREQUENCY
Ban Lung	13	11	Phnom Penh (PP) Sorya, Rith Mony, Thong Ly	morning only
Bangkok	18-23	12	Mekong Express, PP Sorya, Virak Buntham	daily per company
Battambang (day bus)	5-6	6	GST, PP Sorya, Rith Mony, Virak Buntham	several per company
Ho Chi Minh City	8-13	7	Capitol Tour, Mekong Express, PP Sorya, Sapaco, Virak Buntham	several per company until 3pm
Kampot (direct)	5.50-6	3	Capitol Tour, Rith Mony	2 daily per company
Kampot (via Kep)	5.50	4	PP Sorya	7.30am, 9.30am, 2.45pm
Kep	5.25	3	PP Sorya	7.30am, 9.30am, 2.45pm
Koh Kong	5	5½	Olympic Express, PP Sorya, Virak Buntham	2-3 per company until noon
Kompong Cham	5	3	PP Sorya	hourly until 4pm
Kratie	8	6-8	PP Sorya	6.45am, 7.15am, 7.30am, 9.30am, 10.30am
Pakse via Don Det (Laos)	28	12-14	PP Sorya	6.45am
Poipet (day bus)	9-11	8	Capitol Tour, PP Sorya, Rith Mony, Virak Buntham	frequent until noon
Preah Vihear City	10	7	GST, Rith Mony	morning only
Sen Monorom	8	8	PP Sorya	7.30am
Siem Reap	5-8	6	most companies	frequent
Sihanoukville	6-6	5½	Capitol Tour, GST, Mekong Express, PP Sorya, Rith Mony, Virak Buntham	frequent
Stung Treng	12.50	9	PP Sorya	6.45am, 7.30am

Express Van

DESTINATION	COST (US$)	DURATION (HR)	COMPANIES	FREQUENCY
Battambang	10-12	4½	Mekong Express, Golden Bayon	several daily
Kampot	7-8	2	Giant Ibis, Kampot Express, Olympic Express	3 trips per company
Kep	7	2½	Olympic Express	7.15am, 1.30pm
Sen Monorom	10	5½	Kim Seng Express	7am, 7.30am, 11am, 1.30pm
Siem Reap	10-12	5	Golden Bayon, Mekong Express, Mex Hong, Neak Krorhorm, Olympic Express, Seila Angkor	3-5 trips per company
Sihanoukville	10-12	4	CTT Net, Giant Ibis, Golden Bayon, Mekong Express, Mex Hong	2-4 trips per company

Mex Hong Transport (☏023-637 2722) Call for pick-up.

Neak Krorhorm (Map p176; ☏092 966669; 4 St 108)

Seila Angkor (Map p176; ☏077 888080; 43 St 154)

CAR & MOTORCYCLE

Guesthouses and travel agencies can arrange a car and driver from US$25 to US$60 a day, depending on the destination.

SHARE TAXI, PICK-UP & MINIBUS

Share taxis, pick-ups and local minibuses leave Phnom Penh for destinations all over the country. Taxis to Kampot, Kep and Takeo leave from **Psar Dang Kor** (Map p175; Mao Tse Toung Blvd), while packed local minibuses and share taxis

for most other places leave from the northwest corner of Psar Thmei.

Vehicles for the Vietnam border leave from **Chbah Ampeau taxi park** (Map p175; Hwy 1) on the eastern side of Monivong Bridge in the south of town.

Local minibuses and pick-ups aren't much fun and are best avoided when there are larger aircon buses or faster share taxis available, which is pretty much everywhere. However, they will save you a buck or two if you're pinching pennies.

ℹ️ Getting Around

TO/FROM THE AIRPORT & BUS STATIONS

Phnom Penh International Airport is 7km west of central Phnom Penh. An official booth

---

GETTING TO VIETNAM: SOUTHEASTERN BORDERS

Phnom Penh to Chau Doc

The most scenic way to end your travels in Cambodia is to sail the Mekong to Kaam Samnor, about 100km south-southeast of Phnom Penh, cross the border to Vinh Xuong in Vietnam, and proceed to Chau Doc on the Tonlé Bassac River via a small channel or overland.

Various companies do trips all the way through to Chau Doc using a single boat or some combination of bus and boat; they cost US$20 to US$30, depending on the speed of the boat and the level of service. The trip averages about four hours. Backpacker guesthouses and tour companies offer cheaper bus/boat combo trips. All boats depart from Phnom Penh's tourist boat dock (p177).

For more information about crossing this border in the other direction, see p150.

Phnom Penh to Ho Chi Minh City

The original Bavet/Moc Bai crossing between Vietnam and Cambodia has seen steady traffic for two decades.

Getting to the border The easiest way to get to Ho Chi Minh City is to catch an international bus (US$8 to US$13, seven hours) from Phnom Penh. There are several companies making this trip.

At the border Long lines entering either country are not uncommon, but otherwise it's straightforward provided you purchase a Vietnamese visa in advance.

Moving on If you are not on the international bus, it's not hard to find onward transport to HCMC or elsewhere.

For more information about crossing this border in the other direction, see p145.

Takeo to Chau Doc

The remote and seldom-used Phnom Den/Tinh Bien border crossing (open 7am to 5pm) between Cambodia and Vietnam lies about 60km southeast of Takeo town in Cambodia and offers connections to Chau Doc.

Getting to the border Take a share taxi (10,000r), a chartered taxi (US$25) or a *moto* (US$10) from Takeo to the border (48km).

At the border Formalities are minimal here, provided you have a Vietnamese visa.

Moving on On the other side, travellers are at the mercy of Vietnamese *xe om* (motorbike taxi) drivers and taxis for the 30km journey from the border to Chau Doc. Expect to pay somewhere between US$5 and US$10 by bike, more like US$20 for a taxi.

For more information about crossing this border in the other direction, see p150.

outside the airport arrivals area arranges taxis to anywhere in the city for US$9 to US$12, or a *remorque* for a flat US$7. You can get a *remorque* for US$4 and a *moto* for half that if you walk one minute out to the street. Heading to the airport from central Phnom Penh, a taxi/*remorque*/*moto* will cost about US$10/4/2. The journey usually takes around 30 minutes.

If you arrive by bus, chances are you'll be dropped off near Psar Thmei (aka Central Market), a short ride from most hotels and guesthouses. Figure on US$0.50 to US$1 for a *moto*, and US$2 to US$3 for a *remorque*. Prices are about the same from the tourist boat dock on Sisowath Quay, where arriving boats from Vietnam and Siem Reap incite *moto*-madness.

BICYCLE
Simple bicycles can be hired from some guesthouses and hotels from US$1 a day, or contact Vicious Cycle (p178) for something a bit more sophisticated.

CYCLO, MOTO & REMORQUE
Motos are everywhere and the drivers of those hanging out around tourist areas can generally speak good street English. Short rides around the city cost 2000r; it's US$1 to venture out a little further. At night these prices double. To charter one for a day, expect to pay around US$7 to US$10.

Remorques (motorcycle-pulled trailers) usually charge double the price of a *moto*, possibly more if you pile on the passengers. *Cyclos* can be tougher to find but cost about the same as *motos*.

MOTORCYCLE
Exploring Phnom Penh and the surrounding areas on a motorbike is a very liberating experience if you are used to chaotic traffic conditions. You will get what you pay for when choosing a steel steed.

Angkor Motorcycles (Map p176; 012 722098; 92 St 51) Huge selection of trail bikes (day/week rentals US$15/100), plus motorbikes at US$5 to US$7 per day.

Lucky! Lucky! (Map p180; 023-212788; 413 Monivong Blvd) Motorbikes are US$4 to US$7 per day, less for multiple days. Trail bikes from US$12.

New! New! (Map p180; 012 855488; 417 Monivong Blvd) Motorbikes start at US$4 per day, trail bikes from US$12.

Vannak Bikes Rental (Map p176; 46 St 130) High-performance trail bikes up to 600cc for US$15 to US$30 per day, and smaller motorbikes for US$5 to US$7.

TAXI
Taxis are cheap at 3000r per kilometre but don't expect to flag one down on the street.

Call **Global Meter Taxi** (011 311888) or **Choice Taxi** (010 888010, 023-888023) for a pick-up.

AROUND PHNOM PENH
There are several sites close to Phnom Penh that make for interesting excursions.

Tonlé Bati, Phnom Tamao and Phnom Chisor are all near each other on NH2 and make a great full-day *remorque* excursion (US$35) or motorbike ride.

Koh Dach
Known as 'Silk Island' by foreigners, this is actually a pair of islands lying in the Mekong River about 5km northeast of the Japanese Friendship Bridge. They make for an easy half-day DIY excursion for those who want to experience the 'real Cambodia'. The hustle and bustle of Phnom Penh feels light years away here. The name derives from the preponderance of silk weavers who inhabit the islands, and you'll have plenty of chances to buy from them.

Remorque drivers offer half-day tours to Koh Dach; US$12 should do it, but be ready to negotiate. Daily boat tours from the tourist boat dock, departing at 8.30am, 9.30am and 1pm, are another option (minimum four people). If self-driving, cross the Japanese Bridge and follow NH6 for a few kilometres before turning right and picking up a dirt road that's parallel to the river, which leads right to the ferry landing.

Tonlé Bati
Locals love to come to this lake (admission US$3) for picnics, as along the way they can stop off at two 12th-century temples: Ta Prohm and Yeay Peau. Ta Prohm is the more interesting of the two; it has some fine carvings in good condition, depicting scenes of birth, dishonour and damnation.

The well-marked turn-off to Tonlé Bati is on the right, 33km south of central Phnom Penh. The Takeo-bound Phnom Penh Sorya bus (8000r, four daily – shoot for the 7am or the 10.30am one) can drop you here; find a *moto* to the temples (1.8km from the highway). Returning to Phnom Penh can be problematic. The best advice is to buy a ticket in advance on Sorya's Takeo–Phnom Penh bus. Otherwise, hire a *moto*.

CAMBODIA SIEM REAP

Phnom Tamao Wildlife Sanctuary ភ្នំតាម៉ៅ (សួនសត្វ)

This **sanctuary** (adult/child US$5/2; ⊘8am-5pm) for rescued animals is home to gibbons, sun bears, elephants, tigers, deer and a bird enclosure. All were taken from poachers or abusive owners and receive care and shelter here as part of a sustainable breeding program.

Free the Bears (Map p180; www.freethe-bears.org) operates a Bear Keeper for a Day program for those who want to learn more about the Asian black bear and Malayan sun bear. **Wildlife Alliance** (WildAid; www.wildlife-alliance.org) offers a full-day interactive tour to raise funds for Phnom Tamao; donors interact with rescued animals and get to feed various baby animals. All proceeds go towards the rescue and care of wildlife at Phnom Tamao.

The access road to Phnom Tamao is clearly signposted on the right 6.5km south of the turn-off to Tonlé Bati on NH2. If coming by bus, have the driver let you off at the turn-off, where *motos* await to shuttle you the final 5km to the sanctuary.

Phnom Chisor ភ្នំជីស

Some spectacular views of the countryside are on offer from the summit of **Phnom Chisor** (admission levied at the summit US$2), although the landscape screams Gobi Desert during the dry season. This laterite-and-brick temple, dating from the 11th century, with carved sandstone lintels, guards the hilltop's eastern face. From atop the temple's southern stairs, the sacred pool of **Tonlé Om** is visible below.

The access road to Phnom Chisor is signposted (in Khmer) on the left, 12km south of the Phnom Tamao turn-off on NH2. The temple is 4.5km from the highway – *motos* wait at the turn-off.

Udong ឧដុង្គ

Another popular offering among Phnom Penh touts, Udong (the Victorious) served as the capital of Cambodia under several sovereigns between 1618 and 1866. The hill temple of **Phnom Udong** has several interesting stupas and sanctuaries, plus a 20m-high Buddha. At the base of the hill the sprawling **Cambodia Vipassana Dhura** **Buddhist Meditation Centre** (⊘contact Mr Um Sovann 016 883090; www.cambodiavipassana-center.com) offers meditation retreats.

Udong is 37km north of the capital. Take a Phnom Penh Sorya bus bound for Kompong Chhnang (10,000r, one hour to Udong). To return to Phnom Penh flag down a bus on NH5 or take a *moto*/taxi for US$10/40.

SIEM REAP

☑ 063 / POP 135,000

The life-support system for the one and only temples of Angkor, Siem Reap (សៀមរាប) was always destined for great things. Back in the 1960s, Siem Reap (*see*-em ree-*ep*) was the place to be in Southeast Asia and saw a steady stream of the rich and famous. After three decades of slumber, it's well and truly back, reinventing itself as the epicentre of the new Cambodia, with more guesthouses and hotels than temples, and sumptuous spas and world-class wining and dining.

At heart, though, Siem Reap – whose name rather undiplomatically means 'Siamese Defeated' – is still a little charmer, with old French shophouses, shady tree-lined boulevards and a slow-flowing river.

◉ Sights

★**Angkor National Museum** MUSEUM
(សារមន្ទីរអង្គរ; ☑063-966601; www.angkorna-tionalmuseum.com; 968 Charles de Gaulle Blvd; adult/child under 1.2m US$12/6; ⊘8.30am-6pm, to 6.30pm Oct-30) A worthwhile introduction to the glories of the Khmer empire, the state-of-the-art Angkor National Museum will help clarify Angkor's history, religious significance, and cultural and political context. Displays include 1400 exquisite stone carvings and artefacts.

Les Chantiers Écoles SCHOOL
(កសិដ្ឋានស្ត្រី; www.artisansdangkor.com; ⊘7.30am-5.30pm, silk farm 8am-5.30pm) FREE Siem Reap is the epicentre of the drive to revitalise Cambodian traditional culture, which was dealt such a harsh blow by the Khmer Rouge and the years of instability that followed its rule. Les Chantiers Écoles is a school specialising in teaching wood- and stone-carving techniques, traditional silk painting, lacquerware and more to impoverished youngsters. Tours of the workshops are possible when school is in session. On the premises is an impressive shop, **Artisans d'Angkor** (www.artisansdang-

kor.com; ⊙7.30am-6.30pm), that specialises in silks and sculptures.

To see the entire silk-making process, from mulberry trees to silk worms and spinning to weaving, visit Les Chantiers Écoles' **silk farm** (⊙8am-5.30pm), 16km west of town. Shuttle buses leave the school daily at 9.30am and 1.30pm for a free three-hour tour.

Cambodia Landmine Museum MUSEUM
(☑012 598951; www.cambodialandminemuseum. org; admission US$2; ⊙7.30am-5pm) Popular with travellers thanks to its informative displays on one of the country's postwar curses, the nonprofit Cambodia Landmine Museum has a mock minefield where visitors can search for deactivated mines. It's situated about 25km from Siem Reap and 6km south of Banteay Srei temple.

Angkor Butterfly Centre WILDLIFE RESERVE
(សួនមេអំបៅបន្លាយស្រី; ☑097 852 7852; www. angkorbutterfly.com; adult/child US$4/2; ⊙9am-5pm) 🦋 About 1km south of the Cambodia Landmine Museum, near Banteay Srei, this is the largest fully enclosed butterfly centre in Southeast Asia.

Bayon Information Centre INFORMATION CENTRE
(☑092 165083; www.angkor-jsa.org/bic; admission US$2; ⊙8am-4pm Tue, Wed & Fri Sun) This exhibition introduces visitors to the history of the Khmer empire and the restoration projects around Angkor through a series of short films and displays. Set in the beautiful Japanese Team for Safeguarding Angkor (JSA) compound, it's considerably cheaper than the Angkor National Museum, although there is no statuary on display.

Wat Thmei BUDDHIST TEMPLE
(វត្តថ្មី; ⊙6am-6pm) **FREE** On the left fork of the road to Angkor Wat, Wat Thmei has a small memorial stupa containing the skulls and bones of victims of the Khmer Rouge. It also has plenty of young monks eager to practise their English.

🏃 Activities

Golf

For the regulation golf courses, add 25% on top of green fees for clubs, a caddy and buggy.

Angkor Golf Resort GOLF
(☑063-761139; www.angkor-golf.com; green fees US$115) World-class course designed by legendary British golfer Nick Faldo.

Phokheetra Country Club GOLF
(☑063-964600; www.sofitel.com; green fees US$100) Includes an ancient Angkor bridge amid its manicured fairways and greens.

Angkor Putt MINI GOLF
(☑012 302330; www.angkorwatputt.com; adult/child US$5/4; ⊙7.30am-11pm) Navigate mini temples and creative obstacles for 14 holes. Win a beer for a hole-in-one.

Massage & Yoga

Foot massage is a big hit in Siem Reap, hardly surprising given all those steep stairways at the temples. There are half a dozen or more places offering a massage for about US$6 to US$8 an hour on the strip running northwest of Psar Chaa. Some are more authentic than others, so dip your toe in first before selling your sole.

For an alternative foot massage, try a **fish spa**, which sees cleaner fish nibble away at your dead skin – heaven for some, tickly as

---

DON'T MISS

FLIGHT OF THE GIBBON

Angkor is the ultimate backdrop for state-of-the-art zipline experience in Asia. New in 2013, **Flight of the Gibbon Angkor** (☑096 999 9101; www.treetopasia.com; near Ta Nei Temple, Angkor; per person US$99; ⊙7am-5pm) is located inside the Angkor protected area. The course includes 10 ziplines, 21 tree-top platforms, four sky bridges and an abseil finish. A conservation element is included in the project with a pair of gibbons released in the surrounding forest and a plan for more introductions in the future.

If we have one quibble, it would be the high entry price, which does not include the US$20 admission to the temple complex (you pay that separately). However, the price does include an optional transfer to any Siem Reap hotel, plus a lunch before or after the trip near Sra Srang. At the time of writing the price was being discounted to US$79 per person; it was unclear how long the discount would last.

Siem Reap

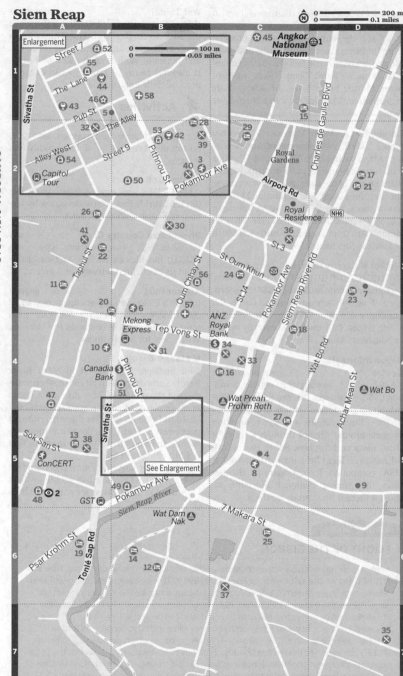

Siem Reap

CAMBODIA SIEM REAP

hell for others. Places have sprung up all over town, including along Pub St.

Bodytune SPA
(☎063-764141; www.bodytune.co.th; 293 Pokambor Ave; ⊙10am-10pm) A lavish outpost of a popular Thai spa, this is a fine place to relax and unwind on the riverfront.

Krousar Thmey MASSAGE
(massage US$7) ✆ Massage by the blind in the same location as its free Tonlé Sap Exhibition.

Lemongrass Garden Spa SPA
(☎012 387385; www.lemongrassgarden.com; 105B Sivatha St; ⊙11am-11pm) Smart spa in a cen-

tral location, offering a range of affordable treatments.

Peace Cafe Yoga YOGA
(☎063-965210; www.peacecafeangkor.org; St 26; per session US$6) Popular community-centre-cum-cafe that has daily yoga sessions at 8.30am and 6.30pm, including Ashtanga and Hatha sessions.

Seeing Hands Massage 4 MASSAGE
(☎012 836487; 324 Sivatha St; per hr fan/air-con US$5/7) ✆ Seeing Hands trains blind people in the art of massage. Watch out for copycats, as some of these are just exploiting the blind for profit.

🎓 Courses

Cooks in Tuk Tuks COOKING COURSE
(☑ 063-963400; www.therivergarden.info; per person US$25) Starts at 10am daily with a visit to Psar Leu market, then returns to the River Garden hotel for a professional class.

Le Tigre de Papier COOKING COURSE
(Pub St; per person US$12) 🍃 Starts at 10am daily and includes a visit to the market. Proceeds go towards supporting Sala Bai Hotel & Restaurant School.

👉 Tours

Beyond TOURS
(www.beyonduniqueescapes.com) Tours to Beng Mealea, Kompong Pluk, cycling trips and cooking classes.

Grasshopper Adventures BICYCLE TOUR
(☑ 012 462165; www.grasshopperadventures.com; 586 St 26; per person from US$39) Rides around the Siem Reap countryside, plus a dedicated temple tour on two wheels.

Happy Ranch HORSE RIDING
(☑ 012 920002; www.thehappyranch.com; 1hr/half-day US$25/56) Explore Siem Reap on horseback, taking in surrounding villages and secluded temples.

Off Track BICYCLE TOUR
(☑ 093-903024; www.kko-cambodia.org; St 20; tours US$35-40) 🍃 Good-cause cycling tours around the paths of Angkor or into the countryside beyond the Western Baray. Proceeds go towards Khmer for Khmer Organisation, which supports education and vocational training.

Pure Countryside Cycling Tour BICYCLE TOUR
(www.pureforkids.org; per person US$22) 🍃 Long half-day tour that takes in local life around Siem Reap, including lunch with a local family. Proceeds support Pure educational and vocational-training projects.

Terre Cambodge TOURS
(☑ 077 448255; www.terrecambodge.com) Remote sites around Angkor, some by bicycle, plus boat trips on the Tonlé Sap Lake.

🛏 Sleeping

Siem Reap now has more hotels and guesthouses than temples and that means there are hundreds to choose from, from simple shacks with shared toilets to sumptuous six-star suites.

Many places offer free pick-up from the airport, port or bus station: email or call ahead. Commission scams abound in Siem Reap so keep your antennae up.

🛏 Psar Chaa Area

This is the liveliest part of town, brimming with restaurants, bars and boutiques. Staying here can be a lot of fun, but it's not the quietest part of town.

★ Ivy Guesthouse 2 GUESTHOUSE $
(☑ 012 800860; www.ivy-guesthouse.com; r US$6-15; 🌀@🌐) An inviting guesthouse with a chill-out area and bar, the Ivy is a lively place to stay. The restaurant is as good as it gets among the guesthouses in town, with a huge vegetarian selection.

Mandalay Inn GUESTHOUSE $
(☑ 063-761662; www.mandalayinn.com; r US$7-18; 🌀@🌐) This smart guesthouse promises Burmese hospitality meets Khmer smiles, offering spotless rooms plus free wi-fi and a rooftop 'gym'. It's a friendly spot.

Downtown Siem Reap Hostel HOSTEL $
(☑ 012 675881; www.downtownsiemreaphostel. hostel.com; Wat Damnak area; dm US$4-6, r US$13-17; 🌀🌐❄) Also sometimes known as Bamboo Garden; the rates here are particularly attractive when you consider there is a small pool in the garden.

Golden Banana BOUTIQUE HOTEL $$
(☑ 063-761259; 063-766655; www.golden-banana. com; B&B r US$22-31, boutique r US$55-136; 🌀@🌐❄) There are now four Golden Bananas occupying this crossroads near Wat Damnak, including the original B&B and a high-rise hotel, plus two boutique hotels under different ownership. We recommend the original B&B or the newer boutique hotels, which offer duplex suites set on two floors. All are gay-friendly.

Steung Siem Reap Hotel HOTEL $$
(☑ 063-965167; www.steungsiemreaphotel.com; Psar Chaa; r from US$63; 🌀@🌐❄) In keeping with the French-colonial air around Psar Chaa, this hotel has high ceilings, louvre shutters and wrought-iron balconies. Three-star rooms feature smart wooden trim.

🛏 Sivatha St Area

The area to the west of Sivatha St includes a good selection of budget guesthouses and midrange boutique hotels.

My Home Tropical
Garden Villa
GUESTHOUSE $

(☎063-760035; www.myhomecambodia.com; r US$12-30; ❄@🖥🌊🚲) Offering hotel standards at guesthouse prices, this is a fine place to rest your head. The decor includes some soft silks and the furnishings are tasteful, plus there's an inviting little swimming pool.

Smiley Guesthouse
GUESTHOUSE $

(☎012 852955; www.smileyguesthouse.com; r US$8-15; ❄@🖥) One of the first guesthouses to undergo a hotel-tastic makeover almost a decade ago, this place has more than 70 rooms set around a garden courtyard.

Garden Village
GUESTHOUSE $

(☎012 217373; www.gardenvillageguesthouse.com; dm US$1, r US$6-13; ❄@🖥) This traditional backpacker hang-out offers some of the cheapest beds in town and is a good place to meet travellers. The rooftop bar is a draw around sunset.

Auberge Mont Royal
HOTEL $$

(☎063-964044; www.auberge-mont-royal.com; r US$32-85; ❄@🖥🌊) Set in a classic colonial-style villa, the Auberge has smart rooms at a smart price, with the swimming pool and spa making it a cut above other offerings in this price bracket.

Encore Angkor Guesthouse
HOTEL $$

(☎063-969400; www.encoreangkor.com; 456 Sok San St; r US$40-60; ❄@🖥🌊) The stylish lobby sets the tone for a budget boutique experience. Rooms include oversized beds and an in-room safe. Their motto was 'just don't tell anyone', but unfortunately we spilled the beans a few years ago.

Sala Bai Hotel &
Restaurant School
HOTEL $$

(☎063-963329; www.salabai.com; Taphul St; r US$15-30; ❄@🖥) 🍴 Immerse yourself in the intimate surrounds of this training-school hotel, where the super staff are ever-helpful. The four rooms include silk wall hangings, woven throw pillows and wicker wardrobes; book ahead.

Park Hyatt Siem Reap
HOTEL $$$

(☎063-966000; www.parkhyatt.com; Sivatha St; r/ste from US$265/765; ❄@🖥🌊) Formerly the funky Hotel de la Paix, Park Hyatt has risen from the renovations and retained much of the personality of its predecessor, albeit at a more luxurious level.

🏛 East Bank

This area is quieter than around Psar Chaa, with plenty of charm near the river.

Seven Candles Guesthouse
GUESTHOUSE $

(☎063-963380; www.sevencandlesguesthouse.com; 307 Wat Bo Rd; r US$10-20; ❄@🖥) 🍴 A good-cause guesthouse, whose profits help a local foundation that seeks to promote education to rural communities. Rooms include hot water, TV and fridge.

Siem Reap Hostel
HOSTEL $

(☎063-964660; www.thesiemreaphostel.com; 10 Makara St; dm US$6-8, r incl breakfast US$20-39; ❄@🖥🌊) Angkor's original full-on backpacker hostel is pretty slick. The dorms are well tended and the rooms are definitely flashpacker, plus there's a covered pool.

Rosy Guesthouse
GUESTHOUSE $

(☎063-965059; www.rosyguesthouse.com; Siem Reap River Rd; r US$8-30; ❄🖥) 🍴 A British-owned establishment whose 13 rooms come with TV and DVD. Has a lively pub downstairs with great grub and hosts regular events to support community causes.

Soria Moria Hotel
BOUTIQUE HOTEL $$

(☎063-964768; www.thesoriamoria.com; Wat Bo Rd; r US$39-63; ❄@🖥🌊) 🍴 This boutique place has attractive rooms with smart bathroom fittings. Fusion restaurant downstairs, open-air hot tub upstairs and a new swimming pool. Promotes local causes to help the community.

La Noria Guesthouse
GUESTHOUSE $$

(☎063-964242; www.lanoriaangkor.com; r US$39-59; ❄@🖥🌊) Long running and lovely La Noria is set in a lush tropical garden with a pretty swimming pool. Rooms have a traditional trim and include a verandah but no TV or fridge.

★La Résidence d'Angkor
RESORT $$$

(☎063-963390; www.residencedangkor.com; Siem Reap River Rd; r from US$280; ❄@🖥🌊) The 54 wood-appointed rooms, among the most tasteful and inviting in town, come with verandahs and huge jacuzzi-sized tubs. The newer wing is ultra-contemporary, as is the sumptuous Kong Kea Spa.

🏛 Riverfront & Royal Gardens

The smart end of town, this is where the royal residence is to be found, along with many of the luxury hotels and boutique resorts.

Shinta Mani
RESORT $$$

(063-761998; www.shintamani.com; Oum Khun St; r US$83-230; ⚹@🕾☀) Contemporary chic designed by renowned architect Bill Bensley, Shinta Mani Resort offers an inviting central pool, while Shinta Mani Club offers more exclusive rooms. Shinta Mani has won several international awards for responsible tourism practices.

Grand Hotel d'Angkor
HOTEL $$$

(063-963888; www.raffles.com; r from US$260; ⚹@🕾☀) The hotel with history on its side, this place has been welcoming guests since 1929, including Charlie Chaplin, Charles de Gaulle, Jackie Kennedy and Bill Clinton. Ensconced in such opulent surroundings, you can imagine what it was like to be a tourist in colonial days.

Victoria Angkor Hotel
HOTEL $$$

(063-760428; www.victoriahotels-asia.com; r from US$150; ⚹@🕾☀) The Victoria is a popular choice for those craving the French touch in Indochine. The classy lobby is the perfect introduction to one of the most impressive courtyard pools in town. The rooms are well finished and many include a striking pool view.

🛏 Further Afield

★Pavillon Indochine
BOUTIQUE HOTEL $$

(012 849681; www.pavillon-indochine.com; r US$55-70, ste US$75-95; ⚹@🕾☀) The Pavillon offers charming colonial-chic rooms set around a small swimming pool. Included in the rates is a *remorque* driver for the day to tour the temples, making it great value.

Samar Villas & Spa
RESORT $$$

(063-762449; www.samarvillas.com; r US$160-300; ⚹@🕾☀) The most boutique of many boutique places in Siem Reap, the Samar offers sumptuous all-wooden suites, each with individual taste and character. Rates include a daily shave for gents and a hand massage for women.

🍴 Eating

Worthy restaurants are sprinkled all around town but Siem Reap's culinary heart is the Psar Chaa area, whose focal point, the Alley, is literally lined with mellow eateries offering great atmosphere. It is wall-to-wall with good Cambodian restaurants, many family owned.

Cheap eats can be found in the small eateries (mains US$1.50-4; ⊘7am-9pm) lining Psar Chaa. For self-caterers, markets sell fruit and veg. Angkor Market (Sivatha St) can supply international treats.

★Green Star
CAMBODIAN $

(www.greenstarrestaurant.org; mains US$2-5; ⊘11.30am-2pm & 5.30-10.30pm Mon-Sat; 🕾) Tucked away in a quiet street behind Wat Damnak is this appealing not-for-profit restaurant supporting former street kids in

---

TOP FIVE: GOOD-CAUSE DINING

Marum (www.marum-restaurant.org; Wat Polanka area; mains US$3.25-6.75; ⊘11am-10pm Mon-Sat; 🕾) Set in a delightful wooden house with a spacious garden, this training restaurant brings the best of Friends (p186) to Siem Reap. Menu highlights include red tree-ant fritters and ginger basil meatballs.

Haven (078-342404; www.haven-cambodia.com; Sok San St; mains US$3-7; ⊘11am-10pm; 🕾) A culinary haven indeed: dine here for the best of East meets West. The fish fillet with green mango is particularly zesty. Proceeds go towards helping young-adult orphans make the step from institution to employment. Book ahead.

Common Grounds (719 St 14; light meals US$3-5; ⊘7am-10pm; 🕾) Sophisticated international cafe with great coffee, homemade cakes, light bites, and free wi-fi and internet terminals. Offers free computer classes and English classes for Cambodians, and supports good causes.

Blossom Cafe (www.blossomcakes.org; St 6; cupcakes US$1.50; ⊘10am-5pm Mon-Sat; 🕾) Cupcakes are elevated to an artform at this elegant cafe. Creative coffees, teas and juices are also available and profits assist Cambodian women in vocational training.

New Leaf Book Cafe (near Psar Chaa; mains US$3-6; ⊘7am-10pm) All profits go towards supporting NGOs working in Siem Reap Province. The menu includes some home favourites, an Italian twist and some local Cambodian specials.

Siem Reap. Authentic Khmer dishes include spicy duck, lemongrass eel and succulent frog.

Sister Srey Cafe
CAFE **$**

(200 Pokambor Ave; mains US$3-6; ⊘7am-7pm Tue-Sun) Friendly Sister Srey offers an ambitious breakfast menu that is perfect after a sunrise at the temples, including eggs Benedelicious. Lunch is Western food with a creative twist, including burgers, wraps and salads.

Blue Pumpkin
CAFE **$**

(Pithnou St; cones US$1.50; ⊘6am-10pm) Upstairs is a world of white minimalism with beds to lounge on and free wi-fi. Light bites, great sandwiches, divine shakes and superb cakes keep them coming.

★ Chanrey Tree
CAMBODIAN **$$**

(www.chanreytree.com; Pokambor Ave; mains US$5-12; ⊘11am-10pm) Cool and contemporary, Chanrey Tree is the new face of Khmer cuisine, combining a stylish setting with expressive presentation while retaining the essentials of traditional Cambodian cooking. Try the roast chicken with honey, rice brandy, young jackfruit and lemongrass.

Sugar Palm
CAMBODIAN **$$**

(www.sugarpalmrestaurant.com; Taphul St; mains US$5-9; ⊘11.30am-3pm & 5.30-10pm Mon-Sat; ☎) Set in a beautiful wooden house, this is an excellent place to sample traditional flavours infused with herbs and spices. Owner-chef Katana taught Gordon Ramsay some tricks during his *Great Escape* shoot.

Chamkar
VEGETARIAN **$$**

(www.chamkar-vegetarian.com; The Alley, mains US$4-8; ⊘11am-11pm, closed lunch Sun; ☎🖉) The name translates as 'farm' at this creative organic restaurant. Asian flavours predominate, such as stuffed pumpkin or vegetable kebabs in black pepper sauce.

FCC Angkor
INTERNATIONAL **$$**

(🖉063-760280; Pokambor Ave; mains US$5-15; ⊘7am-midnight; ☎) This landmark building draws people in from the riverside thanks to a reflective pool, torch-lit dining and a garden bar. Inside, the colonial chic continues with lounge chairs and an open kitchen turning out a range of Asian and international food.

★ Cuisine Wat Damnak
CAMBODIAN **$$$**

(www.cuisinewatdamnak.com; Wat Damnak village; 5/6-course menu US$22/26; ⊘dinner) Set in a traditional wooden house, this is celeb chef Johannes Rivieres' highly regarded restaurant. Seasonal set menus change weekly, plus vegetarian options are available with advance notice.

🍷 Drinking & Nightlife

Siem Reap is now firmly on the nightlife map of Southeast Asia. The Psar Chaa area is a good hunting ground, and one street is now known as 'Pub St': dive in, crawl out.

Many of the high-end hotels offer two-for-one happy hours.

FCC Angkor
BAR

(Pokambor Ave) Well worth stopping by for a jar or two to take in the sophisticated surrounds. Happy hour is from 5pm to 7pm.

Angkor What?
BAR

(Pub St; ⊘5pm-late; ☎) Siem Reap's original bar claims to have been promoting irresponsible drinking since 1998. The happy hour (to 9pm) lightens the mood for later when everyone's bouncing along to indie anthems, sometimes on the tables, sometimes under them.

Mezze Bar
BAR

(www.mezzebarsiemreap.com; St 11; ⊘6pm-late; ☎) One of the hippest bars in Siem Reap, Mezze is located above the madness that surrounds Pub St. Ascend the stairs to a contemporary lounge-bar complete with original art and regular DJs.

Laundry Bar
BAR, NIGHTCLUB

(St 9; ⊘4pm-late; ☎) One of the most alluring bars in town thanks to discerning decor, low lighting and a laid-back soundtrack. Happy hour is 5pm to 9pm.

Miss Wong
BAR

(The Lane; ⊘5pm-late; ☎) Miss Wong carries you back to the chic of 1920s Shanghai. The cocktails are the draw here. A gay-friendly bar.

Warehouse
BAR

(Pithnou St; ⊘10.30am-3am; ☎) A popular bar opposite Psar Chaa, offering indie anthems, table football, a pool table and devilish drinks.

☆ Entertainment

Classical Cambodian dance shows take place all over town, but only a few are worth considering.

GETTING TO THAILAND: SIEM REAP TO BANGKOK

The original Poipet/Aranya Prathet land border crossing (open 7am to 8pm) between Cambodia and Thailand is by far the busiest and the one most people take when travelling between Bangkok and Siem Reap. It has earned itself a bad reputation over the years, with scams galore to help tourists part with their money, especially coming in from Thailand.

Getting to the border Frequent buses and share taxis run from Siem Reap and Battambang to Poipet. Buying a ticket all the way to Bangkok (usually involving a change of buses at the border) can expedite things and save you the hassle of finding onward transport on the Thai side. The 8am through bus to Mo Chit bus station in Bangkok run by Nattakan in Siem Reap costs an inflated US$28, but is the only bus service that allows you to continue to Bangkok on the same bus you board in Siem Reap.

At the border Be prepared to wait in sweltering immigration lines on both sides, especially in the high season. Show up early to avoid the crowds. You can pay a special 'VIP fee' (aka a bribe) of 200B on either side to skip the lines. There is no departure tax to leave Cambodia despite what Cambodian border officials might tell you. Entering Thailand, most nationalities are issued 15-day visa waivers free of charge.

Moving on Minibuses wait just over the border on the Thai side to whisk you to Bangkok (B300, four hours, every 30 minutes). Or make your way 7km to Aranya Prathet by túk-túk (80B) or *sŏrngtăaou* (pick-up truck; 15B), from where there are regular buses to Bangkok's Mo Chit station (223B, five to six hours) between 4am and 6pm. Make sure your túk-túk driver takes you to the main bus station in Aranya Prathet for your 80B, not to the smaller station about 1km from the border (a common scam). The 1.55pm train is another option to Bangkok.

For more information about crossing this border in the other direction, see p403.

★ **Phare** CIRCUS
(The Cambodian Circus; ☎ 015 499480; www.pharecambodiancircus.org; behind Angkor National Museum; adult/child US$15/8, premium seats US$35/18; ⏰ 7.30pm daily) The revered Battambang circus troupe opened a big top in Siem Reap in 2013 and the results have been spectacular. Besides stunningly daring and original acts, Phare's shows carry a subtle yet striking social message. Not to be missed.

La Noria Restaurant PERFORMING ARTS
(☎ 063-964242; show US$6, mains US$4-8) 🌿 For something a bit different, try the Wednesday-evening shadow-puppet show with classical dance at La Noria. Part of the fee is donated to a charity supporting local children.

Temple Club DANCE
(Pub St) Free traditional dance show upstairs from 7.30pm, providing punters order some food and drink from the very reasonably priced menu.

🛍 Shopping

Siem Reap has an excellent selection of Cambodian-made handicrafts. **Psar Chaa** (Old Market) is well stocked. There are bargains to be had if you haggle patiently and humorously. **Angkor Night Market** (www.angkornightmarket.com; ⏰ 4pm-midnight) is packed with silks, handicrafts and souvenirs. Up-and-coming **Alley West** is also a great strip to browse socially responsible fashion boutiques.

Several shops support Cambodia's disabled and disenfranchised, including exquisite Artisans d'Angkor (p194).

Monument Books BOOKSTORE
(Pokambor Ave; ⏰ 9am-9pm) Well-stocked new bookstore near Psar Chaa, with an additional branch at the airport.

Rajana ARTS & CRAFTS
(☎ 063-964744; www.rajanacrafts.org; Sivatha St; ⏰ 9am-9pm Mon-Sat) Sells quirky wooden and metalware objects, silver jewellery and handmade cards. Rajana promotes fair trade and employment opportunities for Cambodians.

Samatoa CLOTHING
(012 285930; www.samatoa.com; Pithnou St;
8am-11pm) Designer clothes in silk with the
option of a tailored fit in 48 hours. Promotes
fair trade and responsible employment.

Senteurs d'Angkor
(063-964860; Pithnou St; 8.30am-9.30pm)
Has a wide-ranging collection of silk, stone
carvings, beauty products, massage oils,
spices, coffees and teas, all sourced locally.

Smateria ACCESSORIES
(www.smateria.com; Alley West; 10am-10pm)
Recycling rocks here, with funky bags made
from construction nets, plastic bags, motorbike seat covers and more. Fair-trade enterprise employing some disabled Cambodians.

Three Seasons CLOTHING
(The Lane; 10am-10pm) Three shops in one
at this new place, including Elsewhere, Zoco
and Keo Kjay, a fair-trade fashion enterprise
helping HIV-positive women earn a living.

Weaves of Cambodia ACCESSORIES
(Angkor Hospital for Children, cnr Oum Chhay St
& St 5; 8am-7pm) Top-quality silk bags,
cushions and scarves. Part of Vientiane-
based American textile designer Carol Cassi-
dy's silk empire, Weaves provides work
and rehabilitation for landmine and polio
victims, widows and orphans out of its studio in Preah Vihear City.

ⓘ Information

Hotels, restaurants and bars can provide the
free *Siem Reap Angkor Visitors Guide* (www.
canbypublications.com) and two handy booklets
produced by Pocket Guide Cambodia.

There are ATMs at the airport and in banks and
minimarts all over central Siem Reap, especially
along Sivatha St. The greatest concentration of
internet shops is along Sivatha St and around
Psar Chaa. Free wi-fi is available at many of the
leading cafes, restaurants and bars, as well as
most guesthouses and hotels.

Angkor Hospital for Children (AHC; 063-
963409; www.angkorhospital.org; cnr Oum
Chhay St & Achar Mean St; 24hr) A paedi-
atric hospital supported by donors. It's free for
anyone under 16, tourists included.

ANZ Royal Bank (Achar Mean St) Offers
credit-card advances and can change travellers cheques in most major currencies. Several
branches and many ATMs (US$5 per with-
drawal) around town.

Canadia Bank (Sivatha St) Offers free credit-
card cash advances and changes travellers
cheques in most major currencies at a 2%
commission. International ATM with no transaction fees.

Main Post Office (Pokambor Ave; 7am-
5.30pm) Offers EMS express international
postal service.

Royal Angkor International Hospital (063-
761888; www.royalangkorhospital.com; Airport
Rd) A new international facility affiliated with
the Bangkok Hospital, so very expensive.

Tourist Police (097-778 0013) At the main
Angkor ticket checkpoint.

U-Care Pharmacy (063-965396; Pithnou St;
8am-9pm) Smart pharmacy and shop, like
Boots in Thailand (and the UK). English spoken.

ⓘ Getting There & Away

AIR

Siem Reap International Airport (063-
761261; www.cambodia-airports.com) is a work
of art set 7km west of the centre and offers
regular connections to most neighbouring Asian
cities, plus **Cambodia Angkor Air** (063-
964488; www.cambodiaangkorair.com) domestic flights to Phnom Penh and Sihanoukville.

CAMBODIA SIEM REAP

TRANSPORT FROM SIEM REAP

DESTINATION	CAR & MOTORBIKE	BUS	BOAT	AIR
Bangkok	8hr	US$12-15, 10hr, frequent	N/A	from US$144, 1hr, 5 daily
Battambang	3hr	US$4-5, 4hr, regular	US$20, 6-8hr, 7am	N/A
Kompong Thom	2hr	US$5, 2½hr, frequent	N/A	N/A
Phnom Penh	5hr	US$5-17, 6hr, fre-quent	US$35, 5hr, 7am	from US$90, 30min, several daily
Poipet	3hr	US$4-5, 4hr, regular	N/A	N/A
Sihanoukville	9hr	US10, 12 hr	N/A	from US$110, 45min

BOAT

Boats for the incredibly scenic trip to Battambang (US$20, five to nine hours depending on water levels) and the faster ride to Phnom Penh (US$35, six hours, August to March only) depart at 7am from the tourist boat dock at Chong Kneas, 11km south of town. Tickets are sold at guesthouses, hotels and travel agencies, including pick-up from your hotel or guesthouse around 6am.

BUS

All buses arrive in and depart from the bus station, which is 3km east of town and about 200m south of NH6. Upon arrival, be prepared for a rugby scrum of eager *moto* drivers greeting the bus.

Tickets are available at guesthouses, hotels, bus offices, travel agencies and ticket kiosks. Some bus companies send a minibus around to pick up passengers at their place of lodging. Buses to all destinations are more frequent in the morning.

Tickets to Phnom Penh via NH6 cost anywhere from US$5 for basic air-con buses to US$17 for the business-class buses run by Giant Ibis.

Several companies offer direct services to Kompong Cham (US$6, five or six hours), Battambang (US$3.75, three hours) and Poipet (US$3.75, three hours). GST has a bus to Anlong Veng (US$4, two hours) and on to Sra Em (for Prasat Preah Vihear; US$10, four hours, 7am).

Most buses to Bangkok involve a change at the border. The only exception is the through bus run by Nattakan (US$28). Advertised trips to Ho Chi Minh City involve a transfer in Phnom Penh.

Bus companies that serve Siem Reap:

Capitol Tour (063-963883)
Giant Ibis (www.giantibis.com)
GST (092 905016)
Mekong Express (063-963662)
Nattakan (078 795333; Sivatha St)
Neak Kror Horm (063-964924)
Phnom Penh Sorya (012 235618)
Rith Mony (012 344377)
Virak Buntham (015 958989)

SHARE TAXI

Share taxis stop along NH6 just north of the bus station. Destinations include Phnom Penh (US$10, five hours), Kompong Thom (US$5, two hours), Sisophon (US$5, two hours) and Poipet (US$7, 2½ hours).

ⓘ Getting Around

From the airport, an official *moto*/taxi costs US$2/7; *remorques* (US$5) are available on the road outside the terminal's parking area.

If arriving by boat, a *moto* into town should cost about US$3 from the dock in Chong Kneas.

From the bus station a *moto/remorque* to the city centre should cost about US$1/2. If you're arriving on a bus service sold by a guesthouse,

---

WORTH A TRIP

FLOATING VILLAGES

Follow the Tonlé Sap River upstream (that's downstream in the wet season!) and eventually it becomes the Tonlé Sap Lake around **Kompong Chhnang**, some 50km north of Udong along NH5.

A short sail from Kompong Chhnang's river port, 2km northeast of the centre on the Tonlé Sap River, leads to a couple of colourful floating villages: **Phoum Kandal**, an ethnic Vietnamese village directly southeast of the boat dock; and the Khmer village of **Chong Kos** a bit further north. Much less commercial than **Chong Kneas** near Siem Reap, they have all the amenities of a mainland village – houses, machine-tool shops, vegetable vendors, a mosque, a petrol station – except that almost everything floats. Hire motorless wooden paddle boats for US$10 per hour at the river port to take you into the heart of these villages.

About 70km northwest of Kompong Chhnang on the NH5, the village of Krakor in Pursat Province is the jumping-off point to another ethnic Vietnamese floating village, **Kompong Luong**. This village shifts with the waters, moving further north as the Tonlé Sap recedes. You can spend the night with a local family in a **homestay** (per night not incl boat ride US$6). From Krakor you need to travel 1km to 6km east on a dirt road, depending on the season, to the tourist boat landing, where you can charter a four-passenger wooden motorboat (US$9 per hour for one to three passengers) to explore the village.

Krakor is about halfway between Phnom Penh and Battambang. Buses or share taxis on the Phnom Penh–Pursat–Battambang run can drop you off in either Kompong Chhnang or Krakor, where local transport awaits to whisk you to the waterfront.

the bus will head straight to a partner guesthouse.

Short *moto* trips around the centre of town cost 2000r or 3000r, more at night. A *remorque* is double again.

Most guesthouses and small hotels can usually help with bicycle rental for about US$2 per day. Motorbike hire is currently prohibited in Siem Reap.

AROUND SIEM REAP

Floating Village of Chong Kneas   ភូមិបណ្ដែតចុងឃ្នាស

The famous floating village of Chong Kneas is an easy excursion to arrange yourself. The village moves depending on the season and you will need to rent a boat to get around it properly.

Unfortunately, Chong Kneas has become somewhat of a zoo in recent years. Large tour groups tend to take over and locals have invented countless scams to separate tourists from their money. Sou Ching, the company that runs the tours, has fixed boat prices at an absurd US$20 per person, plus a US$3 entrance fee. In practice it may be possible to pay just US$20 for the boat shared between several people, or contact **Tara Boat** (☏ 092 957765; www.taraboat.com) for an all-inclusive trip.

In-the-know travellers steer well clear of Chong Kneas, opting for harder-to-reach but more memorable spots like Prek Toal or **Kompong Pluk**, an other-worldly place built on soaring stilts about an hour's boat ride from Chong Kneas.

To get to Chong Kneas from Siem Reap costs US$2 by *moto* each way (more if the driver waits), or US$15 by taxi. The trip takes 20 minutes.

Prek Toal Bird Sanctuary ជម្រកបក្សីព្រែកទាល់

One of three biospheres on Tonlé Sap Lake, **Prek Toal** (admission depending on group size US$25-50) is an ornithologist's fantasy. Rare breeds that nest here in large numbers include the huge lesser and greater adjutant storks, the milky stork and the spot-billed pelican. They build enormous nests and congregate atop treetops in thick droves during the dry season (December to April).

It is also possible to visit from September, but the concentrations may be lower. As water starts to dry up elsewhere, the birds congregate here.

Sam Veasna Center (SVC; ☏ 063-963710; www.samveasna.org), in the Wat Bo area of Siem Reap, offers trips to Prek Toal. The full-day trips cost about US$100 per person for a group of five or more, with additional charges for smaller groups, and include highly trained English-speaking bird guides. **Osmose** (☏ 012 832812; www.osmosetonlesap.net) also runs organised day trips to Prek Toal. These include English-speaking guides and cost US$95 per person with a minimum group of four.

Getting to the sanctuary under your own steam from Siem Reap requires a 20-minute *moto* (US$2 or so) or taxi (US$10 one way) ride to the floating village of Chong Kneas, and then a boat to the environment office in Prek Toal village (around US$55 return, one hour each way). This is where you pay your entrance fee, pick up a Khmer-speaking guide and board a smaller boat to take you into the sanctuary, which is about one hour beyond. Both boat and guide are included in the entrance fee.

Serious twitchers should contact bird specialist SVC about additional trips around Siem Reap and Preah Vihear Province.

TEMPLES OF ANGKOR

Where to begin with Angkor (ប្រាសាទ អង្គរ)? There is no greater concentration of architectural riches anywhere on earth. Choose from the world's largest religious building, Angkor Wat; one of the world's weirdest, Bayon; or the riotous jungle of Ta Prohm. All are global icons and have helped put Cambodia on the map as the temple capital of Asia.

Beyond the big three are dozens more temples, each of which would be the star were it located anywhere else in the region: Banteay Srei, the art gallery of Angkor; Preah Khan, the ultimate fusion temple uniting Buddhism and Hinduism; or Beng Mealea, the *Titanic* of temples suffocating under the jungle. The most vexing part of a visit to Angkor is working out what to see, as there are simply so many spectacular sites. One day at Angkor? Sacrilege! Don't even consider it.

Temples of Angkor

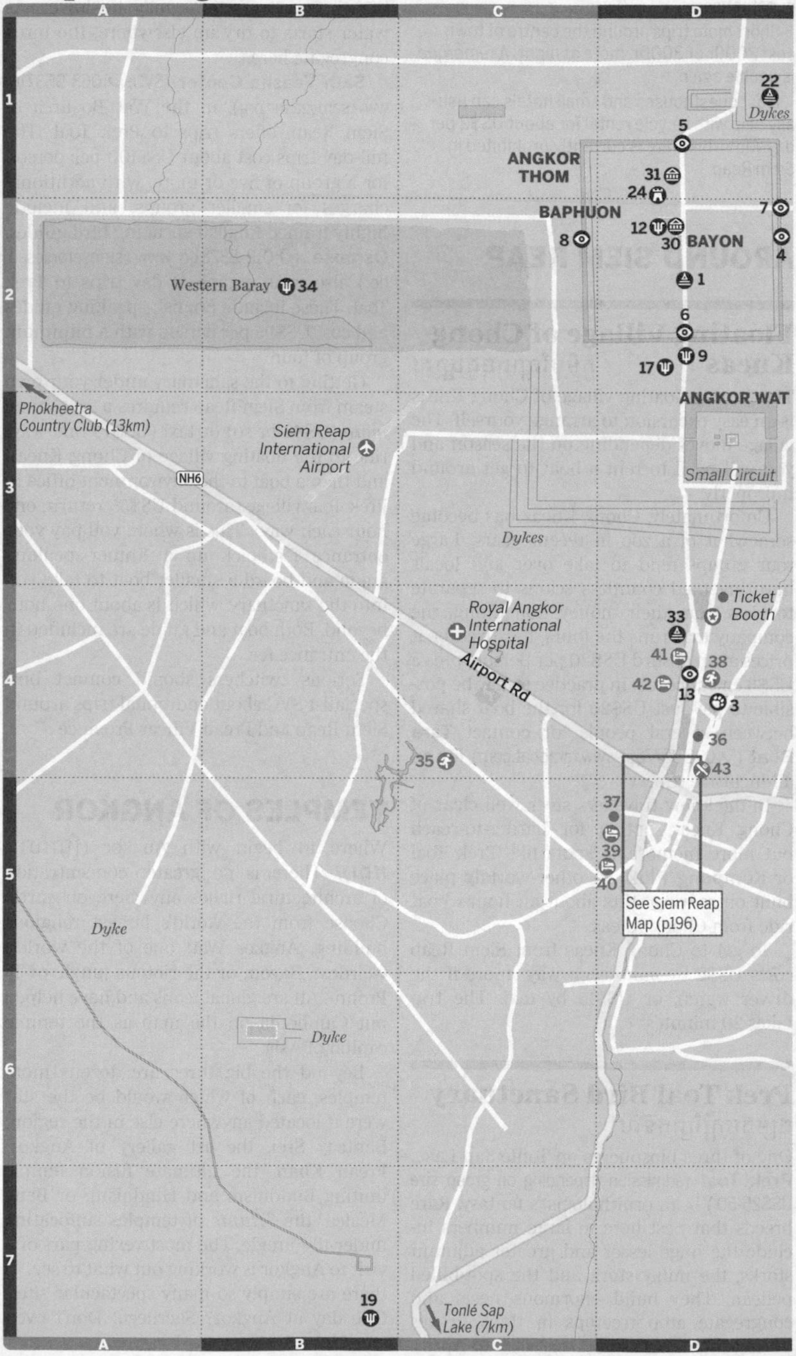

A
B
C
D
1
2
3
4
5
6
7
22
Dykes
5
ANGKOR THOM
31
24
BAPHUON
7
12
8
30
BAYON
4
1
Western Baray
34
6
9
17
ANGKOR WAT
Phokheetra Country Club (13km)
Siem Reap International Airport
NH6
Small Circuit
Dykes
Ticket Booth
Royal Angkor International Hospital
33
41
38
Airport Rd
42
13
3
36
35
43
37
39
40
See Siem Reap Map (p196)
Dyke
Dyke
19
Tonlé Sap Lake (7km)

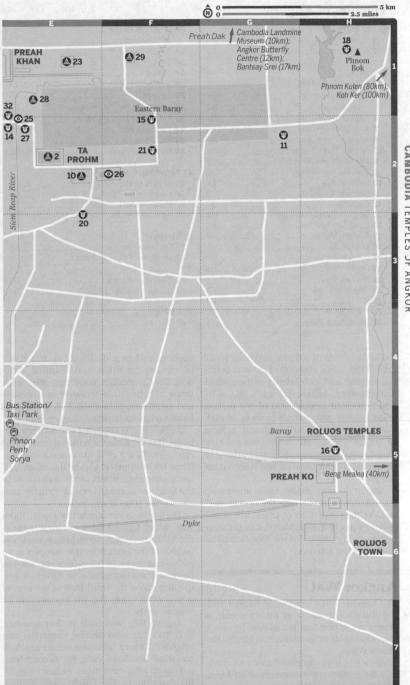

Temples of Angkor

The hundreds of temples surviving today are but the sacred skeleton of the vast political, religious and social centre of the ancient Khmer empire. Angkor was a city that, at its zenith, boasted a population of one million when London was a small town of 50,000. The houses, public buildings and palaces of Angkor were constructed of wood – now long decayed – because the right to dwell in structures of brick or stone was reserved for the gods.

Angkor is one of the most impressive ancient sites on earth, with the epic proportions of the Great Wall of China, the detail and intricacy of the Taj Mahal, and the symbolism and symmetry of the Egyptian pyramids all rolled into one.

Angkor Wat   អង្គរវត្ត

The traveller's first glimpse of Angkor Wat, the ultimate expression of Khmer genius, is simply staggering and is matched by only a few select spots on earth such as Machu Picchu or Petra.

Angkor is, quite literally, heaven on earth: it is the earthly representation of Mt Meru, the Mt Olympus of the Hindu faith and the abode of ancient gods. It's the perfect fusion of creative ambition and spiritual devotion. The Cambodian 'god-kings' of old each strove to better their ancestors in size, scale and symmetry, culminating in the world's largest religious building, Angkor Wat.

Angkor Wat is the heart and soul of Cambodia. It is the Khmers' national symbol, the epicentre of their civilisation and a source of fierce national pride. Unlike the other Angkor monuments, it was never abandoned to the elements and has been in virtually continuous use since it was built.

The temple is surrounded by a moat, 190m wide, which forms a giant rectangle measuring 1.5km by 1.3km. Stretching around the outside of the central temple complex is an 800m-long series of bas-reliefs, designed to be viewed in an anticlockwise direction. Rising 31m above the third level is the central tower, which gives the whole ensemble its sublime unity.

Angkor Wat was built by Suryavarman II (r 1113–52), who unified Cambodia and extended Khmer influence across much of mainland Southeast Asia. He also set himself apart religiously from earlier kings by his devotion to the Hindu deity Vishnu, to whom he consecrated the temple, built around the same time as European Gothic heavyweights such as Westminster Abbey and Chartres.

The sandstone blocks from which Angkor Wat was built were quarried more than 50km away and floated down the Stung Siem Reap on rafts. The logistics of such an operation are mind-blowing.

The upper level of Angkor Wat is once again open to modern pilgrims, but visits are strictly timed to 20 minutes.

Angkor Thom   អង្គរធំ

It is hard to imagine any building bigger or more beautiful than Angkor Wat, but in Angkor Thom the sum of the parts add up to a greater whole. It is the gates that grab you first, flanked by a monumental representation of the Churning of the Ocean of Milk, 54 demons and 54 gods engaged in an epic tug of war on the causeway. Each gate towers above the visitor, the magnanimous faces of the Bodhisattva Avalokiteshvara staring out over the kingdom. Imagine being a peasant in the 13th century approaching the forbidding capital for the first time. It would have been an awe-inspiring yet unsettling experience to enter such a gateway and come face to face with the divine power of the god-kings.

The last great capital of the Khmer empire, Angkor Thom took monumental to a whole new level. Set over 10 sq km it was built in part as a reaction to the surprise sacking of Angkor by the Chams – Jayavarman VII (r 1181–1219) decided that his empire would never again be vulnerable at home. Beyond the formidable walls is a massive moat that would have stopped all but the hardiest invaders in their tracks.

⊙ Sights

★Bayon   BUDDHIST TEMPLE
(បាយ័ន) Right at the heart of Angkor Thom is the Bayon, the mesmerising if slightly mind-bending state temple of Jayavarman VII. It epitomises the creative genius and inflated ego of Cambodia's legendary king. Its 54 Gothic towers are famously decorated with 216 enormous, coldly smiling **faces of Avalokiteshvara** that bear more than a passing resemblance to the great king himself. These huge visages glare down from every angle, exuding power and control with a hint of humanity – precisely the blend required to hold sway over such a vast empire, ensuring that disparate and far-flung populations yielded to the monarch's magnanimous will.

The Bayon is decorated with 1.2km of extraordinary **bas-reliefs** incorporating more than 11,000 figures. The famous carvings on the outer wall of the first level vividly depict everyday life in 12th-century Cambodia.

TEMPLE TALK

Professor Ang Choulean is one of Cambodia's leading experts on anthropology and archaeology and a renowned scholar on Cambodian history. He was awarded the 2011 Grand Fukuoka Prize for his outstanding contribution to Asian culture.

What is the most important Khmer temple? Angkor Thom is the most striking and challenging for archaeologists, since it was a living city, with humans and gods cohabiting there.

What is the most important archaeological site in Cambodia? Sambor Prei Kuk is among the most important for its homogeneity, given the period and its artistic style.

Who is the most important king in Cambodian history? Suryavarman I, who had a real political vision that can be measured by the monuments he built, such as Preah Vihear and Wat Phu.

What is your position on the debate between romance and restoration at Ta Prohm? It is a matter of balance. The trees are most impressive, but maintaining the monument is our duty.

Which other civilisation interests you greatly? Japanese civilisation, as it is so different from Khmer civilisation, which allows me to better understand my culture.

Temples of Angkor

THREE-DAY EXPLORATION

The temple complex at Angkor is simply enormous and the superlatives don't do it justice. This is the site of the world's largest religious building, a multitude of temples and a vast, long-abandoned walled city that was arguably Southeast Asia's first metropolis, long before Bangkok and Singapore got in on the action.

Starting at the Roluos group of temples, one of the earliest capitals of Angkor, move on to the big circuit, which includes the Buddhist-Hindu fusion temple of **1 Preah Khan** and the ornate water temple of **2 Preah Neak Poan**.

On the second day downsize to the small circuit, starting with an atmospheric dawn visit to **3 Ta Prohm**, before continuing to the temple pyramid of Ta Keo, the Buddhist monastery of Banteay Kdei and the immense royal bathing pond of **4 Sra Srang**.

Next venture further afield to Banteay Srei temple, the jewel in the crown of Angkorian art, and Beng Mealea, a remote jungle temple.

Saving the biggest and best until last, experience sunrise at **5 Angkor Wat** and stick around for breakfast in the temple to discover its amazing architecture without the crowds. In the afternoon, explore **6 Angkor Thom**, an immense complex that is home to the enigmatic **7 Bayon**.

Three days around Angkor? That's just for starters.

Bayon
The surreal state temple of legendary king Jayavarman VII, where 216 faces bear down on pilgrims, asserting religious and regal authority.

Terrace of Leper Kin
Preah Palilay
Phimeanakas Temple
Tep Pran
West Gate Angkor Thom
Baphuon Temple
Terrac of the Elephar
7
South Gate Angkor Thom
Phnom Bakheng
Baksei Chamrong
5

Angkor Wat
The world's largest religious building. Experience sunrise at the holiest of holies, then explore the beautiful bas-reliefs – devotion etched in stone.

TOP TIPS

» **Dodging the Crowds** Early morning at Ta Prohm, post sunrise at Angkor Wat and lunchtime at Banteay Srei does the trick.

» **Extended Explorations** Three-day passes can now be used on non-consecutive days over the period of a week but be sure to request this.

Angkor Thom
The last great capital of the Khmer empire conceals a wealth of temples and its epic proportions would have inspired and terrified in equal measure.

Preah Khan
A fusion temple dedicated to Buddha, Brahma, Shiva and Vishnu; the immense corridors are like an unending hall of mirrors.

Preah Neak Poan
If Vegas ever adopts the Angkor theme, this will be the swimming pool; a petite tower set in a lake, surrounded by four smaller ponds.

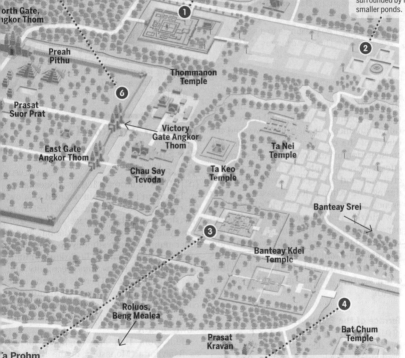

North Gate, Angkor Thom

Preah Pithu

Thommanon Temple

Prasat Suor Prat

Victory Gate Angkor Thom

East Gate Angkor Thom

Chau Say Tevoda

Ta Keo Temple

Ta Nei Temple

Banteay Srei

Banteay Kdei Temple

Roluos, Beng Mealea

Prasat Kravan

Bat Chum Temple

Ta Prohm
Nicknamed the *Tomb Raider* temple; *Indiana Jones* would be equally apt. Nature has run riot, leaving iconic tree roots strangling the surviving stones.

Sra Srang
Once the royal bathing pond, this is the ablutions pool to beat all ablutions pools and makes a good stop for sunset.

TOP ANGKOR EXPERIENCES

➡ See the sun rise over the holiest of holies, **Angkor Wat**, the world's largest religious building.

➡ Contemplate the serenity and splendour of the **Bayon**, its 216 enigmatic faces staring out into the jungle.

➡ Witness nature reclaiming the stones at the mysterious ruin of **Ta Prohm**, the *Tomb Raider* temple.

➡ Stare in wonder at the delicate carvings adorning **Banteay Srei**, the finest seen at Angkor.

➡ Trek deep into the jungle to discover the River of a Thousand Lingas at **Kbal Spean**.

Baphuon   HINDU TEMPLE

(បាពួន) About 200m northwest of the Bayon, the Baphuon is a pyramidal representation of mythical Mt Meru that marked the centre of the city that existed before the construction of Angkor Thom. Restoration efforts were disrupted by the Cambodian civil war and all records were destroyed during the Khmer Rouge years, leaving French experts with the world's largest jigsaw puzzle. The temple was grandly reopened in 2008 but the central structure is still closed to visitors. On the western side, the retaining wall of the second level was fashioned – apparently in the 15th or 16th century – into a reclining Buddha 60m in length.

Terrace of the Elephants   HISTORIC SITE

(ទីលានដំរី) The 350m-long Terrace of the Elephants – decorated with parading elephants towards both ends – was used as a giant viewing stand for public ceremonies and served as a base for the king's grand audience hall. As you stand here, try to imagine the pomp and grandeur of the Khmer empire at its height, with infantry, cavalry, horse-drawn chariots and, of course, elephants parading across the Central Sq in a colourful procession, pennants and standards aloft. Looking on is the god-king, crowned with a gold diadem, shaded by multi-tiered parasols and attended by mandarins and handmaidens.

Terrace of the Leper King   HISTORIC SITE

(ទីលានព្រះគម្លង់) The Terrace of the Leper King, just north of the Terrace of the Elephants, is a 7m-high platform. On top of the platform stands a nude, though sexless, statue, another of Angkor's mysteries. Legend has it that at least two of the Angkor kings had leprosy, and this statue may represent one of them. More likely it is Yama, the god of death, and that the Terrace of the Leper King housed the royal crematorium.

Its front retaining walls are decorated with at least five tiers of meticulously executed carvings of seated *apsaras* (celestial nymphs), kings with short double-edged swords and princesses, the latter adorned with beautiful rows of pearls. At the base on the southern side, there is narrow access to a hidden terrace that was covered up when the outer structure was built. The figures, including *nagas* (mythical serpent-beings), look as fresh as if they had been carved yesterday.

Around Angkor Thom

◉ Sights

★ Ta Prohm   BUDDHIST TEMPLE

(តាព្រហ្ម) The ultimate Indiana Jones fantasy, Ta Prohm is cloaked in dappled shadow, its crumbling towers and walls locked in the slow muscular embrace of vast treeroot systems. If Angkor Wat, the Bayon and other temples are testimony to the genius of the ancient Khmers, Ta Prohm reminds us equally of the awesome fecundity and power of the jungle. There is a poetic cycle to this venerable ruin, with humanity first conquering nature to rapidly create, and nature once again conquering humanity to slowly destroy.

Built from 1186 and originally known as Rajavihara (Monastery of the King), Ta Prohm was a Buddhist temple dedicated to the mother of Jayavarman VII. Ta Prohm is a temple of towers, enclosed courtyards and narrow corridors. Ancient trees tower overhead, their leaves filtering the sunlight and casting a greenish pall over the whole scene. It is the closest most of us will get to experiencing the excitement of the explorers of old.

Phnom Bakheng   HINDU TEMPLE

(ភ្នំបាក់ខែង) Around 400m south of Angkor Thom, this hill's main draw is the sunset view of Angkor Wat, though this has turned into something of a circus, with hundreds of visitors jockeying for space. The temple, built by Yasovarman I (r 889–910), has five tiers with seven levels (including the base and the summit).

Preah Khan BUDDHIST TEMPLE
(ប្រ: ខ័ន្ធ; Sacred Sword) The temple of Preah Khan is one of the largest complexes at Angkor – a maze of vaulted corridors, fine carvings and lichen-clad stonework. Constructed by Jayavarman VII, it covers a very

EXPLORING THE TEMPLES

One Day
If you've got only one day to spend at Angkor, that's unfortunate, but a good itinerary would be Angkor Wat for sunrise, after which you can explore the mighty temple before the crowds arrive. From there, drop by Ta Prohm before breaking for lunch. In the afternoon, explore the temples within the walled city of Angkor Thom and the enigmatic faces of the Bayon in the late afternoon light. Biggest mistake: trying to pack in too much.

Three Days
With three days it's possible to see most of the important sites. One approach is to see as much as you can on the first day or two (as above), then spend the final days visiting other sites such as Roluos and Banteay Srei. Better still is a gradual build-up to the most spectacular places. After all, if you see Angkor Wat first, then a temple like Ta Keo just won't cut it.

One Week
Angkor is your oyster, so relax, enjoy and explore at will. Make sure you visit Beng Mealea and Kbal Spean. Do at least one overnight trip further afield, to Koh Ker, Banteay Chhmar, Sambor Prei Kuk or even Prasat Preah Vihear. For a change of pace, take a boat to the floating village of Kompong Pluk or Prek Toal Bird Sanctuary.

Tickets & Guides
The Angkor **ticket booth** (1-day/3-day/1-week tourist pass US$20/40/60, children under 12 free; ⊙5am-5.30pm) is on the road from Siem Reap to Angkor. Three-day passes can be used on any three days over a one-week period, and one-week passes are valid over the course of a month. Tickets issued after 5pm (for sunset viewing) are valid the next day. Tickets are not valid for Phnom Kulen or Beng Mealea. Get caught ticketless in a temple and you'll be fined US$100.

The **Khmer Angkor Tour Guide Association** (☑063-964347; www.khmerangkor tourguide.com) can arrange certified tour guides in 10 languages (US$25 to US$50 a day).

Eating
All the major temples have some sort of nourishment near the entrance. The most extensive selection of restaurants is opposite the entrance to Angkor Wat. Some excellent local Khmer restaurants line the northern shore of Sra Srang.

Transport
Bicycles are a great way to get to and around the temples, which are linked by flat roads in good shape. Various guesthouses and hotels rent out **White Bicycles** (www.thewhite bicycles.org; per day US$2), and proceeds go to local development projects.

The most popular way to see the temples is the trusty *remorque*. These cost US$15 to US$25 for the day, depending on the destination and number of passengers.

Motos are a popular form of transport around the temples (around US$10 per day, more for distant sites). Drivers accost visitors from the moment they set foot in Siem Reap, but they're often knowledgeable and friendly.

Private cars cost about US$30 a day (more for distant sites), but tend to isolate you from the sights, sounds and smells.

large area, but the temple itself is within a rectangular wall of around 700m by 800m.

Preah Khan is a genuine fusion temple, the eastern entrance dedicated to Mahayana Buddhism with equal-sized doors, and the other cardinal directions dedicated to Shiva, Vishnu and Brahma with successively smaller doors, emphasising the unequal nature of Hinduism.

Unless wet-season conditions preclude it, try to enter via the east gate so the complex unfolds before you as its architects intended, rather than via the west gate, which is all-too-conveniently right on the main road.

Preah Neak Poan   BUDDHIST TEMPLE
(ព្រះនាគព័ន្ធ; Temple of the Intertwined Nagas) Another late 12th-century work of Jayavarman VII, this temple has a large square pool surrounded by four smaller square pools, with a circular 'island' in the middle. Water once flowed into the four pools via four ornamental spouts, in the form of an elephant's head, a horse's head, a lion's head and a human head. It's a safe bet that when the Encore Angkor Casino is eventually but inevitably developed in Las Vegas or Macau, Preah Neak Poan will provide the blueprint for the ultimate swimming complex.

Roluos Group   HINDU TEMPLE
The monuments of Roluos, which served as Indravarman I's (r 877–89) capital, are among the earliest large, permanent temples built by the Khmers and mark the dawn of Khmer classical art. Preah Ko, dedicated to Shiva, has elaborate inscriptions in Sanskrit on the doorposts of each tower and some of the best surviving examples of Angkorian

plasterwork. The city's central temple, Bakong, with its five-tier central pyramid of sandstone, is a representation of Mt Meru.

Roluos is 13km east of Siem Reap along NH6 and can be easily combined with a visit to the stilted village of Kompong Pluk and the nearby flooded forest.

Further Afield

⊙ Sights

★ Banteay Srei   HINDU TEMPLE
(បន្ទាយស្រី) Considered by many to be the jewel in the crown of Angkorian art, Banteay Srei is cut from stone of a pinkish hue and includes some of the finest stone carving anywhere on earth. Begun in AD 967, it is one of the few temples around Angkor not to be commissioned by a king, but by a Brahman, perhaps a tutor to Jayavarman V.

Banteay Srei means 'Citadel of the Women' and it is said that it must have been built by women, as the elaborate carvings are too fine for the hand of a man.

Banteay Srei, 21km northeast of the Bayon and about 32km from Siem Reap, can be visited along with Kbal Spean and the Cambodia Landmine Museum. Transport out to here will cost a little more than the prices quoted for the central temples of Angkor.

Kbal Spean   HINDU SHRINE
(ក្បាលស្ពាន) Kbal Spean is a spectacularly carved riverbed, set deep in the jungle about 50km northeast of Angkor. More commonly referred to in English as the 'River of a Thousand Lingas', it's a 2km uphill walk to

---

BANTEAY CHHMAR

The temple complex of **Banteay Chhmar** (បន្ទាយឆ្មារ; admission US$5) was constructed by Cambodia's most prolific builder, Jayavarman VII (r 1181–1219), on the site of a 9th-century temple. One of a handful of Angkorian sites to feature the towering heads of Avalokiteshvaras, with their enigmatic smiles, the 12th-century temple is also renowned for its intricate carvings.

A pioneering community-based **homestay program** (☏ 012 237605; info@visit banteaychhmar.org; r US$7) 🌱 makes it possible to stay in and around Banteay Chhmar. Rooms come with mosquito nets, fans that run when there's electricity (6pm to 10pm) and downstairs bathrooms. Bikes can be rented for US$2 a day.

Near the temple's eastern entrance, rustic **Banteay Chhmar Restaurant** (mains US$1.50-4) serves tasty Khmer food.

Banteay Chhmar can be visited on a long day trip from Siem Reap, or base youself in Sisophon, 61km south of the temple, where a *moto*/taxi costs US$20/50 return. You *may* be able to find a morning share taxi from Sisophon's Psar Thmei to the temple (15,000r, one hour).

the carvings, which include phallic lingas and Hindu deities. From the carvings you can work your way back down to the **waterfall** to cool off. Carry plenty of water.

Kbal Spean was only 'discovered' in 1969, when ethnologist Jean Boulbet was shown the area by a local hermit; the area was soon off-limits due to the civil war, only becoming safe again in 1998.

At the nearby **Angkor Centre for Conservation of Biodiversity** (www.accb-cambodia.org; donation US$3; ☺tours 1pm Mon-Sat), trafficked animals are nursed back to health.

Phnom Kulen   MOUNTAIN

(ភ្នំគូលែន; admission US$20) The most sacred mountain in Cambodia, Phnom Kulen (487m) is where Jayavarman II proclaimed himself a *devaraja* (god-king) in AD 802, giving birth to Cambodia. It's a popular place of pilgrimage during weekends and festivals; the views it affords are absolutely tremendous.

At no point during a visit to Phnom Kulen should you leave well-trodden paths, as there may be landmines in the area.

Phnom Kulen is 50km from Siem Reap and 15km from Banteay Srei. The road toll is US$20 per foreign visitor; none of this goes towards preserving the site. It is possible to buy a cheaper entrance ticket to Phnom Kulen for US$12 from the City Angkor Hotel in Siem Reap.

Beng Mealea   BUDDHIST TEMPLE

(បឹងមាលា; admission US$5) Built by Suryavarman II to the same floor plan as Angkor Wat, Beng Mealea is the *Titanic* of temples, utterly subsumed by jungle. Nature has well and truly run riot here. Jumbled stones lie like forgotten jewels swathed in lichen, and the galleries are strangled by ivy and vines.

Beng Mealea is about 65km northeast of Siem Reap on a sealed toll road.

Koh Ker   HINDU TEMPLE

(admission US$10) Abandoned to the forests of Preah Vihear Province to the north, Koh Ker, capital of the Angkorian empire from AD 928 to AD 944, is now within day-trip distance of Siem Reap. Most visitors start at **Prasat Krahom**, where impressive stone carvings grace lintels, doorposts and slender window columns. The principal monument is Mayan-looking **Prasat Thom**, a 55m-wide, 40m-high sandstone-faced pyramid whose seven tiers offer spectacular views across the forest. However, access to the top

of Prasat Thom is currently prohibited for safety reasons.

The area around Koh Ker was heavily mined during the war, but by 2008 most mines had been cleared. However, considering what's at stake, it's best to err on the side of caution. Do not stray from previously trodden paths or wander off into the forest.

Koh Ker is 127km northeast of Siem Reap (car hire around US$90, 2½ hours).

Preah Khan   BUDDHIST TEMPLE

(admission US$5) Covering almost 5 sq km in remote Preah Vihear Province, Preah Khan – not to be confused with the temple of the same name at Angkor – is the largest temple enclosure constructed during the Angkorian period, quite a feat when you consider the competition. Thanks to its back-of-beyond location, the site is astonishingly quiet and peaceful. Tragically, much of the enclosure, including the central temple complex, was devastated by looters in the 1990s.

Traditionally, Preah Khan has been the toughest of the remote Angkorian temples to reach, but upgraded provincial highways have improved things. Turn west off smooth NH62 in Svay Pak, about 64km south of Preah Vihear City and 93km north of Kompong Thom. From here an all-season dirt road via Sangkum Thmei commune takes you to Ta Seng, about 56km from the highway, where a new dirt road leads 4km to the temple.

There's no public transport to Preah Khan, so you'll need to hire a *moto* or a taxi in Preah Vihear City or Kompong Thom, or in Siem Reap for an extra-long day trip (possibly combined with Sambor Prei Kuk).

NORTHWESTERN CAMBODIA

Offering highway accessibility and outback adventure in equal measure, northwestern Cambodia stretches from the Cardamom Mountains to the Dangkrek Mountains, with Tonlé Sap Lake at its heart. Battambang attracts the most visitors thanks to an alluring blend of mellowness, colonial-era architecture and excellent day tripping.

Northwestern Cambodia's remote plains and jungles conceal some of the country's most inspired temples, including spectacular Prasat Preah Vihear, declared a World Heritage Site in 2008; 12th-century Banteay

Chhmar, with its trademark Avalokiteshvara faces; and the pre-Angkorian temples of Sambor Prei Kuk near Kompong Thom.

Battambang   បាត់ដំបង

🎴 053 / POP 145,000

The elegant riverside town of Battambang is home to Cambodia's best-preserved French-period architecture. The stunning boat trip from Siem Reap lures travellers here, but it's the remarkably chilled atmosphere that makes them linger. Battambang is an excellent base for exploring nearby temples and villages that offer a real slice of rural Cambodia.

◉ Sights

Colonial-Era Architecture   NOTABLE BUILDINGS
Much of Battambang's special charm lies in its early 20th-century French architecture. Some of the finest colonial buildings are along the waterfront (St 1), especially just south of **Psar Nath**, itself an architectural monument, albeit a modernist one. The two-storey **Governor's Residence**, with its balconies and wooden shutters, is another handsome legacy of the early 1900s. The interior is closed, but you can stroll the grounds.

Phnom Penh–based **KA Architecture Tours** (www.ka-tours.org) has two half-day heritage walks in the historic centre of Battambang available for free on its website. If you're short on time you can do them by bicycle.

LANDMINE ALERT!

Northwestern Cambodia, including the provinces of Banteay Meanchey, Battambang (especially the districts of Samlot and Rotanak Mondol), Oddar Meanchey (Anlong Veng) and Pailin, is one of the most heavily mined places in the world. Demining sites are commonplace, sometimes quite close to the highway, and numerous amputees bear sad tribute to the horror of landmines. Stay well ON the beaten track in these parts. Public roads are OK, but farm roads are risky, and venturing into the region's beautiful forests on foot is definitely not a good idea.

Arts Quarter   NEIGHBOURHOOD
(St 2½) The block of St 2½ that runs south of Psar Nath is Battambang's unofficial arts district. A gaggle of galleries, funky bars and shops has set up. Make a point to have a stroll here and check out the latest happenings.

Battambang Museum   MUSEUM
(សារមន្ទីរបាត់ដំបង; St 1; admission US$1; ⊗8-11am & 2–5.30pm) This small museum displays fine Angkorian lintels and statuary from all over Battambang Province, including Phnom Banan.

Wats   BUDDHIST TEMPLE
Battambang's Buddhist temples survived the Khmer Rouge period relatively unscathed thanks to a local commander who ignored orders from on high. Some of the best are **Wat Phiphétaram**, **Wat Damrey Sar** and **Wat Kandal**.

Train Station   HISTORIC BUILDING
Here the time is always 8.02. Just along the tracks to the south, you can explore a treasure trove of derelict **French-era train repair sheds**, warehouses and rolling stock.

🏃 Activities

Soksabike   CYCLING
(📞012 542019; www.soksabike.com; depending on group size, half day US$19-27, full day US$29-40; ⊗departures 7.30am) 🐟 Based at the cafe Kinyei, Soksabike is a social enterprise aiming to connect visitors with the Cambodian countryside and its people. The daily half-day trip covers about 30km. It includes a fresh coconut, seasonal fruits and a shot of rice wine.

Butterfly Bicycle Tours   CYCLING
(📞089 297070; www.butterflytour.asia; half day depending on group size US$13-17; ⊗departures 7.30am & 1.30pm) This bike-tour operator was started by local students. The Traditional Livelihoods tour draws raves.

Battambang Bike   CYCLING
(📞017 905276; www.thebattambangbike.com; St 2½; tours US$25) A variety of bike tours – the late-afternoon city tour is recommended – plus free weekend 'fun rides'.

Green Orange Kayaks   KAYAKING
(📞017 736166; feda@online.com.kh; half-rental US$12) 🐟 One- to three-person kayaks can be rented for the 8km trip down the Sangker River from Ksach Poy, 8km south of Battambang on the road to Phnom Banan. Home-

DON'T MISS

PHARE PONLEU SELPAK

Battambang's signature attraction is this internationally acclaimed **circus** (☏053-952424; www.phareps.org; adult/student US$10/5), a multi-arts centre for disadvantaged children. Even though they are now running shows in Siem Reap, it's worth timing your visit to Battambang to watch this amazing spectacle where it all began. Performances are at 6.15pm on Monday, Thursday and Saturday, with a Friday show added during the high season.

Phare, as it's known to locals, does a ton of stuff – contrary to popular belief it is not just a circus. It trains musicians, visual artists and performing artists as well. Guests are welcome to walk in during the day to **tour** (admission US$5; ⏱8-11am & 2-5pm) the Phare complex and observe circus, dance, music, drawing and graphic-arts classes. This is definitely five dollars well spent.

To get here from the Vishnu roundabout on NH5, head west for 900m and then turn right (north) and continue another 600m.

stays are available in Ksach Poy through **Green Orange Village Stay Bungalows** (☏012 207957; sothsarin@gmail.com; tr per person US$5). Ask for Ngarm.

Nary Kitchen   COOKING COURSE
(☏012 763950; half-day course US$10) One of a few cooking classes in town, Nary's half-day course includes a visit to the local market, a three-course menu and a keepsake recipe book.

Seeing Hands Massage   MASSAGE
(☏078 337499; St 121; per hr US$6; ⏱7am-10pm) Trained blind masseurs and masseuses offer soothing work-overs.

🛏 Sleeping

The best budget guesthouses are in the centre close to Psar Nath, while most of the nicer boutiques are a short *remorque* ride from the tourist belt in the old quarter.

🛏 City Centre

⭐**Ganesha Family Guesthouse**   GUESTHOUSE $
(☏092 135570; www.ganeshaguesthouse.com; St 1½; dm US$4, r US$10-16; 🖥) This is sort of an upscale backpacker (but not quite flashpacker) place. The en-suite private rooms have attractively tiled bathrooms and plump beds, while the dorms have double-wide beds hung with privacy-protecting linens.

Banan Hotel   HOTEL $
(☏012 739572; www.bananhotel.com; NH5; r with /without breakfast from US$20/15; ❄@🖥🏊) A modern high-rise hotel with Khmer-style

wooden decor, immaculate rooms and extremely friendly service.

Royal Hotel   HOTEL $
(☏016 912034; www.royalhotelbattambang.com; St 115; r with fan US$6-15, with air-con US$10-20; ❄@🖥) Deservedly popular with independent travellers, the Royal has somewhat faded rooms that are nonetheless clean and spacious. It's near the bus offices.

⭐**Sanctuary Villa**   BOUTIQUE HOTEL $$
(☏097 216 7168; www.sanctuarycambodia.com; d/tw incl breakfast US$70/80; ❄@🖥🏊) This intimate poolside boutique in a lush garden has seven attractive villas furnished with traditional woods, tasteful silks and throw rugs. From the White Horse roundabout on NH5 go 500m north and take a right.

Delux Villa   HOTEL $$
(☏077 336373; www.deluxvilla.com; St 4; r incl breakfast US$45-55; ❄🖥🏊) The style is more Cambodian than boutique, but rooms are big and clean (if a bit dark) and the grounds are nice and leafy. Upgrade to a balcony-equipped room around the pool.

🛏 East Bank

Here Be Dragons   HOSTEL $
(☏089 264895; www.herebedragonsbattambang.com; Riverside East; dm US$2, r US$8-10; 🖥) Here bedraggled backpackers find comfy dorm beds and, if they're looking to get their drink on, like-minded souls to swap yarns with at the popular bar. The clean private rooms are a dandy deal. Quiet location next to the riverside park on the East Bank.

Battambang

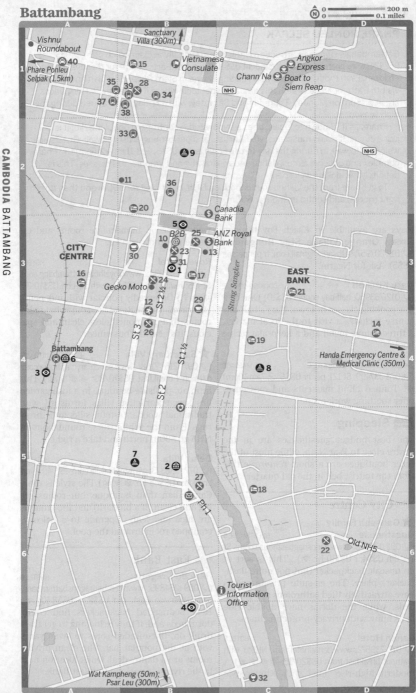

Battambang

◎ Sights

⊕ Activities, Courses & Tours

⊜ Sleeping

✕ Eating

⊖ Drinking & Nightlife

ⓘ Transport

CAMBODIA BATTAMBANG

★ **La Villa** BOUTIQUE HOTEL $$
(☑ 053-730151; www.lavilla-battambang.net; Riverside Rd; d incl breakfast US$65-92; ❋@☎❄) One of the most romantic boutique hotels in Cambodia, this attractive hostelry occupies a French-era villa renovated in vintage 1930s style. It has particularly ugly and tall neighbours, but the ambience and riverside location offset that.

Bambu Hotel HOTEL $$
(☑ 053-953900; www.bambuhotel.com; St 203; r incl breakfast US$70-110; ❋@☎❄) Bambu is in the upper category of Battambang poolside boutiques in both style and price. The spacious Franco-Khmer rooms have gorgeous tiling, stone-inlaid bathrooms, exquisite furniture and private balconies.

Sangker Villa Hotel HOTEL $$
(☑ 097 764 0017; www.sangkervilla.com; off St 203; s/d incl breakfast from US$28/38; ❋☎❄) Sangker Villa lacks the style of Battambang's fancier poolside boutiques, but beats them on price – especially if you're travelling solo. Cosy rooms, cosy pool area and a big, bold bar.

✕ Eating

Cheap dining is available in and around Psar Nath. There's a riverside **night market** (St 1; ◷ 3pm-midnight) opposite the Battambang Museum.

★ **Lonely Tree Cafe** CAFE $
(www.thelonelytreecafe.com; St 121; mains US$2-4; ◷ 10am-10pm; ☎) ✎ Upstairs from the shop of the same name, this uber-cosy cafe serves Khmer food and a few Spanish dishes like *huevos rotos* (broken eggs). Proceeds support cultural preservation and the disabled.

Kinyei CAFE $
(www.kinyei.org; 1 St 1½; mains US$3-4; ◷ 7am-7pm; ☎) ✎ The home base of Soksabike (p216), this tiny cafe hidden at the end of St 1½ offers light bites and what many believe is the best coffee in town. National barista champs have been crowned here.

Fresh Eats Café CAMBODIAN $
(www.mpkhomeland.org; St 2½; mains US$2.50-4; ◷ 9am-9pm Mon-Sat; ☎) ✎ Run by an NGO that helps children whose families have been affected by HIV/AIDS, this little place complements its Khmer specialities with build-your-own baguettes (including a Philly cheesesteak) and pasta.

Vegetarian Foods Restaurant VEGETARIAN $
(St 102; mains 1500-3000r; ◷ 6.30am-5pm; ✎) This hole-in-the-wall eatery serves some of the most delicious vegetarian dishes in

ALL ABOARD THE BAMBOO TRAIN

Battambang's **bamboo train** (1hr ride for 2-plus passengers US$5 per person, for 1 passenger US$10; ☺7am-dusk) is one of the world's all-time classic rail journeys. From O Dambong, on the East Bank 3.7km south of Battambang's old French bridge (Wat Kor Bridge), the train bumps 7km southeast to O Sra Lav along warped, misaligned rails and vertiginous bridges left by the French.

Each bamboo train – known in Khmer as a *norry* – consists of a 3m long wooden frame, covered lengthwise with slats made of ultralight bamboo, that rests on two barbell-like bogies, the aft one connected by fan belts to a 6HP gasoline engine. Pile on 10 or 15 people or up to three tonnes of rice, crank it up and you can cruise along at about 15km/h.

Cambodia, including rice soup, homemade soy milk and 1000r dumplings. Tremendous value.

Bamboo Train Cafe INTERNATIONAL $
(Old NH5; mains 8000-16,000r; ☺7am-10pm) The affable owner ensures this place is always popular. The eclectic menu contains pizzas, pastas, curries and a delicious tofu *amok*.

★ **Jaan Bai** FUSION $$
(☎078 263144; jaanbaibtb@gmail.com; cnr St 1½ & St 2; tapas US$3-4; ☺5-11pm) Battambang deserves a contemporary eating space like Jaan Bai ('rice bowl' in Khmer). The design turns heads with a bright mural outside and some beautiful French-Khmer tilework inside. Likewise, the tapas are successfully bold. It doubles as an art gallery and trains and employs vulnerable youth through the **Cambodian Children's Trust** (www.cambodianchildrenstrust.org).

Cafe Eden CAFE $$
(www.cafeedencambodia.com; 85 St 1; mains US$4-7; ☺7.30am-9pm, closed Tue; ☎) 🍴 Tucked away in a gorgeous colonial shophouse and hung with paintings by local artists, this American-run social enterprise offers a relaxed space for a healthy breakfast or an afternoon drink. Happy hour is from 3pm to 7pm.

Gecko Café INTERNATIONAL $$
(St 3; mains US$5-8; ☺9.30am-10pm; ☎) Battambang's answer to the Foreign Correspondents' Club in Phnom Penh, this has a classic setting in an old French shophouse and a menu that runs the gamut from Mexican to burgers to Asian fusion.

🍷 Drinking & Nightlife

★ **Choco l'art Café** CAFE
(www.chocolartcafe.com; St 117; ☺9am-midnight; ☎) Run with gusto by an arty French-Khmer duo, this gallery-cafe sees foreigners and locals alike gather to drink and eat wonderful bread, pastries and (for breakfast) crêpes. Live music gets going occasionally.

Lotus Bar & Gallery CAFE
(St 2½; ☺11am-late) In a beautifully renovated shophouse, the street-level bar here is a fine place to mingle with all sorts of characters. Upstairs is a gallery.

Riverside Balcony Bar BAR
(cnr St 1 & St 149; mains US$3.50-7.50; ☺4-11pm Tue-Sun) Set in a gorgeous wooden house high above the riverfront, Australian-run Riverside is Battambang's original bar and a mellow place for a sundowner.

ℹ Information

Most backpacker-oriented guesthouses can help arrange guides, transport and just about anything else. The city map that the tourist office hands out details scenic routes to the bamboo train and other attractions outside of town.

ANZ Royal Bank (St 1; ☺8.30am-4pm Mon-Fri) Full international ATM, plus the usual currency services.

B2B (St 2½; ☺24hr) Fast, air-conditioned internet access on Battambang's arty strip.

Canadia Bank (Psar Thom; ☺7.30am-3.30pm Mon-Fri, 7.30-11.30am Sat) Free cash withdrawals and cash advances on plastic.

Handa Emergency Centre & Medical Clinic (☎070 810812, 012 674001; NH5; ☺clinic 9am-3.30pm, emergency 24hr) Has two ambulances and usually a Western doctor or two in residence.

Tourist Information Office (☎012 534177; www.battambang-town.gov.kh; St 1; ☺8-11am & 2-5pm Mon-Fri) Moderately useful office with a great map of Battambang.

ℹ Getting There & Away

BOAT

The riverboat to Siem Reap (US$20, 7am) squeezes through narrow waterways and passes by protected wetlands, taking from five hours in the wet season to nine or more hours at the height of the dry season. Cambodia's most memorable boat trip, it's operated on alternate days by **Angkor Express** (☑ 012 601287) and **Chann Na** (☑ 012 354344). In the dry season, passengers are driven to a navigable section of the river.

BUS

Most bus companies are clustered in the centre just south of the intersection of NH5 and St 4.

Sleeper buses run by Kampuchea Angkor Express are popular to Phnom Penh, but keep in mind it's not a very long trip so arrival at an ungodly hour is a virtual certainty.

For quicker day travel to the capital, consider express minivans run by Golden Bayon Express or Mekong Express (about US$10, 4½ hours).

Bus companies include the following:

Capitol Tour (☑ 053-953040; St 102)

Golden Bayon Express (☑ 070 968966; St 101)

Kampuchea Angkor Express (☑ 017 535015; St 4)

Mekong Express (☑ 088 576 7668; St 3)

Phnom Penh Sorya (☑ 053-953904; St 4)

Ponleu Angkor Khmer (☑ 053-952366; St 4)

Rith Mony (☑ 011 575572; St 102)

TAXI

At the taxi station (NH5), share taxis to Phnom Penh (40,000r, 4½ hours) leave from the southeast corner, while taxis to Poipet (20,000r, 1¾ hours) and Siem Reap (26,000r, three hours) leave from north of the market out on NH5.

Share taxis to Pailin (US$6, 1¼ hours) near the Psar Pruhm–Pong Nam Ron border leave from the east edge of Psar Leu.

ⓘ Getting Around

English- and French-speaking *remorque* drivers are commonplace in Battambang, and all of them are eager to whisk you around on day trips. Figure on US$12 for a half-day trip and US$16 to US$20 for a full day, depending on your haggling skills and the destinations. A *moto* costs about half as much.

A *moto* ride in town costs around 2000r, while a *remorque* ride starts from US$1.

Gecko Moto (☑ 089 924260; www.geckocafe-cambodia.com; St 3; ⊙ 8am-7pm) and Royal Hotel rent out motorbikes for US$7 to US$8 per day. Bicycles are a great way to get around and can be rented at the Royal Hotel, Soksabike and several other guesthouses for about US$2 per day.

Around Battambang

The countryside around Battambang is littered with old temples, bamboo trains and other worthwhile sights. Admission to Phnom Sampeau, Phnom Banan and Wat Ek Phnom costs US$3. If you purchase a ticket at one site, it's valid all day long at the other two.

Phnom Sampeau   ភ្នំសំពៅ

At the summit of this fabled limestone outcrop, 12km southwest of Battambang along NH57 (towards Pailin), a complex of **temples** (admission US$3) affords gorgeous views.

Access to the summit is via a steep staircase or, past the eateries near the entrance at the base of the hill, a cement road. The road up to the summit is too steep for *remorques*.

BUSES FROM BATTAMBANG

DESTINATION	DURATION (HR)	COST (US$)	COMPANIES	FREQUENCY
Bangkok	9	13-14	Capitol Tour, Phnom Penh PP Sorya	7.45am, noon (Capitol), 1pm (PP Sorya)
Kompong Cham	7½	7.50-10	PP Sorya, Rith Mony	both at 9.30am
Pailin	1½	3	Ponleu Angkor Khmer, Rith Mony	1.30pm (PA), 3pm (RM)
Phnom Penh	6	regular/sleeper 5/10	all companies	frequent
Pursat	2	2.50-3	all companies	frequent
Poipet	2¼	3.25	Capitol Tour, Kampuchea Angkor Express, PP Sorya, Rith Mony	7.45am, noon (Capitol), 6.30am (KA), 1pm (PP Sorya), noon (RM)
Siem Reap	4	4-5	most companies	frequent to 2pm

English-speaking *moto* drivers can whisk you up for US$3 return, or take the stairs if you're in need of a workout.

About halfway to the summit via the road, a turn-off leads under a gate and 250m up to the **Killing Caves of Phnom Sampeau**. A golden reclining Buddha lies peacefully next to a glass-walled memorial filled with the bones and skulls of some of the people bludgeoned to death by Khmer Rouge cadres and then thrown through the skylight above.

At the summit of Phnom Sampeau, descend from the **golden stupa**, which dates from 1964 and turn left under the gate decorated with a bas-relief of Eiy Sei (an elderly Buddha). A **deep canyon**, its vertical sides cloaked in greenery, descends 144 steps through a natural arch to a 'lost world'

GETTING TO THAILAND

Samraong to Surin

The O Smach/Chong Chom border crossing connects Cambodia's Oddar Meanchey Province and Thailand's Surin Province.

Getting to the border Share taxis link Siem Reap with Samraong (30,000r, two hours) via NH68. From Samraong, take a *moto* (US$5) or a charter taxi (US$15) for the smooth drive to O Smach (40km, 30 minutes) and its frontier casino zone. A private taxi from Siem Reap all the way to the border should cost US$40 to US$50.

At the border The crossing itself is easy.

Moving on On the Thai side walk to the nearby bus stop, where regular buses depart to Surin throughout the day (60B, 70km, 1½ hours).

For more information about crossing this border in the other direction, see p404

Pailin to Chanthaburi

The laid-back Psar Pruhm/Pong Nam Ron border crossing (open 7am to 8pm) is 102km southwest of Battambang and 18km northwest of Pailin via rapidly improving roads.

Getting to the border From Battambang, the daily Ponleu Angkor Khmer and Rith Mony buses to Pailin continue on to this border. Alternatively, take a share taxi to Pailin from Psar Leu in Battambang, then continue to the border by *moto* (US$5) or private taxi (US$10). Patient travellers might get a share taxi (6000r) to the border from opposite the main market in Pailin, but don't count on it.

At the border You actually pay the true price (US$20) for a Cambodian visa here – rare for a remote crossing. Formalities are extremely straightfoward and quick on both sides.

Moving on Onward transport on the Thai side dries up mid-morning so cross early. In the morning you should be able to find a motorcycle taxi (50B) to the nearby *sŏrngtăaou* station, where two morning minibuses head to Chanthaburi (150B, 1½ hours). Otherwise, you're looking at a private taxi from the border to Chanthaburi bus station (1200B), where you'll find frequent buses to Bangkok.

For more information about crossing this border in the other direction, see p397

Anlong Veng to Chong Sa-Ngam

The remote Choam/Chong Sa-Ngam crossing (open 7am to 8pm) connects Anlong Veng with Thailand's Si Saket Province.

Getting to the border A *moto* from Anlong Veng to the border crossing (16km) costs US$3 or US$4 (more like US$5 in the reverse direction).

At the border Formalities here are straightforward, but note that if you are coming in from Thailand they charge a premium for Cambodian visas on arrival – US$25 instead of the normal US$20. Try to talk them down to the normal rate.

Moving on You should be able to scare up a taxi on the Thai side to take you to the nearest town, Phusing (30 minutes), where buses and *sŏrngtăaou* serve Si Saket and Kantharalak. Or try to hop on a casino shuttle from the border to Phusing, Ku Khan or Si Saket.

For more information about crossing this border in the other direction, see p404.

of stalactites, creeping vines and bats; two Angkorian warriors stand guard.

Every evening at dusk, a thick column of **bats** pours out of a massive cave high up on the north side of the cliff face – the mesmerising display, visible from the base of the cliffs, lasts a good 30 minutes.

Phnom Banan ភ្នំបាណន់

Exactly 358 stone steps lead up a shaded slope to 11th-century **Wat Banan**, 28km south of Battambang, whose five towers are reminiscent of the layout of Angkor Wat. The views are well worth the climb. From the temple, a narrow stone staircase leads south down the hill to three **caves**, which can be visited with a local guide.

Wat Ek Phnom វត្តឯកភ្នំ

This atmospheric, partly collapsed, 11th-century **temple** (admission US$2) is 11km north of Battambang. A lintel showing the Churning of the Ocean of Milk can be seen above the east entrance to the central temple, whose upper flanks hold some fine **bas reliefs**. This is a great place for a picnic.

On the way from Battambang by bicycle or *moto*, it's possible to visit a 1960s **Pepsi bottling plant** (1.2km north of Battambang's ferry landing), frozen in time since 1975 and, 1km further out, the **Slaket crocodile farm**.

Anlong Veng អន្លង់វែង

For almost a decade Anlong Veng was home to the most notorious leaders of Democratic Kampuchea. For those with a keen interest in contemporary Cambodian history, the Khmer Rouge sites in the area are an important, if somewhat disturbing, part of the picture. Anlong Veng is the capital of the remote, dirt-poor province of Oddar Meanchey.

◉ Sights

Ta Mok's House   MUSEUM
(ផ្ទះតាម៉ុក; admission US$2) Pol Pot's military enforcer, Ta Mok, was responsible for thousands of deaths in successive purges during the terrible years of Democratic Kampuchea. Widely known as 'the Butcher', he was arrested in 1999 and died in July 2006 in a Phnom Penh hospital, awaiting trial for genocide and crimes against humanity.

Ta Mok's house is a spartan structure with a bunker in the basement and childish wall murals. It lies east of town on swampy **Ta Mok's Lake**, festooned with the skeletons of dead trees – a fitting monument to the devastation he and his movement left behind. In the middle of the lake, due east from the house, is a small brick structure, an outhouse and all that remains of Pol Pot's residence in Anlong Veng.

The turn-off to Ta Mok's house is about 1km north of the roundabout in the centre of town.

Ta Mok's Grave   MONUMENT
From the turn-off to Ta Mok's house, driving a further 7km north takes you to Tumnup Leu village, where a signposted right turn leads to Ta Mok's Angkorian-style **mausoleum**. Locals come here to light incense and, in a bizarre local tradition, hope his spirit grants them a winning lottery number.

Pol Pot's Cremation Site   HISTORIC SITE
(admission US$2) A few hundred metres before the Thai frontier, under a rusted corrugated-iron roof, is the cremation site of Pol Pot, who was hastily burned in 1998 on a pile of old tyres and rubbish – a fittingly inglorious end, perhaps. In the dry season you can continue east from the border checkpoint along a rugged road to another residence of Ta Mok and, beyond, former houses of Pol Pot and Khieu Samphan.

🛏 Sleeping & Eating

For most people Anlong Veng is an optional stop on the drive from Siem Reap to Prasat Preah Vihear, an hour's drive to east. If you happen to get stuck here for a night, the **Monorom Guesthouse** (☑065-690 0468; r with fan/air-con from US$6/15; ❄ @ 🐱), 200m north of the Dove of Peace roundabout, has adequate if nondescript rooms, or try **Bot Uddom Guesthouse** (☑011 500507; r with fan/air-con from US$7.50/15; ❄ 🐱), a few hundred metres east of the roundabout on the road to Preah Vihear.

Unsigned **Sheang Hai Restaurant** (NH67; mains US$2-6; ⏰5am-9pm), 50m north of the roundabout on the east side of NH67, has the best food in the town centre.

❶ Orientation

The town's focal point is the Dove of Peace roundabout. About 600m north of the roundabout, the NH67 crosses a bridge and continues 16km to the Thai border.

ℹ️ Information

Acleda Bank (🕐 7.30am-2pm Mon-Fri, 7.30am-noon Sat) The only bank in town; has a Visa-only ATM.

ℹ️ Getting There & Around

Rith Mony (NH67) and **Liang US Express** (☑ 092-905026; NH67) have buses to Phnom Penh (US$10, seven hours).

Share taxis to Siem Reap (20,000r, 1½ hours) and Sra Em (20,000r, two hours) are most frequent in the morning.

A *moto* circuit to the Thai border and back, via Ta Mok's house and grave, costs about US$8.

Prasat Preah Vihear

ប្រាសាទព្រះវិហារ

This 800m-long temple (suggested donation US$2-5) – not to be confused with Preah Vihear City (Tbeng Meanchey) some 110km southeast – is the most dramatically situated of all the Angkorian monuments. It sits high atop the Dangkrek escarpment on the Thai border, with stupendous views of Cambodia's northern plains.

Prasat Preah Vihear consists of a series of four cruciform *gopura* (sanctuaries) decorated with exquisite carvings, including some striking lintels. Starting at the **Monumental Stairway**, a walk south takes you to **Gopura IV**, with its early rendition of the Churning of the Ocean of Milk, and finally, perched at the edge of the cliff, **Gopura I**, the Central Sanctuary.

Driving in from Sra Em, your first stop should be the **information centre** (🕐 7am-5.30pm) in the village of Kor Muy. This is where you pay your donation, secure an English-speaking guide if you want one (US$15), and arrange transport via *moto* (US$5 return) or 4WD (US$25 return, maximum six passengers) up the 6.5km temple access road, the final 1.5km of which is extremely steep. Another option is to ascend the hill on foot via the **Eastern Staircase**.

Budget lodging is plentiful in the burgeoning town of Sra Em, 23km south of the

---

MINE YOUR STEP

Stick to well-marked paths, as the Khmer Rouge laid huge numbers of landmines around Prasat Preah Vihear as late as 1998.

---

information centre – try neighbouring **Sok San Guesthouse** (☑ 097 715 3839; s/d with fan US$10/11, air-con from US$14/15; ❄ @ 🛜) or **Raksmey Guesthouse** (☑ 077 516255; r with fan/air-con from US$12/16; ❄ 🛜) 1km west of Sra Em's central roundabout. Eat at **Limy Restaurant** (mains US$3-4.50; 🕐 6am-10pm), the last in a row of restaurants on the right just north of the roundabout (towards Prasat Preah Vihear).

ℹ️ Getting There & Around

With a private car you can get to Prasat Preah Vihear in about 2½ hours from Siem Reap (about US$140 round-trip). It makes much more sense to break up the long trip with a night in Sra Em, which is just 30km from the temple. At Sra Em's central roundabout, you can find a *moto* to the Prasat Preah Vihear information centre in Kor Muy (US$10 return), where another *moto* will take you up to the temple.

Share taxis (US$10, 2½ hours) link Sra Em with Siem Reap. **Liang US Express** has a morning bus from Sra Em to Phnom Penh (US$10, 10 hours) via Preah Vihear City and Kompong Thom. **Rith Mony** (☑ 097 865 6018) has a morning bus to Phnom Penh (US$10, 10 hours) via Siem Reap (20,000r, 3½ hours). Note that buses from Siem Reap or Phnom Penh marked 'Preah Vihear' go only as far as Preah Vihear City and do not continue on to Prasat Preah Vihear.

It used to be possible to get to Prasat Preah Vihear from Thailand, where paved roads from Kantharalak lead almost up to the Monumental Stairway. However, due to the long stand-off between Thailand and Cambodia, access from the Thai side has been forbidden since mid-2008.

Kompong Thom

កំពង់ធំ

☑ 062 / POP 66,000

A bustling commercial centre 130km southeast of Siem Reap, Kompong Thom is mainly a base from which to explore dazzling Sambor Prei Kuk.

🛏️ Sleeping & Eating

Arunras Hotel HOTEL $

(☑ 062-961294; NH6; s/d with fan US$5/8, d with air-con US$15; ❄ 🛜) Dominating the accommodation scene in Kompong Thom, this seven-storey corner establishment has 58 smart, good-value rooms, as well as Kompong Thom's only lift. Also operates the slightly cheaper, 53-room **Arunras Guesthouse** (☑ 012 865935; NH6; s/d with fan US$6/8, air-con US$10/13; ❄ 🛜) next door.

THE FIGHT FOR PRASAT PREAH VIHEAR

Prasat Preah Vihear and the lands surrounding it were ruled by Thailand for several centuries, but were returned to Cambodia during the French protectorate, under the treaty of 1907. In 1959 the Thai military seized the temple from Cambodia and the then prime minister Sihanouk took the dispute to the International Court of Justice (ICJ) in the Hague, gaining worldwide recognition of Cambodian sovereignty in a 1962 ruling.

In July 2008, Prasat Preah Vihear was declared Cambodia's second Unesco World Heritage site. Within a week, Thai troops crossed into Cambodian territory, sparking an armed confrontation that has taken the lives of several dozen soldiers and some civilians on both sides. The Cambodian market at the bottom of the Monumental Stairway, which used to be home to some guesthouses, burned down during an exchange of fire in April 2009. In 2011, exchanges heated up once more and long-range shells were fired into civilian territory by both sides.

In July 2011, the ICJ ruled that both sides should withdraw troops from the area to establish a demilitarised zone. Then in November 2013, the ICJ confirmed its 1962 ruling that the temple belongs to Cambodia, although it declined to define the official borderline, leaving sovereignty of some lands around the temple open to dispute. With a pro-Thaksin (therefore Hun Sen–friendly) government tenuously hanging on to power in Bangkok since August 2011, the border dispute has died down in recent years, but tensions can reignite at any time, especially if the Yellow Shirts regain control in Thailand.

★ **Sambor Village Hotel** BOUTIQUE HOTEL $$
(☏ 062-961391; www.samborvillage.com; Prachea Thepatay St; r/ste US$50/85; ❄@☎⛱) Sambor Village brings boutique to Kompong Thom. Rooms are set in spacious bungalows and the verdant gardens include an inviting pool. It has the best food in town by some measure. Only the service is a let down. Located about 700m east of NH6.

❶ Getting There & Around

Dozens of buses travelling between Phnom Penh (US$5, four hours) and Siem Reap (US$5, two hours) pass through Kompong Thom and can easily be flagged down outside the Arunras Hotel.

Heading north to Preah Vihear City, share taxis (US$5, two hours) depart in the morning only.

Im Sokhom Travel Agency (☏ 012 691527; St 3) rents bicycles (US$1 per day) and motorbikes (US$5 per day).

Around Kompong Thom

Sambor Prei Kuk សំបូរព្រៃគុក

Cambodia's most impressive group of pre-Angkorian monuments, **Sambor Prei Kuk** (www.samborpreikuk.com; admission US$3) encompasses more than 100 brick temples scattered through the forest. Originally called Isanapura, it served as the capital of Chenla during the reign of the early 7th-century King Isanavarman.

Forested and shady, Sambor Prei Kuk has a serene and soothing atmosphere. The main temple area consists of three complexes, each enclosed by the remains of two concentric walls. The principal group, **Prasat Sambor**, is dedicated to Gambhireshvara, one of Shiva's many incarnations (the other groups are dedicated to Shiva himself). **Prasat Yeay Peau** (Prasat Yeai Poeun) feels lost in the forest, its eastern gateway both held up and torn asunder by an ancient tree.

Prasat Tao (Lion Temple), the largest of the Sambor Prei Kuk complexes, boasts excellent examples of Chenla carving in the form of two large, elaborately coiffed stone lions.

Isanborei (☏ 017 936112; www.samborpreikuk.com; dm/d US$4/6) runs a community-based homestay program, offers cooking courses, rents bicycles (US$2 per day) and organises ox-cart rides. It also operates a stable of *remorques* to carry you safely to/from Kompong Thom (US$15 one-way).

The area around the temple entrance, about 500m from the ruins, has shops and outdoor eateries serving surprisingly good Khmer food (mains from US$2).

Sambor Prei Kuk is 30km northeast of Kompong Thom via smooth roads. A round-trip *moto* ride out here should cost US$10, a *remorque* about US$20.

EASTERN CAMBODIA

If it is a walk on the wild side that fires your imagination, then the northeast is calling. It's home to rare forest elephants and freshwater dolphins, and peppering the area are thundering waterfalls, crater lakes and meandering rivers. Trekking, biking, kayaking and elephant adventures are all beginning to take off. The rolling hills and lush forests provide a home to many ethnic minority groups. Do the maths: it all adds up to an amazing experience.

Kompong Cham   កំពង់ចាម

☑ 042 / POP 60,000

This quiet Mekong city, an important trading post during the French period, serves as the gateway to Cambodia's northeast. Most action is on the riverfront. The surrounding province of Kompong Cham is a land of picturesque villages and quiet Mekong meanders. Some of Cambodia's finest silk is woven here.

◉ Sights & Activities

Koh Paen   NEIGHBOURHOOD

For a supremely relaxing bike ride, it's hard to beat Koh Paen. This rural, traffic-free island is connected to the mainland about 600m south of the Mekong bridge by a motorised ferry in the wet season and an elaborate bamboo toll bridge – totally rebuilt from scratch each December – in the dry season.

Wat Nokor   BUDDHIST TEMPLE

(វត្ត ន គរ; admission US$2) The ultimate fusion temple, Wat Nokor is a modern Buddhist pagoda squeezed into the walls of an 11th-century temple of sandstone and laterite. Located about 2.5km west of the bridge over the Mekong in Kompong Cham.

🛏 Sleeping

★ Daly Hotel   HOTEL $

(☑ 042-666 6631; daly.hotel99@gmail.com; d/tw US$18/20, VIP US$40; ❋ 🛜) A newish hotel one block off the river, the Daly is easily the best of the many Khmer-style high-rise hotels in town. Rooms are huge and bright with wall-mounted flat-screen TVs, spick-and-span bathrooms, luscious linens, desks and tea tables.

Mekong Sunrise   GUESTHOUSE $

(☑ 011 449720; bong_tho@yahoo.com; Sihanouk St; r with fan US$5-8, air-con US$12; ❋ 🛜) A backpacker crashpad over a popular riverfront bar-restaurant, Mekong Sunrise has spacious upper-floor rooms with access to a sprawling rooftop. Furnishings are sparse, but it's cheap enough.

🍴 Eating & Drinking

Stalls line the waterfront, selling snacks and cold beers until late in the evening.

★ Smile Restaurant   CAMBODIAN $

(www.bdsa-cambodia.org; Sihanouk St; mains US$3-5; ⊗6.30am-9pm; 🛜) 🍃 This nonprofit restaurant run by the Buddhism and Society Development Association is a big hit with the NGO crowd for its big breakfasts, healthy menu and free wi-fi.

Lazy Mekong Daze   INTERNATIONAL $

(Sihanouk St; mains US$3-5.50; ⊗7.30am-last customer; 🛜) Run by Frank, a Frenchman, this is the go-to place to assemble after dark thanks to a mellow atmosphere, a pool table, a big screen and a range of Khmer, Thai and Western food.

Chaplin's Bar & Restaurant   INTERNATIONAL $$

(Sihanouk St; mains US$3-18; ⊗7am-10pm) For a dash of urban flair in somnolent Kompong Cham, this Scottish-owned, Charlie Chaplin-themed bistro serves excellent Cambodian

BUSES FROM KOMPONG CHAM

DESTINATION	COST (R)	DURATION (HR)	FREQUENCY
Ban Lung	36,000	7	10am
Kratie via Snuol	21,000	4	10.30am, 2pm
Kratie via Chhlong	20,000	2	9.30am
Pakse (Laos)	US$22	12	10am
Phnom Penh	19,000	3	hourly to 3.45pm
Sen Monorom	31,000	5	noon
Siem Reap	24,000	5	7.30am, noon

GETTING TO VIETNAM

Kompong Cham to Tay Ninh

The Trapeang Plong/Xa Mat crossing (open 7am to 5pm) is convenient for those using private transport to travel between northeast Cambodia or Siem Reap and Ho Chi Minh City.

Getting to the border From Kompong Cham take anything heading east on NH7 towards Snuol, and get off at the roundabout in Krek (Kraek) on NH7 55km east-southeast of Kompong Cham. From there, it's 13km south by *moto* (US$3) along NH72 to snoozy Trapeang Plong, marked by a candy-striped road barrier and a few tin shacks.

At the border This border is a breeze; just have your Vietnamese visa ready.

Moving on On the Vietnamese side, motorbikes and taxis go to Tay Ninh, 45km to the south.

Snuol to Binh Long

The Trapeang Sre/Loc Ninh crossing (open 7am to 5pm) is useful for those trying to get straight to Vietnam from Kratie or points north.

Getting to the border First get to the much-maligned junction town of Snuol by bus, share taxi or minibus from Sen Monorom, Kratie or Kompong Cham. In Snuol catch a *moto* (US$5) for the 18km trip southeastward along smooth NH74.

At the border As always you'll need a prearranged visa to enter Vietnam, and US$20 for a visa-on-arrival to enter Cambodia.

Moving on On the Vietnamese side, the nearest town is Binh Long, 40km to the south. Motorbikes wait at the border.

---

food, pizzas and imported steaks in an arty riverfront space. Also has a **guesthouse** (📱 078 688996; reservations@chaplinsguesthouse.com; Sihanouk St; r US$25; ❄️ 🛜) upstairs with some of Kompong Cham's smarter rooms.

ℹ️ Information

Canadia Bank (Preah Monivong Blvd; ⏰ 8am-3.30pm Mon-Fri, 8-11.30am Sat) Free ATM withdrawals, plus free cash advances on credit card.

Mekong Internet (Vithei Pasteur; per hr 1500r; ⏰ 6.30am-10pm) Among a gaggle of internet cafes on Vithei Pasteur.

ℹ️ Getting There & Away

Phnom Penh is 120km southwest. If you are heading north to Kratie or beyond, secure transport via the sealed road to Chhlong rather than taking a huge detour east to Snuol on NH7.

Phnom Penh Sorya (Preah Monivong Blvd) is the most reliable bus company operating out of Kompong Cham. It serves all of the locales listed in the Buses from Kompong Cham table.

Share taxis (US$3.50, 2½ hours) dash to Phnom Penh from the taxi park near the New Market (Psar Thmei). Overcrowded local minibuses also do the run (10,000r).

Morning share taxis and minibuses to Kratie (US$5, 1½ hours) depart when full from the Caltex station (NH7) at the main roundabout, and there are morning minibuses from the taxi park as well.

ℹ️ Getting Around

Figure on US$10/15 or less per day for a *moto*/*remorque* (slightly more if including Wat Maha Leap in your plans). Round-trip *remorque* journeys to Wat Hanchey or Phnom Pros and Phnom Srei are a negotiable US$10.

Guesthouses and restaurants rent motorbikes (US$5 to US$7 per day) and bicycles (US$1 per day).

Around Kompong Cham

Consider hiring an outboard at the boat dock opposite the Mekong Hotel and heading upstream for about 30 minutes to a clutch of idyllic Mekong islands where you'll encounter smiling children and other slices of rural life. It costs about US$40. You could even turn it into a sunset cruise.

Phnom Pros & Phnom Srei ភ្នំប្រុសភ្នំស្រី

'Man Hill' and 'Woman Hill', the subjects of a rich variety of local legends, offer fine views of the countryside, especially during the wet season, and a very strokeable statue of the sacred bull Nandin (Shiva's mount). Phnom Pros is a good place for a cold drink among the inquisitive monkeys that populate the trees. The area between the two hills was once a killing field. A small, gilded brick stupa on the right as you walk from Man Hill to Woman Hill houses a pile of skulls.

The hills are about 7km northwest of town (towards Phnom Penh). Admission is US$2 and includes entry to **Wat Nokor**.

Opposite the entrance to Phnom Pros lies **Cheung Kok** village, home to a local ecotourism initiative run by the NGO **Amica** (www.amica-cambodge.org), aimed at introducing visitors to rural life in Kompong Cham. There is also a small shop in the village selling local handicrafts.

Wat Maha Leap វត្តមហាលាភ

Sacred Wat Maha Leap is one of the last remaining wooden pagodas left in the country, with resplendent gilded columns made out of complete tree trunks. Sadly, the roof collapsed in 2012; a temporary roof had been put in place at the time of our last visit.

The journey to Wat Maha Leap is best done by 40hp outboard from Kompong Cham's boat dock. The scenic one-hour trip along a tributary of the Mekong costs US$50 round-trip, including stops in nearby weaving villages. The trip is only possible from about July to late December. At other times you'll have to go overland – be sure to find a *moto* driver who knows the way. It's 20km by river and almost twice that by road.

Kratie ក្រចេះ

☑ 072 / POP 31,000

Kratie (pronounced *kra-cheh*) is a lively riverside town with a rich legacy of French-era architecture and some of the best Mekong sunsets in Cambodia. A thriving travel hub, it's the natural place to break the overland journey between Kompong Cham and Laos, or to pick up the Mekong Discovery Trail (p230).

◉ Sights & Activities

The riverside road heading south from Wat Roka Kandal towards Chhlong makes for a nice bicycle ride.

Koh Trong ISLAND

Lying just across the water from Kratie is the island of Koh Trong, an almighty sandbar in the middle of the river. Cross here by boat and enjoy a slice of rural island life. Catch the little ferry from the port or charter a local boat (around US$2) to get here. Bicycle rental is available on the island near the ferry landing for US$1, or do the loop around the island on a *moto* (US$2.50) steered by a female *motodup* (*moto* driver) – a rarity for Cambodia.

Dolphin Viewing WILDLIFE

🐟 Fewer than 85 critically endangered freshwater Irrawaddy dolphins (Mekong River dolphin; Latin *Orcaella brevirostris*; Khmer *trey pisaut*), recognisable by their bulbous foreheads and puny dorsal fins, live in the Mekong between Kratie and the Lao border. It is an endangered species throughout Asia; other shrinking populations are in Bangladesh and Myanmar. For more on this rare creature, see www.panda.org/greatermekong.

These gentle mammals can be seen at Kampi, about 15km north of Kratie, on the road to Sambor. A *moto/remorque* should be around US$7/10 return, depending on how long the driver has to wait. Motorboats shuttle visitors out to the middle of the river to view the dolphins at close quarters. It costs US$9 per person for one to two people and US$7 per person for groups of three or four. It is also possible to see them near the Lao border in Stung Treng Province (see Preah Rumkel, p232).

Cycling to Kampi is a fine option. On the way stop off at Phnom Sombok, a 70m-high hill with an active wat and fine Mekong views.

☞ Tours

CRDTours TOURS

(☑ 099 834353; www.crdtours.org; Tonlé Training Center, St 3; ⊙ 8am-noon & 2-5.30pm; 🖻) 🐟 Run by the Cambodian Rural Development Team (CRDT), this company focuses on sustainable tours along the Mekong Discovery Trail. Homestays, volunteer opportunities and various excursions are available on the Mekong island of Koh Pdao, 20km north of Kampi. The typical price is US$40 to US$60 per day, including all meals and tours. Tours and homestays on Koh Preah (near Stung Treng) and Koh Trong are also possible. Bike tours from Kratie to Koh Pdao are another option.

Sorya Kayaking Adventures KAYAKING
(☏090 241148; www.soryakayaking.com; Rue Preah Suramarit) Run by a socially conscious American woman, Sorya has a fleet of eight kayaks and runs half-day and multiday trips (with homestay accommodation) on the Mekong north of Kratie, around Koh Trong, or south of Kratie on the Te River, which sees several Vietnamese floating villages. This is a great way to get close to the dolphins too.

🛏 Sleeping

For something even more relaxed than Kratie, consider staying directly on the island of Koh Trong, where two homestays (US$4 per person) and two midrange guesthouses await.

Tonlé Training Center GUESTHOUSE $
(☏099 834353; www.letonle.org; St 3; r with fan/air-con US$15/30; ❄️🛜) 🌿 Recently opened by CRDT, this guesthouse boasts four rustic but attractive rooms in a beautiful wooden house and delicious food prepared by at-risk program trainees. The rooms share two clean bathrooms.

Silver Dolphin Guesthouse HOSTEL $
(☏012 999810; silver.dolphinbooking@yahoo.com; 48 Rue Preah Suramarit; dm/s/tr US$2/4/12, d US$6-14; ❄️@🛜) Even the cheapest doubles here have a TV, bathroom and some furniture, and the dorm is plenty big, with a soaring ceiling. You can drink and eat both downstairs and upstairs on the riverfront balcony.

Balcony Guesthouse GUESTHOUSE $
(☏016 604036; www.balconyguesthouse.net; Rue Preah Suramarit; s/d without bathroom US$3/6, r with bathroom US$7-20; ❄️@🛜) This long-running backpacker place has good-value rooms and food. Doubles as a popular little bar by night and is gay-friendly.

Star Backpackers GUESTHOUSE $
(☏097 455 3106; starbackpackerskratie@gmail.com; Rue Preah Sihanouk; dm US$2, d US$5-6; ❄️🛜) Young Spanish managers have revived this once-faded backpacker stalwart, installing a rooftop bar and hammock lounge, slapping colourful paint and murals on the walls, and installing a roomy 10-bed dorm room. It's above Tokae Restaurant.

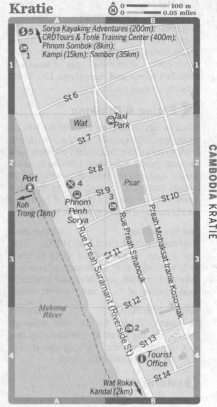

Kratie

🛏 Sleeping
1 Balcony Guesthouse A1
2 Silver Dolphin Guesthouse B4
3 Star Backpackers B2

🍴 Eating
4 Red Sun Falling A2
  Tokae Restaurant .... (see 3)

ℹ Information
5 Canadia Bank A1

Rajabori Villas BOUTIQUE HOTEL $$
(☏012 770150; www.rajabori-kratie.com; r incl breakfast US$52-95; ❄️) This boutique lodge on Koh Trong island has a swimming pool and attractive bungalows. It's located at the northern tip of the island; a private boat from Kratie costs US$4/5 (day/night).

Arun Mekong LODGE $$
(www.arunmekong.wordpress.com; r US$22-27, bungalows US$33) Practically next door to Rajabori Villas at the north end of Koh Trong island, Arun Mekong is a slightly more rustic option, with a nice mix of tastefully furnished rooms and bungalows. Electricity runs only from 6pm to 11pm.

Eating & Drinking

When in Kratie keep an eye out for two famous specialities, sold on the riverfront: *krolan* (sticky rice, beans and coconut milk steamed inside a bamboo tube) and *nehm* (tangy, raw, spiced river fish wrapped in banana leaves). The south end of the *psar* (market) turns into a carnival of barbecue stands hawking meat-on-a-stick by night.

Red Sun Falling INTERNATIONAL $
(Rue Preah Suramarit; mains 7000-14,000r; ⊙ 7am-9pm; 🛜) One of the liveliest spots in town, with a relaxed cafe ambience, a supreme riverfront location, used books for sale and a good selection of Asian and Western meals.

Tokae Restaurant CAMBODIAN $
(St 10; mains US$2-3; ⊙ 6am-11pm; 🛜) Although French-run, the focus at this lively restaurant underneath Star Backpackers is very much on cheap Cambodian food.

ⓘ Information

All of the recommended guesthouses are pretty switched on to travellers' needs. Silver Dolphin Guesthouse has public internet access (per hour 3000r).
Canadia Bank (Rue Preah Suramarit) ATM offering free cash withdrawals, plus currency exchange.

ⓘ Getting There & Around

Kratie is 348km northeast of Phnom Penh (250km via Chhlong) and 141km south of Stung Treng.

Phnom Penh Sorya (📞 081 908005) operates three buses per day to Phnom Penh (US$8, eight hours) along the slow route (via Snuol); Sorya's bus from Laos comes through at roughly 3.30pm and goes to Phnom Penh via the much-shorter Chhlong route (six hours). Sorya buses to Siem Reap involve a change in Suong.

Going the other way, Sorya's bus from Phnom Penh to Pakse, Laos (US$20, eight hours) via Stung Treng collects passengers in Kratie at about 11.30am. Sorya also has a 1pm bus to Ban Lung (US$8, five hours) and a 3pm bus to Stung Treng (US$5, three hours).

Share taxis (US$10) head to Phnom Penh between 6am and 8am, with possible additional departures after lunch. Other destinations include Snuol (10,000r), Kompong Cham (30,000r) and Stung Treng (25,000r). The **taxi park** is just north of the market.

Most guesthouses can arrange bicycle (from US$1) and motorbike (from US$5) hire. An English-speaking *motodup* will set you back US$10 to US$15 per day, a *remorque* about US$25.

Around Kratie

Sambor សំបូរ

Sambor was the site of a thriving pre-Angkorian city during the time of Sambor Prei Kuk and the Chenla empire. Today it has the largest wat in Cambodia, complete with 108 columns, known locally as **Wat Sorsor Moi Roi** (100 Columns Temple).

THE MEKONG DISCOVERY TRAIL

It's well worth spending a couple of days exploring the various bike rides and activities on offer along the **Mekong Discovery Trail** (www.mekongdiscoverytrail.com), an initiative to open up stretches of the Mekong River around Stung Treng and Kratie to community-based tourism. Once managed by the government with foreign development assistance, the project is now being kept alive by private tour companies – mainly Xplore-Asia in Stung Treng and CRDTours in Kratie. It deserves support, as it intends to provide fishing communities an alternative income in order to protect the Irrawaddy dolphin and other rare species on this stretch of river.

There's a great booklet with routes and maps outlining excursions around Kratie and Stung Treng, but you'll be hard pressed to secure your own copy. Ask tour operators if you can photograph theirs. The routes can be tackled by bicycle or motorbike. They range in length from a few hours to several days, with optional overnights in village homestays. Routes criss-cross the Mekong frequently by ferry and traverse several Mekong islands, including Koh Trong.

The **Mekong Turtle Conservation Centre** (☑ 012 712071; www.mekongturtle.com; adult/child US$4/2; ☺ 8.30am-4.30pm) is located within the temple grounds. Established by **Conservation International** (www.conservation.org), it is home to several species of turtle, including the rare Cantor's giant softshell, which can grow to nearly 2m in length. Hatchlings are nurtured here for 10 months before being released in the wild – sometimes with the help of tourists.

To get to Sambor, follow the Kampi road north to Sandan, before veering left along a reasonable 10km stretch of road – it's about 35km in total.

Stung Treng   ស្ទឹងត្រែង

☑ 074 / POP 28,000

Located on the Tonlé San near its confluence with the Mekong, Stung Treng is a dusty city with not much to offer, but perhaps this will change when a new bridge over the Mekong is completed in 2015. The bridge will feed into a new highway running west to Preah Vihear City, cutting about four hours off the journey from northeast Cambodia or southern Laos to Siem Reap.

The main attractions are up near the Lao border, where you can kayak out to a pod of Irrawaddy dolphins then continue downstream on the Mekong along a heavenly stretch of flooded forest.

🛏 Sleeping & Eating

Le Tonlé Tourism Training Centre   GUESTHOUSE $

(☑ 074-973638; www.letonle.org; s/d from US$6/8; 🛜) On the riverfront about 500m west of the ferry dock, this small guesthouse doubles as a training centre to help underprivileged locals. Delicious meals can be ordered in advance.

Riverside Guesthouse   GUESTHOUSE $

(☑ 012 257207; timtysou@gmail.com; r US$5-8; @) Overlooking the riverfront area, the Riverside is a long-time travellers' crossroads with basic rooms and a popular bar-restaurant.

Golden River Hotel   HOTEL $$

(☑ 074-690 0029; www.goldenriverhotel.com; r US$15-35; 🕸@🛜) Still the smartest hotel in town, although that's not saying much. It has the province's only lift and 50 well-appointed rooms with a few quirks. The river-view rooms in front cost a bit more.

Ponika's Palace   INTERNATIONAL $

(mains US$2-5; ☺ 6am-10pm) Need a break from *laab* after Laos? Burgers, pizza and English breakfasts grace the menu here, along with Indian food and wonderful Khmer curries. The affable owner Ponika speaks English.

🛍 Shopping

Mekong Blue   SILK

(មេគង្គប្លូ; ☑ 012 622096; www.mekongblue.com; ☺ 7.30-11.30am & 2-5pm Mon-Sat) 🍃 Part of the Stung Treng Women's Development Centre, Mekong Blue is a silk-weaving centre on the outskirts of town where you can see the entire silk-making process, from rearing silkworms to dyeing and hand-loom weaving. There is a small showroom on site with a selection of exquisite silks on sale, all produced by impoverished and vulnerable weavers. The centre is located about 4km east of town on the riverside road that continues under the bridge.

ℹ Information

Canadia Bank Near the market; has a full international ATM with free withdrawals.

Riverside Guesthouse (☑ 012 257207; timtysou@gmail.com) Specialises in getting people to/from Laos, Siem Reap or just about anywhere else. Also runs boat tours to the Lao border via the resident dolphin pod (US$100/120 for two/four people).

Xplore-Asia (☑ 074-973456, 011 433836; www.xplore-cambodia.com) Doles out brochures, booklets and advice, and tailors one- to several-day cycle-and-kayak combo tours along the Mekong Discovery Trail, including kayaking with the dolphins. Rents out kayaks (US$10 per day), motorbikes (US$10 per day) and sturdy Trek mountain bikes (US$5 per day).

Tourist Information Centre (☑ 074-210001; ☺ 8-11am & 2-7pm; 🛜) Inconveniently located near the new bridge, it's run by the ever-helpful Theany.

ℹ Getting There & Around

Express minibuses with guesthouse pick-ups as early as 4am are the quickest way to Phnom Penh (US$10 to US$13, eight hours). Book through Riverside Guesthouse.

Phnom Penh Sorya (☑ 092 181805) has a 6.30am bus to Phnom Penh (40,000r, nine hours) via Kratie (20,000r, three hours). Sorya's bus from Laos to Phnom Penh comes through Stung Treng around 11.30am.

There is a comfortable tourist van to Ban Lung (US$6, two hours, 8am), with additional morning trips in cramped local minibuses (15,000r, three hours) from the market.

Riverside Guesthouse does minivan trips to Siem Reap via the new highway to Preah Vihear City when there's demand (US$25 per person). These will continue to cross the Mekong by ferry until the new bridge to Thala Boravit is completed.

Riverside Guesthouse also rents out motorbikes (from US$8) and bicycles (US$1 to US$2).

Around Stung Treng

Preah Rumkel អ្នរស្វាយ និងព្រះរំកិល

This small village is emerging as a hotbed of ecotourism thanks to its proximity to the Anlong Cheuteal Irrawaddy dolphin pool near the Lao border. With Ramsar-recognised wetlands, dozens of islands, a rich array of bird life and various rapids and waterfalls cascading down from Laos, this is one of the Mekong River's wildest and most beautiful stretches.

The half-dozen frolicking dolphins in the Anlong Cheuteal pool can easily be sighted from shore in Preah Rumkel. This is the same pool that boats and kayaks out of Don Det and Don Khon in Laos visit. There's a US$2 per person charge to see the dolphins.

Preah Rumkel has an excellent community-based homestay (per person US$3, plus per meal US$3) program.

Hire a long-tail boat in O'Svay or, closer to the Laos border, Anlong Morakot, to explore the area and view the dolphins. Boats cost a negotiable US$25 round-trip to the dolphin pool. Add US$10 if you want to continue upstream to a set of thundering Mekong rapids.

Anlong Morakot is only 4km by *moto* (US$2) from the Lao border. If coming in from Laos, you can arrange for Xplore-Asia (p231) or Riverside Guesthouse (p231) in Stung Treng to pick you up at the border and handle your boat transfer to Preah Rumkel.

Through Xplore-Asia you can also kayak with the dolphins and then paddle downstream to O'Svay – or all the way to Stung Treng via bird-infested flooded forests. A full-day kayak excursion south of O'Svay costs US$65 per person; add US$20 per person to include the boat trip upstream to the dolphin pool and the Mekong rapids.

Ratanakiri Province

Popular Ratanakiri Province is a diverse region of outstanding natural beauty that provides a remote home for a mosaic of minority peoples – Jarai, Tompuon, Brau and Kreung – with their own languages, traditions and customs. Adrenalin activi-

---

GETTING TO LAOS: STUNG TRENG TO SI PHAN DON

The remote Trapeang Kriel/Nong Nok Khiene border (open 6am to 6pm) is 60km north of Stung Treng.

Getting to the border Phnom Penh Sorya (p190), in partnership with Pakse-based Lao operator Sengchalean (☑ 031 212 428) has buses from Phnom Penh straight through to Pakse's 2km (VIP) bus station (US$27, 12 to 14 hours). This bus leaves Phnom Penh at 6.45am, with pick-ups possible in Kompong Cham (around 9.30am), Kratie (around 11.30am) and Stung Treng (around 3pm). The only other option to the border from Stung Treng is a private taxi (US$35 to US$45) or *moto* (US$15 to US$20). Services to Laos from Siem Reap are also possible, with a bus change in Suong.

At the border Both Lao and Cambodian visas are available on arrival. Entering Laos, you'll pay US$35 to US$42 for a visa, depending on nationality, plus a US$2 fee (dubbed either an 'overtime' or a 'processing' fee, depending on when you cross). The bus company wants its cut too, so it charges an extra US$1 to US$2 to handle your paperwork with the border guards. To avoid this fee, insist on doing your own paperwork and go through immigration alone.

Moving on Aside from the Sorya bus, there's virtually zero traffic on either side of the border. If you're dropped at the border, expect to pay 150,000r/50,000K (US$12/4) for a taxi/*sǎhmlór* heading north to Ban Nakasang (for Don Det).

For more information about crossing this border in the other direction, see p346.

ties abound. Swim in clear volcanic lakes, shower under waterfalls, or trek in the vast Virachey National Park – it's all here. Tourism is set to take off, but that is if the lowland politicians and generals don't plunder the place first. Hopefully someone will wake up and smell the coffee – there's plenty of that as well – before it's too late.

Ban Lung បានលុង

☎ 075 / POP 25,000

Affectionately known as *'dey krahorm'* (red earth) after its rust-coloured affliction, Ban Lung provides a popular base for a range of Ratanakiri romps. It is one of the easiest places in Cambodia to arrange a jungle trek and has several beautiful lakes and waterfalls nearby. Members of highland minorities, woven baskets on their backs, come from nearby villages to buy and sell at the market.

◉ Sights

Boeng Yeak Lom LAKE
(បឹងយក្សឡោម; admission US$1) Boeng Yeak Lom is one of the most serene and sublimely beautiful sites in Cambodia. This clear blue crater lake, surrounded by dark-green jungle, is sacred to the indigenous Tompuon peoples. It's a great place to take a dip, although Cambodians jump in fully clothed. A small **Cultural & Environmental Centre** has a modest display on ethnic minorities in the province and hires out life jackets for the young'uns.

To get to Boeng Yeak Lom from Ban Lung head east towards Vietnam for 3km, turn right at the minorities statue and proceed 2km or so. *Motos* charge US$3 return (more if you make them wait), while *remorques* charge up to US$10 return.

Waterfalls WATERFALL
Tucked amid the sprawling cashew and rubber plantations just west of Ban Lung are three waterfalls worth visiting: **Chaa Ong** (admission 2000r), **Ka Tieng** (admission 2000r) and **Kinchaan** (Kachang; admission 2000r). These falls are booming in the wet season but dry up to a trickle in the dry season. One-hour **elephant rides** (US$15/20 for one/two riders) are available near Ka Tieng waterfall.

The turn-offs to all three waterfalls are 200m west of the new bus station, just beyond a Lina petrol station. The Chaa Ong turn-off is on the right (north) side of NH19;

the waterfall is 5.5km from the highway along a dirt road. The turn-off to Ka Tieng and Kinchaan is left of NH19; proceed 5.5km to a fork in the road. Go left 200m to Kinchaan, or right 2.5km to Ka Tieng.

Motos (return US$6 for one waterfall, or US$10 for all three) and *remorques* (US$10/20 for one/three waterfalls) can get you here safely. Visits to all three falls are usually included in tour companies' half- and full-day excursions.

☞ Tours

Overnight treks with nights spent camping or staying in minority villages north of Voen Sai or Ta Veng are popular. Figure on US$45 or US$50 per person per day for a couple (less for bigger groups).

Backpacker Pad, Tree Top Ecolodge and Yaklom Hill Lodge are good at arranging tours, but we recommend using one of the following dedicated tour companies.

Highland Tours TOURS
(☎088 870 3080, 097 658 3841; highland.tour@yahoo.com) Kimi and Horng are husband-wife graduates of the Le Tonlé Tourism Training Centre (p231) in Stung Treng who have moved to the highlands to run a range of tours. Horng is the only female guide in Ratanakiri.

Khieng TOURS
(☎097 923 0923; khamphaykhieng@yahoo.com) Bespectacled Khieng is an indigenous Tompuon guide who runs unique one- to two-night trips in some fairly well-preserved jungle around Lumphat, with overnights in minority villages.

DutchCo Trekking Cambodia TOURS
(☎097 679 2714; www.trekkingcambodia.com) One of the most experienced trekking operators in the province, run by – wait for it – a friendly Dutchman.

Ban Lung

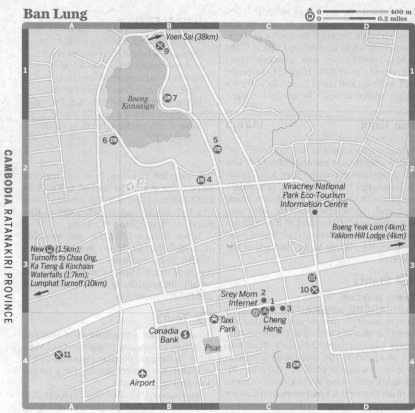

Voen Sai (38km)

Boeng Kansaign

Virachey National Park Eco-Tourism Information Centre

Boeng Yeak Lom (4km); Yaklom Hill Lodge (4km)

New (1.5km); Turnoffs to Chaa Ong, Ka Tieng & Kinchaan Waterfalls (1.7km); Lumphat Turnoff (10km)

Srey Mom Internet

Cheng Heng

Canadia Bank

Taxi Park

Psar

Airport

Ban Lung

Activities, Courses & Tours
1 DutchCo Trekking Cambodia..............C3
2 Highland Tours.....................................C3
3 Parrot Tours C3

Sleeping
4 Backpacker Pad...................................B2
5 Banlung Balcony..................................B2
6 Lakeside Chheng Lok Hotel................A2
7 Terres Rouges Lodge B1
8 Tree Top Ecolodge..............................C4

Eating
9 Coconut Shake Restaurant B1
10 Gecko House..C3
11 Sal's Restaurant & Bar.......................A4

Parrot Tours TOURS
(012 764714; www.jungletrek.blogspot.com) Tours are run by Sitha Nan, a national-park-trained guide with expert local knowledge.

Sleeping

★ Tree Top Ecolodge BUNGALOWS $
(012 490333; www.treetop-ecolodge.com; d US$7, cottage with cold/hot water US$12/15;) Setting the standard for budget digs in the northeast. Here rough-hewn walkways lead to all-wood bungalows with mosquito nets, thatch roofs and verandahs with verdant valley views. Up-to-date travel advice is plentiful, especially for those Laos bound.

Banlung Balcony GUESTHOUSE $
(097 911 0989; www.balconyguesthouse.net; d US$4-7;) Ban Lung's best deal at the bargain-basement end. The rooms are basic but have high ceilings and odour-combating wood floors.

Backpacker Pad HOSTEL $
(092 785259; banlungbackpackerpad@yahoo.com; dm US$2, d with/without bathroom US$5/4;)

Penny pinchers rejoice: it doesn't get cheaper than this. Owner Sophat is a great source of info and runs a tour company.

Lakeside Chheng Lok Hotel HOTEL $
(☑012 957422; lakeside.chhenglokhotel@gmail.com; r with fan/air-con from US$5/15; ✳@🛜❄) The ever-expanding Lakeside has tacked on a swimming pool, a vast new wing and a sister hotel (the Lakeside Hotel, next door) in recent years. A lot to choose from here, from large but generic air-con rooms to barebones fan-cooled rooms.

Yaklom Hill Lodge LODGE $
(☑011 725881; www.yaklom.com; s/d/tr US$10/15/20) 🌿 Ratanakiri's only true ecolodge, staffed by Tompuon, is set amid lush forest near Boeung Yeak Lom, 5km east of Ban Lung's central roundabout. The all-wood bungalows are starting to show their age. Electricity is limited to three hours each evening.

★ **Terres Rouges Lodge** BOUTIQUE HOTEL $$
(☑075-974051; www.ratanakiri-lodge.com; s/d incl breakfast US$46/52, ste US$86-92; ✳@🛜❄) If you're travelling with kids and/or looking for a little more comfort in Ban Lung, staying here is a no-brainer. The fan-cooled standard rooms are done up in classy colonial style, while the sumptuous Balinese-style suites are closer to the 14m pool.

🍴 Eating

Among the guesthouses, Terres Rouges has the most sophisticated menu, while Treetop and Banlung Balcony are also reliable. Waterfront shacks on the lakefront near Coconut Shake Restaurant serve very cheap beer and snacks starting around sunset.

★ **Sal's Restaurant & Bar** INTERNATIONAL $
(mains US$1.75-5) This welcoming restaurant-bar, popular with Ban Lung's small expat community, is the place to come for comfort food from home, including Indian curries, spicy Mexican and great burgers.

Cafe Alee INTERNATIONAL $
(mains US$1.50-5.50; ⏰7am-last customer) Cafe Alee's menu features the full spectrum of Khmer food plus a few token Western dishes – vegie burgers, lasagne, pizza, baguettes, and hearty breakfasts and breads for trekkers. Do try the homemade potato crisps.

Gecko House INTERNATIONAL $
(mains 10,000-20,000r; ⏰8am-10pm; 🛜) This is a charming little restaurant-bar with soft lighting and famously frosty beer mugs. This is a great place by day or night.

Coconut Shake Restaurant CAMBODIAN $
(northeast cnr of Boeng Kansaign; mains 6000-16,000r; ⏰7am-9pm) The best coconut shakes in the northeast cost just 4000r – we drink at least one a day when in Ban Lung. It also has fried noodles and other Khmer fare if you care to sit down and stay.

ℹ Information

Visitors will find their guesthouse or the recommended tour companies to be most useful in the quest for local knowledge.

Canadia Bank Full service bank with fee-free ATM.

Srey Mom Internet (☑097 295 9111; per hr 4000r; ⏰6.30am-10pm) Fan-cooled internet access.

GETTING TO VIETNAM: BAN LUNG TO PLEIKU

The O Yadaw/Le Thanh crossing (open 7am to 5pm) is 64km east of Ban Lung along smooth NH19.

Getting to the border From Ban Lung, guesthouses advertise a 6.30am van to Pleiku (US$12, 3½ hours) involving a change of vehicles at the border. These pick you up at your guesthouse. Alternatively, take a local minibus to O Yadaw from Ban Lung's new bus station, and continue 25km to the border by *moto*. A *moto* from Ban Lung to the border will set you back US$20 (one hour).

At the border Formalities are straightforward and lines nonexistent; just make sure you have a Vietnamese visa.

Moving on On the Vietnamese side of the frontier, the road is nicely paved and *motos* await to take you to Duc Co (20km), where there are buses to Pleiku (15,000d), Quy Nhon and Hoi An.

For more information about crossing this border in the other direction, see p116.

ⓘ Getting There & Away

Ban Lung's new **bus station** (NH19) is on the western outskirts of town, 2.5km east of Ban Lung's main roundabout. All bus departures and most long-distance minibus services depart from here. Tour companies in town usually offer free rides out here with the purchase of a ticket.

Phnom Penh Sorya, Rith Mony and Thong Ly operate early-morning buses to Phnom Penh (US$9 to US$10, 11 hours) via Kratie and Kompong Cham.

Quicker are the speedy express vans that pick you up at your guesthouse and head to Phnom Penh (US$15, eight hours, 6am and 4pm) and Stung Treng (US$6, two hours, around 7.30am). Call Tree Top Ecolodge to arrange an express van pick-up if coming from Phnom Penh. Tree Top is also an expert regarding the ins and outs of getting to Laos and Vietnam.

Long a dirt cattle track known as the 'Death Highway', the road south to Mondulkiri has been upgraded to a sealed highway. It should be ready for prime time upon completion of a bridge over the Srepok River in Lumphat (estimated finish date late 2014). Until that opens, the easiest way to get to Mondulkiri by public transport is to backtrack to Snuol or Kratie and pick up transportation there.

ⓘ Getting Around

Motodups hang out around the market and some double as guides. Figure on US$15 to US$20 per day for a good English-speaking driver-guide. A *moto* to Yeak Lom costs US$3 to US$4 return; to Voen Sai is US$15 return; to any waterfall is about US$6 return.

Cheng Heng (☑ 088 851 6104; ⊗ 6am-8pm) has some 250cc trail bikes for rent (US$25) in addition to a stable of well-maintained smaller motorbikes (US$6 to US$8).

Around Ban Lung

VIRACHEY NATIONAL PARK ឧទ្យានជាតិវីរជ័យ

In this Asean Heritage **park** (admission US$5), one of the largest and wildest protected areas in Cambodia, ecotourism is playing an important role in protecting the park from development. (Cambodian authorities have already sold more remote regions of the park to Vietnamese rubber plantations.)

The park has never been fully explored and is home to a number of rare mammals, including elephants, clouded leopards and sun bears, although your chances of seeing any of these beasts are extremely slim. However, you'll probably hear endangered gibbons and might spot great hornbills, giant ibises, Germain's peacock-pheasants and other rare birds.

The **Virachey National Park Eco-Tourism Information Centre** (☑ 097 896 4995, 075-974013; virachey@camintel.com; ⊗ 8am-noon & 2-5pm) is the exclusive operator of tours within the park boundaries, offering two- to eight-day treks led by English-speaking, park-employed rangers. The signature trek is an eight-day, seven-night **Phnom Veal Thom Wilderness Trek** (1/2 people US$400/350 per person). Prices drop the larger the group.

VOEN SAI វិនសៃ

Located on the banks of Tonlé San, Voen Sai is a cluster of Chinese, Lao and Chunchiet (minority) villages. The Voen Sai area is known for Tompuon cemeteries, but most of them are closed to outsiders these days –

THE REAL GIBBON EXPERIENCE

Conservation International (CI; ☑ in Phnom Penh 023-214627; www.conservation.org) has set up a new project to observe semihabituated yellow-cheeked crested gibbons in the **Voen Sai-Siem Pang Conservation Area** (VSSPCA), just outside the border of Virachey National Park north of Voen Sai. This colony was only discovered in 2010 and is believed to be the world's largest at about 500 groups. Hearing their haunting dawn call echo through the jungle and seeing them swing through the canopy is memorable.

You stay at least one night in the jungle sleeping in hammocks or in a community-based homestay, rising well before dawn to spend time with the gibbons. CI has an exclusive arrangement with the village near the gibbon site to run these tours. The gibbon viewing season runs from November to mid-June (it's too wet at other times). The maximum group size is six. The tours cost US$100 to US$200 per person. Most companies in Ban Lung can arrange these trips on behalf of CI.

The VSSPCA is highly susceptible to the types of illegal and legal logging that have ravaged most of the forests around Ban Lung, so this is money well spent.

RESPONSIBLE TREKKING AROUND RATANAKIRI

Tourism can bring many benefits to highland communities: cross-cultural understanding, improved infrastructure, cheaper market goods, employment opportunities and tourist dollars supporting handicraft industries. However, there are also negatives, such as increased litter and pollutants, domination of the tourism business by lowland Khmers at the expense of highland minorities, and the tendency of tourists to disregard local customs and taboos.

One way to offset the negatives in a big way is to hire indigenous guides for organised treks and other excursions around Ban Lung. Not only does this ensure that your tourist dollars go directly to indigenous communities, it will also enrich your own visit. Indigenous guides can greatly improve your access to the residents of highland communities, who are animists and rarely speak Khmer. They also understand taboos and traditions that might be lost on Khmer.

Tour companies listed in this section can all hire indigenous guides on request. A loose association of Tompuon guides is based at Boeng Yeak Lom lake. They have neither a phone number nor an email so you'll just have to rock up. They can take you on an exclusive tour of several Tompuon villages around Boeng Yeak Lom. You can observe weavers and basket makers in action, learn about animist traditions and eat a traditional indigenous meal of bamboo-steamed fish, fresh vegetables, 'minority' rice and, of course, rice wine.

which is at least partially the result of tourists flaunting behavioural protocols.

At the time of writing, the closest cemetery to Voen Sai open to visitors was an **ethnic Kachah cemetery** in Kaoh Paek, a 45-minute boat ride upriver from Voen Sai. Expect to pay around US$40 for the boat trip from Voen Sai, or about half that from Kachon, 10km upriver (east) of Voen Sai. Tour companies in Ban Lung charge US$50 for an excursion here.

Voen Sai is 39km northwest of Ban Lung on an unsealed but smooth all-weather road. It is easy enough to get here under your own steam on a motorbike or with a vehicle. English-speaking guides ask US$15 or so return to take you out here on a *moto*.

Mondulkiri Province

Mondulkiri (Meeting of the Hills), the original Wild East of the country, is a world apart from the lowlands with not a rice paddy or palm tree in sight. Home to the hardy Bunong people and their noble elephants, this upland area is a seductive mix of grassy hills, pine groves and rainforests of jade green. Conservationists have grand plans for the sparsely populated province but are facing off against loggers, poachers, prospectors and well-connected speculators.

Sen Monorom សែនមនោរម្យ

☑ 073 / POP 10,000

A charming community where the famous hills meet, the area around Sen Monorom is peppered with minority villages and picturesque waterfalls, making it the ideal place to spend some time. Set at more than 800m, the town can get quite chilly so bring warm clothing.

◎ Sights & Activities

As in Ratanakiri, multiday forest treks taking in minority villages are the big draw. We recommend securing indigenous Bunong guides for these trips. They know the forests intimately and can break the ice with the locals in any Bunong villages you visit.

Monorom Falls WATERFALL

FREE A 10m drop into a popular swimming hole, Monorom Falls is lovely if you can beat the crowds. From the west side of the airstrip, head northwest for 2.3km, turn left and proceed 1.5km. A return *moto* costs US$3.

Elephant Valley Project WILDLIFE RESERVE

(☑099 696041; www.elephantvalleyproject.org; ◎Mon-Fri) This popular initiative entices local mahouts to bring their overworked or injured elephants in for some down time or to live permanently. You are not allowed to ride the elephants here. Instead, you simply walk through the forest with them and observe them in their element, learning about elephant behaviour, Bunong culture and forest ecology in the process.

There are two options for visiting the Elephant Valley Project. Option one is a day trip (half/full day US$40/70) on which half the day is spent observing the elephants, the other half, washing them and doing other tasks around the project site. The second option is an overnight stay (dorm US$20, double US$30 to US$50) in exquisite bungalows tucked into the jungle on a ridge overlooking the valley. Meals are included in the price.

It's popular so book well in advance. The maximum amount of day trippers allowed per day is 12. Short- and long-term volunteers who want to help the project while learning mahout skills are welcome.

Elephant Rides
TOURS

You can ride elephants in the villages of **Phulung**, 7km northeast of Sen Monorom, and **Putang**, 9km southwest of town. Treks arranged in Sen Monorom cost US$25 to US$30 per person, including lunch and transport to and from the village. It is also possible to negotiate a longer trek with an overnight stay in a Bunong village, costing US$50 to US$80 per person.

☞ Tours

Bunong Place
TOURS

(☑ 012 474879; www.bunongcenter.org; ☉ 6am-6pm) This NGO-run 'drop-in centre' for Bunong people is a good source of information on sustainable tourism and provides trained Bunong guides for local tours, costing US$15/25 per half/full day, including motorbike. Also sells handicrafts.

Green House
TOURS

(☑ 017 905659; www.greenhouse-tour.blogspot.com) Offers internet access and the most comprehensive tour progam around the province. Besides the normal trekking it also runs full-day mountain-bike tours (about US$20).

🛏 Sleeping

★ Nature Lodge
GUESTHOUSE $

(☑ 012 230272; www.naturelodgecambodia.com; r US$10-30; ☎) Located on a windswept hilltop near town, this quirky resort has attractive, comfortable bungalows with hot showers. The magnificent restaurant/common area has comfy nooks, a pool table and an enviable bar.

Phanyro Guesthouse
GUESTHOUSE $

(☑ 017 770867; r US$8-12; ☎) This is a favourite with visiting volunteers and NGOs, offering a clutch of cottages perched on a ridge overlooking the river valley. Clean with a capital C.

Tree Lodge
BUNGALOWS $

(☑ 097 723 4177; www.treelodge-senmonorom.blogspot.com; r with cold/hot water from US$3/5; ☎) Run by a helpful young family, Tree Lodge targets backpackers with basic (think bed, floor, mosquito net) A-frame huts made from native materials.

Happy Elephant
GUESTHOUSE $

(☑ 097 616 4011; motvil@hotmail.com; d from US$5; ☎) This backpacker special features a half-dozen sturdy cold-water bungalows on a hill behind the pleasingly simple wooden restaurant.

Sovankiri
HOSTEL $

(☑ 097 474 4528; dm US$3, r US$5-8) This central guesthouse offers clean, no-nonsense budget rooms, plus the best Western food in town (fine Khmer food as well).

Mayura Hill Hotel & Resort
HOTEL $$$

(☑ 077 980980; www.mayurahillresort.com; r incl breakfast US$100-120, ste incl breakfast US$150; ❄☎≋) It's considerably overpriced for Cambodia, but if you're looking for a modicum of comfort and boutique-style amenities like imported linens and a modest-sized pool, Mayura is really the only game in town.

✕ Eating & Drinking

All the guesthouses have restaurants. Nature Lodge is probably the best all-rounder for atmosphere and food.

Hefalump Cafe
CAFE $

(☎) 🖉 A collaboration of various NGOs and conservation groups in town, this cafe doubles as a training centre for Bunong people in hospitality. Coffee, tea, cake and sandwiches.

Green House Restaurant & Bar
INTERNATIONAL $

(mains US$1.50-3.50; ☉ 7am-11pm) Popular place for inexpensive Khmer and Western dishes, plus cocktails against a backdrop of ambient reggae beats.

ⓘ Information

Acleda Bank (NH76) Changes major currencies and has a Visa-only ATM.

ⓘ Getting There & Away

Phnom Penh Sorya runs a 7.30am bus to Phnom Penh (US$8, eight hours). Express vans run by Chim Vuth Mondulkiri Express and Kim Seng Express do the trip in 5½ hours (US$10).

Vehicles to Phnom Penh go via Kompong Cham. Any advertised trip to Siem Reap usually involves a change in Suong.

Local minibuses (departing from the taxi park) are the way forward to Kratie (30,000r, four hours). Count on at least one early morning departure and two or three departures around 12.30pm.

See Ban Lung's Getting There & Away section (p236) for information on the new direct route to Ratanakiri. Until that's ready, backtrack to Snuol or Kratie and pick up transportation there.

ⓘ Getting Around

English-speaking *moto* drivers cost about US$15 to US$20 per day. Most guesthouses rent out motorbikes for US$6 to US$8 and a few have bicycles for US$2. **Adventure Rider Asia** (☑078 250350; www.adventurerideriasia.com; NH76; tours per day from US$65) has well-maintained 250cc dirt bikes for rent (US$25).

Around Sen Monorom

The Ho Chi Minh Trail passed through the hills of Mondulkiri and was bombed by the Americans: never touch anything that looks vaguely like unexploded ordnance.

BOU SRAA WATERFALL

This two-tiered **waterfall** (ទឹកជ្រោះប៊ូស្រា; admission 5000r) 33km east of Sen Monorom is famous throughout the country. It's a double-drop waterfall with an upper tier of some 10m and a spectacular lower tier with a thundering 25m drop.

PHNOM PRICH WILDLIFE SANCTUARY

WWF (☑012-776003, 073-690 0096; www.mondulkiritourism.org) has recently helped two villages in this wildlife sanctuary launch projects geared towards giving tourists a glimpse into traditional Bunong lifestyles while improving local livelihoods and protecting the forest.

About 55km north of Sen Monorom on the road to Koh Nhek, the village of **Dei Ey** offers homestays, traditional meals, walking with elephants owned by the local Bunong, and trekking. Prices for a two-day trip start at US$135 for one person and go down substantially with each added person. Included are transport, meals cooked by Bunong, guides and accommodation in the Dei Ey Community Lodge.

There's a similar program in **Sre Y**, about 30km northwest of Sen Monorom. Day trips here involve walking with elephants, followed by a trek to a waterfall, then returning to Sen Monorom on mountain bikes.

Contact Nimith at WWF for details on both projects, which can also be booked through tour operators in Sen Monorom.

SOUTH COAST

Cambodia's south coast is an alluring mix of clear blue water, castaway islands, pristine mangrove forests, time-worn colonial towns and jungle-clad mountains, where bears and elephants lurk. Adventurers will find this region of Cambodia just as rewarding as sunseekers.

MONKEY BUSINESS IN MONDULKIRI

A recent **Wildlife Conservation Society** (WCS; ☑023-219443; www.wcscambodia.org) study estimated populations of 30,500 black-shanked doucs in Mondulkiri's **Seima Protected Forest** and 2600 yellow-cheeked crested gibbons – the world's largest concentration of both species. You can trek into the wild and possibly spot these primates, along with other wild beasts, thanks to an exciting new project supported by the WCS in the Bunong village of Andong Kraloeng, which lies on the highway just 20km southwest of Sen Monorom.

Day treks and overnight trips wind their way through mixed evergreen forest and waterfalls with an excellent chance of spotting the doucs along the way (the gibbons were still being habituated at the time of research).

Registered guides accompany visitors together with local Bunong guides to identify the trails. Sample prices: about US$50 per person for a one-day tour, or US$100 for an overnight tour, including all guides, equipment for overnight stays in hammocks, and food.

For information and bookings, contact Green House in Sen Monorom.

Koh Kong City ក្រុងកោះកុង

📞 035 / POP 35,000

Once Cambodia's Wild West, its frontier economy dominated by smuggling, prostitution and gambling, the city of Koh Kong, capital of the province of the same name, is striding towards respectability as ecotourists scare the sleaze away. The town serves as the gateway to deserted beaches, offshore islands and the lush rainforests of the Koh Kong Conservation Corridor.

👁 Sights & Activities

Koh Kong's main draw is seeking adventure in and around the Cardamom Mountains and the Koh Kong Conservation Corridor.

Wat Neang Kok BUDDHIST TEMPLE

A rocky promontory on the right (western) bank of the Koh Poi River is decorated with **life-size statues** demonstrating the violent punishments that await sinners in the Buddhist hell. This graphic tableau belongs to Wat Neang Kok, a Buddhist temple. To get there, cross the bridge and turn right 600m past the toll booth (*motos* cost 1200r). The statues are 150m beyond the temple.

Peam Krasaop Mangrove Sanctuary WILDLIFE RESERVE

(ជម្រកសត្វព្រៃបឹងគ្រឃ្យាំកនៅព្រាមក្រសោម; mangrove walk admission 5000r; ⏰mangrove walk 6.30am-6pm) 🏖 Anchored to alluvial islands – some no larger than a house – this 260-sq-km sanctuary's millions of magnificent mangroves protect the coast from erosion, serve as a vital breeding and feeding ground for fish, shrimp and shellfish, and provide a home to myriad birds (see www.ramsar.org).

The best way to visit the sanctuary is on a boat tour out of Koh Kong. Alternatively, ride a bicycle or *moto* (return US$5) out to the park entrance, 5.5km southeast of the city centre, where a 600m-long concrete **mangrove walk** wends its way above the briny waters to a 15m observation tower.

👣 Tours

Boat tours are an excellent way to view Koh Kong's many coastal attractions. English-speaking Teur hangs around the boat dock and can help you hire six-passenger (40hp) and three-passenger (15hp) outboards (speedboats). The big draws are Koh Kong Island (big/small boats from US$80/50)

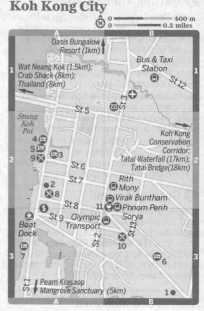

Koh Kong City

and Peam Krasaop Mangrove Sanctuary (US$40/30).

Recommended operators for boat and other tours:

Koh Kong Eco Adventure Tours TOURS

(📞012 707719; www.kohkongecoadventure.com; St 1) Ritthy's excursions include excellent Koh Kong Island boat tours, birdwatching and jungle treks in the Cardamoms.

Blue Moon Guesthouse TOURS
(☑012 946079; bluemoonkohkong@yahoo.com)
Mr Neat offers boat trips and rainforest
overnights in a hammock.

🛏 Sleeping

Koh Kong is becoming a popular holiday
destination for Khmers, so hotels fill up –
and raise their rates – during Cambodian
holidays. The Tatai River, 18km east of town,
has some appealing eco-accommodation options. Also check out the latest accommodation on nearby Koh Kong Island.

★ Koh Kong City Hotel HOTEL $
(☑035-936777; www.kkcthotel.netkhmer.com; St 1;
r US$15-20; ❉@🛜) Ludicrous value for what
you get, rooms include a huge bathroom,
two double beds, 50 TV channels, a full complement of toiletries, free water and – in the
US$20 rooms – glorious river views.

Asian Hotel HOTEL $
(☑035-936667; www.asiankohkong.com; St 1; r
US$15-20; ❉@) A virtual clone of the newer
City Hotel across the street, only with views
of City Hotel instead of the river.

**Paddy's Bamboo
Guesthouse** GUESTHOUSE $
(☑015 533223; ppkohkong@gmail.com; r US$4-8;
🛜) Paddy's targets backpackers with basic
rooms, a balcony for chillin', tours and a pool
table. Shoot for the wood-floored rooms upstairs with shared bathrooms.

PS Guesthouse GUESTHOUSE $
(☑097 729 1600; St 1; r with fan/air-con US$7/12;
❉🛜) A single-storey hotel backing on to
the riverfront, the 18 rooms here are well-
furnished with large beds, flat-screen TVs
and tastefully decorated bathrooms. PS: We
recommend it.

★ Oasis Bungalow Resort RESORT $$
(☑092 228342; http://oasisresort.netkhmer.
com; d/tr US$25/30; ❉🏊) In a quiet rural
area 2km north of the centre, this oa-
sis of calm has a gorgeous infinity pool
with views of the Cardamoms, and five
cheerful, spacious bungalows with all the
amenities. Blue signs point the way from
Acleda Bank.

Koh Kong Bay Hotel BOUTIQUE HOTEL $$
(☑035-936367; www.kohkongbay.com; St 1; r
US$35-90; 🏊) Finally, a relatively upscale
option in the centre. The decor is attractive
and bathrooms include a rain shower. The
pool offers river views and there's a small

spa on site, although the ambience can be
marred by karaoke next door and malodor-
ous scents wafting in from the port area.
Still, terrific value.

🍴 Eating & Drinking

The best cheap food stalls are in the southeast corner of Psar Leu, the main market.
Riverfront food carts sell noodles and cans
of beer for 2000r to 3000r.

Bob's Ice CAFE $
(St 1; mains US$2-5; ⊙7am-10pm; 🛜) Popular
Bob's has a lively location near the riverfront. Don't be fooled by the name, though:
the ice cream is great, but most people here
are drinking chilled beers.

Crab Shack SEAFOOD $
(Koh Yor Beach; mains US$4-8; ⊙11am-9pm) A
family run place over the bridge on Koh
Yor, it's known for perfect sunsets and
heaping portions of fried crab with pepper
(on request).

Japanese Food Maruo JAPANESE $
(mains US$2-7; ⊙11am-10pm) Sushi samples
are just US$1 to US$3 here and set menus
start from just US$5.50. As well as cheap lo-
cal beers, imported sake is available for an
authentic experience.

★ Café Laurent INTERNATIONAL $$
(www.cafelaurent.asia; St 1; mains US$4-15;
⊙11am-10pm; 🛜) This chic, French-style cafe
and restaurant offers refined Khmer cuisine
and Western dishes like lamb stew.

Fat Sam's BAR
(St 3; ⊙7am-11pm) An informal, Welsh-run
bar-restaurant with a decent selection of
beers, fish and chips, pasta, chilli con carne
and more.

ℹ Information

Guesthouses, hotels and pubs are the best
places to get the local low-down.

Thai baht are widely used so there's no urgent
need to change baht into dollars or riel. To do so,
use one of the many mobile-phone shops around
Psar Leu.

Canadia Bank (St 1; ⊙8am-3.30pm Mon-Fri,
to 11.30am Sat) The ATM here accepts most
international plastic and there's no local charge
for withdrawals.

Sen Sok Clinic (☑012 555060; kkpao@camin-
tel.com; St 3, cnr St 5; ⊙24hr) Has doctors
who speak English and French.

CHI PHAT

Once notorious for its loggers and poachers, Chi Phat (សហគមន៍ទេសចរណ៍ជីផាត) is now home to a pioneering **community-based ecotourism project** (CBET; www.chi-phat.org) offering hardy travellers a unique opportunity to explore the Cardamoms ecosystem while contributing to its protection. Visitors can take day treks through the jungle, go sunrise birdwatching by boat, mountain bike to several sets of rapids, and look for monkeys and hornbills with a former poacher as a guide. Also possible are one- to four-night mountain-bike safaris and jungle treks deep into the Cardamoms. In the village, visitors can relax by playing volleyball, badminton or pool with the locals.

Basic accommodation options in Chi Phat include 13 CBET-member guesthouses (doubles US$5) and 10 homestays (singles/doubles US$3/4). Reserve through the **CBET office** (☑035-675 6444; info@chi-phat.org) in Chi Phat.

Chi Phat is on the Preak Piphot River 17km upriver from Andoung Tuek, which is 98km east of Koh Kong on NH48. Any Koh Kong–bound bus can drop you in Andoung Tuek. From Andoung Tuek to Chi Phat it's a two-hour boat journey (about US$30 for the whole boat) or 45-minute motorbike ride (US$7) on an unpaved but smooth road. Call the CBET office to arrange a boat or *moto* in advance.

❶ Getting There & Away

Most buses drop passengers at Koh Kong's unpaved bus station, on the northeast edge of town, where *motos* and *remorques* await, eager to overcharge tourists. Don't pay more than US$1/2 for the three-minute *moto/remorque* ride into the centre.

Rith Mony (☑012 640344; St 3), **Phnom Penh Sorya** (☑077 563447; St 3), **Olympic Transport** (☑011 363678; St 3) and **Virak Buntham** (☑089 998760; St 3) each run two or three buses to Phnom Penh (US$7, six hours, last departure at 11.30am) and one or two trips to Sihanoukville (US$7, five hours). Most Sihanoukville trips involve a transfer, but Rith Mony and Virak Buntham have direct buses around 8am.

Morning trips to Kampot (US$12, five hours) and Kep (US$14, six hours) with Rith Mony and Virak Buntham involve a vehicle change or two. The same two companies offer midday trips to Bangkok with a bus change at the border (US$20, eight hours). There are also trips to Koh Chang (US$14 including ferry) with a change of bus at the border, plus a local ferry to the island.

From the taxi lot next to the bus station, share taxis head to Phnom Penh (US$11, five hours) and occasionally to Sihanoukville (US$10, four hours).

❶ Getting Around

Paddy's Bamboo Guesthouse and Koh Kong Eco Adventure Tours rent out bicycles for US$1 to US$2 per day. Motorbike hire is available from Fat Sam's and from Koh Kong Eco Adventure Tours for US$5.

Koh Kong Conservation Corridor របៀបអភិរក្សខេត្តកោះកុង

Stretching along both sides of NH48 from Koh Kong to the Gulf of Kompong Som, the Koh Kong Conservation Corridor encompasses many of Cambodia's most outstanding natural sites, including the most extensive mangrove forests on mainland Southeast Asia and the southern reaches of the fabled **Cardamom Mountains**, an area of breathtaking beauty and astonishing biodiversity.

The next few years will be critical in determining the future of the Cardamom Mountains. NGOs such as **Conservation International** (CI; www.conservation.org), **Fauna & Flora International** (FFI; www.fauna-flora.org) and **Wildlife Alliance** (www.wildlifealliance.org) are working to help protect the region's 16 distinct ecosystems from loggers and poachers. Ecotourism is playing a huge role in their plans – Wildlife Alliance is promoting several enticing projects in the **Southern Cardamoms Protected Forest** (1443 sq km).

Tatai River & Waterfall ស្ទឹងទឹកធ្លាក់តាតៃ

About 18km east of Koh Kong on NH48, the Phun Daung (Tatai) Bridge spans the Tatai River. Nestled in a lushly forested gorge upstream from the bridge is the Tatai Waterfall, a thundering set of rapids in the wet season, plunging over a 4m rock shelf. Water levels drop in the dry season but you can swim year-round in refreshing pools around the waterfall.

A short kayak away from the waterfall is the supremely tranquil **Rainbow Lodge** (☑ 097 948 5074; www.rainbowlodgecambodia. com; s/d incl all meals from US$50/75). About 6km downriver from the bridge is a more upscale rainforest retreat, the **Four Rivers Floating Ecolodge** (☑ 035-690 0650; www. ecolodges.asia; s/d incl breakfast US$203/239; ☎). Access to both resorts is by boat; call ahead for a free pick-up from the bridge.

The newest accommodation option in the area is **Tatai River Bungalows** (☑ 088 777 0576; www.neptuneadventure-cambodia.com; bungalows US$25-35), where the wood and thatch cottages are equipped with solar power. Activities on offer include kayaking, tubing and trekking.

You can access Tatai Waterfall by car or motorbike. The clearly marked turn-off is about 15km southeast of Koh Kong, or 2.8km northwest of the Tatai Bridge. From Koh Kong, a half-day *moto/remorque* excursion to Tatai Waterfall costs US$10/15 return, or less to go one-way to the bridge. If travelling from Phnom Penh to one of the resorts, tell the driver to let you off at the bridge.

Sihanoukville ក្រុងព្រះសីហនុ

☑ 034 / POP 155,000

Surrounded by white-sand beaches and relatively undeveloped tropical islands, Sihanoukville (aka Kompong Som) is Cambodia's premier seaside resort. While backpackers flock to the party zone of Serendipity Beach, the gorgeous Otres Beach, south of town, has made an incredible comeback and is now equally popular for a more relaxed stay. Meanwhile, the southern islands off Sihanoukville continue to blossom as cradles of castaway cool.

Sihanoukville

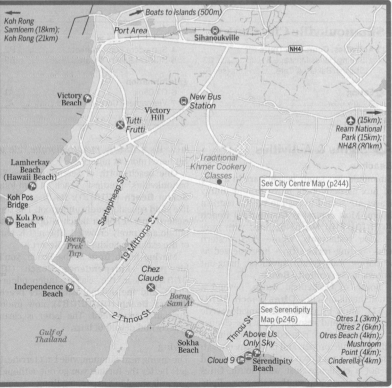

Sihanoukville City Centre

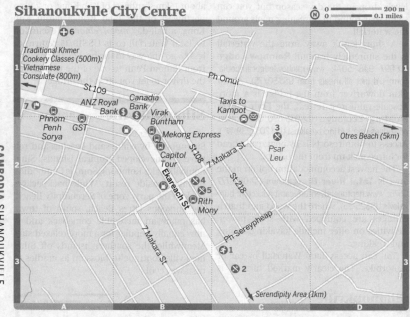

Sihanoukville City Centre

👁️ Sights & Activities

Beaches

Sihanoukville's sandy beaches are in a state of flux as developers move in and murky leases are signed to cash in on the tourism boom. Most central is **Occheuteal Beach** (ឆ្នេរអូរឈើទាល; Map p246), lined with ramshackle restaurants, whose northwestern end – a tiny, rocky strip – has emerged as a happy, easy-going travellers' hang-out known as **Serendipity Beach**.

South of Occheuteal Beach, beyond a small headland, lies **Otres Beach** (ឆ្នេរអូរ ត្រែះ), lined by dozens of bungalow-style restaurants and resorts. Otres has cleaner water and is more relaxed than anything in Sihanoukville proper, and is lengthy enough that finding your own patch of private sand is not a challenge...just walk south. Otres Beach is about 5km south of the Serendipity area. It's a US$2/5 *moto/remorque* ride to get here (more at night).

One beach north of Serendipity lies Sihanoukville's prettiest beach, 1.5km-long **Sokha Beach** (ឆ្នេរសុខា). Its fine, silicon-like sand squeaks loudly underfoot. The tiny eastern end of Sokha Beach is open to the public and rarely crowded. The rest is part of the exclusive Sokha Beach Resort.

Moving north from Sokha Beach, you'll hit pretty **Independence Beach** (ឆ្នេរ ឯករាជ្យ) near the classic Independence Hotel, and the original backpacker beach, **Victory Beach** (ឆ្នេរជយជំនះ), now under Russian management. The latter is clean, orderly and devoid of buzz.

Diving

The diving near Sihanoukville isn't terrific. It gets better the further you go out, although you still shouldn't expect anything on a par with the western Gulf of Thailand or the Andaman Sea. Most serious trips will hit **Koh Rong Samloem**, while overnight trips target the distant islands of **Koh Tang** and **Koh Prins**. Overnight trips cost about US$100 per day including two daily dives, food, accommodation on an island and equipment. Two-tank dives out of Sihanoukville average US$80 including equipment. PADI open-water courses average about US$400 to US$450 – pretty competitive by world standards.

Dive Shop

DIVING

(Map p246; ☑ 034-933664; www.diveshopcambodia.com; Road to Serendipity) PADI five-star dive centre offering National Geographic Diver certification. It has a dive shop on Koh Rong and works closely with Paradise Bungalows.

EcoSea Dive

DIVING

(Map p246; ☑ 034-934631; www.ecoseadive.com; Road to Serendipity) Offers PADI and SSI courses.

Marine Conservation Cambodia

DIVING

(MCC; www.marineconservationcambodia.org) Working to protect the area's reefs and coastal breeding grounds and occasionally has volunteer positions available.

Scuba Nation

DIVING

(Map p246; ☑ 012 604680; www.divecambodia.com; Serendipity St) Longest-running operator in town. Scuba Nation has a comfortable boat for liveaboard trips.

Massage

NGO-trained blind and disabled masseurs deftly ease away the tension at **Seeing Hands Massage 3** (Map p244; 95 Ekareach St; per hr US$6; ☺8am-9pm) 🌿 and **Starfish Bakery & Café** (Map p244; 62 7 Makara St; per hr US$6-10; ☺7am-6pm).

🎓 Courses

Traditional Khmer Cookery Classes

COOKING

(Map p243; ☑ 092 738615; www.cambodiacookeryclasses.com; 335 Ekareach St; per person US$23; ☺10am-2pm Mon-Sat) Teaches traditional culinary techniques in classes with no more than eight participants. Reserve a day ahead.

👉 Tours

Popular day tours go to some of the closer islands and to Ream National Park. Booze cruises are popular.

Eco-Trek Tours

TOUR

(Map p246; ☑ 012 987073; ecotrektourscambodia@yahoo.com; Road to Serendipity; ☺8am-10pm) Associated with the knowledgeable folks at Mick & Craig's guesthouse, this travel agency has information on just about anything. Mountain bikes (US$4 per day) available.

Liberty Ranch

HORSE RIDING

(☑ 016 339774; www.libertyranch-sihanoukville.com; Otres Village; ☺7-11am & 3-6pm) Explore Otres Beach or the surrounding countryside on horseback from US$25 per hour or just US$6 to try a pony.

Party Boat

BOAT TOUR

(Map p246; www.thepartyboat.asia; Serendipity Beach Pier; per person US$25) The Party Boat heads out daily to Koh Rong Samloem, departing at 9.30am and the trip includes snacks, lunch, snorkelling and a free drink. Time it for the full moon party at Saracen Bay on Koh Rong Samloem.

Ravuth Travel

BOAT TOUR

(☑ 012 439292; www.ravuthtravel.blogspot.com; Otres Beach) Located at Otres Beach Resort, Ravuth is one of several operations running daily trips to Koh Ta Kiev/Koh Russei (US$12/15 per person).

GETTING TO THAILAND: KOH KONG TO TRAT

Getting to the border Leaving Cambodia, take a taxi (US$10 plus toll) or *moto* (US$3 plus toll) from Koh Kong across the toll bridge to the border at Cham Yeam/Hat Lek.

At the border Departing Cambodia via the Hat Lek border is actually pretty straightforward, as there are no visa scams for immigration to benefit from. Coming in the other direction and arriving in Cambodia via Hat Lek is a bit of a nightmare, as visa overcharging is common – up to 1000B or more than US$30.

Moving on Once in Thailand, catch a minibus to Trat, from where there are regular buses to Bangkok (from 225B, five to six hours). Arrange onward transport to Ko Chang in Trat.

For more information about crossing this border in the other direction, see p397.

🛏 Sleeping

Most people shoot for the Serendipity area if they want to party, Otres Beach if they want to chill and the islands if they want to get away from it all.

🛏 Serendipity Area

The Road to Serendipity is the main backpacker hang-out, while down the hill tiny Serendipity Beach offers a string of mellow midrange resorts perched over the rocky shoreline. The resort names – Cloud 9, Tranquility, Above Us Only Sky, Aquarium – suggest some supremely mellow vibes. Grab that hookah and pen some verse. Unfortunately, the buzz is partly killed by late-night noise from the nearby clubs. The din isn't too bad, especially the further east you go, but light sleepers may want to bunk elsewhere.

★ Monkey Republic

HOSTEL **$**

(Map p246; ☑ 012 490290; www.monkeyrepublic.info; Road to Serendipity; r US$10-12; @ 🛜) Self-proclaimed 'backpacker central', established in 2005, Monkey Republic quickly rose from the ashes in 2013 following a dramatic fire (no casualities). Smart dorms and an immensely popular bar-restaurant with a happy hour from 6pm to 9pm.

Big Easy

HOSTEL **$**

(Map p246; ☑ 081 943930; www.thebigeasy.asia; Road to Serendipity; dm US$3, r US$6-10; 🛜) The Big Easy is a classic backpacker pad with accommodation, comfort food and a lively bar all rolled into one.

New Sea View Villa

HOTEL **$**

(Map p246; ☑ 092 759753; www.sihanoukville-hotel.com; Serendipity St; r US$10-35; ❄ 🛜) Known more for its food, New Sea View also has popular rooms in a central (almost beachfront) location in the heart of Serendipity.

Utopia

HOSTEL **$**

(Map p246; ☑ 034-934319; www.utopia-cambodia.com; Road to Serendipity; dm US$1-2.50, r US$6-7; @ 🛜 ❄) Dorm beds don't come any cheaper than at this backpacker mecca, including 'luxury' air-con options. The bar is party central.

★ Ropanha Boutique Hotel

BOUTIQUE HOTEL **$$**

(Map p246; ☑ 012 556654; www.ropanha-boutique-hotel.com; 23 Tola St; r US$45-65; ❄ 🛜 ❄) Set around a lush courtyard garden and pool,

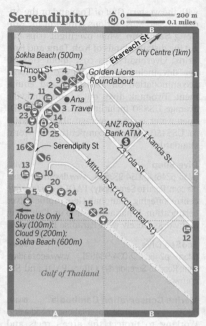

the rooms include flat-screen TVs and accompanying DVD players, plus rain showers in the bathroom. It's exceptional value, although prices may rise a little as the word spreads.

Serendipity Beach Resort

HOTEL **$$**

(Map p246; ☑ 034-938888; www.serendipitybeachresort.com; Serendipity St; r US$35-100; ❄ @ 🛜 ❄) Ignore the ugly duckling exterior, for inside a Serendipity swan awaits. Prices here remain steadfastly cheap given the impressive size and style of the rooms. There is a huge pool, often partially in the shade of the building, and a lift.

Above Us Only Sky

RESORT **$$**

(Map p243; ☑ 089 822318; www.aboveusonlysky-cambodia.com; Serendipity Beach; r incl breakfast with fan/air-con from US$50/55; ❄ 🛜) The bungalows are attractively minimalist inside, but chances are you'll be hangin' on the cosy balcony, where satellite chairs stare seaward. The bar perched over the rocks by the seashore is a gem.

Cloud 9

RESORT **$$**

(Map p243; ☑ 098 215166; www.cloud9bungalows.com; Serendipity Beach; r US$25-100; 🛜) The last place on Serendipity Beach is a fine choice, and not just because it's fur-

Serendipity

thest removed from the club noise. It has a cosy tropical bar and a range of rustic, Khmer-style bungalows with fans and ocean-view balconies.

Reef Resort HOTEL $$
(Map p246; ☑ 034-934281; www.reefresort. kh; Road to Serendipity; d incl breakfast US$40-85; ❋ ⊗ ☎ ⊛) The first somewhat upscale resort to open here, it's a smart choice if you can't live without your mod cons. The generously proportioned rooms afford views of a 12.5m pool, surrounded by a patio and lots of luscious orchids.

Blue Sea Boutique Hotel HOTEL $$
(Map p246; ☑ 034-933999; www.bluesea-boutique. com; Road to Serendipity; r incl breakfast US$50-115; ❋ ⊗ ☎ ⊛) One of the smarter hotels in the Serendipity area, it is tucked away behind a shopping arcade at the top of the hill. Rooms are set in bungalows around a mid-size swimming pool and include more than the average decorative flourish.

🛏 Otres Beach

Most guesthouses are in a cluster about 1km south of Queen Hill Resort, an area known as Otres 1. About 2.5km of empty beach separates this cluster from a smaller, more isolated colony of resorts at the far southern end of the beach, known as Otres 2.

Mushroom Point HOSTEL $
(☑ 078 509079; mushroompoint.otres@gmail. com; Otres 1; dm US$7-10, r US$20-30; ☎) The open-air dorm over the restaurant, with

mosquito-net-draped pods good for two, is a creative masterpiece. The mushie-shaped private bungalows and food get high marks too. There is also now a small annex on the beach.

Otres Orchid GUESTHOUSE $
(☑ 034 633 8484; otres.orchid@yahoo.com; Otres 1; r US$15-20) Cracking value for this popular Otres strip, the Orchid offers a mix of 20 rooms and bungalows at sensible prices.

Wish You Were Here HOSTEL $
(☑ 097 241 5884; http://wishotres.com; Otres 1; r US$10-12, bungalows US$15) The rooms are pretty standard Otres fare, but the bar-restaurant is one of the hippest hang-outs in the Otres area. Lounge around listening to top tunes or order one of the popular wish burgers or barra burgers.

Hacienda HOSTEL $
(☑ 070 814643; haciendaotres@outlook.com; Otres Village; dm US$3, r US$8-15) A great place to escape from it all, Hacienda has bargain dorms (some free after the first night) and a mellow restaurant-bar.

Cinderella RESORT $
(☑ 092 612035; www.cinderella-cambodia.com; Otres 2; bungalows US$15-25; ☎) Way down in the southernmost resort colony, this is your spot if you just want some alone time. The beach is a bit dishevelled here and the A-frame cottages basic, but you can't argue with the beachfront setting.

★ Tamu
BOUTIQUE HOTEL **$$$**

(☏ 088 901 7451; www.tamucambodia.com; Otres 2; r incl breakfast US$110-170; 🌬🕙🔲) A significant statement of confidence in the Otres Beach area, Tamu is an ultra-contemporary boutique hotel offering a range of simple yet stylish rooms set around a courtyard pool, plus a hip beachside restaurant open to all-comers.

🍴 Eating

Sihanoukville's centre of culinary gravity is in the Serendipity area, but the gritty commercial centre also holds a few pleasant surprises.

🍴 Serendipity Area

For romance, nothing beats dining on the water, either at one of the resorts at Serendipity Beach or – more cheaply – in one of the shacks along adjacent Occheuteal Beach. Of the resorts, the best food is found at New Sea View Villa (good for candlelight dinners) and Reef Resort.

Cafe Mango
ITALIAN **$**

(Map p246; Serendipity St; mains US$3-6; ⊙7am-10pm; 🕙) A cracking little Italian cafe turning out wood-fired pizzas, homemade pasta and delicate gnocchi, plus generous US$5 set meals before 6.30pm.

Beachys
BARBECUE **$**

(Map p246; Occheuteal Beach; mains US$2.50-5; ⊙7am-10pm; 🕙) The generous seafood grill at this barbecue shack is fantastic value at US$4. If you aren't up for surf, order turf, a heaped platter of various grilled meats.

★ Sandan
CAMBODIAN **$$**

(Map p246; 2 Thnou St; mains US$4-10; ⊙7am-9pm Mon-Sat; 🕙) 🍴 This superb eatery is loosely modelled on the beloved Phnom Penh restaurant Romdeng. It's an extension of the vocational-training programs for at-risk Cambodians run by local NGO M'lop Tapang. The menu features creative Cambodian cuisine.

Olive & Olive
MEDITERRANEAN **$$**

(Map p246; ☏ 086 283151; Road to Serendipity; mains US$5-15) This new Mediterranean restaurant has been turning heads in Sihanoukville thanks to wood-fired pizzas, homemade pasta, a fine selection of barbecued meats and seafood, and ever-evolving specials.

Mick & Craig's
INTERNATIONAL **$$**

(Map p246; www.mickandcraigs.com; Road to Serendipity; mains US$4-7; ⊙7am-10pm; 🕙) This long-running guesthouse and restaurant is a great place for classic comfort food from around the globe. Two-course Indian meals are just US$6. Thursday and Friday barbecue nights include a rack of ribs.

🍴 Around the City

For Sihanoukville's cheapest dining, head to the food stalls in and around **Psar Leu** (Map p244; 7 Makara St; ⊙7am-9pm) – the vendors across the street, next to the Kampot taxis, are open 24 hours. Options include barbecue chicken, rice porridge or noodles with chicken.

★ Holy Cow
ORGANIC **$**

(Map p244; 83 Ekareach St; mains US$2.50-5; ⊙8.30am-11pm; 🕙🍴) Options at this chic and funky cafe-restaurant include pasta, sandwiches on homemade bread and two vegan desserts, both involving chocolate.

Starfish Bakery & Café
ORGANIC **$**

(Map p244; www.starfishcambodia.org; behind 62 7 Makara St; sandwiches US$2.50-4.50; ⊙7am-6pm; 🕙🍴) 🍴 This relaxing, NGO-run garden cafe specialises in filling Western breakfasts and healthy, innovative sandwiches heavy on Mexican and Middle Eastern flavours. Sells silks and other gifts in a shop upstairs. Income goes to sustainable development projects.

Tutti Frutti
FRENCH **$**

(Map p243; Victory Hill; mains US$3-6; 🕙) On Victory Hill's main drag, this is a seriously good deal, with tasty Khmer mains to supplement rich French offerings, like beef burgundy and *steak haché oeuf au cheval* (egg on beefsteak).

Papa Pippo
ITALIAN **$**

(www.papapippo.com; Otres 1; mains US$3-6.50; ⊙7am-10pm; 🕙) Papa Pippo brings a bit of Italian flair to Otres Beach. The homemade pastas are some of the best on the coast and there are plenty of Tuscan classics on the menu. It's also a popular drinking spot with a quiz night every Tuesday.

Samudera Supermarket
SUPERMARKET **$**

(Map p244; 64 7 Makara St; ⊙6am-10pm) Has a good selection of fruit, vegies and Western favourites, including cheese and wine.

★ **Chez Claude** FRENCH $$

(Map p243; www.claudecambodge.com; above 2 Thnou St; mains US$5-15; 🐱) Dou Dou and Claude are your hosts at this all-wood eyrie – perched high above Sokha Beach – with outstanding French, Vietnamese and Cambodian cuisine, especially seafood. Access is via an innovative tractor-pulled cable car that would make MacGyver proud.

★ **Chez Paou** FRENCH $$

(Otres 1; mains US$4-13; ⊙7am-10pm; 🐱) This is fine dining, Otres-style, where chef specials include stingray cooked on embers with fresh Kampot pepper, prawns flambéed in pastis, and crabs two different ways.

🍷 Drinking & Nightlife

The party tends to start up on the Road to Serendipity before heading downhill (literally and figuratively) to the all-night beach discos along Occheuteal Beach. A few long-standing regular bars remain amid the hostess bars of Victory Hill, but the overall impression is Sinville rather than the more relaxed beach vibe of Sihanoukville.

Some of the aformentioned guesthouses have lively bars, including Monkey Republic (happy hour 6pm to 9pm), the Big Easy (sport and live music) and hedonistic Utopia, with regular US$0.25 beer promotions: yes, that does equal 20 beers for US$5.

Led Zephyr BAR

(Map p246; Road to Serendipity; ⊙7am-midnight) Sihanoukville's premier live-music venue; the house band (and friends from time to time) is rockin' here most nights.

Sessions BAR

(Map p246; Occheuteal Beach; ⊙5pm-1am) An assorted music selection makes Sessions the top sundowner bar on Occheuteal Beach, with the drinking clientele usually lingering well into the evening.

Dolphin Shack BAR

(Map p246; Occheuteal Beach; ⊙5pm-late) Long-running beach shack with a host of specials designed to get you drunk fast, and bevies of beautiful backpackers pouring drinks and passing out flyers.

JJ's Playground BAR

(Map p246; Occheuteal Beach; ⊙5pm-late) Although it has moved down towards the south end of Occheuteal Beach, JJ's remains the go-to spot for those seeking pure late-night debauchery. Have an absinthe shot to get you in the spirit of things, including homegrown Abyss, brewed on nearby Koh Ta Kiev.

Elephant BAR

(Map p246; Serendipity St; ⊙5pm-late) Blink and you'll miss it, this quirky little bar is Cambodia's leading drum 'n' bass venue. It also doubles as a bit of a head shop, with regular homemade treats to put you in the mood for the music.

🛍 Shopping

Tapang HANDICRAFTS

(Map p246; www.mloptapang.org; Serendipity St; ⊙10am-8pm) 🖋 Run by a local NGO that works with at-risk children, this shop sells bags, scarves and good-quality T-shirts. Several other handicrafts shops are nearby.

Let Us Create ARTS & CRAFTS

(Map p246; www.letuscreate.org; Serendipity St; ⊙10am-6pm) Another NGO that works with underprivileged kids; you can buy small paintings and postcards here. The volunteer backpackers are happy to tell you more about the project.

ℹ Information

Internet cafes (4000r per hour) are sprinkled along the Road to Serendipity and, in the city centre, along Ekareach St near Sopheakmongkol St.

Theft is a problem, especially on Occheuteal Beach, so leave your valuables in your room. As in Phnom Penh, drive-by bag snatchings occasionally happen and are especially dangerous when you're riding a *moto*. Hold your shoulder bags tightly in front of you. At night, both men and women should avoid walking alone along dark, isolated beaches and roads.

Ana Travel (Map p246; 📱016 499915; www.anatravelandtours.com; Road to Serendipity; ⊙8am-10pm) Handles Cambodia visa extensions and arranges Vietnam visas the same day.

ANZ Royal Bank (Map p244; 215 Ekareach St; ⊙8am-3.30pm Mon-Fri, to 11.30am Sat) Has a 24-hour ATM. Also offers ATMs at Victory Hill and Serendipity Beach.

Canadia Bank (Map p244; 197 Ekareach St; ⊙8am-3.30pm Mon-Fri, to 11.30am Sat) No fees on ATM withdrawals.

CT Clinic (Map p244; 📱034-936666, 081 886666; 47 Boray Kamakor St; ⊙emergencies 24hr) The best medical clinic in town. Can administer rabies shots and antivenom in the event of a snake bite.

Post Office (Map p244; 19 7 Makara St; ⊙7am-5pm) Across the road from Psar Leu.

❶ Getting There & Away

Sihanoukville is 230km from Phnom Penh along National Highway 4 (NH4), one of Cambodia's most dangerous highways because of heavy truck traffic.

AIR

Cambodia Angkor Airlines (www.cambodia-angkorair.com) has direct daily flights to Sihanoukville from Siem Reap. The airport is 15km east of town, just off NH4. Figure on US$5/10 for a one-way *moto/remorque*.

BUS

All of the major bus companies have frequent connections with Phnom Penh (US$3.75 to US$6, four hours) from early morning until at least 2pm, after which trips are sporadic.

Kampot Tours & Travel runs minibuses to Kampot (US$6, 1½ hours), which continue to Kep (US$10, 2½ hours) and Ha Tien in Vietnam (US$16, five hours). Travel agents can arrange hotel pick-ups.

Virak Buntham and Rith Mony have morning buses to Bangkok (US$25, change buses on the Thai side) via Koh Kong (US$7, four hours). Virak Buntham also has night buses to Siem Reap (US$17, nine hours) at 7pm and 8pm.

Most bus departures originate at the company terminals on Ekareach St and stop at the **new bus station** (Map p243; Mittapheap Kampuchea Soviet St) on the way out of town.

Capitol Tour (Map p244; ☑034-934042; Ekareach St)

Giant Ibis (www.giantibis.com)

GST (Map p244; ☑034-633 9666; Ekareach St)

Kampot Tours & Travel (☑in Kampot 092 125556)

Mekong Express (Map p244; ☑034-934189; Ekareach St)

Phnom Penh Sorya (Map p244; ☑034-933888; Ekareach St)

Rith Mony (Map p244; ☑012 644585; Ekareach St)

Virak Buntham (Map p244; ☑016 754358; Ekareach St)

SHARED TAXI

Cramped share taxis (US$6 per person, US$45 per car) and local minibuses (15,000r) to Phnom Penh depart from the new bus station until about 8pm. Avoid the minibuses if you value things like comfort and your life.

Share taxis to Kampot (US$5, 1½ hours) leave mornings only from an open lot on 7 Makara St, across from Psar Leu. This lot and the new

bus station are good places to look for rides to Koh Kong or the Thai border. If nobody's sharing, expect to pay US$45 to US$60 to the Thai border.

❶ Getting Around

Arriving in Sihanoukville, most buses these days terminate at the new public bus terminal and do not continue to their central terminals. Prices to the Serendipity Beach area from the new bus station are fixed at a pricey US$2/6 for a *moto/remorque*. You can do better by walking out to the street.

A *moto/remorque* should cost about US$1/2 from the city centre to Serendipity.

Motorbikes can be rented from many guesthouses for US$5 to US$7 a day. For fundraising purposes, the police sometimes 'crack down' on foreign drivers. Common violations: no driver's licence, no helmet, and no wing mirrors and driving with the lights on during the day.

Bicycles can be hired from many guesthouses for about US$2 a day, or try Eco-Trek Tours at Mick & Craig's for mountain bikes.

Around Sihanoukville

Ream National Park   សួនឧទ្យានរាម

Just 15km east of Sihanoukville, this large park offers potential trekking in primary forest, invigorating boat trips through coastal mangroves and long stretches of unspoilt beach. This is an easy escape for those looking to flee the crowds of Sihanoukville.

Fascinating two- to three-hour **jungle walks** (per person US$6-10) are led by rangers, most of whom speak English; these are easy to arrange at the **park headquarters** (☑012 875096, 016 767686; ⊙7am-5pm). Hiking unaccompanied is not allowed. Ranger-led **boat trips** (1-5 people US$50) on the **Prek Toeuk Sap Estuary** and its mangrove channels are another option.

To get to some **deserted beaches** on your own, drive south from the park HQ and the airport for about 9km along a sealed road until you get to Ream Naval Base, then follow dirt roads to a series of long white beaches lined with casuarina trees.

The park HQ is opposite Sihanoukville's airport – turn right (south) off NH4 15km east of Sihanoukville. A return trip by *moto* should cost US$8 to US$14, depending on how long you stay.

Southern Islands

They may lack the cachet of Southern Thailand, but the two dozen or so islands that dot the Cambodian coast offer the chance to see what places like Koh Samui and Koh Pha-Ngan were like back in the early days of Southeast Asia overlanding.

This is paradise the way you dreamt it: endless crescents of powdered sugary-soft sand, hammocks swaying in the breeze, photogenic fishing villages on stilts, technicolour sunsets and the patter of raindrops on thatch as you slumber. It seems too good to last – bits of Koh Rong are already getting a tad rowdy. Enjoy it while you can.

❶ Getting There & Away

The logical jumping-off point for the most popular islands is Sihanoukville. Scheduled boat services link Sihanoukville with Koh Rong, Koh Rong Samloem and Koh Sdach. Other islands are reached by private boats, usually owned by the resort you're visiting.

Koh Ta Kiev & Koh Russei កោះតាកៀវ កោះបុស្សី

These two pint-sized islands appear on most island-hopping itineraries out of Sihanoukville, with day trips running from US$12 to US$15, depending on whether you launch from Otres Beach or Serendipity Beach. The islands have accommodation, although both are slated for development.

Koh Ta Kiev has a beautiful long, wide beach and sits just off Ream National Park – the two can easily be combined with overnight stays on the island or in the park.

On Koh Russei (Bamboo Island), plans for a five-star hotel are forcing most simpler resorts to shut down. Day tours out of Sihanoukville bring you here for snorkelling, but there's not much to see.

Koh Rong & Koh Rong Samloem កោះរុង និងកោះរុងសន្ទិម

These deceptively large neighbouring islands are the rapidly emerging pearls of the south coast. They boast isolated white-sand beaches and heavily forested interiors populated by an incredible variety of wildlife.

Plans to turn Koh Rong into a Cambodian version of Thailand's Koh Samui, complete with ring road and airport, have stalled, allowing DIY developers to move in with rustic resorts targeting backpackers.

Koh Rong Samloem is also slowly taking off. Several colonies of bungalows have sprung up on Saracen Bay on the east coast, and more isolated options exist around the island. Saracen Bay also hosts a full-moon party.

🛏 Sleeping & Eating

Most island resorts run their generators from about 6pm to 10.30pm. Most of the isolated resorts or slightly more upscale places have booking offices on the mainland and all are located along the road to Serendipity Beach.

Budget travellers who prefer not to book ahead should head to the biggest concentration of guesthouses at central Koh Tui beach on Koh Rong, where the public boats from Sihanoukville alight.

KOH RONG

Bunna's Place GUESTHOUSE $
(📱086 446515; Koh Tui; dm US$4-5, r US$10) A classic backpacker crashpad with a bustling beach bar and the cheapest dorms in Koh Tui, plus some cheap rooms for those who want a modicum of privacy.

Island Boys/Vagabonds HOSTEL $
(Koh Tui; dm US$6, r from US$10) Two different places under the same ownership offering a similar vibe. Island Boys has a popular bar; Vagabonds has more of a chilled cafe vibe.

Paradise Bungalows BUNGALOWS $$
(📱092 548883; www.paradise-bungalows.com; Koh Tui; bungalows US$35-100) This is the most upscale of the options on Koh Rong's main beach, with its restaurant set up on a hill under a soaring canopy. The 24 bungalows leave little to be desired, although the cheaper ones, curiously, don't face the ocean. The food is scrumptious.

Monkey Island RESORT $$
(📱081 830992; www.monkeyisland-kohrong. com; Koh Tui; bungalows with/without bathroom US$35/25) One of the first resorts to plant its flag on this stretch of Koh Rong, centrally located Monkey Island has a nice mix of stand-alone bungalows and a great bar and restaurant specialising in Thai food.

Treehouse Bungalows BUNGALOWS $$
(📱034-934744; www.treehouse-bungalows.com; Koh Tui; bungalows US$25-35; ❄) Service is indifferent but the bungalows are big and

comfortable and the secluded location around the headland northeast of Koh Rong's main beach is highly appealing. Delicious wood-fired pizza.

KOH RONG SAMLOEM

The Beach Resort　　　RESORT $$
(☑034-666 6106; www.thebeachresort.asia; Saracen Bay; dm US$5, r US$15-85) Koh Rong Samloem's funkiest place to stay, the Beach Resort offers breezy open-air dorms with mosquito nets, plus a great range of beachfront bungalows.

Lazy Beach　　　RESORT $$
(☑017 456536; www.lazybeachcambodia.com; bungalows US$50) Alone on the southwest coast of Koh Rong Samloem, this family-friendly resort features idyllic bungalows with sea-facing balconies and hammocks.

Saracen Bay Resort　　　RESORT $$
(☑016 997047; www.saracenbay-resort-cambodia.com; Saracen Bay; bungalows US$45) Saracen Bay offers solid bungalows with attractive trimmings and great verandah views of the sea. Definitely book ahead, as this place regularly fills up.

Freedom Island Bungalows　　　RESORT $$
(☑034-633 3830; freedom_cambodia@yahoo.com; Saracen Bay; r US$35) Secluded at the north end of Saracen Bay, Freedom has concrete bungalows and a natural freshwater pool. Its big, sturdy boat is the most comfortable way to the islands, especially in rough seas.

❶ Getting There & Away

Koh Rong Island Travel (☑034-934744; http://kohrong-islandtravel.com)I runs two daily boats to/from the port area in Sihanoukville (one-way US$10, 2½ hours); these continue on to Koh Rong Samloem if there's demand.

The new **SEA Cambodia Fastcat** (www.seacambodia.com) departs four times a day from the Serendipity Beach jetty, arriving at Koh Rong in less than one hour (one-way US$13).

Koh Sdach Archipelago　　　កោះស្ដេច

Between Sihanoukville and Koh Kong, just off the southwest tip of **Botum Sakor National Park**, is this modest archipelago of 12 small islands, most of them uninhabited. Access is via the park (private vehicle only) or on the daily slow boat from Sihanoukville to Koh Sdach (US$10, 4½ hours), which

departs around noon (or 8pm in the other direction).

Koh Sdach has the only village of any size and a couple of places to stay, including upscale, Belgian-owned **Belinda Beach Lovely Resort** (☑017 517517; www.belindabeach.com; r incl breakfast US$130; ❀❄). It has four well-appointed concrete bungalows and superb food, but lacks a trophy beach.

A short outboard ride from Koh Sdach is tiny **Koh Totang**, home to **Nomad's Land** (☑011 916171; www.nomadslandcambodia.com; bungalows US$40-135) ❀, a delightfully chilled-out island retreat on a lovely stretch of white beach. The resort is closed from June to October.

Koh Kong　　　កោះកុង

The west coast of Cambodia's largest island shelters seven pristine beaches fringed with coconut palms and lush vegetation, just as you'd expect in a true tropical paradise. At the sixth beach from the north, a narrow channel leads to a Gilligan's Island–style lagoon.

The island, about 25km south of Koh Kong, is not part of any national park and is thus susceptible to rampant development. It recently got its first resort, **Koh Kong Island Resort** (☑035-936371; www.kohkongisland.net; bungalows US$40-90), with a range of rustic all-wooden bungalows.

The best way to get here is on a tour from Koh Kong (full day per person including lunch and snorkelling equipment US$25, or overnight for US$55).

Kampot　　　កំពត
☑ 033 / POP 33,000

There is something about this little charmer that encourages visitors to linger. It might be the lovely riverside setting or the ageing French buildings, or it could be the great little guesthouses and burgeoning bar scene. Whatever the magic ingredient, this is the perfect base from which to explore the abundant natural attractions of Kampot Province. Kampot also produces some of the world's finest pepper (www.kampotpepper.biz).

◎ Sights & Activities

This is not a town where you come and do, but a place to come and feel. Sit on the riverbank and watch the sun set beneath the mountains, or stroll among the town's fine **French shophouses** (in the triangle delineated by 7 Makara St, the central roundabout and the post office).

Kampot Traditional Music School   SCHOOL
(⏰6-9pm Mon-Fri) Visitors are welcome to observe training sessions and/or performances every evening at this school that trains orphaned and disabled children in traditional music and dance.

Seeing Hands Massage 5   MASSAGE
(per hr US$5; ⏰7am-11pm) Blind masseurs and masseuses offer soothing bliss.

🕭 Tours

The big tour is **Bokor Hill Station**, which everybody and their grandmother offers. Excursions also hit the pepper farms and other sights in the countryside around Kampot and nearby Kep.

Some riverside places send boats out on evening **firefly watching** tours. Many a sceptic has returned from these trips in awe.

Bart the Boatman   BOAT TOUR
(☑092 174280) Known simply as Bart the Boatman, this Belgian expat runs original boat tours along the small tributaries of the Kampot River.

Captain Chim's   BOAT TOUR
(☑012 321043) Sunset cruises on a traditional boat cost US$5 per head and include a cold beer – a real bargain. Also offers half-day kayaking trips for US$9.

CAMBODIA KAMPOT

Kampot

◎ Sights

1 Kampot Traditional Music	
School	A3
2 Old Market	A3

🏃 Activities, Courses & Tours

Captain Chim's	(see 11)
3 Kampot Dreamtime Tours	A2
4 Seeing Hands Massage 5	A3

🛏 Sleeping

5 La Java Bleue	A3
6 Magic Sponge	B3
7 Pepper Guesthouse	B3
8 Rikitikitavi	A3
9 The Columns	A3
10 Titch's Place	A2

🍴 Eating

11 Captain Chim's	A2
12 Epic Arts Café	A3
13 Espresso	A2
14 Indo Bar	A3
15 Kampot Fruit Stalls & Little	
Eateries	A2
16 Mea Culpa	A4
17 Night Market	A2
18 Rusty Keyhole	A2

🛍 Shopping

| 19 Kepler's Kampot Books | A3 |
| 20 Tiny Kampot Pillows | A3 |

ℹ Information

| 21 Tourist Information Centre | A2 |

ℹ Transport

22 Giant Ibis	A2
Hua Lian	(see 24)
23 Kampot Express	B2
24 Phnom Penh Sorya	B3

Kampot Dreamtime Tours
BOAT TOUR

(☏089 908417) Runs upmarket countryside trips in air-con vans and wine-and-cheese sunset river cruises in a boat formerly owned by King Norodom Sihanouk.

🛏 Sleeping

You can stay in the centre of the old town or a little out of town in one of several places strung out along the riverbank.

🛏 Old Town

Magic Sponge
GUESTHOUSE $

(☏017 946428; www.magicspongekampot.com; dm US$3, r US$9-15; ☎) This popular backpacker place has a rooftop dorm with impressive through breezes and personalised fans and reading lights. There's well-regarded Indian food and even minigolf in the garden.

Pepper Guesthouse
GUESTHOUSE $

(☏017 822626; guesthousepepper@yahoo.com; r US$5-30; ❄☎) Set in the heart of the backpacker backstreets, Pepper has cheap fan rooms and impressive garden bungalows with rain showers and tasteful decoration.

Titch's Place
GUESTHOUSE $

(☏033-650 1631; titchs.place@yahoo.com; River Rd; dm/r US$3/10; ☎) The only budget crashpad on the riverfront. There are dorm beds aplenty, including single-sex dorms.

★The Columns
BOUTIQUE HOTEL $$

(☏092 932070; www.the-columns.com; 37 Phoum 1 Ouksophear; r incl breakfast US$45-59; ❄☎🅿) Set in a row of thoughtfully restored shophouses near the riverfront, this is the leading boutique hotel in Kampot, with 17 rooms. Blending the classic and the modern, rooms include flat-screen TV, iPod dock, minibar and a safety deposit box.

La Java Bleue
BOUTIQUE HOTEL $$

(☏033-667 6679; www.lajavableue-kampot.fr; Old Quarter; r incl breakfast US$45-60; ❄☎) This is a colonial gem in the centre of town with large, individually decorated rooms and a well-regarded restaurant, including a daily barbecue grill and tender meats.

Rikitikitavi
BOUTIQUE HOTEL $$

(☏012 235102; www.rikitikitavi-kampot.com; River Rd; r incl breakfast US$43-59; ❄☎) On the riverfront, Rikitikitavi has seven of the classiest and most comfortable rooms in town. Also a top restaurant known for its Kampot pepper chicken, slow-cooked curries and fusion salads.

🛏 On the River

★Bodhi Villa
HOSTEL $

(☏012 728884; www.bodhivilla.com; Tuk Chhou Rd; dm US$2.50-3, r US$5-12; ☎) Bodhi is a peaceful hideaway on the opposite bank of the river 2km north of town. There's a good waterfront chill-out bar and a variety of rooms, including one floating bungalow. Live music every Friday from 7.30pm.

Arcadia Backpackers
HOSTEL $

(☏077 219756; www.arcadiabackpackers.com; Tuk Chhou Rd; dm US$3-4, r US$9-10, bungalows US$15-30; ☎) In a secluded riverside setting northwest of town, there is a large bar-restaurant jutting out into the water, plentiful dorms, thatched private bungalows, a rope swing and tubing.

★Les Manguiers
RESORT $$

(☏092 330050; www.mangokampot.com; r US$10-60; @❄☎🅿) This rambling garden complex, on the river 2km north of the new bridge, is rich with activities for kids and adults, including kayaking (single/tandem US$4/6 for two hours), swimming, badminton, pétanque and firefly-watching boat trips (best on a new moon when the phosphorescence peaks).

🍴 Eating & Drinking

Quite a few restaurants line River Rd south of the old French bridge. There are **fruit stalls and little eateries** (⊙7am-10pm) next to Canadia Bank and, nearby, a **night market** (7 Makara St; ⊙4pm-midnight) with both mains and desserts.

Many of the guesthouses are worthy of a meal or two, most notably Rikitikitavi.

★Epic Arts Café
CAFE $

(www.epicarts.org.uk; mains US$2-4; ⊙7am-4pm; ☎) 🖉 A great place for breakfast, homemade cakes or tea, this mellow eatery is staffed by deaf and disabled young people. Profits fund arts workshops for disabled Cambodians.

Espresso
CAFE $

(near Old Market; mains US$3-6; ⊙7am-9pm) A blink-and-you'll-miss-it cafe – we advise you don't blink. The Aussie owners are real foodies and offer fresh specials and the best coffee in town.

Indo Bar
INTERNATIONAL, ASIAN $

(St 726; meals US$2-6; ⊙11am-11pm) A fun and friendly place just up from the river, Indo Bar offers eclectic regional cuisine and the strongest Long Island iced tea in Kampot.

Captain Chim's
CAFE **$**

(mains US$1-3; ⊘7am-10pm; 🛜) Best known for breakfast, but Khmer faves like *loc lak* (peppery stir-fried beef cubes) will fill you up at any time of day. Ask about Cambodian cooking classes or join its bargain booze cruise for sunset every day.

Rusty Keyhole
INTERNATIONAL, CAMBODIAN **$$**

(River Rd; small/large/extra-large ribs US$5/7.50/10; ⊘8am-11pm Nov-May, 11am-11pm Jun-Oct; 🛜) Popular riverfront bar-restaurant serving widely praised food. Order the famous ribs in advance or they may sell out.

Mea Culpa
ITALIAN **$$**

(✍012 504769; www.meaculpakampot.com; pizzas from US$6) The garden restaurant at this guesthouse spins the best pizza in town, straight from a wood-fired oven. Delivery available.

🛍 Shopping

Kepler's Kampot Books
BOOKSTORE

(Old Market; ⊘8am-8pm) This is the place for secondhand books in Kampot, plus pepper, *krama* (checked scarves) and fine T-shirts.

Tiny Kampot Pillows
HANDICRAFTS, CLOTHING

(www.tinykampotpillows.com; 2000 roundabout; ⊘10am-6pm) Textile shop selling pillows in handwoven silk plus plenty of other accessories, from clothing to bags.

ℹ Information

The free and often hilarious *Kampot Survival Guide* takes a tongue-in-cheek look at local expat life.

There's a strip of photocopy shops with internet access southwest of the Durian roundabout on 7 Makara St.

Canadia Bank (⊘8am-3.30pm Mon-Fri, to 11.30am Sat) Has an ATM with no transaction fees and turbo air-con.

Tourist Information Centre (✍033-655 5541; lonelyguide@gmail.com; River Rd; ⊘7am-7pm) The main point of contact for assembling groups for Bokor National Park trips. Also doles out free advice and can arrange transport to area attractions like caves, falls and Kompong Trach.

ℹ Getting There & Away

Rith Mony, Phnom Penh Sorya and Hua Lian sell tickets from offices opposite the Total petrol station near the Four Nagas Roundabout. All three have daily trips to Phnom Penh (US$4 to US$5, 2½ hours) until 1pm or so. Phnom Penh

Sorya and Hua Lian buses go via Kep so they take longer.

Across the street you can catch share taxis (US$6), packed-to-the-gills local minibuses (16,000r) and private taxis (US$40) to Phnom Penh. **Giant Ibis** (www.giantibis.com) and **Kampot Express** (www.kampotexpress.com) run express vans to Phnom Penh (US$8, two hours).

For Sihanoukville, ask your guesthouse to set you up with a minibus service, which can also get you to Koh Kong (usually with at least one bus/van transfer).

A *moto/remorque* to Kep should cost about US$8/12.

ℹ Getting Around

Bicycles are offered to guests for free by many guesthouses, which can also arrange motorbike hire. **Sean Ly** (✍012 944687; ⊘7am-9pm) hires out motorbikes for US$4 and 250cc trail bikes for US$12.

Around Kampot

The limestone hills east towards Kep are honeycombed with fantastic caves, some of which can be explored with the help of local kids and a reliable torch (flashlight).

Surrounded by blazingly beautiful countryside, the temple cave of **Phnom Chhnork** (ភ្នំឆ្នោក; admission US$1; ⊘7am-6pm) is known for its 7th-century (Funan-era) brick

---

ANGKOR BOREI & PHNOM DA

The sleepy town of Takeo, roughly halfway between Kampot and Phnom Penh on NH2, is the jumping-off point for one of Cambodia's great thrill rides: the 20km open-air motorboat ride along Canal No 15, dug in the 1880s, to the impoverished riverine hamlet of Angkor Borei (45 minutes). Angkor Borei is home to a small **archaeological museum** (✍012 201638; admission US$1; ⊘8am-4.30pm) featuring locally discovered Funan- and Chenla-era artefacts. The boat then continues for 15 minutes to **Phnom Da** (admission US$2), spectacularly isolated Mont-St-Michel style by annual floods, which is topped by a temple whose foundations date from the 6th century (the temple itself was rebuilt in the 11th century). Hiring a boat for the trip at Takeo's boat dock costs US$40 return for up to four people.

temple. To get there turn left off NH33 about 5.5km east of Kampot, then go 6km more on a bumpy road. For a return *moto/remorque* ride, count on paying about US$6/10.

Also interesting is **Phnom Sorsia** (ភ្នំសសៀរ, Phnom Sia; ⊙7am-6pm) FREE, 13km southeast of Kampot on the road to Kep, which has a gaudily painted modern temple and several natural caves populated by dense bat colonies.

Bokor National Park
ឧទ្យានជាតិបូរគោ

This 1581-sq-km **national park** (ឧទ្យានជាតិ បូរគោ, Preah Monivong National Park; admission US$5) has impressive wildlife, lush primary forests and a refreshingly cool climate, but is most famous for its once-abandoned French hill station, established atop Phnom Bokor (1080m) in the early 1920s.

Unfortunately it is now becoming more famous for the ugly casino that blights the summit, part of a massive development project that has sadly destroyed the atmosphere of bygone Bokor.

At the park entrance, 7km west of Kampot, an informative **ranger station** has displays about Bokor's fauna, which includes leopards, elephants, bears, gibbons, macaques, slow loris and pangolins. Don't expect to see much wildlife, however, as most of the animals survive by staying in more remote areas and, in addition, are nocturnal.

⊙ Sights & Activities

Until recently the main attraction here was the old French hill station and its grand, four-storey hotel, the **Bokor Palace**, opened in 1925. The hill station was abandoned to the howling winds in the 1970s when Khmer Rouge forces infiltrated the area. The once-grand buildings became eerie, windowless shells.

Bokor Palace was undergoing renovations when we visited and will become part of the new resort city. Other buildings of interest include the squat belfry of the Romanesque-style **Catholic church**, which still holds aloft its cross; and lichen-caked **Wat Sampeau Moi Roi**, which offers tremendous views over the jungle to the coastline below. Wild monkeys like to hang out around the wat. From the wat an 11km trail (four or five hours) leads to two-tiered **Popokvil Falls**.

ℹ Getting There & Around

To visit the park you can take private transport up the new road, or you can join an organised tour. Trekking trips used to be very popular, but treks were recently banned due to all the development underway, a rather surreal scenario, as we have not heard of banning trekking in national parks before. Standard day trips still operate for around US$10 to US$15 per person depending on numbers. Many travellers prefer to rent a motorbike and travel under their own steam.

Kep កែប
📋 036 / POP 10,300

The seaside resort of Kep-sur-Mer is a province-level municipality that consists of little more than a small peninsula facing Bokor National Park and Vietnam's Phu Quoc Island. Famed for its spectacular sunsets and splendid seafood, it was founded as a colonial retreat for the French elite in 1908.

Some find Kep a bit soulless because it lacks a centre and accommodation options are spread out all over the place. Others revel in its sleepy vibe, content to relax at their resort, nibble on crab at the famed Crab Market and poke around the mildewed shells of modernist villas, which still give the town a sort of post-apocalyptic feel.

⊙ Sights & Activities

Kep National Park PARK
(ឧទ្យានជាតិកែប; admission 4000r) The interior of Kep peninsula is occupied by Kep National Park, degraded in recent years by illegal logging but finally guarded by a complement of rangers. An 8km circuit around the park, navigable by foot or mountain bike, starts at the park entrance behind Veranda Natural Resort. Fuel up and grab a map of the park at the **Led Zep Cafe** (⊙9.30am-6pm), which is on the trail 300m into the walk. The map is also reprinted in the ubiquitous *Coastal* guide to Kep and Kampot.

Koh Tonsay (Rabbit Island) ISLAND
(កោះទន្សាយ) Offshore, rustic Koh Tonsay has a lovely beach with several family run clusters of rudimentary bungalows where you can overnight for US$8. Boats to the island (30 minutes) leave from a pier 2.7km east of the Kep Beach roundabout. Your guesthouse can arrange to get you on a boat for around US$7 one way or US$10 per person return. A private boat arranged at the pier costs US$30 one way for up to seven passengers.

Beaches
BEACH

Most of Kep's beaches are too shallow and rocky to make for good swimming. The best is centrally located **Kep Beach**, but it's still somewhat pebbly and tends to fill up with locals on weekends. The best place for sunset viewing is the long wooden pier in front of Knai Bang Chat's **Sailing Club**, where there's also a small but shallow beach.

🛏 Sleeping

Kep meanders along the shoreline for a good 5km, with the resorts situated at intervals along its length. Some of the best options are not on the water but on the other side of the highway in the hills leading up to Kep National Park.

★ Botanica Guesthouse
GUESTHOUSE $

(☑ 097 801 9071; www.kep-botanica.com; NH33A; r with fan US$15-19, with air-con US$23-29; ❄ 🛜 🏊) A little way from the action (if Kep can be said to have any action), Botanica offers exceptional value for money with attractive bungalows boasting contemporary bathrooms. Free bicycles.

Bacoma
GUESTHOUSE $

(☑ 088 411 2424; bacoma@live.com; r US$10-36; 🛜) Cheap and cheerful *rondavels* (round huts) are available in the lush garden and include high ceilings, mosquito nets and a fan, with a generous helping of shared bathrooms.

Tree Top Bungalows
GUESTHOUSE $

(☑ 012 515191; khmertreetop@hotmail.com; r US$5-45; @ 🛜) The highlights here are the towering, stilted, bamboo 'treehouse' bungalows with sea views; each pair shares a bathroom.

Kukuluku Beach Club
GUESTHOUSE $

(☑ 036-630 0150; www.kukuluku-beachclub.com; NH33A; dm US$5-7, r US$15-35; 🛜 🏊) The rooms are nothing special and the pool is tiny, but it's a great place to meet other travellers.

★ Kep Lodge
RESORT $$

(☑ 092 435330; www.keplodge.com; r incl breakfast US$28-70; ❄ 🛜 🏊) An uber-friendly place whose bungalows have thatch roofs, tile floors and verandahs. The grounds are lush, the common area relaxing, the food great and the sunset views outstanding. The turn-off is 600m north of Kep's northern roundabout.

★ Veranda Natural Resort
RESORT $$

(☑ 012 888619; www.veranda-resort.com; d/tr incl breakfast from US$60/68; ❄ 🛜 🏊) This rambling colony of hillside bungalows built of wood, bamboo and stone is up on the hill near the national park entrance. Check out a few rooms because they vary wildly. The food is excellent and sunset views from the restaurant pavilion are stunning. It's constantly expanding and constantly raising prices.

Jasmine Valley Eco-Resort
RESORT $$

(☑ 097 791 7635; www.jasminevalley.com; r incl breakfast US$24-64; 🛜 🏊) ✍ About 2.5km in from the Rabbit Island pier, Jasmine Valley Eco-Resort has funky bungalows raised dramatically amid dense jungle foliage. Green credits include solar power and a natural swimming pool complete with pond critters.

Vine Retreat
LODGE $$

(☑ 036-633 3383; www.thevineretreat.com; r incl breakfast US$25-50; @ 🛜 🏊) ✍ This socially responsible ecolodge is near Chamcar Bei village, 13km northeast of Kep. The eight comfortable rooms, with solar hot water and decent mattresses, look out on an organic farm and a naturally filtered swimming pond. Divine set meals average US$10. To get here from the White Horse Roundabout, head east for 3.5km to a well-marked turn-off on the left.

Knai Bang Chatt
RESORT $$$

(☑ 078 888556; www.knaibangchatt.com; r incl breakfast US$165-325; ❄ @ 🛜 🏊) This ultrachic boutique hotel, occupying a cluster of waterfront villas from the 1960s, has a waterfront infinity pool and its own sailing club. Very classy, although there isn't actually a beach here.

🍴 Eating & Drinking

Eating fresh crab fried with Kampot pepper at the **Crab Market** – a row of wooden waterfront shacks next to a wet fish market – is a quintessential Kep experience. There are lots of great places to choose from. **Kimly** (☑ info 036-904077; Crab Market; mains US$2.50-7; ⏱ 9am-10pm) has a good reputation, with crab prepared 27 different ways, or try the memorably named **Holy Crab**. The crab shacks also serve prawns, squid, fish and terrestrial offerings. You can also buy fresh crab at the crab market and have your guesthouse fry it up.

★ **Sailing Club** FUSION **$$**
(mains US$5-12; ⊘10am-10pm; 🛜) With a small beach, a breezy wooden bar and a wooden jetty poking out into the sea, this is one of Cambodia's top sundowner spots. The Asian fusion food is excellent and you can get your crab fix here too. Happy hour is two-for-one.

Breezes FUSION **$$**
(NH33A; mains US$5-10; ⊘9am-10pm; 🛜) Just 10m from the waterline, this Dutch-owned restaurant boasts sleek furnishings, excellent food and fine views of Koh Tonsay.

Toucan BAR
(Crab Market; snacks US$3-5; ⊘11am-10pm; 🛜) This is the best spot for a drink (or five) once the sun goes down. It has a pool table and usually a few punters propping up the bar until midnight or so (that's late-night for Kep).

ℹ Information

As in Kampot, the best source of information and maps is the *Coastal* guide to Kampot and Kep (www.coastal-cambodia.com). There are no banks or ATMs in Kep.
Anna Tours (✆036-652 3999; ⊘9am-6pm) Organises transport all over Cambodia and on to Vietnam.

Green House (✆089 440161; internet per hr US$1; ⊘9am-6pm) A travel agency with internet access.

ℹ Getting There & Away

Kep is 25km from Kampot and 41km from the Prek Chak–Xa Xia border crossing to Vietnam.
Phnom Penh Sorya and Hua Lian buses link the town with Kampot (US$2, 45 minutes) and Phnom Penh (US$4, four hours, last trips at 2pm). A private taxi to Phnom Penh (three hours) costs US$40 to US$45.
A *moto/remorque* to Kampot costs about US$8/12. Guesthouses can arrange minibus/bus combos to Sihanoukville and Koh Kong.

ℹ Getting Around

Hiring a *remorque* for a full day, including a trip to Kompong Trach and a pepper plantation, costs US$20.
Motorbike rental is US$5 to US$7 per day; ask your guesthouse or any travel agency.

Around Kep

Near the town of Kompong Trach, 28km north of Kep, you'll find **Wat Kiri Sela** (វត្តគិរីសិលា; ⊘7am-6pm), a Buddhist temple built at the foot of **Phnom Kompong Trach**, a dramatic karst formation riddled with over 100 caverns and passageways. From

---

GETTING TO VIETNAM: KEP TO HA TIEN

The Prek Chak/Xa Xia border crossing (open 6am to 5.30pm) has become a popular option for linking Kampot and Kep with Ha Tien and the popular Vietnamese island of Phu Quoc.

Getting to the border The easiest way to get to Prek Chak and on to Ha Tien, Vietnam, is on a bus or van from Sihanoukville (US$16, five hours), Kampot (US$10, two hours) or Kep (US$8, 1½ hours). Several companies ply the Sihanoukville–Kampot–Kep–Ha Tien route.

A more flexible alternative from Phnom Penh or Kampot is to take any bus to Kompong Trach, then a *moto* (about US$3) 15km to the border.

From Kep, tour agencies and guesthouses can arrange a direct *moto* (US$8, 40 minutes), *remorque* (US$13, one hour) or taxi (US$20, 30 minutes). Rates and times are almost double from Kampot.

At the border As always, you need a Vietnamese visa for travel to Phu Quoc, the Mekong Delta and on to Ho Chi Minh City. Pick up *motos* on the Vietnamese side of the border to Ha Tien (7km). You'll save money walking across no-man's land and picking up a *moto* on the other side for US$2 to US$3.

Moving bn Travellers bound for Phu Quoc should arrive in Ha Tien no later than 12.30pm to secure a ticket on the 1pm ferry (230,000d or about US$11, 1½ hours). Extreme early risers may be able to make it to Ha Tien in time to catch the (slower) 8.20am car ferry to Phu Quoc.

For more information about crossing this border in the other direction, see p150.

the wat, an underground passage leads to the centre of a fishbowl-like karst formation, surrounded by vine-draped cliffs and open to the sky. Various stalactite-laden caves shelter reclining Buddhas and miniature Buddhist shrines. There's major **rock-climbing** opportunities around here.

Friendly local kids with torches, eager to put their evening-school English to use, are eager (overeager?) to serve as guides; make sure you tip them if you use them.

❶ Getting There & Away

Kompong Trach makes an easy day trip from Kep or Kampot, or you can hop off the bus on the way to/from Phnom Penh. To get to Wat Kiri Sela, take the dirt road opposite the Acleda Bank for 2km.

UNDERSTAND CAMBODIA

Cambodia Today

Cambodia is at a crossroads in its road to recovery from the brutal years of Khmer Rouge rule. Compare Cambodia today with the dark abyss into which it plunged under the Khmer Rouge and the picture looks optimistic, but look to its more successful neighbours and it's easy to be pessimistic. Cambodia must choose its path: pluralism, progress and prosperity or intimidation, impunity and injustice. The jury is still very much out on which way things will go.

Prime Minister Hun Sen and his Cambodian People's Party (CPP) have dominated the politics of Cambodia since 1979 when the party was installed in power by the Vietnamese. However, in a result that shocked many observers, the 2013 national election saw the united opposition make significant gains in the national assembly.

Or did they win it outright? They claim they did, and have refused to take their seats in the assembly until a fair investigation of widespread election irregularities - some alleged, some proven - takes place. Seven months of sometimes-violent street protests continued to drag on as we went to print. Leading the protests are long-standing opposition leader Sam Rainsy and his one-time rival, Kem Sokha. The two leaders brought their parties together to form the Cambodia National Rescue Party (CNRP) before the 2013 elections.

Many Cambodians hope that both sides will reach a compromise and that in time this surprise result will put pressure on the CPP to introduce much-needed political and electoral reform. The next five years will be very interesting indeed.

History

The good, the bad and the ugly is a simple way to sum up Cambodian history. Things were good in the early years, culminating in the vast Khmer empire, unrivalled in the region during four centuries of dominance. Then the bad set in, from the 13th century, as ascendant neighbours steadily chipped away at Cambodian territory. In the 20th century it turned downright ugly, as a brutal civil war culminated in the genocidal rule of the Khmer Rouge (1975-79), from which Cambodia is still recovering.

Funan & Chenla

The Indianisation of Cambodia began in the 1st century AD as traders plying the sea route from the Bay of Bengal to southern China brought Indian ideas and technologies to what is now southern Vietnam. The largest of the era's nascent kingdoms, known to the Chinese as Funan, embraced the worship of the Hindu deities Shiva and Vishnu and, at the same time, Buddhism.

From the 6th to 8th centuries Cambodia seems to have been ruled by a collection of competing kingdoms. Chinese annals refer to 'Water Chenla', apparently the area around the modern-day town of Takeo, and 'Land Chenla', further north along the Mekong and around Sambor Prei Kuk.

Rise & Fall of Angkor

The Angkorian era lasted from AD 802 to 1432, encompassing periods of conquest, turmoil and retreat, revival and decline, and fits of remarkable productivity.

In 802, Jayavarman II (reigned c 802-50) proclaimed himself a *devaraja* (god-king). He instigated an uprising against Javanese domination of southern Cambodia and, through alliances and conquests, brought the country under his control, becoming the first monarch to rule most of what we now call Cambodia.

In the 9th century, Yasovarman I (r 889–910) moved the capital to Angkor, creating a new centre for worship, scholarship and the arts. After a period of turmoil and conflict, Suryavarman II (r 1113–52) unified the kingdom and embarked on another phase of territorial expansion, waging successful but costly wars against both Vietnam and Champa (an Indianised kingdom that occupied what is now southern and central Vietnam). His devotion to the Hindu deity Vishnu inspired him to commission Angkor Wat.

The tables soon turned. Champa struck back in 1177 with a naval expedition up the Mekong, taking Angkor by surprise and putting the king to death. But the following year a cousin of Suryavarman II – soon crowned Jayavarman VII (r 1181–1219) – rallied the Khmers and defeated the Chams in another epic naval battle. A devout follower of Mahayana Buddhism, it was he who built the city of Angkor Thom.

During the twilight years of the empire, religious conflict and internecine rivalries were rife. The Thais made repeated incursions into Angkor, sacking the city in 1351 and again in 1431, and from the royal court making off with thousands of intellectuals, artisans and dancers, whose profound impact on Thai culture can be seen to this day.

From 1600 until the arrival of the French, Cambodia was ruled by a series of weak kings whose intrigues often involved seeking the protection of either Thailand or Vietnam – granted, of course, at a price.

French Colonialism

The era of yo-yoing between Thai and Vietnamese masters came to a close in 1864, when French gunboats intimidated King Norodom I (r 1860–1904) into signing a treaty of protectorate. An exception in the annals of colonialism, the French presence really did protect the country at a time when it was in danger of being swallowed by its more powerful neighbours.

In 1907 the French pressured Thailand into returning the northwest provinces of Battambang, Siem Reap and Sisophon, bringing Angkor under Cambodian control for the first time in more than a century.

Led by King Norodom Sihanouk (r 1941–55 and 1993–2004), Cambodia declared independence on 9 November 1953.

THE KHMER ROUGE TRIAL

The Vietnamese ousted the Khmer Rouge on 7 January 1979, but it wasn't until 1999 – after two decades of civil war – that serious discussions began about a trial to bring those responsible for the deaths of about two million Cambodians to justice. After lengthy negotiations, agreement was finally reached on establishing a war crimes tribunal to try the surviving leaders of the Khmer Rouge.

It took another decade for the first verdict in the Extraordinary Chambers in the Courts of Cambodia (ECCC) trial. In that time one of the key suspects, the one-legged general Ta Mok ('the Butcher'), died in custody. Case 001, the trial of Kaing Guek Eav, aka Comrade Duch, finally began in 2009. Duch was seen as a key figure as he provided the link between the regime and its crimes in his role as head of S-21 prison. Duch was sentenced to 35 years in 2010, a verdict that was later extended on appeal to life imprisonment.

Case 002 began in November 2011, involving the most senior surviving leaders of the Democratic Kampuchea (DK) era: Brother Number 2 Nuon Chea (age 84); Brother Number 3 and former foreign minister of DK Ieng Sary (age 83); and former DK head of state Khieu Samphan (age 79). Justice may prove elusive, however, due to the slow progress of court proceedings and the advancing age of the defendants. Ieng Sary died in 2013 and his wife and former DK Minister of Social Affairs Ieng Thirith (age 78) was ruled unfit to stand trial because of dementia. Verdicts in Case 002 were due some time in 2014.

Case 003 against head of the DK navy, Meas Muth, and head of the DK air force, Sou Met, is meant to follow Case 002. However, investigations into this case stalled back in 2009 under intense pressure from the Cambodian government, which wanted to draw a line under proceedings with the completion of Case 002. Prime Minister Hun Sen in particular is strongly opposed to Case 003, and few observers give any chance of a third trial actually taking place.

Independence & Civil War

The period after 1953 was one of peace and prosperity, and a time of creativity and optimism. Dark clouds were circling, however, as the war in Vietnam began sucking in neighbouring countries. As the 1960s drew to a close, the North Vietnamese and the Viet Cong were using Cambodian territory in their battle against South Vietnam and US forces, prompting devastating American bombing and a land invasion into eastern Cambodia.

In March 1970, Sihanouk, now serving as prime minister, was overthrown by General Lon Nol, and took up residence in Beijing. Here he set up a government-in-exile that allied itself with an indigenous Cambodian revolutionary movement that Sihanouk had dubbed the Khmer Rouge. This was a defining moment in contemporary Cambodian history: talk to many former Khmer Rouge fighters and they all say that they 'went to the hills' to fight for their monarch and knew nothing of Marxism or Mao.

Khmer Rouge Rule

Upon taking Phnom Penh on 17 April 1975 – two weeks before the fall of Saigon – the Khmer Rouge implemented one of the most radical and brutal restructurings of a society ever attempted. Its goal was to transform Cambodia – renamed Democratic Kampuchea – into a giant peasant-dominated agrarian cooperative, untainted by anything that had come before. Within days, the entire populations of Phnom Penh and provincial towns, including the sick, elderly and infirm, were forced to march into the countryside and work as slaves for 12 to 15 hours a day. Intellectuals were systematically wiped out – having glasses or speaking a foreign language was reason enough to be killed. The advent of Khmer Rouge rule was proclaimed Year Zero.

Leading the Khmer Rouge was Saloth Sar, better known as Pol Pot. As a young man, he won a scholarship to study in Paris, where he began developing the radical Marxist ideas that later metamorphosed into extreme Maoism. Under his rule, Cambodia became a vast slave-labour camp. Meals consisted of little more than watery rice porridge twice a day, meant to sustain men, women and children through a back-breaking day in the fields. Disease stalked the work camps, malaria and dysentery striking down whole families.

Khmer Rouge rule was brought to an end by the Vietnamese, who liberated the almost-empty city of Phnom Penh on 7 January 1979. It is estimated that at least 1.7 million people perished at the hands of Pol Pot and his followers. The **Documentation Center of Cambodia** (DC-Cam; www.dccam.org) records the horrific events of the period.

A Sort of Peace

The Vietnamese installed a new government led by several former Khmer Rouge officers, including current prime minister Hun Sen, who had defected to Vietnam in 1977. In the dislocation that followed liberation, little rice was planted or harvested, leading to a massive famine. The Khmer Rouge continued to wage civil war from remote mountain bases near the Thai border throughout the 1980s. In September 1989 Vietnam, its economy in tatters and eager to end its international isolation, announced the withdrawal of all its forces from Cambodia.

In February 1991 all parties – including the Khmer Rouge – signed the Paris Peace Accords, according to which the UN Transitional Authority in Cambodia (UNTAC) would rule the country for two years. Although UNTAC is still heralded as one of the UN's success stories (elections with a 90% turnout were held in 1993), to many Cambodians who had survived the 1970s it was unthinkable that the Khmer Rouge was allowed to play a part in the process. The Khmer Rouge ultimately pulled out before polling began, but the smokescreen of the elections allowed them to re-establish a guerrilla network throughout Cambodia.

MUST SEE

➡ *The Killing Fields* (1984) The poignant classic about American journalist Sydney Schanberg and his Cambodian assistant both during and after the Khmer Rouge takeover.

➡ *The Last Picture* (2013) Acclaimed filmmaker Rithy Panh uses clay figurines to tell the story of his family's persecution by the Khmer Rouge. In 2014 it became the first Cambodian film to be nominated for an Oscar, for Best Foreign Language Film (French).

CAMBODIA HISTORY

UNTAC is also remembered for causing a significant increase in prostitution and HIV/AIDS.

The last Khmer Rouge hold-outs, including Ta Mok, were not defeated until the capture of Anlong Veng and Prasat Preah Vihear by government forces in the spring of 1998. Pol Pot cheated justice by dying a sorry death near Anlong Veng during that year, and was cremated on a pile of old tyres.

People & Culture

Population

Nearly 15 million people live in Cambodia. With a rapid growth rate of about 2% a year, the population is predicted to reach 20 million by 2025. More than 40% of the population is under the age of 16. According to official statistics, around 96% of the people are ethnic Khmers, making the country the most homogeneous in Southeast Asia, but in reality anywhere between 10% and 20% of the population is of Cham, Chinese or Vietnamese origin. Cambodia's diverse Khmer Leu (Upper Khmer) or Chunchiet (minorities), who live in the country's mountainous regions, probably number between 75,000 and 100,000.

The official language is Khmer, spoken by 95% of the population. English has taken over from French as the second language of choice, although Chinese is growing in popularity. Life expectancy is currently 62 years.

Lifestyle

For many older Cambodians, life is centred on faith, family and food, an existence that has stayed the same for centuries. Faith is a rock in the lives of many older Cambodians, and Buddhism helped them to survive the terrible years and then rebuild their lives after the Khmer Rouge. Family is more than the nuclear family we now know in the West; it's the extended family of third cousins and obscure aunts – as long as there is a bloodline, there is a bond. Families stick together, solve problems collectively, listen to the wisdom of the elders and pool resources. The extended family comes together during times of trouble and times of joy, celebrating festivals and successes, mourning deaths and disappointments. Whether the Cambodian house is big or small, there will be a lot of people living inside.

However, the Cambodian lifestyle is changing as the population gets younger and more urbanized. Cambodia is experiencing its very own '60s swing, as the younger generation stands ready for a different lifestyle to the one their parents had to

NORODOM SIHANOUK, 1922–2012

In his storied career as king, politician and statesman, Norodom Sihanouk, who passed away in 2012, was a lone constant presence in the topsy-turvy world of Cambodian politics. A colourful character with many interests and shifting political positions, he became the prince who stage-managed the close of French colonialism, autocratically led an independent Cambodia, was imprisoned by the Khmer Rouge and, from privileged exile, finally returned triumphant as king, only to abdicate dramatically in 2004.

Sihanouk, born in 1922, was not an obvious contender for the throne. He was crowned in 1941, at just 19 years old, with his education incomplete. By the mid-1960s Sihanouk had been calling the shots in Cambodia for more than a decade. The conventional wisdom was that 'Sihanouk is Cambodia' – his leadership was unassailable. But as government troops battled with a leftist insurgency in the countryside and the economy unravelled, Sihanouk came to be regarded as a liability. His involvement in the film industry and his announcements that Cambodia was 'an oasis of peace' suggested a leader who was losing touch with everyday realities.

Following the Khmer Rouge victory on 17 April 1975, Sihanouk realised he had been used as a Trojan Horse to propel the Khmer Rouge into power and found himself confined to the Royal Palace as a prisoner. He remained there until early 1979 when, on the eve of the Vietnamese invasion, he was flown to Beijing. It was to be more than a decade before Sihanouk finally returned to Cambodia.

Sihanouk never quite gave up wanting to be everything for Cambodia: international statesman, general, president, film director, man of the people. He will be a hard act to follow – the last in a long line of Angkor's god-kings.

swallow. This creates plenty of friction in the cities, as rebellious teens dress as they like, date whoever they wish and hit the town until all hours. More recently this generational conflict spilled over into politics as the Facebook generation helped deliver a shock result that saw the Cambodian Peoples' Party majority slashed in half in the 2013 general elections.

Corruption remains a way of life in Cambodia. It is a major element of the Cambodian economy and exists to some extent at all levels of government. Sometimes it is overt, but increasingly it is covert, with private companies often securing very favourable business deals on the basis of their connections. It seems everything has a price, including ancient temples, national parks and even genocide sites.

Religion

The majority of Khmers (95%) follow the Theravada branch of Buddhism. Buddhism in Cambodia draws heavily on its predecessors, incorporating many cultural traditions from Hinduism for ceremonies such as birth, marriage and death, as well as genies and spirits, such as Neak Ta, which link back to a pre-Indian animist past.

Under the Khmer Rouge, the majority of Cambodia's Buddhist monks were murdered and nearly all of the country's wats (more than 3000) were damaged or destroyed. In the late 1980s, Buddhism once again became the state religion.

Other religions found in Cambodia are Islam, practised by the Cham community; animism, among the hill tribes; and Christianity, which is making inroads via missionaries and Christian NGOs.

Arts

The Khmer Rouge regime not only killed the living bearers of Khmer culture, it also destroyed cultural artefacts, statues, musical instruments, books and anything else that served as a reminder of a past it was trying to efface. The temples of Angkor were spared as a symbol of Khmer glory and empire, but little else survived. Despite this, Cambodia is witnessing a resurgence of traditional arts and a growing interest in cross-cultural fusion.

Cambodia's royal ballet is a tangible link with the glory of Angkor and includes a unique *apsara* (heavenly nymphs) dance. Cambodian music, too, goes back at least as far as Angkor. To get some sense of the

> ### BOTTOMS UP
>
> When Cambodians propose a toast, they usually stipulate what percentage must be downed. If they are feeling generous, it might be just *ha-sip pea-roi* (50%), but more often than not it is *moi roi pea-roi* (100%). This is why they love ice in their beer, as they can pace themselves over the course of the night. Many a *barang* (foreigner) has ended up face down on the table at a Cambodian wedding when trying to outdrink the Khmers without the aid of ice.

music that Jayavarman VII used to like, check out the bas-reliefs at Angkor Wat.

In the mid-20th century a vibrant Cambodian pop music scene developed, but it was killed off (literally) by the Khmer Rouge. After the war, overseas Khmers established a pop industry in the USA and some Cambodian-Americans, raised on a diet of rap, are now returning to their homeland. The Los Angeles based sextet Dengue Fever, inspired by 1960s Cambodian pop and psychedelic rock, is the ultimate fusion band.

The people of Cambodia were producing masterfully sensuous sculptures – more than copies of Indian forms – in the age of Funan and Chenla. The Banteay Srei style of the late 10th century is regarded as a high point in the evolution of Southeast Asian art.

Food & Drink

Some traditional Cambodian dishes are similar to those of neighbouring Laos and Thailand (though not as spicy), others closer to Chinese and Vietnamese cooking. The French left their mark, too.

Thanks to the Tonlé Sap, freshwater fish – often *ahng* (grilled) – are a huge part of the Cambodian diet. The great national dish, *amok,* is fish baked with coconut and lemon grass in banana leaves. *Prahoc* (fermented fish paste) is used to flavour foods, with coconut and lemongrass making regular cameos.

A proper Cambodian meal almost always includes *samlor* (soup), served at the same time as other courses. *Kyteow* is a rice-noodle soup that will keep you going all day. *Bobor* (rice porridge), eaten for breakfast, lunch or dinner, is best sampled with some fresh fish and a dash of ginger.

Beer is immensely popular in the cities, while rural folk drink palm wine, tapped from the sugar palms that dot the landscape. *Tukaloks* (fruit shakes) are mixed with milk, sugar and sometimes a raw egg.

Tap water *must* be avoided, especially in rural areas. Bottled water is widely available but coconut milk is more ecological and may be more sterile.

Environment

The Land

Cambodia's two dominant geographical features are the mighty Mekong River and a vast lake, the Tonlé Sap. The rich sediment deposited during the Mekong's annual wet-season flooding has made central Cambodia incredibly fertile. This low-lying alluvial plain is where the vast majority of Cambodians live – fishing and farming in harmony with the rhythms of the monsoon.

In Cambodia's southwest quadrant, much of the land mass is covered by the Cardamom Mountains and, near Kampot, the Elephant Mountains. Along Cambodia's northern border with Thailand, the plains collide with the Dangkrek Mountains, a striking sandstone escarpment more than 300km long and up to 550m high. One of the best places to get a sense of this area is Prasat Preah Vihear.

TONLÉ SAP: THE HEARTBEAT OF CAMBODIA

During the wet season (June to October), the Mekong River rises dramatically, forcing the Tonlé Sap river to flow northwest into Tonlé Sap (Great Lake). During this period, the lake swells from around 3000 sq km to almost 13,000 sq km, and from the air Cambodia looks like one almighty puddle. An unbelievable 20% of the Mekong's wet-season flow is absorbed by the Tonlé Sap.

As the Mekong falls during the dry season, the Tonlé Sap river reverses its flow, and the lake's floodwaters drain back into the Mekong. This extraordinary process makes the Tonlé Sap an ideal habitat for birds, snakes and turtles, and one of the world's richest sources of freshwater fish.

In the northeastern corner of the country, in the provinces of Ratanakiri and Mondulkiri, the plains give way to the Eastern Highlands, a remote region of densely forested mountains and high plateaus.

Wildlife

Cambodia's forest ecosystems were in excellent shape until the 1990s and, compared with its neighbours, its habitats are still relatively healthy. The years of war took their toll on some species, but others thrived in the remote jungles of the southwest and northeast. Ironically, peace brought increased threats as loggers felled huge areas of primary forest and the illicit trade in wildlife targeted endangered species.

Still, with more than 200 species of mammal, Cambodia has some of Southeast Asia's best wildlife-watching opportunities. Highlights include spotting gibbons and black-shanked doucs (langurs) in Ratanakiri and Mondulkiri provinces, and viewing some of the last remaining freshwater Irrawaddy dolphins in Kratie and Stung Treng provinces.

Globally threatened species that you stand a slight chance of seeing include the Asian elephant, banteng (a wild ox), gaur, clouded leopard, fishing cat, marbled cat, sun bear, Siamese crocodile and pangolin. Asian tigers were once commonplace but are now exceedingly rare – the last sighting was in about 2007.

The country is a birdwatcher's paradise – feathered friends found almost exclusively in Cambodia include the giant ibis, white-shouldered ibis, Bengal florican, sarus crane and three species of vulture. The Siem Reap–based **Sam Veasna Center** (☑063-963710; www.samveasna.org) runs birding trips.

Environmental Issues

Cambodia's pristine environment is a big draw for adventurous ecotourists, but much of it is currently under threat. Ancient forests are being razed to make way for plantations, rivers are being sized up for major hydroelectric power plants and the south coast is being explored by leading oil companies. Places like the Cardamom Mountains are in the front line and it remains to be seen whether the environmentalists or the economists will win the debate.

RESPONSIBLE TRAVEL IN CAMBODIA

Cambodia has been to hell and back and there are many ways in which you can put a little back into the country. Staying longer, travelling further and avoiding package tours is obvious advice. For those on shorter stays, consider spending money in local markets and in restaurants and shops that assist disadvantaged locals.

If trekking in minority villages, pay attention to a few basic rules.

The looting of stone carvings from Cambodia's ancient temples has devastated many temples. Don't contribute to this cultural rape by buying antiquities of any sort – classy reproductions are available in Phnom Penh and Siem Reap, complete with export certificates.

Cambodians dress very modestly and are offended by skimpily dressed foreigners. Just look at the Cambodians frolicking in the sea – most are fully dressed. Wearing bikinis on the beach is fine but cover up elsewhere.

The sexual exploitation of children is now taken very seriously in Cambodia. Report anything that looks like child-sex tourism to the ChildSafe hotlines in **Phnom Penh** (☑ 012 311112), **Siem Reap** (☑ 017 358758) or **Sihanoukville** (☑ 012 478100), or to the national **police hotline** (☑ 023-997919). Tourism establishments that sport the ChildSafe logo have staff trained to protect vulnerable children and, where necessary, intervene.

Organisations with lots of practical ideas for responsible travel:

Cambodia Community-Based Ecotourism Network (www.ccben.org) The official website promoting community-based ecotourism in Cambodia. Browse here for more on projects and initiatives across the country.

ConCERT (☑ 063-963511; www.concertcambodia.org; 560 Phum Stoueng Thmey; ☉ 9am-5pm Mon-Fri) Siem Reap–based organisation 'connecting communities, environment and responsible tourism'.

Friends International (www.friends-international.org) Supports marginalised children and their families and runs the global **ChildSafe** (Map p176; ☑ 023-986601, hotline 012 311112; www.childsafe-cambodia.org; 71 St 174, Phnom Penh; ☉ 8am-5pm Mon-Fri) network to encourage travellers to behave responsibly with children.

The greatest threat is illegal logging, carried out to provide charcoal and timber, and to clear land for cash-crop plantations. The environmental watchdog Global Witness (www.globalwitness.org) publishes meticulously documented exposés on corrupt military and civilian officials and their well-connected business partners.

In the short term, deforestation is contributing to worsening floods along the Mekong, but the long-term implications of deforestation are mind-boggling. Siltation, combined with overfishing and pollution, may lead to the eventual death of Tonlé Sap lake, a catastrophe for future generations of Cambodians.

Throughout the country, pollution is a problem, and detritus of all sorts, especially plastic bags and bottles, can be seen in distressing quantities all over the country.

The latest environmental threat to emerge are dams on the Mekong River.

Environmentalists fear that damming the mainstream Mekong may disrupt the flow patterns of the river and the migratory patterns of fish (including the critically endangered freshwater Irrawaddy dolphin). Work on the Don Sahong (Siphandone) Dam just north of the Cambodia–Laos border has begun, and plans under consideration include the Sambor Dam, a massive 3300MW project 35km north of Kratie.

SURVIVAL GUIDE

❶ Directory A–Z

ACCOMMODATION

Accommodation is great value in Cambodia, just like the rest of the Mekong region. In popular tourist destinations, budget guesthouses generally charge US$5 to US$8 for a room with a cold-water bathroom. Double rooms go as low as US$3 for a room with shared facilities. Dorm beds usually cost US$2 to US$3. Rooms with air-con start at US$10. Spend US$15 or US$20 and you'll be living in style. Spend US$30 and up and we're talking boutique quality with a swimming pool. At the top end you can spend several hundred dollars a night on international-standard luxury digs in Siem Reap and Phnom Penh.

Accommodation is busiest from mid-November to March. There are substantial low-season (May to October) rates available at major hotels in Phnom Penh, Siem Reap and Sihanoukville (although you can only discount a US$5 room so much).

Homestays, often part of a community-based ecotourism project, are a good way to meet the local people and learn about Cambodian life. The **Cambodia Community Based Ecotourism Network** (CCBEN; www.ccben.org) has information on various ecotourism opportunities in Cambodia.

Price Ranges

The following price ranges refer to the cheapest double room on offer, with or without a bathroom, in the high season.

$ less than 79,100r (US$20)

$$ 79,100r to 316,400r (US$20 to US$80)

$$$ more than 316,400r (US$80)

ACTIVITIES

Cambodia is steadily emerging as an ecotourism destination. Activities on offer include:

➡ Rainforest trekking in Ratanakiri, Mondulkiri and the Cardamom Mountains of the south coast

➡ Elephant treks or walking with elephants in Mondulkiri

➡ Scuba diving and snorkelling near Sihanoukville

➡ Cycling around Phnom Penh, in Mondulkiri, along the Mekong Discovery Trail between Kratie and Stung Treng, and around the temples of Angkor

➡ Adventurous dirt biking all over the country (for those with some experience)

BOOKS

A whole bookcase-worth of volumes examines Cambodia's recent history, including the French colonial period, the spillover of the war in Vietnam into Cambodia, the Khmer Rouge years and the wild 1990s. The best include:

➡ *A Dragon Apparent* by Norman Lewis (1951) Classic account of the author's 1950 travels in Indochina.

➡ *First They Killed My Father* by Loung Ung (2001) A personal memoir of Democratic Kampuchea. One of the best of many survivor accounts.

➡ *Cambodia's Curse* by Joel Brinkley (2011) Pulitzer Prize–winning journalist pulls no

punches in his criticism of the government and donors alike.

➡ *Golden Bones* by Sichan Siv (2010) Describes the author's remarkable story from Cambodian refugee in New York to US ambassador to the UN.

➡ *River of Time* by John Swain (1995) Takes readers back to old Indochina, lost to the madness of war.

CUSTOMS REGULATIONS

➡ A 'reasonable amount' of duty-free items is allowed into the country.

➡ Alcohol and cigarettes are on sale at well-below duty-free prices on the streets of Phnom Penh.

➡ It is illegal to take antiquities out of the country.

ELECTRICITY

The usual voltage is 220V, 50 cycles, but power surges and power cuts are common, particularly in the provinces. Electrical sockets are usually two-prong, mostly flat but sometimes round pin.

EMBASSIES & CONSULATES

Some of the embassies located in Phnom Penh:

Australian Embassy (Map p180; ☑023-213413; 16 National Assembly St, Phnom Penh)

French Embassy (Map p175; ☑023-430020; 1 Monivong Blvd, Phnom Penh)

German Embassy (Map p180; ☑023-216381; 76-78 St 214, Phnom Penh)

Lao Embassy (Map p175; ☑023-982632; 15-17 Mao Tse Toung Blvd, Phnom Penh)

Thai Embassy (Map p175; ☑023-726306; 196 Norodom Blvd, Phnom Penh)

UK Embassy (Map p175; ☑023-427124; 27-29 St 75, Phnom Penh)

US Embassy (Map p176; ☑023-728000; 1 St 96, Phnom Penh)

Vietnamese Embassy (Map p175; ☑023-726274; 436 Monivong Blvd, Phnom Penh)

Vietnamese Consulate Battambang (☑053-688 8867; St 3; ◷8-11.30am & 2-4.30pm Mon-Fri); Sihanoukville (Map p244; ☑034-934039; 310 Ekareach St; ◷8am-noon & 2-4pm Mon-Sat)

FOOD

The following price ranges refer to the average price of a main course.

$ less than 20,000r (US$5)

$$ 20,000r to 40,0004 (US$5 to US$10)

$$$ more than 40,000r (US$10)

GAY & LESBIAN TRAVELLERS

Cambodia is a very tolerant country when it comes to sexual orientation and the scene is slowly coming alive in the major cities. But as with heterosexual couples, displays of public affection are a basic no-no. Handy websites include:

Cambodia Out (www.cambodiaout.com) Promoting the GLBT community in Cambodia and the gay-friendly Adore Cambodia campaign.
Sticky Rice (www.stickyrice.ws) Gay travel guide covering Cambodia and Asia.

INSURANCE

Make sure your medical insurance policy covers emergency evacuation: limited medical facilities mean that you may have to be airlifted to Bangkok for problems such as a traffic accident or dengue fever.

Worldwide travel insurance is available at www.lonelyplanet.com/travel_services. You can buy, extend and claim online anytime, even if you're already on the road.

INTERNET ACCESS

Internet access is widespread and there are internet shops in all provincial capitals. Charges range from 1500r to US$2.50 per hour.

Free wi-fi is the rule at pretty much all hotels, guesthouses and cafes in tourist hubs like Phnom Penh, Siem Reap and Battambang, and is usually available in all but the most remote locales.

LEGAL MATTERS

All narcotics, including marijuana, are illegal in Cambodia. However, marijuana is traditionally used in food preparation so you may find it sprinkled across some pizzas.

Many Western countries have laws that make sex offences committed overseas punishable at home.

MAPS

The best all-round map is Gecko's *Cambodia Road Map* at a 1:750,000 scale.

MONEY

➡ Cambodia's currency is the riel, abbreviated in our listings to a lower-case 'r' written after the sum.

➡ The US dollar is accepted everywhere and by everyone, though change may arrive in riel (handy when paying for things such as *moto* rides and drinks).

➡ When calculating change, the US dollar is usually rounded off to 4000r.

➡ Near the Thai border, many transactions are in Thai baht.

➡ Avoid ripped banknotes, which Cambodians often refuse.

ATMs

ATMs that accept debit cards and credit cards are found in all major cities and a growing number of provincial towns and at border crossings.

Machines dispense US dollars or riel. Canadia Bank ATMs charge no transaction fees, although they limit withdrawals on most cards to US$150 per day. ANZ Royal Bank ATMs are friendly to Western plastic, but charge US$5 per transaction.

Bargaining

Bargaining is expected in local markets, when travelling by share taxi or *moto* and, sometimes, when taking a cheap room. The Khmers are not ruthless hagglers, so a persuasive smile and a little friendly quibbling is usually enough to get a good price.

Credit Cards

Top-end hotels, airline offices and upmarket boutiques and restaurants generally accept most major credit cards (Visa, MasterCard, JCB, sometimes American Express), but they usually pass the charges on to the customer, meaning an extra 3% or more on the bill.

Cash advances on credit cards are relatively easy to secure.

Tipping

Tipping is not traditionally expected here, but in a country as poor as Cambodia, a dollar tip (or 5% to 10% on bigger bills) can go a long way.

OPENING HOURS

Government offices Open Monday to Friday from about 8am to 5pm, with a long lunch break, and (sometimes) Saturday morning.
Banks Usually 8am to 3.30pm Monday to Friday, plus Saturday morning.
Markets (psar) Open 6.30am to 5.30pm seven days a week.
Shops About 8am to 7pm daily, sometimes later.

POST

➡ The postal service is hit-and-miss. Letters and parcels sent further afield than Asia can take up to two or three weeks to reach their destination.

➡ Send anything valuable by courier service, such as **EMS** (☑ 023-723511; www.ems.com.kh; Main Post Office, St 13) in Phnom Penh, or from another country.

➡ Ensure postcards and letters are franked before they vanish from your sight.

➡ Phnom Penh's main post office has the most reliable poste restante service.

PUBLIC HOLIDAYS

It is widely believed that Cambodia has more public holidays than any other country on earth.

In addition to the following, the whole country basically shuts down for an entire week for Chaul

Chnam Khmer (Khmer New Year, usually in April) and P'chum Ben (Festival of the Dead, in September or October).

Chinese New Year (January or February) and Bon Om Tuk (Water Festival, October or November) usually mean several days off for the masses as well (although the primary Bon Om Tuk celebration, in Phnom Penh, was cancelled from 2011 to 2013 after a stampede killed hundreds in 2010).

International New Year's Day 1 January
Victory over Genocide Day 7 January
International Women's Day 8 March
International Labour Day 1 May
King's Birthday 13 to 15 May
International Children's Day 1 June
King Mother's Birthday 18 June
Constitution Day 24 September
Coronation Day 29 October
King Father's Birthday 31 October
Independence Day 9 November
International Human Rights Day 10 December

SAFE TRAVEL
Crime

Given the number of guns in Cambodia, there is less armed theft than one might expect. Still, hold-ups and motorcycle theft are a potential danger in Phnom Penh and Sihanoukville. There is no need to be paranoid, just cautious. Walking or riding alone late at night is not ideal, certainly not in rural areas.

Bag snatching has become an increasing problem in Phnom Penh in recent years and the motorbike thieves don't let go, dragging passengers off *motos* and endangering lives. If riding a *moto* carry your shoulder bag in front of you and be careful when riding on *remorques* as well.

Should anyone be unlucky enough to be robbed, it is important to note that the Cambodian police are the best that money can buy! Any help, such as a police report, is going to cost you. The going rate depends on the size of the claim, but anywhere from US$5 to US$50 is a common charge.

Drugs

Be very careful about buying 'cocaine'. Most of what is sold as coke, particularly in Phnom Penh, is actually pure heroin and far stronger than any smack found on the streets back home. Bang that up your hooter and you'll be doing impressions of Uma Thurman in *Pulp Fiction*. See Safe Travel (p492) in the regional Directory for more on drug risks in the Mekong region.

Mines & Mortars

Cambodia is one of the most heavily mined countries in the world, especially in the northwest of the country near the Thai border. Many mined areas are unmarked, so do not stray from well-worn paths and *never*, ever touch any unexploded ordnance (UXO) you come across, including mortars and artillery shells. If you find yourself in a mined area, retrace your steps only if you can clearly see your footprints. If not, stay where you are and call for help. If someone is injured in a minefield, do not rush in to help even if they are crying out in pain – find someone who knows how to enter a mined area safely.

Scams

Most scams are fairly harmless, involving a bit of commission here and there for taxi or *moto* drivers, particularly in Siem Reap.

There have been one or two reports of police set-ups in Phnom Penh, involving planted drugs. This seems to be very rare, but if you fall victim to the ploy, it may be best to pay them off before more police get involved at the local station, as the price will only rise when there are more officials to pay off.

Beggars in places such as Phnom Penh and Siem Reap are asking for milk powder for an infant in arms. Some foreigners succumb to the urge to help, but the beggars usually request the most expensive milk formula available and return it to the shop to split the proceeds after the handover.

Moto and *remorque* drivers will always try to get an extra buck or two out of you. Some price inflation for foreigners is natural, but you are being gouged if they charge three times the prices quoted in this chapter. Fares are pretty cheap and don't tend to rise much year-on-year.

Traffic Accidents

Traffic in Cambodia is chaotic, with vehicles moving in both directions on both sides of the road. Get in a serious accident in a remote area and somehow you'll have to make it to Phnom Penh, Siem Reap or Battambang for treatment. The horn is used to alert other drivers to a vehicle's presence – when walking, cycling or on a motorbike, get out of the way if you hear one honking behind you.

TELEPHONE

Landline area codes appear under the name of each city but in many areas service is spotty. Mobile phones, whose numbers start with 01, 06, 07, 08 or 09, are hugely popular with both individuals and commercial enterprises. Buying a local SIM card is highly recommended to avoid expensive roaming charges. SIM cards are widely available and cost almost nothing. Mobile phone calls and 3G internet access are also quite cheap. Foreigners usually need to present a valid passport to purchase a local SIM card.

If you don't have a phone, the easiest way to make a local call in most urban areas is by heading to one of the many small private booths on the kerbside, with prices around 300r.

For listings of businesses and government offices, check out www.yp.com.kh.

TIME

Cambodia, like Laos, Vietnam and Thailand, is seven hours ahead of Greenwich Mean Time or Universal Time Coordinated (GMT/UTC).

TRAVELLERS WITH DISABILITIES

Although Cambodia has one of the world's highest rates of limb loss (due to mines), the country is not designed for people with impaired mobility. Few buildings have lifts/elevators, footpaths and roads are riddled with potholes, and the staircases and rock jumbles of many Angkorian temples are daunting even for the able-bodied.

Transport-wise, chartering is the way to go and is a fairly affordable option. Also affordable is hired help if you require it, and Khmers are generally very helpful should you need assistance.

VISAS

Visas on Arrival

➜ For most nationalities, one-month tourist visas (US$20) and business visas (US$25) are available on arrival at Phnom Penh and Siem Reap airports and all land border crossings. If you are carrying an African, Asian or Middle Eastern passport, there are some exceptions.

➜ One passport-sized photo is required and you'll be 'fined' US$2 if you don't have one. Citizens of Asean member countries do not require a visa.

➜ Visas are issued extremely quickly at the airports and lines are usually minimal, so it's not really worth paying US$5 extra for an e-visa. However, you might consider the e-visa option if you plan to cross at the Poipet or Koh Kong land borders. Overcharging for visas is rampant at these crossings, and with an e-visa you'll avoid these potential charges.

E-Visas

➜ One-month tourist e-visas cost US$20 plus a US$5 processing fee.

➜ E-visas are available from www.mfaic.gov.kh and take three business days to process.

➜ E-visas can be used at all airports and at the Bavet, Koh Kong and Poipet land border crossings. They cannot be used at the more remote land crossings.

Visa Extensions

➜ Tourist visas can be extended once for one month. If you're planning a longer stay, upon arrival request a one-month business visa (US$25), which can be extended for up to a year through any travel agent in Phnom Penh. Bring a passport photo.

➜ Extensions for 1/3/6/12 months cost about US$45/75/155/285 and take three or four business days.

➜ For one-month extensions, it may be cheaper to do a 'visa run' to Thailand, getting a fresh visa when you cross back into Cambodia.

➜ Overstayers are charged US$5 per day at the point of exit.

Securing Visas for Neighbouring Countries

Vietnam One-month single-entry visas cost US$60/70 for one-day/one-hour processing at the Vietnamese consulates in Phnom Penh, Sihanoukville or Battambang.

Laos Most visitors can obtain a visa on arrival.

Thailand Most visitors do not need a visa.

VOLUNTEERING

Cambodia hosts a huge number of NGOs, some of which do require volunteers from time to time. The best way to find out who is represented in the country is to drop in on the **Cooperation Committee for Cambodia** (CCC; Map p175; ☑ 023-214152; www.ccc-cambodia.org; 9-11 St 476) in Phnom Penh.

Professional Siem Reap–based organisations helping to place volunteers include ConCERT (p265) and **Globalteer** (☑ 063-761802; www.globalteer.org); the latter program involves a weekly charge.

WOMEN TRAVELLERS

Khmer women dress fairly conservatively, and it's best to follow suit, particularly when visiting wats. In general, long-sleeved shirts and long trousers or skirts are preferred. Miniskirts aren't too practical on *motos*, even if – like local women – you ride side-saddle.

Tampons and sanitary napkins are widely available in major cities and provincial capitals, as is the contraceptive pill.

For more advice see Women Travellers (p496) in the regional Directory.

ⓘ Getting There & Away

ENTERING CAMBODIA

Most travellers enter Cambodia by plane or bus, but there are also boat connections from Vietnam via the Mekong River. Formalities at Cambodia's two international airports are extremely straightforward. For details on land and river crossings see the Border Crossings (p484) chapter.

AIRPORT TAXES

There's a tax of US$25 on all international flights out of Cambodia. The airport tax for domestic flights is US$6. Both are now included in the ticket price, so you do not need cash at the airport.

AIR

Cambodia's two major international airports, Phnom Penh International Airport and Siem Reap International Airport, have frequent flights to destinations all over eastern Asia.

Airlines

Air Asia (☑ 023-356011; www.airasia.com) Serves Bangkok and Kuala Lumpur.

Asiana Airlines (☑ 023-890440; www.asiana.co.kr) Serves Seoul from Phnom Penh.

Bangkok Airways (☑ 023-722545; www.bangkokair.com) Serves Bangkok from Phnom Penh and Siem Reap.

Cambodia Angkor Air (☑ 023-212564; www.cambodiaangkorair.com) Serves Bangkok, Ho Chi Minh City and Hanoi.

Cebu Pacific Air (www.cebupacificair.com) Serves Manila from Siem Reap.

China Eastern Airlines (☑ 012-289579; www.ce-air.com) Serves Kunming from Siem Reap.

China Southern Airlines (☑ 023-430877; www.cs-air.com) Serves Guangzhou from Phnom Penh.

Dragon Air (☑ 023-424300; www.dragonair.com) Serves Hong Kong from Phnom Penh.

Eva Air (☑ 023-219911; www.evaair.com) Serves Singapore and Taipei from Phnom Penh.

Jetstar (☑ 023-220909; www.jetstar.com) Serves Singapore from Phnom Penh and Siem Reap.

Korean Air (☑ 023-224047; www.koreanair.com) Serves Seoul from Siem Reap and Phnom Penh.

Lao Airlines (☑ 023-216563; www.laoairlines.com) Serves Vientiane and Luang Prabang.

Malaysia Airlines (☑ 023-426688; www.malaysiaairlines.com) Serves Kuala Lumpur from Phnom Penh.

Myanmar Airways International (☑ 023-881178; www.maiair.com) Serves Yangon.

Shanghai Airlines (☑ 023-723999; www.shanghai-air.com) Serves Shanghai.

Silk Air (☑ 023-426807; www.silkair.com) Serves Singapore and Danang.

Thai Airways (☑ 023-214359; www.thaiair.com) Serves Bangkok from Phnom Penh.

Tigerair (☑ 023-551 5888; www.tigerair.com) Serves Singapore from Phnom Penh.

Vietnam Airlines (☑ 023-363396; www.vietnamair.com.vn) Serves Vientiane.

① Getting Around

AIR

All domestic routes are operated by Cambodia Angkor Air, a monopolistic joint-venture with Vietnam Airlines. The only scheduled domestic flights at the time of writing were:

➔ Phnom Penh–Siem Reap (from US$90, several daily)

➔ Siem Reap–Sihanoukville (from US$110, daily)

BICYCLE

Some guesthouses and hotels rent out bicycles for US$1 to US$2 per day. If you'll be doing lots of cycling, bring along a bike helmet, which can also provide some protection on a *moto*.

Cambodia is a great country for cycle touring, as travelling at gentle speeds allows for lots of interaction with locals. Much of Cambodia is pancake flat or only moderately hilly. Safety, however, is a considerable concern on paved roads, as trucks, buses and cars barrel along at high speeds. Usually flat unpaved trails run roughly parallel to the highways, allowing for a more relaxed journey and much more interaction with the locals.

BOAT

Long-distance public boats are increasingly rare as the roads improve, but fast boats still ply the Tonlé Sap from Phnom Penh to Siem Reap, while smaller boats take on the sublime stretch between Siem Reap and Battambang.

BUS

About a dozen bus companies serve all populated parts of the country. Comfort levels and prices vary wildly, so shop around. Booking bus tickets through guesthouses and travel agents is convenient, but often incurs a commission. Also note that travel agents tend to work with only a handful of preferred companies, thus won't always offer your preferred company and/or departure time, so it pays to shop around.

CAR & MOTORCYCLE

Renting a (self-drive) motorbike is a great way to get around provincial cities and their surrounding sights (although tourists are forbidden from renting motorbikes in Siem Reap). Basic 100cc to 125cc motorbikes are widely available and cheap (about US$5 per day). No-one will ask you for a driver's licence except, occasionally, the police. Make sure you have a strong lock and always leave the bike in guarded parking where possible.

For longer-distance travel, motorcycles and cars offer travellers flexibility to visit out-of-the-way places and to stop when they choose. Cambodia's main national highways (NH) are generally in good shape but can be quite dangerous due to the prevalence of high-speed overtaking/passing.

While major national highways are too heavily trafficked for happy motorcycling, many of Cambodia's less-travelled tracks are perfect for two-wheeled exploration. However, forays on motorcycles into the remote and diabolical roads of the northwest and northeast should only be attempted by experienced riders. In all cases, proceed cautiously, as outside Phnom Penh and Siem Reap medical facilities are rudimentary and ambulances are rare.

LOCAL TRANSPORT

➤ *Motos*, also known as *motodups* (meaning *moto* driver), are small motorcycle taxis. They are a quick way of making short hops around towns and cities. Prices range from 1000r to US$1 or more, depending on the distance and the town. Chartering a *moto* for the day costs between US$7 and US$10, but can cost more if a greater distance is involved or the driver speaks English.

➤ The vehicle known in Cambodia as a *re-morque* (túk-túk) is a roofed, two-wheeled trailer hitched to the back of a motorbike. These generally cost about double what a *moto* costs, but fit more people and are safer and much more comfortable if you've got luggage or it's raining.

➤ Taxis can be ordered via guesthouses and hotels to get around Phnom Penh, Siem Reap and Sihanoukville, and usually cost a bit more than a *remorque*.

➤ A few *cyclos* (pedicabs) can still be seen on the streets of Phnom Penh and Battambang. They are a charming and environmentally friendly, if slow, way to get around, and cost about the same as a *moto*.

➤ Although locals rarely agree on a price in advance for a *moto* or *remorque*, tourists should agree to a price beforehand to avoid any unpleasant surprises. Many drivers will try to charge per passenger. You shouldn't let them do this, although paying an extra dollar or two is fair if you are stuffing six or seven people into a *remorque*.

SHARE TAXI, MINIBUS, PICK-UP & EXPRESS VAN

➤ Share taxis (usually Toyota Camrys) are faster, more flexible in terms of departure times and a bit more expensive than buses. They leave when full, which is usually rather quickly on popular routes. For less-travelled routes, you may have to wait a while before your vehicle fills up, or pay for the vacant seats yourself. Each share taxi carries six or seven passengers, plus the driver. Pay double the regular fare and you get the front seat all to yourself; pay six fares and you've got yourself a private taxi.

➤ Old minibuses serve most provincial routes but are not widely used by Western visitors. They are very cheap but usually extremely overcrowded (you are almost guaranteed to be vomited on).

➤ Pick-up trucks, which are favoured by country folk with oversized luggage (some of it alive), continue to take on the worst roads in Cambodia. Squeeze in the air-con cab or, if you feel like a tan and a mouthful of dust, sit in the back with about 30 locals. They leave when seriously full. Bring a *krama* (scarf), sunscreen and, in the wet season, rain gear.

➤ A newer form of transport, express vans are modern Ford Transit or Toyota Hiace vans that operate on a set schedule between major cities. They cost slightly more than big buses, but are much faster – often too fast for many people's taste. They don't have much legroom either; big buses are considerably more comfortable.

TOURS

It's pretty easy to go it alone in Cambodia. If you prefer the convenience of an organised tour, consider using a tour operator that is trying to put a little something back into the country. Such companies are listed throughout this chapter, or check out the following:

About Asia (☏063-760190; www.aboutasia travel.com) Small bespoke travel company specialising in Siem Reap. Profits help build schools in Cambodia.

Local Adventures (☏023-990460; www.cambodia.nl) Cambodian-based company specialising in off-the-beaten-path tours to the less-visited regions of the country. Assists Cambodian children through the **Cambodian Organisation for Learning and Training** (www.colt-cambodia.org).

PEPY Ride (☏023-222804; www.pepyride.org) Specialist cycling company that runs adventurous bike rides through Cambodia to raise funds to build schools and improve education. Also offers non-cycling trips.

Laos

☎ 856 / POP 6.7 MILLION

Best Places to Eat

➡ Tamarind (p302)

➡ Lao Kitchen (p283)

➡ Le Silapa (p283)

➡ L'Elephant (p302)

Best Places to Stay

➡ Auberge les 3 Nagas (p301)

➡ Apsara (p301)

➡ Inthira Hotel Sikotabang (p329)

➡ Mandala Boutique Hotel (p282)

Why Go?

The 'Land of a Million Elephants' oozes magic the moment you spot a Hmong tribeswoman looming from the mist, trek through a glimmering rice paddy, or hear the sonorous call of one of the country's endangered gibbons. It's a place where it's easy to make a quick detour and find yourself well and truly off the traveller circuit: the snaking Mekong River runs through it all, alongside jagged limestone cliffs and brooding jungle. But it's also a place to luxuriate, pampering yourself like a French colonial in a spa, or chilling under a wood-blade fan in a top-notch Gallic restaurant. Old-world refinement is found in pockets right across the country, especially in languid Vientiane and legendary Luang Prabang.

Laos has also acquitted itself well to green tourism, harnessing forests with excellent treks and tribal homestays. Be it flying along mountain zip-lines, elephant riding, exploring subterranean caves or traversing the jungle via dirt-bike, Laos will indelibly burn itself into your memory.

When to Go
Vientiane

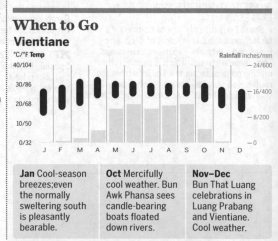

Jan Cool-season breezes; even the normally sweltering south is pleasantly bearable.

Oct Mercifully cool weather. Bun Awk Phansa sees candle-bearing boats floated down rivers.

Nov–Dec Bun That Luang celebrations in Luang Prabang and Vientiane. Cool weather.

Connections

Well-placed Laos is sandwiched between Vietnam, Cambodia, Thailand, Myanmar (Burma) and China. Roads have improved over recent years thanks to the creation of Chinese trade routes, and many ailing public buses have also been updated. Air travel has progressed, with the national carrier, Lao Airlines, enjoying a fleet of nine new planes, better safety records and regular flights to Bangkok, Hanoi, Singapore and Siem Reap; its routes cover the entire country, making it easier than ever to see more in less time.

ITINERARIES

One Week
After spending a few days sampling the Soviet-Franco architecture, sophisticated bars and Asian-fusion cuisine of riverside **Vientiane**, travel north to the unforgettable ancient city of **Luang Prabang** to experience its temples, crumbling villas, pampering spas, myriad monks and Gallic cuisine.

Two Weeks
Fly to **Vientiane**, imbibe its fine accommodation and cuisine for a few days then head north to **Vang Vieng** for climbing, kayaking and tubing in serene karst scenery. Leisurely move on to **Luang Prabang**, the jewel of Southeast Asia and a place so bedecked with charming bakeries, temples, boutiques and restaurants you may not want to leave. After a few days here take a two-day slow boat up the Mekong River to **Huay Xai**, having already booked yourself in for the memorable Gibbon Experience (p323) and an overnight stay in a jungle tree house. If you've got time, head up to **Luang Namtha** for an ecoconscious trek in the wild **Nam Ha National Protected Area** (NPA). From here you can fly back to Vientiane to catch your flight out.

Internet Resources

➡ **Lonely Planet** (www.lonelyplanet.com/laos) Head to the Thorntree forum for the latest news from the road.

➡ **Ecotourism Laos** (www.ecotourismlaos.com) Focusing on trekking, the environment and eco-activities.

➡ **Lao Bumpkin** (www.laobumpkin.blogspot.com) Travel, food and all things Lao.

➡ **Lao National Tourism Authority** (www.tourismlaos.gov.la) Mostly up-to-date travel information from the government.

NEED TO KNOW

➡ **Currency** Kip (K)

➡ **Language** Lao

➡ **Money** Plenty of ATMs in every major town and city

➡ **Visas** 30-day visa available upon arrival

➡ **Mobile phones** Prepay SIM cards available across Laos for as little as 10,000K

Fast Facts

➡ **Area** 236,000 sq km

➡ **Capital** Vientiane

➡ **Emergency** Police ☏191

Exchange Rates

Australia	A$1	7250K
Cambodia	1000r	2020K
Euro Zone	€1	11,020k
Thailand	10B	2470K
UK	£1	13,365K
USA	US$1	8025K
Vietnam	10,000d	3810K

Set Your Budget

➡ **Midrange hotel room** US$20

➡ **Evening meal** US$5–10

➡ **Museum admission** US$1

➡ **Beer** US$1–3 for a big bottle

Laos Highlights

❶ Explore the fabled city of **Luang Prabang** (p295) to find French cuisine, Buddhist temples, colonial villas, stunning river views and some of the best boutique accommodation in Southeast Asia

❷ Take a boat ride through the exhilarating yet spooky 7.5km **Tham Kong Lo** (p326), home to fist-sized spiders and stalactite woods, whilst tackling the three-day 'Loop' by dirt-bike

❸ Zip through the treetops and sleep among the wild things in a cosy jungle tree house on the **Gibbon Experience** (p323) in Huay Xai, Laos' premier eco adventure

❹ Take an ecotrek through some of the wildest, densest jungle in the country, in **Nam Ha National Protected Area** (p317), home to tigers and a rich variety of ethnic tribes

❺ Lower your pulse in the travellers' Mecca of Four Thousand Islands, aka **Si Phan Don** (p341), where the Mekong River turns turquoise and the night air is flecked with fireflies

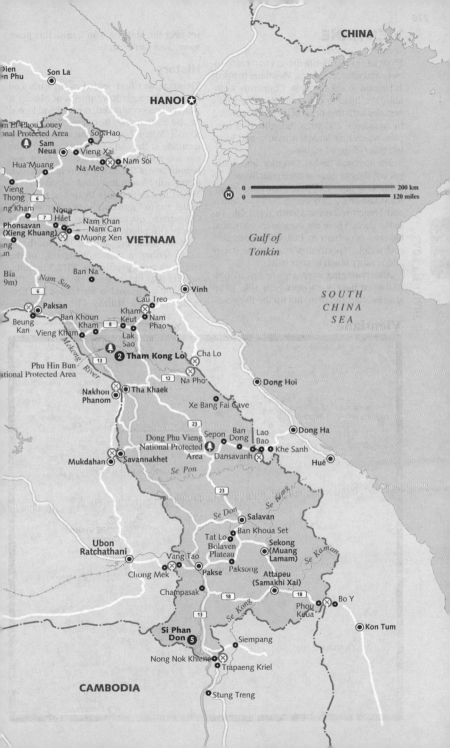

VIENTIANE

021 / POP 237,000

From its sleepy túk-túk drivers to its cafe society and affordable spas, Vientiane (ວຽງຈັນ) is languid to say the least. Eminently walkable, the historic old quarter of Vientiane beguiles with tree-lined boulevards crowded by frangipani and tamarind, glittering temples, wandering Buddhist monks and lunging *naga* (dragon) statues.

For the well-heeled traveller and backpacker, the city acquits itself equally well, be it low-cost digs and street markets, or upscale, jaw-droppingly pretty boutique hotels and French restaurants with reputable Parisian chefs. There are even more cafes and bakeries here than in Luang Prabang, and such a global spectrum of cuisine that it may add another notch to your belt!

After lounging over a novel in an old-fashioned bakery, shopping for silk, swigging Beerlao and drinking up the fiery sunset over the Mekong, you'll miss this place more than you expect.

History

Vientiane was first settled as an early Lao fiefdom. Through 10 centuries of history it was variously controlled, ravaged and looted by the Vietnamese, Burmese, Siamese and Khmer. When Laos became a French protectorate at the end of the 19th century, the city was renamed as the capital, rebuilt, and became one of the classic Indochinese cities, along with Phnom Penh and Saigon (Ho Chi Minh City). By the early 1960s and the onset of the war in Vietnam, the city teemed with CIA agents, madcap Ravens (maverick US Special Ops pilots) and Russian spies.

In 2009 the city hosted the Southeast Asian Games, a major illustration of the country's new profile. In 2012 Vientiane saw its first gay-pride event, and in 2013 the capital enjoyed a visit from US Secretary of State Hillary Clinton. And al-

Vientiane

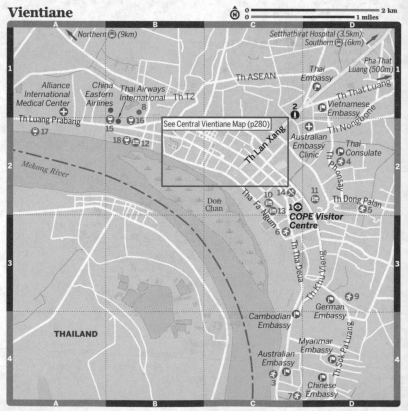

though the newly constructed train line from Thailand to within a few clicks of Laos is still largely useless, China's Kunming to Vientiane express route will be completed over the next few years, at a massive cost to Laos.

◉ Sights

The three main streets parallel to the Mekong – Th Fa Ngoum, Th Setthathirath and Th Samsenthai – are the central inner city of Vientiane and, conveniently, where most of the sights, guesthouses, hotels, restaurants and bars are located.

Pha That Luang   BUDDHIST STUPA

(ພະທາດຫລວງ; Great Sacred Reliquary, Great Stupa; Th That Luang; admission 5000K; ⊗8am-noon & 1-4pm Tue Sun) Svelte and golden Pha That Luang is the most important national monument in Laos, a symbol of Buddhist religion and Lao sovereignty. Legend has it that Ashokan missionaries from India erected a *tâht* (stupa) here to enclose a piece of Buddha's breastbone as early as the 3rd century BC.

Vientiane

Wat Si Saket   BUDDHIST TEMPLE

(ວັດສີສະເກດ; Map p280; cnr Th Lan Xang & Th Setthathirath; admission 5000K; ⊗8am-noon & 1-4pm, closed public holidays) Built between 1819 and 1824 by Chao Anou, Wat Si Saket is believed to be Vientiane's oldest surviving temple. And it shows; this beautiful temple turned national museum is in dire need of a face-lift.

Patuxai   MONUMENT

(ປະຕູໄຊ; Victory Monument; Map p276; Th Lan Xang; admission 5000K; ⊗8am-5pm) Vientiane's Arc de Triomphe replica is a slightly incongruous sight, dominating the commercial district around Th Lan Xang. Officially called 'Victory Monument' *and* commemorating the Lao who died in prerevolutionary wars, it was built in 1969 with cement donated by the USA intended for the construction of a new airport; hence expats refer to it as 'the vertical runway'. Climb to the summit for panoramic views over Vientiane.

Lao National Museum   MUSEUM

(ພິພິດທະພັນປະຫວັດສາດແຫ່ງຊາດລາວ; Map p280; ☎021-212461; Th Samsenthai; admission 10,000K; ⊗8am-noon & 1-4pm) Sadly, this charming French-era building was due to be knocked down and the museum moved to newer premises. Formerly known as the Lao Revolutionary Museum, much of its collection retains an unshakeable revolutionary zeal. Downstairs has a potted account of Khmer culture in the south, accompanied by tools and Buddha statuary; upstairs has ponderous displays that tell the story of the Pathet Lao, peppered with busts of Lenin and Ho Chi Minh.

Xieng Khuan   MUSEUM

(ຊຽງຂວັນ; Suan Phut, Buddha Park; admission 5000K, camera 3000K; ⊗8am-4.30pm) Twenty-five kilometres southeast of Vientiane, eccentric Xieng Khuan thrills with other-worldly Buddhist and Hindu sculptures, and was designed and built in 1958 by Luang Pu, a yogi-priest-shaman who merged Hindu and Buddhist philosophy, mythology and iconography into a cryptic whole.

Bus 14 (8000K, one hour, 24km) leaves the Talat Sao bus station every 15 or 20 minutes throughout the day and goes all the way to Xieng Khuan. Alternatively, charter a túk-túk (200,000K return).

LAOS VIENTIANE

🏃 Activities

Frisbee

Ultimate Frisbee
FRISBEE

(Map p276; American soccer pitch; 12,000K; ⊙6.30pm Mon) Every Monday at 6.30pm aerial wizards meet at the American soccer pitch to play Ultimate Frisbee (two teams of seven players). Check out the Facebook page (Vientiane Ultimate Frisbee) for more info and to arrange a lift with a regular. Mixed boys and girls, Lao and expats. A great way to meet people if you're staying a while.

Bowling

Lao Bowling Centre
BOWLING

(Map p280; ☑021-218661; Th Khun Bulom; per game with shoe hire 16,000K; ⊙9am-midnight) Bright lights, Beerlao and boisterous bowlers are what you'll find here.

Gym

Bee Bee Fitness
GYM

(Map p276; ☑021-315877; opposite the Australian Embassy; 1-day membership 40,000K; ⊙6am-9pm Mon-Fri, 7am-9pm Sat & Sun) Loads of room to enjoy their decent equipment: rowing machines, spinning bikes and weightlifting apparatus. There's also a pool being built, and regular Zumba and Pilates classes, too.

Massage & Herbal Saunas

★ The Spa
MASSAGE

(Map p276; ☑021-285113; www.the-spa-laos.com; Th That Khao; ⊙10am-10pm; 🕾) This restful oasis is the best spa in town (albeit two clicks out), with glacially cool surroundings and a litany of heavenly treatments including head massage (98,000K), oil massage (185,000K) and herbal steam and sauna (110,000K). Two cuboid-faced Persian cats finish off the voluptuous aesthetic.

Oasis
MASSAGE

(Map p280; Th François Ngin; ⊙9am-9pm) Cool, clean and professional, this is an excellent central place to enjoy foot massage (50,000K), Lao-style body massage (60,000K) or a peppermint body scrub (200,000K), among other treatments.

Wat Sok Pa Luang
MASSAGE, SPA

(Map p276; Th Sok Pa Luang; ⊙1-7pm) In the leafy grounds of Wat Sok Pa Luang, a witch's brew of eucalyptus, lemongrass, basil and lime is stirred in a giant cauldron, the fumes of which are then fed into the sauna (20,000K). Traditional massage (40,000K) and meditation class (free) are also available. It's 3km from the city centre. Avoid rush hour between 3pm and 6pm.

Meditation & Yoga

Wat Sok Pa Luang
MEDITATION

(☑021-2311938; Th Sok Pa Luang) Every Saturday from 4pm to 5.30pm, monks lead a session of sitting and walking meditation. Both Lao and foreigners are welcome and there's no charge. There's usually a translator for the question period after the meditation.

Lemongrass Yoga
YOGA

(Map p276; ☑020 5887 2027; www.lemongrass yoga.com; per 90-min class 70,000K; ⊙6.30-8pm Thu, noon-1.30pm Sun) Shelley has been practising for 15 years and teaches hatha yoga one-to-one, or in small groups. The yoga

---

COPE: LIGHT IN THE DARKNESS

An estimated 260 million submunition 'bombies' were dropped on Laos between 1964 and 1973, and 78 million of them failed to explode. Since the end of the war more than 12,000 people have fallen prey to UXO (unexploded ordnance) – many of them children – rendering the work that takes place at the excellent **COPE visitor centre** (Map p280; ☑021-218427; www.copelaos.org; Th Khu Vieng; admission free; ⊙9am-6pm) **FREE** among the most vital in the country.

A 1km bike ride from the city centre, COPE is an inspiring not-for-profit organisation dedicated to supporting the victims of UXO. Since 1992 it has provided clinical mentoring and training programs for local staff in the manufacture of artificial limbs and related rehabilitation activities. There are five COPE centres across Laos where high-tech but low-cost artificial limbs are made, transforming the lives of people who've had to make do with their own improvised limbs.

The recently updated UXO exhibition is fascinating, with photographs portraying the salvaged lives of victims, as well as 'The Cave cinema', a bunker-style screening room showing a number of documentaries. There's also the Karma Café, where you can grab a homemade ice cream and cool off between exploring the centre. Take a free tour around the centre accompanied by an English-speaking guide.

house (number six) is located in the middle of a *soi* (lane) just off of Th Boulichanh in Dongphalan Thong Village. The nearest land mark is Vieng Vang tower, a six-storey business tower which marks the entrance to the *soi*, and is between the Thai consulate and Ton Lam restaurant on Th Boulichanh.

Swimming

There are several places in Vientiane where you can take a cooling dip. You could try **Sengdara Fitness** (Map p276; ☑ 021-452159; 5/77 Th Dong Palan; ☺ 6am-10pm), where a day pass costs 45,000K. Several hotels welcome nonguests, including the beautiful **Settha Palace Hotel** (Map p280; ☑ 021-217581; 6 Th Pangkham; ☺ 7am-8pm) with its decadent pool and surrounding bar, as well as the **Lao Plaza Hotel** (Map p280; ☑ 021-218 800; www.laoplazahotel.com; 63 Th Samsenthai), which is a fair size and also has plenty of loungers (which will set you back 120,000K).

🍴 Courses

Villa Lao COOKING COURSE
(Map p276; ☑ 021-242292; www.villa-lao-guesthouse.com; off Th Nong Douang; half-day class 150,000K) As well as being a guesthouse, Villa Lao offers cooking courses at 9am and 2pm by appointment, involving a trip to the market, preparation of three dishes of your choice, and sampling your creations. The price is per class, so the more people involved the cheaper it will be per person, but to give you an idea it should cost around 150,000K per person.

👉 Tours

Vientiane By Cycle CYCLING TOUR
(Map p276; ☑ 020 5581 2337; www.vientianebycycle.com; full/half day 450,000/350,000K) Run by energised Aline, this tour affords you the chance to experience another side of Vientiane as you meander along its riverfront, through affluent and poor suburbs, and past schools and temples. Starts 8am at **Kong View** (Map p276; ☑ 021-520 522; off Th Luang Prabang; dishes 25,000-70,000K; ☺ 11am-midnight) on the Mekong.

🛏 Sleeping

The old days of shadowy flophouses are out the window, with a raft of elegant boutique hotels and clean, basic guesthouses now on offer.

🛏 Central Vientiane

Vientiane Backpackers Hostel HOSTEL $
(Map p280; ☑ 020 9748 4227; www.vientianebackpackerhostel.com; Th Nokèokoummane; @ 🤶)
A great new hostel with three large fan-cooled dorms. There's a cafe, free vodka after 9pm, laundry services, free wi-fi and bike (10,000K) and scooter rental (70,000K). Bathrooms and showers are modern and clean, while self-catering facilities are more than adequate. Free breakfast, ticketing and visa services, plus friendly European management, make this a worthy option.

Syri 1 Guest House GUESTHOUSE $
(Map p280; ☑ 021-212682; Th Saigon; r 50,000-150,000K; 🕸 @ 🤶) Syri sits on a quiet street and is run by the gentle-natured Air and his family. It's been a traveller fave for many years and with good reason: generously sized rooms (air-con and fan, en suite and shared bathroom), recesses in which to chill, a DVD lounge, bikes for rent, and tailored bike tours of the city. Plus 100% friendly.

Phonethip Guesthouse GUESTHOUSE $
(Map p280; ☑ 021-217239; 72 Th In Paeng; r with fan/air-con US$10/15; 🕸 🤶) With its bubbling water feature and shaded courtyard peppered with swing chairs and spots to relax, this place feels like an escape from the heat and crowds. There's a range of rooms, some – with fridges and TVs – better than others, so look at a few. Friendly owner.

Lao Youth Inn GUESTHOUSE $
(Map p280; ☑ 021-241352; Th François Ngin; r with fan/air-con 60,000/80,000K; 🕸 🤶) There are a couple of mint-green Lao Youth Inns on Th François Ngin, the best one being at the top of the street nearest Th Setthathirath. Rooms are boxy with en suites and polished tiled floors. Useful amenities include ticketing services, bike (10,000K) and scooter (60,000K) rental.

★ Lao Heritage Hotel GUESTHOUSE $$
(Map p280; ☑ 021-265093; Th Phnom Penh; r US$20-25; 🕸 @ 🤶) Like a slice of home, this quirky old Lao house is as friendly as it is appealing, and is undergoing a steady make-over under new management. There's a great new tapas restaurant, while rooms have wood floors, bed runners, TVs and fridges. Rooms 1 and 2 are our favourites. There are plenty of nooks to chill in, too.

Central Vientiane

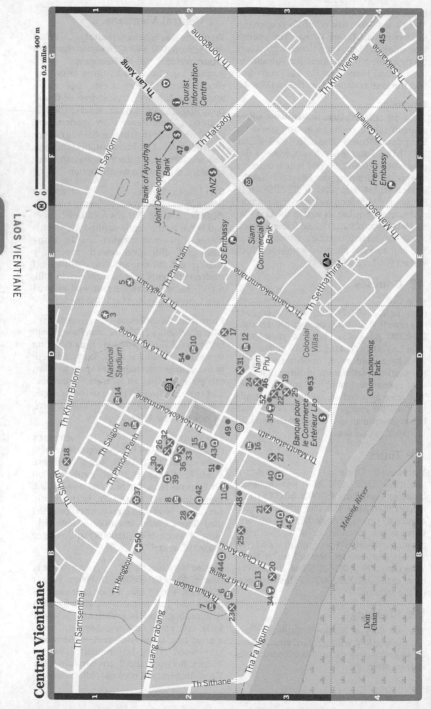

0 0
0.2 miles
400 m

Central Vientiane

★ **Hotel Khamvongsa** HOTEL $$
(Map p280; ☏021-218415; www.hotelkhamvongsa.com; Th Khounboulom; s/d/tr incl breakfast US$35/50/60; ❄☎📶) This lovely French-era building has been stylishly reincarnated as a homey boutique hotel, with belle epoque touches such as glass tear lightshades, chess-tiled floors, and exquisitely simple rooms, softly lit with wood floors and Indo-chic decor. Rooms on the 3rd and 4th floors have masterful views.

Vayakorn Inn HOTEL $$
(Map p280; ☏021-215348; www.vayakorn.biz; 19 Th Hèngbounnoy; r US$35; ❄@📶) On a quiet street, this tasteful hotel is great value given its chandeliered lobby festooned in handicraft and hardwood floors, plus a bijou cafe. Generously sized rooms are impeccably clean with super-fresh linen,

choice art, flat screen TVs, desks and modern en suites. Upper floor rooms have excellent city views.

Mali Namphu Guest House GUESTHOUSE $$
(Map p280; ☏021-215093; www.malinamphu.com; 114 Th Pangkham; s/d/tr incl breakfast 210,000/260,000/350,000K; ❄@📶) On the tailors' street, this old stalwart has fresh, bright rooms wrapped around a leafy courtyard where you also take breakfast. Rooms are fragrant with Lao handicrafts and desks, and enjoy impeccably clean bathrooms and air-con. There's also cable TV.

Lani's House GUESTHOUSE $$
(Map p280; ☏021-215639; www.lanishouse.com; Th Setthathirath; s/d US$50/60; 🅿❄) This tasteful oasis feels like an authentic slice of Indochina; rooms are cool and cozy with wood-blade fans, desks, shabby-chic

armoires, cable TV, fridges, wall hangings, mosquito nets and bamboo-framed beds. Its atmospheric lobby is festooned with handicrafts and stuffed animals.

Auberge Sala Inpeng
GUESTHOUSE $$
(Map p280; ☎ 021-242021; www.salalao.com; Th In Paeng; r incl breakfast US$25-40; ❄️ 🛜 👪) This pretty, unique complex of wood cabanas plus a handsome traditional Laotian house is set in gardens that spill with tamarind and champa flowers. The more grand rooms have a whiff of rustic chic, with en suites and air-con. Staff are as welcoming as a slice of home.

Hotel Beau Rivage Mekong
GUESTHOUSE $$
(Map p276; ☎ 021-243375; www.hbrm.com; Th Fa Ngoum; r with/without view incl breakfast US$67/55; ⊜❄️@🛜) This flamingo-pink boutique hotel still packs a punch, with superb rooms decked in bamboo screens, waffled bedspreads, high ceilings, and a pleasant garden out back. Desirable for couples.

🛏 Out of the Centre

Villa Manoly
GUESTHOUSE $$
(Map p276; ☎ /fax 021-218907; manoly20@hotmail.com; off Th Fa Ngoum; r incl breakfast US$35-45; ❄️ 🖼) A beautifully antiquated house in a garden swimming in mature plants and frangipani flowers, Manoly feels like the sort of place Le Carré might ensconce himself in to write a novel (witness its collection of vintage telephones and typewriters). Nicely furnished rooms, with wood floors, air-con, en suites and bedside lamps, overlook a delightful pool.

★ Mandala Boutique Hotel
BOUTIQUE HOTEL $$$
(Map p276; ☎ 021-214493; www.mandalahotel.asia; off Th Fa Ngoum; r incl breakfast US$80-100; 🅿⊜❄️@🛜👪) Set in an old French villa, Mandala is new and super-chic with lacquered granite floors, flat-screen TVs and dark-wood furniture, which blend perfectly with the aesthetic of its art deco lines. The four-poster beds are possibly the most comfortable in Laos. There's also a natty Asianfusion restaurant in the gardens.

Green Park Hotel
BOUTIQUE HOTEL $$$
(Map p276; ☎ 021-264097; www.greenpark vientiane.com; 248 Th Khu Vieng; r incl breakfast US$145-450; 🅿❄️@🛜🖼👪) This place exudes calm the moment you enter its centre-

piece courtyard, complete with sparkling pool and shaded by sugar palms and frangipani trees. Rooms feature hardwood floors, capacious bathrooms, couches, safety deposit boxes and step-in mosquito nets. The staff are friendly, the breakfast and dinner fantastic; they alone merit the journey here.

✖ Eating

If you were looking to lose a few pounds in Vientiane, forget it. This is a gourmand's heaven, and it's possible to eat your way round the globe from Japan to France – and just about everywhere in between – in a vast selection of top-flight restaurants, as well as informal cafes, juice bars and roadside vendors, who dish up delicious grilled fare.

✖ Around Th Setthathirath, Mekong Riverfront & Nam Phu

Phimphone Market
SELF-CATERING $
(Map p280; 94/6 Th Setthathirath; ⊙7am-9pm Mon-Sat; 🛜) Stocks everything from fresh veg, Western magazines, ice cream, imported French and German salami, bread, biscuits and chocolate, as well as Western toiletries. It also stocks Hobo maps of the city.

Common Ground Café
MEXICAN $
(Map p280; ☎ 020 7872 7183; Th Chao Anou; mains 29,000K; ⊙7am-8pm Mon-Sat; 🛜🍴👪) Find air-con cool in this family-friendly Mexican cafe. It has sofas to read on, plus a cold-selection counter boasting wraps, quesadillas, falafel, salads and homemade cookies.

Khambang Lao Food Restaurant
LAOTIAN $
(Map p280; ☎ 021-217198; 97/2 Th Khounboulom; mains 10,000-70,000K; ⊙11.30am-2.30pm & 5.30-9pm) The Lao food in this joint is worth the wait – expect grub so spicy it leaves a zingy footprint on your palate. Delicious *làhp* (spicy pork salad); roasted Mekong fish; fried frogs' legs; *àw lám*, described on the menu as 'spicy beef stew'; and tasty Luang Prabang–style sausage. Yum!

Istanbul
TURKISH $
(Map p280; ☎ 020 7797 8190; Th François Ngin; mains 20,000-90,000K; ⊙9.30am-10.30pm; 🛜) Istanbul has a colourful menu of doner and shish kebabs as well as favourites such as meatballs, hummus and falafel. Try the Iskender kebab – grilled beef with pepper sauce, yoghurt and green chilli. All meats are fully marinated.

L'Adresse de Tinay FRENCH $$
(Map p280; ☑020 5691 3434; off Th Setthathirath, next to Makphet; mains 130,000K; ☺6-11pm; ☎) Alchemising an eclectic gastro landscape of snails and scrambled eggs, sea bream fillet, beef tenderloin, rack of lamb and rosemary, and to-die-for crème brûleé perfumed with Madagascan vanilla, Chef Tinay is one of the city's top cooks.

Benoni Café ASIAN FUSION $$
(Map p280; ☑021-213334; Th Setthathirath; mains 40,000-50,000K; ☺10am-6pm Mon-Sat) Come lunchtime, Benoni's contemporary interior is packed with NGOs and Lao urbanites, and has a menu that boasts Asian fusion meets Italian cuisine. Super-fresh snacks, salads and pasta dishes; the carbonara is excellent.

Khop Chai Deu ASIAN FUSION $$
(Map p280; ☑021-251564; 54 Th Setthathirath; mains 25,000-60,000K; ☺8am-midnight; ☎☑) Well executed Lao, Thai, Indian and assorted European fare in a handsome old villa spilling with tables and plants. You can pick your live fish from the kitchen and see it a few minutes later on your plate. Upstairs is a cool new low-lit bar.

★ **Le Silapa** FRENCH $$$
(Map p280; ☑021-219689; 88 Th Setthathirath; mains US$20; ☺11am-11pm daily; ☎) Le Silapa is beautiful in its chichi whiteness, complemented by wood floors, a raftered ceiling and bird-cage lights. This, Vientiane's finest Gallic restaurant, features favourites from foie gras to salads, steaks and brain casserole. It's upstairs at the excellent iBeam bar.

✖ Th Samsenthai & Around

★ **Lao Kitchen** LAOTIAN $
(Map p280; ☑021-254332; www.lao-kitchen.com; Th Hengboun; mains 30,000-40,000K; ☺11am-10pm; ☎☑) This superb new Lao restaurant is contemporary, fresh and unfailingly creative in its execution of trad-Lao dishes. Colourful walls dotted with superior photography, indie tunes and decent service complement a menu spanning stews to Luang Prabang sausage (full of vim), *láhp* variations, stir-fried morning glory, and various palate-friendly sorbets.

Pho Dung LAOTIAN $
(Map p280; ☑021-213775; 158 Th Hengboun; noodle soup 12,000-15,000K; ☺6am-2pm) Excellent *f̌er* (rice-noodle soup) diner packed with a melting pot of locals and travellers. Choose from pork-, beef- or chicken-noodle soup. Run by a friendly Vietnamese family, the gargantuan bowls here are served with heaps of optional seasonings and immense plates of fresh vegies and herbs.

PVO VIETNAMESE $
(Map p276; ☑021-454663; off Th Simeuang; mains 18,000K; ☺6am-7pm Mon-Sat, 6am-2pm Sun; ☑) This fresh, no-frills Vietnamese-run eatery is one of the better places in town for lunch, and, in addition to several tasty spring-roll-based Vietnamese dishes (16,000K), PVO does some of the best *kòw jee 'b́a-đê* (baguettes 8000K) in town.

Ban Anou Night Market LAOTIAN $
(Map p280; meals 10,000-15,000K; ☺5-10pm) Setting up on a small street off the north end of Th Chao Anou every evening, this atmospheric open-air market dishes up Lao cuisine, from grilled meats to chilli-based dips with vegetables and sticky rice.

BEST BAKERIES

Le Banneton (Map p280; Th Nokèokoummane; breakfast 45,000K; ☺7am-9pm) Hands-down the country's best croissants, though to get them at their best and before the supply runs out get yourself here first thing in the morning.

Scandinavian Bakery (Map p280; www.scandinavianbakerylaos.com; Nam Phu; mains 10,000 30,000K; ☺7am 9pm; ☎☒) This Vientiane institution is the city's original bakery at which to get your carb fix, with a treasure trove of fresh subs, breakfasts, brownies, muffins, bagels and delicious coffees. When you're done with your main course get stuck into their sweets counter of eclairs, cheesecake and doughnuts.

JoMa Bakery Café (Map p280; Th Setthathirath; mains 29,000K; ☺7am-9pm Mon-Sat; ☎☒) Packed to the gills, Vientiane's busiest, most soothingly cool bakery is a cornucopia of lush salads (25,000K) and bespoke bagels – choose from salami, ham, salmon, turkey, cheese and salad fillings. It also serves tacos, breakfast and soup.

Baguette & Páté Vendor
STREET FOOD $

(Map p280; Th Samsenthai; half/whole baguette 11,000/22,000K; ⊙6am-8pm) Great *kòw jee ʾbá-đê* (baguettes with liver pâté, veg and cream cheese, dripping with sweet chilli sauce). There's no English-language sign here, but the stall is directly on the corner of Th Pangkham and Th Samsenthai.

YuLaLa Cafe
FUSION $$

(Map p280; Th Hengboun; mains 50,000K; ⊙11.30am-2pm & 6-9.30pm Tue-Sun; 🐾) This impeccably clean, restful gem pipes classical music across its wood-floored space and travellers sit cross-legged on cushions (leave yer shoes outside!). Open for lunch and dinner, look out for favourites such as tofu dumplings, stewed eggplant and sautéed salt pork. A little bit of zen to take you from the bustle of the city.

Xayoh
STEAKHOUSE $$

(Map p280; ✉021-261777; www.inthira.com; mains 85,000K; 🐾) Laos' best steakhouse boasts Japanese Kobe steak – soaked in beer it's massaged daily for 30 days before it arrives impossibly tenderised on your plate. At US$100 it's not cheap! There's also a carnivore's delight of cutlets, sirloin, Luang Prabang sausage, slow cooked lamb, plus the challenge to eat a burger as big as your head. Seriously!

🍷 Drinking & Nightlife

The river plays host to a parade of American-style bars. Conveniently, two of the better nightclubs are within walking distance of each other. **Echo** (Map p276; ✉021-213570; Th Samsenthai; ⊙8pm-1am), at the Mercure Hotel, is pretty cool and is popular with Vientiane's beautiful people. Just up the road, **At Home** (Map p276; Th Luang Prabang; ⊙8pm-midnight) thumps with trance and house.

★ Khop Chai Deu
BAR

(Map p280; ✉021-0251564; www.inthira.com; Th Setthathirath) KCD has massively finessed its nocturnal offerings – think low-lit interiors and a sophisticated drinks list, plus more activities than any other bar, such as speed dating and women's arm wrestling. Upstairs on the 3rd floor a new bar has opened; more South Beach, Miami than Vientiane, it's very slick.

Spirit House
COCKTAIL BAR

(Map p276; ✉021-262530; Th Fa Ngoum; cocktails 40,000K; ⊙7am-11pm; 🐾) This traditional Lao house facing the Mekong has a well-stocked bar with enough cocktails on the menu to keep any old boozer smiling. Chilled-out tunes complement the dark woods and comfy couches of its stylish interior.

Bor Pennyang
BAR

(Map p280; ✉020 787 3965; Th Fa Ngoum; ⊙10am-midnight) A cast of locals, expats, bar girls and travellers assemble at this elevated tin-roofed watering hole to watch the sunset over the Mekong. There are easy-on-the-ear Western tunes, pool tables and a huge bar to drape yourself over, as well as sports on TV.

Jazzy Brick
BAR

(Map p280; ✉020 244 9307; Th Setthathirath; ⊙7pm-late; 🐾) With its stylish, exposed-brick interior adorned in old jazz posters, and Coltrane sliding through the low-lit atmosphere, this is perfect for an upscale evening on the tiles. Occasional live Latin and bossa nova.

Noy's Fruit Heaven
JUICE BAR

(Map p280; Th Hengboun; fruit shakes 8000K; ⊙7am-9pm; 🐾🚲) Homely, colourful juice bar with Chinese paper lanterns hanging from the ceiling. Stop in to pick up a few of your five-a-day or decimate your hangover with one of their dragonfruit, coconut, mango, or tomato juice shakes (8000K). They also turn out super-fresh fruit salads and burgers, and rent bikes (10,000K).

☆ Entertainment

By law, entertainment venues close at 11.30pm. Vientiane has movies, cultural shows, a circus, Lao boxing and a clutch of nightclubs to keep you busy, as well as music concerts.

Centre Culturel et de Coopération Linguistique
CINEMA

(French Cultural Centre; Map p280; ✉021-215764; www.ambafrance-laos.org; Th Lan Xang; ⊙9.30am-6.30pm Mon-Fri, to noon Sat) FREE Dance, art exhibitions, literary discussions and live music all take place in this Gallic hive of cultural activity. As well as cult French films (shown Saturday at 7.30pm), the centre also offers French and Lao language lessons.

Anou Cabaret
LIVE MUSIC

(Map p280; ✉021-213 630; cnr Th Hengboun & Th Chao Anou; ⊙8pm-midnight) On the ground floor of the Anou Paradise Hotel, this cabaret has been swinging along for years. It's a funny place, with old crooners and a palpable 1960s feel.

🔒 Shopping

Numerous handicraft and souvenir boutiques are dotted around streets radiating from Nam Phu, particularly Th Pangkham and Th Setthathirath.

★ T'Shop Lai Gallery BEAUTY, HOMEWARES
(Map p280; www.laococo.com/tshoplai.htm; off Th In Paeng; ⊘8am-8pm Mon-Sat, 10-6pm Sun) *Easily Vientiane's finest shopping experience. The first thing you'll notice is the melange of aromas – coconut, aloe vera, honey, frangipani and magnolia – all of which emanate from the body oils, soaps, sprays, perfumes and lip balms that are made and beautifully packaged by self-taught *parfumier,* Michel 'Mimi' Saada.

Next check out the tortoise-shell-inlaid furniture; the old apothecary units beguilingly stocked with illumined antique bottles; plus cards, bangles and fountain pens. These wonderful objets d'art and products are all made by disadvantaged women from sustainable, locally sourced products.

★ Couleur d'Asie FASHION
(Map p280; ☎021-223008; www.couleurdasie. net; 201 Th François Ngin; ⊘9am-5pm Mon-Sat) *Colourful as an artist's palette, this delightful boutique has a range of ladies' dresses, men's linen shirts and boho chemises. They also sell lovely jewellery, bed runners and silk shawls. Upstairs you can see the dresses being made and have one fitted to order.

Camacrafts HANDICRAFTS
(Map p280; www.camacrafts.org; Th Nokèokoummane; ⊘10am-6pm Mon-Sat) *Stocks silk clothes and weavings from Xieng Khuang Province, plus some bed and cushion covers in striking Hmong-inspired designs.

Indochina's Handicrafts HANDICRAFTS
(Map p280; Th Setthathirath; ⊘9am-8pm) This cave of a place would have kept Aladdin quiet with its antique Russian watches, waxed gold and wooden Buddhas, opium pipes, Hmong earrings and bracelets. Upstairs there's a bijou cafe.

Book Café BOOKS
(Map p280; Th Hengboun; ⊘8am-8pm Mon-Fri) Vientiane's best-stocked secondhand book-

shop sells loads of travel guides, thrillers and informative books on Laos' culture and history.

Monument Books BOOKS
(Map p280; 124 Th Nokèokoummane; ⊘9am-8pm Mon-Fri, to 6pm Sat & Sun) Great one-stop shop for glossy magazines, modern classic novels, plus travel guides, thrillers, lush pictorials, as well as a few toys and books for kids.

ℹ️ Information

DANGERS & ANNOYANCES
As Vientiane is one of the most laid-back capitals in the world, you're reasonably safe here. However, during big festivals – when half the country comes to visit – crime goes through the roof, with dangerous drunk-driving (Laos has one of the highest rates of motorcycle-related deaths in the world) and bag-snatching top of the misdemeanours list.

EMERGENCY
Ambulance (☎195)
Fire (☎190)
Police (☎191)
Tourist Police (Map p280; ☎021-251128; Th Lan Xang)

INTERNET ACCESS
There are several internet cafes on Th Setthathirath. Rates are around 6000K per hour with a decent broadband speed. Most have international telephone facilities. Wi-fi is free at most cafes.

True Coffee Internet (Map p280; Th Setthathirath; per hour 8000K; ⊘9am-9pm; 🛜📶) The coolest spot to surf, this cafe also sells Apple accesories and has brownies, yoghurt and fresh juices. Enjoy a latte as you Skype, or use the free wi-fi.

MEDIA
Your only option for local news and upcoming events is the state-censored *Vientiane Times.* French speakers should look for the weekly *Le Rénovateur. Bangkok Post,* the *Economist, Newsweek* and *Time* can also be found in minimarts and bookshops.

MEDICAL SERVICES
Vientiane's medical facilities will do for broken bones and the diagnosis of dengue fever and malaria, but for anything more serious we strongly recommend you cross to Thailand for the **Aek Udon International Hospital** (☎ in Thailand 0 4234 2555; Th Phosri), which can dispatch an ambulance, or in critical situations an airlift, to take you to nearby Udon Thani. The Thai–Lao Friendship Bridge is closed between

10pm and 6am, but Thai/Lao immigration will open for ambulances.

In Vientiane try the following:

Alliance International Medical Center (Map p276; ☎021-513095; Th Luang Prabang) This brand new hospital is fresh, clean and treats basic ailments such as broken bones, and dispenses antibiotics. It is behind the Honda Showroom near Wattay International Airport.

Australian Embassy Clinic (Map p276; ☎021-353840; Th Thadeua; ☺8.30am-5pm Mon-Fri) For nationals of Australia, Britain, Canada, Papua New Guinea and New Zealand only. This clinic's Australian doctor treats minor problems by appointment; it doesn't have emergency facilities. Accepts cash or credit cards. A block southeast of Patuxai.

Poppy's Pharmacy & Beauty (Map p280; ☎030-981 0108; Th Hengboun; ☺8am-10pm) Bright and clean, this modern, well-stocked pharmacy is great for toiletries, cosmetics, sun cream, malaria pills (not Larium), and sleeping tablets for long bus journeys.

Setthathirat Hospital (☎021-351156) This hospital, 6.5km northeast of the city centre, is another option for minor ailments.

MONEY

There are plenty of ATMs in Vientiane, especially along Th Setthathirath. Banks listed here change cash and travellers cheques and issue cash advances (mostly in kip, but occasionally in US dollars and Thai baht) against Visa and/or MasterCard. All are open 8.30am to 3.30pm Monday to Friday.

ANZ (Map p280; ☎021-222700; 33 Th Lan Xang) Main branch has two ATMs and can provide cash advances on Visa or MasterCard for a flat fee of 45,000K. Additional ATMs can be found on Th Setthathirath and Th Fa Ngoum.

Bank of Ayudhya (Map p280; ☎021-214575; 79/6 Th Lan Xang) Cash advances on Visa cards here carry a 1.5% commission.

Banque pour le Commerce Extérieur Lao (BCEL; Map p280; cnr Th Pangkham & Th Fa Ngoum; ☺8.30am-7pm Mon-Fri, to 3pm Sat & Sun) Best rates; longest hours. Exchange booth on Th Fa Ngoum and three ATMs attached to the main building.

Joint Development Bank (Map p280; 75/1-5 Th Lan Xang) Usually charges the lowest commission on cash advances. Also has an ATM.

Siam Commercial Bank (Map p280; 117 Th Lan Xang) ATM and cash advances on Visa.

POST

Post, Telephone & Telegraph (PTT; Map p280; cnr Th Lan Xang & Th Khu Vieng; ☺8am-5pm Mon-Fri, to noon Sat & Sun) Come here for poste restante and stamps.

TOURIST INFORMATION

Tourist Information Centre (NTAL; Map p280; www.ecotourismlaos.com; Th Lan Xang; ☺8.30am-noon & 1.30-4pm) Based in an attractive, easy-to-use room, the centre has descriptions of each province, brochures and some regional maps, plus English-speaking staff who can provide detailed information on visiting Phu Khao Khuay NPA.

TRAVEL AGENCIES

Green Discovery (Map p280; ☎021-264528; www.greendiscoverylaos.com; Th Setthathirath) The country's most respected adventure tours specialist; as well as kayaking, cycling, zip-lining and trekking trips, they can also help with travel arrangements.

Lasi Ticketing (Map p280; ☎021-222851; www.lasiglobal.com; Th François Ngin; ☺8am-5pm Mon-Fri, 8.30am-noon Sat) With helpful English-speaking staff, Lasi sells air, VIP bus and train tickets, and arranges visas for Cambodia and Vietnam. Speak to Miss Pha.

Maison du Cafe (Map p280; ☎020 780 4842, 021-219 743; 119 Th Manthatourath; ☺8am-10pm) Offers ticketing and visa services, and has a few computers for internet use (6000K per hour).

❶ Getting There & Away

AIR

Wattay International Airport is the main transport hub for the rest of the country. Beside it is the rickety domestic terminal.

China Eastern Airlines (Map p276; www.ce-air.com; Th Luang Prabang, Vientiane) Flies daily to Kunming and Nanning.

Lao Air (☎021-513022; www.lao-air.com; Wattay Airport Domestic Terminal; ☺8am-5pm) Operates flights thrice weekly to Sam Neua (US$116) and Sainyabuli (US$90), and twice a week to Phongsali (US$126).

Lao Airlines (Map p280; ☎021-212051; www.laoairlines.com; Th Pangkham, Vientiane; ☺8am-noon & 1-4pm Mon-Sat, to noon Sun) Conducts domestic flights between Vientiane and Huay Xai (US$115, three weekly), Luang Prabang (US$90, 40 minutes, five daily), Luang Namtha (US$115, four weekly), Pakse (US$134, four weekly), Phonsavan (US$90, daily), Savannakhet (US$115, four weekly), Udomxai (US$115, four weekly), and daily international flights between Vientiane and Bangkok (US$170), Chiang Mai (US$165), Hanoi (US$165), Kunming (US$265), Phnom Penh (US$185), Siem Reap (US$185), Ho Chi Minh (US$205) and Guangzhou (US$360). Also has an office at the airport (☎021-512028; Wattay Airport International Terminal; ☺4am-8pm).

BUSES FROM VIENTIANE

Talat Sao Bus Station

DESTINATION	PRICE (K)	DISTANCE (KM)	DURATION (HR)	DEPARTURES
Vang Vieng	30,000	153	4	7am, 9.30am, 1pm, 3pm
Nong Khai	17,000	22	1½	7.30am, 9.30am, 12.40pm, 2.30pm, 3.30pm & 6pm
Udon Thani	22,000	77	2½	8am, 10.30am, 11.30am, 2pm, 4pm, 6pm

Northern Bus Station

DESTINATION	PRICE (K)	DISTANCE (KM)	DURATION (HR)	DEPARTURES
Huay Xai	230,000	869	24	5.30pm
Kunming	610,000	781	30	2pm
Luang Namtha	180,000	676	18	8.30pm
Luang Prabang	110,000	384	11	6.30am, 7.30am, 9am, 11am, 1.30pm, 4pm, 6pm, 7.30pm
	150,000 (VIP)	384	9	7.30pm & 8pm
Udomxai	170,000	578	16–19	6.45am, 1.45pm
Phongsali	190,000	811	28	6.45am
Phonsavan	110,000	374	9–11	6.30am, 8am, 9.30am, 11am, 4pm, 6.40pm (air-con) 8pm
	150,000 (VIP)	374	9–11	8.30pm
Sainyabuli	110,000 (local)	485	14–16	9am, 4pm, 6.30pm
	130,000 (air-con)	485	14–16	6pm
Sam Neua	170,000–190,000	612	15–17	7am, 9.30am, 12.30pm (VIP), 2pm

Southern Bus Station

DESTINATION	PRICE (K)	DISTANCE (KM)	DURATION (HR)	DEPARTURES
Attapeu	140,000 (local)	812	22–24	9.30am, 5.30pm
	200,000 (VIP)	812	22–24	8.30pm
Lak Sao	85,000	334	6–8	5am, 6am, 7am, 8.30pm
Paksan	40,000–50,000	143	3–4	every 30 mins from 7am-5pm
Pakse	140,000	677	14–16	7am-8pm
	180,000 (VIP)	677	9½	9pm
Salavan	150,000 (local)	774	15–20	7.30pm
	180,000 (VIP)	774	15–20	8pm
Savannakhet	75,000 (local)	457	8–11	5.30am, 6am, 7am, 8am, 9am (fan)
	120,000 (VIP)	457	8–10	8.30pm
Tha Khaek	60,000 (local)	332	6	4am, 5am, 6am (fan),
	80,000 (VIP)	332	5	noon & 1pm

Thai Airways International (Map p276; www.thaiairways.com; Th Luang Prabang, Vientiane) Vientiane to Bangkok connections twice daily.

Vietnam Airlines (Map p280; www.vietnamairlines.com; Lao Plaza Hotel, 63 Th Samsenthai, Vientiane; ⊙9am-5pm) Connects Vientiane with Ho Chi Minh City, Hanoi and Phnom Penh, plus Luang Prabang with Hanoi and Siem Reap.

BOAT

Passenger boat services between Vientiane and Luang Prabang have become almost extinct, but a regular slow boat makes the trip from Vientiane to Pak Lai, 115km away. Boats leave Monday, Wednesday and Saturday at 8am (120,000K, about eight hours) from Kiaw Liaw Pier, 3.5km west of the fork in the road where Rte 13 heads north in Ban Kiaw Liaw.

BUS & SŎRNGTĂAOU

Buses use three different stations in Vientiane, all with some English-speaking staff. The **Northern Bus Station** (Th Asiane) is exactly 9km northwest of the centre, and serves all points north of Vang Vieng, including China and some buses to Vietnam.

The **Southern Bus Station** (Rte 13 South), commonly known as Dong Dok Bus Station or just *khíw lot lák kâo* (Km9 bus station), is 9km out of town and serves everywhere south. Buses to Vietnam stop here.

The **Talat Sao Bus Station** is where desperately slow local buses depart for destinations within Vientiane Province, including Vang Vieng, and some more distant destinations, though for these you're better off going to the Northern or Southern stations. International VIP buses to Thailand's Udon Thani (22,000K) leave here roughly every hour. A VIP bus for Bangkok (248,000K) also leaves from here every day at 6pm.

For buses to China, contact **Tong Li Bus Company** (☑021-242657) at the Northern Bus Station. For Vietnam, **S.D.T** (☑021-720175). has buses leaving daily from the Southern Bus Station: for Hanoi (220,000K, 24 hours) via Vinh (180,000K, 16 hours), and for Danang (230,000K) via Hue (200,000K, 19 hours). On Mondays, Thursdays and Sundays they leave at 6pm. For Ho Chi Minh City change at Danang.

❶ Getting Around

Central Vientiane is entirely accessible on foot.

TO/FROM THE AIRPORT

Wattay International Airport is about 4km northwest of the city centre. Fixed-fare airport taxis cost US$10 into town. Alternatively, walk 500m to the airport gate where you can get a shared túk-túk for about 20,000K. Official túk-túk tariffs from the city centre list the airport as a 60,000K ride.

BICYCLE, MOTORCYCLE & CAR

Bicycles can be rented for 10,000K per day from tour agencies and guesthouses. Scooters can be hired on the west side of Th Nokèokoum-mane near the Douang Deuane Hotel. The place directly in front of the hotel rents 110cc bikes for 70,000K per day.

Jules' Classic Rental (Map p280; ☑020 9728 2636; www.bike-rental-laos.com; Th Setthathirath; per day US$35, minimum rental 1 week) With a range of heavy-duty dirt-bikes, owner Thierry can even send your luggage on to your destination (for a charge), or if you're headed far afield and don't want to double back (say Luang Prabang), you can also leave

---

GETTING TO THAILAND: VIENTIANE TO NONG KHAI

Getting to the border The Thai–Lao Friendship Bridge at the Nong Khai/Tha Na Leng border crossing is 22km southeast of Vientiane. The easiest way to cross is on the comfortable Thai–Lao International Bus (22,000k, 90 minutes), which leaves Vientiane's Talat Sao bus station roughly every hour from 7.30am till 6pm, while the VIP bus for Bangkok (248,000K) leaves daily at 6pm. Alternatively catch a taxi (300B) or jumbo (four-wheeled túk-túk seating 12; 250B), or public bus 14 from Talat Sao (15,000K) between 6am and 5.30pm.

Since 2009, it's also possible to cross the brige by train, as tracks have been extended from Nong Khai's train station 3.5km into Laos, terminating at Dongphasy Station, about 13km from central Vientiane. From Nong Khai there are two daily departures (9.30am and 4pm, fan/air-con 20/50B, 15 minutes) and border formalities are taken care of at the respective train stations.

At the border Travellers from most countries can travel visa-free to Thailand.

Moving on From the Thai border catch a túk-túk (60B) to Nong Khai train station where a sleeper train leaves for Bangkok at 6.20pm and costs US$23/37 for a 2nd-class/sleeper ticket. The VIP bus from Talat Sao also goes to Bangkok.

For more information about crossing this border in the other direction, see p417.

the bike there for US$50. Ask for a new bike (helmets provided).

Europcar (Map p280; ☑021-223867; www.europcarlaos.com; Th Setthathirath; ☉8.30am-6.30pm Mon-Fri, 8.30am-1pm Sat & Sun) Hires quality cars (from US$55 per day). You can leave the car at your destination for a charge. Third-party insurance is standard.

TÚK-TÚK

Many túk-túk have a laminated list of vastly inflated tourist prices, and won't budge for less than the price already agreed upon with the other drivers. You can also flag down shared, fixed-route túk-túk (with passengers already in them), which cost around 20,000K, depending on your destination.

AROUND VIENTIANE

Phu Khao Khuay National Protected Area
ສວນອຸດທິຍານແຫ່ງຊາດພູເຂົາ ຄວາຍ

Covering more than 2000 sq km of mountains to the east of Vientiane, Phu Khao Khuay National Protected Area (NPA) is home to three major rivers that flow off a sandstone mountain range and into the Ang Nam Leuk Reservoir. It boasts an extraordinary array of endangered wildlife, including wild elephants, gibbons, Asiatic black bears and clouded leopards.

Detailed information on trekking, accommodation and getting to and from Phu Khao Khuay can be found at the tourist information centre (p286) in Vientiane. Trekking in Phu Khao Khuay costs 160,000K per person per day, and you must also purchase a permit to enter the NPA (50,000K), and contribute to the village fund (50,000K). If trekking from Ban Hat Khai you'll also have to pay for boat transport (70,000K per boat, up to five passengers).

Wild elephants used to make regular appearances near the village of Ban Na, however, sadly, the elephants have now vanished. In 2007 there was an estimated 25-strong herd in Phu Khao Khuay; in 2009, five were killed – stripped of their tusks and hind legs; and in 2010 a further two were recorded dead; according to the Lao Army, they had been electrocuted by lightning. There should still be 18 elephants from the 2007 tally of 25, but their whereabouts are unknown.

Village guides lead one-, two- and three-day treks from Ban Na to Keng Khani (three to four hours one way), through deep forest to the waterfall of Tat Fa (four to five hours) and to the elephant observation tower at Pung Xay (4km). The one-hour trek to this tower is easy, passing by plantations and through the edge of the jungle itself. The tower overlooks a salt lick, which the elephants used to visit regularly. Trekkers sleep in the tower (100,000K per person) beneath a mosquito net on a mattress, and guides cook a tasty local dinner. Despite the absence of the elephants, it's fun.

Homestay-style accommodation is also available for 30,000K per person per night, with an additional 30,000K per person for food. The prices do not include transport from Vientiane and are not negotiable. All money goes to the village and NPA. To contact Ban Na directly, call Lao-speaking Mr Bounthanom.

❶ Getting There & Away

Buses from the Southern Bus Station (p288) in Vientiane leave regularly for Ban Tha Bok and Paksan. For Ban Na get off at Tha Pha Bat near the Km 81 stone; Ban Na is about 2km north.

For Ban Hat Khai, stay on the bus until a turnoff left (north) at Km 92, just before Ban Tha Bok. Then take any passing *sŏrngtǎaou* the 5km to Ban Huay Leuk. Ban Hat Khai is 2km further. For the various waterfalls, find detailed information at www.trekkingcentrallaos.com, or through the tourist information centre (p286) in Vientiane. If you need a bed en route, there are two decent guesthouses in Tha Bok.

Vang Vieng ວັງວຽງ
☑ 023 / POP 30,000

Like a rural scene from an Oriental silk painting, Vang Vieng crouches low over the Nam Song (Song River) with a backdrop of serene cliffs and a tapestry of vivid green paddy fields. Thanks to the iron fist of the Lao government making its presence felt in 2012, the previously toxic party scene has been banished, the river rave bars have been forcibly closed, and the community is recalibrating itself as an outdoor paradise, with some achingly lovely boutique hotels and a raft of adrenalin-inducing, nature-based activities.

For the first time in years Western families and a more mature crowd are visiting to kayak the Nam Song, go caving and climb the karsts. Relief describes the current feel-

Vang Vieng

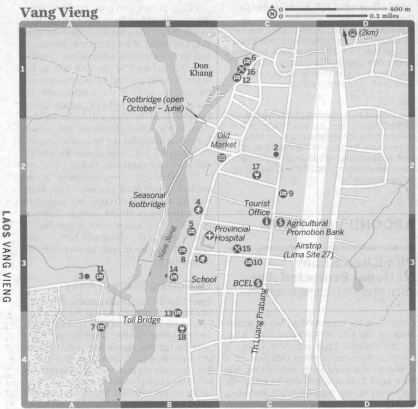

ing of Vang Vieng's inhabitants, with locals glad the town is no longer troubled by thumping music, disrespectful teens and the misconception that anything goes.

Spend a few days here – rent a scooter, take a motorcycle tour, go tubing or trekking – and prepare to manually close your jaw, as you gape at one of Laos' most stunningly picturesque spots.

Sights & Activities

Tubing

Depending on the speed and level of the river, tubing the Nam Song can be a soporific crawl or a speedy glide downstream back to Vang Vieng. It's fantastic fun, but always wear a life jacket when the river runs fast – the currents are lethal even if you're not stoned, and the many stories of travellers who have drowned doesn't make for pleasant reading.

It costs 55,000K to rent a tube plus a 60,000K refundable deposit. Life jackets are available and you can rent a dry bag for 20,000K. The fee includes transport to the tubing drop-off point (3.5km), but keep in mind that you must return the tube before 6pm, otherwise you'll have to pay a 20,000K late fee. If you lose your tube, you have to pay 60,000K. Enjoy!

Kayaking

Kayaking is almost as popular as tubing, and trips typically combine with either visits to caves and villages, optional climbing, cycling and the traverse of a few rapids, the danger of which depends on the speed of the water. There are loads of operators and prices are about US$15 per person per day. Kayaking trips to Vientiane along the Nam Lik (Lik River) are conducted by the excellent Green Discovery (p292), which also runs kayaking adventures on the Nam Song,

Vang Vieng

and involve a lot of paddling. This is only possible post-monsoon, when the water is sufficiently high.

Another useful tour operator for kayaking is VLT (p292).

Rock Climbing

In just a few years the limestone walls around Vang Vieng have gained a reputation as some of the best climbing in Southeast Asia. More than 200 routes have been identified and most have been bolted.

**Adam's Rock
Climbing School**   ROCK CLIMBING
(☑ 020 5501 0832; www.laos-climbing.com; opposite the hospital; half-/full-day climbing 180,000/260,000K, 2-day course US$100; ⊛) The only dedicated climbing outfit in town, with experienced, multilingual guides and sturdy kit.

Hot-Air Ballooning

Best enjoyed first thing in the morning, hot-air ballooning is the perfect way to take in the jaw-dropping scenery. Flights with **Travel With Your Eyes** (☑ 020 9691 82222) take place at 6.30am, 4pm & 4.30pm (US$80) and last approximately 40 minutes. To book contact Mr Vone at VLT (p292).

Caves

After tubing, caving is the town's main attraction. The stunning limestone karst around Vang Vieng is honeycombed with tunnels and caverns. You can buy a map and do the caves yourself, or it's possible to go in an organised group. Wear proper shoes, as the caves are dark and slippery, and absolutely make sure you have your own torch (flashlight), not the dim ones they rent; it's very easy to get lost.

The most famous cave, **Tham Jang** (ຖ້ຳຈັງ; admission 17,000K), south of town, was used as a hideout from marauding Yunnanese Chinese in the early 19th century. A set of stairs leads up to the main cavern entrance. There's also a cool spring at the foot of the cave.

Another popular cave is **Tham Phu Kham** (ຖ້ຳພູຄຳ; Blue Lagoon; admission 10,000K). To reach it, cross the **seasonal bamboo footbridge** (walking/cycling/scooter toll 4000/6000/10,000K) then walk or pedal 6km along a scenic, unsealed road to Ban Na Thong, from where you have to walk 1km to a hill on the northern side of the village. It's a tough final 200m climb, but worth it for a dip in the turquoise pool afterwards.

The **Tham Sang Triangle** is a popular half-day trip that's easy to do on your own. It takes in Tham Sang plus three other caves within a short walk of each other. Begin this odyssey by riding a bike or taking a *sŏrngtăaou* 13km north along Rte 13, turning left a few hundred metres beyond the barely readable Km 169 marker. A rough road leads to the river, where a boatman will ferry you across to Ban Tham Sang for a small fee. **Tham Sang** (ຖ້ຳຊ້າງ; admission 5000K), meaning 'Elephant Cave', is a small cavern containing a few Buddha images and a Buddha 'footprint', plus the elephant-shaped stalactite that gives the cave its name. It's best visited in the morning, when light enters.

From here a signed path takes you 1km northwest through rice fields to the entrances of **Tham Loup** and **Tham Hoi** (combined admission 10,000K). Tham Hoi reportedly continues about 3km into the limestone and an underground lake. About 400m south of Tham Hoi, along a well-used path, **Tham Nam** (ຖ້ຳນ້ຳ; admission 5000K) is the highlight of this trip. This cave is about 500m long and a tributary of the Nam Song flows out of its low entrance. From Tham Nam an easy 1km walk takes you back to Ban Tham Sang.

LAOS VANG VIENG

👉 Tours

★ Green Discovery
ADVENTURE TOUR

(☑023-511230; www.greendiscoverylaos.com; Th Luang Prabang; 1-day cycling tour per person US$37, half-/full-day rock climbing US$27/36, kayaking to Vientiane per person US$53) Green Discovery is Vang Vieng's most reliable operator, offering trekking, kayaking, rafting, rock climbing and caving. From here you can also head out with them to **Nam Lik Jungle Fly** (☑020 5662 2001; www.laosjungle-fly.com). GD's equipment is up to date, plus they have a solid reputation to protect, so safety comes first.

★ Vang Vieng Jeep Tour
ADVENTURE TOURS

(☑020 5443 5747; noedouine@yahoo.fr; Chez Mango; minimum group of 4, per person 120,000K; 🖻) VV Jeep Tour takes in the best of the countryside in friendly Noé's jeep. First he'll take you to a nearby mountain, which you'll gently ascend for an amazing view; next a walk in the paddy fields, followed by a swim in the blue lagoon at Tham Phu Kam; then take a closer look in the cave itself.

VLT
ADVENTURE TOUR

(☑020 5520 8283, 023-511369; www.vangvieng tour.com) VLT is well established and charges US$13 for one day's kayaking, US$22 for one-day mountain-bike trips, and US$33 for one-day treks. Also runs hot-air balloon flights (US$80) at 6.30am, 4pm and 4.30pm every day, lasting 40 minutes. It is a lovely way to see the cliffs, the tapestry of paddy fields and the snaking river below.

🛏 Sleeping

Boutique hotels are increasingly moving in as VV ditches its dreads in favour of a stylish coiffure.

🛏 In Town

★ Champa Lao
GUESTHOUSE $

(☑020 5823 4612; r with/without bath 100,000/70,000K, tr 130,000K; @🖾) This heavily wooded traditional Lao house has basic fan rooms with mosquito nets, and the ambien tgarden restaurant casts off heavenly aromas. There are also bungalows down the bank by the river.

Khamphone Guest House
GUESTHOUSE $

(☑023-511062; r 80,000-120,000K; 🖲) Peach-coloured Khamphone's three buildings offer good-value en suite rooms; the 120,000K options with TV, air-con and fridge are best. Check out the roomier newer building.

Nam Song Garden
GUESTHOUSE $

(☑023-511544; bungalows 50,000-70,000K, 4-bed dm 120,000K; 🖾) At the north end of the town this higgledy-piggledy hillside affair enjoys

---

BIKING IN LAOS

Thanks to improved roads and quality bike operators it's now possible to travel Laos on sturdy, well-maintained motocross bikes with peace of mind; Laos' competent mobile-phone service and the availability of handheld GPS devices also help. With drop-off and luggage-forwarding facilities, it's easy to tackle a slice of your holiday on two wheels.

Hire a bike from Jules' Classic Rental (p288) for the week to take in the north or central Laos, riding through the mountains to Vang Vieng for a few days, before moving on to Luang Prabang and the rest of the north and leaving your bike in Luang Prabang.

Alternatively you can bus it towards Vang Vieng and take a trip with **Uncle Tom's Trail Bike Tour** (☑020 2995 8903; uncletomstrails@hotmail.com; Blue Lagoon Resort, Ban Theua, Ang Nam Ngum; 2-night trip per person US$110) based at the Blue Lagoon resort on the nearby Ang Nam Ngum. Tom can teach you riding skills before taking you on a tailored one-day tour.

If you're thinking of doing Khammuane Province's 'Loop', forget skidding off the road on a wobbly scooter. Mad Monkey Motorbike (p331) has just opened in Tha Khaek, and rents new 250cc Honda dirt-bikes. Better still the owner, DC, can come and get you if you run into trouble in the boonies. Tha Khaek is an excellent base from which to do the Loop and mythic Tham Kong Lo.

And, finally, thanks to the **Midnight Mapper** (☑020 5865 6994; espritdemer@hotmail.com), who's spent the last 10 years tirelessly mapping Laos, you can buy a satellite map off the website and plug it into your GPS gadget (US$50; you'll be mailed the SIM card). Alternatively, you can rent one of his Garmin handheld GPS devices for US$10 per day and plug in your coordinates, so you'll never get lost!

great views from its leafy garden. There's a large room, which sleeps four, and various bungalows with and without bathrooms. Food available (mains 40,000K).

⭐ **Ban Sabai Bungalows** GUESTHOUSE $$
(Xayoh Riverside Bungalows; ☑ 023-511088; www.ban-sabai-bungalows.com; r US$42-54; P ❂ ❄ @ 🔊 ✈) These beautifully hidden cabanas overlook the river and karsts. Imagine manicured lawns bursting with flowers, and cosy rooms with huge beds, chichi decor and slick, modern en suites. There's a pool, a verandah to take in the view, and an elevated, peaceful restaurant. By night, candles flicker and lanterns glow. Perfectly romantic.

Inthira Hotel BOUTIQUE HOTEL $$
(☑ 023-511070; www.inthirahotel.com; Th Luang Prabang; standard/superior/deluxe incl breakfast US$32/43/54; ❂ ❄ @ 🔊 ✈) An oasis of ox-blood red rooms with oblique views of the karsts, Inthira has hardwood floors, upscale furniture, elegant art, bedside lamps and modern, spotless en suites. The restaurant is cool and leafy. Staff are professional.

Elephant Crossing HOTEL $$
(☑ 023-511232; www.theelephantcrossinghotel.com; r 350,000-650,000K; P ❄ @ 🔊 ✈) Set in leafy gardens with an attractive verandah to take breakfast by the river, Elephant has 36 tasteful rooms with glass-panels, spotless en suites, and the whitest of walls. Hmong bed runners, wood floors, air-con, TV and fridge complete the bargain. Ask for a river view.

Thavonsouk Resort HOTEL $$
(☑ 023-511096; www.thavonsouk.com; r incl breakfast 250,000-450,000K; P ❄ @ 🔊 ✈) Beautiful wood-accented rooms burst with light, enjoy full-frontal views of the karsts, and come with waffle quilts, antique beds and the scent of freshly applied beeswax. There's a tempting restaurant, too.

⭐ **Riverside Boutique Resort** BOUTIQUE HOTEL $$$
(☑ 021-511726; www.riversidevangvieng.com; by the toll bridge; r US$123-150; P ❂ ❄ @ 🔊 ✈) Sugar-white and uber-stylish, this beautiful boutique belle is wrapped around a citrus-green pool and garden that looks out onto the karsts. Rooms are gorgeous, with balconies, crisp white sheets, and chic decor. En-

joy a cocktail in the restaurant – if you can tear yourself from the sparkling pool.

🏠 Over the River & Out of Town

Maylyn Guest House GUESTHOUSE $
(☑ 020 5560 4095; jophus_foley@hotmail.com; r 50,000-80,000K; P ❄ 🔊 ✈) Maylyn is a stalwart of peace, has cosy, well-spaced cabanas set in lush gardens and affords possibly the most dramatic views of the karsts. There's a new building with immaculate en suite rooms, a maze of nooks for kids to play in, a pond and a cafe to read in.

Chez Mango GUESTHOUSE $
(☑ 020 5443 5747; www.chezmango.com; r 50,000-70,000K; ❄) Mango is friendly, scrupulously clean and has seven basic but colourful cabanas (some with bathrooms) in its flowery gardens. Run by friendly Frenchman Noé, this makes for a very restful spot. Breakfast is available. He also runs Vang Vieng Jeep Tours (p292) from here. Recommended.

⭐ **Phoudindaeng Organic Farm** GUESTHOUSE $
(☑ 023-511220; www.laofarm.org; dm 30,000K, r 40,000-150,000K, deluxe cliff-facing bungalows 200,000K; P @ 🔊 ✈) 🌿 A few kilometres out of town, by the Nam Song, bungalows here front the soaring cliffs and are sparklingly

clean with mosquito nets, bedside lamps, en suites and verandahs. Up the hill are three eight-bed fan-cooled dorms. There's also a great restaurant – try the mulberry pancakes or mulberry mojitos!

If you have time, ask about volunteering for the permaculture program. There are also art classes for local kids at the weekend and stone painting if you want to lend a hand. Cooking classes here cost US$30.

✕ Eating

Vang Vieng isn't exactly Luang Prabang, but a couple of decent restaurants have recently opened. You'll also find quality restaurants at the top-end hotels.

★ Living Room   ASIAN $
(☑020 5491 9169; next to Champa Lao Guesthouse; ⊗3-11pm) Classy new cafe with a funky sundowner terrace where you can enjoy amazing karst views and a Lao – wait for it – Austrian fusion menu. Fresh juices, shakes (10,000K), soups, tofu, pork schnitzel and really inventive dishes such as spaghetti Vang Vieng – a kind of bolognese meet spicy *làhp* salad. Delicious.

★ The Kitchen   INTERNATIONAL $
(www.inthira.com; Inthira Hotel, Th Luang Prabang; mains 30,000K; ⊗7am-10pm; ☞☑) Striking a fine balance between informality and style, the Kitchen's often packed to the gills and once you've netted the coconut shrimp and steamed fish, you'll understand why. Kitchen also serves pizza, ribs and pasta dishes.

Le Café De Paris   FRENCH $
(mains 20,000-30,000K; ⊗5.30-11.30pm) This place is celebrated for its steak tartare, boeuf bourguignon and hot dog Parisien. A number of red and white wines on the menu, plus the homely decor and friendly, low-lit ambience, make this a worthwhile haunt.

Nam Song Garden   ASIAN FUSION $
(☑023-511 544; ⊗7am-11pm; ☞) This al fresco restaurant makes for a romantic stop from which to gaze at the jagged karsts. The menu is pretty varied, spanning barbecued fish, chicken and meat dishes: breakfasts, *làhp* variations and sweet-and-sour dishes. At the very least pop in here for a sunset cocktail (mojitos 30,000K).

♀ Drinking & Nightlife

Fluid Bar   BAR
(☑020 5929 5840; ☞) Within its riverside walls are original trippy art, mosaics, a relaxing balcony bar, pool table, cool tunes, great grub, a crazy golf course, and a vibrant garden with sun loungers and hammocks. Out of town.

Gary's Irish Bar   IRISH PUB
(☑020 5825 5774; mains 35,000K; ⊗9am-midnight) This is a cool, easy joint to while away an evening listening to indie tunes, playing pool or watching sports on the box. Great full breakfasts, homemade pies and happy hour from 6pm to 10pm.

Kangaroo Sunset Bar   BAR
(☑020 771 4291; mains 35,000K; ⊗8am-11.30pm; ☞) Colourful lanterns and chilled rock and jazz complement a menu of Lao and Western cuisine. It's also well placed for meditative sunset beers by the river.

❶ Information

Visitors die every year from river accidents and while caving, so take care. Theft can also be a problem, with fellow travellers often the culprits.

Despite the 2012 clean up, dope is still around and local police are adept at sniffing out spliffs. If you're caught with a stash of marijuana (or anything else), the normal practice is for police to take your passport and fine you US$500.

Agricultural Promotion Bank (Th Luang Prabang) Exchanges cash only.

BCEL (☑023-511434; Th Luang Prabang; ⊗8.30am-3.30pm) Exchanges cash and travellers cheques, and handles cash advances. Has two ATMs in town.

Post Office (☑023-511009) Beside the old market.

Provincial Hospital (☑023-511604) Has X-ray facilities and is fine for broken bones, cuts and malaria. When we visited, the doctor spoke reasonable English.

Tourist Office (☑023-511707; Th Luang Prabang; ⊗8am-noon, 2-4pm) A useful place to pick up various leaflets on things to do in the local area.

❶ Getting There & Away

From the **bus station** (Rte 13), 2km north of town, minibuses/VIP buses leave for Luang Prabang (110,000/130,00K, six to eight hours, 168km, several daily), Vientiane (fan/minibus/air-con 40,000/60,000/80,000K, three to 4½ hours, 156km, several daily) and Phonsavan

(100,000K, minibus only, six to seven hours, 219km, daily at about 9.30am).

Alternatively, *sŏrngtăaou* (30,000K, 3½ to 4½ hours) leave about every 20 minutes from 5.30am until 4.30pm, and as they're often not full the ride can be quite enjoyable.

Tickets for minibuses and VIP buses are sold at guesthouses, tour agencies and internet cafes in town.

❶ Getting Around

The township is small enough to walk around with ease. Bicycles/mountain bikes can be rented for around 10,000/30,000K a day, while scooters rent for 50,000K per day (automatics cost 70,000K). For cave sites out of town you can charter *sŏrngtăaou* near the old market site – expect to pay around US$10 per trip up to 20km north or south of town.

NORTHERN LAOS

Whether you're here to trek, ride elephants, zip-line, kayak, cycle or try a homestay, a visit to northern Laos is for many the highlight of their Southeast Asian trip. Bordered by China to the far north, Vietnam to the east and Myanmar to the west, there's a fascinating cast of ethnic peoples whose rustic, tribal beliefs are a world away from the Thai-influenced urbanites of Vientiane. Hidden amid this rugged simplicity is Southeast Asia's premier Shangri La, Luang Prabang; with its chic restaurants, photogenic temples and revitalised French villas it's something of an architectural phenomenon. Beyond it are unfettered, dense forests still home to tigers, gibbons and a cornucopia of animals, with a well-established ecotourism framework to take you to their very heart.

Luang Prabang

ຫລວງ ພະ ບາງ

☑ 071 / POP 70,000

This Unesco-protected gem of 33 Buddhist temples is a traveller's dream, with affordable, top-class cuisine and French colonial buildings. There are few places in Southeast Asia that can compete with such a special mix of chic refinement and ancient charm as found on Luang Prabang's hallowed peninsula. The good news is the best things are cheap or free: hiring a bike, chilling by the riverbank, temple-hopping, shopping in the night market, taking a spa or yoga class, and visiting the menthol-blue cascades of Kuang Si. Spend a little more and you can ecotrek, elephant ride or take a cooking course – your choices really are myriad.

The ghosts of the French colonials endure as freshly baked croissants exude aromas from Gallic-style cafes, and old Indochinese mansions are reborn as boutique hotels. Prepare to relax and replot your itinerary: Luang Prabang will effortlessly seduce you.

◉ Sights

Most of the tourist sights are in the old quarter on the peninsula bounded by the Mekong and Nam Khan rivers. Dominating the centre of town, Phu Si is an unmissable landmark. The majority of restaurants, accommodation, tour companies and internet cafes line and radiate from Th Sisavangvong, while additional bars are to be found on Th Kingkitsarat.

★ Royal Palace Museum   MUSEUM
(ພະທາຊະວ້ງຊວງແກວ; Ho Kham; Map p298; ☑ 071 212470; Th Sisavangvong; admission 30,000K; ☺ 8-11.30am & 1.30-4pm Wed-Mon, last entry 3.30pm) The former Royal Palace, built in 1904, was the main residence of King Sisavang Vong (r 1905–59) whose statue stands outside. Note that you must be 'appropriately dressed' to enter, which means no sleeveless shirts or short shorts.

The main palace building is approached from the south. Italian marble steps lead into an entry hall where the centrepiece is the gilded dais of the former Supreme Patriarch of Lao Buddhism. To the right, the king's reception room has walls covered in Gauguinesque canvases of Lao life. A line of centuries-old Khamu metal drums leads back to the main throne room, where the golden trimmed walls are painted deep red and encrusted with a feast of mosaic-work in Japanese coloured mirror glass.

Behind the throne room are the former royal family's residential quarters, left as they were when King Savang Vatthana was forcibly evicted by the communist regime in 1975.

Beneath, but entered from the western side, is a series of exhibition halls used for temporary exhibits. Separate outbuildings display the **Floating Buddha** (Map p298) collection of meditation photographs, and the five-piece **Royal Palace Car Collection** (Map p298), including two 1960s Lincoln Continentals, a rare wing-edged 1958 Edsel Citation, and a dilapidated Citroën DS.

Luang Prabang

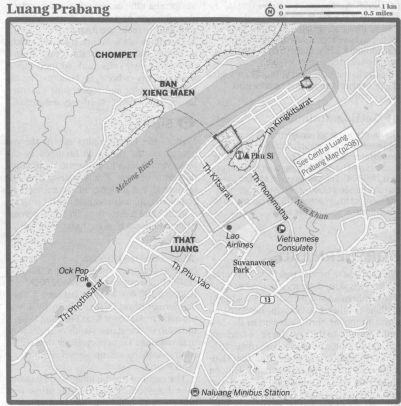

No single treasure in Laos is more histori-cally resonant than the **Pha Bang** (ພະບາງ; Map p298), an 83cm-tall gold-alloy Buddha for which the whole city is named. Its arrival here in 1512 spiritually legitimised the Lan Xang royal dynasty as Buddhist rulers. The Siamese twice carried the Pha Bang off to Thailand (in 1779 and 1827) but it was final-ly restored to Laos by King Mongkut (Rama IV) in 1867. Nearing completion in the southeast corner of the palace gardens, **Wat Ho Pha Bang** (Map p298) is a soaring, multi-roofed temple designed to eventually house the Pha Bang Buddha. For now, however, the Pha Bang lives in an easy-to-miss little room surrounded by engraved elephant tusks and three silk screens embroidered by the former queen. To find it, walk east along the palace's exterior south terrace and peep in between the bars at the eastern end.

Footwear cannot be worn inside the mu-seum, no photography is permitted and you must leave bags in a locker room to the left-hand side of the main entrance.

★ **Phu Si**   HILL

(ພູສີ; Map p298; admission 20,000K; ⊗8am-6pm) A favourite with sunset junkies, the unmiss-able 100m-tall hill of Phu Si is crowned by a 24m gilded stupa called **That Chomsi** (Map p298). Viewed from a distance, especially when floodlit at night, the structure seems to float in the hazy air.

Ascending Phu Si from the north side (329 steps), stop at the decaying **Wat Pa Huak** (Map p298; admission by donation). It has a splendid carved wood Buddha riding Aira-vata, the three-headed elephant from Hindu mythology, and original 19th-century mu-rals in its interior.

Reaching That Chomsi is also possible from the south and east sides. Two such paths climb through large **Wat Siphout-thabat Thippharam** (Map p298) to a curious miniature shrine that protects a **Buddha Footprint** (Map p298) `FREE`. Directly southwest of here a series of new gilded Buddhas are nestled into rocky clefts and niches around **Wat Thammothayalan** (Map p298). The monastery is free to visit if you don't climb beyond to That Chomsi.

★**Wat Xieng Thong**   BUDDHIST TEMPLE
(ວັດຊຽງທອງ; Map p298; off Th Sakkarin; admission 20,000K; ⊗8am-5pm) Luang Prabang's best-known monastery is centred on a 1560 *sǐm* (chapel). Its roofs sweep low to the ground and there's an idiosyncratic 'tree of life' mosaic set on its west exterior wall. Inside, gold stencil work includes dharma wheels on the ceiling and exploits from the life of legendary King Chanthaphanit on the walls.

Dotted around the *sǐm* are several stupas and three compact little chapel halls called *hǎw*. Haw Tai, shaped like a tall tomb, was originally a 'library' but now houses a standing Buddha. The Haw Pa Maan ('success' Buddha sanctuary) remains locked except during the week following Pi Mai. The Haw Tai Pha Sai-nyaat (reclining Buddha sanctuary) was dubbed La Chapelle Rouge – Red Chapel – by the French. It contains an especially rare reclining Buddha that dates from the construction of the temple.

Fronted in especially lavish gilt work, the Hohng Kep Mien is a garage for a ceremonial carriage, designed to carry the huge golden funeral urns of the Lao royalty. This glittering vehicle is festooned with seven red-tongued *naga* snakes.

Wat Wisunarat   BUDDHIST TEMPLE
(ວັດວິຊຸນ; Wat Visoun; Map p298; Th Wisunarat; admission 20,000K; ⊗8am-5pm) Though touted as one of Luang Prabang's oldest operating temples it's actually an 1898 reconstruction of the 1513 original, which was destroyed following Black Flag raids. Peruse the collection of gilded 'Calling for Rain' Buddhas placed here, alongside some medieval ordination stones, for their protection having been rescued from various abandoned or ravaged temples.

★**TAEC**   MUSEUM
(Traditional Arts & Ethnology Centre; Map p298; ☑071-253364; www.teaclaos.org; admission 20,000K; ⊗9am-6pm Tue-Sun) Visiting this professionally presented three-room museum is a must for learning about northern Laos' various hill tribes, especially if planning a trek. There's just enough to inform without overloading a beginner. If you want more information, watch the video or ask to leaf through the books of a small library cabinet in the museum's delightful cafe. TAEC is within a former French judge's mansion, which was among the city's most opulent buildings of the 1920s.

🏃 **Activities**

The best way to really explore the city is by bike, meandering through the peninsula past scenes of monastic life and children playing. Once you've got your bearings, head out beyond Talat Phosy, toward the Kuang Si waterfalls and through some particularly spectacular scenery. Basic/mountain bikes cost 15,000/30,000K per day and can be hired along Th Sisavangvong. For easier journeys, automatic one-gear scooters cost around US$20 per day. Motorcycle rental typically costs US$15 a day or US$20 for 24 hours. **KPTD** (Map p298; ☑071-253447; Th Kitsarat) has a wide range of scooters as well as a Honda CRF (US$65) for motocross riders only.

Luang Prabang is also about pampering, and what better way to ease those trekked-out muscles than sampling the city's affordable spa parlours. Try a basic herbal sauna, or a traditional Lao, Swedish or hot-stone massage (to name a few).

Some of the most popular activities in Luang Prabang are based in the countryside beyond, including trekking, cycling and kayaking tours. Another popular activity is

---

RESPECT THE BAT

The Tak Bat, when apprentice monks form a line down Luang Prabang's Th Sisavangvong to receive alms at dawn, has become a cause for concern. In their hunger for a photogenic keepsake, some Western visitors consider it OK to get uncomfortably close to the monks during this ancient and solemn ceremony. Consider these basic courtesies: observe the ritual in silence and at a respectful distance; only make an offering if it means something personal to you and the food is fresh; and do not make physical contact with the monks or talk to them. Finally, do not follow the monks.

LAOS LUANG PRABANG

Central Luang Prabang

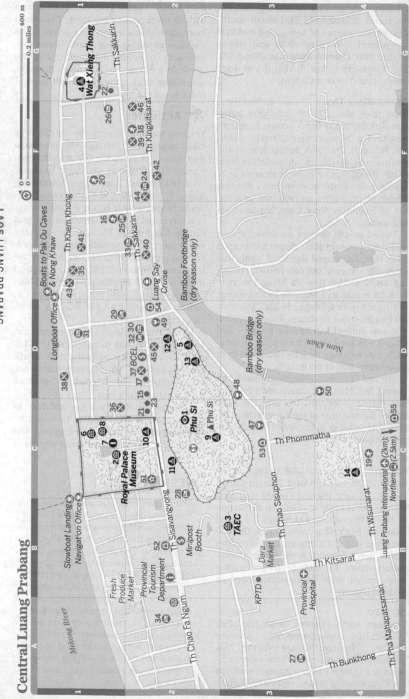

0   0   400 m
0   0.2 miles

Central Luang Prabang

visiting one of the elephant camps beyond town and learning the art of the mahout (elephant trainer) for a day or more.

Luang Prabang Yoga YOGA
(Map p298; ☑020 2388 1771; www.luangprabang yoga.org; Utopia Bar, off Th Phommatha; 30,000K per hr; ⊙7.30am-8.30am Thu-Fri & Sun-Tue, 5.30pm-6.30pm Tue, Thu & Sat; ☏⊕) Based in the lush riverside gardens of Utopia bar, there are daily sessions to clear your cocktail haze and sync your spirit with the city's Buddhist vibe.

Spa Garden MASSAGE, SPA
(Map p298; ☑071-212325; massage 60,000-350,000K, sauna/manicure 30,000/60,000K) Attractive property in a flourishing garden, with various relaxation and detox packages.

Hibiscus Massage MASSAGE
(Map p298; ☑030 923 5079; Th Sakkarin; traditional massage from 60,000K; ⊙10am-10pm) Set in a former gallery in an old French building, Hibiscus wafts chilled tunes through its silk-draped walls while you get pummelled to perfection.

Lao Red Cross MASSAGE, SPA
(Map p298; ☑071-253448; Th Wisunarat; massage 10,000-50,000K; ⊙7am-10.30pm) In traditional (basic!) surroundings of wood rafters, cool fans and stone floors, sample a range of head and body massages, steams, reflexology and aromatherapy. Donations go directly to improving the lives of the poorest villages in Laos.

⚑ Courses

Tamarind COOKING
(Map p298; ☎020 7777 0484; www.tamarind laos.com; Ban Wat Nong; full-day course 270,000K; ◉9am-3pm Mon-Sat) Join Tamarind at its lakeside pavilion for a day's tuition in the art of Lao cuisine, meeting first at its restaurant, before heading to the market for ingredients for classic dishes such as *mok 'bah* (steamed fish in banana leaves). Evening classes are available from 4pm for 200,000K, but there is no market visit included.

**Tum Tum Cheng
Cooking School** COOKING
(Map p298; ☎071-253388; 29/2 Th Sakkarin; full-day course incl cookbook 250,000K) Celebrated chef Chandra teaches you the secrets of his alchemy. Includes a visit to the market to select your vegetables. The day usually starts at 8.30am at the school on the peninsula and finishes at 2pm.

Ock Pop Tok WEAVING
(Map p296; ☎071-212597; www.ockpoptok.com; full-/half-day course US$72/42; ◉8.45am-4pm Mon-Sat) Learn to weave your own scarf and textiles with OckPopTok's classes, as well as its half-day bamboo weaving (US$18). Teachers are master craftspeople, you get to keep your handiwork, and lunch is included. Situated 2km past Phousy market; a free túk-túk will pick you up and take you back.

⚑ Tours

If you have a few days in town, whimsical Tat Kuang Si waterfalls and Pak Ou Caves are well worth a visit. There's a plethora of tour companies down Th Sisavangvong. We recommend **All Lao Travel** (Map p298; ☎071-253522; Th Sisavangvong; ◉8am-10pm) as a one-stop shop for flights, boat and VIP-bus tickets, and visa extensions.

The following operators are good for trekking, rafting, elephant riding and cycling excursions.

Green Discovery ADVENTURE TOURS
(Map p298; ☎071-212093; www.greendiscovery-laos.com; 44/3 Th Sisavangvong) The daddy of ecotourism in Laos offers kayaking, trekking, mountain biking, motorcycling and multiday trips, including motorcycle tours.

Tiger Trail HIKING
(Map p298; ☎071-252655; www.laos-adventures. com; Th Sisavangvong; ◉8.30am-9pm) ⚑ Focusing on socially responsible fair treks benefitting local people, Tiger Trail offers hikes through Hmong and Khamu villages. All tours can be tailored to include kayaking, elephant riding, rafting or mountain biking.

White Elephant HIKING
(Map p298; ☎071-254481; www.white-elephant-adventures-laos.com; Th Sisavangvong) ⚑ White Elephant is hailed for its relationships with remote Hmong and Khamu villages, allowing a deeper insight into ethnic life. You can do this on a trek or by cycle in solid two- and three-day tours. Look out for the BMW motorbike and communist flag.

⚑ Festivals & Events

The two most important annual events in Luang Prabang are **Pii Mai** (Lao or Lunar New Year) in April, when the town is packed to the gills with locals armed with water pistols (book accommodation well in advance), and **Bun Awk Phansa** (End of the Rains Retreat), which sees boat races in October.

⚑ Sleeping

Digs vary from basic guesthouses to five-star hotels and achingly perfect boutique hotels. The most atmospheric place to stay is undoubtedly on the peninsula.

Rates given here are for the high season (October to March). Prices briefly climb higher for Pii Mai (mid-April) and Christmas, but typically fall at least 25% from May.

Paphai Guest House GUESTHOUSE $
(Map p298; ☎071-212752; Th Sisavang Vatthana; r without bathroom 50,000-60,000K; ☎) This place is as cheap and basic as it gets in the old town. Rooms are set in a traditional wooden house near the heart of Th Sisavangvong, and are fan-cooled, rattan-walled and have padlocks on the doors.

Silichit Guest House GUESTHOUSE $
(Map p298; ☎071-212758; Th Sisavang Vatthana; r 80,000-120,000K; ❄☎) A popular place, with boxy, basic rooms finished in traditional Lao style. It's the location that wins you over as it is in the heart of the old town near the Mekong. Try for rooms 4 and 6 upstairs.

Sackarinh Guest House GUESTHOUSE $
(Map p298; ☎071-254412; Th Sisavangvong; r 120,000-150,000K; ❄☎) Hidden down a sidestreet that chokes with flowers, this is a colourful and central option while you get your bearings. Rooms are basic but spacious.

Nora Singh Guesthouse GUESTHOUSE $
(Map p298; ☎071-212033; Th Sisavangvong; r 130,000K; ❄️📶) Tucked away in the lower reaches of Phu Si, this is a likeable little wooden home with just seven guest rooms, which include air-con, hot water and free wi-fi. It feels quite secluded when compared to the main drag, but is just a short stumble away.

★**Xayana Guesthouse** GUESTHOUSE $
(Map p298; ☎071-260680; www.mylaohome. com; Th Hoxieng; dm 40,000K, r from 80,000K; 📶) This budget pad has immaculately clean dorms, with three bathrooms to every eight beds. There's an inviting courtyard out front to hang out, drink coffee and meet other travellers.

Lemon Laos Backpackers HOSTEL $
(Map p298; ☎071-212500; Th Noradet; dm 30,000K; 📶) One of the cheapest crashpads in town, travellers aren't really here for the beds, but to avoid going to bed, as it rumbles on into the early hours. Barbecues and cheap shots add up to a carnival atmosphere.

★**Khoum Xiengthong Guesthouse** GUESTHOUSE $$
(Map p298; ☎071-212906; www.khoumxieng thong.com; Th Sisalernsak; r US$50-70; ❄️📶) Bedecked in tea lights by night, this guesthouse evokes a strong whiff of Indo-chic and nestles around a pretty garden. Stone-floored, white-walled rooms enjoy tapestries and chrome fans; rooms 2 (lower floor) and 5 (upper floor) are vast and include four-poster beds.

Thanaboun Guesthouse GUESTHOUSE $$
(Map p298; ☎071-260606; Th Sisavangvong; r 160,000-280,000K; ❄️@📶) In the heart of town, Thanaboun excels with clean, tastefully finished rooms. Those backing on to the temple grounds are quieter. There's also an internet cafe.

★**Apsara** BOUTIQUE HOTEL $$$
(Map p298; ☎071-254670; www.theapsara.com; Th Kingkitsarat; r incl breakfast US$70-130; ❄️📶) Apsara commands fine views of the sleepy Nam Khan. Its Indochinese lobby is peppered with silk lanterns, and the bar is straight out of an old classic film, while each of the open-plan rooms is individual and artfully designed. From its turquoise walls to its coloured glass Buddhas, everything about this place screams style.

★**Auberge les 3 Nagas** BOUTIQUE HOTEL $$$
(Map p298; ☎071 253888; www.3-nagas.com; Th Sakkarin; r from US$200; ❄️@📶) Bookended by mango trees and a burgundy 1950s Mercedes, this 100-year-old Lao-style building brims with old-world atmosphere (across the road is another wing). Palatial suites sport sink-to-sleep four-poster beds, tannedwood bathrooms and a modern Asian design that fuses with colonial French roots. The service is warmth itself.

Villa Santi HISTORIC HOTEL $$$
(Map p298; ☎071-252157; www.villasantihotel.com; Th Sakkarin; r US$128-288; ❄️📶🏊) This striking old royal building has three very different personalities. The original 19th-century villa, once home to King Sisavang Vong's wife, has just six vast 'royal' suites, plus an upstairs breakfast room with an enviable road-view terrace. Many 'deluxe' (ie standard) rooms are in a central annexe behind.

🍴 Eating

Munching your way through a spectrum of Gallic, international and Lao cuisine is part of the Luang Prabang experience. If you're hankering for a snack of local noodles or fire-grilled meat, head for the night food stalls down Th Chao Phanya Kang. Many of the better restaurants – especially French – are further down the peninsula.

For fresh Mekong fish and delicious local fare, head for one of the many riverside restaurants on Th Khem Khong.

Quick, cheap eats are to be found courtesy of the baguette vendors opposite the tourist office from early morning till sunset.

BIG BROTHER MOUSE

If you want to get involved in improving local literacy, seek out **Big Brother Mouse** (BBM; Map p298; ☎071-254937; www.bigbrothermouse.com; Th Sothiku-man), a home-grown initiative that brings the delights of the written word to infants in remote villages who, for lack of materials, rarely get the chance to read. If a bunch of you sponsor a book party (US$350), you can go with the BBM staff and distribute books. Alternatively, hang out at the BBM office for a couple of hours and read to the kids who attend.

On the Peninsula

★ Le Banneton
BAKERY $

(Map p298; Th Sakkarin; meals 20,000-40,000K; ☺6.30am-6pm; 🛜) Offering the best croissants in Laos, this peaceful cafe is celebrated by pastry buffs. It has a sweet-toothed menu of *pain au chocolat,* fruit shakes, sandwiches, quiches and homemade sorbets.

★ Le Patio
LAOTIAN, INTERNATIONAL $

(Map p298; ☐071-253364; TAEC; sandwiches 30,000K; ☺9am-5.45pm Tue-Sun; 🛜) Sip Phongsali-smoked teas or Lao Arabica espressos and nibble delicious feta-olive baguette sandwiches on a shaded terrace with attractive mountain views. Ethnic minority dishes, such as Akha meatballs and Hmong pork belly, are also available.

Le Café Ban Vat Sene
FRENCH $

(Map p298; Th Sakkarin; mains 30,000K; ☺7.30am-10pm; 🛜) Retro fans whir over an Indochinese scene of flower-shaded lights and stylish refinement. This is the place to work, sip an afternoon pastis and read a paper. French wine, salads, quiche, pasta and pizza...*parfait!*

Xieng Thong Noodle-Shop
LAOTIAN $

(Map p298; Th Sakkarin; noodle soup 15,000K; ☺from 6.30am) The best *kòw ḅeeak sèn* (round rice noodles served in a broth with pieces of chicken or deep-fried crispy pork belly) in town is served from an entirely unexotic shopfront well up the peninsula. Stocks are usually finished by 2pm.

★ Coconut Garden
LAOTIAN, INTERNATIONAL $$

(Map p298; ☐071-260436; Th Sisavangvong; meals 35,000-150,000K; ☺8am-11pm; 🛜🍴) An excellent 100,000K vegetarian set meal provides five top-quality Lao dishes, which allows a single diner to sample the subtle palate of flavours that you'd normally only get from a multiperson feast. International favourites are also available.

Tangor
FUSION $$

(Map p298; ☐071-260761; www.letangor.com; Th Sisavangvong; mains 40,000-80,000K; ☺11am-10pm; 🛜) A gastronomic addition to the Luang Prabang dining scene, Tangor serves beautifully crafted fusion food, blending the best of Lao produce with French flair.

Blue Lagoon
INTERNATIONAL $$

(Map p298; www.blue-lagoon-restaurant.com; mains 75,000-140,000K; ☺10am-10pm; 🛜) A favourite with expats for its lantern-festooned walls, leafy patio and jazz-infused atmosphere. The menu features Luang Prabang sausage, pasta, salads and very tasty *làhp.*

★ L'Elephant Restaurant
FRENCH $$$

(Map p298; www.elephant-restau.com; Ban Wat Nong; mains 80,000-250,000K; ☺11.30am-10pm) The most sophisticated cuisine in the city is found in a renovated villa with wooden floors, stucco pillars, stencilled ochre walls and bags of atmosphere. The Menu du Chasseur (240,000K) includes terrines, soups, duck breast and other Gallic specialities. The buffalo steak tartare is amazing.

Peninsula Riverfronts

Big Tree Café
KOREAN, INTERNATIONAL $

(Map p298; www.bigtreecafe.com; Th Khem Khong; mains 25,000-50,000K; ☺9am-9pm; 🛜) Mouthwatering Korean food. Eat in the cafe – which is full of Adri Berger's alluring Lao photography – or outside on the sun terrace overlooking the Mekong. There's also a choice of Western and Japanese dishes.

Rosella Fusion
FUSION $

(Map p298; Th Kingkitsarat; mains 15,000-35,000K) Established by a former Amantaka bartender, this riverside restaurant offers an innovative selection of affordable fusion flavours. The owner is particularly proud of his bargain cocktails, so consider dropping by for a sundowner before dinner.

Khemkhong View Restaurant
LAOTIAN $

(Map p298; Th Khem Khong; meals 15,000-35,000K; ☺7am-9pm) Split-level Khemkhong View has an extensive menu with choices such as spicy prawn and coconut soup, squid *làhp* (or intestine *làhp* for the more adventurous) and steamed, fermented fish.

Saffron
CAFE $

(Map p298; Th Khem Khong; mains 20,000-35,000K; ☺7am-9pm; 🛜) Perfect for breakfasts, this stylish cafe, hung with lush black-and-white photography, turns out great pasta dishes, serves excellent coffee and has warm service. There's also a choice of interior and al fresco dining.

★ Tamarind
LAOTIAN $$

(Map p298; ☐071-213128; www.tamarindlaos.com; Th Kingkitsarat; mains 25,000-60,000K, set dinners 100,000-150,000K; ☺11am-10pm; 🛜) Chic Tamarind has created its very own strain of 'Mod Lao' cuisine. The à la carte menu boasts delicious sampling platters with bamboo dip, stuffed lemongrass and *meuyang* (DIY parcels of noodles, herbs, fish and chilli pastes, and vegetables).

🍷 Drinking

Mercifully, the ancient city is insulated by an 11.30pm curfew. That said, the following do their valiant best to squeeze as much hedonistic juice from the restrictions as possible.

★ Ikon Klub   BAR
(Map p298; Th Sisavang Vatthana; ⊙5pm-late; 🛜) Ikon is true bohemian, from its shadowy 1930s decor hung with objets d'art and prints of old Hollywood starlets, to the charming Hungarian poetess who runs it. The best mojitos are mixed here, the Bloody Marys are full of vigour, and it makes for a great spot to meet others while listening to cool tunes.

If Bukowski and Bergman were bars and sired a lovechild, it might have looked something like this. Surely the best bar in Laos.

Hive Bar   BAR
(Map p298; Th Kingkitsarat; 🛜) The buzz is back at this stylish den of hidden coves. Out back in the garden there's a dance floor, projector wall and more tables. Check out the excellent ethnic fashion show every night at 7pm, which also features a hip-hop crew. Tapas, happy hour and cocktails.

Utopia   BAR
(Map p298; 🛜) Utopia is all recliner cushions, low-slung tables and hookah pipes. It sounds wrong but works perfectly. Chill over a fruit shake, play a board game or volleyball, or lose yourself in a sea of candles come sunset. Yoga by day, bar snacks by night, this place pulls in the backpacker crowd.

House   BAR
(Map p298; Th Kingkitsarat; 🛜) Fairy-lit House is a tempting stop for a Belgian beer, including Chimay and Duvel. The gardens are pretty, and the snacks and breakfasts are delicious, including *stoofvlees* (beef stew).

☆ Entertainment

Phrolak-Phralam Theatre   TRADITIONAL DANCE
(Map p298; Royal Palace Grounds; tickets 70,000-170,000K; ⊙shows 6pm or 6.30pm Mon, Wed, Fri & Sat) The misleadingly named Royal Lao Ballet puts on slow-moving traditional dances accompanied by a 10-piece Lao 'orchestra'.

Performances last about 1¼ hours and include a Ramayana-based scene. It's worth reading the notes provided at the entrance to have an idea of what's going on.

🛍 Shopping

Handicraft Night Market   MARKET
(Map p298; Th Sisavangvong; ⊙5.30-10pm) Every evening this market assembles along Th Sisavangvong from the Royal Palace Museum to T Kitsarat, and is one of Luang Prabang's biggest tourist lures. Low-lit and quiet, it's devoid of hard selling with tens of dozens of traders selling silk scarves and wall hangings, plus Hmong appliqué blankets, T-shirts, clothing, shoes, silver, bags, ceramics, bamboo lamps and more.

Big Tree Gallery   GALLERY
(Map p298; 🖉071-212262; Th Khem Khong; ⊙9am-10pm) Photographer Adri Berger's compositions of rural Lao are exquisite; nobody captures Laos' honeyed 'magic hour' light like him. His gallery-cum-Korean restaurant has a range of his work on the walls, with prints starting at an affordable US$100.

Pathana Boupha Antique House   ANTIQUES
(Map p298; Th Phommatha) Follow the sweeping stairs in the garden of this impressive old French mansion to discover an Aladdin's cave of antique Buddhas, golden *naga*, silver betel-nut pots, Akha-style bracelets and Hmong necklaces. Also sells fine silk scarves from Sam Neua.

Ock Pop Tok   CLOTHING, HANDICRAFTS
(Map p200; 🖉071 254406; Th Sisavangvong; ⊙8am-9pm) OckPopTok works with a wide range of different tribes to preserve their handicraft traditions. Fine silk and cotton scarves, chemises, dresses, wall hangings and cushion covers make perfect presents.

L'Etranger Books & Tea   BOOKS
(Map p298; Th Kingkitsarat; ⊙8am-10pm Mon-Sat, 10am-10pm Sun) The cheapest spot for secondhand travel books and thrillers. Upstairs there's a comfy lounge-lizard cafe in which to read them. Films shown nightly.

ℹ Information

INTERNET ACCESS
Most cafes and restaurants now offer free wi-fi. Internet cafes are peppered along Th Sisavangvong and charge 100K per minute.

MEDICAL SERVICES

There are plenty of pharmacies in the centre of town.

Provincial Hospital (Map p298; ☑ 071-254025; Ban Naxang; doctor's consultation 100,000K) OK for minor problems but for any serious illnesses consider flying to Bangkok or returning to Vientiane and neighbouring hospitals across the Thai border. Note that the hospital in Luang Prabang charges double for consultations at weekends or anytime after 4pm.

MONEY

BCEL (Map p298; Th Sisavangvong; ☺8.30am-3.30pm Mon-Sat) Changes major currencies in cash or travellers cheques, has a 24-hour ATM and offers cash advances against Visa and MasterCard.

Minipost Booth (Map p298; Th Sisavangvong; ☺7.45am-8.30pm, cash advances 9am-3pm) Changes most major currencies at fair rates and is open daily. After 6pm it's easy to miss, hidden behind market stalls.

POST

Post Office (Map p298; Th Chao Fa Ngum; ☺8.30am-3.30pm Mon-Fri, to noon Sat) Phone calls and Western Union facilities.

TELEPHONE

Most internet cafes in town have Skype and can offer international calls at 2000K per minute or less.

The Minipost Booth (p304) sells mobile-phone SIM cards.

TOURIST INFORMATION

Provincial Tourism Department (Map p298; www.tourismlaos.com; Th Sisavangvong; ☺8am-4pm Mon-Fri) General information on festivals, ethnic groups, maps and leaflets, plus information on buses and boats. Staff speak limited English.

ⓘ Getting There & Away

AIR

Around 4km from the city centre, **Luang Prabang International Airport** (☑ 071-212 173) is decidedly modest, though big expansion plans are afoot. For Bangkok (from US$190, 100 minutes), **Bangkok Airways** (Map p298; www.bangkokair.com) and **Lao Airlines** (Map p296; ☑ 071-212 172; www.laoairlines.com; Th Pha Mahapatsaman) both fly twice daily. Lao Airlines also serves Vientiane (US$101, several daily), Pakse (US$182, daily), Chiang Mai (US$150, daily), Hanoi (US$155, daily) and Siem Reap (US$195, daily). **Vietnam Airlines** (☑ 071-213 049; www.vietnamairlines.com) flies to both Siem Reap (codeshare with Lao Airlines) and Hanoi daily.

BOAT

For slowboats to Pak Beng (110,000K, nine hours, 8am), buy tickets from the **navigation office** (Map p298; ☺8-11am & 2-4pm) behind the Royal Palace. Through-tickets to Huay Xai (220,000K, two days) are also available but you'll have to sleep in Pak Beng; curiously it's slightly cheaper to pay the fare to Pak Beng, then buy the onward section there. The main slowboat landing is directly behind the navigation office but departure points can vary according to river levels.

The more upscale **Luang Say Cruise** (Mekong Cruises; Map p298; ☑ 071-254768; www.luangsay.com; 50/4 Th Sakkarin; cruise US$362-491 depending on the season, single supplement from US$67; ☺9.30am-9.30pm) departs on two-trips rides to Huay Xai from the Xieng Thong jetty opposite Wat Xieng Thong. Rates include an overnight stay at the Luang Say Lodge in Pak Beng.

Fast but uncomfortable – and seriously hazardous – six-person **speedboats** can shoot you up the Mekong to Pak Beng (250,000K, three hours) and Huay Xai (400,000K, seven hours). Boats leave from around 8.30am every morning. The jetty is around 5km north of town: turn west off Rte 13 beside the Km 390 post then head 300m down an unpaved road.

Numerous boats for the Pak Ou Caves depart between 8.30am and lunchtime. A single boat to Nong Khiaw (110,000K, six hours) departs around 8.30am assuming enough people have signed up. Buy tickets at the easily missed little **longboat office** (Map p298; Th Khem Khong).

BUS & SŎRNGTĂAOU

Most interprovincial buses and *sŏrngtăaou* heading north depart from the Northern Bus Station, while southbound vehicles use the Southern Bus Station, 3km south of town. On all these routes the durations can vary wildly during monsoonal weather.

A better option is the **Naluang Minibus Station** (Map p296; ☑ 071-212979; souknasing@hotmail.com; Rte 13, 800m past Km 382) – opposite the Southern Bus Station – which runs minibuses to Nong Khiang, Vang Vieng, Phonsavan, Luang Namtha, Hanoi and Kunming. Although you can travel with one or two people and just turn up in the morning, for less than double the bus fare a great option is to gather your own group and rent a comfortable six-seater minivan. Directly booked through the minibus station, prices are about 1,000,000K to Phonsavan or Vang Vieng and 500,000K to Nong Khiaw, including pick-up from your guesthouse.

Sainyabuli

Buses to Sainyabuli (60,000K, three hours) depart the Southern Bus Station at 9am and 2pm.

Vientiane & Vang Vieng
From the Southern Bus Station there are up to 10 daily Vientiane services (express/VIP 130,000/150,000K, nine to 12 hours) via Vang Vieng between 6.30am and 7.30pm. VIP buses leave at 9am. A plethora of morning minibuses to Vang Vieng (105,000K, seven hours) depart from the Naluang Minibus Station.

Udomxai, Luang Namtha, Nong Khiaw & Sam Neua
For Nong Khiaw (40,000K, four hours), 9am minibuses start from Naluang Minibus Station. Alternatively, from the Northern Bus Station use *sŏrngtăaou* (40,000K) at 9am, 11am and 1pm or the 8.30am bus that continues to Sam Neua (140,000K, 17 hours) via Vieng Thong (110,000K, 10 hours). Another Sam Neua–bound bus (from Vientiane) should pull in sometime around 5.30pm.

China, Udomxai, Phonsavan & Luang Namtha
The sleeper bus to Kunming, China (450,000K, 24 hours) departs from the Southern Bus Station at 7am, sometimes earlier. From the Northern Bus Station buses run to Udomxai (55,000K, five hours) at 9am, noon and 4pm, Luang Namtha (90,000K, nine hours) at 9am and Huay Xai (Borkeo, 120,000K, 15 hours) at 5.30pm and a VIP service at 7pm (145,000K).

For Phonsavan (10 hours) there's an 8.30am minibus (95,000K) from Naluang Minibus Station and an 8am bus (ordinary/express 85,000/105,000K, 10 hours) from the Southern Bus Station.

ⓘ Getting Around
From the airport into town, 4km away, jumbos or minitrucks charge a uniform 50,000K per vehicle; up to six can share the ride. In the reverse direction you can usually pay less.

Most of the town is accessible on foot. Jumbos usually ask foreigners for 20,000K a ride. Scooters cost US$15 per day, and mountain/ordinary bikes cost 50,000/20,000K per day.

Around Luang Prabang

Pak Ou Caves   ຖ້ຳປາກອູ
About 25km upstream on the Mekong and at the mouth of the Nam Ou, the dramatic **Pak Ou Caves** (Tham Ting; admission 20,000K) are set into limestone cliffs and are crammed with hundreds of Buddha images, a kind of statue's graveyard where unwanted images are placed. This pantheon of statuary is split into two levels, with the lower being more impressive. A steep, 10-minute climb up dark slippery steps yields a view of the mysterious *naga* vessel. Bring a torch.

Most boat trips stop at small villages along the way, especially **Ban Xang Hai**. Boatmen call this tourist-dominated place 'Whisky Village', as it's known for its free-flowing *lòw-lów* (rice whisky).

Luang Prabang's longboat office sells return boat tickets to Pak Ou (per person/boat 60,000/400,000K return) taking two hours upstream, 1¼ hours back and allowing around an hour at the caves plus 20 minutes at Ban Xang Hay. Departures are most numerous around 8.30am but generally continue all morning. Travel agencies and guesthouses sell the same tickets for a little more, often including a túk-túk transfer.

Tat Kuang Si   ຕາດກວາງຊີ
Tat Kuang Si (or Kuang Si Falls), 32km from the city, is a tonic for sore eyes, with a multitiered cascade tumbling over limestone formations into menthol-green pools below. The waterfall is set in a beautifully lush, well-manicured **public park** (admission 20,000K), and there's nothing more Eden-like than plunging into the turquoise water to cool off after making the vertiginous ascent.

Just past the entrance are enclosures housing cuddly sun bears at the **Tat Kuang Si Bear Rescue Centre** (www.freethebears. org.au) **FREE**. All have been confiscated from poachers and are kept here in preference to releasing them to the same certain fate.

Túk-túk from Luang Prabang typically charge 200,000K for one person, or from 300,000K for several people for the trip out here. Some folks manage to cobble together an impromptu group by meeting fellow travellers beside the baguette sellers' area near the tourist office. Otherwise you can pay 50,000K per person and let an agency organise a shared vehicle.

Luang Prabang Province

Nong Khiaw   ໜອງຢຽວ
♪ 071
Nestled along the riverbank of the Nam Ou and towered over by forest-clad karsts, beautiful Nong Khiaw is a travellers' haven of cafes, soporific guesthouses and plenty of things to keep you busy. Finally, it's exploiting its handsome outdoor potential with a

range of activities thanks to a couple of great tour providers. Relax with a herbal massage, eat at a couple of tasty restaurants, and stand on the old French bridge at dusk when fabulous star shows turn the deep indigo sky into a pointillist canvas.

Note – the opposite side of the river where most guesthouses are based is called Ban Sop Houn.

🏃 Activities

You can walk by yourself to **Tham Pha Tok**, an enormous, many-levelled cave where villagers hid during the Second Indochina War; just be careful heading down the rickety ladder. To get there, head 2.5km east of the bridge then look for a clearly visible cave mouth in the limestone cliff on the right (it's about 100m from the road). Entry costs 5000K, and it's open from 7.30am to 6.30pm.

Tiger Trail   HIKING, CYCLING
(☑071-252655; www.laos-adventures.com; Delilah's Place) 🌿 This ecoconscious outfit has fair treks around the local area, including one-day trips to the '100 waterfalls' (350,000K per person, group of four). A two-day trek through Hmong villages, incorporating a homestay and clay school visit, costs 500,000K per person, based on at least four travellers.

Green Discovery   HIKING, CYCLING
(☑071-810018; www.greendiscoverylaos.com) GD has several treks and various kayaking options, including a three-day paddle-camping expedition to Luang Prabang (from 1,330,000K per person). A one-day trip starting with a longboat ride to Muang Ngoi Neua then paddling back costs 350,000K per person, assuming four participants in two-person kayaks.

Sabai Sabai   MASSAGE
(Ban Sop Houn; body massage 40,000K, steam bath 15,000K) Has a peaceful Zen-style garden in which to restore the spirit and aching limbs.

🛏 Sleeping

In the low season, prices are definitely negotiable. Look out for the new Mandala Ou Resort, newly opened in the second half of 2013.

Namhoun Guesthouse   GUESTHOUSE $
(☑071-810039; bungalows 50,000-100,000K; 🛜) Cheaper bungalows are set around a small garden behind the family house. Better are the riverside bungalows facing the Nam Ou,

but they come at a premium 100,000K. All rooms have mosquito nets and balconies with the compulsory hammock.

Amphai Guesthouse   GUESTHOUSE $
(☑020 5577 3637; Ban Sop Houn; r 60,000K; 🛜) It lacks the riverfront location of some competitors, but the prices more than reflect this. Rooms are spacious and cool, with clean bathrooms and hot water. A new Indian restaurant has just opened in the downstairs courtyard.

⭐**Nong Kiau Riverside**   GUESTHOUSE $$
(☑020 5570 5000; www.nongkiau.com; Ban Sop Houn; s/d incl breakfast 310,000/350,000K; @🛜) Riverside's elegant bungalows are romantically finished with mosquito nets, ambient lighting, wooden floors and woven bedspreads. Each includes an attractively finished bathroom and a balcony for blissful river views of the looming karsts. The restaurant is surprisingly affordable and has breathtaking views.

Pha Xang Resort   HOTEL $$
(☑071-810014; d US$55; 🛜) Pha Xang offers an upscale collection of bungalows in a quiet part of town near the bus station. The views across to the gnarly peaks are spectacular. Bungalows are finished in wood and rattan, and include a spacious bathroom.

🍴 Eating & Drinking

⭐**Coco Home**
Bar & Restaurant   LAOTIAN, INTERNATIONAL $
(mains 15,000-45,000K; 🛜) Located on the main drag of the west bank, this is the liveliest all-rounder in town, offering dining in an attractive garden setting above the boat dock. The menu includes Lao, Thai and international favourites. Movies are screened upstairs nightly.

Deen   INDIAN $
(Ban Sop Houn; mains 20,000-35,000K; ⊙8.30am-10pm; 🛜) A superb little Indian eatery with wood-fired naan bread, moreish tandoori dishes, zesty curries and a homely atmosphere; Deen is always packed. There's also a bank of computers (internet 15,000K per hour, wi-fi is free).

Hive Bar   BAR
(⊙5pm-late) It may not have quite the buzz of the more famous Hive Bar in Luang Prabang, but it is one of the only late-night

spots in town, offering a free *lòw-lów* (Lao whisky) shot to first-timers.

❶ Information

BCEL Has an ATM at the end of the bridge on the Ban Sop Houn side.

Post Office (☺8.30am-5pm) The tiny post office exchanges baht and US dollars at slightly unfavourable rates.

Tourist Information Office Above the boat landing. Rarely open.

❶ Getting There & Away

BOAT

In the high season, boats heading up the Nam Ou to Muang Ngoi Neua (one way 25,000K, 1¼ hours) leave at 11am and 2pm. Tickets can be bought at an office at the bus station. The 11am boat continues to Muang Khua (120,000K, seven hours) for connections to Phongsali and Dien Bien Phu in Vietnam.

Public boats make the five- to eight-hour trip through striking karst scenery to Luang Prabang. With a minimum of 10 people, tickets cost 110,000K per person. If this is not happening you can charter the boat for 1,500,000K.

BUS & SÖRNGTĂAOU

The journey to Luang Prabang is possible in three hours but in reality usually takes at least four. Minibuses or *sorngtăaou* (40,000K) start at around 9am and 11am, plus there's a minivan (50,000K) at 1pm. Tickets are sold at the bus stand but the 11am service actually starts at the boat office, filling up with folks arriving off the boat(s) from Muang Ngoi. When a boat arrives from Muang Khua there'll usually be additional Luang Prabang minivans departing at around 3pm from the boat office.

For Udomxai, a direct minibus (50,000K, three hours) leaves at 11am. Alternatively take any westbound transport and change at Pak Mong (25,000K, 50 minutes).

Originating in Luang Prabang, the minibus to Sam Neua (130,000K, 12 hours) via Vieng Thong (100,000K, five hours) makes a quick lunch stop in Nong Khiaw around 11.30am. Another Sam Neua bus (arriving from Vientiane) passes through at night.

❶ Getting Around

Bicycle rental makes sense to explore local villages or reach the caves. Town bicycles cost 20,000K per day and mountain bikes cost 30,000K, both available from unsigned **Leh's Place** on the main drag.

Muang Ngoi Neua ເມືອງງອຍເໜືອ

Flanked in all directions by sculpted layers of majestic karsts, this almost roadless village enjoys one of northern Laos' prettiest riverside settings. The one 500m-long 'street' shoots straight from the main monastery towards a dramatic pyramidal tooth of forest-dappled limestone. Short unaided hikes take you into timeless neighbouring villages, while kayaking trips are a great way to savour the memorable Nam Ou, which has its most scenically spectacular stretches either side of the village.

Need to choose between Nong Khiaw and Muang Ngoi Neua? It's a tough call, but generally Nong Khiaw has better accommodation and dining, while Muong Ngoi Neua is more rural and timeless with nearby trekking opportunities.

◉ Sights & Activities

Such is the grandeur of the riverside views that you could happily linger all day just lazing on your balcony or sitting at one of the better-placed restaurant shacks.

Numerous freelance guides offer a wide range of walks to Lao, Hmong and Khamu villages and to regional waterfalls. Prices are remarkably reasonable and some visits, such as to the **That Mok** falls, involve boat rides.

Kayaking is a great way to appreciate the fabulous riverine scenery that stretches both ways along the Nam Ou. **Lao Youth Travel** (☑030 514 0046; www.laoyouthtravel.com; ☺7.30-10.30am & 1.30-6pm) has its own kayaks and is handily located where the boat-landing path passes the two-storey Rainbow House.

🛏 Sleeping

Many guesthouses feature river views, shared cold-water bathrooms, hammocks and attached family-run restaurants.

★**Ning Ning Guest House** GUESTHOUSE $
(☑020 3386 3306; r incl breakfast US$17-20) Nestled around a peaceful garden, Ning Ning is the smartest place in the village, offering immaculate wooden bungalows with mosquito nets, verandahs, en suite bathroom and bed linen, plus the walls are draped with ethnic tapestries. There's a nice restaurant with riverfront views.

Lattanavongsa Guesthouse GUESTHOUSE $
(☑030 514 0770; r from 100,000K) In a palm-filled garden, Lattanavongsa's sun-terraced bungalows enjoy views of the karsts. Inside

rooms are tasteful with house-proud flour-ishes, including gas-fired showers and up-scale linen. There are four rattan bungalows near the river and 12 bungalows above the boat landing.

Aloune Mai Guesthouse   GUESTHOUSE $

(r 70,000K) Not to be confused with rickety Aloune Mai by the river, this hidden gem, found down a dirt track and over a bridge, sits beside a meadow and has 10 fresh rooms in a handsome rattan building with heated showers. There's a little restaurant and stun-ning views of the cliffs on the other side, but no river views.

Bungalows Ecolodge   GUESTHOUSE $

(r 80,000K) Features decent-sized new bun-galows hidden down a side street, with slid-ing shutters that allow you to lie in bed and watch the sky turn amber over the karsts. Tasteful linen, solar-heated showers, mos-quito nets and locally sourced food elevate it above the crowd.

✗ Eating

Well-priced Laotian and Western fare is available in abundance, though there are no gastronomic prodigies here.

★ Riverside Restaurant   LAOTIAN $

(meals 15,000-35,000K; ⊙ 7.30am-10pm) Shaded by a mature mango tree festooned with lanterns, this lively haunt has lovely views of the Nam Ou. The menu encompasses noodles, fried dishes and *làhp*. A real trav-eller magnet, it deserves all the attention it receives.

Phetdavanh Street Buffet   LAOTIAN $

(per person 20,000K; ⊙7pm) Phetdavanh runs an affordable nightly buffet that draws in locals and travellers alike. It sets up on the street around 7pm, serving bar-becued pork, chicken, fish, sticky rice and vegetables.

Nang Phone Keo Restaurant   LAOTIAN $

(mains 10,000-20,000K; ⊙7.30am-9pm) This is a Main St house-restaurant on whose deck you can get Muang Ngoi's most exotic des-sert: a plate of fried bananas flambéed in *lòw-lów*. Also imaginative is the *falang* roll, with peanut butter, banana, sticky rice and honey.

Bee Tree   LAOTIAN $

(mains 15,000-35,000K; ⊙11.30am-11.30pm) Located at the end of the main drag, this barbecue restaurant-cum-beer-garden has a relaxed ambience. Choose from Lao dishes and some comfort food or stroll along here for happy hour cocktails between 5pm and 8pm.

❶ Information

There is now internet access and wi-fi. In emer-gencies you could exchange US dollars at a few of the guesthouses.

Thefts from Muang Ngoi Neua's cheaper guesthouses tend to occur when over-relaxed guests leave flimsy doors and shutters unse-cured or place valuables within easy reach of long-armed pincers – most windows here have no glass.

❶ Getting There & Away

Boats to Nong Khiaw leave at 9am (or when full) and cost 25,000K. Heading north, a 9.30am boat goes most days to Muang Khua (minimum 10 persons, 120,000K, seven hours) for those headed for the Sop Hun–Tay Trang border cross-ing. Buy tickets at the boat office, halfway up the boat landing stairs next to Ning Ning Guest-house. There's a boat to Nong Khiaw from Muang Khua that stops in Muang Ngoi Neua at 1.30pm.

A new road to Nong Khiaw is under construc-tion, so make the most of the delicious isolation.

Xieng Khuang Province

Rainswept and cratered by American bombs that fell by the planeload every eight min-utes for an unbelievable nine years, Xieng Khuang Province will make you either want to stay a while or hotfoot it to the nearest Lao Airlines office. Virtually all of the prov-ince was bombed between 1964 and 1973, and a sense of that tragedy endures today with the pernicious legacy of UXO (unex-ploded ordnance). Despite its alpine land-scape, the shadow of the past looms large, with entire areas still denuded. Most come here to see the mystical Plain of Jars, but there are also several fascinating sites relat-ing to the war that are open to tourists.

Phonsavan   ໂພນສະຫວັນ

♩ 061 / POP 60,000

Phonsavan bears its cratered war scars like an acne-ridden pensioner, while stoic lo-cals make the most of decommissioned un-exploded ordnance (UXO), using it to dec-orate houses and hotel foyers. Touchingly, while other areas of Laos erupt in pockets of sophistication, Phonsavan, like some retro-leaning Muscovite, barely changes. Often mist-shrouded and chilly, with locals gathering collars around weather-beaten faces, this dusty old town (latterly known as Xieng Khouang) has elements of charm if you look past its nondescript, Soviet facade – blame that on its hasty rebuild after it was decimated.

The town is populated by an intriguing cast of Chinese, Vietnamese, Lao and Hmong residents, and is well serviced by an airport, and a handful of guesthouses and restaurants.

◎ Sights

UXO Information Centre　INFORMATION CENTRE
(☑ 061-252004; www.maginternational.org/laopdr; Phonsavan; ⊙ 8am-8pm) **FREE** The centre's photos, slide shows and computer map-program underline the enormity of the UXO problem, plus there are examples of (defused) UXO to ponder. Donations are encouraged: US$12 pays for the clearing of around 10 sq m and qualifies the giver for a commemorative T-shirt.

**Xieng Khouang UXO-Survivors'
Information Centre**　INFORMATION CENTRE
(www.laos.worlded.org; ⊙ 8am-8pm) The insightful Xieng Khouang UXO-Survivors' Information Centre displays prosthetic limbs, wheelchairs and bomb parts and gives harrowing insight into the UXO problem.

Mulberries　SILK FARM
(ປັ້ສາ; ☑ 061-561271; www.mulberries.org; ⊙ 8am-4pm Mon-Sat) This is a fair-trade silk farm that offers interesting free visits, including a complete introduction to the silk-weaving process from cocoon to colourful scarves. It's off Rte 7 just west of the main bus station.

☞ Tours

Amazing Lao Travel　HIKING
(☑ 020 2234 0005; www.amazinglao.com; Rte 7) Runs treks to the jar sites and two-day treks in the mountains, including a homestay in a Hmong village. As ever, the more the merrier, with prices falling for larger groups.

Sousath Travel　GUIDED TOUR
(☑ 061-312031; Rte 7) Sousath offers reliable tours to the Plain of Jars and the Ho Chi Minh Trail as well as homestays in Hmong villages. It also rents motorbikes (100,000K per day). Films are shown nightly at their little office-cum-cafe.

🛏 Sleeping

Kong Keo Guesthouse　GUESTHOUSE $
(☑ 061 211 354; www.kongkeojar.com; r 50,000-80,000K; ⊙📶) The most backpacker-friendly spot in town offers cabins with en suites, as well as a newer block of more comfortable rooms. There is a small bar-restaurant with an open-pit barbecue and occasional guitar strum-alongs. Owner Mr Keo runs excellent tours to the jars, as well as specialised trips.

Nice Guesthouse　GUESTHOUSE $
(☑ 061-312454; vuemany@hotmail.com; r 80,000-110,000K; 📶) With fresh and fragrant rooms, clean bathrooms and firm beds, Nice shows no signs of ageing just yet. Chinese lanterns cast a ruby glow into the chilled night and upstairs rooms include a bathtub.

LAOS XIENG KHUANG PROVINCE

GETTING TO VIETNAM: MUANG KHUA TO DIEN BIEN PHU

Getting to the border The Sop Hun/Tay Trang border in Phongsali Province has now opened as an international entry point to Tay Trang in Vietnam. There are three buses a week bound for Dien Bien Phu leaving from the Lao village of Muang Khua (50,000K, 6.30am, five to six hours). Get there early for a decent seat.

At the border Note, there are no facilities or waiting vehicles at either the Lao or Vietnamese borders (open 8am to 5pm). The nearest ATM in Laos is in Udomxai so bring plenty of dollars. You'll need to organise a Vietnamese visa in advance. Lao visas are available on arrival for US$30 to US$42, depending on your nationality. Bring some photo ID and some extra cash (approx US$5) for administrative costs charged on weekends and holidays.

Moving on Once through the Vietnamese border it's a further 35km to Dien Bien Phu.

For more information about crossing this border in the other direction, see p82.

Phonsavan

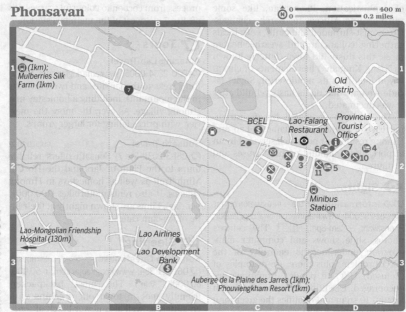

Phonsavan

White Orchid Guesthouse   GUESTHOUSE **$**
(📞061-312403; r incl breakfast 80,000-200,000K;
🌀🛜) The menthol-green walls include clean
en suite bathrooms and welcome blankets.
The higher you ascend, the higher the price

and better the views. Free pick-up from airport or bus station.

★ **Auberge de la
Plaine des Jarres**   CABINS **$$**
(📞030 517 0282; www.plainedesjarres.com; r
US$50-60; @🛜) Hillside elevation, Scotch
pines and Swiss-style wooden interiors give
these inviting all-wood cabins an incongru-
ously alpine feel. There's a great French and
Lao restaurant with a nightly fire and some
panoramic vistas over the town. Rooms
show signs of age, but there are oodles of
charm. It's a 10-minute drive from town.

Phouviengkham Resort   HOTEL **$$**
(📞061-213417; phouviengkham@live.com; r US$65-
85) Tasteful Phouviengkham sits panorami-
cally above town on an isolated hilltop and
has spacious, stylish rooms with Lao cotton
bedspreads and bamboo furnishings.

✗ Eating

Wild *matsutake* mushrooms (*hét wâi*) and
fermented swallows (*nok qan dorng*) are local specialities. Try the **fresh food market**
(⊙6am-5pm). In case you want to avoid an
unpleasant surprise, several Vietnamese restaurants serve dog (*thit chó*).

★**Bamboozle**
Restaurant & Bar INTERNATIONAL $
(Rte 7; meals 15,000-52,000K; ⊘7-10.30am & 3.30-11pm; 🎤) 🍴 The liveliest spot in town after dark, Bamboozle offers a decent range of comfort food, including pizzas, as well as the best of Lao cuisine. A percentage of profits go towards the **Lone Buffalo Foundation** (LBP; www.facebook.com/lonebuffalo), which supports the town's youth.

Nisha Restaurant INDIAN $
(Rte 7; meals 10,000-30,000K; ⊘7am-10pm; ✏) Nisha is one of the best Indian restaurants in northern Laos. The menu includes a wide range of vegetarian options and there's also delicious dosa (flat bread), tikka masala and rogan josh, as well as great lassis.

Simmaly Restaurant LAOTIAN $
(Rte 7; meals 15,000-30,000K; ⊘6am-9pm) Dishes up a tasty line of rice dishes, noodles and spicy meats, including steaming *fĕr*. The pork with ginger is lovely.

Craters Bar & Restaurant INTERNATIONAL $
(Rte 7; meals 20,000-50,000K; ⊘7am-10pm; 🎤) An old-timer popular with NGOs and travellers, Craters has CNN on the tube as you munch through its toasties, soups, burgers, fried chicken, steaks and pizzas.

ⓘ Information

Currency exchange is available at **Lao Development Bank** (⌨061-312188), at **BCEL** (⌨061-213291; Rte 7) and from several travel agents. There are two ATMs along Rte 7.

Don't underestimate the dangers of UXO (unexploded ordnance) in this most heavily bombed of provinces.

Lao-Mongolian Friendship Hospital (⌨061 312 166) Might be able to assist with minor health concerns.

Post Office (⊘8am-4pm Mon-Fri, to noon Sat) Domestic phone service.

Provincial Tourist Office (⌨061-312217) The oddly located tourist office has developed some regional treks. Free maps and leaflets for Phonsavan and Xieng Khuang Province are also available. The yard is crammed full of war junk.

ⓘ Getting There & Away

AIR

Lao Airlines (⌨061-212027; www.laoairlines. com) has daily flights to/from Vientiane (US$101). Sometimes a weekly flight to/from Luang Prabang operates in peak season.

BUS

Longer-distance bus tickets presold by travel agencies typically cost around 40,000K more than standard fares but include a transfer to the bus station, around 4km west of the centre. From here Vietnam-bound buses depart to Vinh (180,000K, 11 hours) at 6.30am on Tuesday, Thursday, Friday and Sunday, continuing seasonally on Mondays to Hanoi (320,000K). For Vientiane (140,000K, 11 hours) there are air-con buses at 7am, 8am, 10.30am, 4.30pm, 6.30pm and a VIP bus (160,000K) at 8pm. These all pass through Vang Vieng, to where there's an additional 7.30am departure (95,000K). For Luang Prabang (10 hours) both minivans (95,000K) and VIP buses (120,000K) depart at 8.30am. There's an 8am bus to Sam Neua (110,000K, eight to 10 hours) plus two Vientiane–Sam Neua buses passing through. A 7.30am bus is timetabled to Paksan (130,000K) on the new road.

Minibuses leave from the centre of town behind Sousath Travel.

ⓘ Getting Around

Túk-túk cost from 10,000K for a short hop to about 20,000K to the airport. **Lao-Falang Restaurant** (⌨020 2221 2456; Rte 7, Phonsavan;

AN ENDURING LEGACY

Between 1964 and 1973, the USA conducted one of the largest sustained aerial bombardments in history, flying 580,344 missions over Laos and dropping two million tonnes of bombs, costing US$2.2 million a day. Around 30% of the bombs dropped on Laos failed to detonate, leaving the country littered with unexploded ordnance (UXO).

For people all over eastern Laos (the most contaminated provinces being Xieng Khuang, Salavan and Savannakhet), living with this appalling legacy has become an intrinsic part of daily life. Since the British **Mines Advisory Group** (MAG; www.mag.org. uk; Rte 7, Phonsavan; ⊘4-8pm) began clearance work in 1994, only a tiny percentage of the quarter of a million pieces in Xieng Khuang and Salavan has been removed. At the current rate of clearance it will take more than 100 years to make the country safe. Visit their UXO Information Centre (p309) to watch a number of late afternoon documentaries including Bomb Harvest (4.30pm), Surviving the Peace (5.50pm) and Bombies (6.30pm).

⊙ 8am-6pm) rents bicycles (40,000K per day) and 100cc motorbikes (100,000K), ideal for reaching a selection of jar sites.

Plain of Jars ທົ່ງໄຫຫີນ

The Plain of Jars represents a huge area of Xieng Khuang scattered with thousands of limestone jars of undetermined age. Thought to be funerary urns, after bones were discovered within them, the jars have been divided into 160 sites, three of which represent the greatest concentration. These are the designated UXO-cleared tourist areas you should visit.

Site 1 (Thong Hai Hin; admission 10,000K), the biggest and most accessible site, is 15km southwest of Phonsavan and features 250 jars, most of which weigh from 600kg to 1 tonne each. The largest jar weighs as much as 6 tonnes and is said to have been the victory cup of mythical King Jeuam, and so is called Hai Jeuam.

Two other jar sites are readily accessible by road from Phonsavan. **Site 2** (Hai Hin Phu Salato; admission 10,000K), about 25km south of town, features 90 jars spread across two adjacent hillsides. Vehicles can reach the base of the hills, then it's a short, steep walk to the jars.

More impressive is 150-jar **Site 3** (Hai Hin Lat Khai; admission 10,000K). It's 7.7km south of Site 2 (or 35km from Phonsavan) on a scenic hilltop near the charming village of **Ban Xiang Di**, where there's a small monastery containing the remains of Buddha images damaged in the war. The site is a 2km hike through rice paddies and up a hill.

❶ Getting There & Away

All three main sites can be visited by rented motorbike from Phonsavan in around five hours, while Site 1 is within bicycle range. Site 1 is just 8km southwest of central Phonsavan, 2.3km west of the Muang Khun road: turn at the signed junction in Ban Hay Hin. For Sites 2 and 3, turn west of the Muang Khun road at just past Km 8. Follow the unpaved road for 10km/14km to find the turnings for Sites 2/3, then follow muddy tracks for 1.5/1.8km respectively.

Alternatively, sign up the night before to join one of several regular guided minibus tours. Most throw in a noodle-soup lunch at Site 3 and a quick stop to see the lumpy rusting remnant of an armoured vehicle at Ban Nakho: its nickname, the 'Russian Tank', exaggerates the appeal.

Huah Phan Province

Rugged and beautiful, Huah Phan is unlike any other province in Laos. Although home to 22 different ethnic groups, including Yao, Hmong, Khamu, Thai Khao and Thai Neua, the strong Vietnamese influence is evident. The province's high altitude means the climate can be cool – even in the hot season – and forested mountains are shrouded in mist. Road journeys to Huah Phan are memorably scenic, described by one local as 'a journey of a million turns'.

Despite the remote border to Vietnam and Hanoi opening to foreigners, this remains one of the least-visited provinces in Laos, which is a great reason to get off the beaten track and come – your exploration will be well rewarded.

Sam Neua ຊຳເຫນືອ

☑ 064 / POP 16,000

A trip to remote Sam Neua, one of Laos' least-visited provincial capitals, rewards with pine-ridged valleys, emerald rice paddies, charcoal-black karsts and the fascinating caves of Vieng Xai. During the Secret War this was a major stronghold of the communist Pathet Lao and there's still a sense

Plain of Jars

0 —— 2 km
0 —— 1 mile

Luang Prabang (260km)

7

Sam Neua (232km)

Bus Station Phonsavan

Airport

Jar Site 1

Ban Hay Hin

Petrol Station Lathang

Muang Khun (16km)

Jar Site 2
Ticket Office

Russian Tank

Ban Lat Khai

Ban Xiang Di Jar Site 3

of this with a Soviet-nodding memorial and Russian hats worn by the old boys in the market. Laos' finest silk scarves are woven here, so keep an eye out for them as you wander the market, and don't miss the eye-opening wet market over the river.

The town is a logical transit point for Vietnam and, at an altitude of roughly 1200m, some warm clothes are advisable in the dry winter period – at least by night and until the thick morning fog burns off.

🛏 Sleeping & Eating

There are plenty of guesthouses in town, with many budget options just across the river from the market.

For cheap *fĕr* (rice noodles), samosas, spring rolls and fried sweet potato, the **market** (⊘6am-6pm) is the place to go.

★ Xayphasouk Hotel   HOTEL $
(📞064-312033; xayphasoukhotel@gmail.com; r 150,000-200,000K; ❄🔊) Currently the smartest hotel in Sam Neua. Rooms are comfortable with piping hot showers, flat-screen TVs, tasteful furnishings and crisp linen, plus free wi-fi.

Bounhome Guest House   GUESTHOUSE $
(📞064-312223; r 60,000-100,000K; 🔊) Plenty of sunlight fills the fine little rooms upstairs in this guesthouse. Their neat interiors have firm, low-set beds, are fan-cooled and include hot-water showers.

Phonchalern Hotel   HOTEL $
(📞064-312192; www.phonechalernhotel.com; r 100,000-120,000K; ❄🔊) This clean and comfortable hotel is a real deal, with TV and fridge in rooms. Try to bag a front-facing room with a balcony overlooking the river.

Dan Nao Muang Xam Restaurant   LAOTIAN $
(mains 15,000-50,000K; ⊘7am-9.30pm) This hole-in-the-wall spot is hardly brimming with atmosphere, but it has the most foreigner-friendly menu in town in concise English. Breakfast includes Cornflakes and a delicious *fĕr*. Dinner includes some excellent rice and soup combinations, plus a steak with al dente vegetables arranged star-like around the plate.

Chittavanh Restaurant   LAOTIAN $
(mains 20,000-40,000K; ⊘7am-9.30pm) Savouring a delicious Chinese fried tofu dish makes it worth braving the reverberant clatter of this cavernous hotel restaurant, where vinyl tablecloths have been nailed into place. Locals eat here as well – always a good sign.

❶ Information

Agricultural Promotion Bank (⊘8am-noon & 1.30-4pm Mon-Fri) Exchanges Thai baht and US dollars at fair rates.

BCEL (⊘8am-3.30pm Mon-Fri) Has a couple of ATMs dispensing kip, plus can exchange most major currencies.

Lao Development Bank (📞064-312171; ⊘8am-4pm Mon-Fri) On the main road 400m north of the bus station on the left; exchanges cash and travellers cheques.

Post Office (⊘8am-4pm Mon-Fri) In a large building directly opposite the bus station. A telephone office at its rear offers international calls.

Provincial Tourist Office (📞064-312567; ⊘8am-noon & 1.30-4pm Mon-Fri) An excellent tourist office with English-speaking staff eager to help.

Tam.com Internet Service (per min 150K; ⊘8am-10pm) A relatively reliable internet cafe.

❶ Getting There & Away

Lao Air (www.lao-air.com) flies to Vientiane on Monday, Wednesday and Friday (915,000K, 1½ hours). The airport is 3km from town.

Set on a hilltop, Sam Neua's main bus station is roughly 1.2km away (túk-túk 8500K) from town. There are three buses a day to Vientiane (170,000K, 22 hours) via Phonsavan (80,000K, eight to 10 hours) at 9am, noon and 2pm. It's a sinuous but beautiful hike through the mountains.

GETTING TO VIETNAM: PHONSAVAN TO VINH

Getting to the border Four direct buses to Vinh (on the Vietnamese side) leave Phonsavan three times per week, crossing at the lonely Nong Haet/Nam Can border (open 8am to noon and 1.30pm to 5pm). The nearest town on the Lao side is Nong Haet.

At the border If entering Vietnam, you'll need to have organised a Vietnamese visa in advance.

Moving on The first town en route to Vinh, 250km away, is Muong Xen, where there's a basic hotel. From here there's also a 4pm bus to Vinh.

For more information about crossing this border in the other direction, see p94.

An additional 8am bus to Vientiane goes via Nong Khiaw (130,000K, 12 hours, 8am) and continues to Luang Prabang (140,000K, 17 hours) and Vang Vieng. If you're heading for Udomxai, take this bus and change at Pak Mong.

Nathong bus station is 1km to the east heading for Vieng Xai. *Sŏrngtăaou* run from here to Vieng Xai (15,000K, 50 minutes, 29km) at 8am, 10am, 11am, 2.30pm and 4pm; the scenery is among the most stunning in Laos. The 'Nameo' (actually the Nam Xoi border post) bus leaves at 8am (30,000K, three hours), and Sam Tai (Xamtay) at 9.30am (50,000K, five hours).

Vieng Xai ဩງໄຊ

🎧 064 / POP 10,000

Set amid valleys patterned with rice paddies and towered over by dramatic karsts, beautiful Vieng Xai seems an unlikely place to have suffered a decade's worth of American air assaults. Its 450 limestone caves provided sanctuary for more than 23,000 people during the Secret War, playing host to bakeries, a hospital, school, a metalwork factory and, more importantly, the political headquarters of the communist Pathet Lao party. As the bombs fell near the virtually unassailable caves, President Kaysone Phomvihane plotted the transformation of his country in a dank grotto, undecorated but for a framed photo of Che Guevara and a few other keepsakes.

About 5km before Vieng Xai keep an eye out for **Tham Nok Ann** (ຖ້ຳນົກແອນ; Nok Ann Cave; admission 10,000K, twin kayak 30,000K; ⊙8am-5pm), a newly opened cave complex you can kayak through.

◎ Sights & Activities

⭐ **Vieng Xai Caves** CAVE
(ຖ້ຳວຽງໄຊ; www.visit-viengxay.com; admission incl audio tour 60,000K) Joining a truly fascinating 18-point tour is the only way to see Vieng Xai's seven most important war-shelter cave complexes, along with several 1970s postwar buildings associated with major liberation heroes. All are set in beautiful yet very natural gardens and backed by fabulous karst scenery. A local guide unlocks each site and can answer basic questions. Meanwhile, an audioguide gives a wealth of first-hand background information and historical context, offering a moving, balanced and uniquely fascinating glimpse of how people struggled on through the war years. The excellent production incorporates original interviews from local survivors and is enlivened with sound effects and accompanying music: the Hendrix-esque soundtrack to the Air America piece is particularly memorable and you may find yourself ducking for cover when the jet fighters screech overhead.

Most caves have minor elements of original furnishings. Some have 'emergency rooms' – air-locked concrete caves-within-caves designed to protect top politburo members from possible chemical or gas attacks (the **Kaysone Phomvihane Cave** still has its air-circulation pump in working order). Almost all the main cave sites are well illuminated but bring a torch (flashlight) if you want to traverse the unadorned **hospital cave** (occasionally flooded).

Steps lead down from the hand-dug **Khamtay Siphandone Cave** to the **Barracks Caves**, extensive natural caverns that would have housed hundreds of conscripted liberation soldiers. Above is the **Artillery Cave** from whose open ledge spotters would watch for incoming American planes. The tour culminates in the **Xanglot Cave**, a wide double-ended cavern that was used as a wedding hall, cinema and even as a theatre. Incredibly, performers from Russia,

---

GETTING TO VIETNAM: SAM NEUA TO THANH HOA

Getting to the border If you're crossing the Na Meo/Nam Xoi border (open 7.30am to 11.30am and 1.30pm to 4.30pm), take the daily bus from Sam Neua's Nathong bus station bound for Thanh Hoa (180,000K, 11 hours, 8am). Buy your ticket at the bus station itself to avoid being overcharged on the bus.

At the border Heading into Vietnam you'll need to have prearranged a visa. There are no ATM facilities at this remote border crossing. On the Lao side there are a couple of restaurants.

Moving on There's a night train from Thanh Hoa to Hanoi departing at 11.30pm and arriving inconveniently at 4am.

For more information about crossing this border in the other direction, see p82.

NAM ET–PHOU LOUEY NATIONAL PROTECTED AREA

In the vast Nam Et–Phou Louey NPA (ປ່າສະຫງວນແຫ່ງຊາດນ້ຳແອດພູເລັຍ) rare civets, Asian golden cats, river otters, white-cheeked crested gibbons and the utterly unique Laotian warty newt (Paramesotriton laoensis) share 4200 sq km of relatively pristine forests with around a dozen tigers. Approximately half is an inaccessible core zone. The remainder includes 98 ethnic minority hamlets. Two-day wildlife-watching excursions have been pioneered to the park's remote Nam Nern field station, a roadless former village site where a campsite and surrounding walking trails have been professionally cleared of UXO. Highlights of the trip include a night-time boat ride 'spotlighting' for animals and day-time guided hikes learning about wildlife tracking. Actually seeing a live tiger is unlikely but there's more hope of spotting sambar and barking deer and for each significant sighting, nearby villages receive a small payment. This is a cleverly thought-out scheme that encourages the local population to work actively against poachers.

Trips are organised through the **NPA office** (☑064-810008; www.namet.org; ⊙8am-noon & 1-4.30pm Mon-Fri) in Vieng Thong but contacting them well in advance is advisable since there's a limit of two departures per week. Tours cost (US$80/100 per person in groups of five/two people) and include guides, cooks, food and camping equipment, with a significant proportion of the fee going into village development funds. The price also includes the 90-minute boat ride from Ban Sonkhua, around 50km east of Vieng Thong on Rte 1. Getting to Ban Sonkhua (not included) is possible on the morning public minibus from Vieng Thong or Phonsavan but be sure to discuss travel arrangements with the organisers.

Paul Eshoo, Lao Ecotourism Consultant

China and Vietnam all managed to mount productions here during the war.

Tours start at 9am and 1pm from the caves office. By arrangement private visits are also possible at other times (costing an extra 50,000K per group), depending on guide availability. Seeing all 18 sites in the three hours available is possible without feeling unduly rushed, assuming you rent a bicycle (available for 10,000/20,000K per tour/day from the caves office) and that you listen to the longer audio tracks while travelling between the sites rather than waiting to arrive before pressing play.

🛏 Sleeping & Eating

Naxay Guesthouse   GUESTHOUSE $
(☑064-314330; r 60,000-80,000K) Opposite the caves office, Vieng Xai's most comfortable option offers bamboo-lined bungalows or concrete cubicles set around a patch of greenery backed by an impressive split-toothed crag. Beds are comfy, hot water flows and the attached beach-style cafe pavilion occasionally serves up food.

ℹ Information

Vieng Xai Cave Tourist Office (☑064-314321; www.visit-viengxay.com; ⊙8-11.30am & 1-4.30pm) Around 1km south of the market,

the caves office organises all cave visits, rents bicycles and has maps, a small book exchange and a useful information board.

ℹ Getting There & Away

Sŏrngtăaou to Sam Neua (15,000K, 50 minutes) leave at 7am, 10am, 1pm, 2.30pm and 4pm from the market. Buses between Sam Neua and Sam Tai, Nam Soi or Thanh Hoa bypass Vieng Xai 1km to the north but will usually stop on request.

Udomxai Province

Home to some of northern Laos' thickest forests, this rugged province is a great place to visit Hmong and Khamu villages. Close to China's Yunnan Province, you'll find 15 ethnic minorities in the area but the dominant group is increasingly the Yunnanese, working in construction and plantation operations. While Udomxai town is undesirable, the surrounding hills are beautiful and shouldn't be overlooked if you have time to trek here.

Udomxai   ອຸດົມໄຊ

☑081 / POP 25,000

Booming Udomxai is a Laos–China trade hub. The absence of a traveller vibe, not to mention the cast of gruff Chinese truck drivers, prostitutes and ugly Soviet-style buildings, puts off many short-term visitors. That said, it takes minimal effort to find the 'real' Laos nearby in the forests and Khmu and Hmong villages.

There's also a well-organised tourist office (p316) with paper-making and cooking courses (both from 100,000K per person), and some great treks and homestays to tempt you to stay longer. Meanwhile **Samlaan Cycling** (☑020 5560 9790; www.samlaancycling.com) runs recommended one-day/multiday cycling tours.

🛏 Sleeping & Eating

There are some decent new options to make your stay a little more enjoyable. Most places are along – or just off – Rte 1.

Saylomen Guesthouse   GUESTHOUSE $
(☑081-211377; r with fan/air-con 60,000/100,000K; ❄) Simple, fair-sized fan rooms with hot water, top sheets and multicoloured coat stands are better value than the average guesthouse around town. Air-con is a good investment in the hot season.

Xayxana Guest House   GUESTHOUSE $
(☑020 5578 0429; off Rte 1; r 70,000-100,000K; ❄ 🗑) Set in a sprawling compound, Xayxana is cool and spacious, with immaculate white rooms, tiled floors and very comfy beds. All rooms come with en suite bathrooms.

★**Villa Keoseumsack**   HOTEL $$
(☑081-312170; Rte 1; r 120,000-200,000K; ❄ 🗑) The town's best-value rooms, with varnished floors, en suites, TVs, Hmong-woven bed runners and freshly plumped pillows. Free wi-fi and a cool reading balcony finish it off. Rooms at the rear are more spacious than those in the main building.

Meuang Neua Restaurant   LAOTIAN $
(mains 20,000-40,000K; ⊙7am-10pm) Relocated to the main strip, this place is popular with the few travellers who stay in Udomxai. The walls are decorated with arabesques and there's an imaginative menu, from salads through pumpkin soup, curry, fish and stir-fries.

★**Cafe Sinouk**   LAOTIAN, INTERNATIONAL $$
(Charming Lao Hotel; mains 20,000-95,000K; 🗑) Sinouk Coffee of Bolaven Plateau fame has ventured north with this stylish restaurant, cafe and bar. The coffee selection is unsur-

prisingly the best in town. Meals include a wide range of Lao and international dishes, including some whole fish to share. Lunch (15,000K) and dinner (20,000K) specials are one-plate value. The garden courtyard features live music at weekends.

ℹ Information

BCEL (☑081-211260; Rte 1) Has an ATM, changes several major currencies and accepts some travellers cheques (2% commission).
Tourist Office (Provincial Tourism Department of Oudomxay; ☑081-211797; www.oudomxay.info; ⊙7.30-11.30am & 1.30-6pm Mon-Fri Apr-Sep, 8am-noon & 1.30-4pm Mon-Fri Oct-Mar) The tourist office organises a selection of treks and tours and sells the GT-Rider Laos maps. The office sometimes opens on weekends, but the hours are irregular.

ℹ Getting There & Away

Lao Airlines (☑081-312047; www.laoairlines.com) flies to Vientiane (one way 695,000K) every Tuesday, Thursday and Saturday.

The bus station at the southwestern edge of town has buses to Luang Prabang (all VIP buses, 55,000K, five hours, 9am, noon and 3pm daily), Nong Khiaw (45,000K, four hours, 9am daily), Pak Beng (40,000K, five hours, 8.30am and 10am daily), Pak Mong (30,000K, 2pm and 4pm daily), Luang Namtha (40,000K, three hours, 8.30am, 11.30am and 3.30pm daily), Muang Khua (35,000K, four hours, 8.30am, 11.30am and 3pm daily), Boten (40,000K, four hours, 8am daily), Phongsali (75,000K, eight to 12 hours, 8.30am daily) and Vientiane (ordinary bus 150,000K, 16 hours, 11am; VIP bus 140,000K, 18 hours, 4pm and 6pm daily).

There are also bus connections to Mengla (China).

Pak Beng   ປາກແບ່ງ

Essentially a one-street town, Pak Beng is the halfway point on the Mekong River between Huay Xai and Luang Prabang. You'll probably stop here for lunch (speedboats) or an obligatory night (two-day slowboats). The town itself is perched on the vertiginous slopes of the riverbank and to call it listless is going overboard – barely a chicken stirs. If you're here for the night there's a couple of plush hotels in which to stay.

There's little in the way of attractions, but the **Mekong Elephant Camp** (☑071-254130) across the Mekong offers elephant rides (prices run from US$40 to US$82) and a chance to see the Dumbos taking their ablutions in the river.

Monsavan Guest House (☑ 084-212619; r from 100,000K; ❄ ☎) has house-proud rooms on the main street close to the boat landing. They feature white walls, a few sticks of furniture and clean bathrooms; upstairs the rooms are better. Nicer still is homely **Villa Santisiouk** (☑ 020 5578 1797; r in low season US$3-12; ❄ ☎) with its warm orange walls, partial wood interiors, tasteful furniture, river views and friendly management. Located at the top of the strip, the **Dockhoun Guesthouse** (☑ 084-212540; dockhoun@hotmail.com; r from 300B; ☎) has inviting rooms with fresh linen and hot-water showers.

For greater comforts, the **Pak Beng Lodge** (☑ 084-212304; www.pakbenglodge.com; r US$84-184; ❄ ☎) and the ecofriendly, traditional **Luang Say Lodge** (☑ 084-212296; www.luangsay.com; r from 700,000K) should satisfy, however the best value upscale digs are found at **Mekong Riverside Lodge** (☑ 020 5517 1068; www.mekongriversidelodge.com; r from US$40; ☎).

Restaurants at the **Bounmee Guesthouse**, **Sarika** or **Sivilai** have great river views. By night, colourful lanterns make **Ounhoan** a favourite. Indian restaurant **Hashan** (☑) also has appealing lighting and decor with good riverviews. **Khopchaideu** is one of the best all-rounders despite the lack of a river view.

A **tourist office** (www.oudomxay.info; ☉ 7am-noon & 2-9pm) up the hill is well endowed with illustrative info and leaflets on things to do including exploring the Chom Ong cave system. There's also a **Lao Development Bank** with an ATM.

The tiny bus station is at the northernmost edge of town with departures to Udomxai (40,000K, four hours) at 9am and 12.30pm.

The downriver slowboat to Luang Prabang departs between 9am and 10am (100,000K, around eight hours). The slowboat for Huay Xai (100,000K, around nine hours) departs at 8am.

Speedboats take around three hours to either Luang Prabang or Huay Xai, costing 180,000K per person.

Luang Namtha Province

Bordered by Myanmar (Burma) and China, this heavily forested province suffered a hammering during the Second Indochina War, particularly its capital, Luang Namtha town. Nowadays it's a mecca for

ecotourism, with award-winning tours into the Nam Ha National Protected Area. If it's trekking, mountain biking, rafting or birdwatching you're seeking, you couldn't have come to a better place. The area is also rich in cultural diversity, with more than 20 ethnic tribes.

Luang Namtha ຫລວງນ້ຳທາ
☑ 086 / POP 21,000

Thanks to its location next to the Nam Ha National Protected Area (one of the largest and the first of Laos' 20 NPAs), Luang Namtha enjoys an influx of intrepid travellers. It also invites exotic appearances from Hmong tribeswomen in full rainbow-hemmed garb at the candle-lit night market. Heavily bombed during the Secret War, the town itself is relatively new, nestled in a valley surrounded by distant mountains, while the original town is some 10km away near the airport. It's a friendly place with plenty of guesthouses, tasty restaurants and a lively market, serviced by banks, internet cafes and cycle-hire shops. Many spend a day pedalling around local waterfalls and temples before setting out into the wilds of Nam Ha NPA.

◉ Sights & Activities

The dense jungle of the **Nam Ha National Protected Area** is home to clouded leopards, gaur and elephants (plus the odd tiger – we know, we met one!). Visiting the NPA involves going on a **trek** with an experienced guide. Guides also offer **rafting**, **canoeing** and **mountain biking** along the Nam Tha River, as well as **homestays**. The **Nam Ha Ecotourism Project** (www.unescobkk.org/culture/our-projects/sustainable-cultural-tourism-and-ecotourism/namha-ecotourism-project) tries to ensure tour operators and villagers work together to provide an authentic experience for trekkers with minimum impact to local communities and the environment.

Places of interest within easy cycling or motorbiking distance include **Wat Ban Vieng Tai** and **Wat Ban Luang Khon**, near the airfield; a hilltop stupa, **That Phum Phuk**, about 4km west of the airfield; a small waterfall about 6km northeast of town past **Ban Nam Dee**; plus a host of Khamu, Lenten, Thai Dam and Thai Lü villages dotted along dirt roads through ricefields. Pick up a map and brochures at the provincial tourism office before setting off.

Luang Namtha

0 200 m
0 0.1 miles

- Golden Stupa (1.3km)
- Ban Nam Dee waterfall (6km); Nam Ha NPA (26km)
- Nam Ha Ecotourism Project
- Phou Iu III Guesthouse (250m)
- Bicycle Shops
- Provincial Tourism Office
- BCEL
- Night Market
- Wat Ban Luang Khon (5km); Wat Ban Vieng Tai (7km); Long Distance (10km)
- That Phum Phuk (4km)
- District Bus Station

Luang Namtha

⊙ Sights
1 Luang Nam Tha Museum A1

⊕ Activities, Courses & Tours
Forest Retreat Laos .... (see 8)
2 Green Discovery................................ B2
3 Nam Ha Ecoguide Service B2
4 Namtha River Experience A2

⊜ Sleeping
5 Adounsiri Guest House A2
6 Royal Hotel A3
7 Zuela Guesthouse A2

⊗ Eating
8 Forest Retreat Gourmet Cafe B2
9 Manychan Guesthouse & Restaurant B2
10 Minority Restaurant A2

Luang Nam Tha Museum   MUSEUM
(ພິພິດທະພັນຫຼວງນໍ້າທາ; admission 5000K;
⊙8.30-11.30am & 1.30-3.30pm Mon-Thu, 8.30-
11.30am Fri) The Museum contains a collection of local anthropological artefacts, such
as ethnic clothing, Khamu bronze drums
and ceramics. There are also a number of
Buddha images and the usual display chron-
icling the Revolution.

Golden Stupa   BUDDHIST STUPA
(admission 5000K) By far Nam Tha's most
striking landmark, the large golden stupa
sits on a steep ridge directly northwest of
town. It gleams majestically when viewed
from afar. Up close, the effect is a bit more
bling, but the views over town are particularly impressive.

⊂ Tours

Green Discovery   ECOTOUR
(☑086-211484; www.greendiscoverylaos.com;
⊙8am-9pm) ✐ The granddaddy of ecotourism in Laos, Green Discovery offers different
tours to those offered by the tourism office
in order to eliminate direct competition and
increase the spread of proceeds.

Forest Retreat Laos   ECOTOUR
(☑020 5568 0031; www.forestretreatlaos.com;
⊙7am-11.30pm) ✐ Based at the Forest Retreat cafe, this ecotourism outfit offers a mix
of jungle adventures, river trips and two-
wheeled exhilaration. It also offers one- to
six-day multi-activity adventures and recruits staff and guides from ethnic-minority
backgrounds where possible.

Nam Ha Ecoguide Service   ECOTOUR
(☑086-211534; ⊙8am-noon & 1.30-8pm) ✐ A
wing of the provincial tourism office. Retains the rights to some of the best trekking
routes.

Namtha River Experience   KAYAKING, RAFTING
(☑086-212047; www.namtha-river-experience-
laos.com; ⊙8am-9pm) ✐ Specialises in kayaking and rafting trips through Khamu and
Lenten villages. Also facilitates homestays.

⊨ Sleeping & Eating

In high season (December to March) the
town gets busy, so it's worth calling ahead to
book a room. If you're here for a few nights
make sure one of them is spent eating at the
night market, which bursts with smoke and
meat crackling on glowing braziers.

★Phou Iu III Guesthouse   GUESTHOUSE $
(☑030 571 0422; www.luangnamtha-oasis-resort.
com; r from 100,000K) Part of the same family as the Phou Iu II in Muang Sing, this
place is cracking value. Bungalows are
spacious and nicely fitted out with lumber
beds, fireplaces and inviting terraces. The
garden is a work in progress, but at this
price it's a steal. It's well-signposted from
the centre of town.

Zuela Guesthouse
GUESTHOUSE $
(📱 020 5588 6694; www.zuela-laos.com; r 60,000-120,000K; ▣ 🗢) Located in a leafy courtyard, Zuela boasts a house built from wood and exposed brick, and has a great restaurant serving 'power breakfasts': pancakes, shakes, salads and chilli-based Akha dishes. Rooms have wooden floors, fans and fresh linen. Zuela also rents scooters and operates an air-con minivan service to Huay Xai.

Adounsiri Guest House
GUESTHOUSE $
(📱 020 2299 1898; adounsiri@yahoo.com; r 60,000-100,000K; 🗢) Located down a quiet street, this homely Lao villa has scrupulously clean rooms with fresh bed linen, tiled floors, and white walls draped in handicrafts. TVs in every room, plus free wi-fi, tea and coffee.

Boat Landing Guest House
RESORT $$
(📱 086-312398; www.theboatlanding.com; r incl breakfast US$40-60) One of the country's original ecolodges, the Boat Landing has riverside acacia groves that hug tastefully finished wooden bungalows, which feature solar-heated showers. It's rustic in places, but the atmosphere more than makes up for the lack of sophistication. Located 7km south of the new town and about 150m off the main road.

Royal Hotel
HOTEL $$
(📱086-212151; d/ste 250,000/350,000K) The Royal is Nam Tha's glitziest hotel. Standard rooms have excellent beds, walk-in showers and elements of modernistic style. The suites come with carpeting and luxurious bathrobes. Staff speak Chinese but not English.

★ Forest Retreat Gourmet Cafe
INTERNATIONAL $
(www.forestretreatlaos.com; mains 20,000-50,000K, pizzas 50,000-90,000K) Famous beyond Luang Namtha for the sheer variety of the menu, Forest Retreat is home away from home. With DIY sandwiches, pastas, wood-fired pizzas, vegetarian risottos and homemade pancakes, it's time to indulge before or after a trek – which they also conveniently organise. Doubles as Bamboo Bar by night with cocktails aplenty.

Minority Restaurant
LAOTIAN $
(mains 15,000-35,000K; ⏱7am-10.30pm) This inviting, wood-beamed restaurant hidden down a little side alley offers the chance to sample typically ethnic dishes from the Khamu, Thai Dam and Akha tribes. If the likes of rattan shoots and banana-flower soup don't appeal, there's also a range of stir-fries.

LAOS LUANG NAMTHA PROVINCE

TONY POE: THE HORROR, THE HORROR

Exceptional secret agent or flipped-out crazoid? CIA Special Ops agent Anthony Poe was every communist guerilla's worst nightmare, famous for going native, à la Colonel Kurtz in *Apocalypse Now*, and collecting Pathet Lao ears and dropping heads on his enemy's porch from a Cessna plane. In many ways he became as savage as the forests where he made his home.

In 1961 Poe was sent to the mountainous north to ignite 'Operation Momentum', an American attempt to repel North Vietnamese forces from Laos as well as providing home-grown resistance to national communist sympathies. His assignment: to train up a crack force of 10,000 hill-tribe warriors. He chose the Hmong: plucky, suspicious of communism and eager to make a trade of guns and money in return for their opium and courage. Poe won the loyalty of his warriors – contravening his paymasters' orders – by fighting beside them and intrepidly attacking enemy-infested strongholds such as Luang Namtha on the Chinese border, risking China's intervention in the Secret War. Furious, the CIA considered its man a liability, their prodigy now a Frankenstein's monster. Pathet Lao ears were stapled by Poe to progress reports and sent to the CIA 'Bubble' in Bangkok. As far as he was concerned: 'War is hell, if you're gonna do it you've gotta do it with gusto.'

After the Pathet Lao victory of 1975 Poe retired to Thailand; a renegade scorned, he would drunkenly shoot off his pistol in Bangkok bars, never forgiving the CIA for yanking him out of Laos before 'the job was done'. The precursor and partial inspiration to Coppola's Kurtz, cinema's most enduring icon of the war in Vietnam, Poe died in 2003.

Boat Landing Restaurant LAOTIAN **$$**
(meals 20,000-150,000K; ⊘7am-8.30pm) Offers some of the most authentic northern Lao cuisine: from five-dish menus for two or three people to one-plate meals, the flavour combinations are divine. If you're baffled by the choice try snacking on a selection of *jqaou* used as dipping sauces for balls of sticky rice.

**Manychan Guesthouse &
Restaurant** LAOTIAN, INTERNATIONAL **$**
(mains 15,000-40,000K; ⊘6.30am-10.30pm; ⊚)
An inviting all-wood interior spills out onto a fairy-lit street terrace and keeps this place among the most popular *falang* venues in town. Wi-fi is free and the menu covers the gamut of possibilities.

ⓘ Information

The provincial tourism office has information on trips, as well as maps and excellent photocopied brochures on responsible tourism, local flora and fauna, local ethnic minorities, customs and etiquette.

BCEL (⊘8.30am-3.30pm Mon-Fri) Changes major currencies (commission free) and travellers cheques (2% commission, minimum US$3), and has a 24-hour ATM.

Provincial Tourism Office (☑086-211534; ⊘8am-noon & 2-5pm) Doubles as Nam Ha Ecoguide Service.

ⓘ Getting There & Away

AIR

Lao Airlines (☑086-312180; www.laoairlines.com) flies to Vientiane (895,000K) daily.

BUS

There are two bus stations. The district bus station is walking distance from the traveller strip. The main long-distance bus station is 10km south of town.

For Nong Khiaw take a Vientiane or Luang Prabang bus and change at Pak Mong.

BOAT

You can reach Huay Xai on a two-day longboat odyssey down the Nam Tha, sleeping en route at a roadless village. For the ride, Luang Namtha agencies charge around US$120 to US$300 per person depending on exact numbers, including accommodation, meals and a tour guide throughout. You might get a better deal from the **boat station** (☑086-312014) beside the Boat Landing Guest House (p319). When river levels are low (January to June), departures start from Na Lae, with agencies providing túk-túk transfers and prearranging a boat.

ⓘ Getting Around

Chartered túk-túk charge 10,000K per person (minimum 40,000K) between the bus station or airport and the town centre. Most agencies and guesthouses sell ticket packages for long-distance buses that include a transfer from the guesthouse and cost around 20,000K above the usual fare.

BUSES FROM LUANG NAMTHA

DESTINATION	COST (K)	DURATION (HR)	STATION	DEPARTURES
Boten	35,000	2	district	6 daily 8am–3.30pm
Huay Xai ('Borkeo')	60,000	4	long distance	9am, 1.30pm bus, 8.30am minibus
Jinghong (China)	90,000	6	long distance	8.30am
Luang Prabang	90,000–100,000	8	long distance	9am bus, 8am minibus
Mengla (China)	50,000	3½	long distance	8am
Muang Long	60,000	4	district	8.30am
Luang Sing	30,000	2	district	6 daily 8am–3.30pm
Na Lae	40,000	3	district	9.30am, noon
Udomxai	40,000	4	long distance	8.30am, noon, 2.30pm
Vieng Phukha	35,000	1½	long distance	9.30am, noon
Vientiane	180,000–200,000	21–24	long distance	8.30am, 2.30pm

GETTING TO CHINA: LUANG NAMTHA TO MENGLA

Getting to the border The Lao immigration post at the Boten/Mohan border crossing (7.30am to 4.30pm Laos time, 8.30am to 5.30pm Chinese time) is a few minutes' walk north of Boten market. Túk-túk shuttle across no-man's land to the Chinese immigration post in Mohan (Bohan) or it's an easy 10-minute walk.

Alternatively, take one of the growing number of handy Laos–China through-bus connections such as Udomxai–Mengla, Luang Namtha–Jinghong and Luang Prabang–Kunming.

At the border Northbound it is necessary to have a Chinese visa in advance.

Moving on From the Chinese immigration post it's a 15-minute walk up Mohan's main street to the stand where little buses depart for Mengla (RMB16, one hour) every 20 minutes or so till mid-afternoon. These arrive at Mengla's bus station No 2. Nip across that city to the northern bus station for Jinghong (RMB42, two hours, frequent till 6pm) or Kunming (mornings only).

Cycling is the ideal way to explore the wats, waterfalls and landscape surrounding Luang Namtha. There are a couple of **bicycle shops** (bicycle per day 10,000-25,000K; motorcycle per day 30,000-50,000K; ☉9am-6.30pm) in front of the Zuela Guesthouse that also rent scooters.

Muang Sing   ເມືອງສິງ

☑081 / POP 10,000

Bordering Myanmar, at the heart of the Golden Triangle, and almost within grasp of the green hills of China, rural Muang Sing has a backwater feel that transports you to a less complicated time. Formerly on the infamous opium trail, it's a sleepy town of wilting, Thai Lü–style houses and, happily, trekking has overtaken smuggling contraband (though tribeswomen may still approach you selling rocks of opium). Hmong, Thai Lü, Akha, Thai Dam and Yao are all seen here in traditional dress at the morning market (get there for dawn), giving the town an exciting frontier feel.

Visitors who venture the extra 60km from Luang Namtha to Muang Sing are rewarded with some of the most scenic, ecoconscious trekking opportunities in the Nam Ha NPA, and if you want to visit ethnic minorities, this is your best bet in Southeast Asia (45% of Muang Sing's population is Akha).

◉ Sights & Activities

The main draw for Muang Sing is its proximity to tribal villages and trekking in Nam Ha NPA. If you're just here to cycle, grab a map (such as Wolfgang Kom's excellent Muang Sing Valley map) from the tourist office, hire a bike and explore on your own.

Tribal Museum   MUSEUM
(admission 5000K; ☉8.30am-4.30pm Mon-Fri, 8-11am Sat) The most distinctive of the old Lao-French buildings is now home to the two-room Tribal Museum, which has costume displays downstairs and six cases of cultural artefacts upstairs. Watching a 40-minute video on the Akha people costs 5000K extra.

Phou Iu Travel   ADVENTURE TOUR
(☑081-400012; www.muangsingtravel.com; ☉7am-7pm) The leading tour operator in Muang Sing, run out of the Phou Iu II Guesthouse, offers well-organised treks around Muang Sing. They also offer treks to the more remote Xieng Khaeng district towards Burma. Check www.adventure-trek-laos.com for details.

🛏 Sleeping & Eating

You'll find most of the guesthouses on the town's main strip. There's not much choice eating-wise; apart from the simple Laotian and Western dishes in the cafes, there's a clutch of *fĕr* shops selling tasty fare.

Thai Lü Guest House   GUESTHOUSE $
(☑086-400375; r 30,000-40,000K) Looking like a backdrop in an old Bruce Lee flick, this creaky wooden building has a certain charm, even if the rattan-walled, squat-loo rooms are uninspiring. The restaurant downstairs (meals 10,000K to 25,000K) serves Thai, Laotian and Western dishes.

Phou Iu II Guesthouse   GUESTHOUSE $$
(☑086-400012; www.muangsingtravel.com; small/medium/large bungalows 100,000/200,000/400,000K) Set around an expansive

Muang Sing

garden, the biggest bungalows have outdoor rock-clad shower spaces. All rooms have comfortable beds, mosquito nets, fans and small verandahs, plus there's an onsite herbal sauna (10,000K) and massage (50,000K per hour). There is also a small restaurant here.

Phunnar Restaurant   LAOTIAN **$**
(Panna Restaurant; mains 15,000-30,000K; ⊘7.30am-8pm) Located in a quiet backstreet, the Phunnar is an airy open-air place for inexpensive fried rice, noodles, *làhp* and soups.

ℹ Information

There's a **Lao Development Bank** (⊘8am-noon & 2-3.30pm Mon-Fri), which changes cash but has no ATM, a **post office** (⊘8am-4pm Mon-Fri) and a lacklustre **tourist office** (⊘8am-4pm Mon-Fri).

ℹ Getting There & Around

From the bus station in the northwest corner of town, *sŏrngtǎaou* depart for Muang Long (40,000K, 1½ hours) at 8am, 11am and 1.30pm. To Luang Namtha (50,000K, two hours, 58km) minibuses leave at 8am, 9am, 11am, 12.30pm, 2pm and 3pm.

   Kalao Motorcycle (per day 80,000K; ⊘8am-5pm), on the road to the main market, rents motorbikes. Bicycle rental (30,000K per day) is available from several main-street agencies and guesthouses.

Bokeo Province

The smallest province in the country – once a major artery on the infamous opium trail of contraband, which was smuggled in and out of the Golden Triangle – these days Bokeo Province is home to a flourishing ecotreasure known as the Gibbon Experience, based in the rugged Bokeo Nature Reserve. Home to a rich biodiversity of large mammals, this area offers great trekking, and you may come across a colourful cast of 34 different ethnic groups.

Huay Xai   ຫ້ວຍຊາຍ

☑ 084 / POP 20,000

A US heroin processing plant was allegedly based here during the Secret War, however, these days the only things trafficked through Huay Xai are travellers en route to Luang Prabang. Separated from Thailand by the cocoa-brown Mekong River, it is for many their first impression of Laos – don't worry, it gets better! The town has some welcoming traveller guesthouses and tasty cafes, and by night its central drag dons fairy lights and fires up roadside food vendors. Huay Xai is also the HQ of the now-fabled Gibbon Experience, the most talked-about environmentally conscious jungle adventure in the country.

🛏 Sleeping

Most guesthouses are on the main street parallel with the river.

★ **Daauw Homestay** HOMESTAY $
(☑ 030 904 1296; www.projectkajsiablaos.org; r 60,000-80,000K) An overnight stay in a bungalow at the Daauw Homestay offers a way to contribute something to women's empowerment and minority rights. As well as accommodation, there is a restaurant-bar, plus a small handicrafts shop. One-week to one-month volunteering positions are available for 850,000K per week, including board and lodging.

Phonetip Guesthouse GUESTHOUSE $
(☑ 084-211084; Th Saykhong; r 50,000-120,000K; ❄ 🛜) Simple, central and clean by budget standards. The cheapest options are just beds in boxes but there's a pleasant road-facing communal area upstairs, if you can grab a seat.

Phonevichith Guesthouse & Restaurant GUESTHOUSE $$
(☑ 084-211765; houayxairiverside.com; Ban Khonekeo; r 600-1000B; ❄ 🛜) Colourful fabrics, fans and kitschy lamps add a little character to the smart rooms, which come with piping-hot showers and air-con. A new wing offers the smartest beds in town, which are verging on 'boutique' standards. The main attraction is the Mekong perch and handy proximity to the slowboat landing.

Riverside Houayxay Hotel HOTEL $$
(☑ 084-211064; riverside_houayxay_laos@hotmail.com; deluxe/riverview r 600/900B) Located

---

THE GIBBON EXPERIENCE

Adrenalin meets conservation in this ecofriendly adventure in the 1060 sq km of Bokeo Nature Reserve wilderness. The **Gibbon Experience** (☑ 084-212021; www.gibbonexperience.org; express 2-day US$190, 3-day classic or waterfall US$290) is essentially a series of navigable 'zip-lines' that criss-cross the canopy of some of Laos' most pristine forest; home to tigers, clouded leopards, black bears and the black-crested gibbon.

Several years ago poaching was threatening the extinction of the black-crested gibbon, but thanks to Animo, a conservation-based tour group, the hunters of Bokeo were convinced to become the forest's guardians.

Laos' most unforgettable adventure, this three-day rush offers the chance to play Tarzan, by spending two nights in soaring tree-houses within thickly forested hills, and swinging high across valleys on incredible zip-lines, some more than 500m long. The guides are helpful, though make sure you're personally vigilant with the knots in your harness. Should it rain, remember you need more time to slow down with your humble brake (a swatch of tyre tread).

For those on the classic experience, there's a good chance of hearing the gibbons' incredible calls. Actually seeing these arboreal athletes is much rarer but some lucky groups do catch a fleeting glimpse. More recently, a faster two-day express trip has been added to the roster for those with less time to spare in the forest canopy. The days also involve a serious amount of trekking; bring a pair of hiking boots and long socks to deter the ever-persistent leeches.

Accommodation is located in unique thatched tree-houses, which are around 40m above the ground and set in natural amphitheatres with spectacular views. Most sleep eight people with bedding laid out beneath large cloth nets, while some tree-houses sleep just two. Well-cooked meals are zip-lined in from one of three rustic kitchens, while coffee, tea and hot chocolate are available in each tree-house. Keeping anything edible in the provided strong box is essential – there are some very large rats with excellent noses! For those who need a little more comfort, the recently added Gibbon Spa option incorporates the best of the 'classic' with gourmet food, improved lodgings and massages.

Whichever option you choose – book weeks in advance – prepayment online through Paypal works well. One day before departure, check in at the Huay Xai Gibbon Experience office (p325). Gloves (essential for using the zip-lines) are sold next door. It's also advisable to bring a torch (flashlight), water bottle and earplugs to deflect the sound of a million crickets. Otherwise leave most of your baggage in the office storeroom – everything you bring you must carry on your back over some steep hikes and on the zip-lines. And, as there's no electricity, don't forget to precharge camera batteries.

just off the main strip and overlooking the mighty Mekong, this is the most upmarket hotel in the centre of town. Rooms are spacious and spotlessly clean. Hot water is on tap, plus there is satellite TV and a minibar.

✗ Eating & Drinking

There are numerous barbecue food stalls (try the one next to BCEL) and cafes to choose from.

BAP Guesthouse   LAOTIAN $
(Th Saykhong; mains 15,000-35,000K; ✐) Run by English-speaking Mrs Changpeng, this wayfarer's fave has an inviting restaurant dishing up snacks, vegetarian dishes and Lao

staples. It's one of the closest spots to Lao immigration so it's good for some arrival or departure fodder.

Maung Ner Cafe   LAOTIAN, INTERNATIONAL $
(Gecko Bar; Th Saykhong; meals 20,000-40,000K; ⊙6.30am-11pm) With its worn turquoise walls adorned in animal horns, Muang Ner remains a popular choice. Mouthwatering *làhp*, Western breakfasts and wood-fired pizzas all complement the welcoming vibe.

Daauw   LAOTIAN $
(mains 20,000-50,000K; ✐) Reminiscent of a Thai island with its chill-out terrace, low cushions and open pit fire, Daauw serves

---

GETTING TO THAILAND

Huay Xai to Chiang Khong

Getting to the border The Lao–Thai Friendship Bridge here was completed in December 2013, and the former boat crossing is now only for locals.

At the border A 15-day Thai visa is automatically granted when entering Thailand; to obtain a 30-day Thai visa, you'll need to arrive in the country by air. The nearest ATM on the Thai side is 2km south.

Moving on Many travellers leave Huay Xai bound for Chiang Rai (365B, 2½ hours) with buses typically leaving from Chiang Khong's bus station every hour from 6am till 5pm. Greenbus (✐ in Thailand 5365 5732; www.greenbusthailand.com) has services to Chiang Mai at 6am, 9am and 11.40am. Several overnight buses for Bangkok (500B to 750B, 10 hours) leave at 3pm and 3.30pm.

Hongsa to Phrae

Getting to the border The Muang Ngeun/Ban Huay Kon border crossing (8am to 5pm) is around 2.5km west of Muang Ngeun junction. Several *sŏrngtăaou* make the run from Hongsa (40,000K, 1½ hours) to Muang Ngeun. Once the new bridge north of Pak Beng is open, there will also be a bus service.

At the border Most nationalities crossing into Thailand receive a visa on arrival.

Moving on From the Thai side, if you don't want to walk your bags across the 1km of no-man's-land you can pay 100B for a motorbike with luggage-carrying sidecar. The Thai border post, Huay Kon, is not quite a village but does have simple noodle shops. The only public transport is a luxurious minibus (✐083-024 3675) to Phrae (160B, five hours) via Nan (100B, three hours) departing from the border post at 11.45am. Northbound it leavto cames the bus stations in Phrae at 6am, and Nan at 8am.

Pak Lai to Loei

Getting to the border The quiet rural Kaen Thao/Tha Li border crossing (8am to 6pm) is the home of yet another (small) Friendship Bridge, this time over the Nam Heuang. From Pak Lai, there are *sŏrngtăaou* to the border post at Kaen Thao at around 10am and noon (40,000K, 1¾ hours).

At the border Most nationalities crossing into Thailand receive a visa on arrival.

Moving on After walking across the bridge you'll have to take a short *sŏrngtăaou* ride (30B) 8km to Tha Li before transferring to another *sŏrngtăaou* (40B) the remaining 46km to Loei, from where there are regular connections to Bangkok and elsewhere.

For more information about crossing these borders in the other direction, see p444.

organic Hmong food, plenty of vegetarian options and whole barbecued Mekong fish or chicken. Linger for 'laojitos' if there's a crowd – a mojito made with *lòw-lów*.

Bar How BAR

(Th Saykhong; meals 20,000-40,000K; ⊗6.30am-11pm; ⊛) The funkiest little bar-restaurant on Huay Xai's main strip, Bar How is a little hole in the wall that serves food by day and plenty of drinks by night. The bar is laden with homemade *lòw-lów* or rice wine, infused with everything from blueberry to tamarind. Try them all if you dare...we did.

ℹ Information

BCEL (Th Saykhong; ⊗8.30am-4.30pm Mon-Fri) 24-hour ATM, exchange facility and Western Union.

Gibbon Experience Office (Th Saykhong)

Lao Development Bank Exchange Booth (⊗8am-5pm) Handy booth right beside the pedestrian immigration window. Most major currencies exchanged into kip. US-dollar bills must be dated 2006 or later.

Tourist Information Office (☑084-211162; Th Saykhong; ⊗8am-4.30pm Mon-Fri) Has free tourist maps of the town and some suggestions for excursions around the town and the province.

ℹ Getting There & Away

AIR

Huay Xai's airport is perched on a hillside 1.5km northwest of the bus station. **Lao Airlines** (☑084-211026; www.laoairlines.com) flies daily to/from Vientiane for 895,000K.

BOAT

Slowboats headed down the Mekong River to Luang Prabang (200,000K per person, two days, not including overnight accommodation) hold about 70 people, but captains try to cram in more than 100. Refuse en masse and a second boat will be drafted in. Boats leave from the boat landing at the north end of town at 11am and stop for one night in Pak Beng (100,000K, six to eight hours). Tickets are available from the boat landing the afternoon before you travel, or from guesthouses.

Speedboats to Pak Beng (160,000K, three hours) and Luang Prabang (360,000K, six hours) leave when full from a landing about 2km south of town, from 8am daily. Buy your ticket at any one of the guesthouses or on arrival at the kiosk above the boat landing. Be aware that deaths are not uncommon given the recklessness of the drivers; if you do choose to go ahead with the trip, bring earplugs and close your eyes.

Slowboats also run to Luang Namtha (1,530,000K to 1,700,000K per boat split between passengers, plus 40,000K each for food and accommodation) via Ban Na Lae.

For any journey take plenty of water, food supplies and padding for your back.

Alternatively, the stylish 40-seat **Luang Say Cruise** (☑020 5509 0718; www.luangsay.com; per person US$362-491, single supplement from US$67; ⊗8am-3pm) includes meals, guides, visits en route and a night's accommodation at the lovely Luang Say Lodge (p317) in Pak Beng.

BUS & SŎRNGTĂAOU

The bus station is 5km east of town. Buses to Luang Prabang (120,000K, 14 to 17 hours) via Luang Namtha and Udomxai depart at 9am, 11.30am, 1pm and 5pm. The 11.30am continues to Vientiane (230,000K, 25 hours), and the 5pm Luang Prabang bus is a VIP service (135,000K). For Udomxai (85,000K, nine hours) there's also an 8.30am service. For Luang Namtha (60,000K, four hours) an additional bus departs at 9am.

Travel-agency minibuses to Luang Namtha leave from central Huay Xai at around 9am (100,000K).

CENTRAL & SOUTHERN LAOS

Steamy rice plains, gothic karst formations, vast forests, coffee-growing plantations and authentic riverine life: all of this beckons en route to and from the border with Cambodia. Ever since Tha Khaek opened her faded colonial petals a few years back, many have been using the town as a picturesque springboard to access Tham Kong Lo, a fantastical 7.5km subterranean cave complex only traversable by boat, and the ragged black karsts of Khammuane Province, home to the Loop, a legendary three-day motorbike adventure. Further south, Savannakhet charms with her old French buildings and trekking options, while close to the hammock-flopping paradise of turquoise-watered Si Phan Don (Four Thousand Islands), you'll find the beautiful Khmer ruins of sleepy Champasak.

Bolikhamsai & Khammuan Provinces

Bolikhamsai and Khammuan form the narrow girdle of Laos, straddling the Annamite Chain, which heads east from Laos to Vietnam, with the Mekong River and Thailand to the west. Due to the presence of the Ho Chi

Minh Trail from Vietnam passing through Laos here, the area was heavily bombed during the Secret War, and the UXO problem is still a major challenge for NGOs.

If you're passing this way to see Tham Kong Lo, languid Tha Khaek is a pleasant base, or nearer still – if you're in a hurry – overnight in the rural village of Ban Kong Lo, literally minutes from the cave.

Paksan ປາກຊັນ

054 / POP 27,000

Sitting at the confluence of Nam San and the Mekong River, Paksan is something of a nonentity and needn't feature on your itinerary unless you're using its international border to cross to Thailand. BK Guest House (054-212638; r 70,000-80,000K; P❈🖥) makes for a budget stop, with clean but small rooms. Midrange, Vietnamese-run Paksan Hotel (054-791333; Rte 13; s/d 100,000/140,000K; P❈🛜), located a little east of the bridge, is probably the best digs on offer, with huge clean rooms that offer air-con, en suites, hot water and TV.

Buses to/from Vientiane stop on Rte 13 outside the Talat Sao (morning market) and leave regularly between 5am and 4.30pm, with most departures in the morning.

Route 8 to Lak Sao

Wind your way through a lost world of jungle and dreamlike rock formations in some

GETTING TO THAILAND: PAKSAN TO BEUNG KAN

Getting to the border Few people use the Mekong Paksan/Beung Kan border crossing. In Paksan follow a sign to the port and Lao border post (open 8am to noon and 1.30pm to 4.30pm). The boat across the Mekong to Bueng Kan takes a few minutes and costs 60B per person, or charter for 480B.

At the border Fifteen-day Thai visas are granted on arrival but check in advance as this is a remote spot seldom used by travellers; to obtain a 30-day Thai visa, you'll need to arrive in the country by air.

Moving on Buses leave Beung Kan in Thailand for Udon Thani and Bangkok.

For more information about crossing this border in the other direction, see p417.

of the country's trippiest landscape. The first major stop is Ban Khoun Kham (also known as Ban Na Hin), 41km east of Rte 13, in the lush Hin Bun valley. The village makes a good base from which to explore Phu Hin Bun National Protected Area. You can also catch your forward bus to Kong Lo village and its ace card: the extraordinary Tham Kong Lo. Community-based treks gear up at Ban Khoun Kham's tourist information centre, just south of the Tat Namsanam entrance.

◉ Sights

Tham Kong Lo CAVE
(106,000K per boat) If you were to realise the ancient Greek underworld (minus the shades and torture), you might end up with Tham Kong Lo. Situated in the 1580-sq-km wilderness of Phu Hin Bun National Protected Area, this 7.5km tunnel, which runs beneath an immense limestone mountain, is unearthly.

Crossing the Nam Hin Bun via rickety suspension bridge you first witness the gaping, ragged mouth of the cave, your breath stolen before you've even entered the eerie, black cavern. Passing into the church-high darkness (100m in some places) by long-tail boat and watching the light of the cave mouth recede is a spooky experience. A section of the cave has now been atmospherically lit, and while your longtail docks in a rocky inlet and you explore a haunting stalactite wood, your imagination will likely be in overdrive: are those Gollum's eyes in the bat-black gloom or a boatman's torch beam?

Once you get to the other side of the cave and stop for refreshments in a nearby shelter, you still have to make the return journey. Remember to bring a decent torch, plus rubber sandals (life-jackets are provided). It costs 105,000K per boat for the return trip (2½ hours, maximum four people). It's best to spend the night near the cave in Kong Lo village (about 1km downstream of the cave mouth), where you'll find restaurants and plenty of guesthouses.

⌂ Sleeping

BAN KHOUN KHAM

Sainamhai Resort RESORT $
(020 233 1683; www.sainamhairesort.com; r 130,000K; P❈🛜) Riverside Sainamhai has a handsome longhouse restaurant (mains 25,000K) and 12 well-maintained rattan-

walled cabanas with private balconies, en suites and clean linen. It's 3km east of Rte 8; follow the sign near the junction of Rte 8 and the road that borders the Theun Hin Bun dam housing compound at the east end of town. Free pick-up from bus station.

Xok Xai Guesthouse GUESTHOUSE $
(☑ 051-233629; Rte 8; r 80,000K; P ❄) Lovely rooms in a traditional house set back off Rte 8, 400m north of the market. Details include spotless varnished floors, thick duvets, TV, air-con, powder-blue curtains and hot-water en suites.

KONG LO VILLAGE & AROUND

Sala Kong Lor GUESTHOUSE $
(☑ 020 5564 5111; www.salalao.com; Ban Tiou; bungalows US$6-30; P) Located 1.5km downstream of Tham Kong Lo, these stilted bungalows range from basic to superior and sit by the Nam Hin Bun. En suite rooms are basic but welcoming, with brick walls, blue bedspreads, mozzie nets, a few sticks of furniture and private balconies from which to enjoy the lush river view.

Chantha Guest House GUESTHOUSE $
(☑ 020 210 0002; Ban Kong Lo; r with/without air-con 100,000/60,000K; P ❄ @ ☎) This Swiss-style accommodation, on the main road to Kong Lo and at the beginning of the village, has 15 cool and well-kept rooms with doubles and twins, plus a dorm that sleeps five people (180,000K). There's a DVD lounge and a small cafe, and the owners are friendly. Temperamental wi-fi.

★ **Auberges Sala Hinboun** GUESTHOUSE $$
(☑ 041 212 445; www.salalao.com; r incl breakfast US$23-29; P) Ten kilometres north of Ban Kong Lo, Sala Hinboun has 12 guacamole-green, homely wood cabanas on stilts. Rooms have gypsy-chic curtains, rattan floors, balconies and comfy beds. The ones facing the river are the largest (US$29), while the smaller ones (US$25) are decent, too. The restaurant has fried fish, roast chicken or even spit-roasted piglet (450,000K).

ℹ Getting There & Away

From Tha Khaek there's a daily 8am and 9am departure for Ban Khoun Kham (50,000K). Alternatively there's a direct daily bus to Kong Lo from Tha Khaek's Talat Phetmany at 7am (80,000K). All transport along Rte 8 stops at Ban Khoun Kham. If you're coming from Vientiane hop off at Vieng Kham and continue by *sŏrngtǎaou* (25,000K, 7am to 7pm) to Ban Khoun Kham.

Buses for Vientiane (75,000K) usually stop between 7am and 10.30am. For Tha Khaek (75,000K, three hours, 143km), there are a couple of buses in the morning; for Lak Sao take any passing bus or *sŏrngtǎaou* (25,000K).

From Ban Khoun Kham to Ban Kong Lo, it's a 20-minute journey by scooter or *sŏrngtǎaou* (25,000K); they leave at 10am, 12.30pm and 3pm. Headed the other way, from Ban Kong Lo to Ban Khoun Kham, *sŏrngtǎaou* depart at 6.30am, 8am and 11am.

Lak Sao ຫລັກຊາວ
☑ 054 / POP 31,400
Deep in logging territory, with trucks rumbling over the Vietnamese border to Vinh, Lak Sao sits in the shadow of handsome karst formations. The town isn't much to look at, but thanks to it being on the Loop and en route to Tham Kong Lo, it's now enjoying a few more passing visitors.

The **Phoutthavong Guest House** (☑ 054-341074; Rte 1E; r 80,000K; P ❄ ☎) has 10 new rooms with shared bathrooms or en suites to choose from. The **Souriya Hotel** (☑ 054-341111; Rte 1E; r 50,000-80,000K; P ❄) is OK for a night, too.

There's a **Lao Development Bank** (Rte 1E) but no internet cafe.

Scheduled buses leave from near the market for Vientiane (85,000K, six to eight hours, 334km) at 5.30am, 6.30am, 8am and 8pm, stopping at Vieng Kham (Thang Beng; 35,000K, 1½ to 2½ hours, 100km), while onward transport to Vieng Kham leaves throughout the day. One bus goes to Tha Khaek (60,000K, six hours, 202km) at 7.30am.

Tha Khaek ທ່າແຂກ
☑ 051 / POP 31,400
This ex-Indochinese trading post is a pleasing melange of crumbling French villas and wilting Chinese merchant shopfronts, and, despite the new bridge over to nearby Thailand, it shows little sign of radical change. Catch a riverside sundowner or wander along the atmospheric streets as dusk's amber light kicks in and douses the old buildings in charm. With its dusty centrepiece fountain and tree-shaded boulevards glowing with braziers, Tha Khaek is reminiscent of Vientiane 15 years ago.

Tha Khaek is also a comfy base from which to visit eerie Tham Kong Lo (p326), or

Tha Khaek

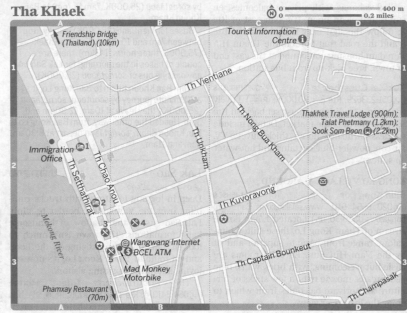

Tha Khaek

🟢 Activities, Courses & Tours
Green Discovery .... (see 4)

🛏 Sleeping
1 Hotel Riveria A2
2 Mekong Hotel A2

🍴 Eating
3 Duc Restaurant A3
4 Inthira Restaurant....................................B3
5 Phavilai Restaurant B3

ℹ Transport
Phavilai Restaurant .... (see 5)

---

experience 'The Loop', the legendary three-day motorbike odyssey. And forget getting to either on rickety scooters: Tha Khaek now has a proper motorbike rental outfit, Mad Monkey Motorbike (p331).

👉 Tours

The tourist information centre (p330), run by reliable **Mr Somkiad** (☑ 030 530 0503, 020 5571 1797; somkiad@yahoo.com), operates various adventures, such as a two-day trek in the Phu Hin Bun NPA, which costs 650,000K per person for a group of four. These treks typically involve a homestay. Ask him too

about the 3km-long newly discovered river cave, **Tham Pa Seuam** (Fish Cave). Slated to open in late 2014, it's similar in scope to Tham Kong Lo, plus, conveniently, it's only 15km away from the town.

Green Discovery ADVENTURE TOUR
(☑ 051-251390; Inthira Hotel, Th Chao Annou; ⏰ 8am-9pm) Has a desk at the Inthira Hotel and runs a range of treks and kayaking excursions in the lush Phu Hin Bun NPA, including to Tham Kong Lo. Cycling, kayaking and a homestay can also be combined.

🛏 Sleeping

⭐ **Thakhek Travel Lodge** GUESTHOUSE $
(☑ 051-212931; thakhektravellodge@gmail. com; Rte 13; dm 30,000K; r 40,000-180,000K; ℗❄@🛜) This travellers' oasis is five minutes east of town and has a spectrum of rooms, from boxy standards to those with elements of Indo-chic. The lodge's centrepiece is a leafy courtyard with a nightly firepit, around which you can swap stories of the Loop. Seven new rooms out back come with slate floors, flat-screen TVs and fridges.

There's also a natty cafe serving up Lao fare such as *làhp*, Western salads and various juices.

Mekong Hotel HOTEL $
(☎051-250777; Th Setthathirat; s/d 130,000/140,000K; [P][✳][@]) This blue, Soviet-inspired monolith has decent rooms that have cable TV, air-con and fresh en suites. There's also a restaurant facing the Mekong.

Thipphachanh Guesthouse GUESTHOUSE $
(☎051-212762; Rte 13; r with fan/air-con 60,000/80,000K; [P][✳]) Despite its dusty location, these digs, based around a courtyard, are fragrantly fresh with white walls, tiled floors, TVs and en suites. There's also clean sheets and blankets for cold nights (do they exist?).

★**Inthira Hotel Sikotabong** HOTEL $$
(☎051-251237; www.inthirahotels.com; Th Chao Annou; r US$29-49; [✳][@]) Set in an old French villa, Inthira, with its pretty facade, offers the most romantic digs in town. Its restaurant fronts the old fountain, and its chic wine-hued rooms are a delight for weary travellers, with exposed brick walls, rain showers, cable TV, dark-wood furniture, air-con and

safety deposit boxes. The best rooms face the street and have balconies.

Hotel Riveria HOTEL $$
(☎051-250000; Th Setthathirat; r US$58-75; [P][⟳][✳][@][@][⟲]) With terrific views of Thailand on one side and even more dramatic vistas of the jagged karsts on the other, this is very much a family/businessperson's choice. Large rooms have king-size beds, TVs, fridges, baths and international-style furniture. Downstairs, there's a decent restaurant with a lovely buffet breakfast and egg station. Professional.

✖ Eating & Drinking

Several baguette vendors can be found on or near Fountain Sq in the morning, and the adjacent riverfront is good for a cheap meal any time. **Duc Restaurant** (Th Setthathirat; meals 15,000K; ◷6am-10pm; ☑), unnamed but for an ETL sign, looks like someone's front room (hung with family photos and portraits of Ho Chi Minh) and serves

LAOS BOLIKHAMSAI & KHAMMUAN PROVINCES

GETTING TO VIETNAM

Lak Sao to Vinh

Getting to the border The Nam Phao/Cau Treo border crossing (open 7am to 4.30pm) is 32km from Lak Sao. Sŏrngtăaou (20,000K, 45 minutes) leave every hour or so from Lak Sao market. Alternatively, direct buses from Lak Sao to Vinh (120,000K, five hours) leave several times a day between noon and 2pm (you may have to change buses at the border).

At the border You'll need to prearrange a visa if heading into Vietnam. There's an exchange booth on the Laos side with ungenerous rates and, inconveniently, the Vietnam border post is another 1km up the road.

Moving on On the Vietnamese side beware of an assortment of piranhas who'll offer to take you to Vinh by minibus for US$30 – it should cost US$5 per person. A metered taxi costs around US$40 while a motorbike fare is 200,000d. Hook up with other travellers to improve bargaining power. These woes can be avoided by taking the direct bus from Lak Sao to Vinh. Once in Vinh take the sleeper train, **Reunification Express** (www.vr.com.vn), direct to Hanoi.

Tha Khaek to Dong Hoi

Getting to the border The Na Phao/Cha Lo border (open 7am to 4pm) is so out of the way it might be better to opt for an easier crossing elsewhere. Transport on either side is slow and scarce, though there's a daily sŏrngtăaou from Tha Khaek (50,000K, 3½ hours, 142km) at 8am bound for Lang Khang, 18km short of the border.

At the border This is a small, sleepy border post. On the Vietnamese side the nearest sizeable city is Dong Hoi. Remember to organise your Vietnamese visa in advance.

Moving on A direct bus from Tha Khaek to Dong Hoi (90,000K, 10 to 14 hours) leaves four times a week at 7pm, making this the easiest way to pass through this border crossing.

For more information about crossing these borders in the other direction, see p94.

delicious *fĕr hàang* (noodle broth), while **Phavilai Restaurant** (Fountain Sq; meals 10,000-15,000K; ☺6am-9pm), though short on charm, is wallet-friendly, with a wide choice of rice and noodles.

Phamxay Restaurant   LAOTIAN $
(Th Setthathirat; ☺8am-12am) Catching whatever breeze is going, this joint sits on the riverfront and covers rice dishes, *láhp* variations, soup, fried shrimp and fried morning glory. Nice place for a sundowner.

★**Inthira Restaurant**   FUSION $$
(Th Chao Anou; mains 45,000K; ☺7am-10pm; 🛜🖉) With its industrial-chic exposed cement walls, low-lit ambience, open-range kitchen and handsome bar stocked with brightly glowing spirits, this is the place to stop for breakfast, lunch or dinner. An Asian fusion menu features delicious *steak au poivre*, *đôm yam* soup, copious salads, curries, stir-fries and very competent burgers. Recommended.

ⓘ Information

BCEL (Th Vientiane) Changes major currencies and travellers cheques, and makes cash advances on Visa. Has three ATMs in town, including one in Fountain Sq, as well as one at the bus station.

Lao Development Bank (Th Vientiane) Cash only – no exchange or Visa advances.

Post Office (Th Kuvoravong) Also offers expensive international phone calls.

Tha Khaek Hospital (cnr Th Chao Anou & Th Champasak) Tha Khaek Hospital is fine for minor ailments or commonly seen problems including malaria and dengue. Seek out English-speaking Dr Bounthavi.

Tourist Information Centre (☎030 530 0503, 020 5571 1797; www.khammuanetourism.com; Th Vientiane; ☺8.30am-5pm) The excellent tourist information centre has plenty of informative pamphlets and sells maps of the town and province. Also runs tours.

Tourist Police (☎051-250610; Fountain Sq) Knows how to write insurance reports (if you can track down an officer).

Wangwang Internet (Fountain Sq; per hr 7000K; ☺7.30am-9.30pm) Offers internet on a few laptops as well as scooter rental (60,000K per day).

ⓘ Getting There & Away

Tha Khaek's **bus station** (Rte 13) is about 3.5km from the centre of town. For Vientiane, buses leave every hour or so between 5.30am and 9am (70,000K, six hours, 332km), as well as a VIP departure at 9.15am (85,000K, six hours) and a sleeper VIP at 1am (85,000K). Any buses going north stop at at Vieng Kham

---

GETTING TO THAILAND

Tha Khaek to Nakhon Phanom

Getting to the border Crossing the Mekong at the Tha Khaek/Nakhon Phanom border crossing is now only possible for locals. Travellers have to use the Friendship bridge, 7km from Tha Khaek. A túk-túk over the bridge carrying two people will cost you 20,000K per person from Tha Khaek's bus station (every half hour). The immigration office on the bridge opens at 6am and closes at 10pm.

At the border A free 15-day visa is granted on entry to Thailand; to obtain a 30-day Thai visa, you'll need to arrive in the country by air. There's an exchange booth and 24hr ATM.

Moving on From the bridge it's a 30B túk-túk ride to Thailand's Nakon Phanom bus station, from where buses leave regularly for Udon Thani and also Bangkok (at 7.30am and from 7pm to 8pm).

Savannakhet to Mukdahan

Getting to the border Regular buses (15,000K, 45 minutes) leave Savannakhet's bus station and cross the new Friendship Bridge for Thailand's Mukdahan between 8am and 7pm.

At the border This is a well-organised, busy border (open 6am to 10pm). A free 15-day tourist visa is given on entering Thailand.

Moving on Onward from Mukdahan, there are five daily buses bound for Bangkok between 5.30pm and 8.15pm.

For more information about crossing these borders in the other direction, see p413.

(Thang Beng; 30,000K, 90 minutes, 102km) and Paksan (40,000K, three to four hours, 193km). There are two daily services to Attapeu (85,000K, 10 hours, 3.30pm and 11pm), Salavan (85,000K, 11pm) and Sekong (75,000K, 10am and 3.30pm).

Southward buses to Savannakhet (30,000K) depart every half hour; for Pakse there's a VIP bus (70,000K, six hours) at 9am and hourly local buses (70,000K). For Vietnam, buses for Hue (120,000K) leave Monday, Tuesday, Wednesday and Saturday at 8am; for Danang (120,000K) every Monday and Friday at 8pm; for Hanoi (160,000K, 17 hours) 8pm on Tuesday and Saturday; and for Dong Hoi (90,000K, 10 hours) every Monday and Friday at 7pm.

If you're headed direct to Don Khong (150,000K, 15 hours, 452km) in Si Phan Don (Four Thousand Islands), a bus from Vientiane stops around 5.30pm.

Sŏrngtǎaou depart every hour or so from Talat Phetmany to Mahaxai Mai (35,000K, 1½ hours, 50km). One also goes direct to Ban Kong Lo (80,000K, four hours) at 7.30am.

Sook Som Boon Bus Terminal (Talat Lak Saam) serves buses into the Khammuane Province interior with *sŏrngtǎaou* leaving every hour between 7.30am and 9.30am for Nyommalat (45,000K, two to three hours, 63km), Nakai (45,000K, 2½ to 3½ hours, 80km) and an 8pm departure for Na Phao (for the Vietnam border; 80,000K, 3½ hours, 142km).

🛈 Getting Around

It should cost about 20,000K to hire a jumbo (motorised three-wheeled taxi) to the bus terminal. Rides around town cost about 15,000K per person.

The one and only place to hire a tough, rollable motocross bike to tackle the Loop (scooters are just not built for the dangerously slippy road) and other adventures is **Mad Monkey Motorbike** (☑ 020 5993 9909, 020 2347 7799; dcn66@hotmail.com; Fountain Sq; 250cc bikes/automatic scooters per day US$38/28, day trips to Tham Kong Lo for a group of 4 per person 300,000K; ☺ 9am-8pm). Run by DC, a friendly German expat, Mad Monkey has two Honda 250cc dirt bikes, and three automatic wide-wheeled scooters. If you break down you can phone DC and, for a price, he'll come and get you and the bike. He can also take you to Tham Kong Lo and back in a day by bus, leaving at 8am and returning at 8pm (300,000K per person for a group of four).

Mr Ku's Motorbike Rental (☑ 020 220 6070; per day 100,000K; ☺ 7.30am-4.30pm), located at Thakhek Travel Lodge, has 110cc Korean bikes for getting around town or to the closer caves, while **Phavilai Restaurant** (Fountain Sq; per day 60,000K; ☺ 6am-9pm) has a few scooters for hire, as does **Wangwang Internet** (☑ 020 5697 8535; Fountain Sq; per day 50,000-60,000K; ☺ 8am-9pm).

Around Tha Khaek

Travellers rave about the Loop, a brilliant three-day motorbike trip through dense jungle, spectrally flooded valleys and gothic karst country, passing via Nakai, Lak Sao, Khoun Kham (Na Hin) and Tham Kong Lo; for details look at the travellers' log at Thakhek Travel Lodge (p328).

Meanwhile, buzz continues in anticipation of trips to the fantastical 9.5km subterranea of Xe Bang Fai Cave, located at the edge of Hin Namno NPA. Even longer than Kong Lo, this underground network boasts some of the tallest caverns and stalagmites of any river cave on earth, not to mention 25cm spiders! This is such a remote location that at present there's no tourist infrastructure to support an independent visit – it's difficult to reach and difficult to evacuate should you run into trouble on the rapids at the entrance or carrying your canoes over the jagged rocks. Tha Khaek tourist information centre (p330) should arrange overnight trips here come 2014.

Also don't miss the myriad caves that can be swum and explored right on Tha Khaek's doorstep. For information, talk to English-speaking Mr Somkiad at Tha Khaek's tourist information centre (p330).

EAST ON ROUTE 12

The first 22km of Rte 12 east of Tha Khaek is an area with several caves, an abandoned railway line and a couple of swimming spots that make a great day trip. All these places can be reached by túk-túk, bicycle or hired motorcycle.

The first cave is Tham Xang (ຖ້ຳຊ້າງ; Elephant Cave; admission 5000K), also known as Tham Pha Ban Tham after the nearby village – Ban Tham. The cave is famous for its stalagmite 'elephant head'. Take the right fork about 2.5km east of the Rte 13 junction and follow the road or, if it's too wet, continue along Rte 12 and turn right (south) onto a dirt road shortly after a bridge.

Back on Rte 12, turn north to Tham Pha Pa (Buddha Cave; admission 5000K; ☺ 8am-noon & 1-4pm), discovered by a villager hunting for bats. It's home to 229 bronze Buddha images, believed to have sat untouched for the last 600 years, and reached by a sturdy staircase that takes you 200m up a cliff face.

LAOS BCLIKHAMSAI & KHAMMUAN PROVINCES

In the rainy season the entrance floods, so you have to take a little boat to get here. It's also possible to go 50m into the mountain by boat along a turquoise river. To get here, take a laterite road north from Rte 12 about 4km after you cross Rte 13. Turn right after about 500m and follow the old railway bed before taking the left fork. The tourist information centre (p330) in Tha Khaek also runs day treks to the cave.

Back on Rte 12 are several other caves. A track heading south for about 400m at Km 14, near the bridge over the Huay Xieng Liap and the village of Ban Songkhone (about 10.5km from Rte 13), leads to the stunning limestone cave Tham Xieng Liap, the entrance of which is at the base of a dramatic 300m-high cliff. Rte 12 continues through a narrow pass (about 11.5km from Rte 13), with high cliffs on either side. Immediately beyond, a track leads north to the holy cave of Tham Sa Pha In (Tham Phanya Inh).

Savannakhet Province

Savannakhet is the country's most populous province and has become an increasingly important trade corridor between Thailand and Vietnam. Most people stop here to experience a bit of Mekong city life and/or to go trekking in the Dong Natad and Dong Phu Vieng protected areas.

Savannakhet ສະຫວັນນະເຂດ

*041 / POP 139,000

Languid and ghostly quiet during the sweltering days that batter the old city's plasterwork, Savannakhet is a beguiling mix of yesteryear coupled with increasingly modern commerce. The best it has to offer is in the historic quarter with its staggering display of decaying early-20th-century French architecture. Leprous and listing, these grand old villas of Indochina's heyday now lie unwanted like aged dames crying out for a makeover. There's little to do in town but amble the riverfront and plonk yourself down in one of a clutch of stylish restaurants and bijou cafes.

That said, there's loads to do nearby. Savannakhet has a dedicated tourist information centre and ecoguide unit, which have myriad trips to tempt you into the nearby NPAs.

◉ Sights

Your best bet is to hire a bicycle and pedal through the cracked streets and along the riverfront, or take a trek in the neighbouring protected areas, organised through Savannakhet's Eco-Guide Unit (p334).

Savannakhet Provincial Museum MUSEUM
(ພິພິດຕະພັນແຂວງສະຫວັນນະເຂດ; Th Khanthabuli; admission 5000K; ⊙ 8-11.30am & 1-4pm Mon-Sat) The Savannakhet Provincial Museum is a good place to see war relics, artillery pieces and inactive examples of the deadly UXO (unexploded ordnance) that has claimed the lives of more than 12,000 Lao since the end of the Secret War.

Musée Des Dinosaures MUSEUM
(ຫໍພິພິດຕະພັນໄດໂນເສົາ; Dinosaur Museum; *041-212597; Th Khanthabuli; admission 5000K; ⊙ 8am-noon & 1-4pm) In 1930, a major dig in a nearby village unearthed 200-million-year-old dinosaur fossils. This enthusiastically run museum is an interesting place to divert yourself for an hour or so. Savannakhet Province is home to five dinosaur sites.

⊨ Sleeping

There are some decent options in town; the following are our favourites.

Souannavong Guest House GUESTHOUSE $
(*041-212600; Th Saenna; r with/without air-con 100,000/70,000K; P※⊛⊛) Unfailingly fresh with clean en suite rooms and an organised reception, this little guesthouse down a quiet street abloom in bougainvillea has wi-fi and bikes to rent. A welcoming spot to stay.

Leena Guesthouse GUESTHOUSE $
(*041-212404; leenaguesthouse@hotmail.com; Th Chaokeen; r 50,000-90,000K; P※@⊛) An oldie but goodie, fairy-lit Leena is something of a motel with kitsch decor in comfortable peach-colored, clean rooms with tiled floors, hot-water showers, TVs and a pleasant breakfast area where you can pick up wi-fi. The air-con rooms are bigger. There's also a cafe.

★ Salsavan Guesthouse GUESTHOUSE $$
(*041-212371; Th Kuvoravong; s/d incl breakfast US$23/28; P※⊛) This beautiful French villa and ex-Thai consulate has all the makings of a boutique hotel. Rooms are large and atmospherically old fashioned with wood floors, mosquito nets and deep-colored walls with shuttered windows and balconies. That said, the en suites are unattractively Soviet

and the place feels like it's in need of invigoration. Outside there's a garden terrace.

Phonepaseud Hotel
HOTEL $$

(☎041-212158; fax 041-212916; Th Santisouk; r US$25-35; P ❄ 🛜) Phonepaseud has a friendly English-speaking owner, a clean lobby and imaginatively tiled and French wallpapered rooms with air-con, TVs, fridges and en suites. The VIP rooms are much larger. Outside there's a *naga*-guarded fountain, mature trees, plenty of plants and a tennis court. Discounts possible in low season.

Daosavanh Resort & Spa Hotel
HOTEL $$$

(☎041-212188; Th Tha He; r US$77-90; P ❄ 🛜 ❄ 🛗) Grand, relatively new and Mekong-facing, this hotel is a slice of international comfort and its kidney-shaped pool is a very welcome boon on sweltering days (which is most days). Rooms are large and immaculate, and there's karaoke, free airport transfers, massage, a gym, and breakfast included.

🍴 Eating & Drinking

With sidewalk cafes and a scattering of French restaurants, the cuisine on offer here is pretty varied. Opposite Wat Sainyaphum the **riverside snack and drink vendors** (⏱5-10pm) are great for sundowners and, as evening approaches, *seen ddat* (Korean-style barbecue) is also available.

★ Chai Dee
JAPANESE, INTERNATIONAL $

(☎020 5988 6767; Th Ratsavongseuk; mains 20,000K; ⏱8.30am-9pm; 🛜 🍽) Run by friendly Moto, this Japanese cafe is a real traveller magnet. And with good reason: there are

rattan mats to lounge on, books to exchange, cool T-shirts for sale and a wide menu of samosas, homemade yoghurt, Thai food and tofu, plus healthy shakes.

★ Lin's Café
INTERNATIONAL $

(Th Latsaphanith; mains 30,000K; ⏱8am-8pm; 🛜🍽) This chic cafe in a former 1930s Chinese merchant's house is on a pretty side street radiating off the old square by St Theresa's Catholic Church. Inside it's a mix of antique and modern furniture, easy tunes, and coffee with attitude. There are also fruit shakes, stir-fries, vegie dishes, breakfasts, fruit salads and *làhp,* and they even make bacon sandwiches!

Xokxay Restaurant
LAOTIAN $

(Th Si Muang; mains 15,000K; ⏱9am-9pm; 🍽) A great hole in the wall on the square near the Catholic church, Xokxay is clean and popular, and dishes up tasty Laotian food, including noodle dishes, fried rice, salads and crispy fried shrimp.

Café Chez Boune
FRENCH $$

(Th Ratsavongseuk; mains 75,000K; ⏱7am-10pm; 🛜) Glacially cool Chez Boune has a French-speaking owner and is deservedly popular with expats. It could be something to do with the decent service and tasty steaks, pasta dishes, lasagna, pork chops and *filet mignon* – all of which are executed with élan.

Dao Savanh
FRENCH $$$

(Th Si Muang; mains 100,000-150,000K, 3-course lunch (cafe) 65,000K; ⏱7am-10pm; 🛜) With its elegant colonial facade, this cool, square-facing place is the city's finest. Fans whir and wine glasses clink as you tuck into a French-

---

GETTING TO VIETNAM: SAVANNAKHET TO DONG HA

Getting to the border Buses for the Dansavanh/Lao Bao border (open 8am to 5pm) leave from Savannakhet (60,000K, five to seven hours) at 7am, 8.30am and 11am, and stop en route at Sepon (50,000K).

At the border It's a 1km walk between the two border posts (hop on a motorbike taxi on the Vietnamese side for 10,000d). Formalities don't take long given that all Vietnamese visas must be issued prior to arrival. There is simple accommodation on both sides of the border.

Moving on A daily 8am bus runs from Savannakhet to Dong Ha (80,000K, about eight hours, 329km), while a daily local bus runs from Savannakhet to Hue (90,000K, 13 hours, 409km); a VIP bus (110,000K, 8 hours, 409km) also runs from Savannakhet to Hue from Monday to Friday at 10.30am. A bus to Danang (110,000K) leaves Tuesday, Thursday and Saturday at 10pm, continuing to Hanoi (200,000K, 24 hours, 650km). No matter what you hear, you will have to change buses at the border.

For more information about crossing this border in the other direction, see p94.

Savannakhet

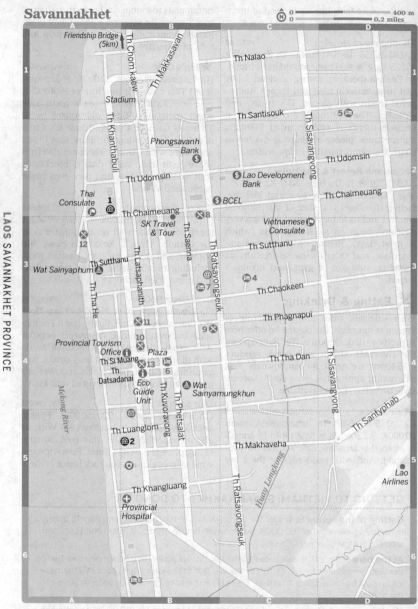

accented menu of soups, grilled entrecôte and lamb chop Provençal. The upstairs restaurant is the classy sister (open evenings only) while downstairs the cafe is open all day with salads, sandwiches and *croque monsieur*.

ⓘ Information

BCEL (Th Ratsavongseuk; ⊙8.30am-4pm) ATM, cash exchange and credit-card advances.

Eco Guide Unit (☑041-214203; www.savannakhet-trekking.com; Th Latsaphanith; ⊙8am-noon & 1-4.30pm Mon-Fri) The industrious eco-guide unit provides information ranging from bookings for treks to Dong Natad PPA and Dong Phu Vieng NPA, to bus times, accommodation, and info on where to get a decent massage or hire a motorbike.

Lao Development Bank (Th Udomsin; ⊘8.30-11.30am & 1.30-3.30pm) Changes cash and offers credit-card advances. Also has an ATM.

Post Office (⊘041-212205; Th Khanthabuli) For calls use an internet cafe instead.

Provincial Hospital (⊘041-212717, 020 260 1993; Th Khanthabuli; ⊘8am-12pm & 1-4pm) Ask for English-speaking Dr Outhon.

Provincial Tourism Office (⊘041-212755; Th Muang Sing; ⊘8-11.30am & 1.30-4.30pm) With helpful city maps and English-speaking staff, plus suggestions of things to do from food to local sights.

SK Travel & Tour (⊘041-300177, 041-300176; Th Chaimeuang; ⊘8am-4pm) Can arrange air tickets.

Tourist Police (⊘041-260173)

ⓘ Getting There & Away

Savannakhet's airport fields daily flights to and from Vientiane (US$128), Pakse (US$75) and Bangkok (US$155). Buy tickets at the **Lao Airlines** (⊘041 212 140; Savannakhet Airport; ⊘6.30am-4.30pm) office.

Savannakhet's bus terminal is 2km north of town on Th Makkasavan. Buses leave for Vientiane (75,000K, nine hours, 470km) hourly from 6am to 11.30am. Thereafter you'll have to catch buses headed to Pakse that pass through Tha Khaek (30,000K, 2½ to four hours, 125km) until 10pm. A sleeper VIP bus to Vientiane (120,000K, six to seven hours) leaves Tha Khaek at 9.30pm.

Heading south, at least 10 buses start here or pass through from Vientiane for Pakse (45,000K, five to six hours, 230km) and a daily bus to Don Khong (80,000K, six to eight hours) at 7pm.

Buses for Dansavanh (60,000K, five to seven hours) on the Lao/Vietnamese border leave at 7am, 8.30am & 11am, stopping at Sepon (50,000K, four to six hours). A daily local bus heads to Hue (90,000K), while a VIP bus (110,00K) runs Monday to Friday at 10.30am. A bus to Danang (110,000K) leaves Tuesday, Thursday and Saturday at 10pm, continuing to Hanoi (200,000K, 24 hours, 650km).

ⓘ Getting Around

A túk-túk to the bus terminal will cost about 20,000K; prices double after dark. The town is fairly sprawled out so it might be a good idea to rent a scooter (70,000K) from Souannavong Guest House (p332). Hire a bike (10,000K) along Th Ratsavongseuk.

East on Route 9

If you're heading east towards Vietnam, there are several places worth stopping at, including **Dong Natad Provincial Protected Area**, just 15km from Savannakhet. The provincial tourism office (p335) runs informative day and overnight treks here, with local guides explaining the myriad uses of the forest, and overnighters staying in a village home. Three-day treks into the remote **Dong Phu Vieng National Protected Area** offer a similar but more extreme experience, staying in Katang villages.

Further east is **Sepon**, with a couple of decent guesthouses. About 20km east of there is **Ban Dong**, a sleepy village on what was once an important branch of the Ho Chi Minh Trail. Today there are a couple of rusting American-built tanks (kids will direct you) that are among the most accessible war relics in southern Laos.

Buses and *sŏrngtăaou* head in both directions along Rte 9 between Savannakhet and Dansavanh; your best bet is to travel in the morning.

Champasak Province

Pakse   ປາກເຊ
⊘031 / POP 75,000

Don't expect Luang Prabang from this dusty, ex-Indochinese capital, but if you're moving north from the escapist Si Phan Don (Four

Pakse

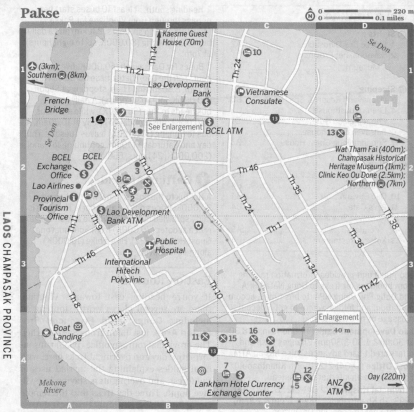

Pakse

◎ Sights
1 Wat Luang..A2

◐ Activities, Courses & Tours
2 Dok Champa Massage...........................B2
3 Green Discovery....................................B2
4 Xplore-Asia..B2

⌂ Sleeping
5 Alisa Guesthouse..................................C4
6 Athena Hotel..D1
7 Lankham Hotel.......................................C4
8 Pakse Hotel..B2

9 Residence Sisouk.................................A2
10 Sabaidy 2 Guesthouse........................C1

⊗ Eating
11 Baguette Vendors................................B4
12 Bolaven Cafe..C4
13 Delta Coffee...D2
14 Friendship Minimart............................C4
15 Jasmine Restaurant............................C4
Lankham Noodle Shop..................(see 7)
16 Mengky Noodle Shop...........................C4
Sinouk Coffee Shop......................(see 9)
17 Xuan Mai Restaurant...........................B2

Thousand Islands) or headed south to Cambodia, chances are you'll stay here a day or two and probably grow to like the place. Thanks to Green Discovery Tree Top Explorer zip-lining adventure, and a more active 'eco' drive from the tourist office, the city is now worth lingering in longer. Pakse is also

close to the beguiling Khmer ruins of Wat Phu in Champasak, and the Bolaven Plateau with its Edenic waterfalls, where many head with a rented scooter.

Central Pakse is bound by the Mekong to the south and by the Se Don (Don River) to the north and west. On and below Rte

13 towards the Mekong are most of Pakse's guesthouses, shops and restaurants. Heading west across Se Don takes you to the northern bus terminal. The southern bus terminal and market are 8km in the opposite direction.

◉ Sights & Activities

There are about 20 wats in Pakse, among which Wat Luang (ວັດຫຼວງ; Th 11) and Wat Tham Fai, both founded in 1935, are the largest. A monastic school at Wat Luang features ornate concrete pillars, carved wooden doors and murals. Behind the *sim* (chapel) is a monks' school.

Wat Tham Fai (ວັດຖ້ຳໄຟ; Rte 13), near the Champasak Palace Hotel, is undistinguished except for its spacious grounds, making it a prime site for temple festivals. It's also known as Wat Pha Bat because there is a small Buddha footprint shrine.

Champasak Historical
Heritage Museum   MUSEUM
(ພິພິດທະພັນເມືອງເດີກປະຫວັດສາດຈຳປາສັກ; Rte 13; admission 10,000K; ⊙8-11.30am & 1-4pm Mon-Fri) This museum has a few interesting artefacts, including three very old Dong Son bronze drums, and a Siam-style sandstone Buddha head dating to the 7th century. Also on display are musical instruments, a scale model of Wat Phu Champasak, and some American UXOs and other weaponry.

Clinic Keo Ou Done   MASSAGE
(Traditional Medicine Hospice; ☑ 020 543 1115, 031-251895; massage 30,000-70,000K, sauna 10,000K; ⊙9am-9pm, sauna 4-9pm) This professional and popular massage centre has an air-con massage room and herbal sauna segregated by gender. To get here, head out of town on Rte 38 and turn right towards Pakse Golf, 1km east of Champasak Grand Hotel.

Dok Champa Massage   MASSAGE
(Th 5; massages from 35,000K, body scrub 200,000K; ⊙9am-10pm) This is the longest-running and still the best massage emporium in the centre of town. Prices are very reasonable for the stylish set-up.

⟲ Tours

Most hotels and guesthouses can arrange day trips to the Bolaven Plateau, Wat Phu Champasak and Si Phan Don. The provincial tourism office (p339) also runs treks.

Green Discovery   ADVENTURE TOURS
(☑ 031-252908; www.greendiscoverylaos.com; Th 10; 2-day Tree Top Explorer tour 2-/4-person group per person US$300/200) Green Discovery's ace card is the Tree Top Explorer adventure in the nearby Dong Hua Sao NPA; think ziplining, canopy walks and jungle trekking. Green Discovery also offers kayaking.

Xplore-Asia   ADVENTURE TOUR
(☑ 031-251983; www.xplore-laos.com; Th 14) Xplore-Asia specialises in multiday adventures, including a variety of options for Mekong River trips to Si Phan Don and on to Cambodia, using boats and/or kayaks. English-speaking guides are US$35 per day.

🛏 Sleeping

★ **Alisa Guesthouse**   HOTEL $
(☑ 031-251555; www.alisa-guesthouse.com; Rte 13; r 110,000K; ❄@🛜) The Alisa offers cleaner and more stylish rooms than anything else in this price range. Rooms have comfy, immaculately made beds, working satellite TV, a fridge and good water pressure. There's also a large fleet of motorbikes for hire. It's well located in the heart of the tourist zone.

Kaesme Guest House   GUESTHOUSE $
(☑ 020 9948 1616; Se Don riverfront; r 30,000-70,000K; ❄🛜) The quiet location and wood deck over the Se Don are the main draws, but the simple rooms, which come with or without bathrooms and air-con, are a great deal. Towels and soap are a nice bonus at these prices.

Lankham Hotel   HOTEL $
(☑ 031-213314; Rte 13; 3-bed dm 40,000K, d with fan/air-con from 60,000/90,000K; ❄🛜) Another popular hotel not known for service,

LAOS CHAMPASAK PROVINCE

the Lankham nonetheless packs 'em in with its central location and cheap prices. Budget rooms are tiny and loud. Pricier air-con rooms are nicer.

Sabaidy 2 Guesthouse
GUESTHOUSE $

(☎031-212992; www.sabaidy2tour.com; Th 24; dm 30,000K, s/d/tr without bathroom 50,000/70,000/114,000K, d with bathroom 85,000-100,000K; @🛜) Good reviews of this place are hard to come by, but it's plenty popular by virtue of its reputation as a backpacker magnet. It's often booked out if you walk in so try booking ahead. The en suite rooms out back are good value.

★Residence Sisouk
BOUTIQUE HOTEL $$

(☎031-214716; www.residence-sisouk.com; cnr Th 9 & Th 11; r US$50-100; ✳🛜) This exquisite boutique occupies a lovely 60-year-old colonial house. The rooms enjoy polished hardwood floors, flat-screen TVs, verandahs, Hmong bed runners, lush photography and fresh flowers everywhere. Breakfast is in the penthouse cafe with 360-degree views (it's closed at other times). Paying extra gets you a bigger, brighter room in front; standard rooms are at the back.

Athena Hotel
HOTEL $$

(☎031-214888; www.athena-pakse.com; Rte 13; r incl breakfast US$60-90; ✳@🛜≋) Easily the most modern and slick hotel in Pakse. The beds are marshmallowy delights, and dimming inlaid ceiling lights let you illuminate them in many ways. The three deluxe rooms ratchet up the luxury factor with humongous flat-screen TVs, bathrobes and big bathtubs, while the refreshing pool is most welcome after a day out on dusty roads. It's about a 10-minute walk from the tourist centre.

Pakse Hotel
HOTEL $$

(☎031-212131; www.paksehotel.com; Th 5; s from 200,000K, d incl breakfast 250,000-450,000K; ✳@🛜) This traditional-luxe hotel towering over central Pakse has a gorgeous lobby and breezy corridors festooned with indigenous sculptures and textiles. The economy rooms are dark and the standard rooms cramped, so upgrade to at least a superior, which brings extras like flat-screen TVs, fancy soaps, designer furniture and Mekong views.

🍴 Eating

Chow down with locals at the **Lankham Noodle Shop** (under the Lankham Hotel, Rte 13; noodles 15,000-25,000K; ☺7am-10pm; 🛜), under the Lankham Hotel, and at the **Mengky Noodle Shop** (Rte 13; meals 8000-15,000K; ☺7am-10pm). Rte 13 in the centre of town is scattered with **baguette vendors** (Rte 13), and by night the braziers light up, selling barbecued chicken and pork. Self-caterers can head to the **Friendship Minimart** (Rte 13; ☺8am-8pm).

★Bolaven Cafe
CAFE $

(www.bolavenfarms.com; Rte 13; mains 20,000-40,000K; ☺7am-9.30pm Mon-Sat; 🛜) Great big coffee-fuelled breakfasts and an extensive menu of Laotian and Thai food as well as sandwiches make it worth a stop here any time of day. Read about Bolaven Farms' interesting history as you eat.

Delta Coffee
CAFE $

(Rte 13; mains 25,000-40,000K; ☺7am-9pm; 🛜) Delta does a lot more than 'Coffee' suggests, including a hearty selection of Italian and Thai dishes. The lasagne, pastas and pizzas are recommended if you've been on a steady diet of sticky rice in the boonies. Delta serves feisty coffee from its plantation near Paksong.

Xuan Mai Restaurant
LAOTIAN, VIETNAMESE $

(Th 5; mains 18,000-30,000K; ☺6am-11.30pm) Vietnamese-run Xuan Mai serves freshly prepared *fer* (rice noodles), *nǎam néuang* (pork balls), *kòw ฿ûn* (white flour noodles with sweet-spicy sauce), fruit shakes and even garlic bread. The house *làhp* (meat salad) is full of zing.

Jasmine Restaurant
INDIAN $

(Rte 13; mains 20,000-30,000K; ☺8am-10pm) Serves up delicious curries and Malaysian fare such as nasi goreng with mutton, plus sizzling chicken tikka masala so tasty you'll be wiping the bowl with their pillow-soft naan.

Sinouk Coffee Shop
CAFE $

(cnr Th 9 & Th 11; dishes 25,000-45,000K; ☺6.30am-8.30pm; 🛜) Attached to the terrific Residence Sisouk hotel, this aromatic cafe is a good breakfast or lunch stop, with sandwiches, salads, pasta, pastries, fresh bread and blasting air-con. Rich Arabica coffee from the Bolaven Plateau is sold by the cup and by the bag.

★Na Dao
FRENCH $$

(☎031-255558; cnr Th 38 & Rte 16W; mains 30,000-180,000K; ☺11am-1.30pm & 6.30-10pm Mon-Sat) Fine French dining has arrived in Pakse. Exiled from Vientiane, the owners migrated south to bring their cultured cuisine to southern Laos. Special moments include a salmon and sea bass carpaccio, Paksong goose with olives, and a five-course menu degustation (185,000K).

Drinking

Wander down the Mekong riverfront and stop at a terrace bar for a beer. Alternatively nurse a bloody Mary on the Parisian-style rooftop Panorama Bar at the Pakse Hotel.

Oay BEER GARDEN
(Th 11; 🛜) Trendy Oay on the Mekong riverfront has occasional live acoustic music and shows football games on a big flat-screen TV.

Information

ATMs are strung out along Rte 13, including an ANZ machine outside **Lankham Hotel** (⊘7am-7pm). The Lankham also has a useful currency-exchange counter that offers decent rates and does cash advances on Visa cards.

BCEL (Th 11; ⊘8.30am-3.30pm Mon-Fri) Changes travellers cheques (1% commission) and gives cash advances on Visa and MasterCard (3%). Its exchange office (Th 11; ⊘8.30am-7pm Mon-Fri, to 3pm Sat & Sun) next door has longer hours. BCEL ATMs are across the city.

International Hitech Polyclinic (VIP Clinic; 📞031-214712; ihpc_lao@yahoo.com; Th 46; ⊘24hr) Adjacent to the public hospital, with English-speaking staff and high standards of care, service and facilities, plus a pharmacy.

Main Post Office (cnr Th 8 & Th 1; ⊘8am-noon & 1-4pm Mon-Fri)

Miss Noy's Internet & Bike Rental (Rte 13; per hour 500K; ⊘7am-8pm) Also rents bicycles and motorbikes.

Police (📞031-212145; Th 10)

Provincial Tourism Office (📞031-212021; Th 11; ⊘8am-noon & 1.30-4pm) The well-organised English-speaking staff can book you onto community-based two- or three-day treks in Se Pian NPA and Phou Xieng Thong NPA.

Unitel (Rte 13; ⊘8am-5pm Mon-Fri, to noon Sat) A convenient stop for a local SIM card if you are just arriving in Laos. Staff can set your smartphone up with 3G internet.

Getting There & Away

AIR

Lao Airlines (📞031-212252; Th 11; ⊘8am-noon & 1-5pm Mon-Fri, 8am-noon Sat) has direct flights from **Pakse International Airport** (📞031-251921) to the following cities in Asia: Vientiane (US$75–135, twice daily), Savannakhet ($US35–65, four weekly), Siem Reap (US$160, daily), Ho Chi Minh City (US$170, four weekly) and Bangkok (US$165, four weekly).

A cheaper way to Bangkok is to travel overland to Ubon Ratchathani and take a budget flight from there.

The airport is 3km northwest of town. A *sǎhmlór* (a slower form of three-wheeled transport than the more zesty *túk-túk*) or *túk-túk* to the airport will cost about 40,000K or 50,000K.

BOAT

A tourist boat motors to Champasak (two hours away) most mornings at 8.30am, provided there are enough passengers (one way per person 70,000K). The return trip from Champasak is at 1.30pm.

GETTING TO THAILAND: PAKSE TO UBON RATCHATHANI

Getting to the border Heading to the busy border (open 6am to 8pm) of Vang Tao/Chong Mek is straightforward if catching a *sǒrngtǎaou* from Pakse (10,000K per person, 75 minutes, 37km). Less stressful is the Thai–Lao International Bus (80,000K, three hours, 126km) direct from Pakse's 2km bus terminal to Ubon's main bus station. Departures in both directions are at 8.30am and 3.30pm. Alternatively, you buy a through ticket to Bangkok (from Pakse 235,000K, 14 hours). This may or may not involve a bus change in Ubon.

At the border There are ATMs on the Thai side, a market and restaurants. You have to walk a bit between the two posts but generally it's hassle free. Free 15-day visas are granted on arrival in Thailand; to obtain a 30-day Thai visa, you'll need to arrive in the country by air.

Moving on A minibus from Chong Mek to Ubon Ratchathani (80km, 1½ hours) costs 100B, while taxi drivers charge between 1000B and 1200B.

For more information about crossing this border in the other direction, see p413.

BUS & SŎRNGTĂAOU

Confusingly, Pakse has several bus and sŏrngtăaou terminals. 'Sleeper' VIP buses leave from the **2km bus station** (VIP Bus Station; ☑ 031-212428; Rte 13, Km2) for Vientiane (170,000K, eight to 10 hours, 677km) every evening. The same bus passes through Tha Khaek (140,000K, 4½ hours) and Savannakhet (140,000K, three hours). The handy Thai–Lao International Bus headed to Bangkok (900B, 8.30am and 3.30pm) and Ubon (80,000K, same bus) also departs from here. It's also possible to buy a combo bus/sleeper train ticket to Bangkok (280,000K) from Pakse travel agents.

From the **northern bus terminal** (Rte 13), sometimes referred to as 'Km 7 bus terminal', agonisingly sweltering local buses crawl north for Savannakhet (40,000K, four to five hours, 277km), Tha Khaek (70,000K, eight to nine hours) and, for those with a masochistic streak, Vientiane (110,000K, 16 to 18 hours), every 40 minutes or so between 6.30am and 4pm. Fancier air-con buses also leave for Vientiane (140,000K, 10 to 12 hours) throughout the day from the southern bus terminal.

For buses or sŏrngtăaou anywhere south or east, head to the **southern bus terminal** (Rte 13), also known as 'Km 8 bus terminal' (it costs 15,000K by túk-túk to get there). For Si Phan Don, transport departs for Muang Khong on Don Khong island (including ferry 40,000K, three hours, 120km) between 8.30am and 3pm, and for Ban Nakasang (for Don Det and Don Khon; 40,000K, three to four hours) hourly between 7.30am and 4pm. A sŏrngtăaou runs to Kiet Ngong (Xe Pian NPA) and Ban Phapho (25,000K, two to three hours) at 1pm.

To the Bolaven Plateau, transport leaves the southern bus terminal for Paksong (25,000K, 90 minutes) hourly between 7am and 4pm, stopping at Tat Fan if you ask. For Tat Lo take the Salavan bus (25,000K, three to four hours, five daily).

Buses leave the southern bus terminal for Vietnam's Danang (180,000K, 18 hours) at 7pm, and Hue (160,000K, 15½ hours) at 6.30pm.

Regular buses and sŏrngtăaou leave Talat Dao Heung (New Market) for Champasak (20,000K, one to two hours).

Mai Linh Express operates a daily minibus service from outside the Saigon Champasak Hotel to Lao Bao (140,000K, 6.30am) on the Vietnamese border. Ask about other fares to Vietnam within the hotel.

🛈 Getting Around

A jumbo to the airport, 3km northwest of town, should cost about 40,000K. Pakse's main attractions are accessible by foot. Bicycles/scooters (around 15,000/50,000K per day) can be hired from Lankham Hotel (p337), which also has Honda Bajas for 240,000K a day – excellent for super-swift day trips to the Bolaven Plateau.

Champasak   จำปาสัก

☑ 031 / POP 14,000

Many eschew arid Pakse for the riverine charms of this lush southern belle – with good reason. Thanks to its silkscreen-style mountain, fringed by emerald rice paddies, and the easy manner of its locals, you may stay a little longer than planned. Among faded colonial villas there's a sprinkling of high-end style with a boutique hotel and a couple of upscale restaurants. Champasak's highpoint though is the picturesque ruins of Wat Phu Champasak, and while it won't wow you like Angkor it's a serene spot to visit. If you're looking for activity beyond the sleepy to and fro of the ferryman and children playing in flower-choked backyards, you may have come to the wrong place.

The town stirs once a year, usually in February, when pilgrims gravitate here for **Bun Wat Phu Champasak**, a three-day Buddhist festival of praying, offerings, traditional music, Thai boxing, comedy shows and cock fights.

Guesthouses are mainly found near the fountain south of Champasak's only roundabout.

👁 Sights & Activities

Wat Phu Champasak   BUDDHIST TEMPLE
(admission 8am-4.30pm 30,000K, 6-8am & 4.30-6pm 40,000K; ⊙ 6am-6pm, museum 8am-4.30pm) The archaeological site itself is divided into six terraces on three main levels joined by a long, stepped promenade, which is flanked by statues of lions and naga. Sanskrit inscriptions and Chinese sources confirm the site has been a place of worship since the mid-5th century. Stretching 1400m up to the slopes of Phu Pasak, the ancient Khmer complex of Wat Phu is small compared with the monumental Angkor-era sites of Cambodia.

Champasak Spa   SPA
(☑ 020 5649 9739; www.champasak-spa.com; ⊙ 10am-noon & 1-7pm) 🍃 Champasak Spa offers a perfect sensual antidote to tired muscles in its fragrant oasis overlooking the Mekong River. Treatments include a foot massage (55,000K), traditional Lao body massage (70,000K) and a herbal massage (95,000K), all of which use organic products.

🛏 Sleeping & Eating

Anouxa Guesthouse
GUESTHOUSE $

(☑031-511006; r with fan 60,000K, with air-con 100,000-200,000K; 🅿🛜) The pricier air-con rooms face the river and have balconies to take advantage of those views. Pleasant interiors, clean bathrooms and decent linen, along with a tempting riverside restaurant, make it worth the splurge. On the main strip.

Thavisab Guesthouse
GUESTHOUSE $

(☑020 5535 4972; r with/without air-con 100,000/50,000K; 🅿) Pleasant rooms with mint-coloured curtains and clean linen located in an airy old house, set back from the river.

Champasak with Love
FUSION $

(mains 20,000-40,000K; ⊙8am-10pm) This Thai-owned eatery has a marvellous riverfront patio. The food tends toward continental and Thai. Bicycle rental is available and the owners may soon open a guesthouse.

Frice and Lujane Restaurant
ITALIAN $$

(mains 40,000-60,000K; ⊙5-9pm) The Italian founder has gone but his legacy, in the form of cuisine inspired by Italy's Friulian alpine region, lives on at this atmospheric restaurant based in a renovated villa. Gnocchi, marinated pork ribs, goulash and homemade sausage grace the menu.

ℹ Getting There & Around

Regular buses and sŏrngtăaou run between Champasak and Pakse (20,000K, one hour) from about 6.30am until 1pm, early morning is busiest.

If you're heading south to Ban Nakasang (for Don Det) or Muang Khong (on Don Khong), get to Ban Lak 30 (on Rte 13), where you can flag down anything going south. Ban Lak 30 sits on a crossroads (marked by a gas station) between Hwy 13 headed south to the Four Thousand Islands, and reached by Rte 140 over the river from Champasak.

Bicycles (per day 15,000K) and scooters (per half/full day 50,000/80,000K) can be hired from guesthouses.

Si Phan Don (Four Thousand Islands) ສີພັນດອນ

☑031

Also known as the Four Thousand Islands, this beguiling archipelago of islets is the emerald jewel towards the end of the Mekong's 4350km journey. Here the river passes around thousands of sandbars sprouting with sugar palms, its colour an electric peacock-green. At night the waters are dotted with the lights of fishing boats and fireflies, the soundtrack provided by braying buffalo and singing cicadas. Activities to keep you occupied include tubing, kayaking, visiting the raging waterfalls and cycling around the three main islands – Don Khong, and sister islands Don Det and Don Khon – spotting the rare Irrawaddy dolphin and, of course, hammock dwelling.

Islands Det and Khon are the best places for hammock flopping and tubing, while neighbour Don Khong is much larger but has less of a traveller scene.

Don Khong ດອນໂຂງ

POP 13,000

Less claustrophobic than islands Det and Khon thanks to its expanse (18km long, 8km wide) and under development, Khong is a sleepy idyll where fishing nets dry in the sun, the turquoise Mekong slips by and locals barely look up from their Beerlao to register your arrival. It tends to be avoided by younger travellers and is good if you're seeking a lower density of *falang*; apart from its little town of Muang Khong, the island is largely unpeopled. Essentially a one-street town, Muang Khong has some lovely hotels and guesthouses in which to stay a few days, plus a couple of decent al fresco restaurants. Take a sunset boat ride to Cambodian waters, read by the river, or hire a bike to explore the island.

🛏 Sleeping & Eating

All of the following are in Muang Khong, on or just back from the riverbank along a 700m stretch. There are few dedicated restaurants worth tweeting about, guesthouses have the best food, with Pon Arena (p343) and Ratana leading the way. Most places serve Don Khong's famous *lòw-lów*, which is often cited as the smoothest in the country.

You'll find all these guesthouses located in Muang Khong.

★Ratana Riverside Guesthouse
GUESTHOUSE $

(☑020 2220 1618, 031-213673; vongdonekhong@hotmail.com; r 100,000K, mains 15,000-40,000K; 🅿🛜) The four comfortable river-facing rooms here enjoy marble floors, balconies,

LAOS SI PHAN DON (FOUR THOUSAND ISLANDS)

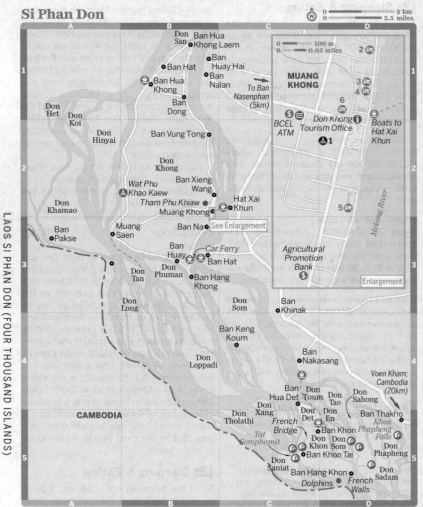

Si Phan Don

LAOS SI PHAN DON (FOUR THOUSAND ISLANDS)

Si Phan Don

⊙ Sights

1 Wat Phuang Kaew D2

⊜ Sleeping

2 Pon Arena Hotel D1

3 Pon's River Guesthouse &
   Restaurant D1

4 Ratana Riverside Guesthouse D1

5 Senesothxeune Hotel D2

6 Villa Kang Khong D1

Siberian air-con and handsome furnishings. Ground-floor rooms have enormous windows close to the road; we advise getting one upstairs. The river-deck restaurant has the best selection of Western food on the island.

Villa Kang Khong   GUESTHOUSE $
(☎ 020 2240 3315; r 50,000-60,000K) The most romantic budget digs in town, this stalwart teak house creaks with uneven floors and nostalgic furnishings. Rooms are basic and fan-cooled, and, with their colourful wood interiors, remind us vaguely of Roma gypsy caravans.

Pon's River Guesthouse & Restaurant
GUESTHOUSE $

(☑020 2227 0037; www.ponarenahotel.com; r 60,000-100,000K; ❉🔊) Pon's original guesthouse gets less TLC since he opened the swish Arena Hotel. The basic rooms, which come in fan and air-con flavours, won't knock you over, but that's OK. The sprawling public balcony in view of the river is the place to hang.

Senesothxeune Hotel
HOTEL $

(☑030 526 0577; www.ssx-hotel.com; r incl breakfast US$45-60, ste US$85; ❉@🔊) This Thaistyle modern hotel has upmarket rooms boasting hardwood floors, TVs, deep baths, milk-white minimalism and a pleasant restaurant with a view of the river through its magnolia-blossoming garden. The pricier rooms have balconies and river views.

★ Pon Arena Hotel
BOUTIQUE HOTEL $$

(☑020 2227 0037, 031-515018; www.ponarena hotel.com; r US$45-85; ❉🔊🔲) This upscale hotel on the river keeps expanding. The most recent addition is a 'Swiss chalet' that sits right on the river and boasts airy rooms with neat wood trim and flat-screens. The 'Mekong view' rooms sit further back and are nicer, while even the mountain-view rooms at the back have granite-inlaid bathrooms, fish-bowl sinks and soft beds.

ℹ Information

One road back from the river, 400m south of Wat Phuang Kaew, the **Agricultural Promotion Bank** (⊗8.30am-3.30pm Mon-Fri) exchanges travellers cheques and cash and has an ATM that works with Visa and MasterCard. There's also a BCEL ATM next to the post office. For medical complaints, the hospital is a little further south of the bank; ask for English- and French-speaking Dr Bounthavi.

The Don Khong **tourism office** (☑020 9784 6464; panhjuki@yahoo.com; ⊗8.30am-4pm Mon-Fri) can organise boats to Don Khon & Don Det (250,000K). The **post office** (⊗8am-noon & 2-4pm Mon-Fri) is just south of the bridge.

ℹ Getting There & Away

From Don Khong to Pakse, buses (60,000K incl ferry, 2½ to three hours, 128km) and *sŏrngtăaou* leave from Hat Xai Khun over the river on the mainland. Be there for 11am. There are regular boats to Hat Xai Khun from Don Khong's Muang Khong town (15,000K).

Boats for Don Det and Don Khon (40,000K, 1½ hours, minimum six passengers) leave when you stump up the cash – boatmen are under the tree near the bridge.

For the Cambodian border, there's usually a 9am minibus connection to Stung Treng, Kratie, Ban Lung, Siem Reap and Phnom Penh.

ℹ Getting Around

Bicycles (10,000K per day) and motorbikes (60,000K per day) can be hired from guesthouses and elsewhere along the main street.

Don Det & Don Khon   ດອນເດດ/ດອນຄອນ

The vast majority of travellers to Si Phan Don end up on these twin islands. Don Det in particular has become more popular among young travellers in recent years, leading some to speculate that it will replace Vang Vieng as the go-to spot in Laos for vice-fuelled excess. That would seem unlikely: there's nothing stronger than grass in the 'happy' snacks sold openly at some bars, and the locals seem to have a genuine desire to keep it that way. Our best guess is that a hippyesque party scene will continue to thrive in Ban Hua Det at the north end of Don Det, but it will never become as depraved as the old Vang Vieng.

Of course there's much more to these two islands than Scooby snacks. Heading south from Ban Hua Det, the guesthouses thin out and the icons of rural island life – fishermen, rice farmers, weavers, buffalo, sugar palms – are on full display. Chill in a hammock, cycle around the islands, or languidly drift downstream in an inner tube amid the turquoise arms of the Mekong. Cross the French bridge to Don Khon and pick up trails that lead through forests and rice fields to hidden rapids, beaches and, off the island's extreme southern tip, frolicking Irrawaddy dolphins.

◉ Sights & Activities

Most sights on Don Khon are accessible on a bicycle hired from just about any guesthouse for 10,000K per day. When you cross the French bridge to Don Khon, you will be asked to pay 25,000K. This covers the entrance fee to Tat Somphamit (p344) (Li Phi Falls).

Full-day and half-day kayaking tours are widely offered. The full-day trips (180,000K per person) take in the dolphin pool and Khon Papaeng Falls; you get picked up before the falls at Don Khon and you and

LAOS SI PHAN DON (FOUR THOUSAND ISLANDS)

your kayaks are transported overland to Ban Hang Khon. **Wonderful Tours** (☑020 5570 5173) is useful.

Renting a kayak to paddle around on your own costs 50,000K per day, but don't go past the French bridge or you'll hit the fast currents that feed into the lethal falls. The same rule applies to inner tubes, which cost 10,000K (avoid during the monsoon when the river runs dangerously quick).

Guesthouses offer sunset boat cruises, full-day island hops, morning birdwatching trips and fishing trips. Prices vary, but figure on 50,000K to 75,000K per person provided you have a few people.

Dolphins   VIEWPOINT
A pod of rare Irrawaddy dolphins hangs out beneath the rapids in a wide pool known as Boong Pa Gooang, off the south tip of Don Khon. Boats are chartered (60,000K, maximum three people) for one-hour trips from the old French landing pier in Ban Hang Khon. Sightings are usual year-round, but the best viewing is from January to May. Try to go early evening or first thing in the morning, when sightings are more regular and the river is at its most scenic.

Tat Somphamit   WATERFALL
(ຕາດສົມພະມິດ; Li Phi Falls; admission 25,000K; ☉ticket booth 8am-5pm) About 1.5km downriver from the French bridge on Don Khon is a raging set of rapids called Tat Somphamit, referred to by just about everyone as Li Phi Falls. Li Phi means 'spirit trap' and locals believe the falls act as just that – a trap for bad spirits (of deceased people and animals) as they wash down the river.

PARADISE RETAINED!

Don Det has distanced itself from its former stoner image by cultivating a range of activities like cycling and kayaking; these days you're more likely to see travellers fishing with locals than buying joints from them. Villagers are grateful for your trade but there are a few things you can do to keep your footprint positive. If partaking a little spliff, be subtle; and please, cover up beyond just a bikini or bathing suit around the island. It's a pain because it's hot, but the Lao find it culturally offensive.

You may notice local fishermen edging out onto the rocks to clear the enormous bamboo traps. During the early rains, a well-positioned trap can catch half a tonne of fish a day.

🛏 Sleeping

Don Det's 'Sunrise Boulevard' on the northern tip is claustrophobic and noisy, but if you want to keep the party going (at least till the 11pm curfew) head here. Much more upscale digs are further south and over on sedate Don Khon.

In low-season expect prices 25% cheaper than listed here.

DON DET

★**Sunset View**   GUESTHOUSE $
(☑020 9788 2978; Sunset Blvd; r 120,000K; 🅿) More of a flashpacker option, the bathrooms are shinier, the living quarters roomier and beds thicker than anywhere else in the area. The riverfront rooms are in a wood house with a common sunset-facing deck that practically hangs over the water.

★**River Garden**   GUESTHOUSE $
(☑020 7770 1860; r 60,000-80,000K; 🛜) Gay-friendly River Garden has rooms set back from the river with a whiff of style: think tidy bathrooms and seductive maroon-stained walls. Opposite is a shaded terrace restaurant. To find it leave Sunrise strip far behind and head toward the French Bridge.

Last Resort   RESORT $
(mrwatkinsonlives@gmail.com; d/tr 50,000/60,000K) It would be hard to match the free-spiritedness of this teepee 'resort', in a field near a friendly village about a 15-minute walk south of the main Sunset Blvd strip. Aussie host Jon grows vegies, bakes bread, loves music consummately and screens movies in the open air. The teepees are utterly unique, and there's a kitchen.

★**Crazy Gecko**   GUESTHOUSE $
(info@crazygecko.ch; r 150,000K; 🛜) Funky Crazy Gecko's four rooms surround a balcony festooned with hammocks, sculptures and random furniture. Bathrooms are shared (for now) and rooms are fragrant and simple. The riverside restaurant across the path is delightful. The guesthouse is between Ban Hua Det and Don Det Village.

Sengthavan Guesthouse & Restaurant   GUESTHOUSE $
(☑020 5613 2696; Sunset Blvd; r 100,000K; 🛜) Probably the best the sunset side has to

DOLPHINS ENDANGERED

The **Irrawaddy dolphin** is one of the Mekong River's most fascinating and endangered creatures. The dark blue to grey cetaceans grow to 2.75m long and are recognisable by their bulging foreheads, perpetual grins and small dorsal fins.

Among the Lao and Khmer, Irrawaddy dolphins are traditionally considered reincarnated humans and there are many stories of dolphins having saved the lives of fishermen or villagers who have fallen into the river or been attacked by crocodiles. These cultural beliefs mean that neither the Lao nor the Khmer intentionally capture dolphins for food or sport.

Gill netting and years of destructive fishing practices have taken their toll. Education and conservation programs continue, but gill netting remains a constant threat – it's now estimated there are fewer than 100 dolphins remaining; prior to the 1970s there were thousands. The surviving few live primarily in several deep-water conservation 'pools' along a 190km stretch of the Mekong between the Lao border and the Cambodian town of Kratie. It is believed that fewer than 10 dolphins now survive in **Boong Pa Gooang**, the 600m-wide, 50m-deep pool where you will be taken to see them.

offer in the budget range, Sengthavan's en suite rooms are fastidiously clean and enjoy uncluttered balcony views of Cambodia. Its low-key cafe has recliner cushions, checked tablecloths and a Lao menu. A few minutes walk south of Ban Hua Det on sunset side.

Dalom Guesthouse GUESTHOUSE $
(☑020 5418 8898; Sunrise Blvd; r with fan/air-con 80,000/160,000K; ❄🤶) This is the best option if you want to be near the centre of the action in Ban Hua Det. If comfort is more important than being right on the river, you'll find good-value fan bungalows in the garden and spiffy air-con rooms in a two-storey concrete structure.

★**Little Eden Guesthouse** GUESTHOUSE $$
(☑030 534 6020; www.littleedenguesthouse dondet.com; Ban Hua Det; standard/deluxe 250,000/320,000K; ❄@🤶) Located in Ban Hua Det, Little Eden is set in lush gardens of sugar palms and betel trees on the northern tip of the island. Fragrant rooms have cool, tiled floors and soft linens. The roomy deluxe rooms, with textile bed runners, white walls, snazzy bathrooms and dark-wood trim, are a substantial upgrade on the fairly basic standard rooms, so consider splurging.

DON KHON

Bounephan Riverside Guesthouse GUESTHOUSE $
(☑031-2710163; r 40,000-60,000K) Choose from basic en suite rooms in a rickety, hammock-strewn wood structure overlooking the river, or slightly spiffier digs across the

road in red-painted wood duplexes at 'Mr Boune's'.

Auberge Sala Done Khone BOUTIQUE HOTEL $$
(☑031-260940; www.saladonekhone.salalao.com; r incl breakfast US$50-60; ❄@🤶❄) In a handsomely renovated French-era hospital, this romantic belle delights with four-poster beds and art deco signatured (if a little faded) rooms. Outside are spotless A-frame bungalows built in classic Lao style with ambient-lit, minimalist interiors, while out on the river the **Sala Phae** (r US$60) wing features equally stylish floating cottages with bio-safe toilets.

Pan's Guesthouse GUESTHOUSE $$
(☑020 9797 8222; www.donkhone.com; garden/ riverfront d 160,000/200,000K, tr 220,000K; ❄@🤶) A range of soporific bungalows finished in solid stained wood with creamy white rattan interiors, immaculate en suites and balconies slung with hammocks. Spring for a riverfront room. A few minutes north of the French Bridge.

🍴 Eating & Drinking

Establishments open for breakfast early, and close anytime around 11pm – some a little later.

★**Four Thousand Sunsets** FUSION $
(Don Khon; mains 30,000-40,000K; 🤶🍴) Auberge Sala Done Khone's floating restaurant boasts white table cloths and an eclectic menu of European, Thai and other Asian fare. Come sunset witness the light cast its amber net over the Mekong.

Rib Shack
AMERICAN $$

(Don Det; per rib 10,000K) Owner Lance slings succulent ribs and sides like 'slaw, potato salad and garlic bread from an aptly named shack in the middle of town. In the thick of the action in Ban Hua Det.

★ Little Eden Restaurant
LAOTIAN, INTERNATIONAL $$

(Ban Hua Det, Don Det; mains 35,000-60,000K; 🛜) Little Eden is one of the archipelago's best places to eat upmarket Laotian and Western cuisine. The eclectic menu features tender New Zealand beef steak, spaghetti Bolognese and fish làhp, to name a few. Warm up with a lòw-lów mojito. In Ban Hua Det.

4000 Island Bar
BAR

(Sunrise Blvd, Don Det) Near the boat landing, this was the most happening place in town when we were there, filling up nightly with youthful travellers eager to munch happy snacks and get their freak on. While it officially closes before midnight, it's likely to stay open unofficially until 1am.

ℹ Information

There is no bank, so take the ferry over to Ban Nakasang, which has a BCEL with an ATM. Little Eden Guesthouse (p345) on Don Det will do cash advances on your card for a 5% commission.

Ban Nakasang is also the place to go for medical and postal services.

ℹ Getting There & Away

Boats regularly leave Don Det for Ban Nakasang (per person/boat 15,000/30,000K). You can charter a private boat to Don Khong from **Paradise Bungalows** (Sunrise Blvd) for 75,000K per person, with a minimum of two people.

For Pakse (70,000K, 2½ to three hours, 148km), buses or sǒrngtǎaou leave Ban Nakasang at around 11am, with a second wave of departures early evening, while túk-túk (40,000K, 3½ hours) leave early morning up until 8am.

Wonderful Tours (p344) organises daily VIP buses, which leave Ban Nakasang at about 9.30am, to Stung Treng, Ban Lung, Kratie, Phnom Penh and Siem Reap in Cambodia, as well as buses to Vietnam's Hue and Danang.

Bolaven Plateau
ພູພຽງບໍລະເວນ

This beautiful landscape of lush forests, rivers, waterfalls and lavender-hued mountains is Laos' principal coffee-growing region. Back in the 19th century the French, looking to maximise the yield of their colony, decided the fertile soil on the 1000m Bolaven Plateau (Phu Phieng Bolaven in Lao) merited being turned into coffee plantations, and enjoying a frothy cappuccino in nearby Pakse, you'll be very glad they did.

The plateau is a centre for several Mon-Khmer ethnic groups, including the Alak, Laven (Bolaven means 'land of the Laven'), Ta-oy, Suay and Katu. The Alak and Katu are known for a water-buffalo sacrifice they perform yearly, usually on a full moon in March. But the main draw are the plateau's several spectacular waterfalls, including the dramatic twin cascades of **Tat Fan**, a few kilometres west of Paksong. The **Tad Fane Resort** (Rte 16, Km38; r incl breakfast US$27-37; 🛜) has tastefully finished log cabanas, sur-

---

GETTING TO CAMBODIA: SOUTHERN LAOS TO STUNG TRENG

Getting to the border The remote Nong Nok Khiene/Trapeang Kriel is a popular crossing on the Indochina overland circuit. From Pakse, catch the Sorya Phnom Penh Transport bus which leaves at 7.30am from the VIP (2km) bus terminal and goes to Phnom Penh (US$27, 12 to 14 hours), with stops to pick up passengers in Don Khong and Don Det. The only other option to the border from Si Phan Don is private transport.

At the border Entering Cambodia, they jack up the price of a 30-day tourist visa to US$25 from the normal US$20. The extra US$5 is called 'tea money', as the poor border guards have been stationed at such a remote crossing. In addition, the Cambodians charge US$2 for a cursory medical inspection upon arrival in the country, and levy a US$2 processing fee upon exit. These fees might be waived if you protest, but don't protest for too long or your bus may leave without you.

Moving on If you're not on a direct bus, head to Stung Treng to catch a bus to Phnom Penh, Siem Reap and Ban Lung. Taxis to Stung Treng from the border cost US$40.

For more information about crossing this border in the other direction, see p232.

> ### GETTING TO VIETNAM: ATTAPEU TO NGOC HOI
>
> **Getting to the border** The Phou Keua/Bo Y border crossing is in far southeastern Attapeu province, 113km southeast of Attapeu town. **Mai Linh Express** (☏ in Attapeu 030-539 0216, in Vietnam 0592-211 211) operates a daily minibus connecting Pakse with Kontum (145,000K) via Paksong, Sekong and Attapeu. It departs at 5.45am from Pakse and reaches Attapeu around 10.30am. From Attapeu it takes around five hours to Kontum and costs 70,000K. Tickets are sold at the Dúc Lôc Hotel.
>
> **At the border** Vietnamese visas must be arranged in advance. Thirty-day visas are granted on arrival in Laos and cost between US$30 and US$42 depending on your nationality.
>
> **Moving on** Once on the Vietnamese side of the border, minibuses continue to Ngoc Hoi, 18km away. There are places to stay in Ngoc Hoi, plus morning departures for a wide range of destinations.
>
> For more information about crossing this border in the other direction, see p116.

rounded by vegetation and overlooking the falls. It offers short treks to the top of the waterfall, but don't attempt this after rain as the near-vertical muddy slopes are lethal.

Tat Lo ຕາດເລາະ

☏ 034

Something of a traveller's secret, about 90km from Pakse on the Salavan road (Rte 20), secluded Tat Lo is a wide waterfall with mint-green pools to swim in. On a baking-hot day it's paradise as you cool off in the icy shallows, accompanied by the sounds of local kids. Accommodation varies from basic and forgettable cabanas to really atmospheric digs at affordable prices. This is a place to chill and is best enjoyed on an overnight visit by scooter from Pakse, giving you the scope to explore the surrounding area.

The nearest cascade to town is **Tat Hang**, which can be seen from the bridge, while **Tat Lo** itself is about 700m upriver via a path leading through Saise Guest House. The spectacular third cascade is **Tat Suong**, about 10km from town and best reached by motorbike or bicycle.

◉ Sights & Activities

For elephant treks (leaving at 8am, 10am, 1pm and 3pm, 100,000K per person) head to Tadlo Lodge.

For any treks around Tat Lo we advise hiring a guide from the Tat Lo Guides Association, operated out of the **Tat Lo Tourism Information Centre** (☏ 020 5445 5907, 034-211528; kouka222@hotmail.com; ☺8am-noon & 1-4.30pm). They can organise half-day and full-day treks as well as homestays.

⌨ Sleeping & Eating

The village is a one-street affair, with most accommodation either side of the bridge (budget places are concentrated on the east side). The best cuisine, not surprisingly, is found at the more upmarket resorts.

★**Saise Guest House & Restaurant** GUESTHOUSE $
(☏ 034-211886; r with fan/air-con from 60,000/180,000K, mains 40,000K-60,000K; ☎) In lush gardens on the west bank of the river, Saise has rooms that range from cheap fan-cooled numbers to sophisticated air-conditioned bungalows. The restaurant is Tat Lo's best, and includes stir-fries, salads and various fish dishes.

★**Fandee** GUESTHOUSE $
(r 50,000-60,000K; ☎) The four raised wood bungalows are sturdy, comfortable and airy, and feature thatched roofs, private porches and pebble-floor, cold-water bathrooms. A communal vibe reigns in the restaurant. It's opposite the tourist office.

Palamy Guesthouse GUESTHOUSE $
(☏ 030 962 0192; r with/without bathroom from 60,000/40,000K; ☎) Overlooking a pretty meadow out back, the better rooms have mosquito nets, terraces with tables and, in some cases, fridges and little lean-to kitchens. The owner, Poh, is an excellent cook so it's well worth dropping in for a meal.

Tadlo Lodge GUESTHOUSE $$
(☏ 034-211885; www.tadlolodge.com; s/d incl breakfast from US$41/47; ☎) Situated above the falls with an Edenic view of the teal-green river, this is a slice of style just where you need it. The main building is finished

in traditional Lao style, with parquet floors and Buddha statuary. Rooms are stylish, with some new bungalows set on the opposite (west) side of the river.

ⓘ Getting There & Away

Tat Lo is 86km northeast of Pakse. Just say 'Tat Lo' at Pakse's southern bus terminal (p340) and you'll be pointed to one of the several morning buses to Salavan that stop at Ban Khoua Set. Regular buses in the morning run from Pakse to Ban Khoua Set (25,000K, two hours) and from Pakse to Paksong (25,000K, 1½ hours). It's a 1.8km walk to Tat Lo from Ban Khoua Set or a swift túk-túk ride (10,000K). Heading to Paksong, get yourself up to Ban Beng, at the junction, and jump on a bus coming through from Salavan.

UNDERSTAND LAOS

Laos Today

Up until early 2008 it was all going extremely well for Laos, with record figures of foreign visitors tuning into the buzz about this little nation, which was fast becoming switched on to responsible ecotourism; newly built hydroelectric power dams; copper and gold mining concessions; and largely foreign investors keen to climb into bed with Laos' natural resources. Then the economic axe fell on the US and those subprime mortgages started impacting every aspect of Laos' attempt, by 2020, to escape its status as one of the 20 poorest nations. Suddenly the foreign investors pulled out because of their own lack of liquidity, and mining concessions collapsed as the price of copper was slashed. Fewer travellers were arriving, too. Through no fault of its own, Laos looked to be heading back to the dark days of stagnation.

Times haven't been easy, but they certainly could have been worse: by 2011, despite global gloom, Laos reported growth of 8%, one of the strongest rates in Asia. And now, as China flourishes, Laos is reaping the rewards of the two countries' close association. China has moved in to grab what it can in return for improving Laos' transport infrastructure. Beijing's Southeast Asian rail network, due to be finished in 2014, will eventually connect the red giant with countries as far afield as Pakistan, India and Singapore, and to achieve this the network will pass directly through Laos. Rte 3, from Kunming to Vientiane, via Luang Prabang, should be ready in the next five years, and, in the next 10 years, it's predicted that travellers will be able to travel at speeds of up to 400km/h through this beautiful green country. How this will impact on this sleepy paradise is anyone's guess, but it's all the more reason for you to visit right now. As US relations begin to improve and the first rumblings of gay expression make themselves heard in the capital, Laos is on one hand embracing the 21st century, while holding fast to its old guard hegemony.

History

Throughout its long history, the inhabitants of modern-day Laos have been subject to the politics and aspirations of more-powerful neighbours in Cambodia, Vietnam, Thailand and China. Even its first taste of nationhood, with the rise of the Lan Xang kingdom, was achieved thanks to Khmer military muscle.

Kingdom of Lan Xang

Before the French, British, Chinese and Siamese drew a line around it, Laos was a collection of disparate principalities subject to an ever-revolving cycle of war, invasion, prosperity and decay. Laos' earliest brush with nationhood was in the 14th century, when Khmer-backed Lao warlord Fa Ngum conquered Wieng Chan (Vientiane). It was Fa Ngum who gave his kingdom the title still favoured by travel romantics and businesses – Lan Xang, or (Land of a) Million Elephants. He also made Theravada Buddhism the state religion and adopted the symbol of Lao sovereignty that remains in use today, the Pha Bang Buddha image, after which Luang Prabang is named. Lan Xang reached its peak in the 17th century, when it was the dominant force in Southeast Asia.

The French

After taking over Annam and Tonkin (modern-day Vietnam) in 1883, the French negotiated with Siam to relinquish its territory east of the Mekong; thus, Laos was born and absorbed into French Indochina.

The country's diverse ethnic make-up and short history as a nation state meant nationalism was slow to form. The first nationalist movement, the Lao Issara (Free Lao), was created to prevent the country's return to French rule after the invading Japanese left at the end of WWII. In 1953 sovereignty was granted to Laos by the French. Internecine struggles followed, with the Pathet Lao (Country of the Lao) army forming an alliance with the Vietnamese Viet Minh, which had also been opposing French rule in its own country. Laos was set to become a stage on which the clash of communist ambition and US anxiety over the perceived Southeast Asian 'domino effect' played itself out.

The Secret War

In 1954 at the Geneva Conference Laos was declared a neutral nation – as such neither Vietnamese nor US forces could cross its borders. Thus began a game of cat and mouse as a multitude of CIA operatives secretly entered the country to train anti-communist Hmong fighters in the jungle. From 1964 to 1973, the US, in response to the Viet Minh funnelling massive amounts of war munitions down the Ho Chi Minh Trail, devastated eastern and northeastern Laos with nonstop carpet-bombing (reportedly a plane load of ordnance dropped every eight minutes). The intensive campaign exacerbated the war between the Pathet Lao and the US-backed Royal Lao Army and, if anything, increased domestic support for the communists.

The US withdrawal in 1973 saw Laos divided up between Pathet Lao and non-Pathet Lao, but within two years the communists had taken over completely and the Lao People's Democratic Republic (PDR) was created under the leadership of Kaysone Phomvihane. Around 10% of Laos' population fled, mostly to Thailand. The remaining opponents of the government – notably tribes of Hmong who fought with and were funded by the CIA – were suppressed or sent to re-education camps for indeterminate periods. It's alleged that two of these camps still endure in the far north, though this is hotly denied.

A New Start

Laos entered the political family of Southeast Asian countries known as Asean in 1997, two years after Vietnam. In 2004 the USA promoted Laos to Normal Trade Relations, cementing the end to a trade embargo in place since the communists took power in 1975. Politically, the Party remains firmly in control. And with neighbours like one-party China and Vietnam, there seems little incentive for Laos to move towards any meaningful form of democracy. While still heavily reliant on foreign aid, Laos has committed to income-generating projects in recent years in a bid to increase its prosperity. Ecotourism is flourishing and the country is enjoying more Western visitors every year. China has recently pulled the financial reins

LAOS HISTORY

OPIUM & YAA BAA (METHAMPHETAMINE)

Up until the introduction of the anti-opium program in 2001, Laos was estimated to produce most of the world's opium. This mantle has since been passed on to Afghanistan, yet in many mountainous regions of northern Laos – far from the reach of doctors – opium is grown as a medicinal drug or painkiller and is used by many tribes. Given its prime location in the heart of the Golden Triangle it's understandable that Laos has often been a pawn and facilitator in the trafficking of drugs intended for the West; during the Secret War the US was allegedly involved in profiteering from opium cultivation. These days the trade of *yaa baa* (methamphetamine) alone is worth US$8.5bn a year to the Golden Triangle.

In 2008 CIA reports based on satellite images suggested opium production had increased by an alarming 78%. However, the trafficking of *yaa baa* gives much more pause for concern; makeshift *yaa baa* laboratories are easily dismantled and discarded by the cooks and Laos and Thailand's porous borders make it very hard to effectively police the movements of major shipments. For corrupt border officials willing to be turned by huge payoffs, there's big money to be made by turning a blind eye and allowing the production and transit of the drug as it is moved through the country to Cambodia, Vietnam and Thailand. In 2011, authorities estimated that nearly one in 60 Thais was a methamphetamine user.

In 2012 a joint operation between China, Thailand, Burma and Laos called 'Mekong Safe' successfully seized almost 10 tonnes of drugs, and more than 2500 suspects were arrested.

on its extensive high-speed rail network across Southeast Asia, with Laos now stepping in and picking up the cost in the form of a US$7.2 billion loan from China. It's a big gamble, but the hope is that it will improve trade, with the rail system passing through the likes of Luang Prabang and Vientiane.

In 2012 the international press started asking embarrassing questions over the disappearance of Sombath Somphone, an award-winning civil society activist and land rights campaigner, with fingers directly pointed at the Lao government as the main culprit. In 2013, in an effort to counterbalance China's growing influence over the region, the Obama administration sent then-Secretary of State Hillary Clinton to broker tighter relations with Laos.

People & Culture

People & Population

As many as 132 ethnic groups make up the people of Laos. Sixty per cent of these people are Lao Loum (lowland Lao); they have the most in common with their Thai neighbours, and it's their cultural beliefs and way of life that are largely known as 'Lao culture'. The remainder are labelled according to the altitude their groups live at: Lao Thai (living in valleys up to an altitude of 400m, composed of Black Thai and White Thai); Lao Thoeng (midlevel mountain slopes, including Khamu, Lamet and Alak); and Lao Soung (living 1000m or more above sea level, including the Hmong, Mien and Akha).

Trying to homogenise the people and psyche of Laos is precarious, as the country is really a patchwork of different beliefs, ranging from animism to the prevailing presence of Theravada Buddhism, often both combined. But certainly there's a commonality in the laid-back attitude you'll encounter. Some of this can be ascribed to Buddhism, with its emphasis on controlling extreme emotions by keeping *jai yen* (cool heart) and making merit – doing good in order to receive good. You'll rarely hear a heated argument, and can expect a level of kindness unpractised to such a national degree in neighbouring countries.

The Lao are very good at enjoying the 'now', and they do this with a mixture of the *bor ʾben nyǎng* (no problem) mentality and a devotion to *móoan* (fun). If a job is *bor móoan* (no fun), it is swiftly abandoned in pursuit of another, even if it means less income. *Kamma* (karma), more than devotion, prayer or hard work, is believed to determine one's lot in life, so the Lao tend not to get too worked up over the future.

Government spending on education amounts to 11.7% of total public spending. Education has improved in recent years, with school enrolment rates at 85%, though many drop out by the time they reach secondary education – the planting and harvesting of crops, especially among the highlands, is seen as more important than education, as the whole family is involved.

Religion

Most lowland Lao are Theravada Buddhists and many Lao males choose to be ordained temporarily as monks, typically spending anywhere from a month to three years at a wat. Indeed, a young man is not considered 'ripe' until he has completed his spiritual term. After the 1975 communist victory, Buddhism was suppressed, but it soon became clear its religious omnipresence was

---

SPIRITS ARE YOU THERE?

The life of a Lao person involves a complex appeasement of spirits through a carousel of sacrifices and rituals designed to protect the supplicant. The *pěe héuan* (good spirits) represent both the guardian spirits of the house and ancestral spirits. In order to promote domestic happiness they're fed with Pepsi, and come crisis time it's their job to recalibrate the troubled household.

In the backyard or garden, you'll often see what look like miniature ornamental temples, the *pa poom* (spirits of the land). Their task is to protect the grounds from any malignant spirits; in Laos the air is thick with them. Before anything is built within their grounds, offerings must be made and permission granted. The same goes for a tree that must be knocked down to make way for a bridge, a field before a harvest...and so on. It's an endless animistic communion between the seen and unseen, the prosaic and the spiritual.

too strong and by 1992 the government relented. However, monks are still forbidden to promote *pĕe* (spirit) worship, which has been officially banned in Laos along with *săinyasàht* (folk magic).

Despite the ban, *pĕe* worship remains the dominant non-Buddhist belief system. Even in Vientiane, Lao citizens openly perform the ceremony called *sukwăn* ('calling of the soul') or *basĕe*, in which the 32 *kwăn* (guardian spirits of the body) are bound to the guest of honour by white strings tied around the wrists.

Outside the Mekong River valley, the *pĕe* cult is particularly strong among tribal Thai. *Mŏr* (priests) who are trained to appease and exorcise troublesome spirits, preside at important festivals and other ceremonies. The Khamu, Hmong and Mien tribes also practise animism.

Arts & Architecture

The true expression of Lao art is found in its religious sculpture, temples and handicrafts. Distinctively Lao is the Calling for Rain Buddha, a standing image with hands held rigidly at his sides. Similarly widespread is the Contemplating the Bodhi Tree Buddha, with crossed hands at the front.

Wats in Luang Prabang feature *sǐm* (chapels), with steep, low roofs. The typical Lao *tâht* (stupa) is a four-sided, curvilinear, spirelike structure. There are also hints of classical architectural motifs entering modern architecture, as with Vientiane's Wattay International Airport.

Many of the beautiful villas from the days of Indochina were torn down by the new regime in favour of harsh Soviet designs, though fortunately there are plenty of villas left, with their distinctive shuttered windows and classic French provincial style.

Traditional Lao art has a more limited range than that of its Southeast Asian neighbours, partly because Laos has a more modest history as a nation state and partly because its neighbours have stolen or burnt what art did exist. Upland crafts include gold- and silver-smithing among the Hmong and Mien tribes, and tribal Thai weaving (especially among the Thai Dam and Thai Lü). Classical music and dance have all but evaporated, partly due to the vapid tentacles of Thai pop and itinerant nature of Laos' young workforce.

Food & Drink

Food

Lao cuisine lacks the variety of Thai food, but there are some distinctive dishes to try. The standard Lao breakfast is *fĕr* (rice noodles), usually served floating in a broth with vegetables and a meat of your choice. The trick is in the seasoning, and Lao people will stir in some fish sauce, lime juice, dried chillies, mint leaves, basil, or one of the wonderful speciality hot chilli sauces that many noodle shops make, testing it along the way.

Làhp is the most distinctively Lao dish, a delicious spicy salad made from minced beef, pork, duck, fish or chicken, mixed with fish sauce, small shallots, mint leaves, lime juice, roasted ground rice and lots and lots of chillies. Another famous Lao speciality is *dąm màhk hung* (known as *sôm đam* in Thailand), a salad of shredded green papaya mixed with garlic, lime juice, fish sauce, sometimes tomatoes, palm sugar, land crab or dried shrimp and, of course, chillies by the handful.

In lowland Lao areas almost every dish is eaten with *kòw nĕeo* (sticky rice), which is served in a small basket. Take a small amount of rice and, using one hand, work it into a bite-sized ball before dipping it into the food.

In main centres, delicious French baguettes are a popular breakfast food. Sometimes they're eaten with condensed milk, or with *kai* (eggs) in a sandwich that also contains Lao-style pâté and vegetables.

As an approximate guide, price ranges listed in this book are less than 40,000K (US$5) for budget places, 40,000K to 80,000K (US$5 to US$10) for midrange, and more than 80,000K (US$10) for top-end places.

Drink

ALCOHOLIC DRINKS

Beerlao remains a firm favourite with 90% of the nation, while officially illegal *lòw-lów* (Lao liquor, or rice whisky) is a popular drink among lowland Lao. It's usually taken neat and offered in villages as a welcoming gesture.

NONALCOHOLIC DRINKS

Water purified for drinking purposes is simply called *nâm deum* (drinking water), whether it's boiled or filtered. All water offered to customers in restaurants or hotels will be purified, and purified water is sold everywhere. Having said that, do be careful of the water you drink – there was an outbreak of E. coli in 2008, so check the ice in your drink originated from a bottle.

Juice bars proliferate around Vientiane and Luang Prabang, and smoothies are usually on the menu in most Western-leaning cafes. Lao coffee is usually served strong and sweet. Lattes and cappuccinos are springing up across the country with pasteurised milk coming from Thailand.

Chinese-style green tea is the usual ingredient in *nâm sáh* or *sáh lôw* – the weak, refreshing tea traditionally served free in restaurants. If you want Lipton-style tea, ask for *sáa hâwn* (hot tea).

Environment

Deforestation & Hydroelectric Power

With a land mass of 236,000 sq km, Laos is a little larger than the UK and, thanks to its relatively small population and mountainous terrain, it's one of the least altered environments in Southeast Asia. Unmanaged vegetation covers an estimated 85% of the country, and 10% of Laos is original-growth forest with some of the most varied and best-preserved ecosystems in Southeast Asia. However, 100 years ago this was closer to 75%, which provides a clear picture of the effects of relentless logging and slash-and-burn farming. The government has clear targets to raise the level of forestation to 70%

by 2020; optimistic perhaps, but thanks to the encouraged (some say forced) relocation of tribes practising slash-and-burn farming to lowland ground, there's a possibility the land may have a chance to regenerate – at least a little.

The same can't be said of areas like Attapeu Province, which has fallen victim to rampant commercial logging since 2005. Once home to dense forests, this Vietnam-bordering province is now denuded in huge areas like a lunar landscape. Just a decade ago Attapeu's remote village of Tahoy was home to a healthy population of tigers; by night they could allegedly be heard roaring at the edge of the forest. However, today, you're more likely to see trucks laden with rare timber openly heading over the border into Thailand. And, although the flooding of lowland forests can be partly justified in line with the national goal of creating dams for hydroelectric power and its subsequent wealth generation (the World Bank estimates that sales of Lao hydropower to Thailand alone could be around US$2 billion per year once new dams are operating to full capacity), it is arguable that the same can't be said for the fierce logging of Attapeu Province. Ironically, furniture makers in Vientiane often complain that they have to buy Lao wood from Thais.

The country's long-term economic goals tend to take precedence over the environment, and, despite its pledge to retain the country's natural riches by creating 20 National Protected Areas (NPAs), the government continues to sacrifice swaths of its land to the industrial logging requirements of China. Furthermore, the Laos army is self-funded, which can often lead to it making

---

TIMBER!

Laos has some of the largest remaining tracts of primary rainforest in mainland Southeast Asia and remains a vulnerable target for foreign companies who have a keen eye on its timber. The Environmental Investigation Agency (EIA) claims that the furniture industry in Vietnam has grown tenfold since 2000, with Laos facilitating the flow of its timber to enable this. An estimated 500,000 cu metres of logs find their way over the border every year. Although an outwardly hard-line approach has been taken against mass logging by the Lao government, the self-funded military and local officials in remote areas can fall prey to bribes.

Forest cover fell from 70% in the 1940s to less than 40% in the early 2000s, with an annual rate of 900 sq km disappearing every year. NPAs (National Protected Areas), which are supposed to be protected under Lao law, are prey to heavy illegal logging, due to the fact that they contain so much commercially valuable timber. An estimated 30% of forest cover will remain in Laos by 2020.

questionable decisions when it comes to granting logging licences and clearing roads as firebreaks.

On the bright side, an estimated half of the country's revenue is generated by tourists, which gives the landscape a limited insurance policy, and the protection of the country's forests is written into Laos' constitution. With an internationally created blueprint to monitor and increase ecotourism there may still be some hope for these wild places. If the country can keep its industrial ambitions in line with its delicate ecosystem, there is a chance Laos will achieve the economic independence it yearns for without squandering its natural heritage.

Wildlife

Laos is home to wild elephants, jackals, Asiatic black bears, black-crested gibbons, langurs, Asian elephants, leopards, tigers, pythons, king cobras, 437 kinds of bird and the rare Irrawaddy dolphin – to name a few! Thanks to some excellent environmentally responsible treks run in a number of the 20 National Protected Areas, there's a chance you'll come into contact with some of Laos' abundant wildlife, be it from the safety of a tree house or perhaps even closer (though hopefully not with one of its big cats, as was the case with one of our authors!).

The wildlife trade is flourishing, driven by the country's neighbours, particularly China, who seek body parts of endangered animals for traditional medicine and aphrodisiac purposes. It's difficult for a father of five living in a forest to turn down a year's wages for killing a tiger, just as it is difficult to police poachers. In certain circumstances an altogether more revolutionary approach has been taken, as in the case of the Gibbon Experience (p323), where former poachers are encouraged to make more money as guides and forest rangers. However, compared with Vietnam and Thailand – much of which is now deforested, urbanised and farmed – the wildlife in Laos is a veritable hothouse of biodiversity.

ASIAN TIGER

Historically, hundreds of thousands of tigers populated Asia, yet today there may be as few as 3000 left in the entire world, occupying a mere 7% of their original range. The survivors in Laos face a constant threat of poaching, habitat loss and conflict with humans. The NPAs in the northeast of Laos,

with deep, intractable forest, are thought to harbour the densest populations. During your trek, look out for tiger scat and deep scratch marks on the trunks of trees; should you hear one you'll know it – it's louder and more resonant than a church organ.

MEKONG CATFISH

Growing up to 3m in length and weighing in at 300kg, the world's largest freshwater fish is unique to the Mekong River. Over the past 10 years or so their numbers have dropped an astonishing 90% due to overfishing and, more pointedly, the building of hydroelectric dams that block their migratory paths. There may only be a few hundred left.

IRRAWADDY DOLPHIN

Beak-nosed and less extroverted than their bottlenose counterparts, these shy and critically endangered mammals inhabit a 190km stretch of the Mekong River between Cambodia and Laos. Recent estimates suggest that between 64 and 76 members survive. The best place to see them in Laos is off the southern tip of Don Khon, where a small pod congregates in a deepwater pool. Gill-net fishing and pollution have wiped out their numbers. During their reign in the late 1970s, the Khmer Rouge used to dynamite them indiscriminately.

BLACK-CRESTED GIBBON

The gibbon is the jungle's answer to Usain Bolt. These heavily poached, soulful animals sing with beautiful voices – usually at dawn – which echo hauntingly around the forest, and majestically race through the canopy quicker than any other ape. Usually males are black and females golden, and, in Laos, they only exist in Bokeo Province (home of The Gibbon Experience (p323)). The black-crested gibbon is one of the world's rarest, most endangered species of gibbon.

SURVIVAL GUIDE

❶ Directory A–Z

ACCOMMODATION

Since the country opened to foreigners in the early 1990s, guesthouses have been steadily multiplying, and most villages that merit a visit will have some form of accommodation. In cities such as Vientiane and Luang Prabang, prices vary wildly, with some truly exceptional boutique hotels that could excite even the most jaded *New*

York Times or Hip Hotels editor. At the other end of the scale, budget digs – usually a room with a fan and sometimes an en suite – are getting better every year. Even though guesthouse prices are rising, they're still unbeatable value when compared with the West; at less than 80,000K (about US$10) a night, who can argue? The cheapest accommodation is in the far north and deepest south.

Prices of low- and high-season accommodation in Laos differ considerably. High season falls between December and February (the cooler months), and is more expensive. All prices listed in this book are for this period, so should you be travelling at another time of year make sure you ask for a discount.

Compared with the West, accommodation in Laos is delightfully cheap; however, this is the developing world and prices are inching up every year as Laos plays catch-up.

Homestays

For more than 75% of Laotians, the 'real Laos' is life in a village. Minority people in villages across the country now welcome travellers into their homes to experience life Lao-style, meaning sleeping, eating and washing as they do. It's not luxury – the mattress will be on the floor and you'll 'shower' by pouring water over yourself from a 44-gallon (170L) drum, while standing in the middle of the yard (take a sarong), but it's exactly this level of immersion that makes a homestay so worthwhile. It's also good to know that the 50,000K you'll pay for bed, dinner and breakfast is going directly to those who need it most.

If you're up for it, remember to pack a torch, flip-flops or sandals, a phrasebook and some photos from home. If you can, give the gift of a children's book from one of the many Big Brother Mouse (p301) outlets.

Price Ranges

Accommodation prices listed are for the high season, for rooms with attached bathroom, unless stated otherwise.

$ less than 160,000K (US$20)
$$ 160,000K to 626,000K (US$20 to US$80)
$$$ more than 626,000K (US$80)

ACTIVITIES
Cycling

With cyclists bringing their own specialised bikes over the border without a hitch, cycling in Laos is becoming an increasingly appropriate way to see the country – leisurely transport for a languid country. Given the low population, Laos' roads are uncongested and many are now sealed, though post-monsoon there are myriad potholes in the best of them. However, if drivers see you in trouble, they are more than likely to stop and help or give you a lift. Alternatively,

should some of those mountains become too back-breaking, just flag down a passing bus or sŏrngtǎaou (literally 'two rows'; a common name for small pick-up trucks with two benches in the back, used as buses/taxis). And – it goes without saying – always bring plenty of water with you.

Off-the-beaten-path places have pretty dire road surfaces, so bring plenty of inner tubes or stock up in Vientiane or Luang Prabang. During the monsoon, mud roads in places such as the Bolaven Plateau churn into a mire of mud.

In cities be careful about leaving bags in the front basket, as passing motorcyclists have been known to lift them, something that seems to be happening more regularly, especially during festivals.

Several companies offer mountain-bike tours, such as from Luang Namtha (Boat Landing Guest House & Restaurant; p319) and Luang Prabang (White Elephant; p300).

Kayaking & Rafting

Kayaking and white-water rafting have taken off and Laos has several world-class rapids, as well as lots of beautiful, although less challenging, waterways. Unfortunately, the industry remains dangerously unregulated and you should not go out on rapids during the wet season unless you are completely confident about your guides and equipment. Vang Vieng has the most options. Green Discovery (p292) has a good reputation.

Rock Climbing

Organised rock-climbing operations are run by Green Discovery (p292) and Adam's Rock Climbing School (p291) in the karst cliffs around Vang Vieng, while Green Discovery (p306) is the only real operator in Nong Khiaw. Vang Vieng has the most established scene, with dozens of climbs ranging from beginner to expert. Nong Khiaw is also gaining repute for its limestone ascents.

Trekking

Where else can you wander through primal forests, past ethnic hill-tribe villages and rare wildlife, the triple canopy towering above you? This is possible largely in a sustainable fashion throughout Laos, thanks to a blueprint drawn up by various international advisors that were determined to help the country retain its natural wealth while harnessing its economic possibilities. Several environmentally and culturally sustainable tours have been developed, allowing you to enter these pristine areas and experience the lives of the indigenous people without exploitation.

These treks are available in several provinces and are detailed at www.ecotourismlaos.com. You can plan to trek from Luang Namtha, Muang Sing, Udomxai, Luang Prabang, Vientiane, Tha Khaek, Savannakhet and Pakse. Treks organised through the provincial tourism offices are the cheapest, while companies such as **Green Discovery** (www.greendiscoverylaos.com) offer more expensive and professional operations.

Tubing

Something of a Lao phenomenon, 'tubing' involves a huge tractor inner tube that carries you downriver. Climb in, sit back and tune out. Do be mindful of how much you drink and what time it is; when the Nam Ou river runs high and swift it's at its most dangerous, and at least one traveller a year loses their life. Vang Vieng is the tubing capital, with Muang Ngoi Neua and Si Phan Don popular runners-up.

BOOKS

Lonely Planet's *Laos* has all the information you'll need for extended travel in Laos, with more detailed descriptions of sights and wider coverage to help you get off the beaten track.

➡ *A Dragon Apparent* (1951) Sees Norman Lewis travelling through the twilight of French Indochina, animating his subjects with atmosphere and pathos, as the colonies are about to be lost.

➡ *The Lao* (2008) Robert Cooper's locally published book (available in Vientiane) is a pithy yet frequently penetrating insight into Lao culture, its psyche and the practicalities of setting up here as an expat.

➡ *The Ravens: Pilots of the Secret War of Laos* (1987) Christopher Robbins' page-turning account of the Secret War and the role of American pilots and the Hmong is an excellent read.

➡ *Shooting at the Moon: The Story of America's Clandestine War in Laos* (1998) Roger Warner's well-respected book exposes the Secret War against the Ho Chi Minh Trail, and the CIA and Hmong role in it.

CUSTOMS REGULATIONS

You can expect borders to be fairly sleepy affairs, and customs officers are not too interested – so long as you're not carrying more than 500 cigarettes and 1L of spirits. If you're caught with drugs, knives or guns on your person, this also may change very quickly.

EMBASSIES & CONSULATES

Australian Embassy (Map p276; ☎021-353800; www.laos.embassy.gov.au; Th Tha Deua, Ban Wat Nak, Vientiane; ◷8:30am-5pm Mon-Fri) Also represents nationals of Canada and New Zealand.

Cambodian Embassy (Map p276; ☎021-314952; Th Tha Deua, Km3, Ban That Khao, Vientiane) Issues visas for US$20.

Chinese Embassy (Map p276; ☎021-315105; http://la.china-embassy.org/eng; Th Wat Nak Nyai, Ban Wat Nak, Vientiane; ◷8-11.30am Mon-Fri) Issues visas in four working days.

French Embassy (Map p280; ☎021-215258; www.ambafrance-laos.org; Th Setthathirath, Ban Si Saket, Vientiane; ◷9am-12.30pm & 2-5.30pm Mon-Fri)

German Embassy (Map p276; ☎021-312110; www.vientiane.diplo.de; Th Sok Pa Luang, Vientiane; ◷9am-noon Mon-Fri)

Myanmar Embassy (Map p276; ☎021-314910; Th Sok Pa Luang, Vientiane) Issues tourist visas in three days for US$20.

Thai Embassy (Map p276; ☎021-214581; www.thaiembassy.org/vientiane; Th Kaysone Phomvihane, Vientiane; ◷8.30am-noon & 1-3.30pm Mon-Fri) Head to the Vientiane consulate (Map p276; ☎021-214581; 15 Th Bourichane, Vientiane; ◷8am-noon & 1-4.30pm) for visa renewals and extensions. Thailand also has a consulate in Savannakhet (☎041 212373; cnr Th Tha He & Th Chaimeuang, Savannakhet), which issues same-day tourist and non-immigrant visas (1000B).

US Embassy (Map p280; ☎021-267000; http://laos.usembassy.gov; Th Bartholomie, Vientiane)

Vietnamese Embassy (Map p276; ☎021-413400; www.mofa.gov.vn/vnemb.la; Th That Luang, Vientiane; ◷8.30am-5.30pm Mon-Fri) Issues tourist visas in three working days for US$45, or in one day for US$60. The Luang Prabang consulate (Map p296; Th Naviengkham, Luang Prabang) issues tourist visas for US$60 in a few minutes or US$45 if you wait a few days. The consulates in Pakse (☎031-214199; www.vietnamconsulate-pakse.org, Th 21, Pakse; ◷7.30-11.30am & 2-4.30pm Mon-Fri) and Savannakhet (☎041-212418; Th Sisavangvong, Savannakhet) issue one-/three-month tourist visas for US$50/60 (one photo, three working days).

GAY & LESBIAN TRAVELLERS

Laos has a liberal attitude towards homosexuality, but a very conservative attitude towards public displays of affection. Gay couples are unlikely to be given frosty treatment anywhere; lesbians won't be bothered, but do expect some strange looks from Lao men. Laos doesn't have an obvious gay scene, though Luang Prabang has Laos' first openly gay bar, Khob Chai (opposite Hive Bar (p303)), and has the rainbow-coloured gay pride flag flying in a few places around town.

INTERNET ACCESS

You can now get internet access in all major towns for around 7000K per hour. Most internet cafes have air-con, fans and also Skype (some with cameras). Wi-fi is widely available in most upmarket bars, hotels and Western-style bakeries.

LEGAL MATTERS

There are virtually no legal services in Laos. If you get yourself in legal strife, contact your embassy in Vientiane, though the assistance it can provide may be limited. For Brits, contact your embassy in Bangkok.

It's against the law for foreigners and Lao to have sexual relations unless they're married. Travellers should be aware that a holiday romance could result in being arrested and deported.

MAPS

The best all-purpose country map available is *Laos* by GT-Rider (http://gt-rider.com), a sturdy laminated affair with several city maps. Look for the 2005 edition or more recent ones.

Hobo Maps has produced a series of decent maps for Vientiane, Luang Prabang and Vang Vieng. These maps are widely available in the relevant destinations.

MONEY

Despite recent nationalistic attempts by the government to impose the Lao kip (K) more rigorously, US dollars and Thai baht are still widely accepted. At the time of research the US dollar was yielding a mere 8000K.

ATMs

ATMs are now proliferating in the main cities, with many spread around Vientiane, Luang Prabang, Pakse, Vang Vieng, Luang Namtha, Phonsavan, Udomxai, Huay Xai and Savannakhet. For a list of all the BCEL ATMs, try www.bcellaos.com/atm locator.php.

Bargaining

With the exception of túk-túk drivers in Vientiane (who are a law unto themselves), most Lao are not looking to rip you off. Take your time when haggling: start lower and gradually meet in the middle.

Cash

Kip notes come in denominations of 500, 1000, 2000, 5000, 10,000, 20,000 and 50,000K; the 50,000K note looks deceptively like the 20,000K note.

Credit Cards

A number of hotels, upmarket restaurants and gift shops in Vientiane and Luang Prabang accept Visa and MasterCard, and to a much lesser extent Amex and JCB. Visa is most widely accepted. Banque pour le Commerce Extérieur Lao (BCEL) branches in Vientiane, Luang Prabang, Vang Vieng, Savannakhet and Pakse offer cash advances/withdrawals on Visa credit/debit cards for a 3% transaction fee.

Moneychangers

US dollars and Thai baht can be exchanged all over Laos. Banks in Vientiane and Luang Prabang – and in some provinces – change euro, Thai baht, UK pounds, Japanese yen, and Canadian, US and Australian dollars. US-dollar travellers cheques can be exchanged in most provincial capitals and usually attract a much better rate than cash.

Generally, the best overall exchange rate is usually offered by BCEL. In rural areas exchange rates can be significantly lower. For the latest rates check www.bcellaos.com.

Travellers Cheques

Banks in most provincial capitals will exchange US-dollar travellers cheques. If you are changing cheques into kip, there is usually no commission, but changing into dollars attracts a minimum 2% charge.

OPENING HOURS

Banks 8.30am to 4pm Monday to Friday
Bars to the officially mandated closing time of 11.30pm or sometimes later
Government offices 8am to 11.30am or noon, and 1pm to 4pm or 5pm, Monday to Friday
Restaurants early to 10pm or 11pm

Most businesses close on Sunday, except restaurants. Shops are often open on weekends.

POST

Postal services from Vientiane are generally reliable, from the provinces less so. If you have valuable items or presents to post home, there is a **Federal Express** (☎ 021-223278; ⊙ 8am-noon & 1-5pm Mon-Fri, 9am-noon Sat) office inside the main post office (p286) compound in Vientiane.

PUBLIC HOLIDAYS

Schools and government offices are closed on these official holidays, and the organs of state move pretty slowly, if at all, during festivals. Most Chinese- and Vietnamese-run businesses close for three days during Vietnamese Tet and Chinese New Year in late January/February. International Women's Day is a holiday for women only.

International New Year 1 January
Army Day 20 January
International Women's Day 8 March
Lao New Year (Bun Pii Mai) 14–16 April
International Labour Day 1 May
International Children's Day 1 June
Bun Nam (Boat Racing Festival) Usually October
Bun Pha That Luang (Full Moon) Early November
Lao National Day 2 December

SAFE TRAVEL

Urban Laos is generally safe. You should still exercise vigilance at night, but thanks to the country's comparatively gentle psyche the likelihood of your being robbed, mugged, harassed or assaulted is much lower than in most Western countries. Since the 1975 revolution, there have been occasional shootings by Hmong guerrillas on Rte 13 between Vang Vieng and Luang Prabang, though it seems calm at the moment and has been since 2003.

In the eastern provinces, particularly Xieng Khuang, Salavan and Savannakhet, UXO (unexploded ordnance) is a hazard. Never walk off well-used paths.

Finally, the transport infrastructure in Laos is barely recognisable compared with what existed just a few years ago. Huge, foreign-funded road construction projects have transformed a network of rough dirt tracks into comparatively luxurious sealed affairs.

TELEPHONE

Laos' country code is ☑ 856. To dial out of the country press ☑ 00 first, or ask for the local mobile operator's cheaper code. For long-distance calls use a post office, Lao Telecom centre (rates vary in these, but in Vientiane are very reasonable) or internet cafes.

As a guide, all mobile-phone numbers have the prefix ☑ 020 followed by seven digits, while the newer WIN Phones (fixed phones without a landline) begin with ☑ 030.

Mobile Phones

With recently improved signals, you can use your own GSM mobile phone in Laos, either on roaming (prohibitively expensive) or by buying a local SIM card for about US$5, then purchasing prepaid minutes for a further US$5. Domestic calls are reasonably cheap. In our experience, Lao Telecom, M-Phone and ETL have the widest network coverage.

TOURIST INFORMATION

The Lao National Tourism Administration (NTAL) and provincial tourism authorities have offices throughout Laos. The offices in Tha Khaek, Savannakhet, Pakse, Luang Namtha, Sainyabuli, Phongsali and Sam Neua are excellent, with well trained staff and plenty of brochures.

NTAL also has three good websites:

Central Laos Trekking www.trekkingcentral laos.com

Ecotourism Laos www.ecotourismlaos.com

Lao National Tourism Administration www.tourismlaos.gov.la

VISAS

Laos issues 30-day tourist visas on arrival at several popular airports and borders. They are available at Vientiane, Luang Prabang and Pakse airports. Visas on arrival cost between US$30 and US$42, payable in US dollars, Lao kip or Thai baht, in cash, depending on what passport you hold. You'll also need two passport photos.

Regulations and prices change regularly, so it's worth checking online or through the traveller grapevine before turning up to some remote border. If you want to be doubly sure, or plan to use a border where visas are not issued, consulates and travel agents in Vietnam, China, Cambodia and Thailand can all issue/arrange visas.

Visa Extensions

Visa extensions cost US$2 per day from the **Immigration Office** (Map p280; ☑ 021-212250; Th Hatsady; ⊗ 8am-4.30pm Mon-Fri), which is in the Ministry of Public Security building in Vientiane. Extensions are available up to a maximum of 30 days. If you overstay your visa, you'll have to pay a fine on departure (US$10 for each day over).

VOLUNTEERING

It's not easy to find short-term volunteer work in Laos. The Organic Mulberry Farm (p293) in Vang Vieng needs volunteers occasionally, as does Big Brother Mouse (p301). If you're professionally skilled as an orthoptist, physio or surgeon, you may be able to work at the **COPE** (ສູນພື້ນຟູຄືນ ພິການບແຫງຊາດ; Map p276; ☑ 021-218427; www. copelaos.org; Th Khu Vieng; ⊗ 9am-6pm) Centre in Vientiane.

WOMEN TRAVELLERS

Stories of women being hassled are few. Lao men are more likely to be a little intimidated by you than anything else. Much of the time any attention will be no more than curiosity, as Western women are so physically different to Lao women.

Remember, you're in a strictly Buddhist country so the revealing of flesh, despite the heat, is seen as cheap and disrespectful. Sarongs and long sleeved T-shirts are a good idea. Lao people will almost never confront you about what you're wearing, but to them wearing a bikini is no different to wandering around in your underwear.

WORK

English teaching is the most common first job for foreigners working in Laos, and schools in Vientiane are often hiring. There is also an inordinate number of development organisations – see www.directoryofngos.org for a full list – where foreigners with technical skills and volunteer experience can look for employment. Ask around.

❶ Getting There & Away

With over a dozen border crossings into Laos, visiting the country has never been easier. Also, the once wobbly Lao Airlines has replaced its ailing fleet with nine new Chinese planes, and is servicing most corners of the country and neighbouring countries with frequent flights.

ENTERING LAOS

It's possible to enter Laos by land and air from Thailand, China, Vietnam and Cambodia. Land borders are often remote and can be quite tough-going with scant transport and accommodation on either side, but the actual frontier crossing itself is usually pretty quick and simple. A 30-day visa is now available at most Laos border crossings.

AIR

There are no intercontinental flights operating to Laos. You can fly into or out of Laos at Vientiane (from or to Cambodia, China, Thailand, Malaysia and Vietnam), Luang Prabang (Cambodia, Thailand and Vietnam) or Pakse (from or to Vietnam, Cambodia and Thailand).

LAND
Border Crossings

Laos has open land borders with Cambodia, China, Thailand and Vietnam, but not Myanmar. Under current rules, 30-day tourist visas are available on arrival at several (but not all) international checkpoints. However, we still recommend checking the **Thorn Tree** (lonelyplanet. com/thorntree) and with other travellers before setting off because things change frequently. Note that many crossings involve changing transport at the border. For details, see the specific border-crossings boxes scattered throughout this chapter.

Car & Motorcycle

If you have your own car or motorcycle, you can import it for the length of your visa after filling in forms and paying fees at the border; it's much easier if you have a carnet. Motorcyclists planning to ride through Laos should check out the wealth of info at www.gt-rider.com.

ⓘ Getting Around

AIR

Lao Airlines (www.laoairlines.com) handles all domestic flights in Laos. Fortunately, its revamped new fleet has slick MA60s, with the airline rapidly improving its safety record. Check the Lao calendar for public festivals before you fly, as it can be difficult getting a seat. In provincial Lao Airlines offices you'll be expected to pay in cash.

Always reconfirm your flights a day before departing, as undersubscribed flights may be cancelled or you could get bumped off the passenger list.

BICYCLE

The light and relatively slow traffic in most Lao towns makes for favourable cycling conditions. Bicycles are available for rent in major tourist destinations, costing around 10,000K per day for a cheap Thai or Chinese model.

BOAT

Given the much-improved trade roads, the days of mass river transport are almost over. The most popular river trip in Laos – the slowboat between Huay Xai and Luang Prabang – remains a daily event. Other popular journeys – between Pakse and Si Phan Don, or between Nong Khiaw and Luang Prabang – are all recommended if you have time. For information on luxury boat charters, try **Asian Oasis** (www.asian-oasis. com), which provides two trips down the Mekong both in the north and south of the country.

River ferries are basic affairs and passengers usually sit, eat and sleep on the wooden decks; it's worth bringing some padding. The toilet (if there is one) is an enclosed hole in the deck at the back of the boat. For shorter river trips, such as Luang Prabang to the Pak Ou Caves, you can easily hire a river taxi.

Between Luang Prabang and Huay Xai, and Xieng Kok and Huay Xai, deafeningly loud and painfully uncomfortable speedboats operate, covering the same distance in six hours as that of a river ferry in two days. Be warned that passengers are killed or injured every year when the boats disintegrate on contact with floating debris, or flip when they hit a standing wave.

BUS & SŎRNGTĂAOU

Long-distance public transport in Laos is either by bus or *sŏrngtăaou*, which are converted trucks or pick-ups with benches down either side. Buses are more frequent and go further. Privately run VIP buses operate on some busier routes, but slow, simple standard buses (occasionally with air-con) remain the norm.

Sŏrngtăaou usually service shorter routes within a given province. Most decent-sized villages have at least one *sŏrngtăaou*, which will run to the provincial capital daily except Sunday, stopping wherever you want.

CAR & MOTORCYCLE

Scooters can be rented for 50,000K to 90,000K a day in Vientiane, Tha Khaek, Savannakhet, Pakse and Luang Namtha. In Vientiane, Luang Prabang, Tha Khaek and Pakse it's also possible to rent dirt bikes for around US$35 per day. Jules' Classic Rental (p288) and Mad Monkey Motorbike (p331) have a range of performance dirt bikes and the former offers the option to rent in Vientiane and drop off in Luang Prabang or Pakse for an additional charge.

Car rental in Laos is a great if relatively costly way of reaching remote places. Europcar (p289) offers vehicles from US$55 per day, charging US$20 extra for an optional driver.

HITCHING

Hitching is possible in Laos, if not common. It's never entirely safe and not recommended, especially for women, as the act of standing beside a road and waving at cars might be misinterpreted.

Northern Thailand

🌐 66 / POP 66.7 MILLION (THAILAND)

Best Places to Eat

➡ nahm (p379)

➡ Khao Soi Lam Duan (p426)

➡ Bao Pradit (p409)

➡ Larp Khom Huay Poo (p434)

➡ Phu-Talay (p398)

Best Places to Stay

➡ Villa Duang Champa (p424)

➡ Keereeta Resort (p398)

➡ Loy La Long (p374)

➡ Kham Pia Homestay (p414)

➡ Boklua View (p443)

Why Go?

Thailand is arguably the 'safest' introduction to Southeast Asia, but this doesn't mean it represents any sort of compromise. In fact, we suspect that the secret of Thailand's popularity, in particular that of its northern half, is that it packs a bit of everything.

Bangkok is one of the most vibrant cities in Southeast Asia, yet if contemporary Thai living is not your thing, you can delve into the country's past at historical parks such as those at Sukhothai or Phanom Rung. Similarly, fresh-air fiends will be satiated by upcountry expeditions ranging from a rafting expedition in Nan to the cliff-top views from Ubon Ratchathani's Pha Taem National Park. And culture junkies can get their fix at a homestay in the country's northeast or via a trek in northern Thailand.

And lest we forget: Thailand also functions as a convenient gateway to Cambodia and Laos. What's not to love?

When to Go
Chiang Mai

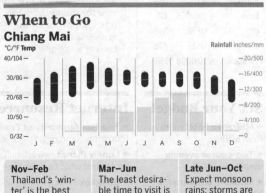

Nov–Feb
Thailand's 'winter' is the best time to visit.

Mar–Jun
The least desirable time to visit is during Thailand's hot season.

Late Jun–Oct
Expect monsoon rains; storms are usually confined to an hour's downpour.

AT A GLANCE

→ **Currency** baht (B)

→ **Language** Thai

→ **Money** ATMs widespread, charge a 150B foreign-account fee; Visa and MasterCard accepted at upmarket places

→ **Visas** Not required for citizens of EU, Australia or USA

→ **Mobile phones** Get inexpensive pre-paid SIM cards for GSM phones; 3G available

Fast Facts

→ **Area (Thailand)** 513,000 sq km

→ **Capital** Bangkok

→ **Country code** ☑66

→ **Emergency** ☑191

Exchange Rates

Australia	A$1	29B
Cambodia	10,000r	80B
Euro Zone	€1	45B
Laos	10,000K	41B
UK	UK£1	54B
USA	US$1	33B
Vietnam	10,000d	15B

Set Your Budget

→ **Midrange hotel room** from 600B

→ **Two-course evening meal** from 150B

→ **Museum entrance** from 100B

→ **Small bottle of beer** from 60B

Connections

Bangkok is one of Southeast Asia's most important air hubs, and has frequent air links to multiple destinations in Cambodia, Laos and Vietnam. Several of Thailand's larger provincial capitals also offer air links to neighbouring countries.

Bus, minivan and train links from Bangkok and eastern, northern and northeastern Thailand lead to numerous land (or sometimes river) border crossings with Cambodia and Laos. Several larger Thai cities (including Bangkok and Chiang Mai) also offer bus links direct to various cities in Cambodia and Laos.

ITINERARIES

One Week

Bangkok is the most likely place to land after a long-haul international flight and is the easiest place to arrange onward travel. Give yourself a couple of days to adjust by exploring the sights in the old royal district of **Ko Ratanakosin** and loading up on souvenirs at the Chatuchak Weekend Market. Experience the urban side of northern Thailand in **Chiang Mai** or **Chiang Rai**. Alternatively, escape cities altogether with a side trip to the beaches of **Ko Chang** or the 'Golden Triangle' village of **Mae Salong**; the former has the advantage of being a skip away from the Cambodian border at **Hat Lek**, while the latter puts you in prime position to cross to Laos at **Chiang Khong**.

Two Weeks

With more time, extend your visit to Thailand's north via a culture- or nature-based excursion such as a trek to the hill-tribe villages that surround **Pai** or a visit to remote **Doi Phu Kha National Park** in Nan. Alternatively, consider a spin through **northeast Thailand**, the country's most traditional rice-growing region. Visit the Khmer ruins at **Phanom Rung** and **Phimai**. Savour the riverine landscape around the parks that make up the **Emerald Triangle** and follow the Mekong River in reverse to laid-back **Nong Khai** before crossing to Laos or Cambodia.

Internet Resources

→ **Tourism Authority of Thailand** (TAT; www. tourismthailand.org) National tourism department.

→ **Lonely Planet** (www.lonelyplanet.com/thailand) Country profile and what to do and see.

→ **Bangkok Post** (www.bangkokpost.com) English-language daily.

→ **Thai Travel Blogs** (www.thaitravelblogs.com) Thailand-based travel blogger.

BANGKOK

📱 02 / POP 8 MILLION

Bangkok's influence stretches beyond the Thai borders into the greater Southeast Asian region due to its prominence as an international transport hub and its manufacturing of entertainment and consumables. You'll need to pass through here to get anywhere else. Encompassing the past, present and future, this sprawwling city is a full-on dose of urban sophistication, megawatt energy and ceaseless chaos, and will tattoo itself onto your travelling skin.

🅾 Sights

🅾 Ko Ratanakosin, Banglamphu & Thonburi

Most of Bangkok's must-sees reside in compact, walkable Ko Ratanakosin, the former royal district.

★ Wat Phra Kaew & Grand Palace
BUDDHIST TEMPLE, HISTORICAL SITE

(วัดพระแก้ว, พระบรมมหาราชวัง; Th Na Phra Lan; admission 500B; ⏰8.30am-4pm; ☷Tha Chang) Also known as the Temple of the Emerald Buddha, **Wat Phra Kaew** (Map p370) is the colloquial name of the vast, fairy-tale compound that, in addition to the eponymous Buddha statue, also includes the former residence of the Thai monarch, the **Grand Palace** (Map p370).

This ground was consecrated in 1782, the first year of Bangkok rule, and is today Bangkok's biggest tourist attraction and a pilgrimage destination for devout Buddhists and nationalists. The 94.5-hectare grounds encompass more than 100 buildings that represent 200 years of royal history and architectural experimentation.

Guides can be hired at the ticket kiosk; ignore offers from anyone outside. An audio guide can be rented for 200B for two hours

Admission for the complex includes same-day entrance to Dusit Palace Park (p369).

★ Wat Pho
BUDDHIST TEMPLE

(วัดโพธิ์ (วัดพระเชตุพน), Wat Phra Chetuphon; Map p370; Th Sanam Chai; admission 100B; ⏰8.30am-6.30pm; ☷Tha Tien) Wat Pho is our personal fave among Bangkok's biggest temples. In fact, the compound incorporates a host of superlatives: the largest reclining Buddha, the largest collection of Buddha images in Thailand and the country's earliest centre for public education.

★ Wat Arun
BUDDHIST TEMPLE

(วัดอรุณฯ; Map p370; www.watarun.net; off Th Arun Amarin; admission 50B; ⏰8am-6pm; ☷cross-river ferry from Tha Tien) Wat Arun is a striking temple named after the Indian god of dawn, Aruna. It looms large on Mae Nam Chao Phraya's west bank, as if it were carved from granite; a closer inspection reveals a mosaic made of broken porcelain covering the imposing 82m Khmer-style *brang* (tower).

At press time, it had been announced that the *brang* would be closed for as long as three years due to renovation. Visitors can enter the compound, but cannot, as in previous years, climb the tower.

Cross-river ferries from Tha Tien run over to Wat Arun every few minutes from 6am to 8pm (3B).

National Museum
MUSEUM

(พิพิธภัณฑสถานแห่งชาติ; Map p370; 4 Th Na Phra Thai; admission 200B; ⏰9am-4pm Wed-Sun; ☷Tha Chang) The National Museum provides a dusty yet interesting overview of Thai art and culture; you'll get more out of the museum on a docent-led **tour** (free with museum admission; ⏰9.30am Wed & Thu).

Museum of Siam
MUSEUM

(สถาบันพิพิธภัณฑ์การเรียนรู้แห่งชาติ; Map p370; www.museumsiam.com; Th Maha Rat; admission 300B; ⏰10am-6pm Tue-Sun; ☷Tha Tien) This fun museum employs a variety of media to explore the origins of the Thai people and their culture via surprisingly modern and engaging exhibits.

Amulet Market
MARKET

(ตลาดพระเครื่องวัดมหาธาตุ; Map p370; Th Maha Rat; ⏰7am-5pm; ☷Tha Chang) The trade at

---

ℹ DRESS FOR THE OCCASION

Thai temples, especially those with a royal connection, are sacred places, and visitors should dress and behave appropriately. Wear shirts with sleeves, long pants or skirts past the knees, and closed-toed shoes. Sarongs and baggy pants are available on loan at the entry area for Wat Phra Kaew & Grand Palace. Shoes should be removed before entering buildings. When sitting in front of a Buddha image, tuck your feet behind you in the 'mermaid' position to avoid the offence of pointing your feet towards a revered figure.

Northern Thailand Highlights

1 Picking up some bargains at Chiang Mai's **Night Bazaar**, **Saturday Walking Street** and **Sunday Walking Street** (p427)

2 Feeling awestruck by the scenery in **Pha Taem National Park** (p415)

3 Cycling around the awesome ruins of Thailand's 'golden age' at **Sukhothai** (p434) and **Si Satchanalai–Chaliang Historical Parks** (p437)

4 Working or living with traditional elephant handlers at northeastern Thailand's **Surin Project** (p405)

5 Getting into the groove of rural northern Thailand in laid-back **Pai** (p432)

6 Beachcombing and jungle trekking on **Ko Chang** (p395)

7 Recover from the hardships of the upcountry in Thailand's modern and decadent capital, **Bangkok** (p361)

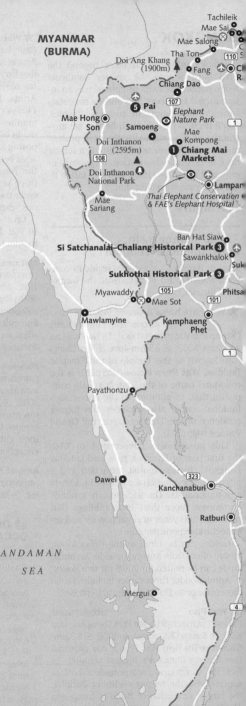

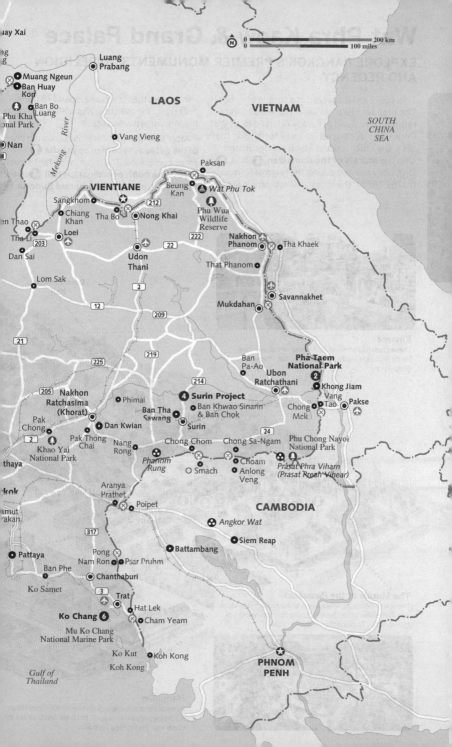

Wat Phra Kaew & Grand Palace

EXPLORE BANGKOK'S PREMIER MONUMENTS TO RELIGION AND REGENCY

This tour can be covered in a couple of hours. The first area tourists enter is the Buddhist temple compound generally referred to as Wat Phra Kaew. A covered walkway surrounds the area, the inner walls of which are decorated with the **murals of the *Ramakian*** ❶ and ❷. Originally painted during the reign of Rama I (r 1782–1809), the murals, which depict the Hindu epic the *Ramayana*, span 178 panels that describe the struggles of Rama to rescu his kidnapped wife, Sita.

After taking in the story, pass through one of the gateways guarded by *yaksha* ❸ to the inner compound. The most important structu here is the ***bòht*, or ordination hall** ❹, whic houses the eponymous **Emerald Buddha** ❺

Kinaree
These graceful half-swan, half-women creatures from Hindu-Buddhist mythology stand outside Prasat Phra Thep Bidon.

Borombhiman Hall

Prasat Phra Thep Bidon

Phra Si Ratana

The Murals of the *Ramakian*
These wall paintings, which begin at the eastern side of the Wat Phra Kaew, often depict scenes more reminiscent of 19th-century Thailand than of ancient India.

Hanuman
Rows of these mischievous monkey deities from Hindu mythology appear to support the lower levels of two sm. *chedi* near Prasat Phra Thep Bidon.

Head east to the so-called Upper Terrace, an elevated area home to the **spires of the three primary *chedi*** ❻. The middle structure, Phra Mondop, is used to house Buddhist manuscripts. This area is also home to several of Wat Phra Kaew's noteworthy mythical beings, including beckoning ***kinaree*** ❼ and several grimacing **Hanuman** ❽.

Proceed through the western gate to the compound known as the Grand Palace. Few of the buildings here are open to the public. The most noteworthy structure is **Chakri Mahaprasat** ❾. Built in 1882, the exterior of the hall is a unique blend of western and traditional Thai architecture.

he Three Spires
ıe elaborate seven-tiered of of Phra Mondop, the ımer-style peak of the Prasat ıra Thep Bidon, and the ıded Phra Si Ratana *chedi* are e tallest structures in the ımpound.

Emerald Buddha
Despite the name, this diminutive statue (it's only 66cm tall) is actually carved from nephrite, a type of jade.

Amarindra Hall

The Death of Thotsakan
The panels progress clockwise, culminating at the western edge of the compound with the death of Thotsakan, Sita's kidnapper, and his elaborate funeral procession

Chakri Mahaprasat
This structure is sometimes referred to as *fa•ràng sài chá•dah* (Westerner in a Thai crown) because each wing is topped by a *mon•dòp*: a spire representing a Thai adaptation of a Hindu shrine.

Dusit Hall

Bòht
(Ordination Hall)
This structure is an early example of the Ratanakosin school of architecture, which combines traditional stylistic holdovers from Ayuthaya along with more modern touches from China and the West.

ıksha
ch entrance the Wat Phra ıew compound is ıtched over by a ıir of vigilant and ırmous *yaksha*, res or giants from ıdu mythology.

Wat Pho

A WALK THROUGH THE BIG BUDDHAS OF WAT PHO

The logical starting place is the main *wí•hǎhn* (sanctuary), home to Wat Pho's centrepiece, the immense **Reclining Buddha ❶**. Apart from its huge size, note the **mother-of-pearl inlays ❷** on the soles of the statue's feet. The interior walls of the *wí•hǎhn* are covered with murals depicting previous lives of the Buddha, and along the south side of the structure are 108 bronze monk bowls; for 20B you can buy 108 coins, each of which is dropped in a bowl for good luck.

Exit the *wí•hǎhn* and head east via the tw **stone giants ❸** who guard the gateway to the rest of the compound. Directly south of these are the four towering **royal *chedi* ❹**.

Continue east, passing through two consecutive **galleries of Buddha**

Phra Ubosot
Built during the reign of Rama I, the imposing *bòht* (ordination hall) as it stands today is the result of renovations dating back to the reign of Rama III (r 1824–51).

Southern *Wí·hǎhn*

Buddha Galleries
The two series of covered hallways that surround the Phra Ubosot feature no fewer than 394 gilded Buddha images, many of whic display classic Ayuthaya or Sukhothai features

Eastern *Wí·hǎhn*

Massage Pavilions
If you're hot and footsore, the two air-conditioned massage pavilions are a welcome way to cool down while experiencing high-quality and relatively inexpensive Thai massage.

Phra Buddha Deva Patimakorn
On an impressive three-tiered pedestal that also holds the ashes of Rama I is this Ayuthaya-era Buddha statue originally brought to the temple by the monarch.

Northern *Wí·hǎhn*

Western *Wí·hǎhn*

AUSTIN BUSH ©

statues **5** linking four *wí•hǎhn*, two of which contain notable Sukhothai-era Buddha statues; these comprise the exterior of **Phra Ubosot** **6**, the immense ordination hall that is Wat Pho's second-most noteworthy structure. The base of the building is surrounded by bas-relief inscriptions, and inside is the notable Buddha statue, **Phra Buddha Deva Patimakorn** **7**.

Wat Pho is often referred to as Thailand's first university, a tradition that continues today in an associated traditional Thai medicine school and, at the compound's eastern extent, two **massage pavilions** **8**.

Interspersed throughout the eastern half of the compound are several additional minor *chedi* and rock gardens.

Royal Chedi
Decorated in coloured tiles in a classic example of Ratanakosin style, these four *chedi* are meant to represent the first four kings of the Chakri dynasty.

Reclining Buddha
Modelled around a brick core 46m long and 15m high and finished in plaster and gold leaf, Wat Pho's Reclining Buddha is an imposing reminder of the Buddha's passing into nirvana (the Buddha's death).

Crocodile Pond

Phra Mondop

Thai Massage Inscriptions

Main Wí•hǎhn

Stone Giants
These huge granite figures – depictions range from Chinese opera characters to Marco Polo – originally arrived in Thailand in the 19th century as ballast aboard Chinese junks.

Mother-Of-Pearl Inlay
The 108 auspicious *lák•sà•nà*, physical characteristics of the Buddha, are depicted on the soles of the feet of the Reclining Buddha.

AUSTIN BUSH ©

Greater Bangkok

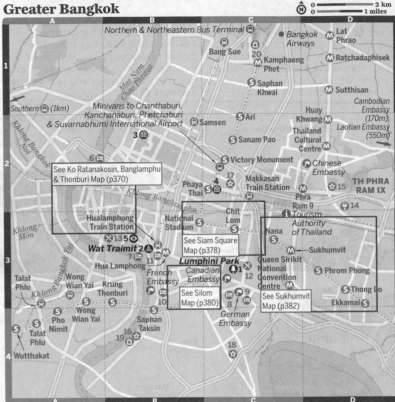

this arcane and fascinating market is based around small talismans prized by collectors, monks, taxi drivers and people in dangerous professions.

Chinatown & Phahurat

Gold shops, towering neon signs and shopfronts spilling out onto the sidewalk – welcome to Chinatown (also known as Yaowarat). The neighbourhood's energy is at once exhilarating and exhausting, and it's fun to explore at night when it's lit up like a Christmas tree and there's lots of street food.

At the western edge of Chinatown is a small but thriving Indian district, generally called Phahurat. Dozens of Indian-owned shops sell all kinds of fabric and clothes.

★ Wat Traimit
BUDDHIST TEMPLE

(วัดไตรมิตร, Temple of the Golden Buddha; Map p368; Th Mitthaphap (Th Traimit); admission 40B; ⏰8am-5pm; ⛴Tha Ratchawong, ⓜHua Lam-

phong exit 1) The attraction at Wat Traimit is undoubtedly the impressive 3m-tall, 5.5-tonne, solid-gold Buddha image, which was 'discovered' some 40 years ago beneath a stucco or plaster exterior, when it fell from a crane while being moved to a new building.

Talat Mai
MARKET

(ตลาดใหม่; Map p368; Soi 6 (Trok Itsaranuphap), Th Yaowarat; ⏰6am-6pm; ⛴Tha Ratchawong, ⓜHua Lamphong exit 1 & taxi) Essentially a narrow covered market squeezed between tall buildings. Even if you're not interested in food the hectic atmosphere and exotic sights and smells here culminate in something of a surreal sensory experience.

Wat Mangkon Kamalawat
BUDDHIST TEMPLE

(วัดมังกรกมลาวาส; Map p370; cnr Th Charoen Krung & Th Mangkon; ⏰6am-6pm; ⛴Tha Ratchawong, ⓜHua Lamphong exit 1 & taxi) FREE

Greater Bangkok

Clouds of incense and the sounds of chanting form the backdrop at this Chinese-style Mahayana Buddhist temple. Dating back to 1871, it's the largest and most important religious structure in the area.

◎ Siam Square

★ Jim Thompson House　HISTORICAL BUILDING
(Map p378; www.jimthompsonhouse.com; 6 Soi Kasem San 2; adult/child 100/50B; ⊙9am-5pm, compulsory tours in English & French every 20min; ⊠klorng boat to Tha Saphan Hua Chang, ⓈNational Stadium exit 1) This jungly compound is the former home of the eponymous American silk entrepreneur. In addition to textiles,

Thompson also collected parts of various derelict Thai homes and had them reassembled in their current location in 1959. His small but splendid Asian art collection and his personal belongings are also on display in the main house.

◎ Silom

★ Lumphini Park　PARK
(สวนลุมพินี; Map p368; bounded by Th Sarasin, Th Phra Ram IV, Th Witthayu (Wireless Rd) & Th Ratchadamri; ⊙4.30am-9pm; ⓂLumphini exit 3, Si Lom exit 1, ⓈSala Daeng exit 3, Ratchadamri exit 2) FREE The best time to visit central Bangkok's largest park is before 7am when legions of Thai-Chinese are practising *taijiquan* (t'ai chi). The park reawakens with the evening's cooler temperatures – aerobics classes collectively sweat to a techno soundtrack. Late at night the borders of the park are frequented by street-walking prostitutes, both male and female.

◎ Other Areas

Suan Pakkad Palace Museum　MUSEUM
(วังสวนผักกาด; Map p368; Th Si Ayuthaya; admission 100B; ⊙9am-4pm; ⓈPhaya Thai exit 4) An overlooked treasure, Suan Pakkad is a collection of eight traditional wooden Thai houses that was once the residence of Princess Chumbon of Nakhon Sawan and before that a lettuce farm – hence the name. Within the stilt buildings are displays of art, antiques and furnishings, and the landscaped grounds are a peaceful oasis complete with ducks, swans and a semi-enclosed garden.

Dusit Palace Park　MUSEUM, HISTORICAL SITE
(วังสวนดุสิต; Map p368; bounded by Th Ratchawithi, Th U Thong Nai & Th Ratchasima; adult/child 100/20B or free with Grand Palace ticket; ⊙9.30am-3.15pm Tue-Sun; ⊠Tha Thewet, ⓈPhaya Thai exit 2 & taxi) Elegant Dusit Palace Park is a former royal palace with serene green space and multiple handicraft museums. The must-see is the 1868 **Vimanmek Teak Mansion**, reputedly the world's largest golden teakwood building.

🏃 Activities

Health Land　THAI MASSAGE
(Map p380; ☎0 2637 8883; www.healthlandspa.com; 120 Th Sathon Neua (North); Thai massage 2hr 500B; ⊙9am-midnight; ⓈSurasak exit 3) A winning formula of affordable prices, expert treatments and pleasant facilities has

Ko Ratanakosin, Banglamphu & Thonburi

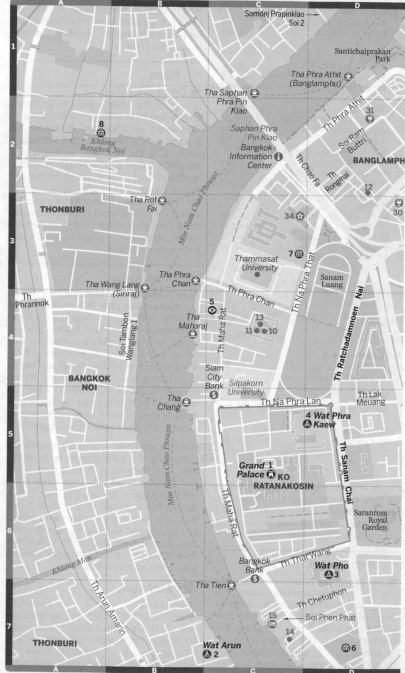

NORTHERN THAILAND BANGKOK

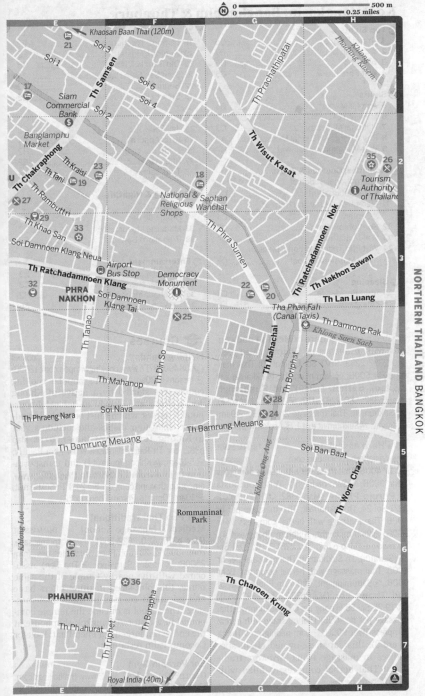

Khaosan Baan Thai (120m)

Soi 3

Soi 1

Th Samsen

Soi 6

Soi 4

Th Prachathipatai

Klong Phadung Kasam

Th Wisut Kasat

21

17

Siam Commercial Bank

Banglamphu Market

Th Chakraphong

Th Kraisi

23

Th Tani

19

Th Rambuttri

27

National & Religious Shops

18

Saphan Wanchat

Th Phra Sumen

Th Ratchadamnoen Nok

35 26

Tourism Authority of Thailand

Th Nakhon Sawan

29

Th Khao San

33

Soi Damnoen Klang Neua

Airport Bus Stop

Democracy Monument

Th Ratchadamnoen Klang

PHRA NAKHON

Soi Damnoen Klang Tai

32

Th Tanao

22

20

Th Lan Luang

Tha Phan Fah (Canal Taxis)

Th Damrong Rak

Khlong Saen Saeb

25

Th Din So

Th Mahanop

Th Mahachai

Th Boriphat

Th Phraeng Nara

Soi Nava

28

24

Th Bamrung Meuang

Th Bamrung Meuang

Soi Ban Baat

Th Wora Chak

Khlong Ong Ang

Rommaninat Park

Khlong Lot

16

Th Charoen Krung

PHAHURAT

36

Th Burapha

Th Phahurat

Th Triphet

Royal India (40m)

9

Ko Ratanakosin, Banglamphu & Thonburi

created a small empire of Health Land centres with branches at **Ekamai** (Map p382; ☏0 2392 2233; 96/1 Soi Ekamai 10; Thai massage 2hr 500B; ☺9am-midnight; ⑤Ekkamai exit 2 & taxi), **Sathon** (p369) and **Sukhumvit** (Map p382; ☏0 2261 1110; 55/5 Soi 21 (Asoke), Th Sukhumvit; Thai massage 2hr 500B; ☺9am-midnight; Ⓜ Sukhumvit exit 1, ⑤Asok exit 5).

Asia Herb Association   THAI MASSAGE
(www.asiaherbassociation.com; Thai massage per hr 400B, Thai massage with herbal compress 1½hr 900B; ☺9am-midnight) With outposts at **Phrom Phong** (Map p382; ☏0 2261 7401; 33/1 Soi 24, Th Sukhumvit; Thai massage per hr 400B, Thai massage with herbal compress 1½hr 900B; ☺9am-midnight; ⑤Phrom Phong exit 4), **Sawadee** (Map p382; ☏0 2261 2201; 20/1 Soi 31 (Sawatdi), Th Sukhumvit; Thai massage per hr 400B, Thai massage with herbal compress 1½hr 900B; ☺9am-midnight; ⑤Phrom Phong e xit 5) and **Thong Lor** (Map p382; ☏0 2392 3631; 58/19-25 Soi 55 (Thong Lor), Th Sukhumvit; Thai massage per hr 400B, Thai massage with herbal compress 1½hr 900B; ☺9am-midnight; ⑤Thong Lo exit 3), this Japanese-owned chain specialises in massage using *ฺbra·kóp*, traditional Thai herbal compresses filled with 18 different herbs.

🎓 Courses

Helping Hands   COOKING
(☏08 4901 8717; www.cookingwithpoo.com; 1200B; ☺lessons 8.30am-1pm) This popular cooking course was started by a native of Khlong Toey's slums and is held in her neighbourhood. Courses, which must be booked in advance, span four dishes and include a visit to **Khlong Toey Market** (ตลาดคลองเตย; Map p382; cnr Th Ratchadaphisek & Th Phra Ram IV; ☺5-10am; Ⓜ Khlong Toei exit 1) and transportation to and from **Emporium** (Map p382; www.emporiumthailand.com; cnr Soi 24 & Th Sukhumvit; ☺10am-10pm; ⑤Phrom Phong exit 2).

**Wat Pho Thai Traditional
Medical & Massage School**   THAI MASSAGE
(Map p370; ☏0 2622 3551; www.watpomassage.com; 392/25-28 Soi Phen Phat; lessons from 2500B; ☺lessons 9am-4pm; ⛴Tha Tien) Associated with the nearby temple of the same name, this pint-sized institute offers basic and advanced courses in traditional massage. The school is outside the temple compound in a restored Bangkok shophouse at the end of unmarked Soi Phen Phat; look for Coconut Palm restaurant.

Sor Vorapin Gym   THAI BOXING
(Map p370; ☏0 2282 3551; www.thaiboxings.com; 13 Th Kasab; per session/month 500/9000B;

lessons 7.30-9.30am & 3-5pm; Tha Phra Athit (Banglamphu)) Specialising in training foreign students of both genders, this gym is sweating distance from Th Khao San.

Wat Mahathat
MEDITATION

(Map p370; 3 Th Maha Rat; Tha Chang) This temple is home to two independently operating meditation centres. The **International Buddhist Meditation Center** (Map p370; 0 2222 6011; Section 5, Wat Mahathat, Th Maha Rat; donations accepted; lessons 7am, 1pm & 6pm; Tha Chang) offers three hour-long daily meditation classes at 7am, 1pm and 6pm, taught by English-speaking Prasuputh Chainikom (Kosalo). The **Meditation Study and Retreat Center** (Map p370; 0 2623 6326; www.mcu.ac.th/IBMC/; Th Maha Rat; donations accepted; Tha Chang) offers a regimented program of meditation.

Festivals & Events

In addition to the national holidays, there's always something going on in Bangkok. Check the website of **TAT** (Tourism Authority of Thailand; www.tourismthailand.org) or the Bangkok Information Center (p387) for exact dates.

Chinese New Year
NEW YEAR

(Jan or Feb) Thai-Chinese celebrate the lunar New Year with a week of housecleaning, lion dances and fireworks. Most festivities centre on Chinatown. Dates vary.

Songkran
NEW YEAR

(13-15 Apr) The Thai New Year has morphed into a water war.

Vegetarian Festival
FOOD

(Sep or Oct) A 10-day Chinese-Buddhist festival whools out yellow bannered streetside vendors serving meatless meals.

Loi Krathong
FULL MOON

(www.loikrathong.net/en; early Nov) A beautiful festival where, on the night of the full moon, small lotus-shaped boats made of banana leaf and containing a lit candle are set adrift on Mae Nam Chao Phraya.

Sleeping

Ko Ratanakosin, Banglamphu & Thonburi

Banglamphu, the neighbourhood that includes the backpacker street of Th Khao San, is a well-padded landing zone for jet-lagged travellers. This doesn't necessarily mean it's the only or even the best place to stay in town, but prices are generally low and standards relatively high. Neighbouring Ko Ratanakosin is seeing an increasing number of boutique-type riverside places.

Fortville Guesthouse
HOTEL $

(Map p370; 0 2282 3932; www.fortvilleguesthouse.com; 9 Th Phra Sumen; r 790-1120B; ; Tha Phra Athit (Banglamphu)) Rooms here are generally small, but the more expensive include perks such as a fridge, balcony and free wi-fi. A quirky, stylish, good-value hotel.

★ Lamphu Treehouse
HOTEL $$

(Map p370; 0 2282 0991; www.lamphutreehotel.com; 155 Wanchat Bridge, off Th Prachathipatai; r incl breakfast 1450-2500B, ste incl breakfast 3600-4900B; ; Tha Phan Fah) Despite the name, this attractive midranger has its feet firmly on land, and represents brilliant value. The wood-panelled rooms are attractive and inviting, and the rooftop bar, pool, internet cafe, restaurant and quiet canal-side location ensure that you may never want to leave.

Feung Nakorn Balcony
HOTEL $$

(Map p370; 0 2622 1100; www.feungnakorn.com; 125 Th Fuang Nakhon; dm incl breakfast 600B; r incl breakfast 1650B, ste incl breakfast 2000-3000B;

> **DON'T MISS**
>
> ## EXPLORING BANGKOK'S CANALS
>
> For an up-close view of the city's famed canals, long-tail boats are available for hire at Tha Chang, Tha Tien, Tha Oriental and Tha Phra Athit (Banglamphu). Trips explore the Thonburi canals Khlong Bangkok Noi and, further south, Khlong Mon, taking in the **Royal Barges National Museum** (พิพิธภัณฑสถาน แห่งชาติ เรือพระราชพิธี (เรือพระที่นั่ง); Map p370; Khlong Bangkok Noi or 80/1 Th Arun Amarin; admission 100B, camera/video 100/200B; 9am-5pm; Tha Saphan Phra Pin Klao), Wat Arun and a riverside temple with fish feeding. Longer trips diverge into Khlong Bangkok Yai, further south, which offers more typical canal scenery, including orchid farms. However, to actually disembark and explore any of these sights, the most common tour of one hour (1000B, up to eight people) is simply not enough time and you'll most likely need 1½ (1300B) or two hours (1500B).

❄ @ 🛜; 🚤 klorng boat to Tha Phan Fah) Located in a former school, the 42 rooms here surround an inviting garden courtyard, and are large, bright and cheery. Amenities such as a free minibar, safe and flat-screen TV are standard, and it has a quiet location away from the strip.

Sam Sen Sam Place
GUESTHOUSE $$

(Map p370; 📞0 2628 7067; www.samsensam. com; 48 Soi 3, Th Samsen; r incl breakfast 590-2500B; ❄ @ 🛜; 🚤 Tha Phra Athit (Banglamphu)) Built almost 100 years ago, this welcoming guesthouse is now a palette of pastels, with 17 rooms sharing names and colours with grapes, bananas, kiwis, peaches and strawberries, among others. The smallest rooms share bathrooms, but all have polished floorboards and teak furnishings.

Sourire
HOTEL $$

(Map p370; 📞0 2280 2180; www.sourirebangkok. com; Soi Chao Phraya Si Phiphat; r incl breakfast 1500-3500B; ❄ @ 🛜; 🚤 Tha Phan Fah) More home than hotel, the 38 rooms here exude a calming, comfortable, matronly feel. To reach the hotel, follow Soi Chao Phraya Si Phiphat to the end and knock on the tall brown wooden door on your left.

★ Arun Residence
HOTEL $$$

(Map p370; 📞0 2221 9158; www.arunresidence. com; 36-38 Soi Pratu Nokyung; r incl breakfast 4000-4200B; ste incl breakfast 5800B; ❄ @ 🛜; 🚤 Tha Tien) The six rooms here manage to feel both homey and stylish, some being tall and loftlike, while others join two rooms

---

KO KRET

Bangkok's easiest green getaway, Ko Kret is an artificial 'island', the result of a canal being dug nearly 300 years ago to shorten an oxbow bend in Mae Nam Chao Phraya. The island is one of Thailand's oldest settlements of Mon people, who were a dominant tribe of central Thailand between the 6th and 10th centuries AD. Today, Ko Kret is known for its rural atmosphere, its distinctive pottery and its busy weekend market.

To get there, take bus 166 from the Victory Monument to Pak Kret, before boarding the cross-river ferry (2B, from 5am to 9pm) from the pier at Wat Sanam Neua.

(the best is the top-floor Arun Suite, with its own balcony). There are also inviting communal areas, including a library, rooftop bar and restaurant.

Old Bangkok Inn
HOTEL $$$

(Map p370; 📞0 2629 1787; www.oldbangkokinn. com; 609 Th Phra Sumen; incl breakfast r 4000-9000B; ❄ @ 🛜; 🚤 klorng boat to Tha Phan Fah) The 10 rooms here occupy unconventional and sometimes cramped spaces, but are all done with class and style, and the enduring vibe is that of the ideal honeymoon hotel.

🛏 Chinatown & Phahurat

Bangkok's Chinatown isn't the most hospitable part of town, but for those who wish to stay off the beaten track it's an area where travellers can remain largely anonymous.

Siam Classic
GUESTHOUSE $

(Map p368; 📞0 2639 6363; 336/10 Trok Chalong Krung; r incl breakfast 500-1200B; ❄ @ 🛜; Ⓜ Hua Lamphong exit 1) This homey-feeling place is just across the street from Bangkok's main train station. Rooms are stylishly bare, while an inviting ground-floor communal area encourages meeting and chatting.

@Hua Lamphong
HOSTEL $

(Map p368; 📞0 2639 1925; www.at-hualamphong. com; 326/1 Th Phra Ram IV; dm 400-450B, r 690-950B; ❄ @ 🛜; 🚤 Tha Ratchawong, Ⓜ Hua Lamphong) Tidy hostel across the street from the train station.

★ Loy La Long
HOTEL $$

(Map p368; 📞0 2639 1390; www.loylalong.com; 1620/2 Th Songwat; incl breakfast dm 1300B, r 2100-4000B; ❄ @ 🛜; 🚤 Tha Ratchawong, Ⓜ Hua Lamphong exit 1 & taxi) The six rooms in this 100-year-old wooden house can claim heaps of personality. And united by breezy, inviting nooks and crannies and a unique location elevated over Mae Nam Chao Phraya, the whole place boasts a hidden, almost secret feel. The only downside is finding it; to get there, proceed to Th Songwat and cut directly through Wat Pathua Khongkha Rachaworawiharn to the river.

🛏 Siam Square

The centre of modern Bangkok, Siam Sq lies conveniently along both BTS lines.

Reno Hotel
HOTEL $$

(Map p378; 📞0 2215 0026; www.renohotel.co.th; 40 Soi Kasem San 1; r incl breakfast 1590-2390B; ❄ @ 🛜 📧; Ⓢ National Stadium exit 1) The rooms here are relatively large, if somewhat dark, and reflect the renovations evident in the lobby and exterior. But the cafe and pool of this Vietnam War–era vet still cling to the past.

Wendy House   HOSTEL $$
(Map p378; ☎ 0 2214 1149; www.wendyguesthouse. com; 36/2 Soi Kasem San 1; r incl breakfast 1100-1490B; ✴ @ 🛜; Ⓢ National Stadium exit 1) Basic, but exceedingly clean and relatively well-stocked (TV, fridge) rooms for this price range.

Siam@Siam   HOTEL $$$
(Map p378; ☎ 0 2217 3000; www.siamatsiam.com; 865 Th Phra Ram I; r incl breakfast 7000-11,200B; ✴ @ 🛜 ☀; Ⓢ National Stadium exit 1) A seemingly random mishmash of colours and industrial/recycled materials result in a style one could only describe as 'junkyard chic' – but in a good way, of course. The rooms, which largely continue the theme, are between the 14th and 24th floors, and offer terrific city views.

🛏 Silom

The city's financial district along Th Silom is not the most charming area of town, but it is conveniently located for nightspots and the BTS and MRT.

Smile Society   HOTEL $$
(Map p380; ☎ 08 1343 1754, 08 1442 5800; www. smilesocietyhostel.com; 30/3-4 Soi 6, Th Silom; dm incl breakfast 420B, r incl breakfast 900-1880B; ✴ @ 🛜; Ⓜ Si Lom exit 2, Ⓢ Sala Daeng exit 1) Part boutique hotel, part hostel, this four-storey shophouse combines small but comfortable and well-equipped rooms and dorms with spotless shared bathrooms. A central location and helpful, English-speaking staff are other perks.

Glow Trinity Silom   HOTEL $$
(Map p380; ☎ 0 2231 5050; www.zinchospital ity.com/glowbyzinc/silom; 150 Soi Phiphat 2; r incl breakfast 1900-2600B, ste incl breakfast 3600B; ✴ @ 🛜 ☀; Ⓢ Chong Nonsi exit 2) Sophisticated-feeling hotel at a midrange price, with modern, tech-equipped rooms and great service.

★ Siam Heritage   HOTEL $$$
(Map p380; ☎ 0 2353 6101; www.thesiamheritage. com; 115/1 Th Surawong; incl breakfast r 2900B, ste 4000-9300B; ✴ @ 🛜 ☀; Ⓜ Si Lom exit 2, Ⓢ Sala Daeng exit 1) The 73 rooms here are decked out in silk and dark woods with genuinely thoughtful design touches, not to mention

considerate amenities. There's an inviting rooftop garden/pool/spa, which, like the rest of the hotel, is looked after by a team of charming and professional staff.

★ Metropolitan by COMO   HOTEL $$$
(Map p368; ☎ 0 2625 3333; www.comohotels.com/ metropolitanbangkok; 27 Th Sathon Tai (South); r incl breakfast, 9220-11,220B, ste incl breakfast 12,200-78,720B; ✴ @ 🛜 ☀; Ⓜ Lumphini exit 2) The exterior of Bangkok's former YMCA has changed relatively little, but a peek inside reveals one of the city's sleekest, sexiest hotels. A recent renovation has all 171 rooms looking better than ever in striking tones of black, white and yellow.

🛏 Sukhumvit

This seemingly endless urban thoroughfare is Bangkok's unofficial International Zone and also boasts much of the city's accommodation, ranging from the odd backpacker hostel to sex tourist hovels and five-star luxury.

NORTHERN THAILAND BANGKOK

BATHROOMLESS IN BANGKOK

If you don't require your own en suite bathroom, Bangkok has heaps of options, ranging from high-tech dorm beds in a brand-new hostel to private bedrooms in an antique wooden house. Some of our picks:

Lub*d (Map p378; ☎ 0 2634 7999; siamsquare.lubd.com; Th Phra Ram I; dm 750B, r 1800-2400B; ✳ @ ☎; Ⓢ National Stadium exit 1) The title is a play on the Thai làp dee, meaning 'sleep well', but the fun atmosphere here might make you want to stay up all night. There's an inviting communal area stocked with games and a bar, and thoughtful facilities ranging from washing machines to a theatre room. If this one's full, there's another branch just off Th Silom (Map p380; ☎ 0 2634 7999; silom.lubd.com; 4 Th Decho; dm 550-650B, r 1400-1800B; ✳ @ ☎; Ⓢ Chong Nonsi exit 2).

NapPark Hostel (Map p370; ☎ 0 2282 2324; www.nappark.com; 5 Th Tani; dm 570-750B; ✳ @ ☎; ⓦ Tha Phra Athit (Banglamphu)) This well-run hostel features dorm rooms of various sizes, all of which boast podlike beds outfitted with power points, mini-TV, reading lamp and wi-fi.

Khaosan Baan Thai (Map p368; ☎ 0 2628 5559; www.khaosanbaanthai.com; 11/1 Soi 3, Th Samsen; r incl breakfast 390-730B; ✳ @ ☎; ⓦ Tha Phra Athit (Banglamphu)) This tiny wooden house holds 10 rooms decked out in cheery pastels and hand-painted bunny pictures.

Silom Art Hostel (Map p380; ☎ 0 2635 8070; www.silomarthostel.com; 198/19-22 Soi 14, Th Silom; dm 400-550B, r 1200-1500B; ✳ @ ☎; Ⓢ Chong Nonsi exit 3) Quirky, artsy, bright and fun, Silom Art Hostel combines recycled materials, bizarre furnishings and colourful kitsch to arrive at a hostel that's quite unlike anywhere else in town.

Saphaipae (Map p368; ☎ 0 2238 2322; www.saphaipae.com; 35 Th Surasak; dm 400-550B, r 1800-2500B; ✳ @ ☎; Ⓢ Surasak exit 1) The bright colours, chunky furnishings and bold murals in the lobby of this new hostel give it the vibe of a day-care centre for travellers – a feel that continues through to the playful communal areas and rooms.

Suneta Hostel Khaosan (Map p370; ☎ 0 2629 0150; www.sunetahostel.com; 209-211 Th Kraisi; dm incl breakfast 440-590B, r incl breakfast 900-1090B; ✳ @ ☎; ⓦ Tha Phra Athit (Banglamphu)) This young hostel is getting rave reviews for its retro-themed design, comfy dorms and friendly service.

S1 Hostel (Map p368; ☎ 0 2679 7777; www.facebook.com/S1hostelBangkok; 35/1-4 Soi Ngam Duphli; dm 330-380B, r 700-1300B; ✳ @ ☎; Ⓜ Lumphini exit 1) A huge new hostel with dorm beds and private rooms decked out in a simple yet attractive primary colour scheme.

Suk 11   HOTEL $

(Map p382; ☎ 0 2253 5927; www.suk11.com; 1/33 Soi 11, Th Sukhumvit; r incl breakfast 500-1600B; ✳ @ ☎; Ⓢ Nana exit 3) Extremely well run and equally popular, this rambling building is an oasis of wood and greenery in the urban jungle that is Th Sukhumvit. The cheaper rooms have shared bathrooms, and although they've somehow managed to stuff nearly 100 rooms in there, you'll still need to book at least two weeks ahead.

Napa Place   HOTEL $$

(Map p382; ☎ 0 2661 5525; www.napaplace. com; 11/3 Soi Napha Sap 2; r incl breakfast 2200-2400B, ste incl breakfast 3400-4100B; ✳ @ ☎; Ⓢ Thong Lo exit 2) The 12 expansive rooms here have been decorated with dark woods from the family's former business and light brown cloths from the hands of Thai weavers. The cosy communal areas couldn't be much different from the suburban living room you grew up in.

Sacha's Hotel Uno   HOTEL $$

(Map p382; ☎ 0 2651 2180; www.sachas.hotel-uno. com; 28/19 Soi 19, Th Sukhumvit; r incl breakfast 1800-2300B; ✳ @ ☎; Ⓜ Sukhumvit exit 1, Ⓢ Asok exit 1) Soi 19 and around are home to a handful of good-value hotels that barely edge into the midrange category, including Uno. Surprisingly sophisticated for this price range, the 56 rooms here are comfortable and equally well equipped for work or play.

Baan Sukhumvit   HOTEL $$

(Map p382; ☎ 0 2258 5630; www.baansukhumvit. com; 392/38-39 Soi 20, Th Sukhumvit; r incl breakfast 1440-1540B; ✳ @ ☎; Ⓜ Sukhumvit exit 1,

S Asok exit 1) This small hotel exudes an appropriately cosy feel. Rooms lack bells and whistles, but are subtly attractive; the more expensive include a bit more space, a bathtub and a safe.

★ **AriyasomVilla** HOTEL $$$

(Map p378; ☑ 0 2254 8880; www.ariyasom.com; 65 Soi 1, Th Sukhumvit; r incl breakfast 5353-11,682B; ✳@🛜☲; S Phloen Chit exit 3) If you can score a reservation, you'll be privy to one of the 24 spacious rooms here, meticulously outfitted with thoughtful Thai design touches and classy antique furniture. There's a spa and an inviting tropical pool; breakfast is vegetarian and is served in the original villa's stunning, glass-encased dining room.

Seven HOTEL $$$

(Map p382; ☑0 2662 0951; www.sleepatseven. com; 3/15 Soi 31, Th Sukhumvit; r incl breakfast 4708-7062B; ✳🛜; S Phrom Phong exit 5) This tiny hotel somehow manages to be chic and homey, stylish and comfortable, Thai and international all at the same time. Each of the five rooms is decked out in a different colour that corresponds to Thai astrology, and thoughtful amenities and friendly service abound.

S31 HOTEL $$$

(Map p382; ☑0 2260 1111; www.s31hotel.com; 545 Soi 31, Th Sukhumvit; r incl breakfast 4000B; ste incl breakfast 7000-60,000B; ✳🛜☲; S Phrom Phong exit 5) The bold patterns and graphics of its interior and exterior make the S31 a fun, young-feeling choice. Thoughtful touches like kitchenettes with large fridge, superhuge beds and free courses (cooking, Thai boxing and yoga) prove that the style also has substance.

✕ Eating

No matter where you go in Bangkok, food is always there. There is so much variety just on the street that you can go days without stepping inside a restaurant. When the need comes for a restaurant, Bangkok's best are the decorless family shops. All the great international cuisines, from French to Japanese, are available too.

✕ Ko Ratanakosin, Banglamphu & Thonburi

The old areas of town near the river are full of simple Thai eats and, because of the traveller presence on and around Th Khao San, Western and vegetarian food as well.

★ **Likhit Kai Yang** NORTHEASTERN THAI $

(Map p370; off Th Ratchadamnoen Nok; mains 30-150B; ☺10am-10pm; 🚤klorng boat to Tha Phan Fah) Located just behind Ratchadamoen Stadium (avoid the rather grotty branch directly next door to the stadium), this decades-old restaurant is where locals come for a quick northeastern Thai-style meal before a Thai boxing match.

★ **Krua Apsorn** THAI $$

(Map p370; www.kruaapsorn.com; Th Din So; mains 65-350B; ☺10.30am-8pm Mon-Sat; 🚤klorng boat to Tha Phan Fah) This homey dining room is a favourite of members of the Thai royal family and, back in 2006, was recognised as Bangkok's Best Restaurant by the *Bangkok Post*. Must-eat dishes include mussels fried with fresh herbs, the decadent crab fried in yellow chilli oil and the *tortilla Española*–like crab omelette.

Shoshana ISRAELI $$

(Map p370; 88 Th Chakraphong; mains 70-240B; ☺10am-midnight; ☑; 🚤Tha Phra Athit (Banglamphu)) Although prices have gone up slightly since it opened back in 1982, Shoshana still puts together a cheap and tasty Israeli meal. Feel safe ordering anything deep-fried – they do an excellent job of it – and don't miss the deliciously garlicky eggplant dip.

> **DON'T MISS**
>
> ## PÀT TAI
>
> Brace yourself, but you should be aware that the fried noodles sold from carts along Th Khao San have nothing to do with the dish known as *pàt tai*. Luckily, less than a five-minute túk-túk (pronounced *dúk dúk;* motorised transport) ride away lies **Thip Samai** (Map p370; 313 Th Mahachai; mains 25-120B; ☺5.30pm-1.30am; 🚤klorng boat to Tha Phan Fah), home to the most legendary *pàt tai* in Bangkok. As elsewhere, a dish here takes the form of thin rice noodles stir-fried with dried and/or fresh shrimp, bean sprouts, tofu, egg and seasonings. For something different, there's Thip Samai's delicate eggwrapped version, or the *pàt tai* fried with *man gûng* (decadent shrimp fat).
>
> Other destinations for *pàt tai* include a vendor at the Soi 38 Night Market (p380), a stall at MBK Food Island (p379) and streetside stalls in Chinatown.

Siam Square

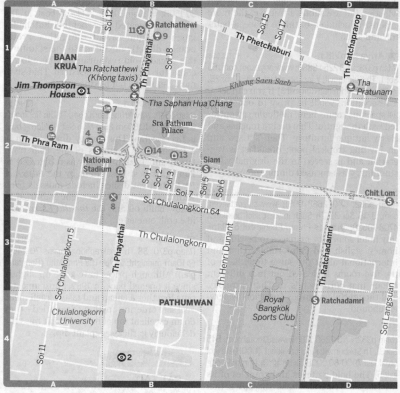

★ **Jay Fai** THAI $$$
(Map p370; 327 Th Mahachai; mains from 400B;
☺3pm-2am Tue-Sun; ⚑klorng boat to Tha Phan
Fah) You wouldn't think so by looking at
her bare-bones dining room, but Jay Fai is
known for serving Bangkok's most expen-
sive *pàt kêe mow* (drunkard's noodles –
wide rice noodles fried with seafood and
Thai herbs). Jay Fai is located in a virtually
unmarked shophouse on Th Mahachai.

✕ Chinatown & Phahurat

When you mention Chinatown, Bangkokians
begin dreaming of noodles, usually prepared
by street vendors lining Th Yaowarat, near
Trok Itsaranuphap (Soi 16, Th Yaowarat), af-
ter dark. Of course, the dining is good in the
Indian district of Phahurat too.

Samsara JAPANESE, THAI $$
(Map p368; 1612 Th Songwat; mains 110-320B;
☺4pm-midnight Tue-Thu, to 1am Fri-Sun; ⓰; ⚑Tha
Ratchawong, Ⓜ Hua Lamphong exit 1 & taxi) Com-
bining Japanese-Thai dishes, Belgian beers
and a retro/artsy atmosphere, Samsara is
easily Chinatown's most eclectic place to
eat. The restaurant is at the end of tiny Soi
Khang Wat Pathum Khongkha, just west of
the temple of the same name.

Thanon Phadungdao
Seafood Stalls THAI $$
(Map p368; cnr Th Phadungdao & Th Yaowarat;
mains 100-600B; ☺4pm-midnight Tue-Sun; ⚑Tha
Ratchawong, Ⓜ Hua Lamphong exit 1 & taxi) After
sunset, these two opposing open-air res-
taurants – each of which claims to be the
original – become a culinary train wreck of
outdoor barbecues, screaming staff, iced sea-
food trays and messy sidewalk seating.

Royal India INDIAN $$
(Map p368; 392/1 Th Chakraphet; mains 70-195B;
☺10am-10pm; ⓰; ⚑Tha Saphan Phut (Memorial
Bridge)) A windowless dining room of 10 ta-

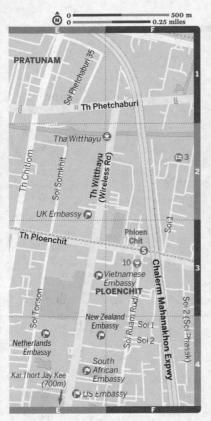

Siam Square

◎ Top Sights
1 Jim Thompson House A1

◎ Sights
2 Chulalongkorn University B4

⬤ Sleeping
3 AriyasomVilla F2
4 Lub*d A2
5 Reno Hotel A2
6 Siam@Siam A2
7 Wendy House B2

✕ Eating
8 MBK Food Island B3

⬤ Drinking & Nightlife
9 Co-Co Walk B1
10 Hyde & Seek F3

⬤ Entertainment
11 Playhouse Theater Cabaret B1

⬤ Shopping
12 MBK Center B2
13 Siam Center B2
14 Siam Discovery Center B2

bles in a dark alley may not be everybody's ideal lunch destination, but this legendary north Indian place continues to draw foodies despite the lack of aesthetics.

✕ Siam Square

If you find yourself hungry in this part of central Bangkok, you're largely at the mercy of shopping-mall food courts and chain restaurants.

★ MBK Food Island   THAI $
(Map p378; 6th fl, MBK Center, cnr Th Phra Ram I & Th Phayathai; mains 35-150B; ⊙10am-10pm; 🖉; ⑤ National Stadium exit 4) The granddaddy of the genre, MBK's expansive food court offers vendors selling dishes from virtually every corner of Thailand and beyond. Exchange cash for a card and head for the tasty vegetarian food stall (stall C8) or the decent northeastern Thai food vendor (C22).

Kai Thort Jay Kee   THAI $$
(Soi Polo Fried Chicken; Map p368; 137/1-3 Soi Sanam Khlii (Soi Polo); mains 40-280B; ⊙11am-9pm; Ⓜ Lumphini exit 3) Although the *sôm đam* (papaya salad), sticky rice and *lâhp* (spicy 'salad' of minced meat) give the impression of a northeastern Thai-style eatery, the restaurant's namesake deep-fried bird is more southern in origin. Regardless, smothered in a thick layer of crispy deep-fried garlic, it is none other than a truly Bangkok experience.

✕ Silom

Office workers swarm the shanty villages of street vendors for lunch, and simple Indian restaurants proliferate towards the western end of Th Silom and Th Surawong.

Chennai Kitchen   INDIAN $
(Map p380; 10 Th Pan; mains 70-150B; ⊙10am-3pm & 6-9pm; 🖉; ⑤ Surasak exit 3) This thimble-sized family-run restaurant near the Hindu temple puts out some of the most solid southern Indian vegetarian food around.

★ nahm   THAI $$$
(Map p368; 🕿 0 2625 3388; www.comohotels.com/metropolitanbangkok/dining/nahm; ground fl, Metropolitan Hotel, 27 Th Sathon Tai (South); set lunch 1100B, set dinner 2000B, mains 180-700B;

Silom

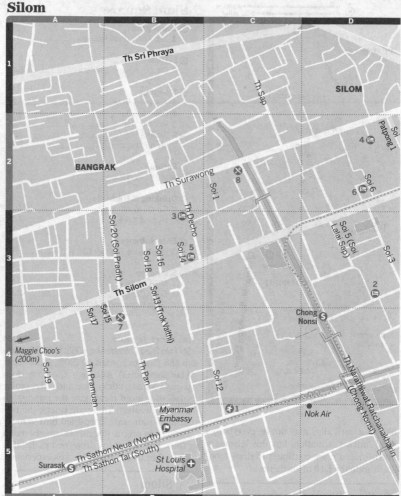

◷ noon-2pm Mon-Fri, 7-10.30pm daily; Ⓜ Lumphini exit 2) Australian chef-author David Thompson is behind what is quite possibly the best Thai restaurant in Bangkok. Using ancient cookbooks as his inspiration, Thompson has given new life to previously extinct dishes. Reservations recommended.

Somboon Seafood　　　　　　　THAI $$$
(Map p380; ☑ 0 2233 3104; www.somboonseafood. com; cnr Th Surawong & Th Narathiwat Ratchanakharin (Chong Nonsi); mains 120-900B; ◷ 4-11.30pm; Ⓢ Chong Nonsi exit 3) Somboon, a busy seafood hall with a reputation far and wide,

is known for doing the best curry-powder crab in town.

✕ Sukhumvit

This avenue is the communal dining room of Bangkok's expat communities.

Soi 38 Night Market　　　　　　THAI $
(Map p382; cnr Soi 38 & Th Sukhumvit; mains 30-60B; ◷ 8pm-3am; Ⓢ Thong Lo exit 4) After a hard night of clubbing on Sukhumvit, this open-air hawker convocation will seem like a shining oasis.

full-flavoured Thai dishes are the results of this tuition. Reservations recommended.

Myeong Ga   KOREAN $$$
(Map p382; ground fl, Sukhumvit Plaza, cnr Soi 12 & Th Sukhumvit; mains 200-950B; ⊙11am-10pm Tue-Sun, 4-10pm Mon; M Sukhumvit exit 3, S Asok exit 2) Located on the ground floor of Sukhumvit Plaza (the multistorey complex also known as Korean Town), this restaurant is the city's best destination for authentic Seoul food. Go for the tasty prepared dishes or, if you've got a bit more time, the excellent, DIY Korean-style barbecue.

Soul Food Mahanakorn   THAI $$$
(Map p382; ☑0 2714 7708; www.soulfoodmaha nakorn.com; 56/10 Soi 55 (Thong Lor), Th Su-khumvit; mains 220-300B; ⊙5.30pm-midnight; ☑; S Thong Lo exit 3) Soul Food gets its buzz from its dual nature as an inviting restaurant – the menu spans tasty interpretations of rustic Thai dishes – and a bar serving deliciously boozy, Thai-influenced cocktails. Reservations are recommended.

🍸 Drinking & Nightlife

Once infamous as an anything-goes nightlife destination, in recent years Bangkok has been edging towards teetotalism with strict regulations limiting the sale of alcohol and increasingly conservative closing times, with most bars closing around

Nasir Al-Masri   MIDDLE EASTERN $$$
(Map p382; 4/6 Soi 3/1, Th Sukhumvit; mains 160-370B; ⊙24hr; ☑; S Nana exit 1) This is Muslim food, with the emphasis on meat, meat and more meat, but the kitchen also pulls off some brilliant vegie *meze* as well.

Bo.lan   THAI $$$
(Map p382; ☑0 2260 2962; www.bolan.co.th; 42 Soi Rongnarong Phichai Songkhram, Soi 26, Th Sukhumvit; set dinner 1980B; ⊙6pm-midnight Tue-Sun; S Phrom Phong exit 4) Bo and Dylan (Bo.lan, a play on words that also means 'ancient') take a scholarly approach to Thai cuisine, and generous set meals featuring

Sukhumvit

NORTHERN THAILAND BANGKOK

SUKHUMVIT

KHLONG TAN

TOBACCO MONOPOLY

Bumrungrad International Hospital

Israeli Embassy

Benjakiti Park

Benjasiri Park

Lake Ratchada

Th Phetchaburi

Kamphaeng Phet 7

Khlong Saen Saab

Th Sukhumvit

Th Ratchadaphisek

Port-Din-Daeng Expwy

Soi 21 (Asoke)

Soi 31 (Sawatdi)

Soi 29 (Lak Khet)

Soi 55 (Thong Lor)

Soi Ekamai

Soi Ekamai 21

Soi Thong Lor 16

Soi Thong Lor 17

Soi Thong Lor 13

Soi Thong Lor 10

Soi Thong Lor 5

Nana (Nana Neua)

Soi Phrom Si 2

Soi Prom Si 1

Soi Prommit

Soi 49

Soi 53

Soi 51

Soi 49

Soi 45

Soi 43

Soi 41

Soi 39

Soi 9

Soi 33

Soi 31

Soi 27

Soi 23

Soi 22

Soi 20

Soi 18

Soi 16

Soi 15

Soi 13

Soi 11

Soi 11/1

Soi 12

Soi 10

Soi 10

Soi 8

Soi 5

Soi 4 (Nana Tai)

Soi 3

Soi 2

Soi 1

Soi 9

Phrom Phong

Asok

Sukhumvit

Nana

Sukhumvit

NORTHERN THAILAND BANGKOK

1am. Likewise, keep in mind that smoking has been outlawed at all indoor (and some quasi-outdoor) entertainment places since 2008.

The trick with nightclubs in Bangkok is to catch the right club on the right night. To find out what is going on, check in with **Dude Sweet** (www.dudesweet.org), organisers of hugely popular monthly parties, or the listings mag **BK** (www.bk.asia-city.com). Cover charges for clubs and discos range from 100B to 600B and usually include a drink. Don't even think about showing up before 11pm, and always bring ID. Most nightclubs close at 2am.

Ko Ratanakosin & Banglamphu

The area around Th Khao San is one of the city's best destinations for a fun night out.

Hippie de Bar   BAR
(Map p370; www.facebook.com/hippie.debar; 46 Th Khao San; ⊙3pm-2am; ⊠Tha Phra Athit (Banglamphu)) Our vote for Banglamphu's best bar, Hippie boasts a funky retro vibe, indoor and outdoor seating, and a soundtrack you're unlikely to hear elsewhere in Top 40–obsessed Bangkok.

Madame Musur   BAR
(Map p370; 41 Soi Ram Buttri; ⊙8am-1am; ⊠Tha Phra Athit (Banglamphu)) Saving you the trip north to Pai, Madame Musur pulls off that elusive combination of northern Thailand-meets-*The Beach*-meets-Th Khao San.

The Club   NIGHTCLUB
(Map p370; www.theclubkhaosan.com; 123 Th Khao San; ⊙10pm-3am; ⊠Tha Phra Athit (Banglamphu)) Located smack dab in the middle of Th Khao San, this cavernlike dance hall hosts a fun mix of locals and backpackers.

Pranakorn Bar   BAR
(Map p370; 58/2 Soi Damnoen Klang Tai; ⊙6pm-midnight; ⊠klorng taxi to Tha Phan Fah) In addition to charming views of old Bangkok, the breezy rooftop of this artsy bar also offers cheap and tasty Thai food.

Siam Square

Co-Co Walk   BAR
(Map p378; 87/70 Th Phayathai; ⊙5pm-midnight; ⑤Ratchathewi exit 2) This covered compound is a smorgasbord of pubs, bars and live music popular with Thai university students.

Hyde & Seek   BAR
(Map p378; www.hydeandseek.com; ground fl, Athenee Residence, 65/1 Soi Ruam Rudi; ⊙11am-1am; ⑤Phloen Chit exit 4) The tasty and comforting English-inspired bar snacks and meals have earned Hyde & Seek the right to call itself a 'gastro bar', but we reckon the real reasons to come are arguably Bangkok's most well-stocked bar and some of the city's tastiest and most sophisticated cocktails.

Silom

★**Moon Bar**   BAR
(Map p368; www.banyantree.com; 61st fl, Banyan Tree Hotel, 21/100 Th Sathon (South) Tai; ⊙5pm-1am; ⓜLumphini exit 2) The Banyan Tree Hotel's Moon Bar kick-started the rooftop trend and, as Bangkok continues to grow at a mad pace, the view from 61 floors up only gets better. Save your shorts and sandals for another locale.

Tapas Room   NIGHTCLUB
(Map p380; 114/17-18 Soi 4, Th Silom; admission 100B; ⊙9pm-2am; ⓜSi Lom exit 2, ⑤Sala Daeng exit 1) Although it sits staunchly at the top of Bangkok's pinkest street, this long-standing two-level disco manages to bring in just about everybody.

Maggie Choo's   BAR
(Map p368; www.facebook.com/maggiechoos; basement, Novotel Bangkok Fenix Silom, 320 Th Silom; ⊙6.30pm-1.30am; ⑤Surasak exit 1) A former bank vault with a Chinatown opium den vibe. Secret passageways. Lounging women in silk dresses. With all this going on, it's easy to forget that the new Maggie Choo's is actually a bar.

Sukhumvit

★**WTF**   BAR
(Map p382; www.wtfbangkok.com; 7 Soi 51, Th Sukhumvit; ⊙6pm-1am Tue-Sun; ⑤Thong Lo exit 3) No, not that WTF – Wonderful Thai Friendship is a funky and friendly neighbourhood bar that, in addition to great drinks and bar snacks, also packs in two floors of gallery space.

Badmotel   BAR
(Map p382; www.facebook.com/badmotel; Soi 55 (Thong Lor), Th Sukhumvit; ⊙5pm-1.30am; ⑤Thong Lo exit 3 & taxi) The new Badmotel combines the modern and the cosmopolitan, and the kitschy and the Thai, in a way that has cultivated a devout Bangkok hipster following.

Tuba   BAR
(Map p382; 34 Room 11-12 A, Soi Ekamai 21, Soi 63 (Ekamai), Th Sukhumvit; ⊙11am-2am; ⑤Ekkamai exit 1 & taxi) Part showroom for over-the-top vintage furniture, part restaurant, part friendly local boozer, this bar certainly doesn't lack in quirk, nor fun.

Grease   NIGHTCLUB
(Map p382; www.greasebangkok.com; 46/12 Soi 49, Th Sukhumvit; ⊙6pm-4am Mon-Sat; ⑤Phrom Phong exit 3 & taxi) Bangkok's newest, hottest club is also one of its biggest – you could get lost in the four floors of dining venues, lounges and dance floors here.

Cheap Charlie's   BAR
(Map p382; Soi 11, Th Sukhumvit; ⊙ 4.30-11.45pm Mon-Sat; Ⓢ Nana exit 3) You're bound to have a mighty difficult time convincing your Thai friends to go to Th Sukhumvit only to sit at this outdoor wooden shack decorated with buffalo skulls and wagon wheels.

Arena 10   NIGHTCLUB
(Map p382; cnr Soi Ekamai 5 & Soi 63 (Ekamai), Th Sukhumvit; Ⓢ Ekkamai exit 2 & taxi) This open-air entertainment zone is the destination of choice for Bangkok's young and beautiful – for the moment at least. Fridays and Saturdays see a 400B entrance fee for foreigners.

🍸 Other Areas

RCA   NIGHTCLUB
(Royal City Avenue; Map p368; Royal City Ave, off Th Phra Ram IX; Ⓜ Phra Ram 9 exit 3 & taxi) Formerly a bastion of the teen scene, this Vegas-like strip has finally graduated from high school and today hosts partiers of every age. Worthwhile destinations include **808 Club** (Map p368; www.808bangkok.com; admission from 300B), **Slim/Flix** (Map p368; www.facebook.com/slimbkk; Royal City Ave, off Th Phra Ram IX; ⊙ 8pm 2am; Ⓜ Phra Ram 9 exit 3 & taxi) and Cosmic Café (p386), and foreigners must pay a 300B entry fee on Fridays and Saturdays.

☆ Entertainment

Shame on you if you find yourself bored in Bangkok. And even more shame if you think the only entertainment options involve the word 'go-go'. Bangkok's nightlife is as diverse as that of virtually any modern city.

Gà·teu·i Cabaret

Over the last few years, *gà·teu·i* (transgender; also spelt *kathoey*) cabaret has emerged to become a staple of the Bangkok tourist

circuit. **Calypso Bangkok** (Map p368; ☑0 2688 1415; www.calypsocabaret.com; Asiatique, Soi 72-76, Th Charoen Krung; admission 1200B; ⊙ show times 8.15pm & 9.45pm; ⛴ shuttle ferry from Tha Sathon (Central Pier)), **Mambo Cabaret** (☑0 2294 7381; www.mambocabaret.com; 59/28 Yannawa Tat Mai; tickets 800-1000B; ⊙ show times 7.15pm & 8.30pm; Ⓢ Chong Nonsi exit 2 taxi) and **Playhouse Theater Cabaret** (Map p378; ☑0 2215 0571; www.playhousethailand.com; basement, Asia Hotel, 296 Th Phayathai; admission 1200B; ⊙ show times 8.15pm & 9.45pm; Ⓢ Ratchathewi exit 1) all host choreographed stage shows featuring Broadway high kicks and lip-synched pop tunes by the most well-endowed dudes you'll find anywhere.

Go-Go Bars

Although technically illegal, prostitution is fully 'out' in Bangkok, and the influence of organised crime and healthy kickbacks means that it will be a long while before the existing laws are ever enforced. Yet, despite the image presented by much of the Western media, the underlying atmosphere of Bangkok's red-light districts is not necessarily one of illicitness and exploitation (although these do inevitably exist), but rather tackiness and boredom.

Patpong (Map p380; Soi Patpong 1 & 2, Th Silom; ⊙ 4pm-2am; Ⓜ Si Lom exit 2, Ⓢ Sala Daeng exit 1), arguably one of the world's most famous red-light districts, earned its notoriety during the 1980s for its wild sex shows involving everything from ping-pong balls to razors to midgets on motorbikes. Today it is more of a circus for curious spectators than sexual deviants. These days, **Soi Cowboy** (Map p382; btwn Soi 21 (Asoke) & Soi 23, Th Sukhumvit; ⊙ 4pm-2am; Ⓜ Sukhumvit exit 2, Ⓢ Asok exit 3) and **Nana Entertainment**

NORTHERN THAILAND BANGKOK

Plaza (Map p382; Soi 4 (Nana Tai), Th Sukhumvit; ☺4pm-2am; ⓢNana exit 2) are the real scenes of sex for hire.

Live Music

★ Brick Bar
LIVE MUSIC
(Map p370; www.brickbarkhaosan.com; basement, Buddy Lodge, 265 Th Khao San; ☺8pm-2am; ⓢTha Phra Athit (Banglamphu)) This basement pub, one of our fave destinations in Bangkok for live music, hosts a nightly revolving cast of bands for an almost exclusively Thai crowd – most of whom will end up dancing on the tables.

Cosmic Café
LIVE MUSIC
(Map p368; www.facebook.com/cosmiccafe.bkk; Block C, Royal City Ave (RCA), off Th Phra Ram IX; ☺8pm-2am Mon-Sat; ⓂPhra Ram 9 exit 3 & taxi) Blessedly more low-key than most places on RCA, Cosmic calls itself a cafe but looks like a bar, and in recent years has become one of Bangkok's better live-music clubs.

Titanium
LIVE MUSIC
(Map p382; www.titaniumbangkok.com; 2/30 Soi 22, Th Sukhumvit; ☺8pm-1am; ⓢPhrom Phong exit 6) Most come to this cheesy 'ice bar' for the chill, the skimpily dressed working girls and the flavoured vodka, but we come for Unicorn, an all-female house band.

Sonic
LIVE MUSIC
(Map p382; www.facebook.com/SonicBangkok; 90 Soi 63 (Ekamai), Th Sukhumvit; ☺6pm-2am; ⓢEkkamai exit 4 & taxi) Drawing a mixture of Thai bands, indie acts, big-name DJs and a painfully hip crowd, Sonic has emerged as Bangkok's hottest venue for live music.

Tawandang German Brewery
LIVE MUSIC
(Map p368; www.tawandang.co.th; cnr Th Phra Ram III & Th Narathiwat Ratchanakharin (Th Chong Nonsi); ☺5pm-1am; ⓢChong Nonsi exit 2 & taxi) It's Oktoberfest all year round at this hangar-sized music hall. The Thai-German food is tasty, the house-made brews are more than potable, and the nightly stage shows make singing along a necessity.

Raintree
LIVE MUSIC
(Map p368; 116/63-64 Th Rang Nam; ☺8pm-2am; ⓢVictory Monument exit 2) This rustic pub is one of the few remaining places in town to hear 'songs for life', Thai folk music with roots in the communist insurgency of the 1960s and '70s.

Thai Boxing

Lumpinee Boxing Stadium (www.muaythailumpinee.net/en/index.php; Th Ram-intra; tickets 3rd class/2nd class/ringside 1000/2000/3000B; ⓂChatuchak Park exit 2 & taxi, ⓢMo Chit exit 3 & taxi) and **Ratchadamnoen Stadium** (Map p370; off Th Ratchadamnoen Nok; tickets 3rd class/2nd class/ringside 1000/1500/2000B; ⊠klorng boat to Tha Phan Fah, ⓢPhaya Thai exit 3 & taxi) host Thailand's biggest *moo·ay tai* matches. Ratchadamnoen hosts the matches on Monday, Wednesday, Thursday and Sunday at 6pm, while Lumpinee hosts matches on Tuesday and Friday at 6.30pm and Saturday at 4pm and 8.30pm.

Traditional Arts Performances

Sala Chalermkrung
THEATRE
(Map p370; ☏0 2222 0434; www.salachalermkrung.com; 66 Th Charoen Krung; tickets 800-1200B; ☺shows 7.30pm Thu & Fri; ⊠Tha Saphan Phut (Memorial Bridge), ⓂHua Lamphong exit 1 & taxi) This art deco Bangkok landmark, a former cinema dating to 1933, is one of the few remaining places where *kŏhn*, masked dance-drama often depicting scenes from the *Ramayana* (the Thai version of India's *Ramayana*), can be witnessed.

National Theatre
THEATRE
(Map p370; ☏0 2224 1342; 2 Th Ratchini; tickets 60-100B; ⊠Tha Chang) Performances of *kŏhn* are held here at 2pm on the first and second Sundays of the month from January to March and July to September, and *lá·kon*, Thai dance-dramas, are held at 2pm on the first and second Sundays of the month from April to June and October to December.

🛍 Shopping

Bangkok is not the place for recovering shopaholics because the temptation to stray from the path is overwhelming. The best of Bangkok's shopping centres line the BTS around Siam Sq. Among your choices are the adjacent **Siam Center** (Map p378; Th Phra Ram I; ☺10am-9pm; ⓢSiam exit 1) and **Siam Discovery Center** (Map p378; cnr Th Phra Ram I & Th Phayathai; ☺10am-9pm; ⓢSiam exit 1), both good places to pick up local clothing labels, and everyman's **MBK Center** (Map p378; www.mbk-center.com; cnr Th Phra Ram I & Th Phayathai; ☺10am-10pm; ⓢNational Stadium exit 4), which is just a few air-conditioners and escalators fancier than a street market.

Chatuchak Weekend Market
MARKET
(Talat Jatujak; Map p368; ☺9am-6pm Sat & Sun; BTS Mo Chit, ⓂChatuchak Park & Kamphaeng Phet) The mother of all markets sprawls over a huge area with 15,000 stalls and an estimated 200,000 visitors a day. Everything

is sold here, from snakes to handicrafts to aisles and aisles of clothes.

Asiatique
MARKET

(Map p368; www.thaiasiatique.com; Soi 72-76, Th Charoen Krung; ⊙4-11pm; ☑shuttle boat from Tha Sathon (Central Pier)) At press time Bangkok's buzziest market, Asiatique takes the form of vast warehouses of commerce next to Mae Nam Chao Phraya. To get here, take one of the frequent shuttle boats from Tha Sathon (Central Pier).

Pak Khlong Market
MARKET

(Flower Market; Th Chakkaphet & Th Atsadang; ⊙24hr; ☑Tha Saphan Phut (Memorial Bridge)) Every night this market near Mae Nam Chao Phraya becomes the city's largest depot for wholesale flowers.

ⓘ Information

ATMs, banks and currency-exchange kiosks are widespread.

DANGERS & ANNOYANCES

Commit these classic rip-offs to memory and join us in our ongoing crusade to outsmart Bangkok's crafty scam artists.

Gem scam If anyone offers you unsolicited advice about a gem sale, you can be sure that there is a scam involved.

Closed today Ignore any 'friendly' local who tells you that an attraction is closed for a Buddhist holiday or for cleaning. These are set-ups for trips to a bogus gem sale.

Túk-túk rides for 10B Say goodbye to your day's itinerary if you climb aboard this ubiquitous scam. These alleged 'tours' bypass all the sights and instead cruise to all the fly-by-night gem and tailor shops that pay commissions.

Flat-fare taxi ride Flatly refuse any driver who quotes a flat fare.

Tourist buses On long-distance vans originating on Th Khao San, well-organised and connected thieves have hours to comb through your bags. This scam has been running for years but is easy to avoid simply by carrying valuables with you on the bus.

Friendly strangers Be wary of smartly dressed men who approach you asking where you're from and where you're going. As the tourist authorities here pointed out, this sort of behaviour is out of character for Thais and should be treated with suspicion.

EMERGENCY

Tourist Police (☑24hr hotline 1155) English-speaking officers.

INTERNET ACCESS

Internet cafes charge 15B to 50B per hour. Wi-fi, mostly free of charge, is becoming more and more ubiquitous around Bangkok. For relatively authoritative lists of wi-fi hotspots in Bangkok, go to www.bkkpages.com or www.stickmanweekly.com/WiFi/BangkokFreeWirelessInternetWiFi.htm.

MEDIA

Bangkok 101 (www.bangkok101.com) A tourist-friendly listings magazine.

Bangkok Post (www.bangkokpost.com) The leading English-language daily with Friday and weekend supplements covering city events.

BK (www.bk.asia-city.com) Online version of Bangkok's best listings magazine.

MEDICAL SERVICES

The following offer 24-hour emergency service, ambulance and English-speaking staff. Prices are high, but so is the quality.

BNH (Map p380; ☑0 2686 2700; www.bnhhospital.com; 9 Th Convent; Ⓜ Si Lom exit 2, ⑤ Sala Daeng exit 2)

Bumrungrad International Hospital (Map p382; ☑0 2667 1000; www.bumrungrad.com; 33 Soi 3, Th Sukhumvit; ⑤Phloen Chit exit 3)

TOURIST INFORMATION

Bangkok Information Center (Map p370; ☑0 2225 7612-4; www.bangkoktourist.com; 17/1 Th Phra Athit; ⊙9am-7pm Mon-Fri, 9am-5pm Sat-Sun; ☑Tha Phra Athit (Banglamphu)) City-specific tourism office provides maps, brochures and directions. Kiosks and booths are found around town; look for the green-on-white symbol of a mahout on an elephant.

Tourism Authority of Thailand (TAT; Map p368; ☑0 2250 5500, nationwide call centre 1672; www.tourismthailand.org; 1600 Th Phetchaburi Tat Mai; ⊙8.30am-4.30pm; Ⓜ Phetchaburi exit 2) Also has offices in Banglamphu (Map p370; ☑0 2283 1500; cnr Th Ratchadamnoen Nok & Th Chakrapatdipong; ⊙8.30am-4.30pm; ☑Tha Phan Fah) and at Suvarnabhumi International Airport (TAT; ☑0 2134 0040; 2nd fl, btwn Gates 2 & 5, Suvarnabhumi International Airport; ⊙24hr).

ⓘ Getting There & Away

The table shows how to get from major destinations and regional hubs from Bangkok; for other destinations, refer to the appropriate chapter. If you're in Bangkok and bound for Cambodia or Laos, it's possible to circumvent air travel altogether. Government buses run direct routes to Cambodia and southern Laos; the route to Siem Reap, via the crossing at Aranya Prathet, is a convenient way to pass this formerly hassle-laden border.

AIR

Bangkok has two airports. **Suvarnabhumi International Airport** (☑0 2132 1888; www.suvarnabhumiairport.com), 30km east of Bangkok, began commercial international and domestic service in September 2006. The airport's name is pronounced *sù·wan·ná·poom,* and it inherited the airport code (BKK) previously used by the old airport at Don Muang. The airport website has practical information in English, as well as real-time details of arrivals and departures.

Bangkok's former international and domestic **Don Muang International Airport** (DMK; ☑ 0 2535 1111; www.donmuangairportonline.com), 25km north of central Bangkok, was retired from commercial service in September 2006, only to reopen later as Bangkok's de facto budget hub.

BUS

Buses using government bus stations are far more reliable and less prone to incidents of theft than those departing from Th Khao San or other tourist centres.

The **Northern & Northeastern Bus Terminal** (Mo Chit; Map p368; ☑ for northeastern routes 0 2936 2852, ext 602/605, for northern routes 0 2936 2841, ext 325/614; Th Kamphaeng Phet; Ⓜ Kamphaeng Phet exit 1 & taxi, Ⓢ Mo Chit exit 3 & taxi) is commonly called *kŏn sòng mŏr chít* (Mo Chit station) – not to be confused with Mo Chit BTS station.

Use the **Eastern Bus Terminal** (Ekamai; Map p382; ☑ 0 2391 2504; Soi 40, Th Sukhumvit; Ⓢ Ekkamai exit 2), accessible via BTS to Ekkamai station, if you are headed to Cambodia via Hat Lek or Chanthaburi. Southern destinations are handled by the **Southern Bus Terminal** (Sai Tai Mai; ☑ 0 2894 6122; Th Boromaratchachonanee) in Thonburi.

MINIVAN

Privately run minivans, called *rót đôo,* are a fast and relatively comfortable way to get between Bangkok and its neighbouring provinces. Minivans depart from various points around the Victory Monument, accessible from the Victory Monument BTS stop.

TRAIN

Bangkok's main train station is **Hualamphong** (☑ 0 2220 4334; off Th Phra Ram IV; Ⓜ Hua Lamphong exit 2), linked to the MRT at Hua Lamphong station. To check timetables and prices for other destinations call the **State Railway of Thailand** (☑ nationwide call centre 1690; www. railway.co.th) or look at its website.

ⓘ Getting Around

Because of parking hassles and traffic jams, hiring a car to get around Bangkok is not recommended.

TO/FROM THE AIRPORT

Bangkok is served by two airports; the vast majority of flights are out of Survarnabhumi International Airport, while the budget airlines operate out of Don Muang International Airport. If

you need to transfer bretween the two, pencil in *at least* an hour of travel, as the two airports are at opposite ends of town. Minivans run between the two airports from 5.30am to 5pm (50B).

Suvarnabhumi International Airport

The following ground transport options leave directly from the Suvarnabhumi terminal to in-town destinations: metred taxis, hotel limousines, airport rail link, private vehicles and some minivans.

Airport Rail Link The elevated train service linking central Bangkok and Suvarnabhumi is comprised of a local service, which makes six stops before terminating at Phaya Thai station (45B, 30 minutes, every 15 minutes from 6am to midnight), connected by a walkway to BTS at Phaya Thai station, and an express service that runs, without stops, between Phaya Thai station and Makkasan (Bangkok City Air Terminal) station and the airport (90B, 15 to 17 minutes, hourly from 6am to midnight).

The Airport Rail Link is on floor B1 of Suvarnabhumi International Airport.

Bus & Minivan The public-transport centre is 3km from Suvarnabhumi and includes a public bus terminal, metred taxi stand and long-term parking. A free airport shuttle bus running both an ordinary and express route connects the transport centre with the passenger terminals. Lines that city-bound tourists are likely to use include bus 554, which stops across from Don Muang International Airport (34B, 24 hours), and minivan lines 551 to Victory Monument BTS station (40B, frequent from 5am to 10pm) and 552 to On Nut BTS station (25B, frequent from 5am to 10pm). From these points, you can continue on public transport or by taxi to your hotel. There are also buses and minivans to destinations including Chanthaburi, Ko Chang and Trat.

Relatively frequent minivans to Don Muang International Airport wait on floor 1, outside door 8 (50B, 40 minutes, from 5.30am to 5pm).

From town, you can take the BTS to On Nut, then from near the market entrance opposite Tesco Lotus take minivan 552 (25B, frequent from 5am to 10pm), or BTS to Victory Monument, then the minivan to Suvarnabhumi.

Taxi As you exit the terminal, ignore the touts and all the signs pointing you to overpriced 'official airport taxis'; instead, descend to floor 1 to join the generally fast-moving queue for a public taxi. Cabs booked through these desks should always use their meter, but they often try their luck so insist by saying 'Meter, please'. Toll charges (paid by passengers) vary between 25B and 60B. Note also that there's an additional 50B surcharge added to all fares departing from the airport, payable directly to the driver.

TRANSPORT FROM BANGKOK

DESTINATION	AIR	BUS	MINIVAN	TRAIN
Aranya Prathet (for Cambodian border)	N/A	N/A	230B, 3½hr, every 40min 4.15am-6.30pm	N/A
Ban Phe (for Ko Samet)	N/A	N/A	200B, 3hr, every 50min 6am-8pm	N/A
Chanthaburi	N/A	214B, 3½ hours, frequent	200B, 3hr, hourly 6am-7.30pm	
Chiang Mai	from 1750B; 1-1½hr; 20 daily (Don Muang); from 1750-2000B; 11 daily (Suvarnabhumi)	438-876B; 9½-11hr; hourly 5.40am-11pm (Northern & Northeastern Bus Terminal)	N/A	231-1454B; 12-15hr; 5 departures 12.45-10pm
Hanoi (Vietnam)	from 2359B; 2hr; 1 daily (Don Muang); from 3495B; 2hr; 6 daily (Suvarnabhumi)	N/A	N/A	N/A
Ho Chi Minh City (Saigon; Vietnam)	from 2550B; 1½hr; 2 daily (Don Muang); from 3495B; 1½hr; 6 daily (Suvarnabhumi)	N/A	N/A	N/A
Luang Prabang (Laos)	from 8305B; 1½-2hr; 3 daily	N/A	N/A	N/A
Nong Khai	N/A	381-762B; 10hr; hourly 8.30-9.45pm (Northern & Northeastern Bus Terminal)	N/A	213-1317B; 12hr; 3 departures 6.30-8.45pm
Pak Chong (for Khao Yai National Park)	N/A	118-150B; 3hr; hourly 5am-7pm (Northern & Northeastern Bus Terminal)	180B; 2½hr; hourly 6am-6pm (from Victory Monument)	N/A
Pakse (Laos)	from 6100B; 2hr 40min; 1.05pm (Suvarnabhumi)	900B; 12hr; 9pm (Northern & Northeastern Bus Terminal)	N/A	N/A
Phnom Penh (Cambodia)	from 1490B; 1hr; 1 daily (Don Muang); from 2965B; 70min; 7 daily (Suvarnabhumi)	N/A	N/A	N/A
Siem Reap (Cambodia; for Angkor Wat)	from 2220B; 70min; 2 daily (Don Muang); from 3365B; 1hr-70min; 8 daily (Suvarnabhumi)	750B; 7hr; 9am (Northern & Northeastern Bus Terminal)	N/A	N/A
Trat	from 2550B; 1hr; 3 daily (Suvarnabhumi)	248-275B; 5½hr; frequent 4-9.45am (Eastern Bus Terminal);	300B; 5hr; hourly 5am-5pm	N/A
Ubon Ratchathani	from 1350B; 70min; 7 daily (Don Muang); from 2350B; 70min; 2 daily (Suvarnabhumi)	600-804B; 10-11hr; hourly 6.40am & hourly 7-10pm (Northern & Northeastern Bus Terminal)	N/A	205-1280B; 8½-12hr; 6 departures 5.45am-10.25pm
Vientiane (Laos)	from 5255B; 1-1¼hr; 8 daily	900B; 10hr; 8pm	N/A	(see Nong Khai)

NORTHERN THAILAND BANGKOK

Don Muang International Airport

Bus & Minivan From outside the arrivals hall, there are two airport bus lines from Don Muang: A1 makes stops at BTS Mo Chit and the Northern & Northeastern Bus Terminal (30B, hourly from 9am to midnight), and A2 makes stops at BTS Mo Chit and BTS Victory Monument (30B, hourly from 9am to midnight).

Relatively frequent minivans also departing from outside the arrivals hall link Don Muang and Suvarnabhumi (50B, 40 minutes, from 5.30am to 5pm).

Public buses stop on the highway in front of the airport. Lines include 29, with a stop at Victory Monument BTS station before terminating at Hualamphong Train Station (24 hours); 59, with a stop near Th Khao San (24 hours); line 538, stopping at Victory Monument BTS station (4am to 10pm); and line 555, bound for Suvarnabhumi International Airport (4am to 11pm); fares are approximately 30B.

Taxi As at Suvarnabhumi, public taxis leave from outside the arrivals hall and there is a 50B airport charge added to the meter fare.

Train The walkway that crosses from the airport to the Amari Airport Hotel also provides access to Don Muang Train Station, which has trains to Hualamphong Train Station every one to 1½ hours from 4am to 11.30am and then roughly every hour from 2pm to 9.30pm (5B to 10B).

BOAT

Once the city's dominant form of transport, public boats still survive along the mighty Mae Nam Chao Phraya and on a few interior *klorng* (canals; also spelt *khlong*).

Canal Routes

Canal taxi boats run along Khlong Saen Saep, from Banglamphu east to Th Ramkhamhaeng. Fares range from 10B to 20B and boats run from approximately 5.30am to 8.30pm (to 7pm on weekends and holidays).

River Routes

Chao Phraya Express Boat (☑ 0 2623 6001; www.chaophrayaexpressboat.com) runs up and down Mae Nam Chao Phraya with boats stopping at different piers depending on their designation: express (from 10B; indicated by yellow, orange or green flags), local (without a flag) and the larger tourist boat (40B per trip) that stops at piers convenient for sightseers. There are also small flat-bottomed boats that do cross-river trips to Thonburi (3B per trip). The main pier (called Tha Sathon or Central Pier) is near Saphan Taksin BTS station, and services run from approximately 6am to 10pm.

BTS & MRT

The elevated **BTS** (☑ 0 2617 7300, tourist information 0 2617 7340; www.bts.co.th), also

known as the Skytrain, whisks you through 'new' Bangkok (Silom, Sukhumvit and Siam Sq). The interchange between the two lines is at Siam station, and trains run frequently from 6am to midnight. Fares vary from 15B to 52B, and most ticket machines only accept coins, but change is available at the information booths.

Bangkok's metro, or **MRT** (www.bangkokmetro.co.th), is most helpful for people staying in the Sukhumvit or Silom areas to reach the train station at Hualamphong. Fares cost 16B to 40B. The trains run frequently from 6am to midnight.

BUS

The city's public bus system is operated by **Bangkok Mass Transit Authority** (☑ 0 2246 0973; www.bmta.co.th); the website is a great source of information on all bus routes, but this doesn't really help the fact that Bangkok's bus system is confusing and generally lacks English. If you're determined, fares for ordinary (fan) buses start at 7B and air-conditioned buses at 10B. Smaller privately operated green buses cost 5B.

TAXI

Although many first-time visitors are hesitant to use them, in general, Bangkok's taxis are new and spacious and the drivers are courteous and helpful, making them an excellent way to get around. All taxis are required to use their meters, which start at 35B, and fares to most places within central Bangkok cost 40B to 80B.

It's generally a good idea to get in moving, rather than parked, taxis, as the latter often refuse to use their meters. Simply exit any taxi that refuses to use the meter.

TÚK-TÚK

Some travellers swear by túk-túk, but most have a hard time bargaining a fair price; know how much it should cost to your destination before soliciting a fare. A short trip on a túk-túk should cost at least 60B.

If a túk-túk driver offers to take you on a sightseeing tour, walk away – it's a touting scheme designed to pressure you into purchasing overpriced goods.

THAILAND'S EASTERN SEABOARD

Bangkok Thais have long escaped the urban grind with weekend escapes to the eastern seaboard. Some of the country's first beach resorts sprang up here, starting a trend that has been duplicated wherever sand meets sea. As the country has become more industrialised, Ko Samet's beaches remain the most spectacular destination within reach of the capital, and Ko Chang and its sister islands, further afield, offer the best 'tropical' ambience in the region.

Just beyond the foothills and the curving coastline is Cambodia, and the east coast provides a convenient cultural link between the two countries. Many of the mainland Thai towns were at some point occupied by the French during the shifting border days of the colonial era. Migrating travellers who take the time to explore lesser-known spots such as Trat will find remnants of Old Siam, tasty market meals and an easy-going prosperity that defines ordinary Thai life.

Ko Samet   เกาะเสม็ด

🖉 038

A tiny island idyll, Ko Samet bobs in the sea with a whole lot of scenery: small sandy coves bathed by clear aquamarine water. You'll have to share all this prettiness with other beach lovers as it's an easy weekend escape from Bangkok.

Ko Samet is part of Ko Laem Ya/Ko Samet National Park and charges all visitors an entrance fee (adult/child 200/100B) upon arrival. The fee is collected at the **National Parks office** (btwn Na Dan & Hat Sai Kaew; ⊙ sunrise-sunset) in Hat Sai Kaew; *sŏrngtăaou* from the pier will stop at the gates for payment. Hold on to your ticket for later inspections.

⦿ Sights & Activities

The northeast part of the island has the most popular and populated beaches. **Hat Sai Kaew** is the widest swathe of sand and thus the busiest with jet skis, karaoke and nightly discos. **Ao Hin Khok** has an unshaved ambience; its beach is smaller, but the backpackers don't seem to mind. **Ao Phai** is another perfectly relaxing bay around the next headland. Further south is **Ao Wong Deuan**, a wide arc of sand filled with bars and mayhem. The further south you go, the more Thai and isolated it becomes.

Bring along mosquito spray as the forest island is home to everyone's favourite blood suckers.

🛏 Sleeping

Though resorts are increasingly replacing bungalows, Ko Samet's accommodation is still refreshingly simple and old-fashioned compared to Thailand's other beach resorts. Weekday rates remain OK value (fan rooms start at 600B), but prices increase at weekends and public holidays, when it is advisable to book ahead.

★ **Tok's**   GUESTHOUSE **$$**
(🖉 0 3864 4073; www.tok-littlehut.com; Ao Hin Khok; r 1500-2000B; 🌢 🛜) One of the top spots on this part of the island, well-maintained villas climb up a landscaped hillside with plenty of shade and flowering plants. The attached bar is popular.

Tubtim Resort   HOTEL **$$**
(🖉 0 3864 4025; www.tubtimresort.com; Ao Phutsa; r 600-3600B; 🌢 @ 🛜) Well-organised place with great nightly barbecues and a range of solid, spacious bungalows of varying quality all close to the same dreamy beach. It's popular with upmarket Thais.

Laem Yai Hut Resort   GUESTHOUSE **$$**
(🖉 0 3864 4282; Hat Sai Kaew; r 1000-2000B; 🌢 🛜) A colourful collection of 25 bunglaows varying in size and age are camped out in a shady garden on the north end of the beach.

Jep's Bungalows   GUESTHOUSE **$$**
(🖉 0 3864 4112; www.jepbungalow.com; Ao Hin Khok; r 300-1800B; 🌢 @ 🛜) If the stars are right, you can still score a very basic fan hut for a mere 300B. But the 600B ones are a far better deal.

Ao Nuan   GUESTHOUSE **$$**
(Ao Nuan; r 600-2500B; 🌢) The inventor of chillaxin' on Ko Samet, quirky Ao Nuan has both very simple wooden bungalows and a few posh ones with air-con and sea views.

Samet Ville Resort   HOTEL **$$$**
(🖉 0 3865 1682; www.sametvilleresort.com; Ao Wai; r 1080-4500B; 🌢 🛜) The only resort at this secluded bay, Samet Ville Resort is an unpretentious place with a range of rooms and cottages that suit most budgets. Ao Wai can be reached from Ban Phe by chartered speedboat.

🍴 Eating & Drinking

Most hotels and guesthouses have restaurants that moonlight as bars after sunset. The food and the service won't blow you away, but there aren't many alternatives.

On weekends Ko Samet is a boisterous night owl with provincial tour groups crooning away on karaoke machines or the young ones slurping down beer and buckets to a techno beat. The bar scene changes depending on who is around but there is usually a

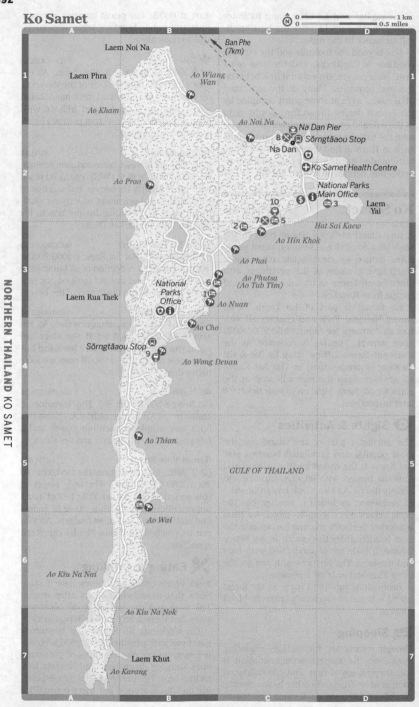

Ko Samet

⬤ Sleeping
1 Ao Nuan..B3
2 Jep's Bungalows C3
3 Laem Yai Hut Resort D2
4 Samet Ville Resort B5
5 Tok's..C2
6 Tubtim Resort B3

✕ Eating
7 Jep's Restaurant C2
8 Rabeang Baan C2

◐ Drinking & Nightlife
9 Baywatch Bar B4
10 Naga Bar C2

crowd on Hat Sai Khao, Ao Hin Khok, Ao Phai and Ao Wong Deuan.

Rabeang Baan THAI $
(Na Dan; dishes 70-120B; ☺8am-10pm) Right by the ferry terminal, this spot has good enough food to make you forget you have to leave the island. It's busier at lunch than dinner.

Jep's Restaurant INTERNATIONAL $
(Ao Hin Khok; mains 60-150B; ☺7am-11pm) Canopied by the branches of an arching tree decorated with pendant lights, this pretty place does a little of everything right on the beach.

Baywatch Bar BAR
(Ao Wong Deuan; beers from 80B) A good spot for after-dark beach-gazing, with a fun crowd and strong cocktails.

Naga Bar BAR
(Ao Hin Khok; beers from 70B) This busy beachfront bar comes with a *moo·ay tai* ring, although the days of drunk foreigners getting battered by the locals are long gone. Instead, you get DJs and lots of whisky and vodka/Red Bull buckets.

ℹ Information
There are several ATMs on Ko Samet, including near the Na Dan pier and Ao Wong Deuan.

Internet terminals or wi-fi are available at hotels on most beaches.

Ko Samet Health Centre (☎0 3861 1123; ☺8.30am-9pm Mon-Fri, 8.30am-4.30pm Sat & Sun) On the main road between Na Dan and Hat Sai Kaew. On-call mobile numbers are posted for after-hours emergencies.

Police Station (☎1155) On the main road between Na Dan and Hat Sai Kaew. There's a substation on Ao Wong Deuan.

ℹ Getting There & Away
Ko Samet is accessed via Ban Phe, in Rayong Province. Buses from Ban Phe's bus station (near Tha Thetsaban) go to/from Bangkok's Eastern Bus Terminal (173B, four hours, hourly 6am to 6pm). Ban Phe also has minivan services to Laem Ngop for boats to Ko Chang (300B, four hours, three departures daily) and Bangkok's Victory Monument (250B, four hours, hourly 7am to 6pm).

There are dozens of piers at Ban Phe, each used by different ferry companies, but they all charge the same fares (one way/return 70/100B, 40 minutes, hourly 8am to 5pm) and dock at Na Dan Pier, the main pier on Ko Samet. The last boat back to the mainland leaves at 6pm. Speedboats charge 200B per person (one way) and will drop you at the beach of your choice, but they only leave when they have enough passengers.

ℹ Getting Around
Green *sŏrngtăaou* meet arriving boats at the pier and provide drop-offs at the various beaches (per person 100B to 400B).

You can rent motorcycles nearly everywhere along the northern half of the island. Expect to pay about 300B per day.

Trat ตราด
☏ 039 / POP 22,000
A major mainland transit point for Ko Chang and coastal Cambodia, Trat's provincial charms are underappreciated. Since your destination is still so far away, why not stay a little longer and enjoy all the things you can't get on the islands: fresh, affordable fruit, tasty noodles; and tonnes of people watching.

◉ Sights
Indoor Market MARKET
The indoor market sprawls east from Th Sukhumvit to Th Tat Mai and has a little bit of everything, especially all the things that you forgot to pack. Without really noticing the difference you will stumble upon the **day market** (Th Tat Mai), selling fresh fruit, vegetables and takeaway food.

⛏ Sleeping & Eating
Trat has many budget hotels housed in traditional wooden houses on and around Th Thana Charoen. You'll find it hard to spend more than if you want to.

Likewise, Trat is all about cheap eats: head to the **day market** on Th Tat Mai for

Trat Province

gah·faa boh·rahn (old-fashioned coffee), the **indoor market** for lunchtime noodles, or the **night market** for a stir-fried dinner.

Ban Jaidee Guest House GUESTHOUSE $
(☑ 08 3589 0839; banjaideehouse@yahoo.com; 6 Th Chaimongkol; r 200B; 🐾) In a charming neighbourhood, this relaxed traditional wooden house has simple rooms with shared bathrooms. It's very popular and booking ahead is essential.

Pop Guest House GUESTHOUSE $
(☑ 0 3951 2392; 1/1 Th Thana Charoen; r 150-600B; 🌸@🐾) Pop is an efficient and expanding – if bland – operation. The many rooms are well-maintained, and the restaurant is OK.

★ **Cool Corner Cafe** INTERNATIONAL-THAI $
(☑ 08 4159 2030; 49-51 Th Thana Charoen; dishes 60-160B; ⏰8am-10pm) This cafe has a degree of sophistication not usually found in provincial towns and serves up a great mix of Thai and Western dishes, as well as beers, coffee and lassis.

❶ Information

Th Sukhumvit runs through town, though it's often referred to as Th Ratanuson.
Bangkok Hospital Trat (☑ 0 3953 2735; www.bangkoktrathospital.com; 376 Moo 2, Th Sukhumvit; ⏰24hr) Best health care in the region. It's about 1km north of the town centre.
Krung Thai Bank (Th Sukhumvit) Has an ATM and currency-exchange facilities.
Police Station (☑1155; cnr Th Santisuk & Th Wiwatthana) A short walk from Trat's centre.
Sawadee@Cafe Net (☑0 3952 0075; Th Lak Meuang; per min 1B; ⏰10am-10pm)

❶ Getting There & Away

Trat's bus station is about 1km north of the centre of town.

Minivans leave from various points along Th Sukhumvit. **Family Tour** (☑08 1940 7380; Th Sukhumvit cnr Th Lak Meuang) has minivans to Bangkok's Victory Monument and Northern & Northeastern Bus Terminal.

The three piers that handle boat traffic to Ko Chang (as well as Ko Kut, Ko Mak and Ko Wai) are located in Laem Ngop, about 30km southwest of Trat. Sŏrngtǎaou to Laem Ngop and the piers

TRANSPORT FROM TRAT

DESTINATION	AIR	BUS	MINIVAN	SÖRNGTǍAOU
Ban Phe (for Ko Samet)	N/A	N/A	200B; 2½hr; hourly 5am-7pm	N/A
Bangkok's Suvarnabhumi International Airport	from 2550B; 1hr; 3 daily	272B; 5-6hr; 5 daily	N/A	N/A
Bangkok's Eastern Bus Terminal	N/A	265B; 5hr; 17 daily	N/A	N/A
Bangkok's Northern & Northeastern Bus Terminal	N/A	272B; 5-6hr; 5 daily	N/A	N/A
Chanthaburi	N/A	80B; 1hr; hourly 7.30am-11.30pm	70B; 50min; frequent 5am-7pm	N/A
Hat Lek (for Cambodia)	N/A	120B; 1½hr; hourly 5am-6pm	N/A	
Laem Ngop (for Ko Chang)	N/A	N/A	N/A	50B; 35-50min

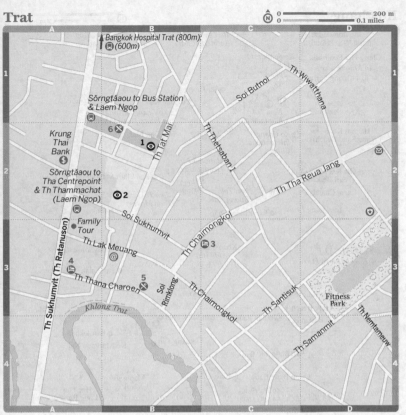

Trat

Trat

⊙ Sights
1 Day Market	B2
2 Indoor Market	B2

🛏 Sleeping
3 Ban Jaidee Guest House	C3
4 Pop Guest House	A3

🍴 Eating
5 Cool Corner Cafe	B3
6 Night Market	B2

leave from two points along Th Sukhumvit (Th Ratanuson): just west of the market and another southwest of the market.

Bangkok Airways (📞 Trat airport 0 3955 1654, Trat airport 0 3955 1655, in Bangkok 0 2265 5555; www.bangkokair.com) operates flights to/from Bangkok. Trat's airport is 40km west of town; taxis there cost 600B.

ⓘ Getting Around

Motorbikes can be rented for 200B a day along Th Sukhumvit near the guesthouse area

Ko Chang เกาะช้าง

📞 039 / POP 5000

With steep, jungle-covered peaks erupting from the sea, picturesque Ko Chang (Elephant Island) retains its remote and rugged spirit despite its current status as a package-tour resort akin to Phuket. The island's swathes of sand are girl-next-door pretty but not beauty-queen gorgeous. Yet what it lacks in sand, it makes up for in an unlikely combination: accessible wilderness with a thriving party scene.

⊙ Sights

Though Ko Chang has accelerated into modernity with some understandable growing pains, the island still has tropically hued

Ko Chang

seas, critter-filled jungles and a variety of water sports for athletic beach bums.

It is mainly the western coast that has been developed for tourism. In the northwest is **Hat Sai Khao (White Sand Beach)**, by far the biggest, busiest and brashest beach. Further south is **Ao Khlong Prao**, an upmarket outpost. The backpacker fave is **Lonely Beach**, which is lonely no more, especially at night. An old-fashioned fishing community is settled around **Ban Bang Bao**. The east coast is largely undeveloped, with only a few low-key spots, like **Hat Yao (Long Beach)**.

Ko Chang's mountainous interior is predominantly protected as a national park. The forest is lush, alive with wildlife and threaded by silver-hued waterfalls. This area is home to **Ban Kwan Chang** (บ้าน ความช้าง; ☑08 1919 3995; changtone@yahoo. com; ☺8am-5pm), the best of the island's three elephant camps.

🏃 Activities

The dive sites near Ko Chang offer a variety of coral, fish and beginner-friendly shallow waters on par with other Gulf of Thailand dive sites. The most pristine diving in the area is around Ko Rang, an uninhabited island protected from fishing by its marine park status. It is reached by boat from Ko Chang.

Diving trips typically cost around 2800B to 3500B. PADI Open Water certification costs 14,500B per person. In recent years, dive shops have remained open during the rainy season (June to September) but visibility and sea conditions can be poor. Recommended dive operators include **BB Divers** (☑0 3955 8040; www.bbdivers.com) and **Lonely Beach Divers** (☑08 0619 0704; www.lonely beachdivers.com).

KayakChang KAYAKING
(☑0 3955 2000; www.kayakchang.com; Amari Emerald Cove Resort, Khlong Prao) KayakChang rents high-end, closed-top kayaks (from 1000B per day) that handle better and travel faster. They also lead one-day and multiday trips (from 2200B) to other islands in the archipelago.

Koh Chang Trekking HIKING, BIRD-WATCHING
(☑08 1588 3324) Bird-watchers should contact Koh Chang Trekking which runs one- and two-day trips (1200B to 1500B) into Mu Ko Chang National Marine Park and hikes to the top of Khao Chom Prasat, two nearby rocky tipped peaks. Prices are for a group of four people.

Sima Massage MASSAGE
(☑08 1489 5171; main road, Khlong Prao; massage per hr 250B; ☺8am-10pm) Across from Tropicana Resort, and regarded by locals as the best massage on the island – quite an accolade in a place where a massage is easier to find than a 7-Eleven.

Courses

Koh Chang Thai Cookery School COOKING
(☑0 3955 7243; Blue Lagoon Bungalows, Khlong Prao) Slices, dices and sautées in a shady open-air kitchen beside the estuary.

Sleeping & Eating

A few places close down during the wet season (May to October) and rates drop precipitously. Consider booking ahead and shopping for online discounts during peak season (November to March), weekends and holidays.

Virtually all of the island's accommodation has attached restaurants with adequate but not outstanding fare. Parties abound on the beaches and range from the older and

---

GETTING TO CAMBODIA

Trat to Koh Kong

Getting to the border From Trat, the closest Thai–Cambodia crossing is the Hat Lek/Charn Yeam crossing. Minivans run to Hat Lek hourly 5am to 6pm (120B, 1½ hours) from Trat's bus station.

At the border The border is open from 7am to 8pm. Visas are available at the border here, but they're a steep 1000B (they are US$20 at other crossings), and payment is only accepted in baht. Ignore anyone who says you require a 'medical certificate' or other paperwork.

Moving on Take a taxi (US$10 plus 6000r for the toll) or moto (unmarked motorcycle taxi; US$3) to Koh Kong town where you can catch a bus (US$7, six hours) or share taxi (US$11, five hours) to Phnom Penh, and buses (US$7, five hours) or share taxis (US$10, four hours) to Sihanoukville.

For more information about crossing this border in the other direction, see p245

Chanthaburi to Pailin

It's possible to cross to Cambodia at the Pong Nam Ron/Psar Pruhn crossing via the eponymous provincial capital of Chanthaburi Province – a less hectic alternative to the crossing at Aranya Prathet, further north.

Getting to the border To Chanthaburi, buses leave from Bangkok's Northern & Northeastern Bus Terminal (214B, 3½ hours, four departures daily) and Eastern Bus Terminal (214B, 3½ hours, frequent), and minivans leave from near the Victory Monument (200B, three hours, hourly from 6am to 7.30pm). In Chanthaburi, minivans leave from a stop across from the River Guest House (150B, 1½ hours, two departures daily).

At the border The border is open from 7am to 8pm, and visas are available upon arrival.

Moving on Take a moto (unmarked motorcycle taxi; US$5), share taxi (6000r) or taxi (US$10) the 18km to Pailin, from where you'll need to connect to one of the frequent share taxis to Battambang (per person $5, 1½ hours). From Battambang, it's possible to continue to Siem Reap by boat, or Phnom Penh by bus. A private taxi from the border to Battambang costs US$40.

For more information about crossing this border in the other direction, see p222.

ⓘ NATIONAL PARK ADMISSION FEE

Parts of Ko Chang are protected and maintained as a national park and you will be required to pay a 200B park entrance fee when visiting some of the waterfalls (entrance fees are stated in the reviews and payable at the site). **National Park headquarters** (☏ 0 3955 5080; Ban Than Mayom; ⊙ 8am-5pm) is on the eastern side of the island near Nam Tok Than Mayom.

Do also be aware that nudity and topless sunbathing are forbidden by law in Mu Ko Chang National Marine Park; this includes all beaches on Ko Chang, Ko Kut, Ko Mak etc.

surlier scene on Hat Sai Khao to the younger and sloppier on Lonely Beach.

Independent Bo's   GUESTHOUSE $
(☏ 08 5283 5581; Hat Sai Khao; r 400-850B; 🅰🅰🅰) Despite the eccentric Scottish owner (no reservations here) this place on the jungle hillside exudes the creative, hippy-ish vibe that Ko Chang used to be famous for. All bungalows are funky and different.

Porn's Bungalows   GUESTHOUSE $
(☏ 08 0613 9266; www.pornsbungalows-kohchang. com; Hat Kaibae; r 550-1500B) Very chilled spot at the far western end of the beach. All bungalows are fan-only. The 900B beachfront bungalows are a great deal.

⭐**Koh Chang Sea Hut**   HOTEL $$
(☏ 08 1285 0570; www.kohchang-seahut.com; Ban Bang Bao; r 2500B; 🅰🅰) Seven luxurious bungalows built on the edge of Bang Bao's pier, each offering near-panoramic views of the bay and a private deck where breakfast is served. There are five rooms here too.

Blue Lagoon Bungalows   GUESTHOUSE $$
(☏ 0 3955 7243; www.kohchangbluelagoon.com; Khlong Prao; r 650-1300B; 🅰🅰🅰🅰) An exceedingly friendly garden spot with a range of bungalows to suit different budgets beside a peaceful estuary. All sorts of amenities, including yoga, cooking school, kids' playground and activities, are on offer too.

⭐**Keereeta Resort**   GUESTHOUSE $$$
(☏ 0 3955 1304; www.keereeta.com; Khlong Prao; r 3500B; 🅰🅰) Only five very special rooms here, all individually colour-themed, huge, secluded and oh-so stylish. Free kayaks for guests to paddle to the beach or the restaurants opposite. Book ahead.

⭐**Phu-Talay**   SEAFOOD $$
(Khlong Prao; 100-320B; ⊙ 10am-10pm) Sensible menu of Ko Chang classics (lots of fish) and far more reasonably priced than many other seafood places.

⭐**Norng Bua**   THAI $$
(Hat Sai Khao; dishes 40-300B; ⊙ 8am-11pm) Always crowded with visiting Thais, a good sign indeed.

ⓘ Information

Internet cafes and banks with ATMs are plentiful on the island, especially in Hat Sai Khao.

Ko Chang Hospital (☏ 0 3952 1657; Ban Dan Mai) Public hospital with a good reputation and affordably priced care; south of the ferry terminal.

Police Station (☏ 0 3958 6191; Ban Dan Mai)

ⓘ Getting There & Away

Whether originating from Bangkok or Cambodia, it is an all-day haul to reach Ko Chang.

Ferries from the mainland leave from either Tha Thammachat, operated by **Koh Chang Ferry** (☏ 0 3955 5188), or Tha Centrepoint, with **Centrepoint Ferry** (☏ 0 3953 8196). Boats from

TRANSPORT TO/FROM KO CHANG

ORIGIN	DESTINATION	BOAT	BUS
Bangkok's Eastern Bus Terminal	Tha Thammachat	N/A	275B; 7hr; 3 daily
Ko Chang	Suvarnabhumi International Airport	N/A	550B; 6-7hr; 3 daily
Tha Centrepoint	Ko Chang	80B; 45min; hourly 6.30am-7pm	N/A
Tha Thammachat	Ko Chang	80B; 30min; every 30min 6.30am-7pm	N/A

BEYOND KO CHANG

Ko Chang is Thailand's second-largest island, and has a mighty reputation, but it's only one of 51 islands in the eponymous archipelago. A handful of these islands are home to accommodation, although most bungalows close during the May-to-September low season when seas are rough and flooding is common.

The islands below can be reached from the mainland, typically from the pier at Laem Ngop, while **Bang Bao Boat** (www.bangbaoboat.com) is the archipelago's inter-island ferry. Boats depart Ko Chang at 9am and arrive at Ko Wai (one way 300B, one hour) and continue on to Ko Mak (one way 400B, one hour) and Ko Kut (700B, three hours). The boats leave from Bang Bao in the southeast of the island.

Ko Kut

All the paradise descriptions apply to Ko Kut: the water is clear, coconut palms outnumber buildings, and an unhurried atmosphere embraces you upon arrival. White sand beaches with aquamarine water are strewn along the western side of the island, while rocky coves and mangrove estuaries make Ko Kut a great destination for snorkelling and kayaking.

You can scrimp your way into the neighbourhood of beautiful **Hat Khlong Chao** by staying at one of the village guesthouses, which are a five- to 15-minute walk to the beach. Families will prefer the midrange options, such as **Dusita** (☑ 08 1707 4546; Ao Ngam Kho; r 1290-2190B; ❀), on Ao Ngam Kho. And if you're itching to splurge, upscale places like **Bann Makok** (☑ 08 1643 9488; www.bannmakok.com; Khlong Yai Ki; r 2800-4000B; ❀ @ ❀) make Ko Kut the place to do it.

Ko Mak

Little Ko Mak is not destined for island super-stardom: the interior is a utilitarian landscape of coconut and rubber plantations and reports of sand flies make visitors a little nervous. But the palm-fringed bays are bathed by gently lapping water and there's a relaxed vibe. The best beach on the island is **Ao Pra** in the west, but it's completely undeveloped and hard to reach. For now, swimming and beach strolling are best on the northwestern bay of **Ao Suan Yai**, a wide arc of sand and looking-glass-clear water.

Most budget guesthouses, such as **Koh Mak Cottage** (☑ 08 1910 2723; Ao Khao; r 400-500B; @), are on Ao Khao, a decent strip of sand on the southwestern side of the island, while the resorts, including **Koh Mak Resort** (☑ 0 3950 1013; www.kohmakresort. com; Ao Suan Yai; r 2800-6800B; ❀ ❀ ❀), sprawl on the more scenic northwestern bay of Ao Suan Yai. There are a handful of family-run restaurants on the main road between Monkey Island and Makathanee Resort.

Ko Rayang

Ko Rayang is a private island with one tiny resort: **Rayang Island Resort** (☑ 0 3950 1000; www.rayang-island.com; r 2500-3800B). Accommodation is basic, but there's potential for snorkelling just outside your door; get there by ferry (170B) from Ko Mak's Tha Makathanee.

Ko Wai

Stunning Ko Wai is teensy and primitive, but is endowed with gin-clear waters, excellent coral reefs for snorkelling and a handsome view across to Ko Chang. Expect to share the bulk of your afternoons with day-trippers but have the remainder of your time in peace.

If you decide to stay, decent bungalows and a restaurant are available at **Ko Wai Pakarang** (☑ 08 4113 8946; www.kohwaipakarang.com; r 600-2200B; ❀ @ ❀).

Tha Thammachat arrive at Tha Sapparot; Centrepoint ferries at a pier down the road.

Bang Bao Boat (www.bangbaoboat.com) operates speedboats between the islands during the high season.

It's possible to go direct to and from Ko Chang from Bangkok's Eastern Bus Terminal and Suvarnabhumi International Airport, via Chanthaburi and Trat.

❶ Getting Around

Shared *sŏrngtăaou* meet arriving boats to shuttle passengers to the various beaches (Hat Sai Khao 100B, Khlong Prao 150B and Lonely Beach 200B). Most hops between neighbouring west coast beaches should cost around 50B to 200B but prices rise after dark.

Businesses along the west coast charge from 200B per day for motorbike hire.

NORTHEASTERN THAILAND

The personality of the northeast (also known as Isan) is much like the hand-loomed silk that the region is famous for. Its cultural patterns – from language to cuisine – were woven from the ancient kingdoms of neighbouring Cambodia and Laos, long before Bangkok defined the current borders. The resulting textile of people is distinct from and slightly foreign to the rest of Thailand. But nationals from modern-day Laos and Cambodia recognise instant kinship with Thai villagers who grow up speaking either Khmer or Lao (depending on the village) and who have preserved common customs and festivals, some of which have since disappeared outside of Isan's borders.

Isan is decidedly off the beaten track with the attendant advantages and disadvantages: English is not widely spoken and travel services are at a minimum. But the reward is an insight into a hardworking and welcoming society.

Nakhon Ratchasima (Khorat)

นครราชสีมา (โคราช)

📞 044 / POP 166,000

This is urban Isan, where the middle class flourishes among sprawling developments and multilane highways. The collection of craft villages and the Khmer ruins at Phimai, outside town, are reasons to tip your hat to Khorat.

◉ Sights

Thao Suranari Monument MONUMENT
(อนุสาวรีย์ท้าวสุรนารี; Th Rajadamnern) FREE
Thao Suranari, wife of the city's assistant governor during the reign of Rama III (r 1824–51), became a hero in 1826 by organising a successful prisoner revolt after Chao Anou of Vientiane had conquered Khorat

---

DON'T MISS

PÀT MÈE KOH·RÂHT

Khorat boasts a local variation on *pàt tai* known as *pàt mèe koh·râht*, which is made with a local-style rice noodle. Hunker down to a plate along with Isan's other specialities at **Wat Boon Night Bazaar** (Th Chumphon; ⊘5-9.30pm).

---

during his rebellion against Siam. As one version of the legend has it, she convinced the women to seduce the Lao soldiers and then the Thai men launched a surprise attack, which saved the city.

Her monument sits photogenically in front of **Chumphon Gate**, the only original gate left standing: the other three are recent rebuilds. It was a part of the city walls erected in 1656 by French technicians on the orders of Ayuthaya King Narai. The little white building north of this gate that resembles the old fortifications is **Suranari Hall** (Th Chumphon; ⊘9am-6pm Tue-Sun) FREE, a museum of sorts with a cool diorama and even cooler sculpted mural creatively depicting the famous battle.

Maha Viravong National Museum MUSEUM
(พิพิธภัณฑสถานแห่งชาติมหาวีรวงศ์; Th Rajadamnern; admission 50B; ⊘9am-4pm Wed-Sun) Though the collection at this seldom-visited museum is very small, it's also very good. There's ancient pottery (don't miss sneaking a peak at what's stored in the back) and a variety of Buddha images spanning the Dvaravati to Rattanakosin eras.

🍴 Sleeping & Eating

★ **Sansabai House** HOTEL $
(📞0 4425 5144; www.sansabai-korat.com; Th Suranaree; r 300-550B; 🅿️➆❄️🐾) Walk into the welcoming lobby and you half expect the posted prices to be a bait-and-switch ploy. But no, all rooms are bright and cheerful and come with good mattresses, mini-fridges and little balconies.

Thai Inter Hotel HOTEL $$
(📞0 4424 7700; www.thaiinterhotel.com; Th Yommarat; r incl breakfast 750-850B; 🅿️❄️@🛜) This little hotel tries to be hip by patching together an odd mix of styles, and it pretty much pulls it off. The lobby is homey and the rooms are comfy. It's got a good (though not so quiet) location near decent restaurants and bars.

★ **Rabieng Kaew** THAI $$
(Th Yommarat; dishes 80-300B; ⊘11am-5pm; 🅿️) This lovely spot has an antique-filled dining room and a leafy garden in back. But it's not all about the atmosphere. The food, big dishes meant to be shared, is simply excellent.

ℹ️ Information

Klang Plaza 2 shopping centre has a **Bangkok Bank** (Th Jomsurangyat; ⊘10am-8pm) (changes cash only) open daily until 8pm, on the 5th

Nakhon Ratchasima (Khorat)

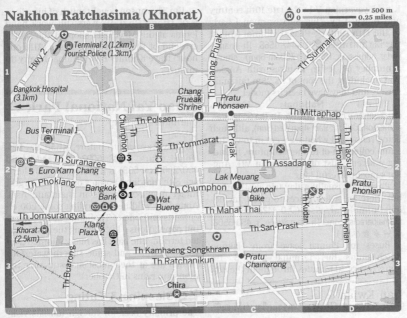

floor. There are more extended-hours **banks** (Th Mittaphap) at the Mall.

Walk two or three blocks and you're bound to pass an internet cafe.

Bangkok Hospital (☑ 0 4442 9999; Th Mittaphap)

Tourism Authority of Thailand (TAT; ☑ 0 4421 3666; tatsima@tat.or.th; Th Mittaphap; ⊕8.30am-4.30pm) Next to Sima Thani Hotel.

Tourist Police (☑ 0 4434 1777; Hwy 2) Opposite Bus Terminal 2.

ⓘ Getting There & Away

There are two bus terminals in Nakhon Ratchasima. **Bus Terminal 1** (☑ 0 4424 2899; Th Burin) in the city centre serves towns within the province and VIP buses to Bangkok. Buses to other destinations, plus more Bangkok buses, use **Bus Terminal 2** (bor kŏr sŏr sŏrng; ☑ 0 4429 5271; Hwy 2), off Hwy 2.

Many trains pass through Khorat's **train station** (☑ 0 4424 2044), but buses are faster. To check timetables and prices for other destinations call the **State Railway of Thailand** (☑ nationwide call centre 1690; www.railway.co.th) or look at its website.

ⓘ Getting Around

Túk-túk and motorcycle taxis cost between 40B and 70B to most places around town. **Euro Karn Chang** (☑ 08 8355 9393; 239-241 Th

Nakhon Ratchasima (Khorat)

⊙ Sights

1 Chumphon Gate	B2
2 Maha Viravong National Museum	B3
3 Suranari Hall	B2
4 Thao Suranari Monument	B2

⊜ Sleeping

5 Sansabai House	A2
6 Thai Inter Hotel	D2

⊗ Eating

7 Rabieng Kaew	C2
8 Wat Boon Night Bazaar	D2

Suranaree; ⊕8am-5pm Mon-Sat) and **Jompol Bike** (☑ 08 1955 2838; Th Chumphon; ⊕8am-5.30pm) hire motorcycles.

Around Nakhon Ratchasima

Phimai   พิมาย

One of Thailand's finest surviving Khmer temples sits at the heart of this innocuous little town, 60km northeast of Nakhon Ratchasima. Originally started by Khmer

King Jayavarman V in the late 10th century and finished by King Suryavarman I early in the 11th century, **Prasat Phimai** (อุทยานประวัติศาสตร์พิมาย; ☎0 4447 1568; Th Anantajinda; admission 100B; ⊙7.30am-6pm) shares a number of design features with Angkor Wat, including the roof of its 28m-tall main shrine, and may have been its model.

Phimai National Museum (พิพิธภัณฑสถานแห่งชาติพิมาย; Th Tha Songkhran; admission 100B; ⊙9am-4pm Wed-Sun), although being renovated when we were in town, has a fine collection of Khmer sculpture, including a serene bust of Jayavarman VII, Angkor's most powerful king.

Phimai is usually a day-trip destination, but there are a few places to crash, including **Phimai Paradise** (☎0 4428 7565; www.phimaiparadise.com; Th Samairujee; r 450-650B; P⊖❄@☎≋).

Buses for Phimai leave from Nakhon Ratchasima's Bus Terminal 2 (50B, 1½ hours) every 20 minutes throughout the day.

Dan Kwian & Pak Thong Chai ด่านเกวียน/ปักธงชัย

South of Nakhon Ratchasima are two of Thailand's most successful craft villages. **Dan Kwian** is known for its rough textured pottery often fired with a rustlike hue. Frequent buses (14B, 30 minutes) run from near Khorat's south city gate.

Jim Thompson bought much of his silk in **Pak Thong Chai**. Weavers still work hand looms at the Macchada shop, at the southern end of the main road. Buses (21B, one hour) leave Khorat's Bus Terminal 1 every 30 minutes.

Khao Yai National Park

อุทยานแห่งชาติเขาใหญ่

☎044

An easy escape into nature, **Khao Yai National Park**; ☎08 6092 6529; adult/child 400/200B, car 50B) is a Unesco World Heritage Site that incorporates one of the largest intact monsoon forests in mainland Asia. Abundant wildlife – including some 200 elephants and one of Thailand's largest hornbill populations – lives among the park's varied terrain. The park has many kilometres of trekking trails and some superb waterfalls (which are at their most majestic after the monsoon rains in October).

Sleeping & Eating

The primary base for foreign tourists visiting the park is the town of Pak Chong, where hotels and guesthouses arrange park tours. You can also visit the park independently without your own transport.

Restaurants line Th Thanarat, the main conduit to the park, and the park itself has

TRANSPORT FROM NAKHON RATCHASIMA (KHORAT)

DESTINATION	BUS	MINIVAN	TRAIN
Aranya Prathet (for Cambodia)	165B; 4hr; 5 daily 5.30am-5.30pm	N/A	N/A
Bangkok	171-320B; 3½ hours; frequent	N/A	50-1010B; 5-7hr; 9 daily
Chiang Mai	473-710B; 12-13hr; 11 daily 3am-8.30pm	N/A	N/A
Nang Rong (for Phanom Rung Historical Park)	75-95B; 2hr; frequent	75B; 1½hr; frequent 5am-8pm	N/A
Nong Khai	220-435B; 6hr; frequent	N/A	64-301B; 6½hr; 2 daily
Pak Chong (for Khao Yai National Park)	60-80B; 1hr; frequent	N/A	54-168B; 1hr; 5 daily
Surin	136-175B; 4hr; 6 daily 7am-7.20pm	N/A	N/A
Trat	324B; 8hr; 1am, 11.15am & 9pm	N/A	N/A
Ubon Ratchathani	286-445B; 5-6hr; 14 daily 8am-1am	N/A	58-1068B; 5-6hr; 9 daily
Vientiane (Laos; must have visa)	540B; 6½hr; 12.30am	N/A	(see Nong Khai)

GETTING TO CAMBODIA: BANGKOK TO SIEM REAP

Getting to the border The easiest way to get from Bangkok to Siem Reap overland is the direct bus departing from the Northern & Northeastern Bus Terminal that crosses at the Aranya Prathet/Poipet crossing. The through-service bus trips sold on Th Khao San and elsewhere in Bangkok seem cheap and convenient, but they haven't been nicknamed 'scam buses' for nothing, and if you use them you run the risk of being hassled and ripped off, often quite aggressively.

If you choose to do the trip in stages (much cheaper than the direct bus), you can get from Bangkok to the border town of Aranya Prathet (aka Aran) by bus from Bangkok's Northern & Northeastern Bus Terminal, by bus or minivan from Bangkok's Eastern Bus Terminal, by bus from Suvarnabhumi International Airport's bus station, by minivan from Victory Monument, or by 3rd-class train (only the 5.55am departure will get you there early enough to reach Siem Reap the same day) from Hualamphong Train Station. Aran also has bus services about every one or two hours from other cities in the area including Nakhon Ratchasima (Khorat) and Surin. All minivans plus some buses go all the way to the Rong Kluea Market next to the border, so there's no need to stop in Aranya Prathet city. Otherwise, you'll need to take a *sŏrngtăaou* (15B), motorcycle taxi (60B) or túk-túk (80B) the final 7km to the border.

At the border The border is open 7am to 8pm daily, and visas are available upon arrival. Be prepared to wait in sweltering immigration lines on both sides – waits of two or more hours are not uncommon, especially in the high season. You can pay a special 'VIP fee' (aka a bribe) of 200B on either side to skip the lines. There are many persistent scammers on the Thai side trying to get you to buy your Cambodia visa through them, but no matter what they might tell you, there's no reason to get visas anywhere except the border.

After getting stamped out of Thailand – a completely easy and straightforward process – follow the throng to Cambodian immigration and find the 'Visa on Arrival' sign if you don't already have a visa. Entering Cambodia you should not have to pay more than the US$20 visa fee, but again they will likely try to charge you at least 100B extra as a 'stamp' or 'overtime' fee. You don't need to pay this, but if you don't they will make you wait a while before they stamp your passport.

Moving on From Poipet, there are relatively convenient connections to Battambang, Phnom Penh and Siem Reap. Avoid the overpriced taxis that hang out near the roundabout by the border, and the similar Poipet Tourist Passenger International Terminal, situated 9km east of town. Touts will try to shepherd you towards the international tourist terminal, where rates for onward buses and share taxis cost double the local rate. Alternatively, walk or take a *moto* (unmarked motorcycle taxi; 2000r) to the bus company offices near the main market, one block north of Canadia Bank off NH5, or the nearby bus station. The vast majority of buses depart in the morning (before 10.30am). If you can't get a bus, just take a share taxi – these also depart from the NH5 around Canadia Bank – onward to Siem Reap (seat/whole taxi US$5/35), Battambang (seat/whole taxi US$4.25/30) or Phnom Penh (seat/whole taxi US$8/42). The taxis that hang out near the roundabout by the border tend to charge tourists at least double.

For more information about crossing this border in the other direction, see p202.

restaurants at all busy locations, with most closing around 6pm.

★ Greenleaf Guesthouse   GUESTHOUSE $

(☑ 0 4436 5073; www.greenleaftour.com; Th Thanarat, Km 7.5; r 200-300B; ℗ 🛜) Step past the slightly chaotic common areas and you'll be surprised by the good-value rooms (with cold-water private bathrooms) at the back of this long-running family-owned place.

Park Lodging   CAMPING GROUND

(☑ 0 2562 0760; www.dnp.go.th/parkreserve; tents 150-400B; r & bungalows 800-3500B; 30% discount Mon-Thu) The Department of National Parks provides a range of clean, simple lodgings scattered through the park, starting at

GETTING TO CAMBODIA

Surin to Samraong

Getting to the border Because of Cambodia's casinos, there are plenty of minivans (60B, 1½ hours, frequent) from Surin's bus terminal to the border at Chong Chom.

At the border The border is open from 7am to 8pm. Cambodian officials will try to get you to pay for your visa in baht - usually 1000B. If you insist on paying in dollars you should be able to pay close to the real price of US$20.

Moving on Taxis are readily available to take you to Siem Reap (1600B to 2500B, depending on your negotiation skills, 2½ hours), or take a moto (US$5) to Samraong, where morning share taxis depart to Siem Reap (US$7.50, two hours).

Chong Sa-Ngam to Anlong Veng

This border crossing in Sri Saket province sees very little traffic, despite the road to Siem Reap being in excellent shape, because it can't be done by public transport.

Getting to the border Cambodian casinos occasionally run free shuttles to this border from a host of Thai towns, including Ku Khan (45 minutes), Si Sa Ket (1¼ hours) and Kantharalak (1½ hours), but schedules are sporadic. Otherwise, make your way by bus to Phusing, which is 30 minutes from the border by taxi, motorcycle taxi or casino shuttle.

At the border The border is open from 7am to 8pm. Entering Cambodia, note that they charge a premium for visas on arrival – US$25 instead of the normal US$20. You could try talking them down to the normal rate.

Moving on Motos are readily available at the border to take you 16km to Anlong Veng (US$5, with optional stops at the Khmer Rouge sites on the way). In Anlong Veng share taxis do the run to Siem Reap (20,000r, 1½ hours).

For more information about crossing these borders in the other direction, see p222.

800B for two people. Camping is 150B per person with tents and bedding included.

❶ Getting There & Away

To reach Khao Yai you need to connect to Pak Chong, which is on the highway between Bangkok (108B to 150B, 2½ hours) and Nakhon Ratchasima (Khorat; 60B to 80B, one hour). There are also minivans to/from Bangkok's Victory Monument (180B, 2½ hours, hourly from 8am to 8pm). Pak Chong is also on the train line, but trains are slower than the bus, especially if coming from Bangkok.

Sŏrngtăaou travel the 30km from Pak Chong to the park's northern gate (40B, 45 minutes, frequently from 6am to 5pm). It's another 14km to the visitor centre and Thai families piled into pick-up trucks often offer a lift. Some shops on Pak Chong's main road hire motorcycles.

Phanom Rung & Around

🗐 044

The ruins at Phanom Rung Historical Park constitute Thailand's largest and best-restored Khmer monuments. The rice-growing regions surrounding the park are peppered with dozens of minor Khmer ruins, although many are little more than jumbled piles of laterite block.

◉ Sights

A 150B combo ticket allows entry to Phanom Rung and Muang Tam at a 50B discount.

★ Phanom Rung

Historical Park   KHMER RUIN
(☑0 4466 6251; admission 100B, combined ticket with Prasat Muang Tam 150B; ⊙6am-6pm) Crowning the summit of a spent volcano, this sanctuary, originally erected as a Hindu monument to Shiva between the 10th and 13th centuries, sits a good 70 storeys above the paddy fields below.

Prasat Muang Tam   KHMER RUIN
(admission 100B; ⊙6am-6pm) In the little village of Khok Meuang, this restored Khmer temple is an ideal bolt-on to any visit to Phanom Rung, which is only 8km to the north-west. The whole complex (another shrine to Shiva) is surrounded by laterite walls, within

which are four lotus-filled reservoirs, each guarded by whimsical five-headed *naga*.

🛏 Sleeping

Phanom Rung can be undertaken as a day trip from Nakhon Ratchasima (Khorat) or Surin. But the closest place to lay your head is the town of Nang Rong, which also has vehicle and guide hire. Nang Rong is in Buriram Province and is accessible by bus from Khorat and Surin.

The village of Khok Muang, near Prasat Muang Tam, runs a **homestay** (☑08 9070 8889; per person with 3 meals 500B) program. Another overnight option is **Tanyaporn Guesthouse** (☑08 7431 3741; r 350-500B; 🅿❄❋🛜), southwest of the ruins.

⭐**P California Inter Hostel** GUESTHOUSE $ (☑08 1808 3347; www.pcalifornianangrong.webs. com; Th Sangkakrit; s 250-500B, d 300-600B; 🅿❄❋🛜) This great place on the east side of town offers bright, nicely decorated rooms with good value in all price ranges. English-speaking owner Khun Wicha is a wealth of knowledge about the area and leads tours. A motorcycle taxi from the bus station costs 50B.

The Park HOTEL $$ (☑0 4463 3778; www.theparknangrong.com; Th Praditpana; r 590-1000; 🅿❄❋🛜) One of several new midrange hotels in Nang Rong, The Park is the loveliest, with all of its fairly priced rooms around a quiet, lovely garden. It's southeast of the bus station.

❶ Getting There & Away

Phanom Rung is not directly accessible from Isan's major towns. Those coming from or heading to Ubon Ratchathani (263B, 4½ hours, hourly), Surin (80B, two hours, every 30 minutes), Nakhon Ratchasima (Khorat; 75B to 95B, two hours, hourly), Pak Chong (122B, 2½ hours, hourly) or Bangkok (231B to 275B, five hours, hourly) have the option of getting off at Ban Tako, a well-marked turn-off about 14km east of Nang Rong and waiting for one of the buses or *sŏrngtăaou* from Nang Rong, or just taking a motorcycle taxi (300B return) all the way to Phanom Rung.

To get to the historical park from Nang Rong, hop on a *sŏrngtăaou* (25B, 30 minutes, every 30 minutes) that leaves from the old market at the east end of town and goes to Ban Ta Pek, where motorcycle taxi drivers charge 200B to Phanom Rung including waiting time.

Motorcycle-taxi drivers will add Prasat Muang Tam onto Phanom Rung for about 150B.

Surin & Around

📞044 / POP 42,000

A distinct Cambodian influence has long infiltrated the border into Surin, which was once the western frontier of the Angkor kingdom and later a safe refuge for Cambodians fleeing conflict in their homeland. Today the province is known for elephants and silk weaving, and the provincial capital of the same name is a good base for visiting nearby craft villages and Khmer ruins.

👁 Sights & Activities

Craft Villages HANDICRAFTS The province's distinct textiles reflect many Khmer influences and use natural dyes and delicate silk fibres. **Ban Tha Sawang** is one of the country's most famous weaving centres, specialising in the intensive handwoven *pâh yók torng*, which requires four weavers, as well as more mainstream varieties. The village is 8km west of Surin city via Rte 4026, and *sŏrngtăaou* (15B, 20 minutes) run regularly from the market in Surin.

Eighteen kilometres north of Surin via Rtes 214 and 3036 are **Ban Khwao Sinarin** and **Ban Chok**, which are known for silk and silver respectively, though you can buy some of both in each village. Big blue *sŏrngtăaou* to Ban Khwao Sinarin (25B, 30 minutes, hourly) park on an unnamed soi between the fountain and the train station – look for the 'Osram' signs.

⭐**Surin Project** ELEPHANT ENCOUNTER (☑08 4482 1210; www.surinproject.org) If you'd like to spend some quality time with Surin's elephants, sign up for a course at this excellent centre, where options range from an

---

DON'T MISS

ELEPHANT ROUNDUP

Surin's biggest tourist draw is the **Elephant Roundup**, celebrated in November with 10 days of pachyderm pageantry. On the last weekend, there's a buffet spread set out for the creatures and a mock battle involving hundreds of elephants re-enacting their roles as war machines. Tickets for the show start at 40B, but VIP seats (500B) come with shade and English commentary.

hour of elephant bathing (400B) to week-long volunteering stints (13,000B). A homestay (per person 200B, meals 50-100B) program is also available.

Surin Project is located in the Suai village of Ban Ta Klang. *Sŏrngtăaou* run from Surin's bus terminal (60B, 1½ hours, hourly), with the last one returning at 4pm.

🛏 Sleeping & Eating

⭐ Baan Chang Ton   HOMESTAY $
(☑08 7459 8962; www.baanchangton.com; Th Suriyarart; r 400-500B; 🅿🌀❄@📶) This old wooden house is quite simple (shared bathrooms, mattresses on the floor, and air-conditioning in only one room) but the atmosphere makes it special. It's on a mostly quiet side street south of *săh·lah glahng* (provincial hall).

Surin Majestic Hotel   HOTEL $$
(☑0 4471 3980; www.surinmajestic.com; Th Jitrbumrung; r incl breakfast 1200-1400B, ste 2200-4500B; 🅿🌀❄@📶🏊) The rooms here are nothing special, but they can fetch these high prices because they're the best in town and there are also plenty of extras, including a swimming pool and fitness room. It's next to the bus station in the heart of town.

Petmanee 2   NORTHEASTERN THAI $
(Th Murasart; dishes 20-80B; ☉9am-3pm) This simple spot south of Ruampaet Hospital by Wat Salaloi (look for the large chicken grill) is Surin's most famous purveyor of *sôm·dam* and *gài yâhng* (grilled chicken).

Night Market   NORTHEASTERN THAI $
(Th Krungsri Nai; ☉5-10pm) A block south of the fountain, this good night market whips up Thai and Isan dishes.

❶ Information

Most banks in Surin are on Th Thesaban, south of the train station.

Ruampaet Hospital (☑0 4451 3192; Th Thesaban 1)

Tourism Authority of Thailand (TAT; ☑0 4451 4447; tatsurin@tat.or.th; Th Thesaban 1; ☉8.30am-4.30pm) Across from Ruampaet Hospital.

❶ Getting There & Away

Surin's **bus terminal** (☑0 4451 1756; Th Jitrbumrung) and **train station** (cnr Th Nong Toom & Th Thawasan) are both near the centre of town. To check timetables and prices for other destinations for the latter, call the **State Railway of Thailand** (☑nationwide call centre 1690; www.railway.co.th) or look at its website.

Ubon Ratchathani อุบลราชธานี

☑045 / POP 107,000

A veritable metropolis among the rice fields, Ubon Ratchathani (better known as Ubon) claims a deep cultural connection with neighbouring Laos. The city can appear bland but its riverine area along Mae Nam Mun, Thailand's second-longest waterway, is a textbook example of laid-back living.

◎ Sights & Activities

The main thing Thai visitors want to see is the 7cm-tall Phra Kaew Busarakham (Topaz Buddha) in the *bòht* (chapel) at **Wat Si Ubon Rattanaram** (วัดศรีอุบลรัตนาราม; Th Uparat; ☉dawn-dusk) **FREE**. Most foreign visitors are more fascinated by **Wat Thung Si Meuang** (วัดทุ่งศรีเมือง; Th Luang; ☉dawn-dusk) **FREE**, which has a photogenic *hŏr drai* (Tripitaka library) on stilts in the middle of a pond and **Wat Jaeng** (วัดแจ้ง; Th Nakhonban; ☉dawn-dusk) **FREE** with its adorable little Lan Xang–style chapel.

Ubon Ratchathani National Museum   MUSEUM
(พิพิธภัณฑสถานแห่งชาติอุบลราชธานี; Th Kheuan Thani; admission 100B; ☉9am-4pm Wed-Sun) Oc-

---

TRANSPORT FROM SURIN

DESTINATION	BUS	MINIVAN	TRAIN
Aranya Prathet	234B; 6hr; 5 daily	N/A	N/A
Bangkok	272-543B; 7hr; frequent	N/A	73-1146B, 7-9hr; 9 daily
Chong Chom (for Cambodia)	N/A	60B; 1½ hours; frequent	N/A
Nakhon Ratchasima (Khorat)	125-175B; 4hr; every 30min	N/A	N/A
Ubon Ratchathani	105-200B; 3hr; every 2hr	N/A	31-382B; 2-4hr; 10 daily

Ubon Ratchathani

cupying the former city hall, this is a very informative museum with plenty on show, from Dvaravati-era Buddhist ordination-precinct stones to Ubon textiles.

Ubon Ratchathani Art & Culture Centre   MUSEUM
(ศูนย์ศิลปวัฒนธรรมกาญจนาภิเษกฯ; Th Jaeng Sanit; ⊙8.30am-4.30pm Mon-Sat) FREE The museum in the lower level of this striking contemporary Isan-design tower at Rajabhat University is more scattershot than the National Museum, but there are some interesting cultural displays, particularly of houses and handicrafts.

🛏 Sleeping & Eating

★**Sri Isan Hotel**   HOTEL **$**
(📞0 4526 1011; www.sriisanhotel.com; Th Ratchabut; r incl breakfast 450-800B; 🅿❄✳@🛜) The exception to the rule of Isan's typically uninspired budget hotels. The rooms are

Ubon Ratchathani

◎ Top Sights
1 Wat Thung Si Meuang C3

◎ Sights
2 Ubon Ratchathani National
    Museum A3
3 Wat Jaeng B1
4 Wat Si Ubon Rattanaram A3

🛏 Sleeping
5 Sri Isan Hotel B4

🍴 Eating
6 Porntip Gai Yang Wat Jaeng B1
7 Rung Roj B1

🛍 Shopping
8 Camp Fai Ubon C2
9 Grass-Root B3
10 Punchard A2
11 Punchard B3
12 Rawang Thang B3
13 Walking Street Market B3

TRANSPORT FROM UBON RATCHATHANI

DESTINATION	AIR	BUS	TRAIN
Bangkok	from 1350B; 65min; 9 daily	420-603B; 8½-10hr; frequent	95-1280B; 8½-12hr; 6 daily
Mukdahan	N/A	75-135B; 3½hr; every 30min	N/A
Nakhon Ratchasima	N/A	286-445B; 5-6hr; 14 daily	58-186B; 5h; 7 daily
Nang Rong (for Phanom Rung Historical Park)	N/A	263B; 4½; hourly	N/A
Pakse (Laos)	N/A	200B; 3hr; 9.30am & 3.30pm	N/A
Surin	N/A	105-200B; 3hr; every 2hr	30-100B; 3hr; 10 daily

small, and rather ordinary compared to the lobby (look at several before deciding), and the air-conditioning takes a while to cool them down, but Sri Isan has a great location for exploration and it's good for the price.

★ **Outside Inn**   GUESTHOUSE $$
(☑ 08 8581 2069; www.theoutsideinnubon.com; Th Suriyat; r incl breakfast 450-790B; P 🌀 🌀 🌀) The rooms here are large and comfy, though the 450B rate only gets you ceiling fans instead of air-con. It's a long walk to the town's main attractions, but bikes (50B per day) and motorcycles (250B to 300B per day) can be hired and *sŏrngtăaou* 10 can deliver you from the bus station.

★ **Rung Roj**   THAI $
(Th Nakhonban; dishes 45-280B; ☺ 9.30am-8.30pm; 🌀) What this Ubon institution lacks in service, it more than makes up for with excellent food using family recipes and only fresh ingredients. It's the restaurant with the bold plate, fork and spoon sign.

Porntip Gai Yang
Wat Jaeng   NORTHEASTERN THAI $
(Th Saphasit; dishes 20-130B; ☺ 8am-8pm) This is considered by many to be Ubon's premier purveyor of *gài yâhng, sôm·đam,* sausages and other classic Isan foods.

🛍 Shopping

The speciality of Ubon Province is natural-dyed, hand-woven cotton and you'll find a fantastic assortment at **Grass-Root** (Th Yutthaphan; ☺ 10am-5pm) and **Camp Fai Ubon** (Th Thepyothi; ☺ 8.30am-5pm). **Punchard** (Th Ratchabut; ☺ 8am-7pm) and **Punchard 2** (Th Pha Daeng; ☺ 9am-7pm) stock a wider array of handicrafts.

★ **Rawang Thang**   HANDICRAFTS
(Th Kheuan Thani; ☺ 8am-8pm Mon-Thu, 8am-9pm Fri-Sun) In addition to Ubon cotton, this Isan-themed shop sells fun and funky T-shirts, pillows, postcards, picture frames and assorted bric-a-brac, most made and designed by the friendly husband-and-wife owners. They can fill you in on all things Ubon.

Walking Street Market   MARKET
(Th Ratchabut; ☺ 6-11pm Fri-Sun) This fun, youthful market takes over Th Ratchabut on weekends.

ℹ Information

Ying Charoen Park (Th Ratchathani; ☺ 10.30am-7pm), near Rajabhat university, has the extended-hours banks nearest to downtown.

Tourism Authority of Thailand (TAT; ☑ 0 4524 3770; tatubon@tat.or.th; Th Kheuan Thani; ☺ 8.30am-4.30pm) Has helpful staff.

Ubonrak Thonburi Hospital (☑ 0 4526 0285; Th Phalorangrit) 4-hour casualty department.

ℹ Getting There & Away

Ubon's airport is about 1km north of the city; a taxi costs only 100B. **Thai Airways International** (THAI; ☑ 0 4531 3340; www.thaiairways.com) flies to/from Bangkok's Suvarnabhumi International Airport, while **Air Asia** (☑ 0 2515 9999; www.airasia.com) and **Nok Air** (☑ 0 2900 9955; www.nokair.com) fly to/from Bangkok's Don Muang International Airport.

Ubon's **bus terminal** (☑ 0 4531 6085) is north of the town centre, just off Th Chayangkun, accessible via *sŏrngtăaou* 2, 3 and 10.

The **train station** (☑ 0 4532 1588) is in Warin Chamrap; take *sŏrngtăaou* 2 from Ubon. To check timetables and prices for other destinations call the **State Railway of Thailand** (☑ nationwide call centre 1690; www.railway.co.th) or look at its website.

Mukdahan & Around

☑ 042 / POP 32,000

A ho-hum river town, Mukdahan went from forgettable to integral thanks to the 2006 opening of the Thai-Lao Friendship Bridge 2, which links northeastern Thailand to the Lao city of Savannakhet.

⊙ Sights

Talat Indojin   MARKET
(ตลาดอินโดจีน; ☺8am-6pm) Most Thai tour groups on their way to Laos and Vietnam make a shopping stop at this market for cheap food, clothing, and assorted trinkets from China and Vietnam, and silk and cotton fabrics made in Isan.

Hor Kaew Mukdahan   MUSEUM
(หอแก้วมุกดาหาร; Th Samut Sakdarak; admission 50B; ☺8am-6pm) The nine-sided base of this eye-catching 65m-tall tower has a good museum with displays on the eight ethnic groups of the province. There are great views and a few more historical displays in 'The 360° of Pleasure in Mukdahan by the Mekong' room up at the 50m level.

🛏 Sleeping & Eating

Ban Rim Suan   HOTEL $
(☑0 4263 2980; www.banrimsuan.weebly.com; Th Samut Sakdarak; r 350B; P ➾ ✻ @ ☞) You can't call it lovely, but the owners have made some effort to liven things up here and that helps make this the best budget deal in town.

★ Riverview Maekhong Hotel   HOTEL $$
(☑0 4263 3323; Th Samran Chaikhongthi, r 650B; P ✻ @ ☞) This funky place south of Talat Indojin has good rooms and a great location. Add the friendly staff, free bikes and wooden terrace overlooking the river and it's our favourite place in Mukdahan.

★ Bao Pradit   NORTHEASTERN THAI $
(Th Samran Chaikhongthi; dishes 30-280B; ☺10am-10pm; ☞) It's a bit of a trek south of the centre (look for the Coke sign), but this is a real Isan restaurant with dishes including *gôy kài mót daang* (raw beef with lemon, chilli, fish sauce and red ant eggs) and *gaang wǎi* (rattan curry).

Night Market   THAI, VIETNAMESE $
(Th Song Nang Sathit; ☺4-9pm) Mukdahan's night market has all the Thai and Isan classics, but it's the Vietnamese vendors that set it apart.

ℹ Getting There & Away

Mukdahan's **bus terminal** (☑0 4263 0486) is on Rte 212, west of town. To get there from the centre catch a yellow *sǒrngtǎaou* (10B, 6am to 5pm) running west along Th Phitak Phanomkhet.

Nakhon Phanom   นครพนม

☑ 042 / POP 35,000

In Sanskrit-Khmer, Nakhon Phanom means 'City of Hills', but it refers to the hills across the river in Laos. The fabulous views befit this somnolent town, as does the scattering of graceful French colonial buildings.

⊙ Sights

Nakhon Phanom's **temples** have a distinctive style. This was once an important town in the Lan Xang empire and later a vivid Vietnamese and French influence added to the mix. The Tourism Authority of Thailand office (p410) has a good city map for a DIY architectural tour.

Ho Chi Minh's House   MUSEUM
(บ้านโฮจิมินห์; ☑0 4252 2430; entry by donation; ☺dawn-dusk) The Vietnamese community in Ban Na Chok village, about 3.5km west of town, has built a replica of Udon Thani's Uncle Ho's House, the simple wooden house where Ho Chi Minh sometimes stayed (1928–29) while planning his resistance movement. There are more displays, some labelled in English, in the Ho Chi Minh Museum (☑08 0315 4630; admission free; ☺8am-4pm), a bit to the northwest at the community centre.

Former Governor's Residence Museum   MUSEUM
(จวนผู้ว่าราชการจังหวัดนครพนม (หลังเก่า); Th Sunthon Wijit; ☺9am-5pm Wed-Sun) **FREE** This museum fills a beautifully restored 1925 mansion with photos of old Nakhon Phanom,

---

TRANSPORT FROM MUKDAHAN

DESTINATION	BUS	MINIVAN
Bangkok	420-533B; 10; frequent 5-8pm	N/A
Nakhon Phanom	N/A	80B; 2hr; every 30min
Ubon Ratchathani	75-135B; 3½hr; every 30min	105B; 2½hr; every 30min

many labelled in English, while in the back are displays about the Illuminated Boat Procession.

✷✷ Festivals & Events

Lai Reua Fai CULTURAL
(Illuminated Boat Procession; ◷ late Oct/early Nov) The city pays its respect to the Mekong with the annual Illuminated Boat Procession. Giant bamboo rafts decorated with thousands of handmade lanterns are set afloat, followed by a week of festivities including boat races and music competitions. Everything in town gets booked up during this period.

🛏 Sleeping & Eating

You're likely to meet the Vietnamese-style baguette sandwich at some of the river promenade restaurants.

SP Residence HOTEL **$**
(📞0 4251 3500; Th Nittayo; r 450-800B; P⊕❄@🛜) Plain but modern, the rooms here are less institutional than the exterior and hallways would lead you to believe, and for just a few extra baht it's better than the city's older hotels in this price range.

TC Apartment HOTEL **$$**
(📞0 4251 2212; Th Sunthon Wijit; r incl breakfast 690B; P⊕❄🛜) One of many new hotels in Nakhon Phanom, TC gets our vote as the best of the bunch for its central location and big river views from the balconies.

Indochina Market THAI **$**
(Th Sunthon Wijit; ◷7am-7pm) The balcony fronting this small food court has choice seats that frame the mountain views.

Luk Tan INTERNATIONAL-THAI **$**
(Th Bamrung Meuang; dishes 39-149B; ◷5-10pm Wed-Sun) This quirky little spot does Thai-style steaks and fa·ràng favourites including some delicious mashed potatoes. Owner Bai-Tong is a great source of local advice.

ℹ Information

Tourism Authority of Thailand (TAT; 📞0 4251 3490; tatphnom@tat.or.th; Th Sunthon Wijit; ◷8.30am-4.30pm) Covers Nakhon Phanom, Sakon Nakhon and Mukdahan Provinces.

ℹ Getting There & Away

Air Asia (📞0 2515 9999; www.airasia.com) and **Nok Air** (📞0 2900 9955; www.nokair.com) fly daily to/from Bangkok's Don Muang International Airport (from 2600B, 40 minutes). An airport shuttle drops passengers at any in-town hotel for 100B per person.

Nakhon Phanom's **bus terminal** (📞0 4251 3444; Th Fuang Nakhon) is west of the town centre.

Nong Khai หนองคาย

📞042 / POP 61,500
A riverside darling, Nong Khai lounges along the leafy banks of the Mekong River, enjoying the river view and its proximity to the Friendship Bridge, an important border crossing for travellers en route to Laos. The town has cultivated one of Isan's few guesthouse scenes and boasts a surreal sculpture park that concretes religious visions into 3-D.

◉ Sights & Activities

★**Sala Kaew Ku** SCULPTURE PARK
(admission 20B; ◷8am-6pm) One of Thailand's most enigmatic attractions is this fantastical sculpture park inspired by a mystic shaman. The larger-than-life sculptures depict the Hindu and Buddhist deities and stories (examples include a pack of anthropomorphic dogs, a 25m-high Buddha statue and a Wheel of Life, which you enter through a giant mouth) and represent one of Thailand's most striking examples of modern religious art.

TRANSPORT FROM NAKHON PHANOM

DESTINATION	AIR	BUS	MINIVAN
Bangkok	from 1000B; 70min; 1 daily	447-893B; 11-12hr; frequent 7-8am & 5-7pm	N/A
Mukdahan	N/A	N/A	80B; 2½hr;
Nong Khai	N/A	210B; 6½hr; 4 daily	N/A
Tha Khaek (Laos)	N/A	70-75B; 2hr; 8 daily 8am-5pm	N/A
Ubon Ratchathani	N/A	229B; 4½hr; 7am	162B; 4hr; 7 daily
Udon Thani	N/A	170-220B; 4½hr; frequent	N/A

Central Nong Khai

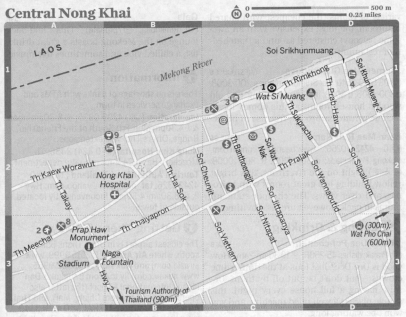

All buses headed east from Nong Khai pass the road leading to Sala Kaew Ku (10B), which is about 2km east of town and is also known as Wat Kaek. It's about a five-minute walk from the highway. Chartered túk-túk should cost 150B return with a one-hour wait or you can bike it in about 30 minutes.

Wat Pho Chai BUDDHIST TEMPLE
(วัดโพธิ์ชัย; Th Phochai; ⊙7am-7.30pm) FREE
Luang Po Phra Sai, a large Lan Xang–era Buddha image awash with gold, bronze and precious stones, sits at the hub of Nong Khai's holiest temple.

Tha Sadet Market MARKET
(ตลาดท่าเสด็จ; Th Rimkhong; ⊙8.30am-6pm)
Offers the usual mix of clothes, electronic equipment, food and assorted bric-a-brac, most of it imported from Laos and China, but there are also a few shops selling quirky quality stuff.

Volunteering in Nong Khai VOLUNTEERING
Nong Khai has also sprouted grassroots volunteer organisations, like **Isara** (☎0 4246 0827; www.isara.org) and **Open Mind Projects** (☎08 7233 5734; www.openmind-projects.org), which place travellers in teaching and volunteering positions in and around Nong Khai.

Central Nong Khai

🛏 Sleeping

Catering to the steady flow of backpackers heading to Laos, Nong Khai's budget offerings are the best in Isan.

★ **Mut Mee Garden Guesthouse** GUESTHOUSE $
(☎0 4246 0717; www.mutmee.com; Soi Mutmee; r 180-1500B; ❄❅☎) Occupying a sleepy stretch of the Mekong, Nong Khai's budget old-timer has a relaxing garden and a huge

variety of rooms (the cheapest with shared bathroom, the most expensive with an awesome balcony) clustered around a thatched-roof restaurant.

Joomemalee Guesthouse GUESTHOUSE $
(☑08 5010 2540; Soi Srikhunmuang; s 200-300B, d 300-450B, q 800B; P🖳❄🕸🛜) Filling two old wooden houses, rooms at this homey locale include private bathroom; free use of bikes.

Baan Mae Rim Nam HOTEL $$
(☑0 4242 0256; www.baanmaerimnam.com; Mekong Promenade; d 500-700B, tr 800-1000B; 🖳❄🛜) Right on the riverfront, this bright yellow building has great rooms with balconies and river views. The cheaper standard rooms in back, however, are less inviting.

✖ Eating & Drinking

★ Dee Dee Pohchanah THAI $
(Th Prajak; dishes 45-250B; ⊘10.30am-2am) How good is Dee Dee? Just look at the dinnertime crowds – but don't be put off by them. Despite having a full house every night, this simple place is a well-oiled machine and you won't be waiting long.

★ Saap Lai NORTHEASTERN THAI $
(Th Meechai; dishes 25-150B; ⊘7am-8pm) For excellent *gài yâhng, sôm·dam* and other Isan foods, follow your nose to this no-frills shop.

Daeng Namnuang VIETNAMESE $
(Th Rimkhong; dishes 60-130B; ⊘8am-8pm; P🛜) This massive river restaurant has grown into an Isan institution, and hordes of out-of-towners head home with car boots and carry-on bags stuffed with *năam new·ang* (pork spring rolls).

Gaia BAR
(Th Rimkhong; ⊘7pm-late) This laid-back lounge on the Mekong boasts a great drinks list, a chilled vibe and sometimes live music.

❶ Information
There is no shortage of banks with ATMs and exchange services in town.

Immigration (☑0 4299 0935; ⊘8.30am-noon & 1-4.30pm Mon-Fri) South of the Friendship Bridge. Offers Thai visa extensions.

Nong Khai Hospital (☑0 4241 3456; Th Meechai) Has a 24-hour casualty department.

Tourism Authority of Thailand (TAT; ☑0 4242 1326; tat_nongkhai@yahoo.com; Hwy 2; ⊘8.30am-4.30pm) Inconveniently located outside of town.

❶ Getting There & Away
The closest airport is in Udon Thani, 55km south, where **Air Asia** (☑0 2515 9999; www.airasia.com) and **Nok Air** (☑0 2900 9955; www.nokair.com) fly to/from Bangkok's Don Muang International Airport (the latter also operates a flight to/from Chiang Mai), and **Thai Airways International** (THAI; ☑0 4531 3340; www.thaiairways.com) flies to/from Bangkok's Suvarnabhumi International Airport. **Udonkaew Tour** (☑0 4241 1530; Th Pranang Cholpratan; ⊘8.30am-5.30pm) runs minivans from Nong Khai to the airport (per person 150B).

Nong Khai's bus terminal is just off Th Prajak, about 1.5km from the main pack of riverside guesthouses.

Nong Khai train station (☑0 4241 1592) is 2km west of downtown. To check timetables and prices for other destinations call the **State Railway of Thailand** (☑ nationwide call centre 1690; www.railway.co.th) or look at its website.

TRANSPORT FROM NONG KHAI

DESTINATION	AIR	BUS	MINIVAN	TRAIN
Bangkok	from 1500B; 1hr; 13 daily (from Udon Thani)	380-762B; 11hr; frequent	N/A	103-1317B; 11½hr; 3 daily
Chiang Mai	from 2199B; 80min; 3 daily (from Udon Thani)	666-888B; 12hr; 10 daily	N/A	N/A
Loei	N/A	130B; 6½hr; 7.30am	N/A	N/A
Nakhon Phanom	N/A	210B; 6½hr; 4 daily	N/A	N/A
Udon Thani	N/A	40-45B; 1hr; every 30min	50B; 45min; hourly	11-175B; 1hr; 3 daily
Vang Vieng (Laos)	N/A	270B; 4hr; 10am	N/A	N/A
Vientiane (Laos)	N/A	55-60B; 1hr; 6 daily	N/A	20-30B; 15min; 9am & 2.45pm

GETTING TO LAOS: SOUTHERN BORDERS

Mukdahan to Savannakhet

This crossing can also be used as a relatively convenient corridor to Vietnam. Note that, since the construction of the Thai-Lao Friendship Bridge 2 in 2006, non-Thai and non-Lao citizens are no longer allowed to cross between Mukdahan and Savannakhet by boat.

Getting to the border Buses to Savannakhet (50B, hourly from 7.30am to 7pm) depart from Mukdahan's bus terminal and the trip will take from one to two hours depending on the length of the immigration queues.

At the border The border is open from 6am to 10pm; Lao visas are available on arrival.

Moving on Savannakhet's airport has connections to Vientiane (895,000K, 55 minutes), and its bus terminal has connections to Vientiane (75,000K, eight to 11 hours) approximately every 30 minutes from 6am to 11.30am, and a sleeper VIP at 9.30pm (120,000K, six to eight hours); otherwise you'll have to catch buses from Pakse that also stop at Tha Khaek (30,000K, 2½ to four hours) until 10pm.

There are also buses bound for Vietnam, with destinations including Dong Ha (80,000K, seven hours), departing at 8am on even-numbered dates; Hue (90,000-110,000K, 13 hours, 10.30am and 10pm); and Danang (110,000K, 10 hours) on Tuesday, Thursday and Saturday at 10pm, continuing to Hanoi (200,000K, about 24 hours).

For more information about crossing this border in the other direction, see p330.

Ubon Ratchathani to Pakse

Getting to the border Almost every traveller coming through the Chong Mek/Vang Tao crossing uses the direct Ubon Ratchathani-Pakse buses (200B, three hours, 9.30am and 3.30pm), which wait long enough to buy Lao visas at the border. Otherwise, Chong Mek's little bus terminal serves *sŏrngtăaou* from Phibun Mangsahan (40B, one hour, frequent) and minivans from Ubon (100B, 1¼ hours, every 30 minutes) via Phibun (50B). It's nearly 1km from the bus station to the border: motorcycle taxis and túk-túk charge 20B.

At the border The border is open from 6am to 8pm; Lao visas are available upon arrival.

Moving on If you're not on the international bus, Pakse is about an hour away in one of the frequent *sŏrngtăaou* that run there until 4pm (10,000K). Pakse's five bus stations have relatively frequent connections to most other parts of Laos, and the airport has connections to Vientiane, Savannakhet, Siem Reap (Cambodia) and Ho Chi Minh City (Vietnam).

For more information about crossing this border in the other direction, see p339.

Nakhon Phanom to Tha Khaek

Passenger ferries cross the Mekong to Tha Khaek in Laos, but they're for Thai and Lao citizens only. All others must use the Thai-Lao Friendship Bridge 3, north of the city. This crossing can also be used to access Vietnam.

Getting to the border Buses from Nakhon Phanom's bus station to Tha Khaek run between 8am and 5pm (70B to 75B, two hours, eight daily).

At the border The border is open from 6am to 10pm; Lao visas are available on arrival.

Moving on Tha Khaek's bus station, about 3.5km from the centre of town, has buses bound north to Vientiane (70,000K to 85,000K, six hours, hourly 4am to midnight) and south to Savannakhet (30,000K, two to three hours, every 30 minutes), Pakse (70,000K, six to seven hours, hourly) and Attapeu (85,000K, 10 hours, 3.30pm and 11pm).

If you're heading to Vietnam, a bus for Hue (120,000K) leaves every Monday, Tuesday, Wednesday, Saturday and Sunday at 8pm. There are also departures for Danang (120,000K) every Monday and Friday at 8pm, and for Hanoi (160,000K) at 8pm on Tuesday and Saturday.

For more information about crossing this border in the other direction, see p330.

River Road: Nong Khai to Loei

The River Rd (Th Kaew Worawut) west of Nong Khai is lined by flood-plain fields of tobacco, tomatoes and chillies and leads to a series of sleepy market towns and hamlets that hardly make a blip on the national radar.

Mainly a day trip from Nong Khai, **Tha Bo** makes its money by using its noodle – the production of noodles that is. A large Vietnamese population has cornered the rice-noodle industry, a handmade process that occurs on the west side of town near the hospital. From about 5am to 10am you can watch people at the factories making the noodles, and then around 2pm they start the cutting. Afterwards the hairlike strands are set out to dry in the sun.

A yellow bus runs regularly between Nong Khai's bus station and Tha Bo (27B, one hour, every 30 minutes), taking the scenic riverside route.

At a scenic stretch of the Mekong where giant boulders rise out of the watery depths, **Wat Hin Mak Peng** (วัดหินหมากเป้ง; ⊘ 6am-7pm) **FREE** is hidden away in a cool bamboo grove. The monks here have taken ascetic vows in addition to the standard 227 precepts, eating only once a day and wearing robes sewn by hand from torn pieces of cloth. The current abbot requests that visitors dress politely: no shorts or sleeveless tops.

The temple is midway between Si Chiangmai and Sangkhom. Sangkhom-bound buses from Nong Khai (50B, 2¼ hours) pass the wát, and then it's a longish walk.

Seductively sleepy, the little town of **Sangkhom** is a convenient layover between Nong Khai and Loei. The town looks out at the Lao island of Don Klang Khong (as per border agreements, all river islands belong to Laos) and the river dominates life here. Just after the wet season, the town's main attractions are its waterfalls: the three-tiered **Nam Tok Than Thip**, 13km west of Sang-

---

OFF THE BEATEN TRACK

BEUNG KAN & AROUND

From Nakhon Phanom, the river-fronting road loops around the northeastern hump of Thailand to **Beung Kan**, a dusty riverside pit stop. During the dry season the Mekong recedes here to its narrowest point along the Thailand–Laos border. Beyond river trivia and the **Thai-Lao Market** every Tuesday and Friday morning, the area surrounding Beung Kan has a few untouristed attractions that might waylay curious visitors.

If you decide to stay, the Mekong-facing **Maenam Hotel** (✆ 0 4249 1051; Th Chansin; r 400-450B; P ⊛ ❉ @ 🖝) has the best views in town. Many restaurants set up tables along the riverside promenade at dinnertime.

Buses to Nong Khai (100B to 150B, 3½ hours, eight daily), Nakhon Phanom (140B, 3½ hours, four daily) and Udon Thani (130B to 150B, 4½ hours, 12 daily) park near the old clock tower. Beung Kan is also a legal border crossing into Laos.

Planted on a giant sandstone outcrop southeast of Beung Kan, **Wat Phu Tok** (วัดภู ทอก; Isolated Mountain Temple; ⊘ 6am-5pm, closed 10-16 Apr) **FREE** is a forest monastery known for its meditative isolation. Seven levels of stairs scramble up the mountain past shrines and monastic residences built in caves and clutching at cliffs. The final flight represents the last ascent to enlightenment and rewards climbers with vistas over the surrounding countryside.

Túk-túk in Beung Kan can be hired for the return journey to/from Wat Phu Tok for about 800B. It's cheaper to take a bus from Beung Kan to Ban Siwilai (30B, 45 minutes) where túk-túk drivers will do it for 350B. If you catch an early bus to Beung Kan, Wat Phu Tok can be visited as a day trip from Nong Khai, although there's no need to backtrack since buses from Siwilai go to Udon Thani (140B, four hours, last bus 4.45pm).

Another nearby attraction is the 186-sq-km **Phu Wua Wildlife Reserve**, home to several herds of elephants. The reserve can be easily visited through the excellent **Kham Pia Homestay** (✆ 08 7861 0601, 0 4241 3578; www.thailandwildelephanttrekking. com; per r 200B, meals 50-90B). Buses between Nong Khai (150B, 3½ hours) and Nakhon Phanom (130B, three hours) will drop you off at the Ban Don Chik highway junction, 3km away.

EMERALD TRIANGLE

A tourism-brochure conceit, the Emerald Triangle refers to the tri-border area of Thailand, Laos and Cambodia. On the Thai side, this new moniker has been bestowed on most of Ubon Ratchathani Province and some of Si Saket Province.

In the northeastern part of Ubon Province, the Mae Nam Mun (Mun River) joins the Mekong River just before it does an oxbow into Laos. The geographic confluence of the two rivers occurs at **Khong Jiam**, where Thais come to see 'Mae Nam Song Si' (Two-Coloured River). In the wet season the bicoloured merger is visible from the shore, but is best seen in a boat (200B to 350B). Since 2005 the famous and unexplained *naga* fireball phenomenon (p416) has appeared here.

Up the Mekong from Khong Jiam is **Pha Taem National Park** (☑ 0 4531 8026; admission 200B), whose centrepiece is a long cliff with views over to Laos and a collection of prehistoric rock paintings that are at least 3000 years old. Mural subjects include fish traps (which look similar to the conical ones still used today), *blah bèuk* (giant Mekong catfish), elephants, human hands and geometric designs.

You can catch a bus from Ubon to Khong Jiam (80B, 2½ hours) at 2pm, but there's no public transport to Pha Taem National Park. You can, however, rent a motorcycle (per day 200B to 300B) from guesthouses in Khong Jiam.

khom (2km off Rte 211), is the most spectacular but **Nam Tok Than Thong**, 11km east of Sangkhom, is easier to get to and has a swimmable pool at the bottom. It dries up around April.

Sangkhom's veteran lodge, **Bouy Guesthouse** (☑ 0 4244 1065; toy_bgh@hotmail.com; Rte 211; s 250-280B, d 280-300B, r with air-con 500B; P❄✿@☎) has a few simple huts with hammock-strung decks overlooking the river. The hotel **Poopae Ruenmaithai** (☑ 0 4244 1088, Rte 211, r 700-1500B, P⊖✿@☎) is more modern.

To Sangkhom, there are three buses a day from Nong Khai (60B, three hours), the earliest of those continuing to Loei (70B, 3½ hours).

Loei   เลย
☑ 042
The city of Loei is a necessary transport hub but not nearly as endearing as its remote and mountainous countryside, much of which is sparsely inhabited and not easily cultivated. If you need to spend the night, try **Sugar Guest House** (☑ 08 9711 1975; www.sugarguesthouse.blog.com; Soi 2, Th Wisut Titep; r 200-380B; P⊖✿@☎), the cheapest and friendliest place in town.

Loei's **bus terminal** (☑ 0 4283 3586) is about 1km south of the centre of town. There are frequent departures to Bangkok (440B to 697B, 11 hours), and buses to Chiang Mai (409B to 570B, 10 hours, four daily), Nakhon Ratchasima (290B, six hours, hour-

ly), Nong Khai (130B, seven hours, 6am) and Udon Thani (100B, three hours, half-hourly).

Nok Air (☑ 0 2900 9955; www.nokair.com) connects Loei and Bangkok's Don Muang International Airport twice daily (from 1700B, 1¼ hours).

Chiang Khan   เชียงคาน
☑ 042
Virtually overnight, what was once a sleepy little-known riverside town full of traditional timber houses became a trendy destination for Thais, and now tour buses arrive in Chiang Khan daily.

The Mekong River at this point is reaching its final dramatic stretch of mountainous impediments before it slumps eastward into the flat plateau of greater Isan and beyond. The flood plain of the river is Loei's most fertile area and has the greatest population concentration. You'll see farmers and merchants frolicking at **Kaeng Khut Khu**, a series of rapids about 5km downstream from town. This is a popular recreation spot in the dry season. Most guesthouses arrange 1½-hour boat trips (around 1000B for up to 10 people) to the rapids.

Chiangkhan Riverview Guesthouse (☑ 08 0741 8055; 277 Th Chai Khong; r 300-800B; ⊖✿☎) has rooms with fan and air-con, shared and private bathrooms, and a mix of old and new construction. The friendly owners of the seven-room **Huean Yai Bab** (☑ 0 4282 1705; 340 Th Chai Khong; r incl breakfast 1500-1800B; P⊖✿☎) have combined historic touches with modern stylings.

GREAT BALLS OF FIRE

Methane gas? Drunken Lao soldiers? Clever monks? Or perhaps the fiery breath of the sacred *naga*, a serpentlike being that populates folkloric waterways throughout Southeast Asia. Since 1983 (or for ages, depending on who you ask), the sighting of the *bâng fai pá yah nâhk* (loosely translated, '*naga* fireballs') has been an annual event along the Mekong River. Sometime in the early evening, at the end of the Buddhist Rains Retreat (October), which coincides with the 15th waxing moon of the 11th lunar month, small reddish balls of fire shoot from the Mekong River and float a hundred or so metres into the air before vanishing without a trace. Most claim the *naga* fireballs are soundless, but others say a hissing can be heard if one is close enough to where they emerge from the surface of the river. Most Thai and Lao see the event as a sign that resident *naga* are celebrating the end of the holiday.

There are many theories about the fireballs. One, which aired on a Thai exposé-style TV program, claimed that Lao soldiers taking part in festivities on the other side of the Mekong were firing their rifles into the air. Interestingly, the reaction to the TV program was a storm of protest from both sides of the river. Some suggest that a mixture of methane gas and phosphane, trapped below the mud on the river bottom, somehow reaches a certain temperature at exactly that time of year and is released. Many simply assume that some monks have found a way to make a 'miracle'. The latter was the premise behind a 2002 comedy film entitled *Sìp Hâh Kâm Deuan Sìp-èt* (Fifteenth Waxing Moon of the Eleventh Lunar Month), released with English subtitles under the peculiar title *Mekhong Full Moon Party*.

Natural or manufactured, *naga* fireballs have become big business in Nong Khai Province, and curious Thais from across the country converge at various spots on the banks of the Mekong for the annual show. Little Phon Phisai, the locus of fireball-watching, hosts some 40,000 guests. Special buses (cheap or free) make the return trip to Nong Khai city, and several hotels run their own buses where you'll get a guaranteed seat. Mut Mee Garden Guesthouse (p411) sails its boat there and back (2800B, including lunch and dinner).

If you don't come with the right mindset, you'll likely be disappointed. The fireball experience is more than just watching a few small lights rise from the river; it's mostly about watching Thais watching a few small lights rise from the river. And even if the *naga* doesn't send his annual greeting on the day you come (it's sometimes delayed by a day due to the vagaries of calculating the arrival of the full moon), it will still be an interesting experience.

Sŏrngtăaou to Loei (35B, 1¼ hours) depart about every 15 minutes in the early morning from a stop on Rte 201. From a terminal 300m south, there are also eight buses bound for Nakhon Ratchasima (Khorat; 326B, seven hours). Three companies, departing from offices around town in the morning and evening, make the run direct to Bangkok (351B to 756B, 10 hours).

No transport runs direct to Nong Khai. The quickest way there is via Loei and Udon Thani, but for the scenic river route take a Loei-bound *sŏrngtăaou* south to Ban Tad (20B, 30 minutes), where you can catch the bus to Nong Khai that leaves Loei at 6am. Another option is to hire a car (about 700B) to take you to Pak Chom where there are buses to Nong Khai at 10am and 3pm (80B, four hours).

NORTHERN THAILAND

With much of today's Thailand resembling relatively flat farmland, it is surprising to encounter the mist-shrouded peaks and valleys that crown the northern reaches of Thailand. Traders and migrants from Asia's mountainous interior trickled through the river valleys bringing with them commerce and cultural attributes now geopolitically partitioned into the Yunnan Province of China, Shan state in Myanmar and the various provinces of northern Thailand. These migration routes were a southern spur of the so-called Asian silk route and these mountains are the final southeastern stretch of the great Himalayan range that acted as both a barrier and a conduit. The most enduring symbol of northern Thailand's connection to such seemingly foreign locales as the Tibetan highlands are the minority hill tribes, some of whom claim Tibetan origin but have now dispersed throughout the high-altitude valleys of the region hoping to preserve their traditional way of life.

The history and culture of northern Thailand was shaped by the Lanna kingdom (literally 'Million Rice Fields'), which is believed to have originated near present-day Chiang Saen, a border town on the west bank of the Mekong River. In the 13th century, the kingdom migrated south through Chiang Rai and finally settled in Chiang Mai. It prospered through cooperation with Sukhothai and other city-state neighbours until its defeat in 1556 by the Burmese. The occupation lasted 200 years until the Thai military leader Phaya Taksin began his campaign to push out the Burmese after the fall

GETTING TO LAOS: CENTRAL BORDERS

Beung Kan to Paksan

Getting to the border Beung Kan can be reached via bus or minivan from Nong Khai (100B to 150B, 2½ to 3½ hours, eight daily), or by bus from Nakhon Phanom (140B, 3½ hours, four daily). The border is 2.5km northwest of town; a túk-túk will cost about 60B. Boats (per person 60B) cross the Mekong (minimum eight people or by charter for 480B).

At the border The Lao border post is open from 8am to noon and 1.30pm to 4.30pm, although note that Lao visas are not available upon arrival.

Moving on Túk-túk wait on the Lao shore, though the highway and Paksan's hotels are an easy walk from the landing. From Paksan, buses leave from Rte 13 outside the market area for Vientiane (30,000K, three to four hours) between 6.05am and 4.30pm. All buses heading south from Vientiane pass through Paksan about two hours after leaving the capital; you can hop on near the morning market.

For more information about crossing this border in the other direction, see p326

Nong Khai to Vientiane

The site of the original Thai-Lao Friendship Bridge, the Nong Khai/Tha Na Long border crossing is one of the busiest Thai border crossings.

Getting to the border If you already have your Lao visa, the easiest way to reach Vientiane is the direct bus from Nong Khai's bus terminal (55B to 60B, one hour, six daily).

If you plan to get your visa at the border (open from 6am to 10pm), take a túk-túk there; expect to pay 100B from the bus station, but you can pay 60B from the town centre or train station. Unless you're travelling in a large group, there's no good reason to use a visa service agency, so don't let a driver take you to one. Bring some photo ID and extra cash (approx US$5) for administrative costs charged on weekends and holidays.

You can also go to Laos by train (there are immigration booths at both stations) though not to Vientiane, so we recommend against doing this. The 15-minute ride (20B to 30B, departs 9am and 2.45pm) drops you in Thanaleng (aka Dongphasay) station just over the bridge, leaving you at the mercy of túk-túk drivers who charge extortionate prices.

At the border After getting stamped out of Thailand, you can take the minibuses (20B to 30B) that carry passengers across the bridge to the hassle-free, but sometimes busy, Lao immigration checkpoint, where visas are available upon arrival.

Moving on A local bus (15,000K), minivans (100B), túk-túk (250B) and taxis (300B) ply the remaining 20km to Vientiane.

For more information about crossing this border in the other direction, see p288

Loei to Pak Lai

The quiet rural Tha Li/Kaen Thao border is the home of yet another (but smaller) Friendship Bridge, this time over Nam Heuang.

Getting to the border Sŏrngtăaou run the 46km between Loei and Tha Li (30B), from where you'll need another sŏrngtăaou for the remaining 8km to the border (40B).

At the border The border is open from 8am to 6pm; Lao visas are available upon arrival.

Moving on From Kaen Thao, there are two daily sŏrngtăaou to Pak Lai (40,000K, 1¾ hours), from where two daily sŏrngtăaou ply the dusty route to Sainyabuli (80,000K, four hours), and there's a daily bus to Vientiane (100,000K, six hours, 9am).

For more information about crossing this border in the other direction, see p324

of Ayuthaya. Once 'liberated', the former Lanna kingdom was beholden to the new Thai kingdom based in Bangkok and never again regained its independence, though its modern descendants continue to speak a unique regional dialect and maintain old food ways and religious traditions.

Chiang Mai เชียงใหม่

☑ 053 / POP 150,000

Chiang Mai is beloved by Thais and tourists for its (relatively) cool climate and its enduring connections to its past as the capital of the northern Thai kingdom of Lanna. It is a city of temples and culture classes and a gateway to the great outdoors of the northern mountains.

◉ Sights

Temples in Town

Chiang Mai's many temples are famous for their distinctive regional architectural styles: intricate woodcarvings, colourful murals and steeply pitched roofs.

★ **Wat Phra Singh**   BUDDHIST TEMPLE
(วัดพระสิงห์; Th Singharat; admission 20B; ⊙6am-6pm) Chiang Mai's most revered temple, Wat Phra Singh draws pilgrims and sightseers for its resident Buddha and its classic Lanna art and architecture. Visitors should dress modestly (clothing covering shoulders and knees). The temple owes its fame to the resident Buddha, Phra Singh (Lion Buddha), housed in a small chapel at the back of the compund.

Wat Chedi Luang   BUDDHIST TEMPLE
(วัดเจดีย์หลวง; Th Phra Pokklao; donations appreciated; ⊙6am-6pm) The huge ruined *chedi* (religious monument, often containing Buddha relics) at Wat Chedi Luang either collapsed during an earthquake in 1545 or from cannon fire in 1775 during the recapture of Chiang Mai from the Burmese. A partial restoration has preserved its 'ruined' look while ensuring it doesn't crumble further.

Wat Phan Tao   BUDDHIST TEMPLE
(วัดพันเถา; Th Phra Pokklao; donations appreciated; ⊙6am-6pm) This pretty little temple evokes mist-shrouded forests and the largess of the teak trade, and the large, old teak *wí-hǎhn* (sanctuary) here is one of Chiang Mai's unsung treasures.

Wat Chiang Man   BUDDHIST TEMPLE
(วัดเชียงมั่น; Th Ratchaphakhinai; donations appreciated; ⊙6am-6pm) Wat Chiang Man is believed to be the oldest *wát* within the city walls and was erected by King Mengrai, Chiang Mai's founder, in 1296. Two famous Buddha images (Phra Sila and the Crystal Buddha) are kept here in a glass cabinet inside the smaller sanctuary to the right of the main chapel.

Temples Outside Town

Wat Doi Suthep   BUDDHIST TEMPLE
(Doi Suthep-Pui National Park; admission 30B) One of Thailand's most famous temples, Wat Suthep overlooks the whole city from its mountainside perch. The temple contains many fine examples of Lanna art and architecture as well as the frequently photographed gold-plated *chedi,* topped by a five-tiered umbrella and enshrining a famous Buddha relic.

Wat U Mong   BUDDHIST TEMPLE
(วัดอุโมงค์; Soi Wat U Mong, Th Khlong Chonprathan; donations appreciated; ⊙6am-6pm) The forest temple of Wat U Mong, dating from Mengrai's rule, has brick-lined tunnels supposedly fashioned around 1380 for a clairvoyant monk; some are still open for exploration.

Wat Suan Dok   BUDDHIST TEMPLE
(วัดสวนดอก; Th Suthep; donations appreciated; ⊙6am-6pm) Built in a forest grove in 1373, Wat Suan Dok contains a 500-year-old bronze Buddha image and colourful *jataka* (past-life stories of the Buddha) murals, but the scenic sunsets over the collection of royal *chedi* are the biggest attraction.

Museums

Lanna Folklife Museum   MUSEUM
(พิพิธภัณฑ์พื้นถิ่นล้านนา; Th Phra Pokklao; adult/child 90/40B; ⊙8.30am-5pm Tue-Sun) Life-size dioramas explain northern Thai religious beliefs and customs, temple paraphernalia and symbolism, traditional crafts and other features of ordinary life. The displays have artistic merit and informative English signage and the atmospheric building, once a former royal residence and later used by the court system, is a pleasure to stroll around. Combination tickets to nearby museums are available.

Chiang Mai National Museum   MUSEUM
(พิพิธภัณฑสถานแห่งชาติเชียงใหม่; ☑ 0 5322 1308; www.thailandmuseum.com; off Th Superhighway;

admission 100B; ◐ 9am-4pm Wed-Sun) Operated by the Fine Arts Department, this museum is the primary caretaker of Lanna artefacts and northern Thai history. The museum is a nice complement to the municipally run **Chiang Mai City Arts & Cultural Centre** (หอศิลปวัฒนธรรมเชียงใหม่; ☎0 5321 7793; Th Phra Pokklao; adult/child 90/40B; ◐ 8.30am-5pm Tue-Sun) with more art and artefacts that extend beyond the city limits. The best curated section is **Lanna art**, which displays a selection of Buddha images in all styles.

🏃 Activities

Massage

Ban Hom Samunphrai   MASSAGE
(☎0 5381 7362; www.homprang.com; Saraphi; steam bath 200B, massage 600-1300B) Maw Hom ('Herbal Doctor'), a licensed herb practitioner and massage therapist, runs a traditional herbal steam bath, once a common feature of rural villages. Traditional Thai massage can be added for an upcountry 'spa' session. It is 9km from Chiang Mai near the McKean Institute.

Lila Thai Massage   MASSAGE
(Th Phra Pokklao; massage 200-600B; ◐10am-10pm) Established by the director of the Chiang Mai women's prison, Lila Thai offers post-release employment to the inmates who participated in the prison's massage training program. There are now five branches in the old city and a full menu of massage treatments.

Ping River Trips

Scorpion Tailed River Cruise   RIVER CRUISE
(☎08 1960 9398; www.scorpiontailedrivercruise.com; Th Charoenrat; ticket 500B) This river cruise focuses on the history of the Mae Ping (Ping River) using traditional-style craft,

---

DON'T MISS

PARTYING WITH GHOSTS

The otherwise uninteresting town of Dan Sai has developed a local festival so colourful and outlandish that for three days in June (sometimes July) the town is overrun with something akin to the drunken revelry of Carnival and the ghouls of Halloween.

The raucous **Phi Ta Khon Festival** coincides with the more subdued Buddhist holy day of Bun Phra Wet (Phra Wet Festival, also known as Bun Luang), honouring the penultimate life of the Buddha, Phra Wessandara (often shortened in Thai to Phra Wet) According to the story, when the prince returned to his city the village spirits were so happy that they joined with the human inhabitants in a parade. Most observations of Bun Phra Wet include silk-clad merit-makers intently listening to recitations of the *Mahavessantara Jataka* (past-life stories of the Buddha), which are supposed to enhance the listener's chances of being reborn in the lifetime of the next Buddha.

But Dan Sai's unique twist is the peculiar re-enactment of Phra Wet's return and the participation of the spirits. Villagers don clothing and wild 'spirit' costumes and masks for a day of *lâo kôw* (whisky)-fuelled dancing full of sexual innuendo. The revelries culminate with the launching of rockets (a popular fertility ritual in Isan believed to appease the guardian spirits for bountiful rains). The next day, the crowd proceeds to the temple to listen to sermons.

The origins of the festival are not known but some theorise that it is an offshoot of the spirit worship of the ethnic Tai Dam tribe. The dates for the festival are divined by Jao Phaw Kuan, a local spirit medium who invites Phra Upakud (an enlightened monk who transformed himself into a block of white marble to live eternally on the bottom of Mae Nam Mun) to come to town. Phra Upakud is believed to protect the town from evil spirits.

A couple of villages just outside of Dan Sai run a **homestay** (☎08 9077 2080; dm/tw/tr 150/550/700B, meals 70B), organised by some local English teachers. Everything can be arranged at **Kawinthip Hattakham** (กวินทิพย์หัตถกรรม; Th Kaew Asa; ◐8am-7pm), a craft shop in town that sells authentic Phi Ta Khon masks and other festival-related souvenirs.

Buses between Loei (65B to 79B, 1½ hours) and Phitsanulok (73B to 102B, three hours) stop in Dan Sai near the junction of Th Kaew Asa and Rte 2013 every couple of hours.

Central Chiang Mai

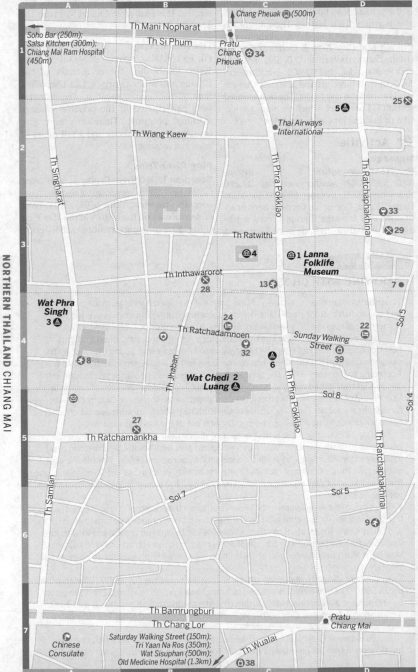

Chang Pheuak (500m)

Th Mani Nopharat

Th Si Phum

Pratu Chang Pheuak 34

Soho Bar (250m);
Salsa Kitchen (300m);
Chiang Mai Ram Hospital
(450m)

5 25

Th Wiang Kaew

Thai Airways
International

Th Phra Pokklao

Th Singharat

Th Ratchaphakhinai

33

29

Th Ratwithi

4 1 Lanna
Folklife
Museum

Th Inthawarorot

28

13 7

Soi 5

Wat Phra
Singh
3

24

Th Ratchadamnoen

22

Sunday Walking
Street

32 39

8

6

Th Jhaban

Wat Chedi 2
Luang

Th Phra Pokklao

Soi 8

Soi 4

27

Th Ratchamankha

Soi 7

Soi 5

Th Samlan

9

Th Ratchaphakhinai

Th Bamrungburi

Th Chang Lor

Pratu
Chiang Mai

Chinese
Consulate

Saturday Walking Street (150m);
Tri Yaan Na Ros (350m);
Wat Sisuphan (500m);
Old Medicine Hospital (1.3km)

Th Wualai

38

NORTHERN THAILAND CHIANG MAI

0 400 m
0 0.2 miles

Th Muang Samut

Th Wichayanon

US Consulate

Th Charoenrat

14

Mae Nam Ping

McCormick Hospital (1.5km)

Th Kaew Nawarat

Baan Orapin (200m);
Riverside Bar & Restaurant (500m)

Th Taiwang

Th Ratchawong

Th Praisani

Th Chang Moi

Mae Ping River Cruise (600m);
Baan Kaew Guest House (1.5km)

Th Chaiyaphum

Soi 9

Soi 8

Soi 7

Soi 1

21

Soi 2

Soi 6

31

Soi 5

15 Wat Dokaueng

18 23

20

16

Soi 1

Soi 2

Th Chang Moi Kao

Th Khang Mehn

Air Asia

Pratu Tha Phae

19

Th Tha Phae

Soi 2

Soi 4

Soi 3

Soi 5

Th Kamphaeng Din

17

10

12

Soi 6

Th Chang Khlan

Soi 1

Soi 1

37

Soi 2

30

Soi 2

11

26

Chiang Mai Night Bazaar

36

Soi 6

Th Loi Kroh

Riverside House (400m)

35

Soi Anusan

Soi 1

Soi 2

Th Moon Muang

Th Kotchasan

Wat Sai Moon Myanmar

Th Si Donchai

Baan Kaew Guest House (500m);
French Consulate (500m)

Central Chiang Mai

known as scorpion-tailed boats. Informative cruises (five daily) last one to 1½ hours.

Mae Ping River Cruises   RIVER CRUISE
(☑ 0 5327 4822; www.maepingrivercruise.com; 133 Th Charoen Prathet, Wat Chaimongkhon) Offers daytime cruises (450B, two hours) in roofed long-tail boats. The boats stop at a small farm for fruit snacks after touring the countryside. The Thai dinner cruise (550B, two hours, daily at 7pm) offers a set menu.

Trekking
Most Chiang Mai–based trekking outfits offer the same type of tour: a one-hour minibus ride to Mae Taeng or Mae Wang (depending on the duration of the trip), a brief hike to an elephant camp, a one-hour elephant ride to a waterfall, another hour rafting down a river and an overnight in or near a hill-tribe village. One-day treks usually cost around 1000B, while multiday treks (three days and two nights) cost 1500B. Both prices include transport, guide and lunch; in the case of overnight trips, the price also includes lodging.

Other Activities
Flight of the Gibbon   ZIPLINING
(☑ 0 5301 0660; www.treetopasia.com; 29/4-5 Th Kotchasan; 3hr tour 3400B) ⌀ This adventure outfit in Chiang Mai started the zipline craze a few years ago. Nearly 5km of wire with 33 staging platforms are strung through the forest canopy some 1300m above sea level.

**Chiang Mai Rock Climbing
Adventures**   ROCK CLIMBING
(CMRCA; ☑08 6911 1470; www.thailandclimbing.com; 55/3 Th Ratchaphakhinai; climbing course 3000-4000B) CMRCA maintains many of the climbing routes at Crazy Horse Buttress (also known as 'The Crack'). Tours teach introductory and fundamental rock climbing, bouldering and caving.

Siam River Adventures   RAFTING
(☑08 9515 1917; www.siamrivers.com; 17 Th Ratwithi; tours from 1800B) With more than a decade of experience, this white-water rafting outfit has a well-regarded safety reputation. Trips can be combined with elephant trekking and village overnight stays. It also operates kayak trips.

Chiang Mai Mountain Biking &
Kayaking MOUNTAIN BIKING
(☑ 08 1024 7046, 0 5381 4207; www.chiangmaikay
aking.com; 1 Th Samlan; tours 1550-2000B) A variety of guided mountain biking and kayaking
trips head into the jungles and rivers, respectively, for fresh air, a good workout and
mountain scenery.

🎋 Courses

Buddhist Meditation

International Buddhism Center MEDITATION
(IBC; ☑ 0 5329 5012; www.fivethousandyears.
org; Wat Phra That Doi Suthep) Headquartered
within the temple grounds at **Doi Suthep**
(วัดพระธาตุดอยสุเทพ; Th Huay Kaew, Doi Suthep;
admission 30B; ⊙ 6am-6pm), this centre offers
beginner to advanced meditation retreats,
lasting from three to 21 days.

Wat Sisuphan MEDITATION
(☑ 0 5320 0332; 100 Th Wualai; ⊙ 5.30-9pm Tue,
Thu & Sat) This temple south of the old city

offers an introduction to meditation using
the four postures: standing, walking, sitting
and lying down.

Wat Suan Dok Meditation
Retreat MEDITATION
(☑ 08 4609 1357; www.monkchat.net; Th Suthep;
⊙ Tue & Wed) The Buddhist university affiliated with Wat Suan Dok conducts a two-day
meditation retreat. Check the website for
more details.

Cooking

Several guesthouses, such as Gap's House,
also offer cookery courses. Most courses cost
about 1000B per day.

Asia Scenic Thai Cooking COOKING
(☑ 0 5341 8657; www.asiascenic.com; 31 Soi 5,
Th Ratchadamnoen; courses 900-1000B) Khun
Gayray's cooking school has expanded to include an out-of-town farm location as well
as its original in-town spot for those with
less time.

TREKKING IN NORTHERN THAILAND

Thousands of visitors trek into the hills of northern Thailand each year hoping to see fantastic mountain scenery, interact with hilltribe cultures and ride elephants. Most come with an Indiana Jones sense of adventure but leave with disappointment: the actual walk through the jungle lasted less than an hour, the hill-tribe villagers were unin- terested in the lowlanders and the other trekkers were boring. To avoid disappointment, consider the following:

➡ Talk to people who've just returned from a trek about their experience. This is also a great way to source a good guide.

➡ Make sure that your guide is licensed; Chiang Mai's TAT office (p427) has a list of accredited guides and agencies.

➡ Do your homework: ask how many people will be in the group, exactly what the trip entails, and exactly when the tour begins and ends. Is everything – food, transport – included in the fee?

➡ The best time to trek is from November to February. Outside of these months, rain, smoke and heat can be considerable obstacles.

When visiting hill-tribe villages:

➡ Don't hand out candy, pens or other small gifts. If you want to give a gift, talk to your guide beforehand about donating to the local school or health centre.

➡ Dress modestly no matter how hot and sweaty you are.

➡ Always ask for permission when taking photos.

➡ Show respect for religious symbols and rituals.

➡ Set a good example to hill-tribe youngsters by not using drugs.

Chiang Mai is not the only base for hill-tribe treks in northern Thailand, but it is the most accessible and one of the cheapest. For those looking for something different, Chiang Dao and Tha Ton are two scenic towns north of Chiang Mai that have fewer tourists and a variety of small-scale trekking options. Other somewhat less commercial trekking des- tinations include the areas around Chiang Rai, and Mae Hong Son and Nan Provinces.

DON'T MISS

MONK CHAT

If you're curious about Buddhism, many Chiang Mai temples offer 'monk chat', during which monks get to practise their English by fielding questions from visitors about religion, rituals and life in the monastery.

Wat Suan Dok (p418) has a dedicated room just beyond the main sanctuary hall and holds its chats from 5pm to 7pm, Monday, Wednesday and Friday. Wat Sisuphan (p423) holds its sessions from 5.30pm to 7pm just before its meditation course. Wat Chedi Luang (p418) has a table under a shady tree where monks chat from 9am to 6pm daily.

Remember that it is respectful to dress modestly: cover your shoulders and knees. Women should take care not to touch the monks or their belongings, or to pass anything directly to them.

Chiang Mai Thai Cookery School   COOKING
(☑ 0 5320 6388; www.thaicookeryschool.com; 47/2 Th Moon Muang; course 1450B) One of Chiang Mai's first cooking schools holds classes in a rural setting outside of Chiang Mai.

Traditional Thai Massage

Thai Massage School of Chiang Mai   MASSAGE, YOGA
(TMC; ☑ 0 5385 4330; www.tmcschool.com; 203/6 Th Chiang Mai-Mae Jo; basic courses 6500-7500B) Northeast of town, this well-known school offers a government-licensed massage curriculum. There are three foundation levels and an intensive teacher-training program.

Old Medicine Hospital   MASSAGE
(OMH; ☑ 0 5327 5085; www.thaimassageschool. ac.th; 78/1 Soi Siwaka Komarat, Th Wualai; courses 5000-6000B) The government-accredited curriculum is very traditional, with a northern-Thai slant, and was one of the first to develop massage training for foreigners.

☆☆ Festivals & Events

Flower Festival   AGRICULTURAL
(☉ early Feb) This agricultural celebration is held over a three-day period and includes displays of flower arrangements, cultural performances and beauty pageants.

Songkran   NEW YEAR
(☉ mid-Apr) The traditional Thai New Year is celebrated in Chiang Mai with boozy enthusiasm. It is virtually impossible to stay dry during the five days of this festival.

Loi Krathong   RELIGIOUS
(☉ Oct/Nov) Northern Thais call this festival Yi Peng, and celebrate by launching illuminated lanterns into the night sky.

🛏 Sleeping

Most of Chiang Mai's budget guesthouses are clustered on either side of the east moat, and most will arrange free transport from the bus or train station if you call.

🛏 In Town

★ **Awanahouse**   GUESTHOUSE $
(☑ 0 5341 9005; www.awanahouse.com; 7 Soi 1, Th Ratchadamnoen; r 375-1000B; ❋ ❂ ❂ ❂) Popular with families, this multistorey building has bright and well-decorated rooms, ranging from basic to just right. The ground-level pool and the rooftop chill-out area are added bonuses.

Gap's House   GUESTHOUSE $
(☑ 0 5327 8140; www.gaps-house.com; 3 Soi 4, Th Ratchadamnoen; r 550-850B; ❋ ❂) A matron among guesthouses, good old Gap's still has a jungle-like garden and budget rooms in old-fashioned wooden houses. Bring your mozzie spray. No advance reservations.

Nice Apartments   GUESTHOUSE $
(☑ 0 5321 8290; 15 Soi 1, Th Ratchadamnoen; r 400-500B; ❋) This low-rise is a decent deal with clean rooms and a central location. The service is friendly and the shaded outdoor seating is the perfect perch to plot the day.

★ **Sri Pat Guest House**   GUESTHOUSE $$
(☑ 0 5321 8716; 16 Soi 7, Th Moon Muang; r 1000-1400B; ❋ ❂ ❂) A standout in the flashpacker category, Sri Pat has just the right dose of personality. Rooms have sunny dispositions, celadon-coloured tiles, folksy cotton drapes and balconies.

★ **Villa Duang Champa**   HOTEL $$
(☑ 0 5332 7199; http://duangchampa.com; 82 Th Ratchadamnoen; r from 1500B; ❋ ❂) Duang Champa is an excellent small hotel in a heritage-style building. Rooms are pretty enough to be in a design magazine, with minimalist modern furnishings. Stick to

the hotel as the dark, cramped guesthouse rooms are not a good deal.

TJR Boutique House
HOTEL **$$**

(☏0 5332 6525; Soi 1, Th Moon Muang; r 1000-1200B; ❋@🛜) A new apartment-style hotel, TJR has huge rooms, huge beds and bathrooms with tubs. Street-facing rooms get views of the mountain.

Mini Cost
HOTEL **$$**

(☏0 5341 8787; www.minicostcm.com; 19/4 Soi 1, Th Ratchadamnoen; r 1000B; ❋@🛜) This apartment-style building has contemporary rooms, comfy beds and more couches and chaise longues than you could ever sit on. It delivers midrange comfort at a modest price.

Tamarind Village
HOTEL **$$$**

(☏0 5341 8896-9; www.tamarindvillage.com; 50/1 Th Ratchadamnoen; r from 7000B; ❋🛜🏊🛜) One of the first of the 'Lanna revival' hotels in Chiang Mai, Tamarind Village recreates the quiet spaces of a temple on the grounds of an old tamarind orchard.

Outside Town Centre

★ Riverside House
GUESTHOUSE **$**

(☏0 5324 1860; www.riversidehousechiangmai.com; 101 Th Chiang Mai-Lamphun; r 550-1500B; ❋@🛜🏊🛜) Near the Saphan Lek (Iron Bridge), clean and spacious rooms populate a pretty garden with pool. Rates rise with amenities including TV and fridge.

★ Sakulchai
HOTEL **$**

(☏0 5321 1982; Soi Plubpueng, Th Huay Kaew; r 590-790B; ❋🛜) The neighbourhood has zero ambience but this multistorey hotel has midrange standards at budget prices. Rooms are large and new with all the mod cons.

★ Baan Kaew Guest House
GUESTHOUSE **$**

(☏0 5327 1606; www.baankaew-guesthouse.com; 142 Th Charoen Prathet; r 680-800B; ❋🛜🛜) This two-storey, apartment-style place is a good honest deal in a quiet part of town. Rooms have all the basics plus small balconies to enjoy the spacious garden.

★ Baan Orapin
B&B **$$**

(☏0 5324 3677; www.baanorapin.com; 150 Th Charoenrat; r 2400-3600B; ❋@🛜) It's a family affair at Baan Orapin – a pretty garden compound anchored by a stately teak house – which has been in the family since 1914. Luxurious guest residences (a total of 15 rooms) are in separate and modern buildings spread throughout the property.

★ Mo Rooms
HOTEL **$$**

(☏0 5328 0789; www.morooms.com; 263/1-2 Th Tha Phae; r 2800-3500B; ❋@🛜) This art-concept hotel has 12 rooms, individually decorated by local artists according to the Chinese zodiac. The rooms are quirky endeavours with funky beds, angular windows and 'art you can live in'.

Tri Yaan Na Ros
BOUTIQUE HOTEL **$$$**

(☏0 5327 3174; www.triyaannaros.com; 156 Th Wualai; r from 3675B; ❋🛜) A superb honeymoon candidate, this boutique hotel creates a romantic reconstruction of the past with its artfully restored house, galleried chambers and narrow walkways. There are only eight rooms and the owner is charming.

✗ Eating

You won't lack for dining variety in Chiang Mai, as the city has an increasingly diverse assortment for grazing.

WORTH A TRIP

DOKMAI GARDEN

For flower enthusiasts and plant geeks who collect floral trivia, **Dokmai Garden** (☏08 7187 5787; Hang Dong; admission 300B, tour 1200-1900B; ☺Jan-Jun) is a private botanical garden outside Chiang Mai that preserves and propagates native flora and floral knowledge. The garden contains over 1000 plants and their friends, including bees, birds and butterflies. Basic admission allows visitors to wander around the garden reading the informative signs that give the plants' scientific names and cultural applications. Their guided tours offer more in-depth discussions.

Call ahead to make an appointment. The garden is about 30 minutes south of Chiang Mai airport and can be reached by chartered transport (about 300B); you may need to contact the garden to provide specific directions to the driver.

Blue Diamond VEGETARIAN $

(35/1 Soi 9, Th Moon Muang; mains 70-150B; ⏰7am-9pm Mon-Sat; 🛜🌿) Chock-full of fresh produce and baked goods, this backpacker kitchen is a jack-of-all-health-trends: big salads sopped up with slices of bread, veg stir-fries and great breakfasts.

★New Delhi INDIAN $$

(Th Ratwithi; mains 150-280B; ⏰11am-10pm) This basic eatery serves up some of Chiang Mai's best Indian food – lots of complex flavours without the oily afterglow.

★Salsa Kitchen MEXICAN $$

(Th Huay Kaew; mains 150-220B; ⏰11am-11pm) Baja-style Mexican earns high praise for its fresh and zesty dishes served in super-sized portions. It's an expat favourite but Thais dig it too, and it's often busy in the evening.

Heuan Phen NORTHERN THAI $$

(📷0 5327 7103; 112 Th Ratchamankha; mains 80-200B; ⏰11am-10pm) True northern food is difficult to find in a restaurant setting, but this tourist-friendly place does its best to introduce visitors to regional specialities.

Riverside Bar & Restaurant INTERNATIONAL-THAI $$

(Th Charoenrat; dishes 100-200B; ⏰10am-1am) This rambling set of wooden buildings has been the most consistently popular riverside place for over 20 years. It's right on the river just 300m north of Saphan Nawarat.

Chez Marco Restaurant & Bar FRENCH $$

(📷0 5320 7032; 15/7 Th Loi Kroh; mains 150-350B; ⏰5.30pm-midnight Mon-Sat) Chez Marco catapults past the ho-hum tourist joints with top-notch French fare and reasonable prices. Homemade bread, duck dishes and tuna carpaccio are just some of the specialities.

🍷 Drinking & Nightlife

Most Chiang Mai bars are open from about 5pm to midnight.

Zoe In Yellow BAR

(40/12 Th Rathwithi; ⏰5pm-2am) Everybody's party pal, Zoe is a beer garden, club and live music venue. Start off in the garden for sobriety cure-alls then stumble over to the dance floor with your new-found confidence.

Beer Republic BAR

(Soi 11, Th Nimmanhaemin; ⏰5pm-midnight Tue-Sun) Fifteen draught beers keep the hop-sippers happy at this upscale beer bar in trendy Nimman. It is packed and chummy.

Writer's Club & Wine Bar BAR

(141/3 Th Ratchadamnoen; ⏰10am-midnight) Run by a former foreign correspondent, this bar and restaurant is popular with expats, including current and retired writers, and anybody else who wanders by.

The Pub PUB

(189 Th Huay Kaew; ⏰7am-midnight) In an old Tudor-style house surrounded by a big garden, this venerable institution recreates the atmosphere of an English country pub with history to boot. It's a couple of hundred metres past Th Nimmanhaemin on the west side of Th Huay Kaew.

UN Irish Pub PUB

(24/1 Th Ratwithi; ⏰10am-midnight) Chiang Mai's leading pub ambassador, this is *the* place for international sport matches and Thursday quiz nights.

Soho Bar BAR

(www.sohochiangmai.com; 20/3 Th Huay Kaew; ⏰5pm-midnight) Personality is on tap at this cosy shopfront bar. It is gay-friendly but all-inclusive and the affable owners attract a steady supply of regulars and newcomers with cheerful chats and cold drinks.

John's Place BAR

(Th Moon Muang; ⏰10am-midnight) This old-school spot dominates the triangular wedge of Th Ratchamankha and Soi 2 with neon and beer bellies. Climb the stairs to the roof deck where a cold beer is good company at sunset.

DON'T MISS

KÔW SOY

Kôw soy, wheat-and-egg noodles in a rich curry broth served with sides of crunchy pickled vegies and spicy chilli condiment, is a Chiang Mai speciality. Th Faham, past Saphan Nakhon Ping, is Chiang Mai's *kôw soy* ghetto and is home to **Khao Soi Lam Duan** (Th Faham; dishes 50-70B) and **Khao Soi Samoe Jai** (Th Faham; dishes 50-70B), two of the city's most legendary destinations for the dish. In town, locals flock to the bowls served at **Kow Soy Siri Soy** (Th Inthawarorot; mains 40-50B; ⏰7am-3pm Mon-Fri).

DON'T MISS

CHIANG MAI'S MARKETS

Arguably one of Chiang Mai's biggest tourist draws is its **Night Bazaar** (Th Chang Khlan; ⊘7pm-midnight). The legacy of Yunnanese trading caravans that stopped in Chiang Mai along the ancient trade route between Simao (in China) and Mawlamyine (on Myanmar's Gulf of Martaban coast), the modern trade has shifted to the usual tourist souvenirs. In true market fashion, vendors form a gauntlet along the footpath of Th Chang Khlan from Th Tha Phae to Th Loi Kroh. In between are dedicated shopping buildings: the Chiang Mai Night Bazaar Building is filled mainly with antique and handicraft shops. Across the street is the **Galare Night Bazaar** selling upmarket clothes and home decor. The **Anusan Night Bazaar** (Anusan Night Market; Th Chang Khlan; ⊘5-10pm) is less claustrophobic and filled with tables of vendors selling knitted caps, carved soaps and other cottage-industry goods.

A more relaxed and local shopping experience has been cultivated at Chiang Mai's two weekly walking street markets. The **Saturday Walking Street** (Th Wualai; ⊘4pm-midnight Sat), in the historic silversmith district, and the **Sunday Walking Street** (Th Ratchadamnoen; ⊘4pm-midnight Sun), in the heart of the old city, turn the normally busy streets into pedestrian-only bazaars with colourful stalls selling cottage-industry wares, hill-tribe crafts and tasty local food.

☆ Entertainment

★ Sudsanan   LIVE MUSIC
(Th Huay Kaew; ⊘5pm-2am) Down a dark driveway near Kad Suan Kaew, this old wooden house is filled with characters and songs. Mainly acoustic bands jog from samba to *pleng pêu·a chee·wít* ('songs for life') and the eclectic crowd bows solemnly during tear-jerking songs.

North Gate Jazz Co-Op   LIVE MUSIC
(Th Si Phum) This tight little jazz club packs in more musicians, both local and foreign, than patrons, especially for its Tuesday open-mic night.

❶ Information

You will stumble across banks and ATMs on seemingly every street you visit in Chiang Mai.

EMERGENCY

Tourist Police (☑0 5324 7318, 24hr emergency 1155; Th Faham; ⊘6am-midnight) Has a volunteer staff of foreign nationals who speak a variety of languages. It's on the eastern side of the river, just south of the superhighway.

INTERNET ACCESS

Guesthouses, restaurants and cafes in Chiang Mai have free wi-fi access. A few guesthouses and cafes still have internet-enabled terminals though these are quickly disappearing.

MEDIA

Chiangmai Mail (www.chiangmai-mail.com) Weekly English-language newspaper covering local and regional news and politics.

Citylife (www.chiangmainews.com) Lifestyle magazine profiling restaurants, bars, local culture, politics and people; also has a classified section.

Guidelines Living (www.guidelineschiangmai.com) Monthly lifestyle magazine that features business profiles plus respectable historical essays and bilingual (Thai and English) articles.

MEDICAL SERVICES

Chiang Mai Ram Hospital (☑0 5322 4880; www.chiangmairam.com; 8 Th Bunreuangrit) The most modern hospital in town.

McCormick Hospital (☑0 5392 1777; www.mccormick.in.th; 133 Th Kaew Nawarat) Former missionary hospital; good for minor treatments.

TOURIST INFORMATION

Tourism Authority of Thailand (TAT; ☑0 5327 6140; www.tourismthailand.org; Th Chiang Mai-Lamphun; ⊘8.30am-4.30pm) English-speaking staff provide maps and recommendations for tour guides. It's just over Saphan Lek on the eastern side of the river. At the time of writing the office had temporarily relocated to 164/94-95 Th Chang Khlan while a new building was being constructed on the original site.

❶ Getting There & Away

AIR

Regularly scheduled flights arrive into and depart from Chiang Mai International Airport. The airport is 3km south of the centre of the old city; airport taxis cost a flat 120B, and from any point within the city you can charter a túk-túk or *rót daang* ('red car') to the airport for about 60B to 80B.

In addition to the destinations below, there are also direct flights to domestic destinations including Hat Yai, Ko Samui, Krabi, Mae Hong Son, Mae Sot, Phitsanulok and Phuket; and international destinations including Beijing, Guangzhou, Hong Kong, Kuala Lumpur, Kunming, Macau, Seoul, Singapore, Taipei, Wuhan and Yangon.

Air Asia (☑0 5323 4645; www.airasia.com; 416 Th Phae; ☉10am-8pm) Flies to Bangkok's Don Muang International Airport.

Bangkok Airways (☑0 5328 9338; www. bangkokair.com; Room A & B, Kantary Terrace, 44/1 Soi 12, Th Nimmanhaemin; ☉8.30am-noon & 1-6pm Mon-Sat) Flies daily to Bangkok's Suvarnabhumi International Airport.

Lao Airlines (☑0 5322 3401; www.laoairlines. com; Ground fl, Nakornping Condominium, 2/107 Th Huay Kaew; ☉8.30am-5pm Mon-Fri, to noon Sat) Flies to/from Luang Prabang (Laos).

Kan Air (☑0 5328 3311; www.kanairlines. com; 2nd fl, Chiang Mai International Airport; ☉8am-5.30pm) Flies to/from Pai and Nan.

Nok Air (☑0 5392 2183; www.nokair.com; 2nd fl, Chiang Mai International Airport; ☉8am-5pm) Flies to Bangkok's Don Muang International Airport and Udon Thani.

Thai Airways International (THAI; ☑0 2356 1111, 0 5321 1044; www.thaiair.com; 240 Th Phra Pok Klao; ☉8.30am-4.30pm Mon-Fri) Flies to Bangkok's Suvarnabhumi International Airport.

BUS

There are two bus stations in Chiang Mai. **Chang Pheuak Bus Terminal** (Th Chang Pheuak) is north of the old city and primarily handles destinations within Chiang Mai Province. **Arcade Bus Station** (Th Kaew Nawarat), 3km northeast of the old city, handles most long-distance routes. From the town centre, a túk-túk or chartered *sŏrngtăaou* to the Arcade terminal should cost about 50B to 60B.

TRAIN

Chiang Mai's **train station** (Th Charoen Muang) is 2.5km east of the old city. To check timetables and prices for destinations not indicated below, call the **State Railway of Thailand** (☑free hotline 1690; www.railway.co.th) or look at its website.

ⓘ Getting Around

Red *sŏrngtăaou*, known locally as *rót daang* ('red cars'), cruise the city and function like shared taxis: flag one down, tell them your destination and they'll nod if they're going that way. They might pick up another fare if the stops are en route. Short trips should cost 20B per person, longer trips from 40B.

Túk-túk only do charters. Short trips start at 40B; longer trips 60B. At night túk-túk drivers often ask an inflated 100B for return trips from the riverside restaurants to the old city.

Traffic is a bit heavy, but Chiang Mai is small enough that everything is accessible by bike. Rentals cost 30B to 50B a day from guesthouses and various places along the east moat.

Around Chiang Mai

North of Chiang Mai the province becomes mountainous and rugged as it bumps against Myanmar's frontier. Among the highlights are the beautiful Mae Sa Valley

TRANSPORT FROM CHIANG MAI

DESTINATION	AIR	BUS	MINIVAN	TRAIN
Bangkok	from 1750B; 1½hr; frequent	438-876B; 9-10hr; frequent	N/A	231-881B, 12hr, 5-6 daily
Chiang Khong	N/A	190-351B; 6½hr; 2 daily	N/A	N/A
Chiang Rai	N/A	144-288B; 3-4hr; hourly	N/A	N/A
Luang Prabang (Laos)	5000B; 1hr; 6 weekly	1200B; 20hr; 2 daily	N/A	N/A
Mae Sai	N/A	182-364B; 5hr; 2-3 daily	N/A	N/A
Nakhon Ratchasima	N/A	600-700B; 12hr, 11 daily	N/A	N/A
Nan	N/A	225-451B; 6hr; 10 daily	N/A	N/A
Pai	from 1990B; 20min; daily	138B; 4hr; hourly	150B; 3hr; hourly	N/A
Sukhothai	N/A	239-308B; 5-6hr; 6 daily	N/A	N/A
Udon Thani	from 2500B; 1½hr, daily	444-666B; 12hr; 2 daily	N/A	N/A

EASY RIDER

One of the increasingly popular ways of exploring northern Thailand is from the saddle of a rented motorcycle. Despite the obvious risks of driving in Thailand, motorcycle touring is one of the best ways to explore the countryside at your own pace, and provides the opportunity to leave the beaten track at any moment.

Unless you're specifically intending to go off-road or plan on crossing unpaved roads during the wet season, it's highly unlikely you'll need one of the large dirt bikes you'll see for rent in Chiang Mai. The automatic transmission 110cc to 150cc scooterlike motorcycles found across Thailand are fast and powerful enough for most roads. Rental prices in Chiang Mai start at about 200B per day for a 125cc Honda Wave/Dream, all the way to 1500B per day for a Honda CB1000.

A good introduction to motorcycle touring in northern Thailand is the 100km Samoeng loop, which can be tackled in half a day. The route extends north from Chiang Mai and follows Rtes 107, 1096 and 1269, passing through excellent scenery and ample curves, providing a taste of what a longer ride up north will be like. The 470km Chiang Rai loop, which passes through scenic Fang and Tha Ton along Rtes 107, 1089 and 118, is another popular ride that can be broken up with a stay in Chiang Rai. The classic northern route is the Mae Hong Son loop, a 950km ride that begins in Chiang Mai and takes in Rte 1095's 1864 curves with possible stays in Pai, Mae Hong Son and Mae Sariang, before looping back to Chiang Mai via Rte 108.

The best source of information on motorcycle travelling in the north, not to mention publishers of a series of terrific motorcycle touring-based maps, is **Golden Triangle Rider** (www.gt-rider.com). Their website includes heaps of information on renting bikes (including recommended hire shops in Chiang Mai and Chiang Rai) and bike insurance, plus a variety of suggested tours with maps and an interactive forum.

and the forested peaks around Chiang Dao. This region is particularly apt for some self-guided exploration.

Mae Sa Valley & Samoeng
แม่สา/สะเมิง

📙 053

One of the easiest mountain escapes, the 100km Mae Sa–Samoeng route makes a good day trip with private transport or a country getaway with an overnight stay in Samoeng.

Head north of Chiang Mai on Rte 107 (Th Chang Pheuak) towards Mae Rim, then left onto Rte 1096. The road becomes more rural but there's a steady supply of tour-bus attractions: orchid farms, butterfly parks, snake farms, you name it.

Only 6km from the Mae Rim turn-off, **Nam Tok Mae Sa** (adult/child 100/50B, car 30B) is a picturesque waterfall that's a favourite weekend getaway for locals.

The road starts to climb and twist after the waterfall entrance. Not far past an elephant camp is the **Queen Sirikit Botanic Gardens** (📙0 5384 1333; www.qsbg.org; Rte 1096; adult/child 100/50B; ⊙8.30am-4.30pm), featuring a shorn mountainside displaying 227 hectares of various exotic and local flora for conservation and research purposes.

After the botanic gardens the road climbs into the fertile Mae Sa Valley, once a high-altitude basin for growing opium poppies.

Sitting at the western edge of the valley, **Proud Phu Fah** (📙0 5387 9389; www.proudphufah.com; Rte 1096, Km17, r 2500-4000B; 🌸@🛜🏊) is a small boutique hotel with creature-comfort villas designed to give the illusion of sleeping amid the great outdoors. The open-air restaurant serves healthy Thai food (mains 150B to 250B) with a panoramic view of the valley.

Eventually the road spirals down into Samoeng, a pretty Thai village. If you want to stay overnight, try the rather run-down **Samoeng Resort** (📙0 5348 7074; Rte 6033; r 500-800B; 🌸). To get here take Rte 1349 from Samoeng (a right-hand turn in the town).

Only part of the route is accessible via public transport. Sŏrngtǎaou go to Samoeng (70B, 2¾ hours, two morning departures) from the Chang Pheuak Bus Terminal in Chiang Mai.

WORTH A TRIP

PACHYDERM PARTNERS

Thailand's iconic animal has not fared well in the modern age. After the logging ban, these forest fellers faced unemployment, exploitation and the near extinction of the ma-hout tradition. Recently Thais have begun a homegrown campaign to give the elephants a safe working environment in semi-wild sanctuaries or ecotourism programs. The following are a few of the country's campaigners:

➡ **Elephant Nature Park** (☎ 0 5381 8754; www.elephantnaturepark.org; 1 Th Ratchamankha; 1-/2-day tour 2500/5800B) ✐ is run by Khun Lek (Sangduan Chailert), who has won numerous awards for her elephant sanctuary in the Mae Taeng valley, 60km from Chiang Mai. The forested area provides a semi-wild environment for elephants rescued from abusive situations or retired from a lifetime of work. Visitors wash the elephants and watch the herd but there is no show or riding. Volunteer opportunities are available. Transportation from Chiang Mai is included in a visit to the Elephant Nature Park.

➡ ★ **Thai Elephant Conservation Center** (TECC; ☎ 0 5482 9333; www.thailandelephant. org; Rte 11; adult/child 170/110B; ⊙ elephant bathing 9.45am & 1.15pm, public shows 10am, 11am & 1.30pm), 70km southeast of Chiang Mai, covers the usual elephant encounters (shows, bathing, rides and mahout training) but uses the proceeds from the tourist program to underwrite medical treatment for sick elephants. The **elephant show** (⊙ 10am, 11am & 1.30pm) is less of a circus and more of a historical showing of how elephants were used in the timber industry. Its **mahout training program** (☎ 0 5424 7875; from 3500B) is one of Thailand's most popular and runs from one to 10 days. Next door but not associated, **FAE's Elephant Hospital** (Friends of the Asian Elephant; ☎ 08 1914 6113; www. elephant-soraida.com; off Rte 11; admission by donation; ⊙ 8am-5pm) is a functioning medical facility for injured elephants. There are no guided tours, but devout fans can stop by to make charitable donations.

The Thai Elephant Conservation Center and FAE's Elephant Hospital can be reached by any Lampang-bound bus or *sǒrngtǎaou* (30B to 70B, 40 minutes) from Chiang Mai. Let the driver know where you are headed and get off at the Km 28 marker.

Chiang Dao   เชียงดาว

☑ 060

In a lush, jungle setting and slammed up against the limestone cliffs of a mighty *doi*, Chiang Dao is a very popular escape from the steaming urban plains of Chiang Mai.

Chiang Dao town isn't much but a dusty crossroads that hosts a colourful **Tuesday morning market** (⊙ 7am-noon 1st & 3rd Tue of the month), when hill tribes come to sell their wares. The more charming part of town is 5km west along the road that leads to Tham Chiang Dao (Chiang Dao Cave).

◉ Sights

Tham Chiang Dao   CAVE
(ถ้ำเชียงดาว, Chiang Dao Cave; admission 40B) In the heat of the day, the coolest place in town is the Chiang Dao Cave, a complex said to extend some 10km to 14km into Doi Chiang Dao. There are four interconnected caverns that are open to the public. Tham Phra Non (360m) is the initial segment and is electrically illuminated and can be explored on your own. To explore the other caves – Tham

Mah (735m), Tham Kaew (474m) and Tham Nam (660m) – we recommend that you hire a guide with a pressurised gas lantern (100B for up to five people), not because you aren't intrepid enough to go solo, but because the guide service provides income for the local villagers.

Doi Chiang Dao   MOUNTAIN
(ดอยเชียงดาว, Doi Luang) Part of the Doi Chiang Dao National Park, Doi Chiang Dao pokes into the heavens at 2195m above sea level. From the summit, reachable by a two-day hike, the views are spectacular. The southern side of the mountain is believed to be one of the most accessible spots in the world to see the giant nuthatch and Hume's pheasant. **Bird-watching** and **overnight treks** can be arranged through local guesthouses.

🛏 Sleeping & Eating

There is a daily food market off the main street.

Hobby Hut   GUESTHOUSE $
(☎ 08 0034 4153; r from 250B) Chiang Dao's cheapest backpacker choice, Hobby Hut has

simple A-frame huts with shared bathrooms surrounded by rice fields. Meals with the family are available.

★**Chiang Dao Nest** GUESTHOUSE $$
(☑08 6017 1985; http://nest.chiangdao.com; r 895-1500B; @ 🛜 🛋) The simple bungalows here get the basics right – comfy beds, privacy and immaculate interiors. Those closest to the restaurant have terrific views from the rickety rear porches.

★**Chiang Dao Nest** INTERNATIONAL $$$
(☑0 6017 1985; mains 300-500B; ⊗6am-10pm) Wicha, the owner and chef, received her culinary training in the UK and creates a menu that reflects the seasons.

ℹ **Getting There & Around**

Buses to Chiang Dao (40B, 1½ hours, six daily) leave from Chiang Mai's Chang Pheuak Bus Terminal. The buses arrive and depart from Chiang Dao's bus station from where *sŏrngtăaou* drivers charge 150B to deliver passengers to guesthouses on the cave road. Buses also travel to Fang (60B).

Some guesthouses rent mountain bikes for 100B a day.

Fang & Tha Ton ฝาง/ท่าตอน

☑053
For most people Fang is just a road marker on the way to Tha Ton, the launching point for river trips to Chiang Rai. If you do hang around this large, bustling town, there are some quiet backstreets lined with little shops in wooden buildings and the Shan/Burmese-style **Wat Jong Paen** (near the New Wiang Kaew Hotel), which has an impressive stacked-roof *wí·hăhn*. Along the main street in Fang there are banks offering currency exchange and ATMs.

The petite settlement of **Tha Ton** is plonked on the banks of a pretty bend of Mae Nam Kok, which is lined by a few riverside restaurants and the boat launch for river trips to Chiang Rai. There is a **tourist police office** (☑1155) near the bridge on the boat-dock side.

👁 **Sights & Activities**

Wat Tha Ton BUDDHIST TEMPLE
(☑0 5345 9309; www.wat-thaton.org) In Tha Ton, this temple sprawls up the side of a wooded hill. There are nine different levels and each level affords stunning views of the mountainous valley towards Myanmar, the plains of Tha Ton and the winding river.

Hill-tribe Trekking ADVENTURE SPORTS
(tours from 1000B) Tha Ton has a very low-key personality and does little to promote itself as a tourism destination, but within 20km of the town there are six hill-tribe villages inhabited by Palaung, Black Lahu, Akha, Karen and Yunnanese people. Treks can be arranged through any of Tha Ton's guesthouses.

🛏 **Sleeping & Eating**

Most visitors who do stay overnight prefer to stay in Tha Ton.

Sappaya Guesthouse GUESTHOUSE $
(☑08 0792 8725; r 400-500B) This newcomer is a friendly and breezy spot with simple, shared bathrooms in a two-storey terraced house. There are shared kitchen facilities, lots of local information and an outgoing host.

★**Old Tree's House** HOTEL $$
(☑08 5722 9002; www.oldtreeshouse.net; bungalows 1200-1400B; ❄🛜🛋) This French-Thai operation is a cleverly designed mini-resort, with luxury bungalows sitting in a pretty garden with lots of nooks and crannies. It's 400m past Tha Ton, and signed off the road.

Chankasen THAI $
(209 Rimnumkok; mains 60-80B; ⊗10am-8pm) The food is fine at this friendly, entrepreneurial Thai spot, but the real puller is the

TRANSPORT FROM FANG & THA TON

DESTINATION	BOAT	BUS	SÖRNGTĂAOU
Bangkok	N/A	600B; 14hr; 4 daily	N/A
Chiang Dao	N/A	63B; 2hr; 7 daily	N/A
Chiang Mai	N/A	90B; 4hr; 7 daily	N/A
Chiang Rai	350B; 3-5hr; 12.30pm	N/A	N/A
Fang (from Tha Ton)	N/A	30B; 30min; 7 daily	25B; 30min; frequent
Mae Salong	N/A	N/A	60B; 1½hr; 3 daily

seating right on the river. It is conveniently located right alongside the boat dock.

Sunshine Cafe
CAFE $

(mains 60-110B; ⏲8am-3pm) This is the place to come for freshly brewed coffee in the morning. It also does a wide selection of Western breakfasts including muesli, fresh fruit and yoghurt. It is on the main road, just before the bridge.

ℹ️ Getting There & Away

The bus stop in Tha Ton is across the bridge from town. The passenger boats to Chiang Rai are also availble for charter (2200B, up to six people).

Pai
ปาย

📞 053 / POP 2000

The hippie trail is alive and well in Pai (pronounced more like the English 'bye' not 'pie'), a cool, moist corner of a mountain-fortressed valley. A solid music, art and New Age scene has settled in along with the town's more permanent population of Shan, Thai and Muslim Chinese, though in the high season Pai can feel more like Ko Pha-Ngan without a beach. Diluting the fa·ràng factor are visiting Thais from Bangkok and Chiang Mai, who pop in for a long weekend in the country.

◎ Sights & Activities

Tuckered out on temples? Pai is lean on sights and high on activities, from hikes to massages. Treks start at about 800B per day, while rafting excursions start at about 1200B.

Ban Santichon
VILLAGE

(บ้านสันติชน) About 4km outside of Pai, a small market, restaurants serving Yunnanese food, tea tasting, pony rides, a tacky recreation of the Great Wall of China and a **mountaintop viewpoint** (Ban Santichon; admission 20B; ⏲4.30am-6pm) make the former KMT village of Ban Santichon not unlike a Chinese-themed Disneyland.

Tha Pai Hot Springs
HOT SPRINGS

(บ่อน้ำร้อนท่าปาย; adult/child 200/100B; ⏲7am-6pm) Across Mae Nam Pai and 7km southeast of town via a paved road is this well-kept local park. A scenic stream flows through the park; the stream mixes with the hot springs in places to make pleasant bathing areas.

Pai Adventure
RAFTING

(📞0 5369 9385; www.thailandpai.net; 28 Th Chai-songkhram; ⏲8am-10pm) The one- to two-day white-water rafting trips offered by this recommended outfit can be combined with trekking and other activities.

Pai Traditional Thai Massage
MASSAGE

(PTTM; 📞0 5369 9121; www.pttm1989.com; 68/3 Soi 1, Th Wiang Tai; massage per 1/1½/2hr 180/270/350B, sauna per visit 100B, 3-day massage course 2500B; ⏲9am-9pm) This long-standing and locally owned outfit offers very good northern Thai massage, as well as a sauna (cool season only) where you can steam yourself in sà·mǔn·prai (medicinal herbs). Three-day massage courses begin every Monday and Friday and last three hours per day.

🎓 Courses

Pai Traditional Thai Massage also runs massage courses.

Pai Cookery School
COOKING

(📞08 1706 3799; Th Wanchalerm; lessons 600-750B; ⏲lessons 11am-1.30pm & 2-6.30pm) With a decade of experience, this outfit offers a variety of courses spanning three to five dishes. The afternoon course involves a trip to the market for ingredients.

🛏️ Sleeping

Accommodation can be tight during the Thai tourist season of December to January, and prices drop by as much as 60% during the low season.

🛏️ In Town

Tayai's Guest House
GUESTHOUSE $

(📞0 5369 9579; off Th Raddamrong; r & bungalows 200-500B; ❄🅿) Simple but clean fan and air-con rooms and bungalows in a leafy compound just off the main drag.

Pai Country Hut
HOTEL $

(📞08 7779 6541; www.facebook.com/paicountry bungalows; Ban Mae Hi; bungalows incl breakfast 200-500B; 🅿) The bamboo bungalows here are utterly simple, but are tidy and most have bathrooms and inviting hammocks.

Baan Pai Village
HOTEL $$

(📞0 5369 8152; www.baanpaivillage.com; 88 Th Wiang Tai; bungalows incl breakfast 1000-1900B; ❄@🅿) This well-maintained place has a collection of 21 wooden bungalows set

Pai

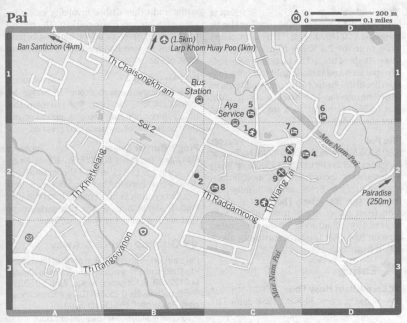

among winding garden pathways. Huge low-season discounts are available.

Breeze of Pai Guesthouse HOTEL $$
(☑ 08 1998 4597; suthasinee.svp@gmail.com; Soi Wat Pa Kham; r 400B, bungalows 800B; ✸ 🛜) This well-groomed compound near the river consists of nine attractive and spacious rooms and six large A-frame bungalows. A loyal customer base means you'll probably have to book ahead.

★ Rim Pai Cottage HOTEL $$$
(☑ 0 5369 9133; www.rimpaicottage.com; Th Chaisongkhram; bungalows 1200-4000B; ✸🛜) The homelike bungalows here are spread out along a secluded and beautifully wooded section of Mae Nam Pai. There are countless cosy riverside corners to relax in and a palpable village-like feel about the whole place.

🛏 Outside of Town

Spicypai Backpackers HOTEL $
(☑ 08 5263 5147; Mae Yen; dm 100-150B, bungalows 500B; ✸@🛜) The bamboo dorms here look like they could have featured in an episode of *Survivor*. Communal areas ranging from kitchen to fire pit continue the rustic feel, and there are a few air-con bungalows for those with loftier standards. It's about 750m

Pai

🔾 **Activities, Courses & Tours**
1 Pai Adventure	C2
2 Pai Cookery School	B2
3 Pai Traditional Thai Massage	C2

🛏 **Sleeping**
4 Baan Pai Village	D2
5 Breeze of Pai Guesthouse	C1
6 Pai Country Hut	D1
7 Rim Pai Cottage	D2
8 Tayai's Guest House	C2

🍴 **Eating**
9 Ping's Burger Queen	C2
10 Witching Well	C2

east of Mae Nam Pai, just off the road that leads to Tha Pai Hot Springs.

★ Bueng Pai Farm GUESTHOUSE $$
(☑ 08 9265 4768; www.paifarm.com; Ban Mae Hi; bungalows 500-2000B; 🛜✉) Uniting yoga enthusiasts and fisherfolk, the 12 simple bungalows here are strategically and attractively positioned between a functioning farm and a vast pond stocked with freshwater fish. Bueng Pai is 2.5km from Pai, off the road that leads to Tha Pai Hot Springs; look for the sign.

★ **Pairadise** HOTEL $$
(☑ 0 5369 8065; www.pairadise.com; Ban Mae Hi; bungalows 800-1400B; ❈ 🤶) This neat resort looks over the Pai Valley from atop a ridge just outside of town. The bungalows are stylish, spacious and include gold leaf lotus murals, beautiful rustic bathrooms and terraces with hammocks. The hotel is about 750m east of Mae Nam Pai; look for the sign just after the bridge.

Phu Pai HOTEL $$$
(☑ 0 5306 5111; www.phupai.com; Mae Na Theung; bungalows incl breakfast 2000-3500B; ❈ 🤶 ❈) Views are the focus here, with most bungalows edging rice fields and an infinity pool framing the Pai Valley. The hotel is about 4km from the centre of town off the road to Mae Hong Son; look for the well-posted turn-off just after the airport runway, about 1.3km from Pai.

✗ Eating

★ **Larp Khom Huay Poo** NORTHERN THAI $
(Ban Huay Pu; mains 30-70B; ⏲9am-8pm) The house special here is *làhp kôo·a,* minced meat (beef or pork) fried with local herbs and spices. The restaurant is on the road to Mae Hong Son, about 1km north of town, just past the well-posted turn-off to Sipsongpanna.

★ **Yunnanese Restaurant** CHINESE $
(no roman-script sign; mains 30-180B; ⏲8am-8pm) This open-air place in the Chinese village of Ban Santichon serves the traditional dishes of the town's Yunnanese residents. There are several dishes using unique local crops and other dishes involving exotic ingredients such as black chicken. The restaurant is in an open-air adobe building behind the giant rock in Ban Santichon, about 4km west of Pai.

Witching Well INTERNATIONAL $
(www.witchingwellrestaurant.com; Th Wiang Tai; mains 75-140B; ⏲7am-11pm; 🤶 🖋) In town, this buzzy foreigner-run place is good for authentic sandwiches, pasta and pastries.

Ping's Burger Queen AMERICAN $
(Th Wiang Tai; mains 60-80B; ⏲2-10pm) Burgers are huge in Pai, and of the various vendors, we're certain that Ping does the best job. Everything is homemade, from the soft, slightly sweet buns to the rich garlic mayo that accompanies the thick-cut fries.

❶ Getting There & Away

Pai's airport is around 1.5km north of town along Rte 1095 and offers a daily connection to Chiang Mai (1990B, 20 minutes) on **Kan Air** (☑ 0 5369 9955, nationwide 0 2551 6111; www.kanairlines.com; Pai Airport; ⏲8.30am-5pm).

To Chiang Mai, buses (80B, three to four hours, noon) and minivans (150B, three hours, hourly from 7am to 4.30pm) leave from Pai's tiny **bus station** (Th Chaisongkhram).

Aya Service (☑ 0 5369 9888; www.ayaservice.com; 22/1 Th Chaisongkhram; bikes per 24hr 100-400B; ⏲8am-9pm) also runs air-con minivan buses to Chiang Mai (150B, three hours, hourly from 8am to 4.30pm), Chiang Rai (550B, six hours, 5.30am) and Chiang Khong (650B, seven hours, 6pm).

Sukhothai สุโขทัย

📍 055 / POP 37,000

The Khmer empire extended its influence deep into modern-day Thailand before a formidable rival arose in 1257 to undermine the distant throne's frontier. Naming its capital Sukhothai (Rising Happiness), the ascendant kingdom claimed lands as far north as Vientiane and began to define a cohesive Thai identity by developing a distinctive Thai alphabet as well as architecture and art. All this was accomplished in 150 years, before Sukhothai was superseded by Ayuthaya to the south.

◉ Sights & Activities

Sukhothai Historical Park HISTORICAL SITE
(อุทยานประวัติศาสตร์สุโขทัย) Designated a Unesco World Heritage Site, Sukhothai's

---

DRINKING IN PAI 101

There are dozens of bars in Pai – too many to list here – and given the fickleness of the local drinking scene, few are likely to be still around by the time this goes to print. Instead, here's a cheat sheet to downtown Pai's drinking scene: most of the open-air and VW van–based cocktail bars are along Th Chaisongkhram; Th Wiang Tai is where you'll find the largely indoor, live music places; Th Rangsiyanon is where most of the 'guesthouse' style restaurant-bars are located; and a knot of open-air reggae-style bars can be found at the eastern end of Th Raddamrong, just across the bridge.

historical park, also known as *meuang gòw* (old city), contains 21 historic sites that lie within the old wall, with another 70 within a 5km radius. Thailand's Loi Krathong festival is thought to have originated here and is celebrated in November with much historic fanfare.

The park is 12km west of New Sukhothai, home to the bulk of the area's accommodation and restaurants. The two areas are linked by frequent *sŏrngtăaou* (30B, 30 minutes, from 6am to 5.30pm) from the south side of Th Jarot Withithong west of Poo Restaurant. Within the old city, bicycles (per day 30B) are a great way to explore the grounds and can be hired near the park entrance. **Cycling Sukhothai** (☎08 5083 1864, 0 5561 2519; www.cycling-sukhothai.com; off Th Jarot Withithong; half-/full day 650/750B, sunset tour 350B) offers educational bike tours of the area.

➡ Central Zone
(admission 100B, plus per bicycle/motorcycle/car 10/30/50B; ⏰6.30am-7pm Sun-Fri, to 9pm Sat) This is the historical park's main zone and is home to what are arguably some of the park's most well-preserved and impressive ruins. Near the entrance, **Ramkhamhaeng National Museum** (พิพิธภัณฑสถานแห่งชาติรามคำแหง; admission 150B; ⏰9am-4pm) provides a modest collection of Sukhothai-era artefacts.

The crown jewel of the old city, **Wat Mahathat**, is one of the best examples of Sukhothai architecture, typified by the classic lotus-bud stupa that features a conical spire topping a square-sided structure on a three-tiered base. Some of the orignal Buddha images remain, including a 9m standing Buddha among the broken columns.

Wat Si Sawai, just south of Wat Mahathat, has three Khmer-style prang and a picturesque moat. **Wat Sa Si** is a classically simple Sukhothai-style temple set on an island. **Wat Trapang Thong**, next to the museum, is reached by the footbridge crossing the large, lotus-filled pond that surrounds it.

➡ Northern Zone
(admission 100B, plus per bicycle/motorcycle/car 10/30/50B; ⏰7.30am-5.30pm) This zone, 500m north of the old city walls, is easily reached by bicycle.

In the northwestern corner, **Wat Si Chum** contains a massive seated Buddha tightly squeezed into an open, walled *mon·dòp* (the small square-sided building with a spire in a wát). Somewhat isolated to the north of the city, Wat Phra Pai Luang is similar in style to **Wat Si Sawai**, but the *Ƀrahng* (tower) are larger.

➡ Western Zone
(admission 100B, plus per bicycle/motorcycle/car 10/30/50B; ⏰8am-4.30pm) The western zone is the most expansive. **Wat Saphan Hin** is on a hill 3km west of the old city walls, and features a 12.5m-high standing Buddha image looking back towards Sukhothai.

Elsewhere, the large, bell-shaped stupa at **Wat Chang Lom**, to the east, is supported by 36 elephants sculpted into its base.

Sleeping

Many guesthouses offer free wi-fi, free use of bicycles and free pick-up from the bus terminal.

New Sukhothai

TR Room & Bungalow GUESTHOUSE **$**
(☎0 5561 1663; www.sukhothaibudgetguesthouse.com; 27/5 Th Prawet Nakhon; r 250-450B, bungalows 400-550B; ❄@📶) The rooms here are basic and lack character, but figure among the tidiest we've encountered in northern Thailand. For those needing leg room, there are five wooden bungalows out back.

Sabaidee House HOTEL **$**
(☎0 5561 6303; www.sabaideehouse.com; 81/7 Th Jarot Withithong; r 200-600B; ❄📶) This cheery guesthouse in a semi-rural setting spans seven attractive bungalows and rooms in the main structure. Sabaidee is off Th Jarot Withithong about 200m before the intersection with Rte 101; look for the sign.

Lotus Village HOTEL **$$**
(☎0 5562 1484; www.lotus-village.com; 170 Th Ratchathani; r incl breakfast 720-1200B, bungalows incl breakfast 1000-2850B; ❄@📶) Village is an apt label for this peaceful compound of wooden bungalows elevated over lotus ponds. Smaller, mostly fan-cooled rooms in a wooden building are also available, and an attractive Burmese/Indian design theme runs through the entire place.

At Home Sukhothai GUESTHOUSE **$$**
(☎0 5561 0172; www.athomesukhothai.com; 184/1 Th Vichien Chamnong; r incl breakfast 400-800B; ❄@📶) Located in the 50-year-old childhood home of the proprietor, the simple but

---

DON'T MISS

GǑO·AY ĐĔE·O SÙ·KǑH·TAI

Sukhothai's signature dish is gǒo·ay đĕe·o sù·kǒh·tai (Sukhothai-style noodles), which features a slightly sweet broth with different types of pork, ground peanuts and thinly sliced green beans. The dish is available at **Jayhae** (Th Jarot Withithong; dishes 25-40B; ⊙8am-4pm) and **Ta Pui** (Th Jarot Withithong, no roman-script sign; dishes 25-35B; ⊙7am-3pm), located across from each other on Th Jarot Withithong, about 1.3km west of Mae Nam Yom.

---

comfortable rooms – both those fan-cooled in the original structure and the newer air-con ones – really do feel like home.

★ **Ruean Thai Hotel**　　　HOTEL **$$$**
(☑ 0 5561 2444; www.rueanthaihotel.com; 181/20 Soi Pracha Ruammit; r incl breakfast 1480-4200B; ❉@🛜🏊) At first glance, you may mistake this eye-catching complex for a Buddhist temple. The rooms on the upper level follow a distinct Thai theme, while the poolside rooms are slightly more modern, and there's a concrete building with simple air-con rooms out the back.

🛏 Sukhothai Historical Park

Vitoon Guesthouse　　　GUESTHOUSE **$**
(☑ 0 5569 7045; www.vitoonguesthouse.com; 49 Rte 12; r 300-900B; ❉@🛜) The better of the two budget options within walking distance of the old city, the fan rooms here are OK, but the air-con rooms, in a newer building, are spotless and represent a good deal.

Orchid Hibiscus Guest House　　HOTEL **$$**
(☑ 0 5563 3284; orchid_hibiscus_guest _house@ya hoo.com; 407/2 Rte 1272; r/bungalows 900/1300B;

❉@🛜🏊) This collection of rooms and bungalows is set in relaxing, manicured grounds with a swimming pool as a centrepiece and the self-professed 'amazing breakfast' (100B) as a highlight. Orchid Hibiscus is on Rte 1272 about 500m off Rte 12 – the turn-off is between the Km 48 and Km 49 markers.

🍴 Eating & Drinking

A wise choice for cheap eats is New Sukhothai's tiny **night market** (Th Jarot Withithong; mains 30-60B; ⊙6-11pm).

Dream Café　　　THAI **$$**
(86/1 Th Singhawat; mains 120-250B; 🅿) A meal at Dream Café is like dining in an antique shop. Eclectic but tasteful furnishings and knick-knackery abound, staff are equal parts competent and friendly, and, most importantly of all, the food is good.

Chopper Bar　　　BAR
(Th Prawet Nakhon; mains 30-150B; ⊙10am-12.30am; 🛜) Both travellers and locals congregate at this restaurant/bar from morning till hangover for food, drinks and live music. Take advantage of Sukhothai's cool evenings on the rooftop terrace.

ℹ Information

Sukhothai Hospital (☑ 0 5561 0280; Th Jarot Withithong) Located just west of New Sukhothai.

Tourism Authority of Thailand (TAT; ☑ 0 5561 6228, nationwide 1672; Th Jarot Withithong; ⊙8.30am-4.30pm) Near the bridge in New Sukhothai, this new office has a pretty good selection of maps and brochures.

Tourist Police (☑ 1155; Rte 12)

ℹ Getting There & Away

Sukhothai's airport is 27km north of town.
Bangkok Airways (☑ 0 5564 7224, nationwide

TRANSPORT FROM SUKHOTHAI

DESTINATION	AIR	BUS	MINIVAN	SǑRNGTǍAOU
Bangkok	2490B; 1hr; 2 daily	279-416B; 6-7hr; every 30min 7.50am-10.40pm	N/A	N/A
Chiang Mai	N/A	239-308B; 5-6hr; every 30min 6.15am-5.30pm	N/A	N/A
Chiang Rai	N/A	266B; 9hr; 4 departures 6.40-11.30am	N/A	N/A
Nan	N/A	202B; 4hr; 3pm & 4pm	N/A	N/A
Sukhothai Historical Park	N/A	N/A	N/A	30B; 30min; frequent 6am-5.30pm

1771; www.bangkokair.com; Sukhothai Airport; ⊙7.30am-5.30pm) operates flights to/from Bangkok's Suvarnabhumi International Airport. There is a **minivan service** (☑0 5564 7220; Sukhothai Airport; 180B) between the airport and New Sukhothai.

The **bus terminal** (☑0 5561 4529; Rte 101) is 1km northwest of New Sukhothai.

❶ Getting Around

A motorcycle taxi between here and central new Sukhothai should cost around 50B, or you can hop on any *sŏrngtăaou* bound for Sukhothai Historical Park, which make a stop at the bus station on their way out of town.

Poo Restaurant (24/3 Th Jarot Withithong; ⊙11am-midnight) and several guesthouses hire motorcycles.

Around Sukhothai

Si Satchanalai–Chaliang Historical Park
อุทยานประวัติศาสตร์ศรีสัชนาลัย

Set amid rolling mountains 56km north of Sukhothai, Si Satchanalai and Chaliang were a later extension of the Sukhothai empire. The 13th- to 15th-century ruins in the historical park are in the same basic style as those in Sukhothai Historical Park, but the setting is more rural and covers a 720-hectare area.

The **Si Satchanalai zone** (admission 100B, plus car 50B; ⊙8am-5pm) contains the vast majority of ruins. An **information centre** (⊙8.30am-5pm) distributes free park maps and has a small historical exhibit. Bikes (30B) can be rented near the entrance gate. **Wat Chedi Jet Thaew** has seven rows of stupas in classic Sukhothai style. **Wat Chang Lom** has a *chedi* surrounded by Buddha statues set in niches and guarded by the fine remains of elephant buttresses. Climb to the top of the hill supporting **Wat Khao Phanom Phloeng** for a view over the town and river.

Head east along the riverside for 2km to Chaliang, where you'll find **Wat Phra Si Ratana Mahathat** (วัดพระศรีรัตนมหาธาตุ; admission 20B; ⊙8am-4.30pm), a very impressive temple with well-preserved *chedi* and a variety of seated and standing Buddhas.

The third zone, which stretches 5km north of Si Satchanalai, is home to more than 200 **kilns**. Several of the old kilns have been carefully excavated and can be viewed along with original pottery samples at the **Si Satchanalai Centre for Study & Preservation of Sangkhalok Kilns** (ศูนย์ศึกษาและอนุรักษ์เตาสังคโลก; admission 100B; ⊙8.30am-5pm).

The ruins can be visited as a day trip from Sukhothai.

Si Satchanalai–Chaliang Historical Park is off Rte 101 between Sawankhalok and Ban Hat Siaw. From New Sukhothai, take a Si Satchanalai bus (46B, 1½ hours, 11am) or one of three buses to Chiang Rai (46B) at 6.40am, 9am and 11.30am, and ask to get off at *'meuang gòw'* (old city). The last bus back to New Sukhothai leaves at 4.30pm.

Chiang Rai   เชียงราย

☑053 / POP 67,000

Well-groomed Chiang Rai is more liveable than visitable, as it lacks any major tourist attractions. But the cosy city is a geat spot for arranging hill-tribe treks with companies that try harder than most to help the host tribes.

⦿ Sights

Oub Kham Museum   MUSEUM
(พิพิธภัณฑ์อูบคำ; www.oubkhammuseum.com; Th Nakhai; adult/child 300/100B; ⊙8am-5pm) This slightly zany museum houses an impressive collection of paraphernalia from virtually every corner of the former Lanna kingdom. The items, some of which truly are one of a kind, range from a monkey-bone food taster used by Lanna royalty to an impressive carved throne from Chiang Tung, Myanmar.

The Oub Kham Museum is 2km west of the town centre and can be a bit tricky to find; túk-túk will go there for about 50B.

Hilltribe Museum & Education Center   MUSEUM
(พิพิธภัณฑ์และศูนย์การศึกษาชาวเขา; www.pdacr.org; 3rd fl, 620/25 Th Thanalai; admission 50B; ⊙9am-6pm Mon-Fri, 10am-6pm Sat & Sun) This museum and cultural centre is a good place to visit before undertaking any hill-tribe trek. Run by the nonprofit Population & Community Development Association (PDA), the displays are underwhelming in their visual presentation, but contain a wealth of information on Thailand's various tribes and the issues that face them.

Wat Phra Kaew   BUDDHIST TEMPLE
(วัดพระแก้ว; Th Trairat; ⊙temple 7am-7pm, museum 9am-5pm) FREE Originally called Wat Pa Yia (Bamboo Forest Monastery) in the

Chiang Rai

Dusit Island

Chiang Rai

⊙ Sights

⊕ Activities, Courses & Tours

🛏 Sleeping

✗ Eating

⊕ Drinking & Nightlife

local dialect, this is the city's most revered Buddhist temple. The main prayer hall is a medium-sized, well-preserved wooden structure. The octagonal *chedi* behind it dates from the late 14th century and is in typical Lanna style. The adjacent two-storey wooden building is a **museum** housing various Lanna artefacts.

🏃 Activities

Nearly all travel agencies, guesthouses and hotels in Chiang Rai offer trekking trips. Rates range from 2500B to 6500B per person for two people for a two-night trek. Generally everything from accommodation to transport and food is included.

Mirror Foundation   TREKKING
(✆ 0 5373 7616; www.thailandecotour.org) Although its rates are higher, trekking with this nonprofit NGO helps support the training of its local guides.

PDA Tours & Travel   TREKKING
(☑0 5374 0088; www.pda.or.th/chiangrai/pack
age_tour.htm; 3rd fl, Hilltribe Museum & Education
Center, 620/25 Th Thanalai; ⊙9am-6pm Mon-Fri,
10am-6pm Sat & Sun) One- to three-day treks
are available through this NGO.

Rai Pian Karuna   TREKKING
(☑08 7186 7858, 08 2195 5645; www.facebook.
com/raipiankaruna) This new, community-
based social enterprise conducts one- and
multiday treks and homestays at Akha, Lahu
and Lua villages in Mae Chan, north of Chiang Rai.

Sleeping

In Town

Baan Warabordee   HOTEL $
(☑0 5375 4488; baanwarabordee@hotmail.com;
59/1 Th Sanpannard; r 500-600B; ✲🞔) A delightful small hotel has been made from this
modern three-storey Thai villa. Rooms come
decked out in dark woods and light cloths,
and are equipped with air-con, fridge and
hot water.

Moon & Sun Hotel   HOTEL $
(☑0 5371 9279; www.moonandsun-hotel.com;
632 Th Singhaclai; r incl breakfast 500-600B, ste
incl breakfast 800B; ✲🞔) Bright and spar-
kling clean, this little hotel offers large
modern rooms. Some feature four-poster
beds, while all come with desk, cable TV
and refrigerator.

Baan Rub Aroon   GUESTHOUSE $$
(☑0 5371 1827; www.baanrubaroon.net; 893
Th Ngam Meuang; r incl breakfast 550-1000B;
✲@🞔) The rooms in this handsome villa,
located just west of the city centre, aren't as
charming as the exterior suggests, and most
share bathrooms, but it's a good choice if
you're looking for a quiet homey stay.

Outside Town Centre

★**Bamboo Nest de
Chiang Rai**   GUESTHOUSE $$
(☑08 9953 2330, 08 1531 6897; www.bamboo
nest-chiangrai.com; bungalows incl breakfast 650-
1300B) Bamboo Nest takes the form of simple but spacious bamboo huts perched on a
hill overlooking tiered rice fields 23km from
Chiang Rai. The only electricity is provided
by solar panels, so leave your laptops in the
city and instead take part in activities that
range from birdwatching to hiking.

Free transport to/from Chiang Rai is
available for two nights or more.

Ben Guesthouse   GUESTHOUSE $$
(☑0 5371 6775; www.benguesthousechiangrai.
com; 351/10 Soi 4, Th Sankhongnoi; r 350-850B, ste
1500-3000B; ✲@🞔🞔) This absolutely spot-
less compound has a bit of everything, from
fan-cooled cheapies to immense suites, not
to mention a pool. It's 1.2km from the centre
of town, at the end of Soi 4 on Th Sankhong-
noi (the street is called Th Sathanpayabarn
where it intersects with Th Phahonyothin) –
a 60B túk-túk ride.

WORTH A TRIP

WAT RONG KHUN & BAAN DUM

Seen from a distance, **Wat Rong Khun** (วัดร่องขุ่น; White Temple, off Asia 1 Hwy; ⊙8am-
5pm Mon-Fri, 8am-5.30pm Sat & Sun) FREE appears to be made of glittering porcelain; a
closer look reveals that the appearance is due to a combination of whitewash and clear-
mirrored chips. Inside, instead of the traditional Buddha life scenarios, the artist has
painted contemporary scenes representing samsara (the realm of rebirth and delusion)
via images such as a plane smashing into the Twin Towers and, oddly enough, Keanu
Reeves as Neo from The Matrix.

Wat Rong Khun is about 13km south of Chiang Rai. To get to the temple, hop on one
of the regular buses that run from Chiang Rai to Chiang Mai or Phayao (20B).

A rather sinister counterpoint to Wat Rong Khun, **Baan Dum** (Black House; off Asia
1 Hwy; ⊙9am-noon & 1-5pm) FREE unites several quasi-traditional structures, most of
which are stained black and ominously decked out with animal pelts and bones. Other
buildings include white, breast-shaped bedrooms, dark phallus-decked bathrooms, and
a bone- and fur-lined 'chapel'.

Baan Dum is 13km north of Chiang Rai in Nang Lae; any Mae Sai–bound bus will drop
you off there for around 20B.

Legend of Chiang Rai HOTEL $$$

(✆0 5391 0400; www.thelegend-chiangrai.com; 124/15 Th Kohloy; r incl breakfast 3900-5900B, bungalow incl breakfast 8100-12,900B; ✳@☎☎) One of the few hotels in town to boast a riverside location, this upscale resort feels like a traditional Lanna village. Rooms feel romantic and luxuriously understated with furniture in calming creams and rattan. The hotel is about 500m north of Th Singhaclai.

Eating & Drinking

Th Jetyod is Chiang Rai's rather tacky drinking strip.

★Lung Eed NORTHERN THAI $

(Th Watpranorn; mains 40-100B; ⊙11.30am-9pm Mon-Sat) There's an English-language menu on the wall, but don't miss the sublime *lâhp gài*, minced chicken fried with herbs and topped with crispy deep-fried chicken skin, shallots and garlic. The restaurant is on Th Watpranorn about 100m from the intersection with the Superhighway.

Khao Soi Phor Jai NORTHERN THAI $

(Th Jetyod, no roman-script sign; mains 30-60B; ⊙7.30am-5pm) Phor Jai serves mild but tasty bowls of the eponymous curry noodle dish, as well as a few other northern Thai staples.

Nam Ngiaw Paa Nuan VIETNAMESE, THAI $

(Vietnamese Restaurant; Th Sanpannard, no roman-script sign; mains 10-120B; ⊙9am-5pm) This quasi-concealed place serves a unique and delicious mix of Vietnamese and northern Thai dishes.

BaanChivitMai Bakery CAFE

(www.baanchivitmai.com; Th Prasopsook; ⊙8am-9pm Mon-Sat; ☎) In addition to a very well prepared cup of local joe, you can snack on

TRANSPORT FROM CHIANG RAI

DESTINATION	AIR	BOAT	BUS	MINIVAN
Ban Pasang (for Doi Mae Salong)	N/A	N/A	25B; 30min; frequent 6am-8pm (Inter-Provincial Bus Station)	N/A
Bangkok	from 2135B; 1¼hr; 5 daily	N/A	487-980B; 11-12hr; hourly 7-9.40am & 5-7.30pm (new bus station)	N/A
Chiang Khong	N/A	N/A	65B; 2hr; frequent 6am-5pm (Inter-Provincial Bus Station)	N/A
Chiang Mai	N/A	N/A	144-288B; 3-7hr; hourly 6.30am-7.30pm (new bus station); 144-288B; 7hr; frequent 6.30am-noon (Inter-Provincial Bus Station)	N/A
Fang	N/A	N/A	92B; 2½hr; 8am (new bus station)	N/A
Luang Prabang (Laos)	N/A	N/A	950B; 16hr; 1pm (new bus station)	N/A
Mae Sai (for Mae Salong)	N/A	N/A	39B; 1½hr; frequent 6am-8pm (Inter-Provincial Bus Station)	46B; 1½hr; frequent 6.30am-6pm (Inter-Provincial Bus Station)
Nan	N/A	N/A	164B; 6hr; 9.30am (Inter-Provincial Bus Station)	N/A
Nakhon Ratchasima (Khorat)	N/A	N/A	514-771B; 12-13hr; 5 daily (new bus station)	N/A
Sop Ruak (Golden Triangle)	N/A	N/A	N/A	50B; 2hr; hourly 6.20am-5.40pm (Inter-Provincial Bus Station)
Sukhothai	N/A	N/A	300B; 8hr; hourly 7.30am-2.30pm (new bus station)	N/A
Tha Ton	N/A	350B; 4hr; 10.30am	N/A	N/A

amazingly authentic Swedish-style sweets (and Western-style meals and sandwiches) at this popular bakery.

❶ Information

You'll have no problem finding banks and internet access along Th Phahonyothin.

Overbrook Hospital (☑ 0 5371 1366; www.overbrookhospital.com; Th Singhaclai) English is spoken at this modern hospital.

Tourism Authority of Thailand (TAT; ☑ 0 5374 4674, nationwide 1672; tatchrai@tat.or.th; Th Singhaclai; ⊙8.30am-4.30pm) English is limited, but staff here do their best to give advice, and can provide a small selection of maps and brochures.

Tourist Police (☑ 0 5374 0249, nationwide 1155; Th Utarakit; ⊙24hr) English is spoken and police are on stand-by 24 hours a day.

❶ Getting There & Away

Chiang Rai International Airport (☑ 0 5379 8000), also known as Mae Fah Luang, is approximately 8km north of the city. **Air Asia** (☑ 0 5379 3543, nationwide 0 2515 9999; www.airasia.com; ⊙8am-9pm) and **Nok Air** (☑ 0 5379 3000, nationwide 1318; www.nokair.co.th; ⊙8am-7pm) fly to Bangkok's Don Muang International Airport, while **Thai Airways International** (THAI; ☑ 0 5379 8202, nationwide 0 2356 1111; www.thaiair.com; ⊙8am-8pm) flies to Bangkok's Suvarnabhumi International Airport. Taxis run into town from the airport for 200B. From town, a metred trip with Chiang Rai Taxi will cost around 120B.

Passenger boats ply Mae Nam Kok between Chiang Rai and Tha Ton, in Chiang Mai, departing from **CR Pier** (☑ 0 5375 0009; ⊙6am-4.30pm), 2km northwest of town, via Th Kraisorasit; a túk-túk to the pier should cost about 60B.

Buses bound for destinations within Chiang Rai Province, as well as a couple of minivans and mostly slow fan-cooled buses bound for a handful of destinations in northern Thailand, depart from the **Provincial Bus Station** (Th Prasopsook) in the centre of town. If you're heading beyond Chiang Rai (or are in a hurry), you'll have to go to the **new bus station** (☑ 0 5377 3989), 5km south of town on Rte 1 (Asia 1 Hwy); frequent *sŏrngtǎaou* linking it and the Inter-Provincial Bus Station run from 6am to 6.30pm (15B, 15 minutes).

Golden Triangle

The tri-country border of Thailand, Myanmar and Laos is known as the Golden Triangle. For more on this region, see p442.

Sop Ruak   สบรวก

☑ 053

This small, riverside village has been dubbed the official 'centre of the Golden Triangle', and in addition to **Phra Chiang Saen Si Phaendin** (พระเชียงแสนสีแผ่นดิน; Rte 1290; ⊙7am-9pm) FREE, a giant Buddha statue that straddles a boatlike platform, is home to two opium-related museums. The **House of Opium** (บ้านฝิ่น; www.houseofopium.com; Rte 1290; admission 50B; ⊙7am-7pm) has a small display of poppy cultivation and opium paraphernalia, while 1km north of Sop Ruak is the royally sponsored **Hall of Opium** (หอฝิ่น; Rte 1290; admission 200B; ⊙8.30am-4pm Tue-Sun), an impressive facility with multimedia exhibits on the history and effects of opium on individuals and society.

Long-tail boat trips (1hr cruise max 5 people per boat 400B; ⊙6am-6pm) on the Mekong River can be arranged at one of various piers. The typical trip involves a circuit upriver for a view of the Myanmar casino hotel and a stop at the Lao island of Don Sao.

The only reason to stay overnight in or around Sop Ruak is to take advantage of some of northern Thailand's best upscale lodgings. The **Four Seasons Tented Camp** (☑ 0 5391 0200; www.fourseasons.com; tent per night, all-inclusive 79,000-89,000B; ❉@⊛⊛) has 15 luxurious tents that are decked out in colonial-era safari paraphernalia, and guests are encouraged to participate in daily activities ranging from mahout training to spa treatments.

Budget accommodation, such as **Chiang Saen Guest House** (☑ 0 5365 0196; 45/2 Th Rimkhong; r & bungalows 100-500B; ❉⊛), is available in Chiang Saen, 9km south.

From Sop Ruak, there are frequent *sŏrngtǎaou* to Chiang Saen (20B, from 7am to noon). Minivans to Chiang Rai (50B, one hour, hourly from 6am to 5pm) wait in the parking lot west of Phra Chiang Saen Si Phaendin.

Mae Salong   แม่สลอง

☑ 053 / POP 25,000

For a taste of China without crossing any international borders, head to this atmospheric village perched on the back hills of Chiang Rai. Originally founded by KMT fighters escaping Myanmar (Burma) in the 1960s, it's a great place to kick back for a couple of days, and the surrounding area is ripe for exploration.

NORTHERN THAILAND GOLDEN TRIANGLE

THE GOLDEN TRIANGLE, YESTERDAY & TODAY

In historical terms, the Golden Triangle refers to an area, stretching thousands of square kilometres into Myanmar, Laos and Thailand, within which the opium trade was once prevalent. From the early 20th century to the 1980s, the Golden Triangle was the world's biggest grower of *Papaver somniferum*, the poppy that produces opium. Poverty and lack of infrastructure and governance in the largely rebel-controlled areas meant that growing poppies and transporting opium proceeded virtually unchecked, eventually making its way around the world as refined heroin.

Undoubtedly the single most significant player in the Golden Triangle drug trade was Khun Sa, a Shan/Chinese warlord dubbed the 'Opium King' by the Western press. Starting in the mid-1970s from his headquarters in Chiang Rai Province, Khun Sa, his Shan United Army (SUA), ex-KMT fighters in Mae Salong and other cohorts in the region formed a partnership that would eventually claim a virtual monopoly of the world's opium trade.

In 1988, after having been the victim of two unsuccessful assassination attempts, Khun Sa offered to sell his entire crop of opium to the Australian government for AUS$50 million a year, claiming that this would essentially end the world's entire illegal trade in heroin. He made a similar offer to the US, but was dismissed by both. With a US DEA bounty of US$2 million on his head, in 1996 Khun Sa surrendered to Myanmar officials. They refused to extradite him to the US, and Khun Sa eventually died in Yangon in 2007.

Khun Sa's surrender seemed to be the last nail in the coffin of the Golden Triangle opium trade. Land dedicated to poppy cultivation in the region hit an all-time low in 1998, and since the early 21st century Afghanistan's Golden Crescent has replaced the region as the world's pre-eminent producer of opium. But a recent report by the United Nations Office of Drugs and Crime claims that the trade has spiked yet again – most likely due to increased demand from China – and in 2012 Myanmar alone was thought to have produced 10% of the world's opium.

However, most agree that the contemporary Golden Triangle drug trade has shifted from opium to methamphetamines. Manufactured in Myanmar in factories with alleged links to the United Wa State Army, the drug, known in Thai as *yah bâh* (crazy drug) has become the new scourge of the region, and footage of tweaked-out users holding hostages was a Thai news staple in the early 2000s. Although recent efforts to eradicate methamphetamines by Thai authorities have led to higher prices, trafficking and use are thought to have increased.

The area's opium days are (mostly) long gone, but hoteliers and tour operators in Chiang Rai have been quick to cash in on the name by rebranding the tiny village of Sop Ruak as 'the Golden Triangle'. The name is undoubtedly meant to conjure up images of illicit adventure, exotic border areas and opium caravans, but these days the only caravan you're likely to see is the endless parade of buses carrying package tourists. Sop Ruak's opium is fully relegated to museums, and even the once beautiful natural setting has largely been obscured by ATMs, stalls selling tourist tat and the seemingly never-ending loud announcements from the various temples. And perhaps most tellingly, Khun Sa's formerly impenetrable headquarters in Ban Thoet Thai are today a low-key tourist attraction.

⊙ Sights & Activities

A tiny but interesting **morning market** convenes from 6am to 8am at the T-intersection near Shin Sane Guest House. An **all-day market** forms at the southern end of town, and unites vendors selling hill-tribe handicrafts, shops selling tea and a few basic restaurants.

To soak up the great views from **Wat Santikhiri** go past the market and ascend 718 steps (or drive if you have a car). The wát is of the Mahayana tradition and Chinese in style.

Shin Sane Guest House and Little Home Guesthouse have free maps showing approximate **trekking** routes to Akha, Lisu, Mien, Lahu and Shan villages in the area. Nearby Akha and Lisu villages are less than half a day's walk away.

Shin Sane Guest House arranges **horseback treks** to four nearby villages for 500B for about three or four hours.

🛏 Sleeping & Eating

All accommodation and restaurants are on, or just off, the main road.

Little Home Guesthouse GUESTHOUSE **$$**
(☑0 5376 5389; www.maesalonglittlehome.com; bungalows 800B; @📶) Located behind a wooden house near the market intersection is this handful of great-value bungalows.

Baan Hom Muen Li HOTEL **$$**
(☑0 5376 5271; osmanhouse@hotmail.com; no roman-script sign; r incl breakfast 1000-2000B; ✱📶) Located in the middle of town, this stylish place consists of 14 rooms decked out in modern and classic Chinese themes.

Sweet Maesalong CAFE **$**
(mains 45-155B; ⊙8.30am-5pm; 📶) If you require more caffeine than the local tea leaves can provide, stop by this modern cafe with an extensive menu of coffee drinks using local beans. Located more or less in the middle of town.

Salema Restaurant MUSLIM-CHINESE **$$**
(mains 30-250B; ⊙7am-8pm) One of the friendliest restaurants in town also happens to be the most delicious. Salema does tasty Muslim-Chinese dishes, and is at the southern end of town.

❶ Information

There is an ATM at the Thai Military Bank opposite Khumnaiphol Resort, at the southern end of town. An **internet cafe** (per hr 20B; ⊙9am-11pm) can be found next door.

❶ Getting There & Away

To get to Mae Salong by bus, take a Mae Sai–bound bus or minivan from Chiang Rai to Ban Pasang (20B to 25B, 30 minutes, every 20 minutes from 6am to 8pm). From Ban Pasang, blue *sŏrngtăaou* head up the mountain to Mae Salong when full (60B, one hour, from 6am to 5pm). To get back to Ban Pasang, *sŏrngtăaou* park near Mae Salong's lone 7-Eleven. *Sŏrngtăaou* stop running at around 5pm but you can charter one in either direction for about 500B.

You can also reach Mae Salong by road from Tha Ton. Yellow *sŏrngtăaou* bound for Tha Ton stop near Little Home Guesthouse at 8.20am, 10.20am, 12.20pm and 1.50pm (60B, one hour).

Chiang Khong เชียงของ

☑053 / POP 12,000

A lively border town, Chiang Khong sits at a crucial crossroads in the history of the region. For most of its history, Chiang Khong was a remote but important market town for local hill tribes (including local Mien and White Hmong) and then developed a bustling business as a travellers' gateway to Laos starting in the 1990s.

The nearby village of **Ban Hat Khrai**, 1.5km south of Chiang Khong, is a riverside fishing village that has long harvested the *blah beuk* (giant Mekong catfish; *Pangasianodon gigas* to ichthyologists). This catfish is one of the largest freshwater fish in the world and can measure 2m to 3m in length and weigh up to 300kg. The fish is technically endangered, though fishing is still allowed during the annual migration period between late April and June.

In Chiang Khong, several banks have branches with ATMs and foreign-exchange services.

There is no shortage of lodging in town, much of it near the river and geared towards the budget market such as **PP Home** (Baan

---

OFF THE BEATEN TRACK

BAN BO LUANG บ้านบ่อหลวง

Ban Bo Luang (also known as Ban Bo Kleua, or Salt Well Village) is a picturesque Htin village southeast of Doi Phu Kha National Park where the long-standing occupation has been the extraction of salt from local salt wells. The village is a good base for exploring Doi Phu Kha National Park (p446) and **Khun Nan National Park** (อุทยานแห่งชาติขุน น่าน; ☑0 5477 8140; adult/child 100/50B; ⊙8am-4.30pm), the latter with a 2km walk from the visitor centre that ends in a viewpoint looking over local villages and nearby Laos, acommodation (bungalows 800B to 1600B) and a basic restaurant.

The town's best accommodation is **Boklua View** (☑08 1809 6392; www.bokluaview. com; r & bungalows incl breakfast 1850B; ✱📶), an attractive and well-run hillside resort overlooking the village and the Nam Mang that runs through it. There are a few small restaurants serving basic dishes in Ban Bo Luang.

To reach the village, you must first take a bus or *sŏrngtăaou* to Pua (50B, two hours, hourly from 7am to 5pm). Get off at the 7-Eleven then cross the highway to board one of the three daily *sŏrngtăaou* (80B, one hour) that depart at 9am, 10.30am and 12.30pm.

GETTING TO LAOS: NORTHERN BORDERS

Chiang Khong to Huay Xai

Since the completion of the Thai-Lao Friendship Bridge 4 in late 2013, the former boat crossing across the Mekong is only for locals.

Getting to the border The bridge is 11km south of Chiang Khong, a 200B túk-túk ride from town.

At the border The border is open from 6am to 10pm. After going through the usual formalities on the Thai side, board the bus (20B to 30B) that crosses the bridge to Lao immigration, where visas are available on arrival.

Moving on On the Lao side, túk-túk charge 80B per person to Huay Xai. Destinations from Huay Xai's bus station include Luang Namtha (350B, 4½ hours, 9am and 12.30pm), Luang Prabang (700B to 900B, 12 hours, 2pm and 5pm), Udomxai (500B to 700B, nine hours, 3pm) and Vientiane (1800B, 24 hours, 3pm).

If time is on your side, the daily slow boat (950B, 10.30am) to Luang Prabang takes two days, including a night in the village of Pak Beng. Booking tickets through a Chiang Khong–based agent such as **Easy Trip** (☏ 0 5365 5174, 08 6997 7246; www.discoverylaos. com; 183 Th Sai Klang; ⊗ 8.30am-6pm) costs slightly more, but they arrange tickets for you, and provide transport from your guesthouse to the bridge and a boxed lunch for the boat ride. Avoid the noisy fast boats (1600B, six to seven hours, frequent 9am to 11am) as there have been reports of bad accidents.

Lao Airlines (☏ local +856 8421 1026, nationwide +856 2121 2051; www.laoairlines.com) operates a flight from Huay Xai to Vientiane every Wednesday for US$100.

If you already hold a Chinese visa, it's also possible to go directly to China from Chiang Khong. After obtaining a 30-day Laos visa on arrival in Huay Xai, simply board one of the buses bound for Mengla (1900B, eight hours, 10am Monday to Saturday) or Kunming (2500B, 18 hours, 10am Monday to Saturday), which are both in China's Yunnan Province.

Nan to Hongsa

The Ban Huay Kon/Muang Ngeun border crossing is 140km north of Nan.

Getting to the border To Ban Huay Kon, there are four daily minivans departing from Nan's bus station at 5am, 6.50am, 8am and 9.30am (100B, three hours). If you miss one of these, the only other option is to hop on a bus from Nan to Pon (85B, 2½ hours, hourly from 6am to 6pm), at which point you'll need to transfer to the infrequent *sŏrngtăaou* that go the remaining 30km to Ban Huay Kon (100B, one hour, from 9am to 6pm).

At the border The border is open from 8am to 6pm. On the Lao side, foreigners can purchase a visa on arrival.

Moving on You can then proceed 2.5km to the Lao village of Muang Ngeun, where you could stay at the **Phouxay Guesthouse** (☏ 020 2214 2826; r 60,000K). Or, if you're heading onward, go to the tiny **Passenger Car Station** (☏ 020 244 4130, 020 245 0145) beside the market, from where *sŏrngtăaou* leave for Hongsa (40,000K, 1½ hours) between 2pm and 4pm. Once the new bridge north of Pak Beng is open, there will also be a bus service and ostensibly, more frequent transport links.

For more information about crossing these borders in the other direction, see p324.

Pak Pon; ☏ 0 5365 5092; baanpakpon@hotmail. co.th; off Th Sai Klang; r 350-600B; ✴@☎) and **Ban Tammila** (☏ 0 5379 1234; www.baantammi-la.com; 113 Th Sai Klang; r & bungalows 400-650B; ✴☎). **Khao Soi Pa Orn** (Soi 6, Th Sai Klang, no roman-script sign; mains 15-30B; ⊗8am-4pm) does an excellent local noodle dish; look for the gigantic highway pillar at the eastern end of Soi 6.

Buses depart frequently for Chiang Mai (144B to 288B, three hours, from 8am 5.30pm) and Chiang Rai (65B, 2½ hours, from 4.30am to 3.45pm), with a few departures to Bangkok (688B to 963B, 14 hours) between 3pm and 4pm.

Boats taking up to five passengers can be chartered up the Mekong River to Chiang Saen for 2000B.

Nan   น่าน

054 / POP 20,000

Due to its remote location, Nan is not the kind of destination most travellers are going to stumble upon. And its largely featureless downtown isn't going to inspire many postcards home. But if you've taken the time to get here, you'll be rewarded by a city rich in both culture and history. Nan Province also has a low-key outdoor adventure scene, and the border at Ban Huay Kon makes the province a possible gateway to Laos.

Sights

Wat Phumin   BUDDHIST TEMPLE
(วัดภูมินทร์; cnr Th Suriyaphong & Th Pha Kong; ⊙daylight hours) FREE Nan's most famous Buddhist temple is celebrated for its exquisite murals that were executed during the late 19th century by a Thai Lü artist named Thit Buaphan.

Nan National Museum   MUSEUM
(พิพิธภัณฑสถานแห่งชาติน่าน; Th Pha Kong; admission 100B; ⊙9am-4pm Wed-Sun) Housed in the 1903 vintage palace of Nan's last two feudal lords, this museum first opened its doors in 1973. In terms of collection and content, it's one of the country's better provincial museums, and has English labels for most items.

Activities

White-water rafting along Mae Nam Wa, in northern Nan, is popular, but only possible when the water level is high (September to December), and is said to be best during the early part of the wet season.

Nan Touring   RAFTING
(08 1961 7711; www.nantouring.com; 11/12 Th Suriyaphong; 3 days & 2 nights per person 5500B; ⊙9am-5pm) Offers a variety of rafting trips for groups of at least five people.

Tours

Nan Seeing Tour   CYCLING TOURS
(08 1472 4131; www.nanseeingtour.com; Th Sumon Thewarat; bike tours per person 2/3 days 2250/4550B; ⊙8am-7pm) This locally owned outfit conducts two-wheeled expeditions in and around Nan.

Sleeping & Eating

The town's **night market** (Th Pha Kong; mains 30-60B; ⊙5-11pm) and its Saturday **walking street** (Th Sumon Thewarat; ⊙5-10pm Sat) offer decent food stall options.

Fah Place   HOTEL $
(0 5471 0222; 237/8 Th Sumon Thewarat; r 350-500B; ❄☎) The rooms here are spacious and have been decorated with attractive teak furniture, including the kind of puffy inviting beds you'd expect at places that charge several times this much.

★ Pukha Nanfa Hotel   HOTEL $$$
(0 5477 1111; www.pukhananfahotel.com; 369 Th Sumon Thewarat; r 2500-4600B; ❄@☎) Rooms at this charming boutique are cosy and classy, with aged wood accentuated by touches such as local cloth, handicrafts and art, and the place is conveniently located and has more-than-capable staff.

Pu Som Restaurant   NORTHERN THAI $
(203/1 Th Khamyot, no roman-script sign; mains 35-90B; ⊙10am-10pm) The emphasis here is on meat, served in the local style as *lâhp* or *néu·a nêung* (beef steamed over herbs and served with an incredibly delicious galangal-based dip). There's no English-language sign; look for the 'est cola' banner.

NORTHERN THAILAND NAN

TRANSPORT FROM NAN

DESTINATION	AIR	BUS	MINIVAN	SŎRNGTĂAOU
Ban Huay Kon (for border with Laos)	N/A	N/A	100B; 3hr; 4 daily 5-9.30am	N/A
Bangkok	2190B; 1½hr; 2 daily	420-820B; 10-11hr; frequent	N/A	N/A
Chiang Mai	N/A	225-451B; 6hr; frequent	N/A	N/A
Chiang Ra	N/A	181B; 6hr; 9am	N/A	N/A
Pon (Lao border)	N/A	85B; 2½hr; hourly 6am-6pm	N/A	N/A
Pua (for Ban Bo Luang and Doi Phu Kha National Park)	N/A	N/A	N/A	50B; 2hr; hourly 7am-5pm

Hot Bread INTERNATIONAL-THAI $
(38/1-2 Th Suriyaphong; mains 25-130B; ⊘7am-4pm; 🖉) This retro-themed cafe and restaurant has a generous menu of Western-style breakfast dishes – including the eponymous and delicious homemade bread – and other Western and Thai items.

ℹ Information

You shouldn't have any trouble locating banks and/or internet in Nan, particularly along Th Sumon Thewarat.

Tourist Information Centre (🖉0 5475 1169; Th Pha Kong; ⊘8.30am-noon & 1-4.30pm) Opposite Wat Phumin, hidden behind vendors and coffee shops, is this helpful information centre.

ℹ Getting There & Away

Nok Air (🖉08 8263 2012, nationwide 1318; www.nokair.co.th; Nan Airport; ⊘7.30am-7pm) is the only airline operating out of Nan, with flights to/from Bangkok's Don Muang International Airport. **Nan Taxi** (🖉08 4617 0777) does airport transfers for about 100B per person.

From Nan, all buses, minivans and *sŏrngtăao* leave from the bus station at the southwestern edge of town. A motorcycle taxi between the station and the centre of town costs 30B.

Around Nan

Doi Phu Kha National Park อุทยานแห่งชาติดอยภูคา

This **national park** (🖉0 2562 0760, 08 2194 1349; www.dnp.go.th; admission 200B) is centred on 2000m-high Doi Phu Kha, the province's highest peak. There are several Htin, Mien, Hmong and Thai Lü villages in the park and vicinity, as well as a couple of caves and waterfalls, and endless opportunities for forest walks.

The park offers a variety of **bungalows** (🖉0 2562 0760; www.dnp.go.th; bungalow 2-7 people 300-2500B), and there is a nearby restaurant and basic shop.

To reach the national park by public transport you must first take a bus or *sŏrngtăaou* to Pua (50B, two hours, hourly from 7am to 5pm). Get off at the 7-Eleven then cross the highway to board one of the three daily *sŏrngtăaou* (80B, one hour) that depart at 9am, 10.30am and 12.30pm.

UNDERSTAND THAILAND

Thailand Today

Smartphones everywhere, cars instead of motorcycles and the need for immigrant labour – there is no doubt about it, Thailand is getting richer. In 2011, the World Bank upgraded the country's category from a lower-middle economy to an upper-middle income economy, a designation based on per capita gross national income (GNI). In 2012, Thailand's GNI was US$5210, more than double what it was a decade ago.

Yet cyclical political instability remains a lingering and legitimate threat to Thailand's economic success. Following the 2006 coup d'état (the 18th in 70 years), which ousted then Prime Minister, Thaksin Shinawatra, there have been six prime ministers and an increasing sense of social division in Thai society.

Much of this is due to the sometimes violent protests by the Yellow Shirts, made up of the educated elite aligned with the monarchy and the military, and the Red Shirts, comprised of the predominantly rural-based supporters of the exiled prime minister. In 2008, Yellow Shirt protestors shut down the country's major international airports for two weeks, and in 2010, opposition Red Shirt protestors staged a two-month siege of Bangkok's central shopping district that ended in violent clashes with the military. In late 2013 and early 2014, tensions flared yet again when Yellow Shirt protestors took to Bangkok's streets, taking over key parts of town and blocking parliamentary elections in an effort to force the Thaksin-linked government to stand down.

Thais in the political middle are fatigued from the political discord, which undermines a deep-seated sense of a unified 'Thai-ness' and a cultural aversion to displays of violence and anger. Many also resent the perceived stress upon whom the political bickering and societal division have burdened their beloved monarch, Bhumibol Adulyadej. Now 86 years old, he is the world's longest-serving king and is essentially worshipped by his subjects. But as his health has declined, his role in the society at large has diminished. He has been hospitalised since September 2009 and his public appearances are so rare that they make laudatory coverage in Thai national news.

Losing the king will be a national tragedy: he has ruled for more than 60 years and defined through his life what many regard as the modern Thai man (educated, philanthropic family-oriented and even stylish). The heir apparent, his son the Crown Prince Vajiralongkorn, has assumed many of the royal duties his father previously performed, but the ongoing political problems complicate a smooth transfer of crown from father to son.

On the upside, prospects for Thailand's border areas, formerly irksome hotspots of instability, are starting to look more positive. At the end of 2015, the Asean Economic Community (AEC) will unite the association's 10 Southeast Asian countries into a liberalised marketplace where goods, services, capital and labour are shared across borders with little or no country-specific impediments. Open borders and improved infrastructure between Thailand's neighbouring countries have already come as a result of the AEC. Although Thailand's lengthy border with Myanmar (Burma) remains home to an estimated 130,000 refugees, there's hope that Myanmar's recent moves towards democracy, coupled with a lull in sectarian conflict, may finally allow some refugees to return home. And in late 2013, Thailand and Cambodia came close to reaching an agreement regarding ownership of the long-disputed and violently contested Prasat Phra Viharn (in Khmer, Prasat Preah Vihear), a Khmer-era temple straddling the border.

History

Rise of Thai Kingdoms

It is believed that the first Thais migrated here from modern-day Yunnan and Guangxi, China, settling into small riverside farming communities.

By the 13th and 14th centuries, what is considered the first Thai kingdom, Sukhothai, began to chip away at the crumbling Angkor empire. The third Sukhothai king, Ramkhamhaeng, developed a Thai writing system and built Angkor-inspired temples that defined early Thai art.

Sukhothai was soon eclipsed by another emerging power, Ayuthaya, which was established in present-day Thailand's central plains in 1350. This new centre developed

NORTHERN THAILAND HISTORY

THE KING

His image present everywhere from towering roadside billboards to the country's money, King Bhumibol Adulyadej is not only Thailand's longest-reigning monarch, but also the longest-reigning living monarch in the world. Known in English as Rama IX (the ninth king of the Chakri dynasty), Bhumibol Adulyadej was born in 1927 in the USA, where his father Prince Mahidol was studying medicine at Harvard University.

Fluent in English, French, German and Thai, Bhumibol ascended the throne in 1946 following the death of his brother Rama VIII (King Ananda Mahidol; r 1935–46), who reigned for just over 11 years before dying under mysterious circumstances.

An ardent jazz composer and saxophonist when he was younger, Rama IX has hosted jam sessions with the likes of jazz greats Woody Herman and Benny Goodman. The king is also recognised for his extensive development projects, particularly in rural areas of Thailand. For an objective English-language biography of the king's accomplishments, *King Bhumibol Adulyadej: A Life's Work* (Nicholas Grossman and Dominic Faulder, 2010) is available in most Bangkok bookstores.

Rama IX and Queen Sirikit have four children: Princess Ubol Ratana (b 1951), Crown Prince Maha Vajiralongkorn (b 1952), Princess Mahachakri Sirindhorn (b 1955) and Princess Chulabhorn (b 1957).

After more than 60 years in power, and having recently reached his 86th birthday, Rama IX is preparing for his succession. The king has spent most of the last few years in hospital, and the Crown Prince has performed most of the royal ceremonies the king would normally perform, such as presiding over the Royal Ploughing Ceremony, changing the attire on the Emerald Buddha and handing out academic degrees at university commencements.

Along with nation and religion, the monarchy is very highly regarded in Thai society – negative comment about the king or any member of the royal family is a social as well as legal taboo.

DOS & DON'TS

➡ Because Thai money bears a picture of the king, don't step on a dropped bill to prevent it from blowing away.

➡ Stand respectfully for the national anthem, which is played at 8am and 6pm.

➡ Rise for the royal anthem, which is played in cinemas before every screening.

➡ Don't get a tattoo of the Buddha, as the culture ministry is seeking to ban the practice and it is viewed as being sacrilegious.

➡ Greet people with a smile and a cheery *sà·wàt·dee kráp* if you're male or *sà·wàt·dee kâ* if you're female.

➡ Bring a gift if you're invited to a Thai home and take off your shoes when you enter.

➡ Lower your head slightly when passing between two people having a conversation or when passing near a monk.

➡ Dress modestly (cover to the elbows and the ankles) for temple visits and always remove your shoes when you enter any building that contains a Buddha image.

➡ Never step over someone or his personal belongings.

➡ Avoid tying your shoes to the outside of your backpack where they might accidentally brush against someone.

into a cosmopolitan port on the Asian trade route courted by European nations attracted to the region for commodities and potential colonies, though the small nation managed to thwart foreign takeovers. For 400 years Ayuthaya dominated most of present-day Thailand until the Burmese destroyed the capital in 1767.

The Thais eventually rebuilt their capital in present-day Bangkok and established the Chakri dynasty, which continues to occupy the throne today. As Western imperialism marched across the region, King Mongkut (Rama IV; r 1851–68) and his son and successor King Chulalongkorn (Rama V; r 1868–1910) successfully steered Thailand into the modern age without becoming a colonial vassal.

A Struggling Democracy

In 1932 a peaceful coup converted Thailand into a constitutional monarchy loosely based on the British model. Nearly half a century of political chaos followed. During the mid-20th century, a series of anticommunist military dictators wrestled each other for power, successfully suppressing democratic representation and civil rights. Student protests in the 1970s called for a reinstatement of a constitution and the end of military rule. In October 1976, a demonstration on the campus of Thammasat University in Bangkok was quashed by the military, resulting in deaths and injuries. Many activists went underground to join armed communist insurgency groups hiding in the northeast.

In the 1980s and 1990s there were slow steps towards democracy and even a return to a civilian government. During these tumultuous times, Rama IX defined a new political role for the monarchy, as a paternal figure who restrained excesses in the interests of all Thais.

Economic & Political Roller Coaster

During the 1990s, Thailand was one of the so-called tiger economies that imploded in 1997, leading to a recession that lasted nearly three years. Thailand's convalescence progressed remarkably well and it pulled an 'early exit' from the International Monetary Fund's loan package in mid-2003.

The ambitious and charismatic billionaire Thaksin Shinawatra became prime minister in 2001 on a populist platform. He delivered on his promises for affordable health care and village development funds, which won him diehard support among the working class, especially in the impoverished northeast.

He and his party swept to victory in the 2005 election but his popularity plummeted due to a host of corruption charges.

Rumours of his unabated ambitions – to interrupt or even usurp the eventual transfer of the crown from father to son – filtered into the general public, sparking mass protests organised by political rivals and those viewed as loyal to the crown. Behind the scenes Thaksin had earned very powerful enemies as he attempted to eradicate the role that the military continued to play in the government by replacing key appointments with his own loyalists.

On 19 September 2006, army chief Sonthi Boonyaratglin led a bloodless military coup, and Thaksin fled the country to avoid corruption charges. Political and social instability dominated the next five years, culminating in the 2011 election victory of the Pheu Thai Party, headed by Thaksin's younger sister, Yingluck Shinawatra. In 2013, an effort by Yingluck's government to grant amnesty to her brother, thus ostensibly allowing him to return to Thailand, infuriated the opposition, who took to the streets. Months-long blockades of central Bangkok followed, which a violence-prone snap election in early 2014 failed to disperse.

People & Culture

People

Thais are master chatters and will have a shopping list of questions: where are you from, are you married, do you have children? Occasionally they get more curious and want to know how much you weigh or how much money you make; these questions to a Thai are matters of public record and aren't considered impolite.

Thais are laid-back, good-natured people who live by a philosophy of sà·nùk (fun), and every task is measured on the sà·nùk meter. Thais believe strongly in the concept of 'saving face', that is, avoiding confrontation and endeavouring not to embarrass themselves or other people. All relationships follow simple lines of social rank defined by age, wealth, status, and personal and political power.

About 75% of citizens are ethnic Thais, further divided by geography (north, central, south and northeast). Each group speaks its own Thai dialect and to an extent practises regional customs. Politically and economically the central Thais are dominant.

People of Chinese ancestry, many of whom have been in Thailand for generations, make up over 14% of the population. Other large minority groups include Vietnamese in the east, Khmer in parts of the northeast, Lao spread throughout the north and northeast, and Muslim Malays in the far south. Smaller non-Thai-speaking groups include the hill tribes living in the northern mountains.

Religion

Country, family and daily life are all married to Theravada Buddhism (as opposed to the Mahayana schools found in East Asia and the Himalaya). Every Thai male is expected to become a monk for a short period in his life since a family earns great merit when a son 'takes robe and bowl'.

More evident than the philosophical aspects of Buddhism is the everyday fusion with animist rituals. Monks are consulted to determine an auspicious date for a wedding or the likelihood of success for a business. Spirit houses are constructed outside buildings and homes to encourage the guardian spirits to bring good fortune to the site. Food, drink and furniture are all offered to the spirits to smooth daily life.

Roughly 95% of the population practises Buddhism, but there is a significant Muslim community, especially in southern Thailand.

Arts

Classical central Thai music features an incredible array of textures and subtleties, hair-raising tempos and pastoral melodies. Among the more common instruments is the *ȟȟ*, a woodwind instrument with a reed mouthpiece; it is heard prominently at Thai boxing matches. A bowed instrument, similar to examples played in China and Japan, is called the *sor*. The *rá·nâht èhk* is a bamboo-keyed percussion instrument

NORTHERN THAILAND PEOPLE & CULTURE

CLASSIC THAI MOVIES

➡ *6ixtynin9* (1997)

➡ *Yam Yasothon* (2005)

➡ *Ruang Rak Noi Nid Mahasan* (*Last Life in the Universe*; 2003)

➡ *Fah Talai Jone* (*Tears of the Black Tiger*; 2000)

➡ *Uncle Boonmee Who Can Recall His Past Lives* (2010)

resembling the Western xylophone, while the *klòo·i* is a wooden flute. This traditional orchestra originated as an accompaniment to classical dance-drama and shadow theatre, but these days it can be heard at temple fairs and concerts.

In the north and northeast there are several popular wind instruments with multiple reed pipes, which function basically like a mouth-organ. Chief among these is the *kaan*, which originated in Laos; when played by an adept musician, it sounds like a rhythmic, churning calliope organ.

The best example of modern Thai music is the rock group Carabao, which has been performing for more than 30 years. Another major influence was a 1970s group called Caravan. It created a modern Thai folk style known as *pleng pêu·a chee·wít* ('songs for life'), which features political and environmental topics. In the 1990s, a respectable alt-rock scene emerged thanks to the likes of Modern Dog and Loso.

On an international scale, Thailand has probably distinguished itself more in traditional religious sculpture than in any other art form. Thailand's most famous sculptural output has been its bronze Buddha images, coveted the world over for their originality and grace.

Temple architecture symbolises elements of the religion. A steeply pitched roof system tiled in green, gold and red represents the Buddha (the Teacher), the Dhamma (Dharma in Sanskrit; the Teaching) and the Sangha (the fellowship of followers of the Teaching).

The traditional Thai theatre consists of dance-dramas using either human dancers or puppets to act out the plot. *Kŏhn* is formal masked dance-drama depicting scenes from the *Ramakian* (the Thai version of India's *Ramayana*) and originally performed only for the royal court; *lá·kon* is a general term covering several types of dance-dramas (usually for nonroyal occasions), as well as Western theatre; *lí·gair* is a partly improvised, often bawdy folk play featuring dancing, comedy, melodrama and music; and *lá·kon lék* is puppet theatre.

Food & Drink

Welcome to a country where it is cheaper and tastier to eat out than to cook at home. Markets, pushcart vendors, makeshift stalls, open-air restaurants – prices stay low and cooks become famous in all walks of life for a particular dish.

Take a walk through the day markets to see mounds of clay-coloured pastes moulded into pyramids like art supplies. These are the backbone for Thai *gaang* (curries) and are made of finely ground herbs and seasonings. The paste is taken to home kitchens and thinned with coconut milk and decorated with vegetables and meat to make a meal. Although it is the consistency of soup, *gaang* is ladled onto a plate of rice instead of eaten directly out of the bowl.

For breakfast and for snacks, Thais nosh on *gŏo·ay dĕe·o*, rice noodle soup with chicken or pork and vegetables. There are two primary types of noodles to choose from: *sên lék* (thin) and *sên yài* (wide and flat). Before you dig in, add to taste a few teaspoons of the provided spices: dried red chilli, sugar, fish sauce and vinegar. Now you have the true taste of Thailand in front of you.

Not sure what to order at some of the popular dinner restaurants? Reliable favourites are *yam ꝫlah mèuk* (spicy squid salad with mint leaves, coriander and Chinese celery), *đôm yam gûng* (a tart, herbal soup with prawns, often translated as 'hot and sour soup') or its sister *đôm kàh gài* (coconut soup with chicken and galangal).

Thais are social eaters: meals are rarely taken alone and dishes are meant to be shared. Usually a small army of plates will be placed in the centre of the table, with individual servings of rice in front of each diner. The protocol goes like this: ladle a spoonful of food at a time onto your plate of rice. Using the spoon like a fork and your fork like a knife, steer the food (with the fork) onto your spoon, which enters your mouth.

Environment

Like all countries with a high population density, there is enormous pressure on Thailand's ecosystems: 50 years ago about 70% of the countryside was forest, it's now 28%. In response to environmental degradation, the Thai government has created a large number of protected areas since the 1970s. Following devastating floods, exacerbated by soil erosion, logging was banned in 1989.

Though Thailand has a better record than most of its neighbours at protecting endangered species, corruption hinders the efforts and the country is a popular conduit for the illegal wildlife trade.

SURVIVAL GUIDE

❶ Directory A–Z

ACCOMMODATION

Thailand offers a wide variety of good-value accommodation. The budget range runs from around 200B for basic rooms (shared bathrooms and fan cooled), while for 400B you'll get air-con and private bathroom. In Bangkok and Chiang Mai, the midrange begins at about 1000B and has become more stylish and interesting these days. In the rest of the country you'll start getting midrange quality at around 600B but the hotels tend to be old and poorly maintained. Top-end in small towns starts above 1500B and in Bangkok above 3000B. Prices listed in this chapter are high-season rates.

A two-tiered pricing system has been used to determine the accommodation price ranges (budget, midrange, top end).

Bangkok & Chiang Mai

$ less than 1000B (US$30)
$$ 1000B to 3000B (US$30 to US$90)
$$$ more than 3000B (US$90)

Elsewhere

$ less than 600B (US$20)
$$ 600B to 1500B (US$20 to US$45)
$$$ more than 1500B (US$45)

BOOKS

➡ *Chronicle of Thailand* (2010; William Warren and Nicholas Grossman)
➡ *Sacred Tattoos of Thailand* (2011; Joe Cummings)
➡ *Very Thai* (2013; Philip Cornwell-Smith)
➡ *The Arts of Thailand* (1998; Steve Van Beek)
➡ *Thai Folk Wisdom: Contemporary Takes on Traditional Proverbs* (2010; Tulaya Pornpiriyakulchai and Jane Vejjajiva)

CUSTOMS REGULATIONS

The **customs department** (www.customs.go.th) maintains a helpful website with specific information about customs regulations. Thailand allows the follow items to enter duty free:
➡ reasonable amount of personal effects (clothing and toiletries)
➡ professional instruments
➡ 200 cigarettes
➡ 1L of wine or spirits

Thailand prohibits the import of the following items:

➡ firearms and ammunition (unless registered in advance with the police department)
➡ illegal drugs
➡ pornographic media

When leaving Thailand, you must obtain an export licence for any antiques, reproductions or newly cast Buddha images (except personal amulets). Submit two front-view photos of the object(s), a photocopy of your passport, along with the purchase receipt and the object(s) in question, to the **Department of Fine Arts** (☏ 0 2628 5032). Allow four days for the application and inspection process to be completed.

EMBASSIES & CONSULATES

Foreign embassies are in Bangkok; some nations also have consulates in Chiang Mai, as indicated below.

Australian Embassy (Map p380; ☏ 0 2344 6300; www.thailand.embassy.gov.au/bkok/home.html; 37 Th Sathon Tai (South), Bangkok; ⊗ 8.30am-4.30pm Mon-Fri; M Lumphini exit 2)

Cambodian Embassy (☏ 0 2957 5851; 518/4 Th Pracha Uthit/Soi Ramkhamhaeng 39, Bangkok; ⊗ 9am-noon Mon-Fri; M Phra Ram 9 exit 3 & taxi)

Canadian Embassy (Map p368; ☏ 0 2646 4300; www.canadainternational.gc.ca; 15th fl, Abdulrahim Pl, 990 Th Phra Ram IV, Bangkok; ⊗ 7.30am-12.15pm & 1-4.15pm Mon-Thu, to 1pm Fri; M Si Lom exit 2, S Sala Daeng exit 4)

Canadian Consulate (☏ 0 5385 0147; 151 Superhighway, Tambon Tahsala, Chiang Mai)

Chinese Embassy (Map p368; ☏ 0 2245 7044; www.fmprc.gov.cn; 57 Th Ratchadaphisek, Bangkok)

Chinese Consulate (☏ 0 5327 6125; chiang mai.chineseconsulate.org; 111 Th Chang Lor, Tambon Haiya, Chiang Mai)

French Embassy (Map p368; ☏ 0 2657 5100; www.ambafrance-th.org; 35 Soi 36, Th Charoen Krung, Bangkok; ⊗ 8.30am-noon Mon-Fri; ▣ Tha Oriental)

French Consulate (☏ 0 5328 1466; 138 Th Charoen Prathet, Chiang Mai)

German Embassy (Map p368; ☏ 0 2287 9000; www.bangkok.diplo.de; 9 Th Sathon Tai (South), Bangkok; ⊗ 8.30-11am Mon-Fri; M Lumphini exit 2)

Irish Consulate (Map p380; ☏ 0 2632 6720; www.irelandinthailand.com; 4th fl, Thaniya Bldg, 62 Th Silom, Bangkok; ⊗ 8.30am-12.30pm Mon-Fri; M Si Lom exit 2, S Sala Daeng exit 1)

Israeli Embassy (Map p382; ☏ 0 2204 9200; bangkok.mfa.gov.il; 25 Soi 19, Th Sukhumvit, Ocean Tower 2, 25th fl, Bangkok)

Laotian Embassy (☏ 0 2539 6678; www.laoembassybkk.com; Th Ramkamhaeng,

NORTHERN THAILAND DIRECTORY A–Z

502/1-3 Soi Sahakarnpramoon, Pracha Uthit/Soi 39, Bangkok)

Myanmar Embassy (Map p380; ☑0 2233 7250; www.myanmarembassybkk.com; 132 Th Sathon Neua (North), Bangkok; ☺9am-4.30pm (embassy), 9am-noon & 1-3pm Mon-Fri (visa section); ⑤Surasak exit 3)

Netherlands Embassy (Map p378; ☑0 2309 5200; thailand.nlembassy.org; 15 Soi Tonson, Bangkok; ☺8.30-11.30am Mon-Wed, 8.30-11.30am & 1.30-3pm Thu (consular office); ⑤Chit Lom exit 4)

New Zealand Embassy (Map p378; ☑0 2254 2530; www.nzembassy.com/thailand; 14th fl, M Thai Tower, All Seasons Pl, 87 Th Witthayu (Wireless Rd), Bangkok; ☺8am-noon & 1-2.30pm Mon-Fri; ⑤Phloen Chit exit 5)

South African Embassy (Map p378; ☑0 2659 2900; www.dirco.gov.za; 87 Th Witthayu (Wireless Rd), 12th A fl, M Thai Tower, All Seasons Pl, Bangkok)

UK Embassy (Map p378; ☑0 2305 8333; www.gov.uk/government/world/organisations/british-embassy-bangkok; 14 Th Witthayu (Wireless Rd), Bangkok; ☺8am-4.30pm Mon-Thu, to 1pm Fri; ⑤Phloen Chit exit 5)

UK Consulate (☑0 5326 3015; www.british-consulate.net; 198 Th Bamrungrat, Chiang Mai)

US Embassy (Map p378; ☑0 2205 4049; http://bangkok.usembassy.gov; 95 Th Witthayu (Wireless Rd), Bangkok)

US Consulate (☑0 5310 7700; chiangmai.usconsulate.gov; 387 Th Wichayanon, Chiang Mai)

Vietnamese Embassy (Map p378; ☑0 2251 5838, 0 2251 5836; www.vietnamembassy-thailand.org; 83/1 Th Witthayu (Wireless Rd), Bangkok)

FOOD

As an approximate guide, prices for main dishes when eating out in Thailand are:

$ less than 150B (US$4.50)

$$ 150B to 350B (US$4.50 to US$11)

$$$ more than 350B (US$11)

GAY & LESBIAN TRAVELLERS

Thai culture is relatively tolerant of both male and female homosexuality. However, public displays of affection – whether heterosexual or homosexual – are frowned upon. Utopia (p385) posts lots of Thailand information for gay and lesbian visitors and publishes a guidebook to the kingdom for homosexuals.

INSURANCE

A travel-insurance policy to cover theft, loss and medical problems is a good idea. There is a wide variety of policies available, so check the small print. Be sure that the policy covers ambulances or an emergency flight home.

Some policies specifically exclude 'dangerous activities', which can include scuba diving, motorcycling or even trekking. A locally acquired motorcycle licence is not valid under some policies.

Worldwide travel insurance is available at www.lonelyplanet.com/travel-insurance. You can buy, extend and claim online any time – even if you're already on the road.

INTERNET ACCESS

As more and more people travel with mobile devices, internet cafes have begun to disappear. Some guesthouses still have computer terminals, however, charging between 60B to 150B an hour, depending on how much competition there is. Wi-fi is becoming commonplace in guesthouses, restaurants and cafes.

LEGAL MATTERS

In general, Thai police don't hassle tourists, unless you are caught holding drugs. If it's a small amount, you might be able to get away with paying a 'fine', but traffickers are certain to end up in prison.

If you're arrested for any offence, the police will let you make a phone call to your embassy, if you have one, or to a friend or relative if not. Thai law does not presume an indicted detainee to be either 'guilty' or 'innocent' but rather a 'suspect', whose guilt or innocence will be decided in court. Trials are usually speedy.

The **tourist police** (☑1155) usually speak English, and offer a range of assistance from providing road conditions during floods to assistance if you've been ripped off or robbed.

MAPS

ThinkNet (www.thinknet.co.th) produces high-quality, bilingual city and country maps, including interactive-map CDs.

MONEY

The unit of Thai currency is the baht, which is divided into 100 satang; coins include 25-satang and 50-satang pieces and baht in 1B, 2B, 5B and 10B coins. Notes are in 20B (green), 50B (blue), 100B (red), 500B (purple) and 1000B (beige). Rarely are other currencies accepted.

Occasionally high-end hotels in Bangkok will quote prices in US dollars; when this is the case we've followed suit. Also note that in certain border sections we've quoted dollars or the local currency when Thai baht is not accepted.

ATMs & Credit Cards

Debit and ATM cards issued by your home bank can be used at ATMs, which are widespread, to withdraw cash (in Thai baht only). Thai ATMs now charge a 150B foreign-transaction fee on top of whatever currency conversion and out-of-network fees your home bank charges. Cards can also be used for purchases at many shops, hotels and restaurants. The most commonly accepted cards are Visa and MasterCard. Top-end hotels will accept Amex.

Moneychangers

Banks and private moneychangers (only found in popular tourist destinations) give the best exchange rates and hotels give the worst. Since banks charge commission and duty for each travellers cheque cashed, use large denominations. British pounds and euros are second to the US dollar in general acceptability.

OPENING HOURS

The following are standard hours for different types of businesses in Thailand. All government offices and banks are closed on public holidays.

Banks 9.30am to 3.30pm Monday to Friday; ATMs accessible 24 hours.

Bars & Nightclubs Bars 6pm to midnight (officially); closing times vary due to local enforcement of curfew laws; bars close during elections and certain religious public holidays. Nightclubs 8pm to 2am; closing times vary due to local enforcement of curfew laws.

Government offices 8.30am to 4.30pm Monday to Friday; some close for lunch (noon to 1pm), while others are open Saturday (9am to 3pm).

Restaurants 10am to 10pm; some specialise in morning meals and close by 3pm.

Stores Local stores 10am to 6pm daily; department stores 10am to 10pm daily. In some small towns, local stores close on Sunday.

PHOTOGRAPHY

Memory cards for digital cameras are generally widely available in the more popular formats and are available in the electronic sections of most shopping malls.

Be considerate when taking photographs of the locals. Learn how to ask politely in Thai and wait for an embarrassed nod. In some of the regularly visited hill-tribe areas be prepared for the photographed subject to ask for money in exchange for a picture. Some hill tribes will not allow you to point a camera at them.

POST

Thailand has an efficient postal service. Typical provincial post offices keep the following hours: 8.30am to 4.30pm weekdays and 9am to noon on Saturdays. Larger main post offices in provincial capitals may also be open for a half-day on Sundays.

PUBLIC HOLIDAYS

Government offices and banks close on the following days:

1 January New Year's Day

February (date varies) Makha Bucha, Buddhist holy day

6 April Chakri Day, commemorating the founder of the Chakri dynasty, Rama I

13–14 April Songkran Festival, traditional Thai New Year and water festival

5 May Coronation Day, commemorating the 1946 coronation of HM the King and HM the Queen

1 May Labour Day

May/June (date varies) Visaka Bucha, Buddhist holy day

July (date varies) Asanha Bucha, Buddhist holy day

12 August Queen's Birthday

23 October Chulalongkorn Day

October/November (date varies) Ork Phansaa, the end of Buddhist 'lent'

5 December King's Birthday

10 December Constitution Day

31 December New Year's Eve

SAFE TRAVEL

Thailand is not a dangerous country, but there are a few common scams and things to watch out for. For Bangkok-specific scams see p387.

Try not to get into an argument with a Thai, especially if alcohol is involved. While foreigners might see a verbal argument as sport, Thais view it as a loss of face and have been known to respond with excessive and unpredictable violence. Especially untrustworthy are the off-duty police officers who are still armed even in civilian settings; there have been several incidents of altercations between foreigners and off-duty police, typically at bars, that have resulted in gun homicides.

Women also need to take care of themselves when travelling or visiting bars alone. Flirtation for the fun of it can often be misunderstood by Thais and can result in unwanted advances or unpredictable retribution if interest isn't mutual.

TELEPHONE

The telephone country code for Thailand is ☑ 66 and is used when calling the country from abroad. All Thai telephone numbers are preceded by a '0' if you're dialling domestically (the '0' is omitted when calling from overseas). After the initial '0', the next three numbers represent the provincial area code, which is now integral to the telephone number. If the initial '0' is followed by an '8' or a '9', then you're dialling a mobile phone.

The standard International Direct Dial prefix is ☑ 001. Economy rates are available with ☑ 007, ☑ 008 and ☑ 009, all of which use Voice over Internet Protocol (VoIP), with varying but adequate sound quality.

NORTHERN THAILAND DIRECTORY A–Z

Dial ☑ 100 for operator-assisted international calls or reverse-charges (or collect) calls. Alternatively contact your long-distance carrier for their overseas operator number, a toll-free call, or try ☑ 001 9991 2001 from a CAT phone and ☑ 1 800 000 120 from a TOT phone.

The easiest phone option in Thailand is to acquire a mobile (cell) phone equipped with a local SIM card. Thailand is on the GSM network and mobile phone providers include AIS (1 2 Call), DTAC and True Move. You have two hand-phone options: you can buy a mobile phone in Thailand at one of the urban shopping malls or phone stores near the markets in provincial towns. Or you can use an imported phone that isn't SIM-locked (and one that supports the GSM network). To get started, buy a SIM card of a particular carrier, which includes an assigned telephone number. Once your phone is SIM-enabled you can buy minutes with prepaid phonecards. SIM cards and refill cards (usually sold in 300B to 500B denominations) can be bought from 7-Elevens throughout the country. Thailand finally has a 3G network and True Move is offering 4G LTE coverage in Bangkok.

TIME

Thailand's time zone is seven hours ahead of GMT/UTC (London).

TOILETS

Increasingly the Asian-style squat toilet is less of the norm in Thailand. There are still specimens in rural places, but the Western-style toilet is becoming more prevalent and appears wherever foreign tourists can be found.

THAILAND'S IMMIGRATION OFFICES

The following are two common immigration offices where visa extensions and other formalities can be addressed. Remember to dress in your Sunday best when doing official business in Thailand and do all visa business yourself (don't hire a third party). For all types of visa extensions, bring along two passport-sized photos and one copy each of the photo and visa pages of your passport.

Bangkok Immigration Office (☑ 0 2141 9889; Bldg B, Government Center, Soi 7, Th Chaeng Watthana; ⊗ 8.30am-noon & 1-4.30pm Mon-Fri; ⬛ Mo Chit & access by taxi)

Chiang Mai Immigration Office (☑ 0 5320 1755; chiangmaiimm.com; Th Mahidon; ⊗ 8.30am-4.30pm Mon-Fri)

Even in places where sit-down toilets are installed, the septic system may not be designed to take toilet paper. In such cases there will be a waste basket where you're supposed to place used toilet paper and feminine hygiene products. Some modern toilets also come with a small spray hose – Thailand's version of the bidet.

TOURIST INFORMATION

The helpful **Tourism Authority of Thailand** (TAT; www.tourismthailand.org) has 35 offices throughout the country. Most staff speak English. Check TAT's website for a list of overseas offices, plus plenty of tourism information.

VISAS

Thailand's **Ministry of Foreign Affairs** (www. mfa.go.th) oversees immigration and visa issues. In the past five years there have been new rules nearly every year regarding visa extensions; the best online monitor is **Thaivisa** (www. thaivisa.com).

Citizens of 41 countries (including most European countries, Australia, New Zealand and the USA) can enter Thailand at no charge. These citizens are issued a 30-day visa if they arrive by air or 15 days by land.

If you need more time in the country, apply for a 60-day tourist visa prior to arrival at a Thai embassy or consulate abroad. Rules enacted in 2011 state that hotel reservation and documentation of return flight are required for this, but the consensus at writing time is that these rules weren't being enforced across the board.

If you overstay your visa, the penalty is 500B per day, with a 20,000B limit; fines can be paid at any official exit point or at the Bangkok immigration office.

You can extend your stay, for the normal fee of 1900B, at an immigration office. Those issued with a standard stay of 15 or 30 days can extend their stay for seven to 10 days (depending on the immigration office), if the extension is handled before the visa expires. The 60-day tourist visa can be extended by up to 30 days at the discretion of Thai immigration authorities.

VOLUNTEERING

There are many wonderful volunteering organisations in Thailand that provide meaningful work and cultural engagement. Volunteer Work Thailand (www.volunteerworkthailand.org) maintains a database of opportunities.

WOMEN TRAVELLERS

Attacks and rapes are not common in Thailand, but incidents do occur. If you return home from a bar alone, be sure to have your wits about you. Avoid accepting rides from strangers late at night or travelling around in isolated areas by yourself – common sense stuff that might escape your notice in a new environment filled with hospitable people.

ⓘ Getting There & Away

Flights, tours and train tickets can be booked online at www.lonelyplanet.com/bookings.

ENTERING THAILAND

Entry procedures for Thailand, by air or by land, are straightforward: you'll have to show your passport, and you'll need to present completed arrival and departure cards.

AIR

Bangkok is *the* air-travel hub for mainland Southeast Asia and airfares are quite competitive. Carriers operating to the international destinations covered in this book include:

Air Asia (☑ nationwide call centre 0 2515 9999; www.airasia.com) Bangkok's Don Muang International Airport to Hanoi (Vietnam), Ho Chi Minh City (Saigon; Vietnam), Phnom Penh (Cambodia) and Siem Reap (Cambodia).

Bangkok Airways (☑ 1771; www.bangkokair. com) Bangkok's Suvarnabhumi International Airport to Luang Prabang (Laos), Phnom Penh (Cambodia), Siem Reap (Cambodia) and Vientiane (Laos).

Cambodia Angkor Air (☑ in Bangkok 0 2655 4747; www.cambodiaangkorair.com) Bangkok's Suvarnabhumi International Airport to Phnom Penh (Cambodia) and Siem Reap (Cambodia).

Lao Airlines (☑ in Bangkok 0 2236 9822; www. laoairlines.com) Bangkok's Suvarnabhumi International Airport to Luang Prabang (Laos), Pakse (Laos), Savannakhet (Laos) and Vientiane (Laos); Chiang Mai International Airport to Luang Prabang (Laos).

Qatar Airways (☑ in Bangkok 0 2259 2701; www.qatarairways.com) Bangkok's Suvarnabhumi International Airport to Hanoi (Vietnam).

Thai Airways International (THAI; ☑ 0 2356 1111; www.thaiair.com) Bangkok's Suvarnabhumi International Airport to Luang Prabang (Laos), Hanoi (Vietnam), Ho Chi Minh City (Saigon; Vietnam), Phnom Penh (Cambodia) and Vientiane (Laos).

Turkish Airlines (☑ in Bangkok 0 2231 0300; www.turkishairlines.com) Bangkok's Suvarnabhumi International Airport to Ho Chi Minh City (Saigon; Vietnam).

LAND
Border Crossings

See p484 for more detail on the region's border crossings. In addition to those detailed in this book, Northern Thailand also shares borders with Myanmar (Burma) at Mae Sai, in Chiang Rai Province, and Mae Sot, in Tak Province.

Cambodia Cambodian tourist visas are available at most borders for US$20, though some borders charge 1500B. Bring a passport photo and ignore the runner boys who claim that you'll need a health certificate or other medical paperwork for additional fees.

Laos It is fairly hassle-free to cross into Laos from crossings in northern Thailand and northeastern Thailand. Lao visas (US$35 to US$50) can be obtained on arrival at most borders and applications require a passport photo.

ⓘ Getting Around

AIR

Hopping around Thailand by air can be quite affordable. Airlines with routes to the domestic destinations mentioned in this chapter include: Air Asia, flying from Bangkok's Don Muang International Airport to Chiang Mai, Chiang Rai, Nakhon Phanom, Ubon Ratchathani and Udon Thani; **Bangkok Airways** (Map p368; ☑1771; www.bangkokair.com), flying from Suvarnabhumi International Airport to Chiang Mai, Sukhothai, Trat and Udon Thani; and Thai Airways International, flying from Suvarnabhumi to Chiang Mai, Chiang Rai, Ubon Ratchathani and Udon Thani. Also flying are:

Kan Air (☑ 0 2551 6111; www.kanairlines.com) Chiang Mai International Airport to Pai.

Nok Air (☑1318; www.nokair.co.th) Bangkok's Don Muang International Airport to Chiang Mai, Chiang Rai, Loei, Mukdahan, Nakhon Phanom, Nan, Ubon Ratchathani and Udon Thani; Chiang Mai International Airport to Udon Thani.

BICYCLE

Single-geared bicycles are available for rent in most tourist towns from around 30B per day. Higher-quality mountain bikes are sometimes available for around 150B per day. Touring the country is also a doable activity as the roads are well sealed and lodging is available along the way.

BOAT

The true Thai river transport is the long-tail boat (*reu·a hǎhng yow*), so-called because the propeller is mounted at the end of a long driveshaft extending from the engine. Boats are a common (and highly recommended) means of travel in Bangkok and, to a lesser degree, along the Mekong River in the far north.

BUS & MINIVAN

The bus network in Thailand is prolific and reliable. The Thai government subsidises the Transport Company (*bò·rí·sàt kǒn sòng*), usually abbreviated to Baw Khaw Saw (BKS). Every city and town in Thailand linked by bus has a BKS station, even if it's just a patch of dirt by the side of the road. We do not recommend using bus companies that operate directly out of tourist centres, like Bangkok's Th Khao San, because of repeated instances of theft and commission-seeking stops.

The cheapest buses are the fan-cooled *rót tam·má·dah* that stop in every town and for every waving hand along the way, but this class of bus is a dying breed. Most services are in faster air-con buses, called *rót aa*. Longer routes offer 2nd-class and 1st-class air-con services; the latter have toilets and better air-con. VIP and Super VIP buses have fewer seats, and hostesses serve snacks.

Minivans are increasingly becoming the middle-class option. Minivans are run by private companies and because their vehicles are smaller, they can depart from in-town (instead of the out-of-town bus stations) and can sometimes deliver guests directly to their hotel.

CAR & MOTORCYCLE

Cars, 4WDs or vans can be rented in most large cities. Always verify (ask to see the dated documents) that the vehicle is insured for liability before signing a contract. An International Driving Permit is necessary to drive vehicles in Thailand, but this is rarely enforced for motorcycle hire.

Thais drive on the left-hand side of the road (most of the time!). The main rule to be aware of is that smaller vehicles always yield to bigger ones.

Motorcycle travel is a popular way to get around Thailand. Dozens of places along the guesthouse circuit rent motorbikes for as little as 150B a day. Motorcycle rental usually requires that you leave your passport, and many provinces require you to wear a helmet.

Recommended car-rental agencies:

Avis (www.avisthailand.com)

North Wheels (www.northwheels.com)

Thai Rent A Car (www.thairentacar.com)

LOCAL TRANSPORT
Motorcycle Taxi

Many cities have motorcycle taxis. Rather than cruise the streets they cluster near busy intersections. Fares range from 10B to 50B.

Sähm·lór & Túk-Túk

Sähm·lór, meaning 'three wheels', are pedal rickshaws. The motorised version is called túk-túk because of the throaty cough their two-stroke engines make. In tourist centres, Bangkok especially, many túk-túk drivers are unscrupulously greedy, inflating fares or diverting passengers to places that pay commissions.

You must bargain and agree on a fare before accepting a ride, but in many towns there is a de facto fixed fare anywhere in town.

Sŏrngtăaou

Sŏrngtăaou (literally, two rows) are small pickups with a row of seats down each side. In most towns *sŏrngtăaou* serve as public buses running fixed routes.

TOURS

The better tour companies build their own Thailand itineraries from scratch and choose their local suppliers based on which best serve these itineraries. Many are now offering 'voluntourism' programs, which means that you might buy lunch for an orphanage, visit a hospital or teach an English class in addition to sightseeing. If you're looking for alternative travelling experiences, volunteering is also an option.

Asian Trails (www.asiantrails.info) Tour operator that runs programs for overseas brokers; trips include a mix of on- and off-the-beaten-path destinations.

Hands Up Holidays (www.handsupholidays.com) Volunteer tourism and village sightseeing programs.

I-to-I (www.i-to-i.com) Volunteer tourism and gap-year programs.

Intrepid Travel (www.intrepidtravel.com) Specialises in small-group travel geared towards young people.

Isan Explorer (www.isanexplorer.com) Custom tours to the northeast.

Tour de Thailand (www.tourdethailand.com) Charity bike ride organiser covering touring routes throughout the country.

Tours with Kasma Loha-Unchit (www.thaifoodandtravel.com) Thai cookbook author offers personalised 'cultural immersion' tours of Thailand.

TRAIN

The **State Railway of Thailand** (SRT; ☑1690; www.railway.co.th) has four main lines (northern, southern, northeastern and eastern) branching out from Bangkok. Trains are comfortable, but almost always slower and less frequent than buses.

Trains are often heavily booked, so it's wise to reserve well ahead, especially the Bangkok–Chiang Mai overnight trip. You can make bookings at any train station (English is usually spoken) and, for a small fee, through some Bangkok travel agencies.

First-class, 2nd-class and 3rd-class cabins are available on most trains, but each class varies considerably depending on the type of train (rapid, express or ordinary). First class is a private cabin. Second class has individually reclining seats; depending on the train, some cabins have air-con. Non-air-conditioned 3rd class is spartan with bench seating.

Overnight trains have sleeping berths in 1st and 2nd class. Single 1st-class cabins are not available, so if you're travelling alone you may be paired with another passenger.

Understand
the Mekong
Region

The Mekong Region Today

Rewind just a generation and Cambodia, Laos and Vietnam were pariah states, scarred by decades of war and boycotted by much of the Western world. Despite the region's communist history, its leaders proved themselves to be open to Western economic models as they balanced Eastern communism with Western capitalism. Touchdown today and the bad old days seem but a footnote in history. Like the river that runs through it, the Mekong region is well and truly going places.

Best In Print

The Quiet American (Graham Greene, 1955) Seminal anti-war novel set in the 1950s as the French empire is collapsing.

The Lover (Marguerite Duras, 1984) Semi-autobiographical tale of a young girl in love with a local scion in French colonial Vietnam.

Phaic Tan: Sunstroke on a Shoestring (2004) Ultimate spoof guidebook pokes fun at locals, travellers and guidebook authors.

Best on Film

Apocalypse Now (1979) Francis Ford Coppola's masterpiece is one of the most savage indictments of war ever seen on screen.

The Killing Fields (1984) Iconic film about the Khmer Rouge period, focusing on photographer Dith Pran's relationship with journalist Sidney Schanberg.

Platoon (1986) Based on the first-hand experiences of director Oliver Stone, it follows a young recruit to the Vietnam War.

Uncle Boonmee Who Can Recall His Past Lives (2010) Terminally ill Thai man explores ghosts of his past in Apichatpong Weerasethakul's Palme d'Or winner.

Spirit of Cooperation

Much of the region is closer than it has been for some time thanks to the Association of Southeast Asian Nations (Asean). At the end of 2015, the Asean Economic Community (AEC) will unite the association's 10 Southeast Asian countries into a liberalised marketplace where trade moves freely. Things are moving especially fast in the Mekong region. Major cross-border highways are being built. Railroad track is being laid down or rehabilitated. New border posts are being installed and old ones upgraded. Airlines are expanding their interregional routes. There's even talk of a single-visa policy for foreign visitors to the region, although this appears to be some ways off.

Needless to say improved infrastructure is having a profound effect on tourism, as it makes it that much easier to get around. This may disappoint old-timers for whom the epic journey by longboat or pickup tuck was an inherent part of travel in the region. Ultimately, however, improved accessibility puts more tourist dollars in remote communities and helps some locals escape poverty. Meanwhile you can still dial up those epic journeys, you just need to venture more off-the-beaten track to do so.

Big Brother

As the nations of the Mekong region draw closer together through Asean, the elephant in the room continues to be China. Beijing exerts political and economic influence on the region as it spends some of its enormous surplus in Laos and Cambodia. Apart from the obvious investment in infrastructure such as roads, dams and plantations, this has two significant effects. Firstly, Chinese aid comes with few strings attached, meaning that roads, plantations and dams are built by Chinese companies with little or no concern for local people or environments. Secondly, having China as a major source of funding and as a political role model is unlikely to encourage the Lao and Cambodian governments to adopt democratic reforms.

Chinese investment in the region rankles environmentalists and democracy watchdogs – not to mention Vietnam. Relations between Vietnam and China have traditionally been frosty. On the plus side trade is booming, albeit it's more one-way than the Vietnamese would like. However, the Spratly Islands, rich in oil deposits, remain a potential flashpoint, with both nations claiming sovereignty. There have been regular protests in Hanoi against the Chinese occupation of the islands. Meanwhile both Cambodia and Vietnam are at loggerheads with Laos and China over the construction of upstream dams on the Mekong River, which could severely impact fish stocks downstream.

Season of Protest

Over in Thailand, politics has been getting very shirty, as hordes of opposition protesters come and go from the capital with alarming regularity. Red Shirts support exiled former Prime Minister Thaksin Shinawatra and are mostly drawn from provincial northern and eastern Thailand. Yellow Shirts support the royal family and the established elite and are generally from Bangkok and central Thailand. As we went to print, the Red Shirts were tenuously holding on to power under the leadership of Thaksin's younger sister, Yingluck. But another round of Yellow Shirt protests was wreaking havoc in Bangkok and threatening the Shinawatra dynasty.

In Cambodia, protesters have hit the streets of Phnom Penh over alleged improprieties in the 2013 national elections. Although ostensibly democratic, Cambodia has effectively been under the rule of one party – Prime Minister Hun Sen's Cambodia People's Party (CPP) – since 1979. However, against all expectations the united opposition made significant gains in the National Assembly in 2013. Indeed the opposition claimed that it had narrowly won the election and was cheated out of victory by the CPP. Six months after the contested election, the opposition still had refused to take up its seats in the National Assembly and street protests continued.

Such public expressions of discontent are not seen in Vietnam and Laos, which are still old-school, one-party states.

POPULATION: **182.5 MILLION**

AREA: **1,262,165 SQ KM**

HIGHEST POINT: **MT FAN SI PAN, VIETNAM (3,144M)**

BIGGEST CITIES: **BANGKOK (8 MILLION), HO CHI MINH CITY (7.4 MILLION)**

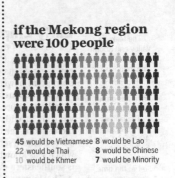

if the Mekong region were 100 people

45 would be Vietnamese   8 would be Lao
22 would be Thai   8 would be Chinese
10 would be Khmer   7 would be Minority

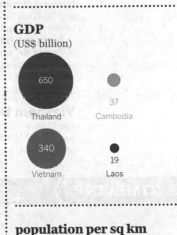

GDP
(US$ billion)

650 Thailand

37 Cambodia

340 Vietnam

19 Laos

population per sq km

CAMBODIA   VIETNAM   LAOS

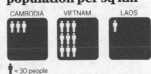

🧍 ≈ 30 people

History

This vibrant region has a history as long and dramatic as the Mekong River that cuts through its heart. The Mekong played host to some of the most brutal wars of the 20th century and the bloodiest revolutions. However, calmer waters lie ahead, as the region is peaceful and relatively stable for the first time in generations.

The Mekong Valley and Khorat Plateau were inhabited as far back as 10,000 years ago, and rice was grown in northeastern Thailand as early as 4000 BC. China, by contrast, was still growing millet at the time.

Early Empire

The history of this great region is also the history of two great civilisations colliding. China and India may be making headlines today as the emerging giants of the 21st century, but it is old news. They have long been great powers and have historically influenced the Mekong region, from art and architecture to language and religion.

Indian culture was disseminated through much of the Mekong region via contact with seafaring Indian merchants calling at trading settlements along the coast of present-day Thailand, Cambodia and Vietnam. Some of these settlements were part of nascent kingdoms, the largest of which was known as Funan to the Chinese, and occupied much of what is southeastern Cambodia today.

The Funanese constructed an elaborate system of canals both for transportation and the irrigation of rice. The principal port city of Funan was Oc-Eo in the Mekong Delta and excavations here reveal contact between Funan and Indonesia, Persia and even the Mediterranean.

Funan was famous for its refined art and architecture, and its kings embraced the worship of Hindu deities Shiva and Vishnu and, concurrently, Buddhism. The *linga* (phallic totem) was the focus of ritual and an emblem of kingly might, a feature that was to evolve further in the Angkorian cult of the god king.

Vietnam Under Occupation

The Chinese ruled Vietnam for 1000 years, introducing Confucianism, Taoism and Mahayana Buddhism to Vietnam, as well as a written character system. Meanwhile, the Indians brought Theravada Buddhism.

TIMELINE	4200 BC	c 2000 BC	c AD 100
	Cave dwellers capable of making pots inhabit caves around Laang Spean; archaeological evidence suggests the vessels these people were making are similar to those made in Cambodia today.	The Bronze Age Dong Son culture emerges in the Red River Delta around Hanoi. It's renowned for its rice cultivation and the production of bronzeware, including drums and gongs.	The process of Indianisation begins in the Mekong region, the religions, language, sculpture and culture of India taking root through maritime contact with Cambodia.

Monks carried with them the scientific and medical knowledge of these two great civilisations, and Vietnam was soon producing its own great doctors, botanists and scholars.

In the early 10th century, the Tang dynasty in China collapsed. The Vietnamese seized the initiative and launched a revolt against Chinese rule in Vietnam. In 938 popular patriot Ngo Quyen finally vanquished the Chinese armies at a battle on the Bach Dang River, ending a millennium of Chinese rule. However, it was not the last time the Vietnamese would tussle with their mighty northern neighbour.

From the 11th to 13th centuries, Vietnamese independence was consolidated under the enlightened emperors of the Ly dynasty. During the Ly dynasty many enemies, including the Chinese, the Khmer and the Cham, launched attacks on Vietnam, but all were repelled.

The Rise of Chenla

From the 6th century the Funan kingdom's importance as a port of call declined, and Cambodia's population gradually settled along the Mekong and Tonlé Sap rivers, where the majority remains today.

Chinese records refer to the rise of the Chenla empire, divided into 'water Chenla' (lower) and 'land Chenla' (upper). Water Chenla was located around Angkor Borei and the temple mount of Phnom Da; and land Chenla in the upper reaches of the Mekong River and east of Tonlé Sap lake, around Sambor Prei Kuk, one of the first great temple cities of the Mekong region.

What is certain is that the people of the lower Mekong were well known to the Chinese, and the region was becoming gradually more cohesive. Before long the fractured kingdoms of Chenla would merge to become the greatest empire in Southeast Asia.

The Khmer Empire

A popular place of pilgrimage for Khmers today is the sacred mountain of Phnom Kulen, to the northeast of Angkor, and home to an inscription that tells us that in 802 Jayavarman II proclaimed himself a 'universal monarch', or a *devaraja* (god king). Jayavarman set out to bring the region under his control through alliances and conquests. He was the first monarch to rule all of what we call Cambodia today, and the first of a long succession of kings who presided over the Southeast Asian empire that was to leave the stunning legacy of Angkor.

The Romans of Asia

The Khmers built massive irrigation systems and a sophisticated network of highways to connect the outposts of their empire – much like the Romans did. Roads fanned out from Angkor, connecting the capital with

There are few surviving contemporary accounts of Angkor, but Chinese emissary Chou Ta Kuan lived there in 1296 and his observations have been republished as *The Customs of Cambodia*, a fascinating insight into that period.

245	600	802	938
The Chinese Wei emperor sends a mission to the countries of the Mekong region and is told that a barbarous but rich country called Funan exists in the Delta region.	The first inscriptions are committed to stone in Cambodia in ancient Khmer, offering historians the first contemporary accounts of the pre-Angkorian period other than from Chinese sources.	Jayavarman II proclaims independence from Java, marking the start of the Khmer empire of Angkor, which controls much of the Mekong region from the 10th to 13th centuries.	The Chinese are expelled from Vietnam after 1000 years of occupation, as Ngo Quyen leads his people to victory in the battle of Bach Dang River, luring the Chinese ships onto sharpened stakes.

satellite cities such as Ayuthaya and Phimai in Thailand and as far away as Wat Phu in southern Laos.

From 1113, King Suryavarman II embarked on another phase of expansion, waging wars against Champa and Vietnam. He is immortalised in Cambodia as the king who, in his devotion to the Hindu deity Vishnu, bequeathed the world the majestic temple of Angkor Wat.

Enter Sandstone Man

Suryavarman II had brought Champa to heel and reduced it to vassal status. In 1177 the Chams struck back with a naval expedition up the Mekong and into Tonlé Sap lake. They took the city of Angkor by surprise and put King Dharanindravarman II to death. A year later a cousin of Suryavarman II gathered forces and defeated the Chams in another naval battle. The new leader was crowned Jayavarman VII in 1181.

A devout follower of Mahayana Buddhism, Jayavarman VII built the city of Angkor Thom and many other massive monuments visited by tourists around Angkor today. Immortalised in sandstone and on T-shirts, Jayavarman is deified by many Cambodians as their greatest leader, a populist who promoted equality, and a socially conscious leader who built schools and hospitals for his people.

The Fall

Some scholars maintain that decline was on the horizon at the time Angkor Wat was built, when the Angkorian empire was at the height of its remarkable productivity. There are indications that the irrigation network was overworked and slowly starting to silt up due to the massive

Southeast Asian kingdoms were not states in the modern sense, with fixed frontiers, but varied in extent. Outlying *meuang* (principalities or city-states) might transfer their allegiance elsewhere when the centre was weak. This is why scholars prefer the term 'mandala', meaning 'circle of power'.

THE MONGOLS IN THE MEKONG

The marauding Mongols left an indelible mark on the peoples of the Mekong as they initiated a major shift in the balance of power in the region.

In 1253, Kublai Khan, grandson of Genghis, attacked the Thai state of Nan Chao, which was located in Xishuangbanna in the south of Yunnan. Thais had already been migrating south for several centuries, and settling in parts of Laos and northern Thailand. However, the sacking of their capital provoked a mass exodus and brought the Thais into conflict with the waning Khmer empire. The Mongol empire evaporated into the dust of history, but with the sacking of the Thai capital, the die was cast: it was the Thais versus the Khmers, a conflict that has persisted through the centuries to the present day.

In 1288, Kublai Khan planned to attack Champa and demanded the right to cross Vietnamese territory. The Vietnamese refused, but the Mongol hordes – all half a million of them – pushed ahead, seemingly invulnerable. However, they met their match in the legendary general Tran Hung Dao. He defeated them in the battle of Bach Dang River, one of the most celebrated scalps among many the Vietnamese have taken.

1049	1113	1238	1353
Suryavarman I annexes the Dravati kingdom of Lopburi in Thailand and widens his control of Cambodia, stretching the empire to perhaps its greatest extent.	Suryavarman II commences the construction of Angkor Wat in Cambodia, the mother of all temples and the world's largest religious building; it is dedicated to Vishnu and designed as Suryavarman's funerary temple.	Sukhothai (Land of Rising Happiness) is born, considered the first Thai kingdom in what is contemporary Thailand. It begins to exert pressure on the ailing Khmer empire.	Lao prince Fa Ngum is sponsored by his Khmer father-in-law on an expedition to conquer the new Thai kingdoms, declaring himself leader of Lan Xang Hom Khao (Land of a Million Elephants and the White Parasol).

deforestation that had taken place in the heavily populated areas to the north and east of Angkor.

Following the reign of Jayavarman VII, temple construction effectively ground to a halt, largely because public works quarried local sandstone into oblivion and the population was left exhausted. The state religion reverted to Hinduism for a century or more and outbreaks of iconoclasm saw Buddhist sculpture vandalised or altered.

The Thais grew in strength and made repeated incursions into Angkor, finally sacking the city in 1431. During this period, perhaps drawn by the opportunities for sea trade with China and fearful of the increasingly bellicose Thais, the Khmer elite began to migrate to the Phnom Penh area. Angkor was abandoned to pilgrims, holy men and the elements.

The Golden Age of Siam

Several Thai principalities in the Mekong valley united in the 13th and 14th centuries to create Sukhothai (Land of Rising Happiness). Thai princes wrested control of the territory from the Khmers, whose all-powerful empire at Angkor was slowly disintegrating. Sukhothai is considered by the Thais to be the first true Thai kingdom. It was annexed by Ayuthaya in 1376, by which time a national identity of sorts had been forged.

The Thai kings of Ayuthaya grew very powerful in the 14th and 15th centuries, taking over the former Khmer strongholds in present-day central Thailand. Even though the Khmers had been their adversaries in battle, the Thai kings of Ayuthaya adopted many facets of Khmer culture, including court customs and rituals, language and culture. The cultural haemorrhage that took place with the sacking of Angkor in 1431 continues to strain relations between the two neighbours. Some Thais claim Angkor as their own, while the Khmers bemoan the loss of Khmer kickboxing, classical Khmer dance and Khmer silk to the all-powerful Thai brand.

Angkor's loss was Ayuthaya's gain and it went on to become one of the greatest cities in Asia. It's been said that London, at the time, was a village in comparison. The kingdom sustained an unbroken monarchical succession through 34 reigns from King U Thong (r 1350–69) to King Ekathat (r 1758–67).

> 'Among the Asian nations, the Kingdom of Siam is the greatest. The magnificence of the Ayuthaya court is incomparable.'
>
> *Engelbert Kaempfer, 1690*

Lan Xang, the Birth of Laos

As the power of Sukhothai grew, the ascendant Thais began to exert more pressure on the Khmers. The Cambodian court looked around for an ally, and found one in Fa Ngum, an exiled Lao prince who was being educated at Angkor.

1431	1516	1560	1767
The expansionist Thais sack Angkor definitively, carting off most of the royal court, including nobles, priests, dancers and artisans, to Ayuthaya. It's an irrevocable spiritual and cultural loss to Cambodia.	Portuguese traders land at Danang, sparking the start of European interest in Vietnam. They set up a trading post in Faifo (present-day Hoi An) and introduce Catholicism to the Vietnamese.	King Setthathirat moves the capital of Lan Xang (modern-day Laos) from Luang Prabang to Viang Chan, today known as Vientiane.	Following several centuries of military rivalry, the Burmese sack the Thai capital of Ayuthaya, forcing its relocation to Thonburi, then to the present-day location of Bangkok.

King Jayavarman VIII married Fa Ngum to a Khmer princess and offered him an army of more than 10,000 troops. He pushed north to wrest the middle Mekong from the control of Sukhothai and its allied Lanna kingdom. By 1353 he declared himself king of Lan Xang Hom Khao, meaning 'land of a million elephants and the white parasol'. This was really the last hurrah of the declining Khmer empire and quite probably served only to weaken Angkor and antagonise the Thais.

Within 20 years of its birth, Lan Xang had expanded eastward to pick off parts of a disintegrating Champa and along the Annamite Mountains in Vietnam. Fa Ngum earned the sobriquet 'The Conqueror' because of his constant preoccupation with warfare. Theravada Buddhism became the state religion in Lan Xang when King Visounarat accepted the Pha Bang, a gold Buddha image, from his Khmer sponsors.

Vietnamese Expansion

The Chinese seized control of Vietnam once more in the early 15th century, carting off the national archives and some of the country's intellectuals to China – this was an irreparable loss to Vietnamese civilisation. The poet Nguyen Trai (1380–1442) wrote of this period: 'Were the water of the Eastern Sea to be exhausted, the stain of their ignominy could not be washed away; all the bamboo of the Southern Mountains would not suffice to provide the paper for recording all their crimes.'

In 1418, wealthy philanthropist Le Loi rallied the people against the Chinese. Upon victory in 1428, Le Loi declared himself Emperor Le Thai To, the first in the long line of the Le dynasty. To this day, Le Loi is highly revered as one of the country's all-time national heroes. Le Loi and his successors launched a campaign to take over Cham lands to the south, wiping the kingdom of Champa from the map, and parts of eastern Laos were forced to kowtow to the might of the Vietnamese.

The Dark Ages

The glorious years of the Khmer empire and the golden age of Ayuthaya were no guarantee of future success and the 18th century proved a time of turmoil. This was the dark ages when the countries of the Mekong were convulsed by external threats and internal intrigue.

The Continuing Decline of Cambodia

From 1600 until the arrival of the French in 1863, Cambodia was ruled by a series of weak kings who were forced to seek the protection – at a price – of either Thailand or Vietnam. In the 17th century, assistance from the Nguyen lords of southern Vietnam was given on the condition

By naming his kingdom Lan Xang Hom Khao, Fa Ngum was making a statement. Elephants were the battle tanks of Southeast Asian warfare, so to claim to be the kingdom of a million elephants was to issue a warning to surrounding kingdoms: 'Don't mess with the Lao!'

1772	1802	1834	1864
Cambodia is caught between the powerful Vietnamese and Siamese; the latter burn Phnom Penh to the ground, another chapter in the story of inflamed tensions that persist today.	Emperor Gia Long takes the throne to reign over a united Vietnam for the first time in decades, and the Nguyen dynasty is born, ruling until 1945.	The Vietnamese take control of much of Cambodia during the reign of Emperor Minh Mang and begin a slow revolution to 'teach the barbarians their customs'.	The French force Cambodia into a Treaty of Protectorate, which ironically does prevent the small kingdom being wiped off the map by its more powerful neighbours, Thailand and Vietnam.

THE LOST KINGDOM OF CHAMPA

The Hindu kingdom of Champa emerged around Vietnam's present-day Danang in the late 2nd century AD. Like Funan, it adopted Sanskrit as a sacred language and borrowed heavily from Indian art and culture. By the 8th century Champa had expanded southward to include what is now Nha Trang and Phan Rang. The Cham were a bellicose bunch who conducted raids along the entire coast of Indochina, and thus found themselves in a perpetual state of war with the Vietnamese to the north and the Khmers to the south. Ultimately this cost them their kingdom, as they found themselves squeezed between two great powers.

that Vietnamese be allowed to settle in what is now the Mekong Delta region of Vietnam, at that time part of Cambodia and today still referred to by the Khmers as Kampuchea Krom (Lower Cambodia).

In the west, the Thais controlled the provinces of Battambang and Siem Reap from 1794; by the late 18th century they had firm control of the Cambodian royal family.

The Threat of Burma

Meanwhile, the so-called golden age of Ayuthaya was starting to lose its shine. In 1765 the Burmese laid siege to the capital for two years and the city fell. Everything sacred to the Thais was destroyed, including temples, manuscripts and religious sculpture. The Thais vented their frustrations on their Lao neighbours. If the 17th century had been Lan Xang's very own golden age, the first Lao unified kingdom began to unravel by the end of the century. The country split into the three kingdoms of Luang Prabang, Viang Chan (Vientiane) and Champasak.

Civil War in Vietnam

In a dress rehearsal for the tumultuous events of the 20th century, Vietnam found itself divided in half through much of the 17th and 18th centuries. It wasn't until the dawn of a new century, in 1802, that Nguyen Anh proclaimed himself Emperor Gia Long, thus beginning the Nguyen dynasty. For the first time in two centuries, Vietnam was united, with Hue as its new capital city.

The French Protectorate

Marco Polo was the first European to cross the Mekong and penetrate the east. In the following centuries many more Europeans followed in his wake, trading in ports as diverse as Ayuthaya and Faifo (Hoi An). However, it was France that was to ultimately claim much of the region as its own.

Between 1944 and 1945, the Viet Minh received funding and arms from the US Office of Strategic Services (OSS; the CIA today). When Ho Chi Minh declared independence in 1945, he had OSS agents at his side and borrowed liberally from the American Declaration of Independence.

1883	1893	1907	1930
The French impose the Treaty of Protectorate on the Vietnamese, bringing together Tonkin in the north, Annam in the centre and Cochinchina in the south, marking the start of 70 years of colonial control.	France gains sovereignty over all Lao territories east of the Mekong, thus consolidating its control over the Mekong region as part of its colony of Indochina.	French authorities negotiate the return of Siem Reap, Battambang and Preah Vihear to Cambodia, under Siamese control since 1794; Laos loses out as territory to the west of the Mekong is conceded in the deal.	Ho Chi Minh establishes the Indochinese Communist Party; it splits into three national communist forces – the Viet Minh in Vietnam, the Khmer Rouge in Cambodia and the Pathet Lao in Laos.

SORROW
OF WAR

The concept of 'protectorate' was often employed as a smokescreen by European colonial powers in order to hide their exploitative agenda. However, for the weak and divided kingdoms of Cambodia and Laos, French intervention came not a moment too soon. Both were starting to feel the squeeze as expansionist Thailand and Vietnam carved up their territory. Were it not for the French, it is quite plausible that Cambodia and Laos would have gone the way of Champa, a mere footnote in history, a people without a homeland.

Indochina is Born

France's military activity in Vietnam began in 1847, when the French Navy attacked Danang harbour in response to Emperor Thieu Tri's suppression of Catholic missionaries. Saigon was seized in early 1859 and, in 1862, Emperor Tu Duc signed a treaty that gave the French the three eastern provinces around Saigon.

Cambodia succumbed to French military might in 1864, when French gunboats intimidated King Norodom I (r 1860–1904) into signing a Treaty of Protectorate. In Laos, the same technique was employed with much success. In 1893 a French warship forced its way up the Chao Phraya river to Bangkok and trained its guns on the palace. Under duress, the Siamese agreed to transfer all territory east of the Mekong to France and Laos became part of Indochina.

In 1883 the French attacked Hue and imposed the Treaty of Protectorate on the imperial court of Vietnam. The Indochinese Union proclaimed by the French in 1887 may have ended the existence of an independent Vietnamese state, but active resistance continued in various parts of the country for the duration of French rule.

For a human perspective on the North Vietnamese experience during the war, read *The Sorrow of War* by Bao Ninh, a poignant tale of love and loss that shows the soldiers from the North had the same fears and desires as most American GIs.

The Thais Hold Out

The Thais are proud of their independent history and that they were never colonised. Successive Thai kings courted the Europeans while maintaining their neutrality. It was an ambiguous relationship, best summed up by King Mongkut: 'Whatever they have invented or done, we should know of and do, we can imitate and learn from them, but do not wholeheartedly believe in them.'

The French were able to exert some influence over the Thais, convincing Siam to return the northwest provinces of Battambang, Siem Reap and Sisophon to Cambodia in 1907 in return for concessions of Lao territory. This returned Angkor to Cambodian control.

In the end, it was less the Thai manoeuvring that kept the country independent, but the realisation by the British in Burma (present-day Myanmar) and the French in Indochina that a buffer zone would prevent open warfare.

1939	1941	1945	1953
Following a nationalist coup by a pro-fascist military leadership, Siam changes its name to Thailand in an effort to cement control of the Thai peoples in the Mekong region, choosing to side with Japan in WWII.	Japan sweeps through mainland Southeast Asia during WWII, occupying French Indochina in cooperation with pro-Vichy France colonial authorities and winning Thailand's support in return for the promise of territory.	Ho Chi Minh proclaims Vietnamese independence on 2 September in Ba Dinh Sq in Hanoi, but the French have other ideas, sparking 30 years of warfare, first against the French, later the Americans.	Cambodia and Laos go it alone with independence from France; almost insignificant sacrifices as the colonial power attempts to cling to control in Vietnam.

Communism & WWII

The first Marxist grouping in Indochina was the Vietnam Revolutionary Youth League, founded by Ho Chi Minh in Canton, China, in 1925. This was succeeded in February 1930 by the Vietnamese Communist Party, part of the Indochinese Communist Party (ICP).

As the desire for independence grew in Vietnam, the communists proved adept at tuning into the frustrations and aspirations of the population, and effectively channelling their demands for fairer land distribution.

War Gamesmanship

In WWII Japanese forces occupied much of Asia, and Indochina was no exception. With many in France collaborating with the occupying Germans, the French in Indochina ended up on the side of the Japanese.

In 1941, Ho formed the League for the Independence of Vietnam, much better known as the Viet Minh. Receiving assistance from the US government, Ho resisted the Japanese/French alliance and carried out extensive political activities throughout the war. Ho was pragmatic, patriotic and populist, and understood the need for national unity.

A False Dawn

As events unfolded in Europe, the French and Japanese fell out and the Viet Minh saw its opportunity to strike. By the spring of 1945, the Viet Minh controlled large parts of Vietnam. On 2 September 1945 Ho Chi Minh declared independence. Throughout this period, Ho wrote no fewer than eight letters to US president Harry Truman and the US State Department asking for US aid, but received no replies.

Having prevailed in Europe, the French wasted no time returning to Indochina, making the countries 'autonomous states within the French

Hitch a ride with Michael Herr and his seminal work *Dispatches*. A correspondent for *Rolling Stone* magazine, Herr tells it how it is, as some of the darkest events of the war in Vietnam unfold around him, including the siege of Khe Sanh.

SIAM REBORN AS THAILAND

Siam transformed itself from an absolute monarchy to a constitutional monarchy in a bloodless coup in 1932. Under nationalist military leader Phibul Songkhram, the country veered in a fascist direction, changing its name to Thailand in 1939 and siding with the Japanese in WWII in order to seize back Cambodian and Lao territory returned to French Indochina in 1907.

Changing the name of the country from Siam to Thailand was a political masterstroke, as Siamese exclusivity was abolished and everyone was welcome to be a part of the new Thai family, including ethnic minorities and Laotians detached from their homeland by colonial intrigue.

1954	1955	1956	1959
French forces surrender en masse to Viet Minh fighters at Dien Bien Phu on 7 May, marking the end of colonial rule in Indochina.	Cambodia's King Norodom Sihanouk abdicates to enter a career in politics; he founds the Sangkum Reastr Niyum (People's Socialist Community) and wins the election with ease.	Vietnam remains divided at the 17th parallel into communist North Vietnam, under the leadership of Ho Chi Minh, and 'free' South Vietnam, under the rule of President Ngo Dinh Diem.	The Ho Chi Minh Trail, which had been in existence for several years during the war against the French, reopens for business and becomes the main supply route to the South for the next 16 years.

Union', but retaining de facto control. French general Jacques Philippe Leclerc pompously declared: 'We have come to reclaim our inheritance.'

In the north, Chinese Kuomintang troops were fleeing the Chinese communists and pillaging their way southward towards Hanoi. Ho tried to placate the Chinese, but as the months of Chinese occupation dragged on, he decided 'better the devil you know' and accepted a temporary return of the French.

War with the French

In the face of determined Vietnamese nationalism, the French proved unable to reassert their control. Despite massive US aid and the existence of significant indigenous anticommunist elements, it was an unwinnable war. As Ho said to the French at the time, 'You can kill 10 of my men for every one I kill of yours, but even at those odds you will lose and I will win.'

The whole complexion of the First Indochina War changed with the 1949 victory of communism in China. As Chinese weapons flowed to the Viet Minh, the French were forced onto the defensive. After eight years of fighting, the Viet Minh controlled much of Vietnam and neighbouring Laos. On 7 May 1954, after a 57-day siege, more than 10,000 starving French troops surrendered to the Viet Minh at Dien Bien Phu. This was a catastrophic defeat that brought an end to the French colonial adventure in Indochina. The following day, the Geneva Conference opened to negotiate an end to the conflict, but the French had no cards left to bring to the table.

Independence for Cambodia & Laos

In 1941 Admiral Jean Decoux placed 19-year-old Prince Norodom Sihanouk on the Cambodian throne, assuming he would be naive and pliable. As he grew in stature, this proved to be a major miscalculation. In 1953 King Sihanouk embarked on his 'royal crusade': his travelling campaign to drum up international support for his country's independence.

Independence was proclaimed on 9 November 1953 and recognised by the Geneva Conference of May 1954. In 1955 Sihanouk abdicated, afraid of being marginalised amid the pomp of royal ceremony. The 'royal crusader' became 'citizen Sihanouk' and vowed never again to return to the throne.

Laos was granted independence at the same time. The tragedy for Laos was that when, after two centuries, the independent Lao state was reborn, it was conceived in the nationalism of WWII, nourished during the agony of the First Indochina War and born into the Cold War. Thus, from its inception, the Lao state was torn by ideological division, which the Lao tried mightily to overcome, but which was surreptitiously stoked by outside interference.

For a full Cambodian history, from humble beginnings in the prehistoric period through the glories of Angkor and right up to the present day, seek out a copy of *The History of Cambodia* by David Chandler.

1962	1964	1965	1968
The International Court rules in favour of Cambodia in the long-running dispute with Thailand over Preah Vihear, perched on the Dangkrek Mountains; it continues to create friction between the neighbours today.	The US begins secret bombing of Laos to try to disrupt North Vietnamese supplies to the guerrilla war in South Vietnam; Air America takes off, the CIA airline allegedly funded by opium and heroin smuggling.	The first US marines wade ashore at Danang as the war in Vietnam hots up, and the Americans commit ground troops to avoid the very real possibility of a communist victory.	The Viet Cong launches the Tet Offensive, a synchronised attack throughout the South that catches the Americans unaware. Iconic images of this are beamed into households all over the USA.

A 'SOLUTION' TO THE INDOCHINA PROBLEM

The Geneva Conference of 1954 was designed to end the conflict in Indochina, but the Vietnamese had done a good job of that with their comprehensive defeat of French forces at Dien Bien Phu. Resolutions included: the temporary division of Vietnam into two zones at the Ben Hai River (near the 17th Parallel); the free passage of people across the 17th parallel for a period of 300 days; and the holding of nationwide elections on 20 July 1956.

Laos and Cambodia were broadly neglected. In Laos two northeastern provinces (Hua Phan and Phongsali) were set aside as regroupment areas for Pathet Lao ('Land of the Lao', or communist) forces. No such territory was set aside in Cambodia, so a group of 1000 Cambodian communists travelled north to Hanoi where they were to remain for the best part of two decades. When they returned to Cambodia to help the revolution in the early 1970s, most were purged under orders from Pol Pot, who viewed them as ideologically contaminated by the Vietnamese.

The War in Vietnam

The 1954 Geneva Accords resulted in two Vietnams. Ho Chi Minh led the communist northern zone, while the South was ruled by Ngo Dinh Diem, a fiercely anticommunist Catholic. Nationwide elections scheduled for 1956 were never held, as the Americans and the South rightly feared that Ho Chi Minh would win easily.

During the first few years of his rule, Diem consolidated power effectively. During Diem's 1957 official visit to the USA, President Eisenhower called him the 'miracle man' of Asia. As time went on Diem became increasingly tyrannical in dealing with dissent.

In the early 1960s, the South was rocked by anti-Diem unrest led by university students and Buddhist clergy. The US decided Diem was a liability and threw its support behind a military coup. A group of young generals led the operation in November 1963. Diem was to go into exile, but the generals got overexcited and both Diem and his brother were killed. He was followed by a succession of military rulers who continued his erratic policies and dragged the country deeper into war.

War Breaks Out

The North's campaign to 'liberate' the South had begun in late 1950s with the creation of the National Liberation Front (NLF), nicknamed the Viet Cong (VC) by the Americans. By early 1965, Hanoi was sending regular North Vietnamese Army (NVA) units down the Ho Chi Minh Trail and the Saigon government was on its last legs. To the Americans, Vietnam was the next domino and could not topple. It was clearly time for the

As WWII drew to a close, Japanese rice requisitions, in combination with floods and breaches in the dikes, caused a horrific famine in which two million of northern Vietnam's 10 million people starved to death.

1969	1970	1973	1975
US President Richard Nixon authorises the secret bombing of Cambodia as an extension of the war in Vietnam; the campaign continues until 1973, killing up to 250,000 Cambodians.	Cambodian leader Norodom Sihanouk is overthrown in a coup engineered by his general Lon Nol and cousin Prince Sirik Matak, thus beginning Cambodia's bloody descent into civil war and genocide.	All sides in the Vietnam conflict sign the Paris Peace Accords on 27 January 1973, supposedly bringing an end to the war in Vietnam, but it's actually a face-saving deal for the US to 'withdraw with honour'.	The Khmer Rouge enters Phnom Penh on 17 April, implementing one of the bloodiest revolutions in history; North Vietnamese forces take Saigon on 30 April, renaming it Ho Chi Minh City; Vietnam is reunified.

BOMBS

Americans to 'clean up the mess', as one of Lyndon Johnson's leading officials put it.

For the first years of the conflict, the American military was boldly proclaiming victory upon victory, as the communist body count mounted. However, the Tet Offensive of 1968 brought an alternative reality into the homes of the average American. On the evening of 31 January, as Vietnam celebrated the Lunar New Year, the VC launched a series of strikes in more than 100 cities and towns, including Saigon. As the TV cameras rolled, a VC commando team took over the courtyard of the US embassy in central Saigon. The Tet Offensive killed about 1000 US soldiers and 2000 Army of the Republic of Vietnam (ARVN) troops, but VC losses were more than 10 times higher, at around 32,000 deaths. For the VC the Tet Offensive ultimately proved a success: it made the cost of fighting the war unbearable for the Americans.

Simultaneously, stories began leaking out of Vietnam about atrocities and massacres carried out by US forces against unarmed Vietnamese civilians, including the infamous My Lai Massacre. This helped turn the tide against the war, and antiwar demonstrations rocked American university campuses and spilled onto the streets.

Tricky Dick's Exit Strategy

Richard Nixon was elected president in 1968 in part because of a promise that he had a 'secret plan' to end the war. Nixon's strategy called for 'Vietnamisation', which meant making the South Vietnamese fight the war without US troops.

The 'Christmas bombing' of Haiphong and Hanoi at the end of 1972 was meant to wrest concessions from North Vietnam at the negotiating table. Eventually, the Paris Peace Accords were signed by the US, North Vietnam, South Vietnam and the VC on 27 January 1973, which provided for a ceasefire, the total withdrawal of US combat forces and the release of 590 US prisoners of war (POWs).

The End is Nigh

In January 1975 the North Vietnamese launched a massive ground attack across the 17th parallel using tanks and heavy artillery. Whole brigades of ARVN soldiers disintegrated and fled southward, joining hundreds of thousands of civilians clogging Hwy 1. The North Vietnamese pushed on to Saigon and on the morning of 30 April 1975 their tanks smashed through the gates of Saigon's Independence Palace (now called Reunification Palace). The long war was over, Vietnam was reunited and Saigon was renamed Ho Chi Minh City.

During the US bombing of 1964–73, some 13 million tonnes of bombs – equivalent to 450 times the energy of the atomic bomb used on Hiroshima – were dropped on the Indochina region. This equates to 265kg for every man, woman and child in Vietnam, Cambodia and Laos.

1978	1986	1989	1991
Vietnam invades Cambodia on Christmas Day in response to border attacks; the Khmer Rouge is overthrown weeks later; a decade-long war between communist 'brothers' begins.	*Doi moi* (economic reform), Vietnam's answer to *perestroika* and the first step towards re-engaging with the West, is launched with a rash of economic reforms.	Vietnamese forces pull out of Cambodia in the face of dwindling support from the Soviet Union under the leadership of reform-minded President Gorbachev; Vietnam is at peace for the first time in decades.	The Paris Peace Accords are signed in which all Cambodian parties (including, controversially, the Khmer Rouge) agree to participate in free and fair elections supervised by the UN, held in 1993.

Reunification

Vietnam may have been united, but it would take a long time to heal the scars of war. Damage from the fighting extended from unmarked minefields to war-focused, dysfunctional economies; from a chemically poisoned countryside to a population that had been physically or mentally battered.

The party decided on a rapid transition to socialism in the South, but this proved disastrous for the economy. Reunification was accompanied by widespread political repression. Despite repeated promises to the contrary, hundreds of thousands of people who had ties to the previous regime had their property confiscated and were rounded up and imprisoned without trial in forced-labour camps, euphemistically known as re-education camps.

Sideshow: the Civil War in Cambodia

The 1950s were seen as Cambodia's golden years and Sihanouk, now as prime minister, successfully maintained Cambodia's neutrality into the 1960s. However, with the war in Vietnam raging across the border, Cambodia was being sucked slowly into the vortex.

By 1969 the conflict between the Cambodian army and leftist rebels had become more serious, as the Vietnamese sought sanctuary deeper in Cambodia. In March 1970, while Sihanouk was on a trip to France, he was overthrown in a coup by General Lon Nol, his army commander. Sihanouk took up residence in Beijing and formed an alliance with the Cambodian communists, nicknamed the Khmer Rouge (Red Khmer), who exploited this partnership to gain new recruits.

On 30 April 1970, US and South Vietnamese forces invaded Cambodia in an effort to flush out thousands of Viet Cong and North Vietnamese troops. The Vietnamese communists withdrew deeper into Cambodia.

The Secret Bombing

In 1969, the US began a secret program of bombing suspected communist base camps in Cambodia. For the next four years, until bombing was halted by the US Congress in August 1973, huge areas of the eastern half of the country were carpet bombed by US B-52s, killing thousands of civilians and turning hundreds of thousands more into refugees.

Despite massive US military and economic aid, Lon Nol never succeeded in gaining the initiative against the Khmer Rouge. Large parts of the countryside fell to the rebels and many provincial capitals were cut off from Phnom Penh. On 17 April 1975, Phnom Penh surrendered to the Khmer Rouge.

Author and documentary film-maker John Pilger was ripping into the establishment long before Michael Moore rode into town. Get to grips with his hard-hitting views on the war in Vietnam at www.johnpilger.com.

For the full story on how Cambodia was sucked into hell, read *Sideshow: Kissinger, Nixon and the Destruction of Cambodia* by William Shawcross.

1997	1998	1999	2001
Asian financial crisis grips the Mekong region; Cambodia is convulsed by a coup and becomes a pariah once more; Laos and Myanmar (Burma) join Asean (Association of Southeast Asian Nations).	Following a government push on the Khmer Rouge's last stronghold at Anlong Veng, Pol Pot dies on 15 April 1998; rumours swirl around Phnom Penh about the circumstances of his death.	Cambodia finally joins Asean after a two-year delay, taking its place among the family of Southeast Asian nations welcoming the country back to the world stage.	Telecommunications tycoon Thaksin Shinawatra is elected prime minister of Thailand, setting the country on a divisive course.

The Land of a Million Irrelevants

War correspondents covering the conflict in Indochina soon renamed Lan Xang (ie Laos) the land of a million irrelevants. However, the on-going conflict was very relevant to the Cold War and the great powers were playing out their power struggles on this most obscure of stages. Successive governments came and went so fast they needed a revolving door in the national assembly.

Upcountry, large areas fell under the control of communist forces. The US sent troops to Thailand, in case communist forces attempted to cross the Mekong, and it looked for a time as if the major commit-ment of US troops in Southeast Asia would be to Laos rather than Vietnam. Both the North Vietnamese and the Americans were jockey-ing for strategic advantage, and neither was going to let Lao neutrality get in the way.

By mid-1972, when serious peace moves got under way, some four-fifths of Laos was under communist control. Unlike Cambodia and Viet-nam, the communists were eventually able to take power without a fight. City after city was occupied by the Pathet Lao (communist forces) and in August 1975 they marched into Vientiane unopposed.

François Bizot was kidnapped by the Khmer Rouge, interrogated by Comrade Duch and is believed to be the only foreigner to have been released. Later he was holed up in the French embassy in April 1975. Read his harrow-ing story in *The Gate*.

The Khmer Rouge & Year Zero

Upon taking Phnom Penh, the Khmer Rouge implemented one of the most radical and brutal restructurings of a society ever attempted; its goal was to transform Cambodia into a Maoist, peasant-dominated agrar-ian cooperative. Within days of the Khmer Rouge coming to power the entire population of the capital, including the sick, elderly and infirm, was forced to march out to the countryside. Disobedience of any sort of-ten brought immediate execution. The advent of Khmer Rouge rule was proclaimed Year Zero. Currency was abolished and postal services were halted. The country was cut off from the outside world.

THE SECRET WAR IN LAOS

Before his assassination in 1963, President John F Kennedy gave the order to recruit a force of 11,000 Hmong under the command of Vang Pao. They were trained by several hundred US and Thai Special Forces advisers and supplied by Air America, all under the supervision of the CIA. The secret war had begun.

In 1964 the US began its air war over Laos. According to official figures, the US dropped 2,093,100 tonnes of bombs in 580,944 sorties. The total cost was US$7.2 billion, or US$2 million a day for nine years. No one knows how many people died, but one-third of the population of 2.1 million became internal refugees.

2004	2004	2004	2006
King Sihanouk abdi-cates for a second time in Cambodia, closing the chapter on 63 years as monarch, politician and statesman, and is succeeded by his son King Sihamoni.	The first US com-mercial flight since the end of the Vietnam War touches down in Ho Chi Minh City, as US-Vietnamese busi-ness and tourism links mushroom.	Indian Ocean tsunami kills over 5000 people in Thailand and damages tourism and fishing industries.	Thailand's revered King Bhumibol celebrates 60th year on the throne; Thaksin gov-ernment is overthrown in a coup and the prime minister forced into exile.

Counting the Cost of Genocide

It is still not known exactly how many Cambodians died at the hands of the Khmer Rouge during the three years, eight months and 20 days of its rule. Two million or one-third of the population is a realistic estimate.

Hundreds of thousands of people were executed by the Khmer Rouge leadership, while hundreds of thousands more died of famine and disease. Some zones were better than others, some leaders fairer than others, but life for the majority was one of unending misery and suffering. Cambodia had become a 'prison without walls', as some survivors referred to it at this time.

The Khmer Rouge detached the Cambodian people from all they held dear: their families, their food and their faith. Nobody cared for the Khmer Rouge by 1978, but nobody had an ounce of strength to fight back...except the Vietnamese.

The Vietnamese Move In

Repeated attacks on Vietnamese border villages by the Khmer Rouge forced Vietnam to respond. Defying China, Vietnamese forces entered Cambodia on Christmas Day 1978. They succeeded in driving the Khmer Rouge from power on 7 January 1979 and set up a pro-Hanoi regime in Phnom Penh.

The demise of the Khmer Rouge proved to be a false dawn, as the country was gripped by a disastrous famine that killed hundreds of thousands more who had struggled to survive the Khmer Rouge. Caught in the crossfire of Cold War politics, even the relief effort was about political point scoring and organisations had to choose whether to work with the UN and the 'free world' on the Thai border or the Vietnamese and their Soviet allies in Phnom Penh.

Liberation of Cambodia from the Khmer Rouge resulted in years of Vietnamese occupation and a long civil war that drained both countries.

Reversal of Fortune

The communist cooperatives in Indochina were a miserable failure and caused almost as much suffering as the wars that had preceded them. Pragmatic Laos was the first to liberalise in response to the economic stagnation, and private farming and enterprise were allowed as early as 1979. However, the changes came too late for the Lao royal family and the last king and queen are believed to have died of malnutrition and disease in a prison camp sometime in the late 1970s.

Vietnam was slower to evolve, but the arrival of President Mikhail Gorbachev in the Soviet Union meant *glasnost* (openness) and *perestroika* (restructuring) were in, and radical revolution was out. *Doi moi* (economic reforms) were experimented with in Cambodia and introduced to Vietnam. As the USSR scaled back its commitments to the communist world,

Several of the current crop of Cambodian leaders were previously members of the Khmer Rouge, including Prime Minister Hun Sen and Head of the Senate Chea Sim, although there is no evidence to implicate them in mass killings.

2010	2010	2010	2011
Comrade Duch, aka Kaing Guek Eav, former commandant of the notorious S-21 prison in Phnom Penh, becomes first Khmer Rouge leader convicted of crimes against humanity.	Red Shirt, pro-Thaksin activists occupy central Bangkok for two months; military crackdown results in 91 deaths.	The Prime Minister of the Lao PDR, Bouasone Bouphavanh, resigns after more than four years in office, catching political observers off guard.	Cambodia and Thailand trade blows over the ancient border temple of Prasat Preah Vihear on the Dangkrek Mountains; Asean attempts to broker a lasting settlement.

the far-flung outposts were the first to feel the pinch. The Vietnamese decided to unilaterally withdraw from Cambodia in 1989, as they could no longer afford the occupation. The party in Vietnam was on its own and needed to reform to survive. Cambodia and Laos would follow its lead.

A New Beginning

You may be wondering what happened to Thailand in all of this? Well, compared with the earth-shattering events unfolding in Indochina, things were rather dull. Thailand profited as its neighbours suffered, providing air bases and logistical support to the Americans during the war in Vietnam. As the war and revolution consumed a generation in Cambodia, Laos and Vietnam, Thailand's economy prospered and democracy slowly took root, although coups remain common currency right up to the present day – largely because of the divisiveness of billionaire tycoon Thaksin Shinawatra, who served as prime minister from 2001 to 2006 before being ousted by the military and forced into exile. The power struggle between Thaksin's 'red shirt' supporters and their 'yellow shirt' opponents has dominated the headlines in Thailand for the better part of a decade. Meanwhile, southern Thailand continues to be gripped by an Islamic insurgency that has claimed hundreds of lives.

Cambodia was welcomed back to the world stage in 1991 with the signing of the Paris Peace Accords, which set out a UN roadmap to free and fair elections. There have been many hiccups along the way, including coups and a culture of impunity, but Cambodia has come a long way from the dark days of the Khmer Rouge. Democracy is hardly flourishing, corruption most certainly is, but life is better for many than it has been for a long time. Attempts to bring the surviving Khmer Rouge leadership to trial continue to stumble along.

Vietnam has followed the Chinese road to riches, taking the brakes off the economy while keeping a firm hand on the political steering wheel. With only two million paid-up members of the Communist Party and around 90 million Vietnamese, it is a road they must follow carefully. However, the economy has been booming since the the country joined the World Trade Organisation in 2006. Industry and manufacturing have led the way, along with tourism – the country welcomed more than 7.5 million visitors in 2013, up from 5 million in 2010.

In Laos, hydroelectric power is a big industry and looks set to subsidise the economy in the future. On the flip side, illegal logging remains a major problem, as in Cambodia, with demand for timber in China, Thailand and Vietnam driving the destruction. Tourism has good prospects and Laos is carving a niche for itself as the ecotourism destination of Southeast Asia.

Like the river that binds them, the countries of the Mekong region have a turbulent past and an uncertain future.

RIVER OF TIME

Jon Swain's *River of Time* (1995) takes the reader back to an old Indochina, partly lost to the madness of war, and includes first-hand accounts of the French embassy stand-off in the first days of the Khmer Rouge takeover.

2011	2012	2013	2013
Red Shirts back in power as Yingluck Shinawatra becomes Thailand's first female prime minister.	Cambodia's former King Norodom Sihanouk dies a national hero.	Vietnam War hero General Giap, seen as an antidote to the country's corrupt modern-day leadership, dies. Millions pay their respects.	Cambodia's opposition party surprisingly wins 45% of vote in Cambodia's elections, but cries foul and protestors take to the streets claiming widespread voting irregularities.

People & Culture

The Mekong region is not known as Indochina for nothing. Geographically it is the land in between China and India. China has shaped the destiny of Vietnam and continues to cast a shadow over the Mekong region. India exported its great religions, language, culture and sculpture to Cambodia, Laos and Thailand. With a millennium of influence from two of the world's great civilisations, it is hardly surprising to find such a dynamic variety of culture in the Mekong region today.

Lifestyle

A typical day in the Mekong region starts early. Country folk tend to rise before dawn, woken by the cry of cockerels and keen to get the most out of the day before the sun heats up. This habit has spilled over into the towns and cities and many urban dwellers rise at the crack of dawn for a quick jog, a game of badminton or some tai chi moves. Breakfast comes in many flavours, but Chinese congee (rice soup) and noodle soups are universally popular.

Food is almost as important as family in this part of the world and that is saying something. Long lunch breaks are common (and common sense, as they avoid the hottest part of the day). The working day winds down for some around 5pm and the family will try to come together for dinner and trade tales about their day. Traditionally, life in the Mekong region has revolved around family, fields and faith, the rhythm of rural existence continuing for centuries. For the majority of the population still living in the countryside, these constants have remained unchanged, with several generations sharing the same roof, the same rice and the same religion.

But in recent decades these rhythms have been jarred by war and ideology, as peasants were dragged from all they held dear to fight in civil wars, or were herded into cooperatives as communism tried to assert itself as the moral and social beacon in the lives of the people. But Buddhism is back and for many older Mekong residents the temple or pagoda remains an important pillar in their lives. Traditionally rural agrarian societies, the race is on for the move to the cities. Thailand experienced the growing pains first, and now Cambodia, Laos and Vietnam are witnessing a tremendous shift in the balance of population, as increasing numbers of young people desert the fields in search of those mythical streets paved with gold or, more commonly, jammed with motorbikes.

Around 18 million Khmers live in Cambodia, Thailand and Vietnam.

People

As empires came and went, so too did the populations, and many of the countries in the Mekong region are far less ethnically homogenous than their governments would have us believe. It wasn't only local empire building that had an impact, but colonial meddling, which left a number of people stranded beyond their borders. There are Lao and Khmer in Thailand, Khmer in Vietnam, Thai (Dai) in Vietnam and Chinese everywhere. No self-respecting Mekong town would be complete without a Chinatown.

The mountains of the Mekong region provide a home for a mosaic of minority groups, often referred to as hill tribes. Many of these groups migrated from China and Tibet and have settled in areas that lowlanders considered too challenging to cultivate. Colourful costumes and unique traditions draw increasing numbers of visitors to their mountain homes. The most popular areas to visit local hill tribes include Mondulkiri and Ratanakiri Provinces in Cambodia, Luang Nam Tha and Muang Sing in northern Laos, Chiang Mai and Chiang Rai in northern Thailand, and Sapa and Bac Ha in northern Vietnam.

> The Mekong region is home to around 45 million Thais, concentrated in Thailand, Laos, Vietnam and Yunnan.

Population growth varies throughout the Mekong region. Developed Thailand embraced family planning decades ago and Vietnam has adopted a Chinese model of sorts with a two-child policy in lowland areas. Cambodia and Laos have the highest birth rates and large families remain the rule rather than the exception out in the countryside.

Chinese

Many of the great cities of the Mekong region have significant Chinese communities, and in the case of capitals like Bangkok and Phnom Penh people of at least some Chinese ancestry may make up half the population. The Chinese are much more integrated in the Mekong region than in places like Indonesia, and continue to contribute to the economy through investment and initiative.

With one eye on history, the Vietnamese are more suspicious of the Chinese than most, even though, culturally, the Vietnamese have much in common with the Chinese. Vietnam was occupied by China for more than a thousand years and the Chinese brought with them their religion, philosophy and culture. Confucianism and Taoism were introduced and still form the backbone of Vietnamese religion, together with Buddhism.

Kinh (Vietnamese)

Despite the Chinese view that the Vietnamese are 'the ones that got away', the Vietnamese existed in the Red River Delta area long before the first waves of Chinese arrived some 2000 years ago. The Kinh make up about 90% of the population of Vietnam. Centuries ago, the Vietnamese began to push southward in search of cultivable land and swallowed the kingdom of Champa before pushing on into the Mekong Delta and picking off pieces of a decaying Khmer empire. As well as occupying the coastal regions of Vietnam, the lowland Kinh have been moving into the mountains to take advantage of new opportunities in agriculture, industry and tourism.

> The Mekong region is home to around 85 million Kinh, most living in Vietnam, Cambodia and Laos.

Khmer (Cambodian)

The Khmer have inhabited Cambodia since the beginning of recorded history around the 2nd century AD, long before the Thais and Viet-

---

FACE IT

Face, or more importantly the art of not making the locals lose face, is an important concept to understand in Asia. Face is all in Asia, and in the Mekong region it is above all. Having 'big face' is synonymous with prestige. All families, even poor ones, are expected to have big wedding parties and throw their money around like it is water in order to gain face. This is often ruinously expensive, but that is far less important than 'losing face'. And it is for this reason that foreigners should never lose their tempers with the locals; this will bring unacceptable 'loss of face' to the individual involved and end any chance of a sensible solution to the dispute. Take a deep breath and keep your cool. If things aren't always going according to plan, remember that in countries like Cambodia and Laos, tourism is a relatively new industry.

namese arrived in the southern Mekong region. During the subsequent centuries, the culture of Cambodia was influenced by contact with the civilisations of India and Java.

Cambodia was the cultural staging post for the Indianisation of the Mekong region. Indian traders brought Hinduism and Buddhism around the 2nd century and with these came the religious languages of Sanskrit and Pali; Sanskrit forming the root of modern Khmer, Lao and Thai. They also brought their art and architecture, which was redefined so effectively by the ancient Khmers before spreading into Laos and Thailand.

During the glory years of Angkor, Hinduism was the predominant religion, but from the 15th century Theravada Buddhism was adopted and most Khmers remain devoutly Buddhist today, their faith being an important anchor in the struggle to rebuild their lives following the rule of the Khmer Rouge. The Cambodian population went to hell and back during those brutal times when it is believed as much as one-third of the population perished.

Lao

Laos is often described as less a nation-state than a conglomeration of tribes and languages. The Lao traditionally divide themselves into four broad families – Lao Loum, Lao Thai, Lao Thoeng and Lao Soung – roughly defined by the altitude at which they live and their cultural proclivities. The Lao government has an alternative three-way split, in which the Lao Thai are condensed into the Lao Loum group. This triumvirate is represented on the back of every 1000 kip bill, in national costume, from left to right: Lao Soung, Lao Loum and Lao Thoeng.

Foreign ethnographers carrying out field research in Laos have identified anywhere from 49 to 132 different ethnic groups.

Thai

Thais make up about 75% of the population of Thailand, although this group is commonly broken down into four subgroups: Central Thais or Siamese who inhabit the Chao Phraya delta, the Thai Lao of northeastern Thailand, the Pak Thai of southern Thailand, and northern Thais. Each group speaks its own dialect and to a certain extent practises customs unique to its region. Politically and economically, the Central Thais are the dominant group, although they barely outnumber the Thai Lao.

Minority Groups

There are many other important minority groups in the region, some rendered stateless by the conflicts of the past, others recent migrants to the region, including the many hill tribes.

Cham

The Cham people originally occupied the kingdom of Champa in south-central Vietnam and their beautiful brick towers dot the landscape from Danang to Phan Rang. Victims of a historical squeeze between Cambodia and Vietnam, their territory was eventually annexed by the expansionist Vietnamese. Originally Hindu, they converted to Islam in the 16th and 17th centuries and many migrated to Cambodia. Today there are small numbers of Cham in Vietnam and as many as half a million in Cambodia, all of whom continue to practise a flexible form of Islam. The Cham population has intermarried over the centuries with migrating Malay seafarers, introducing an additional ethnic background into the mix.

There are around 12 million Lao people living across the Mekong region, in Laos, Thailand and Cambodia.

Hmong

The Hmong are one of the largest hill tribes in the Mekong region, spread through much of northern Laos, northern Vietnam and Thailand. As some of the last to arrive in the region in the 19th century, they were left with the highest and harshest lands from which to eke out their existence. They soon made the best of a bad deal and opted for opium cultivation, which brought them into conflict with mainstream governments during the 20th century.

Hmong groups are usually classified by their colourful clothing, including Black Hmong, White Hmong, Red Hmong and so on. The brightest group is the Flower Hmong of northwest Vietnam, living in villages around Bac Ha. There may be as many as one million Hmong in the Mekong region, half of them living in the mountains of Vietnam.

Dzao

The Dzao (also known as Yao or Dao) are one of the largest and most colourful ethnic groups in Vietnam and are also found in Laos, Thailand and Yunnan. The Dzao practise ancestor worship of spirits, or *ban ho* (no relation to Uncle Ho), and hold elaborate rituals with sacrifices of pigs

---

LIFE AMONG THE MINORITIES

One of the highlights of a visit to the Mekong region is an encounter with one of the many ethnic minority groups inhabiting the mountains. Many wear incredible costumes, and so elaborate are some of these that it's easy to believe minority girls learn to embroider before they can walk.

While some of these minorities number as many as a million people, it is feared that other groups have dwindled to as few as 100. The areas inhabited by each group are often delineated by altitude, with more recent arrivals settling at a higher altitude. Each hill tribe has its own language, customs, mode of dress and spiritual beliefs. Some groups are caught between medieval and modern worlds, while others have assimilated into modern life.

Most groups share a rural, agricultural lifestyle which revolves around traditional rituals. Most hill-tribe communities are seminomadic, cultivating crops such as rice and using slash-and-burn methods, which have taken a toll on the environment. Hill tribes have among the lowest standards of living in the region and lack access to education, health care and even minimum-wage jobs. While there may be no official discrimination system, cultural prejudice against hill-tribe people ensures they remain at the bottom of the ladder. Put simply, life is a struggle for most minority people.

Tourism can bring many benefits to highland communities: cross-cultural understanding, improved infrastructure, cheaper market goods, employment opportunities and tourist dollars supporting handicraft industries. However, there are also negatives, such as increased litter and pollutants, dependency on tourist dollars, and the erosion of local values and practices. Here are some tips on having a positive effect when visiting minority communities:

➡ Where possible, hire indigenous guides – they understand taboos and traditions that might be lost on lowland guides.

➡ Always ask permission before taking photos of tribespeople.

➡ Don't show up for 15 minutes and expect to be granted permission to take photos – invest some time in getting to know the villagers first.

➡ Don't touch totems or sacred items hanging from trees.

➡ Avoid cultivating a tradition of begging, especially among children.

➡ Avoid public nudity and don't undress near an open window.

➡ Don't flirt with members of the opposite sex.

➡ Taste traditional wine if you are offered it, especially during a ceremony.

➡ Dress modestly.

➡ Don't buy village treasures, such as altar pieces or totems.

and chickens. The Dzao are famous for their elaborate dress. Women's clothing typically features intricate weaving and silver-coloured beads and coins – the wealth of a woman is said to be in the weight of the coins she carries. Their long flowing hair, shaved above the forehead, is tied up into a large red or embroidered turban.

Karen

The Karen are the largest hill tribe in Thailand, numbering more than 300,000. There are four distinct groups, the Skaw Karen (White Karen), Pwo Karen, Pa-O Karen (Black Karen) and Kayah Karen (Red Karen). Unmarried women wear white and kinship remains matrilineal. Most Karen live in lowland valleys and practise crop rotation.

Economy

Life for many in the Mekong region has undergone a profound transition in the space of a generation, even if the politics hasn't always come along for the ride. Laos and Vietnam are one-party states which tolerate no opposition. But communism, the mantra for a generation, has taken a back seat to capitalism and the rush to embrace the market. The result is a contradictory blend of ultraliberal economics and ultraconservative politics that has left many inhabitants confused about the country in which they live. They have the freedom to make money but not the basic freedom to voice a political opinion. And the more the average person engages with the outside world – through business, tourism, the internet – the harder this paradox is to swallow.

Corruption remains a cancer throughout the Mekong region. Despite the best intentions of a small minority, the worst intentions of many a politician continue to cost the Mekong countries hundreds of millions of dollars in lost assets. Vietnam has started tackling corruption head on with high-profile executions and prison sentences. Senior party officials have even been put away, but cronyism and nepotism remain alive and well. Laos suffers from corruption, but the small size of the economy has kept enrichment to a minimum for now.

In Cambodia, corruption has been elevated to an art form. When asked to sum up the country's problems in three words, former World Bank head James Wolfensohn famously once said, 'Corruption, corruption, corruption.' Global anti-corruption watchdog Transparency International (TI) ranked Cambodia as the 160th most corrupt country in the world out of 175 surveyed in 2013, behind such luminaries as the Democratic Republic of Congo and Tajikistan. Laos ranked 140th, Vietnam 116th and Thailand 102nd.

According to most observers, corruption in Thailand worsened under Thaksin Shinawatra, who created a new blend by mixing business and politics to turn the country into 'Shinawatra Plc'. Ultimately it backfired and he was overthrown, but with his younger sister Yingluck Shinawatra in power it appears to be business as usual again – Thailand's corruption ranking in the 2013 TI ranking was 14 places worse than in 2012. By contrast, Laos improved by 20 places, while Vietnam registered a modest improvement.

Since shaking off the shadow of Marxist theory, the economies of the Mekong region have been some of the fastest growing in the world. As the global economic crisis continues to unfold, nobody is certain what is in store for the export-oriented region. The Mekong countries were quick to plug themselves into the global economy and now they are likely to share the shock of its continuing collapse. However, the impact may be mild compared to the West, with economies having to settle for sluggish growth rather than experiencing a full-blown recession. For now their

For an in-depth look at the beauty of Angkorian-era sculpture and its religious, cultural and social context, seek out a copy of *Sculpture of Angkor and Ancient Cambodia: Millennium of Glory*.

fate is tied to that of the rest of the world, although China may unseat the US as the model of choice for sound economic management in the region.

Thailand is the regional powerhouse with a strong economy underpinned by manufacturing, handicrafts, tourism and agriculture. Vietnam is fast catching up and, like Thailand, is now a major manufacturing centre for automotive assembly and hi-tech gadgetry. Agriculture remains a major industry, with Thailand and Vietnam going head to head for the title of world's largest rice exporter.

The economies of Cambodia and Laos are much smaller by comparison. Cambodia relies heavily on the textile industry and tourism to drive its economy, but agro-industries such as rubber and palm oil are growing fast and traditional agriculture and fishing remain very important to the average person. In Laos, the export of hydropower is big business and, if not too contradictory, ecotourism is one of the fastest-growing sectors.

Religion

The dominant religions of Southeast Asia have absorbed many traditional animistic beliefs of spirits, ancestor worship and the power of the celestial planets in bringing about good fortune. The Mekong region's spiritual connection to the realm of magic and miracles commands more respect, even among intellectual circles, than the remnants of paganism in Western Christianity. Locals erect spirit houses in front of their homes, while ethnic Chinese set out daily offerings to their ancestors, and almost everyone visits the fortune teller.

Although the majority of the population has only a vague notion of Buddhist doctrines, they invite monks to participate in life-cycle ceremonies, such as funerals and weddings. Buddhist pagodas are seen by many as a physical and spiritual refuge from an uncertain world.

Ancestor Worship

Ancestor worship dates from long before the arrival of Confucianism or Buddhism. Ancestor worship is based on the belief that the soul lives on after death and becomes the protector of its descendants. Because of the influence the spirits of one's ancestors exert on the living, it is considered not only shameful for them to be upset or restless, but downright dangerous.

Animism

Both Hinduism and Buddhism fused with the animist beliefs already present in the Mekong region before Indianisation. Local beliefs didn't

---

CAO DAISM

A fascinating fusion of East and West, Cao Daism (Dai Dao Tam Ky Pho Do) is a syncretic religion born in 20th-century Vietnam that contains elements of Buddhism, Confucianism, Taoism, native Vietnamese spiritualism, Christianity and Islam – as well as a dash of secular enlightenment thrown in for good measure. The term Cao Dai (meaning high tower or palace) is a euphemism for God. There are an estimated two to three million followers of Cao Daism worldwide.

Cao Daism was founded by the mystic Ngo Minh Chieu (also known as Ngo Van Chieu; born 1878), who began receiving revelations in which the tenets of Cao Dai were set forth.

All Cao Dai temples observe four daily ceremonies: at 6am, noon, 6pm and midnight. If all this sounds like just what you've been waiting for, read more on the official Cao Dai site: www.caodai.org. The most impressive Cao Dai temple is at Tay Ninh, near Ho Chi Minh City.

THE LUNAR CALENDAR

Astrology has a long history in China and Vietnam (plus in the Chinese communities of Cambodia, Laos and Thailand), and is intricately linked to religious beliefs. There are 12 zodiacal animals, each of which represents one year in a 12-year cycle. If you want to know your sign, look up your year of birth in the following chart. Don't forget that the Chinese/Vietnamese New Year falls in late January or early February. If your birthday is in the first half of January, it will be included in the zodiac year before the calendar year of your birth. To check the Gregorian (solar) date corresponding to a lunar date, pick up any Vietnamese or Chinese calendar.

Rat (generous, social, insecure, idle) 1924, 1936, 1948, 1960, 1972, 1984, 1996, 2008

Cow (stubborn, conservative, patient) 1925, 1937, 1949, 1961, 1973, 1985, 1997, 2009

Tiger (creative, brave, overbearing) 1926, 1938, 1950, 1962, 1974, 1986, 1998, 2010

Rabbit (timid, affectionate, amicable) 1927, 1939, 1951, 1963, 1975, 1987, 1999, 2011

Dragon (egotistical, strong, intelligent) 1928, 1940, 1952, 1964, 1976, 1988, 2000, 2012

Snake (luxury seeking, secretive, friendly) 1929, 1941, 1953, 1965, 1977, 1989, 2001

Horse (emotional, clever, quick thinker) 1930, 1942, 1954, 1966, 1978, 1990, 2002

Goat (charming, good with money, indecisive) 1931, 1943, 1955, 1967, 1979, 1991, 2003

Monkey (confident, humorous, fickle) 1932, 1944, 1956, 1968, 1980, 1992, 2004

Rooster (diligent, imaginative, needs attention) 1933, 1945, 1957, 1969, 1981, 1993, 2005

Dog (humble, responsible, patient) 1934, 1946, 1958, 1970, 1982, 1994, 2006

Pig (materialistic, loyal, honest) 1935, 1947, 1959, 1971, 1983, 1995, 2007

simply fade away, but were incorporated into the new religions. The purest form of animism is practised among the ethnic minorities or hill tribes of the region

Buddhism

The sedate smile of the Buddhist statues decorating the landscapes and temples characterise the nature of the religion in Southeast Asia. Religious devotion within the Buddhist countries is highly individualistic, omnipresent and nonaggressive, with many daily rituals rooted in the indigenous religions of animism and ancestor worship.

Buddhism, like all great religions, has been through a messy divorce, and arrived in the Mekong region in two flavours. Mahayana Buddhism (northern school) proceeded north into Nepal, Tibet, China, Korea, Mongolia, Vietnam and Japan, while Theravada Buddhism (southern school) took the southern route through India, Sri Lanka, Myanmar (Burma), Thailand, Cambodia and Laos.

Every Buddhist male is expected to become a monk for a short period in his life, optimally between the time he finishes school and starts a career or marries. Men or boys under 20 years of age may enter the Sangha (the monkhood or the monastic community) as novices. Nowadays, men may spend less than one month to accrue merit as monks.

Mahayana Buddhists believe in Bodhisattvas, who are Buddhas that attain nirvana but postpone their enlightenment to stay on earth to save their fellow beings.

Christianity

Catholicism was introduced to the region in the 16th century by missionaries. Vietnam has the highest percentage of Catholics (8% to 10% of the population) in Southeast Asia outside the Philippines.

THE RAMAYANA

The literary epic of the Ramayana serves as the cultural fodder for traditional art, dance and shadow puppetry throughout the region. In this epic Hindu legend, Prince Rama (an incarnation of the Hindu god Vishnu) falls in love with beautiful Sita and wins her hand in marriage by successfully stringing a magic bow. Before the couple settle down to marital bliss, Rama is banished from his kingdom and his wife is kidnapped by the demon king, Ravana, and taken to the island of Lanka. With the help of the Monkey King, Hanuman, Sita is rescued, but a great battle ensues. Rama and his allies defeat Ravana and restore peace and goodness to the land. The Ramayana is known as the Reamker in Cambodia or the Ramakien in Laos and Thailand.

Hinduism

Hinduism ruled the spiritual lives of Mekong dwellers more than 1500 years ago, and the great Hindu empire of Angkor built magnificent monuments to their pantheon of gods. The primary representations of the one omnipresent god include Brahma (the creator), Vishnu (the preserver) and Shiva (the destroyer and reproducer).

The forgotten kingdom of Champa was profoundly influenced by Hinduism and many of the Cham towers, built as Hindu sanctuaries, contain *lingas* (phallic symbols representing Shiva) that are still worshipped by ethnic Vietnamese and ethnic Chinese alike.

Islam

Southeast Asians converted to Islam to join a brotherhood of spice traders and to escape the inflexible caste system of earlier Hindu empires. The Chams may be Muslims, but in practice they follow a localised adaptation of Islamic theology and law. Though Muslims usually pray five times a day, the Chams pray only on Fridays and observe Ramadan (a month of dawn-to-dusk fasting) for only three days.

For a virtual tour of Thai Buddhist architecture around the region, visit www.orientalarchitecture.com.

Taoism

Taoism originated in China and is based on the philosophy of Laotse (The Old One), who lived in the 6th century BC. Little is known about Laotse and there is some debate as to whether or not he actually existed. Taoist philosophy emphasises contemplation and simplicity. The ideal is returning to the Tao (the Way, or the essence of which all things are made), and it emphasises the importance of Yin and Yang.

Tam Giao

Over the centuries, Confucianism, Taoism and Buddhism have fused with popular Chinese beliefs and ancient Vietnamese animism to create Tam Giao (Triple Religion). When discussing religion, most Vietnamese people are likely to say that they are Buddhist, but when it comes to family or civic duties they are likely to follow the moral and social code of Confucianism, and will turn to Taoist concepts to understand the nature of the cosmos.

Survival Guide

Border Crossings

During the bad old days of communism and the Cold War, there were pretty much no land borders open to foreigners in the Mekong region. Times have changed and there are now dozens of border crossings connecting the neighbouring countries of the region. Before making a long-distance trip, be aware of border closing times, visa regulations and any transport scams. Border details change regularly, so ask around or check the Lonely Planet Thorntree (www.lonelyplanet.com/thorntree).

Visa on Arrival

Visas (or in the case of Thailand, visa waivers) are available on arrival at some borders but not at others. As a general rule of thumb, visas are available at the land borders of Cambodia, Laos and Thailand, and are not available at Vietnam border crossings.

The exceptions to the above are at the Laos–Vietnam border. Entering Laos, visas on arrival are available only at Dansavanh, Nam Phao, Nong Haet, Phou Keua and Sop Hun.

Opening Hours

Most borders are open during the core hours of 7am to 6pm. However, some popular crossings are open later in the evening, while more remote crossings might close for lunch or at 5pm. Be wary of buses that arrive at the border in the middle of the night and are forced to wait around until the border opens, adding hours to the journey time.

Scams & Extra Fees

Some of the immigration police at land border crossings have a reputation for petty extortion. Especially at remote Cambodian and Lao border stations, travellers are occasionally asked for an 'immigration fee' or an overtime surcharge – 'tea money' as it's sometimes called.

To avoid being scammed, be aware of the proper fees and study up on the tricks you are likely to face at the border you are crossing. The Poipet (C)/Aranya Prathet (T) and Cham Yeam (C)/Hat Lek (T) borders are particularly scam-ridden.

It's generally easier to exit overland than it is to enter, and extra charges generally occur upon entry rather than on exit.

Changing Money

There are few legal money-changing facilities at some of the more remote border crossings, so be sure to have some small-denomination US dollars. The black market is also an option for local currencies, but black marketeers have a well-deserved reputation for short-changing and outright theft.

Private Vehicles

The general rule is that you can get private vehicles into Cambodia, Laos and Thailand, but forget about driving into or out of Vietnam. However, some Vietnamese motorbike-tour companies do have permission to cross the border between Laos and Vietnam.

Crossing between Cambodia, Laos and Thailand, you'll want to make sure to have all of your vehicle's paperwork in order. Before setting out, check with the embassy of your target country to see if you need additional permissions and documents.

New Border Developments

In Thailand, the big news is that there is now a direct through bus from Bangkok to Siem Reap, Cambodia, run by Nattakan. These buses are a hassle-free way to navigate the scam-laden Aranya Prathet/Poipet border, but of course they cost a bit more.

On the Thailand–Laos border, a third 'Friendship Bridge' over the Mekong opened in 2011. It connects Nahkon Phanom in Thailand with Tha Kaek in Laos. In late 2013, a fourth Friendship Bridge opened, connecting Chiang Khong in Thailand with Huay Xai in Laos. Both were formerly boat crossings.

Laos is seeing some serious infrastructure improvements as part of a regional drive to improve transport links between Thailand and Vietnam. A major four-lane highway from Paksong (on the Bolaven Plateau in Southern Laos) to the Vietnamese frontier should be completed during the lifetime of this book; this highway will shorten the route from Ubon Ratchathani, Thailand, to the Vietnamese port of Danang. A new border crossing at Dak Cheung (Laos), east of

Border Crossings

Sekong, will be part of the equation. The Chong Mek/ Vang Tao border post near Ubon Ratchathani is also being expanded.

Crossings with Other Countries

Thailand/Malaysia

You can cross the border by road into Malaysia at:

➡ Kanger (T)/Padang Besar (M)

➡ Sadao (T)/Bukit Kayu Hitam (M)

➡ Betong (T)/Keroh (M)

➡ Sungai Kolok (T)/Rantau Panjang (M)

➡ Tak Bai (T)/Pengkalan Kubor (M)

The train route into Malaysia is on the Hat Yai–Alor Setar–Butterworth route, which crosses the border at Kanger (T)/Padang Besar (M).

On the west coast, the crossing between Satun (T) to Pulau Langkawi (M) is made by boat.

Thailand/Myanmar (Burma)

There are three legal crossings: Mae Sai (T) to Tachileik (My); Ranong (T) to Kawthoung (My); and Mae Sot (T) to Myawaddy (My).

Be sure to have a valid Myanmar visa when exiting and be prepared for unexpected charges from Myanmar officials at the border when crossing into Thailand.

MEKONG REGION BORDERS AT A GLANCE

From Cambodia

TO	BORDER CROSSING	CONNECTING TOWNS	VISA ON ARRIVAL	MORE INFO
Laos	Trapeang Kriel (C)/Nong Nok Khiene (L)	Stung Treng (C)/Si Phan Don (L)	Yes	p232
Thailand	Poipet (C)/Aranya Prathet (T)	Siem Reap (C)/Bangkok (T)	Yes	p202
Thailand	Cham Yeam (C)/Hat Lek (T)	Koh Kong (C)/Trat (T)	Yes	p245
Thailand	O Smach (C)/Chong Chom (T)	Samraong (C)/Surin (T)	Yes	p222
Thailand	Psar Pruhm (C)/Pong Nam Ron (T)	Pailin (C)/Chanthaburi (T)	Yes	p222
Thailand	Choam (C)/Chong Sa-Ngam (T)	Anlong Veng (C)/Chong Sa-Ngam (T)	Yes	p222
Vietnam	Bavet (C)/Moc Bai (V)	Phnom Penh (C)/HCMC (V)	No	p192
Vietnam	Kaam Samnor (C)/Vinh Xuong (V)	Phnom Penh (C)/Chau Doc (V)	No	p192
Vietnam	Prek Chak (C)/Xa Xia (V)	Kep (C)/Ha Tien (V)	No	p258
Vietnam	Phnom Den (C)/Tinh Bien (V)	Takeo (C)/Chau Doc (V)	No	p192
Vietnam	O Yadaw (C)/Le Thanh (V)	Ban Lung (C)/Pleiku (V)	No	p235
Vietnam	Trapeang Sre (C)/Loc Ninh (V)	Snuol (C)/Binh Long (V)	No	p227
Vietnam	Trapeang Plong (C)/Xa mat (V)	Kompong Cham (C)/ Tay Ninh (V)	No	p227

From Laos

TO	BORDER CROSSING	CONNECTING TOWNS	VISA ON ARRIVAL	MORE INFO
Cambodia	Nong Nok Khiene (L)/Trapeang Kriel (C)	Si Phan Don (L)/Stung Treng (C)	Yes	p232
China	Boten (L)/Mohan (Ch)	Luang Namtha (L)/Mengla (Ch)	No	p321
Thailand	Tha Na Long (L)/Nong Khai (T)	Vientiane (L)/Nong Khai (T)	Yes	p288
Thailand	Paksan (L)/Beung Kan (T)	Paksan (L)/Beung Kan (T)	Yes	p326
Thailand	Huay Xai (L)/Chiang Khong (T)	Huay Xai (L)/Chiang Rai (T)	Yes	p324
Thailand	Tha Khaek (L)/Nakhon Phanom (T)	Tha Khaek (L)/Nakhon Phanom (T)	Yes	p330
Thailand	Savannakhet (L)/Mukdahan (T)	Savannakhet (L)/Mukdahan (T)	Yes	p330
Thailand	Vang Tao (L)/Chong Mek (T)	Pakse (L)/Ubon Ratchathani (V)	Yes	p339
Thailand	Kaen Thao (L)/Tha Li (T)	Pak Lai (L)/Loei (T)	Yes	p324
Thailand	Muang Ngeun (L)/Ban Huay Kon (T)	Hongsa (L)/Phrae (T)	Yes	p324
Vietnam	Dansavanh (L)/Lao Bao (V)	Savannakhet (L)/Dong Ha (V)	No	p333
Vietnam	Phou Keua (L)/Bo Y (V)	Attapeu (L)/Kon Tum (V)	No	p347
Vietnam	Na Phao (L)/Cha Lo (V)	Tha Khaek (L)/Dong Hoi (V)	No	p329
Vietnam	Nong Haet (L)/Nam Can (V)	Phonsavan (L)/Vinh (V)	No	p313
Vietnam	Nam Phao (L)/Cau Treo (V)	Lak Sao (L)/Vinh (V)	No	p329
Vietnam	Na Meo (L)/Nam Soi (V)	Sam Neua (L)/Thanh Hoa (V)	No	p314
Vietnam	Sop Hun (L)/Tay Trang (V)	Muang Khua (L)/Dien Bien Phu (V)	No	p309

MEKONG REGION BORDERS AT A GLANCE

From Thailand

TO	BORDER CROSSING	CONNECTING TOWNS	VISA ON ARRIVAL	MORE INFO
Cambodia	Aranya Prathet (T)/ Poipet (C)	Bangkok (T)/Siem Reap (C)	Yes	p403
Cambodia	Hat Lek (T)/Cham Yeam (C)	Trat (T)/Koh Kong (C)	Yes	p397
Cambodia	Chong Chom (T)/O Smach (C)	Surin (T)/Samraong (C)	Yes	p404
Cambodia	Pong Nam Ron (T)/Psar Pruhm (C)	Chanthaburi (T)/Pailin (C)	Yes	p397
Cambodia	Chong Sa-Ngam (T)/Choam (C)	Chong Sa-Ngam (T)/Anlong Veng (C)	Yes	p404
Laos	Nong Khai (T)/Tha Na Long (L)	Nong Khai (T)/Vientiane (L)	Yes	p417
Laos	Beung Han (T)/Paksan (L)	Beung Han (T)/Paksan (L)	No	p417
Laos	Chiang Khong (T)/Huay Xai (L)	Chiang Rai (T)/Huay Xai (L)	Yes	p444
Laos	Nakhon Phanom (T)/Tha Khaek (L)	Nakhon Phanom (T)/Tha Khaek (L)	Yes	p413
Laos	Mukdahan (T)/Savannakhet (L)	Mukdahan (T)/Savannakhet (L)	Yes	p413
Laos	Chong Mek (T)/Vang Tao (L)	Ubon Ratchathani (T)/Pakse (L)	Yes	p413
Laos	Tha Li (T)/Kaen Thao (L)	Loei (T)/Pak Lai (L)	Yes	p417
Laos	Ban Huay Kon (T)/Muang Ngeun (LL)	Nan (T)/Hongsa (L)	Yes	p444

From Vietnam

TO	BORDER CROSSING	CONNECTING TOWNS	VISA ON ARRIVAL	MORE INFO
Cambodia	Moc Bai (V)/Bavet (C)	Ho Chi Minh City (V)/Phnom Penh (C)	Yes	p146
Cambodia	Vinh Xuong (V)/Kaam Camnor (C)	Chau Doc (V)/Phnom Penh (C)	Yes	p150
Cambodia	Xa Xia (V)/Prek Chak (C)/	Ha Tien (V)/Kep (C)	Yes	p150
Cambodia	Tinh Bien (V)/Phnom Den (C)	Chau Doc (V)/Takeo (C)	Yes	p150
Cambodia	Le Thanh (V)/O Yadaw (C)	Pleiku (V)/Ban Lung (C)	Yes	p116
China	Lao Cai (V)/Hekou (Ch)	Hanoi (V)/Kunming (Ch)	No	p74
China	Dong Dang (V)/Pingxiang (Ch)	Lang Son (V)/Pingxiang (Ch)	No	p74
China	Mong Cai (V)/Dongxing (Ch)	Mong Cai (V)/Dongxing (Ch)	No	p74
Laos	Lao Bao (V)/Dansavanh (L)	Dong Ha (V)/Savannakhet (L)	Yes	p94
Laos	Bo Y (V)/Phou Keua (L)	Kon Tum (V)/Attapeu (L)	Yes	p116
Laos	Nam Can (V)/Nong Haet (L)	Vinh (V)/Phonsavan (L)	Yes	p94
Laos	Cau Treo (V)/Nam Phao (L)	Vinh (V)/Vieng Khan (L)	Yes	p94
Laos	Nam Xoi (V)/Na Meo (L)	Thanh Hoa (V)/Sam Neua (L)	No	p82
Laos	Tay Trang (V)/Sop Hun (L)	Dien Bien Phu (V)/Muang Khua (L)	Yes	p82

Directory A–Z

Accommodation

The Mekong region has something for everyone – from dives to the divine – and we cover them all. Although costs vary slightly across the region, accommodation in the Mekong region is almost always great value, especially compared with the West.

Important points to note:

➤ We've quoted prices in the local currency or US dollars based on the preferred currency of the particular property.

➤ Accommodation prices quoted are high season.

➤ Expect low-season discounts of up to 50% in touristy areas.

➤ Some hotels add 25% to high-season prices over Christmas, New Year and Chinese New Year (Tet in Vietnam); advance reservations are strongly recommended during these times.

➤ Assume that a fan will be provided if there is no air-con.

➤ Most top-end hotels levy a tax of 10% and a service charge of 5%, displayed as ++ ('plus plus') on the bill.

➤ Power outages are common in some towns; higher-end hotels will be equipped with generators.

➤ Many hotels post a small sign warning guests not to leave cameras, money, passports and other valuables in the room. Although there's no reason to be too paranoid, it's best to heed this warning. Higher-end hotels have safety boxes.

Camping

With the exception of the national parks in Thailand and some high-end experiences in Cambodia, Laos and Vietnam, the opportunities for general camping are limited.

Homestays

Homestays are a popular option in parts of the Mekong region, but some countries are more flexible than others about the concept. Homestays are well established in parts of Thailand and Vietnam, and many treks through minority areas in the far north include a night with a local family to learn about their lifestyle.

Homestays are also becoming more popular in Cambodia and Laos, where they are integral components of several popular community-based tourism programs. Many visitors also end up staying with local families when motorbiking in remote areas. For more on homestays, see individual country chapters.

BOOK YOUR STAY ONLINE

For more reviews by Lonely Planet authors, check out http://lonelyplanet.com/hotels/. You'll find independent reviews, as well as recommendations on the best places to stay. Best of all, you can book online.

YOU WANT MASSAGE?

Karaoke clubs and massage parlours are ubiquitous throughout the region. Sometimes this may mean an 'orchestra without instruments', or a healthy massage to ease a stiff body. However, more often than not, both these terms are euphemisms for some sort of prostitution. There may be some singing or a bit of shoulder tweaking going on, but ultimately it is just a polite introduction to something naughtier. Legitimate karaoke and legitimate massage do exist in the bigger cities, but as a general rule of thumb, if the place looks sleazy, it probably is.

Activities

There are plenty of activities to keep visitors busy in the Mekong region: go on the water, go under the water, crank up the revs on a motorbike or cruise down a slope on a mountain bike – the possibilities abound. Thailand is the adventure capital of the region, with Vietnam fast catching up, but every country has something to offer. For more on outdoor activities and adventures in the region, see p24.

Children

Children can live it up in the Mekong region, as they are always the centre of attention and almost everybody wants to play with them. This goes double for exotic-looking foreign children from faraway lands, who become instant celebrities wherever they go.

For the full picture on surviving and thriving on the road, check out Lonely Planet's *Travel with Children*, which contains useful advice on how to cope on the road, with a focus on travel in developing countries. There is also a rundown on health precautions for kids and advice on travel during pregnancy.

Safety & Amenities

➡ Child safety features, such as safety seats or boosters for vehicles, are virtually nonexistent in the Mekong region. This is a deal-breaker for some parents. Others are happy following the example of local families and hold smaller children on their laps.

➡ Boats usually have life jackets, but often lack child sizes, so if you are going to be doing a lot of boat travel pack a kiddie life jacket. These can also be bought in most cities, although they rarely meet international standards.

➡ Cot beds (cribs) are available in international-

standard midrange and top-end hotels, but not elsewhere.

➡ Baby formula and nappies (diapers) are available at minimarts and supermarkets in larger towns and cities, but the sizes are usually smallish, small and smaller.

➡ Nappy-rash cream is sold at pharmacies.

➡ Breastfeeding in public is quite common, so there is no need to worry about crossing a cultural boundary.

➡ High chairs in restaurants and nappy-changing facilities in public restrooms are hard to come by outside the major cities.

Children's Highlights

BEACHES

Cambodia and Thailand have the most shallow and child-friendly waters, on the warm Gulf of Thailand.

In Vietnam, Hoi An combines culture with cavorting on the sand, Nha Trang has fun boat trips, and the older kids can windsurf or sandboard in Mui Ne.

Note that most Vietnamese beaches face the South China Sea, which attracts some bigger rip tides, so watch your kids closely.

WILDLIFE

Wildlife-viewing highlights include the following:

➡ Kayaking or boating with rare Irrawaddy dolphins in Laos and Cambodia.

➡ Various opportunities to view primates in rainforests across the region.

➡ Animal rescue centres such as **Phnom Tamao Wildlife Sanctuary** (adult/child US$5/2; ☺8am-5pm) near Phnom Penh.

➡ Sustainable elephant initiatives around Lampang and Chiang Mai in Thailand, Luang Prabang and Champasak in Laos and Mondulkiri in Cambodia.

TEMPLES

Modern Buddhist temples are a delight for children. Shimmering gold Buddhas, shiny stupas, animal statues and the occasional monkey give the little ones plenty of visual stimulation (just keep their eyes averted from potentially scary demons).

The ruins of ancient temples serve as fun playgrounds for children. There are ruins all over the region, especially in northeastern Thailand, southern Laos and Cambodia. Hilltop temples abound, and some have forested hills and cool cave shrines to explore.

TOP DESTINATIONS FOR KIDS

Bangkok (p361 The City of Angels does a surprising cameo as the City of Little Angels, although you have to seek out the experiences. Think boat rides on the *khlong* (canals), shopping centres with aquariums and wax museums.

Luang Prabang (p295) While its cultural credentials draw mature visitors in their thousands, Luang Prabang has plenty to offer younger visitors, including kayaking, cycling and elephant encounters. The waterfalls are also a hit thanks to jungle bathing opportunities.

Siem Reap (p194) If the children are Indiana Jones fans, look no further than the temples of Angkor. Ta Prohm and Preah Khan have the jungle, Bayon has the weirdness and Angkor Wat has the proportions. Siem Reap is also loaded with alternative activities for kids.

Ko Chang (p392) Elephant rides, waterfalls and jungle treks combined with heavenly beaches.

Customs Regulations

Customs regulations vary little around the region. Drugs and firearms are strictly prohibited – a lengthy stay in prison is a common sentence.

INSURANCE ALERT!

Do not visit the Mekong region without medical insurance. Hospitals are often basic, particularly in remote areas. Anyone with a serious injury or illness may require emergency evacuation to Bangkok or Hong Kong. With an insurance policy costing no more than the equivalent of a few bottles of beer a day, this evacuation is free. Without an insurance policy, it will cost US$10,000 or more.

Discount Cards

The International Student Identity Card (ISIC) is the official student card, but is of limited use in the Mekong region. Some domestic and international airlines provide discounts to ISIC cardholders, but because knock-offs are so readily available, the cards carry little power.

Electricity

Most countries work on a voltage of 220V to 240V at 50Hz (cycles); note that 240V appliances will happily run on 220V. You should be able to pick up adaptors in markets and electrical shops in most of the main towns and cities.

Embassies & Consulates

It's important to realise what your own embassy – the embassy of the country of which you are a citizen – can and can't do to help if you get into trouble:

➡ Generally speaking, it won't be much help in emergencies if the trouble you're in is remotely your own fault.

➡ Remember that you are bound by the laws of the country you are in. Your embassy will not be sympathetic if you end up in jail after committing a crime locally, even if such actions are legal in your own country.

➡ In genuine emergencies you might get some assistance, but only if other channels have been exhausted.

Food

This is arguably the best region in the world when it comes to sampling the local cuisine. The food of China, Thailand and Vietnam needs no introduction, but Laotian and Khmer cuisine is also a rewarding experience. Food is fantastic value throughout the region. Street snacks start from as little as US$0.50, meals in local restaurants start at US$1.50 and even a serious spread at a decent restaurant will only be in the US$10 to US$20 range.

For an overview of Vietnamese cuisine see p159; for Cambodian food see p263; for Laotion food p351; and for Thai food p447.

Gay & Lesbian Travellers

Thailand, Cambodia and Laos have the most progressive attitudes towards homosexuality. While same-sex displays of affection are part of most Asian cultures, be discreet and respectful of the local culture. Extra vigilance should be practised in Vietnam, where authorities have arrested people on charges of suspected homosexual activities. There is not usually a problem with same-sex couples checking into rooms throughout the region, as it is so common among travellers.

Check out **Utopia Asian Gay & Lesbian Resources** (www.utopia-asia.com) for more information on gay and lesbian travel in Asia. Other links with useful pointers for gay travellers include www.gayguide.net and www.asiaout.com.

Insurance

A travel insurance policy to cover theft, loss and medical problems is essential. Worldwide travel insurance is available at www.lonelyplanet.com/travel_services. You can buy, extend and claim online anytime – even if you're already on the road.

A few considerations to keep in mind when purchasing insurance:

➡ Some policies specifically exclude 'dangerous activities', which can include

THE NATIONAL DISH

If there's just one dish you try, make it one of these. These are the dishes that capture the cuisine of the country in a single serving. Enjoy.

Cambodia *Amok* (baked fish in coconut leaves).

Laos *Làp* (spicy salad with meat or fish).

Thailand *Đôm yam gûng* (hot and sour soup with shrimp).

Vietnam *Pho bo* (rice noodle soup with beef).

scuba diving, motorcycling and even trekking.

➡ A locally acquired motorcycle licence is not valid under some policies.

➡ Check that the policy covers ambulance rides and emergency flights home.

Internet Access

You won't have trouble finding internet access or free wi-fi, at least in cities and touristy areas. 3G connections are also cheap and functional. A few concerns:

➡ Vietnam regularly blocks access to social networking sites, including Facebook. Learn to navigate the ways around such blocks if you feel the need to drop travel-related science on the interweb.

➡ Cambodian islands generally lack wi-fi (and mobile phone coverage for that matter), as do most national parks and similarly remote areas, particularly in Laos.

➡ Connection speeds aren't always the best but, hey, being on the internet at all in this neck of the woods is a bonus, right?

Legal Matters

Be sure to know the national laws before unwittingly committing a crime. In all of the Mekong region countries, using or trafficking drugs carries stiff punishments that are enforced, even if you're a foreigner.

If you are the victim of a crime, contact the tourist police, if available; they are usually better trained to deal with foreigners and foreign languages than the regular police force.

Maps

Good maps of Indochina, including Bangkok and Northeast Thailand, include Nelles *Vietnam, Laos & Cambodia* map at a scale of 1:1,500,000.

Money

Most experienced travellers will carry their money in a combination of US dollars and credit/bank cards. You'll always find situations in which one or the other cannot be used, so it pays to carry both. Euros are harder to change in a pinch, and it's difficult to cash travellers cheques outside of big cities.

ATMs

➡ In most large cities ATMs are widespread, but most charge at least US$3 per transaction, with withdrawal limits of about US$250 per withdrawal. Some banks offer free withdrawals.

➡ Banks back home charge for withdrawals overseas, so get some sort of premium account that negates such charges.

Credit Cards

Credit cards are widely accepted in the region. Thailand leads the way, where almost anything can be paid for with plastic. However, things dry up beyond major tourist centres or bigger towns, so don't rely exclusively on credit cards.

It is quite common for the business to pass on the commission (usually 3%) to the customer in Cambodia, Laos and Vietnam, so check if there is an additional charge before putting it on the plastic. Also check your monthly bills carefully in case some scamster clones your card while you are paying for something on your travels.

MAKING YOUR MONEY GO FURTHER

Many parts of the Mekong region remain mired in poverty. Support local businesses by buying locally made products. Eat in local restaurants where possible and dine in villages rather than taking picnics from town. Use local guides for remote regions, including indigenous minority peoples. Consider the option of homestays where they are available and support national park programs by visiting one of the many protected areas in the region.

When bargaining for goods or transport, remember the aim is not to get the lowest possible price, but one that's acceptable to both you and the seller. Coming on too strong or arguing over a few cents does nothing to foster positive feelings towards foreign visitors. Don't ask the price unless you're interested in actually buying it. If you become angry or visibly frustrated then you've lost the bargaining game.

Begging is common in many countries of the region and the tug on the shirtsleeve can become tiresome for visitors after a time. However, try to remember that many of these countries have little in the way of a social-security net. It is best to keep denominations small to avoid foreigners becoming even more of a target than they already are. Avoid giving money to children, as it is likely going straight to a 'begging pimp' or family member. Food is an option, but better still is to make a donation to one of the many local organisations trying to assist in the battle against poverty.

Exchanging Money

The US dollar is the currency of choice in the Mekong region. It is widely accepted as cash in Cambodia, Laos and Vietnam, and can be easily exchanged in Thailand. Other major currencies are also widely accepted by banks and exchange bureaus, but the rates get worse the further you are from a major city. The Thai baht is also accepted throughout Laos and in parts of western Cambodia.

Tipping

Tipping is not a traditional practice but is greatly appreciated, particularly in the poorer countries of the region where salaries remain low. Locals sometimes don't tip, but tourism has introduced the concept to hotels and restaurants, as well as to tour guides and drivers.

Travellers Cheques

Travellers cheques can be a pain to cash in the Mekong region, but if you must, get your cheques in US dollars and in large denominations, say US$100 or US$50, to avoid heavy per-cheque commission fees.

Photography

➡ Photography equipment and flash memory are widely available in urban areas.

➡ Ask for permission before taking photos of hill-tribe villagers, as many seriously object to being photographed.

➡ If you're after some tips, check out Lonely Planet's *Travel Photography: A Guide to Travel Photography*, written by travel photographer Richard l'Anson.

Post

Postal services are generally reliable across the region. Of course, it's always better to leave important mail and parcels for the big centres such as Bangkok and Hanoi.

There's always an element of risk in sending parcels home by sea, though as a rule they eventually reach their destination. If it's something of value, it's worth considering air freight – better still, register the parcel or send it by courier. Don't send cash or valuables through government postal systems.

Poste restante is widely available throughout the region and is the best way of receiving mail. When getting people to write to you, ask them to leave plenty of time for mail to arrive and to print your name very clearly.

Public Holidays

➡ Chinese New Year (or Tet in Vietnam) is the one holiday common to all countries and can have a big impact on travel plans, as businesses close and all forms of transport are booked out.

➡ Cambodia, Laos and Thailand celebrate their own new year at the same time in the middle of April. Each country shuts down for business for at least a week, and mass water fights break out in Thailand and Laos.

Safe Travel

Commissions

It could be the taxi driver, it might be the bus driver or even the friendly tout who latches on to you at the train station. Commissions are part and parcel of life in Asia, and the Mekong region is no exception. Thailand is getting better, while Cambodia and Vietnam are arguably getting worse. Laos doesn't have much of a problem just yet. Many places in the region refuse to pay commissions to touts, and hence you might be told a certain hotel or guesthouse is closed. Don't believe it unless you have seen it with your own eyes.

Drugs

The risks associated with recreational drug use and distribution have grown to the point where all visitors should exercise extreme caution even in places with illicit reputations. A spell in a local prison can be truly torturous. Even worse, you could become the next in a long line of tourists who have succumbed to a bad batch of cocaine or *yaba*.

Pollution & Noise

Pollution is a growing problem in the major cities of the region. Bangkok has long been famous as a place to

---

YABA DABA DO? YABA DABA DON'T!

Watch out for *yaba*, the 'crazy' drug from Thailand, known as *yama* in Cambodia, and also, rather ominously, as the Hindu god of death. Known as ice or crystal meth back home, it's not just any old diet pill from the pharmacist, but homemade meta-amphetamines produced in labs in Myanmar (Burma), Cambodia, Laos, Thailand and elsewhere. The pills are often laced with toxic substances, such as mercury, lithium or whatever else the maker can find. *Yaba* is a dirty drug and more addictive than users would like to admit, provoking powerful hallucinations, sleep deprivation and psychosis. Steer clear of the stuff unless you plan on an indefinite extension to your trip to the Mekong region.

chew the air rather than inhale. However, Ho Chi Minh City (Saigon) and Phnom Penh also have problems of their own. Laos remains blissfully pollution-free for the most part.

Remember the movie *Spinal Tap*? The soundtrack of the cities in this region is permanently cranked up to 11. Not just any noise, but a whole lot of noises that just never seem to stop. At night there is most often a competing cacophony from motorbikes, discos, cafes, video arcades, karaoke lounges and restaurants. If your hotel is near any or all of these, it may be difficult to sleep. Fortunately most noise subsides around 10pm or 11pm, as few places stay open much later than that. Unfortunately, however, locals are up and about from around 5am onwards.

One last thing...don't forget the earplugs.

Queues

What queues? Most locals in the Mekong region don't queue, they mass in a rugby scrum, pushing towards the counter. When in Rome... This is first-seen, first-served, so take a deep breath, muscle your way to the front and wave your passport or papers as close to the counter as you can.

Scams

Every year Lonely Planet gets hundreds of letters and emails from hapless travellers reporting that they've been scammed in this region. In almost all cases there are two culprits involved: a shrewd scam artist and the traveller's own greed.

Two perennial scams involve card games and gemstones. If someone asks you to join a card game be extremely wary. If the game involves money, walk away – it's almost certainly rigged. As for gemstones, if there really were vast amounts of money to be made by sell-

THE ABUSE OF INNOCENCE

The sexual abuse of children by foreign paedophiles is a serious problem in some parts of the Mekong region. Many child prostitutes are sold into the business by relatives. These sex slaves are either trafficked overseas or forced to cater to domestic demand and local sex-tourism operators.

Fear of contracting HIV/AIDS from mature sex workers has led to increasing exploitation of (supposedly as-yet uninfected) children. Unicef estimates that there are close to one million child prostitutes in Asia – one of the highest figures in the world.

Paedophiles are treated as criminals in the region and several have served or are serving jail sentences as a result. Many Western countries have introduced legislation that sees nationals prosecuted in their home country for having underage sex abroad. Visitors can do their bit to fight this menace by keeping an eye out for suspicious behaviour on the part of foreigners. Don't ignore it. Try to pass on any relevant information such as the name and nationality of the individual to the embassy concerned.

End Child Prostitution & Trafficking (Ecpat; www.ecpat.net) is a global network aimed at stopping child prostitution, child pornography and the trafficking of children for sexual purposes, and has affiliates in most Western countries. **Childsafe International** (www.childsafe-international.org), operating out of Cambodia, now covers Laos and Thailand as well, and aims to educate businesses and individuals to be on the lookout for children in vulnerable situations.

ing gems back home, savvy businesspeople would have a monopoly on the market already. Don't believe the people who say that they support their global wanderings by reselling gemstones; in reality they support themselves by tricking unsuspecting foreigners.

Other common scams include having your rented bicycle or motorbike 'stolen' by someone with a duplicate key; and dodgy drug deals that involve police extortion. There are many more scams so it pays to keep your antennae up during a trip through the Mekong region.

Theft

Theft in this part of the world is usually by stealth rather than by force. Keep your money and valuables in a money belt worn under-

neath your clothes. Be alert to the possible presence of snatch thieves, who will whisk a camera or a bag off your shoulder. Don't store valuables in easily accessible places such as packs that are stored in the luggage compartment of buses, or the front pocket of daypacks.

Violent theft is very rare but occurs from time to time – usually late at night and after the victim has been drinking. Be careful when walking alone late at night and don't fall asleep in taxis.

Always be diplomatically suspicious of overfriendly locals. Don't accept gifts of food or drinks from someone you don't know. In Thailand, thieves have been known to drug travellers for easier pickings.

HAPPINESS IS A STATE OF MIND

'Don't worry, be happy' could be the motto for the Mekong region, but in some backpacker centres the term 'happy' has taken on a completely different connotation. Seeing the word 'happy' in front of 'shake', 'pizza' or anything else does not, as one traveller was told, mean it comes with extra pineapple. The extra is usually marijuana, added in whatever quantity the shake-maker deems fit. For many travellers 'happy' is a well-understood alias, but there are others who innocently down their shake or pizza only to spend the next 24 hours floating in a world of their own.

Finally, don't let paranoia ruin your trip. With just a few sensible precautions most travellers make their way without incident.

Unexploded Ordnance (UXO) & Landmines

The legacy of war lingers on in Cambodia, Laos and Vietnam in the form of undetonated bombs and explosives. Be careful walking off the trail in areas near the Laos–Vietnam border or around the DMZ (Demilitarised Zone).

Cambodia suffers the additional affliction of landmines, some 4 to 6 million of them according to surveys. Many of these are located in border areas with Thailand in the north and west of the country, but it pays to stick to marked paths anywhere in Cambodia.

Violence

Violence against foreigners is pretty rare and is not something you should waste much time worrying about, but if you do get into a flare-up with some locals, swallow your pride and back down. You are the outsider. You don't know how many friends they have nearby, how many weapons they are carrying or how many years they have studied kickboxing.

Websites

Travel advisories are government-run websites that update nationals on the latest security situation in any given country, including the countries of the Mekong region. They are useful for checking out dangerous countries or during dangerous events, but these official sites tend to be pretty conservative to cover themselves, stressing dangers where many would feel they don't always exist.

Australia (www.dfat.gov.au/travel)

Canada (www.voyage.gc.ca)

New Zealand (www.safetravel.govt.nz)

UK (www.fco.gov.uk/travel)

USA (www.travel.state.gov)

Telephone

For country-specific information on landlines, phone cards, mobile phone networks and international dialling codes, see the individual country directories.

The following rules apply to the entire region:

➡ Calls over the internet using Skype or another voice-over-internet protocol (VOIP) are the way forward, and there is plenty of infrastructure in place – both 3G and wi-fi – to make it happen.

➡ Roaming is bad for you! Do not be that idiot who cluelessly yaks his way around the world and returns home to a US$3000 phone bill. Instead, buy a local SIM card, configure it for 3G, and call home for pennies via VOIP.

➡ Some phones are 'locked' by the issuing company back home, but most telephone shops in the Mekong region can 'unlock' them in seconds for a small charge.

➡ Mobile phone coverage usually extends to all but the most remote areas in the Mekong region.

Time

Cambodia, Laos, Thailand and Vietnam are seven hours ahea of Greenwich Mean Time or Universal Time Coordinated (GMT/UTC). When it is midday in Bangkok or Hanoi, it is 10pm the previous evening in San Francisco, 1am in New York, 5am in London, 6am in Paris and 3pm in Sydney.

Tourist Information

All the countries in the Mekong region have government-funded tourist offices with varying degrees of usefulness. Thailand offers by far the most efficient tourism information service. When it comes to the rest, better information is often available from dedicated internet sites, guesthouses and travellers cafes, or your fellow travellers, rather than through the state-run tourist offices.

Travellers with Disabilities

Travellers with serious disabilities will likely find the Mekong region a challenging place to travel. Inconveniences include the following:

→ chaotic traffic

→ lack of lifts in smaller hotels

→ high kerbs and uneven pavements (sidewalks) that are routinely blocked by parked motorbikes and footstalls

→ an almost complete lack of disabled-friendly public amenities, even in big cities and major tourist hubs.

→

On the positive side, most people in the region are helpful towards foreigners, and local labour is cheap if you need someone to accompany you at all times. Most guesthouses and small hotels have ground-floor rooms that are reasonably easy to access.

Dus and train travel is tough, but rent a private vehicle with a driver and almost anywhere can become accessible.

The Travellers With Disabilities forum on Lonely Planet's **Thorn Tree** (www. lonelyplanet.com) is a good place to seek the advice of other disabled travellers.

International organisations that can provide information on mobility-impaired travel include:

Accessible Journeys (☑610-521 0339; www.disabilitytravel.com)

Mobility International USA (☑541-343-1284; www. miusa.org; PO Box 10767, Eugene, Oregon)

RADAR (www.radar.org.uk) UK-based umbrella organisation for voluntary groups for people with disabilities.

Society for Accessible Travel & Hospitality (SATH; ☑212-447-7284; www.sath. org; 347 5th Ave, Suite 610, New York)

Visas

Generally, the following rules of thumb apply no matter which border you are crossing:

→ For Thailand, citizens of most Western countries are issued a 30-day visa waiver if they arrive by air, or a 15-day waiver if they arrive by land (a 'waiver' means they do not need a visa for the period of the waiver).

→ For Cambodia and Laos, 30-day visas are issued upon arrival at both airports and land borders.

→ For Vietnam, it is always necessary to arrange a visa in advance.

Get your visas as you go rather than all at once before you leave home; they are often easier and cheaper to get in neighbouring countries and visas are only valid within a certain time period, which could interfere with an extended trip.

Procedures for extending a visa vary from country to country. In some cases, extensions are quite complicated, in others they're a mere formality. Remember the most important rule: treat visits to embassies, consulates and borders as formal occasions and look smart for them.

You do not need to show an onward ticket to obtain a visa or enter the countries of the Mekong region, even though some do have such rules on the book.

Volunteering

There are fewer opportunities for volunteering than one might imagine there would be in a region that remains predominantly poor. This is partly due to the sheer number of professional development workers based here, and development is a pretty lucrative industry these days.

The other avenue is professional volunteering through an organisation back home that offers one- or two-year placements in the region. One of the largest is **Voluntary Service Overseas** (VSO; www.vso.org.uk) in the UK, but other countries have their own organisations, including: **US Peace Corps** (www.peacecorps.gov), **VSO Canada** (www.vsocan. org), **Australian Volunteers**

RESPONSIBLE TRAVEL TIPS

Some basic behavioural rules to follow when travelling in the Mekong region:

→ Respect local dress standards, particularly at religious sites. Always remove your shoes before entering a temple, as well as any hat or head covering.

→ Nude sunbathing is considered totally inappropriate.

→ Learn the local greetings in each country – and use them.

→ Monks are not supposed to touch or be touched by women.

→ No matter how high your blood pressure rises, do not raise your voice or show signs of aggression. This will lead to a loss of face.

→ Don't leave a pair of chopsticks sitting vertically in a rice bowl – they can look like the incense sticks that are burned for the dead.

→ The people of the Mekong region like to keep a clean house; it's customary to remove shoes when entering a home.

International (www.austra
lianvolunteers.com) and **Volunteer Service Abroad**
(VSA; www.vsa.org.nz). **I-to-I**
(www.i-to-i.com) runs volunteer tourism and gap-year
programs. The UN also operates its own volunteer program; details are available at
www.unv.org. Other general
volunteer sites with links all
over the place include www.
worldvolunteerweb.org and
www.volunteerabroad.com.

Women Travellers

While travel in the Mekong
region for women is generally
safe, there are several things
visitors can do to make it
hassle free.

Keep in mind that mod-
esty in dress is culturally
important across all Southeast Asia. Causes for com-
motion include wearing the
ever-popular midriff T-shirt
that inadvertently sends the
message that you're a prostitute. At the beach, save the
topless sunbathing for home
rather than this conservative
region of the world. This is
particularly important when
travelling from Thailand to
Cambodia or Laos. Thailand
may be very Westernised
with an 'anything goes'
atmosphere, but Cambodia
and Laos are much more
traditional. Walking around
Angkor or Luang Prabang
dressed like you are going
to a full-moon party won't
impress the locals.

There's no question about
it: solo women make inviting targets for thieves, and
countless female travellers
have been the victim of
bag-snatching incidents and
worse in places like Phnom
Penh. Women should be
on guard especially when
returning home late at night
or arriving in a new town at
night.

While physical assault is
rare, local men often consider foreign women exempt
from their own society's rules
of conduct regarding mem-
bers of the opposite sex.
Use common sense about
venturing into dangerous-
looking areas, particularly
alone or at night. If you do
find yourself in a tricky situation, try to extricate yourself
as quickly as possible – hopping into a taxi or entering a
business establishment and
asking them to call a cab is
often the best solution.

Treat overly friendly strangers, both male and female,
with a good deal of caution.

Many travellers have
reported small peepholes in
the walls and doors of cheap
hotels, some of which operate as boarding houses or
brothels (often identified by
their advertising 'day use'
rates). If you can, move on
to another guesthouse or
hotel.

Work

The main opportunities for
people passing through the
region are teaching Eng-
lish (or another European
language), landing a job in
tourism or starting a small
business such as a bar or
restaurant.

Teaching English This is the
easiest way to support yourself in the Mekong region. For
short-term gigs, the large cities
such as Bangkok, Ho Chi Minh
City and Phnom Penh have a
lot of language schools and a
high turnover. **Payaway** (www.
payaway.co.uk) provides a handy
online list of language schools
and volunteer groups looking
for recruits for its regional
programs.

Tourism Most of these jobs
deservedly go to locals, but there
are opportunities for wannabe
guesthouse or hotel managers,
bartenders, chefs and so on. This
can be a pretty memorable way
to pass a few months in a different culture.

Small-business start-up If
you elect to go this route tread
with caution. Many a foreigner
has been burned in the region.
Sometimes it's an unscrupulous
partner, other times it's the local
girlfriend, or boyfriend, who
changes their mind and goes it
alone. Sometimes the owners
burn out themselves, drinking
the profits of the bar or dabbling
in drugs. Do your homework
regarding ownership laws and
legal recourse in the event of
a dispute. That said, there are
many success stories in the
region, where people came for a
holiday and built an empire.

Transitions Abroad (www.
transitionsabroad.com) and its
namesake magazine cover all
aspects of overseas life, including landing a job in a variety of
fields. The website also provides
links to other useful sites and
publications for those living
abroad.

Transport

GETTING THERE & AWAY

Entering the Region

All the countries in the region have international airports, but Bangkok is far and away the most important hub. There are long-haul flights linking Hanoi and Ho Chi Minh City (Saigon) to Europe and North America, but Phnom Penh and Vientiane are only accessible via a regional gateway such as Bangkok, Hong Kong or Singapore.

When it comes to land borders, Thailand is linked to Malaysia for those visiting more of Southeast Asia. Myanmar (Burma) looks like a tantalising option for overland travel to India, but this is not currently permitted. Both Laos and Vietnam share borders with China for those heading deeper into Asia or planning an epic overland trip to or from Europe.

Flights, cars and tours can be booked online at www.lonelyplanet.com/bookings.

Passport

To enter the Mekong region countries, your passport must be valid for at least six months from your date of entry, even if you're only staying for a few days. You may be refused entry if your passport doesn't have enough blank pages available for a visa.

Air

Tickets

➡ The major gateways for budget flights in Southeast Asia are Bangkok, Kuala Lumpur and Singapore.

➡ Other popular jumping-off points for flights into the Mekong region are Guangzhou, Hong Kong, Seoul, Taipei and Tokyo.

➡ Bangkok is the best place to shop for onward tickets and tickets around the Mekong region.

➡ When researching and buying tickets on the internet, try flight-comparison sites like kayak.com or skyscanner.net.

➡ Note that some popular budget airlines, such as Air Asia, are not covered by online travel and flight-comparison sites, so it pays to check the airline websites separately.

Other useful sites for booking tickets in the Mekong region:

Lonely Planet (www.lonelyplanet.com)

STA Travel (www.statravel.com) Leading student travel agency with cheap fares, plus separate websites for the UK, Australia and New Zealand.

CLIMATE CHANGE & TRAVEL

Every form of transport that relies on carbon-based fuel generates CO_2, the main cause of human-induced climate change. Modern travel is dependent on , which might use less fuel per per person than most cars but travel much greater distances. The altitude at which aircraft emit gases (including CO_2) and particles also contributes to their climate change impact. Many websites offer 'carbon calculators' that allow people to estimate the carbon emissions generated by their journey and, for those who wish to do so, to offset the impact of the greenhouse gases emitted with contributions to portfolios of climate-friendly initiatives throughout the world. Lonely Planet offsets the carbon footprint of all staff and author travel.

AIR PASSES

Major air alliances like Star Alliance and OneWorld offer Asia air passes that provide discounts on open-jaw itineraries to several destinations within Asia. Often your trip must originate in the USA, Europe or Australia to avail yourself of these; contact individual airlines or a travel agent for more info.

Bucket shops, consolidators and online search engines offer cheap tickets to the region. If Asia is one of many stops on a global tour, consider a round-the-world (RTW) ticket, which allows a certain number of stops within a set time period as long as you don't backtrack.

Land

The land borders between the Mekong region and the rest of Asia include the Lao and Vietnamese northern borders with China and the frontier that Thailand shares with Malaysia and Myanmar.

There are only two international trains into the region:

➡ The twice-weekly international service between Hanoi and Beijing.

➡ Direct services from Singapore and Kuala Lumpur to Bangkok via Butterworth (Malaysia) and Hat Yai (Thailand).
From Vietnam you can also take local trains to the towns

of Lang Son and Lao Cai near the Chinese border.

There are also two daily bus services from Hanoi to Nanning, involving a change of buses at the border. Reports from Nanning-bound travellers indicate that the bus is less hassle and quicker than travelling by train.

See the Border Crossings chapter (p484) for more on entering the region overland.

Sea

Apart from a few cruises that call at ports in Thailand, Vietnam and, occasionally, Cambodia, there are no real options for travelling to the Mekong region by sea.

Tours

There was a time when prearranged tours were a near necessity in countries like Cambodia and Laos. The situation has changed dramatically and it is now much easier to organise your own trip. Budget and midrange travellers in particular can go it alone, as arrangements are cheap and easy on the ground. Travelling independently, you'll put more money into local pockets and have a richer travel experience.

Think twice about prebooking a Mekong trip with a global tour company based in your home country, as you'll generally pay a premium

compared with using a company based in the Mekong region. In many cases, once you've landed in the region, you'll simply be passed off to the global company's local partner.

If you prefer the security and ease of a tour, you'll find scores of experienced, competent local tour companies on the ground in the region, ready to tailor a trip to your needs. This could be anything from a one-day Angkor Wat excursion to a multiweek trail-biking expedition in the highlands of Vietnam and Laos. We recommend competent local tour companies throughout this book.

GETTING AROUND

Air

Air travel is a mixed bag in the Mekong region. Some routes to/from/within Thailand are now a real bargain, as no-frills regional carriers such as **Air Asia** (www.airasia. com) and **Nok Air** (www. nokair.com) offer heavily discounted fares. However, on many other routes, there may only be one carrier and prices are high.

Flights can usually be booked online easily enough, especially for budget airlines, or you can book through one of the region's myriad travel agents.

Air Passes

The national airlines of Southeast Asian countries frequently run promotional deals from select Western cities or for regional travel.

Bangkok Airways (www. bangkokair.com) offers a Discovery Pass (in conjunction with Lao Airlines), which includes domestic coupons for US$88 in Thailand and US$70 in Laos, plus international coupons from US$120

SURVIVING THE STREETS

Wherever you roam in the region, you'll have to cross some busy streets eventually, so if you don't want to wind up like a bug on a windscreen, pay close attention to a few pedestrian survival rules. Foreigners frequently make the mistake of thinking that the best way to cross a busy street in the Mekong region is to run quickly across, but this could get you creamed. Most locals cross the street slowly – very slowly – giving the motorbike drivers sufficient time to judge their position so they can pass on either side. They won't stop or even slow down, but they will try to avoid hitting you. Just don't make any sudden moves.

per sector (US$200 for longer distances).

Bicycle

Touring Southeast Asia on a bicycle has been steadily growing in popularity.

Thailand Used as a base by many long-distance cyclists to head into Indochina for some challenging adventures.

Vietnam Traffic is relatively light away from National Hwy 1A, buses take bicycles and the entire coastal route is feasible, give or take a few hills.

Cambodia and Laos Road conditions can make two-wheeling more challenging, but light traffic, especially in Laos, makes pedalling more pleasant than elsewhere.

Parts and Services International standard bicycles and components can be bought in Bangkok and Phnom Penh, but most cyclists bring their own.

Shipping Bikes Bicycles can travel by air; ask about extra charges and any shipment specifications.

Boat

As roads in the region improve, boats are less a factor than they once were, but they are still popular on a few routes and in certain particularly remote areas they remain a necessity.

Thailand In the far north there are boat connections between Chiang Saen and Jinghong in Yunnan.

Laos The leisurely Luang Say cruise is a fine way to link Huay Xai and Luang Prabang with a night in Pak Beng. For those on a budget there are plenty of public boats running this way.

Cambodia The boat ride from Siem Reap to Battambang is spectacular, and you can also get from Siem Reap to Phnom Penh by boat.

Cambodia to Vietnam There are also various fast, slow and luxury boats plying the Mekong

MOTORCYCLE TIPS

Most Asians are so adept at driving and riding on motorcycles that they can balance the whole family on the front bumper, or even take a quick nap as a passenger. Foreigners unaccustomed to motorcycles are not as graceful. If you're riding on the back of a motorcycle remember to relax. For balance hold on to the back bar, not the driver's waist. Tall people should keep their long legs tucked in as most drivers are used to shorter passengers. Women (or men) wearing skirts should always ride side-saddle and collect longer skirts so that they don't catch in the wheel or drive chain. Enjoy the ride.

between Phnom Penh/Siem Reap and Chau Doc, Vietnam, for those who want to explore the Mekong Delta without backtracking to Ho Chi Minh City.

Cruising Luxury river cruises are popular along the Mekong in Laos and between Cambodia and Vietnam. Halong Bay is another popular spot for boat cruises. Companies specialising in upscale boat cruises include:

Compagnie Fluviale du Mekong (www.cfmekong.com)

Heritage Line (www.heritage-line.com)

Indochina Sails (www.indochinasails.com)

Pandaw Cruises (www.pandaw.com)

Bus

Bus travel has become a great way to get around with improved roads throughout the region. Most land borders are crossed via bus; these either travel straight through the two countries with a stop for border formalities, or require a change of buses at the appropriate border towns.

➡ Thailand offers by far the most comfortable buses.

➡ Cambodia and Vietnam have a pretty impressive network of buses connecting major cities, although these dry up in remote areas.

➡ Buses in Laos are reasonable on the busiest

routes, but pretty poor elsewhere.

➡ Theft does occur on some long-distance buses; keep all valuables on your person, not in a stowed bag.

Car & Motorcycle

Self-drive car hire is possible in Thailand and in some areas of Laos and Cambodia.

Laos and Cambodia offer brilliant motorbiking for experienced riders, not forgetting the incredible mountain roads of northern Vietnam. Motorbikes are widely available for hire. Road conditions vary within the region:

➡ Thailand has an excellent road network with plenty of well-signposted, well-paved roads.

➡ Vietnam has decent roads, but self-drive is not possible.

➡ Laos and Cambodia road conditions vary, although sealed roads are now the norm.

Driving Licence

If you are planning to drive a car, get an International Driving Permit (IDP) from your local automobile association before you leave your home country; IDPs are inexpensive and valid for one year.

Hiring a smaller motorbike generally doesn't require a licence.

Hiring 250cc or larger bikes may require a licence, especially in Thailand.

Hire

➤ Self-drive car hire is mainly an option in Thailand, plus a few places hire out vehicles in Cambodia and Laos.

➤ Cars with drivers are available at very reasonable rates in all countries of the region.

➤ Guesthouses rent motorcycles cheaply throughout the region, usually for around US$5 to US$10 a day.

➤ 250cc dirt bikes are also widely available in the region and are a lot of fun if you know how to handle them.

MOTORBIKE CHECKLIST

Before taking a hired motorbike out on the road, perform the following routine safety checks:

➤ Look at the tyres for treads.

➤ Check for oil leaks.

➤ Test the brakes.

➤ Make sure the headlights and tail lights work and that you know how to turn them on.

A decent helmet that fits is highly recommended. These can be hard to come by on the ground, so consider bringing your own if you are going to be doing a lot of two-wheeling.

Other gear-related tips to improve both safety and comfort during those long days in the saddle:

➤ If your helmet doesn't have a visor, then wear goggles, glasses or sunglasses to keep bugs, dust and other debris out of your eyes.

➤ Long trousers, long-sleeved shirts, gloves and shoes are highly recommended as protection against sunburn and as a second skin if you fall.

➤ Pack wet weather gear, especially in the rainy season.

Insurance

Purchasing insurance is highly recommended when you hire a motorcycle. The more reputable motorcycle-hire places will always offer insurance.

Without insurance you are responsible for anything that happens to the bike. To be absolutely clear about your liability, ask for a written estimate of the replacement cost for a similar bike.

Insurance for a hired car is also necessary. Be sure to ask the car-hire agent about liability and damage coverage.

Road Rules

Basically, there aren't many, and arguably none. Drive cautiously. An incredible number of lives are lost on roads in this region every year, particularly around major holidays.Your odds of surviving are better if you heed the following rules:

➤ Size matters and the biggest vehicle wins by default, regardless of circumstances – might makes right on the road.

➤ The middle of the road is typically used as an invisible third lane, even if there is oncoming traffic.

➤ The horn is used to notify other vehicles that you intend to pass them.

➤ Be particularly careful about children on the road, as they often live and play on the sides of even the busiest highways.

➤ Slow down if you see livestock near the road; hit a cow on a motorbike and you'll both be hamburger.

Hitching

Hitching is never entirely safe in any country in the world and we do not recommend it.

FARE'S FAIR?

This is the million-dong question: 'Am I being quoted the right fare or are they completely ripping me off?' Well, there's no easy answer, but here are some guidelines to help you navigate the maze.

Air Fares usually fixed, although web fares differ depending on when you book and what dates you want to travel.

Train Fixed, although naturally there are different prices for different classes.

Bus Usually fixed if you buy the ticket from the point of departure, but there is a chance you'll be overcharged if you board the bus along the way. Buying through a travel agent or guesthouse usually incurs a small commission.

Boat Fixed for ferries or hydrofoils, but not for small local boats or some tourist boats.

Minibus and sŏrngtăaou Generally fixed, though overcharging tourists is not unheard of.

Cyclo (pedicab), motorbike taxi and túk-túk Most definitely not fixed. Any local transport prices given here are indicative; the actual price of a ride depends on the wiliness of the driver and your bargaining skills. It's best to agree on a price with your driver before setting off.

Travellers who decide to hitch should understand that they are taking a small but potentially serious risk. People who do choose to hitch will be safer if they travel in pairs and let someone know where they are planning to go.

Locals do flag down private and public vehicles for a lift, but some sort of payment is usually expected.

Local Transport

In the Mekong region, anything motorised is often modified to carry passengers.

Túk-túk The favoured form of transportation for tourists in Thailand, Cambodia and, increasingly, Laos. In Thailand and Laos túk-túk (or *đúk đúk*) are high-octane three-wheeled chariots, while in Cambodia they take the form of comfy little trailers pulled by motorbikes. For the Cambodian version we use the term *remorque* (or *remork*) instead of túk-túk in this book.

Motorcycle Taxi Ubiquitous in Cambodia, Thailand and Vietnam, but rarer in Laos. However, in Laos motorised *săhmlór* (three wheelers, or motorbikes with a sidecar) are becoming popular.

Sŏrngtǎaou The main form of public transport in provincial Laos and Thailand, these are flatbed or pick up trucks kitted out with bench seating. They generally ply fixed routes but are also usually available for private hire.

Taxis Metered taxis are common in Thai and Vietnamese cities and can be flagged down on the street easily enough. They are remarkably cheap (about US$2 for a short ride), but be on the lookout for rigged meters in Vietnam. Taxis in Laos and Cambodia are generally not metered and must be ordered by phone or through your guesthouse.

Pedicab The old-fashioned bicycle rickshaw still survives in Cambodia and Vietnam, where it's known as a *cyclo*. In Laos they are *săhmlór*, often motorised.

Public Bus Bangkok, Hanoi and Ho Chi Minh City have efficient bus networks, but there is no such thing in Phnom Penh or Vientiane.

Metro Bangkok boasts a state-of-the-art light-rail and underground system that make zipping around town feel like time travel.

Animals Beasts of burden still make up a percentage of the local transport in very remote areas, and it is possible to ride an ox cart through remote parts of Cambodia and Laos in the wet season.

Tours

Trail-bike touring is a regional speciality, and we list several tour operators in the individual country chapters. Hanoi-based **Explore Indochina** (www.exploreindochina.com) is one company that does cross-border trips into Laos and sometimes Cambodia.

The following cover the whole of the Mekong with a range of general tours:

Exotissimo (www.exotissimo. com) Runs a wide range of tours throughout the Mekong region, including cycling, trekking, golfing – you name it.

Handspan Travel (www. handspan.com) Vietnam-based Handspan dips into Laos and Cambodia with bicycle tours and more.

Journeys Within (☎063-964748; www.journeys-within. com) A boutique tourism company based in Siem Reap that offers various cross-border trips in addition to appealing trips within Cambodia. Operates a charitable arm helping schools and communities.

Spice Roads (www. spiceroads.com) Specialises in cycling tours of the Mekong region.

Stray Asia (www.straytravel. asia) 'Hop-on hop-off' travel passes and budget-friendly adventure tours across Thailand, Laos, Cambodia and Vietnam.

Train

Thailand and Vietnam Both have efficient railway networks, including the option of comfortable air-con sleeper berths.

Cambodia Has a rail system, but it's being rehabilitated and passenger services are not offered.

Laos Has no railway at all, save a short link to Thailand via the Friendship Bridge to Nong Khai.

Cross-border trains There are no cross-border trains between Mekong countries. Thai trains serve the Thai border towns of Nong Khai (for crossing into Laos), Aranya Prathet (for crossing into Cambodia) and Ubon Ratchathani (for crossing into Laos).

Health

Travellers tend to worry about contracting infectious diseases when in the tropics, but infections are a rare cause of serious illness or death in travellers. Pre-existing medical conditions such as heart disease, and accidental injury (especially traffic accidents), account for most life-threatening problems. Becoming ill in some way, however, is relatively common. The advice given here is a general guide and does not replace the advice of a doctor trained in travel medicine.

BEFORE YOU GO

Medications

➡ Pack medications in their original, clearly labelled containers.

➡ A letter from your physician describing medical conditions and medications, including generic names, is a good idea.

➡ If carrying syringes or needles, be sure to have a physician's letter stating their medical necessity.

➡ If taking any regular medication, bring a double supply in case of loss or theft.

➡ In most Mekong region countries, you can buy many medications over the counter without a doctor's prescription, but it can be difficult to find some of the newer drugs.

Insurance

Even if you're fit and healthy, don't travel without health insurance. Bills of more than US$100,000 are not uncommon if you need emergency evacuation. Some things to keep in mind when choosing an insurer:

➡ Declare any existing medical conditions, as the insurance company *will* check if the problem is pre-existing and will not pay up if undeclared.

➡ Adventure activities such as rock climbing sometimes require extra cover.

➡ If your health insurance doesn't cover you for medical expenses abroad, consider getting extra insurance.

➡ Find out in advance if the insurance plan will make direct payments to providers or reimburse later for overseas health expenditures.

➡ Even if you have a direct-pay plan, many hospitals in the Mekong region expect payment up front in cash. Exceptions are the big hospitals in Bangkok and International SOS clinics in Phnom Penh, Ho Chi Minh City (Saigon) and elsewhere.

Vaccinations

If you plan to get vaccinated before your trip, consider the following:

➡ Specialised travel-medicine clinics are the best source of information, as they stock all available vaccines and can give specific recommendations for each region.

➡ Doctors will take into account factors such as past vaccination history, length of trip, activities and existing medical conditions.

➡ Most vaccines don't produce immunity until at least two weeks after they're given.

➡ Ask for an International Certificate of Vaccination (otherwise known as the yellow booklet), which will list all vaccinations given.

Recommended Vaccinations

The World Health Organization (WHO) recommends the following vaccinations for travellers to the Mekong region:

Adult diphtheria and tetanus Single booster recommended if you haven't had one in the previous 10 years.

Hepatitis A Provides almost 100% protection for up to a year; a booster after 12 months provides at least another 20 years' protection.

Hepatitis B Now considered routine for most travellers. Given as three shots over six months. A rapid schedule is also available, as is a combined vaccination with hepatitis A. Lifetime protection occurs in 95% of people.

Measles, mumps and rubella (MMR) Two doses of MMR are required unless you have had the diseases. Many young adults require a booster.

Polio Only one booster is required as an adult for lifetime protection.

Typhoid Recommended unless your trip is less than a week long and only to developed cities. The vaccine offers around 70% protection, lasts for two to three years and comes as a single shot.

Required Vaccinations

The only vaccine required by international regulations is for yellow fever. Proof of vaccination is only required if you have visited a country in the yellow-fever zone within the six days before entering the Mekong region. If travelling to the Mekong region from Africa or South America, check to see if proof of vaccination is required. It is only likely to be an issue if flying directly from an affected country to a major gateway such as Bangkok.

Medical Checklist

Recommended items for a personal medical kit:

➡ antibacterial cream, eg Muciprocin

➡ antibiotics for diarrhoea, such as Norfloxacin or Ciprofloxacin; for bacterial diarrhoea Azithromycin; for giardiasis or amoebic dysentery Tinidazole

➡ antifungal cream, eg Clotrimazole

➡ antihistamine – there are many options, eg Cetirizine for daytime and Promethazine for night

➡ anti-inflammatory such as Ibuprofen

➡ antiseptic, eg Betadine

➡ antispasmodic for stomach cramps, eg Buscopan

➡ contraceptives

➡ decongestant, eg Pseudoephedrine

➡ DEET-based insect repellent

➡ diarrhoea treatment – consider an oral rehydration solution (eg Gastrolyte), diarrhoea 'stopper' (eg Loperamide) and antinausea medication (eg Prochlorperazine)

➡ first-aid items such as scissors, plasters, bandages, gauze, thermometer (but not one with mercury), sterile needles and syringes, safety pins and tweezers

➡ indigestion medication, eg Quickeze or Mylanta

➡ paracetamol

➡ Permethrin to impregnate clothing and mosquito nets

➡ steroid cream for allergic or itchy rashes, eg 1% to 2% hydrocortisone

➡ sunscreen and hat

➡ throat lozenges

➡ thrush (vaginal yeast infection) treatment, eg Clotrimazole pessaries or Diflucan tablet

➡ Ural or equivalent if you're prone to urinary infections

Websites

There is a wealth of travel health advice on the internet.

➡ **Lonely Planet** (www. lonelyplanet.com) A good place to start.

➡ **World Health Organization** (www.who.int/ith) Publishes a superb book called *International Travel & Health*, which is revised annually and is available online at no cost.

➡ **MD Travel Health** (www. mdtravelhealth.com) Provides complete travel health

recommendations for every country and is updated daily.

➡ **Centers for Disease Control & Prevention** (CDC; www.cdc.gov) Good source of general information.

Further Reading

Lonely Planet's *Healthy Travel – Asia & India* is a handy pocket-sized book that is packed with useful information, including pretrip planning, emergency first aid, immunisation and disease information, and what to do if you get sick on the road. Other recommended references include *Traveller's Health* by Dr Richard Dawood and *Travelling Well* by Dr Deborah Mills; check out www.travellingwell.com.au.

IN THE MEKONG REGION

Availability & Cost of Health Care

If you think you may have a serious disease, especially malaria, do not waste time – travel to the nearest quality facility to receive attention. Bangkok is a popular medical-tourism destination, with a few world-class hospitals that provide excellent care. In other Mekong capitals the best options are clinics that cater specifically to travellers and expats. These are more expensive than local medical facilities, but provide several advantages:

➡ They provide a superior standard of care (usually).

➡ They liaise with insurance companies should you require evacuation.

➡ They understand the local system and are aware of the safest local hospitals and best specialists.

Infectious Diseases

Cutaneous Larva Migrans

Risk All countries, but most common on beaches of Thailand

Cause Dog hookworm

Symptoms Intensely itchy rash that starts as a small lump, then slowly spreads in a linear fashion

Treatment Medications; should not be cut out or frozen

Dengue

Risk All countries; most common in cities

Cause Mosquito-borne (day and night)

Symptoms High fever, severe headache and body ache (dengue used to be known as breakbone fever); sometimes a rash and diarrhoea

Treatment No specific treatment, just rest and paracetamol; do not take aspirin as it increases the likelihood of haemorrhaging. See a doctor to be diagnosed and monitored

Prevention Insect-avoidance measures (both day and night)

Filariasis

Risk All countries, but rare in travellers (common in the local population)

Cause Mosquito-borne

Prevention Insect-avoidance measures

Hepatitis A

Risk Very common in all countries

Cause Food- and water-borne virus

Symptoms Infects the liver, causing jaundice (yellow skin and eyes), nausea and lethargy

Treatment No specific treatment, just allow time for the liver to heal

Prevention All travellers to the Mekong region should be vaccinated against hepatitis A

Hepatitis B

Risk All countries. In some parts of the Mekong region, up to 20% of the population carry hepatitis B, and usually are unaware of this

Cause Spread by body fluids, including sexual contact

Long-Term Consequences Possible liver cancer and cirrhosis, among others

Prevention Vaccination (it's the only STD that can be prevented by vaccination)

Hepatitis E

Risk All countries, but far less common than Hepatitus A

Cause Contaminated food and water

Symptoms Similar symptoms to hepatitis A

Consequences Severe in pregnant women, can result in the death of both mother and baby

Prevention Currently no vaccine; follow safe eating and drinking guidelines

HIV

Risk All countries; Vietnam has worst and most rapidly increasing HIV problem in region

Cause Heterosexual sex is main method of transmission in region

Consequences One of the most common causes of death in people under the age of 50 in Thailand

Influenza (flu)

Risk All countries; present year-round

Symptoms High fever, muscle aches, runny nose, cough and sore throat

Consequences Can be very severe in people over the age of 65 or in those with underlying medical conditions such as heart disease or diabetes

Treatment Rest and paracetamol

Prevention Vaccination recommended for at-risk individuals

Japanese B Encephalitis

Risk All countries, but highest in Thailand and Vietnam; rare in travellers but infects at least 50,000 locals each year, mostly in rural areas

Cause Mosquito-borne

Treatment No treatment

Consequences A third of infected people will die while another third will suffer permanent brain damage

Prevention Vaccination recommended for travellers spending more than one month outside of cities

Malaria

Risk All countries, mainly in rural areas

Cause Mosquito-borne parasite

Symptoms Fever; headache, diarrhoea, cough or chills may also occur; diagnosis can only be made by taking a blood sample

Prevention Two-pronged strategy: mosquito avoidance and antimalarial medications

Measles

Risk Mild risk in all countries

Cause Highly contagious bacterial infection, spread via coughing and sneezing

Symptoms Starts with a high fever and rash

Treatment No specific treatment

Prevention Most people born before 1966 are immune as they had the disease in childhood. Routine vaccination for children has been available since 1963

Meliodosis

Risk Cambodia, Laos and Thailand. Rare in travellers, but in some parts of northeast Thailand up to 30% of the local population is infected

Cause Skin coming into contact with contaminated soil

Symptoms Very similar to tuberculosis

Treatment Medications

Prevention No vaccine

Rabies

Risk Common in most regions

Cause Bite or lick from infected animal – most commonly a dog or monkey

Consequences Uniformly fatal

Treatment If an animal bites you, gently wash wound with soap and water, apply iodine-based antiseptic and imme-

WEIGHING THE RISKS OF MALARIA

For such a serious and potentially deadly disease, there is an enormous amount of misinformation concerning malaria. You must get expert advice about whether your trip will actually put you at risk. Many parts of the Mekong region, particularly city and resort areas, have minimal to no risk of malaria, and the risk of side effects from the prevention tablets may outweigh the risk of actually getting the disease. For most rural areas in the region, however, the risk of contracting the disease far outweighs the risk of any tablet side effects. Remember that malaria can be fatal. Before you travel, seek medical advice on the right medication and dosage for you.

There are two strategies to malaria prevention: avoiding mosquito bites and taking antimalarial medication.

Mosquito Prevention

Travellers are advised to take the following steps:

➡ Use a DEET-based insect repellent on exposed skin. Wash off at night, as long as you are sleeping under a mosquito net. Natural repellents such as citronella can be effective, but must be applied more frequently than products containing DEET.

➡ Sleep under a mosquito net that is impregnated with Permethrin.

➡ Choose accommodation with screens and fans (if not air-conditioned).

➡ Impregnate clothing with Permethrin in high-risk areas.

➡ Wear long sleeves and trousers in light colours.

➡ Use mosquito coils.

➡ Spray your room with insect repellent before going out for your evening meal.

Antimalarials

Most people who catch malaria are taking inadequate or no antimalarial medication. A variety of medications are available.

Derivatives of Artesunate Not suitable as a preventive medication. They are useful treatments under medical supervision.

Chloroquine and Paludrine combination Limited effectiveness in most of the Mekong region. Common side effects include nausea (40% of people) and mouth ulcers. Generally not recommended.

Doxycycline Broad-spectrum antibiotic, ingested daily, that has the added benefit of helping to prevent a variety of tropical diseases, including leptospirosis, tick-borne disease, typhus and meliodosis. Potential side effects include photosensitivity (a tendency to sunburn), thrush in women, indigestion, heartburn, nausea and interference with the contraceptive pill. More serious side effects include ulceration of the oesophagus. You can help prevent this by taking your tablewt with a meal and a large glass of water, and never lying down within half an hour of taking it. It must be taken for four weeks after leaving the risk area.

Lariam (Mefloquine) Weekly tablet that suits many people. Has received much bad press, some of it justified, some not. Serious side effects are rare but include depression, anxiety, psychosis and seizures. Anyone with a history of depression, anxiety, other psychological disorders or epilepsy should not take Lariam. Considered safe in the second and third trimesters of pregnancy. Tablets must be taken for four weeks after leaving the risk area.

Malarone Combines Atovaquone and Proguanil. Side effects are uncommon and mild, usually nausea and headache. Best tablet for scuba divers and for those on short trips to high-risk areas. Must be taken for one week after leaving the risk area.

A final option is to take no preventive tablets but to have a supply of emergency medication should you develop the symptoms of malaria. This is less than ideal, and you'll need to get to a good medical facility within 24 hours of developing a fever. If you choose this option the most effective and safest treatment is Malarone (four tablets once daily for three days).

STD PRIMER

Sexually transmitted diseases (STDs) most common in the Mekong region include herpes, warts, syphilis, gonorrhoea and chlamydia. People carrying these diseases often have no signs of infection. Condoms will prevent gonorrhoea and chlamydia but not warts or herpes. If after a sexual encounter you develop any rash, lumps, discharge, or pain when passing urine, seek immediate medical attention. If you have been sexually active during your travels, have an STD check on your return home.

diately seek medical advice and commence post-exposure treatment. If you are not pre-vaccinated you will need to receive rabies immunoglobulin as soon as possible

Prevention Pre-travel vaccination simplifies post-bite treatment

Schistosomiasis

Risk All countries

Cause Tiny parasite that enters the skin after swimming in contaminated water

Symptoms Travellers usually only get a light infection and are asymptomatic. If you are concerned, you can be tested three months after exposure. On rare occasions, travellers may develop 'Katayama fever'. This occurs some weeks after exposure, as the parasite passes through the lungs and causes an allergic reaction – symptoms are coughing and fever

Treatment Medications

Strongyloides

Risk Common in travellers to Cambodia, Laos and Thailand

Cause Parasite transmitted by skin contact with soil

Symptoms Unusual skin rash called *larva currens* – a linear rash on the trunk that comes and goes. Most people don't have other symptoms until their immune system becomes severely suppressed, when the parasite can cause an overwhelming infection

Treatment Medications

Tuberculosis

Risk All countries; rare in travellers, more common in medical and aid workers who have significant contact with local population

Symptoms Fever, cough, weight loss, night sweats and tiredness

Prevention Vaccination usually only given to children under the age of five; adults at risk are recommended to have pre- and post-travel TB testing

Typhoid

Risk All countries

Cause Spread via food and water

Symptoms Serious bacterial infection results in high and slowly progressive fever, headache; may be accompanied by a dry cough and stomach pain. Diagnosis requires a blood test

Treatment Antibiotics

Prevention Vaccination recommended for all travellers spending more than one week in the Mekong region, or travelling outside of the major cities. Be aware that vaccination is not 100% effective so you must still be careful with what you eat and drink

Typhus

Risk All countries, but rare in travellers

Cause Flea bite (murine typhus) or mite bite (scrub typhus)

Symptoms Fever, muscle pains and a rash

Prevention Insect-avoidance measures; doxycycline

Traveller's Diarrhoea

Traveller's diarrhoea is by far the most common problem that affects travellers – between 30% and 50% of people will suffer from it within two weeks of starting their trip. In more than 80% of cases, traveller's diarrhoea is caused by bacteria (there are numerous potential culprits), and therefore responds promptly to treatment with antibiotics. Treatment will depend on your situation – how sick you are, how quickly you need to get better, where you are and so on.

Traveller's diarrhoea is defined as the passage of more than three watery bowel actions within 24 hours, plus at least one other symptom such as fever, cramps, nausea, vomiting or feeling generally unwell.

Treatment consists of staying well hydrated; rehydration solutions such as Gastrolyte are the best for this. Antibiotics such as Norfloxacin, Ciprofloxacin or Azithromycin will kill the bacteria quickly.

Loperamide is just a 'stopper' and doesn't get to the cause of the problem. It can be helpful, for example, if you have to go on a long bus ride. Don't take Loperamide if you have a fever, or blood in your stools. Seek medical attention quickly if you do not respond to an appropriate antibiotic. You should always seek reliable medical care if you have blood in your diarrhoea.

Amoebic Dysentery

Amoebic dysentery is very rare in travellers but is often misdiagnosed by poor-quality labs in the Mekong region.

Symptoms Similar to bacterial diarrhoea, ie fever, bloody diarrhoea and generally feeling unwell

Consequences If left untreated, complications such as liver or gut abscesses can occur

Treatment Tinidazole or Metronidazole to kill the parasite in your gut, and then a second drug to kill the cysts

Giardiasis

Giardia lamblia is a relatively common parasite in travellers.

Symptoms Nausea, bloating, excess gas, fatigue, intermittent diarrhoea

Treatment Tinidazole the top choice, with Metronidazole being a second option. The parasite will eventually go away if left untreated but this can take months

Environmental Hazards

Air Pollution

→ Increasing problem in most of the Mekong region's major cities, particularly vehicle pollution.

→ Causes minor respiratory problems such as sinusitis, dry throat and irritated eyes.

→ If you have severe respiratory problems speak with your doctor before travelling to any heavily polluted urban centres.

Diving

→ Divers should ensure their insurance covers them for decompression illness – get specialised dive insurance through an organisation such as **Divers Alert Network** (DAN; www.danseap.org).

Food

Eating in restaurants is the biggest risk factor for contracting traveller's diarrhoea. Ways to avoid diarrhoea include:

→ Eat only freshly cooked food, and avoid shellfish and food that has been sitting around in buffets.

→ Peel all fruit, cook vegetables and soak salads in iodine water for at least 20 minutes.

→ Eat in busy restaurants where there is a high turnover of customers.

Heat

Many parts of the Mekong region are hot and humid throughout the year. For most people it takes at least two weeks to adapt to the hot climate. Swelling of the feet and ankles is common, as are muscle cramps caused by excessive sweating. To minimise the adjustment pains, try the following:

→ Avoid dehydration and excessive activity in the heat.

→ Take it easy when you first arrive.

→ Drink rehydration solution or eat salty food.

→ Don't eat salt tablets (they only aggravate the gut).

HEAT EXHAUSTION

Dehydration is the main contributor to heat exhaustion. Recovery is usually rapid, but it is common to feel weak for some days afterwards.
Symptoms include:

→ weakness
→ headache
→ irritability
→ nausea or vomiting
→ sweaty skin
→ fast, weak pulse
→ normal or slightly elevated body temperature.

Recommended treatment:

→ getting out of the heat and/or sun

→ fanning or applying cool wet cloths to the skin

→ lying flat with legs raised and rehydrating with water containing a quarter of a teaspoon of salt per litre.

HEATSTROKE

Heatstroke is a serious medical emergency. Symptoms come on suddenly and include:

→ weakness
→ nausea
→ body hot and dry; body temperature more than 41°C
→ dizziness, confusion, loss of coordination, seizures, and eventually collapse and loss of consciousness.
Treatment:

→ Seek medical help and commence cooling by getting out of the heat, removing clothes, fanning and applying cool, wet cloths or ice to body, especially to the groin and armpits.

PRICKLY HEAT

This is a common skin rash in the tropics, caused by sweat being trapped under the skin. The result is an itchy rash of tiny lumps.
Treatment:

→ Move out of the heat and into an air-conditioned area for a few hours.

→ Take cool showers.

→ Use locally bought prickly heat powder.

→ Creams and ointments clog the skin so they should be avoided.

DRINKING WATER

→ Never drink tap water.

→ Bottled water is generally safe – check the seal is intact at purchase.

→ Boiling water is the most efficient method of purifying it.

→ The best chemical purifier is iodine. It should not be used by pregnant women or those people who suffer with thyroid problems.

→ Water filters should filter out viruses. Ensure your filter has a chemical barrier such as iodine and a small pore size, ie less than four microns.

Insect Bites & Stings

Bedbugs Don't carry disease but their bites are very itchy. Live in the cracks of furniture and walls and then migrate to the bed at night to feed on you. Treat the itch with an antihistamine.

Lice Inhabit various parts of your body but most commonly your head and pubic area. Transmission is via close contact with an infected person. Lice can be difficult to treat and you may need numerous applications of an anti-lice shampoo such as Permethrin. Pubic lice are usually contracted from sexual contact.

Ticks Contracted in rural areas. Commonly found behind the ears, on the belly and in armpits. If you have had a tick bite and experience symptoms such as a rash at the site of the bite or elsewhere, or fever or muscle aches, you should see a doctor. Doxycycline prevents tick-borne diseases.

Leeches Found in humid rainforest areas. Do not transmit any disease but bites are often intensely itchy for weeks afterwards and become infected easily. Apply an iodine-based antiseptic to any leech bite to help prevent infection.

Bee and wasp stings Mainly a problem for people who are allergic to them. Anyone with a serious bee or wasp allergy should carry an injection of adrenalin (eg an Epipen) for emergency treatment.

Jellyfish Mostly not dangerous, just irritating. First aid for jellyfish stings involves pouring vinegar onto the affected area to neutralise the poison. Do not rub sand or water onto the stings. Take painkillers, and if you feel ill in any way after being stung seek medical advice. Take local advice if there are dangerous jellyfish around and keep out of the water.

Parasites

Numerous parasites are common in local populations in the Mekong region; however, most of these are rare in travellers.

➡ Two rules for avoiding parasitic infections: wear shoes and avoid eating raw food, especially fish, pork and vegetables.

➡ A number of parasites are transmitted via the skin by walking barefoot, including strongyloides, hookworm and cutaneous *larva migrans*.

Skin Problems

There are two skin problems that commonly affect travellers:

Fungal rashes These occur in moist areas that get less air, such as the groin, armpits and between the toes. It starts as a red patch that slowly spreads and is usually itchy. Treatment involves keeping the skin dry, avoiding chafing and using an antifungal cream such as Clotrimazole or Lamisil.

Infected cuts and scratches These are common in humid climates. Take meticulous care of any cuts and scratches to prevent complications such as abscesses. Immediately wash all wounds in clean water and apply antiseptic. If you develop signs of infection, such as increasing pain and redness, see a doctor. Divers and snorkellers should be particularly careful with coral cuts as they can be easily infected.

Snakes

The Mekong region is home to many species of both poisonous and harmless snakes. Some rules on avoiding and treating snake bites:

➡ Assume that all snakes are poisonous and never try to catch one.

➡ Always wear boots and long pants if walking in an area that may have snakes.

➡ First aid in the event of a snakebite involves pressure immobilisation via an elastic bandage firmly wrapped around the affected limb, starting at the bite site and working up towards the chest. The bandage should not be so tight that the circulation is cut off, and the fingers or toes should be kept free so the circulation can be checked. Immobilise affected limb with a splint and carry the victim to medical attention.

➡ Do not use tourniquets or try to suck the venom out.

➡ Antivenin is available for most species in the urban centres of Thailand or Vietnam, but not readily available in Cambodia and Laos.

Sunburn

Even on a cloudy day sunburn can occur rapidly. Some tips on dealing with the searing tropical sun:

➡ Always use a strong sunscreen (at least factor 30), making sure to reapply after a swim.

➡ Wear a wide-brimmed hat and sunglasses outdoors.

➡ Avoid lying in the sun during the hottest part of the day (10am to 2pm).

➡ If you become sunburnt, stay out of the sun until you have recovered, apply cool compresses and take painkillers for the discomfort. One percent hydrocortisone cream applied twice daily is also helpful.

Language

This chapter offers basic vocabulary to help you get around the countries covered in this book. Read our coloured pronunciation guides as if they were English, and you'll be understood. Some of the phrases have both polite and informal forms – these are indicated by the abbreviations 'pol' and 'inf'. The abbreviations 'm' and 'f' indicate masculine and feminine gender respectively.

KHMER

In our pronunciation guides, vowels and vowel combinations with an h at the end are pronounced hard and aspirated (with a puff of air).

The symbols are read as follows: aa as the 'a' in 'father'; a and ah shorter and harder than aa; i as in 'kit'; uh as the 'u' in 'but'; ii as the 'ee' in 'feet'; eu like 'oo' (with the lips spread flat); euh as eu (short and hard); oh as the 'o' in 'hose' (short and hard); ow as in 'glow'; u as the 'u' in 'flute' (short and hard); uu as the 'oo' in 'zoo'; ua as the 'ou' in 'tour'; uah as ua (short and hard); œ as 'er' in 'her' (more open); ie as the 'oo in 'beer' (without the 'r'); e as in 'they'; ai as in 'aisle'; ae as the 'a' in 'cat'; ay as ai (slightly more nasal); ey as in 'prey'; o as the 'ow' in 'cow'; av like a nasal ao (without the 'v'); euv like a nasal eu (without the 'v'); ohm as the 'ome' in 'home'; am as the 'um' in 'glum'; ih as the 'ee' in 'teeth' (short and hard); eh as the 'a' in 'date' (short and hard); awh as the 'aw' in 'jaw' (short and hard); and aw as the 'aw' in 'jaw'.

Some consonant combinations in our pronunciation guides are separated with an apostrophe for ease of pronunciation, eg 'j-r' in j'rook and 'ch-ng' in ch'ngain. Also note that k is pronounced as the 'g' in 'go'; kh as the 'k' in 'kind'; p as the final 'p' in 'puppy'; ph as the 'p' in 'pond'; r as in 'rum' but hard and rolling; t as the 't' in 'stand'; and th as the 't' in 'two'.

WANT MORE?

For in-depth language information and handy phrases, check out Lonely Planet's Southeast Asia Phrasebook. You'll find it at **shop.lonelyplanet.com**, or you can buy Lonely Planet's iPhone phrasebooks at the Apple App Store.

Basics

Hello.	ជម្រាបសួរ	johm riab sua
Goodbye.	លាសិនហើយ	lia suhn hao-y
Excuse me./ Sorry.	សូមទោស	sohm toh
Please.	សូម	sohm
Thank you.	អរគុណ	aw kohn
Yes.	បាទ/ចាស	baat/jaa (m/f)
No.	ទេ	te

What's your name?

អ្នកឈ្មោះអ្វី?   niak ch'muah ei

My name is ...

ខ្ញុំឈ្មោះ...   kh'nyohm ch'muah ...

Accommodation

I'd like a room ...	ខ្ញុំសុំបន្ទប់...	kh'nyohm sohm bantohp ...
for one person	សម្រាប់ មួយនាក់	samruhp muy niak
for two people	សម្រាប់ ពីរនាក់	samruhp pii niak

How much is it per day?

តម្លៃមួយថ្ងៃ   damlay muy th'ngay
ប៉ុន្មាន?   pohnmaan

Numbers – Khmer

1	មួយ	muy
2	ពីរ	pii
3	បី	bei
4	បួន	buan
5	ប្រាំ	bram
6	ប្រាំមួយ	bram muy
7	ប្រាំពីរ	bram pii
8	ប្រាំបី	bram bei
9	ប្រាំបួន	bram buan
10	ដប់	dawp

Eating & Drinking

Do you have a menu in English?

មានម៉ឺនុយជា | mien menui jea
ភាសាអង់គ្លេសទេ? | piasaa awnglay te

I'm vegetarian.

ខ្ញុំតមសាច់ | kh'nyohm tawm sait

The bill, please.

សូមគិតលុយ | sohm kuht lui

beer	ប៊ីយ៉ែរ	bii-yœ
coffee	កាហ្វេ	kaa fey
tea	តែ	tai
water	ទឹក	teuk

Emergencies

Help!

ជួយខ្ញុំផង! | juay kh'nyohm phawng

Call the police!

ជួយហៅប៉ូលិសមក! | juay hav polih mao

Call a doctor!

ជួយហៅគ្រូពេទ្យមក! | juay hav kruu paet mao

Where are the toilets?

បង្គន់នៅឯណា? | bawngkohn neuv ai naa

Shopping & Services

How much is it?

នេះថ្លៃប៉ុន្មាន? | nih th'lay pohnmaan

That's too much.

ថ្លៃពេក | th'lay pek

I'm looking for the ...

ខ្ញុំរក... | kh'nyohm rohk ...

bank	ធនាគារ	th'niakia
market	ផ្សារ	p'saa
post office	«ប្រៃសណីយ៍	praisuhnii
public telephone	ទូរស័ព្ទ សាធារណៈ	turasahp saathiaranah

Transport & Directions

Where is a/the ...?

...នៅឯណា? | ... neuv ai naa

bus stop

ចំណតឡានឈ្នួល | jamnawt laan ch'nual

train station

ស្ថានីយរថភ្លើង | s'thaanii roht plœng

When does the ... leave?

...ចេញម៉ោង b'unman? | ... jein maong pohnmaan

boat	ទូក	duk
bus	ឡានឈ្នួល	laan ch'nual
train	រថភ្លើង	roht plœng
plane	យន្តហោះ	yohn hawh

LAO

Lao is a tonal language, meaning that many identical sounds are differentiated only by changes in the pitch of a speaker's voice. Pitch variations are relative to the speaker's natural vocal range, so that one person's low tone isn't necessarily the same pitch as another person's. There are six tones in Lao, indicated in our pronunciation guides by accent marks on letters: low tone (eg dęe), high (eg héu·a), rising (eg săhm), high falling (eg sŏw) and low falling (eg kŏw). Note that no accent mark is used for the mid tone (eg het).

The pronunciation of vowels goes like this: i as in 'it'; ee as in 'feet'; ai as in 'aisle'; ah as the 'a' in 'father'; a as the short 'a' in 'about'; aa as in 'bad'; air as in 'air'; er as in 'fur'; eu as in 'sir'; u as in 'put'; oo as in 'food'; ow as in 'now'; or as in 'jaw'; o as in 'phone'; oh as in 'toe'; ee·a as in 'lan'; oo·a as in 'tour'; ew as in 'yew'; and oy as in 'boy'.

Most consonants correspond to their English counterparts. The exceptions are đ (a hard 't' sound, a bit like 'dt') and b (a hard 'p' sound, a bit like 'bp').

In our pronunciation guides, the hyphens indicate syllable breaks in words, eg àng-gít

(English). Some syllables are further divided with a dot to help you pronounce compound vowels, eg kĕe·an (write).

coffee	ກາແຝ	gạh-fáir
tea	ຊາ	sáh
water	ນ້ຳດື່ມ	nâm deum

Basics

Hello.	ສະບາຍດີ	sábại-dĕe
Goodbye.	ສະບາຍດີ	sábại-dĕe
Excuse me./ Sorry.	ຂໍໂທດ	kŏr tôht
Please.	ກະລຸນາ	ga-lú-náh
Thank you.	ຂອບໃຈ	kòrp jại
Yes./No.	ແມນ/ບໍ່	maan/bor

What's your name?
ເຈົ້າຊື່ຫຍັງ   jôw seu nyăng

My name is ...
ຂ້ອຍຊື່ ...   kòy seu ...

Accommodation

| hotel | ໂຮງແຮມ | hóhng háam |
| guesthouse | ທີ່ຮັບແຂກ | hŏr hap káak |

Do you have a room?
ມີຫ້ອງບໍ່   mée hòrng bor

single room
ຫ້ອງນອນຕຽງດຽວ   hòrng nórn đĕe·ang dee·o

double room
ຫ້ອງນອນຕຽງຄູ່   hòrng nórn đĕe·ang koo

How much ...?	... ເທົ່າໃດ	... tŏw dại
per night	ຄືນລະ	kéun-la
per week	ອາທິດລະ	ạh-tit-la

Eating & Drinking

What do you have that's special?
ມີຫຍັງພິເສດບໍ່   mée nyăng pi-sèt bor

I'd like to try that.
ຂ້ອຍຢາກລອງກິນເບິ່ງ   kòy yàhk lórng gịn berng

I eat only vegetables.
ຂ້ອຍກິນແຕ່ຜັກ   kòy gịn đaa pák

Please bring the bill.
ຂໍແຊັກແດ່   kŏr saak daa

| beer | ເບຍ | bẹe·a |

Emergencies

| Help! | ຊ່ວຍແດ່ | soo·ay daa |
| Go away! | ໄປເດີ້ | bại dêr |

Call the police!
ຊ່ວຍເອີ້ນຕຳລວດແດ່   soo·ay êrn đam-lòo·at daa

Call a doctor!
ຊ່ວຍຕາມທານໝໍ ໃຫ້ແດ່   soo·ay đạhm hăh mŏr hài daa

I'm lost.
ຂ້ອຍຫລົງທາງ   kòy lŏng táhng

Where are the toilets?
ຫ້ອງນ້ຳຢູ່ໃສ   hòrng nâm yoo să

Shopping & Services

I'm looking for ...
ຂ້ອຍຊອກຫາ ...   kòy sòrk hăh ...

How much (for) ...?
... ເທົ່າໃດ   ... tow dại

The price is very high.
ລາຄາແພງຫລາຍ   láh-káh páang lăi

I want to change money.
ຂ້ອຍຢາກປ່ຽນເງິນ   kòy yàhk bee·an ngérn

bank	ທະນາຄານ	ta-náh-káhn
pharmacy	ຮ້ານຂາຍຢາ	hâhn kăi yạh
post office	ໄປສະນີ	bại-sá-née
	ໂຮງສາຍ	hóhng săi

Numbers – Lao		
1	ໜຶ່ງ	neung
2	ສອງ	sŏrng
3	ສາມ	săhm
4	ສີ່	see
5	ຫ້າ	hàh
6	ຫົກ	hók
7	ເຈັດ	jét
8	ແປດ	bàat
9	ເກົ້າ	gŏw
10	ສິບ	síp

Transport & Directions

Where is the ...?
... ยู่ใส ... yòo săi

How far?
ไกเท่าใด kai tow dai

I'd like a ticket.
ข้อยยฑากได้ตี๋ kòy yàhk dâi bĕe

What time will the ... leave?
... จะออกจักโมงๆ ... já òrk ják móhng

boat	เรือ	héu·a
bus	ลิฉเม	lot máir
minivan	ลิฉตู้	lot đôo
plane	เรือบิน	héu·a bǐn

THAI

In Thai the meaning of a syllable may be altered by means of tones. In standard Thai there are five tones: low (eg bàht), mid (eg dee), falling (eg mâi), high (eg máh) and rising (eg săhm). The range of all tones is relative to each speaker's vocal range, so there is no fixed 'pitch' intrinsic to the language.

In our pronunciation guides, the hyphens indicate syllable breaks within words, and for ease of pronunciation some compound vowels are further divided with a dot, eg mêu·a·rai (when).

The vowel a is pronounced as in 'about', aa as the 'a' in 'bad', ah as the 'a' in 'father', ai as in 'aisle', air as in 'flair' (without the 'r'), eu as the 'er' in 'her' (without the 'r'), ew as in 'new' (with rounded lips), oh as the 'o' in 'toe', or as in 'torn' (without the 'r') and ow as in 'now'.

Note also the pronunciation of the following consonants: b (a hard 'p' sound, almost like a 'b', eg in 'hip-bag'); đ (a hard 't' sound, like a sharp 'd', eg in 'mid-tone'); and r (as in 'run' but flapped; often pronounced like 'l').

Basics

Hello.	สวัสดี	sà·wàt·dee
Goodbye.	ลาก่อน	lah gòrn
Excuse me.	ขออภัย	kŏr à·pai
Sorry.	ขอโทษ	kŏr tôht
Please.	ขอ	kŏr
Thank you.	ขอบคุณ	kòrp kun
Yes.	ใช่	châi
No.	ไม่	mâi

What's your name?
คุณชื่ออะไร kun chêu à-rai

My name is ...
ผม/ดิฉัน pŏm/dì-chăn
ชื่อ... chêu ... (m/f)

Accommodation

Where's a ...? ... อยู่ที่ไหน ... yòo têe năi

campsite	ค่ายพักแรม	kâi pák raam
guesthouse	บ้านพัก	bâhn pák
hotel	โรงแรม	rohng raam
youth hostel	บ้าน	bâhn
	เยาวชน	yow-wá-chon

Do you have มีห้อง ... mee hôrng ...
a ... room? ไหม măi

single	เดี่ยว	dèe·o
double	เตียงคู่	đee·ang kôo

Eating & Drinking

What would you recommend?
คุณแนะนำอะไรบ้าง kun náa-nam à-rai bâhng

I'd like (the menu), please.
ขอ (รายการ kŏr (rai gahn
อาหาร) หน่อย ah-hăhn) nòy

I don't eat (red meat).
ผม/ดิฉันไม่กิน pŏm/dì-chăn mâi gin
(เนื้อแดง) (néu·a daang) (m/f)

Cheers!
ไชโย chai-yoh

Please bring the bill.
ขอบิลหน่อย kŏr bin nòy

beer	เบียร์	bee·a
coffee	กาแฟ	gah-faa
tea	ชา	chah
water	น้ำดื่ม	nám dèum

Emergencies

Help!	ช่วยด้วย	chôo·ay dôo·ay
Go away!	ไปให้พ้น	bai hâi pón

Numbers – Thai

1	หนึ่ง	nèung
2	สอง	sŏrng
3	สาม	săhm
4	สี่	sèe
5	ห้า	hâh
6	หก	hòk
7	เจ็ด	jèt
8	แปด	bàat
9	เก้า	gôw
10	สิบ	sìp

I'm lost.
ผม/ดิฉัน
หลงทาง   pŏm/dì-chăn
     lŏng tahng (m/f)

Call the police!
เรียกตำรวจหน่อย   rêe-ak đam-ròo-at nòy

Call a doctor!
เรียกหมอหน่อย   rêe-ak mŏr nòy

I'm ill.
ผม/ดิฉันป่วย   pŏm/dì-chăn bòo-ay (m/f)

Where are the toilets?
ห้องน้ำอยู่ที่ไหน   hôrng nám yòo têe năi

Shopping & Services

I'd like to buy ...
อยากจะซื้อ ...   yàhk jà séu ...

How much is it?
เท่าไร   tôw-rai

That's too expensive.
แพงไป   paang bai

Transport & Directions

Where's ...?
... อยู่ที่ไหน   ... yòo têe năi

What's the address?
ที่อยู่คืออะไร   têe yòo keu à-rai

Can you show me (on the map)?
ให้ดู (ในแผนที่)   hâi doo (nai păan têe)
ได้ไหม   dâi măi

A ... ticket, please.	ขอตั๋ว ...	kŏr đŏo-a ...
one-way	เที่ยวเดียว	têe-o dee-o
return	ไปกลับ	bai glàp
boat	เรือ	reu-a
bus	รถเมล์	rót mair
plane	เครื่องบิน	krêu-ang bin
train	รถไฟ	rót fai

VIETNAMESE

Vietnamese is written in a Latin-based phonetic alphabet, which was declared the official written form in 1910.

In our pronunciation guides, a is pronounced as in 'at', aa as in 'father', aw as in 'law', er as in 'her', oh as in 'doh!', ow as in 'cow', u as in 'book', uh as in 'but' and uhr as in 'fur' (without the 'r'). We've used dots (eg dee·úhng) to separate the combined vowel sounds. Note also that d is pronounced as in 'stop', đ as in 'dog', and ğ as in 'skill'.

Vietnamese uses a system of tones to make distinctions between words – so some vowels are pronounced with a high or low pitch. There are six tones in Vietnamese, indicated in the written language (and in our pronunciation guides) by accent marks on the vowel: mid (ma), low falling (mà), low rising (mả), high broken (mã), high rising (má) and low broken (mạ). The mid tone is flat.

The variation in vocabulary between the Vietnamese of the north and the south is indicated by (N) and (S) respectively.

Basics

Hello.	*Xin chào.*	sin jòw
Goodbye.	*Tạm biệt.*	daạm bee·yht
Excuse me./ Sorry.	*Xin lỗi.*	sin lõy
Please.	*Làm ơn.*	laàm ern
Thank you.	*Cảm ơn.*	ğaảm ern
Yes.	*Vâng./Dạ.* (N/S)	vuhng/ yạ
No.	*Không.*	kawm

What's your name?
Tên là gì?   den laà zeè

My name is ...
Tên tôi là ...   den doy laà ...

LANGUAGE VIETNAMESE

Accommodation

Where's a ...? *Đâu có ... ?* đoh ğó ...

campsite *nơi cắm trại* ner·ee ğǔhm chại

hotel *khách sạn* kaák sạan

guesthouse *nhà khách* nyaà kaák

I'd like a ... *Tôi muốn ...* doy moo·úhn ...

single room *phòng đơn* fòm dern

double room *phòng giường đôi* fòm zuhr·èrng đọy

How much is it per ...? *Giá bao nhiêu một ...?* zaá bow nyee·oo mạwt ...

night *đêm* đem

person *người* nguhr·eè

Eating & Drinking

I'd like the menu.
Tôi muốn thực đơn. doy moo·úhn tụhrk đern

What's the speciality here?
Ở đây có món gì đặc biệt? ẻr day kó món zeè dụhk bee·ụht

I'm a vegetarian.
Tôi ăn chay. doy uhn jay

I'd like ...
Xin cho tôi ... sin jo doy ...

Cheers!
Chúc sức khoẻ! júp súhrk kwả

The bill, please.
Xin tính tiền. sin díng dee·ùhn

beer *bia* bi·a

coffee *cà phê* ğaà fe

tea *chè/trà (N/S)* jà/chaà

water *nước* nuhr·érk

wine *rượu nho* zee·ọọ nyo

Emergencies

Help!
Cứu tôi! ğuhr·oó doy

Leave me alone!
Thôi! toy

I'm lost.
Tôi bị lạc đường. doi beẹ lạak đuhr·èrng

Please call the police.
Làm ơn gọi công an. laàm ern gọy ğawm aan

Please call a doctor.
Làm ơn gọi bác sĩ. laàm ern gọy baák seẽ

I'm ill.
Tôi bị đau. doy beẹ đoh

Where is the toilet?
Nhà vệ sinh ở đâu? nyaà vẹ sing ẻr đoh

Shopping & Services

I'd like to buy ...
Tôi muốn mua ... doy moo·úhn moo·uh ...

How much is this?
Cái này giá bao nhiêu? ğaí này zaá bow nyee·oo

It's too expensive.
Cái này quá mắc. ğaí này gwaá múhk

bank *ngân hàng* nguhn haàng

market *chợ* jẹr

post office *bưu điện* buhr·oo đee·ụhn

tourist office *văn phòng hướng dẫn du lịch* vuhn fòm huhr·érng zũhn zoo lịk

Transport & Directions

Where is ...?
... ở đâu? ... ẻr đoh

What is the address?
Địa chỉ là gì? đee·ụh cheẻ laà zeè

Can you show me (on the map)?
Xin chỉ giùm (trên bản đồ này). sin jeẻ zùm (chen baản dàw này)

I'd like a ... ticket. *Tôi muốn vé ...* doy moo·úhn vá ...

one way *đi một chiều* đee mạt jee·oò

return *khứ hồi* kúhr haw·eẻ

boat *thuyền* twee·ùhn

bus *xe buýt* sa beét

plane *máy bay* máy bay

train *xe lửa* sa lủhr·uh

Numbers – Vietnamese

1	*một*	mạwt
2	*hai*	hai
3	*ba*	baa
4	*bốn*	báwn
5	*năm*	nuhm
6	*sáu*	sóh
7	*bảy*	bảy
8	*tám*	dúhm
9	*chín*	jín
10	*mười*	muhr·eè

GLOSSARY

This glossary is a list of Cambodian (C), Lao (L), Thai (T) and Vietnamese (V) terms you may come across in the Mekong region.

ao dai (V) – traditional Vietnamese tunic and trousers

APEC – Asia-Pacific Economic Cooperation

apsara (C) – heavenly nymphs or angelic dancers

Asean – Association of Southeast Asian Nations

baasii (L) – sometimes written as 'basi' or 'baci'; a ceremony in which the 32 khwǎn are symbolically bound to the participant for health and safety

baht (T) – the Thai unit of currency

baray (C) – ancient reservoir

BE (L, T) – Buddhist Era

boeng (C) – lake

BTS (T) – Bangkok Transit System (Skytrain)

bun (L) – festival

buu dien (V) – post office

Cao Daism (V) – Vietnamese religious sect

Cham (C, V) – ethnic minority descended from the people of Champa; a Hindu kingdom dating from the 2nd century BC

chedi (T) – see stupa

Chenla (C, L, V) – Pre-Angkorian Khmer kingdom covering parts of Cambodia, Laos and Vietnam

Chunchiet (C) – ethnolinguistic minority

CPP (C) – Cambodian People's Party

cyclo (C, V) – bicycle rickshaw

devaraja (C) – god king

DMZ (V) – the misnamed Demilitarised Zone, a strip of land that once separated North and South Vietnam

dong (V) – the Vietnamese unit of currency

duong (V) – road, street; abbreviated as 'Ð'

Ecpat – End Child Prostitution & Trafficking

faràng (T) – Western, Westerner; foreigner

Funan (C, V) – first Khmer kingdom, located in Mekong Delta area

HCMC (V) – Ho Chi Minh City (Saigon)

Hoa (V) – ethnic Chinese, the largest single minority group in Vietnam

Indochina – Vietnam, Cambodia and Laos, the French colony of Indochine; the name derives from Indian and Chinese influences

Isan (T) – general term used for northeastern Thailand

jataka (C, L, T) – stories of the Buddha's past lives, often enacted in dance-drama

jumbo (L) – a motorised three-wheeled taxi, sometimes called a túk-túk

karst – limestone peaks with caves, underground streams and potholes

khao (T) – hill, mountain

khlong (T) – canal

Khmer (C) – ethnic Cambodians; Cambodian language

Khmer Rouge (C) – literally Red Khmers, the commonly used name for the Cambodian communist movement responsible for the genocide in the 1970s

khwǎn (L) – guardian spirits of the body

Kinh (V) – the Vietnamese language

kip (L) – the Lao unit of currency

ko (T) – island

koh (C) – island

krama (C) – chequered scarf

lákhon (C, T) – classical dance-drama

linga (C, L, T, V) – phallic symbol

mae nam (L, T) – river

Mahayana – literally, 'Great Vehicle'; a school of Buddhism that extended the early Buddhist teachings; see also Theravada

meuang (L, T) – city

MIA (C, L, V) – missing in action, usually referring to US personnel

Montagnards (V) – highlanders, mountain people; specifically the ethnic minorities inhabiting remote areas of Vietnam

moto (C) – motorcycle taxi

Mt Meru – the mythical dwelling place of the Hindu gods, symbolised by the Himalayas

múan (L) – fun, which the Lao believe should be present in all activities

muay thai (T) – Thai boxing

nâam (L, T) – water, river

naga (C, L, T) – mythical serpent-being

NTAL (L) – National Tourism Administration of Lao

NVA (V) – North Vietnamese Army

Pali – ancient Indian language that, along with Sanskrit, is the root of Khmer, Lao and Thai

Pathet Lao (L) – literally, 'Country of Laos'; both a general term for the country and the common name for the Lao communist military during the civil war

phansăa (T) – Buddhist lent
phnom (C) – mountain
phu (L) – hill or mountain
POW – prisoner of war
prasat (C, T) – tower, temple
psar (C) – market

quan (V) – urban district
quoc ngu (V) – Vietnamese alphabet

Ramakian (T) – Thai version of the Ramayana
Ramayana – Indian epic story of Rama's battle with demons
Reamker (C) – Khmer version of the Ramayana
remorque (C) – (or remork) a motorised three-wheeled pedicab
riel (C) – the Cambodian unit of currency
roi nuoc (V) – water puppetry
rót fai fáa (T) – Skytrain; BTS

săhmlór (T) – three-wheeled pedicab
Sanskrit – ancient Hindu language that, along with Pali, is the root of Khmer, Lao and Thai
sànùk (T) – fun
soi (L, T) – lane, small street
song (L, V) – river
Songkran (T) – Thai New Year, held in mid-April
sŏrngtăaou (L, T) – small pick-up truck with two benches in the back
SRV (V) – Socialist Republic of Vietnam (Vietnam's official name)
stung (C) – small river
stupa – religious monument, often containing Buddha relics

talat (L) – market
Tam Giao (V) – literally, 'triple religion'; Confucianism, Taoism and Buddhism fused over time with popular Chinese beliefs and ancient Vietnamese animism
Tao (V) – the Way; the essence of which all things are made
TAT (T) – Tourism Authority of Thailand
tat (L) – waterfall
Tet (V) – Lunar New Year
thâat (L) – Buddhist stupa, reliquary; also written as 'that'
thànŏn (L, T) – road, street, avenue; abbreviated as 'Th'
Theravada – a school of Buddhism found in Cambodia, Laos and Thailand; this school confined itself to the early Buddhist teachings unlike Mahayana
tonlé (C) – major river
tripitaka (T) – Buddhist scriptures
túk-túk (L, T) – motorised săhmlór

UNDP – United Nations Development Programme
UXO (C, L, V) – unexploded ordnance

VC (V) – Viet Cong or Vietnamese Communists
vihara (C) – temple sanctuary

wâi (L, T) – palms-together greeting
wat (C, L, T) – Buddhist temple-monastery
wíhăhn (T) – sanctuary, hall, dwelling

xe om (V) – motorbike taxi (also Honda om)
xich lo (V) – see cyclo

Behind the Scenes

SEND US YOUR FEEDBACK

We love to hear from travellers – your comments keep us on our toes and help make our books better. Our well-travelled team reads every word on what you loved or loathed about this book. Although we cannot reply individually to your submissions, we always guarantee that your feedback goes straight to the appropriate authors, in time for the next edition. Each person who sends us information is thanked in the next edition – the most useful submissions are rewarded with a selection of digital PDF chapters.

Visit **lonelyplanet.com/contact** to submit your updates and suggestions or to ask for help. Our award-winning website also features inspirational travel stories, news and discussions.

Note: We may edit, reproduce and incorporate your comments in Lonely Planet products such as guidebooks, websites and digital products, so let us know if you don't want your comments reproduced or your name acknowledged. For a copy of our privacy policy visit lonelyplanet.com/privacy.

OUR READERS

Many thanks to the travellers who used the last edition and wrote to us with helpful hints, useful advice and interesting anecdotes: Alex Wheeler, Alexandra Guillemin, Allan Cowin, Alwin Quispel, Angela Summers, Ann Troy, Anna Cecilia Hüttmann, Anna Maria Ståhle, Anthony Huszar, Barbara Kuiters, Benjamin Boudard, Claudia Arends, Diane Flint, Dominika Hadolova, Hans Gubler, Jacqueline Griffiths, James Kersey, Jan Quinlan, Jane Margaret Sprackling, Jimmy Videle, Jon Martin, Juu Moua, Kerry Doyle, Klara Avsenik, Kristina Dahmen, Krystyna Deuss, Leo Binh, Margit Fröhlich, Mark Snoeij, Michiel Brus, Mika Morrissey, Nicole Uttinger, Philippe Desmarais, Pia Zellweger-Balzer, Robin de Graaf, Ruth Orli Mosser, Sarah-Rose Williams, Stuart Cameron, Summer Lewis, Susan Doel, Suzanne Stolwijk, Teea Kemppinen.

AUTHOR THANKS

Greg Bloom

The cumulative knowledge of my gang (both real and Twitter-based) in Phnom Penh was elemental in writing this book. Special shout-outs to Jared for the Ratanakiri hook-ups; to Lonely Planet colleague Nick for general Cambodia wisdom; and to the likes of @HayleyFlack. In Phnom Penh Zach, Joe and Barry tagged along on several gruelling Phnom Penh bar crawls, while Lucy teamed up on the restaurant research. Thanks to Anna, apple of my eye, for being my 'travel with children' guinea pig in places such as Anlong Veng, Preah Vihear, Stung Treng and Ratanakiri; and to Ofie for helping out with Anna on our epic road trip.

Austin Bush

A massive shout out to Lonely Planeteers for life Ilaria Walker and Bruce Evans, super cartographer Diana Von Holdt, and coordinating author Greg Bloom, not to mention the kind folks on the ground in Thailand.

Iain Stewart

Thanks to Vinh Vu, Chien, Dzung, Neil and Caroline, Mark Wyndham, Ben and Bich, Howard and Deborah Limbert, the Nha Trang boys, and Mark and Jason in Ho Chi Minh City. And to Greg Bloom and my co-authors, Ilaria Walker and all the Lonely Planet editors and cartographers for their professionalism and help on this title.

Richard Waters

Special thanks go to Alex for his zeal and generosity, as well as to Vianney for his much needed wisdom, Elizabeth for her fiery Bloody Marys at the inspiring Icon Bar, Mr Somkiad for his patience, DC for fixing my bike, Thierry for the sturdy Baja, Lao Heritage Hotel, Scandi Bakery for keeping me awake, Don Duvall for his excellent help, photographer Adri Berger, and as ever to the Lao people who make me wonder why the rest of the planet can't possess a little more of their gentle essence.

ACKNOWLEDGMENTS

Climate map data adapted from Peel MC, Finlayson BL & McMahon TA (2007) 'Updated World Map of the Köppen-Geiger Climate Classification', Hydrology and Earth System Sciences, 11, 1633¬44.

Illustrations pp90-1, pp210-11, pp364-5 and p366-7 by Michael Weldon.

Cover photograph: Buddhist ceremony in a Cambodian temple; Pascal Deloche, Corbis.

THIS BOOK

This fourth edition of Lonely Planet's *Vietnam, Cambodia, Laos & Northern Thailand* guidebook was written by Greg Bloom, Austin Bush, Iain Stewart and Richard Waters. Original research for Vietnam was conducted by Iain Stewart, Brett Atkinson, Damian Harper and Nick Ray; for Cambodia by Nick Ray and Greg Bloom; for Laos by Nick Ray, Greg Bloom and Richard Waters; and for Northern Thailand by Austin Bush, China Williams, Tim Bewer and David Eimer. The previous edition of this book was coordinated by Nick Ray, working with Greg, Austin, Iain and Richard.

This guidebook was commissioned in Lonely Planet's Melbourne office, and produced by the following:

Commissioning Editor
Ilaria Walker

Coordinating Editors
Elin Berglund, Paul Harding

Senior Cartographer
Diana Von Holdt

Book Designer
Mazzy Prinsep

Assisting Editors Michelle Bennett, Penny Cordner, Anne Mulvaney, Katie O'Connell, Chris Pitts

Assisting Cartographers
Jeff Cameron, Rachel Imeson, Alison Lyall

Cover Researcher
Naomi Parker

Language Content
Branislava Vladisavljevic

Thanks to Anita Banh, Sasha Baskett, Ryan Evans, Larissa Frost, Mark Griffiths, Genesys India, Jouve India, Anne Mason, Catherine Naghten, Karyn Noble, Lorna Parkes, Martine Power, Dianne Schallmeiner, Luna Soo, Angela Tinson

Index

Map Legend

Sights

- Beach
- Bird Sanctuary
- Buddhist
- Castle/Palace
- Christian
- Confucian
- Hindu
- Islamic
- Jain
- Jewish
- Monument
- Museum/Gallery/Historic Building
- Ruin
- Sento Hot Baths/Onsen
- Shinto
- Sikh
- Taoist
- Winery/Vineyard
- Zoo/Wildlife Sanctuary
- Other Sight

Activities, Courses & Tours

- Bodysurfing
- Diving
- Canoeing/Kayaking
- Course/Tour
- Skiing
- Snorkelling
- Surfing
- Swimming/Pool
- Walking
- Windsurfing
- Other Activity

Sleeping

- Sleeping
- Camping

Eating

- Eating

Drinking & Nightlife

- Drinking & Nightlife
- Cafe

Entertainment

- Entertainment

Shopping

- Shopping

Information

- Bank
- Embassy/Consulate
- Hospital/Medical
- Internet
- Police
- Post Office
- Telephone
- Toilet
- Tourist Information
- Other Information

Geographic

- Beach
- Hut/Shelter
- Lighthouse
- Lookout
- Mountain/Volcano
- Oasis
- Park
- Pass
- Picnic Area
- Waterfall

Population

- Capital (National)
- Capital (State/Province)
- City/Large Town
- Town/Village

Transport

- Airport
- Border crossing
- Bus
- Cable car/Funicular
- Cycling
- Ferry
- Metro/MRT station
- Monorail
- Parking
- Petrol station
- Skytrain/Subway station
- Taxi
- Train station/Railway
- Tram
- Underground station
- Other Transport

Note: Not all symbols displayed above appear on the maps in this book

Routes

- Tollway
- Freeway
- Primary
- Secondary
- Tertiary
- Lane
- Unsealed road
- Road under construction
- Plaza/Mall
- Steps
- Tunnel
- Pedestrian overpass
- Walking Tour
- Walking Tour detour
- Path/Walking Trail

Boundaries

- International
- State/Province
- Disputed
- Regional/Suburb
- Marine Park
- Cliff
- Wall

Hydrography

- River, Creek
- Intermittent River
- Canal
- Water
- Dry/Salt/Intermittent Lake
- Reef

Areas

- Airport/Runway
- Beach/Desert
- Cemetery (Christian)
- Cemetery (Other)
- Glacier
- Mudflat
- Park/Forest
- Sight (Building)
- Sportsground
- Swamp/Mangrove

OUR STORY

A beat-up old car, a few dollars in the pocket and a sense of adventure. In 1972 that's all Tony and Maureen Wheeler needed for the trip of a lifetime – across Europe and Asia overland to Australia. It took several months, and at the end – broke but inspired – they sat at their kitchen table writing and stapling together their first travel guide, *Across Asia on the Cheap*. Within a week they'd sold 1500 copies. Lonely Planet was born.

Today, Lonely Planet has offices in Franklin, London, Melbourne, Oakland, Beijing and Delhi, with more than 600 staff and writers. We share Tony's belief that 'a great guidebook should do three things: inform, educate and amuse'.

OUR WRITERS

Greg Bloom

Coordinating Author, Cambodia After five years in Manila, Greg crossed the pond to 'small town' Phnom Penh in 2008. Since then he has covered virtually every inch of Cambodia for Lonely Planet, from Koh Kong to Sen Monorom and Ban Lung to Anlong Veng. He also dipped a toe into Southern Laos for this book, returning to the Land of a Million Elephants for the first time in 15 years. When not writing about Southeast Asia for Lonely Planet, Greg might be found kicking around the former Soviet Union (he was editor of the *Kyiv Post* in another life) or running around Asia's ultimate frisbee fields. Read about his trips at www.mytripjournal.com/bloomblogs. Greg also wrote the Plan Your Trip section, the Understand features and the Survival Guide.

Read more about Greg at:
lonelyplanet.com/thorntree/profiles/gbloom4

Austin Bush

Northern Thailand Austin came to Thailand in 1999 as part of a language study programme hosted by Chiang Mai University. The lure of city life, employment and spicy food eventually led him to Bangkok. City life, employment and spicy food have managed to keep him there since. Austin is a native of Oregon and a writer and photographer who often focuses on food. Samples of his work can be seen at www.austinbushphotography.com.

Read more about Austin at:
lonelyplanet.com/thorntree/profiles/osten_th

Iain Stewart

Vietnam Iain first visited Vietnam when all foreigners were presumed to be Soviets. He has returned many times since to write several editions of Lonely Planet's *Vietnam*. Highlights on this trip were travelling with mate Vinh and his family, the swim-through caves of Phong Nha, mountain biking around Dalat, hanging out in Hoi An, bar-hopping in Ho Chi Minh City and the silence of Con Dao.

Read more about Iain at:
lonelyplanet.com/thorntree/profiles/stewpot

Richard Waters

Laos Richard is an award-winning journalist and works for the *Independent, Sunday Times, Wanderlust* and *National Geographic Traveller*. He lives with his fiancée and two kids in the Cotswolds. Laos is one of his favourite countries in the world; his journeys there started in '99 as a traveller, his next as a journalist taking him into the forbidden Special Zone investigating the Hmong guerrilla survivors of the Secret War. The people and endless allure of the country have kept him coming back ever since. This will be his eighth Lonely Planet book on Laos. He's also authored a thriller set in Laos, *Black Buddha*, which is published on Kindle. To read more of his travel journalism visit: www.richardwaters.co.uk.

Published by Lonely Planet Publications Pty Ltd
ABN 36 005 607 983
4th edition – Aug 2014
ISBN 978 1 74220 583 0
© Lonely Planet 2014 Photographs © as indicated 2014
10 9 8 7 6 5 4 3 2 1
Printed in China